ISBN 978-1-5278-3874-1
PIBN 10892005

INDEX

TO THE

PROBATE RECORDS .

OF THE

COUNTY OF WORCESTER,

MASSACHUSETTS,

FROM JULY 12, 1731, TO JULY 1, 1881.

SERIES A.

PREPARED UNDER THE SUPERVISION OF

GEORGE H. HARLOW,

REGISTER OF PROBATE AND INSOLVENCY FOR THE COUNTY OF WORCESTER.

WORCESTER, MASS.
OLIVER B. WOOD, PUBLISHER.
1898.

PRESS OF OLIVER B. WOOD,
LAW PRINTER,
WORCESTER, - MASSACHUSETTS.

Year.	Name.	Residence.	Nature.	Case.
	ABBOT and ABBOTT,			
1875	Abbie M.	Holden,	Guardianship,	1
1810	Abijah	Paxton,	Administration,	2
1804	Abner	Grafton,	Administration,	3
1806	Abner	Grafton,	Guardianship,	4
1853	Alanson M.	Worcester,	Administration,	5
1876	Alice	Fitchburg,	Guardianship,	6
1876	Annie F.	Worcester,	Adoption,	7
1877	Augusta	Worcester,	Administration,	8
1871	Azubah R.	West Brookfield,	Will,	9
1853	Benjamin	Holden,	Administration,	10
1876	Bertha	Fitchburg,	Guardianship,	11
1849	Betsey	Holden,	Administration,	12
1770	Betty	Andover,	Guardianship,	13
1876	Calva	Fitchburg,	Guardianship,	14
1813	Chenery	Holden,	Guardianship,	15
1731	Daniel	Woodstock,	Will,	16
1741	Daniel	Woodstock,	Will,	17
1792	Daniel	Brookfield,	Administration,	18
1775	Ebenezer	Shrewsbury,	Administration,	19
1843	Edward F.	Comeant, Ohio,	Guardianship,	20
1872	Florence, etc.	Spencer,	Administration,	21
1875	Frederick L.	Worcester,	Guardianship,	22
1748	George	Woodstock,	Guardianship,	23
1761	George, Jr.	Hardwick,	Administration,	24
1867	Helen F.	Putnam, Iowa,	Guardianship,	25
1813	Hollice	Holden,	Guardianship,	26
1843	Hollice C.	Comeant, Ohio,	Guardianship,	27
1822	Horace	Westborough,	Guardianship,	28
1875	Ida J. G.	Worcester,	Guardianship,	29
1777	Isaac	Shrewsbury,	Guardianship,	30
1771	Jacob	Brookfield,	Will,	31
1879	Jacob J.	Northbridge,	Administration,	32
1850	Jairus	Brookfield,	Will,	33
1865	James	West Brookfield,	Administration,	34
1878	James	Fitchburg,	Administration,	35
1813	Jarvis	Holden,	Guardianship,	36
1843	Jason	Boylston,	Will,	37
1876	Jennie C.	Worcester,	Guardianship,	38
1827	Jesse	Brookfield,	Will,	39
1799	John	Holden,	Will,	40
1806	John C.	Grafton,	Guardianship,	41
1825	John C.	Grafton,	Administration,	42
1777	John M.	Shrewsbury,	Guardianship,	43
1805	Jonathan	Brookfield,	Will,	44

(1)

	ABBOT AND ABBOTT,			
1813	Lemuel	Holden,	Administration,	45
1867	Lemuel	Blackstone,	Administration,	46
1777	Lewis	Shrewsbury,	Guardianship,	47
1862	Lewis	Brookfield,	Will,	48
1806	Mariot	Grafton,	Guardianship,	49
1792	Martha	Shrewsbury,	Will,	50
1806	Nancy	Grafton,	Guardianship,	51
1830	Nancy	Grafton,	Guardianship,	52
1834	Nancy	Grafton,	Administration,	52
1879	Paul W.	Northbridge,	Guardianship,	53
1785	Peter	Brookfield,	Will,	54
1875	Phillip S.	Worcester,	Guardianship,	55
1772	Ruth	Brookfield,	Administration,	56
1749	Samuel	Hardwick,	Administration,	57
1765	Samuel	Hardwick,	Guardianship,	58
1856	Samuel	Leominster,	Will,	59
1819	Samuel S.	Grafton,	Guardianship,	60
1748	Sarah	Woodstock,	Guardianship,	61
1806	Stillman	Grafton,	Guardianship,	62
1813	Susanna A.	Holden,	Guardianship,	63
1880	Susannah A.	Holden,	Administration,	64
1853	Timothy, Jr.	Grafton,	Administration,	65
1851	Waldo	New York, N. Y.,	Guardianship,	66
1842	Warren S.	Worcester,	Will,	67
1806	William T.	Grafton,	Guardianship,	68
1875	Zillah C.	Holden,	Guardianship,	69
1871	ABERCROMBIE, Ella	Worcester,	Guardianship,	70
1851	Otis	Lunenburg,	Will,	71
1875	ABORN, Reuben	Oxford,	Will,	72
1747	ABRAHAM, Andrew, Jr.	Grafton,	Will,	73
1785	David	Grafton,	Will,	74
1878	ACERES, Bessie M.	Charlestown,	Adoption, etc.,	75
1880	ACKLEY, Mary A.	Fitchburg,	Administration,	76
1840	ADAMS, Aaron	Grafton,	Guardianship,	77
1847	Aaron	Paxton,	Guardianship,	78
1877	Aaron	Leicester,	Administration,	79
1864	Abby J.	North Brookfield,	Guardianship,	80
1822	Abel F.	Lunenburg,	Guardianship,	81
1869	Abel F.	Fitchburg,	Will,	82
1801	Abigail	Spencer,	Administration,	83
1881	Abigail H.	Milford,	Will,	84
1860	Abigail L.	Northbridge,	Will,	85
1834	Abner	Northbridge,	Will,	86
1809	Abraham	Brookfield,	Administration,	87

(2)

YEAR.	NAME.	RESIDENCE.	NATURE.	CASE.
1839	ADAMS, Achsah	Athol,	Guardianship,	88
1826	Adaline	Brookfield,	Guardianship,	89
1865	Adaline E.	Charlton,	Administration,	90
1871	Addie L.	Webster,	Guardianship,	91
1858	Addie M.	Gardner,	Guardianship,	92
1823	Adelpha	Brookfield,	Guardianship,	93
1747	Adonijah	Worcester,	Administration,	94
1825	Alason	Mendon,	Guardianship,	95
1850	Alason	Blackstone,	Administration,	95
1853	Alice	Oakham,	Guardianship,	96
1858	Alice	Harvard,	Administration,	97
1864	Alice	Oakham,	Administration,	98
1875	Alice	Barre,	Administration,	99
1834	Alma A.	Milford,	Guardianship,	100
1838	Almira	Oxford,	Guardianship,	101
1865	Alpheus	Northbridge,	Administration,	102
1815	Alvin T.	Westborough,	Guardianship,	103
1822	Amasa	Brookfield,	Administration,	104
1830	Amasa	Sturbridge,	Administration,	105
1844	Amasa	Brookfield,	Guardianship,	106
1881	Amasa	Brookfield,	Administration,	107
1852	Ame	Harvard,	Will,	108
1819	Amos	Rutland,	Administration,	109
1823	Amos	Brookfield,	Administration,	110
1864	Amos	Brookfield,	Administration,	111
1881	Amos T.	Hubbardston,	Partition,	112
1782	Andrew	Grafton,	Will,	113
1818	Andrew	New Braintree,	Guardianship,	114
1841	Andrew	Grafton,	Will,	115
1853	Andrew	Auburn,	Guardianship,	116
1835	Anna	Hubbardston,	Administration,	117
1866	Arathusa E.	Webster,	Guardianship,	118
1804	Arnold	Northbridge,	Guardianship,	119
1881	Arnold	Barre,	Will,	120
1801	Artemas	Spencer,	Guardianship,	121
1823	Artemas	Spencer,	Administration,	122
1868	Asa F.	Milford,	Administration,	123
1879	Asa S.	Athol,	Administration,	124
1855	Asahel	Milford,	Will,	125
1829	Augustus	Sutton,	Guardianship,	126
1865	Augustus	Leicester,	Will,	127
1867	Augustus E.	Brookfield,	Guardianship,	128
1831	Austin	Sturbridge,	Guardianship,	129
1785	Benjamin	Brookfield,	Will,	130
1827	Benjamin	Northbridge,	Will,	131

(3)

Year.	Name.	Residence.	Nature.	Case.
1829	ADAMS, Benjamin	North Brookfield,	Will,	132
1837	Benjamin	Uxbridge,	Administration,	133
1843	Benjamin	Winchendon,	Administration,	134
1843	Benjamin	Winchendon,	Partition,	134
1843	Benjamin	Winchendon,	Guardianship,	135
1853	Benjamin	Winchendon,	Administration,	135
1822	Benjamin, Jr.	North Brookfield,	Guardianship,	136
1877	Benjamin F.	West Brookfield,	Will,	137
1851	Betsey	Northbridge,	Will,	138
1865	Betsey	Brookfield,	Will,	139
1868	Betsey	Dudley,	Adoption, etc.,	140
1874	Betsey	Spencer,	Will,	141
1779	Betty	Fitchburg,	Guardianship,	142
1867	Carrie A.	West Brookfield,	Guardianship,	143
1874	Carrie M.	Worcester,	Guardianship,	144
1880	Catherine	Brookfield,	Administration,	145
1773	Charles	Worcester,	Administration,	146
1878	Charles	North Brookfield,	Will,	147
1864	Charles A.	Athol,	Administration,	148
1864	Charles E.	Spencer,	Guardianship,	149
1864	Charles F.	Brookfield,	Guardianship,	150
1865	Charles W.	Milford,	Guardianship,	151
1833	Charlotte E.	Unknown,	Sale Real Estate,	152
1844	Clarinda R.	Oakham,	Guardianship,	153
1850	Clark	Charlton,	Administration,	154
1862	Cora	Athol,	Adoption, etc.,	155
1861	Cordelia M.	Gardner,	Administration,	156
1838	Cornelia	Oxford,	Guardianship,	157
1866	Cylena	Charlton,	Administration,	158
1844	Cyrus	Northbridge,	Will,	159
1815	Daniel	Barre,	Administration,	160
1833	Daniel	Rutland,	Will,	161
1856	Daniel	Northbridge,	Will,	162
1873	Daniel	Gardner,	Administration,	163
1815	Daniel P.	Westborough,	Guardianship,	164
1816	Daniel P.	Barre,	Guardianship,	165
1848	Daniel W.	Spencer,	Guardianship,	166
1746	Darius	Woodstock,	Administration,	167
1879	Darius	Hubbardston,	Administration,	168
1801	David	Spencer,	Partition,	169
1815	David	Spencer,	Administration,	170
1825	David	Spencer,	Guardianship,	171
1848	David	Spencer,	Administration,	172
1849	David	Spencer,	Partition,	172
1880	David	Brookfield,	Administration,	173

Year.	Name.	Residence.	Nature.	Case.
1873	ADAMS, David N.	Westborough,	Will,	174
1834	David S.	Milford,	Guardianship,	175
1836	Dudley W.	Winchendon,	Guardianship,	176
1804	Ebenezer	Ashburnham,	Guardianship,	177
1830	Ebenezer	Ashburnham,	Administration,	178
1804	Ebenezer T.	Ashburnham,	Will,	179
1870	Ednah	Woodstock, Conn.,	Guardianship,	180
1753	Edward	Grafton,	Guardianship,	181
1865	Edward S.	Milford,	Guardianship,	182
1831	Edwin	Sturbridge,	Guardianship,	183
1877	Edwin G.	Templeton,	Will,	184
1823	Eleazer	Brookfield,	Will,	185
1836	Elias	Northbridge,	Guardianship,	186
1842	Elias	Spencer,	Pension,	187
1845	Elias A.	Northbridge,	Guardianship,	188
1865	Elihu	Douglas,	Administration,	189
1818	Elijah	Hubbardston,	Administration,	190
1842	Elijah	Hubbardston,	Administration,	191
1871	Elijah	Brookfield,	Will,	192
1760	Eliphalet	Westborough,	Administration,	193
1878	Elisha	Rutland,	Administration,	194
1804	Eliza	Ashburnham,	Guardianship,	195
1848	Eliza J.	Spencer,	Guardianship,	196
1797	Elizabeth	Grafton,	Guardianship,	197
1844	Elizabeth	Grafton,	Will,	198
1850	Elizabeth	Lunenburg,	Administration,	199
1824	Emeline	Brookfield,	Guardianship,	200
1847	Emeline J.	Brookfield,	Administration,	201
1863	Emery G.	Spencer,	Guardianship,	202
1834	Emily	Milford,	Guardianship,	203
1856	Emily E.	Northbridge,	Administration,	204
1840	Emma	Leominster,	Administration,	205
1866	Emma I.	Milford,	Guardianship,	206
1818	Ephraim	New Braintree,	Guardianship,	207
1822	Ephraim	Brookfield,	Will,	208
1832	Ephraim	Northbridge,	Guardianship,	209
1862	Ephraim	Worcester,	Administration,	210
1811	Eunice	Sutton,	Guardianship,	211
1841	Eveline	Charlton,	Guardianship,	212
1825	Ezra	Brookfield,	Administration,	213
1874	E. G.	Leominster,	Will,	214
1801	Fanny	Spencer,	Guardianship,	215
1826	Fanny	Brookfield,	Guardianship,	216
1866	Fanny	Brookfield,	Administration,	217
1878	Fanny A.	Uxbridge,	Will,	218

YEAR.	NAME.	RESIDENCE.	NATURE.	CASE.
1844	ADAMS, Fatima	Brookfield,	Guardianship,	219
1875	Fergus L.	North Brookfield,	Guardianship,	220
1865	Fisher	Milford,	Administration,	221
1874	Flora N.	Rindge, N. H.,	Guardianship,	222
1874	Florence M.	Worcester,	Guardianship,	223
1801	Francis	Spencer,	Guardianship,	224
1802	Francis	Northbridge,	Will,	225
1863	Francis	Spencer,	Administration,	226
1875	Frank C.	Hopedale,	Guardianship,	227
1873	Frank G.	Worcester,	Guardianship,	228
1859	Frank S.	Westborough,	Guardianship,	229
1863	Frederick H.	Spencer,	Guardianship,	230
1869	Frederick J. B.	Worcester,	Adoption, etc.,	231
1785	George	Westminster,	Guardianship,	232
1832	George	Uxbridge,	Will,	233
1838	George	Uxbridge,	Guardianship,	234
1875	George	North Brookfield,	Guardianship,	235
1873	George A.	Worcester,	Administration,	236
1880	George A.	Webster,	Administration,	237
1864	George D.	Spencer,	Guardianship,	238
1865	George K.	Northborough,	Guardianship,	239
1869	George P.	Fitchburg,	Guardianship,	240
1865	George S.	Milford,	Guardianship,	241
1839	George T.	Athol,	Guardianship,	242
1868	George W.	Millbury,	Administration,	243
1815	Hannah	Westborough,	Guardianship,	244
1844	Hannah	Barre,	Guardianship,	245
1845	Hannah	Barre,	Administration,	245
1832	Hannah J.	Northbridge,	Guardianship,	246
1868	Hannah M.	Shrewsbury,	Guardianship,	247
1852	Harriet M.	Sterling,	Administration,	248
1865	Hattie	Northborough,	Guardianship,	249
1867	Hattie W.	Brookfield,	Guardianship,	250
1860	Helen	Spencer,	Guardianship,	251
1832	Henry	Northbridge,	Guardianship,	252
1844	Henry	Brookfield,	Guardianship,	253
1826	Henry H.	Brookfield,	Guardianship,	254
1872	Henry H.	Brookfield,	Administration,	255
1881	Henry H.	Gardner,	Partition,	256
1804	Hepze	Ashburnham,	Guardianship,	257
1869	Herbert T.	Hubbardston,	Guardianship,	258
1881	Herbert T.	Gardner,	Partition,	259
1824	Hiram	Brookfield,	Guardianship,	260
1879	Homer M.	Hubbardston,	Administration,	261
1857	Horace	Grafton,	Guardianship,	262

YEAR.	NAME.	RESIDENCE.	NATURE.	CASE.
1881	ADAMS, Horace M.	Templeton,	Partition,	263
1881	H. Augustus	Hubbardston,	Partition,	264
1872	Ida L.	Milford,	Guardianship,	265
1840	Ira	Brookfield,	Administration,	266
1815	Isaac, Jr.	Westborough,	Administration,	267
1815	Isaac V.	Westborough,	Guardianship,	268
1834	Isabella L.	Milford,	Guardianship,	269
1811	Israel	Sutton,	Will,	270
1829	Issachar	Hubbardston,	Will,	271
1827	Jacob	Northbridge,	Guardianship,	272
1858	Jacob	Northbridge,	Will,	273
1738	James	Holliston,	Guardianship,	274
1776	James	New Braintree,	Administration,	275
1804	James	Sutton,	Will,	276
1843	James	Barre,	Will,	277
1848	James	Rutland,	Administration,	278
1850	James	Blackstone,	Guardianship,	279
1857	James	Barre,	Will,	280
1864	James	Spencer,	Administration,	281
1865	James D.	Oxford,	Administration,	282
1858	James H.	Gardner,	Guardianship,	283
1865	James H.	Millbury,	Administration,	284
1847	Jane E.	Paxton,	Guardianship,	285
1850	Jasper	Southborough,	Will,	286
1869	Jemison	Oxford,	Will,	287
1827	Jesse	Brookfield,	Will,	288
1870	Jessie	Woodstock, Conn.,	Guardianship,	289
1872	Jessie	Brookfield,	Guardianship,	290
1839	Joel	Athol,	Guardianship,	291
1841	Joel	Charlton,	Administration,	292
1735	John	Worcester,	Will,	293
1796	John	Northbridge,	Will,	294
1805	John	Brookfield,	Guardianship,	295
1813	John	New Braintree,	Will,	296
1827	John, 2d	Northbridge,	Administration,	297
1843	John	Worcester,	Administration,	298
1843	John	Worcester,	Pension,	299
1844	John	Oakham,	Guardianship,	300
1857	John	Brookfield,	Administration,	301
1876	John	Hubbardston,	Will,	302
1881	John	Hubbardston,	Partition,	303
1845	John F.	Boston,	Guardianship,	304
1815	John G.	Westborough,	Guardianship,	305
1864	John M.	Spencer,	Guardianship,	306
1848	John P.	Spencer,	Guardianship,	307

(7—SERIES A.)

YEAR.	NAME.	RESIDENCE.	NATURE.	CASE.
1862	ADAMS, John Q.	Worcester,	Guardianship,	308
1858	John S.	Gardner,	Administration,	309
1879	John W.	Hubbardston,	Guardianship,	310
1881	John W.	Hubbardston,	Partition,	311
1802	Jonathan	Shrewsbury,	Will,	312
1813	Jonathan	Barre,	Administration,	313
1813	Jonathan	Lunenburg,	Will,	314
1843	Jonathan	Lunenburg,	Will,	315
1844	Jonathan	Lunenburg,	Pension,	316
1745	Jonathan, Jr.	Grafton,	Administration,	317
1778	Joseph	Fitchburg,	Administration,	318
1801	Joseph	Spencer,	Guardianship,	319
1805	Joseph	Uxbridge,	Guardianship,	320
1835	Joseph	Uxbridge,	Will,	321
1836	Joseph	Uxbridge,	Pension,	322
1836	Joseph	Winchendon,	Administration,	323
1867	Joseph	Grafton,	Administration,	324
1845	Joseph O.	Boston,	Guardianship,	325
1876	Joseph S.	Harvard,	Will,	326
1828	Josiah	Douglas,	Administration,	327
1867	Josiah	Shrewsbury,	Will,	328
1837	Josiah A.	Uxbridge,	Guardianship,	329
1823	Jude	Brookfield,	Administration,	330
1866	Judson	Northbridge,	Will,	331
1816	Julia	Barre,	Guardianship,	332
1841	Julia A.	Charlton,	Guardianship,	333
1836	Laura	Northbridge,	Guardianship,	334
1845	Laura A.	Boston,	Guardianship,	335
1813	Laurinda M.	Brookfield,	Guardianship,	336
1780	Lemuel	Brookfield,	Guardianship,	337
1823	Levi	Brookfield,	Guardianship,	338
1848	Levi	Spencer,	Will,	339
1860	Levi	North Brookfield,	Will,	340
1848	Levi H.	Spencer,	Guardianship,	341
1853	Liberty	Brookfield,	Guardianship,	342
1870	Liberty	Brookfield,	Will,	342
1864	Lois	Northbridge,	Administration,	343
1864	Lois B.	Harvard,	Will,	344
1844	Lorin	Brookfield,	Guardianship,	345
1838	Loring	Oxford,	Guardianship,	346
1862	Louisa	Charlestown,	Adoption, etc.,	347
1855	Lucius A.	Providence, R. I.,	Guardianship,	348
1811	Lucy	Sutton,	Guardianship,	349
1844	Lucy	Douglas,	Administration,	350
1872	Lucy	Hubbardston,	Administration,	351

Year.	Name.	Residence.	Nature.	Case.
1822	ADAMS, Lucy Ann	Lunenburg,	Guardianship,	352
1815	Luke	Barre,	Guardianship,	353
1753	Lydia	Grafton,	Guardianship,	354
1804	Lydia	Ashburnham,	Guardianship,	355
1845	Lydia	Northbridge,	Guardianship,	356
1875	Lyman	North Brookfield,	Guardianship,	357
1864	Mabel V.	Brookfield,	Guardianship,	358
1864	Marcia A.	Worcester,	Will,	359
1872	Margaret	Spencer,	Administration,	360
1828	Maria	Northbridge,	Guardianship,	361
1847	Maria C.	Paxton,	Guardianship,	362
1867	Maria F.	Northbridge,	Guardianship,	363
1797	Martha	Worcester,	Will,	364
1863	Martha A.	Brookfield,	Guardianship,	365
1863	Martha A.	Brookfield,	Administration,	366
1772	Mary	Worcester,	Will,	367
1804	Mary	Ashburnham,	Guardianship,	368
1815	Mary	Ashburnham,	Administration,	369
1831	Mary	Sturbridge,	Guardianship,	370
1828	Mary A.	Northbridge,	Guardianship,	371
1834	Mary E.	Milford,	Guardianship,	372
1850	Mary E.	Charlton,	Guardianship,	373
1855	Mary E.	Providence, R. I.,	Guardianship,	374
1870	Mary E.	Athol,	Guardianship,	375
1864	Mary K.	Spencer,	Guardianship,	376
1860	Mary M.	Northbridge,	Guardianship,	377
1863	Mary M.	Spencer,	Guardianship,	378
1866	Mary O.	Millbury,	Guardianship,	379
1845	Mary P.	Boston,	Guardianship,	380
1836	Maxwell	Winchendon,	Guardianship,	381
1860	Maxwell	Winchendon,	Administration,	382
1820	Melvin	Athol,	Guardianship,	383
1843	Meriam	Brookfield,	Will,	384
1844	Meriam	Brookfield,	Pension,	385
1813	Michal	Brookfield,	Will,	386
1877	Minnie	Boston,	Adoption, etc.,	387
1868	Minnie C.	Millbury,	Guardianship,	388
1864	Morton S.	Brookfield,	Guardianship,	389
1787	Moses	Uxbridge,	Guardianship,	390
1811	Moses	Sutton,	Guardianship,	391
1827	Moses	Northbridge,	Guardianship,	392
1834	Moses	Milford,	Administration,	393
1839	Moses	Grafton,	Will,	394
1851	Moses	Brookfield,	Will,	395
1854	Moses	Milford,	Partition,	396

YEAR.	NAME.	RESIDENCE.	NATURE.	CASE.
1874	ADAMS, Moses	Northbridge,	Will,	396
1854	Moses H.	Grafton,	Administration,	397
1769	Nathan	Weston,	Guardianship,	398
1825	Nathan	Barre,	Administration,	399
1860	Nathan	Northbridge,	Administration,	400
1761	Nathaniel	Westborough,	Guardianship,	401
1776	Nathaniel	Worcester,	Will,	402
1823	Nathaniel	Ashburnham,	Administration,	403
1829	Nathaniel	Grafton,	Will,	404
1833	Nathaniel	Northbridge,	Will,	405
1803	Nehemiah	Northbridge,	Will,	406
1810	Nehemiah	Northbridge,	Guardianship,	407
1810	Nehemiah	Spencer,	Guardianship,	408
1874	Nellie E.	Rindge, N. H.,	Guardianship,	409
1877	Newell	Milford,	Guardianship,	410
1879	Newell	Milford,	Administration,	410
1804	Olive	Northbridge,	Guardianship,	411
1832	Olive	Grafton,	Will,	412
1804	Oliver	Harvard,	Administration,	413
1815	Oliver	Westborough,	Guardianship,	414
1856	Oliver	Northborough,	Administration,	415
1865	Oliver Q.	Northborough,	Guardianship,	416
1865	Oliver W.	Oxford,	Administration,	417
1860	Otis	Grafton,	Will,	418
1874	Palmer	Oakham,	Guardianship,	419
1875	Palmer	Oakham,	Will,	419
1807	Patty	Spencer,	Guardianship,	420
1863	Patty	Grafton,	Administration,	421
1807	Persis	Spencer,	Guardianship,	422
1813	Persis N.	Brookfield,	Guardianship,	423
1762	Peter	Westborough,	Guardianship,	424
1824	Phebe	Brookfield,	Guardianship,	425
1813	Polly H.	Brookfield,	Guardianship,	426
1830	Reuben	Ward,	Guardianship,	427
1838	Reuben	Oxford,	Will,	428
1838	Reuben	Oxford,	Guardianship,	429
1848	Reuben	Westminster,	Administration,	430
1848	Reuben	Westminster,	Pension,	431
1869	Richard F.	Fitchburg,	Guardianship,	432
1839	Rosanna	Athol,	Guardianship,	433
1874	Roxanna A.	Northbridge,	Administration,	434
1828	Rufus	Worcester,	Administration,	435
1830	Rufus	Worcester,	Guardianship,	436
1843	Rufus	Worcester,	Guardianship,	437
1850	Rufus	Worcester,	Guardianship,	438

YEAR.	NAME.	RESIDENCE.	NATURE.	CASE.
1864	ADAMS, Rufus	Spencer,	Administration,	439
1865	Rufus	Northborough,	Guardianship,	440
1848	Ruth	Brookfield,	Will,	441
1851	Sally	Oxford,	Administration,	442
1878	Sally	Grafton,	Will,	443
1834	Sally A.	Milford,	Guardianship,	444
1758	Samuel	Sutton,	Guardianship,	445
1829	Samuel	Grafton,	Will,	446
1841	Samuel	Lancaster,	Administration,	447
1845	Samuel	Northbridge,	Guardianship,	448
1854	Samuel	Northbridge,	Administration,	449
1873	Samuel	Spencer,	Will,	450
1855	Samuel J.	Providence, R. I.,	Guardianship,	451
1815	Sanford	Westborough,	Guardianship,	452
1880	Sanford	Westborough,	Will,	453
1833	Sarah	Spencer,	Administration,	454
1834	Sarah	Brookfield,	Guardianship,	455
1856	Sarah A.	Harvard,	Administration,	456
1881	Schuyler	Barre,	Administration,	457
1824	Selinda	Brookfield,	Guardianship,	458
1839	Seth R.	Portland, Me.,	Administration,	459
1847	Sidney	Princeton,	Administration,	460
1783	Silas	Brookfield,	Guardianship,	461
1832	Silence	Northbridge,	Guardianship,	462
1858	Solomon	West Brookfield,	Administration,	463
1841	Solon S.	Charlton,	Guardianship,	464
1871	Solon S.	New Garden, Pa.,	Administration,	465
1815	Sophia	Barre,	Guardianship,	466
1844	Sophia	Worcester,	Will,	467
1877	Sophia	Barre,	Administration,	468
1804	Stephen	Ashburnham,	Guardianship,	469
1847	Stephen	Paxton,	Administration,	470
1858	Susan	Uxbridge,	Administration,	471
1879	Susan	Spencer,	Guardianship,	472
1873	Susan M.	New Braintree,	Administration,	473
1840	Susannah	Uxbridge,	Administration,	474
1864	Susie	Unknown,	Adoption, etc.,	475
1872	Sylvanus	Milford,	Will,	476
1871	Thomas E.	Versailles, Ky.,	Guardianship,	477
1831	Thomas J.	Westborough,	Administration,	478
1877	Thomas R.	Ashburnham,	Administration,	479
1814	Timothy	Athol,	Administration,	480
1872	Victoria A.	Brookfield,	Guardianship,	481
1865	Villroy	Brookfield,	Guardianship,	482
1868	Waldo	Oxford,	Will,	483

Year.	Name.	Residence.	Nature.	Case.
1876	ADAMS, Walter	Ashburnham,	Will,	484
1874	Walter F.	Rindge, N. H.,	Guardianship,	485
1847	Warren	Upton,	Administration,	486
1828	Welcome	Sutton,	Administration,	487
1841	Wellington W.	Charlton,	Guardianship,	488
1856	West	Worcester,	Administration,	489
1825	William	Brookfield,	Administration,	490
1829	William	Leominster,	Guardianship,	491
1834	William	Brookfield,	Guardianship,	492
1853	William	Brookfield,	Administration,	493
1871	William	North Brookfield,	Administration,	494
1872	William	North Brookfield,	Partition,	494
1872	William	West Brookfield,	Will,	495
1853	William E.	Brookfield,	Guardianship,	496
1866	William E.	Millbury,	Guardianship,	497
1864	William H.	Spencer,	Guardianship,	498
1826	William J.	Brookfield,	Guardianship,	499
1880	William J.	Brookfield,	Administration,	500
1871	Willie G.	Webster,	Guardianship,	501
1852	Windsor	Brookfield,	Change of Name,	502
1867	Winthrop M.	Brookfield,	Administration,	503
1801	Zabdiel	Lunenburg,	Will	504
1814	Zabdiel B.	Lunenburg,	Administration,	505
1852	Zeruiah	Winchendon,	Will,	506
1852	Zilpah	Westminster,	Administration,	507
1881	ADAMSON, Fidelia	Barre,	Administration,	508
1880	James	Barre,	Will,	509
1872	Sylvia	Barre,	Will,	510
1863	ADDISON, Thomas L.	Templeton,	Administration,	511
1874	AGAN, Francis	Nova Scotia,	Adoption, etc.,	512
1876	AHERN, David	Webster,	Administration,	513
1874	Michael H.	Milford,	Administration,	514
1871	Thomas M.	Worcester,	Guardianship,	515
1773	AIKEN, Atwood	Hardwick,	Guardianship,	516
1773	Bethsheba	Hardwick,	Guardianship,	517
1864	Brigham	Hardwick,	Administration,	518
1805	David	Hardwick,	Will,	519
1852	David	Hardwick,	Will,	520
1880	Emily S.	Worcester,	Administration,	521
1773	Israel	Hardwick,	Guardianship,	522
1773	Jerusha	Hardwick,	Guardianship,	523
1768	John	Hardwick,	Administration,	524
1773	John	Hardwick,	Guardianship,	525
1810	John	Hardwick,	Will,	526
1836	John	Deering, N. H.,	Guardianship,	527

(12)

YEAR.	NAME.	RESIDENCE.	NATURE.	CASE.
1854	AIKEN, John	Hardwick,	Will,	528
1875	Lewis	Hardwick,	Will,	529
1880	Nancy P.	Worcester,	Administration,	530
1877	Patty	Hardwick,	Will,	531
1773	Samuel	Hardwick,	Guardianship,	532
1773	Solomon	Hardwick,	Guardianship,	533
1872	AINLEY, Sarah	Spencer,	Administration,	534
1797	AINSWORTH, Allis	Brookfield,	Guardianship,	535
1837	Amos	Brookfield,	Administration,	536
1844	Bemsley	Brookfield,	Administration,	537
1858	Charles E.	Sturbridge,	Guardianship,	538
1851	Charles W.	Milford,	Administration,	539
1808	Chester	Brookfield,	Guardianship,	540
1841	Chester	Brookfield,	Administration,	541
1841	Chester H.	Brookfield,	Guardianship,	542
1841	Danforth	Brookfield,	Guardianship,	543
1858	Danforth	Sturbridge,	Administration,	544
1807	Daniel	Brookfield,	Administration,	545
1741	Edward	Woodstock,	Will,	546
1864	Elam W.	Millbury,	Will,	547
1858	Ethelin	Milford,	Guardianship,	548
1831	Eunice	Brookfield,	Administration,	549
1797	Fanny	Brookfield,	Guardianship,	550
1855	Henry L.	Worcester,	Guardianship,	551
1872	Henry O.	Brookfield,	Administration,	552
1862	Henry W.	Northbridge,	Administration,	553
1864	Henry W.	Millbury,	Administration,	554
1853	James G.	Barre,	Guardianship,	555
1864	James G.	Barre,	Administration,	556
1797	John	Brookfield,	Guardianship,	557
1842	John, 2nd	Brookfield,	Administration,	558
1797	Justin	Brookfield,	Guardianship,	559
1797	Lemuel	Brookfield,	Administration,	560
1841	Leonard A.	Brookfield,	Guardianship,	561
1853	Lura Francis	Barre,	Guardianship,	562
1860	Mary E.	Athol,	Guardianship,	563
1867	Mary E.	Athol,	Adoption, etc.,	564
1855	Mary J.	Worcester,	Guardianship,	565
1841	Mary Jane	Brookfield,	Guardianship,	566
1868	Mason	Barre,	Will,	567
1856	Merrick E.	Athol,	Will,	568
1813	Moses	Petersham,	Administration,	569
1859	Moses	Athol,	Administration,	570
1854	Nathan	Worcester,	Administration,	571
1841	Pamelia F.	Brookfield,	Guardianship,	572

YEAR.	NAME.	RESIDENCE.	NATURE.	CASE.
1797	AINSWORTH, Rebecca	Brookfield,	Guardianship,	573
1841	Sarah J.	Brookfield,	Guardianship,	574
1876	Susan A.	Athol,	Administration,	575
1790	Thomas	Brookfield,	Guardianship,	576
1793	Thomas	Brookfield,	Administration,	577
1812	Walter	Sturbridge,	Guardianship,	578
1841	Warren	Brookfield,	Guardianship,	579
1877	William A.	Brookfield,	Guardianship,	580
1853	William F.	Barre,	Will,	581
1877	AITKIN, Thomas S.	Clinton,	Administration,	582
1875	AKINS, Willie H.	Leicester,	Adoption, etc.,	583
1803	ALBEE, Aaron	Dudley,	Administration,	584
1879	Abby T.	Dana,	Administration,	585
1778	Abel	Mendon,	Guardianship,	586
1817	Abel	Milford,	Will,	587
1817	Abel	Milford,	Guardianship,	588
1873	Abel	Milford,	Administration,	589
1874	Abel	Milford,	Partition,	589
1869	Abigail	Milford,	Administration,	590
1845	Albert	Milford,	Guardianship,	591
1845	Alfred	Milford,	Guardianship,	592
1863	Alice C.	Dudley,.	Guardianship,	593
1878	Allen	Milford,	Administration,	594
1827	Almira	Charlton,	Guardianship,	595
1814	Alpheus	Uxbridge,	Guardianship,	596
1810	Amos	Milford,	Guardianship,	597
1859	Anderson B.	Milford,	Administration,	598
1810	Anna	Milford,	Guardianship,	599
1827	Asa	Charlton,	Guardianship,	600
1843	Asa	Charlton,	Administration,	601
1845	Augustus C.	Milford,	Guardianship,	602
1761	Barzilla	Mendon,	Guardianship,	603
1755	Benjamin	Mendon,	Will,	604
1758	Benjamin	Mendon,	Administration,	605
1862	Celia A.	Douglas,	Guardianship,	606
1860	Charles	Dudley,	Adoption, etc.,	607
1879	Charles E.	Dudley,	Change of Name,	608
1778	Chloe	Mendon,	Guardianship,	609
1790	Chloe	Milford,	Guardianship,	610
1817	Chloe H.	Milford,	Guardianship,	611
1846	Clarence L.	Mendon,	Guardianship,	612
1845	Clark	Milford,	Will,	613
1879	Clifton E.	Dana,	Adoption, etc.,	614
1848	Dorcas E.	Charlton,	Guardianship,	615
1848	Edwin	Charlton,	Guardianship,	616

YEAR.	NAME.	RESIDENCE.	NATURE.	CASE.
1856	ALBEE, Edwin W.	Northbridge,	Guardianship,	617
1848	Elizabeth	Blackstone,	Guardianship,	618
1863	Ella C.	Dudley,	Guardianship,	619
1865	Ellis	Uxbridge,	Will,	620
1831	Enos	Mendon,	Guardianship,	621
1873	Eunice B.	Milford,	Will,	622
1880	George N.	Worcester,	Administration,	623
1848	George W.	Charlton,	Guardianship,	624
1799	Gideon	Milford,	Will,	625
1823	Gideon	Milford,	Guardianship,	626
1832	Hannah	Milford,	Administration,	627
1848	Henry	Charlton,	Guardianship,	628
1834	Henry B.	Mendon,	Administration,	629
1845	Henry C.	Milford,	Guardianship,	630
1856	Henry F.	Northbridge,	Guardianship,	631
1856	Herbert J.	Northbridge,	Guardianship,	632
1834	Hezekiah	Charlton,	Administration,	633
1836	Izanna	Milford,	Guardianship,	634
1784	James	Milford,	Will,	635
1795	James	Uxbridge,	Will,	636
1814	James	Uxbridge,	Will,	637
1814	James	Uxbridge,	Guardianship,	638
1832	James	Milford,	Partition,	635
1830	Jesse	Mendon,	Administration,	639
1843	John	Charlton,	Guardianship,	640
1819	Joseph	Oxford,	Will,	641
1859	Joseph	Douglas,	Administration,	642
1880	Joseph	Milford,	Will,	643
1778	Laban	Mendon,	Guardianship,	644
1856	Laura F.	Northbridge,	Guardianship,	645
1831	Lemira	Mendon,	Guardianship,	646
1827	Leonard	Charlton,	Guardianship,	647
1859	Lovett	Milford,	Will,	648
1863	Lydia A.	Dudley,	Guardianship,	649
1761	Margarett	Mendon,	Guardianship,	650
1837	Martha	Dudley,	Will,	651
1856	Mary F.	Northbridge,	Guardianship,	652
1832	Nathan	Milford,	Administration,	653
1817	Obadiah H.	Milford,	Guardianship,	654
1858	Obadiah W.	Milford,	Administration,	655
1781	Olive	Milford,	Guardianship,	656
1863	Oliver A.	Dudley,	Guardianship,	657
1829	Otis	Milford,	Will,	658
1848	Persis N.	Charlton,	Guardianship,	659
1761	Rachel	Mendon,	Guardianship,	660

Year.	Name.	Residence.	Nature.	Case.
1778	ALBEE, Rachel	Mendon,	Guardianship,	661
1808	Rachel	Grafton,	Administration,	662
1857	Rachel T.	Northbridge,	Administration,	663
1832	Sabra	Milford,	Guardianship,	664
1832	Sabrina	Milford,	Guardianship,	665
1776	Seth	Mendon,	Administration,	666
1833	Seth	Milford,	Will,	667
1845	Seth	Milford,	Guardianship,	668
1755	Stephen	Mendon,	Guardianship,	669
1781	Susanna	Milford,	Guardianship,	670
1855	Thompson T.	Northbridge,	Administration,	671
1832	Timothy	Milford,	Administration,	672
1862	Washington M.	Douglas,	Administration,	673
1848	Wesley	Blackstone,	Guardianship,	674
1842	Willard	Charlton,	Administration,	675
1848	Willard	Warwick, R. I.,	Will,	676
1827	Willard, Jr.	Charlton,	Guardianship,	677
1832	Zebina	Milford,	Guardianship,	665
1866	ALBERT, James, Jr.	Brookfield,	Guardianship,	678
1866	ALBRO, Isaac	Worcester,	Administration,	679
1879	ALDEN, Austin H.	Auburn,	Administration,	680
1879	Charles A.	Auburn,	Guardianship,	681
1879	Frank H.	Auburn,	Guardianship,	682
1878	Luther	Templeton,	Administration,	683
1869	Marshall	Templeton,	Administration,	684
1841	Silas	Templeton,	Administration,	685
1826	ALDIS, Hannah	Mendon,	Will,	686
1809	ALDRICH, Aaron	Douglas,	Will,	687
1828	Aaron	Douglas	Guardianship,	688
1849	Aaron	Douglas,	Administration,	689
1874	Abbie A.	Uxbridge,	Guardianship,	690
1787	Abel	Uxbridge,	Will,	691
1841	Abel	Uxbridge,	Will,	692
1844	Abel	Mendon,	Will,	693
1810	Abel, Jr.	Uxbridge,	Administration,	694
1737	Abigail	Uxbridge,	Guardianship,	695
1877	Abigail	Uxbridge,	Will,	696
1877	Abigail	Webster,	Administration,	697
1879	Abigail L.	Sutton,	Guardianship,	698
1844	Abzada E.	Uxbridge,	Guardianship,	699
1874	Addison S.	Northbridge,	Guardianship,	700
1879	Adeline	Grafton,	Administration,	701
1867	Agnes A.	Worcester,	Adoption, etc.,	702
1876	Agnes H.	Mendon,	Adoption, etc.,	703
1825	Ahaz	Northbridge,	Administration,	704

(16)

Year.	Name.	Residence.	Nature.	Case.
1847	ALDRICH, Albert	Grafton,	Guardianship,	705
1860	Albert	Grafton,	Administration,	706
1857	Albert A.	Grafton,	Guardianship,	707
1852	Albert C.	Uxbridge,	Guardianship,	708
1831	Albert G.	Hallowell, Me.,	Administration,	709
1814	Alexander	Northbridge,	Will,	710
1867	Alice A.	Northbridge,	Guardianship,	711
1830	Allen	Uxbridge,	Guardianship,	712
1834	Allen	Mendon,	Administration,	713
1836	Allen D.	Mendon,	Guardianship,	714
1809	Alpheus	Upton,	Guardianship,	715
1821	Almira	Mendon,	Guardianship,	716
1821	Amos	Cumberland, R. I.,	Will,	717
1863	Amos C.	Oxford,	Will,	718
1879	Anah C.	Sutton,	Administration,	719
1842	Ann E.	New York, N. Y.,	Guardianship,	720
1837	Ann Maria B.	Northbridge,	Guardianship,	721
1803	Anna	Uxbridge,	Guardianship,	722
1821	Anna	Mendon,	Guardianship,	723
1838	Anna	Bolton,	Will,	724
1838	Anna	Northbridge,	Will,	725
1877	Anna A.	Milford,	Administration,	726
1855	Anna J.	Northbridge,	Guardianship,	727
1871	Annie J.	Northbridge,	Will,	728
1793	Arnold	Uxbridge,	Guardianship,	729
1825	Artemas	Uxbridge,	Will,	730
1778	Asahel	Uxbridge,	Will,	731
1844	Asahel, 2d	Uxbridge,	Administration,	732
1844	Asahel F.	Uxbridge,	Guardianship,	733
1875	Austin J.	Northbridge,	Administration,	734
1826	Barbara	Douglas,	Guardianship,	735
1807	Baruch	Cumberland, R. I.,	Will,	736
1851	Baylies W.	Uxbridge,	Guardianship,	737
1812	Benjamin	Uxbridge,	Will,	738
1832	Benoni	Mendon,	Administration,	739
1828	Betsey	Douglas,	Guardianship,	740
1836	Betsey W.	Mendon,	Guardianship,	741
1808	Brown	Northbridge,	Administration,	742
1844	Calvin	Oxford,	Will,	743
1817	Chalkley	Douglas,	Guardianship,	744
1773	Charles	Mendon,	Administration,	745
1847	Charles	Grafton,	Administration,	746
1842	Charles A.	New York, N. Y.,	Guardianship,	747
1838	Charles B.	Northbridge,	Guardianship,	748
1841	Charlotte	Douglas,	Guardianship,	749

(17)

Year.	Name.	Residence.	Nature.	Case.
1869	ALDRICH, Cheney	Worcester,	Administration,	750
1874	Cheney	Uxbridge,	Guardianship,	751
1815	Chiron	Mendon,	Guardianship,	752
1847	Cyrus D.	Grafton,	Guardianship,	753
1817	Dan	Cumberland, R. I.,	Administration,	754
1812	Daniel	Douglas,	Will,	755
1820	Daniel	Northbridge,	Guardianship,	756
1837	Daniel	Millbury,	Will,	757
1829	Daniel H.	Northbridge,	Guardianship,	758
1867	Daniel H.	Northbridge,	Will,	759
1871	Daniel H.	Uxbridge,	Administration,	760
1876	Daniel W.	Westborough,	Will,	761
1771	David	Mendon,	Will,	762
1803	David	Uxbridge,	Guardianship,	763
1817	David	Uxbridge,	Guardianship,	764
1828	David	Northbridge,	Administration,	765
1842	David	Northbridge,	Partition,	765
1737	Deborah	Uxbridge,	Guardianship,	766
1808	Dennis	Mendon,	Guardianship,	767
1817	Dorcas	Douglas,	Guardianship,	768
1864	Easick	Thompson, Conn.,	Will,	769
1834	Ebenezer	Mendon,	Guardianship,	770
1842	Ebenezer	Mendon,	Will,	770
1853	Ebenezer	Grafton,	Administration,	771
1844	Edmund H.	Uxbridge,	Guardianship,	772
1875	Edward	Woodstock, Conn.,	Will,	773
1857	Edward H.	Grafton,	Guardianship,	774
1847	Edward R.	Grafton,	Guardianship,	775
1853	Edwin	Cumberland, R. I.,	Foreign Sale,	776
1839	Edwin A.	Uxbridge,	Guardianship,	777
1857	Effie M.	Providence, R. I.,	Guardianship,	778
1851	Eleanor W.	Uxbridge,	Guardianship,	779
1820	Eliza B.	Northbridge,	Guardianship,	780
1737	Elizabeth	Uxbridge,	Guardianship,	781
1793	Elizabeth	Uxbridge,	Guardianship,	782
1796	Elizabeth	Uxbridge,	Will,	783
1841	Elizabeth	Douglas,	Guardianship,	784
1872	Elizabeth	Douglas,	Will,	785
1874	Elizabeth C.	Mendon,	Change of Name,	786
1860	Ella A.	Winchendon,	Guardianship,	787
1879	Ella M.	Grafton,	Guardianship,	788
1876	Ellen F.	Fitchburg,	Will,	789
1867	Ellen M.	Northbridge,	Guardianship,	790
1793	Ellis	Uxbridge,	Guardianship,	791
1838	Ellis	Northbridge,	Administration,	792

Year.	Name.	Residence.	Nature.	Case.
1838	ALDRICH, Emeline	Northbridge,	Guardianship,	793
1852	Emeline	Douglas,	Administration,	794
1867	Emma F.	Northbridge,	Guardianship,	795
1873	Emma F.	Northbridge,	Will,	796
1852	Emma I.	Uxbridge,	Guardianship,	797
1869	Emma I.	Oxford,	Guardianship,	798
1834	Enoch	Uxbridge,	Administration,	799
1826	Ephraim	Uxbridge,	Will,	800
1795	Esek	Northbridge,	Guardianship,	801
1793	Eunice	Uxbridge,	Guardianship,	802
1840	Ezra	Douglas,	Administration,	803
1829	Fanny	Douglas,	Guardianship,	804
1872	Frances	Westmoreland, N. H.,	Adoption, etc.,	805
1870	Frances M.	Webster,	Guardianship,	806
1847	Franklin A.	Grafton,	Guardianship,	807
1795	Gardner	Northbridge,	Will,	808
1797	George	Mendon,	Will,	809
1848	George	Worcester,	Will,	810
1849	George C.	Northbridge,	Guardianship,	811
1847	George H.	Grafton,	Guardianship,	812
1838	George S.	Uxbridge,	Guardianship,	813
1841	George T.	Douglas,	Guardianship,	814
1844	George W.	Worcester,	Administration,	815
1862	George W.	Douglas,	Guardianship,	816
1839	Gilbert	Uxbridge,	Guardianship,	817
1840	Grosvenor	Uxbridge,	Guardianship,	818
1874	Grosvenor	Uxbridge,	Administration,	819
1874	Grosvenor	Uxbridge,	Guardianship,	820
1822	Gustavus	Mendon,	Administration,	821
1796	Hannah	Mendon,	Guardianship,	822
1862	Hannah	Blackstone,	Will,	823
1843	Hannah I.	Mendon,	Guardianship,	824
1879	Hannah K.	Grafton,	Administration,	825
1855	Hannibal S.	Westborough,	Administration,	826
1841	Harriet	Douglas,	Guardianship,	827
1850	Harriet	Uxbridge,	Administration,	828
1841	Harrison G.	Charlton,	Guardianship,	829
1866	Hattie	Webster,	Guardianship,	830
1878	Henry C.	Uxbridge,	Administration,	831
1879	Herbert A.	Sutton,	Guardianship,	832
1874	Horatio	Uxbridge,	Administration,	833
1880	Hosea	Charlton,	Administration,	834
1880	Hosea	Uxbridge,	Administration,	835
1820	Huldah	Northbridge,	Guardianship,	836
1869	Huldah	Northbridge,	Will,	837

Year.	Name.	Residence.	Nature.	Case.
1820	ALDRICH, Ira	Bolton,	Administration,	838
1874	Ira	Uxbridge,	Administration,	839
1879	Ira E.	Grafton,	Guardianship,	840
1788	Isaac	Upton,	Will,	841
1815	Israel	Bow, N. H.,	Will,	842
1831	Israel	Douglas,	Will,	843
1838	Jabez	Mendon,	Administration,	844
1753	Jacob	Mendon,	Will,	845
1777	Jacob	Uxbridge,	Will,	846
1868	Jacob	Uxbridge,	Administration,	847
1841	James M.	Douglas,	Guardianship,	848
1869	Jennie I.	Oxford,	Guardianship,	849
1781	Jeremiah	Northbridge,	Will,	850
1795	Jesse	Northbridge,	Guardianship,	851
1830	Jesse	Douglas,	Administration,	852
1845	Jesse	Uxbridge,	Administration,	853
1869	Jesse	Northbridge,	Guardianship,	854
1880	Jesse	Northbridge,	Administration,	854
1811	Jirah	Douglas,	Administration,	855
1796	Joab	Mendon,	Will,	856
1839	Joel	Uxbridge,	Will,	857
1758	John	Uxbridge,	Administration,	858
1792	John	Northbridge	Will,	859
1825	John	Douglas,	Administration,	860
1826	John	Douglas,	Guardianship,	861
1833	John	Douglas,	Partition,	860
1838	John	Northbridge,	Will,	862
1826	John, Jr.	Northbridge,	Administration,	863
1846	John A.	Uxbridge,	Guardianship,	864
1852	John A.	Uxbridge,	Administration,	865
1840	John M.	Charlton,	Administration,	866
1841	John M.	Charlton,	Guardianship,	867
1863	John M.	Milford,	Guardianship,	868
1878	John M.	Worcester,	Administration,	869
1844	John W.	Uxbridge,	Guardianship,	870
1737	Jonathan	Uxbridge,	Guardianship,	871
1862	Jonathan	Worcester,	Will,	872
1738	Joseph	Uxbridge,	Guardianship,	873
1788	Joseph	Uxbridge,	Will,	874
1793	Joseph	Uxbridge,	Guardianship,	875
1825	Joseph	Douglas,	Administration,	876
1828	Joseph	Douglas,	Guardianship,	877
1838	Joseph	Douglas,	Will,	878
1846	Joseph	Uxbridge,	Will,	879
1846	Joseph	Uxbridge,	Guardianship,	880

(20)

YEAR.	NAME.	RESIDENCE.	NATURE.	CASE.
1862	ALDRICH, Joseph	Douglas,	Partition,	876
1874	Joseph	Northbridge,	Will,	881
1851	Joseph C.	Cumberland, R. I.,	Will,	882
1790	Joshua	Uxbridge,	Will,	883
1850	Joshua	Uxbridge,	Guardianship,	884
1857	Judith	Uxbridge,	Administration,	885
1863	Julia M.	Milford,	Guardianship,	886
1869	Lamond	Uxbridge,	Administration,	887
1839	Leander H.	Uxbridge,	Guardianship,	888
1842	Levi M.	Charlton,	Guardianship,	889
1847	Lewis	Grafton,	Guardianship,	890
1857	Lewis	Grafton,	Administration,	891
1840	Lois	Douglas,	Guardianship,	892
1793	Lovell	Uxbridge,	Guardianship,	893
1829	Lucina P.	Douglas,	Guardianship,	894
1839	Lucina P.	Burrillville, R. I.,	Administration,	895
1866	Lucy D.	Winchendon,	Administration,	896
1804	Luke	Mendon,	Administration,	897
1815	Luke	Mendon,	Will,	898
1867	Luke	Mendon,	Will,	899
1824	Lydia	Uxbridge,	Will,	900
1842	Lyman	Northbridge,	Will,	901
1855	Lyman	Northbridge,	Administration,	902
1874	Lyman P.	Northbridge,	Guardianship,	903
1856	Madison M.	Worcester,	Will,	904
1801	Marcus	Milford,	Guardianship,	905
1807	Marcus	Milford,	Administration,	906
1860	Marcus A.	Winchendon,	Guardianship,	907
1845	Marcus M.	Mendon,	Guardianship,	908
1855	Marcus M.	Northbridge,	Guardianship,	909
1864	Marcus M.	Northbridge,	Administration,	910
1820	. Marcy	Northbridge,	Guardianship,	911
1869	Maria	Northbridge,	Administration,	912
1777	Mark	Mendon,	Administration,	913
1829	Martha	Bolton,	Guardianship,	914
1850	Martha	Bolton,	Will,	915
1878	Martha B.	Upton,	Administration,	916
1821	Mary	Uxbridge,	Will,	917
1829	Mary	Douglas,	Administration,	918
1832	Mary	Mendon,	Guardianship,	919
1842	Mary	Northbridge,	Will,	920 .
1853	Mary	Cumberland, R. I.,	Foreign Sale,	921
1867	Mary	Oxford,	Administration,	922
1869	Mary B.	Westborough,	Will,	923
1839	Mary J.	Uxbridge,	Guardianship,	924

(21)

Year	Name.	Residence.	Nature	Case.
1774	ALDRICH, Mehitable	Mendon,	Administration,	925
1877	Melecent F.	Upton,	Administration,	926
1870	Milla	Blackstone,	Will,	927
1793	Molly	Uxbridge,	Guardianship,	928
1826	Molly	Douglas,	Guardianship,	929
1762	Moses	Mendon,	Will,	930
1853	Moses	Cumberland, R. I.,	Foreign Sale,	931
1841	Mowry A.	Charlton,	Guardianship,	932
1860	Nancy	Winchendon,	Guardianship,	933
1786	Nathan	Uxbridge,	Administration,	934
1872	Nathan	Uxbridge,	Will,	935
1874	Nathan	Woodstock, Conn.,	Foreign Will,	936
1815	Nathan C.	Mendon,	Guardianship,	937
1866	Nathan C.	Mendon,	Will,	938
1840	Nathaniel	Uxbridge,	Administration,	939
1843	Nathaniel	Uxbridge,	Partition,	939
1803	Nehemiah	Uxbridge,	Will,	940
1803	Nehemiah	Uxbridge,	Guardianship,	941
1812	Noah	Douglas,	Will,	942
1829	Noah	Douglas,	Will,	943
1814	Obadiah	Uxbridge,	Will,	944
1793	Olive	Uxbridge,	Guardianship,	945
1838	Olive	Northbridge,	Guardianship,	946
1776	Oliver	Douglas,	Guardianship,	947
1838	Orrice C.	Northbridge,	Guardianship,	948
1874	Otis	Blackstone,	Will,	949
1871	Paine	Worcester,	Administration,	950
1855	Pardon	Grafton,	Guardianship,	951
1857	Pardon	Grafton,	Will,	951
1858	Pardon	Grafton,	Partition,	951
1847	Pardon W.	Grafton,	Guardianship,	952
1796	Patience	Mendon,	Guardianship,	953
1834	Paul	Northbridge,	Will,	954
1874	Paul	Blackstone,	Administration,	955
1858	Peleg	Northbridge,	Will,	956
1748	Peter	Uxbridge,	Will,	957
1772	Peter	Mendon,	Guardianship,	958
1799	Peter	Northbridge,	Will,	959
1817	Phebe	Douglas,	Guardianship,	960
1826	Phebe	Douglas,	Guardianship,	961
1836	Phebe A.	Mendon,	Guardianship,	962
1827	Phila	Uxbridge,	Will,	963
1762	Philip	Mendon,	Guardianship,	964
1821	Phinehas	Mendon,	Administration,	965
1879	Phœbe	Mendon,	Administration,	966

Year.	Name.	Residence.	Nature.	Case.
1817	ALDRICH, Pliny	Douglas,	Guardianship,	967
1841	Prudence	Douglas,	Guardianship,	968
1796	Rachel	Northbridge,	Guardianship,	969
1841	Rachel	Mendon,	Will,	970
1793	Relief	Uxbridge,	Guardianship,	971
1777	Rizpah	Mendon,	Guardianship,	972
1796	Robert	Cumberland, R. I.,	Will,	973
1879	Robert E.	Sutton,	Guardianship,	974
1877	Rosa E. E.	Oxford,	Adoption, etc.,	975
1826	Roxalana	Douglas,	Guardianship,	976
1857	Royal	Oxford,	Will,	977
1833	Rufus	Mendon,	Administration,	978
1834	Rufus	Mendon,	Pension,	979
1835	Rufus	Mendon,	Partition,	978
1838	Rufus M.	Northbridge,	Guardianship,	980
1803	Ruth	Uxbridge,	Guardianship,	981
1829	Ruth	Douglas,	Guardianship,	982
1847	Sally	Blackstone,	Administration,	983
1869	Sally	Worcester,	Administration,	984
1877	Sally	Uxbridge,	Administration,	985
1832	Sally Ann	Mendon,	Administration,	986
1737	Samuel	Uxbridge,	Guardianship,	987
1766	Samuel	Upton,	Will,	988
1814	Samuel	Northbridge,	Will,	989
1820	Samuel	Northbridge,	Will,	990
1846	Samuel T.	Uxbridge,	Guardianship,	991
1855	Samuel T.	Northbridge,	Guardianship,	992
1873	Samuel T.	Northbridge,	Will,	993
1844	Samuel W.	Northbridge,	Administration,	994
1857	Samuel W.	Grafton,	Guardianship,	995
1867	Samuel W.	Northbridge,	Guardianship,	996
1778	Sarah	Uxbridge,	Will,	997
1795	Sarah	Northbridge,	Guardianship,	998
1815	Sarah	Mendon,	Guardianship,	999
1838	Sarah	Mendon,	Will,	1000
1862	Sarah	Uxbridge,	Will,	1001
1877	Sarah	Keene, N. H.,	Foreign Will,	1002
1839	Sarah D.	Uxbridge,	Guardianship,	1003
1867	Sarah E.	Northbridge,	Guardianship,	1004
1867	Savel	Uxbridge,	Administration,	1005
1815	Scammel	Mendon,	Guardianship,	1006
1869	Scammell	Mendon,	Will,	1007
1737	Seth	Uxbridge,	Will,	1008
1775	Seth	Uxbridge,	Will,	1009
1818	Seth	Uxbridge,	Will,	1010

Year.	Name.	Residence.	Nature.	Case.
1839	ALDRICH, Seth	Douglas,	Administration,	1011
1865	Seth	Uxbridge,	Will,	1012
1824	Seth, Jr.	Uxbridge,	Will,	1013
1763	Silas	Mendon,	Guardianship,	1014
1838	Silas	Mendon,	Guardianship,	1015
1804	Simeon	Petersham,	Administration,	1016
1879	Smith	Blackstone,	Will,	1017
1778	Solomon	Dudley,	Administration,	1018
1844	Solomon C.	Uxbridge,	Guardianship,	1019
1841	Sophia	Douglas,	Guardianship,	1020
1870	Sophia W.	Worcester,	Will,	1021
1795	Stephen	Northbridge,	Will,	1022
1855	Stephen	Uxbridge,	Will,	1023
1879	Susan F.	Sutton,	Guardianship,	1024
1863	Susan S.	Milford,	Guardianship,	1025
1836	Sylvanus A.	Mendon,	Guardianship,	1026
1881	Sylvanus B.	Upton,	Administration,	1027
1870	Sylvester W.	Northbridge,	Guardianship,	1028
1832	Tamar	Mendon,	Administration,	1029
1874	Theodore W.	Mendon,	Change of Name,	1030
1826	Thomas	Holden,	Administration,	1031
1876	Thomas	Uxbridge,	Guardianship,	1032
1880	Thomas H.	Uxbridge,	Change of Name,	1033
1843	Tiddeman	Mendon,	Guardianship,	1034
1809	Timothy	Upton,	Administration,	1035
1858	Welcome	Sutton,	Will,	1036
1868	Welcome	Northbridge,	Will,	1037
1821	Wheeler	Mendon,	Guardianship,	1038
1879	Wheeler	Upton,	Administration,	1039
1879	Wheeler	Uxbridge,	Will,	1040
1839	Willard	Uxbridge,	Will,	1041
1840	William	Worcester,	Guardianship,	1042
1843	William	Mendon,	Will,	1043
1873	William	Uxbridge,	Will,	1044
1832	William A.	Mendon,	Guardianship,	1045
1838	William H.	Mendon,	Guardianship,	1046
1843	William II.	Mendon,	Guardianship,	1047
1863	William H.	Milford,	Guardianship,	1048
1870	William II.	Northbridge,	Guardianship,	1049
1857	William T.	Grafton,	Guardianship,	1050
1795	Willis	Northbridge,	Guardianship,	1051
1866	Wilson W.	Smithfield, R. I.,	Administration,	1052
1879	Winfield W.	Sutton,	Guardianship,	1053
1795	Winter	Northbridge,	Guardianship,	1054
1799	Winter	Northbridge,	Administration,	1055

1795	ALDRICH, Zacheus	Northbridge,	Guardianship,	1056
1880	ALEXANDER, Alfred L.	Fitchburg,	Administration,	1057
1876	Amy	Webster,	Administration,	1058
1804	Asa	Westminster,	Guardianship,	1059
1804	Calvin	Westminster,	Guardianship,	1060
1852	Cincinnatus	Worcester,	Administration,	1061
1837	Dan	Mendon,	Guardianship,	1062
1857	Eleanor	Brookfield,	Guardianship,	1063
1837	Elias	Mendon,	Guardianship,	1064
1871	Everett T.	Worcester,	Guardianship,	1065
1840	Ezekiel	Upton,	Administration,	1066
1746	Francis	Lunenburg,	Will,	1067
1870	Frank E.	Worcester,	Will,	1068
1838	James, Jr.	Shrewsbury,	Will,	1069
1873	Jennie F.	Providence, R. I.,	Guardianship,	1070
1828	John	Milford,	Guardianship,	1071
1753	Joseph	Mendon,	Administration,	1072
1840	Joseph W.	Upton,	Guardianship,	1073
1867	Lucy	Worcester,	Guardianship,	1074
1837	Mason	Mendon,	Guardianship,	1075
1823	Perez	Western,	Administration,	1076
1804	Polly	Westminster,	Guardianship,	1077
1837	Rhoda	Mendon,	Guardianship,	1078
1840	Silas L.	Upton,	Guardianship,	1079
1841	Silvia A.	Mendon,	Guardianship,	1080
1840	Thirza	Upton,	Administration,	1081
1837	Timothy, Jr.	Mendon,	Administration,	1082
1762	William	Mendon,	Guardianship,	1083
1788	William	Lunenburg,	Will,	1084
1817	William	Upton,	Will,	1085
1783	ALFRED, Joanna	Lancaster,	Will,	1086
1857	ALGER, Abiel	Winchendon,	Will,	1087
1867	Benjamin	Winchendon,	Administration,	1088
1863	Edward	Winchendon,	Administration,	1089
1871	Franklin	Winchendon,	Guardianship,	1090
1870	George	Winchendon,	Will,	1091
1849	George W.	Winchendon,	Administration,	1092
1831	James	Oxford,	Administration,	1093
1833	James	Oxford,	Guardianship,	1094
1836	James	Oxford,	Administration,	1095
1856	James	Oxford,	Partition,	1093
1864	Leonidas	Fitchburg,	Administration,	1096
1879	Nathan	Winchendon,	Will,	1097
1822	Seth	Mendon,	Will,	1098
1873	Sylvia	Winchendon,	Administration,	1099

Year.	Name.	Residence.	Nature.	Case.
1850	ALGER, Warren	Winchendon,	Guardianship,	1100
1867	William B.	Winchendon,	Guardianship.	1101
1826	ALLARD, Achsah	Gerry,	Guardianship,	1102
1778	Andrew	Holden,	Administration,	1103
1779	Andrew	Holden,	Guardianship,	1104
1826	Banister	Gerry,	Guardianship,	1105
1862	Charles W.	Ashburnham,	Administration,	1106
1826	Christopher D.	Gerry,	Guardianship,	1107
1842	Deliza	Southbridge,	Will,	1108
1842	Eliza A.	Southbridge,	Guardianship,	1109
1826	Horace	Gerry,	Guardianship,	1110
1779	Isaac	Holden,	Guardianship,	1111
1842	Jane E.	Southbridge,	Guardianship,	1112
1826	Mary Ann	Gerry,	Guardianship,	1113
1826	Sam'l Richardson	Gerry,	Guardianship,	1114
1826	Sam'l Ross	Gerry,	Guardianship,	1115
	ALLEN AND ALLYN,			
1761	Aaron	Petersham,	Guardianship,	1116
1794	Aaron	Sturbridge,	Will,	1117
1818	Aaron	Sturbridge,	Will,	1118
1827	Abel	Sturbridge,	Will,	1119
1786	Abigail	Rutland,	Guardianship,	1120
1814	Abigail	Worcester,	Will,	1121
1829	Abigail	Oakham,	Will,	1122
1838	Abigail	Barre,	Will,	1123
1865	Abijah	Millbury,	Will,	1124
1880	Abilener	Worcester,	Will,	1125
1765	Abner	Sutton,	Guardianship,	1126
1806	Abner	Hubbardston,	Guardianship,	1127
1820	Abner	Charlton,	Administration,	1128
1830	Abner	Sturbridge,	Will,	1129
1839	Abner	Western,	Will,	1130
1841	Abner	Hubbardston,	Administration,	1131
1854	Abner	Princeton,	Administration,	1132
1857	Adelia C.	Medway,	Guardianship,	1133
1870	Albert	Millbury,	Administration,	1134
1880	Alexander H.	Mendon,	Administration,	1135
1850	Alfred M.	Worcester,	Guardianship,	1136
1867	Alice G.	Leominster,	Guardianship,	1137
1840	Alman	Princeton,	Will,	1138
1830	Alvan	Milford,	Will,	1139
1840	Alvan	Spencer,	Administration,	1140
1841	Alvan	Spencer,	Guardianship,	1141
1860	Alvan	Worcester,	Administration,	1142
1863	Alvan	Charlton,	Administration,	1143

Year.	Name.	Residence.	Nature.	Case.
	ALLEN and ALLYN,			
1859	Alvin	Mendon,	Administration,	1144
1840	Amazonia	Hubbardston,	Guardianship,	1145
1816	Ambrose	Barre,	Guardianship,	1146
1861	Amos C.	Blackstone,	Administration,	1147
1871	Amos C.	Blackstone,	Guardianship,	1148
1878	Amos C.	Worcester,	Administration,	1149
1837	Ann W.	Mendon,	Guardianship,	1150
1776	Anna	Sutton,	Guardianship,	1151
1810	Anna	Barre,	Guardianship,	1152
1810	Anna	Brookfield,	Guardianship,	1153
1832	Anna	Brookfield,	Administration,	1154
1847	Anna	Rutland,	Administration,	1155
1861	Anne B.	Sturbridge,	Will,	1156
1835	Arnold	North Brookfield,	Administration,	1157
1856	Arnold L.	Shrewsbury,	Will,	1158
1836	Artemas	Brookfield,	Administration,	1159
1837	Artemas	Brookfield,	Partition,	1159
1842	Artemas	Brookfield,	Guardianship,	1160
1863	Arthur W.	Hubbardston,	Guardianship,	1161
1787	Asa	Holden,	Guardianship,	1162
1853	Asa	Charlton,	Will,	1163
1879	Asa M.	Worcester,	Administration,	1164
1834	Ashbel	Spencer,	Administration,	1165
1842	Augusta M.	Brookfield,	Guardianship,	1166
1878	Augustus T.	Dudley,	Will,	1167
1879	Austin	Sturbridge,	Administration,	1168
1826	Belary T.	Hardwick,	Guardianship,	1169
1772	Benjamin	Western,	Will,	1170
1832	Benjamin, 2d	Rutland,	Administration,	1171
1873	Benjamin	Spencer,	Will,	1172
1806	Betsy	Hubbardston,	Guardianship,	1173
1815	Betsy	Mendon,	Will,	1174
1844	Betsy	Milford,	Administration,	1175
1881	Betsey	Brookfield,	Guardianship,	1176
1875	Betsy B.	Sturbridge,	Administration,	1177
1857	Breck	Hubbardston,	Administration,	1178
1786	Caleb	Mendon,	Administration,	1179
1838	Caleb	Sturbridge,	Guardianship,	1180
1839	Caleb	Sturbridge,	Pension,	1181
1786	Caleb (V.)	Mendon,	Guardianship,	1182
1863	Calvin	Hubbardston,	Administration,	1183
1801	Candice	Barre,	Guardianship,	1184
1823	Caroline	Athol,	Guardianship,	1185
1856	Caroline E.	Millbury,	Guardianship,	1186

YEAR.	NAME.	RESIDENCE.	NATURE.	CASE.
	ALLEN and ALLYN,			
1867	Caroline L.	Oakham,	Guardianship,	1187
1850	Caroline M.	Worcester,	Guardianship,	1188
1868	Caroline M.	Shrewsbury,	Administration,	1189
1849	Charles	Southbridge,	Administration,	1190
1869	Charles	Worcester,	Will,	1191
1873	Charles	Worcester,	Administration,	1192
1850	Charles D.	Worcester,	Guardianship,	1193
1845	Charles G.	Barre,	Guardianship,	1194
1839	Charles H.	Brookfield,	Guardianship,	1195
1849	Charles H.	Sturbridge,	Guardianship,	1196
1877	Charles L.	Worcester,	Administration,	1197
1865	Charles Y.	Worcester,	Guardianship,	1198
1870	Charlotte	Brookfield,	Administration,	1199
1848	Charlotte L.	Rutland,	Guardianship,	1200
1837	Charlotte M.	Lunenburg,	Guardianship,	1201
1859	Clarinda	West Brookfield,	Administration,	1202
1877	Clarinda H.	Grafton,	Administration,	1203
1873	Clarissa	Barre,	Administration,	1204
1870	Clarissa W.	Dudley,	Administration,	1205
1876	Collins	Oxford,	Administration,	1206
1757	Cumings	Petersham,	Guardianship,	1207
1767	Daniel	Athol,	Guardianship,	1208
1776	Daniel	Sutton,	Administration,	1209
1799	Daniel	Brookfield,	Will,	1210
1810	Daniel	Barre,	Guardianship,	1211
1876	Daniel	West Brookfield,	Will,	1212
1877	Daniel W.	West Boylston,	Administration,	1213
1876	Darius	Spencer,	Administration,	1214
1799	David	Hardwick,	Will,	1215
1820	David	Petersham,	Guardianship,	1216
1823	David	Petersham,	Administration,	1216
1835	David	Hardwick,	Will,	1217
1857	David	Leominster,	Administration,	1218
1874	David A.	Worcester,	Change of Name,	1219
1877	David A.	Winchendon,	Administration,	1220
1853	Delphia	Sturbridge,	Will,	1221
1820	Dennison R.	Barre,	Guardianship,	1222
1823	Dolly M.	Athol,	Guardianship,	1223
1779	Dorcas	Shrewsbury,	Will,	1224
1818	Dwight	Sturbridge,	Guardianship,	1225
1869	Dwight D.	Worcester,	Administration,	1226
1770	Ebenezer	Lancaster,	Will,	1227
1812	Ebenezer	Lancaster,	Will,	1228
1860	Eden	Charlton,	Administration,	1229

Year.	Name.	Residence.	Nature.	Case.
	ALLEN and ALLYN,			
1787	Edward	Brookfield,	Will,	1230
1776	Eleazer	Sutton,	Guardianship,	1231
1851	Eli	Warren,	Administration,	1232
1786	Elijah	Rutland,	Administration,	1233
1870	Elijah	Leominster,	Will,	1234
1784	Eliphalet	Sturbridge,	Administration,	1235
1793	Elisha	Princeton,	Administration,	1236
1818	Elisha	Sturbridge,	Administration,	1237
1816	Eliza	Barre,	Guardianship,	1238
1869	Eliza J.	Worcester,	Guardianship,	1239
1814	Elizabeth	Hubbardston,	Guardianship,	1240
1849	Elizabeth D.	Chelsea,	Guardianship,	1241
1839	Elizabeth L.	Brookfield,	Guardianship,	1242
1837	Elizabeth P.	Lunenburg,	Guardianship,	1243
1868	Elmer Rogene	Oakham,	Adoption, etc.,	1244
1735	Elnathan	Shrewsbury,	Administration,	1245
1805	Elnathan	Shrewsbury,	Will,	1246
1845	Emary	Douglas,	Will,	1247
1864	Emeline D.	Worcester,	Administration,	1248
1842	Emery H.	Brookfield,	Guardianship,	1249
1876	Emery H.	Brookfield,	Administration,	1250
1865	Emily T.	Worcester,	Guardianship,	1251
1788	Enos	Paxton,	Administration,	1252
1828	Ephraim	Rutland,	Administration,	1253
1848	Ephraim	Hubbardston,	Will,	1254
1857	Ephraim	Hubbardston,	Administration,	1255
1849	Erastus	Charlton,	Administration,	1256
1811	Ethan	Sturbridge,	Administration,	1257
1871	Ethan	Worcester,	Will,	1258
1765	Eunice	Sutton,	Guardianship,	1259
1810	Eunice	Brookfield,	Guardianship,	1260
1833	Eunice	Brookfield,	Will,	1261
1858	Eunice	West Brookfield,	Will,	1262
1858	Eunice	North Brookfield,	Will,	1263
1813	Ezra	Milford,	Administration,	1264
1815	Ezra	Mendon,	Guardianship,	1265
1849	Ezra A.	Milford,	Administration,	1266
1793	Frances	Royalston,	Will,	1267
1870	Frances	Brookfield,	Administration,	1268
1880	Frances A.	Worcester,	Administration,	1269
1843	Frances Ann	Lunenburg,	Administration,	1270
1837	Frances N.	Lunenburg,	Guardianship,	1271
1832	Frances W.	Brattleborough, Vt.,	Foreign Sale,	1272
1861	Francis A.	West Brookfield,	Guardianship,	1273

(29)

Year.	Name.	Residence.	Nature.	Case.
	ALLEN AND ALLYN,			
1871	Francis D.	Sturbridge,	Administration,	1274
1853	Frank H.	Gardner,	Guardianship,	1275
1878	Frank W.	Warren,	Change of Name,	1276
1810	George	Brookfield,	Guardianship,	1277
1855	George	Gardner,	Administration,	1278
1876	George	Sutton,	Administration,	1279
1862	George A.	Burrillville, R. I.,	Administration,	1280
1874	George A.	Leominster,	Administration,	1281
1859	George C.	Barre,	Guardianship,	1282
1845	George E.	Barre,	Guardianship,	1283
1842	George H.	Brookfield,	Guardianship,	1284
1845	George S.	Barre,	Administration,	1285
1833	George W.	Brookfield,	Guardianship,	1286
1837	George W.	Sturbridge,	Guardianship,	1287
1839	George W.	Brookfield,	Administration,	1286
1871	George W.	West Brookfield,	Will,	1288
1853	Georgianna	Gardner,	Guardianship,	1289
1768	Hannah	Sutton,	Administration,	1290
1787	Hannah	Holden,	Guardianship,	1291
1813	Hannah	Sturbridge,	Will,	1292
1813	Hannah	Sturbridge,	Guardianship,	1293
1823	Hannah	Barre,	Will,	1294
1830	Hannah	Holden,	Will,	1295
1867	Hannah B.	Leominster,	Guardianship,	1296
1844	Harmonia	Sturbridge,	Will,	1297
1823	Harriet	Athol,	Guardianship,	1298
1880	Harriet W.	West Brookfield,	Will,	1299
1867	Harry T.	Worcester,	Guardianship,	1300
1865	Harvey	North Brookfield,	Administration,	1301
1814	Haskell	Barre,	Guardianship,	1302
1871	Hattie S.	Blackstone,	Guardianship,	1303
1875	Hellen L.	Barre,	Guardianship,	1304
1849	Henry	Sturbridge,	Will,	1305
1875	Henry N.	Barre,	Guardianship,	1306
1787	Hepsibah	Holden,	Guardianship,	1307
1842	Hepza	Holden,	Will,	1308
1862	Hezekiah	Sturbridge,	Will,	1309
1823	Hiram H.	Athol,	Guardianship,	1310
1852	Horace	Sturbridge,	Will,	1311
1820	Horatio	Barre,	Guardianship,	1312
1858	Irene	Shrewsbury,	Will,	1313
1844	Isaac	Bolton,	Will,	1314
1853	Isaac	West Brookfield,	Will,	1315
1879	Isaac G.	Sturbridge,	Administration,	1316

ALLEN AND ALLYN,

YEAR.	NAME.	RESIDENCE.	NATURE.	CASE.
1783	Israel	Shrewsbury	Will,	1317
1817	Israel	Sterling,	Will,	1318
1799	Jacob	Brookfield,	Guardianship,	1319
1799	James	Brookfield,	Guardianship,	1320
1823	James	Athol,	Administration,	1321
1836	James	Lunenburg,	Administration,	1322
1840	James	Spencer,	Pension,	1323
1855	James	Athol,	Administration,	1324
1858	James	Barre,	Will,	1325
1863	James	West Brookfield,	Administration,	1326
1872	James	Blackford City, Mont.,	Administration,	1327
1874	James C.	Worcester,	Change of Name,	1328
1852	James E.	West Boylston,	Guardianship,	1329
1842	James H.	Hubbardston,	Guardianship,	1330
1763	Jason	Brookfield,	Guardianship,	1331
1778	Jason	Brookfield,	Administration,	1332
1867	Jeannie C.	Leominster,	Guardianship,	1333
1861	Jennie F.	West Brookfield,	Guardianship,	1334
1846	Jerusha	Brookfield,	Will,	1335
1787	Jesse	Holden,	Administration,	1336
1787	Jesse	Holden,	Guardianship,	1337
1816	Jesse	Oakham,	Will,	1338
1765	John	Sutton,	Guardianship,	1339
1780	John	Oxford,	Administration,	1340
1788	John	Brookfield,	Guardianship,	1341
1803	John	Sturbridge,	Administration,	1342
1809	John	Brookfield,	Will,	1343
1811	John	Barre,	Will,	1344
1814	John	Barre,	Guardianship,	1345
1847	John	Brookfield,	Will,	1346
1863	John	Hubbardston,	Will,	1347
1865	John	Worcester,	Administration,	1348
1760	John, Jr.	Sutton,	Administration,	1349
1808	John, Jr.	Brookfield,	Administration,	1350
1879	John A.	Barre,	Administration,	1351
1865	John B.	Worcester,	Guardianship,	1352
1852	John D.	West Boylston,	Guardianship,	1353
1867	John E.	Oakham,	Guardianship,	1354
1843	John P.	Sturbridge,	Administration,	1355
1863	John P.	Barre,	Administration,	1356
1821	Jonas	Barre,	Administration,	1357
1822	Jonas	Royalston,	Administration,	1358
1826	Jonas	Hardwick,	Guardianship,	1359
1876	Jonas	Barre,	Will,	1360

YEAR.	NAME.	RESIDENCE.	NATURE.	CASE.
	ALLEN AND ALLYN,			
1750	Jonathan	Douglas,	Guardianship,	1361
1822	Jonathan	Barre,	Will,	1362
1871	Jonathan	Worcester,	Administration,	1363
1871	Jonathan	West Brookfield,	Guardianship,	1364
1876	Jonathan	West Brookfield,	Administration,	1364
1843	Jonathan W.	Oakham,	Administration,	1365
1793	Joseph	Hardwick,	Will,	1366
1802	Joseph	Mendon,	Will,	1367
1810	Joseph	Brookfield,	Guardianship,	1368
1822	Joseph	Hardwick,	Will,	1369
1825	Joseph	Brookfield,	Guardianship,	1370
1827	Joseph	Worcester,	Will,	1371
1834	Joseph	Hardwick,	Administration,	1372
1873	Joseph	Northborough,	Will,	1373
1783	Joseph, Jr.	Worcester,	Guardianship,	1374
1835	Joseph C.	Sturbridge,	Administration,	1375
1851	Joseph P.	West Boylston,	Administration,	1376
1852	Joseph P.	West Boylston,	Guardianship,	1377
1837	Joseph W.	Worcester,	Administration,	1378
1851	Josiah	Barre,	Will,	1379
1845	Josiah H.	Barre,	Guardianship,	1380
1870	Josiah W.	Worcester,	Administration,	1381
1857	Julia	Leominster,	Will,	1382
1851	Julia A. T.	Mendon,	Change of Name,	1383
1857	Julia B.	Medway,	Guardianship,	1384
1849	Julia D.	Sturbridge,	Guardianship,	1385
1871	Justus E.	Blackstone,	Guardianship,	1386
1875	Katie	Leominster,	Guardianship,	1387
1810	Keziah	Westborough,	Will,	1388
1866	Lambert	Worcester,	Administration,	1389
1852	Levi	Milford,	Administration,	1390
1782	Lewis	Leicester,	Administration,	1391
1853	Lewis	Northborough,	Will,	1392
1863	Lewis	Oakham,	Administration,	1393
1810	Liberty	Brookfield,	Guardianship,	1394
1865	Liberty	Shrewsbury,	Will,	1395
1827	Liberty B.	Brookfield,	Administration,	1396
1839	Liberty W.	Brookfield,	Guardianship,	1397
1859	Lilla A.	Barre,	Guardianship,	1398
1849	Lois	Sturbridge,	Administration,	1399
1813	Loren	Sturbridge,	Guardianship,	1400
1813	Louisa	Sturbridge,	Guardianship,	1401
1815	Lucinda	Mendon,	Guardianship,	1402
1861	Lucinda S.	Mendon,	Administration,	1403

(32)

Year.	Name.	Residence.	Nature.	Case.
	ALLEN and ALLYN,			
1880	Lucius S.	Worcester,	Will,	1404
1844	Lucy	Warren,	Administration,	1405
1844	Lucy	Warren,	Pension,	1406
1845	Lucy E.	Barre,	Guardianship,	1407
1867	Lucy M.	Oakham,	Guardianship,	1408
1837	Luther	Sterling,	Will,	1409
1815	Lydia	Mendon,	Will,	1410
1850	Lyman	Northborough,	Administration,	1411
1874	Margaret	Hanover, Conn.,	Adoption, etc.,	1412
1856	Margaret N.	Millbury,	Guardianship,	1413
1841	Martha A.	Spencer,	Guardianship,	1414
1861	Martha E.	West Brookfield,	Guardianship,	1415
1850	Martha L.	Worcester,	Guardianship,	1416
1852	Martha N.	West Boylston,	Guardianship,	1417
1817	Mary	Worcester,	Administration,	1418
1830	Mary	Brookfield,	Will,	1419
1838	Mary	Barre,	Guardianship,	1420
1853	Mary	Winchendon,	Administration,	1421
1857	Mary	Hubbardston,	Guardianship,	1422
1865	Mary	Barre,	Administration,	1420
1877	Mary	Fitchburg,	Administration,	1423
1820	Mary A.	Charlton,	Guardianship,	1424
1850	Mary E.	Worcester,	Guardianship,	1425
1852	Mary E.	West Boylston,	Guardianship,	1426
1863	Mary L.	Hubbardston,	Guardianship,	1427
1822	Mary S.	Hardwick,	Guardianship,	1428
1835	Mary S.	Hardwick,	Will,	1428
1823	Mary W.	Athol,	Guardianship,	1429
1825	Mehitable	Royalston,	Will,	1430
1841	Mehitable G.	Spencer,	Guardianship,	1431
1879	Melvin	Auburn,	Will,	1432
1848	Mercy	Sturbridge,	Administration,	1433
1837	Minerva E.	Mendon,	Guardianship,	1434
1857	Miriam	Barre,	Will,	1435
1786	Molly	Rutland,	Guardianship,	1436
1811	Moses	West Boylston,	Administration,	1437
1841	Moses	Sturbridge,	Will,	1438
1843	Moses	Hardwick,	Will,	1439
1746	Myron W.	Lowell,	Guardianship,	1440
1806	Nabby	Hubbardston,	Guardianship,	1441
1768	Nathan	Petersham,	Guardianship,	1442
1814	Nathan	Brookfield,	Administration,	1443
1831	Nathan	Barre,	Administration,	1444
1770	Nathaniel	Shrewsbury,	Will,	1445

(33)

YEAR.	NAME.	RESIDENCE.	NATURE.	CASE.
	ALLEN AND ALLYN,			
1838	Nathaniel	Grafton,	Administration,	1446
1800	Nehemiah	Oakham,	Will.	1447
1811	Nehemiah	Barre,	Will,	1448
1822	Nehemiah	Sturbridge,	Administration,	1449
1861	Nehemiah	Barre,	Administration,	1450
1864	Nehemiah	Barre,	Partition,	1450
1845	Noah	Shrewsbury,	Administration,	1451
1765	Obadiah	Sutton,	Guardianship,	1452
1781	Obadiah	Shrewsbury,	Will,	1453
1814	Oren	Sturbridge,	Administration,	1454
1871	Orlando F.	Blackstone,	Guardianship,	1455
1799	Otis	Brookfield,	Guardianship,	1456
1866	Otis	Barre,	Will,	1457
1877	Pamelia	Millbury,	Will,	1458
1847	Pardon	Warren,	Will,	1459
1835	Parker	Sturbridge,	Administration,	1460
1864	Patience G.	Webster,	Will,	1461
1818	Patty	Sturbridge,	Guardianship,	1462
1787	Pelatiah	Holden,	Guardianship,	1463
1820	Pelatiah	Holden,	Administration,	1464
1865	Perley	Sturbridge,	Will,	1465
1835	Persis	Brookfield,	Will,	1466
1823	Phebe A.	Athol,	Guardianship,	1467
1856	Philinda	Hardwick,	Guardianship,	1468
1803	Polly	Sturbridge,	Guardianship,	1469
1809	Polly	Brookfield,	Guardianship,	1470
1854	Prudence	Millbury,	Will,	1471
1839	Rachel	Worcester,	Will,	1472
1819	Reuben	Sturbridge,	Administration,	1473
1823	Reuben	Hardwick,	Administration,	1474
1858	Reuel C.	Milford,	Administration,	1475
1853	Robert	Mendon,	Will,	1476
1880	Ruby B.	Warren,	Administration,	1477
1810	Sally	Brookfield,	Guardianship,	1478
1816	Sally	Barre,	Guardianship,	1479
1855	Sally	Sterling,	Will,	1480
1799	Samuel	Northborough,	Will,	1481
1809	Samuel	Barre,	Administration,	1482
1810	Samuel	Barre,	Guardianship,	1483
1829	Samuel	Barre,	Administration,	1484
1830	Samuel	Worcester,	Will,	1485
1875	Samuel	Shrewsbury,	Will,	1486
1832	Samuel A.	Brattleborough, Vt.,	Foreign Sale,	1487
1864	Samuel H.	Grafton,	Will,	1488

(34)

YEAR.	NAME.	RESIDENCE.	NATURE.	CASE.
	ALLEN and ALLYN,			
1757	Sarah	Lancaster,	Administration,	1489
1863	Sarah	Leominster,	Will,	1490
1840	Sarah A.	Hubbardston,	Guardianship,	1491
1842	Sarah C.	Brookfield,	Guardianship,	1492
1823	Sarah P.	Athol,	Guardianship,	1493
1850	Seraph	New Braintree,	Administration,	1494
1834	Silas	Shrewsbury,	Will,	1495
1840	Silas	Leominster,	Administration,	1496
1873	Silas	Northborough,	Will,	1497
1763	Simeon	Sutton,	Guardianship,	1498
1803	Simeon	Sturbridge,	Guardianship,	1499
1806	Simeon	Hubbardston,	Administration,	1500
1844	Simeon	Sturbridge,	Will,	1501
1881	Simon	Paxton,	Will,	1502
1878	Simon B.	Grafton,	Administration,	1503
1776	Solomon	Sutton,	Guardianship,	1504
1785	Stephen	Grafton,	Will,	1505
1847	Sumner	Rutland,	Administration,	1506
1842	Susannah	Brookfield,	Guardianship,	1507
1807	Thankful	Shrewsbury,	Administration,	1508
1813	Timothy	Sturbridge,	Will,	1509
1817	Timothy	Millbury,	Administration,	1510
1856	Timothy B.	Millbury,	Administration,	1511
1860	Walter A.	West Brookfield,	Administration,	1512
1876	Waterman	Oxford,	Will,	1513
1879	Wilber	Spencer,	Administration,	1514
1852	Willard	Westminster,	Administration,	1515
1876	Willard E.	Worcester,	Will,	1516
1757	William	Grafton,	Will,	1517
1810	William	Barre,	Guardianship,	1518
1879	William C.	Worcester,	Administration,	1519
1823	William E.	Barre,	Guardianship,	1520
1878	William E.	Worcester,	Change of Name,	1521
1852	William P.	Gardner,	Administration,	1522
1876	William R.	Worcester,	Administration,	1523
1875	William T.	Leominster,	Will,	1524
1863	Willie	Fitchburg,	Guardianship,	1525
1878	Willie E.	Worcester,	Change of Name,	1526
1815	Willis	Mendon,	Guardianship,	1527
1808	Zebadiah	Barre,	Administration,	1528
1810	Zebadiah	Barre,	Guardianship,	1529
1826	Zebadiah	Barre,	Administration,	1530
1840	Zebadiah	Brookfield,	Administration,	1531
1842	Zebadiah	Brookfield,	Guardianship,	1532

	ALLEN and ALLYN,			
1845	Zenas C.	Barre,	Guardianship,	1533
1859	Zenas C.	Barre,	Administration,	1534
1820	Zilpha	Charlton,	Guardianship,	1535
1874	ALLEY, Frederick H.	Lunenburg,	Guardianship,	1536
1874	Joseph	Lunenburg,	Administration,	1537
1807	ALLIS, Sarah	Western,	Will,	1538
	ALLTON and ALTON,			
1866	John	Thompson, Conn.,	Administration,	1539
1778	William	Charlton,	Will,	1540
1836	AMBACH, Justina C.	Mendon,	Administration,	1541
1862	AMBLER, Ann S.	Milford,	Will,	1542
1872	Jeremiah D.	Milford,	Will,	1543
1839	Nathan	Millbury,	Guardianship,	1544
1862	AMES, Alfaretta V.	Athol,	Guardianship,	1545
1862	Andrew J.	Athol,	Guardianship,	1546
1874	Caroline	Berlin,	Administration,	1547
1822	Clarissa	Rutland,	Guardianship,	1548
1820	Daniel	Boylston,	Will,	1549
1840	Davis	Sturbridge,	Administration,	1550
1872	Edwin H.	Worcester,	Adoption, etc.,	1551
1840	Edwin J.	Sturbridge,	Guardianship,	1552
1872	Elijah	Charlton,	Administration,	1553
1840	Emily R.	Sturbridge,	Guardianship,	1554
1875	Eugene	Royalston,	Adoption, etc.,	1555
1880	Fannie M.	Westminster,	Will,	1556
1840	Hannah J.	Sturbridge,	Guardianship,	1557
1840	Harriet A.	Sturbridge,	Guardianship,	1558
1840	Hiram H.	Sturbridge,	Guardianship,	1559
1872	Horace H.	Worcester,	Administration,	1560
1874	Jacob	Fitchburg,	Will,	1561
1870	Joel	Fitchburg,	Administration,	1562
1810	John	Rutland,	Will,	1563
1811	John	Rutland,	Guardianship,	1564
1816	John	Barre,	Will,	1565
1840	John D.	Sturbridge,	Guardianship,	1566
1826	John P.	Barre,	Administration,	1567
1878	Joseph L.	Worcester,	Administration,	1568
1862	Juniatta C.	Athol,	Guardianship,	1569
1867	Laura J.	Fitchburg,	Administration,	1570
1863	Lucinda	Webster,	Will,	1571
1821	Lucy	Boylston,	Guardianship,	1572
1868	Luther	West Boylston,	Administration,	1573
1859	Martha	Lunenburg,	Will,	1574
1821	Mary	Boylston,	Guardianship,	1575

Year.	Name.	Residence.	Nature.	Case.
1822	AMES, Melissa	Rutland,	Guardianship,	1576
1853	Miriam	Southbridge,	Will,	1577
1871	Polly W.	West Boylston,	Administration,	1578
1866	Winifred	Worcester,	Adoption, etc.,	1579
	AMIDON, AMMIDOWN AND AMYDOWN,			
1755	Abigail	Hardwick,	Guardianship,	1580
1850	Adolphus	Southbridge,	Administration,	1581
1797	Allis	Hardwick,	Guardianship,	1582
1840	Andrew J.	Southbridge,	Guardianship,	1583
1836	Betsey	Southbridge,	Guardianship,	1584
1799	Caleb	Charlton,	Administration,	1585
1822	Caleb	Southbridge,	Administration,	1586
1855	Caleb	Southbridge,	Administration,	1587
1814	Callina	Dudley,	Guardianship,	1588
1825	Calvin	Southbridge,	Will,	1589
1822	Carlo	Southbridge,	Guardianship,	1590
1834	Carlo ·	Southbridge,	Administration,	1591
1869	Catherine H.	Southbridge,	Guardianship,	1592
1797	Cephrona	Hardwick,	Guardianship,	1593
1873	Dan	Ashford, Conn.,	Administration,	1594
1875	Debeann	Southbridge,	Will,	1595
1827	Deborah	Southbridge,	Will,	1596
1880	Deborah	Southbridge	Administration,	1597
1822	Deliza	Southbridge,	Guardianship,	1598
1842	Deliza	Southbridge,	Will,	1599
1802	Ebenezer	Dudley,	Administration,	1600
1803	Ebenezer	Dudley,	Guardianship,	1601
1865	Ebenezer D.	Southbridge,	Will,	1602
1865	Ebenezer D.	Southbridge,	Guardianship,	1603
1828	Elbridge	Southbridge,	Guardianship,	1604
1827	Elizabeth	Oxford,	Administration,	1605
1873	Elizabeth	Ashford, Conn.,	Administration,	1606
1875	Emeline S.	Southbridge,	Administration,	1607
1786	Ephraim	Oxford,	Administration,	1608
1865	Fanny L.	Southbridge,	Guardianship,	1609
1850	George A.	Southbridge,	Guardianship,	1610
1755	Hannah	Hardwick,	Guardianship,	1611
1797	Hannah	Hardwick,	Guardianship,	1612
1872	Hannah	Douglas,	Administration,	1613
1869	Henry C.	Southbridge,	Will,	1614
1862	Holdridge	Southbridge	Will,	1615
1789	Ichabod	Mendon,	Will,	1616
1838	Jedediah	Paxton,	Will,	1617
1813	Jeremiah	Oxford,	Will,	1618

YEAR.	NAME.	RESIDENCE.	NATURE.	CASE.
	AMIDON, AMMIDOWN AND AMYDOWN,			
1755	John	Hardwick,	Will,	1619
1755	John	Hardwick,	Guardianship,	1620
1814	John	Dudley,	Will,	1621
1814	John	Dudley,	Guardianship,	1622
1825	John	Hardwick,	Administration,	1623
1838	John	Southbridge,	Partition,	1621
1848	John	Southbridge,	Administration,	1624
1848	John	Southbridge,	Guardianship,	1625
1862	John	Hardwick,	Administration,	1626
1840	John P.	Southbridge,	Guardianship,	1627
1840	Jonathan P.	Southbridge,	Administration,	1628
1840	Judson	Southbridge,	Guardianship,	1629
1814	Julia	Dudley,	Guardianship,	1630
1835	Julina	Southbridge,	Will,	1631
1870	Lewis	Southbridge,	Administration,	1632
1874	Lewis	Southbridge,	Partition,	1632
1865	Lucian M.	Southbridge,	Guardianship,	1633
1854	Lucius E.	Southbridge,	Guardianship,	1634
1854	Lucius H.	Southbridge,	Administration,	1635
1865	Lucy	Webster,	Administration,	1636
1865	Lura J.	Hardwick,	Adoption, etc.,	1637
1835	Luther	Southbridge,	Will,	1638
1878	Luther	Southbridge,	Administration,	1639
1865	Malcolm	Southbridge,	Administration,	1640
1850	Marcus M.	Southbridge,	Guardianship,	1641
1876	Mila	Worcester,	Administration,	1642
1854	Nancy	Southbridge,	Administration,	1643
1814	Olive	Douglas,	Guardianship,	1644
1837	Olive	Southbridge,	Will,	1645
1848	Oliver	Southbridge,	Administration,	1646
1848	Oliver F.	Southbridge,	Guardianship,	1647
1828	Otis	Southbridge,	Will,	1648
1828	Otis	Southbridge,	Guardianship,	1649
1747	Philip	Oxford,	Will,	1650
1755	Philip	Hardwick,	Guardianship,	1651
1796	Philip	Hardwick,	Administration,	1652
1802	Phillip	Mendon,	Will,	1653
1878	Rebekah	Southbridge,	Will,	1654
1860	Ruth	Charlton,	Administration,	1655
1871	Salem R.	Toledo, O.,	Guardianship,	1656
1797	Sally	Hardwick,	Guardianship,	1657
1803	Samuel	Dudley,	Guardianship,	1658
1827	Samuel	Oxford,	Administration,	1659

Year.	Name.	Residence.	Nature.	Case.
	AMIDON, AMMIDOWN and AMYDOWN,			
1861	Samuel	Douglas,	Administration,	1660
1755	Sarah	Hardwick,	Guardianship,	1661
1847	Sarah	Southbridge,	Administration,	1662
1840	Sarah B.	Southbridge,	Guardianship,	1663
1840	Susan E.	Southbridge,	Guardianship,	1664
1869	William H.	Webster,	Guardianship,	1665
1866	AMSDEN, Albert A.	Petersham,	Guardianship,	1666
1773	Barzaleel	Petersham,	Guardianship,	1667
1852	Bezaleel	Dana,	Will,	1668
1862	Burrell	Dana,	Administration,	1669
1864	Carrie M.	Athol,	Guardianship,	1670
1843	Charles E.	Petersham,	Will,	1671
1864	Charles F.	Athol,	Guardianship,	1672
1868	C. Ellsworth	Athol,	Guardianship,	1673
1821	Daniel	Petersham,	Administration,	1674
1766	David	Southborough,	Will,	1675
1864	David	Petersham,	Administration,	1676
1850	Ebenezer	Dana,	Administration,	1677
1831	Ellis P.	Petersham,	Guardianship,	1678
1760	Ephraim	Leicester,	Administration,	1679
1864	Fenno E.	Athol,	Guardianship,	1680
1864	Festus F.	Athol,	Will,	1681
1864	Frances B.	Athol,	Guardianship,	1682
1866	Frank A.	Petersham,	Guardianship,	1683
1864	Frederick E.	Athol,	Guardianship,	1684
1869	Frederick W.	Dana,	Administration,	1685
1817	Galon	Southborough,	Guardianship,	1686
1868	Hero M.	Athol,	Guardianship,	1687
1767	Isaac	Rutland,	Administration,	1688
1770	Isaac	Rutland,	Guardianship,	1689
1772	Jacob	Petersham,	Administration,	1690
1773	Jacob	Petersham,	Guardianship,	1691
1830	Jacob	Dana,	Administration,	1692
1843	Jacob	Dana,	Administration,	1693
1773	Joel	Petersham,	Guardianship,	1694
1843	Joel F.	Dana,	Guardianship,	1695
1827	John	Southborough,	Administration,	1696
1831	Lauriston	Petersham,	Guardianship,	1697
1817	Lee	Southborough,	Guardianship,	1698
1864	Linda H.	Athol,	Guardianship,	1699
1831	Lucinda	Petersham,	Guardianship,	1700
1849	Lucy	Southborough,	Administration,	1701
1874	Lucy	Petersham,	Will,	1702

(39—SERIES A.)

Year.	Name.	Residence.	Nature.	Case.
1863	AMSDEN, Luther	Dana,	Will,	1703
1797	Mary	Petersham,	Will,	1704
1864	Mary E.	Athol,	Guardianship,	1705
1869	Nellie L.	Dana,	Guardianship,	1706
1832	Silas	Southborough,	Administration,	1707
1816	Sukey	Lancaster,	Guardianship,	1708
1878	Susie E.	Clinton,	Adoption, etc.,	1709
1811	Thomas	Dana,	Administration,	1710
1867	Warren H.	Athol,	Will,	1711
1843	Washington H.	Dana,	Guardianship,	1712
1833	Willard	Southborough,	Will,	1713
1872	ANASTASE, Pasquall	Worcester,	Change of Name,	1714
1869	ANDERSON, Abbie E.	New Braintree,	Guardianship,	1715
1843	Almeda	Hardwick,	Guardianship,	1716
1880	Almira	Hardwick,	Will,	1717
1833	Anna	New Braintree,	Will,	1718
1765	Charity	Lancaster,	Will,	1719
1869	Charles	New Braintree,	Will,	1720
1879	Charles	Sturbridge,	Will,	1721
1865	Eunice	Templeton,	Will,	1722
1874	James	Sutton,	Will,	1723
1822	John	New Braintree,	Will,	1724
1849	John	Templeton,	Administration,	1725
1871	John F.	Athol,	Will,	1726
1868	Sarah E.	Thompson, Conn.,	Administration,	1727
1850	Susannah	Templeton,	Will,	1728
1842	Timothy P.	Hardwick,	Administration,	1729
1867	William	Hardwick,	Will,	1730
1868	Willie H.	Thompson, Conn.,	Guardianship,	1731
1841	(No name given)	Petersham,	Guardianship,	1732
1876	ANDRE, Frederick	Webster,	Administration,	1733
1823	ANDREWS, Alonzo	Fitchburg,	Guardianship,	1734
1760	Anna	Worcester,	Guardianship,	1735
1873	Annie M.	Leicester,	Adoption, etc.,	1736
1834	Asa	Millbury,	Will,	1737
1844	Asa	Boylston,	Will,	1738
1844	Asa, 2d	Millbury,	Administration,	1739
1859	Asaph	Shrewsbury,	Will,	1740
1812	Benjamin	Worcester,	Administration,	1741
1821	Caleb A.	Westborough,	Guardianship,	1742
1877	Caroline A.	Leominster,	Administration,	1743
1838	Catharine F.	Westborough,	Guardianship,	1744
1877	Cynthia L.	Southborough,	Will,	1745
1823	Daniel	Fitchburg,	Guardianship,	1746
1826	Daniel	Boylston,	Will,	1747

Year.	Name.		Residence.	Nature.	Case.
1838	ANDREWS, Daniel		Boylston,	Administration,	1748
1820	Dennis		Boylston,	Will,	1749
1862	Edward A.		Shrewsbury,	Administration,	1750
1869	Eleanor S.		Worcester,	Administration,	1751
1857	Elizabeth		Warren,	Administration,	1752
1858	Elizabeth		Warren,	Pension,	1753
1871	Eunice		Southborough,	Will,	1754
1864	Ferdinand		Boylston,	Administration,	1755
1844	Frederick		Boylston,	Guardianship,	1756
1804	George		Westborough,	Guardianship,	1757
1831	George		Westborough,	Will,	1758
1863	George B.		Fitchburg,	Guardianship,	1759
1873	Georgianna M.		North Bridgewater,	Adoption, etc.,	1760
1871	Herbert W.		Fitchburg,	Guardianship,	1761
1873	Ida M.		Shrewsbury,	Guardianship,	1762
1852	James		Worcester,	Administration,	1763
1861	Jeremiah		Fitchburg,	Administration,	1764
1822	John		Boylston,	Will,	1765
1872	John		Worcester,	Administration,	1766
1874	John		Fitchburg,	Will,	1767
1879	John		Boylston,	Administration,	1768
1823	Joshua		Milford,	Administration,	1769
1852	Jotham		Boylston,	Will,	1770
1823	Leander		Fitchburg,	Guardianship,	1771
1838	Lucius C.		Westborough,	Guardianship,	1772
1876	Lucius C.		Westborough,	Administration,	1773
1817	Lucy		Boylston,	Administration,	1774
1874	Lucy M.		New Braintree,	Will,	1775
1823	Lysander		Fitchburg,	Guardianship,	1776
1860	Mary E.		Warren, R. I.,	Guardianship,	1777
1847	Mary K.		New London, Conn.,	Foreign Sale,	1778
1814	Mary M.		Lancaster,	Guardianship,	1779
1823	Nancy		Fitchburg,	Guardianship,	1780
1822	Nathan		Fitchburg,	Administration,	1781
1845	Nathaniel		Westborough,	Will,	1782
1857	Otis C.		Northbridge,	Guardianship,	1783
1862	Patty		Westborough,	Administration,	1784
1857	Pembroke H.		Northbridge,	Guardianship,	1785
1823	Porter		Fitchburg,	Guardianship,	1786
1789	Robert		Boylston,	Will,	1787
1862	Robert		Boylston,	Will,	1788
1866	Sabrina		Petersham,	Guardianship,	1789
1855	Sally		Warren,	Guardianship,	1790
1760	Samuel		Worcester,	Administration,	1791
1785	Samuel		Westborough,	Administration,	1792

YEAR.	NAME.	RESIDENCE.	NATURE.	CASE.
1814	ANDREWS, Samuel	Lancaster,	Will,	1793
1838	Stephen	Westborough,	Guardianship,	1794
1794	Thomas	Boylston,	Administration,	1795
1824	Thomas	Westborough,	Will,	1796
1823	Thomas D.	Boylston,	Guardianship,	1797
1838	Thomas E.	Westborough,	Administration,	1798
1838	Thomas E.	Westborough,	Guardianship,	1799
1844	Trial	Milford,	Administration,	1800
1806	Turel	Unknown,	Guardianship,	1801
1874	Willard	Boylston,	Administration,	1802
1871	(No name given)	Dalton,	Adoption, etc.,	1803
1879	ANGELL, Brown	Burrillville, R. I.,	Foreign Will,	1804
1825	Charles	Douglas,	Guardianship,	1805
1840	Charles A.	Douglas,	Guardianship,	1806
1859	Cyrus	Leominster,	Change of Name,	1807
1869	Edwin E.	Petersham,	Guardianship,	1808
1827	George	Southbridge,	Administration,	1809
1825	Nelson	Douglas,	Guardianship,	1810
1855	Randall	Smithfield, R. I.,	Will,	1811
1865	Rhoades	Pomfret, Conn.,	Administration,	1812
1818	Rufus	Sutton,	Administration,	1813
1845	Stephen B.	Westborough,	Administration,	1814
1825	Ziba	Douglas,	Administration,	1815
	ANGIER AND ANGER,			
1846	Anna	Shrewsbury,	Guardianship,	1816
1858	Anna	Shrewsbury,	Administration,	1816
1869	Austin	Worcester,	Will,	1817
1839	Benjamin	Shrewsbury,	Administration,	1818
1838	Calvin	Southborough,	Administration,	1819
1816	Charles	Southborough,	Administration,	1820
1870	Charles	Southbridge,	Administration,	1821
1845	Elizabeth	Southborough,	Administration,	1822
1850	Gabriel P.	Worcester,	Administration,	1823
1793	John	Southborough,	Will,	1824
1838	Marshall B.	Southborough,	Guardianship,	1825
1807	Mary	Southborough,	Will,	1826
1856	Mary	Worcester,	Administration,	1827
1869	ANGLUN, Daniel	Worcester,	Administration,	1828
1831	ANNETS, Mary	Southborough,	Guardianship,	1829
1831	William	Southborough,	Will,	1830
1872	ANSELLO, Joseph	Worcester,	Change of Name,	1831
1864	ANSON, Frederick S.	Milford,	Guardianship,	1832
1877	Manning, W.	Uxbridge,	Will,	1833
1841	(No name given)	Petersham,	Guardianship,	1834

Year.	Name.	Residence.	Nature.	Case.
	ANTHONY AND ANTONY,			
1839	Abigail P.	Uxbridge,	Guardianship,	1835
1871	Arnold	Worcester,	Administration,	1836
1834	Benjamin	Paxton,	Administration,	1837
1835	Benjamin H.	Paxton,	Guardianship,	1838
1827	Caleb	Paxton,	Administration,	1839
1828	Caleb	Paxton,	Partition,	1839
1835	Charles	Paxton,	Guardianship,	1840
1874	Elisha	Uxbridge,	Guardianship,	1841
1877	Elisha	Uxbridge,	Administration,	1841
1841	Hezekiah	Paxton,	Will,	1842
1828	Isaac	Paxton,	Partition,	1843
1828	Jacob	Paxton,	Partition,	1844
1864	Jerome F.	Uxbridge,	Administration,	1845
1881	Joseph	Paxton,	Administration,	1846
1835	Rebecca	Paxton,	Will,	1847
1844	Reuben	Uxbridge,	Administration,	1848
1853	Smith W.	Milford,	Administration,	1849
1862	APPERSON, James	Worcester,	Administration,	1850
1880	APPLEBY, Mary A.	Oxford,	Will,	1851
1795	APPLETON, Joseph	Brookfield,	Administration,	1852
1795	Mary A.	Brookfield,	Guardianship,	1853
1795	Nabby E.	Brookfield,	Guardianship,	1854
1795	Phineas	Brookfield,	Guardianship,	1855
1795	Sally H.	Brookfield,	Guardianship,	1856
1872	Samuel A.	Southborough,	Guardianship,	1857
1795	William	Brookfield,	Guardianship,	1858
1872	ARBET, Florence	Spencer,	Administration,	1859
1878	ARBING, Mabel	Unknown,	Adoption, etc.,	1860
1784	ARCHER, Benjamin	Uxbridge,	Administration,	1861
1872	Charles F.	Worcester,	Change of Name,	1862
1872	Charles T. W.	Worcester,	Change of Name,	1863
1839	Rosilinda	Lunenburg,	Guardianship,	1864
1878	ARCHIBALD, Alfred G.	Petersham,	Guardianship,	1865
1850	Asa	Leominster,	Will,	1866
1878	Everett W.	Petersham,	Guardianship,	1867
1878	Herbert H.	Petersham,	Guardianship,	1868
1877	John H.	Petersham,	Administration,	1869
1878	Joseph F.	Petersham,	Guardianship,	1870
1782	ARG, Nathaniel	Athol,	Administration,	1871
	ARMES see ARMS.			
1870	ARMINGTON, William P.	St. Johnsbury, Vt.,	Guardianship,	1872
1871	ARMITAGE, John	Auburn,	Will,	1873
1872	ARMOR, Hannah	Mendon,	Guardianship,	1874

Year	Name.	Residence.	Nature	Case.
	ARMS AND ARMES,			
1838	Elizabeth G.	Petersham,	Guardianship,	1875
1838	Hutchins H.	Petersham,	Guardianship,	1876
1825	Josiah L.	Petersham,	Guardianship,	1877
1867	Lathrop	Southbridge,	Administration,	1878
1867	Mary	Southbridge	Guardianship,	1879
1838	Sophia H.	Petersham,	Guardianship,	1880
1867	William H.	Southbridge,	Guardianship,	1881
1855	ARMSBY, Benjamin W.	Sutton,	Administration,	1882
1818	Enos	Sutton,	Will,	1883
1878	Harriet E.	Sutton,	Administration,	1884
1879	Horace	Millbury,	Administration,	1885
1858	Joshua	Sutton,	Administration,	1886
1873	Joshua M. C.	Worcester,	Administration,	1887
1873	Lewis	Millbury,	Will,	1888
1875	Mary B.	Millbury,	Administration,	1889
1859	Sarah	Sutton,	Administration,	1890
1734	ARMSTRONG, Martha	Roxbury,	Administration,	1891
1879	ARNOLD, Abby	Royalston,	Guardianship,	1892
1793	Abigail	Shrewsbury,	Administration,	1893
1869	Abigail	Uxbridge,	Will,	1894
1872	Abigail	Paxton,	Administration,	1895
1845	Abigail F.	Burrillville, R. I.,	Guardianship,	1896
1835	Ahab	Leicester,	Administration,	1897
1845	Albert T.	Burrillville, R. I.,	Guardianship,	1898
1877	Alpha	Royalston,	Will,	1899
1822	Amasa	Mendon,	Administration,	1900
1880	Anna L.	Worcester,	Guardianship,	1901
1808	Betsey	Lancaster,	Guardianship,	1902
1839	Charles	Douglas,	Guardianship,	1903
1875	Charles J.	Worcester,	Guardianship,	1904
1842	Charlotte	Douglas,	Administration,	1905
1875	Cyrus	Worcester,	Administration,	1906
1841	Daniel	Thompson, Conn.,	Will,	1907
1872	Dwight E.	Fitchburg,	Guardianship,	1908
1839	Eber	Douglas,	Administration,	1909
1860	Edward M.	Douglas,	Guardianship,	1910
1826	Elisha	Uxbridge,	Will,	1911
1845	Emeline H.	Burrillville, R. I.,	Guardianship,	1912
1878	Emma I.	Douglas,	Administration,	1913
1805	Esek	Western,	Administration,	1914
1847	Frances	Southborough,	Guardianship,	1915
1872	Frank A.	Fitchburg,	Guardianship,	1916
1875	Freddie J.	Worcester,	Guardianship,	1917
1845	George L.	Burrillville, R. I.,	Guardianship,	1918

Year.	Name.	Residence.	Nature.	Case.
1783	ARNOLD, Gideon	Mendon,	Guardianship,	1919
1875	Harry W.	Worcester,	Guardianship,	1920
1860	Ira W.	Douglas,	Guardianship,	1921
1847	Jackson	Southborough,	Will,	1922
1875	James H.	Lancaster,	Administration,	1923
1838	John	Burrillville, R, I.,	Will,	1924
1777	Joseph	Grafton,	Will,	1925
1865	Joseph T.	Royalston,	Will,	1926
1876	Julia A.	Worcester,	Guardianship,	1927
1862	Laura B.	Fitchburg,	Adoption, etc.,	1928
1880	Leora F.	Douglas,	Guardianship,	1929
1847	Lorren,	Southborough,	Guardianship,	1930
1839	Louisa M.	Douglas,	Guardianship,	1931
1808	Lucy	Lancaster,	Guardianship,	1932
1847	Lucy	Southborough,	Guardianship,	1933
1877	Luther L.	Woodstock, Conn.,	Foreign Will,	1934
1868	Lydia	Dudley,	Will,	1935
1860	Lyman T.	Douglas,	Guardianship,	1936
1831	Maria	Southborough,	Guardianship,	1937
1808	Mary	Lancaster,	Guardianship,	1938
1825	Mary	Smithfield, R. I.,	Administration,	1939
1844	Mary J.	Sterling,	Guardianship,	1940
1839	Mercy A.	Douglas,	Guardianship,	1941
1845	Mowry A.	Burrillville, R. I.,	Guardianship,	1942
1875	Nellie F.	Worcester,	Guardianship,	1943
1811	Olive	Western,	Guardianship,	1944
1860	Oliver	Paxton,	Will,	1945
1868	Oliver	West Brookfield,	Will,	1946
1854	Olney	Douglas,	Will,	1947
1826	Olney R.	Dudley,	Will,	1948
1881	Phila	Sutton,	Will,	1949
1839	Prudence	Douglas,	Guardianship,	1950
1881	Ralph	Douglas,	Adoption, etc.,	1951
1827	Richard	Thompson, Conn.,	Administration,	1952
1850	Richard	Sturbridge,	Will,	1953
1864	Rufus	Sterling,	Administration,	1954
1808	Samuel	Lancaster,	Guardianship,	1955
1808	Sarah	Lancaster,	Guardianship,	1956
1845	Sarah S.	Burrillville, R. I.,	Guardianship,	1957
1844	Silas W.	Sterling,	Administration,	1958
1869	Smith R.	Burrillville, R. I.,	Administration,	1959
1850	Stephen	Burrillville, R. I.,	Administration,	1960
1845	Stephen, Jr.,	Burrillville, R. I.,	Guardianship,	1961
1870	Sumner C.	Douglas,	Administration,	1962
1810	Thankful	Western,	Guardianship,	1963

Year.	Name.	Residence.	Nature.	Case.
1852	ARNOLD, Thomas	Lunenburg,	Administration,	1964
1875	Walter W.	Worcester,	Guardianship,	1965
1832	Willard	Oxford,	Administration,	1966
1879	Willard	Royalston,	Guardianship,	1967
1805	William	Lancaster,	Administration,	1968
1873	William E.	Fitchburg,	Administration,	1969
1862	William H.	West Brookfield,	Will,	1970
1847	William J.	Southborough,	Guardianship,	1971
1875	Willie E.	Worcester,	Guardianship,	1972
1868	ARTHUR, Janet	Clinton,	Administration,	1973
1851	ARVINE, Earlliss	Worcester,	Guardianship,	1974
1851	Freeling	Worcester,	Guardianship,	1975
1851	Kazlitt	Worcester,	Will,	1976
1857	ASH, Francis	Worcester,	Administration,	1977
1857	ASHBY, Edwin R.	North Brookfield,	Administration,	1978
1857	Emma J.	North Brookfield,	Guardianship,	1979
1871	ASHWORTH, Charles H.	Blackstone,	Guardianship,	1980
1846	Robert	Fitchburg,	Administration,	1981
1876	ASPINWALL, Betsey	Brookfield,	Administration,	1982
1875	Catherine	Warren,	Administration,	1983
1843	ATHERTON, Abigail M., etc.	Fitchburg,	Guardianship,	1984
1790	Achsa	Bolton,	Guardianship,	1985
1843	Ann F.	Fitchburg,	Guardianship,	1986
1880	Annes	Harvard,	Will,	1987
1790	Asenath	Bolton,	Guardianship,	1988
1752	Benjamin	Billerica,	Administration,	1989
1786	Benjamin	Bolton,	Administration,	1990
1826	Benjamin	Bolton,	Administration,	1991
1847	Caroline F.	Fitchburg,	Guardianship,	1992
1840	Charles	Harvard,	Administration,	1993
1842	Charles	Harvard,	Partition,	1993
1827	Charles L.	Bolton,	Guardianship,	1994
1847	Charlotte M.	Fitchburg,	Guardianship,	1995
1869	Clara	Leominster,	Guardianship,	1996
1831	David	Harvard,	Will,	1997
1849	David	Sturbridge,	Administration,	1998
1880	David	Worcester,	Will,	1999
1847	Elbridge G.	Fitchburg,	Administration,	2000
1758	Eliakim	Harvard,	Guardianship,	2001
1787	Eliakim	Bolton,	Administration,	2002
1827	Eliza	Harvard,	Guardianship,	2003
1742	Elizabeth	Harvard,	Guardianship,	2004
1792	Eunice	Bolton,	Administration,	2005
1758	Ezra	Harvard,	Guardianship,	2006
1776	Ezra	Ashburnham,	Administration,	2007

(46)

Year.	Name.	Residence.	Nature.	Case.
1790	ATHERTON, Ezra	Bolton,	Guardianship,	2008
1843	Frances A.	Fitchburg,	Guardianship,	2009
1827	Galen	Harvard,	Guardianship,	2010
1875	George	Harvard,	Will,	2011
1742	Hannah	Harvard,	Guardianship,	2012
1847	Henry M.	Fitchburg,	Guardianship,	2013
1827	Henry W.	Harvard,	Guardianship,	2014
1822	Israel	Lancaster,	Administration,	2015
1755	John	Harvard,	Administration,	2016
1843	John L.	Fitchburg,	Guardianship,	2017
1793	Jonathan	Bolton,	Administration,	2018
1735	Joseph	Harvard,	Administration,	2019
1742	Joseph	Harvard,	Guardianship,	2020
1789	Joseph	Harvard,	Administration,	2021
1881	Llewellyn	Gardner,	Administration,	2022
1869	Lucius	Leominster,	Guardianship,	2023
1758	Lydia	Harvard,	Guardianship,	2024
1827	Martha	Harvard,	Guardianship,	2025
1815	Mary	Bolton,	Administration,	2026
1869	Mary	Leominster,	Guardianship,	2027
1873	Mary	Worcester,	Administration,	2028
1879	Mary	Lancaster,	Administration,	2029
1843	Mary A.	Fitchburg,	Guardianship,	2030
1840	Mary D.	Harvard,	Guardianship,	2031
1827	Miranda	Bolton,	Guardianship,	2032
1848	Nelson A.	Fitchburg,	Administration,	2033
1813	Oliver	Harvard,	Will,	2034
1827	Oliver H.	Harvard,	Guardianship,	2035
1869	Otis	Leominster,	Administration,	2036
1859	Otis R.	Lancaster,	Will,	2037
1742	Patience	Harvard,	Guardianship,	2038
1790	Patience	Harvard,	Guardianship,	2039
1843	Percy	Fitchburg,	Administration,	2040
1764	Peter	Harvard,	Will,	2041
1784	Peter	Harvard,	Administration,	2042
1790	Phebe	Bolton,	Guardianship,	2043
1826	Philemon	Harvard,	Administration,	2044
1827	Rachel	Harvard,	Guardianship,	2045
1867	Rebecca	Sturbridge,	Will,	2046
1881	Rodney L.	Gardner,	Guardianship,	2047
1807	Samuel	Harvard,	Administration,	2048
1758	Sarah	Harvard,	Guardianship,	2049
1867	Shepard F.	Fitchburg,	Administration,	2050
1758	Thomas	Harvard,	Guardianship,	2051
1758	William	Harvard,	Guardianship,	2052

YEAR.	NAME.	RESIDENCE.	NATURE.	CASE.
1845	ATHERTON, William M.	Harvard,	Administration,	2053
1872	ATKINS, Orstella H.	Westborough,	Guardianship,	2054
1876	Solomon	Worcester,	Will,	2055
1881	ATKINSON, Frank F.	Upton,	Guardianship,	2056
1881	Minnie M.	Upton,	Guardianship,	2057
1864	Ruth W.	Worcester,	Administration,	2058
1881	Walter E.	Upton,	Guardianship,	2059
1832	ATWOOD, Alfred	Barre,	Guardianship,	2060
1860	Amaziah.	Southborough,	Will,	2061
1832	Barnabas	Barre,	Administration,	2062
1759	Benjamin	Mendon,	Administration,	2063
1841	Charles F.	Barre,	Guardianship,	2064
1879	Clara E.	Lowell,	Sale Real Est.,	2065
1841	Cyrus W.	Barre,	Guardianship,	2066
1875	David F.	Worcester,	Administration,	2067
1829	Doane	Sturbridge,	Administration,	2068
1879	Edith H.	Worcester,	Guardianship,	2069
1860	Edward S.	Chelsea,	Guardianship,	2070
1814	Eldad	Milford,	Will,	2071
1870	Electa J.	Millbury,	Will,	2072
1879	Emma L.	Worcester,	Guardianship,	2073
1856	Esther	Oxford,	Administration,	2074
1859	Gratee	Barre,	Administration,	2075
1830	Harriet	Sturbridge,	Guardianship,	2076
1879	Herbert L.	Lowell,	Sale Real Est.,	2077
1860	Horace F.	Chelsea,	Guardianship,	2078
1800	John	Gerry,	Will,	2079
1841	John H.	Barre,	Guardianship,	2080
1825	Justus	North Brookfield,	Administration,	2081
1826	Lucinda	North Brookfield,	Guardianship,	2082
1832	Lucius	Barre,	Guardianship,	2083
1839	Marshall W.	Barre,	Administration,	2084
1830	Mary	Sturbridge,	Guardianship,	2085
1860	Mary F.	Chelsea,	Guardianship,	2086
1879	Minnie S.	Lowell,	Sale Real Est.,	2087
1881	Nancy	Worcester,	Administration, .	2088
1830	Orville	Sturbridge,	Guardianship,	2089
1862	Otis	Barre,	Administration,	2090
1848	Stephen	Nashua, N. H.,	Administration,	2091
1861	Thomas	Barre,	Administration,	2092
1872	Warren D.	Fitchburg,	Administration,	2093
1830	William	Sturbridge,	Guardianship,	2094
1869	AULD, Caroline M.	Worcester,	Guardianship,	2095
1814	AUSTIN, Betsey	Lunenburg,	Guardianship,	2096
1773	Daniel	Lunenburg,	Will,	2097

YEAR.	NAME.	RESIDENCE.	NATURE.	CASE.
1803	AUSTIN, Daniel	Lunenburg,	Guardianship,	2098
1773	Daniel, Jr.	Lunenburg,	Administration,	2099
1856	Ella M.	Athol,	Guardianship,	2100
1877	Haskell	Fitchburg,	Will,	2101
1880	Hattie E.	Worcester,	Guardianship,	2102
1856	Horace B.	Athol,	Administration,	2103
1856	Horace W.	Athol,	Guardianship,	2104
1814	James	Lunenburg,	Guardianship,	2105
1863	Jennie M.	Gardner,	Guardianship,	2106
1802	John	Lunenburg,	Administration,	2107
1878	Lizzie M.	Oakham,	Adoption, etc.,	2108
1866	Nathan	Woodstock, Conn.,	Will,	2109
1802	Phebe	Lunenburg,	Administration,	2110
1847	Richard T.	Lunenburg,	Will,	2111
1875	Robert B.	Worcester,	Will,	2112
1880	Sampson	Worcester,	Will,	2113
1803	Samuel	Lunenburg,	Guardianship,	2114
1832	Samuel	Glastonbury, Conn.,	Foreign Will,	2115
1879	Samuel	Worcester,	Administration,	2116
1813	Timothy	Lunenburg,	Administration,	2117
1814	Timothy	Lunenburg,	Guardianship,	2118
1859	Warren	Spencer,	Administration,	2119
1861	AVERY, Amos H.	Ashburnham,	Administration,	2120
1859	Daniel	Worcester,	Administration,	2121
1872	David C.	Millbury,	Administration,	2122
1878	Frank F.	Millbury,	Guardianship,	2123
1878	George L.	Millbury,	Guardianship,	2124
1824	Joseph	Holden,	Administration,	2125
1861	Joseph	Worcester,	Administration,	2126
1878	Lucy B.	Millbury,	Guardianship,	2127
1842	Mary	Boylston,	Will,	2128
1842	Samuel	Holden,	Administration,	2129
1873	Sarah	Worcester,	Administration,	2130
1878	Walter C.	Millbury,	Guardianship,	2131
1854	AVIS, Henry	Spencer,	Administration,	2132
1854	Richard	Spencer,	Administration,	2133
	AXTELL AND AXTEL,			
1825	Adeline	Grafton,	Guardianship,	2134
1871	Alice B.	Kirkwood, Mo.,	Partition,	2135
1871	Charles R.	Kirkwood, Mo.,	Partition,	2136
1851	Chloe	Grafton,	Will,	2137
1871	Hannah	Grafton,	Will,	2138
1808	Henry	Douglas,	Administration,	2139
1791	John	Alstead, N. H.,	Guardianship,	2140
1871	Lillie H.	Kirkwood, Mo.,	Partition,	2141

Year.	Name.	Residence.	Nature.	Case.
	AXTELL AND AXTEL,			
1817	Mary	Grafton,	Will,	2142
1807	Rebecca	Northbridge,	Will,	2143
1803	Sabra	Unknown,	Guardianship,	2144
1825	Seth J.	Grafton,	Guardianship,	2145
1880	Seth J.	Grafton,	Will,	2146
1750	Thomas	Grafton,	Will,	2147
1798	Thomas	Grafton,	Administration,	2148
1819	Thomas	Grafton,	Administration,	2149
1824	Thomas	Grafton,	Administration,	2150
1871	Thomas	Kirkwood, Mo.,	Partition,	2151
1825	Thomas R.	Grafton,	Guardianship,	2152
1871	Tunie E.	Kirkwood, Mo.,	Partition,	2153
1816	William	Sutton,	Administration,	2154
1871	Willie	Kirkwood, Mo.,	Partition,	2155
	AYRES, AYRE AND AIRS,			
1823	Adaline	North Brookfield,	Guardianship,	2156
1837	Adaline W.	Oakham,	Guardianship,	2157
1855	Amos	North Brookfield,	Administration,	2158
1785	Benjamin	Brookfield,	Administration,	2159
1786	Benjamin	Brookfield,	Guardianship,	2160
1881	Charles H. D.	Charlestown,	Adoption, etc.,	2161
1823	Charlotte	North Brookfield,	Guardianship,	2162
1850	Clarissa	North Brookfield,	Will,	2163
1822	Cyrus	North Brookfield,	Administration,	2164
1823	Cyrus	North Brookfield,	Guardianship,	2165
1871	Daniel W.	North Brookfield,	Guardianship,	2166
1747	Ebenezer	Hardwick,	Administration,	2167
1796	Eliphalet	New Braintree,	Will,	2168
1823	Eliza	North Brookfield,	Guardianship,	2169
1747	Elizabeth	Brookfield,	Will,	2170
1874	Elizabeth M.	Petersham,	Adoption, etc.,	2171
1874	Emilia	Worcester,	Will,	2172
1878	Emma A.	North Brookfield,	Administration,	2173
1876	Emma J.	Webster,	Administration,	2174
1823	Eunice	North Brookfield,	Guardianship,	2175
1850	Francis W.	Douglas,	Will,	2176
1837	Freelove	North Brookfield,	Administration,	2177
1834	Hazel	North Brookfield,	Administration,	2178
1867	Horace	Worcester,	Will,	2179
1840	Increase	North Brookfield,	Will,	2180
1762	Jabez	Brookfield,	Will,	2181
1748	John	Brookfield,	Guardianship,	2182
1739	John	Brookfield,	Will,	2183
1745	John	Brookfield,	Administration,	2184

YEAR.	NAME.	RESIDENCE.	NATURE.	CASE.
	AYRES, AYRE AND AIRS,			
1841	Jonas	North Brookfield,	Administration,	2185
1860	Jonathan J.	North Brookfield,	Will,	2186
1748	Joseph	Hardwick,	Guardianship,	2187
1760	Joseph	New Braintree,	Guardianship,	2188
1786	Joseph	Brookfield,	Guardianship,	2189
1815	Jude	North Brookfield,	Will,	2190
1838	Lucy H.	Grafton,	Guardianship,	2191
1786	Mary	Brookfield,	Guardianship,	2192
1875	Mary	North Brookfield,	Administration,	2193
1796	Moses	Brookfield,	Will,	2194
1844	Moses	New Braintree,	Will,	2195
1869	Moses	New Braintree,	Will,	2196
1870	Myron N.	Petersham,	Adoption, etc.,	2197
1860	Nahum	New Braintree,	Will,	2198
1809	Onesiphorus	Brookfield,	Will,	2199
1880	Perley	Oakham,	Will,	2200
1787	Persis	Brookfield,	Guardianship,	2201
1787	Relief	Brookfield,	Guardianship,	2202
1778	Solomon	Hardwick,	Guardianship,	2203
1823	Sophronia	North Brookfield,	Guardianship,	2204
1852	Suza	North Brookfield,	Will,	2205
1767	William	Brookfield,	Administration,	2206
1789	William	Brookfield,	Will,	2207
1815	William	North Brookfield,	Will,	2208
1823	William	North Brookfield,	Guardianship,	2209
1835	William	North Brookfield,	Will,	2210
1871	William A.	Worcester,	Administration,	2211
1871	William H.	North Brookfield,	Will,	2212
	BABBIT AND BABBITT,			
1815	Abigail	Petersham,	Guardianship,	2213
1849	Albion	Worcester,	Guardianship,	2214
1849	Almira	Worcester,	Guardianship,	2215
1843	Avery B.	Barre,	Administration,	2216
1776	Benjamin	Brookfield,	Administration,	2217
1880	Bertha B.	Hubbardston,	Guardianship,	2219
1815	Charles	Petersham,	Guardianship,	2219
1849	Charles	Worcester,	Guardianship,	2220
1843	Charles A.	Barre,	Guardianship,	2221
1864	Charles A.	Barre,	Guardianship,	2222
1843	Dennis	Barre,	Guardianship,	2223
1815	Edward	Petersham,	Will,	2224
1815	Edward	Petersham,	Guardianship,	2225
1849	Edward	Worcester,	Administration,	2226
1849	Edward	Worcester,	Guardianship,	2227

Year.	Name.	Residence.	Nature.	Case.
	BABBIT and BABBITT,			
1815	Eliza	Petersham,	Guardianship,	2228
1864	Eliza	Dana,	Administration,	2229
1799	Erasmus	Sturbridge,	Administration,	2230
1782	Erasmus, Jr.	Sturbridge,	Guardianship,	2231
1825	Ezra	Dana,	Administration,	2232
1815	Fanny	Petersham,	Guardianship,	2233
1864	George F.	Barre,	Guardianship,	2234
1782	Henry	Sturbridge,	Guardianship,	2235
1856	Jonathan	Dana,	Administration,	2236
1815	Joseph F.	Petersham,	Guardianship,	2237
1815	Laban S.	Petersham,	Guardianship,	2238
1815	Levi	Petersham,	Guardianship,	2239
1827	Lewis	Dana,	Guardianship,	2240
1864	Lizzie N.	Barre,	Guardianship,	2241
1827	Louisa	Dana,	Guardianship,	2242
1878	Lyman D.	Athol,	Will,	2243
1849	Lysander C.	Worcester,	Guardianship,	2244
1782	Mary	Sturbridge,	Guardianship,	2245
1815	Mary	Petersham,	Guardianship,	2246
1864	Mary A.	Barre,	Guardianship,	2247
1858	Polly	Harvard,	Guardianship,	2248
1856	Rinaldo	Dana,	Guardianship,	2249
1851	Sarah	Barre,	Administration,	2250
1856	Sarah E.	Dana,	Guardianship,	2251
1875	Sewell	Athol,	Administration,	2252
1843	Susan M.	Barre,	Guardianship,	2253
1782	Thomas	Sturbridge,	Guardianship,	2254
1813	Thomas	Brookfield,	Administration,	2255
1843	Warren E.	Barre,	Guardianship,	2256
1880	William S.	Hubbardston,	Administration,	2257
1836	BABCOCK, Abram	Berlin,	Trustee,	2258
1874	Abram	Berlin,	Administration,	2259
1836	Benjamin	Princeton,	Administration,	2260
1842	Catharine	Dana,	Guardianship,	2261
1826	David R.	Fitchburg,	Guardianship,	2262
1826	Eliza	Fitchburg,	Guardianship,	2263
1826	Enos	Fitchburg,	Guardianship,	2264
1852	Ephraim	Berlin,	Administration,	2265
1864	Ephraim	Berlin,	Administration,	2266
1863	Eunice	Berlin,	Administration,	2267
1853	George E.	Bolton,	Guardianship,	2268
1838	Hepsibah	Boylston,	Guardianship,	2269
1826	Jerusha	Fitchburg,	Guardianship,	2270
1853	Jesse W.	Bolton,	Guardianship,	2271

YEAR.	NAME.	RESIDENCE.	NATURE.	CASE.
1825	BABCOCK, John	Fitchburg,	Administration,	2272
1826	John	Fitchburg,	Guardianship,	2273
1864	John D.	Berlin,	Guardianship,	2274
1845	John S.	Dana,	Administration,	2275
1838	Jonas	Northborough,	Administration,	2276
1859	Josiah	Berlin,	Administration,	2277
1852	Josiah C.	Bolton,	Administration,	2278
1841	Leonard	Princeton,	Will,	2279
1843	Leonard G.	Worcester,	Guardianship,	2280
1851	Martha Ann	Berlin,	Guardianship,	2281
1851	Martha Ann	Berlin,	Administration,	2281
1843	Mary L.	Worcester,	Guardianship,	2282
1838	Miriam	Northborough,	Administration,	2283
1836	Patience	Berlin,	Trustee,	2284
1837	Peter	Boylston,	Administration,	2285
1842	Polly S.	Dana,	Will,	2286
1881	Priscilla	Berlin,	Will,	2287
1844	Reuben	Northborough,	Administration,	2288
1826	Sarah	Fitchburg,	Guardianship,	2289
1864	Sarah E.	Bolton,	Guardianship,	2290
1826	Susan	Fitchburg,	Guardianship,	2291
1838	Wheeler	Boylston,	Guardianship,	2292
1821	William	Berlin,	Administration,	2293
1827	William	Berlin,	Partition,	2293
1861	William	Berlin,	Will,	2294
1874	BABSON, James M.	Clinton,	Will,	2295
	BACHELER AND BACHELOR			
	see BATCHELLER.			
1864	BACK, Arthur J.	Worcester,	Administration,	2296
1868	Ellen E.	Sturbridge,	Guardianship,	2297
1868	Ida E.	Sturbridge,	Guardianship,	2298
1868	Mary E.	Sturbridge,	Administration,	2299
1859	BACON, Abbie I.	Worcester,	Guardianship,	2300
1872	Abby I.	Charlton,	Administration,	2301
1777	Abigail	Barre,	Guardianship,	2302
1818	Abigail	Southbridge,	Guardianship,	2303
1847	Abigail	Gardner,	Will,	2304
1783	Abijah	Sutton,	Administration,	2305
1843	Adalaide	Charlton,	Guardianship,	2306
1773	Alsena	Dudley,	Guardianship,	2307
1827	Anna	Petersham,	Will,	2308
1838	Arna	Westminster,	Administration,	2309
1858	Arthur B.	Warren,	Guardianship,	2310
1855	Asa	Charlton,	Administration,	2311
1858	Berthier	Warren,	Administration,	2312

YEAR.	NAME.	RESIDENCE.	NATURE.	CASE.
1843	BACON, Charlotte S.	Charlton,	Guardianship,	2313
1875	Cyril L.	Dudley,	Will,	2314
1841	Cyrus	Charlton,	Administration,	2315
1843	Cyrus V.	Charlton,	Guardianship,	2316
1813	Daniel	Charlton,	Administration,	2317
1814	Daniel	Barre,	Guardianship,	2318
1834	Daniel	Charlton,	Will,	2319
1866	Daniel F.	Southbridge,	Will,	2320
1754	David	Sutton,	Guardianship,	2321
1850	David	Templeton,	Administration,	2322
1771	Ebenezer	Dudley,	Will,	2323
1772	Ebenezer	Dudley,	Administration,	2324
1773	Ebenezer	Dudley,	Guardianship,	2325
1827	Ebenezer	Petersham,	Will,	2326
1860	Edward	Westminster,	Will,	2327
1836	Elisha	Barre,	Administration,	2328
1832	Eliza	Barre,	Guardianship,	2329
1754	Elizabeth	Sutton,	Guardianship,	2330
1846	Ellen U.	Sutton,	Guardianship,	2331
1859	Elmer A.	Southbridge,	Guardianship,	2332
1868	Emogene L.	Sturbridge,	Guardianship,	2333
1798	Ephraim	Barre,	Will,	2334
1815	Ephraim	Barre,	Administration,	2335
1825	Ephraim	Southbridge,	Will,	2336
1828	Ephraim	Southbridge,	Partition,	2336
1837	Ephraim S.	Sutton,	Administration,	2337
1849	Eunice	Templeton,	Will,	2338
1873	Fiske	Charlton,	Will,	2339
1842	Frances	Warren,	Guardianship,	2340
1808	Francis S.	Gardner,	Guardianship,	2341
1860	George	Charlton,	Will,	2342
1839	George H.	Warren,	Guardianship,	2343
1842	George I.	Warren,	Guardianship,	2344
1854	Hannah W.	Millbury,	Administration,	2345
1843	Hellen M.	Charlton,	Guardianship,	2346
1843	Henrii E.	Charlton,	Guardianship,	2347
1870	Henry S.	Southbridge,	Administration,	2348
1880	Ira P.	Millbury,	Administration,	2349
1827	Jacob B.	Southbridge,	Guardianship,	2350
1755	James	Rutland,	Guardianship,	2351
1859	James O.	Southbridge,	Guardianship,	2352
1842	Jepthah, Jr.	Warren,	Administration,	2353
1839	Jerome H.	Warren,	Guardianship,	2354
1877	Jerusha C.	Worcester,	Administration,	2355
1830	Joel	Barre,	Administration,	2356

(54)

YEAR.	NAME.	RESIDENCE.	NATURE.	CASE.
1776	BACON, John	Dudley,	Administration,	2357
1777	John	Barre,	Guardianship,	2358
1803	John, 2d	Barre,	Will,	2359
1818	John	Charlton,	Administration,	2360
1828	John	Barre,	Will,	2361
1872	John E.	Worcester,	Will,	2362
1807	Jonathan	Dudley,	Administration,	2363
1815	Jonathan	Charlton,	Administration,	2364
1815	Jonathan	Dudley,	Administration,	2365
1868	Jonathan C.	Sturbridge,	Administration,	2366
1747	Joseph	Woodstock,	Guardianship,	2367
1746	Joseph	Woodstock,	Administration,	2368
1808	Joseph	Gardner,	Administration,	2369
1750	Josiah	Rutland,	Administration,	2370
1776	Josiah	Barre,	Administration,	2371
1841	Josiah	Barre,	Will,	2372
1841	. Josiah	Barre,	Pension,	2373
1846	Julia M.	Sutton,	Guardianship,	2374
1846	Julius E.	Sutton,	Guardianship,	2375
1818	Liberty	Southbridge,	Guardianship,	2376
1843	Louisa M.	Charlton,	Guardianship,	2377
1841	Lucius A.	Worcester,	Guardianship,	2378
1841	Lucius F.	Worcester,	Administration,	2379
1827	Lucy	Sutton,	Guardianship,	2380
1842	Lucy A.	Warren,	Guardianship,	2381
1841	Lucy Ann	Worcester,	Guardianship,	2382
1840	Luther	Southbridge,	Administration,	2383
1864	Martha E.	Webster,	Administration,	2384
1880	Martin	Worcester,	Administration,	2385
1776	Mary	Dudley,	Guardianship,	2386
1777	Mary	Barre,	Guardianship,	2387
1839	Mary A.	Warren,	Guardianship,	2388
1866	Mary C.	Southbridge,	Guardianship,	2389
1842	Mary I.	Warren,	Guardianship,	2390
1861	Mary L.	Charlton,	Administration,	2391
1843	Massena P.	Charlton,	Guardianship,	2392
1846	Maturin	Southbridge,	Administration,	2393
1830	Miles	Uxbridge,	Will,	2394
1828	Molly	Southbridge,	Administration,	2395
1831	Nancy M.	Harvard,	Guardianship,	2396
1832	Nathan	Barre,	Guardianship,	2397
1837	Olive L.	Barre,	Guardianship,	2398
1848	Olivia	Oxford,	Will,	2399
1848	Olivia	Oxford,	Pension,	2400
1859	Otis A.	Southbridge,	Will,	2401

YEAR.	NAME.	RESIDENCE.	NATURE.	CASE.
1838	BACON, Patience	Templeton,	Administration,	2402
1762	Philip	Woodstock,	Administration,	2403
1852	Polaski	Worcester,	Administration,	2404
1822	Priscilla	Dudley,	Administration,	2405
1747	Rebecca	Woodstock,	Guardianship,	2406
1781	Reuben	Brookfield,	Guardianship,	2407
1781	Robert	Brookfield,	Guardianship,	2408
1820	Rufus	Sutton,	Administration,	2409
1846	Rufus	Sutton,	Administration,	2410
1858	Rufus F.	Warren,	Administration,	2411
1754	Ruth	Sutton,	Guardianship,	2412
1869	Ruth	Spencer,	Administration,	2413
1839	Ruth C.	Warren,	Guardianship,	2414
1871	Sabra E.	Holden,	Administration,	2415
1773	Samuel	Dudley,	Guardianship,	2416
1827	Samuel	Sturbridge,	Administration,	2417
1838	Samuel	Templeton,	Will,	2418
1855	Samuel	Worcester,	Will,	2419
1868	Samuel	Harvard,	Administration,	2420
1831	Sarah	Dudley,	Administration,	2421
1846	Sarah A.	Sutton,	Guardianship,	2422
1831	Sarah F.	Harvard,	Guardianship,	2423
1842	Sarah L.	Warren,	Guardianship,	2424
1747	Simeon	Woodstock,	Guardianship,	2425
1831	Sophia A.	Harvard,	Guardianship,	2426
1842	Susan C.	Warren,	Guardianship,	2427
1868	Theresa M.	Sturbridge,	Guardianship,	2428
1856	Tileston	Oakham,	Administration,	2429
1783	Timothy	Sutton,	Administration,	2430
1868	Uriah E.	Sturbridge,	Guardianship,	2431
1827	William	Uxbridge,	Administration,	2432
1827	William, Jr.	Sutton,	Guardianship,	2433
1876	William E.	Barre,	Guardianship,	2434
	BADCOCK see also BABCOCK.			
1826	Henry E.	Bolton,	Guardianship,	2435
1826	Hepsibah	Berlin,	Administration,	2436
1821	Nathan	Fitchburg,	Administration,	2437
1826	Nathan	Bolton,	Administration,	2438
1801	William	Northborough,	Will,	2439
1825	BAGG, Adaline	Princeton,	Guardianship,	2440
1825	Augusta	Princeton,	Guardianship,	2441
1825	Eunice	Princeton,	Guardianship,	2442
1825	Harriet	Princeton,	Guardianship,	2443
1824	Henry	Princeton,	Administration,	2444
1825	Henry H.	Princeton,	Guardianship,	2445

Year.	Name.	Residence.	Nature.	Case.
1825	BAGG, James H.	Princeton,	Guardianship,	2446
1825	Sukey	Princeton,	Guardianship,	2447
1873	BAGLEY, Charles H.	Fitchburg,	Administration,	2448
	BAILEY, BAYLEY AND BAYLIES,			
1862	Abigail	Sterling,	Administration,	2449
1872	Addie A.	Sterling,	Guardianship,	2450
1843	Addison	Sterling,	Guardianship,	2451
1841	Adelia M.	Milford,	Guardianship,	2452
1856	Adolphus	Worcester,	Administration,	2453
1880	Albert	Southbridge,	Will,	2454
1852	Alden	Sterling,	Administration,	2455
1874	Alice N.	Southbridge,	Guardianship,	2456
1859	Alma	Sterling,	Administration,	2457
1864	Almond F.	Worcester,	Administration,	2458
1826	Alpheus	Uxbridge,	Administration,	2459
1834	Amelia O.	Milford,	Guardianship,	2460
1831	Amherst	Berlin,	Administration,	2461
1873	Ann H.	Milford,	Administration,	2462
1866	Anna R.	Milford,	Guardianship,	2463
1790	Barnibas	Berlin,	Will,	2464
1853	Barzillai	Southbridge,	Will,	2465
1874	Belle M.	Athol,	Change of Name,	2466
1876	Belle M.	Athol,	Adoption,	2466
1791	Benjamin	Berlin,	Will,	2467
1831	Benjamin	Lunenburg,	Pension,	2468
1843	Benjamin	Sterling,	Will,	2469
1852	Benjamin	Bolton,	Will,	2470
1862	Benjamin M.	Auburn, Ill.,	Guardianship,	2471
1785	Bethiah	Berlin,	Guardianship,	2472
1853	Betsey	Harvard,	Administration,	2473
1867	Carrie I.	Fitchburg,	Guardianship,	2474
1811	Catharine	Berlin,	Will,	2475
1834	Charles A.	Milford,	Guardianship,	2476
1870	Charles E.	Sterling,	Administration,	2477
1875	Charles H.	Fitchburg,	Adoption, etc.,	2478
1877	Charles W.	Montpelier, Vt.,	Administration,	2479
1867	Charles W. O.	Townsend,	Adoption, etc.,	2480
1874	Clarissa	Southbridge,	Will,	2481
1860	Cynthia	Sterling,	Administration,	2482
1752	Daniel	Bolton,	Guardianship,	2483
1757	Daniel	Bolton,	Administration,	2484
1834	Daniel M.	Milford,	Guardianship,	2485
1805	Ebenezer	Berlin,	Administration,	2486
1831	Ebenezer F.	Fitchburg,	Guardianship,	2487
1862	Edward G.	Fitchburg,	Guardianship,	2488

BAILEY, BAYLEY AND BAYLIES

YEAR.	NAME.	RESIDENCE.	NATURE.	CASE.
1862	Edward M.	Auburn, Ill.,	Guardianship,	2489
1818	Elizabeth	Berlin,	Will,	2490
1842	Elizabeth	Auburn,	Administration,	2491
1862	Elizabeth M.	Auburn, Ill.,	Guardianship,	2492
1854	Ellen A.	Worcester,	Guardianship,	2493
1858	Ellen G.	Worcester,	Guardianship,	2494
1772	Ephraim	Northborough,	Guardianship,	2495
1848	Ephraim	Uxbridge,	Administration,	2496
1835	Frances A.	Bolton,	Guardianship,	2497
1872	Frank E.	Milford,	Guardianship,	2498
1808	Frederick	Sturbridge,	Will,	2499
1859	F. Sawyer	West Boylston,	Administration,	2500
1840	George E.	Sterling,	Administration,	2501
1870	George E.	Clinton,	Administration,	2502
1869	George I.	Milford,	Adoption, etc.,	2503
1837	George L.	Berlin,	Guardianship,	2504
1849	George M.	Uxbridge,	Guardianship,	2505
1848	George N.	Dudley,	Guardianship,	2506
1834	George T.	Milford,	Guardianship,	2507
1865	George T.	Milford,	Will,	2508
1831	Goldsmith	Fitchburg,	Guardianship,	2509
1862	Goldsmith F.	Fitchburg,	Will,	2510
1821	Hannah	Sturbridge,	Will,	2511
1843	Hannah W.	Sterling,	Guardianship,	2512
1841	Harriet M.	Sterling,	Guardianship,	2513
1859	Henrietta	Uxbridge,	Administration,	2514
1872	Holloway	Northborough,	Will,	2515
1870	Horace	Westborough,	Will,	2516
1876	Huldah R.	Worcester,	Will,	2517
1814	Isaac	Ward,	Will,	2518
1865	James	Holden,	Will,	2519
1841	James D.	Milford,	Guardianship,	2520
1875	James F.	Warren,	Will,	2521
1856	James H.	Holden,	Administration,	2522
1848	James J.	Dudley,	Guardianship,	2523
1875	James W.	Brookfield,	Administration,	2524
1785	Jedediah	Berlin,	Guardianship,	2525
1835	Jonas	Sterling,	Guardianship,	2526
1842	Jonas	Sterling,	Will,	2527
1842	Jonas	Sterling,	Pension,	2528
1813	Jonathan	Lunenburg,	Will,	2529
1862	Joseph M.	Auburn, Ill.,	Guardianship,	2530
1798	Josiah	Lunenburg,	Will,	2531
1858	Josiah	Fitchburg,	Administration,	2532

BAILEY, BAYLEY and BAYLIES,

Year	Name	Residence	Nature	Case
1785	Levi	Berlin,	Guardianship,	2533
1862	Lucinda M.	Auburn, Ill.,	Guardianship,	2534
1867	Lucy	Fitchburg,	Administration,	2535
1855	Lydia	Dudley,	Will,	2536
1860	Lyman	Dudley,	Administration,	2537
1862	Margaret A.	Auburn, Ill.,	Guardianship,	2538
1843	Maria	Sterling,	Guardianship,	2539
1843	Mark	Sterling,	Guardianship,	2540
1874	Martha	Sterling,	Will,	2541
1860	Martha E.	Sterling,	Guardianship,	2542
1866	Mary A.	Milford,	Guardianship,	2543
1872	Milton	Sterling,	Administration,	2544
1835	Moses	Sterling,	Administration,	2545
1844	Moses M.	Sterling,	Guardianship,	2546
1850	Nathaniel	Sterling,	Administration,	2547
1833	Nathaniel M.	Sterling,	Administration,	2548
1831	Nicholas	Uxbridge,	Will,	2549
1854	Nicholas	Uxbridge,	Partition,	2549
1836	Noah	Worcester,	Pension,	2550
1864	Olive T.	Douglas,	Administration,	2551
1834	Orson	Bolton,	Administration,	2552
1851	Paul	Sterling,	Administration,	2553
1873	Pauline	Milford,	Adoption, etc.,	2554
1859	Sampson	Sterling,	Will,	2555
1874	Samuel E.	Worcester,	Will,	2556
1868	Samuel H.	Lunenburg,	Administration,	5557
1791	Sarah	Sterling,	Will,	2558
1827	Sarah	Uxbridge,	Guardianship,	2559
1857	Sarah	Uxbridge,	Will,	2560
1858	Sarah A.	Worcester,	Guardianship,	2561
1862	Sarah A.	Auburn, Ill.,	Guardianship,	2562
1803	Sibilla	Berlin,	Administration,	2563
1793	Silas	Berlin,	Will,	2564
1840	Silas	Northborough,	Will,	2565
1858	Silas	Princeton,	Will,	2566
1860	Silas	Worcester,	Will,	2567
1844	Sophronia E.	Sterling,	Guardianship,	2568
1815	Stephen	Berlin,	Will,	2569
1861	Stephen	West Brookfield,	Administration,	2570
1834	Thomas B.	Milford,	Guardianship,	2571
1844	Thomas B.	Sterling,	Guardianship,	2572
1745	Timothy	Bolton,	Administration,	2573
1780	Timothy	Bolton,	Administration,	2574

BAILEY, BAYLEY AND BAYLIES,

Year	Name	Residence	Nature	Case
1837	Timothy	Berlin,	Administration,	2575
1834	William	Milford,	Administration,	2576
1834	William H.	Milford,	Guardianship,	2577

BAIRD see also BEARD.

Year	Name	Residence	Nature	Case
1821	Betsey	Worcester,	Guardianship,	2578
1816	Daniel	Worcester,	Guardianship,	2579
1819	Daniel	Worcester,	Will,	2579
1821	Daniel	Worcester,	Guardianship,	2580
1821	James S.	Worcester,	Guardianship,	2581
1829	Jane R.	Ward,	Guardianship,	2582
1834	Mary	Ward,	Administration,	2583
1821	Sally	Worcester,	Guardianship,	2584
1829	Samuel E.	Ward,	Guardianship,	2585
1819	Thomas	Ward,	Will,	2586
1829	Thomas	Ward,	Will,	2587
1828	Thomas, Jr.	Ward,	Administration,	2588
1829	Thomas N.	Ward,	Guardianship,	2589
1842	BAKER, Abigail	Sterling,	Administration,	2590
1842	Abigail	Sterling,	Pension,	2591
1852	Adin F.	Westminster,	Guardianship,	2592
1875	Albert T.	Leicester,	Will,	2593
1877	Alfred S.	Worcester,	Administration,	2594
1864	Alice F.	Sutton,	Guardianship,	2595
1870	Amos	Westminster,	Administration,	2596
1855	Amos S.	Dudley,	Administration,	2597
1871	Angie M.	Fitchburg,	Administration,	2598
1783	Anna	Sturbridge,	Guardianship,	2599
1865	Anna N.	Upton,	Adoption, etc.,	2600
1849	Annie	Phillipston,	Will,	2601
1816	Artemas	Petersham,	Administration,	2602
1850	Artemas D.	Shrewsbury,	Will,	2603
1769	Asa	Shrewsbury,	Guardianship,	2604
1777	Asa	Shrewsbury,	Administration,	2605
1866	Asa	Worcester,	Administration,	2606
1852	Asaph	Westminster,	Guardianship,	2607
1864	Austin S.	Sutton,	Guardianship,	2608
1790	Benjamin	Shrewsbury,	Will,	2609
1803	Benjamin	Berlin,	Will,	2610
1838	Benoni	Sterling,	Pension,	2611
1880	Betsey W.	Millbury,	Will,	2612
1872	Beulah	Shrewsbury,	Will,	2613
1847	Brad	Douglas,	Administration,	2614
1833	Bradford	Douglas,	Guardianship,	2615
1860	Byron E.	Templeton,	Guardianship,	2616

YEAR.	NAME.	RESIDENCE.	NATURE.	CASE.
1864	BAKER, Calvin L.	Sutton,	Administration,	2617
1864	Calvin W.	Sutton,	Guardianship,	2618
1812	Charles	Gerry,	Guardianship,	2619
1813	Charles	Gerry,	Will,	2619
1826	Charles	Phillipston,	Administration,	2620
1878	Charles F.	Worcester,	Administration,	2621
1852	Charles R.	Westminster,	Guardianship,	2622
1873	Chloe	Templeton,	Will,	2623
1821	Cinthia	Westminster,	Guardianship,	2624
1755	Cornelius	Grafton,	Guardianship,	2625
1769	Daniel	Shrewsbury,	Guardianship,	2626
1872	Daniel H.	Phillipston,	Will,	2627
1858	Darius	Dudley,	Administration,	2628
1858	Darius W.	Dudley,	Guardianship,	2629
1864	David	Hubbardston,	Will,	2630
1880	David A.	Worcester,	Administration,	2631
1822	Delphia	Mendon,	Will,	2632
1813	Dinah	Berlin,	Will,	2633
1877	Dwight L.	Charlton,	Guardianship,	2634
1872	Eber	Westminster,	Administration,	2635
1816	Edward	Petersham,	Guardianship,	2636
1819	Edward	Petersham,	Will,	2637
1864	Edward F.	Upton,	Guardianship,	2638
1783	Elizabeth	Sturbridge,	Guardianship,	2639
1858	Ella	Dudley,	Guardianship,	2640
1864	Ella A.	Sutton,	Guardianship,	2641
1874	Ella A.	Worcester,	Adoption, etc.,	2642
1853	Ellen E.	Athol,	Guardianship,	2643
1852	Elmore	Westminster,	Administration,	2644
1864	Elvira L.	Sutton,	Guardianship,	2645
1858	Emma	Dudley,	Guardianship,	2646
1855	Emma J.	Dudley,	Guardianship,	2647
1771	Esther	Oxford (Gore),	Administration,	2648
1874	Eunice R.	Westminster,	Administration,	2649
1844	Ezra	Gardner,	Guardianship,	2650
1867	Ezra	Gardner,	Administration,	2650
1858	Frances M.	Dudley,	Guardianship,	2651
1862	Francis	Petersham,	Administration,	2652
1850	Francis F.	Worcester,	Guardianship,	2653
1874	Francis L.	Gardner,	Administration,	2654
1875	Frank A.	Dudley,	Guardianship,	2655
1872	Frank L.	Worcester,	Administration,	2656
1869	Frank S.	Worcester,	Guardianship,	2657
1858	Franklin P.	Dudley,	Guardianship,	2658
1840	George	Uxbridge,	Guardianship,	2659

YEAR.	NAME.	RESIDENCE.	NATURE.	CASE.
1854	BAKER, George	Douglas,	Will,	2660
1861	George	Gardner,	Will,	2661
1881	George	Ashburnham,	Will,	2662
1873	George C.	Westminster,	Guardianship,	2663
1863	George H.	Templeton,	Administration,	2664
1873	George W.	Charlton,	Guardianship,	2665
1751	Gideon	Grafton,	Administration,	2666
1843	Hannah	Dudley,	Administration,	2667
1798	Harriet	Upton,	Guardianship,	2668
1858	Harriet E.	Dudley,	Guardianship,	2669
1869	Healy	Worcester,	Administration,	2670
1854	Healy T.	Worcester,	Guardianship,	2671
1859	Healy T.	Worcester,	Administration,	2671
1858	Henrietta	Dudley,	Guardianship,	2672
1798	Hillal	Upton,	Administration,	2673
1837	Hollis	Westminster,	Administration,	2674
1854	Huldah F.	Hubbardston,	Guardianship,	2675
1836	Jacob	Dudley,	Administration,	2676
1837	Jacob	Dudley,	Partition,	2676
1837	Jacob	Dudley,	Guardianship,	2677
1877	James H.	Worcester,	Will,	2678
1846	Jared, Jr.	Worcester,	Administration,	2679
1853	Jeanet Y.	Athol,	Guardianship,	2680
1873	Jennie	Charlton,	Guardianship,	2681
1838	Jesse	Lunenburg,	Will,	2682
1847	Joel	Westminster,	Administration,	2683
1852	Joel	Westminster,	Will,	2684
1760	John	Petersham,	Administration,	2685
1767	John	Shrewsbury,	Will,	2686
1809	John	Charlton,	Guardianship,	2687
1811	John	Shrewsbury,	Will,	2688
1819	John	Douglas,	Will,	2689
1851	John	Charlton,	Guardianship,	2690
1854	John S.	Westborough,	Guardianship,	2691
1783	Joseph	Sturbridge,	Guardianship,	2692
1784	Joseph	Sturbridge,	Will,	2693
1821	Joseph	Westminster,	Guardianship,	2694
1862	Joseph	Phillipston,	Will,	2695
1809	Joseph C.	Charlton,	Will,	2696
1858	Joseph P.	Phillipston,	Administration,	2697
1828	Leonard	Leicester,	Administration,	2698
1816	Levi	Phillipston,	Guardianship,	2699
1825	Levi	Phillipston,	Will,	2700
1852	Levi	Westminster,	Guardianship,	2701
1879	Levi	Charlton,	Administration,	2702

YEAR.	NAME.	RESIDENCE.	NATURE.	CASE.
1840	BAKER, Lois	Uxbridge,	Administration,	2703
1855	Louisa A.	Brookfield,	Administration,	2704
1872	Louisa E.	Templeton,	Administration,	2705
1858	Louisa M.	Dudley,	Guardianship,	2706
1857	Lovell	Grafton,	Will,	2707
1860	Lucas L.	Templeton,	Guardianship,	2708
1865	Lucretia M.	Upton,	Administration,	2709
1867	Lucretia S.	Warren,	Administration,	2710
1778	Lucy	Westborough,	Guardianship,	2711
1862	Lucy M.	Phillipston,	Guardianship,	2712
1847	Luke	Rutland,	Administration,	2713
1778	Lydia	Westborough,	Guardianship,	2714
1831	Manasseh	Uxbridge,	Administration,	2715
1838	Martha A.	Lunenburg,	Guardianship,	2716
1813	Mary	Westminster,	Will,	2717
1821	Mary	Westminster,	Guardianship,	2718
1853	Mary	Westminster,	Administration,	2719
1880	Mary C.	Worcester,	Guardianship,	2720
1864	Mary E.	Upton,	Guardianship,	2721
1880	Mary E.	Vergennes, Vt.,	Administration,	2722
1880	Mary G.	Worcester,	Will,	2723
1838	Mary L.	Lunenburg,	Guardianship,	2724
1798	Melita	Upton,	Guardianship,	2725
1867	Mercy	Dudley,	Administration,	2726
1876	Milton	Worcester,	Will,	2727
1818	Nancy	Shrewsbury,	Guardianship,	2728
1866	Nancy	Worcester,	Administration,	2729
1873	Nancy	Charlton,	Will,	2730
1777	Nathan	Norwich, Conn.,	Guardianship,	2731
1878	Nathan	Auburn,	Administration,	2732
1822	Nathan, Jr.	Westminster,	Administration,	2733
1854	Nathan H.	Westborough,	Guardianship,	2734
1868	Nellie F.	Woonsocket, R. I.,	Guardianship,	2735
1878	Oliver	Auburn,	Administration,	2736
1848	Phila	Mendon,	Will,	2737
1809	Polly	Charlton,	Guardianship,	2738
1815	Preserved	Ward,	Administration,	2739
1877	Quincy	Hubbardston,	Administration,	2740
1836	Reuben	Lunenburg,	Administration,	2741
1769	Reubin	Shrewsbury,	Guardianship,	2742
1809	Richard	Westminster,	Administration,	2743
1864	Richard	Royalston,	Will,	2744
1870	Richard	Gardner,	Will,	2745
1854	Roxa E.	Hubbardston,	Guardianship,	2746
1822	Sally	Westminster,	Guardianship,	2747

Year.	Name.	Residence.	Nature.	Case.
1859	BAKER, Sally	Phillipston,	Will,	2748
1880	Sally D.	Hubbardston,	Will,	2749
1795	Samuel	Berlin,	Will,	2750
1778	Sarah	Westborough,	Guardianship,	2751
1821	Sarah	Westminster,	Guardianship,	2752
1860	Sibbel	Templeton,	Administration,	2753
1826	Silas	Phillipston,	Dower,	2754
1777	Solomon	Westborough,	Administration,	2755
1821	Stephen M.	Westminster,	Guardianship,	2756
1837	Susanna	Douglas,	Will,	2757
1769	Thomas	Shrewsbury,	Will,	2758
1811	Thomas	Upton,	Administration,	2759
1842	Thomas	Gardner,	Will,	2760
1858	Thomas G.	Bolton,	Administration,	2761
1810	Thomas M.	Upton,	Administration,	2762
1850	Thomas M.	Upton,	Will,	2763
1821	William	Westminster,	Guardianship,	2764
1838	William	Lunenburg,	Guardianship,	2765
1878	William L.	Charlton,	Will,	2766
1864	William S.	Upton,	Administration,	2767
1854	BALCH, Adaline A.	Leominster,	Guardianship,	2768
1854	Er	Leominster,	Will,	2769
1876	Francis	Leominster,	Will,	2770
1854	Francis E.	Leominster,	Guardianship,	2771
1854	Harriet E.	Leominster,	Guardianship,	2772
1772	Josiah	Douglas,	Administration,	2773
1852	Lizzie F.	Boston,	Guardianship,	2774
1867	Susan B.	Leominster,	Administration,	2775
	BALCOM, BALCOLM, BALCOMB, BALCOME and BALKCOM,			
1838	Aaron	Douglas,	Guardianship,	2776
1865	Abigail	Winchendon,	Guardianship,	2777
1833	Alanson	Mendon,	Administration,	2778
1849	Amos	Douglas,	Guardianship,	2779
1849	Amos	Douglas,	Will,	2780
1855	Amos	Douglas,	Administration,	2781
1880	Ann M.	Douglas,	Will,	2782
1878	Betsey D.	Worcester,	Will,	2783
1834	Bezaleel	Douglas,	Administration,	2784
1834	Bezaleel	Douglas,	Pension,	2785
1837	Catharine	Templeton,	Will,	2786
1825	Clark	Douglas,	Administration,	2787
1844	David	Douglas,	Will,	2788
1838	David, Jr.	Douglas,	Administration,	2789
1839	David H.	Douglas,	Administration,	2790

**BALCOM, BALCOLM, BALCOMB,
BALCOME AND BALKCOM,**

Year.	Name.	Residence.	Nature.	Case.
1875	Dudley	Douglas,	Administration,	2791
1828	Ebenezer	Douglas,	Guardianship,	2792
1836	Ebenezer	Douglas,	Administration,	2793
1852	Edward L.	Douglas,	Administration,	2794
1737	Elijah	New Sherborn,	Guardianship,	2795
1769	Elijah	Douglas,	Guardianship,	2796
1868	Elizabeth S.	Worcester,	Administration,	2797
1852	Franklin C.	Douglas,	Guardianship,	2798
1823	Gideon	Winchendon,	Administration,	2799
1833	Hannah, etc.	Oxford,	Guardianship,	2800
1880	Herbert A.	Douglas,	Guardianship,	2801
1837	Jemima	Douglas,	Administration,	2802
1856	Jesse	Douglas,	Administration,	2803
1838	Joel C.	Douglas,	Guardianship,	2804
1732	Joseph	New Sherborn,	Will,	2805
1737	Joseph	New Sherborn,	Guardianship,	2806
1797	Joseph	Douglas,	Administration,	2807
1827	Joseph	Templeton,	Administration,	2808
1864	Judson	Grafton,	Administration,	2809
1826	Lincoln	Winchendon,	Guardianship,	2810
1857	Luther C.	Douglas,	Administration,	2811
1862	Lydia	Oxford,	Administration,	2812
1833	Manson	Douglas,	Guardianship,	2813
1860	Manson P.	Douglas,	Administration,	2814
1852	Manilla C.	Douglas,	Guardianship,	2815
1737	Mary	New Sherborn,	Guardianship,	2816
1769	Mary	Douglas,	Guardianship,	2817
1838	Mary	Douglas,	Guardianship,	2818
1850	Mary	Douglas,	Will,	2819
1867	Mary K.	Douglas,	Administration,	2820
1853	Mary L.	Douglas,	Guardianship,	2821
1861	Minerva S.	Douglas,	Adoption, etc.,	2822
1865	Moses	Douglas,	Will,	2823
1876	Myron J.	Oxford,	Administration,	2824
1832	Peter	Douglas,	Administration,	2825
1839	Prudence	Douglas,	Guardianship,	2826
1826	Sabrina	Winchendon,	Guardianship,	2827
1737	Samuel	New Sherborn,	Guardianship,	2828
1783	Samuel	Douglas,	Will,	2829
1853	Samuel	Douglas,	Administration,	2830
1737	Sarah	New Sherborn,	Guardianship,	2831
1849	Sibil	Douglas,	Guardianship,	2832
1867	Sumner	Bridgeport, Conn.,	Administration,	2833

**BALCOM, BALCOLM, BALCOMB,
BALCOME AND BALKCOM,**

Year	Name	Residence	Nature	Case
1839	Wellington	Douglas,	Guardianship,	2834
1839	Willard W.	Douglas,	Guardianship,	2835
1857	William N.	Douglas,	Guardianship,	2836
1860	BALDWIN, Abby Maria	Lunenburg,	Guardianship,	2837
1813	Abel	Fitchburg,	Will,	2838
1816	Abigail	Spencer,	Administration,	2839
1840	Abigail	Templeton,	Guardianship,	2840
1871	Addie E.	Kirkwood, Mo.,	Partition,	2841
1840	Althine	Templeton,	Guardianship,	2842
1850	Anna	Leicester,	Guardianship,	2843
1851	Anna	Leicester,	Will,	2844
1873	Arthur E.	Royalston,	Guardianship,	2845
1789	Asa	Templeton,	Guardianship,	2846
1811	Asa	Spencer,	Will,	2847
1830	Asenath	Fitchburg,	Guardianship,	2848
1868	Belle M.	Schoharie, N. Y.,	Administration,	2849
1873	Belle M.	Royalston,	Guardianship,	2850
1874	Belle M.	Athol,	Change of Name,	2851
1876	Belle M.	Athol,	Adoption,	2851
1820	Benjamin	Leicester	Administration,	2852
1789	Betsey	Templeton,	Guardianship,	2853
1830	Calvin	Fitchburg,	Guardianship,	2854
1785	Catherine	Worcester,	Guardianship,	2855
1870	Charles	Sterling,	Administration,	2856
1879	Charles	Southborough,	Administration,	2857
1839	Charles W.	Templeton,	Guardianship,	2858
1830	Daniel P.	Fitchburg,	Guardianship,	2859
1782	David	Spencer,	Guardianship,	2860
1784	David	Spencer,	Administration,	2860
1830	David	Fitchburg,	Administration,	2861
1873	Dolly W.	Templeton,	Will,	2862
1830	Edah	Fitchburg,	Guardianship,	2863
1839	Eden	Templeton,	Will,	2864
1840	Eden	Templeton,	Guardianship,	2865
1873	Eden	Athol,	Will,	2866
1873	Eden	Royalston,	Guardianship,	2867
1826	Eden, Jr.	Templeton,	Administration,	2868
1839	Eden A.	Templeton	Guardianship,	2869
1849	Edward	Worcester,	Guardianship,	2870
1820	Elizabeth	Winchendon,	Guardianship,	2871
1824	Elizabeth	Winchendon,	Administration,	2872
1849	Elizabeth	Leicester,	Will,	2873
1853	Ellen M.	Spencer,	Guardianship,	2874

YEAR.	NAME.	RESIDENCE.	NATURE.	CASE.
1879	BALDWIN, Ellen M.	Spencer,	Administration,	2875
1870	Flora I.	Sterling,	Guardianship,	2876
1870	Frank L.	Fitchburg,	Guardianship,	2877
1866	Freddie	Ashburnham,	Guardianship,	2878
1874	George S.	Fitchburg,	Administration,	2879
1860	Hannah C.	Lunenburg,	Guardianship,	2880
1853	Harriet A.	Spencer,	Guardianship,	2881
1790	Henry	Shrewsbury,	Administration,	2882
1790	Henry	Shrewsbury,	Guardianship,	2883
1872	Henry	Shrewsbury,	Administration,	2884
1790	Henry, Jr.	Shrewsbury,	Administration,	2885
1864	Hubbard H.	Winchendon,	Administration,	2886
1779	James	Leicester,	Will,	2887
1814	James	Leicester,	Will,	2888
1850	James H.	Shrewsbury,	Guardianship,	2889
1788	Jeduthan	Brookfield,	Will,	2890
1848	Jemima	Leicester,	Administration,	2891
1820	Jerusha	Winchendon,	Guardianship,	2892
1841	Jerusha	Fitchburg,	Administration,	2893
1834	John E.	Templeton,	Guardianship,	2894
1852	John W.	Spencer,	Guardianship,	2895
1761	Jonathan	Leicester,	Administration,	2896
1788	Jonathan	Templeton,	Administration,	2897
1789	Jonathan	Templeton,	Guardianship,	2898
1841	Jonathan	Templeton,	Guardianship,	2899
1841	Jonathan, 2d	Templeton,	Administration,	2900
1790	Joseph	Spencer,	Administration,	2901
1804	Joseph	Spencer,	Guardianship,	2902
1820	Joseph	Winchendon,	Guardianship,	2903
1878	Katie	Unknown,	Adoption, etc.,	2904
1837	Levi	Spencer,	Administration,	2905
1837	Levi	Spencer,	Pension,	2906
1841	Louisa J.	Templeton,	Guardianship,	2907
1841	Lucia O.	Templeton,	Guardianship,	2908
1789	Lucy	Templeton,	Guardianship,	2909
1788	Luke	Brookfield,	Guardianship,	2910
1836	Lydia	Leicester,	Will,	2911
1864	Marcus M.	Sterling,	Administration,	2912
1792	Martha	Shrewsbury,	Will,	2913
1865	Martha M.	Leicester,	Administration,	2914
1785	Mary	Worcester,	Guardianship,	2915
1879	Mary A.	Royalston,	Guardianship,	2916
1879	Mary E.	Royalston,	Administration,	2917
1852	Mary M.	Spencer,	Guardianship,	2918
1880	Mary N.	Templeton,	Administration,	2919

YEAR.	NAME.	RESIDENCE.	NATURE.	CASE.
1850	BALDWIN, Mehitable	Leicester,	Guardianship,	2920
1789	Nabby	Templeton,	Guardianship,	2921
1871	Nancy	Spencer,	Will,	2922
1784	Nathan	Worcester,	Will,	2923
1794	Nathan	Shrewsbury,	Guardianship,	2924
1847	Nathan	Leicester,	Administration,	2925
1850	Nathan	Shrewsbury,	Administration,	2926
1876	Nellie	Unknown,	Adoption, etc.,	2927
1789	Polly	Templeton,	Guardianship,	2928
1790	Polly	Shrewsbury,	Guardianship,	2929
1834	Polly	Templeton,	Administration,	2930
1870	Reuben B.	Fitchburg,	Administration,	2931
1847	Rhoda	Leicester,	Administration,	2932
1848	Rhoda	Leicester,	Guardianship,	2933
1849	Rhoda	Leicester,	Administration,	2933
1864	Rosetta H. L.	Winchendon,	Guardianship,	2934
1830	Roxanna	Fitchburg,	Guardianship,	2935
1789	Sally	Templeton,	Guardianship,	2936
1817	Samuel	Spencer,	Guardianship,	2937
1832	Samuel	Winchendon,	Will,	2938
1832	Samuel	Winchendon,	Guardianship,	2939
1837	Samuel	Leicester,	Will,	2940
1853	Simon	Spencer,	Administration,	2941
1814	Tamar	Leicester,	Administration,	2942
1844	Tilly	Phillipston,	Administration,	2943
1819	William	Winchendon,	Will,	2944
1820	William	Winchendon,	Guardianship,	2945
1851	William	Spencer,	Administration,	2946
1873	Winnie A.	Royalston,	Guardianship,	2947
1873	Winnie A.	Athol,	Adoption, etc.,	2948
1824	Zorobabel	Spencer,	Administration,	2949
1878	BALENTINE, Thomas	Millbury,	Will,	2950
	BALKCOM see BALCOM.			
1818	BALL, Aaron A.	Berlin,	Guardianship,	2951
1799	Abel	Northborough,	Guardianship,	2952
1810	Abel	Northborough,	Will,	2953
1849	Abigail S.	Leicester,	Guardianship,	2954
1764	Abraham	Brookfield,	Guardianship,	2955
1775	Abraham	Templeton,	Administration,	2956
1826	Adaline A.	Rutland,	Guardianship,	2957
1835	Addison	Petersham,	Guardianship,	2958
1833	Adonijah	Athol,	Will,	2959
1828	Adonijah, Jr.	Athol,	Administration,	2960
1829	Alonzo	Athol,	Guardianship,	2961
1870	Alvin	Berlin,	Administration,	2962

YEAR.	NAME.	RESIDENCE.	NATURE.	CASE.
1838	BALL, Amaziah	Sterling,	Administration,	2963
1867	Amos	Princeton,	Will,	2964
1829	Ann Sophia	Athol,	Guardianship,	2965
1858	Arminda E.	Holden,	Administration,	2966
1818	Barnabas B.	Berlin,	Guardianship,	2967
1868	Barnabas B.	Boylston,	Release,	2968
1764	Benjamin	Brookfield,	Guardianship,	2969
1795	Benjamin	Westborough,	Guardianship,	2970
1795	Benjamin	Westborough,	Will,	2971
1832	Benjamin	Grafton,	Administration,	2972
1843	Benjamin H.	Westborough,	Guardianship,	2973
1860	Benjamin L.	Northborough,	Administration,	2974
1875	Betsey S.	Princeton,	Administration,	2975
1865	Betsey T.	Milford,	Will,	2976
1813	Brigham	North Brookfield,	Guardianship,	2977
1750	Caleb	Leicester,	Guardianship,	2978
1877	Camelia H. E.	Holden,	Will,	2979
1850	Caroline L.	Milford,	Guardianship,	2980
1858	Charles A.	Holden,	Guardianship,	2981
1866	Charles E.	Spencer,	Administration,	2982
1858	Charles J.	Holden,	Administration,	2983
1876	Charles J.	Holden,	Guardianship,	2984
1829	Chester A.	Athol,	Guardianship,	2985
1777	Daniel	Spencer,	Guardianship,	2986
1854	Daniel	Spencer,	Administration,	2987
1759	David	Southborough,	Will,	2988
1870	Dennis W.	Fitchburg,	Guardianship,	2989
1871	Densmore	Boylston,	Administration,	2990
1783	Ebenezer	Northborough,	Administration,	2991
1857	Edward B.	Northborough,	Will,	2992
1853	Edward W.	Worcester,	Guardianship,	2993
1871	Edwin S.	Oxford,	Administration,	2994
1863	Eleanor	Athol,	Will,	2995
1762	Eleazer	Concord,	Guardianship,	2996
1765	Eleazer	Spencer,	Will,	2997
1766	Eleazer	Rutland,	Will,	2998
1772	Eleazer	Rutland,	Guardianship,	2999
1777	Eleazer	Spencer,	Guardianship,	3000
1826	Eleazer	Rutland,	Administration,	3001
1827	Eleazer	Rutland,	Partition,	3001
1865	Eli G.	Milford,	Will,	3002
1856	Elijah, Jr.	Shrewsbury,	Administration,	3003
1856	Elijah D.	Shrewsbury,	Guardianship,	3004
1815	Elizabeth	Bolton,	Guardianship,	3005
1853	Elizabeth	Northborough,	Will,	3006

YEAR.	NAME.	RESIDENCE.	NATURE.	CASE.
1856	BALL, Elliot H.	Shrewsbury,	Guardianship,	3007
1865	Ema B.	Milford,	Guardianship,	3008
1858	Emma E.	Holden,	Guardianship,	3009
1835	Eunice	Athol,	Administration,	3010
1818	Everlina	Athol,	Guardianship,	3011
1865	E. J.	Milford,	Guardianship,	3012
1843	Francis	Sterling,	Guardianship,	3013
1834	Francis A.	Athol,	Guardianship,	3014
1873	Frank A.	Clinton,	Guardianship,	3015
1836	George S.	Berlin,	Guardianship,	3016
1835	George W.	Shrewsbury,	Guardianship,	3017
1856	Georgiana A.	Shrewsbury,	Guardianship,	3018
1876	Gertrude A.	Holden,	Guardianship,	3019
1812	Gilman	Westborough,	Guardianship,	3020
1764	Hannah	Brookfield,	Guardianship,	3021
1801	Hannah	Northborough,	Guardianship,	3022
1818	Hannah A.	Athol,	Guardianship,	3023
1859	Helen M.	Gardner,	Guardianship,	3024
1860	Henrietta J.	Holden,	Guardianship,	3025
1877	Henry	Milford,	Administration,	3026
1830	Henry A.	Grafton,	Guardianship,	3027
1879	Henry H.	Webster,	Administration,	3028
1856	Henry S.	Shrewsbury,	Guardianship,	3029
1871	Hollis	Worcester,	Will,	3030
1757	Isaac	Southborough,	Guardianship,	3031
1759	Isaac	Worcester,	Guardianship,	3032
1817	Jacob	Athol,	Administration,	3033
1756	James	Westborough,	Will,	3034
1784	James	Shrewsbury,	Administration,	3035
1863	James	Northborough,	Administration,	3036
1834	Jane M. G.	Athol,	Guardianship,	3037
1768	Jemima	Northborough,	Guardianship,	3038
1829	Joel	Rutland,	Guardianship,	3039
1756	John	Worcester,	Will,	3040
1756	John	Westborough,	Guardianship,	3041
1757	John	Worcester,	Guardianship,	3042
1765	John	Spencer,	Guardianship,	3043
1775	John	Spencer,	Administration,	3044
1777	John	Spencer	Guardianship,	3045
1801	John	Northborough,	Administration,	3046
1825	John	Westborough,	Will,	3047
1838	John	Westminster,	Administration,	3048
1838	John	Westminster,	Pension,	3049
1870	John	Leicester,	Administration,	3050
1811	John, Jr.	Westborough,	Administration,	3051

YEAR.	NAME.	RESIDENCE.	NATURE.	CASE.
1864	BALL, Jonah	Boylston,	Administration,	3052
1755	Jonas	Southborough,	Guardianship,	3053
1759	Jonas	Worcester,	Guardianship,	3054
1807	Jonas	Southborough,	Will,	3055
1844	Jonas	Southborough,	Will,	3056
1847	Jonas	Northborough,	Will,	3057
1860	Jonas	Holden,	Administration,	3058
1860	Jonas	Holden,	Partition,	3058
1757	Jonathan	Southborough,	Guardianship,	3059
1759	Jonathan	Worcester,	Guardianship,	3060
1757	Joseph	Southborough,	Guardianship,	3061
1759	Joseph	Worcester,	Guardianship,	3062
1757	Josiah	Worcester,	Guardianship,	3063
1791	Josiah	Milford,	Will,	3064
1835	Josiah	Milford,	Will,	3065
1869	Josiah	Holden,	Administration,	3066
1834	Jotham	Holden,	Will,	3067
1871	Laura A.	Boylston,	Guardianship,	3068
1849	Lawson	Leicester,	Will,	3069
1819	Lazarus	Milford,	Guardianship,	3070
1853	LeRoy D,	Worcester,	Guardianship,	3071
1876	Lillian L.	Holden,	Guardianship,	3072
1795	Lucy	Westborough,	Guardianship,	3073
1835	Lucy	Westborough,	Guardianship,	3074
1849	Lucy	Worcester,	Guardianship,	3075
1862	Lucy	Worcester,	Pension,	3076
1871	Lucy	Leicester,	Administration,	3077
1835	Lucy A.	Petersham,	Guardianship,	3078
1861	Lucy H. E.	Worcester,	Will,	3079
1818	Lucy M.	Berlin,	Guardianship,	3080
1856	Lucy O.	Shrewsbury,	Guardianship,	3081
1795	Lydia	Westborough,	Guardianship,	3082
1866	Lydia	Northborough,	Will,	3083
1818	Lydia M.	Berlin,	Guardianship,	3084
1875	Mabel H.	Worcester,	Adoption, etc.,	3085
1875	Mabel S.	Worcester,	Adoption, etc.,	3086
1870	Manassah S.	Boylston,	Will,	3087
1836	Mark	Berlin,	Guardianship,	3088
1757	Martha	Southborough,	Guardianship,	3089
1879	Martha F.	Berlin,	Administration,	3090
1756	Mary	Worcester,	Guardianship,	3091
1772	Mary	Rutland,	Guardianship,	3092
1812	Mary	Westborough,	Guardianship,	3093
1872	Mary	Holden,	Guardianship,	3094
1873	Mary	Boylston,	Will,	3095

YEAR.	NAME.	RESIDENCE.	NATURE.	CASE.
1875	BALL, Mary	Northborough,	Will,	3096
1849	Mary E.	Leicester,	Guardianship,	3097
1873	Mary E.	Spencer,	Administration,	3098
1859	Mary L.	Gardner,	Administration,	3099
1856	Mary S.	Shrewsbury	Guardianship,	3100
1865	May T.	Milford,	Guardianship,	3101
1777	Mehitabel	Spencer,	Guardianship,	3102
1877	Melinda A.	Holden,	Guardianship,	3103
1880	Micah R.	Princeton,	Will,	3104
1820	Moses	Athol,	Will,	3105
1799	Nahum	Northborough,	Guardianship,	3106
1811	Nahum	W. Cambridge,	Guardianship,	3107
1814	Nahum	Northborough,	Administration,	3108
1833	Nahum	Southborough,	Administration,	3109
1849	Nahum W.	Northborough,	Administration,	3110
1836	Nancy	Berlin,	Guardianship,	3111
1860	Nancy	Lunenburg,	Administration,	3112
1756	Nathan	Worcester,	Guardianship,	3113
1768	Nathan	Northborough,	Administration,	3114
1768	Nathan	Northborough,	Guardianship,	3115
1805	Nathan	Bolton,	Will,	3116
1838	Nathan	Northborough,	Will,	3117
1838	Nathan	Northborough,	Partition,	3117
1866	Nixon	Southborough,	Will,	3118
1818	Oliver M.	Berlin,	Guardianship,	3119
1827	Oliver M.	Boylston,	Administration,	3120
1877	Oscar F.	Holden,	Adoption, etc.,	3121
1755	Peter	Southborough,	Administration,	3122
1734	Phinehas	Watertown,	Guardianship,	3123
1772	Phinehas	Rutland,	Guardianship,	3124
1854	Phinehas	Winchendon,	Will,	3125
1756	Rebecca	Southborough,	Guardianship,	3126
1792	Reuben	Unknown,	Guardianship,	3127
1873	Richard	Worcester,	Will,	3128
1854	Richard C.	Princeton,	Administration,	3129
1855	Robert	Dana,	Administration,	3130
1826	Sally	Westborough,	Administration,	3131
1757	Samuel	Southborough,	Guardianship,	3132
1826	Samuel	Rutland,	Administration,	3133
1859	Samuel A.	Gardner	Administration,	3134
1777	Sarah	Spencer,	Guardianship,	3135
1793	Sarah	Northborough,	Administration,	3136
1829	Sarah F.	Athol,	Guardianship,	3137
1879	Sarah M.	Spencer,	Administration,	3138
1856	Sarah Z.	Shrewsbury,	Guardianship,	3139

YEAR.	NAME.	RESIDENCE.	NATURE.	CASE.
1757	BALL, Silas	Southborough,	Guardianship,	3140
1764	Silas	Brookfield,	Guardianship,	3141
1787	Silas	Southborough,	Administration,	3142
1826	Silas R.	Rutland,	Guardianship,	3143
1798	Stephen	Northborough,	Administration,	3144
1850	Stephen	Northborough,	Will,	3145
1854	Stephen	Northborough,	Partition,	3145
1762	Submitt	Concord,	Guardianship,	3146
1843	Sukey	Boylston,	Guardianship,	3147
1809	Susanna	Northborough,	Administration,	3148
1777	Sybel	Spencer,	Guardianship,	3149
1735	Thomas	Uxbridge,	Guardianship,	3150
1760	Thomas	Brookfield,	Administration,	3151
1764	Thomas	Brookfield,	Guardianship,	3152
1768	Thomas	Bolton,	Will,	3153
1812	Thomas	Brookfield,	Will,	3154
1853	Warren	Worcester,	Administration,	3155
1870	Willard	Fitchburg,	Will,	3156
1815	William	Bolton,	Guardianship,	3157
1815	William	Boylston,	Will,	3158
1850	William E.	Milford,	Will,	3159
1865	William E.	Milford,	Guardianship,	3160
1861	Zenas	Milford,	Will,	3161
1843	BALLARD, Abigail	Lancaster,	Will,	3162
1834	Abigail R.	Lancaster,	Guardianship,	3163
1876	Alfred M.	Worcester,	Partition,	3164
1876	Arthur H.	Worcester,	Partition,	3165
1770	Benjamin	Lancaster,	Administration,	3166
1856	Carrie A.	Worcester,	Adoption, etc.,	3167
1868	Charles D.	Sturbridge,	Administration,	3168
1834	Charles H.	Lancaster,	Guardianship,	3169
1794	Ebenezer	Brookfield,	Will,	3170
1853	Eliphas	Lancaster,	Administration,	3171
1845	Elizabeth	Westminster,	Administration,	3172
1864	Elsey S.	Leominster,	Guardianship,	3173
1856	Eunice A.	Holden,	Adoption, etc.,	3174
1858	Fannie L.	Worcester,	Adoption, etc.,	3175
1830	Henry	Lancaster,	Administration,	3176
1838	Jeremiah	Lancaster,	Will,	3177
1770	John	Oxford,	Guardianship,	3178
1826	John	Lancaster,	Will,	3179
1840	John	Grafton,	Administration,	3180
1763	Jonathan	Oxford,	Will,	3181
1799	Josiah	Lancaster,	Will,	3182
1834	Louisa C.	Lancaster,	Guardianship,	3183

YEAR.	NAME.	RESIDENCE.	NATURE.	CASE.
1802	BALLARD, Lyman	Brookfield,	Guardianship,	3184
1857	Ruth B.	Dudley,	Administration,	3185
1841	Sally	Lancaster,	Administration,	3186
1834	Sarah E.	Lancaster,	Guardianship,	3187
1834	Thirza B.	Lancaster,	Guardianship,	3188
1838	Thomas	Lancaster,	Will,	3189
1864	William	Lancaster,	Administration,	3190
	BALLOU AND BALOU,			
1880	Almon	Blackstone,	Guardianship,	3191
1873	Arnold	Worcester,	Will,	3192
1868	Emma E.	Wrentham,	Adoption, etc.,	3193
1877	George C.	Woonsocket, R. I.,	Administration,	3194
1853	Hannah	Blackstone,	Will,	3195
1804	Hephzibah	Mendon,	Will,	3196
1871	Mabel M.	Winchendon,	Adoption, etc.,	3197
1875	Madge D.	Grafton,	Adoption, etc.,	3198
1860	Nella	Sutton,	Administration,	3199
1876	Otis D.	Woonsocket, R. I.,	Foreign Will,	3200
1848	Russell	Swanzey, N. H.,	Will,	3201
1880	Sarah	Uxbridge,	Administration,	3202
1866	Seth	Blackstone,	Administration,	3203
1881	Silas	Blackstone,	Administration,	3204
1876	Warren J.	Cumberland, R. I.,	Foreign Will,	3205
1839	BANCROFT, Aaron	Worcester,	Will,	3206
1872	Alonzo H.	Athol,	Guardianship,	3207
1873	Amanda F.	Auburn,	Will,	3208
1818	Amasa	Gardner,	Guardianship,	3209
1849	Betsey	Ashburnham,	Administration,	3210
1869	Betsey	Auburn,	Will,	3211
1881	Carl K.	Phillipston,	Adoption, etc.,	3212
1860	Charles	Athol,	Will,	3213
1872	Charles O.	Athol,	Administration,	3214
1782	David	Ward,	Will,	3215
1869	Ella	Worcester,	Guardianship,	3216
1864	Frank C.	Lancaster,	Guardianship,	3217
1872	George	Auburn,	Administration,	3218
1873	Gustavus C.	Worcester,	Administration,	3219
1866	Harrison	Petersham,	Will,	3220
1818	Harvey M.	Gardner,	Guardianship,	3221
1860	Henry K.	Auburn,	Administration,	3222
1863	Hervey	Auburn,	Will,	3223
1779	Jacob	Reading,	Guardianship,	3224
1869	James A.	Worcester,	Guardianship,	3225
1822	John C.	Worcester,	Will,	3226
1824	Jonas	Ward,	Administration,	3227

Year.	Name.	Residence.	Nature.	Case.
1860	BANCROFT, Jonas	Auburn,	Administration,	3228
1826	Jonathan	Gardner,	Administration,	3229
1840	Jonathan	Gardner,	Will,	3230
1839	Joseph	Millbury,	Pension,	3231
1870	Joseph	Millbury,	Administration,	3232
1846	Kendall	Auburn,	Will,	3233
1873	Laura E.	Auburn,	Guardianship,	3234
1875	Leonard	Rutland,	Administration,	3235
1870	Lizzie A.	Worcester,	Guardianship,	3236
1881	Martha	Worcester,	Guardianship,	3237
1849	Martin H.	Worcester,	Administration,	3238
1844	Mary	Worcester,	Will,	3239
1844	Mary	Auburn,	Administration,	3240
1818	Mary A.	Gardner,	Guardianship,	3241
1876	Mary G.	Milford,	Guardianship,	3242
1876	Mortimer	Upton,	Administration,	3243
1797	Moses	Sutton,	Will,	3244
1862	Myron J.	Millbury,	Administration,	3245
1867	Nancy	Worcester,	Administration,	3246
1870	Nathan S.	Worcester,	Guardianship,	3247
1881	Nathan W.	Worcester,	Administration,	3248
1765	Nathaniel	Reading,	Guardianship,	3249
1809	Nathaniel	Gerry,	Will,	3250
1879	N. Rebecca	Worcester,	Will,	3251
1862	Peter M.	Worcester,	Administration,	3252
1818	Sally W.	Gardner,	Guardianship,	3253
1868	Samuel N.	Auburn,	Administration,	3254
1849	Sarah	Worcester,	Guardianship,	3255
1875	Sarah	Worcester,	Will,	3256
1818	Smyrna	Gardner,	Administration,	3257
1840	Smyrna O.	Gardner,	Guardianship,	3258
1818	Smyrna W.	Gardner,	Guardianship,	3259
1880	Smyrna W.	Gardner,	Administration,	3260
1829	Solomon	Millbury,	Administration,	3261
1872	Tarbell	Lancaster,	Will,	3262
1776	Timothy	Lunenburg,	Administration,	3263
1834	Timothy	Ward,	Will,	3264
1875	Timothy	Worcester,	Will,	3265
1854	Timothy W.	Worcester,	Administration,	3266
1855	Timothy W.	Worcester,	Guardianship,	3267
1818	Viola	Gardner,	Guardianship,	3268
1835	William	Dana,	Pension,	3269
1879	William H.	Petersham,	Administration,	3270
1873	Willis H.	Auburn,	Guardianship,	3271
1779	BANGS, Azariah	Barre,	Will,	3272

YEAR.	NAME.	RESIDENCE.	NATURE.	CASE.
1852	BANGS, Edmund	Barre,	Administration,	3273
1818	Edward	Worcester,	Will,	3274
1838	Edward D.	Worcester,	Will,	3275
1818	Elijah	Hardwick,	Will,	3276
1855	Elijah	Hardwick,	Will,	3277
1798	Enoch	Barre,	Will,	3278
1852	George	Barre,	Guardianship,	3279
1821	Hannah	Barre,	Will,	3280
1789	Judith Fox	Barre,	Guardianship,	3281
1789	Nathaniel	Barre,	Guardianship,	3282
1853	Patty	Barre,	Will,	3283
1789	Sarah	Barre,	Guardianship,	3284
1881	Watson	Barre,	Will,	3285
	BANISTER AND BANNISTER,			
1848	Aaron	Spencer,	Administration,	3286
1879	Addie T.	Worcester,	Guardianship,	3287
1841	Andrew	Brookfield,	Administration,	3288
1841	Andrew	Brookfield,	Pension,	3289
1839	Antoinette T.	Worcester,	Guardianship,	3290
1815	Barzillai	Southborough,	Will,	3291
1815	Caleb S.	Southborough,	Guardianship,	3292
1857	Charles H.	Brookfield,	Guardianship,	3293
1874	Eli B.	Boylston,	Administration,	3294
1857	Emma	Worcester,	Adoption, etc.,	3295
1852	Fanny	Spencer,	Will,	3296
1811	Francis B.	Newburyport,	Foreign Sale,	3297
1857	Francis W.	Brookfield,	Guardianship,	3298
1864	George S.	Westborough,	Will,	3299
1822	John	Shrewsbury,	Administration,	3300
1758	Joseph, Jr.	Brookfield,	Administration,	3301
1815	Joseph G.	Southborough,	Guardianship,	3302
1839	Julius K.	Worcester,	Guardianship,	3303
1879	Kate	Worcester,	Administration,	3304
1861	Linus	West Brookfield,	Administration,	3305
1839	Marcella L.	Worcester,	Guardianship,	3306
1826	Martha F.	Richmond, N. Y.,	Foreign Sale,	3307
1870	Mary A.	Worcester,	Administration,	3308
1826	Mary A. M. W.	Richmond, N. Y.,	Foreign Sale,	3309
1826	Mary H.	Shrewsbury,	Guardianship,	3310
1825	Nathan	Boylston,	Will,	3311
1846	Nathan	Southborough,	Administration,	3312
1879	Nettie J.	Worcester,	Guardianship,	3313
1865	Samuel	Worcester,	Will,	3314
1819	Seth	Brookfield,	Will,	3315
1822	Seth	Brookfield,	Guardianship,	3316

YEAR.	NAME.	RESIDENCE.	NATURE.	CASE.
	BANISTER and BANNISTER,			
1858	Seth	Boylston,	Will,	3317
1861	Seth W.	Brookfield,	Administration,	3318
1835	Solomon	Brookfield,	Will,	3319
1835	Solomon	Brookfield,	Pension,	3320
1839	Susan S.	Worcester,	Guardianship,	3321
1811	William B.	Newburyport,	Foreign Sale,	3322
1857	William B.	Brookfield,	Guardianship,	3323
1875	BANKS, Robert	Westborough,	Administration,	3324
	BANNISTER see BANISTER.			
1877	BAPTISTE, Ephraim	Worcester,	Guardianship,	3325
	BARBER and BARBOUR,			
1807	Allen	Worcester,	Guardianship,	3326
1832	Asa	Worcester,	Administration,	3327
1867	Benjamin	Worcester,	Will,	3328
1873	Benjamin A.	Worcester,	Guardianship,	3329
1858	Charles A.	Upton,	Administration,	3330
1873	Charles E.	Westminster,	Guardianship,	3331
1873	Charles J.	Gardner,	Administration,	3332
1845	Charles N.	Milford,	Guardianship,	3333
1806	Ebenezer	Worcester,	Administration,	3334
1879	Eliot	Grafton,	Administration,	3335
1853	Emily	Athol,	Adoption, etc.,	3336
1873	Eva R.	Westminster,	Guardianship,	3337
1847	Francis	Worcester,	Administration,	3338
1875	Frank	Templeton,	Guardianship,	3339
1864	Frank W.	Worcester,	Guardianship,	3340
1871	George W.	Worcester,	Guardianship,	3341
1843	Henry D.	Worcester,	Guardianship,	3342
1864	Henry P.	Worcester,	Guardianship,	3343
1812	James	Worcester,	Will,	3344
1845	James	Milford,	Administration,	3345
1807	Joel	Worcester,	Guardianship,	3346
1810	Joel	Worcester,	Administration,	3347
1777	John	Worcester,	Will,	3348
1822	John	Thompson, Conn.,	Administration,	3349
1792	John, Jr.	Worcester,	Administration,	3350
1874	John P.	Winchendon,	Will,	3351
1807	Joseph	Worcester,	Guardianship,	3352
1811	Joseph	Worcester,	Will,	3353
1871	Josephine A.	Worcester,	Guardianship,	3354
1870	Josephine M.	Athol,	Administration,	3355
1807	Levi	Worcester,	Guardianship,	3356
1874	Levi H.	Worcester,	Administration,	3357
1807	Lydia	Worcester,	Guardianship,	3358

	BARBER AND BARBOUR,			
1857	Maria	Worcester,	Guardianship,	3359
1871	Martha B.	Worcester,	Guardianship,	3360
1812	Mary	Worcester,	Administration,	3361
1876	Mary	Mendon,	Will,	3362
1807	Nancy	Worcester,	Guardianship,	3363
1864	Nancy	Milford,	Will,	3364
1812	Nathan	Berlin,	Will,	3365
1843	Reuel	Worcester,	Administration,	3366
1769	Robert	Worcester,	Will,	3367
1744	Robert, Jr.	Westfield,	Guardianship,	3368
1807	Samuel	Worcester,	Guardianship,	3369
1790	Sarah	Worcester,	Will,	3370
1853	Sarah	Athol,	Administration,	3371
1870	Silas	Worcester,	Will,	3372
1875	Silas	Templeton,	Administration,	3373
1875	Silas A.	Templeton,	Guardianship,	3374
1845	Thomas	Worcester,	Guardianship,	3375
1845	Thomas	Worcester,	Will,	3376
1873	Walter R.	Milford	Administration,	3377
1879	William T.	Worcester,	Administration,	3378
1871	BARCLAY, John	Spencer,	Will,	3379
1847	BARD, Aron	Lunenburg,	Will,	3380
	BARDEEN, BARDINE, BARDEN AND BARDENS,			
1859	Charles W.	Fitchburg,	Guardianship,	3381
1799	Daniel	Harvard,	Administration,	3382
1859	George E.	Fitchburg,	Guardianship,	3383
1854	George W.	Millbury,	Adoption,	3384
1770	James	Uxbridge,	Administration,	3385
1859	Mary E. S.	Fitchburg,	Guardianship,	3386
1770	Moses	Uxbridge,	Guardianship,	3387
1770	Stephen	Uxbridge,	Guardianship,	3388
1833	Thomas	Harvard,	Will,	3389
1859	William T.	Fitchburg,	Will,	3390
	BARDWELL AND BORDWELL,			
1848	Eliza Jane	Grafton,	Guardianship,	3391
1870	Emeline	Southbridge,	Change of Name,	3392
1879	Frederick R.	Worcester,	Administration,	3393
1865	George W.	Upton,	Administration,	3394
1866	Horatio	Oxford,	Will,	3395
1843	Lydia	New Braintree,	Administration,	3396
1863	BARKER, Anna H.	Fitchburg,	Guardianship,	3397
1832	Anne	Southbridge,	Will,	3398
1855	Betsey	Grafton,	Administration,	3399

Year.	Name.	Residence.	Nature.	Case.
1853	BARKER, Calvin	Millbury,	Administration,	3400
1838	Calvin W.	Millbury,	Guardianship,	3401
1807	Clarissa	Worcester,	Guardianship,	3402
1807	Eliza	Worcester,	Guardianship,	3403
1852	Eliza A.	Fitchburg,	Guardianship,	3404
1864	Hiram	Worcester,	Administration,	3405
1846	Isabella G.	Richmond, Va.,	Guardianship,	3406
1776	Jane	Upton,	Will,	3407
1870	Joel	Fitchburg,	Will,	3408
1829	John	Leominster,	Administration,	3409
1835	John H.	Grafton,	Administration,	3410
1807	Jonathan	Worcester,	Administration,	3411
1813	Joseph	Gardner,	Guardianship,	3412
1813	Joseph	Gardner,	Administration,	3413
1838	Lucy Ann	Millbury,	Guardianship,	3414
1813	Martha	Gardner,	Guardianship,	3415
1852	Martha M.	Fitchburg,	Guardianship,	3416
1813	Mary	Gardner,	Guardianship,	3417
1844	Mary E.	Grafton,	Guardianship,	3418
1852	Mary L.	Fitchburg,	Guardianship,	3419
1777	Nathan	Princeton,	Guardianship,	3420
1865	Pliny L.	Leominster,	Guardianship,	3421
1875	Reuben	Rutland,	Administration,	3422
1802	Robert	Lancaster,	Will,	3423
1881	Samuel D.	Worcester,	Administration,	3424
1856	Thomas H.	Fitchburg,	Administration,	3425
1757	William	Upton,	Will,	3426
1804	William	Worcester,	Administration,	3427
1828	BARLOW, Asahel	Warren,	Guardianship,	3428
1857	Charles F.	Southbridge,	Adoption,	3429
1863	Charles F.	Hardwick,	Guardianship,	3430
1878	Charles F.	Southbridge,	Administration,	3431
1806	Eliakim	Brookfield,	Will,	3432
1867	Elmer C.	West Brookfield,	Guardianship,	3433
1867	Eugene T.	West Brookfield,	Guardianship,	3434
1867	Frank W.	West Brookfield,	Guardianship,	3435
1863	Fred C.	Hardwick,	Guardianship,	3436
1828	Huldah	Warren,	Guardianship,	3437
1856	Ira F.	Southbridge,	Administration,	3438
1867	James M.	Hardwick,	Administration,	3439
1850	John	Hardwick,	Administration,	3440
1863	John H.	Hardwick,	Guardianship,	3441
1862	Sarah C.	Southbridge,	Will,	3442
1827	Silas	Brookfield,	Administration,	3443
1830	Susanna	Hardwick,	Will,	3444

Year.	Name.	Residence.	Nature.	Case.
1867	BARLOW, Sylvanus T.	West Brookfield,	Administration,	3445
1863	Willard W.	Hardwick,	Guardianship,	3446
1813	William	Brookfield,	Administration,	3447
1872	William	Milford,	Adoption, etc.,	3448
1827	Wyatt	Hardwick,	Will,	3449
1856	Wyatt	Hardwick,	Administration,	3450
1870	BARNARD, Abigail	Northborough,	Administration,	3451
1861	Amory	Northborough,	Administration,	3452
1831	Ann A. S.	Lancaster,	Guardianship,	3453
1855	Annas	Leominster,	Administration,	3454
1857	Benjamin	Harvard,	Will,	3455
1875	Betsey	Auburn,	Administration,	3456
1851	Caroline	Worcester,	Guardianship,	3457
1813	Daniel	Northborough,	Administration,	3458
1828	David	Harvard,	Will,	3459
1850	Ebenezer L.	Worcester,	Administration,	3460
1804	Edmund	Westminster,	Administration,	3461
1805	Edmund	Westminster,	Guardianship,	3462
1851	Edward L.	Worcester,	Guardianship,	3463
1864	Edward L.	Worcester,	Administration,	3464
1851	Eliza	Worcester,	Guardianship,	3465
1837	Elizabeth	Northborough,	Will,	3466
1863	Elizabeth	North Brookfield,	Will,	3467
1868	Emory	Harvard,	Administration,	3468
1833	Ephraim	Northborough,	Administration,	3469
1851	Frederick J.	Worcester,	Guardianship,	3470
1864	George E.	Worcester,	Administration,	3471
1875	Hannah C.	Worcester,	Will,	3472
1862	Harriet V. A.	Harvard,	Will,	3473
1831	Henry B.	Lancaster,	Guardianship,	3474
1851	Henry S.	Berlin,	Guardianship,	3475
1788	Isaac	Worcester,	Administration,	3476
1862	Jemima	Harvard,	Will,	3477
1808	Joab	Harvard,	Guardianship,	3478
1871	Joab	Bolton,	Will,	3479
1808	Joel	Harvard,	Guardianship,	3480
1871	Joel	Bolton,	Will,	3481
1796	John	Berlin,	Guardianship,	3482
1830	John	Worcester,	Will,	3483
1873	John	Worcester,	Will,	3484
1862	John G.	Auburn,	Will,	3485
1832	Josiah	Berlin,	Administration,	3486
1808	Jotham	Harvard,	Administration,	3487
1808	Levi	Harvard,	Guardianship,	3488
1853	Lewis	Worcester,	Administration,	3489

(8o)

YEAR.	NAME.	RESIDENCE.	NATURE.	CASE.
1851	BARNARD, Lewis H.	Berlin,	Will,	3490
1839	Lucy	Harvard,	Administration,	3491
1850	Lucy	Harvard,	Administration,	3492
1866	Lucy	Sterling,	Will,	3493
1856	Luther	Northborough,	Administration,	3494
1843	Martha	Berlin,	Administration,	3495
1844	Martha	Berlin,	Pension,	3496
1844	Mary	Harvard,	Will,	3497
1862	Mary A.	Harvard,	Guardianship,	3498
1871	Mary A.	Sterling,	Administration,	3499
1841	Oliver H.	Berlin,	Administration,	3500
1794	Phebe	Worcester,	Guardianship,	3501
1865	Phinehas	Harvard,	Will,	3502
1805	Polly	Westminster,	Guardianship,	3503
1807	Sally	Leicester,	Will,	3504
1831	Samuel	Harvard,	Will,	3505
1813	Sarah	Leicester,	Guardianship,	3506
1834	Sarah	Worcester,	Administration,	3507
1839	Sarah	Leicester,	Will,	3508
1862	Susan J. M.	Harvard,	Guardianship,	3509
1813	William	Leicester,	Guardianship,	3510
	BARNES AND BARNS,			
1734	Aaron	Brookfield,	Guardianship,	3511
1794	Aaron	Brookfield,	Administration,	3512
1823	Aaron	Berlin,	Administration,	3513
1783	Aaron, Jr.	Brookfield,	Guardianship,	3514
1859	Abby M.	Worcester,	Guardianship,	3515
1814	Abigail	Brookfield,	Will,	3516
1734	Abigaill	Brookfield,	Guardianship,	3517
1857	Adams P.	Worcester,	Will,	3518
1855	Adelaide H.	Worcester,	Guardianship,	3519
1872	Adoniram J.	North Brookfield,	Guardianship,	3520
1845	Albert H.	Brookfield,	Guardianship,	3521
1865	Alfred	Thompson, Conn.,	Will,	3522
1870	Alfred W.	Fitchburg,	Guardianship,	3523
1863	Alice E.	Spencer,	Guardianship,	3524
1867	Allen A.	Westminster,	Guardianship,	3525
1858	Anna J.	Northborough,	Guardianship,	3526
1855	Arabella S.	Worcester,	Guardianship,	3527
1877	Artemas	Worcester,	Administration,	3528
1811	Asa	Brookfield,	Administration,	3529
1857	Asa	West Brookfield,	Will,	3530
1854	Asenath M.	Berlin,	Guardianship,	3531
1854	Baxter	Worcester,	Administration,	3532
1864	Baxter	West Brookfield,	Administration,	3533

YEAR.	NAME.	RESIDENCE.	NATURE.	CASE.
	BARNES AND BARNS,			
1820	Bela	Spencer,	Guardianship,	3534
1878	Benjamin	Millbury,	Will,	3535
1863	Betsey	Berlin,	Will,	3536
1864	Betsey	West Brookfield,	Administration,	3537
1871	Bridget	Southborough,	Guardianship,	3538
1871	Catharine	Southborough,	Guardianship,	3539
1876	Catharine	Thompson, Conn.,	Administration,	3540
1872	Catherine L.	North Brookfield,	Guardianship,	3541
1811	Charles	Leicester,	Guardianship,	3542
1826	Charles	Westminster,	Guardianship,	3543
1867	Charles A.	Westminster,	Guardianship,	3544
1845	Charles E.	Brookfield,	Guardianship,	3545
1868	Charles J.	Athol,	Administration,	3546
1877	Clarinda	Hardwick,	Administration,	3547
1748	Comfort	Brookfield,	Guardianship,	3548
1748	Comfort	Brookfield,	Will,	3549
1844	Daniel	Hubbardston,	Will,	3550
1854	Daniel	Berlin,	Administration,	3551
1814	David	Spencer	Will,	3552
1827	David	Hubbardston,	Administration,	3553
1828	David	Hubbardston,	Guardianship,	3554
1837	David	Hubbardston,	Partition,	3553
1839	David	Boylston,	Will,	3555
1854	David	Berlin,	Guardianship,	3556
1875	David	Hubbardston,	Will,	3557
1814	David, Jr.	Spencer,	Administration,	3558
1846	David B.	Westminster,	Guardianship,	3559
1846	David B.	Westminster,	Administration,	3560
1812	Dinah	Boylston,	Administration,	3561
1797	Dorothy	Brookfield,	Guardianship,	3562
1827	Dorothy	North Brookfield,	Administration,	3563
1872	Edith J.	West Brookfield,	Guardianship,	3564
1875	Edward	Worcester,	Guardianship,	3565
1874	Edwin M.	Dudley,	Guardianship,	3566
1872	Elbridge E.	North Brookfield,	Guardianship,	3567
1824	Eleanor	Berlin,	Guardianship,	3568
1845	Electa J.	Brookfield,	Guardianship,	3569
1773	Elijah	Brookfield,	Guardianship,	3570
1837	Elijah H.	Templeton,	Administration,	3571
1860	Eliza A.	Chelsea,	Adoption, etc.,	3572
1827	Eliza W.	Western,	Guardianship,	3573
1748	Elizabeth	Brookfield,	Guardianship,	3574
1824	Elizabeth	Berlin,	Guardianship,	3575
1854	Elizabeth F.	Auburn,	Guardianship,	3576

(S2)

YEAR.	NAME.	RESIDENCE.	NATURE.	CASE.
	BARNES AND BARNS,			
1845	Elizabeth R.	Brookfield,	Guardianship,	3577
1872	Ellen J.	North Brookfield,	Guardianship,	3578
1866	Elvira	Hardwick,	Will,	3579
1854	Emma O.	Auburn,	Guardianship,	3580
1854	Eva C.	Auburn,	Guardianship,	3581
1875	Ezra C.	West Brookfield,	Guardianship,	3582
1874	Fanny	Worcester,	Administration,	3583
1862	Fanny B.	West Brookfield,	Will,	3584
1869	Florence E.	Westminster,	Guardianship,	3585
1807	Fortunatus	Berlin,	Will,	3586
1855	Frances S.	Worcester,	Guardianship,	3587
1796	Francis	Brookfield,	Administration,	3588
1813	Francis	Westminster,	Administration,	3589
1828	Francis	North Brookfield,	Administration,	3590
1826	Franklin	Westminster,	Guardianship,	3591
1847	Frederick	Brookfield,	Will,	3592
1864	Gardner F.	Worcester,	Administration,	3593
1849	George B.	Lancaster,	Guardianship,	3594
1838	George E.	Dudley,	Guardianship,	3595
1866	George H.	Barre,	Administration,	3596
1846	George M.	Westminster,	Guardianship,	3597
1734	Hannah	Brookfield,	Guardianship,	3598
1748	Hannah	Brookfield,	Guardianship,	3599
1864	Hannah	Berlin,	Will,	3600
1845	Harriet W.	Brookfield,	Guardianship,	3601
1874	Hattie F.	Dudley,	Guardianship,	3602
1879	Henry	Northborough,	Administration,	3603
1874	Herbert W.	Dudley,	Guardianship,	3604
1832	Homer	Royalston,	Guardianship,	3605
1797	Hubbard	Brookfield,	Guardianship,	3606
1827	Hubbard	North Brookfield,	Administration,	3607
1858	Irving A.	Worcester,	Guardianship,	3608
1866	Irving A.	Worcester,	Will,	3609
1849	James B.	Lancaster,	Will,	3610
1872	James F.	West Brookfield,	Administration,	3611
1846	James H.	Westminster,	Guardianship,	3612
1864	James H.	Fitchburg,	Guardianship,	3613
1874	James L.	Dudley,	Guardianship,	3614
1748	John	Brookfield,	Guardianship,	3615
1789	John	Brookfield,	Administration,	3616
1815	John	Paxton,	Administration,	3617
1826	John	Western,	Administration,	3618
1827	John	Western,	Guardianship,	3619
1843	John	Brookfield,	Will,	3620

Year.	Name.	Residence.	Nature.	Case.
	BARNES AND BARNS,			
1852	John	Oxford,	Will,	3621
1871	John	Southborough,	Guardianship,	3622
1876	John	Worcester,	Will,	3623
1845	John W.	Brookfield,	Guardianship,	3624
1867	John W.	Westminster,	Guardianship,	3625
1797	Jonah	Brookfield,	Guardianship,	3626
1830	Jonas	Hardwick,	Administration,	3627
1844	Jonas R.	Brookfield,	Administration,	3628
1797	Jonathan	Brookfield,	Guardianship,	3629
1797	Jonathan	Brookfield,	Administration,	3630
1748	Joseph	Brookfield,	Guardianship,	3631
1859	Joseph	Worcester,	Administration,	3632
1859	Josephine E.	Worcester,	Guardianship,	3633
1843	Josiah	Dudley,	Will,	3634
1843	Josiah	Dudley,	Pension,	3635
1826	Leonard	Westminster,	Guardianship,	3636
1872	Lillian E.	West Brookfield,	Guardianship,	3637
1855	Linda M.	Worcester,	Guardianship,	3638
1836	Lois	Boylston,	Administration,	3639
1872	Lorenzo	North Brookfield,	Guardianship,	3640
1865	Lovina	Warren,	Administration,	3641
1874	Lucian M.	Dudley,	Administration,	3642
1734	Lucy	Brookfield,	Guardianship,	3643
1828	Lucy	Hubbardston,	Guardianship,	3644
1838	Lucy	Milford,	Administration,	3645
1870	Lucy	Worcester,	Will,	3646
1748	Lydia	Brookfield,	Guardianship,	3647
1811	Lydia	New Braintree,	Administration,	3648
1820	Lydia	Spencer,	Guardianship,	3649
1811	Lydia E.	Leicester,	Guardianship,	3650
1849	Marina	Lancaster,	Guardianship,	3651
1854	Martha	Berlin,	Guardianship,	3652
1859	Martha	Berlin,	Guardianship,	3653
1858	Martha W.	Worcester,	Administration,	3654
1734	Mary	Brookfield,	Guardianship,	3655
1748	Mary	Brookfield,	Guardianship,	3656
1820	Mary	Spencer,	Guardianship,	3657
1826	Mary	Westminster,	Guardianship,	3658
1843	Mary	Hardwick,	Will,	3659
1872	Mary	Lancaster,	Will,	3660
1854	Mary A.	Auburn,	Guardianship,	3661
1859	Mary A.	Worcester,	Guardianship,	3662
1872	Mary A.	North Brookfield,	Guardianship,	3663
1824	Mary E.	Berlin,	Guardianship,	3664

YEAR.	NAME.	RESIDENCE.	NATURE.	CASE.
	BARNES AND BARNS,			
1867	Mary E.	Westminster,	Guardianship,	3665
1849	Mary M.	Lancaster,	Guardianship,	3666
1865	Mary M.	Brookfield,	Guardianship,	3667
1869	Merrick	Westminster,	Administration,	3668
1748	Miriam	Brookfield,	Guardianship,	3669
1748	Moses	Brookfield,	Guardianship,	3670
1802	Moses	Brookfield,	Will,	3671
1835	Moses	Brookfield,	Will,	3672
1854	Moses	West Brookfield,	Will,	3673
1859	Myron E.	Shrewsbury,	Guardianship,	3674
1857	Nancy	Auburn,	Administration,	3675
1819	Nathan	North Brookfield,	Administration,	3676
1784	Noah	Brookfield,	Will,	3677
1797	Noah	Brookfield,	Guardianship,	3678
1811	Olive	Leicester,	Guardianship,	3679
1806	Oliver	Boylston,	Administration,	3680
1847	Oliver	Boylston,	Will,	3681
1826	Patience	North Brookfield,	Will,	3682
1838	Patience	Hardwick,	Guardianship,	3683
1869	Persis	Brookfield,	Administration,	3684
1818	Peter	Sutton,	Administration,	3685
1854	Phenton	Auburn,	Will,	3686
1824	Phineas	Unknown,	Sale Real Est.,	3687
1734	Rachell	Brookfield,	Guardianship,	3688
1792	Richard	Westborough,	Administration,	3689
1834	Sabra E.	Bolton,	Guardianship,	3690
1820	Sally	Spencer,	Guardianship,	3691
1733	Samuel	Brookfield,	Administration,	3692
1762	Samuel	Leicester,	Will,	3693
1804	Samuel	Spencer,	Guardianship,	3694
1811	Samuel	Spencer,	Administration,	3695
1814	Samuel	Westminster,	Guardianship,	3696
1820	Samuel	Spencer,	Guardianship,	3697
1878	Samuel	Spencer,	Administration,	3698
1870	Samuel S.	Worcester,	Guardianship,	3699
1877	Samuel S.	Worcester,	Administration,	3699
1858	Samuel W.	Shrewsbury,	Administration,	3700
1748	Sarah	Brookfield,	Guardianship,	3701
1878	Sarah B.	Westminster,	Administration,	3702
1830	Sarah E.	North Brookfield,	Guardianship,	3703
1842	Sarah E.	Worcester,	Guardianship,	3704
1864	Sewell	Westminster,	Administration,	3705
1874	Solomon L.	West Brookfield,	Administration,	3706
1869	Stella L.	Westminster,	Guardianship,	3707

Year	Name.	Residence.	Nature	Case.
	BARNES AND BARNS,			
1826	Sullivan	Westminster,	Administration,	3708
1870	Sumner S.	Worcester,	Guardianship,	3709
1877	Sumner S.	Worcester,	Administration,	3709
1863	Susan B.	Spencer,	Guardianship,	3710
1871	Susannah	North Brookfield,	Will,	3711
1761	Thomas	Brookfield,	Administration,	3712
1797	Thomas	Brookfield,	Guardianship,	3713
1851	Thomas	North Brookfield,	Administration,	3714
1820	Wait	Boylston,	Pension,	3715
1855	Walter H.	Worcester,	Guardianship,	3716
1830	Welcome	Berlin,	Will,	3717
1803	William	Brookfield,	Guardianship,	3718
1853	William	Berlin,	Administration,	3719
1875	William	Westminster,	Administration,	3720
1868	Wilson A.	Athol,	Guardianship,	3721
1825	Zebulon	Brookfield,	Administration,	3722
1835	BARNEY, Nathaniel	Nantucket,	Trustee,	3723
1869	Ozias	Southborough,	Administration,	3724
	BARNS see BARNES.			
1861	BARNUM, Charles H.	Springfield,	Adoption,	3725
1841	Ephraim	Brookfield,	Guardianship,	3726
1816	BARR, Asa	New Braintree,	Guardianship,	3727
1829	Deborah	New Braintree,	Will,	3728
1815	Elizabeth P.	New Braintree,	Guardianship,	3729
1868	Eunice	New Braintree,	Will,	3730
1822	George	New Braintree,	Will,	3731
1862	Hiram	Spencer,	Administration,	3732
1818	James	New Braintree,	Will,	3733
1814	James, Jr.	New Braintree,	Administration,	3734
1864	James F.	West Brookfield,	Guardianship,	3735
1815	James H.	New Braintree,	Guardianship,	3736
1815	John	New Braintree,	Will,	3737
1866	John A.	Spencer,	Administration,	3738
1866	John A.	Spencer,	Pension,	3739
1865	Lydia E.	Sturbridge,	Guardianship,	3740
1829	Matthew	New Braintree,	Administration,	3741
1815	Micah R.	New Braintree,	Guardianship,	3742
1864	Orlando S.	West Brookfield,	Guardianship,	3743
1816	Phineas W.	New Braintree,	Guardianship,	3744
1874	Phinehas W.	Petersham,	Will,	3745
1816	Priscilla A.	New Braintree,	Guardianship,	3746
1816	Roxana	New Braintree,	Guardianship,	3747
1879	Sally T.	Spencer,	Administration,	3748
1815	Sarah A.	New Braintree,	Guardianship,	3749

YEAR.	NAME.	RESIDENCE.	NATURE.	CASE.
	BARRELL AND BERRELL,			
1852	Abigail	Westminster,	Administration,	3750
1855	Charles W.	Westminster,	Guardianship,	3751
1865	Charles W.	Ashburnham,	Will,	3752
1841	Elmer	Ashburnham,	Guardianship,	3753
1807	Fanny	Westminster,	Guardianship,	3754
1807	John	Westminster,	Guardianship,	3755
1841	John	Ashburnham,	Administration,	3756
1841	John F.	Ashburnham,	Guardianship,	3757
1806	Luther	Westminster,	Administration,	3758
1807	Luther	Westminster,	Guardianship,	3759
1854	Luther	Westminster,	Will,	3760
1807	Nabby L.	Westminster,	Guardianship,	3761
1875	Nahum	Westminster,	Will,	3762
1807	Nelson	Westminster,	Guardianship,	3763
1841	Nelson	Ashburnham,	Guardianship,	3764
1871	Nelson D., etc.	Barre,	Administration,	3765
1841	Otis	Ashburnham,	Guardianship,	3766
1855	Theodore	Westminster,	Guardianship,	3767
1877	Walter H.	Ashburnham,	Adoption, etc.,	3768
1860	William	Ashburnham,	Will,	3769
	BARRETT AND BARRITT,			
1869	Albert	New Braintree,	Administration,	3770
1779	Alford	Barre,	Guardianship,	3771
1821	Almira	Sturbridge,	Guardianship,	3772
1851	Almira E.	Ashburnham,	Guardianship,	3773
1793	Amasa	Sturbridge,	Guardianship,	3774
1879	Anna M.	Barre,	Guardianship,	3775
1858	Arthur C.	Lancaster,	Guardianship,	3776
1786	Benjamin	Brookfield,	Will,	3777
1851	Benjamin	West Brookfield,	Administration,	3778
1851	Benjamin	West Brookfield,	Pension,	3779
1815	Benjamin P.	Brookfield,	Administration,	3780
1871	Danforth K.	Worcester,	Guardianship,	3781
1866	Daniel	Thompson, Conn.,	Will,	3782
1872	Edward	Milford,	Guardianship,	3783
1793	Elizabeth	Sturbridge,	Guardianship,	3784
1851	Elizabeth F.	Ashburnham,	Guardianship,	3785
1870	Ellen M.	Killingly, Conn.,	Foreign Sale,	3786
1815	Elmira	Sturbridge,	Guardianship,	3787
1796	Ephraim	Sturbridge,	Administration,	3788
1881	Eva E.	Worcester,	Guardianship,	3789
1837	Finis	Bolton,	Guardianship,	3790
1851	Francis J.	Ashburnham,	Administration,	3791
1789	Gaius	Brookfield,	Will,	3792

YEAR.	NAME.	RESIDENCE.	NATURE.	CASE.
	BARRETT AND BARRITT,			
1863	Hannah	Burrillville, R. I.,	Guardianship,	3793
1879	Henrietta F.	Barre,	Guardianship,	3794
1826	Henry	Paris, N. Y.,	Foreign Sale,	3795
1863	Henry	Sturbridge,	Guardianship,	3796
1863	Henry W.	Burrillville, R. I.,	Guardianship,	3797
1876	Isabella T.	Fitchburg,	Adoption, etc.,	3798
1873	Jabez	Bolton,	Administration,	3799
1866	Joanna	Putnam, Conn.,	Foreign Will,	3800
1822	Joel	Ashburnham,	Guardianship,	3801
1821	Joel, Jr.	Ashburnham,	Will,	3802
1842	Joel A.	Ashburnham,	Guardianship,	3803
1775	John	Hutchinson,	Administration,	3804
1779	John	Barre,	Guardianship,	3805
1872	John A.	Milford,	Guardianship,	3806
1871	John H.	Worcester,	Guardianship,	3807
1854	Jonas H.	Ashburnham,	Will,	3808
1849	Jonathan	Northborough,	Will,	3809
1850	Jonathan	Northborough,	Pension,	3810
1737	Joseph	Grafton,	Administration,	3811
1808	Joseph	Sturbridge,	Administration,	3812
1849	Joseph	Barre,	Will,	3813
1853	Joseph	Lancaster,	Will,	3814
1872	Joseph	Worcester,	Administration,	3815
1808	Joseph, Jr.	Sturbridge,	Administration,	3816
1783	Levi	Templeton,	Guardianship,	3817
1881	Lincoln W.	Worcester,	Administration,	3818
1879	Lois	Lancaster,	Administration,	3819
1860	Louisa	West Brookfield,	Administration,	3820
1875	Lucy	Bolton,	Administration,	3821
1873	Lucy S.	Bolton,	Guardianship,	3822
1779	Lydia	Barre,	Guardianship,	3823
1861	Marcus	Auburn,	Administration,	3824
1869	Maria M.	Southbridge,	Guardianship,	3825
1822	Martha	Brookfield,	Will,	3826
1737	Mary	Grafton,	Guardianship,	3827
1858	Mary A.	Lancaster,	Guardianship,	3828
1872	Mary A.	Milford,	Guardianship,	3829
1854	Mary S.	Ashburnham,	Guardianship,	3830
1872	Michael F.	Milford,	Guardianship,	3831
1846	Moses	Lancaster,	Will,	3832
1858	Moses	Lancaster,	Administration,	3833
1858	Moses H.	Lancaster,	Guardianship,	3834
1793	Nancy	Sturbridge.	Guardianship,	3835
1815	Nancy	Sturbridge,	Guardianship,	3836

BARRETT AND BARRITT,

YEAR.	NAME.	RESIDENCE.	NATURE.	CASE.
1817	Oliver	Bolton,	Will,	3837
1867	Oliver	Barre,	Will,	3838
1877	Phebe	Barre,	Will,	3839
1869	Polly	Southbridge,	Administration,	3840
1815	Rebecca	Sturbridge,	Guardianship,	3841
1847	Rebeckah	Lancaster,	Will,	3842
1793	Rhoda	Sturbridge,	Guardianship,	3843
1876	Ruth B.	Brookfield,	Administration,	3844
1852	Samuel	Ashburnham,	Administration,	3845
1872	Samuel	Lancaster,	Will,	3846
1847	Samuel P.	Lancaster,	Administration,	3847
1737	Sarah	Grafton,	Guardianship,	3848
1834	Sarah	Bolton,	Will,	3849
1873	Sarah	Lancaster,	Administration,	3850
1879	Sarah E.	Barre,	Guardianship,	3851
1842	Selah W.	Hardwick,	Guardianship,	3852
1826	Solomon	Paris, N. Y.,	Foreign Sale,	3853
1826	Sophronia	Paris, N. Y.,	Foreign Sale,	3854
1792	Thomas	Sturbridge,	Administration,	3855
1832	Thomas	Webster,	Administration,	3856
1800	Timothy	Paxton,	Administration,	3857
1871	Townsend	Ashburnham,	Administration,	3858
1826	Violetta	Paris, N. Y.,	Foreign Sale,	3859
1850	Willard S.	Hardwick,	Administration,	3860
1879	William O.	Barre,	Guardianship,	3861
1809	Zacheus	Templeton,	Will,	3862
1759	BARRICK, William	Shrewsbury,	Guardianship,	3863

BARRITT see BARRETT.

YEAR	NAME	RESIDENCE	NATURE	CASE
1785	BARRON, Lucy	Petersham,	Guardianship,	3864
1837	Mehitable	Westminster,	Administration,	3865
1860	Moses II.	Leominster,	Will,	3866
1754	Nathan	Bolton,	Guardianship,	3867
1785	Polly	Petersham.	Guardianship,	3868
1785	Prescott	Petersham,	Guardianship,	3869
1785	Stephen	Petersham,	Guardianship,	3870
1785	Thomas	Petersham,	Guardianship,	3871
1784	William	Petersham.	Administration,	3872
1785	William A.	Petersham,	Guardianship,	3873
1867	BARROWS, Albert B.	Westborough,	Guardianship,	3874
1876	Alfred J.	Mendon,	Guardianship,	3875
1879	Alice E.	Brookfield,	Adoption, etc.,	3876
1867	Anna R.	Westborough,	Guardianship,	3877
1843	Augustus	Worcester,	Guardianship,	3878
1863	Charles S.	Worcester,	Adoption, etc.,	3879

YEAR.	NAME.	RESIDENCE.	NATURE.	CASE.
1876	BARROWS, Charles S.	Worcester,	Change of Name,	3880
1855	Enoch	Dana,	Will,	3881
1856	Ethan A.	Webster,	Administration,	3882
1853	Jane	Clinton,	Adoption, etc.,	3883
1810	John	Barre,	Administration,	3884
1867	Lillian S.	Westborough,	Guardianship,	3885
1843	Mary	Boylston,	Will,	3886
1845	Rufus	Worcester,	Administration.	3887
1859	Sarah E.	Worcester,	Guardianship,	3888
1854	BARRUS, Jane L.	West Boylston,	Adoption, etc.,	3889
1867	BARRY, Agnes A.	Worcester,	Adoption, etc.,	3890
1868	Benjamin W. A.	Bolton,	Will,	3891
1881	Ellen	Worcester,	Administration,	3892
1875	John	Blackstone,	Will,	3893
1880	Richard	Worcester,	Change of Name,	3894
1858	Roswell	Gardner,	Administration,	3895
1878	Sarah	Gardner,	Administration,	3896
1852	BARSTOW, Charles	North Brookfield,	Will,	3897
1860	George H.	Loda, Ill.,	Guardianship,	3898
1860	Hattie L.	Loda, Ill.,	Guardianship,	3899
1867	Mary E.	Oxford,	Administration,	3900
1870	BARTHOLOMEW, Adolphus	Barre,	Will,	3901
1874	Gardner	Hardwick,	Will,	3902
1869	Martha A.	Hardwick,	Administration,	3903
1862	Nelson	Oxford,	Administration,	3904
1873	Persis	Hardwick,	Administration,	3905
	BARTHRICK see BATHRICK.			
1775	BARTLETT, Aaron	Brookfield,	Administration,	3906
1840	Abel	Leominster,	Guardianship,	3907
1820	Abigail	Westminster,	Guardianship,	3908
1830	Abigail	Westminster,	Administration,	3908
1792	Abner	Brookfield,	Administration,	3909
1795	Abner	Brookfield,	Guardianship,	3910
1875	Ada M.	Grafton,	Guardianship,	3911
1829	Adam	Berlin,	Administration,	3912
1841	Adonijah	Rutland,	Will,	3913
1835	Albert	Shrewsbury,	Guardianship,	3914
1857	Alic	Preston, Conn.,	Guardianship,	3915
1880	Alony A.	Worcester,	Administration,	3916
1881	Amos	Webster,	Administration,	3917
1841	Andrew J.	Hubbardston,	Guardianship,	3918
1797	Anna	Sutton,	Guardianship,	3919
1817	Antipas	Northborough,	Will,	3920
1835	Artemas	Holden,	Will,	3921
1864	Arthur I.	Paxton,	Administration,	3922

YEAR.	NAME.	RESIDENCE.	NATURE.	CASE.
1865	BARTLETT, Ashley	Northborough,	Will,	3923
1832	Avilda	North Brookfield,	Administration,	3924
1818	Avilda	North Brookfield,	Guardianship,	3925
1857	Azubah	Worcester,	Will,	3926
1857	Azubah	Worcester,	Pension,	3927
1806	Bathsheba	Brookfield,	Administration,	3928
1852	Benjamin B.	Royalston,	Will,	3929
1821	Bethuel	Hardwick,	Administration,	3930
1835	Betsey	Shrewsbury,	Guardianship,	3931
1854	Betsey	Berlin,	Administration,	3932
1854	Bridget	Webster,	Administration,	3933
1839	Broughton	Hubbardston,	Guardianship,	3934
1839	Butler	Rutland,	Guardianship,	3935
1840	Caroline	Leominster,	Guardianship,	3936
1865	Caty	Worcester,	Will,	3937
1877	Charles	Rutland,	Administration,	3938
1870	Charles D.	Southbridge,	Guardianship,	3939
1863	Charles P.	Paxton,	Will,	3940
1870	Clarissa	Northborough,	Will,	3941
1860	Clarissa M.	Northborough,	Administration,	3942
1853	Cora V.	Royalston,	Guardianship,	3943
1867	Cynthia R.	Lexington,	Adoption, etc.,	3944
1854	Damaris	Princeton,	Administration,	3945
1840	Damarus	Leominster,	Guardianship,	3946
1780	Daniel	Brookfield,	Guardianship,	3947
1802	Daniel	Rutland,	Will,	3948
1819	Daniel	Westminster,	Will,	3949
1780	Darius	Brookfield,	Guardianship,	3950
1878	David	Lunenburg,	Will,	3951
1870	David N.	Southbridge,	Administration,	3952
1877	Deborah	Warren,	Administration,	3953
1829	Dwight	Brookfield,	Administration,	3954
1870	Eddy N.	Southbridge,	Guardianship,	3955
1857	Edmund D.	Hubbardston,	Administration,	3956
1854	Edward B.	Northborough,	Administration,	3957
1850	Edwards	Leominster,	Guardianship,	3958
1861	Eleazer	Webster,	Administration,	3959
1818	Elias	North Brookfield,	Guardianship,	3960
1788	Elijah	Brookfield,	Will,	3961
1840	Elijah	Brookfield,	Will,	3962
1824	Elijah, Jr.	Brookfield,	Administration,	3963
1839	Elisha	Hubbardston,	Guardianship,	3964
1839	Eliza A.	Hardwick,	Guardianship,	3965
1846	Elizabeth	Uxbridge,	Administration,	3966
1863	Emeline A.	Oakham,	Administration,	3967

YEAR.	NAME.	RESIDENCE.	NATURE.	CASE.
1857	BARTLETT, Emma	Preston, Conn.,	Guardianship,	3968
1874	Emma A.	Worcester,	Administration,	3969
1761	Ephraim	Brookfield,	Will,	3970
1871	Ephraim W.	Worcester,	Will,	3971
1835	Esther	Unknown,	Trustee,	3972
1840	Eunice	Leominster,	Guardianship,	3973
1841	Eunice	Rutland,	Administration,	3974
1851	Ezekiel C.	Winchendon,	Administration,	3975
1864	Francis T.	Brookfield,	Administration,	3976
1870	Frederick L.	Southbridge,	Guardianship,	3977
1870	George A.	Southbridge,	Guardianship,	3978
1852	George L.	Mendon,	Administration,	3979
1859	George N.	Webster,	Administration,	3980
1877	George O.	Worcester,	Administration,	3981
1851	Hamilton M.	Winchendon,	Guardianship,	3982
1835	Harriet	Shrewsbury,	Guardianship,	3983
1832	Harriet M.	Brookfield,	Guardianship,	3984
1832	Harrison G. O.	Brookfield,	Guardianship,	3985
1872	Hattie P.	Leominster,	Will,	3986
1835	Henry	Shrewsbury,	Guardianship,	3987
1870	Henry E.	Southbridge,	Guardianship,	3988
1853	Herbert C.	Royalston,	Guardianship,	3989
1845	Hiram P.	Brookfield,	Guardianship,	3990
1864	Ida L.	Paxton,	Guardianship,	3991
1804	Ira	Royalston,	Administration,	3992
1795	Isaac	Holden,	Will,	3993
1860	Isaac	Worcester,	Administration,	3994
1868	James O.	Douglas,	Administration,	3995
1877	Jane M.	Brookfield,	Administration,	3996
1864	Joel	Northborough,	Administration,	3997
1778	John	Sutton,	Administration,	3998
1832	John	Royalston,	Administration,	3999
1840	John	Leominster,	Guardianship,	4000
1864	John	Berlin,	Will,	4001
1817	John H.	Sutton,	Administration,	4002
1808	Jonas	Marlborough,	Will,	4003
1837	Jonas	Royalston,	Will,	4004
1838	Jonas	Northborough,	Administration,	4005
1841	Jonas	Hubbardston,	Guardianship,	4006
1789	Jonathan	Northborough,	Will,	4007
1830	Jonathan	Northborough,	Administration,	4008
1831	Jonathan	Berlin,	Guardianship,	4009
1867	Jonathan	Northborough,	Administration,	4010
1777	Joseph	Brookfield,	Guardianship,	4011
1837	Joseph	Hubbardston,	Administration,	4012

YEAR.	NAME.	RESIDENCE.	NATURE.	CASE.
1851	BARTLETT, Josephine E.	Winchendon,	Guardianship,	4013
1797	Josiah	Sutton,	Guardianship,	4014
1835	Jotham	Shrewsbury,	Administration,	4015
1844	Jotham	Northborough,	Will,	4016
1862	Laura B.	Fitchburg.	Adoption, etc.,	4017
1856	Leander	Fitchburg,	Administration,	4018
1848	Levi	Rutland,	Guardianship,	4019
1850	Levi	Rutland,	Administration,	4019
1877	Levi	Rutland,	Administration,	4020
1877	Levi	Southbridge,	Administration,	4021
1864	Lizzie M.	Brookfield,	Guardianship,	4022
1846	Lois	Lancaster,	Administration,	4023
1846	Lois	Lancaster,	Pension,	4024
1875	Lottie G.	Grafton,	Guardianship,	4025
1828	Larcina	Dudley,	Administration,	4026
1839	Lucy M.	Hardwick,	Guardianship,	4027
1845	Lucy P.	Brookfield,	Guardianship,	4028
1838	Luke	Hardwick,	Administration,	4029
1795	Luther	Brookfield,	Guardianship,	4030
1838	Luther	Leominster,	Administration,	4031
1840	Luther	Leominster,	Guardianship,	4032
1875	Mariah M.	Templeton,	Administration,	4033
1832	Martha S.	Brookfield,	Guardianship,	4034
1859	Martha W.	Northborough,	Guardianship,	4035
1769	Mary	Brookfield,	Will,	4036
1814	Mary	Northborough,	Administration,	4037
1822	Mary	Northborough,	Will,	4038
1841	Mary	Leominster,	Administration,	4039
1841	Mary	Hubbardston,	Guardianship,	4040
1852	Mary	Northborough,	Administration,	4041
1858	Mary	New Braintree,	Administration,	4042
1868	Mary	Webster,	Administration,	4043
1878	Mary	Berlin,	Administration,	4044
1870	Mary S.	Southbridge,	Guardianship,	4045
1872	Maryette	Webster,	Will,	4046
1776	Mathew	Brookfield,	Administration,	4047
1864	Melzar A.	Paxton,	Guardianship,	4048
1870	Miriam	Webster,	Will,	4049
1878	Nancy	Southborough,	Administration,	4050
1821	Nathan	Royalston,	Will,	4051
1868	Nathan S.	Douglas,	Administration,	4052
1793	Nathaniel	Brookfield,	Will,	4053
1779	Obadiah	Brookfield,	Administration,	4054
1795	Obadiah	Brookfield,	Guardianship,	4055
1795	Persis	Brookfield,	Guardianship.	4056

YEAR.	NAME.	RESIDENCE.	NATURE.	CASE.
1784	BARTLETT, Richard	Sutton,	Will,	4057
1804	Richard	Ward,	Administration,	4058
1791	Roger	Sterling,	Administration,	4059
1840	Sampson	Leominster,	Guardianship,	4060
1868	Sampson	Princeton,	Will,	4061
1873	Sarah	Bolton,	Administration,	4062
1755	Silas	Unknown,	Guardianship,	4063
1866	Silvia ·	Leominster,	Guardianship,	4064
1835	Solomon	Shrewsbury,	Guardianship,	4065
1824	Stephen	Dudley,	Will,	4066
1870	Stephen	Winchendon,	Will,	4067
1775	Thomas	Brookfield,	Will,	4068
1818	Thomas	North Brookfield,	Guardianship,	4069
1858	Uriah	Sterling,	Administration,	4070
1871	Varnum	Blackstone,	Will,	4071
1840	Whipple	North Brookfield,	Administration,	4072
1818	William	North Brookfield,	Guardianship,	4073
1829	William	Templeton,	Guardianship,	4074
1835	William	Brookfield,	Pension,	4075
1863	William	Troy, N. Y.,	Administration,	4076
1850	William B.	Bolton,	Will,	4077
1870	William F.	Southbridge	Guardianship,	4078
1831	William H.	Berlin,	Guardianship,	4079
1864	William H.	Brookfield	Guardianship,	4080
1871	William H.	Brookfield,	Will,	4081
1875	William H.	Grafton,	Will,	4082
1866	William H. H.	Chicago, Ill.,	Administration,	4083
1856	William L.	Fitchburg,	Guardianship,	4084
1815	Wyman	North Brookfield,	Administration,	4085
1819	Wyman	North Brookfield,	Partition,	4085
1874	BARTON, Aaron S.	Greenville, N. H.	Foreign Will,	4086
1840	Abigail J.	Milbury,	Guardianship,	4087
1840	Adeline	Millbury,	Guardianship,	4088
1879	Adeline L.	Millbury,	Guardianship,	4089
1869	Ann E.	Worcester,	Administration,	4090
1858	Benjamin F.	Worcester,	Administration,	4091
1869	Bethana B.	Newport, N. H.,	Sale Real Est.,	4092
1875	Betsey R.	Oxford,	Will,	4093
1776	Bezaleel	Royalston,	Administration,	4094
1836	Caleb	Leicester,	Pension,	4095
1858	Charles U.	North Brookfield,	Will,	4096
1850	Elbridge	Oxford,	Administration,	4097
1840	Eleanor	Millbury,	Guardianship,	4098
1853	Elizabet	Leicester,	Will,	4099
1860	Emerson	Worcester,	Administration,	4100

YEAR.	NAME.	RESIDENCE.	NATURE.	CASE.
1840	BARTON, George	Millbury,	Guardianship,	4101
1878	George E.	Worcester,	Will,	4102
1867	Georgianna	Worcester,	Guardianship,	4103
1814	Harlem	Charlton,	Guardianship,	4104
1823	Harlem	Dudley,	Administration,	4105
1854	Harriet N.	Fitchburg,	Change of Name,	4106
1866	Henry A.	Worcester,	Administration,	4107
1869	Hiram	Unknown,	Sale Real Est.,	4108
1867	Ira M.	Worcester,	Will,	4109
1770	Isaac	Oxford,	Administration,	4110
1808	Jedediah	Sutton,	Will,	4111
1859	John	Worcester,	Administration,	4112
1839	John F.	Millbury,	Administration,	4113
1834	Joseph T.	Charlton,	Administration,	4114
1773	Joshua	Sutton,	Administration,	4115
1792	Joshua	Spencer,	Administration,	4116
1881	Joyce W.	Worcester,	Administration,	4117
1850	Lewis	Millbury,	Guardianship,	4118
1852	Lucretia	Charlton,	Administration,	4119
1853	Lucretia	Charlton,	Pension,	4120
1869	Lucy W.	Worcester,	Will,	4121
1870	Malcolm W.	Worcester,	Administration,	4122
1754	Mary	Sutton,	Guardianship,	4123
1840	Mary	Millbury,	Guardianship,	4124
1876	Mary A.	Dudley,	Administration,	4125
1859	Mary E.	Shrewsbury,	Guardianship,	4126
1872	Mary H.	Worcester,	Administration,	4127
1848	Mehitable	Sutton,	Guardianship,	4128
1869	Nancy	Worcester,	Administration,	4129
1812	Perley	Oxford,	Guardianship,	4130
1849	Reuben	Millbury,	Administration,	4131
1871	Rice	Oxford,	Administration,	4132
1845	Rufus	Millbury,	Guardianship,	4133
1854	Rufus	Millbury,	Administration,	4134
1850	Rufus, Jr.	Millbury,	Administration,	4135
1732	Samuel	Oxford,	Will,	4136
1813	Sibley	Charlton,	Administration,	4137
1862	Stephen	Oxford,	Will,	4138
1837	Theron H.	Millbury,	Guardianship,	4139
1813	William	Charlton,	Administration,	4140
1841	William	Charlton,	Guardianship,	4141
1837	William S.	Millbury,	Guardianship,	4142
1817	William T.	Charlton,	Guardianship,	4143
1866	William T.	Webster,	Will,	4144
1801	BASCOM, Clarissa	Western,	Guardianship,	4145

Year.	Name.	Residence.	Nature.	Case.
1879	BASCOM, Frank P.	Clinton,	Adoption, etc.,	4146
1780	Lydia	Western,	Guardianship,	4147
1801	Peace	Western,	Guardianship,	4148
1805	Polly	Western,	Guardianship,	4149
1816	Priscilla E.	Templeton,	Guardianship,	4150
1779	Samuel	Western,	Administration,	4151
1823	Samuel	Western,	Administration,	4152
1787	Thomas	Western,	Administration,	4153
1811	BASEY, Clement	Sutton,	Administration,	4154
1838	BASLINGTON, Abraham S.	Brookfield,	Guardianship,	4155
1838	George	Brookfield,	Administration,	4156
1838	George O.	Brookfield,	Guardianship,	4157
1838	Luther S.	Brookfield,	Guardianship,	4158
1838	William E.	Brookfield,	Guardianship,	4159
1879	BASS, Susan	Winchendon,	Administration,	4160
1788	BASSA, Clement	Rutland,	Guardianship,	4161
1870	BASSETT, Adoniram J.	Webster,	Guardianship,	4162
1817	Alvin	Hardwick,	Guardianship,	4163
1879	Alvin	Hardwick,	Will,	4164
1868	Ann	Uxbridge,	Will,	4165
1873	Anne	Uxbridge,	Administration,	4166
1855	Charles E.	West Brookfield,	Guardianship,	4167
1831	Cyrus	Royalston,	Administration,	4168
1878	Edward, etc.	Boston,	Adoption, etc.,	4169
1867	Elias	Athol,	Administration,	4170
1877	Elizabeth S.	Barre,	Administration,	4171
1839	Franklin	Hardwick,	Administration,	4172
1869	Helen L.	Athol,	Guardianship,	4173
1852	Isaac	Barre,	Pension,	4174
1835	James U.	Hardwick,	Guardianship,	4175
1870	Jane	Killingly, Conn.,	Administration,	4176
1828	Jason	Sutton,	Administration,	4177
1855	John I.	Worcester,	Administration,	4178
1837	Joseph	Uxbridge,	Administration,	4179
1876	Joseph	Millbury,	Administration,	4180
1877	Joseph P.	Barre,	Administration,	4181
1847	Joshua	Holden,	Will,	4182
1856	Lewis	Holden,	Administration,	4183
1816	Lydia	Hardwick,	Will,	4184
1834	Massa	Hardwick,	Administration,	4185
1864	Preston	Holden,	Will,	4186
1870	Ruthella	Webster,	Guardianship,	4187
1870	Samuel W.	Webster,	Guardianship,	4188
1867	Sarah	Grafton,	Will,	4189

YEAR.	NAME.	RESIDENCE.	NATURE.	CASE.
1858	BASSETT, Susan	Killingly, Conn.,	Administration,	4190
1847	William	Hardwick,	Administration,	4191
1835	William S.	Hardwick,	Guardianship,	4192
1878	BASTIAN, Minot V.	Clinton,	Adoption, etc.,	4193
1846	BASTOW, Sumner	Oxford,	Will,	4194
1871	Tamar E.	Oxford,	Administration,	4195
	BATCHELLER, BATCHELLOR, BATCHELDER, BATCHELOR, BACHELER, BACHELOR,			
1812	Aaron	Northbridge,	Guardianship,	4196
1834	Aaron	Douglas,	Administration,	4197
1855	Aaron A.	Fitchburg,	Guardianship,	4198
1796	Abigail	Brookfield,	Guardianship,	4199
1813	Abraham	Sutton,	Administration,	4200
1834	Abraham	Sutton,	Administration,	4201
1871	Alma M.	Leominster,	Guardianship,	4202
1832	Amos	Sutton,	Will,	4203
1880	Amos	Sutton,	Administration,	4204
1861	Anne M.	Northbridge,	Change of Name,	4205
1875	Annie	Douglas,	Guardianship,	4206
1862	Asa	Royalston,	Will,	4207
1859	Augusta L.	Douglas,	Guardianship,	4208
1761	Benjamin	Brookfield,	Administration,	4209
1761	Benjamin	Brookfield,	Guardianship,	4210
1881	Benjamin L.	Sutton,	Administration,	4211
1855	Betsey A.	Fitchburg,	Guardianship,	4212
1835	Chandler	Upton,	Guardianship,	4213
1854	Charles H.	Upton,	Will,	4214
1872	Charlotte	Northbridge,	Administration,	4215
1859	Clifford H.	Worcester,	Adoption,	4216
1862	Clifford H.	Worcester,	Change of Name,	4216
1862	Clifford H.	Worcester,	Guardianship,	4217
1874	Clifford L.	Upton,	Guardianship,	4218
1829	Daniel	Western,	Administration,	4219
1868	Daniel	Athol,	Administration,	4220
1835	Daniel W.	Upton,	Guardianship,	4221
1805	David	Northbridge,	Will,	4222
1823	David	Oxford,	Administration,	4223
1866	Elhanan	Sutton,	Administration,	4224
1855	Eli M.	Northbridge,	Guardianship,	4225
1820	Elijah	Charlton,	Will,	4226
1823	Elijah	Charlton,	Administration,	4227
1834	Eliza A.	Northbridge,	Guardianship,	4228
1867	Eliza R. E.	Mt. Pleasant, S. C.,	Administration,	4229

YEAR.	NAME.	RESIDENCE.	NATURE.	CASE.
	BATCHELLER, BATCHELLOR, BATCHELDER, BATCHELOR, BACHELER, BACHELOR,			
1799	Elizabeth	Brookfield,	Administration,	4230
1846	Enoch	Upton,	Will,	4231
1847	Enoch	Upton,	Pension,	4232
1862	Enoch	Upton,	Will,	4233
1827	Ezra	North Brookfield,	Will,	4234
1870	Ezra	North Brookfield,	Will,	4235
1855	Ezra D.	North Brookfield,	Change of Name,	4236
1871	Fanny C.	Brooklyn, N. Y.,	Guardianship,	4237
1878	Fenner	Douglas,	Will,	4238
1875	Francis H.	Douglas,	Guardianship,	4239
1871	Frederick A. P.	Leominster,	Will,	4240
1796	Galen	Brookfield,	Guardianship,	4241
1852	George C.	Grafton,	Guardianship,	4242
1869	George S.	Royalston,	Guardianship,	4243
1761	Hannah	Brookfield,	Guardianship,	4244
1838	Hannah	Sutton,	Will,	4245
1868	Hervey J.	North Brookfield,	Administration,	4246
1852	Hiram W.	Grafton,	Guardianship,	4247
1867	Holland N.	Mt. Pleasant, S. C.,	Administration,	4248
1761	Huldah	Brookfield,	Guardianship,	4249
1761	Jacob	Brookfield,	Guardianship,	4250
1841	Jairus H.	Sutton,	Guardianship,	4251
1835	Jeremiah	Douglas,	Pension,	4252
1875	Jeremiah	Douglas,	Administration,	4253
1844	Joel	Northbridge,	Administration,	4254
1761	John	Brookfield,	Guardianship,	4255
1765	John	Brookfield,	Administration,	4256
1795	John	Brookfield,	Administration,	4257
1843	John	Millbury,	Administration,	4258
1824	Jonathan	Upton,	Will,	4259
1797	Joseph	Grafton,	Will,	4260
1866	Joseph E.	Dansville, N. Y.,	Guardianship,	4261
1841	Josiah	Northbridge,	Administration,	4262
1879	Laura G.	Northbridge,	Administration,	4263
1864	Levi	Upton,	Will,	4264
1830	Lewis	Sutton,	Administration,	4265
1871	Lucinda	Sutton,	Will,	4266
1878	Luthera C.	North Brookfield,	Will,	4267
1761	Lydia	Brookfield,	Guardianship,	4268
1843	Lydia	Douglas,	Administration,	4269
1843	Lydia	Douglas	Pension,	4270
1850	Lydia	Sutton,	Will,	4271

BATCHELLER, BATCHELLOR,
BATCHELDER, BATCHELER,
BATCHELOR, BACHELOR,

YEAR.	NAME.	RESIDENCE.	NATURE.	CASE.
1872	Lysander	Fitchburg,	Administration,	4272
1817	Mark	Sutton,	Will,	4273
1847	Mark	Grafton,	Will,	4274
1860	Mark J.	Westborough,	Will,	4275
1872	Mary A.	Northbridge,	Will,	4276
1880	Mary Ann	Grafton,	Administration,	4277
1829	Mary L.	Western,	Guardianship,	4278
1852	Mary L.	Grafton,	Guardianship,	4279
1866	Mary L.	Dansville, N. Y.,	Guardianship,	4280
1874	Mary T.	Upton,	Guardianship,	4281
1796	Matilda	Brookfield,	Guardianship,	4282
1865	Mehitable	Grafton,	Administration,	4283
1796	Melvin	Brookfield,	Guardianship,	4284
1851	Moses L.	Grafton,	Administration,	4285
1841	Nancy M.	Northbridge,	Guardianship,	4286
1880	Nettie I.	Sutton,	Guardianship,	4287
1874	Nina C.	Upton,	Guardianship,	4288
1873	Ollis	Northbridge,	Will,	4289
1846	Orlando	Sutton,	Guardianship,	4290
1862	Orlando W.	Sutton,	Administration,	4291
1796	Orpha	Brookfield,	Guardianship,	4292
1822	Orrin D.	Sturbridge,	Guardianship,	4293
1869	Otis	Upton,	Will,	4294
1796	Pamela	Brookfield,	Guardianship,	4295
1829	Pamela P.	Western,	Guardianship,	4296
1855	Pamelia	Northbridge,	Administration,	4297
1812	Perley	Grafton,	Will,	4298
1873	Polly	Sutton,	Administration,	4299
1860	Prentiss J.	Westborough,	Guardianship,	4300
1879	Prudence	Northbridge,	Administration,	4301
1827	Rachel	Northbridge,	Will,	4302
1880	Rebecca T.	Sutton,	Guardianship,	4303
1859	Sally	Millbury,	Will,	4304
1796	Samuel	Royalston,	Administration,	4305
1860	Sarah V.	Westborough,	Guardianship,	4306
1840	Simeon	Sutton,	Administration,	4307
1833	Simeon, Jr.	Sutton,	Administration,	4308
1848	Stephen	Royalston,	Administration,	4309
1865	Stephen F.	Northbridge,	Will,	4310
1877	Susan E.	Warren,	Administration,	4311
1796	Thiel	Brookfield,	Guardianship,	4312
1861	Warren	Sutton,	Guardianship,	4313

BATCHELLER, BATCHELLOR,
BATCHELDER, BATCHELER,
BATCHELOR, BACHELOR,

1877	Warren	Sutton,	Administration,	4313
1841	Warren J.	Northbridge,	Guardianship,	4314
1853	Willard,	North Brookfield,	Administration,	4315
1818	William, Jr.	Douglas,	Will,	4316
1852	William A.	Grafton,	Guardianship,	4317
1829	William G.	Western,	Guardianship,	4318
1864	Zeri	Northbridge,	Will,	4319
1808	BATEMAN, Charles	Harvard,	Guardianship,	4320
1852	George H.	Harvard,	Guardianship,	4321
1808	Harriot	Harvard,	Guardianship,	4322
1808	John	Harvard,	Guardianship,	4323
1808	Jonas	Harvard,	Guardianship,	4324
1852	Jonas	Harvard,	Administration,	4325
1808	Jonas, Jr.	Harvard,	Guardianship,	4326
1808	Polly	Harvard,	Guardianship,	4327
1808	Rebecca	Harvard,	Guardianship,	4328
1877	William F.	Harvard,	Administration,	4329
1852	BATES, Abigail E.	Barre,	Guardianship,	4330
1873	Addie L.	Webster,	Guardianship,	4331
1842	Alanson	Webster,	Will,	4332
1873	Alanson	Webster,	Will,	4333
1866	Alfred	Worcester,	Administration,	4334
1836	Anson	Barre,	Will,	4335
1848	Asa	Phillipston,	Administration,	4336
1852	Azubah	Phillipston,	Administration,	4337
1793	Benjamin	Mendon,	Guardianship,	4338
1867	Benjamin	Mendon,	Will,	4339
1797	Betsey	Gerry,	Guardianship,	4340
1866	Charles S.	Sutton,	Administration,	4341
1856	Clement E.	Swansey, N. H.,	Guardianship,	4342
1842	Comfort M.	Webster,	Guardianship,	4343
1813	David	Hardwick,	Will,	4344
1831	David	Westborough,	Guardianship,	4345
1863	Elijah	North Brookfield,	Administration,	4346
1843	Elizabeth	Southbridge,	Guardianship,	4347
1869	Elizabeth A.	Oakham,	Administration,	4348
1869	Elizabeth A.	Oakham,	Pension,	4349
1881	Emory	Phillipston,	Administration,	4350
1859	Ezra L.	Phillipston,	Will,	4351
1864	Fanny K.	Norwalk, O.,	Guardianship,	4352
1852	Francis G.	Barre,	Guardianship,	4353
1797	Frank	Gerry,	Guardianship,	4354

Year.	Name.	Residence.	Nature.	Case.
1837	BATES, Franklin	Barre,	Guardianship,	4355
1870	Franklin	VirginsBay,Cent.Am.,	Administration,	4356
1873	Frederick O.	Webster,	Guardianship,	4357
1797	George	Gerry,	Guardianship,	4358
1829	George	Mendon,	Administration,	4359
1876	George	Mendon,	Administration,	4360
1836	George A.	Barre,	Guardianship,	4361
1869	George F.	Hardwick,	Guardianship,	4362
1852	George H.	Barre,	Guardianship,	4363
1870	Grace A.	Brookfield,	Guardianship,	4364
1793	Hannah	Mendon,	Guardianship,	4365
1837	Henry	Barre,	Guardianship,	4366
1870	Henry T.	Brookfield,	Administration,	4367
1870	Henry W.	Brookfield,	Guardianship,	4368
1874	Ida F.	Providence, R. I.,	Guardianship,	4369
1869	Ira D.	Hardwick,	Guardianship,	4370
1789	Isaac	Mendon,	Will,	4371
1795	Jacob	Thompson, Conn.,	Will,	4372
1872	Jacob	Webster,	Guardianship,	4373
1872	Jacob	Webster,	Administration,	4373
1793	Jedediah	Mendon,	Guardianship,	4374
1857	Jedediah	Mendon,	Administration,	4375
1836	John	Barre,	Guardianship,	4376
1863	John	Thompson, Conn.,	Foreign Will,	4377
1870	John	Sterling, Ill.,	Administration,	4378
1873	John	Dudley,	Will,	4379
1865	John, Jr.	Dudley,	Administration,	4380
1869	John A.	Hardwick,	Guardianship,	4381
1793	Joseph	Mendon,	Administration,	4382
1793	Joseph	Mendon,	Guardianship,	4383
1856	Joseph	Southbridge,	Administration,	4384
1793	Joshua	Mendon,	Guardianship,	4385
1856	Junius D.	Swansey, N. H.,	Guardianship,	4386
1869	Kimball K.	Webster,	Administration,	4387
1879	Laban	Mendon,	Will,	4388
1874	Lavinia	Webster,	Will,	4389
1778	Levina	Upton,	Guardianship,	4390
1842	Loran	Webster,	Guardianship,	4391
1872	Lydia E.	Webster,	Administration,	4392
1876	Marietta B.	Webster,	Administration,	4393
1824	Martha	Mendon,	Will,	4394
1797	Mercy	Gerry,	Guardianship,	4395
1777	Micah	Upton,	Administration,	4396
1863	Myra E.	North Brookfield,	Guardianship,	4397
1857	Noah	Athol,	Administration,	4398

Year.	Name.	Residence.	Nature.	Case.
1869	BATES, Oscar W.	Hardwick,	Guardianship,	4399
1860	Peter	Mendon,	Will,	4400
1793	Rebecca	Mendon,	Guardianship,	4401
1880	Samuel H.	Santa Rosa, Cal.,	Administration,	4402
1861	Sarah	Fitchburg,	Administration,	4403
1863	Smith G.	Northbridge,	Will,	4404
1842	Sumner	Webster,	Guardianship,	4405
1865	Thomas S.	North Brookfield,	Administration,	4406
1852	Welcome	Barre,	Administration,	4407
1852	Welcome C.	Barre,	Guardianship,	4408
1831	Zealous	Westborough,	Administration,	4409
	BATHRICK and BARTHRICK,			
1778	Anor	Lunenburg,	Guardianship,	4410
1857	Betsey	Ashburnham,	Will,	4411
1825	Curtis	Westborough,	Guardianship,	4412
1778	Daniel	Lunenburg,	Guardianship,	4413
1794	David	Westborough,	Administration,	4414
1825	David	Westborough,	Guardianship,	4415
1880	Edward A.	Northbridge,	Guardianship,	4416
1825	Edwin	Westborough,	Guardianship,	4417
1825	Elizabeth	Westborough,	Guardianship,	4418
1828	Elmer	Westborough,	Administration,	4419
1878	George L.	Northbridge,	Administration,	4420
1871	Harriet F.	Northbridge,	Will,	4421
1828	Jason	Upton,	Administration,	4422
1812	John	Westborough,	Guardianship,	4423
1861	John	Lunenburg,	Guardiauship,	4424
1825	Jonathan	Westborough,	Will,	4425
1880	Judson H.	Northbridge,	Guardianship,	4426
1833	Levi	Westborough,	Administration,	4427
1829	Levi A.	Westborough,	Guardianship,	4428
1829	Maltina M.	Westborough,	Guardianship,	4429
1873	Martha	Westminster,	Administration,	4430
1829	Nancy A.	Westborough,	Guardianship,	4431
1857	Reuben	Ashburnham,	Guardianship,	4432
1873	Reuben	Ashburnham,	Administration,	4432
1829	Roxana S.	Westborough,	Guardianship,	4433
1778	Sarah	Lunenburg,	Guardianship,	4434
1824	Solomon	Westborough,	Will,	4435
1777	Stephen	Lunenburg,	Will,	4436
1881	Stephen	Westminster,	Will,	4437
1874	BATT, Almira L.	Leominster,	Guardianship,	4438
1874	Mary D.	Leominster,	Guardianship,	4439
1874	William M.	Leominster,	Guardianship,	4440

Year.	Name.	Residence.	Nature.	Case.
1872	BATTELLE, Anna P.	Worcester,	Will,	4441
1872	Mary F.	Worcester,	Administration,	4442
1875	BATTEN, Joseph	Fitchburg,	Will,	4443
1879	BATTERSBY, Ada L.	Petersham,	Adoption, etc.,	4444
1866	BATTERSON, Charles E.	Clinton,	Guardianship,	4445
1866	Emma E.	Clinton,	Guardianship,	4446
1866	George F.	Clinton,	Guardianship,	4447
	BATTEY see BATTY.			
1813	BATTLES, Betsey	Fitchburg,	Guardianship,	4448
1848	Betsey	Fitchburg,	Trustee,	4449
1769	Content	Leominster,	Guardianship,	4450
1812	David	Fitchburg,	Administration,	4451
1813	David	Fitchburg,	Guardianship,	4452
1868	David	Fitchburg,	Administration,	4453
1857	Elbridge D.	Fitchburg,	Administration,	4454
1813	Elmira	Fitchburg,	Guardianship,	4455
1769	James	Leominster,	Guardianship,	4456
1769	John	Leominster,	Guardianship,	4457
1761	Joseph	Leominster,	Administration,	4458
1848	Joseph	Fitchburg,	Trustee,	4459
1813	Lucy	Grafton,	Administration,	4460
1813	Lucy	Fitchburg,	Guardianship,	4461
1769	Mabel	Leominster,	Guardianship,	4462
1769	Pricilla	Leominster,	Guardianship,	4463
1769	Rachel	Leominster,	Guardianship,	4464
1813	Rebecca	Fitchburg,	Guardianship,	4465
1880	Samuel	Fitchburg,	Administration,	4466
1813	Sarah A.	Fitchburg,	Guardianship,	4467
	BATTY and BATTEY,			
1880	Frank E.	Oxford,	Guardianship,	4468
1880	Lafayette E.	Oxford,	Administration,	4469
1880	Lafayette L.	Oxford,	Guardianship,	4470
1880	Mary A.	Oxford,	Guardianship,	4471
1881	BAUER, Peter	Leicester,	Guardianship,	4472
1827	BAXTER, Isaac	Spencer,	Administration,	4473
1842	John	Spencer,	Guardianship,	4474
1754	Joseph	Mendon,	Administration,	4475
1842	Lydia	Spencer,	Will,	4476
1821	Moses	Rutland,	Will,	4477
1816	Richard	Princeton,	Will,	4478
1846	Stephen	Western,	Will,	4479
1842	William	Spencer,	Guardianship,	4480
	BAYLEY see BAILEY.			
	BAYLIES see BAILEY.			
1855	BEACH, Priscilla	Bennington, Vt.,	Administration,	4481

(103)

Year.	Name.	Residence.	Nature.	Case.
1809	BEADENT, Jesse	Hardwick,	Guardianship,	4482
	BEAL and BEALS,			
1846	Alfred S.	Palmer,	Guardianship,	4483
1846	Caroline A.	Palmer,	Guardianship,	4484
1762	Daniel	Mendon,	Administration,	4485
1846	Edwin C.	Palmer,	Guardianship,	4486
1827	Eunice	Royalston,	Administration,	4487
1851	Foster E. L.	Lunenburg,	Guardianship,	4488
1833	Huldah	Hardwick,	Administration,	4489
1763	John	Sturbridge,	Guardianship,	4490
1821	Jonathan	Winchendon,	Guardianship,	4491
1834	Jonathan	Upton,	Administration,	4492
1834	Jonathan	Upton,	Guardianship,	4493
1849	Jonathan S.	Phillipston,	Guardianship,	4494
1857	Jonathan S.	Hubbardston,	Administration,	4495
1861	Joseph	Winchendon,	Will,	4496
1769	Joshua	Mendon,	Guardianship,	4497
1769	Josiah	Mendon,	Guardianship,	4498
1821	Madison	Winchendon,	Guardianship,	4499
1769	Mehitable	Mendon,	Guardianship,	4500
1821	Nathaniel	Winchendon,	Guardianship,	4501
1880	Olive	Worcester,	Guardianship,	4502
1880	Olive	Worcester,	Will,	4502
1769	Samuel	Mendon,	Guardianship,	4503
1827	Samuel	Hardwick,	Will,	4504
1821	Samuel, Jr.	Winchendon,	Guardianship,	4505
1859	Samuel R.	Uxbridge,	Administration,	4506
1876	Seraph	Providence, R. I.,	Foreign Will,	4507
1846	Solomon	Palmer,	Guardianship,	4508
1849	Stephen	Phillipston,	Administration,	4509
1821	Stower	Winchendon,	Will,	4510
1834	Thomas	Royalston,	Pension,	4511
1873	Thomas	Winchendon,	Administration,	4512
1821	Wilder	Winchendon,	Guardianship,	4513
1876	William C.	Worcester,	Administration,	4514
	BEAMAN and BEEMAN,			
1845	Aaron	Northborough,	Administration,	4515
1792	Abel	Leominster,	Guardianship,	4516
1815	Abraham	Westborough,	Will,	4517
1872	Artemas	Westborough,	Will,	4518
1811	Betsey	West Boylston,	Guardianship,	4519
1865	Charles W.	Fitchburg,	Guardianship,	4520
1792	Damaris	Leominster,	Guardianship,	4521
1778	David	Royalston,	Guardianship,	4522
1785	David	Leominster,	Administration,	4523

BEAMAN AND BEEMAN,

YEAR.	NAME.	RESIDENCE.	NATURE.	CASE.
1758	Deborah	Bolton,	Will,	4524
1853	Dolly	Sterling,	Administration,	4525
1853	Dolly	Sterling,	Pension,	4526
1870	Edwin D.	Princeton,	Administration,	4527
1870	Edwin J.	Princeton,	Guardianship,	4528
1750	Eleazer	Westborough,	Administration,	4529
1771	Elijah	Lancaster,	Administration,	4530
1876	Eliza C.	Winchendon,	Partition,	4531
1852	Ella S.	Sterling,	Guardianship,	4532
1852	Elory B.	Sterling,	Administration,	4533
1852	Emma C.	Sterling,	Guardianship,	4534
1757	Ephraim	Shrewsbury,	Guardianship,	4535
1805	Ephraim	Boylston,	Will,	4536
1806	Ephraim	Princeton,	Guardianship,	4537
1868	Eunice	Princeton,	Will,	4538
1811	Ezra	West Boylston,	Administration,	4539
1847	Ezra	Sterling,	Administration,	4540
1863	Ezra	West Boylston,	Administration,	4541
1745	Gamaliel	Lancaster,	Will,	4542
1777	Gamaliel	Royalston,	Administration,	4543
1833	Gideon	Sterling,	Administration,	4544
1833	Gideon	Sterling,	Pension,	4545
1878	Harriet E.	Princeton,	Guardianship,	4546
1865	Helen L.	Templeton,	Guardianship,	4547
1757	Jabez	Shrewsbury,	Administration,	4548
1812	Jabez	West Boylston,	Administration,	4549
1852	Jane	Sterling,	Guardianship,	4550
1806	Joanna	Princeton,	Guardianship,	4551
1763	John	Lancaster,	Will,	4552
1848	John	Westborough,	Administration,	4553
1804	Jonas	Princeton,	Administration,	4554
1867	Jonas	Princeton,	Will,	4555
1867	Jonas W.	Princeton,	Guardianship,	4556
1822	Joseph	Westminster,	Administration,	4557
1757	Lois	Shrewsbury,	Guardianship,	4558
1813	Mary	West Boylston,	Administration,	4559
1852	Mary	Sterling,	Guardianship,	4560
1870	Mary L.	Princeton,	Guardianship,	4561
1852	Moses S.	Sterling,	Guardianship,	4562
1869	Nabby W.	Jaffrey, N. H.,	Foreign Will,	4563
1865	Olive	Westborough,	Administration,	4564
1881	Persis	Westborough,	Administration,	4565
1815	Persis M.	West Boylston,	Administration,	4566
1803	Phineas	Sterling,	Will,	4567

	BEAMAN and BEEMAN,			
1830	Phineas	Princeton,	Will,	4568
1848	Phineas	Princeton,	Administration,	4569
1839	Rebecca	Princeton,	Pension,	4570
1806	Sally	Princeton,	Guardianship,	4571
1848	Samuel B.	Princeton,	Guardianship,	4572
1852	Sarah	Sterling,	Guardianship,	4573
1811	Silas	West Boylston,	Administration,	4574
1873	Susannah	Westborough,	Administration,	4575
1824	Tamar	West Boylston,	Will,	4576
1777	Thomas	Petersham,	Absentee,	4577
1869	Warren H.	Athol,	Guardianship,	4578
1758	Zerviah	Lancaster,	Guardianship,	4579
	BEAMIS see BEMIS.			
1859	BEAN, Charles	Worcester,	Guardianship,	4580
1874	George W.	Northbridge,	Guardianship,	4581
1874	Hazen O.	Northbridge,	Will,	4582
1859	Lucas P.	Worcester,	Administration,	4583
1867	Minnietta M.	Ashburnham,	Adoption, etc.,	4584
1874	Wilford A.	Northbridge,	Guardianship,	4585
	BEARD see also BAIRD.			
1857	Abigail	Harvard,	Pension,	4586
1850	Asa	Nashville, N. H.	Foreign Will,	4587
1866	Emily L., etc.	Sterling,	Guardianship,	4588
1866	Emma L.	Sterling,	Guardianship,	4588
1873	Ezra K.	Harvard,	Will,	4589
1865	George H.	Fitchburg,	Administration,	4590
1857	Hepsebeth	Gardner,	Will,	4591
1871	Jonas H.	Worcester,	Administration,	4592
1843	Jonathan	Harvard,	Will,	4593
1843	Jonathan	Harvard,	Pension,	4594
1857	Lucinda	Gardner,	Will,	4595
1865	Mary A.	Sterling,	Will,	4596
1873	Mary E.	Worcester,	Guardianship,	4597
1870	Sarah J.	Harvard,	Guardianship,	4598
1866	William R.	Sterling	Guardianship,	4599
1872	BEATY, Charles H.	Worcester,	Administration,	4600
	BEAUDETTE and BODET,			
1878	David	Worcester,	Administration,	4601
1863	Eli	Athol,	Administration,	4602
1872	Marie R. D.	Worcester,	Will,	4603
1878	Napoleon	Worcester,	Guardianship,	4604
1880	BEAUMONT, Betty	Oxford,	Will,	4605
1877	BEAUREGARD, Victor	Milford,	Guardianship,	4606

1877	BEAVEN, Samuel	Clinton,	Will,	4607
1880	BEBOO, Felix	Woonsocket, R. I.,	Will,	4608
1866	BECK, Catharine	Hardwick,	Adoption,	4609
1869	BECKWITH, Alvah A.	Fitchburg,	Will,	4610
1837	Charles	Fitchburg,	Administration,	4611
1837	Charles L.	Fitchburg,	Guardianship,	4612
1814	Elliott	Hardwick,	Administration,	4613
1814	Fanny	Hardwick,	Guardianship,	4614
1877	Mindwell A.	Fitchburg,	Will,	4615
1837	Sarah L.	Fitchburg,	Guardianship,	4616
1871	BEDARD, John	Northbridge,	Adoption, etc.,	4617
1877	BEECHER, Jane E.	Southbridge,	Guardianship,	4618
1870	Katherine E.	North Brookfield,	Will,	4619
1875	Smith	Southbridge,	Will,	4620
1877	William A.	Southbridge,	Administration,	4621
	BEEMAN see BEAMAN.			
	BEERS AND BIERS,			
1879	Adaline	Leicester,	Will,	4622
1826	Albert	Worcester,	Guardianship,	4623
1843	Alphonso	Leicester,	Will,	4624
1826	Jefferson	Charlton,	Guardianship,	4625
1838	Laura A.	Leicester,	Guardianship,	4626
1838	Liberty	Leicester	Administration,	4627
1838	Liberty	Leicester,	Guardianship,	4628
1877	Liberty	Spencer,	Administration,	4629
1838	Mary H.	Leicester,	Guardianship,	4630
1838	Matilda M.	Leicester,	Guardianship,	4631
1844	Polly	Charlton,	Guardianship,	4632
1825	Richard	Leicester,	Guardianship,	4633
1838	Tamason M.	Leicester,	Guardianship,	4634
1868	BEESO, Michael	Millbury,	Administration,	4635
1838	BEETON, George W.	Westborough,	Will,	4636
1789	John	Westborough,	Will,	4637
1816	John	Westborough,	Will,	4638
1810	Martha	Westborough,	Will,	4639
1875	BEHLING, Andrew	Webster,	Will,	4640
1865	BELCHER, Andrew	Unknown,	Adoption, etc.,	4641
1873	Clara E.	Spencer,	Guardianship,	4642
1873	Frank W.	Spencer,	Guardianship,	4643
1873	George W.	Spencer,	Guardianship,	4644
1858	Harvey	North Brookfield,	Will,	4645
1877	Henry A.	North Brookfield,	Partition,	4646
1778	Jeremiah	Lunenburg,	Administration,	4647
1824	Joshua H.	Shrewsbury,	Guardianship,	4648
1873	William H.	Spencer,	Guardianship,	4649

Year.	Name.	Residence.	Nature.	Case.
1756	BELDING, Silas	Hardwick,	Will,	4650
1861	BELKNAP, Alonzo B.	Sutton,	Administration,	4651
1863	Annah	Sturbridge,	Will,	4652
1777	Deborah	Shrewsbury,	Guardianship,	4653
1879	Deliverance F.	Southbridge	Administration,	4654
1777	Ebenezer	Shrewsbury,	Guardianship,	4655
1869	Emma J.	Milford,	Guardianship,	4656
1850	Irving M.	Byron, Ill.,	Foreign Sale,	4657
1869	James R.	Milford,	Guardianship,	4658
1764	Jedediah	Holden,	Administration,	4659
1842	John	Sterling,	Administration,	4660
1764	Joseph	Holden,	Guardianship,	4661
1777	Loisa	Shrewsbury,	Guardianship,	4662
1872	Lowell	Westborough,	Will,	4663
1869	Lyman E.	Milford,	Guardianship,	4664
1764	Martha	Holden,	Guardianship,	4665
1858	Mary	Sterling,	Will,	4666
1850	Mary Adeline	Byron, Ill.,	Foreign Sale,	4667
1861	Melissa A.	Sutton,	Guardianship,	4668
1818	Peter	Sturbridge,	Will,	4669
1847	Peter	Sturbridge,	Administration,	4670
1875	Polly	Clinton,	Administration,	4671
1850	Sarah Jane	Byron, Ill.,	Foreign Sale,	4672
1777	Silence	Shrewsbury,	Guardianship,	4673
1764	Stephen	Holden,	Guardianship,	4674
1777	Submit	Shrewsbury,	Guardianship,	4675
1764	Zedikiah	Holden,	Guardianship,	4676
1866	BELL, Alice	Boston,	Adoption, etc.,	4677
1864	Anna O.	Oakham,	Will,	4678
1812	Anne	Oakham,	Guardianship,	4679
1871	Elizabeth	Milford,	Administration,	4680
1763	Isabel	New Braintree,	Will,	4681
1811	James	Oakham,	Administration,	4682
1864	James	Bolton,	Will,	4683
1880	Jane	Lancaster	Will,	4684
1749	John	Brookfield,	Administration,	4685
1765	John	Brookfield,	Guardianship,	4686
1776	John	Brookfield	Administration,	4687
1812	Melinda	Oakham,	Guardianship,	4688
1873	Melinda	Oakham,	Will,	4689
1812	Patty	Oakham,	Guardianship,	4690
1812	Polly	Oakham,	Guardianship,	4691
1809	Simson	Brookfield,	Will,	4692
1849	Thomas	West Brookfield,	Administration,	4693

| --- | --- | --- | --- | --- |
1876	BELL, William	Lancaster,	Administration,	4694
1767	BELLENGER, John	Brookfield,	Will,	4695
1769	Silence	Brookfield,	Administration,	4696
1857	BELLOWS, Abigail P.	Shrewsbury	Administration,	4697
1854	Absalom	Paxton,	Administration,	4698
1845	Achsah S.	Westborough,	Guardianship,	4699
1825	Albert J.	Worcester,	Guardianship,	4700
1795	Amasa	Hubbardston,	Administration,	4701
1795	Amasa	Hubbardston,	Guardianship,	4702
1819	Amasa	Hubbardston,	Administration,	4703
1870	Arthur L.	Webster,	Guardianship,	4704
1795	Asa	Hubbardston,	Guardianship,	4705
1812	Asa	Western,	Guardianship,	4706
1870	Asa F.	Southborough,	Guardianship,	4707
1835	Asahel	Worcester,	Administration,	4708
1812	Betsey	Western,	Guardianship,	4709
1812	Calvin	Western,	Administration,	4710
1812	Calvin	Western,	Guardianship,	4711
1759	Charles	Holden,	Guardianship,	4712
1823	Charles D.	Westborough,	Guardianship,	4713
1837	Charles D.	Westborough,	Administration,	4714
1825	Christopher W.	Worcester,	Guardianship,	4715
1823	Daniel	Westborough,	Administration,	4716
1754	David	Southborough,	Administration,	4717
1812	Edson W.	Western,	Guardianship,	4718
1798	Elijah	Princeton,	Will,	4719
1820	Elizabeth	Hubbardston,	Guardianship,	4720
1812	Elvira	Western,	Guardianship,	4721
1825	Emeline A.	Worcester,	Guardianship,	4722
1807	Ezekiel	Paxton,	Administration,	4723
1815	Ezekiel	Oakham,	Administration,	4724
1852	Ezekiel D.	Worcester,	Administration,	4725
1864	George L.	Worcester,	Administration,	4726
1870	George N.	Webster,	Guardianship,	4727
1824	Hannah	Worcester,	Will,	4728
1825	Hannah M.	Worcester,	Guardianship,	4729
1857	Harrison B.	Westborough,	Administration,	4730
1759	Hepzibeth	Holden,	Guardianship,	4731
1845	Horace E.	Westborough,	Guardianship,	4732
1747	Isaac	Southborough,	Administration,	4733
1811	Isaac	Hubbardston,	Will,	4734
1878	Isaac	Hubbardston,	Will,	4735
1880	Isaac	Paxton,	Guardianship,	4736
1810	James	Southborough,	Will,	4737
1869	James	Smithfield, R. I.,	Administration,	4738

YEAR.	NAME.	RESIDENCE.	NATURE.	CASE.
1759	BELLOWS, Jane	Holden,	Guardianship,	4739
1876	Jefferson	Grafton,	Administration,	4740
1874	Jennie E.	Paxton,	Adoption,	4741
1772	John	Southborough,	Will,	4742
1826	John	Shrewsbury,	Administration,	4743
1854	John	Paxton,	Guardianship,	4744
1854	John	Paxton,	Administration,	4744
1817	John, Jr.	Shrewsbury,	Administration,	4745
1820	John W.	Hubbardston,	Guardianship,	4746
1826	John W.	Shrewsbury,	Guardianship,	4747
1848	Jonas	Brookfield,	Administration,	4748
1757	Jonathan	Southborough,	Will,	4749
1759	Jonathan	Westborough,	Administration,	4750
1759	Joseph	Holden,	Guardianship,	4751
1759	Joseph	Holden,	Administration,	4752
1767	Joseph	Southborough,	Guardianship,	4753
1817	Jotham	Southborough,	Will,	4754
1826	Leonard	Shrewsbury,	Guardianship,	4755
1826	Lucretia	Shrewsbury,	Guardianship,	4756
1838	Luke	Westborough,	Guardianship,	4757
1826	Luther	Shrewsbury,	Guardianship,	4758
1856	Lydia	Shrewsbury	Administration,	4759
1856	Lydia	Shrewsbury,	Pension,	4760
1872	Lyman	Worcester,	Administration,	4761
1823	Mary A.	Westborough,	Guardianship,	4762
1782	Moses	Southborough,	Will,	4763
1859	Newell	Westborough,	Administration,	4764
1856	Permelia	Southborough,	Will,	4765
1812	Polly	Western,	Guardianship,	4766
1812	Rebecca	Western,	Guardianship,	4767
1759	Reuben	Westborough,	Guardianship,	4768
1759	Ruth	Holden,	Guardianship,	4769
1873	Sally	Paxton,	Will,	4770
1826	Samuel A.	Shrewsbury,	Guardianship,	4771
1823	Simeon	Westborough,	Administration,	4772
1838	Stephen	Southborough,	Pension,	4773
1853	Stephen	Shrewsbury,	Will,	4774
1853	Stephen H.	Shrewsbury,	Guardianship,	4775
1860	Susan H.	Worcester,	Administration,	4776
1870	Susan H.	Worcester,	Administration,	4777
1845	Susan M.	Westborough,	Guardianship,	4778
1822	Timothy	Southborough,	Will,	4779
1812	Webster	Western,	Guardianship,	4780
1821	Willard	Southborough,	Administration,	4781
1878	Zalmon	Paxton,	Will,	4782

YEAR.	NAME.	RESIDENCE.	NATURE.	CASE.
1876	BELVAL, John B.	Millbury,	Foreign Will,	4783
1879	BELYEA, Adaline A.	Worcester,	Partition,	4784
1872	Samuel	Clinton,	Will,	4785
	BEMIS, BEMISS AND BEAMIS,			
1850	Abel	Winchendon,	Will,	4786
1780	Abigail	Spencer,	Guardianship,	4787
1829	Abigail	Harvard,	Guardianship,	4788
1875	Abigail	Spencer,	Administration,	4789
1840	Abijah	Spencer,	Administration,	4790
1877	Agnes M.	Worcester,	Guardianship,	4791
1825	Albert T.	Royalston,	Guardianship,	4792
1857	Albion F.	Brookfield,	Guardianship,	4793
1851	Almira	Spencer,	Administration,	4794
1839	Almira A.	Spencer,	Guardianship,	4795
1881	Alonzo A.	Spencer,	Guardianship,	4796
1860	Alpha	Spencer,	Administration,	4797
1839	Amasa, 2d	Spencer,	Administration,	4798
1842	Amasa	Spencer,	Will,	4799
1843	Amasa	Spencer,	Pension,	4800
1845	Amasa	Spencer,	Guardianship,	4801
1831	Amasa, Jr.	Spencer,	Administration,	4802
1862	Amos	Spencer,	Administration,	4803
1845	Angeline	Spencer,	Guardianship,	4804
1854	Angeline	Charlton,	Administration,	4805
1790	Anna	Spencer,	Guardianship,	4806
1857	Anna H.	Spencer,	Guardianship,	4807
1881	Anna J.	Spencer,	Guardianship,	4808
1843	Asa	Spencer,	Administration,	4809
1846	Asa	Spencer,	Guardianship,	4810
1850	Asa	Spencer,	Will,	4811
1823	Asahel	Westborough,	Guardianship,	4812
1832	Asahel	Southborough,	Administration,	4813
1811	Asaph	Leicester,	Guardianship,	4814
1823	Asaph	North Brookfield,	Administration,	4815
1854	Austin	Spencer,	Guardianship,	4816
1862	Austin F.	Brookfield,	Administration,	4817
1788	Barnard	Spencer,	Will,	4818
1856	Betsey	Spencer,	Administration,	4819
1876	Carrie B.	Worcester,	Guardianship,	4820
1790	Catharine	Spencer,	Guardianship,	4821
1829	Catharine	Harvard,	Guardianship,	4822
1840	Cemantha G.	Royalston,	Guardianship,	4823
1811	Cephas	Leicester,	Guardianship,	4824
1829	Cephas	North Brookfield,	Administration,	4825
1880	Chandler	Spencer,	Will,	4826

	BEMIS, BEMISS AND BEAMIS,			
1842	Charles	Barre,	Administration,	4827
1840	Charles E.	Spencer,	Guardianship,	4828
1843	Charles H.	Barre,	Guardianship,	4829
1876	Cheney	Spencer,	Will,	4830
1836	Chloe	Spencer,	Guardianship,	4831
1870	Cora E.	Spencer,	Guardianship,	4832
1853	Danforth	Spencer,	Administration,	4833
1836	David	Spencer,	Administration,	4834
1843	Dexter	Mississippi,	Administration,	4835
1814	Dolly	Spencer,	Administration,	4836
1807	Edmund	Westminster,	Administration,	4837
1836	Edward	Spencer,	Guardianship,	4838
1846	Edward	Spencer,	Guardianship,	4839
1861	Edward	Spencer,	Will,	4840
1876	Edward	Worcester,	Administration,	4841
1876	Edward P.	Worcester,	Guardianship,	4842
1857	Edward W.	Brookfield,	Guardianship,	4843
1844	Edwin A.	Spencer,	Guardianship,	4844
1790	Elias	Spencer,	Guardianship,	4845
1812	Elias	Spencer,	Guardianship,	4846
1845	Elias	Spencer,	Administration,	4847
1845	Elias	Spencer,	Guardianship,	4848
1837	Elias T.	Worcester,	Guardianship,	4849
1791	Elijah	Spencer,	Guardianship,	4850
1798	Elijah	Spencer,	Administration,	4851
1808	Elisha	Southborough,	Administration,	4852
1817	Elisha	Southborough,	Administration,	4853
1852	Elisha	Southborough,	Will,	4854
1849	Elizabeth	Spencer,	Guardianship,	4855
1843	Ellen Maria	Barre,	Guardianship,	4856
1851	Emma A.	Spencer,	Guardianship,	4857
1851	Emma N.	North Brookfield,	Guardianship,	4858
1790	Esther	Spencer,	Guardianship,	4859
1857	Francis A.	Brookfield,	Guardianship,	4860
1863	Franklin	Spencer,	Will,	4861
1881	Fred A.	Spencer,	Guardianship,	4862
1849	Frederick A.	Spencer,	Guardianship,	4863
1880	Freeland	Sturbridge,	Administration,	4864
1836	George	Spencer,	Guardianship,	4865
1849	George II.	Brookfield,	Administration,	4866
1839	George L.	Spencer,	Guardianship,	4867
1791	Hannah	Spencer,	Guardianship,	4868
1848	Hannah	Spencer,	Administration,	4869
1848	Hannah	Spencer,	Pension,	4870

BEMIS, BEMISS AND BEAMIS,

YEAR.	NAME.	RESIDENCE.	NATURE.	CASE.
1836	Harriet Elizabeth	Spencer,	Guardianship,	4871
1830	Harriet E.	North Brookfield,	Guardianship,	4872
1843	Harriet E.	Barre,	Guardianship,	4873
1825	Harriet J.	Royalston,	Guardianship,	4874
1848	Henry M.	Spencer,	Guardianship,	4875
1855	Henry W.	Spencer,	Guardianship,	4876
1830	Hiram M.	North Brookfield,	Guardianship,	4877
1836	Horace	Spencer,	Guardianship,	4878
1845	Horace	Spencer,	Guardianship,	4879
1851	Ida A.	North Brookfield,	Guardianship,	4880
1861	Isaac	Spencer,	Administration,	4881
1867	Jacob	Southborough,	Will,	4882
1843	James H.	Barre,	Guardianship,	4883
1849	Janette	Spencer,	Guardianship,	4884
1780	Jemima	Spencer,	Guardianship,	4885
1829	Jemima	Brookfield,	Will,	4886
1836	Jesse	Spencer,	Will,	4887
1836	Jesse	Spencer,	Pension,	4888
1849	Jesse	Mobile, Ala.,	Administration,	4889
1822	John	Sturbridge,	Guardianship,	4890
1835	John	Sturbridge,	Administration,	4891
1835	John	Sturbridge,	Pension,	4892
1837	John	Worcester,	Administration,	4893
1843	John	Barre,	Guardianship,	4894
1853	John	Spencer,	Administration,	4895
1870	John	Barre,	Administration,	4896
1876	John S.	Spencer,	Administration,	4897
1840	John W.	Royalston,	Guardianship,	4898
1790	Jonas	Spencer,	Administration,	4899
1831	Jonas	Royalston,	Will,	4900
1846	Jonas	Spencer,	Will,	4901
1846	Jonas	Spencer,	Pension,	4902
1824	Jonas, Jr.	Royalston,	Administration,	4903
1823	Joseph	Spencer,	Will,	4904
1840	Joseph P.	Royalston,	Guardianship,	4905
1789	Joshua	Spencer,	Administration,	4906
1812	Joshua	Spencer,	Guardianship,	4907
1835	Joshua	Spencer,	Will,	4908
1836	Joshua	Spencer,	Guardianship,	4909
1822	Joshua, Jr.	Spencer,	Administration,	4910
1848	Joshua E.	Spencer,	Guardianship,	4911
1851	Joshua E.	North Brookfield,	Will,	4912
1812	Lewis	Spencer,	Guardianship,	4913

Year.	Name.	Residence.	Nature.	Case.
	BEMIS, BEMISS AND BEAMIS,			
1856	Lewis	Spencer,	Administration,	4914
1853	Lucelia A.	North Brookfield,	Will,	4915
1843	Lucretia W.	Barre,	Guardianship,	4916
1871	Lucy	Spencer,	Will,	4917
1867	Lucy G.	Spencer,	Administration,	4918
1865	Lura	Barre,	Guardianship,	4919
1831	Lyman	Spencer,	Administration,	4920
1862	Lyman A.	Charlton,	Guardianship,	4921
1845	Maria A.	Spencer,	Guardianship,	4922
1812	Martin	Spencer,	Guardianship,	4923
1845	Martin	Spencer,	Guardianship,	4924
1847	Martin	Spencer,	Administration,	4925
1847	Mary	Spencer,	Administration,	4926
1840	Mary E.	Spencer,	Guardianship,	4927
1854	Mary L.	Spencer,	Guardianship,	4928
1855	Mary L.	Spencer,	Guardianship,	4929
1840	Mary S.	Royalston,	Guardianship,	4930
1808	Mehitable	Spencer,	Administration,	4931
1791	Molly	Spencer,	Guardianship,	4932
1790	Moses	Spencer,	Guardianship,	4933
1840	Moses	Spencer,	Guardianship,	4934
1840	Nahum	Royalston,	Administration,	4935
1847	Nathan	Spencer,	Will,	4936
1856	Nathan	Spencer,	Administration,	4937
1840	Nathaniel	Spencer,	Will,	4938
1863	Nathaniel	Brookfield,	Will,	4939
1811	Nathaniel, Jr.	Leicester,	Guardianship,	4940
1862	Oscar R.	Spencer,	Administration,	4941
1838	Otis	Spencer,	Administration,	4942
1853	Otis	Spencer,	Will,	4943
1855	Otis	Spencer,	Guardianship,	4944
1848	Pamelia K.	Spencer,	Guardianship,	4945
1812	Persis	Spencer,	Guardianship,	4946
1822	Phebe	Spencer,	Guardianship,	4947
1864	Phebe	Southborough,	Will,	4948
1867	Phineas	Dudley,	Will,	4949
1793	Phinehas	Spencer,	Guardianship,	4950
1834	Phinehas	Grafton,	Pension,	4951
1831	Polly	Southborough,	Guardianship,	4952
1822	Prudence	Spencer,	Guardianship,	4953
1779	Reuben	Spencer,	Will,	4954
1794	Reubin	Spencer,	Guardianship,	4955
1849	Reubin	Spencer,	Will,	4956
1877	Reubin	Winchendon,	Administration,	4957

YEAR.	NAME.	RESIDENCE.	NATURE.	CASE.
	BEMIS, BEMISS AND BEAMIS,			
1840	Ruth A.	North Brookfield,	Guardianship,	4958
1839	Ruth E.	Spencer,	Guardianship,	4959
1812	Sally	Spencer,	Guardianship,	4960
1793	Samuel	Spencer,	Administration,	4961
1869	Samuel F.	Brookfield,	Administration,	4962
1791	Sarah	Spencer,	Administration,	4963
1845	Sarah	Spencer,	Guardianship,	4964
1852	Sarah	North Brookfield,	Administration,	4965
1847	Sarah C.	Burke, Vt.,	Guardianship,	4966
1863	Silas	Barre,	Administration,	4967
1828	Stephen	Harvard,	Will,	4968
1837	Susan	Worcester,	Guardianship,	4969
1843	Susan	Barre,	Guardianship,	4970
1879	Susan M.	Barre,	Will,	4971
1830	Susanna	Southborough,	Administration,	4972
1878	Sylvia.S.	Royalston,	Adoption, etc.,	4973
1865	Theodore	Barre,	Guardianship,	4974
1755	Thomas	Westminster,	Administration,	4975
1757	Thomas	Westminster,	Guardianship,	4976
1850	Thomas H.	Brookfield,	Guardianship,	4977
1876	Tyler	Paxton,	Will,	4978
1857	Waldo	Brookfield,	Administration,	4979
1881	Wallace L.	Spencer,	Guardianship,	4980
1837	Willard	Worcester,	Guardianship,	4981
1801	William	Westminster,	Will,	4982
1811	William	Leicester,	Guardianship,	4983
1835	William	Spencer,	Administration,	4984
1835	William	Westminster,	Administration,	4985
1836	William	Spencer,	Guardianship,	4986
1855	William	Spencer,	Will,	4987
1873	William	Fitchburg,	Will,	4988
1881	William	Ashburnham,	Will,	4989
1876	William C.	Worcester,	Guardianship,	4990
1829	William L.	Harvard,	Guardianship,	4991
1840	Windsor C.	North Brookfield,	Guardianship,	4992
1805	Zaccheus	Westminster,	Will,	4993
1868	BENCHLEY, Albert F.	Worcester,	Administration,	4994
1867	Albert L.	Worcester,	Administration,	4995
1870	Albertina	Worcester,	Guardianship,	4996
1870	Eleanora I.	Worcester,	Guardianship,	4997
1872	James H.	Worcester,	Administration,	4998
1863	BENDER, Hannah	North Brookfield,	Will,	4999
1869	Jacob	Webster,	Administration,	5000

YEAR.	NAME.	RESIDENCE.	NATURE.	CASE.
1841	BENDER, Sarah	Bolton,	Will,	5001
1832	BENEDICT, Elizabeth H.	Millbury,	Guardianship,	5002
1832	Margaret H.	Millbury,	Guardianship,	5003
1881	Truman	New Haven, Conn.,	Foreign Will,	5004
1839	William G.	Millbury,	Guardianship,	5005
1833	William M.	Millbury,	Trustee,	5006
1847	William M.	Millbury,	Administration,	5007
1880	BENJAMIN, Clara S.	Brookfield,	Will,	5008
1819	Daniel	Ashburnham,	Administration,	5009
1880	Edith	Brookfield,	Guardianship,	5010
1772	Elizabeth	Shrewsbury,	Will,	5011
1880	Florence E.	Fitchburg,	Change of Name,	5012
1880	Frank E.	Fitchburg,	Change of Name,	5013
1819	Irene	Ashburnham,	Guardianship,	5014
1819	Louisa	Ashburnham,	Guardianship,	5015
1879	Mary J.	Fitchburg,	Administration,	5016
1879	Samuel H.	Fitchburg,	Will,	5017
	BENNETT AND BENNITT,			
1861	Abel	Westminster,	Administration,	5018
1762	Abigail	Leominster,	Guardianship,	5019
1843	Abigail K.	Lunenburg,	Guardianship,	5020
1784	Abner	Shrewsbury,	Guardianship,	5021
1859	Abram	Fitchburg,	Administration,	5022
1836	Albert C.	Northbridge,	Guardianship,	5023
1843	Albert P.	Mendon,	Will,	5024
1868	Albert T.	Mendon,	Guardianship,	5025
1815	Alfred	Leominster,	Guardianship,	5026
1862	Allen R.	Danvers,	Adoption, etc.,	5027
1762	Bathsheba	Lancaster,	Administration,	5028
1762	Bathsheba	Leominster,	Guardianship,	5029
1814	Calvin	Leominster,	Administration,	5030
1815	Calvin W.	Leominster,	Guardianship,	5031
1849	Catharine C.	Brookfield,	Guardianship,	5032
1815	Charles F.	Leominster,	Guardianship,	5033
1874	Charles H.	Worcester,	Administration,	5034
1881	Darius	Blackstone,	Will,	5035
1822	David	Lunenburg,	Administration,	5036
1825	David	Hubbardston,	Administration,	5037
1867	David	Hubbardston,	Administration,	5038
1762	Demaras	Leominster,	Guardianship,	5039
1784	Elias	Shrewsbury,	Guardianship,	5040
1825	Elias	Sterling,	Administration,	5041
1765	Elisha	Lancaster,	Guardianship,	5042
1769	Elisha	Lancaster,	Administration,	5043
1815	Eliza	Leominster,	Guardianship,	5044

YEAR.	NAME.	RESIDENCE.	NATURE.	CASE.
	BENNETT AND BENNITT,			
1779	Elizabeth	Lancaster,	Administration,	5045
1845	Elizabeth	Royalston,	Pension,	5046
1847	Emeline E.	Brookfield,	Guardianship,	5047
1847	Emery W.	Brookfield,	Guardianship,	5048
1756	Ephraim	Holden,	Will,	5049
1877	Eugene A.	Leominster,	Will,	5050
1862	Eva A.	West Boylston,	Guardianship,	5051
1804	Ezra	Spencer,	Administration,	5052
1843	Freedom R.	Lunenburg,	Guardianship,	5053
1872	George	Webster,	Administration,	5054
1872	Hannah	Hubbardston,	Will,	5055
1872	Hannah	Hubbardston,	Will,	5056
1862	Helen G.	West Boylston,	Guardianship,	5057
1789	Hezekiah	Shirley,	Guardianship,	5058
1804	Hosea	Spencer,	Guardianship,	5059
1820	Hosea	Mendon,	Guardianship,	5060
1824	Hosea	Mendon,	Administration,	5060
1762	Isaac	Leominster,	Guardianship,	5061
1807	Isaac	Spencer,	Guardianship,	5062
1807	Jacob	Spencer,	Guardianship,	5063
1875	Jacob H.	Holden,	Administration,	5064
1815	James	Leominster,	Guardianship,	5065
1839	James	Lunenburg,	Administration,	5066
1847	James H.	Ashburnham,	Administration,	5067
1871	Jeremiah F.	Unknown,	Sale of Real Est.,	5068
1764	Joanna	Harvard,	Administration,	5069
1750	John	Lancaster,	Guardianship,	5070
1761	John	Lancaster,	Will,	5071
1762	John	Leominster,	Guardianship,	5072
1765	John	Lancaster,	Guardianship,	5073
1777	John	Lancaster,	Administration,	5074
1806	John	Leominster,	Administration,	5075
1818	John	Grafton,	Will,	5076
1748	John, Jr.	Lancaster,	Administration,	5077
1773	Jonathan	Shrewsbury,	Guardianship,	5078
1784	Jonathan	Shrewsbury,	Administration,	5078
1754	Joseph	Lancaster,	Will,	5079
1766	Josiah	Harvard,	Guardianship,	5080
1783	Josiah	Shrewsbury,	Will,	5081
1790	Josiah	Boylston,	Administration,	5082
1820	Lemuel	Boylston,	Pension,	5083
1862	Lillian V.	West Boylston,	Guardianship,	5084
1765	Lois, etc.	Lancaster,	Guardianship,	5085
1765	Louis	Lancaster,	Guardianship,	5085

YEAR.	NAME.	RESIDENCE.	NATURE.	CASE.
	BENNETT AND BENNITT.			
1843	Luceba T.	Lunenburg,	Guardianship,	5086
1843	Lucinda L.	Lunenburg,	Guardianship,	5087
1880	Lucy	Royalston,	Administration,	5088
1850	Luther	Worcester,	Administration,	5089
1875	Margaret L.	Uxbridge,	Will,	5090
1771	Mary	Lancaster,	Guardianship,	5091
1843	Mary	Lunenburg,	Guardianship,	5092
1847	Mary A.	Brookfield,	Guardianship,	5093
1871	Mary L.	Worcester,	Sale Real Est.,	5094
1762	Moses	Harvard,	Administration,	5095
1835	Nancy	Boylston,	Will,	5096
1760	Nathan	Leominster,	Administration,	5097
1814	Nathan	Fitchburg,	Administration,	5098
1843	Orin M. C.	Lunenburg,	Guardianship,	5099
1784	Patience	Shrewsbury,	Guardianship,	5100
1779	Percis	Shrewsbury,	Guardianship,	5101
1765	Prudence	Lancaster,	Administration,	5102
1753	Rachell	Sutton,	Guardianship,	5103
1843	Richard S.	Lunenburg,	Guardianship,	5104
1843	Richard S.	Lunenburg,	Administration,	5104
1829	Robert	Northbridge,	Will,	5105
1804	Rufus	Spencer,	Guardianship,	5106
1852	Rufus	Northbridge,	Will,	5107
1862	Rufus	West Boylston,	Administration,	5108
1836	Rufus A.	Northbridge,	Guardianship,	5109
1856	Russell	Blackstone,	Will,	5110
1868	Russell	Mendon,	Will,	5111
1742	Samuel	Shrewsbury,	Will,	5112
1818	Samuel C.	Grafton,	Guardianship,	5113
1860	Samuel C.	Grafton,	Administration,	5114
1784	Thomas	Shrewsbury,	Guardianship,	5115
1841	Thomas	Winchendon,	Will,	5116
1815	Thomas S.	Leominster,	Guardianship,	5117
1881	Thomas S.	Leominster,	Will,	5118
1807	Timothy	Spencer,	Guardianship,	5119
1807	Whipple	Spencer,	Guardianship,	5120
1769	William	Harvard,	Guardianship,	5121
1839	William	Westborough,	Guardianship,	5122
1863	William	Hubbardston,	Administration,	5123
1881	William	Hubbardston,	Administration,	5124
1832	William H.	Brookfield,	Guardianship,	5125
1814	William H.	Brookfield,	Administration,	5126
1827	BENSON, Aaron	Douglas,	Will,	5127
1778	Abigail	Mendon,	Guardianship,	5128

YEAR.	NAME.	RESIDENCE.	NATURE.	CASE.
1803	BENSON, Abner	Hubbardston,	Administration,	5129
1879	Achsah A.	Blackstone,	Will,	5130
1848	Adaline M.	Blackstone,	Will,	5131
1865	Albert	Killingly, Conn.,	Administration,	5132
1853	Alonzo L.	Upton,	Guardianship,	5133
1869	Alphonso	Worcester,	Administration,	5134
1783	Amasa	Uxbridge,	Guardianship,	5135
1837	Amasa	Mendon,	Administration,	5136
1847	Amasa	Northbridge,	Will,	5137
1865	Ann E.	Blackstone,	Administration,	5138
1802	Benjamin	Northbridge,	Will,	5139
1805	Benjamin	Northbridge,	Guardianship,	5140
1815	Benjamin	Northbridge,	Administration,	5141
1853	Benjamin L.	Upton,	Guardianship,	5142
1761	Benoni	Mendon,	Will,	5143
1783	Benoni	Uxbridge,	Guardianship,	5144
1806	Benoni	Mendon,	Will,	5145
1845	Charles	Blackstone,	Administration,	5146
1845	Charles E.	Blackstone,	Guardianship,	5147
1853	Charles H.	Upton,	Guardianship,	5148
1857	Charles S.	Sturbridge,	Guardianship,	5149
1863	Charles S.	Sturbridge,	Administration,	5150
1783	Chloe	Uxbridge,	Guardianship,	5151
1847	David	Sturbridge,	Administration,	5152
1877	Edgar O.	Northbridge,	Guardianship,	5153
1853	Edwin	Sturbridge,	Administration,	5154
1859	Edwin R.	Blackstone,	Guardianship,	5155
1876	Edwin R.	Windsor Locks, Conn.,	Will,	5156
1830	Ellis	Douglas,	Administration,	5157
1877	Erastus O.	Northbridge,	Administration,	5158
1833	Gardner A.	Northbridge,	Administration,	5159
1844	George E.	Mendon,	Guardianship,	5160
1870	George E.	Blackstone,	Administration,	5161
1853	George H.	Upton,	Guardianship,	5162
1832	George T.	Uxbridge,	Guardianship,	5163
1831	Hannah	Northbridge,	Administration,	5164
1832	Hannah J.	Uxbridge,	Guardianship,	5165
1855	Harriet	Blackstone,	Will,	5166
1859	Harrison	Uxbridge,	Will,	5167
1853	Heman C.	Upton,	Guardianship,	5168
1777	Henry	Mendon,	Administration,	5169
1778	Henry	Mendon,	Guardianship,	5170
1878	Henry H.	Blackstone,	Administration,	5171
1821	Henry S.	Mendon,	Administration,	5172
1844	Henry S.	Mendon,	Guardianship,	5173

Year.	Name.	Residence.	Nature.	Case.
1861	BENSON, Henry S.	Blackstone,	Will,	5174
1778	Isaac	Dudley,	Guardianship,	5175
1844	James H.	Mendon,	Guardianship,	5176
1869	Jane	Grafton,	Administration,	5177
1854	Jared	Blackstone,	Will,	5178
1778	Joanna	Dudley,	Guardianship,	5179
1778	Joanna	Mendon,	Guardianship,	5180
1818	John	Mendon,	Administration,	5181
1842	John	Uxbridge,	Will,	5182
1763	Joseph	Mendon,	Will,	5183
1777	Joseph	Dudley,	Administration,	5184
1778	Joseph	Dudley,	Guardianship,	5185
1786	Joseph	Sturbridge,	Will,	5186
1853	Joseph E.	Upton,	Guardianship,	5187
1878	Laurette V. H., etc.	Bruce, Ill.,	Guardianship,	5188
1856	Lewis	Sturbridge,	Will,	5189
1853	Loring	Upton,	Will,	5190
1878	Lottie E.	Bruce, Ill.,	Guardianship,	5191
1866	Lovina	Blackstone,	Will,	5192
1864	Lucretia T.	Uxbridge,	Administration,	5193
1806	Martha	Northbridge,	Administration,	5194
1847	Mary J.	Northbridge,	Guardianship,	5195
1877	Mary J.	Northbridge,	Guardianship,	5196
1869	Mary W.	Mendon,	Will,	5197
1853	Mellen	Blackstone,	Will,	5198
1820	Phila	Mendon,	Guardianship,	5199
1853	Prince A.	Upton,	Guardianship,	5200
1785	Prudence	Mendon,	Will,	5201
1778	Rachel	Mendon,	Guardianship,	5202
1855	Sally	Blackstone,	Will,	5203
1848	Sarah	Northbridge,	Administration,	5204
1861	Sarah	Blackstone,	Administration,	5205
1874	Sarah	Princeton,	Will,	5206
1869	Stephen S.	Blackstone,	Will,	5207
1778	Susanna	Mendon,	Guardianship,	5208
1778	Sybel	Mendon,	Guardianship,	5209
1778	Tirzah	Mendon,	Guardianship,	5210
1806	Truelove	Northbridge,	Guardianship,	5211
1847	Willard	Oxford,	Administration,	5212
1838	William H.	Mendon,	Guardianship,	5213
1859	William H.	Blackstone,	Administration,	5214
1827	BENT, Alphonso	Rutland, Vt.,	Guardianship,	5215
1798	David	Rutland,	Will,	5216
1822	David	Rutland, Vt.,	Foreign Sale,	5217
1798	Elizabeth	Southborough,	Administration,	5218

YEAR	NAME.	RESIDENCE.	NATURE.	CASE.
1855	BENT, Florence B.	Worcester,	Adoption, etc.,	5219
1813	Joel	Barre,	Administration,	5220
1803	John	Southborough,	Will,	5221
1785	Josiah	Petersham,	Administration,	5222
1817	Martha	Rutland,	Will,	5223
1879	Mary, etc.	Holden,	Will,	5224
1856	Nathaniel T.	Worcester,	Administration,	5225
1879	Polly	Holden,	Will,	5226
1798	Samuel B.	Rutland,	Guardianship,	5227
1830	Samuel W.	Spencer,	Guardianship,	5228
1834	BENTHALL, John	Sterling,	Administration,	5229
1880	BENTON, Charles P.	Worcester,	Administration,	5230
1824	Jonas	Sturbridge,	Guardianship,	5231
1834	Jonas	Brookfield,	Pension,	5232
1860	Lucy	Westminster,	Will,	5233
1851	Lysander W.	Templeton,	Administration,	5234
1853	Lysander W.	Templeton,	Guardianship,	5235
1853	L. Sibbel	Templeton,	Guardianship,	5236
1875	BENWAY, Austin	Webster,	Will,	5237
1879	Teophiele	Oxford,	Will,	5238
1877	BERCUME, Lewis N.	Spencer,	Guardianship,	5239
1866	BERGEN, Mary E.	Leicester,	Change of Name,	5240
1860	BERGERON, Lewis	Spencer,	Administration,	5241
	BERGMAN AND BERGMANN,			
1878	Francis J.	Clinton,	Administration,	5242
1878	Jessie M.	Clinton,	Guardianship,	5243
1878	Joseph	Clinton,	Guardianship,	5244
1878	BERIGAN, John	Worcester,	Will,	5245
1855	BERNARD, David A.	Worcester,	Administration,	5246
1855	Dwight W.	Worcester,	Guardianship,	5247
1767	George	Princeton,	Administration,	5248
1869	George H.	Worcester,	Administration,	5249
1873	John N.	Northborough,	Administration,	5250
	BERRELL see BARRELL.			
1874	BERRIAN, Aaron O. D.	Barre,	Guardianship,	5251
1876	BERRY, Abram J.	Charlton,	Guardianship,	5252
1858	Albert	Gardner,	Guardianship,	5253
1833	Benjamin	Royalston,	Administration,	5254
1827	Daniel	Dudley,	Guardianship,	5255
1852	Ellen L.	Worcester,	Guardianship,	5256
1865	Fanny C.	Worcester,	Guardianship,	5257
1827	Francis O.	Dudley,	Guardianship,	5258
1865	Frank S.	Worcester,	Guardianship,	5259
1793	George	Oakham,	Will,	5260
1876	George A.	Charlton,	Guardianship,	5261

Year.	Name.	Residence.	Nature.	Case.
1858	BERRY, Hannah M.	Gardner,	Guardianship,	5262
1876	Henry J.	Charlton,	Guardianship,	5263
1874	Ira	Charlton,	Administration,	5264
1876	Ira B.	Charlton,	Guardianship,	5265
1827	John	Dudley,	Guardianship,	5266
1876	John W.	Charlton,	Guardianship,	5267
1878	Louisa	Worcester,	Will,	5268
1872	Lucy	Hardwick,	Administration,	5269
1876	Nellie	Charlton,	Guardianship,	5270
1826	Oloff	Dudley,	Administration,	5271
1827	Samuel	Dudley,	Guardianship,	5272
1876	Sarah A.	Charlton,	Guardianship,	5273
1864	Scotto	Hardwick,	Will,	5274
1852	Susan C.	Worcester,	Guardianship,	5275
1872	BERTODY, Lucretia D.	Leicester,	Will,	5276
1840	Thomas D.	Leicester,	Guardianship,	5277
1784	BETTERLEY, George	Boston,	Guardianship,	5278
1875	George T. J.	Winchendon,	Will,	5279
1878	Laura W.	Winchendon,	Will,	5280
1748	BETTY, John	Worcester,	Administration,	5281
1832	BICKFORD, Charles E.	Gardner,	Guardianship,	5282
1867	Charles W.	Gardner,	Guardianship,	5283
1876	David P.	Gardner,	Administration,	5284
1855	Ebenezer	Gardner,	Administration,	5285
1826	Edmund	Gardner,	Administration,	5286
1841	Elisha	Gardner,	Guardianship,	5287
1864	Elmer E.	Ashburnham,	Guardianship,	5288
1867	Franklin P.	Gardner,	Guardianship,	5289
1881	George W.	Gardner,	Guardianship,	5290
1867	Imogene F.	Gardner,	Guardianship,	5291
1832	Lydia	Gardner,	Guardianship,	5292
1864	Lydia S.	Paxton,	Sale Real Est.,	5293
1832	Nancy	Gardner,	Guardianship,	5294
1827	Oliver E.	Gardner,	Guardianship,	5295
1864	Orion W.	Unknown,	Sale Real Est.,	5296
1863	Sarah W.	Worcester,	Guardianship,	5297
1832	William	Gardner,	Will,	5298
1858	William	Barre,	Administration,	5299
1863	William M.	Worcester,	Will,	5300
1863	William O.	Gardner,	Administration,	5301
1867	BICKNELL, Benjamin C.	Mendon,	Administration,	5302
1870	Erastus	Woodstock, Conn.,	Administration,	5303
1824	Jetson	Lunenburg,	Administration,	5304
1826	Joseph	Lunenburg,	Will,	5305
1872	Mary A.	Worcester,	Guardianship,	5306

YEAR.	NAME.	RESIDENCE.	NATURE.	CASE.
1867	BICKNELL, Susan P.	Mendon,	Administration,	5307
	BIERS see BEERS.			
	BIGELOW, BIGLOW AND BIGLO,			
1780	Abel	Lancaster,	Will,	5308
1821	Abel	West Boylston,	Administration,	5309
1840	Abel	Athol,	Will,	5310
1774	Abigail	Brookfield,	Guardianship,	5311
1808	Abigail	Brookfield,	Will,	5312
1827	Abigail	Athol,	Guardianship,	5313
1860	Abijah	Worcester,	Will,	5314
1802	Abraham	Sterling,	Administration,	5315
1875	Abraham M.	Grafton,	Will,	5316
1829	Adeline E.	Paxton,	Guardianship,	5317
1867	Alfred F.	North Brookfield,	Guardianship,	5318
1880	Alfred S.	Leicester,	Administration,	5319
1780	Amariah	Shrewsbury,	Will,	5320
1787	Amariah	Boylston,	Administration,	5321
1777	Amasa	Westborough,	Guardianship,	5322
1872	Amasa	New Braintree,	Administration,	5323
1784	Andrew,	Shrewsbury,	Guardianship,	5324
1834	Andrew	Boylston,	Administration,	5325
1848	Andrew L.	Charlton,	Guardianship,	5326
1840	Ann E.	Rutland,	Guardianship,	5327
1875	Anne G.	Worcester,	Will,	5328
1852	Arathusa	Phillipston,	Will,	5329
1804	Arethusa	Gerry,	Guardianship,	5330
1829	Artemas E.	Paxton,	Guardianship,	5331
1872	Arthur M.	Grafton,	Guardianship,	5332
1845	Asa	Westminster,	Will,	5333
1771	Asahel	Westborough,	Guardianship,	5334
1783	Asahel	Shrewsbury,	Guardianship,	5335
1844	Augusta	Charleston, S. C.,	Will,	5336
1778	Augustus	Worcester,	Guardianship,	5337
1869	Augustus	Fitchburg,	Administration,	5338
1873	Aurel	Hubbardston,	Administration,	5339
1826	Benjamin	Berlin,	Guardianship,	5340
1880	Benson	Westminster,	Will,	5341
1879	Betsey	North Brookfield,	Will,	5342
1827	Betsey E.	Athol,	Guardianship,	5343
1777	Catherine	Westborough,	Guardianship,	5344
1878	Catherine P.	Worcester,	Administration,	5345
1783	Charles	Shrewsbury,	Guardianship,	5346
1783	Charles	Shrewsbury,	Administration,	5347
1828	Charles	Lancaster,	Administration,	5348
1851	Charles	Petersham,	Administration,	5349

YEAR.	NAME.	RESIDENCE.	NATURE.	CASE.
	BIGELOW, BIGLOW AND BIGLO,			
1863	Charles	Grafton,	Will,	5350
1863	Charles A.	Grafton,	Guardianship,	5351
1868	Charles B.	Clinton,	Guardianship,	5352
1862	Charles D.	Sterling,	Guardianship,	5353
1864	Charles F.	West Boylston,	Administration,	5354
1837	Charles H.	Watertown,	Guardianship,	5355
1869	Charles O.	Barre,	Guardianship,	5356
1849	Charles P.	Holden,	Guardianship,	5357
1878	Charles P.	Worcester,	Administration,	5358
1827	Charles W.	Athol,	Guardianship,	5359
1877	Charles W.	Clinton,	Guardianship,	5360
1830	Christopher B.	Berlin,	Administration,	5361
1877	Clarissa N.	Clinton,	Administration,	5362
1770	Cornelius	Westborough,	Administration,	5363
1776	Daniel	Worcester,	Administration,	5364
1802	Daniel	Harvard,	Administration,	5365
1806	Daniel	Petersham,	Will,	5366
1810	David	Worcester,	Will,	5367
1866	David B.	Worcester,	Administration,	5368
1840	David E.	Rutland,	Guardianship,	5369
1769	Delight	Stow,	Guardianship,	5370
1851	Dennis	West Boylston,	Will,	5371
1758	Ebenezer	Lancaster,	Administration,	5372
1871	Edward B.	Grafton,	Will,	5373
1854	Edward H.	Worcester,	Sale of Real Est.,	5374
1762	Eleazer	Westminster,	Will,	5375
1859	Elijah	Douglas,	Administration,	5376
1865	Elijah	Grafton,	Administration,	5377
1814	Elisha	Westminster,	Will,	5378
1868	Eliza M.	Paxton,	Guardianship,	5379
1881	Elizabeth A.	Worcester,	Guardianship,	5380
1857	Ella J.	Rutland,	Guardianship,	5381
1780	Elnathan	Shrewsbury,	Guardianship,	5382
1851	Emeline E.	Paxton,	Guardianship,	5383
1867	Emma J.	North Brookfield,	Guardianship,	5384
1837	Ephraim	West Boylston,	Administration,	5385
1857	Erving E.	Rutland,	Guardianship,	5386
1840	Esther	Athol,	Guardianship,	5387
1867	Eugene F.	North Brookfield,	Guardianship,	5388
1839	Eunice	West Boylston,	Guardianship,	5389
1861	Eunice	Athol,	Administration,	5390
1798	Ezra	Boylston,	Guardianship,	5391
1824	Frances M.	Barre,	Guardianship,	5392
1798	Francis	Boston,	Administration,	5393

BIGELOW, BIGLOW AND BIGLO,

YEAR.	NAME.	RESIDENCE.	NATURE.	CASE.
1854	Francis E.	Worcester,	Guardianship,	5394
1880	Francis E.	West Boylston,	Will,	5395
1872	Francis W. W.	Boylston,	Will,	5396
1857	Fred C.	Rutland,	Guardianship,	5397
1879	Freeman	Oxford,	Will,	5398
1867	George	Boylston,	Administration,	5399
1827	George A.	Athol,	Guardianship,	5400
1844	George A.	New Braintree,	Guardianship,	5401
1859	George C.	Worcester,	Will,	5402
1841	George F.	Leicester,	Guardianship,	5403
1865	George L.	West Boylston,	Administration,	5404
1829	George N.	Paxton,	Guardianship,	5405
1862	George P.	Worcester,	Guardianship,	5406
1849	George T.	Holden,	Guardianship,	5407
1807	Gershom	Royalston,	Will,	5408
1852	Gilbert F.	Petersham,	Guardianship,	5409
1843	Guilford D.	Harvard,	Guardianship,	5410
1778	Hannah	Worcester,	Guardianship,	5411
1798	Hannah	Boston,	Guardianship,	5412
1808	Hannah	Petersham,	Guardianship,	5413
1840	Hannah	Gardner,	Will,	5414
1848	Hannah	Worcester,	Administration,	5415
1848	Hannah	Worcester,	Pension,	5416
1874	Hannah	Worcester,	Administration,	5417
1840	Hannah L.	Athol,	Guardianship,	5418
1861	Hannah L.	Athol,	Administration,	5419
1852	Harriet	Petersham,	Guardianship,	5420
1827	Harriet M.	Athol,	Guardianship,	5421
1870	Harriet S.	Shrewsbury,	Will,	5422
1843	Helen L.	Harvard,	Guardianship,	5423
1837	Helen M.	Watertown,	Guardianship,	5424
1844	Helen M.	New Braintree,	Guardianship,	5425
1871	Henry	Westborough,	Will,	5426
1840	Henry A.	Athol,	Guardianship,	5427
1859	Henry A.	Athol,	Will,	5428
1877	Henry F.	Clinton,	Guardianship,	5429
1844	Henry H.	New Braintree,	Guardianship,	5430
1767	Hepzibah	Brookfield,	Guardianship,	5431
1830	Horace	Berlin,	Guardianship,	5432
1868	Horatio N.	Clinton,	Administration,	5433
1877	Horatio N.	Clinton,	Guardianship,	5434
1844	Humphrey	Sutton,	Pension,	5435
1869	Isaac	Barre,	Administration,	5436
1843	Isaac L.	Fitzwilliam, N. H.,	Guardianship,	5437

Year.	Name.	Residence.	Nature.	Case.

BIGELOW, BIGLOW AND BIGLO,

Year.	Name.	Residence.	Nature.	Case.
1874	Isabella F.	Worcester,	Guardianship,	5438
1807	Ithamar	Paxton,	Administration,	5439
1861	Ithamar	Paxton,	Administration,	5440
1822	Jabez	Westminster,	Will,	5441
1800	Jacob	New Braintree,	Will,	5442
1783	James	Shrewsbury,	Guardianship,	5443
1872	James S.	Paxton,	Will,	5444
1852	Jane	Brookfield,	Guardianship,	5445
1854	Jane L.	West Boylston,	Adoption, etc.,	5446
1767	Jason	Brookfield,	Will,	5447
1768	Jason	Brookfield,	Guardianship,	5448
1810	Jason	Worcester,	Guardianship,	5449
1826	Jason	North Brookfield,	Will,	5450
1854	Jason	Harvard,	Administration,	5451
1856	Jason	North Brookfield,	Administration,	5452
1880	Jennie L.	Leicester,	Guardianship,	5453
1877	Jesse	Webster,	Will,	5454
1852	Jesse W.	Brookfield,	Administration,	5455
1777	Job	Westborough,	Administration,	5456
1878	Job S.	Fitchburg,	Guardianship,	5457
1879	Job S.	Fitchburg,	Administration,	5457
1783	John	Shrewsbury,	Guardianship,	5458
1829	John	Westminster,	Administration,	5459
1843	John	Worcester,	Administration,	5460
1843	John	Worcester,	Pension,	5461
1872	John	North Brookfield,	Will,	5462
1829	John F.	Paxton,	Guardianship,	5463
1848	John J.	Charlton,	Administration,	5464
1847	John T.	Oxford,	Guardianship,	5465
1858	John T.	Oakham,	Will,	5466
1768	Jonas	Brookfield,	Guardianship,	5467
1843	Jonas	North Brookfield,	Administration,	5468
1844	Jonas	North Brookfield,	Pension,	5469
1861	Jonas	North Brookfield,	Will,	5470
1774	Joseph	Spencer,	Administration,	5471
1783	Joseph	Shrewsbury,	Will,	5472
1783	Joseph	Shrewsbury,	Guardianship,	5473
1801	Joseph	Boylston,	Administration,	5474
1854	Joseph	Rutland,	Will,	5475
1758	Joshua	Sutton,	Administration,	5476
1788	Joshua	Worcester,	Guardianship,	5477
1790	Joshua	Worcester,	Will,	5477
1850	Josiah	Phillipston,	Administration,	5478
1803	Jotham	Gerry,	Will,	5479

YEAR.	NAME.	RESIDENCE.	NATURE.	CASE.
	BIGELOW, BIGLOW AND BIGLO,			
1863	Judith T.	Worcester,	Administration,	5480
1865	Julia A.	Grafton,	Guardianship,	5481
1869	Julia E.	Barre,	Guardianship,	5482
1822	Lambert	Westborough,	Administration,	5483
1874	Lawrence G.	Worcester,	Guardianship,	5484
1856	Lawson,	North Brookfield,	Guardianship,	5485
1856	Lawton	North Brookfield,	Guardianship,	5486
1780	Levi	Shrewsbury,	Guardianship,	5487
1833	Levi	West Boylston,	Administration,	5488
1859	Lewis	Worcester,	Administration,	5489
1876	Lewis R.	Rutland,	Guardianship,	5490
1840	Lois O.	Rutland,	Guardianship,	5491
1804	Lucinda	Gerry,	Guardianship,	5492
1875	Lucinda G.	Worcester,	Will,	5493
1871	Lucinda R.	Rutland,	Administration,	5494
1767	Lucy	Brookfield,	Guardianship,	5495
1777	Lucy	Westborough,	Guardianship,	5496
1783	Lucy	Shrewsbury,	Guardianship,	5497
1847	Luke	Westborough,	Administration,	5498
1860	Luke	Westminster,	Will,	5499
1873	Luke	Lancaster,	Will,	5500
1871	Luther H.	Worcester,	Will,	5501
1848	Lydia	North Brookfield,	Will,	5502
1849	Lydia	North Brookfield,	Pension,	5503
1862	Lydia	Boylston,	Administration,	5504
1862	Lydia	Boylston,	Pension,	5505
1835	Lydia L.	Boylston,	Guardianship,	5506
1847	Marshall S.	Leicester,	Administration,	5507
1848	Martha	West Boylston,	Will,	5508
1840	Martha J.	Rutland,	Guardianship,	5509
1783	Mary	Shrewsbury	Guardianship,	5510
1872	Mary	Worcester,	Will,	5511
1827	Mary A.	Athol,	Guardianship,	5512
1874	Mary A.	North Brookfield,	Administration,	5513
1875	Mary A.	Bolton,	Guardianship,	5514
1843	Mary E.	Fitzwilliam, N. H.,	Guardianship,	5515
1856	Mary E. A.	Phillipston,	Guardianship,	5516
1871	Mary K.	Worcester,	Administration,	5517
1867	Mary L.	North Brookfield,	Guardianship,	5518
1844	Mary R.	New Braintree,	Guardianship,	5519
1853	Mary S.	Worcester,	Sale of Real Est.,	5520
1869	Melona C.	Paxton,	Administration,	5521
1840	Merrill H.	Rutland,	Guardianship,	5522
1857	Merrill H.	Rutland,	Administration,	5523

BIGELOW, BIGLOW AND BIGLO,

1808	Nancy	Petersham,	Guardianship,	5524
1829	Nancy J.	Paxton,	Guardianship,	5525
1810	Olive	Boylston,	Will,	5526
1824	Olive S.	Barre,	Guardianship,	5527
1866	Owen A.	Webster,	Guardianship,	5528
1875	Patty	North Brookfield,	Administration,	5529
1798	Persis	Boylston,	Guardianship,	5530
1848	Persis	Paxton,	Will,	5531
1856	Persis	Petersham,	Will,	5532
1868	Phebe M.	Paxton,	Guardianship,	5533
1798	Polly	Boston,	Guardianship,	5534
1840	Prudence A.	Rutland,	Guardianship,	5535
1873	Ralph E.	Paxton,	Will,	5536
1856	Rebecca	Boylston,	Will,	5537
1840	Rhoena E.	Athol,	Guardianship,	5538
1861	Rhoena E.	Athol,	Administration,	5539
1840	Richard S.	Athol,	Guardianship,	5540
1861	Richard S.	Athol,	Will,	5541
1769	Roger	Stow,	Guardianship,	5542
1801	Roger	Winchendon,	Administration,	5543
1852	Ruth C.	Leicester,	Will,	5544
1796	Samuel	Shrewsbury,	Will,	5545
1833	Samuel	New Braintree,	Administration,	5546
1836	Samuel	Petersham,	Pension,	5547
1787	Samuel, Jr.	Shrewsbury,	Administration,	5548
1867	Samuel F.	North Brookfield,	Administration,	5549
1868	Samuel L.	Worcester,	Guardianship,	5550
1777	Sarah	Westborough,	Guardianship,	5551
1780	Sarah	Shrewsbury,	Guardianship,	5552
1865	Sarah	Harvard,	Administration,	5553
1840	Sarah E.	Athol,	Guardianship,	5554
1861	Sarah E.	Athol,	Administration,	5555
1835	Sarah F.	Boylston,	Guardianship,	5556
1769	Silas	Paxton,	Administration,	5557
1829	Silas	Paxton,	Administration,	5558
1837	Silas	Worcester,	Administration,	5559
1775	Solomon	Shrewsbury,	Administration,	5560
1783	Solomon	Shrewsbury,	Guardianship,	5561
1840	Solon	Athol,	Guardianship,	5562
1861	Solon	Athol,	Administration,	5563
1778	Sophia	Worcester,	Guardianship,	5564
1798	Sukey	Boylston,	Guardianship,	5565
1875	Susan M.	Royalston,	Administration,	5566
1868	Susan W.	Leominster,	Administration,	5567

YEAR.	NAME.	RESIDENCE.	NATURE.	CASE.
	BIGELOW, BIGLOW AND BIGLO,			
1863	Sylvia A.	Grafton,	Guardianship,	5568
1877	Tabitha M.	Rutland,	Will,	5569
1810	Thaddeus	Rutland,	Will,	5570
1869	Thankful M.	Barre,	Guardianship,	5571
1837	Thomas	Douglas,	Administration,	5572
1865	Thomas	Harvard,	Administration,	5573
1790	Timothy	Worcester,	Administration,	5574
1857	Walter	Worcester,	Will,	5575
1880	Walter	Worcester,	Will,	5576
1870	Walter B.	Worcester,	Guardianship,	5577
1872	Walter B.	Worcester,	Administration,	5577
1876	Walter S.	Worcester,	Administration,	5578
1820	William	Templeton,	Administration,	5579
1827	William	Athol,	Administration,	5580
1849	William	Phillipston,	Administration,	5581
1849	William A.	Holden,	Guardianship,	5582
1840	William B.	Athol,	Guardianship,	5583
1861	William B.	Athol,	Administration,	5584
1868	William H.	Westminster,	Change of Name,	5585
1875	Winsor H.	Bolton,	Administration,	5586
1873	BIGGS, Nelson	Leicester,	Guardianship,	5587
	BIGLO AND BIGLOW see BIGELOW.			
	BILL AND BILLS,			
1781	Joseph	Worcester,	Administration,	5588
1858	Samuel	Mendon,	Administration,	5589
1865	Sarah	Douglas,	Administration,	5590
1866	Susan	Clinton,	Administration,	5591
	BILLINGS AND BILLING.			
1859	Aaron	Worcester,	Administration,	5592
1878	Abigail K.	Sutton,	Guardianship,	5593
1812	Adaline	Hardwick,	Guardianship,	5594
1859	Agnes A.	Worcester,	Adoption, etc.,	5595
1843	Allen	Worcester,	Administration,	5596
1776	Artemas	Northborough,	Administration,	5597
1804	Asahel	Hardwick,	Administration,	5598
1804	Caty	Lunenburg,	Guardianship,	5599
1855	Charles	Fitchburg,	Administration,	5600
1860	Charles A.	Ashburnham,	Guardianship,	5601
1872	Charles A.	Ashburnham,	Guardianship,	5602
1836	Charlotte	Ashburnham,	Guardianship,	5603
1799	Daniel	Hardwick,	Will,	5604
1810	Daniel	Hardwick.	Administration,	5605
1833	David	Hardwick,	Administration,	5606
1804	Diana	Hardwick,	Guardianship,	5607

BILLINGS and BILLING,

YEAR.	NAME.	RESIDENCE.	NATURE.	CASE.
1836	Dolly	Ashburnham,	Guardianship,	5608
1812	Dwight	Hardwick,	Guardianship,	5609
1803	Elisha	Hardwick,	Will,	5610
1866	Emma S.	Northborough,	Guardianship,	5611
1858	Eunice	Lunenburg,	Will,	5612
1844	Frances (A.)	Dana,	Guardianship,	5613
1866	Francis E.	Northborough,	Guardianship,	5614
1851	George A.	Worcester,	Guardianship,	5615
1874	George F.	Westborough,	Guardianship,	5616
1860	George H.	Ashburnham,	Guardianship,	5617
1804	Hannah	Lunenburg,	Guardianship,	5618
1854	Hannah E.	Fitchburg,	Administration,	5619
1851	Harriet G.	Worcester,	Guardianship,	5620
1851	Hiram H.	Worcester,	Guardianship,	5621
1829	Horace	Lancaster,	Guardianship,	5622
1874	H. L.	Westborough,	Guardianship,	5623
1846	James	Ashburnham,	Administration,	5624
1834	John	Lunenburg,	Will,	5625
1836	John	Ashburnham,	Guardianship,	5626
1848	John H.	Ashburnham,	Guardianship,	5627
1860	John H.	Ashburnham,	Will,	5628
1820	Jonathan	Hardwick,	Will,	5629
1843	Joseph F.	Lancaster,	Guardianship,	5630
1834	Joshua	Ashburnham,	Administration,	5631
1843	Josiah	Lancaster,	Administration,	5632
1829	Josiah, Jr.	Lancaster,	Guardianship,	5633
1874	Josie D.	Westborough,	Guardianship,	5634
1817	Julia	Charlton,	Guardianship,	5635
1860	Leafy M.	Ashburnham,	Guardianship,	5636
1817	Lewis	Charlton,	Guardianship,	5637
1850	Lorenzo	Worcester,	Administration,	5638
1834	Lucius F.	Hardwick,	Guardianship,	5639
1804	Lucy	Lunenburg,	Guardianship,	5640
1860	Lucy	Lunenburg,	Administration,	5641
1829	Luther	Lancaster,	Guardianship,	5642
1843	Luther	Lunenburg,	Administration,	5643
1829	Lydia W.	Lancaster,	Guardianship,	5644
1829	Martha F.	Lancaster,	Guardianship,	5645
1834	Mary A.	Hardwick,	Guardianship,	5646
1866	Mary E.	Grafton,	Administration,	5647
1874	Nellie A.	Westborough,	Guardianship,	5648
1835	Reuben	Fitchburg,	Will,	5649
1870	Reuben	Fitchburg,	Will,	5650
1763	Richard	Hardwick,	Guardianship,	5651

BILLINGS AND BILLING,

1817	Sally	Charlton,	Guardianship,	5652
1872	Sally H.	Eau Pleine, Wis.,	Administration,	5653
1778	Samuel	Hardwick,	Will,	5654
1808	Samuel	Charlton,	Guardianship,	5655
1812	Samuel	Hardwick,	Guardianship,	5656
1828	Samuel	Lunenburg,	Administration,	5657
1868	Samuel.	Worcester,	Will,	5658
1878	Sarah J.	Athol,	Change of Name,	5659
1875	Sibyl A.	Grafton,	Administration,	5660
1873	Sophia	Lunenburg,	Will,	5661
1818	Stephen	Hardwick,	Administration,	5662
1804	Theodosia	Hardwick,	Guardianship,	5663
1880	Thomas	Leominster,	Will,	5664
1812	Timothy	Hardwick,	Administration,	5665
1812	Timothy R.	Hardwick,	Guardianship,	5666
1817	Willard	Charlton,	Guardianship,	5667
1808	William	Charlton,	Guardianship,	5668
1817	William	Charlton,	Administration,	5669
1843	William E.	Dana,	Administration,	5670
1844	William H.	Dana,	Guardianship,	5671
1854	William H.	Millbury,	Administration,	5672

BILLS see BILL.

BINNEY AND BINNY,

1795	Benjamin	Kent Co., Md.,	Will,	5673
1845	Mary P.	West Boylston,	Administration,	5674
1855	BIRCHARD, Eliphalet	Lebanon, Conn.,	Will,	5675
1838	BIRD, Abner	North Brookfield,	Administration,	5676
1878	Alice M.	Sturbridge,	Guardianship,	5677
1812	Bailey	Sterling,	Guardianship,	5678
1857	Bailey	Fitchburg,	Administration,	5679
1878	Enoch	Sturbridge,	Will,	5680
1855	Eliza	North Brookfield,	Will,	5681
1878	Lillian F.	Sturbridge,	Guardianship,	5682
1826	Mary	North Brookfield,	Administration,	5683
1873	Sally H.	Worcester,	Administration,	5684
1878	Willie O.	Sturbridge,	Guardianship,	5685
1870	BIRMINGHAM, Catharine	Milford,	Guardianship,	5686
1870	James	Milford,	Guardianship,	5687
1870	Margaret	Milford,	Guardianship,	5688
1870	Patrick	Milford,	Guardianship,	5689
1870	Thomas	Milford,	Guardianship,	5690

BIRON see BYRON.

BISCO AND BISCOE,

1843	Adeline	Leicester,	Guardianship,	5691

YEAR.	NAME.	RESIDENCE.	NATURE.	CASE.
	BISCO AND BISCOE,			
1843	Alden	Leicester,	Will,	5692
1879	Arthur G.	Westborough,	Will,	5693
1865	Bathsheba	Grafton,	Will,	5694
1877	Eliza A.	Spencer,	Will,	5695
1881	Foster	Spencer,	Will,	5696
1837	Jacob	Spencer,	Administration,	5697
1837	Jacob	Spencer,	Guardianship,	5698
1808	John	Spencer,	Will,	5699
1812	John	Spencer,	Administration,	5700
1879	Laura A.	Marietta, O.,	Foreign Will,	5701
1843	Laurinda	Leicester,	Guardianship,	5702
1876	Ruth W.	Leicester,	Administration,	5703
1875	BISHOP, Almina	Worcester,	Administration,	5704
1878	George A.	Leominster,	Administration,	5705
1879	George W.	Leominster,	Guardianship,	5706
1879	Lillie J.	Leominster,	Guardianship,	5707
1878	Martha D.	Woodstock, Conn.,	Administration,	5708
1859	BISP, Henry	Milford,	Administration,	5709
1878	BIXBY, Albert	Milford,	Administration,	5710
1787	Asa	Barre,	Will,	5711
1856	Austin	Barre,	Will,	5712
1833	Clark S.	Barre,	Guardianship,	5713
1820	Joel	Worcester,	Administration,	5714
1741	Jonathan	Sutton,	Guardianship,	5715
1791	Jonathan	Barre,	Guardianship,	5716
1859	Lucy	Brookfield,	Will,	5717
1859	Lucy	Brookfield,	Pension,	5718
1876	Luther	Westborough,	Administration,	5719
1850	Mary	Millbury,	Pension,	5720
1863	Mary	Thompson, Conn.,	Foreign Will,	5721
1869	Melissa A.	Fitchburg,	Administration,	5722
1768	Mephibosheth	Winchendon,	Administration,	5723
1778	Nathaniel	Winchendon,	Administration,	5724
1791	Patty	Barre,	Guardianship,	5725
1868	Phebe	Webster,	Administration,	5726
1788	Rebekah	Sutton,	Will,	5727
1833	Roxana	Barre,	Guardianship,	5728
1791	Salmon	Barre,	Guardianship,	5729
1741	Sampson	Sutton,	Guardianship,	5730
1789	Sampson	Barre,	Administration,	5731
1741	Samuel	Sutton,	Administration,	5732
1809	Samuel	Sutton,	Will,	5733
1848	Samuel	Millbury,	Pension,	5734
1851	Samuel	Millbury,	Administration,	5735

YEAR.	NAME.	RESIDENCE.	NATURE.	CASE.
1741	BIXBY, Solomon	Sutton,	Guardianship,	5736
1802	Solomon, 2d	Sturbridge,	Administration,	5737
1859	Susan	Holden,	Administration,	5738
1832	Wesson	Barre,	Administration,	5739
1864	BLACK, Amos R.	Worcester,	Administration,	5740
1839	Archibald	Barre,	Administration,	5741
1841	Charles	Holden,	Guardianship,	5742
1877	Cyrus B.	Princeton,	Adoption, etc.,	5743
1792	Daniel	Holden,	Will,	5744
1841	Eliza	Holden,	Guardianship,	5745
1805	Elizabeth	Barre,	Administration,	5746
1846	Elizabeth	Barre,	Administration,	5747
1785	George	Barre,	Guardianship,	5748
1803	George	Oakham,	Will,	5749
1841	George	Holden,	Guardianship,	5750
1871	George C.	Worcester,	Administration,	5751
1753	Henry	Boston,	Guardianship,	5752
1863	Henry E.	Holden,	Guardianship,	5753
1846	Isabella	Barre,	Administration,	5754
1824	James	Barre,	Will,	5755
1833	James A.	Barre,	Guardianship,	5756
1841	James D.	Holden,	Guardianship,	5757
1879	James T.	Sturbridge,	Adoption, etc.,	5758
1797	John	Barre,	Administration,	5759
1804	Josiah	Barre,	Will,	5760
1841	Lucy	Holden,	Guardianship,	5761
1843	Lucy R.	Milford,	Administration,	5762
1797	Mariot	Barre,	Guardianship,	5763
1753	Marmaduke	Rutland,	Will,	5764
1841	Mary	Holden,	Guardianship,	5765
1879	Mary A.	Sturbridge,	Adoption, etc.,	5766
1797	Sarah C.	Barre,	Guardianship,	5767
1841	Simon	Holden,	Administration,	5768
1868	Simon	Holden,	Will,	5769
1770	William	Oakham,	Will,	5770
1849	William	Barre,	Administration,	5771
1879	BLACKER, Alice L.	Worcester,	Guardianship,	5772
1738	BLACKMAN, Ephraim	Stratford, Conn.,	Guardianship,	5773
1842	Nathan	Charlton,	Administration,	5774
1826	Susanna	Worcester,	Will,	5775
	BLACKMAR, BLACKMER AND BLACKMORE,			
1863	Charles	Charlton,	Will,	5776
1851	Charles H.	Holden,	Guardianship,	5777
1872	Daniel G.	Worcester,	Administration,	5778

BLACKMAR, BLACKMER and BLACKMORE,

Year	Name	Residence	Nature	Case
1851	Dexter M.	Holden,	Guardianship,	5779
1868	Dexter M.	Worcester,	Guardianship,	5780
1851	Emeline L.	Holden,	Guardianship,	5781
1859	Francis A.	Hardwick,	Guardianship,	5782
1867	Franklin	Dana,	Administration,	5783
1865	George E.	Athol,	Guardianship,	5784
1853	Harrison R.	Dana,	Guardianship,	5785
1858	Hosea	Dana,	Administration,	5786
1850	Hubbard V.	Holden,	Administration,	5787
1853	Jacob S.	Dana,	Guardianship,	5788
1815	John	Western,	Administration,	5789
1817	John	Western,	Guardianship,	5790
1847	Lauriston E.	Dana,	Guardianship,	5791
1855	Lauriston E.	Dana,	Administration,	5792
1817	Lewis	Western,	Guardianship,	5793
1853	Lewis W.	Dana,	Guardianship,	5794
1847	Lorenzo S.	Dana,	Guardianship,	5795
1873	Luther	Worcester,	Administration,	5796
1851	Mary A.	Holden,	Guardianship,	5797
1873	Mary A.	Hardwick,	Administration,	5798
1881	Mary J.	North Brookfield,	Administration,	5799
1817	Melinda	Western,	Guardianship,	5800
1854	Moses	Holden,	Administration,	5801
1874	Ruth	Charlton,	Administration,	5802
1829	Sally	Western,	Guardianship,	5803
1786	Simeon	Western,	Administration,	5804
1853	Solomon	Dana,	Will,	5805
1836	Solomon, Jr.	Dana,	Guardianship,	5806
1842	Theophilus	Charlton,	Administration,	5807
1872	Theophilus	Charlton,	Will,	5808
1844	Warren	Dana,	Administration,	5809
1877	BLAIN, Mary J.	West Boylston,	Adoption, etc.,	5810
1778	BLAINEY, Jedediah	Ward,	Administration,	5811
1870	BLAIR, Alvah	Warren,	Will,	5812
1857	Charles	Worcester,	Will,	5813
1844	Deborah	Brookfield,	Will,	5814
1731	Elizabeth	Framingham,	Guardianship,	5815
1844	Ezekiel	Warren,	Will,	5816
1880	E. Elizabeth	Worcester,	Guardianship,	5817
1773	Francis	Western,	Administration,	5818
1874	George S.	West Brookfield,	Will,	5819
1798	Huldah	Worcester,	Will,	5820
1797	Increase	Worcester,	Administration,	5821

Year.	Name.	Residence.	Nature.	Case.
1756	BLAIR, James	New Braintree,	Will,	5822
1807	James	Spencer,	Guardianship,	5823
1823	James	Western,	Will,	5824
1872	James	West Brookfield,	Will,	5825
1731	John	Framingham,	Guardianship,	5826
1773	John	Western,	Guardianship,	5827
1796	John	Western,	Administration,	5828
1798	John	Worcester,	Guardianship,	5829
1859	John	Southbridge,	Administration,	5830
1802	Joseph	Brookfield,	Will,	5831
1804	Joseph	Worcester,	Will,	5832
1854	Joseph	West Brookfield,	Administration,	5833
1880	Joshua B.	Worcester,	Guardianship,	5834
1879	Lucien A.	Warren,	Administration,	5835
1839	Marcy	Barre,	Guardianship,	5836
1768	Mary	New Braintree,	Administration,	5837
1868	Mary	West Brookfield,	Administration,	5838
1807	Polly	Spencer,	Guardianship,	5839
1834	Reuben	Brookfield,	Pension,	5840
1731	Robert	Framingham,	Guardianship,	5841
1736	Robert	Shrewsbury,	Guardianship,	5842
1773	Robert	Western,	Guardianship,	5843
1837	. Robert	Worcester,	Will,	5844
1848	Roswell	Warren,	Administration,	5845
1831	Samuel	Western,	Will,	5846
1731	Samuell	Framingham,	Guardianship,	5847
1840	Solomon	Brookfield,	Pension,	5848
1731	William	Framingham,	Guardianship,	5849
1746	William	Shrewsbury,	Guardianship,	5850
1789	William	Worcester,	Administration,	5851
1854	William	Rutland,	Guardianship,	5852
1874	BLAISDELL, Parritt	Worcester,	Will,	5853
1844	BLAKE, Angenette	New York, N. Y.,	Guardianship,	5854
1811	Barnum	Westborough,	Administration,	5855
1816	Benjamin	Mendon,	Will,	5856
1836	Benjamin	Princeton,	Administration,	5857
1880	Caroline B.	Worcester,	Administration,	5858
1859	Charles F.	Worcester,	Change of Name,	5859
1864	Charles L.	Worcester,	Administration,	5860
1866	Clara E.	Athol,	Guardianship,	5861
1826	Daniel	North Brookfield,	Guardianship,	5862
1859	Eben D.	Northborough,	Administration,	5863
1834	Elias	Holden,	Administration,	5864
1850	Elihu	Westborough,	Will,	5865
1839	Eliza A.	Worcester,	Administration,	5866

Year.	Name.	Residence.	Nature.	Case.
1876	BLAKE, Ellen	Worcester,	Guardianship,	5867
1826	Ellis	Mendon,	Guardianship,	5868
1794	Ellis G.	Worcester,	Administration,	5869
1817	Francis	Worcester,	Administration,	5870
1857	Hannah	Westborough,	Will,	5871
1866	Harriet M.	Athol,	Guardianship,	5872
1844	Harvey B.	New York, N. Y.,	Guardianship,	5873
1866	Helen A.	Athol,	Guardianship,	5874
1795	Increase	Worcester,	Administration,	5875
1783	James	Mendon,	Will,	5876
1797	James	Oakham,	Will,	5877
1827	James	Oakham,	Administration,	5878
1871	James B.	Worcester,	Administration,	5879
1837	Jeremiah	Holden,	Administration,	5880
1869	Joel	Holden,	Administration,	5881
1872	John	Worcester,	Administration,	5882
1873	John M.	Leominster,	Guardianship,	5883
1824	Jonathan	New Braintree,	Administration,	5884
1804	Joseph	Uxbridge,	Will,	5885
1876	Louisa	Worcester,	Guardianship,	5886
1876	Lowell E.	Worcester,	Guardianship,	5887
1845	Lydia	Mendon,	Administration,	5888
1876	Mabel	Worcester,	Guardianship,	5889
1819	Marshall H.	Westborough,	Guardianship,	5890
1863	Marshall H.	Westborough,	Administration,	5891
1867	Mary	Vernon, Vt.,	Adoption, etc.,	5892
1844	Mary E.	New York, N. Y.,	Guardianship,	5893
1826	Nancy	North Brookfield,	Guardianship,	5894
1828	Nancy M.	Holden,	Guardianship,	5895
1872	Nancy P. H.	Worcester,	Will,	5896
1840	Nelson	Brookfield,	Guardianship,	5897
1828	Oliver	Holden,	Administration,	5898
1849	Ruth	Westborough,	Administration,	5899
1827	Sally	North Brookfield,	Administration,	5900
1857	Sarah D.	Boston,	Miscellaneous,	5901
1785	Simeon	Mendon,	Administration,	5902
1841	Susan	Brookfield,	Guardianship,	5903
1844	Susan O.	New York, N. Y.,	Guardianship,	5904
1866	William H.	Westborough,	Administration,	5905
1826	BLANCHARD, Abel	Harvard,	Administration,	5906
1825	Albert C.	Brookfield,	Guardianship,	5907
1874	Albert C.	Brookfield,	Will,	5908
1845	Amasa	Sturbridge,	Guardianship,	5909
1868	Ann M.	Douglas,	Administration,	5910
1812	Babbitt	Petersham,	Guardianship,	5911

Year.	Name.	Residence.	Nature.	Case.
1812	BLANCHARD, Betsey	Petersham,	Guardianship,	5912
1851	Betsey	Harvard,	Administration,	5913
1842	Calvin D.	Harvard,	Guardianship,	5914
1871	Cyrus D.	Fitchburg,	Will,	5915
1826	Dexter	Charlton,	Administration,	5916
1881	Douglas F.	Uxbridge,	Will,	5917
1756	Elizabeth	Gore,	Guardianship,	5918
1800	Elizabeth	Harvard,	Administration,	5919
1876	Elizabeth	Harvard,	Guardianship,	5920
1891	Elizabeth	Harvard,	Administration,	5920
1878	Emma H.	Worcester,	Guardianship,	5921
1863	Hosea	Winchendon,	Administration,	5922
1745	Isaac	Lancaster,	Administration,	5923
1813	James	Charlton,	Administration,	5924
1842	John	Harvard,	Will,	5925
1875	John	Harvard,	Will,	5926
1787	Joseph	Harvard,	Will,	5927
1789	Joseph	Sutton,	Guardianship,	5928
1875	Joseph	Uxbridge,	Will,	5929
1878	Joseph	Leominster,	Administration,	5930
1842	Josephine H.	Harvard,	Guardianship,	5931
1756	Josiah	Gore,	Guardianship,	5932
1832	Julia A.	Charlton,	Guardianship,	5933
1832	Lorin	Charlton,	Guardianship,	5934
1789	Lucy B.	Sutton,	Guardianship,	5935
1875	Lucy W.	Brookfield,	Will,	5936
1876	Margaret B.	Harvard,	Will,	5937
1875	Margaret J.	Harvard,	Guardianship,	5938
1842	Mary A.	Harvard,	Guardianship,	5939
1834	Moses	Charlton,	Administration,	5940
1865	Nancy	Northborough,	Will,	5941
1842	Nathaniel	Harvard,	Guardianship,	5942
1865	Parley	Brookfield,	Administration,	5943
1856	Peter	Charlton,	Administration,	5944
1812	Pliny	Petersham,	Guardianship,	5945
1858	Ruth M.	Palatka, Fla.,	Guardianship,	5946
1825	Samuel	Millbury,	Will,	5947
1842	Sarah A.	Harvard,	Guardianship,	5948
1811	Seth	Petersham,	Administration,	5949
1833	Simon	Harvard,	Administration,	5950
1833	Simon	Harvard,	Pension,	5951
1792	Stephen	Sturbridge,	Will,	5952
1855	Stephen	Millbury,	Will,	5953
1786	Thomas	Sutton,	Administration,	5954
1878	Vianna L.	Worcester,	Will,	5955

YEAR.	NAME.	RESIDENCE.	NATURE.	CASE.
1818	BLANCHARD, William	Lancaster,	Will,	5956
1825	William	Brookfield,	Will,	5957
	BLANDIN AND BLANDING,			
1835	Elisha	Oxford,	Administration,	5958
1835	Elisha	Oxford,	Pension,	5959
1836	Francis	Oxford,	Administration,	5960
1836	Francis	Oxford,	Pension,	5961
1820	George	Oxford,	Pension,	5962
1878	Nancy W.	Hubbardston,	Administration,	5963
1832	Shubel	Royalston,	Will,	5964
1862	BLANKENHORN, Catherine	Worcester,	Administration,	5965
1839	BLASHFIELD, Bathsheba	Sturbridge,	Will,	5966
1812	BLISS, Aaron	Western,	Administration,	5967
1849	Aaron	Royalston,	Will,	5968
1852	Aaron	Warren,	Will,	5969
1879	Abby G.	West Brookfield,	Administration,	5970
1852	Abel	Royalston,	Administration,	5971
1852	Abel H.	Royalston,	Guardianship,	5972
1881	Abner A.	Warren,	Administration,	5973
1881	Alvin B.	Warren,	Will,	5974
1863	Anna	Royalston,	Guardianship,	5975
1848	Asenath P.	Worcester,	Administration,	5976
1869	Benjamin W.	Royalston,	Administration,	5977
1815	Caroline	Royalston,	Guardianship,	5978
1855	Caroline F.	West Brookfield,	Guardianship,	5979
1881	Caroline P. F.	West Brookfield,	Administration,	5980
1880	Charles	Warren,	Will,	5981
1857	Charles W.	Milford,	Adoption, etc.,	5982
1815	Daniel	Royalston,	Guardianship,	5983
1863	Daniel	Royalston,	Will,	5984
1866	Daniel	Warren,	Change of Name,	5985
1872	Daniel	Warren,	Guardianship,	5986
1866	Daniel J.	Warren,	Change of Name,	5987
1787	David	Western,	Guardianship,	5988
1856	David	West Brookfield,	Administration,	5989
1815	Dorothy	Royalston,	Guardianship,	5990
1871	Edward	Berlin,	Will,	5991
1852	Eliza A.	Grafton,	Guardianship,	5992
1873	Elizabeth B.	Athol,	Will,	5993
1841	Frances L.	Worcester,	Guardianship,	5994
1864	Herbert F.	Milford,	Guardianship,	5995
1876	Ida M.	Worcester,	Adoption, etc.,	5996
1826	Isaac	Western,	Will,	5997
1846	James H.	Fitchburg,	Administration,	5998
1787	Jemima	Western,	Guardianship,	5999

YEAR.	NAME.	RESIDENCE.	NATURE.	CASE.
1853	BLISS, Jesse	West Brookfield,	Administration,	6000
1862	Joel	Warren,	Will,	6001
1787	Jonathan	Western,	Guardianship,	6002
1863	Joseph	Royalston,	Administration,	6003
1847	Levi	West Brookfield,	Guardianship,	6004
1867	Levi	West Brookfield,	Administration,	6004
1852	Mary Louise	Warren,	Guardianship,	6005
1852	Nathan	Royalston,	Will,	6006
1852	Nathan	Royalston,	Pension,	6007
1829	Noah	Warren,	Will,	6008
1787	Oliver	Western,	Guardianship,	6009
1848	Oliver	Warren,	Will,	6010
1852	Orvis L.	Grafton,	Administration,	6011
1815	Polly	Royalston,	Guardianship,	6012
1871	Renselaer	North Brookfield,	Will,	6013
1869	Roswell	Berlin,	Administration,	6014
1876	Rufus D.	Warren,	Administration,	6015
1862	Ruth	Royalston,	Will,	6016
1786	Samuel	Western,	Administration,	6017
1842	Samuel	Brookfield,	Will,	6018
1867	Samuel	Worcester,	Will,	6019
1873	Samuel	West Brookfield	Administration,	6020
1841	Samuel A.	Worcester,	Administration,	6021
1803	Solomon	Western,	Will,	6022
1855	Sylvanus J.	West Brookfield,	Administration,	6023
1868	Theodore H.	Worcester,	Guardianship,	6024
1815	Timothy, Jr.	Royalston,	Administration,	6025
1870	William H.	Hardwick,	Guardianship,	6026
1855	William W.	Worcester,	Administration,	6027
	BLODGET, BLODGETT AND BLOGGET,			
1807	Abner	Sturbridge,	Administration,	6028
1869	Alden	Warren,	Will,	6029
1878	Alton	Fitchburg,	Will,	6030
1854	Amos	Templeton,	Administration,	6031
1832	Angelina	Royalston,	Guardianship,	6032
1836	Charles	Worcester,	Administration,	6033
1825	Elias	Westminster,	Administration,	6034
1825	Elias	Westminster,	Guardianship,	6035
1837	Eunice L.	Royalston,	Guardianship,	6036
1863	Franklin	Worcester,	Guardianship,	6037
1837	George	Royalston,	Administration,	6038
1837	George S.	Royalston,	Guardianship,	6039
1879	Grace E.	Templeton,	Guardianship,	6040
1825	Harriet	Westminster,	Guardianship,	6041

YEAR.	NAME.	RESIDENCE.	NATURE.	CASE.
	BLODGET, BLODGETT AND BLOGGET,			
1824	Isaac	Westminster,	Will,	6042
1812	James	Westminster,	Administration,	6043
1837	Julius P.	Royalston,	Guardianship,	6044
1876	Julius P.	Leominster,	Administration,	6045
1825	Lucy	Westminster,	Guardianship,	6046
1825	Mary	Westminster,	Guardianship,	6047
1865	Mary	Union, Conn.,	Will,	6048
1793	Nathaniel	Chesterfield, N. H.,	Guardianship,	6049
1825	Sarah	Westminster,	Guardianship,	6050
1832	Selah	Royalston,	Guardianship,	6051
1871	Susan M.	North Brookfield,	Administration,	6052
1832	Susanna	Royalston,	Guardianship,	6053
1877	Williard	Sturbridge,	Administration,	6054
1742	Zacheus	Litchfield,	Guardianship,	6055
1865	Ziba, etc.	Worcester,	Administration,	6056
1865	Zibora A.	Worcester,	Administration,	6056
1862	BLOOD, Anne W.	Fitchburg,	Will,	6057
1859	Charles F.	Worcester,	Change of Name,	6058
1875	Charles H.	Hubbardston,	Guardianship,	6059
1881	Charles H.	Fitchburg,	Guardianship,	6060
1870	Charlotte	Charlton,	Administration,	6061
1879	Eben P.	Sterling,	Administration,	6062
1830	Edmund	Bolton,	Administration,	6063
1847	Eli	Charlton,	Guardianship,	6064
1826	Elijah	Charlton,	Administration,	6065
1869	Eliza A.	Southbridge,	Administration,	6066
1878	Eliza J.	Sterling,	Administration,	6067
1867	Elizabeth L.	Leominster,	Will,	6068
1867	Emma J.	Worcester,	Guardianship,	6069
1876	Eunice	North Brookfield,	Will,	6070
1875	Frederick E.	Hubbardston,	Guardianship,	6071
1867	George	Worcester,	Administration,	6072
1827	Hannah	Berlin,	Administration,	6073
1880	John	Worcester,	Administration,	6074
1820	Joseph	Charlton,	Administration,	6075
1875	Julia A.	Hubbardston,	Administration,	6076
1872	Mabel E.	Hubbardston,	Guardianship,	6077
1858	Marshall	Leominster,	Administration,	6078
1872	Martha H.	Worcester,	Administration,	6079
1875	Mary C.	Hubbardston,	Administration,	6080
1877	Mary E.	Charlton,	Administration,	6081
1839	Moses	China, N. Y.,	Administration,	6082
1801	Nathaniel	Charlton,	Will,	6083
1861	Nellie P.	Upton,	Adoption, etc.,	6084

Year	Name	Residence	Nature	Case
1858	BLOOD, Oliver H.	Worcester,	Administration,	6085
1875	Otis	Worcester,	Administration,	6086
1842	Reuben	Sterling,	Pension,	6087
1877	Reuben	Sterling,	Will,	6088
1768	Richard	Charlton,	Will,	6089
1820	Richard	Charlton,	Administration,	6090
1848	Samuel	Harvard,	Pension,	6091
1869	Samuel J.	Charlton,	Will,	6092
1881	Thomas C.	Fitchburg,	Guardianship,	6093
1848	William	Berlin, Conn.,	Administration,	6094
1880	BLOS, John C.	Worcester,	Administration,	6095
1881	Minnie H.	Worcester,	Guardianship,	6096
1881	William J.	Worcester,	Guardianship,	6097
1880	BLUNT, Ellen E.	Worcester,	Adoption, etc.,	6098
1742	Ezekiel	Oxford,	Guardianship,	6099
1747	Ezekiel	Sutton,	Administration,	6100
1759	Hannah	Sturbridge,	Guardianship,	6101
1755	John	Sturbridge,	Will,	6102
1761	Martha	Sturbridge,	Guardianship,	6103
1759	Ruth	Sturbridge,	Guardianship,	6104
1881	BOAK, William	Southbridge,	Will,	6105
	BOARDMAN AND BORDMAN,			
1872	Abbie B.	Williamstown,	Adoption, etc.,	6106
1877	Abner	Millbury,	Administration,	6107
1880	Amelia R.	Millbury,	Guardianship,	6108
1849	Charles	Worcester,	Will,	6109
1880	Delia E.	Millbury,	Guardianship,	6110
1880	Eliza	Millbury,	Guardianship,	6111
1880	Flora D.	Millbury,	Guardianship,	6112
1849	Harriet T.	Worcester,	Guardianship,	6113
1841	John	Douglas,	Will,	6114
1875	John	Leicester,	Will,	6115
1858	Joseph F.	Westborough,	Administration,	6116
1870	Maria A.	Westborough,	Will,	6117
1880	Mary	Millbury,	Guardianship,	6118
1875	Teresa S.	Worcester,	Administration,	6119
1858	BODELL, John B.	Leominster,	Administration,	6120
	BODET see BEAUDETTE.			
1863	BODWELL, Philander	Worcester,	Will,	6121
1871	BOHONAN, Abbie M.	Fitchburg,	Guardianship,	6122
1877	Agnes P.	Fitchburg,	Adoption, etc.,	6123
1877	BOHRING, Lizzie	Boston,	Adoption, etc.,	6124
	BOICE AND BOIES see BOYCE.			
1873	BOLAND, Patrick J.	Worcester,	Will,	6125

YEAR.	NAME.	RESIDENCE.	NATURE.	CASE.
1878	BOLEN, Patrick H.	Worcester,	Administration,	6126
1879	BOLIO, Elizabeth	Worcester,	Administration,	6127
1870	King	Worcester,	Will,	6128
1753	BOLSTER, Isaac	Uxbridge,	Administration,	6129
1753	Isaac	Uxbridge,	Guardianship,	6130
1869	Isaac	Charlton,	Administration,	6131
1866	Jerome B.	Blackstone,	Administration,	6132
1856	Lorin O.	Oxford,	Administration,	6133
1762	Mary	Uxbridge,	Guardianship,	6134
1791	Mary	Uxbridge,	Administration,	6134
1793	Richard	Douglas,	Guardianship,	6135
1821	Richard	Douglas,	Administration,	6136
1753	William	Uxbridge,	Guardianship,	6137
	BOLTON (see also BOULTON.)			
1871	Aaron S.	Westminster,	Administration,	6138
1880	Albert A.	Phillipston,	Administration,	6139
1839	Christopher	Gardner,	Guardianship,	6140
1835	Ebenezer	Gardner,	Will,	6141
1850	Ebenezer	Gardner,	Administration,	6142
1880	Henry E.	West Boylston,	Administration,	6143
1838	Horatio N.	Gardner,	Administration,	6144
1871	Jackson M.	Westminster,	Guardianship,	6145
1819	Nathaniel	Oakham,	Guardianship,	6146
1868	Nellie E.	Westminster,	Adoption, etc.,	6147
1844	Ransom	Gardner,	Administration,	6148
1839	Sidney	Gardner,	Guardianship,	6149
1864	Sidney	Gardner,	Guardianship,	6150
1871	Sidney	Gardner,	Administration,	6150
1796	BOND, Abraham	Westborough,	Will,	6151
1807	Amasa	Sutton,	Guardianship,	6152
1878	Amasa	Millbury,	Administration,	6153
1848	Amos	North Brookfield,	Will,	6154
1857	Amy E.	North Brookfield,	Administration,	6155
1877	Annie E.	Worcester,	Guardianship,	6156
1784	Benjamin	Leicester,	Will,	6157
1812	Benjamin	Leicester,	Administration,	6158
1813	Benjamin	Leicester,	Administration,	6159
1832	Cary H.	Leicester,	Administration,	6160
1864	Charles A.	Charlton,	Guardianship,	6161
1833	Chauncey	Shrewsbury,	Will,	6162
1833	David F.	Boylston,	Administration,	6163
1832	David T.	Hardwick,	Administration,	6164
1861	Eber	Leicester,	Will,	6165
1776	Edward	Leicester,	Will,	6166
1807	Eliza	Sutton,	Guardianship,	6167
1871	Eliza	Worcester,	Administration,	6168

YEAR.	NAME.	RESIDENCE.	NATURE.	CASE.
1866	BOND, Ellen M.	Sturbridge,	Guardianship,	6169
1851	Emery	Millbury,	Will,	6170
1866	Estes	Sturbridge,	Will,	6171
1820	Experience	Leicester,	Guardianship,	6172
1855	Fanny M.	Oxford,	Guardianship,	6173
1877	Fanny P.	Worcester,	Guardianship,	6174
1870	Flora S.	Sutton,	Guardianship,	6175
1831	Francis H.	Bolton,	Guardianship,	6176
1852	George	Leicester,	Will,	6177
1853	Henry	Northbridge,	Administration,	6178
1838	Jacob	Leicester,	Will,	6179
1854	Jane E.	Worcester,	Guardianship,	6180
1856	Jane S.	Wilkesbarre, Pa.,	Guardianship,	6181
1764	John	Rutland,	Administration,	6182
1769	John	Lancaster,	Will,	6183
1837	John	Boylston,	Administration,	6184
1846	John B.	Worcester,	Guardianship,	6185
1853	John B.	Worcester,	Will,	6185
1865	John L.	Warren,	Will,	6186
1806	Jonas, Jr.	Sutton,	Administration,	6187
1794	Jonathan	Boylston,	Will,	6188
1821	Jonathan	Boylston,	Will,	6189
1874	Jonathan	Charlton,	Administration,	6190
1796	Joseph	Westborough,	Guardianship,	6191
1838	Joseph	Leicester,	Guardianship,	6192
1850	Joseph	Leicester,	Administration,	6193
1863	Joseph	Worcester,	Will,	6194
1856	Josephine	Wilkesbarre, Pa.,	Guardianship,	6195
1869	Josephine E.	Kingston, Pa.,	Administration,	6196
1853	Josiah	Shrewsbury,	Administration,	6197
1853	Laura A.	Shrewsbury,	Guardianship,	6198
1799	Loice	Westminster,	Guardianship,	6199
1860	Louisa	Leicester,	Administration,	6200
1862	Lydia	Leicester,	Will,	6201
1879	Marcus	Oxford,	Administration,	6202
1867	Martin L.	Charlton,	Guardianship,	6203
1835	Mary A. R.	Hardwick,	Guardianship,	6204
1846	Mary E.	Leicester,	Guardianship,	6205
1865	Mary J.	Charlton,	Administration,	6206
1846	Moses	Sterling,	Administration,	6207
1807	Nancy	Sutton,	Guardianship,	6208
1771	Nathaniel	Sturbridge,	Administration,	6209
1813	Oliver	Leicester,	Guardianship,	6210
1832	Oliver B.	Leicester,	Administration,	6211
1807	Polly	Sutton,	Guardianship,	6212

YEAR.	NAME.	RESIDENCE.	NATURE.	CASE.
1835	BOND, Polly	Westborough,	Guardianship,	6213
1877	Relief	Westminster,	Will,	6214
1799	Reuhiu	Westminster,	Guardianship,	6215
1819	Richard	Leicester,	Administration,	6216
1838	Richard	Leicester,	Will,	6217
1846	Rufus	Leicester,	Administration,	6218
1835	Sally	North Brookfield,	Guardianship,	6219
1860	Sally	Leicester,	Will,	6220
1854	Samuel F.	Worcester,	Guardianship,	6221
1873	Samuel F.	Worcester,	Will,	6222
1813	Sewall	Leicester,	Guardianship,	6223
1831	Thaddeus	Westminster,	Will,	6224
1830	Thomas	North Brookfield,	Guardianship,	6225
1830	Thomas	North Brookfield,	Will,	6225
1835	Thomas	North Brookfield,	Guardianship,	6226
1866	Thomas C.	Charlton,	Will,	6227
1864	Warren H.	Charlton,	Guardianship,	6228
1813	William	Leicester,	Guardianship,	6229
1842	William	Sutton,	Will,	6230
1875	William	Leicester,	Will,	6231
1864	William J.	Charlton,	Administration,	6232
1875	BONN, Joseph D.	Grafton,	Administration,	6233
	BONNAR AND BONNER,			
1866	Auerlix	Grafton,	Guardianship,	6234
1864	Charles	Worcester,	Guardianship,	6235
1864	Cornelius	Worcester,	Guardianship,	6236
1864	Edward	Worcester,	Guardianship,	6237
1866	Josephine	Grafton,	Guardianship,	6238
1864	Margaret	Worcester,	Guardianship,	6239
1866	Mary	Grafton,	Guardianship,	6240
1874	Nellie	Worcester,	Adoption, etc.,	6241
1866	Peter	Grafton,	Guardianship,	6242
1867	BONNEVILLE, Joseph	Worcester,	Adoption, etc.,	6243
1863	BONNEY, Fanny M.	Hardwick,	Guardianship,	6244
1839	Frances	Templeton,	Guardianship,	6245
1801	Job	Hardwick,	Administration,	6246
1804	Job	Hardwick,	Guardianship,	6247
1838	Warren	Templeton,	Administration,	6248
1804	William	Hardwick,	Guardianship,	6249
1852	William	Hardwick,	Will,	6250
1874	BONZEY, Frank A.	Millbury,	Guardianship,	6251
1874	John A.	Millbury,	Administration,	6252
1866	Peter	Auburn,	Guardianship,	6253
1864	BOOMER, George B.	Castle Rock, Mo.,	Administration,	6254
1837	James	Charlton,	Will,	6255

YEAR.	NAME.	RESIDENCE.	NATURE.	CASE.
1837	BOOMER, James	Charlton,	Pension,	6256
1865	BOOTH, Adeline J.	Worcester,	Guardianship,	6257
1858	Ellen	Blackstone,	Guardianship,	6258
1865	James	Worcester,	Administration,	6259
1865	James A.	Worcester,	Guardianship,	6260
1865	John W.	Worcester,	Guardianship,	6261
1865	Mary E.	Worcester,	Guardianship,	6262
1869	BOOTMAN, Frederick W.	Worcester,	Guardianship,	6263
1869	Nellie F.	Worcester,	Guardianship,	6264
1863	William O.	Worcester,	Administration,	6265
1808	BORDEN, Asa	Charlton,	Will,	6266
1874	Benjamin C.	New Braintree,	Administration,	6267
1820	Ebenezer	Charlton,	Guardianship,	6268
1824	Ebenezer	Charlton,	Administration,	6268
1857	Jane F.	New Braintree,	Guardianship,	6269
1865	Jane W.	New Braintree,	Will,	6270
1815	John	New Braintree,	Will,	6271
1835	Mary	New Braintree,	Guardianship,	6272
1834	Samuel	New Braintree,	Administration,	6273
1857	Samuel A.	New Braintree,	Guardianship,	6274
1818	Stephen	New Braintree,	Guardianship,	6275
1827	Stephen	New Braintree,	Administration,	6275
	BORDMAN see BOARDMAN.			
1864	BORDO, Alexander	Millbury,	Guardianship,	6276
1864	Levi	Millbury,	Guardianship,	6277
1864	Mary J.	Millbury,	Guardianship,	6278
	BORDWELL see BARDWELL.			
1861	BORMAN, Charles	Templeton,	Administration,	6279
1873	BOSLEY, Alice A. J.	Worcester,	Guardianship,	6280
1873	Joseph E. H.	Worcester,	Guardianship,	6281
1873	Margaret A. E.	Worcester,	Guardianship,	6282
1873	William F.	Worcester,	Guardianship,	6283
1856	BOSWELL, Thirzy	Leominster,	Administration,	6284
1870	BOSWORTH, Alonzo	West Boylston,	Administration,	6285
1866	Amos B.	Royalston,	Administration,	6286
1828	Ann M.	Upton,	Guardianship,	6287
1866	Carrie L.	Warren,	Guardianship,	6288
1865	Charles F.	Sturbridge,	Administration,	6289
1866	Charles O.	Warren,	Guardianship,	6290
1871	Chilson	Royalston,	Administration,	6291
1859	Chloe	Grafton,	Administration,	6292
1858	Cyrus	Mobile, Ala.,	Will,	6293
1873	David	Upton,	Will,	6294
1870	Edward A.	West Boylston,	Guardianship,	6295
1871	Eliza	Woodstock, Conn.,	Foreign Will,	6296

YEAR.	NAME.	RESIDENCE.	NATURE.	CASE.
1869	BOSWORTH, Eller A.	Dana,	Guardianship,	6297
1828	George H.	Upton,	Guardianship,	6298
1865	Harrison T.	Upton,	Administration,	6299
1866	James	Royalston,	Guardianship,	6300
1859	John	Royalston,	Administration,	6301
1840	Jonas	Petersham,	Administration,	6302
1819	Jonathan	Royalston,	Administration,	6303
1831	Jonathan	Royalston,	Administration,	6304
1832	Jonathan	Winchendon,	Guardianship,	6305
1826	Mary	Winchendon,	Guardianship,	6306
1862	Mary M.	Fitchburg,	Guardianship,	6307
1870	Milton H.	West Boylston,	Guardianship,	6308
1869	Nelson	Dana,	Administration,	6309
1850	Ruth	Grafton,	Administration,	6310
1850	Ruth	Grafton,	Pension,	6311
1879	Stephen L.	Upton,	Administration,	6312
1874	Sylvanus	Grafton,	Administration,	6313
1837	William	Petersham,	Administration,	6314
1846	William	Winchendon,	Administration,	6315
1872	BOTHAM, Lovina C.	Southbridge,	Administration,	6316
1854	Sanford	Wales,	Guardianship,	6317
1872	BOTHWELL, Ernst S.	North Brookfield,	Guardianship,	6318
1814	John	Oakham,	Will,	6319
1855	Melinda	Oakham,	Will,	6320
1851	Reuben	Oakham,	Will,	6321
1878	BOTTOM, Jedd	Killingly, Conn.,	Foreign Will,	6322
1870	BOTTOMLY, Booth	Leicester,	Administration,	6323
1870	Florence B.	Worcester,	Guardianship,	6324
1847	Jerome	Leicester,	Guardianship,	6325
1877	Martha P.	Leicester,	Administration,	6326
1876	Miranda, etc.	Worcester,	Will,	6327
1876	Miranda D.	Worcester,	Will,	6327
1880	Samuel	Leicester,	Will,	6328
1865	Thomas	Leicester,	Will,	6329
	BOUGHTELL see BOUTELLE.			
1881	BOUGHTON, Alice E.	Lunenburg,	Adoption, etc.,	6330
	BOULTON, (see also BOLTON.)			
1879	Elmer H.	Southbridge,	Guardianship,	6331
1879	George	Southbridge,	Administration,	6332
1877	Julia A.	Derby, Conn.,	Partition,	6333
1880	Julia A.	Derby, Conn.,	Foreign Will,	6334
1822	BOUNDS, Daniel T.	Oxford,	Guardianship,	6335
1735	John	Sutton,	Administration,	6336
1819	John	Oxford,	Will,	6337
1822	John	Oxford,	Guardianship,	6338

YEAR.	NAME.	RESIDENCE.	NATURE.	CASE.
1736	BOUNDS, Ruth	Sutton,	Guardianship,	6339
1822	Sarah	Oxford,	Guardianship,	6340
1822	Susannah	Oxford,	Guardianship,	6341
1822	West	Oxford,	Guardianship,	6342
1868	BOUTEATTE, Charles	Southbridge,	Will,	6343
1871	Cordilla	Southbridge,	Guardianship,	6344
1871	James	Southbridge,	Administration,	6345
1871	Louisa	Southbridge,	Guardianship,	6346
1871	Odile	Southbridge,	Guardianship,	6347
1871	Rosilda	Southbridge,	Guardianship,	6348
	BOUTELLE, BOUTELL, BOUGH- TELL AND BOWTLE,			
1813	Abigail	Fitchburg,	Guardianship,	6349
1856	Alpheus	Fitchburg,	Administration,	6350
1818	Asaph	Fitchburg,	Administration,	6351
1819	Asaph	Fitchburg,	Guardianship,	6352
1823	Betsey	Leominster,	Guardianship,	6353
1813	Caroline	Fitchburg,	Guardianship,	6354
1813	Catharine	Fitchburg,	Guardianship,	6355
1823	Charles	Leominster,	Guardianship,	6356
1823	Cynthia	Leominster,	Guardianship,	6357
1816	David	Fitchburg,	Administration,	6358
1848	Dorothy	Fitchburg,	Administration,	6359
1819	Eliza	Fitchburg,	Guardianship,	6360
1816	Enoch	Leominster,	Will,	6361
1877	Frank L.	Fitchburg,	Administration,	6362
1868	George W.	Athol,	Guardianship,	6363
1819	Hannah	Fitchburg,	Guardianship,	6364
1868	Harry F.	Athol,	Guardianship,	6365
1752	James	Leominster,	Will,	6366
1814	James	Fitchburg,	Guardianship,	6367
1822	James	Leominster,	Will,	6368
1868	James	Athol,	Will,	6369
1870	James	Leominster,	Will,	6370
1783	Jedediah	Sutton,	Guardianship,	6371
1837	John	Leominster,	Pension,	6372
1814	John H.	Fitchburg,	Guardianship,	6373
1823	Josiah	Leominster,	Guardianship,	6374
1814	Josiah W.	Fitchburg,	Guardianship,	6375
1752	Kendal	Leominster,	Guardianship,	6376
1819	Kendall	Fitchburg,	Will,	6377
1813	Kendall, Jr.	Fitchburg,	Administration,	6378
1815	Lucretia	Fitchburg,	Guardianship,	6379
1855	Lydia	Fitchburg,	Will,	6380
1867	Mary E.	Fitchburg,	Administration,	6381

Year.	Name.	Residence.	Nature.	Case.
	BOUTELLE, BOUTELL, BOUGH- TELL AND BOWTLE,			
1819	Mary W.	Fitchburg,	Guardianship,	6382
1813	Nathaniel	Fitchburg,	Administration,	6383
1813	Nathaniel S.	Fitchburg,	Guardianship,	6384
1869	Nathaniel S.	Fitchburg,	Will,	6385
1813	Philena	Fitchburg,	Guardianship,	6386
1813	Polly	Fitchburg,	Guardianship,	6387
1813	Polly	Fitchburg,	Guardianship,	6388
1824	Relief	Leominster,	Administration,	6389
1769	Samuel	Sutton,	Will,	6390
1783	Samuel	Sutton,	Guardianship,	6391
1816	Sarah	Leominster,	Guardianship,	6392
1864	Sarah	Leominster,	Will,	6393
1815	Sarah A.	Fitchburg,	Guardianship,	6394
1813	Sarah W.	Fitchburg,	Guardianship,	6395
1870	Sarah W.	Fitchburg,	Guardianship,	6396
1881	Sarah W.	Fitchburg,	Will,	6396
1815	Susan	Fitchburg,	Guardianship,	6397
1813	Susannah W.	Fitchburg,	Guardianship,	6398
1823	Thomas	Leominster,	Guardianship,	6399
1866	Thomas	Fitchburg,	Administration,	6400
1869	Thomas R.	Fitchburg,	Will,	6401
1810	Timothy	Leominster,	Will,	6402
1816	Timothy	Leominster,	Guardianship,	6403
1835	Timothy L.	Leominster,	Guardianship,	6404
1797	William	Leominster,	Will,	6405
1870	William	Leominster,	Administration,	6406
1780	BOUTWELL, Alpheus	Sutton,	Guardianship,	6407
1876	George S.	Lunenburg,	Administration,	6408
1798	James	Leominster,	Will,	6409
1866	Marshall	Lunenburg,	Will,	6410
1771	Samuel	Sutton,	Administration,	6411
1863	Sewel	Lunenburg,	Will,	6412
1875	BOUTILLIER, Thomas L., etc.	St. Henry, Que.,	Foreign Will,	6413
	BOWDEN see BOWDOIN,			
1847	BOWDITCH, Asa	Uxbridge,	Administration,	6414
1877	Sarah	Leicester,	Guardianship,	6415
	BOWDOIN AND BOWDEN.			
1865	James	New Braintree,	Will,	6416
1859	Samuel	Sturbridge,	Administration,	6417
1870	Stella V.	Boston,	Adoption, etc.,	6418
1845	BOWEN, Abigail	Hardwick,	Administration,	6419
1863	Alfred S.	Sturbridge,	Will,	6420
1874	Alice L.	Royalston,	Adoption, etc.,	6421

YEAR.	NAME.	RESIDENCE.	NATURE.	CASE.
1877	BOWEN, Alonzo D.	North Brookfield,	Administration,	6422
1819	Arathusa	Hardwick,	Guardianship,	6423
1875	Arnold	Milford,	Administration,	6424
1870	Barnwell	Brookfield,	Will,	6425
1814	Betsey B.	Sturbridge,	Guardianship,	6426
1881	Charles	Worcester,	Will,	6427
1866	Clayton A.	Leominster,	Guardianship,	6428
1848	Cynthia	Brookfield,	Guardianship,	6429
1857	Ebenezer H.	Worcester,	Will,	6430
1852	Edwin W.	Brookfield,	Administration,	6431
1819	Eliza	Hardwick,	Guardianship,	6432
1866	Eliza	Upton,	Guardianship,	6433
1852	Ellen M.	Brookfield,	Guardianship,	6434
1881	Elsie A.	Brookfield,	Will,	6435
1865	Esther M.	Millbury,	Will,	6436
1872	George	Worcester,	Administra'n, etc.,	6437
1839	Henry	Brookfield,	Guardianship,	6438
1866	James H.	Upton,	Guardianship,	6439
1779	John	Princeton,	Absentee,	6440
1866	John W.	Upton,	Guardianship,	6441
1818	Levina	Sturbridge,	Will,	6442
1876	Martha M.	West Brookfield,	Administration,	6443
1866	Mary	Upton,	Guardianship,	6444
1793	Mehitabel	Brookfield,	Will,	6445
1792	Nathaniel H.	Brookfield,	Guardianship,	6446
1807	Peter	Brookfield,	Administration,	6447
1814	Polly N.	Sturbridge,	Guardianship,	6448
1857	Priscilla J.	Paxton,	Guardianship,	6449
1814	Rachel	Brookfield,	Will,	6450
1807	Rebecca	Brookfield,	Guardianship,	6451
1829	Rebecca	Spencer,	Administration,	6452
1814	Samuel D.	Sturbridge,	Guardianship,	6453
1790	Silas	Brookfield,	Will,	6454
1818	Silvester	Hardwick,	Administration,	6455
1819	Silvester	Hardwick,	Guardianship,	6456
1831	Sylvanus	Upton,	Administration,	6457
1842	Thomas	Northbridge,	Will,	6458
1813	William	Sturbridge,	Administration,	6459
1873	William C.	Brookfield,	Administration,	6460
1852	Windsor A.	Brookfield,	Change of Name,	6461
1854	Zenus	Paxton,	Will,	6462
1875	BOWERS, Abel	Leominster,	Will,	6463
1869	Edward M.	Charlton,	Guardianship,	6464
1869	Ervin W.	Charlton,	Guardianship,	6465
1851	Francis A.	Harvard,	Guardianship,	6466

YEAR.	NAME.	RESIDENCE.	NATURE.	CASE.
1864	BOWERS, George H.	Berlin,	Administration,	6467
1876	Harriet E.	Seymour, Ind.,	Administration,	6468
1875	Herman H.	Milford,	Will,	6469
1793	Jerathmeel	Leominster,	Will,	6470
1796	Joel	Harvard,	Guardianship,	6471
1851	Joel	Harvard,	Will,	6472
1796	Joshua	Harvard,	Administration,	6473
1796	Joshua	Harvard,	Guardianship,	6474
1836	Josiah	Lancaster,	Will,	6475
1836	Josiah	Lancaster,	Pension,	6476
1796	Polly	Harvard,	Guardianship,	6477
1876	Rosanna W.	Leominster,	Will,	6478
1880	Rufus G.	Leominster,	Guardianship,	6479
1796	Sally	Harvard,	Guardianship,	6480
1881	Sarah A.	Worcester,	Guardianship,	6481
1868	BOWKER, Aaron H.	Winchendon,	Will,	6482
1828	Abigail	Winchendon,	Guardianship,	6483
1843	Abigail	Templeton,	Will,	6484
1819	Abigail H.	Hopkinton,	Guardianship,	6485
1841	Alfred	Templeton,	Administration,	6486
1817	Alpha	Milford,	Guardianship,	6487
1830	Ann M.	Milford,	Guardianship,	6488
1764	Asa	Shrewsbury,	Administration,	6489
1787	Asa	Southborough,	Will,	6490
1800	Asa	Gerry,	Administration,	6491
1803	Asa	Gerry,	Guardianship,	6492
1825	Asa	Winchendon,	Administration,	6493
1789	Benjamin	Petersham,	Guardianship,	6494
1803	Betsy	Gerry,	Guardianship,	6495
1866	Charles	Royalston,	Administration,	6496
1872	Charles A.	Winchendon,	Guardianship,	6497
1858	Charles H.	Fitchburg,	Guardianship,	6498
1858	Charlotte	Fitchburg,	Pension,	6499
1871	Chloe	Winchendon,	Guardianship,	6500
1863	Daniel	Winchendon,	Administration,	6501
1879	Dicea A.	Athol,	Will,	6502
1773	Edmund	Hopkinton,	Guardianship,	6503
1841	Edmund	Milford,	Will,	6504
1841	Edmund	Milford,	Pension,	6505
1854	Edward B.	Barre,	Administration,	6506
1852	Eli	Milford,	Administration,	6507
1811	Eliza	Milford,	Guardianship,	6508
1819	Eliza	Hopkinton,	Guardianship,	6509
1861	Eliza	Milford,	Will,	6510
1838	Elizabeth	Petersham,	Will,	6511

YEAR.	NAME.	RESIDENCE.	NATURE.	CASE.
1838	BOWKER, Elizabeth	Petersham,	Pension,	6512
1866	Elizabeth	Winchendon,	Administration,	6513
1867	Ella M.	Athol,	Adoption, etc.,	6514
1878	Elliott A.	Milford,	Will,	6515
1872	Emily S.	Worcester,	Will,	6516
1870	Ephraim S.	Gardner,	Administration,	6517
1828	Esther	Winchendon,	Guardianship,	6518
1817	Ethan	Milford,	Administration,	6519
1817	Ethan L.	Milford,	Guardianship,	6520
1855	Ethan L.	Milford,	Will,	6521
1782	Eunice	Shrewsbury,	Will,	6522
1835	Ezekiel	Petersham,	Pension,	6523
1782	Ezra	Shrewsbury,	Will,	6524
1870	Fannie	Southbridge,	Guardianship,	6525
1858	George	Fitchburg,	Administration,	6526
1858	George M.	Fitchburg,	Guardianship,	6527
1830	George S.	Milford,	Guardianship,	6528
1843	Hannah	Winchendon,	Pension,	6529
1845	Hannah	Winchendon,	Administration,	6530
1870	Henry	Southbridge,	Guardianship,	6531
1783	Hesadiah	Shrewsbury,	Will,	6532
1836	Horatio E.	Westminster,	Guardianship,	6533
1830	Ira	Milford,	Administration,	6534
1860	James	Worcester,	Administration,	6535
1870	Jennie	Southbridge,	Guardianship,	6536
1765	John	Westborough,	Administration,	6537
1797	John	Petersham,	Will,	6538
1862	John	Phillipston,	Will,	6539
1871	John	Petersham,	Administration,	6540
1781	John, Jr.	Petersham,	Administration,	6541
1872	John B.	Winchendon,	Guardianship,	6542
1858	John H.	Winchendon,	Will,	6543
1838	Jonathan	Templeton,	Administration,	6544
1861	Jonathan	Templeton,	Will,	6545
1811	Josiah	Northborough,	Will,	6546
1819	Levett H.	Hopkinton,	Guardianship,	6547
1828	Lois	Winchendon,	Guardianship,	6548
1868	Lois	Winchendon,	Administration,	6549
1871	Losina F.	Swansey, N. H.,	Foreign Will,	6550
1789	Lucy	Petersham,	Guardianship,	6551
1803	Lucy	Gerry,	Guardianship,	6552
1826	Luther	Winchendon,	Administration,	6553
1846	Luther	Winchendon,	Guardianship,	6554
1789	Lydia	Petersham,	Guardianship,	6555
1803	Lydia	Gerry,	Guardianship,	6556

Year.	Name.	Residence.	Nature.	Case.
1871	BOWKER, Marcellus	Winchendon,	Guardianship,	6557
1819	Mary G.	Hopkinton,	Guardianship,	6558
1870	Mary T.	Fitchburg,	Will,	6559
1874	Milton	Fitchburg,	Administration,	6560
1863	Nancy A.	Royalston,	Guardianship,	6561
1868	Nancy E.	Royalston,	Administration,	6562
1861	Nathaniel	Royalston,	Will,	6563
1867	Persis	Winchendon,	Administration,	6564
1811	Ralph	Milford,	Administration,	6565
1817	Ralph W.	Milford,	Guardianship,	6566
1803	Sally	Gerry,	Guardianship,	6567
1849	Sarah J.	Gardner,	Sale Real Est.,	6568
1863	Sarah J.	Manchester, N. H.,	Administration,	6569
1833	Stephen B.	Royalston,	Will,	6570
1871	Sullivan	Winchendon,	Will,	6571
1803	Susanna	Gerry,	Guardianship,	6572
1803	Thomas	New Braintree,	Guardianship,	6573
1819	Uriah	Hopkinton,	Guardianship,	6574
1867	Warren H.	Athol,	Will,	6575
1847	William	Winchendon,	Will,	6576
1870	William	Southbridge,	Guardianship,	6577
1863	William H.	Phillipston,	Guardianship,	6578
1870	Willie	Southbridge,	Guardianship,	6577
1803	Windsor	Gerry,	Guardianship,	6579
1873	BOWLES, Elizabeth	New York, N. Y.,	Administration,	6580
1864	Henry E.	Unknown,	Inventory,	6581
1799	Josiah	Harvard,	Will,	6582
1796	William	Lancaster,	Administration,	6583
1857	BOWMAN, Charles D.	Oxford,	Will,	6584
1868	Daniel	Westborough,	Administration,	6585
1828	Elijah	Westborough,	Administration,	6586
1867	Elmer	Westborough,	Administration,	6587
1867	Gilbert	Westborough,	Will,	6588
1762	James	Westborough,	Administration,	6589
1881	Jane	Westborough,	Will,	6590
1815	Joseph	Northborough,	Administration,	6591
1852	Joseph	New Braintree,	Will,	6592
1866	Levi	Westborough,	Administration,	6593
1871	Lorania A.	Westborough,	Administration,	6594
1857	Louise J.	Oxford,	Guardianship,	6595
1835	Nathaniel	Westborough,	Will,	6596
1878	Samuel S.	Grafton,	Will,	6597
1747	Samuell	Worcester,	Administration,	6598
1859	Simeon	Clinton,	Administration,	6599
1831	Sophia	Westborough,	Guardianship,	6600

Year.	Name.	Residence.	Nature.	Case.
1854	BOWMAN, Sophia	Westborough,	Administration,	6601
1764	Thankfull	Westborough,	Guardianship,	6602
	BOWTLE see BOUTELLE.			
	BOYCE, BOICE AND BOIES,			
1860	Adaline A.	Worcester,	Administration,	6603
1790	Asa	Mendon,	Will,	6604
1734	Benjamin	Mendon,	Guardianship,	6605
1782	Benjamin	Sutton,	Will,	6606
1787	Benjamin	Mendon,	Will,	6607
1734	Bothya	Mendon,	Guardianship,	6608
1837	Cadis	Royalston,	Administration,	6609
1819	Clarinda	Worcester,	Guardianship,	6610
1813	Eliza	Leicester,	Guardianship,	6611
1878	Elliot	Spencer,	Will,	6612
1819	Faustine	Worcester,	Guardianship,	6613
1734	John	Mendon,	Guardianship,	6614
1790	John	Oxford,	Administration,	6615
1817	John	Barre,	Administration,	6616
1846	John	Worcester,	Administration,	6617
1864	John	Worcester,	Will,	6618
1878	John F.	Worcester,	Will,	6619
1734	Jonathan	Mendon,	Guardianship,	6620
1746	Jonathan	Mendon,	Administration,	6621
1794	Jonathan	Mendon,	Will,	6622
1819	Lucy P.	Worcester,	Guardianship,	6623
1740	Lydia	Mendon,	Guardianship,	6624
1734	Margarett	Mendon,	Guardianship,	6625
1799	Patrick	Western,	Guardianship,	6626
1852	Phebe R.	Worcester,	Will,	6627
1734	Samuell	Mendon,	Guardianship,	6628
1867	Sarah E.	Spencer,	Adoption, etc.,	6629
1734	William	Mendon,	Guardianship,	6630
1739	William	Mendon,	Will,	6631
1756	BOYD, Alexander	Boston,	Guardianship,	6632
1861	Alice M.	Oakham,	Guardianship,	6633
1827	Cheney	New Braintree,	Will,	6634
1829	Cheney	Oakham,	Guardianship,	6635
1861	Danforth	Oakham,	Will,	6636
1829	Danforth R.	Oakham,	Guardianship,	6637
1861	Frederick	Oakham,	Guardianship,	6638
1879	Hattie E., etc.	North Brookfield,	Administration,	6639
1880	Henry	Worcester,	Administration,	6640
1824	James	Oakham,	Will,	6641
1829	James	Oakham,	Guardianship,	6642
1780	John	Brookfield,	Will,	6643

YEAR.	NAME.	RESIDENCE.	NATURE.	CASE.
1828	BOYD, John	Oakham,	Administration,	6644
1844	John	Shrewsbury,	Administration,	6645
1829	Julia	Oakham,	Guardianship,	6646
1829	Mary J.	Oakham,	Guardianship,	6647
1829	Rebecca	Oakham,	Guardianship,	6648
1856	Sally	Shrewsbury,	Administration,	6649
1780	Samuell	Worcester,	Guardianship,	6650
1861	Susan E.	Oakham,	Guardianship,	6651
1855	Susan W.	Shrewsbury,	Will,	6652
1864	BOYDEN, Abby F.	Grafton,	Guardianship,	6653
1835	Abigail	Sturbridge,	Guardianship,	6654
1817	Adaline	Oakham,	Guardianship,	6655
1784	Alvin	Ward,	Guardianship,	6656
1841	Amasa	Oakham,	Administration,	6657
1836	Amos	Mendon,	Guardianship,	6658
1836	Amos	Mendon,	Administration,	6659
1784	Asa	Ward,	Guardianship,	6660
1817	Betsey	Oakham,	Guardianship,	6661
1831	Betsey	Spencer,	Administration,	6662
1876	Charlotte	New Braintree,	Administration,	6663
1857	Comfort	Holden,	Will,	6664
1782	Daniel	Ward,	Will,	6665
1801	Daniel	Holden,	Administration,	6666
1817	Daniel	Oakham,	Will,	6667
1783	Darius	Ward,	Administration,	6668
1862	David	Worcester,	Administration,	6669
1862	David	Worcester,	Guardianship,	6670
1861	Dwight	Bolton,	Will,	6671
1774	Eli	Rutland District,	Guardianship,	6672
1829	Eliza J.	Spencer,	Guardianship,	6673
1814	Elizabeth	Ward,	Will,	6674
1784	Esther	Ward,	Guardianship,	6675
1813	Eunice	Sturbridge,	Guardianship,	6676
1813	Experience	Sturbridge,	Guardianship,	6677
1860	Frank	Worcester,	Administration,	6678
1862	Frank W.	Worcester,	Guardianship,	6679
1778	Hannah	Worcester,	Guardianship,	6680
1864	Harriet	New Braintree,	Will,	6681
1862	Henry P.	Worcester,	Guardianship,	6682
1822	Herman	Hubbardston,	Will,	6683
1827	Horace	Worcester,	Guardianship,	6684
1817	Jane	Oakham,	Guardianship,	6685
1773	John	Worcester,	Administration,	6686
1795	John	Sturbridge,	Will,	6687
1828	John	Spencer,	Administration,	6688

YEAR.	NAME.	RESIDENCE.	NATURE.	CASE.
1829	BOYDEN, John	Spencer,	Guardianship,	6689
1834	John, 2d	Sturbridge,	Administration,	6690
1835	John	Sturbridge,	Guardianship,	6691
1857	John	Brookfield,	Will,	6692
1757	Joseph	Worcester,	Administration,	6693
1774	Joseph	Worcester,	Guardianship,	6694
1812	Joseph	Sturbridge,	Will,	6695
1770	Joshua	Rutland District,	Will,	6696
1771	Joshua	Rutland District,	Guardianship,	6697
1813	Julia M.	Sturbridge,	Guardianship,	6698
1774	Katharine	Rutland District,	Guardianship,	6699
1784	Levinah	Ward,	Guardianship,	6700
1855	Lucy	Gardner,	Will,	6701
1861	Martha	Northborough,	Will,	6702
1774	Mary	Rutland District,	Guardianship,	6703
1784	Mary	Ward,	Guardianship,	6704
1839	Mary	Douglas,	Guardianship,	6705
1771	Micah	Rutland District,	Administration,	6706
1817	Milton	Oakham,	Guardianship,	6707
1850	Mindwell C.	Holden,	Administration,	6708
1853	Moses	New Braintree,	Will,	6709
1818	Moses	Barre,	Administration,	6710
1835	Nancy	Sturbridge,	Guardianship,	6711
1759	Nathaniel	Worcester,	Guardianship,	6712
1879	Octavia T.	Worcester,	Administration,	6713
1835	Olive	Sturbridge,	Guardianship,	6714
1838	Patience	Holden,	Guardianship,	6715
1813	Paul	Sturbridge,	Administration,	6716
1777	Peter	Worcester,	Will,	6717
1839	Peter	Douglas,	Administration,	6718
1867	Peter	Leominster,	Will,	6719
1784	Priscilla	Ward,	Guardianship,	6720
1877	Roxana S.	Leominster,	Will,	6721
1837	Sally	Mendon,	Will,	6722
1846	Samuel	Auburn,	Will,	6723
1870	Samuel	Leominster,	Will,	6724
1878	Samuel	Oxford,	Administration,	6725
1848	Samuel F.	Northborough,	Guardianship,	6726
1813	Silas	Sturbridge,	Guardianship,	6727
1813	Warren	Sturbridge,	Guardianship,	6728
1836	William W.	Mendon,	Guardianship,	6729
	BOYINGTON see BOYNTON.			
	BOYLE AND BOYLES,			
1863	Abby M. E.	Princeton,	Guardianship,	6730
1876	Ann	Fitchburg,	Guardianship,	6731

YEAR.	NAME.	RESIDENCE.	NATURE.	CASE.
	BOYLE AND BOYLES,			
1876	Edward	Fitchburg,	Guardianship,	6732
1863	Henry	Princeton,	Administration,	6733
1863	Hezekiah E.	Princeton,	Guardianship,	6734
1877	James	Worcester,	Will,	6735
1876	James M.	Blackstone,	Guardianship,	6736
1876	John	Blackstone,	Administration,	6737
1877	John	Auburn,	Will,	6738
1878	Kate	Springfield,	Adoption, etc.,	6739
1867	Luke	Worcester,	Administration,	6740
1876	Mary J.	Fitchburg,	Administration,	6741
1875	Michael	Fitchburg,	Administration,	6742
1878	Paul	Worcester,	Will,	6743
1876	Thomas F.	Blackstone,	Guardianship,	6744
1875	Thomas J.	Worcester,	Will,	6745
1876	Winifred I.	Fitchburg,	Guardianship,	6746
1867	BOYLSTON, Alicia B.	Princeton,	Will,	6747
1847	John L.	Princeton,	Will,	6748
1881	Sally	Princeton,	Will,	6749
1868	Ward N.	Princeton,	Guardianship,	6750
1870	Ward N.	Princeton,	Will,	6750
1827	BOYNES, Harriet	Rutland,	Guardianship,	6751
1858	Nancy	Sturbridge,	Administration,	6752
	BOYNTON AND BOYINGTON,			
1811	Abiel	West Boylston,	Administration,	6753
1876	Alfred W.	Royalston,	Administration,	6754
1869	Alonzo	Paxton,	Guardianship,	6755
1869	Alonzo	Paxton,	Administration,	6755
1843	Asa	West Boylston,	Administration,	6756
1864	Benjamin	Westborough,	Will,	6757
1760	Benoni	Lunenburg,	Administration,	6758
1831	Betsey	Sterling,	Administration,	6759
1797	Caleb	Northbridge,	Administration,	6760
1849	Caroline	Troy, N. Y.,	Guardianship,	6761
1863	Charles H.	Lunenburg,	Guardianship,	6762
1868	Charles H.	Lunenburg,	Administration,	6763
1881	Charles W.	West Boylston,	Administration,	6764
1818	Clarissa	Spencer,	Guardianship,	6765
1858	Curtis J.	West Brookfield,	Administration,	6766
1845	Daniel	Winchendon,	Administration,	6767
1868	David	Paxton,	Administration,	6768
1815	David A.	Lunenburg,	Guardianship,	6769
1863	David B.	Lunenburg,	Guardianship,	6770
1861	David F.	Paxton,	Administration,	6771
1822	Dolly M.	Winchendon,	Guardianship,	6772

YEAR.	NAME.	RESIDENCE.	NATURE.	CASE.
	BOYNTON AND BOYINGTON,			
1843	Dolly M.	West Boylston,	Guardianship,	6773
1856	Dorothy,	Fitchburg,	Will,	6774
1815	Ebenezer	Paxton,	Will,	6775
1849	Edwin M.	Troy, N. Y.,	Guardianship,	6776
1807	Eleanor	Leicester,	Will,	6777
1865	Elizabeth R.	Templeton,	Administration,	6778
1820	Elizabeth S.	Sterling,	Guardianship,	6779
1868	Emma E.	Worcester,	Guardianship,	6780
1812	Ephraim	Sterling,	Administration,	6781
1820	Ephraim	Sterling,	Administration,	6782
1815	Eunice	Lunenburg,	Guardianship,	6783
1835	Ezra	Paxton,	Administration,	6784
1841	Frances A. P.	Lunenburg,	Guardianship,	6785
1849	Francis H.	Troy, N. Y.	Guardianship,	6786
1863	George W.	Lunenburg,	Guardianship,	6787
1817	Hannah	Paxton,	Administration,	6788
1836	Hannah G.	Paxton,	Guardianship,	6789
1745	Hilkiah	Lunenburg,	Will,	6790
1774	Jedediah	Royalston,	Administration,	6791
1799	Jeremiah	Holden,	Administration,	6792
1750	Jewell	Lunenburg,	Guardianship,	9793
1759	Jewet	Petersham,	Will,	6794
1867	John	Leominster,	Administration,	6795
1843	John J.	West Boylston,	Guardianship,	6796
1820	John S.	Sterling,	Guardianship,	6797
1801	Jonathan	Lunenburg,	Will,	6798
1814	Jonathan	Fitchburg,	Will,	6799
1820	Joseph	Winchendon,	Will,	6800
1858	Lewis J.	Paxton,	Administration,	6801
1774	Lucy	Royalston,	Guardianship,	6802
1779	Lucy	Winchendon,	Guardianship,	6803
1873	Lyman W.	Clinton,	Administration,	6804
1843	Manda M. F.	West Boylston,	Guardianship,	6805
1841	Maria A.	Lunenburg,	Guardianship,	6806
1878	Mary	Waterbury, Conn.,	Administration,	6807
1834	Nathan	Westborough,	Administration,	6808
1815	Otis	Lunenburg,	Guardianship,	6809
1836	Persis F.	Paxton,	Guardianship,	6810
1876	Phebe	Paxton,	Administration,	6811
1836	Phebe S.	Paxton,	Guardianship,	6812
1818	Reuben	Spencer,	Administration,	6813
1822	Sally A.	Winchendon,	Guardianship,	6814
1820	Sally N.	Sterling,	Guardianship,	6815
1779	Sarah	Winchendon,	Guardianship,	6816

Year.	Name.	Residence.	Nature.	Case.
	BOYNTON and BOYINGTON,			
1841	Sarah E.	Lunenburg,	Guardianship,	6817
1778	Stephen	Winchendon,	Administration,	6818
1800	Stephen	Lunenburg,	Will,	6819
1841	Stephen	Lunenburg,	Will,	6820
1779	Susanna	Winchendon,	Guardianship,	6821
1815	William	Lunenburg,	Administration,	6822
1841	William S.	Lunenburg,	Guardianship,	6823
1784	Zacheus	Lancaster,	Will,	6824
1861	BOYT, Sarah	West Brookfield,	Will,	6825
	BRABROOK and BRAYBROOK,			
1864	Adaline	Bolton,	Guardianship,	6826
1841	Albert	Leominster,	Guardianship,	6827
1851	Charles P.	Chelsea,	Guardianship,	6828
1743	Comfort	Brookfield,	Guardianship,	6829
1755	Comfort	Brookfield,	Will,	6830
1841	George T.	Leominster,	Guardianship,	6831
1746	Hepzibah	Brookfield,	Administration,	6832
1762	Hepzibah	Lancaster,	Guardianship,	6833
1742	Joseph	Brookfield,	Administration,	6834
1762	Joseph	Lancaster,	Guardianship,	6835
1851	Julia E.	Chelsea,	Guardianship,	6836
1851	Mary F.	Chelsea,	Guardianship,	6837
1747	William	Brookfield,	Guardianship,	6838
1758	William	Lancaster,	Administration,	6839
1841	William	Leominster,	Administration,	6840
1848	William F.	Lancaster,	Will,	6841
1851	William F.	Chelsea,	Guardianship,	6842
	BRACKET and BRACKETT,			
1791	Aaron	Gore,	Administration,	6843
1837	Aaron	Sturbridge,	Administration,	6844
1866	Almira	Worcester,	Administration,	6845
1875	Almira	Southbridge,	Will,	6846
1866	Amos	Worcester,	Administration,	6847
1861	Asa	Webster,	Will,	6848
1812	Ebenezer	Dudley,	Administration,	6849
1860	George T.	Harvard,	Adoption, etc.,	6850
1872	Gilbert M.	Worcester,	Administration,	6851
1876	Huldah	Webster,	Administration,	6852
1756	John	Dudley,	Administration,	6853
1801	John	Dudley,	Will,	6854
1831	John	Dudley,	Administration,	6855
1881	Prince	Webster,	Will,	6856
1861	Rebecca	Webster,	Will,	6857
1818	Sally N.	Upton,	Guardianship,	6858
1876	Samantha	Webster,	Will,	6859

YEAR.	NAME.	RESIDENCE.	NATURE.	CASE.
	BRACKET AND BRACKETT,			
1856	Stephen	Southbridge,	Administration,	6860
1860	BRADBURY, Cora	Boston,	Adoption, etc.,	6861
1770	Jacob	Dudley,	Administration,	6862
1856	James	Webster,	Administration,	6863
1878	Sarah E.	Milford,	Adoption, etc.,	6864
1847	BRADEEN, Charles	Gardner,	Guardianship,	6865
·1837	BRADFORD, Caroline	Southbridge,	Guardianship,	6866
1852	Caroline	Southbridge,	Will,	6867
1875	Cora E.	Uxbridge,	Adoption, etc.,	6868
1855	Edwin T.	Southbridge,	Guardianship,	6869
1855	Ella B.	Southbridge,	Guardianship,	6870
1855	Emily C.	Southbridge,	Guardianship,	6871
1855	Fanny C.	Southbridge,	Guardianship,	6872
1876	Frank	Bolton,	Will,	6873
1869	Frank W.	Worcester,	Adoption, etc.,	6874
1878	George	Woodstock, Conn.,	Administration,	6875
1839	Henry	Southbridge,	Guardianship,	6876
1855	John A.	Millbury,	Guardianship,	6877
1871	Jonathan C.	Milford,	Will,	6878
1878	Lillian A.	Milford,	Guardianship,	6879
1855	Lucinda	Millbury,	Guardianship,	6880
1878	Milton	Woodstock, Conn.,	Administration,	6881
1835	William	Southbridge,	Administration,	6882
1855	William H.	Southbridge,	Guardianship,	6883
1876	William H.	Worcester,	Administration,	6884
1866	BRADISH, Charlotte P.	Worcester,	Will,	6885
1842	Hannah	Worcester,	Will,	6886
1872	Harvey	Upton,	Will,	6887
1870	Jonas	Templeton,	Administration,	6888
1876	Polly D.	Upton,	Will,	6889
1880	Samuel S.	West Brookfield,	Will,	6890
1880	BRADLEY, Alexander	Barre,	Will,	6891
1877	Anthony	West Brookfield,	Administration,	6892
1869	Fanny S.	Worcester,	Guardianship,	6893
1875	George H.	Grafton,	Guardianship,	6894
1875	Hugh F.	Grafton,	Guardianship,	6895
1864	Jane H.	Royalston,	Administration,	6896
1874	Jeremiah	Royalston,	Administration,	6897
1842	Jerome	Lancaster,	Guardianship,	6898
1840	John	Worcester,	Administration,	6899
1872	John	Grafton,	Administration,	6900
1869	John E.	Worcester,	Guardianship,	6901
1875	Joseph A.	Grafton,	Guardianship,	6902
1842	Levantia	Lancaster,	Guardianship,	6903

Year.	Name.	Residence.	Nature.	Case.
1859	BRADLEY, Margery	Worcester,	Will,	6904
1842	Ophelia	Lancaster,	Guardianship,	6905
1874	Owen	Milford,	Will,	6906
1842	Robert M.	Lancaster,	Will,	6907
1779	BRADSHAW, Benjamin	Brookfield,	Administration,	6908
1810	Eleazer	Brookfield,	Will,	6909
	BRADSTREET AND BROAD-STREET,			
1767	Abigail	Lunenburg,	Guardianship,	6910
1757	Jonathan	Lunenburg,	Will,	7911
1767	Mary	Lunenburg,	Guardianship,	6912
1767	Olive	Lunenburg,	Guardianship,	6913
1767	Phebe	Lunenburg,	Guardianship,	6914
1767	Reliefe	Lunenburg,	Guardianship,	6915
1761	Samuel	Lunenburg,	Administration,	6916
1767	Vastic	Lunenburg	Guardianship,	6917
1859	BRADY, John	Worcester,	Administration,	6918
1858	John C.	Worcester,	Guardianship,	6919
1858	Louisa S.	Worcester,	Guardianship,	6920
1858	Mary F.	Worcester,	Guardianship,	6921
1855	BRAGG, Arial	Milford,	Will,	6922
1867	Arial	Milford,	Administration,	6923
1852	Benjamin	Royalston,	Administration,	6924
1853	Benjamin L.	Royalston,	Guardianship,	6925
1870	Charles S.	Milford,	Guardianship,	6926
1853	Cynthia R.	Royalston,	Guardianship,	6927
1766	Ebenezer	Shrewsbury,	Will,	6928
1790	Ebenezer	Petersham,	Administration,	6929
1870	Ebenezer	Lancaster,	Guardianship,	6930
1874	Ebenezer	Lancaster,	Administration,	6930
1868	Ebenezer G.	Lancaster,	Will,	6931
1868	Edward A.	Grafton,	Adoption, etc.,	6932
1862	Erastus W.	Westborough,	Administration,	6933
1869	Herman	Milford,	Guardianship,	6934
1832	Isaac	Petersham,	Guardianship,	6935
1790	James	Brookfield,	Guardianship,	6936
1832	James	Petersham,	Guardianship,	6937
1819	John	Shrewsbury,	Will,	6938
1852	John H.	Royalston,	Will,	6939
1797	Lois	Shrewsbury,	Guardianship,	6940
1822	Lois	Worcester,	Guardianship,	6941
1870	Lottie A.	Milford,	Guardianship,	6942
1870	Luther C.	Milford,	Guardianship,	6943
1833	Martin	Petersham,	Administration,	6944
1853	Mary S.	Royalston,	Guardianship,	6945

YEAR.	NAME.	RESIDENCE.	NATURE.	CASE.
1797	BRAGG, Molly	Shrewsbury,	Guardianship,	6946
1830	Molly	Worcester,	Will,	6947
1777	Moses	Brookfield,	Administration,	6948
1866	Nancy	Milford,	Will,	6949
1818	Nathaniel	Royalston,	Will,	6950
1851	Nathaniel	Royalston,	Will,	6951
1832	Patty	Petersham,	Guardianship,	6952
1872	Polly K.	Royalston,	Administration,	6953
1828	Samuel	Petersham,	Guardianship,	6954
1788	Sarah	Shrewsbury,	Will,	6955
1797	Sarah	Shrewsbury,	Guardianship,	6956
1832	Sarah	Shrewsbury,	Will,	6957
1853	Sarah P. P.	Royalston,	Guardianship,	6958
1797	Timothy	Shrewsbury,	Administration,	6959
	BRAHANEY AND BRAHENEY,			
1873	Catherine	Northbridge,	Guardianship,	6960
1873	Celia	Northbridge,	Guardianship,	6961
1873	Daniel	Upton,	Administration,	6962
1873	Ellen E.	Northbridge,	Guardianship,	6963
1873	Hugh	Lancaster,	Will,	6964
	BRAINARD see BRAYNARD.			
1830	BRAMAN, Amasa	Millbury,	Administration,	6965
1849	Anson	Worcester,	Will,	6966
1864	Cynthia	Worcester,	Administration,	6967
1816	Daniel	Petersham,	Administration,	6968
1846	Mary	Millbury,	Will,	6969
1846	William S.	Uxbridge,	Administration,	6970
1864	BRANDT, Henry S.	Warren,	Administration,	6971
1853	BRANNON, Catherine	Worcester,	Administration,	6972
1865	William	Milford,	Administration,	6973
1853	BRANSFIELD, Ellen	Paxton,	Administration,	6974
1876	BRASSEL, Bridget	Southbridge,	Administration,	6975
1797	BRASTOW, Betsey	Uxbridge,	Guardianship,	6976
1797	Nabby	Uxbridge,	Guardianship,	6977
1797	Sally	Uxbridge,	Guardianship,	6978
1783	BRATTLE, William	Cambridge,	Absentee,	6979
1874	BRAY, Annie E.	Worcester,	Adoption, etc.,	6980
1865	Charles C.	Boylston,	Administration,	6981
1872	Dennis	Fitchburg,	Will,	6982
	BRAYBROOK see BRABROOK.			
	BRAYNARD AND BRAINARD,			
1833	Susan A.	Princeton,	Guardianship,	6983
1873	BRAYTON, David	Worcester,	Will,	6984
1816	Hannah	Douglas,	Will,	6985
1838	Mary	Berlin,	Administration,	6986

YEAR.	NAME.	RESIDENCE.	NATURE.	CASE.
1835	BRAZER, Samuel	Worcester,	Will,	6987
1872	BRECK, Catharine	Hardwick,	Guardianship,	6988
1872	George R.	Southborough,	Administration,	6989
1813	John	Barre,	Administration,	6990
1824	John	Sterling,	Administration,	6991
1875	Julia A.	Sterling,	Administration,	6992
1863	Moses T.	Worcester,	Administration,	6993
1865	Osgood B.	Worcester,	Administration,	6994
1863	Sarah J.	Worcester,	Guardianship,	6995
1863	Susan R.	Worcester,	Guardianship,	6996
1865	BRECKINBRIDGE, Louisa V.	Charlton,	Will,	6997
1826	Mary	Leicester,	Guardianship,	6998
1881	BREED, Andrews	Lancaster,	Will,	6999
1863	BREEN, Dennis	Webster,	Guardianship,	7000
1864	Edward, etc.	Southborough,	Administration,	7001
1879	Margaret	Worcester,	Will,	7002
1879	BREHM, Margaret	Worcester,	Administration,	7003
	BRENNAN AND BRENNEN,			
1871	James	New Braintree,	Administration,	7004
1875	John F.	Millbury,	Guardianship,	7005
1869	Robert	Worcester,	Administration,	7006
1875	Sarah M.	Millbury,	Guardianship,	7007
1874	Thomas	Milford,	Partition,	7008
1871	William	Fitchburg,	Administration,	7009
1838	BREWER, Abijah	Northborough,	Will,	7010
1851	Alonzo P.	Worcester,	Guardianship,	7011
1851	Anna M.	Worcester,	Guardianship,	7012
1879	Anna R.	Clinton,	Adoption, etc.,	7013
1782	Betsey	Watertown,	Guardianship,	7014
1845	Charles	Petersham,	Guardianship,	7015
1879	Charles N.	Southborough,	Administration,	7016
1861	Clarissa	Shrewsbury,	Administration,	7017
1779	Ebenezer	Shrewsbury,	Guardianship,	7018
1851	Edward T.	Worcester,	Guardianship,	7019
1764	Elisha	Sherburn,	Guardianship,	7020
1764	Elizabeth	Sherburn,	Guardianship,	7021
1782	Elizabeth	Watertown,	Guardianship,	7022
1872	Ella F.	Worcester,	Guardianship,	7023
1861	Eunice	Petersham,	Will,	7024
1771	Hannah	Brookfield,	Guardianship,	7025
1881	Hannah R.	Athol,	Administration,	7026
1851	Henrietta L.	Worcester,	Guardianship,	7027
1852	Henry	Boylston,	Will,	7028
1872	Henry C.	Boylston,	Administration,	7029
1830	James	Boylston,	Will,	7030

YEAR.	NAME.	RESIDENCE.	NATURE.	CASE.
1859	BREWER, James	Clinton,	Administration,	7031
1831	Joel	Southborough,	Administration,	7032
1836	Joel	Southborough,	Will,	7033
1829	John	Worcester,	Administration,	7034
1836	John	Spencer,	Will,	7035
1850	John	Worcester,	Administration,	7036
1851	John G.	Worcester,	Guardianship,	7037
1877	Jonas	Royalston,	Will,	7038
1764	Jonathan	Sherburn,	Guardianship,	7039
1833	Joseph	Boylston,	Administration,	7040
1768	Josiah	Worcester,	Will,	7041
1826	Lewis	Royalston,	Administration,	7042
1872	Lydia	Royalston,	Will,	7043
1874	Lyman	Spencer,	Will,	7044
1782	Mary	Watertown,	Guardianship,	7045
1853	Mary A.	North Brookfield,	Guardianship,	7046
1876	Mary C.	Clinton,	Adoption, etc.,	7047
1872	Mary W.	Worcester,	Guardianship,	7048
1764	Moses	Sherburn,	Guardianship,	7049
1862	Moses	Southborough,	Administration,	7050
1875	Nellie	Northborough,	Guardianship,	7051
1877	Nellie	Boylston,	Will,	7052
1800	Peter	Southborough,	Will,	7053
1859	Peter	Southborough,	Administration,	7054
1851	Polly	Southborough,	Will,	7055
1857	Rufus	Milford,	Will,	7056
1872	Ruth A.	Worcester,	Guardianship,	7057
1870	Samuel R.	Barre,	Administration,	7058
1771	Sarah	Brookfield,	Guardianship,	7059
1838	Sarah A.	Boylston,	Guardianship,	7060
1881	Sarah C.	North Brookfield,	Will,	7061
1870	Sarah D.	Royalston,	Administration,	7062
1855	Simeon	Worcester,	Will,	7063
1864	Simeon D.	Fitchburg,	Administration,	7064
1865	S. L. W.	Worcester,	Sale Real Estate,	7065
1879	Thomas	Northbridge,	Administration,	7066
1873	Thomas J.	Worcester,	Will,	7067
1777	William, Jr.	Shrewsbury,	Administration,	7068
1853	William Henry H.	Spencer,	Guardianship,	7069
1865	William M.	Unknown,	Sale Real Estate,	7070
1880	William P.	Spencer,	Administration,	7071
1873	BREWSTER, Charles O., Jr.	Brookfield,	Guardianship,	7072
1873	Le Roy S.	Webster,	Will,	7073
1873	Lewis	Brookfield,	Guardianship,	7074
1871	Lucy	Southbridge,	Will,	7075

1874	BREWSTER, Mary D.	Brookfield,	Administration,	7076
1873	Mary J.	Brookfield,	Guardianship,	7077
1873	Sophia L.	Brookfield,	Guardianship,	7078
1873	Walter S.	Brookfield,	Guardianship,	7079
1873	William L.	Brookfield,	Guardianship,	7080
	BRIANT see BRYANT.			
1785	BRIARD, Nicholas	Shrewsbury,	Administration,	7081
1855	BRICK, Enoch	Gardner,	Administration,	7082
1866	Elijah	Gardner,	Will,	7083
1853	Francis	Gardner,	Guardianship,	7084
1853	Harriet S.	Gardner,	Guardianship,	7085
——	Sally	Gardner,	Guardianship,	7086
1877	Sarah	Gardner,	Administration,	7087
1849	BRIDE, Sarah	Spencer,	Will,	7088
1870	BRIDEN, Bridget	Worcester,	Guardianship,	7089
1870	Charles	Worcester,	Guardianship,	7090
1870	Dennis	Worcester,	Guardianship,	7091
1870	Frank	Worcester,	Guardianship,	7092
1870	James	Worcester,	Guardianship,	7093
1875	John	Worcester,	Administration,	7094
1870	Mary A.	Worcester,	Guardianship,	7095
	BRIDGE and BRIDGES,			
1843	Alvira J.	Leicester,	Guardianship,	7096
1852	Annis	Harvard,	Will,	7097
1853	Annis E.	Harvard,	Guardianship,	7098
1825	Arba	Western,	Guardianship,	7099
1876	Arba	Warren,	Will,	7100
1749	Benjamin	Southborough,	Guardianship,	7101
1774	Benjamin	Harvard,	Guardianship,	7102
1797	Benjamin	Winchendon,	Administration,	7103
1828	Benjamin	Milford,	Administration,	7104
1829	Benjamin A.	Milford,	Guardianship,	7105
1862	Benjamin F.	Sturbridge,	Guardianship,	7106
1869	Betsey	Worcester,	Administration,	7107
1864	Charlotte	Rutland,	Will,	7108
1825	Delia	Western,	Guardianship,	7109
1817	Dexter	Western,	Administration,	7110
1808	Ebenezer	Harvard,	Administration,	7111
1827	Edmund	Rutland,	Guardianship,	7112
1832	Edmund	Rutland,	Administration,	7112
1853	Eliakim H.	Harvard,	Guardianship,	7113
1794	Elijah	Spencer,	Guardianship,	7114
1873	Eliza	Hardwick,	Guardianship,	7115
1843	Emery	Leicester,	Administration,	7116
1811	George	Harvard,	Guardianship,	7117

Year	Name.	Residence.	Nature.	Case.
	BRIDGE and BRIDGES,			
1825	George	Western,	Guardianship,	7118
1854	Georgianna	Gardner	Adoption, etc.,	7119
1817	Gideon	North Brookfield,	Will,	7120
1862	Hackaliah	Sturbridge,	Administration,	7121
1816	Hadassah	Western,	Guardianship,	7122
1739	Hakaliah	Southborough,	Administration,	7123
1749	Hakaliah	Southborough,	Guardianship,	7124
1833	Isaac	Harvard	Administration,	7125
1746	James	Southborough,	Guardianship,	7126
1798	James	Worcester,	Administration,	7127
1805	James	Southborough,	Will,	7128
1774	Jeremiah	Harvard,	Guardianship,	7129
1783	John	Harvard,	Guardianship,	7130
1825	John	Western,	Guardianship,	7131
1863	John	Gardner,	Administration,	7132
1876	John	West Brookfield,	Will,	7133
1853	John A.	Harvard,	Administration,	7134
1825	Jonathan	Western,	Administration,	7135
1817	Josiah	Southborough,	Will,	7136
1824	Keziah	North Brookfield,	Administration,	7137
1846	Martin	Leicester,	Will,	7138
1825	Mary	Western,	Guardianship,	7139
1832	Mary	Phillipston,	Administration,	7140
1838	Mary	Rutland,	Will,	7141
1829	Mary E.	Milford,	Guardianship,	7142
1749	Nathan	Southborough,	Guardianship,	7143
1809	Nathan	Southborough,	Will,	7144
1854	Nathan	Southborough,	Will,	7145
1876	Nettie C.	Hardwick,	Guardianship,	7146
1835	Patty	Rutland,	Guardianship,	7147
1872	Patty W.	Southborough,	Will,	7148
1797	Richard P.	Petersham,	Administration,	7149
1765	Samuel	Marblehead,	Guardianship,	7150
1799	Samuel	Worcester,	Will,	7151
1831	Samuel L.	Swansey, N. H.,	Guardianship,	7152
1749	Sarah	Southborough,	Guardianship,	7153
1764	Sarah	Southborough,	Guardianship,	7154
1805	Silas	Sturbridge,	Guardianship,	7155
1829	Solomon	Lancaster,	Administration,	7156
1832	Thomas H.	Harvard,	Guardianship,	7157
1816	Timothy P.	Western,	Administration,	7158
1843	Urania E.	Leicester,	Guardianship,	7159
1853	Vienna L.	Harvard,	Guardianship,	7160
1805	William	Rutland,	Administration,	7161

YEAR.	NAME.	RESIDENCE.	NATURE.	CASE.
	BRIDGE AND BRIDGES,			
1829	William	Spencer,	Administration,	7162
1833	William, Jr.	Southborough,	Guardianship,	7163
1848	BRIERLY, Benjamin	Millbury,	Administration,	7164
1868	Elizabeth	Millbury,	Administration,	7165
1849	John	Milwaukee, Wis.,	Administration,	7166
1855	John	Worcester,	Will,	7167
1855	Mary	Southbridge,	Administration,	7168
1846	BRIGDEN, Joseph	Worcester,	Will,	7169
1774	Thomas	Westminster,	Will,	7170
1852	BRIGGS, Abraham	Worcester,	Guardianship,	7171
1874	Albert	Oakham,	Administration,	7172
1833	Amos	Petersham,	Will,	7173
1870	Anthony T.	Worcester,	Guardianship,	7174
1805	Bowers	Oxford,	Administration,	7175
1881	Carrie D.	Worcester,	Sep. Support,	7176
1870	Clarence M.	Athol,	Guardianship,	7177
1861	Cornelius W.	Webster,	Guardianship,	7178
1806	Elijah	Northbridge,	Administration,	7179
1880	Eva	Mendon,	Adoption, etc.,	7180
1870	Florence V.	Athol,	Guardianship,	7181
1852	Hannah	Worcester,	Guardianship,	7182
1854	Hannah	Worcester,	Administration,	7182
1877	Hannah	Dana,	Administration,	7183
1877	Hannah P.	Upton,	Administration,	7184
1881	Horace S.	Worcester,	Sep. Support,	7185
1837	Isaac	Athol,	Will,	7186
1832	Jacob	Athol,	Administration,	7187
1802	Job	Dana,	Will,	7188
1852	Levi	Athol,	Will,	7189
1863	Lewis R.	Templeton,	Administration,	7190
1861	Lucius H.	Webster,	Guardianship,	7191
1834	Lydia	Athol,	Will,	7192
1809	Mercy	Sutton,	Will,	7193
1874	Moses	Athol,	Will,	7194
1877	Nathan G.	Petersham,	Guardianship,	7195
1818	Rufus	Charlton,	Administration,	7196
1854	Rufus	Worcester,	Guardianship,	7197
1874	Rufus	Spencer,	Guardianship,	7198
1869	Russell	Worcester,	Administration,	7199
1879	Sarah P.	Millbury,	Administration,	7200
1855	Silas	Douglas,	Administration,	7201
1823	Simeon	Charlton,	Guardianship,	7202
1870	Tyler M.	Athol,	Administration,	7203
1827	Wilder	Templeton,	Administration,	7204

Year.	Name.	Residence.	Nature.	Case.
1870	BRIGGS, Willie K.	Athol,	Guardianship,	7205
1785	Zephaniah	Northborough,	Administration,	7206
1768	BRIGHAM, Aaron	Grafton,	Will,	7207
1860	Abigail	Templeton,	Will,	7208
1823	Abner	Princeton,	Administration,	7209
1813	Abraham	Northborough,	Administration,	7210
1858	Abraham	Berlin,	Administration,	7211
1872	Abram	Fitchburg,	Administration,	7212
1859	Adolphus	Shrewsbury,	Administration,	7213
1863	Albert	Westborough,	Guardianship,	7214
1878	Alden	Oakham,	Will,	7215
1847	Alice	Northborough,	Pension,	7216
1853	Alice	Westborough,	Guardianship,	7217
1768	Amariah	Grafton,	Guardianship,	7218
1843	Amariah	Millbury,	Pension,	7219
1876	Ann	Berlin,	Administration,	7220
1789	Anna	Grafton,	Guardianship,	7221
1805	Anna	Brookfield,	Guardianship,	7222
1847	Anna	Oxford,	Administration,	7223
1848	Anna	Barre,	Will,	7224
1849	Anna	Barre,	Pension,	7225
1746	Antipas	Grafton,	Administration,	7226
1802	Artemas	Northborough,	Will,	7227
1818	Artemas	Northborough,	Guardianship,	7228
1859	Artemas	Northborough,	Adoption, etc.,	7229
1847	Artemas A.	Worcester,	Guardianship,	7230
1794	Asa	Princeton,	Administration,	7231
1795	Asa	Princeton,	Guardianship,	7232
1809	Asa	Princeton,	Guardianship,	7233
1824	Asa	Princeton,	Guardianship,	7234
1856	Asa	Northborough,	Administration,	7235
1809	Asenath	Brookfield,	Guardianship,	7236
1821	Azubah	Berlin,	Guardianship,	7237
1869	Baker	Southborough,	Will,	7238
1817	Barnabas	North Brookfield,	Administration,	7239
1852	Benajah	Fitchburg,	Will,	7240
1831	Benjamin	Shrewsbury,	Administration,	7241
1876	Bertha M.	Mendon,	Adoption, etc.,	7242
1870	Bertham F.	Westborough,	Guardianship,	7243
1806	Betsey	Southborough,	Guardianship,	7244
1809	Betsey	Princeton,	Guardianship,	7245
1840	Betsey	Hubbardston,	Guardianship,	7246
1875	Betsey C.	Westborough,	Will,	7247
1848	Bryant	Westborough,	Administration,	7248
1866	Calvin	Worcester,	Will,	7249

| --- | --- | --- | --- | --- |
1870	BRIGHAM, Carrie G.	Westborough,	Guardianship,	7250
1816	Catharine M.	Westborough,	Guardianship,	7251
1824	Charles	Princeton,	Guardianship,	7252
1836	Charles	Westborough,	Guardianship,	7253
1871	Charles	Grafton,	Will,	7254
1842	Charles A.	Westborough,	Guardianship,	7255
1860	Charles A.	Worcester,	Guardianship,	7256
1852	Charles D.	Worcester,	Will,	7257
1862	Charles E.	Boylston,	Guardianship,	7258
1864	Charles L.	Charlton,	Administration,	7259
1864	Charles L.	Brookfield,	Administration,	7260
1861	Clarissa A.	Northborough,	Adoption, etc.,	7261
1842	Clarissa E.	Westborough,	Guardianship,	7262
1816	Dana W.	Westborough,	Guardianship,	7263
1831	Dana W.	Westborough,	Administration,	7263
1750	David	Westborough,	Will,	7264
1824	David	Shrewsbury,	Will,	7265
1851	David	Westborough,	Will,	7266
1876	Delia A.	Templeton,	Administration,	7267
1863	Dexter P.	Westborough,	Guardianship,	7268
1768	Dorothy	Grafton,	Administration,	7269
1869	Dorothy P.	Leominster,	Will,	7270
1871	Drusilla D.	Northborough,	Administration,	7271
1765	Ebenezer	Westborough,	Will,	7272
1772	Ebenezer	Westborough,	Guardianship,	7273
1852	Ebenezer	Southborough,	Will,	7274
1806	Edmund	Westborough,	Will,	7275
1840	Edmund	Templeton,	Will,	7276
1841	Edmund	West Boylston,	Administration,	7277
1858	Edmund T.	Shrewsbury,	Will,	7278
1827	Edward	Petersham,	Administration,	7279
1868	Edward	Westborough,	Will,	7280
1870	Edward F.	Thompson, Conn.,	Administration,	7281
1877	Edward M.	Worcester,	Administration,	7282
1816	Eli	Upton,	Administration,	7283
1865	Eli	Sterling,	Will,	7284
1804	Elijah	Southborough,	Administration,	7285
1816	Elijah	Westborough,	Administration,	7286
1808	Elisha	Brookfield,	Will,	7287
1795	Elizabeth	Princeton,	Guardianship,	7288
1821	Elizabeth	Berlin,	Guardianship,	7289
1855	Elizabeth	Leominster,	Administration,	7290
1863	Ella S.	Westborough,	Guardianship,	7291
1845	Ellen	West Boylston,	Guardianship,	7292
1875	Ellen S.	Westborough,	Administration,	7293

YEAR.	NAME.	RESIDENCE.	NATURE.	CASE.
1845	BRIGHAM, Elliot F.	West Boylston,	Guardianship,	7294
1871	Elmer	Westborough,	Administration,	7295
1815	Emerson	Hubbardston,	Guardianship,	7296
1849	Ephraim	Southborough,	Administration,	7297
1861	Ephraim	Westborough,	Administration,	7298
1853	Eugene F.	Oakham,	Adoption, etc.,	7299
1858	Eunice	Worcester,	Administration,	7300
1841	Eunice E.	West Boylston,	Guardianship,	7301
1788	Ezekiel	Grafton,	Administration,	7302
1848	Ezekiel	Grafton,	Will,	7303
1809	Fanny	Brookfield,	Guardianship,	7304
1881	Fanny	Southborough,	Administration,	7305
1850	Francis A.	Southborough,	Guardianship,	7306
1878	Frank E.	Oakham,	Change of Name,	7307
1859	Franklin W.	Shrewsbury,	Guardianship,	7308
1841	Frederic	West Boylston,	Guardianship,	7309
1878	Frederick	Warren,	Administration,	7310
1808	George	Southborough,	Administration,	7311
1842	George B.	Westborough,	Administration,	7312
1870	George B.	Westborough,	Guardianship,	7313
1831	George C.	Westborough,	Guardianship,	7314
1845	George T.	West Boylston,	Guardianship,	7315
1862	Georgiana	Boylston,	Guardianship,	7316
1814	Gersham	Westborough,	Will,	7317
1858	Hannah L.	Berlin,	Guardianship,	7318
1839	Harriet	Worcester,	Guardianship,	7319
1841	Harriet A.	Southborough,	Guardianship,	7320
1842	Harriet A.	Westborough,	Guardianship,	7321
1845	Harriet A.	West Boylston,	Guardianship,	7322
1842	Harriet D.	Westborough,	Guardianship,	7323
1877	Harrison F.	Westborough,	Administration,	7324
1852	Helen A.	Worcester,	Guardianship,	7325
1809	Henderson	Northborough,	Administration,	7326
1831	Henrietta A.	Westborough,	Guardianship,	7327
1858	Henrietta D.	Berlin,	Guardianship,	7328
1844	Henrietta F.	New York, N. Y.,	Guardianship,	7329
1829	Henry	Barre,	Will,	7330
1853	Henry	Northborough,	Will,	7331
1863	Henry	Rutland,	Will,	7332
1841	Henry, Jr.	Northborough,	Guardianship,	7333
1881	Herbert E.	Hubbardston,	Partition,	7334
1869	Holloway	Northborough,	Administration,	7335
1810	Horace	Milford,	Administration,	7336
1839	Hosea	Worcester,	Administration,	7337
1864	(Infant daughter)	Charlton,	Guardianship,	7338

Year.	Name.	Residence.	Nature.	Case.
1825	BRIGHAM, Isaac	Milford,	Administration,	7339
1858	Isaac	Milford,	Will,	7340
1831	Ivers J.	Westborough,	Guardianship,	7341
1834	Jabez	Worcester,	Will,	7342
1796	James	Brookfield,	Will,	7343
1864	James D.	Charlton,	Guardianship,	7344
1877	Jane A.	Westborough,	Guardianship,	7345
1853	Jane M.	Westborough,	Guardianship,	7346
1848	Jane S.	Westborough,	Guardianship,	7347
1847	Jason S.	Worcester,	Guardianship,	7348
1862	Jemima	Boylston,	Will,	7349
1873	Jennie M.	Northborough,	Guardianship,	7350
1796	Jesse	Northborough,	Will,	7351
1809	Joel	Brookfield,	Guardianship,	7352
1828	Joel	Leominster,	Dower,	7353
1767	John	Shrewsbury,	Will,	7354
1795	John	Princeton,	Guardianship,	7355
1806	John	Princeton,	Guardianship,	7356
1818	John	Gerry,	Will,	7357
1839	John	Oxford,	Will,	7358
1864	John H.	Charlton,	Guardianship,	7359
1870	John L.	Westborough,	Guardianship,	7360
1827	Jonah	Northborough,	Will,	7361
1790	Jonas	Westborough,	Will,	7362
1872	Jonas B.	Westborough,	Will,	7363
1772	Joseph	Westborough,	Guardianship,	7364
1836	Joseph	Shrewsbury,	Administration,	7365
1838	Joseph	Westborough,	Administration,	7366
1873	Joseph D.	Princeton,	Administration,	7367
1873	Joseph F.	Boylston,	Administration,	7368
1831	Joshua B.	Westborough,	Guardianship,	7369
1870	Josiah	Westborough,	Will,	7370
1836	Lavina V.	Princeton,	Guardianship,	7371
1860	Lily	Worcester,	Guardianship,	7372
1876	Lincoln	Westborough,	Will,	7373
1870	Lizzie J.	Grafton,	Adoption, etc.,	7374
1805	Loring	Brookfield,	Guardianship,	7375
1824	Louisa	Princeton,	Guardianship,	7376
1802	Lovell	Northborough,	Guardianship,	7377
1849	Lovell	West Boylston,	Administration,	7378
1840	Lowell	Southborough,	Administration,	7379
1849	Lowell	Westborough,	Will,	7380
1844	Lucien F.	New York, N. Y.,	Guardianship,	7381
1812	Lucinda	West Boylston,	Guardianship,	7382
1768	Lucy	Grafton,	Guardianship,	7383

YEAR.	NAME.	RESIDENCE.	NATURE.	CASE.
1861	BRIGHAM, Lucy	Shrewsbury,	Administration,	7384
1866	Lucy	Boylston,	Administration,	7385
1768	Lydia	Grafton,	Guardianship,	7386
1789	Lydia	Grafton,	Guardianship,	7387
1809	Lydia	Brookfield,	Guardianship,	7388
1858	Marion	Berlin,	Guardianship,	7389
1841	Martha E.	Southborough,	Guardianship,	7390
1772	Mary	Westborough,	Guardianship,	7391
1809	Mary	Brookfield,	Guardianship,	7392
1852	Mary	Boylston,	Will,	7393
1871	Mary	Winchendon,	Administration,	7394
1860	Mary A.	Worcester,	Guardianship,	7395
1836	Mary E.	Princeton,	Guardianship,	7396
1863	Mary E.	Grafton,	Guardianship,	7397
1876	Mary E.	Worcester,	Administration,	7398
1873	Mary J.	Westborough,	Guardianship,	7399
1874	Mary M.	Winchendon,	Guardianship,	7400
1772	Mehitable	Westborough,	Guardianship,	7401
1795	Mehitable	Westborough,	Will,	7402
1802	Michael	Brookfield,	Administration,	7403
1789	Milecent	Grafton,	Guardianship,	7404
1768	Moses	Grafton,	Guardianship,	7405
1770	Moses	Westborough,	Guardianship,	7406
1770	Moses	Westborough,	Administration,	7407
1802	Moses	Northborough,	Guardianship,	7408
1806	Moses	Northborough,	Administration,	7409
1860	Nahum B.	Worcester,	Administration,	7410
1804	Nancy	Northborough,	Guardianship,	7411
1847	Nancy	Worcester,	Will,	7412
1864	Nancy J.	Charlton,	Guardianship,	7413
1784	Nathan	Southborough,	Will,	7414
1870	Nathaniel	Northborough,	Administration,	7415
1875	Nellie A.	Westborough,	Administration,	7416
1868	Nellie E.	Fitchburg,	Adoption, etc.,	7417
1861	Oliver M.	Grafton,	Will,	7418
1875	Orra E.	Boylston,	Guardianship,	7419
1872	Otis	Westborough,	Will,	7420
1873	Otis L.	Southborough,	Administration,	7421
1881	O. Augusta	Hubbardston,	Partition,	7422
1804	Patty	Northborough,	Guardianship,	7423
1869	Paul	Berlin,	Administration,	7424
1836	Persis E.	Westborough,	Guardianship,	7425
1831	Peter W.	Westborough,	Administration,	7426
1802	Phineas	Westborough,	Administration,	7427
1880	Phineas F.	Worcester,	Administration,	7428

YEAR.	NAME.	RESIDENCE.	NATURE.	CASE.
1770	BRIGHAM, Phinehas	Westborough,	Guardianship,	7429
1836	Pierpont	Westborough,	Will,	7430
1876	Pierpont D.	Southborough,	Will,	7431
1877	Polly	Sterling,	Administration,	7432
1870	Polly M.	Westborough,	Administration,	7433
1768	Rebecca	Grafton,	Guardianship,	7434
1876	Rebeckah B.	Fitchburg,	Administration,	7435
1817	Robert B.	Worcester,	Will,	7436
1837	Robert M.	Petersham,	Guardianship,	7437
1874	Rockwood	Chattanooga, Tenn.,	Administration,	7438
1874	Rosa A.	Boylston,	Guardianship,	7439
1875	Rosa A.	Boylston,	Administration,	7439
1814	Ruth	Southborough,	Administration,	7440
1831	Ruth	Southborough,	Administration,	7441
1795	Sally	Princeton,	Guardianship,	7442
1860	Sally	Brookfield,	Administration,	7443
1860	Sally	Millbury,	Will,	7444
1861	Sally	Millbury,	Pension,	7445
1824	Sally M.	Princeton,	Guardianship,	7446
1806	Samuel	Southborough,	Guardianship,	7447
1872	Samuel	Southborough,	Will,	7448
1842	Samuel A.	Westborough,	Guardianship,	7449
1847	Samuel A.	Shrewsbury,	Will,	7450
1875	Samuel R.	Westborough,	Administration,	7451
1803	Sarah	Southborough,	Will,	7452
1825	Sarah	Westborough,	Will,	7453
1841	Sarah	Southborough,	Will,	7454
1847	Sarah E.	Worcester,	Guardianship,	7455
1870	Sarah M.	West Brookfield,	Will,	7456
1831	Sereno L.	Westborough,	Guardianship,	7457
1876	Seth	Brookfield,	Administration,	7458
1791	Silas	Shrewsbury,	Administration,	7459
1838	Silas	Southborough,	Will,	7460
1836	Silas O.	Southborough,	Guardianship,	7461
1841	Solomon	Grafton,	Administration,	7462
1863	Sophronia	Petersham,	Administration,	7463
1812	Stephen	West Boylston,	Administration,	7464
1817	Stephen	Westborough,	Will,	7465
1821	Stephen	Princeton,	Will,	7466
1862	Stephen B.	Boylston,	Administration,	7467
1846	Stephen P.	Worcester,	Administration,	7468
1861	Susan	Grafton,	Will,	7469
1873	Susan H.	Worcester,	Administration,	7470
1816	Susan W.	Westborough,	Guardianship,	7471
1826	Susan W.	Westborough,	Administration,	7472

YEAR.	NAME.	RESIDENCE.	NATURE.	CASE.
1879	BRIGHAM, Sybil	Berlin,	Will,	7473
1870	Sylvanus	Brookfield,	Administration,	7474
1858	Sylvester,	Westborough,	Will,	7475
1804	Taylor,	Southborough,	Guardianship,	7476
1878	Theodore F.	Westborough,	Administration,	7477
1769	Thomas	Grafton,	Administration,	7478
1821	Thomas	Berlin,	Administration,	7479
1808	Tilly	Brookfield,	Administration,	7480
1865	Tilly	Brookfield,	Will,	7481
1775	Timothy	Southborough,	Will,	7482
1875	Trowbridge	Southborough,	Will,	7483
1805	Tyler	Brookfield,	Guardianship,	7484
1875	Walter	Westborough,	Guardianship,	7485
1858	Wealthy	Milford,	Guardianship,	7486
1860	Wealthy	Milford,	Administration,	7486
1877	Willard	Winchendon,	Administration,	7487
1834	William	Southborough,	Will,	7488
1834	William	Grafton,	Administration,	7489
1836	William	Princeton,	Guardianship,	7490
1853	William	Westborough,	Administration,	7491
1859	William	Unknown,	Trustee,	7492
1853	William C.	Westborough,	Guardianship,	7493
1845	William E.	Millbury,	Administration,	7494
1860	William H.	Worcester,	Guardianship,	7495
1858	William R.	Worcester,	Administration,	7496
1837	Winslow	Northborough,	Will,	7497
1837	Winslow	Northborough,	Pension,	7498
1774	BRIGHT, Henry	Spencer,	Administration,	7499
1830	BRIMHALL, Ann E.	Oakham,	Guardianship,	7500
1876	Caroline N.	Clinton,	Administration,	7501
1829	Elisha	Oakham	Administration,	7502
1830	Eunice	Oakham,	Administration,	7503
1813	Joel	Oakham,	Guardianship,	7504
1813	Jonas	Oakham,	Guardianship,	7505
1856	Jonas	Oakham,	Administration,	7506
1817	Joshua	Oakham,	Administration,	7507
1812	Samuel	Oakham,	Administration,	7508
1828	Susan H.	Oakham,	Guardianship,	7509
1839	Sylvanus	Hardwick,	Will,	7510
1875	BRINKMAN, Almina	Westminster,	Administration,	7511
1852	John	Gardner,	Guardianship,	7512
1867	John	Gardner,	Administration,	7513
1851	Nancy	Gardner,	Will,	7514
1875	BRINLEY, George	Hartford, Conn.,	Foreign Will,	7515

Year.	Name.	Residence.	Nature.	Case.
	BRITTON and BRITTAN,			
1831	Ansil N.	Princeton,	Guardianship,	7516
1867	Bradford	Ashburnham,	Administration,	7517
1831	Catharine	Princeton,	Guardianship,	7518
1870	Daniel W.	Fitchburg,	Administration,	7519
1879	Ida S.	Milford,	Guardianship,	7520
1760	John	Southborough,	Will,	7521
1798	John	Lancaster,	Administration,	7522
1824	Josiah	Rutland,	Guardianship,	7523
1831	Josiah	Princeton,	Guardianship,	7524
1863	Josiah	Worcester,	Will,	7525
1872	Josiah P.	Leominster,	Will,	7526
1793	Luther	Oxford,	Guardianship,	7527
1783	Samuel	Rutland,	Administration,	7528
1829	William	Princeton,	Administration,	7529
1831	William W.	Princeton,	Guardianship,	7530
1854	BRIZZEE, Emily M.	Unknown,	Adoption, etc.,	7531
1779	BROAD, Amos	Holden,	Guardianship,	7532
1867	Amos W.	West Boylston,	Administration,	7533
1878	Arthur H.	West Boylston,	·Administration,	7534
1838	Asa	Holden,	Administration,	7535
1861	Asa	Holden,	Administration,	7536
1839	Charles	Holden,	Guardianship,	7537
1839	Dexter	Holden,	Guardianship,	7538
1857	Dexter	Chicago, Ill.,	Administration,	7539
1816	Elisha	Barre,	Administration,	7540
1779	Elizabeth	Holden,	Guardianship,	7541
1779	Enos	Holden,	Guardianship,	7542
1878	Erastus	West Boylston,	Will,	7543
1877	Horace N.	West Boylston,	Administration,	7544
1869	Ira	Holden,	Will,	7545
1779	John	Holden,	Guardianship,	7546
1836	John	Barre,	Guardianship,	7547
1840	Joseph	Barre,	Administration,	7548
1779	Josiah	Holden,	Will,	7549
1799	Lucy	Barre,	Administration,	7550
1878	Mabel S.	West Boylston,	Guardianship,	7551
1875	Martha B.	Worcester,	Administration,	7552
1839	Roxa	Holden,	Guardianship,	7553
1779	Sarah	Holden,	Guardianship,	7554
1870	Sarah D.	Chicago, Ill.,	Guardianship,	7555
1839	Sylva	Holden,	Guardianship,	7556
1786	Thaddeus	Barre,	Guardianship,	7557
1868	Willard	Barre,	Administration,	7558
1778	William	Westborough,	Administration,	7559

YEAR.	NAME.	RESIDENCE.	NATURE.	CASE.
1877	BROADBENT, Albert	Blackstone,	Guardianship,	7560
1868	Annie	Worcester,	Guardianship,	7561
1867	Benjamin	Worcester,	Administration,	7562
1869	Emeline	Charlton,	Will,	7563
1875	Jane	Blackstone,	Administration,	7564
1878	Jeremiah	Worcester,	Administration,	7565
1852	Joseph	Southbridge,	Will,	7566
1868	Josephine	Worcester,	Guardianship,	7567
1851	Mary	Southbridge,	Administration,	7568
1877	Samuel W.	Blackstone,	Guardianship,	7569
1868	Sarah J.	Worcester,	Guardianship,	7570
1821	BROADERS, Barnabas	Westborough,	Guardianship,	7571
1785	Jacob	Westborough,	Administration,	7572
1847	Jacob	Westborough,	Administration,	7573
	BROADSTREET see BRADSTREET.			
1807	BROCAS, John	Shrewsbury,	Guardianship,	7574
1874	Mary K.	Shrewsbury,	Will,	7575
1851	BROCK, Fidelia	Athol,	Administration,	7576
1878	Isaac Z.	Athol,	Administration,	7577
1880	Peter	Milford,	Will,	7578
1879	BROCKLEBANK, Ethel S.	Fitchburg,	Adoption, etc.,	7579
1878	BROCKWAY, George H.	Lancaster,	Partition,	7580
1865	Hattie F.	Berlin,	Adoption, etc.,	7581
1878	James W.	Unknown,	Partition,	7582
1878	John L.	Boston,	Partition,	7583
1878	Lorenzo H.	Clinton,	Partition,	7584
1880	Martin J.	Milford,	Will,	7585
1877	Tilley	Lancaster,	Administration,	7586
1878	Willard H.	Boston,	Partition,	7587
1879	BRODERICK, Frances	Oxford,	Guardianship,	7588
1879	Sarah F.	Oxford,	Guardianship,	7589
1869	BROGAN, Ann	Sturbridge,	Guardianship,	7590
1869	James	Sturbridge,	Administration,	7591
1869	James	Sturbridge,	Guardianship,	7592
1869	Joseph	Sturbridge,	Guardianship,	7593
1856	Michael	So. Kingston, R. I.,	Administration,	7594
1869	Michael	Sturbridge,	Guardianship,	7595
1869	Patrick	Sturbridge,	Guardianship,	7596
1820	BROMFIELD, Henry	Harvard,	Administration,	7597
1857	BRONSDON, Lila M.	Athol,	Adoption,	7598
1875	BRONSON, Alfred R.	Worcester,	Administration,	7599
1830	Willis B.	Milford,	Will,	7600
1809	BROOKS, Aaron	Petersham,	Guardianship,	7601
1847	Aaron	Petersham,	Will,	7602

(175—SERIES A.)

YEAR.	NAME.	RESIDENCE.	NATURE.	CASE.
1845	BROOKS, Aaron, Jr.	Petersham,	Will,	7603
1873	Abby C.	Holden,	Administration,	7604
1845	Abby M.	Petersham,	Guardianship,	7605
1785	Agness	Worcester,	Guardianship,	7606
1845	Albert	Belfast, Me.,	Foreign Sale,	7607
1847	Alden	Ashburnham,	Administration,	7608
1815	Ammi	Sterling,	Administration,	7609
1823	Ann	Lunenburg,	Guardianship,	7610
1832	Ann	Worcester,	Guardianship,	7611
1793	Anna	Worcester,	Guardianship,	7612
1875	Arthur J.	Leominster,	Guardianship,	7613
1782	Asa	Western,	Guardianship,	7614
1852	Asa	Westminster,	Will,	7615
1852	Asa	Westminster,	Guardianship,	7616
1855	Asa, 2d	Westminster,	Administration,	7617
1859	Asa	Blackstone,	Will,	7618
1876	Asa	Westminster,	Administration,	7616
1812	Ashley	Bolton,	Guardianship,	7619
1782	Benjamin	Western,	Guardianship,	7620
1809	Betsey	Petersham,	Guardianship,	7621
1877	Betsey	Warren,	Administration,	7622
1845	Caroline A.	Belfast, Me.,	Foreign Sale,	7623
1820	Caroline E.	Westminster,	Guardianship,	7624
1855	Caroline W.	Westminster,	Guardianship,	7625
1798	Charles	Princeton,	Will,	7626
1874	Charles	Leominster,	Administration,	7627
1875	Charles	Leominster,	Guardianship,	7628
1845	Charles A.	Newport, Me.,	Foreign Sale,	7629
1866	Charles G.	Rockdale, N. Y.,	Guardianship,	7630
1859	Charles S.	New Braintree,	Change of Name,	7631
1845	Charlotte	Belfast, Me.,	Foreign Sale,	7632
1880	Cynthia	Gardner,	Administration,	7633
1875	Daniel	Leominster,	Guardianship,	7634
1819	Dexter	Sterling	Guardianship,	7635
1768	Ebenezer	Grafton,	Will,	7636
1779	Ebenezer	Grafton,	Guardianship,	7637
1821	Ebenezer	Sterling,	Administration,	7638
1810	Ebenezer	Sterling,	Will,	7639
1777	Edward	Western,	Administration,	7640
1845	Edward K.	Newport, Me.,	Foreign Sale,	7641
1870	Edwin A.	Templeton,	Guardianship,	7642
1847	Edwin H.	Winchendon,	Guardianship,	7643
1817	Edwin L. B.	Worcester,	Guardianship,	6644
1832	Elijah	Worcester,	Guardianship,	7645
1843	Elijah	Grafton,	Will,	7646

YEAR.	NAME.	RESIDENCE.	NATURE.	CASE.
1830	BROOKS, Elijah B.	Grafton,	Guardianship,	7647
1879	Elijah B.	Grafton,	Administration,	7648
1869	Elijah F.	Worcester,	Will,	7649
1845	Elisha	Princeton,	Guardianship,	7650
1866	Elisha	Princeton,	Administration,	7650
1839	Eliza A.	Templeton,	Guardianship,	7651
1825	Elizabeth	Worcester,	Guardianship,	7652
1855	Ellen E.	Westminster,	Guardianship,	7653
1875	Emily	Leominster,	Guardianship,	7654
1846	Emily A.	Gardner,	Guardianship,	7655
1825	Enoch	Princeton,	Will,	7656
1859	Enoch	Princeton,	Will,	7657
1779	Ephraim	Grafton,	Guardianship,	7658
1823	Ephraim	Barre,	Administration,	7659
1874	Erastus M.	Dana,	Administration,	7660
1863	Esther	Sturbridge,	Administration,	7661
1817	Eunice	Westminster,	Administration,	7662
1828	Eunice	Barre,	Administration,	7663
1785	Ezra	Westminster,	Guardianship,	7664
1843	Ezra	Westminster,	Administration,	7665
1839	Francis A.	Petersham,	Guardianship,	7666
1851	Frederick B.	Worcester,	Guardianship,	7667
1809	George	Petersham,	Guardianship,	7668
1823	George	Ashburnham,	Guardianship,	7669
1846	George	Gardner,	Guardianship,	7670
1785	Hannah	Westminster,	Guardianship,	7671
1817	Hannah	Worcester,	Guardianship,	7672
1848	Hannah	Templeton,	Administration,	7673
1854	Hannah	Ashford, Conn.,	Will,	7674
1825	Hannah J.	Worcester,	Guardianship,	7675
1845	Hannah M.	Newport, Me.,	Foreign Sale,	7676
1881	Hannah S.	Winchendon,	Will,	7677
1875	Hattie L.	Leominster,	Guardianship,	7678
1844	Helon,	Sterling,	Administration,	7679
1857	Henry	Petersham,	Administration,	7680
1851	Horace E.	Worcester,	Guardianship,	7681
1827	Isaac	Westminster,	Administration,	7682
1869	Isaac	Templeton,	Will,	7683
1817	Ivers	Westminster,	Guardianship,	7684
1790	Jacob	Northborough,	Administration,	7685
1839	Jacob	Northborough,	Administration,	7686
1845	James W.	Petersham,	Guardianship,	7687
1833	Jemima	Sterling,	Guardianship,	7688
1840	Jemima	Sterling,	Administration,	7689
1811	Joel	Grafton,	Will,	7690

YEAR.	NAME.	RESIDENCE.	NATURE.	CASE.
1828	BROOKS, Joel	Grafton,	Administration,	7691
1841	Joel	Gardner,	Will,	7692
1846	Joel	Gardner,	Guardianship,	7693
1857	Joel	Petersham,	Will,	7694
1864	Joel	Ashburnham,	Administration,	7695
1877	Joel	Gardner,	Administration,	7696
1784	John	Westminster,	Administration,	7697
1789	John	Sterling,	Administration,	7698
1809	John	Petersham,	Guardianship,	7699
1825	John	Sterling,	Administration,	7700
1845	John	Petersham,	Guardianship,	7701
1845	John	Winchendon,	Administration,	7702
1847	John	Winchendon,	Administration,	7703
1858	John	Athol,	Will,	7704
1859	John	Athol,	Administration,	7705
1863	John	Princeton,	Administration,	7706
1870	John, Jr.	Templeton,	Guardianship,	7707
1817	John A.	Worcester,	Guardianship,	7708
1824	John B.	Lunenburg,	Guardianship,	7709
1834	John B.	Lunenburg,	Administration,	7710
1867	John H.	Princeton,	Will,	7711
1830	John T.	Grafton,	Guardianship,	7712
1787	Jonas	Athol,	Administration,	7713
1807	Jonas	Westminster,	Administration,	7714
1823	Jonas	Ashburnham,	Guardianship,	7715
1859	Jonas	Winchendon,	Administration,	7716
1865	Jonas	Princeton,	Will,	7717
1866	Jonas II.	Rockdale, N. Y.,	Guardianship,	7718
1777	Jonathan	Lancaster,	Will,	7719
1779	Joseph	Grafton,	Guardianship,	7720
1837	Joseph	Upton,	Guardianship,	7721
1857	Joseph	Upton,	Will,	7722
1832	Joseph S.	Holden,	Guardianship,	7723
1878	Josephine	Unknown,	Adoption, etc.,	7724
1860	Josephine B.	Petersham,	Guardianship,	7725
1847	Levi	Winchendon,	Guardianship,	7726
1873	Levi	Claremont, N. H.,	Foreign Sale,	7727
1863	Levi W.	Winchendon,	Administration,	7728
1867	Lizzie E.	Templeton,	Guardianship,	7729
1865	Lizzie L.	Lancaster,	Guardianship,	7730
1817	Lucinda	Worcester,	Guardianship,	7731
1860	Lucius E.	Petersham,	Guardianship,	7732
1826	Lucy	Westminster,	Administration,	7733
1875	Lucy	Princeton,	Administration,	7734
1875	Lucy	Templeton,	Will,	7735

YEAR.	NAME.	RESIDENCE.	NATURE.	CASE.
1864	BROOKS, Lucy C.	Boston,	Adoption, etc.,	7736
1785	Lydia	Westminster,	Guardianship,	7737
1865	Maria A.	Petersham,	Guardianship,	7738
1860	Martha E.	Petersham,	Guardianship,	7739
1845	Martha W.	Petersham,	Guardianship,	7740
1782	Mary	Western,	Guardianship,	7741
1808	Mary	Princeton,	Administration,	7742
1828	Mary	Sterling,	Administration,	6743
1847	Mary	Winchendon,	Guardianship,	7744
1861	Mary	Lunenburg,	Guardianship,	7745
1876	Mary	Worcester,	Administration,	7746
1860	Mary A. E.	Petersham,	Guardianship,	7747
1875	Mary E.	Leominster,	Administration,	7748
1845	Mary I.	Newport, Me.,	Foreign Sale,	7749
1839	Mary J.	Templeton,	Guardianship,	7750
1845	Mary J.	Belfast, Me.,	Foreign Sale,	7751
1817	Mary M.	Worcester,	Guardianship,	7752
1875	Melissa	Leominster,	Guardianship,	7753
1829	Milton	Sterling,	Administration,	7754
1779	Molly	Grafton,	Guardianship,	7755
1823	Nancy	Ashburnham,	Guardianship,	7756
1868	Nancy D.	Princeton,	Will,	7757
1830	Nancy G.	Grafton,	Guardianship,	7758
1844	Nancy J.	Princeton,	Guardianship,	7759
1817	Nathaniel	Worcester,	Guardianship,	7760
1838	Nathaniel	Worcester,	Will,	7761
1850	Nathaniel	Worcester,	Administration,	7762
1805	Noah	Grafton,	Will,	7763
1809	Oliver	Petersham,	Guardianship,	7764
1831	Parnell	Lunenburg,	Administration,	7765
1779	Peter	Grafton,	Administration,	7766
1779	Peter	Grafton,	Guardianship,	7767
1803	Peter	Upton,	Will,	7768
1867	Phineas	Petersham,	Administration,	7769
1809	Polly	Petersham,	Guardianship,	7770
1819	Prosper	Western,	Administration,	7771
1784	Rebecca	Ashburnham,	Guardianship,	7772
1833	Rebecca	Sterling,	Guardianship,	7773
1782	Reuben	Western,	Guardianship,	7774
1838	Royal T.	Templeton,	Administration,	7775
1828	Ruth	Westminster,	Guardianship,	7776
1784	Sally	Ashburnham,	Guardianship,	7777
1817	Sally	Westminster,	Guardianship,	7778
1863	Sally	Westminster,	Guardianship,	7779
1807	Samuel, 2nd	Worcester,	Administration,	7780

YEAR.	NAME.	RESIDENCE.	NATURE.	CASE.
1808	BROOKS, Samuel	Princeton,	Guardianship,	7781
1810	Samuel	Westminster,	Will,	7782
1817	Samuel	Worcester,	Will,	7783
1817	Samuel	Westminster,	Guardianship,	7784
1832	Samuel	Worcester,	Guardianship,	7785
1840	Samuel	Princeton,	Will,	7786
1865	Samuel	Ashburnham,	Administration,	7787
1865	Samuel	Holden,	Will,	7788
1872	Samuel	Ashburnham,	Administration,	7789
1779	Sarah	Grafton,	Guardianship,	7790
1782	Sarah	Western,	Guardianship,	7791
1866	Sarah	Princeton,	Will,	7792
1875	Sarah	Templeton,	Will,	7793
1868	Sarah M.	Southborough,	Will,	7794
1839	Sarah W.	Templeton,	Guardianship,	7795
1822	Sewell	Ashburnham,	Administration,	7796
1843	Sewell	Princeton,	Administration,	7797
1827	Sidney	Sterling,	Will,	7798
1815	Silas	Winchendon,	Administration,	7799
1846	Silas	Gardner,	Administration,	7800
1856	Silas	Worcester,	Will,	7801
1784	Stephen	Ashburnham,	Guardianship,	7802
1784	Stephen	Ashburnham,	Administration,	7803
1822	Stephen	Worcester,	Will,	7804
1836	Stephen	Templeton,	Administration,	7805
1864	Stephen T.	Templeton,	Administration,	7806
1847	Sumner	Winchendon,	Guardianship,	7807
1846	Sylvanus	Gardner,	Guardianship,	7808
1823	Thomas	Lunenburg,	Administration,	7809
1823	Walter	Ashburnham,	Guardianship,	7810
1846	Webster	Gardner,	Guardianship,	7811
1777	William	Lancaster,	Guardianship,	7812
1777	William	Lancaster,	Will,	7813
1823	William	Ashburnham,	Guardianship,	7814
1863	William	Ashburnham,	Will,	7815
1865	William	Winchendon,	Administration,	7816
1875	William'	Leominster,	Guardianship,	7817
1869	William B.	Winchendon,	Will,	7818
1852	William C.	Worcester,	Change of Name,	7819
1819	William D.	Sterling,	Administration,	7820
1869	William H.	Worcester,	Guardianship,	7821
1866	BROPHY, Eliza	Worcester,	Administration,	7822
	BROSNIHAN AND BROSNAHAN,			
1865	Honorah	Worcester,	Will,	7823
1872	John	Westminster,	Will,	7824

YEAR.	NAME.	RESIDENCE.	NATURE.	CASE.
	BROSNIHAN AND BROSNAHAN,			
1871	John J.	Worcester,	Administration,	7825
1872	Margaret	Westminster,	Guardianship,	7826
1872	Mary	Westminster,	Guardianship,	7827
1871	Thomas M.	Worcester,	Will,	7828
1738	BROUGHTON, Copia	Lancaster,	Guardianship,	7829
1738	Patience	Lancaster,	Guardianship,	7830
1738	Sarah	Lancaster,	Guardianship,	7831
1880	BROUILLET, Jean B.	West Boylston,	Adoption,	7832
1873	BROW, Peter	Spencer,	Will,	7833
1821	BROWN, Aaron	Southbridge,	Administration,	7834
1856	Abby P.	Grafton,	Guardianship,	7835
1880	Abby R.	Fitchburg,	Administration,	7836
1864	Abel	Milford,	Guardianship,	7837
1788	Abigail	Worcester,	Guardianship,	7838
1793	Abigail	Royalston,	Guardianship,	7839
1815	Abigail	Western,	Guardianship,	7840
1826	Abigail	Lunenburg,	Administration,	7841
1860	Abigail	Winchendon,	Guardianship,	7842
1867	Abigail	Templeton,	Will,	7843
1874	Abigail	Petersham,	Administration,	7844
1815	Abigail R.	Lunenburg,	Guardianship,	7845
1813	Abijah	Sturbridge,	Administration,	7846
1826	Abijah	Charlton,	Guardianship,	7847
1842	Abijah	Charlton,	Administration,	7848
1822	Abraham	Sutton,	Administration,	7849
1856	Ada	Worcester,	Guardianship,	7850
1856	Ada I.	Worcester,	Adoption, etc.,	7851
1866	Addie O.	Winchendon,	Guardianship,	7852
1846	Adelaide	Charlton,	Guardianship,	7853
1864	Adeline A.	Worcester,	Administration,	7854
1851	Alanson C.	Fitchburg,	Administration,	7855
1854	Albert	Worcester,	Administration,	7856
1879	Albert W.	Worcester,	Administration,	7857
1801	Alexander	Charlton,	Will,	7858
1853	Allen	Holden,	Administration,	7859
1853	Allen	Holden,	Guardianship,	7860
1856	Almira A.	West Boylston,	Guardianship,	7861
1871	Alonzo F.	Westminster,	Administration,	7862
1846	Alonzo J.	Douglas,	Guardianship,	7863
1814	Alvan	Oxford,	Administration,	7864
1867	Alvin G.	Southbridge,	Administration,	7865
1860	Alvin M.	Gardner,	Guardianship,	7866
1868	Amanda	Winchendon,	Administration,	7867
1803	Amos	Gerry,	Guardianship,	7868

YEAR.	NAME.	RESIDENCE.	NATURE.	CASE.
1829	BROWN, Amos	Fitchburg,	Guardianship,	7869
1848	Amos	Worcester,	Will,	7870
1854	Amos	Fitchburg,	Will,	7871
1854	Amos	Phillipston,	Administration,	7872
1869	Amos	Charlton,	Administration,	7873
1877	Amos	Fitchburg,	Administration,	7874
1805	Amos H.	Winchendon,	Guardianship,	7875
1859	Amos H.	Winchendon,	Will,	7876
1788	Andrew	Dudley,	Administration,	7877
1841	Andrew	Holden,	Pension,	7878
1874	Ann	Worcester,	Administration,	7879
1849	Ann E.	Worcester,	Guardianship,	7880
1854	Ann E.	Worcester,	Administration,	7881
1793	Anna	Royalston,	Guardianship,	7882
1876	Anna D.	Westborough,	Will,	7883
1788	Arad	Worcester,	Guardianship,	7884
1803	Arathusa	Gerry,	Guardianship,	7885
1836	Arathusa	Northborough,	Administration,	7886
1856	Arethusa	Phillipston,	Administration,	7887
1797	Artemas	Winchendon,	Guardianship,	7888
1803	Artemas	Winchendon,	Guardianship,	7889
1833	Artemas	Phillipston,	Administration,	7890
1857	Artemas	Templeton,	Administration,	7891
1869	Artemas H.	Royalston,	Will,	7892
1879	Arthur W.	Gardner,	Will,	7893
1817	Asa	Hubbardston,	Administration,	7894
1818	Asa	Hubbardston,	Guardianship,	7895
1835	Asa	Fitchburg,	Administration,	7896
1855	Asaph	Winchendon,	Administration,	7897
1846	Augustus	Blackstone,	Administration,	7898
1857	Azuba A.	Hubbardston,	Guardianship,	7899
1774	Benjamin	Sturbridge,	Will,	7900
1792	Benjamin	Winchendon,	Administration,	7901
1803	Benjamin	Gerry,	Guardianship,	7902
1804	Benjamin	Westminster,	Guardianship,	7903
1808	Benjamin	Sterling,	Will,	7904
1808	Benjamin	Sterling,	Guardianship,	7905
1848	Benjamin	Milford,	Will,	7906
1853	Benjamin	Fitchburg,	Will,	7907
1863	Benjamin	Templeton,	Will,	7908
1847	Benjamin F.	Grafton,	Guardianship,	7909
1863	Benjamin F.	Templeton,	Guardianship,	7910
1836	Benjamin L., etc.	Northborough,	Guardianship,	7911
1851	Benjamin S. H.	Royalston,	Administration,	7912
1881	Bertha C.	Templeton,	Guardianship,	7913

Year.	Name.	Residence.	Nature.	Case.
1879	BROWN, Bertha E.	Lunenburg,	Guardianship,	7914
1869	Bessie A.	Barre,	Adoption, etc.,	7915
1837	Bethiah	West Boylston,	Pension,	7916
1788	Betsey	Worcester,	Guardianship,	7917
1797	Betsey	Winchendon,	Guardianship,	7918
1841	Betsey	Hubbardston,	Guardianship,	7919
1868	Betsey H.	Southbridge,	Administration,	7920
1865	Betsey S.	Douglas,	Administration,	7921
1873	Beulah M.	Grafton,	Administration,	7922
1842	Brigham	Leicester,	Administration,	7923
1758	Caleb	Harvard,	Administration,	7924
1838	Caroline	Charlton,	Guardianship,	7925
1847	Caroline S.	Blackstone,	Guardianship,	7926
1861	Carrie B.	Leominster,	Adoption, etc.,	7927
1880	Catherine	Royalston,	Administration,	7928
1797	Caty	Winchendon,	Guardianship,	7929
1808	Caty	Sterling,	Guardianship,	7930
1838	Celestina	Charlton,	Guardianship,	7931
1809	Charles	Charlestown,	Guardianship,	7932
1837	Charles	Charlton,	Administration,	7933
1838	Charles	Charlton,	Pension,	7934
1845	Charles	Charlton,	Administration,	7935
1856	Charles	West Boylston,	Administration,	7936
1866	Charles	Upton,	Administration,	7937
1880	Charles	Brookfield,	Guardianship,	7938
1864	Charles D.	Winchendon,	Administration,	7939
1856	Charles E.	Worcester,	Guardianship,	7940
1870	Charles E.	Worcester,	Administration,	7941
1865	Charles H.	Upton,	Change of Name,	7942
1842	Charles M.	Winchendon,	Guardianship,	7943
1851	Charles P.	Grafton,	Administration,	7944
1880	Charlotte A.	Templeton,	Will,	7945
1838	Chloe	Charlton,	Guardianship,	7946
1876	Chloe	Webster,	Will,	7947
1872	Chloe A.	Charlton,	Guardianship,	7948
1854	Christopher	Ashburnham,	Guardianship,	7949
1865	Clara S.	Douglas,	Guardianship,	7950
1808	Clarissa	Sterling,	Guardianship,	7951
1838	Clarissa E.	Charlton,	Guardianship,	7952
1844	Clark	Grafton,	Administration,	7953
1839	Clark J.	Rutland,	Administration,	7954
1846	Clovis G.	Douglas,	Guardianship,	7955
1838	Cynthia	Charlton,	Guardianship,	7956
1847	Cyrus	Templeton,	Will,	7957
1875	Dana	Hubbardston,	Administration,	7958

Year.	Name.	Residence.	Nature.	Case.
1793	BROWN, Daniel	Royalston,	Administration,	7959
1809	Daniel	Mendon,	Administration,	7960
1870	Daniel	Worcester,	Will,	7961
1856	Daniel C.	Grafton,	Guardianship,	7962
1880	Daniel R.	Athol,	Administration,	7963
1790	David	Winchendon,	Will,	7964
1801	David	Charlton,	Will,	7965
1816	David	Worcester,	Will,	7966
1872	David	Southbridge,	Guardianship,	7967
1856	David W.	Grafton,	Administration,	7968
1832	Deborah	Petersham,	Will,	7969
1865	Deidamia	Leicester,	Administration,	7970
1880	Della M.	Athol,	Guardianship,	7971
1876	Dexter	West Boylston,	Will,	7972
1785	Dorothy	Princeton,	Guardianship,	7973
1865	Dudley	Blackstone,	Administration,	7974
1772	Ebenezer	Sutton,	Guardianship,	7975
1832	Ebenezer	Charlton,	Administration,	7976
1834	Ebenezer	Hubbardston,	Administration,	7977
1849	Ebenezer	Oxford,	Administration,	7978
1871	Ebenezer	Hubbardston,	Administration,	7979
1867	Edgar A.	Southbridge,	Guardianship,	7980
1846	Edith	Shrewsbury,	Guardianship,	7981
1848	Edith	Shrewsbury,	Administration,	7981
1853	Edward	Holden,	Guardianship,	7982
1851	Edward P.	Fitchburg,	Guardianship,	7983
1827	Edwards	Oakham,	Guardianship,	7984
1829	Edwards	Oakham,	Administration,	7985
1856	Edwin	Worcester,	Guardianship,	7986
1860	Edwin M.	Gardner,	Guardianship,	7987
1836	Elbridge	Sterling,	Guardianship,	7988
1869	Elbridge S.	Lunenburg,	Administration,	7989
1747	Eleazer	Rutland,	Administration,	7990
1815	Eli	Western,	Guardianship,	7991
1831	Eli	Western,	Administration,	7992
1768	Elihu	Douglas,	Guardianship,	7993
1840	Elihu	Uxbridge,	Will,	7994
1861	Elijah	New York, N. Y.,	Administration,	7995
1791	Elioner	Worcester,	Guardianship,	7996
1858	Elisha	Upton,	Will,	7997
1857	Eliza J.	Hubbardston,	Guardianship,	7998
1872	Eliza J.	Gardner,	Guardianship,	7999
1853	Eliza P.	Winchester, N. H.,	Administration,	8000
1813	Elizabeth	Princeton,	Administration,	8001
1820	Elizabeth	Fitchburg,	Will,	8002

YEAR.	NAME.	RESIDENCE.	NATURE.	CASE.
1847	BROWN, Elizabeth	Holden,	Guardianship,	8003
1865	Elizabeth	Milford,	Will,	8004
1828	Elizabeth D.	Lunenburg,	Guardianship,	8005
1853	Elizabeth D.	Fitchburg,	Will,	8006
1760	Elizabeth L.	Worcester,	Guardianship,	8007
1857	Ella	Oxford,	Administration,	8008
1865	Ellen M.	Douglas,	Guardianship,	8009
1815	Elvira E.	Lunenburg,	Guardianship,	8010
1856	Emily	Worcester,	Guardianship,	8011
1837	Emily L.	Webster,	Guardianship,	8012
1874	Emma C. E.	Worcester,	Administration,	8013
1867	Emma L.	Oxford,	Guardianship,	8014
1863	Emma R.	Worcester,	Guardianship,	8015
1825	Enoch	Lunenburg,	Administration,	8016
1870	Enoch	Douglas,	Administration,	8017
1815	Enoch D.	Lunenburg,	Guardianship,	8018
1866	Ernest F.	Millbury,	Guardianship,	8019
1803	Esther	Winchendon,	Will,	8020
1827	Esther	Oakham,	Guardianship,	8021
1793	Eunice	Royalston,	Guardianship,	8022
1828	Eunice	Oakham,	Administration,	8023
1851	Eunice E.	Boylston,	Guardianship,	8024
1867	Everett A. R.	Southbridge,	Guardianship,	8025
1801	Ezekiel	Dudley,	Administration,	8026
1801	Ezekiel	Dudley,	Guardianship,	8027
1870	Ezekiel H.	Phillipston,	Will,	8028
1878	Ezekiel P.	Mendon,	Administration,	8029
1878	Ezra P.	Worcester,	Will,	8030
1857	Fidelia T.	Webster,	Guardianship,	8031
1815	Frances	Western,	Guardianship,	8032
1847	Francis A.	Blackstone,	Guardianship,	8033
1874	Francis W.	Uxbridge,	Adoption, etc.,	8034
1873	Franklin	Winchendon,	Administration,	8035
1847	Franklin S.	West Boylston,	Guardianship,	8036
1864	Frederic C.	Worcester,	Will,	8037
1866	Frederick E.	Millbury,	Guardianship,	8038
1857	Frederick L.	Hubbardston,	Guardianship,	8039
1837	Frederick P.	Phillipston,	Guardianship,	8040
1840	Freeman	Hubbardston,	Administration,	8041
1876	Genieve E.	Placerville, Cal.,	Guardianship,	8042
1826	George	Westminster,	Guardianship,	8043
1854	George	Ashburnham,	Administration,	8044
1854	George	Ashburnham,	Guardianship,	8045
1859	George	Blackstone,	Will,	8046
1866	George	Winchendon,	Administration,	8047

YEAR.	NAME.	RESIDENCE.	NATURE.	CASE.
1868	BROWN, George	Southborough,	Guardianship,	8048
1865	George A.	Douglas,	Guardianship,	8049
1847	George B.	West Boylston,	Guardianship,	8050
1862	George E.	Blackstone,	Guardianship,	8051
1863	George E.	Leicester,	Administration,	8052
1844	George L.	Douglas,	Guardianship,	8053
1836	George R.	Winchendon,	Guardianship,	8054
1859	George W.	Galesburg, Ill.,	Administration,	8055
1865	George W.	Holden,	Administration,	8056
1865	Gideon	Webster,	Administration,	8057
1835	Gilson	Sterling,	Administration,	8058
1867	Grace	Sutton,	Administration,	8059
1846	Greenleaf D.	Douglas,	Guardianship,	8060
1760	Hannah	Worcester,	Guardianship,	8061
1859	Hannah	Templeton,	Administration,	8062
1836	Hannah B.	Sterling,	Guardianship,	8063
1876	Hannah H.	Oxford,	Administration,	8064
1856	Hannah P.	Grafton,	Guardianship,	8065
1879	Harriet	Gardner,	Will,	8066
1826	Harriet K.	Rutland,	Guardianship,	8067
1805	Harvey	Brookfield,	Guardianship,	8068
1864	Hattie A.	Leicester,	Adoption, etc.,	8069
1876	Henry	Charlton,	Guardianship,	8070
1877	Henry	Charlton,	Administration,	8070
1867	Henry E.	Templeton,	Administration,	8071
1876	Hermon	Westminster,	Will,	8072
1804	Hezekiah	Winchendon,	Administration,	8073
1865	Hezekiah	Winchendon,	Will,	8074
1815	Homer	Lunenburg,	Guardianship,	8075
1867	Hopestill	Upton,	Will,	8076
1880	Horace P.	Grafton,	Will,	8077
1804	Hori	Brookfield,	Guardianship,	8078
1826	Huldah	Westminster,	Guardianship,	8079
1857	Huldah	Winchendon,	Will,	8080
1801	Ira	Brookfield,	Guardianship,	8081
1880	Ira II.	Berlin,	Administration,	8082
1872	Isaac	Providence, R. I.,	Foreign Will,	8083
1852	Isaac L.	Oxford,	Administration,	8084
1763	Isaiah	Holden,	Guardianship.	8085
1849	Jacob	Leominster,	Administration,	8086
1750	James	Rutland,	Will,	8087
1778	James	Worcester,	Will,	8088
1797	James	Winchendon,	Guardianship,	8089
1819	James	Oakham,	Will,	8090
1827	James	Oakham,	Guardianship,	8091

YEAR.	NAME.	RESIDENCE.	NATURE.	CASE.
1835	BROWN, James	Warren,	Will,	8092
1839	James	Princeton,	Will,	8093
1866	James	Worcester,	Administration,	8094
1872	James	Southbridge,	Guardianship,	8095
1872	James	Oakham,	Will,	8096
1878	James	Princeton,	Administration,	8097
1856	James S.	Worcester,	Guardianship,	8098
1842	Jane M.	Brookfield,	Guardianship,	8099
1804	Jemima	Westminster,	Administration,	8100
1879	Jennie P.	Winchendon,	Will,	8101
1875	Jeremiah	Charlton,	Will,	8102
1864	Jerusha D.	Hubbardston,	Will,	8103
1815	Joel	Western,	Administration,	8104
1851	Joel	Boylston,	Will,	8105
1761	John	Douglas,	Administration,	8106
1770	John	Holden,	Guardianship,	8107
1787	John	Leicester,	Guardianship,	8108
1788	John	Worcester,	Guardianship,	8109
1791	John	Holden,	Guardianship,	8110
1793	John	Royalston,	Guardianship,	8111
1801	John	Dudley,	Guardianship,	8112
1803	John	Bolton,	Administration,	8113
1813	John	Douglas,	Administration,	8114
1820	John	Sterling,	Administration,	8115
1834	John	Webster,	Will,	8116
1854	John	Northbridge,	Guardianship,	8117
1856	John	Douglas,	Administration,	8118
1864	John	Charlton,	Guardianship,	8119
1868	John	West Boylston,	Administration,	8120
1821	John A.	Westminster,	Guardianship,	8121
1860	John A.	Worcester,	Guardianship,	8122
1865	John A.	Webster,	Administration,	8123
1812	John F.	Fitchburg,	Administration,	8124
1878	John G.	Athol,	Will,	8125
1832	John M.	Paxton,	Will,	8126
1836	John N. W.	Sterling,	Guardianship,	8127
1851	John P.	Ashburnham,	Administration,	8128
1845	John S.	Sutton,	Will,	8129
1842	Jonah	Douglas,	Pension,	8130
1772	Jonas	Sutton,	Will,	8131
1814	Jonas	Millbury,	Guardianship,	8132
1827	Jonas	Rutland,	Administration,	8133
1874	Jonas	Petersham,	Administration,	8134
1879	Jonas	Petersham,	Will,	8135
1866	Jonas B.	Princeton,	Will,	8136

YEAR.	NAME.	RESIDENCE.	NATURE.	CASE.
1821	BROWN, Jonathan	Westminster,	Will,	8137
1840	Jonathan	Gardner.	Will,	8138
1860	Jonathan	Gardner,	Administration,	8139
1876	Jonathan P.	North Brookfield,	Administration,	8140
1803	Joseph	Oxford,	Guardianship,	8141
1812	Joseph	Fitchburg,	Guardianship,	8142
1814	Joseph	Petersham,	Will,	8143
1822	Joseph	Oxford,	Will,	8144
1826	Joseph	Westminster,	Guardianship,	8145
1826	Joseph	Westminster,	Administration,	8146
1849	Joseph	Sterling,	Guardianship,	8147
1849	Joseph	Oxford,	Will,	8148
1861	Joseph	Northbridge,	Guardianship,	8149
1871	Joseph	Oxford,	Will,	8150
1846	Josephine M.	Douglas,	Guardianship,	8151
1859	Josephine M.	Galesburg, Ill.,	Guardianship,	8152
1793	Joshua	Royalston,	Guardianship,	8153
1774	Joshua C.	Sturbridge,	Guardianship,	8154
1835	Joshua I.	Charlton,	Administration,	8155
1808	Joshua M.	Belchertown,	Guardianship,	8156
1758	Josiah	Brookfield,	Guardianship,	8157
1758	Josiah	Mendon,	Guardianship,	8158
1814	Josiah	Millbury,	Administration,	8159
1828	Josiah	Sturbridge,	Guardianship,	8160
1836	Josiah	Winchendon,	Will,	8161
1837	Josiah	Bolton,	Administration,	8162
1839	Josiah	Webster,	Will,	8163
1844	Josiah	Sturbridge,	Administration,	8160
1853	Josiah	Stow,	Will,	8164
1860	Josiah	Fitchburg,	Will,	8165
1849	Josiah L.	Worcester,	Guardianship,	8166
1831	Josiah P.	West Boylston,	Administration,	8167
1762	Jude	Brookfield,	Guardianship,	8168
1851	Julia P.	Boylston,	Guardianship,	8169
1840	Juliann	Smithfield,	Guardianship,	8170
1854	Justus	Ashburnham,	Guardianship,	8171
1875	Kendall L.	Worcester,	Administration,	8172
1815	Learned	Oxford,	Guardianship,	8173
1867	Leonard	Phillipston,	Administration,	8174
1814	Levi	Lancaster,	Guardianship,	8175
1828	Levi	Western,	Guardianship,	8176
1836	Levi	Fitchburg,	Guardianship,	8177
1854	Levi H.	Blackstone,	Guardianship,	8178
1870	Lewis B.	Bolton,	Will,	8179
1834	Lois	Webster,	Guardianship,	8180

YEAR.	NAME.	RESIDENCE.	NATURE.	CASE.
1835	BROWN, Lois	Webster,	Administration,	8180
1881	Louis M.	Templeton,	Guardianship,	8181
1807	Louisa	Sturbridge,	Guardianship,	8182
1838	Louisa	Charlton,	Guardianship,	8183
1857	Louisa P.	Hardwick,	Guardianship,	8184
1846	Lucien	Charlton,	Guardianship,	8185
1851	Lucinda	Fitchburg,	Guardianship,	8186
1846	Lucinda W.	Charlton,	Guardianship,	8187
1836	Lucius	Northborough,	Guardianship,	8188
1826	Lucy	Westminster,	Guardianship,	8189
1862	Lucy	Sturbridge,	Will,	8190
1863	Lucy	Worcester,	Will,	8191
1872	Lucy A.	Gardner,	Guardianship,	8192
1851	Lucy S.	Boylston,	Guardianship,	8193
1772	Luke	Worcester,	Administration,	8194
1777	Luke	Worcester,	Will,	8195
1788	Luke	Worcester,	Guardianship,	8196
1760	Luke, Jr.	Worcester,	Guardianship,	8197
1846	Lumen	Charlton,	Guardianship,	8198
1857	Lurah	Hubbardston,	Guardianship,	8199
1808	Luther	Belchertown,	Guardianship,	8200
1774	Lydia	Sturbridge,	Guardianship,	8201
1788	Lydia	Worcester,	Guardianship,	8202
1803	Lydia	Gerry,	Guardianship,	8203
1805	Lydia	Douglas,	Administration,	8204
1868	Lydia	Oxford,	Will,	8205
1841	Lyman	Hubbardston,	Guardianship,	8206
1854	Marcus M.	Blackstone,	Guardianship,	8207
1791	Margarett	Worcester,	Guardianship,	8208
1879	Marshall D.	Paxton,	Administration,	8209
1851	Martha	Fitchburg,	Guardianship,	8210
1856	Martha J.	Grafton,	Guardianship,	8211
1866	Martha W.	Winchendon,	Will,	8212
1804	Mary	Bolton,	Guardianship,	8213
1815	Mary	Oxford,	Guardianship,	8214
1838	Mary	Worcester,	Administration,	8215
1843	Mary	Harvard,	Will,	8216
1844	Mary	Webster,	Pension,	8217
1847	Mary	Blackstone	Guardianship,	8218
1848	Mary	Worcester,	Guardianship,	8219
1859	Mary	Paxton,	Administration,	8220
1860	Mary	Lunenburg,	Will,	8221
1873	Mary	West Brookfield,	Adoption, etc.,	8222
1839	Mary A.	Rutland,	Guardianship,	8223
1847	Mary A.	Holden,	Guardianship,	8224

Year.	Name.	Residence.	Nature.	Case.
1880	BROWN, Mary A.	Sutton,	Administration,	8225
1877	Mary C.	Worcester,	Administration,	8226
1881	Mary E.	Worcester,	Administration,	8227
1863	Mary F.	Fitchburg,	Will,	8228
1879	Mary F.	Lunenburg,	Guardianship,	8229
1828	Mary J.	Lunenburg,	Guardianship,	8230
1853	Mary J.	Fitchburg,	Will,	8231
1854	Mary J.	Ashburnham,	Guardianship,	8232
1856	Mary L.	Worcester,	Guardianship,	8233
1865	Mary M.	Wethersfield, Conn.,	Administration,	8234
1865	Mary R.	Douglas,	Guardianship,	8235
1874	Mary S.	Worcester,	Administration,	8236
1826	Mary S. C.	Rutland,	Guardianship,	8237
1881	Mary W.	Hubbardston,	Administration,	8238
1838	Menellia	Charlton,	Guardianship,	8239
1842	Mercy	Phillipston,	Administration,	8240
1803	Meriam	Oxford,	Guardianship,	8241
1874	M. Minerva	North Brookfield,	Administration,	8242
1826	Moses	Oakham,	Administration,	8243
1827	Moses	Oakham,	Guardianship,	8244
1877	Moses D.	Charlton,	Administration,	8245
1880	Myron	Brookfield,	Guardianship,	8246
1881	Myron L.	Templeton,	Guardianship,	8247
1808	Nabby	Sterling,	Guardianship,	8248
1836	Nancy	Fitchburg,	Guardianship,	8249
1854	Nancy	Phillipston,	Administration,	8250
1852	Nancy H.	Worcester,	Administration,	8251
1839	Nancy M.	Rutland,	Guardianship,	8252
1827	Nathan	Oakham,	Guardianship,	8253
1835	Nathan	Oakham,	Will,	8254
1841	Nathan	Southbridge,	Pension,	8255
1873	Nathan	Lancaster,	Guardianship,	8256
1877	Nathan	Lancaster,	Administration,	8256
1798	Nathaniel	Petersham,	Administration,	8257
1811	Nathaniel	Dana,	Guardianship,	8258
1842	Nathaniel	Brookfield,	Administration,	8259
1861	Nathaniel	Worcester,	Will,	8260
1772	Nathaniel R.	Leominster,	Guardianship,	8261
1813	Nathaniel S.	Worcester,	Administration,	8262
1864	Nellie	Webster,	Adoption, etc.,	8263
1838	Nelson T.	Charlton,	Guardianship,	8264
1873	Nettie A.	Warren,	Administration,	8265
1854	Octavius L.	Ashburnham,	Guardianship,	8266
1797	Olive	Winchendon,	Guardianship,	8267
1808	Olive	Sterling,	Guardianship,	8268

YEAR.	NAME.	RESIDENCE.	NATURE.	CASE.
1812	BROWN, Olive	Unknown,	Guardianship,	8269
1847	Olive	West Boylston,	Administration,	8270
1878	Olive H.	Stoneham,	Partition,	8271
1756	Oliver	Mendon,	Administration,	8272
1768	Oliver	Douglas,	Guardianship,	8273
1771	Oliver	Douglas,	Guardianship,	8274
1858	Oliver	Hubbardston,	Administration,	8275
1857	Oliver H.	Hubbardston,	Guardianship,	8276
1871	Oratus S.	Webster,	Will,	8277
1854	Orrin	Blackstone,	Administration,	8278
1832	Patty	Paxton,	Will,	8279
1841	Pearson	Fitchburg,	Will,	8280
1829	Peter	Lunenburg,	Will,	8281
1812	Philemon	Lunenburg,	Administration,	8282
1860	Philenia	Grafton,	Will,	8283
1827	Phillip	Oxford,	Will,	8284
1812	Polly	Fitchburg,	Guardianship,	8285
1849	Polly	Rutland,	Will,	8286
1795	Prudence	Sterling,	Administration,	8287
1849	Prudence S.	Leicester,	Guardianship,	8288
1825	Rebecca	Princeton,	Will,	8289
1871	Rebecca	Dudley,	Administration,	8290
1876	Reuben	Harvard,	Will,	8291
1819	Rhoda	Oakham,	Administration,	8292
1768	Robert	Douglas,	Guardianship,	8293
1791	Robert	Worcester,	Guardianship,	8294
1875	Roxana J.	Sutton,	Guardianship,	8295
1814	Ruhama	Millbury,	Guardianship,	8296
1804	Ruth	Dudley,	Will,	8297
1855	Ruth	Princeton,	Administration,	8298
1855	Ruth	Princeton,	Pension,	8299
1793	Sally	Rutland,	Guardianship,	8300
1801	Sally	Charlton,	Guardianship,	8301
1826	Sally	Westminster,	Guardianship,	8302
1849	Sally	Phillipston,	Administration,	8303
1871	Sally	West Boylston,	Administration,	8304
1871	Sally	Fitchburg,	Guardianship,	8305
1830	Salome	Oakham,	Administration,	8306
1738	Samuel	Mendon,	Administration,	8307
1757	Samuel	Shrewsbury,	Administration,	8308
1760	Samuel	Worcester,	Guardianship,	8309
1768	Samuel	Douglas,	Guardianship,	8310
1785	Samuel	Worcester,	Administration,	8311
1788	Samuel	Worcester,	Guardianship,	8312
1793	Samuel	Paxton,	Will,	8313

Year.	Name.	Residence.	Nature.	Case.
1801	BROWN, Samuel	Charlton,	Guardianship,	8314
1803	Samuel	Unknown,	Guardianship,	8315
1816	Samuel, 2d	Sterling,	Administration,	8316
1834	Samuel	Sterling,	Will,	8317
1834	Samuel	Sterling,	Pension,	8318
1837	Samuel	Charlton,	Administration,	8319
1847	Samuel	West Boylston,	Will,	8320
1854	Samuel	Winchendon,	Administration,	8321
1864	Samuel	Gardner,	Guardianship,	8322
1833	Samuel, Jr.	Winchendon,	Administration,	8323
1838	Samuel A.	Charlton,	Guardianship,	8324
1837	Samuel C.	Webster,	Guardianship,	8325
1836	Samuel F.	Northborough,	Guardianship,	8326
1875	Samuel H.	Westborough,	Administration,	8327
1876	Samuel S.	Winchendon,	Administration,	8328
1833	Samuel W.	Winchendon,	Guardianship,	8329
1758	Sarah	Mendon,	Guardianship,	8330
1866	Sarah	Worcester,	Administration,	8331
1856	Sarah D.	Worcester,	Guardianship,	8332
1861	Sarah F.	Northbridge	Guardianship,	8333
1871	Sarah J.	Blackstone,	Guardianship,	8334
1849	Sarah M.	Worcester,	Guardianship,	8335
1880	Sarah M.	Fitchburg,	Administration,	8336
1855	Seth	Winchendon,	Guardianship,	8337
1871	Seth	Winchendon,	Will,	8338
1841	Sewall	Hubbardston,	Guardianship,	8339
1758	Silas	Mendon,	Guardianship,	8340
1846	Silas A.	Douglas,	Guardianship,	8341
1878	Simeon	Webster,	Will,	8342
1846	Simeon A.	Douglas,	Guardianship,	8343
1857	Sophia	Oxford,	Will,	8344
1875	Sophia A.	Worcester,	Administration,	8345
1815	Sophrina	Western,	Guardianship,	8346
1856	Stephen	Grafton,	Will,	8347
1864	Sukey	Lunenburg,	Administration,	8348
1846	Sullivan R.	Douglas,	Guardianship,	8349
1861	Susan A.	Northbridge,	Guardianship,	8350
1815	Sylvanus	Oxford,	Guardianship,	8351
1862	Sylvanus	Douglas,	Administration,	8352
1857	Sylvester	Paxton,	Will,	8353
1837	Tarissa E.	Phillipston,	Guardianship,	8354
1770	Thaddeus	Holden,	Guardianship,	8355
1803	Thaddeus	Phillipston,	Administration,	8356
1836	Theodore	Sterling,	Guardianship,	8357
1852	Theodore	Leicester,	Guardianship,	8358

Year.	Name.	Residence.	Nature.	Case.
1879	BROWN, Theophilus	Worcester,	Will,	8359
1751	Thomas	Brookfield,	Administration,	8360
1756	Thomas	Lunenburg,	Administration,	8361
1777	Thomas	Worcester,	Will,	8362
1795	Thomas	Sterling,	Will,	8363
1844	Thomas	Bolton,	Guardianship,	8364
1857	Thomas B.	Bolton,	Administration,	8365
1808	Thomas H.	Sterling,	Guardianship,	8366
1866	Thomas H.	Hubbardston,	Administration,	8367
1763	Timothy	Holden,	Will,	8368
1804	Timothy	Westminster,	Guardianship,	8369
1878	Timothy	Westminster,	Will,	8370
1858	Turner C.	Dudley,	Guardianship,	8371
1846	Uriah	Grafton,	Administration,	8372
1871	Walter R.	Royalston,	Administration,	8373
1865	Walter W.	Douglas,	Guardianship,	8374
1839	Warren C.	Rutland,	Guardianship,	8375
1865	Willard	Worcester,	Administration,	8376
1865	Willard, Jr.	Worcester,	Administration,	8377
1756	William	Brookfield,	Guardianship,	8378
1771	William	Lancaster,	Guardianship,	8379
1772	William	Oxford,	Administration,	8380
1780	William	Northbridge,	Will,	8381
1789	William	Worcester,	Administration,	8382
1793	William	Brookfield,	Administration,	8383
1802	William	Framingham,	Partition,	8384
1807	William	Brookfield,	Guardianship,	8385
1810	William	Fitchburg,	Will,	8386
1852	William	Sutton,	Administration,	8387
1853	William	Hubbardston,	Administration,	8388
1854	William	Ashburnham,	Guardianship,	8389
1860	William	Winchendon,	Will,	8390
1860	William	Lunenburg,	Will,	8391
1869	William	Worcester,	Will,	8392
1870	William	Leominster,	Will,	8393
1870	William	Brookfield,	Guardianship,	8394
1794	William, Jr.	Worcester,	Administration,	8395
1812	William A.	Fitchburg,	Guardianship,	8396
1842	William C.	Winchendon,	Administration,	8397
1857	William C.	Dudley,	Will,	8398
1837	William E.	Webster,	Guardianship,	8399
1857	William E.	Hubbardston,	Guardianship,	8400
1853	William F.	Phillipston,	Guardianship,	8401
1875	William H.	Boston,	Adoption, etc.,	8402
1814	William L.	Douglas,	Guardianship,	8403

YEAR.	NAME.	RESIDENCE.	NATURE.	CASE.
1879	BROWN, William L.	Lunenburg,	Administration,	8404
1880	William R.	Athol,	Guardianship,	8405
1865	William T.	Leicester,	Will,	8406
1756	Zachariah	Brookfield,	Guardianship,	8407
1756	Zachariah	Brookfield,	Will,	8408
1828	BROWNELL, Elizabeth	Charlton,	Administration,	8409
1864	BROWNING, Albert H.	Hubbardston,	Guardianship,	8410
1865	Alice C.	Templeton,	Guardianship,	8411
1819	Almira	Rutland,	Guardianship,	8412
1875	Andrew J.	Dudley,	Guardianship,	8413
1863	Asa B.	Hubbardston,	Administration,	8414
1810	Asaph	Hubbardston,	Guardianship,	8415
1837	Betsey B.	Hubbardston,	Guardianship,	8416
1875	Charles	Spencer,	Administration,	8417
1875	Charles C.	Dudley,	Guardianship,	8418
1864	Charles G.	Hubbardston,	Guardianship,	8419
1875	Christopher	Dudley,	Will,	8420
1813	Daniel	Rutland,	Administration,	8421
1877	Dorcas T.	Dudley,	Will,	8422
1864	Edgar A.	Hubbardston,	Guardianship,	8423
1866	Edward P.	Worcester,	Guardianship,	8424
1810	Eliza	Hubbardston,	Guardianship,	8425
1869	Eliza	Newbury, O.,	Administration,	8426
1866	Emma J.	Barre,	Guardianship,	8427
1852	Franklin	Hardwick,	Administration,	8428
1860	Franklin J.	Hardwick,	Guardianship,	8429
1861	Frederick	Hardwick,	Administration,	8430
1780	George	Rutland,	Guardianship,	8431
1810	George	Hubbardston,	Guardianship,	8432
1815	George	Rutland,	Guardianship,	8433
1845	George	Webster,	Administration,	8434
1837	George D.	Hubbardston,	Guardianship,	8435
1865	George D.	Templeton,	Administration,	8436
1845	George H.	Webster,	Guardianship,	8437
1865	George H.	Templeton,	Guardianship,	8438
1875	Hannah A.	Dudley,	Guardianship,	8439
1862	Harriet S.	Hardwick,	Guardianship,	8440
1860	Helen M.	Hardwick,	Guardianship,	8441
1872	Henry H.	Hubbardston,	Guardianship,	8442
1865	Herbert L.	Templeton,	Guardianship,	8443
1749	James	Rutland,	Will,	8444
1770	James	Rutland,	Administration,	8445
1808	James	Rutland,	Will,	8446
1820	James	Rutland,	Administration,	8447
1837	James	Hubbardston,	Administration,	8448

YEAR.	NAME.	RESIDENCE.	NATURE.	CASE.
1837	BROWNING, James	Hubbardston,	Guardianship,	8449
1871	James	Hardwick,	Will,	8450
1865	James W.	Petersham,	Guardianship,	8451
1749	John	Rutland,	Guardianship,	8452
1809	John	Hubbardston,	Will,	8453
1812	John	Rutland,	Will,	8454
1813	John	Rutland,	Guardianship,	8455
1837	John	Hubbardston,	Guardianship,	8456
1859	John	Hubbardston,	Administration,	8457
1780	Joseph	Rutland,	Guardianship,	8458
1810	Joshua	Hubbardston,	Guardianship,	8459
1837	Josiah	Hubbardston,	Guardianship,	8460
1846	Lewis H.	Blackstone,	Administration,	8461
1864	Lucius H.	Hubbardston,	Guardianship,	8462
1810	Lucy	Hubbardston,	Guardianship,	8463
1864	Lyman W.	Hubbardston,	Guardianship,	8464
1845	Mareon	Rutland,	Guardianship,	8465
1813	Margaret	Rutland,	Administration,	8466
1749	Martha	Rutland,	Guardianship,	8467
1780	Martha	Rutland,	Guardianship,	8468
1845	Martha A.	Rutland,	Guardianship,	8469
1862	Mary A.	Hardwick,	Will,	8470
1866	Mary L.	Worcester,	Guardianship,	8471
1845	Mary S.	Rutland,	Guardianship,	8472
1877	Nellie F.	Spencer,	Guardianship,	8473
1780	Rebecca	Rutland,	Guardianship,	8474
1810	Rebecca	Hubbardston,	Guardianship,	8475
1876	Rebecca	Rutland,	Guardianship,	8476
1846	Reuben	Rutland,	Administration,	8477
1864	Richardson H.	Paxton,	Administration,	8478
1862	Sally	Spencer,	Administration,	8479
1749	Samuel	Rutland,	Guardianship,	8480
1784	Samuel	Rutland,	Administration,	8481
1848	Samuel	Rutland,	Guardianship,	8482
1867	Sarah E.	Rutland,	Adoption, etc.,	8483
1864	Sarah L.	Hubbardston,	Guardianship,	8484
1837	Sibel M.	Hubbardston,	Guardianship,	8485
1810	Susan	Hubbardston,	Guardianship,	8486
1864	Susan E.	Hubbardston,	Guardianship,	8487
1755	Tristram	Rutland,	Will,	8488
1812	Tristram	Rutland,	Guardianship,	8489
1866	Walter E.	Worcester,	Guardianship,	8490
1806	William	Rutland,	Will,	8491
1858	William	Hardwick,	Will,	8492
1845	William A.	Abington, Conn.,	Foreign Sale,	8493

YEAR.	NAME.	RESIDENCE.	NATURE.	CASE.
1875	BROWNING, William J.	Dudley,	Guardianship,	8494
1760	BRUCE, Abigail	Southborough,	Guardianship,	8495
1790	Abigail	Brookfield,	Guardianship,	8496
1805	Abigail	Templeton,	Guardianship,	8497
1758	Abijah,	Grafton,	Guardianship,	8498
1767	Abner	Grafton,	Guardianship,	8499
1823	Anna	Shrewsbury,	Will,	8500
1824	Anna	Berlin,	Administration,	8501
1771	Artemas	Westborough,	Guardianship,	8502
1764	Benjamin	Grafton,	Guardianship,	8503
1758	Charles	Grafton,	Administration,	8504
1785	Charles	Brookfield,	Administration,	8505
1790	Charles	Brookfield,	Guardianship,	8506
1871	Charles	Athol,	Will,	8507
1850	Charles S.	Petersham,	Administration,	8508
1779	Daniel	Bolton,	Will,	8509
1760	David	Southborough,	Guardianship,	8510
1772	David	Southborough,	Guardianship,	8511
1877	Dexter	West Brookfield,	Will,	8512
1767	Eli	Grafton,	Guardianship,	8513
1839	Eli	Templeton,	Administration,	8514
1799	Eliza	Grafton,	Guardianship,	8515
1847	Eliza J.	Oxford,	Guardianship,	8516
1810	Elizabeth	Grafton,	Administration,	8517
1847	Emily C.	Oxford,	Guardianship,	8518
1759	Ephraim	Westborough,	Administration,	8519
1839	Esther	Phillipston,	Pension,	8520
1804	Eunice	Grafton,	Will,	8521
1812	Freeman	Templeton,	Guardianship,	8522
1768	George	Mendon,	Administration,	8523
1788	George	Leicester,	Administration,	8524
1880	Hannah	Berlin,	Will,	8525
1824	John	Hardwick,	Will,	8526
1865	John	West Boylston,	Administration,	8527
1808	John M.	Templeton,	Guardianship,	8528
1803	Jonathan	Shrewsbury,	Administration,	8529
1805	Jonathan	Templeton,	Guardianship,	8530
1816	Jonathan	Northborough,	Will,	8531
1870	Jonathan	Northborough,	Administration,	8532
1749	Joseph	Mendon,	Administration,	8533
1799	Joseph	Grafton,	Will,	8534
1799	Joseph	Grafton,	Guardianship,	8535
1758	Josiah	Southborough,	Administration,	8536
1760	Josiah	Southborough,	Guardianship,	8537
1805	Josiah	Templeton,	Will,	8538

YEAR.	NAME.	RESIDENCE.	NATURE.	CASE.
1873	BRUCE, Julia A.	Oxford,	Administration,	8539
1880	Leha G.	Berlin,	Guardianship,	8540
1847	Lott W.	Oxford,	Administration,	8541
1790	Lucy	Brookfield,	Guardianship,	8542
1807	Lucy	Northborough,	Guardianship,	8543
1837	Lucy E.	Northborough,	Guardianship,	8544
1807	Lydia	Northborough,	Guardianship,	8545
1868	Lydia G.	Oxford,	Will,	8546
1868	L. Ellen	Templeton,	Will,	8547
1877	Nathan	Southborough,	Administration,	8548
1859	Olive	Westminster,	Will,	8549
1814	Otis	Marlborough,	Guardianship,	8550
1853	Otis	Northborough,	Will,	8551
1877	Phebe S.	West Boylston,	Administration,	8552
1733	Roger	Southborough,	Will,	8553
1748	Roger	Holden,	Guardianship,	8554
1818	Roger	North Brookfield,	Will,	8555
1742	Samuel	Holden,	Administration,	8556
1830	Samuel	Westminster,	Will,	8557
1799	Sarah	Grafton,	Guardianship,	8558
1817	Sarah	Grafton,	Administration,	8559
1806	Silas	Northborough,	Administration,	8560
1807	Silas	Northborough,	Guardianship,	8561
1816	Silas	Templeton,	Guardianship,	8562
1836	Silas	Northborough,	Administration,	8563
1854	Silas	Templeton,	Pension,	8564
1767	Simeon	Grafton,	Guardianship,	8565
1810	Simeon	Gerry,	Administration,	8566
1796	Simon	Grafton,	Administration,	8567
1807	Solomon B.	Northborough,	Guardianship,	8568
1790	Stephen	Leicester,	Guardianship,	8569
1854	Susan B.	Northborough,	Will,	8570
1807	Susanna B.	Northborough,	Guardianship,	8571
1879	Sylvanus	Berlin,	Will,	8572
1744	Thomas	Bolton,	Administration,	8573
1877	William S.	Grafton,	Administration,	8574
1749	Zeruiah	Bolton,	Guardianship,	8575
1871	BRUNNELL, Henry	Worcester,	Administration,	8576
1807	BRUNSON, Mary	Mendon,	Guardianship,	8577
1805	Willis	Mendon,	Will,	8578
1807	Willis	Mendon,	Guardianship,	8579
1865	BRUSO, Charles	Worcester,	Administration,	8580
1879	Joseph	West Boylston,	Will,	8581
	BRYANT AND BRIANT,			
1850	Abigail	Leicester,	Administration,	8582

Year.	Name.	Residence.	Nature.	Case.
	BRYANT and BRIANT,			
1850	Abigail	Leicester,	Pension,	8583
1841	Albert	Royalston,	Guardianship,	8584
1818	Alfred S.	Westborough,	Guardianship,	8585
1802	Allis	Leicester,	Guardianship,	8586
1874	Anna	Phillipston,	Administration,	8587
1865	Arnold	Holden,	Administration,	8588
1858	Artemas	Petersham,	Administration,	8589
1829	Asaph	Sutton,	Administration,	8590
1845	Betsey	Rutland,	Administration,	8591
1833	Charles	Oakham,	Guardianship,	8592
1835	Christopher N.	Westborough,	Guardianship,	8593
1864	Consider	Sutton,	Administration,	8594
1781	David	Leicester,	Guardianship,	8595
1833	David	Oakham,	Guardianship,	8596
1841	David	Leicester,	Will,	8597
1850	Edward W.	Worcester,	Guardianship,	8598
1872	Eleanor	Northbridge,	Guardianship,	8599
1850	Elizabeth C.	Princeton,	Guardianship,	8600
1841	Eunice H.	Royalston,	Guardianship,	8601
1853	Finette L.	Athol,	Adoption, etc.,	8602
1854	Finette L.	Athol,	Guardianship,	8602
1870	Francis A.	Paxton,	Change of Name,	8603
1876	Frederick J.	Athol,	Will,	8604
1850	George	Princeton,	Guardianship,	8605
1869	George	Worcester,	Adoption, etc.,	8606
1865	George E.	Templeton,	Guardianship,	8607
1876	George W.	Templeton,	Will,	8608
1860	Hannah	Princeton,	Will,	8609
1859	Harriet A.	Rutland,	Guardianship,	8610
1826	Harrison	Petersham,	Guardianship,	8611
1875	Ida E.	Bolton,	Guardianship,	8612
1802	Ira	Leicester,	Guardianship,	8613
1875	Ira	Worcester,	Will,	8614
1836	Isaac	Rutland,	Administration,	8615
1836	Isaac	Rutland,	Pension,	8616
1858	Isaac	Rutland,	Administration,	8617
1781	Jacob	Leicester,	Will,	8618
1838	James M.	Templeton,	Administration,	8619
1850	James T.	Worcester,	Guardianship,	8620
1825	Joel	Petersham,	Administration,	8621
1802	John	Leicester,	Guardianship,	8622
1833	John	Oakham,	Will,	8623
1865	John	Princeton,	Administration,	8624
1833	John F.	Oakham,	Guardianship,	8625

YEAR.	NAME.	RESIDENCE.	NATURE.	CASE.
	BRYANT AND BRIANT,			
1850	John W.	Princeton,	Guardianship,	8626
1781	Jonathan	Leicester,	Guardianship,	8627
1802	Jonathan	Leicester,	Will,	8628
1853	Jonathan	Athol,	Administration,	8629
1781	Joseph	Leicester,	Guardianship,	8630
1874	Joseph	Paxton,	Will,	8631
1841	Lucian	Royalston,	Administration,	8632
1794	Lydia	Petersham,	Guardianship,	8633
1874	Lydia T.	Barre,	Administration,	8634
1802	Lyman	Leicester,	Guardianship,	8635
1877	Melinda	Leicester,	Will,	8636
1818	Melinda A.	Westborough,	Guardianship,	8637
1861	Myra A.	Princeton,	Guardianship,	8638
1875	Myra A.	Princeton,	Administration,	8639
1794	Nahum	Petersham,	Guardianship,	8640
1848	Nathan	Templeton,	Will,	8641
1803	Noyes	Petersham,	Guardianship,	8642
1856	Noyes	Westborough,	Administration,	8643
1811	Polly	Dana,	Administration,	8644
1879	Rachel	Winchendon,	Guardianship,	8645
1853	Richard	Athol,	Administration,	8646
1860	Rufus	Petersham,	Administration,	8647
1793	Samuel	Petersham,	Administration,	8648
1794	Samuel	Petersham,	Guardianship,	8649
1818	Samuel W.	Westborough,	Guardianship,	8650
1757	Seth	Shrewsbury,	Administration,	8651
1844	Shubael	Sutton,	Guardianship,	8652
1841	Solon	Royalston,	Guardianship,	8653
1789	Thomas	Petersham,	Will,	8654
1821	Timothy	Harvard,	Administration,	8655
1850	Walter A.	Worcester,	Guardianship,	8656
1850	Walter A.	Worcester,	Will,	8657
1861	Warren H.	Princeton,	Guardianship,	8658
1777	William	Petersham,	Administration,	8659
1866	William E., Jr.	Rutland,	Administration,	8660
1835	William H.	Westborough,	Guardianship,	8661
1885	BRYDON, Clara E.	Worcester,	Foreign Guard.,	8662
1885	Francis J.	Worcester,	Foreign Guard.,	8663
1876	James J.	Worcester,	Administration,	8664
1885	Robert E.	Worcester,	Foreign Guard.,	8665
1872	BRYSON, Florence E.	Sturbridge,	Guardianship,	8666
1872	Walter D.	Sturbridge,	Guardianship,	8667
1866	BUCK, Abbie	North Brookfield,	Administration,	8668
1876	Alice M. C.	Warren,	Adoption, etc.,	8669

YEAR.	NAME.	RESIDENCE.	NATURE.	CASE.
1870	BUCK, Charles	Westborough,	Will,	8670
1868	Charles M.	Southborough,	Administration,	8671
1871	Delia L.	Southborough,	Guardianship,	8672
1862	Ellen O.	Milford,	Guardianship,	8673
1864	Ernest	Millbury,	Adoption, etc.,	8674
1868	Fostina A.	Southborough,	Guardianship,	8675
1868	Francena E.	Southborough,	Guardianship,	8676
1868	Harriet M.	Southborough,	Guardianship,	8677
1871	Isaac	Leominster,	Administration,	8678
1872	John	Millbury,	Will,	8679
1871	John W.	Southborough,	Administration,	8680
1868	Jonathan	Sturbridge,	Administration,	8681
1777	Joshua	Sutton,	Guardianship,	8682
1827	Joshua	Ward,	Will,	8683
1876	Laura	West Boylston,	Will,	8684
1871	Leona B.	Southborough,	Guardianship,	8685
1744	Mary	Sutton,	Guardianship,	8686
1864	Mary	Millbury,	Administration,	8687
1766	Peter	Worcester,	Guardianship,	8688
1874	Pliny	West Boylston,	Administration,	8689
1807	Rachel	Ward,	Will,	8690
1761	Samuel	Sutton,	Will,	8691
1803	Samuel	Sutton,	Will,	8692
1863	Silas	Sterling,	Will,	8693
1869	Welcome W.	Southbridge,	Administration,	8694
1772	BUCKINGHAM, Jonas	Rutland,	Will,	8695
1876	BUCKLEY, Charles I.	Worcester,	Guardianship,	8696
1881	Cornelius	Worcester,	Will,	8697
1876	Elizabeth A.	Worcester,	Guardianship,	8698
1876	Emma	Worcester,	Guardianship,	8699
1875	Honora	Worcester,	Administration,	8700
1877	Honora	Templeton,	Administration,	8701
1878	Lizzie S.	Northbridge,	Adoption, etc.,	8702
1876	Louis H.	Worcester,	Guardianship,	8703
1877	Margaret	Templeton,	Administration,	8704
1877	Margaret	Templeton,	Administration,	8705
1863	Martha	Leicester,	Administration,	8706
1875	Thomas	Leicester,	Will,	8707
1874	Timothy	Gardner,	Will,	8708
1876	William T.	Worcester,	Administration,	8709
1873	BUCKLIN, Emerson	Ashburnham,	Administration,	8710
1800	Hannah	Northbridge,	Guardianship,	8711
1800	Nabby	Northbridge,	Guardianship,	8712
1798	Nathaniel	Northbridge,	Administration,	8713
1800	Nathaniel	Northbridge,	Guardianship,	8714

YEAR.	NAME.	RESIDENCE.	NATURE.	CASE.
1800	BUCKLIN, Sally	Northbridge,	Guardianship,	8715
1800	Simon	Northbridge,	Guardianship,	8716
1800	Stephen	Northbridge,	Guardianship,	8717
1833	BUCKMAN, Darius	Athol,	Will,	8718
1786	BUCKMINSTER, Barns	Barre,	Guardianship,	8719
1745	Elizabeth	Brookfield,	Guardianship,	8720
1745	Hannah	Brookfield,	Guardianship,	8721
1782	Joseph	Rutland,	Guardianship,	8722
1792	Joseph	Rutland,	Will,	8723
1801	Lucinda	Rutland,	Guardianship,	8724
1745	Mary	Brookfield,	Guardianship,	8725
1745	Samuel	Brookfield,	Guardianship,	8726
1765	Sarah	Brookfield,	Guardianship,	8727
1745	Susanah	Brookfield,	Guardianship,	8728
1765	Thomas	Brookfield,	Will,	8729
1786	William	Barre,	Will,	8730
1782	William S.	Rutland,	Guardianship,	8731
	BUCKNAM AND BUCKNUM,			
1811	Clarissa	Unknown,	Guardianship,	8732
1783	Daniel	Sutton,	Will,	8733
1811	Darius	Athol,	Guardianship,	8734
1747	Jeremiah	Sutton,	Guardianship,	8735
1746	Ruth	Sutton,	Guardianship,	8736
1744	Stephen	Sutton,	Administration,	8737
1875	BUDDING, Benjamin Q.	Worcester,	Administration,	8738
1869	BUELL, George S.	Worcester,	Trus. Sale R'l Est.,	8739
1869	Samuel K.	Worcester,	Trus. Sale R'l Est.,	8740
1874	Samuel K.	Worcester,	Partition,	8741
1863	BUFFINGTON, Amasa F.	Milford,	Guardianship,	8742
1876	Amasa F.	Douglas,	Administration,	8743
1863	Edgar A.	Milford,	Guardianship,	8744
1863	Gilbert H.	Milford,	Guardianship,	8745
1878	John H.	Barrington, R. I.,	Foreign Will,	8746
1877	BUFFUM, Abbie W. S.	Leominster,	Administration,	8747
1864	Amos	Templeton,	Administration,	8748
1830	Benjamin	Douglas,	Will,	8749
1866	Benjamin	Uxbridge,	Will,	8750
1878	Benjamin	Providence, R. I.,	Trustee,	
1879	Benjamin	Warwick, R. I.,	Foreign Will,	8751
1874	Betsey A.	Templeton,	Administration,	8752
1836	Elizabeth	Leominster,	Administration,	8753
1864	Elsie E.	Templeton,	Guardianship,	8754
1872	Emma J.	Worcester,	Guardianship,	8755
1868	George R.	Douglas,	Guardianship,	8756
1868	Harriet	Douglas,	Guardianship,	8757

YEAR.	NAME.	RESIDENCE.	NATURE.	CASE.
1868	BUFFUM, James P.	Douglas,	Guardianship,	8758
1874	Moses	Oxford,	Administration,	8759
1838	Phebe	Douglas,	Will,	8760
1832	Sally	Uxbridge,	Guardianship,	8761
1869	Thomas M.	Burrillville, R. I.,	Administration,	8762
1879	BUGBEE, Amos H.	Fitchburg,	Guardianship,	8763
1870	Bernajah	Webster,	Administration,	8764
1868	Charles A.	Southbridge,	Guardianship,	8765
1877	Daniel	Sutton,	Will,	8766
1874	Edward	Worcester,	Guardianship,	8767
1871	Elizabeth	Webster,	Partition,	8768
1874	Ella	Worcester,	Guardianship,	8769
1874	George	Worcester,	Guardianship,	8770
1874	James	Worcester,	Guardianship,	8771
1827	Jason	Dudley,	Administration,	8772
1867	Lyman	Worcester,	Administration,	8773
1738	Mary	Woodstock,	Will,	8774
1866	Patrick H.	Ashford, Conn.,	Administration,	8775
1743	Samuel	Woodstock,	Ag'm't of Set'm't,	8776
1839	Stephen	Worcester,	Administration,	8777
1880	BUGGY, Elizabeth	Sturbridge,	Administration,	8778
1874	BUKER, William F.	Worcester,	Will,	8779
1876	BULL, Abby D.	Harvard,	Guardianship,	8780
1878	Trumbull	Harvard,	Administration,	8781
	BULLAN see BULLEN.			
1870	BULLARD, Abby S.	Oakham,	Administration,	8782
1848	Abigail	Shrewsbury,	Administration,	8783
1826	Abijah,	Sturbridge,	Administration,	8784
1818	Adin	Oakham,	Administration,	8785
1840	Amasa	Holden,	Guardianship,	8786
1832	Amasa C.	Holden,	Guardianship,	8787
1865	Amasa C.	West Brookfield,	Will,	8788
1825	Amos	Athol,	Administration,	8789
1825	Amos	Athol,	Guardianship,	8790
1850	Amos	Barre,	Administration,	8791
1796	Arba	Brookfield,	Guardianship,	8792
1824	Arha	Rutland,	Administration,	8793
1826	Arba	Rutland,	Guardianship,	8794
1865	Arthur M.	Sturbridge,	Administration,	8795
1796	Asenath	Brookfield,	Guardianship,	8796
1881	Augustus H.	Worcester,	Administration,	8797
1857	Baalis	Bellingham,	Sp'cfic Perf'rm'ce,	8798
1837	Baruck	Uxbridge,	Administration,	8799
1837	Baruck	Uxbridge,	Pension,	8800
1802	Benjamin	Paxton,	Administration,	8801

YEAR.	NAME.	RESIDENCE.	NATURE.	CASE.
1862	BULLARD, Benjamin	Westborough,	Administration,	8802
1797	Bethiah	Milford,	Administration,	8803
1839	Betsey	Petersham,	Administration,	8804
1833	Burleigh	Southborough,	Administration,	8805
1848	Charles F.	Orange,	Guardianship,	8806
1861	Clarissa	Oakham,	Guardianship,	8807
1803	Daniel	Brookfield,	Will,	8808
1825	Daniel	Athol,	Guardianship,	8809
1875	Ede	Westborough,	Administration,	8810
1845	Edwin P.	Westborough,	Guardianship,	8811
1880	Egbert G.	Worcester,	Guardianship,	8812
1858	Elijah	Sutton,	Administration,	8813
1849	Elizabeth	Worcester,	Administration,	8814
1836	Ellen	Wendell,	Guardianship,	8815
1839	Ellen B.	Southborough,	Guardianship,	8816
1863	Elvira J.	Worcester,	Guardianship,	8817
1848	Emma E.	Orange,	Guardianship,	8818
1855	Eva M.	Holliston,	Guardianship,	8819
1818	Ezekiel W.	Oakham,	Guardianship,	8820
1848	Frances E.	Orange,	Guardianship,	8821
1845	Francis H.	Westborough,	Guardianship,	8822
1827	Franklin	Westborough,	Guardianship,	8823
1870	Franklin	Westborough,	Will,	8824
1870	Hammond	Auburn,	Administration,	8825
1845	Hannah E.	Westborough,	Guardianship,	8826
1845	Hannah J.	Westborough,	Will,	8827
1852	Harriet H.	Berlin,	Guardianship,	8828
1849	Harriot E.	Winchendon,	Guardianship,	8829
1845	Hartwell	Westborough,	Administration,	8830
1831	Henry	Holden,	Will,	8831
1865	Henry	West Brookfield,	Administration,	8832
1871	Hermon	Auburn,	Administration,	8833
1826	Horace	Rutland,	Guardianship,	8834
1864	Ira B.	Sutton,	Administration,	8835
1763	Isaac	Rutland District,	Will,	8836
1764	Isaac	Rutland District,	Guardianship,	8837
1818	James M.	Oakham,	Guardianship,	8838
1852	James M.	Berlin,	Guardianship,	8839
1871	James P.	Holden,	Will,	8840
1836	Jane	Wendell,	Guardianship,	8841
1852	Jane M.	Berlin,	Guardianship,	8842
1875	Jason	West Boylston,	Administration,	8843
1850	Joel	Berlin,	Administration,	8844
1860	Joel	Oakham,	Administration,	8845
1862	Joel	Oakham,	Partition,	8845

Year.	Name.	Residence.	Nature.	Case.
1796	BULLARD, John	Brookfield,	Administration,	8846
1796	John	Brookfield,	Guardianship,	8847
1826	John	Rutland,	Guardianship,	8848
1861	John	Oakham,	Guardianship,	8849
1876	John	Shrewsbury,	Administration,	8850
1796	Jonathan	Oakham,	Administration,	8851
1839	Joseph	Southborough,	Administration,	8852
1872	Joseph	Sutton,	Will,	8853
1795	Joshua	Milford,	Administration,	8854
1796	Josiah	Milford,	Guardianship,	8855
1860	Josiah P.	Milford,	Guardianship,	8856
1864	Judith B.	Berlin,	Will,	8857
1796	Julia	Brookfield,	Guardianship,	8858
1871	Julia A.	Hartford, Conn.,	Will,	8859
1872	Juliana	Grafton,	Administration,	8860
1879	J. Parker	Milford,	Administration,	8861
1764	Lemuel	Rutland District,	Guardianship,	8862
1777	Lemuel	Barre,	Guardianship,	8863
1871	Levi C.	Holden,	Administration,	8864
1796	Lewis	Milford,	Guardianship,	8865
1764	Lucy	Rutland District,	Administration,	8866
1769	Lucy	Rutland District,	Guardianship,	8867
1834	Lucy A.	Oakham,	Guardianship,	8868
1796	Lydia	Milford,	Guardianship,	8869
1796	Lyman	Brookfield,	Guardianship,	8870
1840	Lyman	Spencer,	Administration,	8871
1849	Malachi, Jr.	Winchendon,	Administration,	8872
1834	Martin	Oakham,	Guardianship,	8873
1861	Martin	Westborough,	Administration,	8874
1774	Mary	Rutland District,	Guardianship,	8875
1825	Mary	Athol,	Guardianship,	8876
1833	Mary	Sutton,	Administration,	8877
1872	Mary A.	Sutton,	Guardianship,	8878
1852	Mary C. J.	Berlin,	Guardianship,	8879
1847	Mary J.	Southborough,	Administration,	8880
1861	Moses	Princeton,	Will,	8881
1861	Nancy	Princeton,	Administration,	8882
1796	Nathan	Milford,	Guardianship,	8883
1846	Nathan	Berlin,	Pension,	8884
1755	Nathaniel	Worcester,	Administration,	8885
1809	Olive	Brookfield,	Will,	8886
1818	Patty	Oakham,	Guardianship,	8887
1841	Peter	Worcester,	Will,	8888
1796	Phila	Brookfield,	Guardianship,	8889
1809	Polly	Brookfield,	Guardianship,	8890

YEAR.	NAME.	RESIDENCE.	NATURE.	CASE.
1829	BULLARD, Ruth	Oakham,	Administration,	8891
1827	Sally C.	Westborough,	Guardianship,	8892
1830	Samuel	Shrewsbury,	Administration,	8893
1795	Sarah	Barre,	Will,	8894
1826	Silas	Oakham,	Will,	8895
1880	Sophia	Holden,	Will,	8896
1861	Susannah	Barre,	Will,	8897
1865	Sylvester G.	West Brookfield,	Guardianship,	8898
1863	Walter H.	Worcester,	Guardianship,	8899
1851	William	Oakham,	Will,	8900
1861	William H.	Oakham,	Guardianship,	8901
1865	William H.	Oakham,	Administration,	8902
	BULLEN AND BULLAN,			
1802	Elizabeth	Western,	Will,	8903
1822	Stephen	Charlton,	Will,	8904
1838	Stephen	Charlton,	Will,	8905
1813	BULLOCK, Abigail	Sturbridge,	Guardianship,	8906
1812	Benjamin	Sturbridge,	Administration,	8907
1812	Benjamin	Sturbridge,	Guardianship,	8908
1845	Benjamin	Sturbridge,	Administration,	8909
1819	Calvin	Princeton,	Will,	8910
1850	Charles A.	Fitchburg,	Administration,	8911
1863	Esther	Royalston,	Will,	8912
1844	George W.	Mendon,	Administration,	8913
1813	Haskett U.	Sturbridge,	Guardianship,	8914
1813	Horatio	Sturbridge,	Guardianship,	8915
1875	Horatio	Sturbridge,	Administration,	8916
1845	James B.	Sturbridge,	Guardianship,	8917
1845	Lothrop L.	Sturbridge,	Guardianship,	8918
1868	Louisa L.	Sturbridge,	Administration,	8919
1856	Mary	Worcester,	Administration,	8920
1813	Mary A.	Sturbridge,	Guardianship,	8921
1873	Mary Ann	Sturbridge,	Will,	8922
1818	Molton	Royalston,	Will,	8923
1851	Olive	Royalston,	Administration,	8924
1878	Rebecca H.	Leicester,	Administration,	8925
1851	Richmond	Providence, R. I.,	Will,	8926
1858	Rufus	Royalston,	Will,	8927
1850	Rufus A.	Fitchburg,	Guardianship,	8928
1864	Rufus H.	Royalston,	Administration,	8929
1854	Thomas	Worcester,	Administration,	8930
1813	William	Sturbridge,	Guardianship,	8931
1828	William	Sturbridge,	Administration,	8932
1829	William H.	Sturbridge,	Guardianship,	8933
1874	BULLOUGH, James	Accrington, Eng.,	Administration,	8934

YEAR.	NAME.	RESIDENCE.	NATURE.	CASE.
1756	BUMSO, Samuel	Westborough,	Administration,	8935
1878	BUNDY, Danford H.	Worcester,	Administration,	8936
1838	Elizabeth	Charlton,	Will,	8937
1880	George H.	Grafton,	Administration,	8938
1873	Lucretia	Worcester,	Administration,	8939
1778	BUNN, Abby	Brookfield,	Guardianship,	8940
1778	Hannah	Brookfield,	Guardianship,	8941
1778	Keziah	Brookfield,	Guardianship,	8942
1778	Matthew	Brookfield,	Guardianship,	8943
1775	Nathaniel	Brookfield,	Administration,	8944
1778	Nathaniel	Brookfield,	Guardianship,	8945
1778	Polly	Brookfield,	Guardianship,	8946
1778	Sarah	Brookfield,	Guardianship,	8947
1819	BURBANK, Abijah	Millbury,	Administration,	8948
1869	Alfred	Lancaster,	Guardianship,	8949
1806	Asahel	Brookfield,	Guardianship,	8950
1894	Betsey	Athol,	Guardianship,	8951
1863	Caroline A.	Worcester,	Adoption, etc.,	8952
1851	Charles E.	Sterling,	Guardianship,	8953
1851	Charles W.	Sterling,	Administration,	8954
1854	Charles W.	Worcester,	Guardianship,	8955
1774	Daniel	Sutton,	Will,	8956
1794	Daniel	Athol,	Guardianship,	8957
1816	Daniel	Oakham,	Will,	8958
1859	David	Worcester,	Administration,	8959
1849	Elizabeth	Warren,	Will,	8960
1849	Elizabeth	Warren,	Pension,	8961
1851	Emma A.	Sterling,	Guardianship,	8962
1869	Emma L.	Lancaster,	Guardianship,	8963
1866	Eunice E.	Worcester,	Administration,	8964
1876	Fanny	Warren,	Will,	8965
1852	Frances I.	Warren,	Guardianship,	8966
1875	George	Warren,	Administration,	8967
1880	George G.	Worcester,	Will,	8968
1854	George L.	Worcester,	Guardianship,	8969
1864	Harriot	Worcester,	Sale of Real Est.,	8970
1859	Henry	Worcester,	Guardianship,	8971
1758	Isaac	Sutton,	Will,	8972
1878	James L.	Worcester,	Will,	8973
1859	Jane E.	Worcester,	Guardianship,	8974
1851	John, 2d	Warren,	Administration,	8975
1852	John	Warren,	Will,	8976
1853	John F.	Worcester,	Administration,	8977
1837	John G.	Fitchburg,	Guardianship,	8978
1848	John G.	Worcester,	Administration,	8979

YEAR.	NAME.	RESIDENCE.	NATURE.	CASE.
1828	BURBANK, Levi	Lancaster,	Guardianship,	8980
1794	Luke	Athol,	Guardianship,	8981
1869	Luther	Lancaster,	Guardianship,	8982
1823	Maria	Oakham,	Guardianship,	8983
1852	Maria L.	Warren,	Guardianship,	8984
1823	Mary	Millbury,	Will,	8985
1852	Mary R.	Warren,	Guardianship,	8986
1855	Mary R.	Warren,	Administration,	8987
1794	Nabby	Athol,	Guardianship,	8988
1823	Nancy	Oakham,	Guardianship,	8989
1854	Nancy	Oakham,	Will,	8990
1819	Nathaniel	Lancaster,	Will,	8991
1855	Nathaniel	Lancaster,	Guardianship,	8992
1794	Polly	Athol,	Guardianship,	8993
1859	Ruth	Worcester,	Guardianship,	8994
1875	Salmon	Athol,	Will,	8995
1869	Samuel W.	Lancaster,	Administration,	8996
1794	Thomas	Athol,	Administration,	8997
1825	Thomas	Western,	Administration,	8998
1863	William T.	Worcester,	Administration,	8999
1868	BURBECK, Mary G.	Uxbridge,	Will,	9000
1768	BURCH, Thomas	Mendon,	Will,	9001
	BURDEN and BURDON,			
1878	Aaron	Blackstone,	Will,	9002
1879	Amos	Sutton,	Partition,	9003
1881	Amos	Sutton,	Administration,	9004
1847	Bilottee	Mendon,	Pension,	9005
1794	Consider	Middleborough,	Guardianship,	9006
1879	Cyrus	Charlton,	Guardianship,	9007
1809	Daniel	Charlton,	Guardianship,	9008
1809	David	Charlton,	Guardianship,	9009
1849	Emeline	Southbridge,	Guardianship,	9010
1879	Emeline	Southbridge,	Administration,	9010
1866	Harriet N.	Oxford,	Administration,	9011
1858	Isaac	Worcester,	Administration,	9012
1800	Jesse	Charlton,	Administration,	9013
1763	John	Sutton,	Will,	9014
1778	Jonathan	Sutton,	Guardianship,	9015
1854	Jonathan	Sutton,	Administration,	9016
1871	Louise A.	Sutton,	Administration,	9017
1831	Lyman	Sutton,	Will,	9018
1848	Mary	Sutton,	Administration,	9019
1876	Polly	Sutton,	Administration,	9020
1864	Rufus	Sutton,	Will,	9021
1879	Sally	Sutton,	Partition,	9022

	BURDEN AND BURDON,			
1865	Salmon	Sutton,	Will,	9023
1857	Sarah	Oxford,	Administration,	9024
1873	BURDITT, Alfred F.	Leominster,	Guardianship,	9025
1828	Charles F.	Leominster,	Guardianship,	9026
1846	Charles F.	Lancaster,	Guardianship,	9027
1873	Fannie C.	Leominster,	Guardianship,	9028
1873	Helen E.	Leominster,	Guardianship,	9029
1873	James H.	Leominster,	Guardianship,	9030
1873	Jerome S.	Leominster,	Will,	9031
1802	Jesse, Jr.	Hubbardston,	Administration,	9032
1844	John	Leominster,	Will,	9033
1856	John	Clinton,	Will,	9034
1828	Lucinda	Leominster,	Guardianship,	9035
1828	Luke H.	Leominster,	Guardianship,	9036
1828	Mary Ann	Leominster,	Guardianship,	9037
1871	Nathan	Clinton,	Will,	9038
1778	Thomas	Lancaster,	Administration,	9039
1810	William	Hubbardston,	Administration,	9040
1769	BURGE, Joanna	Bolton,	Guardianship,	9041
1768	Samuel	Bolton,	Administration,	9042
1769	Samuel	Bolton,	Guardianship,	9043
1769	Susannah	Bolton,	Guardianship,	9044
	BURGES AND BURGESS,			
1852	Abba M.	Bolton,	Guardianship,	9045
1852	Abigail S.	Bolton,	Guardianship,	9046
1795	Caleb	Bolton,	Guardianship,	9047
1872	Danforth	Thompson, Conn.,	Administration,	9048
1808	Ebenezer	Harvard,	Will,	9049
1789	Elizabeth	Bolton,	Will,	9050
1873	Elizabeth F.	Westborough,	Will,	9051
1861	Eunice R.	Bolton,	Administration,	9052
1859	George M.	Blackstone,	Administration,	9053
1852	Harriet B.	Bolton,	Guardianship,	9054
1840	Isaac	Harvard,	Administration,	9055
1868	Ivers	Ashburnham,	Administration,	9056
1833	Jonathan	Harvard,	Administration,	9057
1828	Joseph	Douglas,	Administration,	9058
1849	Joseph	Douglas,	Pension,	9059
1844	Joseph F.	Ashburnham,	Will,	9060
1825	Loammi	Harvard,	Administration,	9061
1863	Lois G.	Ashburnham,	Will,	9062
1785	Luther	Hardwick,	Administration,	9063
1871	Luther	Sturbridge,	Administration,	9064
1857	Lydia	Spencer,	Pension,	9065

YEAR.	NAME.	RESIDENCE.	NATURE.	CASE.
	BURGES AND BURGESS,			
1868	Mariette	Clinton,	Guardianship,	9066
1806	Nathaniel	Hardwick,	Administration,	9067
1852	Nathaniel	Bolton,	Administration,	9068
1880	Prudence	Worcester,	Administration,	9069
1862	Sally	Sterling,	Will,	9070
1785	William	Bolton,	Administration,	9071
1792	William	Bolton,	Guardianship,	9072
1858	William H.	Fitchburg,	Administration,	9073
	BURKE AND BURK,			
1873	Ann	Clinton,	Guardianship,	9074
1873	Bridget	Clinton,	Guardianship,	9075
1850	Catharine	Worcester,	Guardianship,	9076
1870	Catharine	Milford,	Guardianship,	9077
1854	Edmund	Worcester,	Administration,	9078
1870	Francis J.	Milford,	Guardianship,	9079
1830	James	New Braintree,	Administration,	9080
1849	James	Worcester,	Administration,	9081
1868	James	Clinton,	Guardianship,	9082
1873	James	Clinton,	Guardianship,	9083
1876	James	Clinton,	Administration,	9084
1870	James W.	Milford,	Guardianship,	9085
1870	John	Milford,	Guardianship,	9086
1871	John	Worcester,	Guardianship,	9087
1873	John	Fitchburg,	Administration,	9088
1876	John B.	Winchendon,	Administration,	9089
1874	John M.	Worcester,	Partition,	9090
1868	John W.	Clinton,	Guardianship,	9091
1871	Julia	Worcester,	Guardianship,	9092
1874	Julia M.	Worcester,	Partition,	9093
1867	Katharine	Clinton,	Administration,	9094
1871	Margaret	Worcester,	Administration,	9095
1872	Margaret	Clinton,	Administration,	9096
1866	Martin	Ireland,	Adoption,	9097
1869	Martin	Worcester,	Administration,	9098
1870	Mary	Milford,	Guardianship,	9099
1871	Mary	Worcester,	Guardianship,	9100
1874	Mary	Worcester,	Partition,	9101
1868	Mary A.	Clinton,	Guardianship,	9102
1871	Michael	Worcester,	Administration,	9103
1874	Michael	Worcester,	Partition,	9104
1872	Michael S. J.	Clinton,	Administration,	9105
1871	Morgan	Worcester,	Guardianship,	9106
1874	Morgan	Worcester,	Partition,	9107
1861	Patrick	Milford,	Will,	9108

	BURKE AND BURK,			
1870	Patrick	Milford,	Will,	9109
1871	Patrick	Worcester,	Guardianship,	9110
1873	Patrick	Clinton,	Guardianship,	9111
1874	Patrick	Worcester,	Partition,	9112
1880	Patrick	Clinton,	Will,	9113
1873	Richard	Clinton,	Guardianship,	9114
1873	Thomas	Clinton,	Guardianship,	9115
1873	William	Clinton,	Guardianship,	9116
	BURLEIGH AND BURLEY,			
1833	Betsey	Grafton,	Administration,	9117
1848	John O.	East Douglas,	Administration,	9118
1863	Joseph B.	Union, Conn.,	Administration,	9119
1865	Mary E.	Oxford,	Administration,	9120
1841	Samuel	Sturbridge,	Administration,	9121
1821	BURLING, Elizabeth W.	Worcester,	Will,	9122
1866	BURLINGAME, Abraham	Killingly, Conn.,	Will,	9123
1871	Alice	Webster,	Administration,	9124
1872	Asa W.	Worcester,	Guardianship,	9125
1858	Benjamin	Charlton,	Guardianship,	9126
1858	Chauncey C.	Charlton,	Guardianship,	9127
1858	Ebenezer,	Charlton,	Administration,	9128
1858	Elizabeth	Charlton,	Guardianship,	9129
1875	Emily J.	Worcester,	Administration,	9130
1858	George A.	Charlton,	Guardianship,	9131
1872	Harris	Worcester,	Guardianship,	9132
1858	Henrietta	Charlton,	Guardianship,	9133
1872	Maria	Worcester,	Guardianship,	9134
1858	Mary F.	Charlton,	Guardianship,	9135
1834	Sarah	Charlton,	Will,	9136
1762	BURNAL, Samuel	Dudley,	Administration,	9137
	BURNAM see BURNHAM.			
1840	BURNAP, Ahijah	Millbury,	Will,	9138
1840	Abijah	Millbury,	Pension,	9139
1844	Abijah	Paxton,	Administration,	9140
1844	Ama	Paxton,	Guardianship,	9141
1849	Amy D.	Paxton,	Will,	9142
1809	Annis P	Fitchburg,	Guardianship,	9143
1868	Aurelia C.	New Braintree,	Will,	9144
1864	Berthiah	Sutton,	Administration,	9145
1844	Caroline E.	Paxton,	Guardianship,	9146
1868	Charles E.	Fitchburg,	Will,	9147
1844	Cylinda W.	Paxton,	Guardianship,	9148
1756	David	Southborough,	Administration,	9149
1871	Deney	Sutton,	Administration,	9150

YEAR.	NAME.	RESIDENCE.	NATURE.	CASE.
1820	BURNAP, Ebenezer	Ward,	Administration,	9151
1820	Ebenezer T.	Ward,	Guardianship,	9152
1827	Edmund, etc.	Fitchburg,	Administration,	9153
1827	Edward, etc.	Fitchburg,	Administration,	9153
1820	Erasmus L.	Ward,	Guardianship,	9154
1756	Hannah	Southborough,	Guardianship,	9155
1807	Jacob	Fitchburg,	Will,	9156
1809	Jacob	Fitchburg,	Guardianship,	9157
1869	James	Sutton,	Will,	9158
1840	Jerome J.	Millbury,	Guardianship,	9159
1864	John	Sutton,	Administration,	9160
1809	Joseph	Fitchburg,	Guardianship,	9161
1844	Julia C.	Paxton,	Guardianship,	9162
1860	Lewis	Sutton,	Administration,	9163
1871	Lucy M.	Sutton,	Administration,	9164
1820	Mary H.	Ward,	Guardianship,	9165
1830	Mary H.	Ward,	Will,	9166
1840	Mary W.	Millbury,	Guardianship,	9167
1875	Matilda	Charlton,	Will,	9168
1869	Nancy M.	Leominster,	Guardianship,	9169
1855	Polly	Fitchburg,	Administration,	9170
1855	Polly	Fitchburg,	Pension,	9171
1842	Samuel	Fitchburg,	Administration,	9172
1756	Sarah	Southborough,	Guardianship,	9173
1868	Stillman	Fitchburg,	Administration,	9174
1828	Timothy	Sutton,	Administration,	9175
1858	Timothy	Sutton,	Administration,	9176
1869	Warren S.	Leominster,	Guardianship,	9177
1844	Willard A.	Paxton,	Guardianship,	9178
	BURNE see BURNS.			
1880	BURNELL, George F.	Boylston,	Adoption, etc.,	9179
1748	Hannah	Dudley,	Guardianship,	9180
1745	John	Dudley,	Administration,	9181
1748	Samuell	Dudley,	Guardianship,	9182
1762	Samuell	Woodstock, Conn.,	Administration,	9183
	BURNET AND BURNETT,			
1773	Barsheba	Oxford,	Guardianship,	9184
1858	Calvin A.	Leicester,	Administration,	9185
1824	Charles R.	Southborough,	Administration,	9186
1875	Clarissa	Winchendon,	Administration,	9187
1867	Clark	Holden,	Administration,	9188
1845	Eliza B.	Southborough,	Guardianship,	9189
1865	Harriet K.	Leicester,	Administration,	9190
1845	Harriet M.	Southborough,	Guardianship,	9191
1845	Joel	Southborough,	Administration,	9192

BURNET AND BURNETT,

1758	John	Oxford,	Guardianship,	9193
1758	John	Oxford,	Administration,	9194
1773	John	Hardwick,	Administration,	9195
1845	Luther	Oxford,	Will,	9196
1841	Luther, Jr.	Worcester,	Guardianship,	9197
1850	Luther, Jr.	Oxford,	Administration,	9197
1845	Waldo J.	Southborough,	Guardianship,	9198
1868	BURNEY, Anna R.	Fitchburg,	Adoption,	9199
1868	Auretta E.	Fitchburg,	Adoption,	9200
1870	Frederick W.	Fitchburg,	Adoption,	9201
1870	Helen A.	Fitchburg,	Adoption,	9202
1868	Isabella M.	Fitchburg,	Adoption,	9203
1868	Mabel H.	Fitchburg,	Adoption,	9204
1877	Samuel	Templeton,	Will,	9205

BURNHAM AND BURNAM,

1818	Anna	Lunenburg,	Will,	9206
1858	Clarence H.	Southbridge,	Guardianship,	9207
1863	George W.	Smithfield, R. I.,	Administration,	9208
1870	Ida G.	Bolton,	Guardianship,	9209
1870	Ida G.	Bolton,	Adoption, etc.,	9210
1813	Joshua	Lunenburg,	Will,	9211
1842	Lyman	Mendon,	Administration,	9212
1800	Robert	Fitchburg,	Will,	9213
1855	Roxana	Grafton,	Administration,	9214

BURNS, BURN, BURNE, BYRNE AND BYRNES,

1871	Alanson E.	Sutton,	Guardianship,	9215
1857	Alexander, etc.	Southbridge,	Administration,	9216
1874	Carrie	Holden,	Guardianship,	9217
1865	Charles E.	Grafton,	Guardianship,	9218
1864	Daniel	Westborough,	Guardianship,	9219
1857	Dorothy	Southbridge,	Guardianship,	9220
1874	Eugene	Milford,	Guardianship,	9221
1865	Eugene A.	Grafton,	Guardianship,	9222
1795	Fortain	Grafton,	Will,	9223
1869	Frederick J.	Worcester,	Guardianship,	9224
1869	Frederick J.	Worcester,	Adoption, etc.,	9225
1865	George E.	Grafton,	Administration,	9226
1877	George F.	Millbury,	Guardianship,	9227
1871	George H.	Sutton,	Guardianship,	9228
1881	Hannah	Clinton,	Guardianship,	9229
1874	Isabella	Holden,	Guardianship,	9230
1871	James G.	Sutton,	Guardianship,	9231
1864	Jeremiah	Worcester,	Administration,	9232

Year.	Name.	Residence.	Nature.	Case.
	BURNS, BURN, BURNE, BYRNE **AND BYRNES,**			
1857	John	Southbridge,	Guardianship,	9233
1874	John	Holden,	Guardianship,	9234
1874	John	Holden,	Administration,	9235
1875	John	Clinton,	Will,	9236
1877	John	Worcester,	Guardianship,	9237
1878	John	Clinton,	Administration,	9238
1881	John J.	Clinton,	Guardianship,	9239
1869	J. Edward	Worcester,	Guardianship,	9240
1877	Kate	Worcester,	Guardianship,	9241
1879	Martin	Clinton,	Partition,	9242
1864	Mary	Southborough,	Guardianship,	9243
1874	Mary	Holden,	Guardianship,	9244
1880	Mary	Athol,	Will,	9245
1881	Mary	Clinton,	Guardianship,	9246
1875	Mary A.	Blackstone,	Guardianship,	9247
1869	Mary F.	Worcester,	Guardianship,	9248
1862	Mary L.	Boston,	Adoption, etc.,	9249
1874	Michael	Holden,	Guardianship,	9250
1877	Michael	Worcester,	Guardianship,	9251
1879	Michael, etc.	Clinton,	Partition,	9252
1879	Michael J.	Clinton,	Partition,	9252
1881	Patrick F.	Clinton,	Guardianship,	9253
1861	Peter	Bolton,	Administration,	9254
1875	Richard	Grafton,	Administration,	9255
1857	Samuel	Southbridge,	Administration,	9256
1877	Sarah	Worcester,	Guardianship,	9257
1857	Thomas	Southbridge,	Guardianship,	9258
1867	William	Worcester,	Administration,	9259
1874	William	Blackstone,	Will,	9260
1881	No name given	Gardner,	Adoption, etc.,	9261
1835	**BURNSIDE, Samuel M.**	Worcester,	Trustee,	9262
1850	Samuel M.	Worcester,	Will,	9263
1871	Sophia D. F.	Worcester,	Administration,	9264
1815	Thomas	Westborough,	Will,	9265
1864	**BURPEE, Abbie L.**	Princeton,	Guardianship,	9266
1864	Alice A.	Princeton,	Guardianship,	9267
1822	Andrew	Sterling,	Guardianship,	9268
1827	Andrew	Sterling,	Administration,	9269
1881	Asenath	Leominster,	Will,	9270
1859	Catharine	Templeton,	Administration,	9271
1833	Ebenezer	Sterling,	Administration,	9272
1836	Elijah	Sterling,	Pension,	9273
1834	Elizabeth	Sterling,	Administration,	9274

Year.	Name.	Residence.	Nature.	Case.
1835	BURPEE, Elizabeth	Sterling,	Administration,	9275
1817	Jeremiah	Sterling,	Will,	9276
1822	Jeremiah	Sterling,	Administration,	9277
1853	Joel	Sterling,	Administration,	9278
1854	Jonathan	Sterling,	Will,	9279
1877	Julia A. F.	Sterling,	Partition,	9280
1846	Luke	Sterling,	Guardianship,	9281
1856	Margaret	Sterling,	Administration,	9282
1817	Martin, Jr.	Lancaster,	Guardianship,	9283
1827	Moses	Sterling,	Will,	9284
1757	Nathan	Lancaster,	Administration,	9285
1830	Nathan	Sterling,	Administration,	9286
1856	Nathan	Sterling,	Administration,	9287
1871	Rebekah	Lancaster,	Will,	9288
1791	Samuel	Sterling,	Will,	9289
1828	Samuel	Templeton,	Administration,	9290
1863	Solomon J.	Princeton,	Administration,	9291
1878	Sophronia A.	Leominster,	Administration,	9292
1855	Stephen	Winchendon,	Administration,	9293
1780	Thomas	Lancaster,	Will,	9294
1838	BURR, Augusta N.	Millbury,	Guardianship,	9295
1859	Dolly	Ashburnham,	Administration,	9296
1838	Eliza P.	Millbury,	Guardianship,	9297
1872	Heman M.	Leicester,	Will,	9298
1793	John	Winchendon,	Administration,	9299
1797	John	Winchendon,	Guardianship,	9300
1813	John	Winchendon,	Guardianship,	9301
1838	Marcia J.	Millbury,	Guardianship,	9302
1850	Marcus	Milford,	Will,	9303
1837	Newton	Millbury,	Administration,	9304
1868	Pyam	Ashburnham,	Will,	9305
1797	Samuel	Winchendon,	Guardianship,	9306
1838	Sarah E.	Millbury,	Guardianship,	9307
1881	William H. P.	Millbury,	Guardianship,	9308
	BURRAGE AND BURRIDGE,			
1849	Anna C.	Fitchburg,	Guardianship,	9309
1849	Charles E	Fitchburg,	Guardianship,	9310
1862	Charles E.	Leominster,	Administration,	9311
1844	Charles W.	Leominster,	Guardianship,	9312
1878	Emory	Leominster,	Will,	9313
1848	George N.	Lunenburg,	Guardianship,	9314
1877	George S.	Leominster,	Administration,	9315
1844	Hannah	Lunenburg,	Guardianship,	9316
1848	Harriet A. B.	Lunenburg,	Guardianship,	9317
1874	Hattie M.	Leominster,	Guardianship,	9318

	BURRAGE AND BURRIDGE,			
1848	John	Lunenburg,	Administration,	9319
1844	John B.	Lunenburg,	Guardianship,	9320
1848	John W.	Lunenburg,	Guardianship,	9321
1856	Josiah	Leominster,	Will,	9322
1844	Martha A.	Leominster,	Guardianship,	9323
1827	Mary C.	Leominster,	Guardianship,	9324
1844	Mary J.	Leominster,	Guardianship,	9325
1851	Mary J.	Leominster,	Administration,	9326
1849	Mary W.	Fitchburg,	Administration,	9327
1858	Roxana	Leominster,	Administration,	9328
1875	Ruth K.	Leominster,	Administration,	9329
1820	William	Leominster,	Administration,	9330
1844	William	Leominster,	Will,	9331
1844	William	Lunenburg,	Administration,	9332
1825	William, Jr.	Leominster,	Will,	9333
1844	William F.	Leominster,	Guardianship,	9334
1875	William F.	Leominster,	Will,	9335
	BURRELL see BURRILL.			
	BURRIDGE see BURRAGE.			
	BURRILL AND BURRELL,			
1869	Asenath	Putnam, Conn.,	Will,	9336
1838	Charles O.	Mendon,	Guardianship,	9337
1837	Dormand	Mendon,	Administration,	9338
1838	Hansa M.	Mendon,	Guardianship,	9339
1864	John	Westminster,	Administration,	9340
1838	Lafayette	Mendon,	Guardianship,	9341
1838	Malissa M.	Mendon,	Guardianship,	9342
1838	Marvellous B.	Mendon,	Guardianship,	9343
	BURROUGHS AND BURROWS,			
1869	Catherine	Brookfield,	Administration,	9344
1869	David	Warren,	Will,	9345
1841	Francis	Spencer,	Administration,	9346
1826	John	Western,	Guardianship,	9347
1826	Mildred	Western,	Guardianship,	9348
1874	Samuel R.	Warren,	Will,	9349
1826	Wealthy	Western,	Guardianship,	9350
1869	BURSLEY, Evander C.	Northbridge,	Guardianship,	9351
1836	Samuel	Paxton,	Guardianship,	9352
1847	BURT, Asa	Millbury,	Administration,	9353
1874	Benjamin	Northbridge,	Will,	9354
1847	Caroline F.	Millbury,	Guardianship,	9355
1874	Chloe	Sutton,	Guardianship,	9356
1832	David	Sutton,	Administration,	9357
1874	David	Northbridge,	Administration,	9358

Year.	Name.	Residence.	Nature.	Case.
1764	BURT, Ebenezer	Mendon,	Will,	9359
1861	Ebenezer	Athol,	Will,	9360
1846	Eli	Oakham,	Administration,	9361
1847	Elizabeth A.	Millbury,	Guardianship,	9362
1862	Ellis	Sutton,	Administration,	9363
1875	George	Northbridge,	Administration,	9364
1824	Hannah	Harvard,	Will,	9365
1870	Jane D.	Northbridge,	Adoption, etc.,	9366
1872	Jeremiah J.	Millbury,	Administration,	9367
1858	John	New Braintree,	Will,	9368
1847	John S.	Sutton,	Administration,	9369
1735	Jonas	Stow,	Guardianship,	9370
1819	Joseph	Barre,	Will,	9371
1864	Juliet	Sutton,	Guardianship,	9372
1864	Julius	Sutton,	Guardianship,	9373
1872	Laura, etc.	Sutton,	Guardianship,	9374
1872	Laura N., etc.	Sutton,	Guardianship,	9374
1872	Linda	Sutton,	Adoption, etc.,	9375
1872	Linda, etc.	Sutton,	Guardianship,	9376
1866	Martha E.	Oakham,	Guardianship,	9377
1879	Mason	Northbridge,	Administration,	9378
1872	Melinda R.	Sutton,	Guardianship,	9379
1833	Nathaniel	Worcester,	Will,	9380
1864	Samuel	Sutton,	Administration,	9381
1881	Sanford	Sutton,	Administration,	9382
1872	Sarah L.	Sutton,	Administration,	9383
1735	Sybell	Rutland,	Administration,	9384
1811	William	Harvard,	Will,	9385
1847	William M.	Millbury,	Guardianship,	9386
1850	BURTON, Daniel A.	Douglas,	Guardianship,	9387
1873	Eliza A.	Grafton,	Will,	9388
1839	BUSH, Ann S.	Templeton,	Guardianship,	9389
1847	Avery	Oakham,	Administration,	9390
1826	Calvin	Bolton,	Administration,	9391
1847	Charles	Oakham,	Guardianship,	9392
1872	Charles W.	Gardner,	Will,	9393
1779	David	Shrewsbury	Absentee,	9394
1858	Elizabeth	Westborough,	Guardianship,	9395
1860	Elizabeth	Westborough,	Will,	9395
1760	George	Lancaster,	Administration,	9396
1767	George	Shrewsbury,	Will,	9397
1847	George A.	Oakham,	Guardianship,	9398
1840	Hervey F.	Oakham,	Guardianship,	9399
1803	Jesse	Templeton,	Will,	9400
1757	John	Shrewsbury,	Will,	9401

YEAR.	NAME.	RESIDENCE.	NATURE.	CASE.
1758	BUSH, John	Shrewsbury,	Will,	9402
1779	John	Shrewsbury,	Absentee,	9403
1816	John	Worcester,	Will,	9404
1847	John	Oakham,	Guardianship,	9405
1837	Jonathan	Bolton,	Pension,	9406
1756	Joseph	Shrewsbury,	Administration,	9407
1786	Joseph	Brookfield,	Will,	9408
1847	Joseph	Oakham,	Guardianship,	9409
1863	Joseph	Oakham,	Administration,	9410
1778	Jotham	Shrewsbury,	Administration,	9411
1838	Jotham	Boylston,	Will,	9412
1879	Jotham	Boylston,	Guardianship,	9413
1847	Julian H.	Oakham,	Guardianship,	9414
1779	Levi	Shrewsbury,	Guardianship,	9415
1779	Lucy	Shrewsbury,	Guardianship,	9416
1877	Maria H.	Gardner,	Administration,	9417
1779	Martha	Shrewsbury,	Guardianship,	9418
1792	Martha	Shrewsbury,	Will,	9419
1869	Mary R.	Brookfield,	Will,	9420
1798	Micah	Bolton,	Will,	9421
1779	Persis	Shrewsbury,	Guardianship,	9422
1765	Ruth	Shrewsbury,	Will,	9423
1838	Silas	Templeton,	Administration,	9424
1880	Wilder	Northborough	Administration,	9425
1846	William	Spencer,	Will,	9426
1879	BUSHNELL, Charlotte A.	Sturbridge,	Administration,	9427
1874	Eleazer	Lisbon, Conn.,	Administration,	9428
1881	Gerard	Templeton,	Administration,	9429
1790	BUSS, Aaron	Lunenburg,	Will,	9430
1825	Charles	Leominster,	Guardianship,	9431
1847	Charles	Holden,	Guardianship,	9432
1734	Ebenezer	Lancaster,	Guardianship,	9433
1801	Ebenezer	Sterling,	Will,	9434
1833	Ebenezer	Sterling,	Administration,	9435
1868	Ebenezer	Sterling,	Will,	9436
1863	Elisha G.	Clinton,	Administration,	9437
1734	John	Lancaster,	Administration,	9438
1776	John	Lunenburg,	Will,	9439
1825	John, 2nd	Leominster,	Guardianship,	9440
1845	John	Leominster,	Will,	9441
1846	John	Leominster,	Pension,	9442
1824	John, Jr.	Leominster,	Administration,	9443
1878	John L.	Leominster,	Administration,	9444
1734	Jonathan	Lancaster,	Guardianship,	9445
1745	Jonathan	Leominster,	Guardianship,	9446

Year.	Name.	Residence.	Nature.	Case.
1762	BUSS, Jonathan	Lancaster,	Guardianship,	9447
1772	Jonathan	Leominster,	Administration,	9448
1847	Joshua B.	Holden,	Guardianship,	9449
1836	Keziah	Sterling,	Will,	9450
1836	Lucius W.	Rutland,	Guardianship,	9451
1825	Mary E.	Leominster,	Guardianship,	9452
1867	Minnie F.	Providence, R. I.,	Guardianship,	9453
1836	Perna H.	Rutland,	Guardianship,	9454
1766	Peter	Boston,	Guardianship,	9455
1785	Prudence	Leominster,	Guardianship,	9456
1840	Ruhamah	Sterling,	Administration,	7457
1825	Sally R.	Leominster,	Guardianship,	9458
1853	Sarah	Leominster,	Pension,	9459
1865	Sarah	Sterling,	Administration,	9460
1827	Silas	Sterling,	Will,	9461
1734	Stephen	Lancaster,	Guardianship,	9462
1790	Stephen	Leominster,	Administration,	9463
1825	Susan E.	Leominster,	Guardianship,	9464
1830	BUTLER, Abigail	Boylston,	Guardianship,	9465
1843	Abigail	Boylston,	Administration,	9465
1858	Abigail	Oxford,	Administration,	9466
1859	Abigail	Milford,	Administration,	9467
1822	Abijah	Leominster,	Administration,	9468
1873	Adams	Southborough,	Administration,	9469
1874	Albert	Douglas,	Partition,	9470
1854	Amos J.	Boylston,	Administration,	9471
1736	Asa	Lancaster,	Guardianship	9472
1880	Berzalda	Worcester,	Will,	9473
1880	Catharine	Worcester,	Will,	9474
1794 .	Damarus	Bolton,	Guardianship,	9475
1822	Ebenezer	Boylston,	Will,	9476
1868	Ebenezer	Winchendon,	Will,	9477
1867	Edmund	Milford,	Administration,	9478
1813	Elizabeth	Lancaster,	Guardianship,	9479
1873	Elizabeth N.	Northborough,	Administration,	9480
1868	Ella L.	Worcester,	Adoption, etc.,	9481
1865	Ellen	Mendon,	Adoption, etc.,	9482
1838	Emeline	Webster,	Guardianship,	9483
1794	Ephraim	Bolton,	Guardianship,	9484
1813	Eunice	Lancaster,	Will,	9485
1818	Gracia	Oakham,	Administration,	9486
1808	Hannah	Dudley,	Guardianship,	9487
1736	Isaac	Lancaster,	Guardianship,	9488
1814	Israel	Lancaster,	Administration,	9489
1736	James	Lancaster,	Administration,	9490

Year.	Name.	Residence.	Nature.	Case.
1808	BUTLER, James	Dudley,	Guardianship,	9491
1813	James	Lancaster,	Guardianship,	9492
1828	James	Oxford,	Administration,	9493
1838	James	Webster,	Guardianship,	9494
1880	Joanna F.	Worcester,	Administration,	9495
1736	John	Lancaster,	Guardianship,	9496
1742	Jolm	Bolton,	Guardianship,	9497
1813	John	Oakham,	Will,	9498
1824	John	Oxford,	Administration,	9499
1813	John E.	Lancaster,	Guardianship,	9500
1810	John N.	Leominster,	Guardianship,	9501
1744	Lucy	Lunenburg,	Guardianship,	9502
1822	Lucy	Leominster,	Guardianship,	9503
1880	Margaret B.	Leicester,	Will,	9504
1838	Mary	Webster,	Guardianship,	9505
1846	Mary	Rutland,	Foreign Sale,	9506
1864	Mary F.	Worcester,	Adoption,	9507
1880	Mary F.	Worcester,	Guardianship,	9508
1736	Merriam	Lancaster,	Guardianship,	9509
1736	Nathan	Lancaster,	Guardianship,	9510
1760	Nathaniel	Bolton,	Administration,	9511
1736	Patience	Lancaster,	Guardianship,	9512
1857	Peter	Oxford,	Will,	9513
1807	Phineas	Leominster,	Guardianship,	9514
1810	Phineas	Leominster,	Administration,	9514
1808	Polly	Dudley,	Guardianship,	9515
1744	Rachell	Lunenburg,	Guardianship,	9516
1838	Samuel C.	Webster,	Administration,	9517
1823	Simeon	Leominster,	Administration,	9518
1795	Simon	Leominster,	Will,	9519
1802	Simon	Lancaster,	Will,	9520
1813	Simon	Lancaster,	Guardianship,	9521
1880	Sophia S.	Oxford,	Will,	9522
1822	Sophronia	Leominster,	Guardianship,	9523
1878	Thomas	Worcester,	Administration,	9524
1875	Thomas L.	St. Henry, Quebec,	Foreign Will,	9525
1818	Walter	Oakham,	Guardianship,	9526
1825	Walter	Oakham,	Administration,	9527
1741	William	Lunenburg,	Administration,	9528
1794	William	Bolton,	Will,	9529
1794	William	Bolton,	Guardianship,	9530
1868	BUTMAN, Benjamin	Worcester,	Guardianship,	9531
1872	Benjamin	Worcester,	Will,	9531
1864	George F.	Worcester,	Will,	9532
1876	Maria	Worcester,	Will,	9533

| --- | --- | --- | --- | --- |
1758	BUTMAN, Samuel	Sutton,	Will,	9534
1867	BUTTERFIELD, Arthur D.	Leominster,	Guardianship,	9535
1862	Candace	Worcester,	Will,	9536
1867	Catharine L.	Fitchburg,	Will,	9537
1873	Deborah	Bolton,	Administration,	9538
1867	Edwin G.	Leominster,	Guardianship,	9539
1756	Isaac	Westford,	Guardianship,	9540
1756	Jonas	Westford,	Guardianship,	9541
1853	Wallace W.	Fitchburg,	Guardianship,	9542
1864	Wallace W.	Westminster,	Administration,	9542
1853	Warren S.	Fitchburg,	Administration,	9543
	BUTTERICK see BUTTRICK.			
1854	BUTTERS, Abel	Lunenburg,	Administration,	9544
1832	James	Lunenburg,	Administration,	9545
1855	J. Franklin	Barre,	Administration,	9546
1871	Mary	Lunenburg,	Will,	9547
1863	BUTTERWORTH, Anna A.	Fitchburg,	Guardianship,	9548
1877	Eliza	Worcester,	Guardianship,	9549
1880	Eliza	Worcester,	Administration,	9549
1863	Frank	Warren,	Guardianship,	9550
1870	Jonathan	Worcester,	Will,	9551
1849	BUTTON, Barbara	Worcester,	Will,	9552
	BUTTRICK AND BUTTERICK,			
1829	Abner	Sterling,	Guardianship,	9553
1857	Adell L.	Sterling,	Guardianship,	9554
1881	Allen G.	Lancaster,	Adoption, etc.,	9555
1867	Francis	Sterling,	Will,	9556
1857	George	Sterling,	Administration,	9557
1857	George F.	Sterling,	Guardianship,	9558
1829	Hannah	Sterling,	Guardianship,	9559
1830	Hannah W.	Sterling,	Administration,	9560
1872	Hiram	Barre,	Guardianship,	9561
1863	Hiram N.	Winchendon,	Administration,	9562
1809	Jonathan	Sterling,	Administration,	9563
1825	Jonathan	Lancaster,	Will,	9564
1880	Lorinda	Winchendon,	Will,	9565
1865	Luella	Sterling,	Guardianship,	9566
1876	Sarah J. P.	Fitchburg,	Will,	9567
1844	William	Harvard,	Administration,	9568
1876	William F.	Fitchburg,	Administration,	9569
1881	BUTTS, Harriet N. G.	Milford,	Will,	9570
1869	BUXTON, Andrew	North Brookfield,	Will,	9571
1793	Anna	Barre,	Guardianship,	9572
1817	Chloe	Mendon,	Guardianship,	9573
1869	Charles W.	West Brookfield,	Guardianship,	9574

YEAR.	NAME.	RESIDENCE.	NATURE.	CASE.
1784	BUXTON, Daniel	Barre,	Administration,	9575
1784	Daniel	Barre,	Guardianship,	9576
1817	Eliza	Mendon,	Guardianship,	9577
1843	Emeline O.	Sutton,	Guardianship,	9578
1839	Enos	North Brookfield,	Administration,	9579
1843	Enos J.	Sutton,	Guardianship,	9580
1869	Etta J.	West Brookfield,	Guardianship,	9581
1867	Frank H.	Worcester,	Guardianship,	9582
1871	Gertrude F.	Worcester,	Guardianship,	9583
1867	Ida F.	Worcester,	Guardianship,	9584
1871	Iola E.	Worcester,	Guardianship,	9585
1817	Joel	Mendon,	Guardianship,	9586
1777	John	Sutton,	Guardianship,	9587
1794	John	Barre,	Guardianship,	9588
1817	John	Mendon,	Guardianship,	9589
1843	John	Sutton,	Administration,	9590
1767	Joseph	Rutland District,	Administration,	9591
1777	Joseph	Sutton,	Administration,	9592
1782	Joseph	Sutton,	Guardianship,	9593
1817	Leonard	Mendon,	Guardianship,	9594
1784	Lucy	Barre,	Guardianship,	9595
1879	Pearl P.	Milford,	Adoption, etc.,	9596
1811	Peleg	Mendon,	Administration,	9597
1857	Rebecca	Northborough,	Will,	9598
1859	Rebecca L.	Worcester,	Administration,	9599
1859	Rufus	Charlton,	Administration,	9600
1843	Submit	Sutton,	Guardianship,	9601
1876	Warren R.	Worcester,	Administration,	9602
1879	William B.	Worcester,	Will,	9603
1881	BUZZELL, Charles O.	Worcester,	Guardianship,	9604
1881	Florence E.	Worcester,	Guardianship,	9605
1881	John P.	Clinton,	Will,	9606
1881	Mary A.	Worcester,	Administration,	9607
1866	BYAM, Charlie L.	Winchendon,	Adoption, etc.,	9608
1830	Lydia	Templeton,	Guardianship,	9609
1813	Mary	Templeton,	Will,	9610
1807	Phineas	Templeton,	Will,	9611
1820	Samuel	Templeton,	Guardianship,	9612
1821	Samuel	Templeton,	Will,	9613
1830	Samuel	Templeton,	Will,	9612
1820	Samuel, Jr.	Templeton,	Guardianship,	9614
1830	Samuel W.	Templeton,	Guardianship,	9615
1878	Sylvia A.	Fitzwilliam, N. H.,	Adoption, etc.,	9616
1759	Thomas	Mendon,	Administration,	9617

YEAR.	NAME.	RESIDENCE.	NATURE.	CASE.
	BYRON AND BIRON,			
1875	Annie	Ashburnham,	Guardianship,	9618
1875	Carrie	Ashburnham,	Guardianship,	9619
1875	Etta	Ashburnham,	Guardianship,	9620
1875	George	Ashburnham,	Guardianship,	9621
1875	Katie	Ashburnham,	Guardianship,	9622
1875	Lizzie	Ashburnham,	Guardianship,	9623
1860	Lucy	Grafton,	Guardianship,	9624
1875	Mary	Ashburnham,	Guardianship,	9625
	CADORET AND CADRETTE,			
1880	Alexis C.	Worcester,	Administration,	9626
1880	Edmund	Worcester,	Guardianship,	9627
1880	Joseph	Worcester,	Guardianship,	9628
1871	Josephine	Sturbridge,	Guardianship,	9629
1880	Minnie	Worcester,	Guardianship,	9630
1871	Silermy	Sturbridge,	Guardianship,	9631
1864	**CADWELL, Ebenezer**	Northbridge,	Will,	9632
1837	John	Northbridge,	Administration,	9633
1867	**CADY, Almond C.**	Grafton,	Guardianship,	9634
1875	Charles L.	Southbridge,	Guardianship,	9635
1879	Daniel R.	Westborough,	Will,	9636
1862	David	Clinton,	Administration,	9637
1866	Flora A. J.	Oxford,	Guardianship,	9638
1867	George H.	Grafton,	Guardianship,	9639
1868	Harriet	Warren,	Administration,	9640
1842	Henry A.	Mendon,	Guardianship,	9641
1881	Jessie A.	Grafton,	Adoption, etc.,	9642
1875	John	Blackstone,	Will,	9643
1865	Loren W.	Oxford,	Administration,	9644
1863	Lucinda	Northbridge,	Will,	9645
1842	Mary A. M.	Mendon,	Guardianship,	9646
1856	Mary C.	Somers, Conn.,	Administration,	9647
1853	Mary S.	Westborough,	Guardianship,	9648
1875	Newton C.	Southbridge,	Administration,	9649
1842	Rebecca	Mendon,	Guardianship,	9650
1865	Rosabelle	Millbury,	Adoption,	9651
1857	Sally	Thompson, Conn.,	Administration,	9652
1862	Samuel R.	Northbridge,	Administration,	9653
1842	Sarah F.	Mendon,	Guardianship,	9654
1842	Seth D.	Mendon,	Guardianship,	9655
1866	William C.	Oxford,	Guardianship,	9656
1865	**CAHILL, Bridget**	Blackstone,	Will,	9657
1867	Daniel	Spencer,	Guardianship,	9658
1867	David	Spencer,	Guardianship,	9659
1876	Dennis	Worcester,	Partition,	9660

YEAR.	NAME.	RESIDENCE.	NATURE.	CASE.
1879	CAHILL, Elizabeth	Worcester,	Administration,	9661
1863	James	Uxbridge,	Administration,	9662
1877	Mary	Worcester,	Administration,	9663
1870	Patrick	Blackstone,	Will,	9664
1879	Patrick	Worcester,	Administration,	9665
1879	Sabina	Worcester,	Administration,	9666
	CAIN (see also KANE).			
1869	Charles H.	Ashburnham,	Guardianship,	9667
1874	Jeremiah	North Brookfield,	Guardianship,	9668
1875	John	Blackstone,	Administration,	9669
1879	Joseph	Milford,	Administration,	9670
1874	Margaret B.	North Brookfield,	Guardianship,	9671
1873	Martin	Worcester,	Administration,	9672
1874	Mary A.	North Brookfield,	Guardianship,	9673
1879	Mary E.	North Brookfield,	Guardianship,	9674
1874	Michael	North Brookfield,	Administration,	9675
1871	Patrick	North Brookfield,	Will,	9676
1866	Philip	Southbridge,	Administration,	9677
1876	Phillip	Spencer,	Will,	9678
1877	Sarah	Southbridge,	Administration,	9679
1877	Thomas	Fitchburg,	Will,	9680
1878	Thomas	Worcester,	Administration,	9681
1879	Thomas	Leicester,	Will,	9682
1869	William E.	Ashburnham,	Guardianship,	9683
1839	CALDWELL, Abigail C.	Fitchburg,	Guardianship,	9684
1866	Ann	Dudley,	Administration,	9685
1767	Anna	Rutland,	Guardianship,	9686
1783	Anna	Barre,	Administration,	9687
1789	Benjamin	Barre,	Guardianship,	9688
1811	Benjamin	Barre,	Will,	9689
1842	Charles B.	Lunenburg,	Guardianship,	9690
1859	Charlotte E.	Fitchburg,	Guardianship,	9691
1839	Edmund C.	Fitchburg,	Guardianship,	9692
1842	Edward T.	Lunenburg,	Guardianship,	9693
1859	Elliot L.	Fitchburg,	Guardianship,	9694
1859	Emily M.	Fitchburg,	Guardianship,	9695
1873	Enoch	Fitchburg,	Will,	9696
1784	Ephraim	Barre,	Administration,	9697
1806	Ezra	Barre,	Guardianship,	9698
1865	Frances	Lunenburg,	Will,	9699
1783	George	Barre,	Administration,	9700
1847	George	Barre,	Administration,	9701
1806	Harriet	Barre,	Guardianship,	9702
1825	Harriet	Barre,	Sale Real Estate,	9703
1823	Jacob	Lunenburg,	Inventory,	9704

YEAR.	NAME..	RESIDENCE.	NATURE.	CASE.
1843	CALDWELL, Jacob	Lunenburg,	Will,	9705
1763	James	Rutland District,	Administration,	9706
1767	James	Rutland District,	Guardianship,	9707
1782	James	Barre,	Guardianship,	9708
1880	Jane	Dudley,	Will,	9709
1784	John	Barre,	Guardianship,	9710
1807	John	Barre,	Will,	9711
1859	John	Fitchburg,	Administration,	9712
1782	John, Jr.	Barre,	Administration,	9713
1839	John A.	Fitchburg,	Guardianship,	9714
1829	John C.	Barre,	Administration,	9715
1841	Jonathan P.	Lunenburg,	Administration,	9716
1806	Joseph	Barre,	Guardianship,	9717
1806	Joseph	Barre,	Guardianship,	9718
1808	Joseph	Barre,	Will,	9719
1806	Levi	Barre,	Guardianship,	9720
1859	Louisa W.	Fitchburg,	Guardianship,	9721
1806	Lucinda	Barre,	Guardianship,	9722
1806	Mary	Barre,	Guardianship,	9723
1825	Mary	Barre,	Administration,	9724
1828	Mary	Barre,	Administration,	9725
1829	Mary	Barre,	Administration,	9726
1864	Mary	Lunenburg,	Administration,	9727
1818	Mary F.	Barre,	Guardianship,	9728
1795	Matthew	Barre,	Administration,	9729
1865	Mehitable	Barre,	Will,	9730
1814	Moses	Barre,	Guardianship,	9731
1824	Moses	Barre,	Administration,	9731
1806	Nathan	Barre,	Guardianship,	9732
1818	Nathan	Barre,	Guardianship,	9733
1832	Nathan	Barre,	Guardianship,	9733
1838	Nathan	Barre,	Administration,	9733
1862	Nathaniel	Worcester,	Guardianship,	9734
1806	Sally	Barre,	Guardianship,	9735
1806	Samuel	Barre,	Guardianship,	9736
1767	Sarah	Rutland District,	Guardianship,	9737
1820	Sarah	Barre,	Administration,	9738
1839	Sarah E.	Fitchburg,	Guardianship,	9739
1806	Sarah S.	Barre,	Guardianship,	9740
1805	Seth	Barre,	Administration,	9741
1806	Seth	Barre,	Guardianship,	9742
1870	Seth	Worcester,	Administration,	9743
1767	Submit	Rutland District,	Guardianship,	9744
1825	Sylvia	Barre,	Sale of Real Est.,	9745
1767	William	Rutland District,	Guardianship,	9746

| --- | --- | --- | --- | --- |
1805	CALDWELL, William	Worcester,	Administration,	9747
1806	William	Barre,	Will,	9748
1806	William	Barre,	Guardianship,	9749
1814	William	Barre,	Administration,	9750
1838	William	Worcester,	Guardianship,	9751
1859	William M.	Fitchburg,	Guardianship,	9752
1862	William O.	Worcester,	Guardianship,	9753
1808	CALEF, Lucy	Westminster,	Guardianship,	9754
1787	CALHOON, James	Petersham,	Administration,	9755
1854	CALL, Elam	Northborough,	Administration,	9756
	CALLAHAN, CALLIHAN AND CALLAGHAN,			
1868	Bridget	Warren,	Administration,	9757
1880	Bridget, etc.	Southbridge,	Will,	9758
1849	Dennis	Millbury,	Guardianship,	9759
1854	Eliza	Clinton,	Guardianship,	9760
1878	Elizabeth	Worcester,	Will,	9761
1860	Francis	Burrillville, R. I.,	Administration,	9762
1779	Frederick W.	Boston,	Guardianship,	9763
1858	Jeremiah T.	Millbury,	Administration,	9764
1849	John	Millbury,	Administration,	9765
1849	Thomas	Millbury,	Guardianship,	9766
1768	CALLAM, Caleb	Mendon,	Will,	9767
1800	Daniel	Mendon,	Administration,	9768
1869	William J.	Holden,	Administration,	9769
1848	CALLIGAN, James	Worcester,	Administration,	9770
1878	CALLON, Caroline	Sturbridge,	Change of Name,	9771
1851	CALVERT, Edward	Southbridge,	Will,	9772
1880	Tamerline	Southbridge,	Administration,	9773
	CAMBEL see CAMPBELL.			
1876	CAMBRIDGE, Ida M.	Lowell,	Adoption, etc.,	9774
1869	CAMERON, Donald	Clinton,	Administration,	9775
1881	CAMP, Francis A. S.	Leominster,	Will,	9776
	CAMPBELL AND CAMBEL,			
1752	Abraham	Marlborough,	Guardianship,	9777
1783	Alexander	Oxford,	Administration,	9778
1830	Alexander	Oxford,	Administration,	9779
1879	Alice H.	Barre,	Guardianship,	9780
1851	Ami B.	Worcester,	Guardianship,	9781
1837	Anna	Shrewsbury,	Pension,	9782
1818	Archibald	Oxford,	Administration,	9783
1819	Archibald	Oxford,	Guardianship,	9784
1819	Benjamin F.	Oxford,	Guardianship,	9785
1819	Celia E.	Oxford,	Guardianship,	9786
1802	Charles	Charlton,	Guardianship,	9787

Year.	Name.	Residence.	Nature.	Case.
	CAMPBELL and CAMBEL,			
1744	Daniel	Rutland,	Administration,	9788
1795	Duncan	Oxford,	Administration,	9789
1796	Elizabeth	Lancaster,	Guardianship,	9790
1783	Esther	Oxford,	Will,	9791
1850	Ezra B.	Worcester,	Administration,	9792
1871	Franklin	Worcester,	Adoption, etc.,	9793
1873	Franklin	Worcester,	Adoption, etc.,	9793
1851	George S.	Worcester,	Guardianship,	9794
1851	Horace W.	Worcester,	Guardianship,	9795
1825	James	Worcester,	Administration,	9796
1879	James	Worcester,	Will,	9797
1819	James B.	Oxford,	Guardianship,	9798
1841	Jeremiah	Hardwick,	Will,	9799
1850	Jeremiah	Hardwick,	Administration,	9800
1796	Job	Lancaster,	Guardianship,	9801
1759	John	Oxford,	Guardianship,	9802
1761	John	Oxford,	Will,	9803
1791	John	Lancaster,	Will,	9804
1822	John	Fitchburg,	Administration,	9805
1796	Joseph	Lancaster,	Guardianship,	9806
1879	Martin	Lancaster,	Will,	9807
1796	Mary	Lancaster,	Guardianship,	9808
1819	Mary B.	Oxford,	Guardianship,	9809
1851	Mary E.	Worcester,	Guardianship,	9810
1833	Phineas	Lunenburg,	Administration,	9811
1796	Rogers	Lancaster,	Guardianship,	9812
1796	Sally	Lancaster,	Guardianship,	9813
1843	Samuel	Oxford,	Administration,	9814
1825	Stearns	Oxford,	Administration,	9815
1856	Sylvanus	Spencer,	Administration,	9816
1796	Thomas	Lancaster,	Guardianship,	9817
	CANADA see KENNEDY.			
1879	CANIFF, Mabel	Princeton,	Adoption, etc.,	9818
	CANNON and CANON,			
1874	Ann	Milford,	Administration,	9819
1880	Ann	Clinton,	Guardianship,	9820
1752	Cornelius	New Braintree,	Administration,	9821
1757	Cornelius	New Braintree,	Guardianship,	9822
1880	Dominick	Clinton,	Guardianship,	9823
1848	Ellen	Worcester,	Guardianship,	9824
1848	James	Worcester,	Guardianship,	9825
1757	Jesse	New Braintree,	Guardianship,	9826
1768	Jesse	New Braintree,	Guardianship,	9827
1757	John	New Braintree,	Guardianship,	9828

Year.	Name.	Residence.	Nature.	Case.
	CANNON and CANON,			
1880	John	Clinton,	Administration,	9829
1757	Keziah	New Braintree,	Guardianship,	9830
1848	Maria	Worcester,	Guardianship,	9831
1880	Maria	Clinton,	Guardianship,	9832
1837	Mary	Dana,	Will,	9833
1757	Mehitabell	New Braintree,	Guardianship,	9834
1768	Mehitable	New Braintree,	Guardianship,	9835
1879	Patrick	Clinton,	Will,	9836
1880	Patrick	Clinton,	Guardianship,	9837
1757	Philip	New Braintree,	Guardianship,	9838
1757	Simeon	New Braintree,	Guardianship,	9839
1847	Thomas	Worcester,	Administration,	9840
1880	CANNOVAN, Patrick, Jr.	Webster,	Administration,	9841
1876	CANTARA, Ata T.	Spencer,	Guardianship,	9842
1813	CANTERBURY, George	Sturbridge,	Guardianship,	9843
1813	Harry	Sturbridge,	Guardianship,	9844
1863	Ira	Gardner,	Administration,	9845
1812	John	Sturbridge,	Administration,	9846
1813	John	Sturbridge,	Guardianship,	9847
1813	Phebe	Sturbridge,	Guardianship,	9848
1813	Polly	Sturbridge,	Guardianship,	9849
1870	Sylvia	Worcester,	Will,	9850
1877	CAOUETTE, Sophia	Douglas,	Administration,	9851
1848	CAPEN, Abraham	Spencer,	Administration,	9852
1877	Alfred	Charlton,	Administration,	9853
1818	Betsey	Dana,	Administration,	9854
1873	Charles B.	Southborough,	Administration,	9855
1855	Daniel	Spencer,	Will,	9856
1868	Dwight	Lebanon, Ill.,	Foreign Sale,	9857
1848	Ebenezer	Spencer,	Guardianship,	9858
1863	Ebenezer	Leicester,	Administration,	9859
1868	Ida M.	Lebanon, Ill.,	Foreign Sale,	9860
1833	James	Spencer,	Administration,	9861
1833	James	Spencer,	Pension,	9862
1833	James	Spencer,	Guardianship,	9863
1848	James	Spencer,	Guardianship,	9864
1824	James, Jr.	Spencer,	Administration,	9865
1855	Lydia	Spencer,	Administration,	9866
1874	Martha E.	Southborough,	Guardianship,	9867
1833	Melinda	Spencer,	Guardianship,	9868
1833	Nancy	Spencer,	Guardianship,	9869
1879	Nancy	Brookfield,	Administration,	9870
1848	Susan M.	Spencer,	Guardianship,	9871
1804	Timothy	Spencer,	Administration,	9872

Year.	Name.	Residence.	Nature.	Case.
1834	CAPEN, Timothy	Spencer,	Administration,	9873
1834	Timothy	Spencer,	Pension,	9874
1813	CAPET, Lewis	Uxbridge,	Guardianship,	9875
1880	CAPRON, Alice H.	Uxbridge,	Guardianship,	9876
1880	Anna L.	Uxbridge,	Guardianship.	9877
1877	Annie H.	Uxbridge,	Guardiauship,	9878
1875	Bertha F.	Hartford, Conn.,	Guardianship,	9879
1880	Catharine B.	Uxbridge,	Will,	9880
1880	Catherine M.	Uxbridge,	Guardianship,	9881
1816	Celia	Mendon,	Guardianship,	9882
1812	Charles	Uxbridge,	Administration,	9883
1837	Charles	Uxbridge,	Guardianship,	9884
1880	Charles F.	Uxbridge,	Guardianship,	9885
1836	Charles S.	Uxbridge,	Will,	9886
1875	Clara D.	Hartford, Conn.,	Guardianship,	9887
1815	David T.	Uxbridge,	Guardianship,	9888
1840	Edmund	Mendon,	Administration,	9889
1859	Effingham L.	Worcester,	Will,	9890
1816	Elizabeth	Mendon,	Guardianship,	9891
1839	Elizabeth R.	Uxbridge,	Guardianship,	9892
1836	John	Uxbridge,	Will,	9893
1880	John L.	Uxbridge,	Guardianship,	9894
1879	John W.	Uxbridge,	Will,	9895
1855	Josephine A.	Uxbridge,	Administration,	9896
1877	Laura E.	Uxbridge,	Guardianship,	9897
1877	Lovina W.	Northbridge,	Administration,	9898
1856	Lydia B.	Worcester,	Will,	9899
1815	Maria	Uxbridge,	Guardianship,	9900
1816	Mary	Mendon,	Guardianship,	9901
1839	Mary A.	Uxbridge,	Guardianship,	9902
1816	Nathaniel	Mendon,	Will,	9903
1816	Phebe	Mendon,	Guardianship,	9904
1814	Pliny E.	Uxbridge,	Guardiauship,	9905
1880	Roswell M.	Uxbridge,	Guardianship,	9906
1837	Sarah W.	Uxbridge,	Guardianship,	9907
1840	Sarah W.	Uxbridge,	Administration,	9908
1816	William	Mendon,	Guardianship,	9909
1875	William C.	Hartford, Conn.,	Guardianship,	9910
1875	William C.	Uxbridge,	Administration,	9911
1880	CARBERRY, Elizabeth J.	Westborough,	Sep. Support,	9912
1880	James T.	Unknown,	Sep. Support,	9913
1881	CARDER, Grant C.	Chicago, Ill.,	Foreign Sale,	9914
1870	CAREW, Francis M.	West Brookfield,	Will,	9915
	CAREY and CARY,			
1870	Alice E.	Fitchburg,	Sale Real Est.,	9916

(228)

CAREY AND CARY,

YEAR.	NAME.	RESIDENCE.	NATURE.	CASE.
1873	Ann J.	Southbridge,	Guardianship,	9917
1808	Avery	Brookfield,	Guardianship,	7918
1878	Betsey	Webster,	Administration,	9919
1835	Caroline R.	Ward,	Guardianship,	9920
1866	Catharine	Thompson, Conn.,	Administration,	9921
1848	Eliza	Brookfield,	Guardianship,	9922
1848	Ephraim	Brookfield,	Guardianship,	9923
1836	Freelove	North Brookfield,	Guardianship,	9924
1875	George	Sterling,	Administration,	9925
1870	Henry	Shrewsbury,	Administration,	9926
1870	Henry F.	Fitchburg,	Administration,	9927
1877	Ida M.	Worcester,	Guardianship,	9928
1870	James	Fitchburg,	Administration,	9929
1875	James	Spencer,	Guardianship,	9930
1872	Johanna	Worcester,	Administration,	9931
1859	John	Boston,	Adoption, etc.,	9932
1873	John	Southbridge,	Will,	9933
1878	John	Westminster,	Guardianship,	9934
1809	Jonathan	Brookfield,	Guardianship,	9935
1807	Josiah	Brookfield,	Administration,	9936
1873	Lucretia	Shrewsbury,	Will,	9937
1808	Luther	Brookfield,	Guardianship,	9938
1825	Luther	Brookfield,	Administration,	9939
1809	Lydia	Brookfield,	Guardianship,	9940
1848	Lydia	Brookfield,	Guardianship,	9941
1862	Malikey	Westminster,	Administration,	9942
1866	Martha	Auburn,	Administration,	9943
1835	Martha E.	Ward,	Guardianship,	9944
1880	Mary	Worcester,	Will,	9945
1825	Mary A.	Brookfield,	Guardianship,	9946
1871	Mary A.	Mendon,	Guardianship,	9947
1871	Michael F.	Mendon,	Guardianship,	9948
1809	Mordecai	Brookfield,	Guardianship,	9949
1876	Mordecai	Brookfield,	Will,	9950
1875	Patrick	Worcester,	Administration,	9951
1832	Peter	Shrewsbury,	Will,	9952
1835	Preston M,	Ward,	Guardianship,	9953
1848	Sarah	Brookfield,	Guardianship,	9954
1868	Thomas	Mendon,	Will,	9955
1809	Thomas H.	Brookfield,	Guardianship,	9956
1828	William	Shrewsbury,	Administration,	9957
1836	William A.	North Brookfield,	Guardianship,	9958
1869	William J.	Worcester,	Administration,	9959
1834	Zebulon	Ward,	Administration,	9960

| --- | --- | --- | --- | --- |
	CAREY AND CARY,			
1847	Zebulon	Brookfield,	Administration,	9961
	CARGILL AND CARGEL,			
1753	Benjamin	Mendon,	Guardianship,	9962
1813	Benjamin	Dudley,	Will,	9963
1872	Calista L.	Millbury,	Administration,	9964
1753	James	Mendon,	Will,	9965
1875	Joel W.	Leicester,	Administration,	9966
1787	Lucretia	Dudley,	Administration,	9967
1877	Olive W.	Leicester,	Administration,	9968
1872	Walter B.	Millbury,	Guardianship,	9969
1881	CARKIN, Martha J. W.	Brookfield,	Administration,	9970
	CARLEN AND CARLIN,			
1857	Hugh	Northborough,	Administration,	9971
1874	Joseph A.	Worcester,	Administration,	9972
1861	Peter	Burlington, Vt.,	Guardianship,	9973
	CARLISLE AND CARLILE,			
1857	Charles	Worcester,	Administration,	9974
1769	David	Lunenburg,	Will,	9975
1854	James	Worcester,	Administration,	9976
1857	Warren T.	Worcester,	Guardianship,	9977
	CARLTON AND CARLETON,			
1779	Abraham	Lunenburg,	Will,	9978
1871	Alfred O.	Fitchburg,	Guardianship,	9979
1881	Amy P.	Barre,	Guardianship,	9980
1871	Annie A.	Fitchburg,	Guardianship,	9981
1827	Benjamin	Sutton,	Will,	9982
1875	Bertha A.	Milford,	Adoption, etc.,	9983
1869	Charlotte	Shrewsbury,	Administration,	9984
1787	Clark	Lunenburg,	Will,	9985
1864	Ella J.	Ashburnham,	Guardianship,	9986
1847	Eri	Fitchburg,	Will,	9987
1838	Frances S.	Lancaster,	Guardianship,	9988
1872	Frank E.	Worcester,	Guardianship,	9989
1870	Henry	Worcester,	Change of Name,	9990
1872	Ira	Fitchburg,	Administration,	9991
1856	James S.	Sutton,	Administration,	9992
1864	Joseph	Ashburnham,	Administration,	9993
1878	Joseph E.	Worcester,	Administration,	9994
1872	Lewis	Rutland,	Administration,	9995
1870	Mary L.	Worcester,	Change of Name,	9996
1858	Moses	Lancaster,	Will,	9997
1826	Silas	Sutton,	Administration,	9998
1851	Silas G.	Millbury,	Administration,	9999
1856	Walter E.	Lunenburg,	Administration,	10000

YEAR.	NAME.	RESIDENCE.	NATURE.	CASE.
	CARLTON AND CARLETON,			
1860	William	Fitchburg,	Will,	10001
1865	William H.	Brookfield,	Change of Name,	10002
1849	CARLY, Mary	Lunenburg,	Will,	10003
1849	Mary	Lunenburg,	Pension,	10004
1878	CARNES, James	West Brookfield,	Will,	10005
1869	CARNEY, Catharine G.	Spencer,	Adoption, etc.,	10006
1873	Edmund	Spencer,	Guardianship,	10007
1873	Ellen	Spencer,	Guardianship,	10008
1873	John	Spencer,	Guardianship,	10009
1873	Kate	North Brookfield,	Guardianship,	10010
1865	Margaret	Webster,	Administration,	10011
1870	Mary L.	Worcester,	Change of Name,	10012
1870	Michael	Worcester,	Change of Name,	10013
1870	Patrick	Worcester,	Administration,	10014
1872	Patrick	Webster,	Will,	10015
1875	Patrick	Gardner,	Administration,	10016
1876	Thomas	Leominster,	Administration,	10017
1879	CARON, Honory M.	Spencer,	Adoption, etc.,	10018
1748	CARPENTER, Abigail	Woodstock,	Guardianship,	10019
1814	Abigail	Uxbridge,	Guardianship,	10020
1829	Abigail	Sutton,	Guardianship,	10021
1803	Abner P.	Upton,	Guardianship,	10022
1814	Abraham	Uxbridge,	Guardianship,	10023
1877	Alice T.	Brookfield,	Guardianship,	10024
1871	Amy	Sturbridge,	Administration,	10025
1874	Ann D.	Brookfield,	Administration,	10026
1804	Anna	Sutton,	Will,	10027
1808	Anna	Sturbridge,	Guardianship,	10028
1877	Antionette	Brookfield,	Guardianship,	10029
1854	Asenath D.	Southbridge,	Guardianship,	10030
1829	Betsey	Sutton,	Guardianship,	·10031
1839	Betsey	Sutton,	Administration,	10032
1849	Betsey	Brookfield,	Administration,	10033
1847	Caroline E.	Charlton,	Guardianship,	10034
1875	Charles	Milford,	Administration,	10035
1860	Charlie E.	Charlton,	Guardianship,	10036
1852	Cynthia	Thompson, Conn.,	Administration,	10037
1867	Cynthia	Milford,	Administration,	10038
1860	Cynthia M. S.	Worcester,	Administration,	10039
1851	Daniel S.	Grafton,	Will,	10040
1748	Daniell	Woodstock,	Guardianship,	10041
1880	David	Bolton,	Will,	10042
1823	Ebenezer	Northbridge,	Administration,	10043
1820	Edmund	Douglas,	Will,	10044
1848	Edmund	Douglas,	Will,	10045

Year.	Name.	Residence.	Nature.	Case.
1860	CARPENTER, Edmund	Douglas,	Administration,	10046
1878	Edwin R.	Uxbridge,	Administration,	10047
1867	Elias	Sturbridge,	Will,	10048
1808	Elijah	Sturbridge,	Will,	10049
1814	Elijah	Hardwick,	Will,	10050
1748	Eliphalett	Woodstock,	Administration,	10051
1803	Elisha	Upton,	Guardianship,	10052
1789	Elisha	Sutton,	Will,	10053
1814	Eliza	Uxbridge,	Guardianship,	10054
1849	Eliza S.	Warren,	Guardianship,	10055
1869	Elizabeth M.	Charlton,	Guardianship,	10056
1863	Ella F.	Milford,	Guardianship,	10057
1877	Elva E.	Brookfield,	Guardianship,	10058
1877	Emma E.	Milford,	Guardianship,	10059
1869	Emma L.	Charlton,	Guardianship,	10060
1846	Ephraim L.	Woodstock, Conn.,	Administration,	10061
1871	Ephraim W.	Providence, R. I.,	Foreign Will,	10062
1860	Estes R.	Charlton,	Guardianship,	10063
1876	Frank N.	Warren,	Guardianship,	10064
1863	Frank O.	Milford,	Guardianship,	10065
1803	George	Upton,	Guardianship,	10066
1864	George	Uxbridge,	Administration,	10067
1864	George A.	Milford,	Guardianship,	10068
1829	Harriet D.	Sutton,	Guardianship,	10069
1849	Harvey S.	Warren,	Guardianship,	10070
1872	Harvey S.	Warren,	Guardianship,	10071
1876	Harvey S.	Warren,	Administration,	10071
1869	Henry L.	Charlton,	Administration,	10072
1854	Henry L. M.	Southbridge,	Guardianship,	10073
1876	Herbert B.	Warren,	Guardianship,	10074
1832	Ira	Sturbridge,	Administration,	10075
1814	Isaac	Uxbridge,	Guardianship,	10076
1743	Isaiah	Douglas,	Administration,	10077
1747	Isaiah	Douglas,	Guardianship,	10078
1860	James A.	Upton,	Adoption, etc.,	10079
1849	Jane E.	Warren,	Guardianship,	10080
1747	John	Douglas,	Guardianship,	10081
1869	John	Uxbridge,	Administration,	10082
1877	John B.	Brookfield,	Guardianship,	10083
1851	John S.	Leicester,	Guardianship,	10084
1866	John S.	Stafford, Conn.,	Foreign Will,	10085
1747	Jonah	Douglas,	Guardianship,	10086
1829	Jonathan	Sutton,	Guardianship,	10087
1837	Jonathan	Northbridge,	Administration,	10088
1771	Joseph	Hardwick,	Guardianship,	10089

Year.	Name.	Residence.	Nature.	Case.
1813	CARPENTER, Joseph	Uxbridge,	Administration,	10090
1814	Joseph	Uxbridge,	Guardianship,	10091
1840	Joseph R.	Northbridge,	Administration,	10092
1861	Josephine	Milford,	Guardianship,	10093
1826	Julia	Brookfield,	Guardianship,	10094
1877	Lena L.	Brookfield,	Guardianship,	10095
1829	Lucretia O.	Sutton,	Guardianship,	10096
1861	Luke	Milford,	Guardianship,	10097
1875	Lydia	Rutland,	Administration,	10098
1829	Maranda	Sutton,	Guardianship,	10099
1829	Maria W.	Sutton,	Guardianship,	10100
1860	Marjara	Douglas,	Administration,	10101
1877	Martha A.	Milford,	Guardianship,	10102
1837	Mary A.	Northbridge,	Guardianship,	10103
1876	Mary G.	Warren,	Guardianship,	10104
1854	Mercy	Southbridge,	Will,	10105
1866	Mitty P.	Woodstock, Conn.,	Foreign Will,	10106
1861	Nahum B.	Milford,	Guardianship,	10107
1829	Nancy	Sutton,	Guardianship,	10108
1770	Nathan	Hardwick,	Will,	10109
1839	Nathaniel	Douglas,	Will,	10110
1840	Nathaniel	Douglas,	Guardianship,	10111
1872	Nelson	Warren,	Administration,	10112
1808	Oliver	Sturbridge,	Guardianship,	10113
1809	Oliver	Brookfield,	Will,	10114
1826	Oliver	Brookfield,	Will,	10115
1826	Oliver	Brookfield,	Guardianship,	10116
1858	Oliver	Milford,	Administration,	10117
1880	Onetto J.	Worcester,	Administration,	10118
1861	Oscar B.	Milford,	Guardianship,	10119
1861	Otis	Milford,	Guardianship,	10120
1814	Perrin	Uxbridge,	Guardianship,	10121
1860	Phebe J.	Douglas,	Guardianship,	10122
1835	Pliny	Douglas,	Administration,	10123
1802	Reuben	Upton,	Administration,	10124
1803	Reuben	Upton,	Guardianship,	10125
1860	Roxalana J.	Douglas,	Guardianship,	10126
1803	Sally	Upton,	Guardianship,	10127
1836	Sally	Sutton,	Administration,	10128
1826	Samuel	Sutton,	Will,	10129
1874	Samuel	Uxbridge,	Will,	10130
1747	Sarah	Douglas,	Guardianship,	10131
1815	Sarah	Brookfield,	Will,	10132
1842	Sarah	Hardwick,	Administration,	10133
1829	Sarah F.	Sutton,	Guardianship,	10134

Year.	Name.	Residence.	Nature.	Case.
1803	CARPENTER, Seth P.	Upton,	Guardianship,	10135
1847	Simeon	Sutton,	Will,	10136
1874	Simon	Charlton,	Will,	10137
1828	Tiley	Sutton,	Administration,	10138
1860	Walter E.	Douglas,	Guardianship,	10139
1803	Welcome	Upton,	Guardianship,	10140
1860	Wilder	Charlton,	Guardianship,	10141
1748	William	Woodstock,	Guardianship,	10142
1829	William	Sutton,	Guardianship,	10143
1864	Willie	Milford,	Guardianship,	10144
1874	Zacheus G.	Rutland,	Guardianship,	10145
1874	Zacheus G.	Rutland,	Will,	10145
1880	CARR, Charles A.	Douglas,	Guardianship,	10146
1876	Edward C.	Worcester,	Guardianship,	10147
1864	Elizabeth	Lancaster,	Guardianship,	10148
1864	Ellen	Lancaster,	Guardianship,	10149
1864	George	Spencer,	Adoption, etc.,	10150
1856	Harriet M.	Lancaster,	Guardianship,	10151
1860	Hiram J.	Southborough,	Administration,	10152
1833	James	Leicester,	Administration,	10153
1856	Leonard E.	Lancaster,	Guardianship,	10154
1859	Loammi B.	Northbridge,	Guardianship,	10155
1872	Lois	Upton,	Will,	10156
1864	Lucy	Lancaster,	Guardianship,	10157
1856	Lyman A.	Lancaster,	Guardianship,	10158
1864	Mary	Lancaster,	Guardianship,	10159
1870	Mayhew V.	Southborough,	Guardianship,	10160
1854	Phebe	Blackstone,	Administration,	10161
1869	Rhoda P.	Bricksburg, N. J.,	Administration,	10162
1848	Ruth	Blackstone,	Administration,	10163
1859	Samuel A.	Northbridge,	Guardianship,	10164
1874	Walter V.	Westminster,	Will,	10165
1864	William D.	Lancaster,	Administration,	10166
1790	CARRARY, Stephen	Uxbridge,	Will,	10167
1758	CARREAN, Gloud	Worcester,	Will,	10168
	CARREL AND CARRELL see CARROLL.			
1863	CARRICO, Charles H.	Worcester,	Guardianship,	10169
1863	George A.	Worcester,	Guardianship,	10170
1863	Joshua W.	Worcester,	Administration,	10171
1871	Lucy M.	Worcester,	Guardianship,	10172
1863	William F.	Worcester,	Guardianship,	10173
	CARRIEL see CARROLL.			
1878	CARRIERE, Peter, etc.	Millbury,	Administration,	10174
1866	CARRIGAN, James	Northborough,	Administration,	10175
	CARRIL see CARROLL.			

Year.	Name.	Residence.	Nature.	Case.

CARROLL, CARREL, CARRELL, CARRIL AND CARRIEL,

1863	Annis D.	Fitzwilliam, N. H.,	Foreign Sale,	10176
1767	Asa	Sutton,	Guardianship,	10177
1867	Charles E.	Barre,	Guardianship,	10178
1759	Daniel	Sutton,	Will,	10179
1767	Daniel	Sutton,	Guardianship,	10180
1803	Eli	Templeton,	Guardianship,	10181
1863	Eliza A.	Fitzwilliam, N. H.,	Foreign Sale,	10182
1879	Eliza A.	Royalston,	Will,	10183
1863	Emery A.	Fitzwilliam, N. H.,	Foreign Sale,	10184
1874	Henry	Worcester,	Administration,	10185
1879	James S.	Worcester,	Guardianship,	10186
1811	Jeduthan	Sutton,	Administration,	10187
1875	Johanna	Gardner,	Administration,	10188
1823	John	Sutton,	Will,	10189
1877	John	Worcester,	Will,	10190
1879	John F.	Worcester,	Guardianship,	10191
1817	Jonathan	Sutton,	Guardianship,	10192
1841	Jonathan	Sutton,	Administration,	10193
1803	Joseph	Sutton,	Administration,	10194
1867	Malcolm W.	Fitzwilliam, N. H.,	Foreign Sale,	10195
1867	Margaret	Barre,	Guardianship,	10196
1878	Maurice	Gardner,	Administration,	10197
1767	Mary	Sutton,	Administration,	10198
1842	Nancy	Sutton,	Guardianship,	10199
1755	Nathaniel	Palmer,	Guardianship,	10200
1816	Nathaniel	Sutton,	Administration,	10201
1817	Nathaniel	Sutton,	Guardianship,	10202
1878	Nellie M.	Worcester,	Guardianship,	10203
1863	Nelson S.	Fitzwilliam, N. H.,	Foreign Sale,	10204
1862	Owen	Milford,	Administration,	10205
1874	Owen	Barre,	Administration,	10206
1880	Patrick	Worcester,	Administration,	10207
1867	Patrick J.	Barre,	Administration,	10208
1841	Polly	Sutton,	Administration,	10209
1829	Rebekah	Millbury,	Will,	10210
1826	Sally	Mendon,	Guardianship,	10211
1759	Samuel	Sutton,	Will,	10212
1796	Samuel	Royalston,	Administration,	10213
1797	Samuel	Royalston,	Guardianship,	10214
1757	Samuel, Jr.	Sutton,	Administration,	10215
1867	Solomon	Grafton,	Will,	10216
1797	Timothy	Royalston,	Guardianship,	10217
1863	Timothy D.	Fitzwilliam, N. H.,	Foreign Sale,	10218

Year.	Name.	Residence.	Nature.	Case.
1869	CARRUTH, Alfred J.	Petersham,	Administration,	10219
1833	Arza	Petersham,	Guardianship,	10220
1842	Augusta	Paxton,	Guardianship,	10221
1841	Benjamin M.	Barre,	Guardianship,	10222
1875	Bennery A.	Clinton,	Guardianship,	10223
1873	Caleb H.	Clinton,	Administration,	10224
1881	Charles	Barre,	Administration,	10225
1869	Charles A.	Petersham,	Guardianship,	10226
1870	Clarence E.	Northborough,	Guardianship,	10227
1865	Clarinda	Northborough,	Administration,	10228
1812	Elijah	Barre,	Guardianship,	10229
1847	Elijah	Barre,	Administration,	10230
1850	Ellen M.	Petersham,	Guardianship,	10231
1870	Everett H.	Northborough,	Guardianship,	10232
1869	Fanny E.	Petersham,	Guardianship,	10233
1858	Francis	North Brookfield,	Will,	10234
1875	Frederick W.	Clinton,	Guardianship,	10235
1847	George J.	Barre,	Guardianship,	10236
1847	Henry	Barre,	Guardianship,	10237
1872	Hiram	North Brookfield,	Will,	10238
1869	Ida E.	Petersham,	Guardianship,	10239
1847	James	Phillipston,	Will,	10240
1831	James H.	Barre,	Guardianship,	10241
1772	John	Northborough,	Will,	10242
1829	John, 2d	Barre,	Administration,	10243
1841	John	Barre,	Administration,	10244
1842	John	Northborough,	Will,	10245
1849	John	Petersham,	Administration,	10246
1847	John L.	Barre,	Guardianship,	10247
1827	Jonas	Petersham,	Will,	10248
1851	Jonas	Petersham,	Administration,	10249
1850	Jonas A.	Petersham,	Guardianship,	10250
1812	Joseph	Barre,	Guardianship,	10251
1830	Joseph	Northborough,	Administration,	10252
1862	Levi W.	Winchendon,	Administration,	10253
1869	Lucy E.	Petersham,	Guardianship,	10254
1860	Lutheria D.	Athol,	Administration,	10255
1842	Lydia	Northborough,	Guardianship,	10256
1841	Maria	Barre,	Guardianship,	10257
1827	Martha	Barre,	Administration,	10258
1852	Martha	Petersham,	Administration,	10259
1847	Martha A.	Barre,	Guardianship,	10260
1866	Mary F.	North Brookfield,	Will,	10261
1880	Mary P.	North Brookfield,	Will,	10262
1833	Molly	Petersham,	Will,	10263

YEAR.	NAME.	RESIDENCE.	NATURE.	CASE.
1827	CARRUTH, Nathan	North Brookfield,	Will,	10264
1813	Nathan, Jr.	North Brookfield,	Administration,	10265
1864	Russell	Phillipston,	Trustee,	10266
1812	Samuel	Barre,	Administration,	10267
1841	Sarah M.	Barre,	Guardianship,	10268
1868	Theophilus	Northborough,	Administration,	10269
1772	William	Northborough,	Guardianship,	10270
1799	William	Barre,	Administration,	10271
1865	CARSON, Robert	Worcester,	Administration,	10272
1873	Simon J.	Oxford,	Guardianship,	10273
1865	CARTER, Abbie S.	Leominster,	Administration,	10274
1790	Abel	Lancaster,	Will,	10275
1844	Abel	Leominster,	Administration,	10276
1741	Abigail	Dudley,	Guardianship,	10277
1767	Abigail	Lancaster,	Guardianship,	10278
1801	Abigail	Dudley,	Will,	10279
1816	Abigail	Lancaster,	Guardianship,	10280
1826	Abigail	Leominster,	Will,	10281
1856	Abigail	Lancaster,	Will,	10282
1864	Abigail K.	Leominster,	Administration,	10283
1874	Ada L.	Clinton,	Guardianship,	10284
1852	Adeline E.	Leominster,	Guardianship,	10285
1864	Adaline E.	Leominster,	Administration,	10286
1869	Adelle M.	Lancaster,	Guardianship,	10287
1869	Albert H.	Lancaster,	Guardianship,	10288
1853	Alpheus	Lancaster,	Administration,	10289
1869	Alpheus H.	Worcester,	Administration,	10290
1869	Amanda E.	Leominster,	Guardianship,	10291
1815	Amory	Berlin,	Administration,	10292
1815	Amory	Berlin,	Guardianship,	10293
1869	Andrew L.	Leominster,	Guardianship,	10294
1881	Ann A.	Leominster,	Administration,	10295
1849	Ann E.	Lancaster,	Guardianship,	10296
1869	Ann J.	Leominster,	Guardianship,	10297
1830	Anna	Leominster,	Administration,	10298
1851	Anna	Leominster,	Administration,	10299
1860	Anna B.	Westborough,	Guardianship,	10300
1856	Artemas	Portland, Me.,	Administration,	10301
1850	Asa	Berlin,	Administration,	10302
1852	Asaph	Westminster,	Will,	10303
1849	Azubah C.	Barre,	Will,	10304
1879	Bartimus	Leominster,	Will,	10305
1804	Benjamin	Dudley,	Guardianship,	10306
1867	Benjamin G.	Barre,	Administration,	10307
1860	Betsey	Leominster,	Administration,	10308

(237)

1830	CARTER, Betsey T.	Lancaster,	Guardianship,	10309
1859	Calvin	Lancaster,	Will,	10310
1814	Caroline	Uxbridge,	Guardianship,	10311
1826	Caroline	Lancaster,	Guardianship,	10312
1847	Caroline I.	Leominster,	Guardianship,	10313
1847	Catherine S.	Leominster,	Guardianship,	10314
1861	Cephas	Northbridge,	Will,	10315
1826	Chandler	Berlin,	Guardianship,	10316
1804	Charles	Dudley,	Guardianship,	10317
1869	Charles E.	Leominster,	Guardianship,	10318
1860	Charles S.	Northborough,	Guardianship,	10319
1871	Charles W.	Worcester,	Will,	10320
1852	Danforth	Berlin,	Administration,	10321
1815	Daniel	Berlin,	Guardianship,	10322
1820	Daniel	Milford,	Administration,	10323
1821	Daniel	Milford,	Guardianship,	10324
1824	Daniel	Berlin,	Administration,	10325
1868	Daniel A.	Lancaster,	Administration,	10326
1855	Darius	Hardwick,	Guardianship,	10327
1820	David	Leominster,	Guardianship,	10328
1767	Deborah	Lancaster,	Guardianship,	10329
1855	Dolly	Berlin,	Administration,	10330
1853	Dolly E.	Berlin,	Guardianship,	10331
1869	Edward W.	Leominster,	Guardianship,	10332
1871	Eli	Lancaster,	Guardianship,	10333
1812	Elias	Fitchburg,	Guardianship,	10334
1814	Elijah	Fitchburg,	Administration,	10335
1813	Elisha	Leominster,	Administration,	10336
1843	Elisha	Leominster,	Administration,	10337
1737	Elizabeth	Lancaster,	Guardianship,	10338
1738	Elizabeth	Lancaster,	Guardianship,	10339
1783	Elizabeth	Sutton,	Guardianship,	10340
1865	Elizabeth	Fitchburg,	Administration,	10341
1844	Emeline	Millbury,	Guardianship,	10342
1869	Emily L.	Lancaster,	Guardianship,	10343
1798	Ephraim	Lancaster,	Will,	10344
1816	Ephraim	Lancaster,	Guardianship,	10345
1817	Ephraim	Leominster,	Will,	10346
1827	Ephraim	Lancaster,	Administration,	10347
1857	Eunice L.	Leominster,	Will,	10348
1785	Ezbon	Dudley,	Guardianship,	10349
1803	Ezbon	Dudley,	Administration,	10350
1848	Ferdinand	Auburn,	Guardianship,	10351
1869	Francis W.	Leominster,	Guardianship,	10352
1863	Frank E.	Sturbridge,	Guardianship,	10353

YEAR.	NAME.	RESIDENCE.	NATURE.	CASE.
1869	CARTER, Frank H.	Lancaster,	Guardianship,	10354
1773	Frederick	Leominster,	Guardianship,	10355
1860	George	Westborough,	Will,	10356
1869	George A.	Leominster,	Guardianship,	10357
1804	George E.	Dudley,	Guardianship,	10358
1860	George I.	Berlin,	Guardianship,	10359
1865	George S.	Blackstone,	Guardianship,	10360
1873	Gertrude M.	Leominster,	Adoption, etc.,	10361
1872	Grace M.	Leominster,	Adoption, etc.,	10362
1825	Hannah	Millbury,	Guardianship,	10363
1844	Hannah	Millbury,	Guardianship,	10364
1877	Hannah D.	Leominster,	Will,	10365
1825	Harriet	Millbury,	Guardianship,	10366
1816	Henry	Lancaster,	Guardianship,	10367
1874	Henry A.	Leominster,	Guardianship,	10368
1850	Henry G.	Barre,	Guardianship,	10369
1873	Herbert B.	Leominster,	Guardianship,	10370
1869	Herbert J.	Leominster,	Guardianship,	10371
1875	Herbert J.	Leominster,	Administration,	10372
1834	Horatio	Leominster,	Administration,	10373
1815	Ira	Berlin,	Guardianship,	10374
1859	Ira	Berlin,	Administration,	10375
1850	Israel F.	Berlin,	Guardianship,	10376
1850	Ivory	Berlin,	Administration,	10377
1737	James	Lancaster,	Guardianship,	10378
1800	James	Lancaster,	Will,	10379
1817	James	Lancaster,	Will,	10380
1820	James	Fitchburg,	Administration,	10381
1826	James	Lancaster,	Guardianship,	10382
1853	James	Leominster,	Administration,	10383
1849	James G.	Lancaster,	Administration,	10384
1871	James H.	Leominster,	Will,	10385
1814	Jane	Fitchburg,	Guardianship,	10386
1851	Jane E.	Berlin,	Guardianship,	10387
1855	Jared	Hardwick,	Guardianship,	10388
1762	Jemima	Lancaster,	Guardianship,	10389
1820	Jerome S.	Leominster,	Guardianship,	10390
1874	Jerome S.	Leominster,	Administration,	10391
1766	John	Lancaster,	Administration,	10392
1767	John	Lancaster,	Guardianship,	10393
1812	John	Leominster,	Administration,	10394
1816	John	Lancaster,	Administration,	10395
1820	John	Leominster,	Guardianship,	10396
1824	John	Fitchburg,	Will,	10397
1830	John, 2nd	Lancaster,	Will,	10398

(239—SERIES A.)

YEAR.	NAME.	RESIDENCE.	NATURE.	CASE.
1832	CARTER, John	Lancaster,	Guardianship,	10399
1841	John	Lancaster,	Administration,	10399
1852	John	Petersham,	Administration,	10400
1875	John	Petersham,	Change of Name,	10401
1875	John A.	Petersham,	Change of Name,	10402
1843	John G.	Berlin,	Guardianship,	10403
1858	John O.	Dana,	Administration,	10404
1762	Jonas	Lancaster,	Guardianship,	10405
1799	Jonathan	Leominster,	Will,	10406
1821	Jonathan	Leominster,	Administration,	10407
1824	Jonathan	Leominster,	Administration,	10408
1762	Joseph	Lunenburg,	Administration,	10409
1857	Joseph	Harvard,	Administration,	10410
1873	Joseph S.	Leominster,	Guardianship,	10411
1783	Joshua	Sutton,	Administration,	10412
1846	Joshua	Millbury,	Administration,	10413
1846	Joshua	Millbury,	Pension,	10414
1738	Josiah	Lancaster,	Guardianship,	10415
1812	Josiah	Leominster,	Will,	10416
1830	Julia A. D.	Lancaster,	Guardianship,	10417
1850	Laura E.	Berlin,	Guardianship,	10418
1832	Leonard	Westminster,	Guardianship,	10419
1849	Leonard	Boylston,	Administration,	10420
1850	Leonard	Boylston,	Guardianship,	10421
1879	Lewis	Berlin,	Administration,	10422
1870	Louisa	Leominster,	Will,	10423
1773	Lucinda	Leominster,	Guardianship,	10424
1867	Lucinda	Lancaster,	Will,	10425
1804	Lucretia	Dudley,	Guardianship,	10426
1846	Lucy	Leominster,	Administration,	10427
1876	Lucy	Leominster,	Administration,	10428
1875	Lucy S.	Berlin,	Administration,	10429
1777	Lucy W.	Sudbury,	Guardianship,	10430
1867	Luke W.	Leominster,	Guardianship,	10431
1877	Luke W.	Leominster,	Administration,	10431
1865	Luther	Berlin,	Administration,	10432
1820	Lydia	Leominster,	Guardianship,	10433
1850	Lydia A.	Boylston,	Guardianship,	10434
1876	Margaret	Uxbridge,	Administration,	10435
1838	Martha	Lancaster,	Administration,	10436
1826	Martha L.	Lancaster,	Guardianship,	10437
1816	Mary	Lancaster,	Guardianship,	10438
1820	Mary	Leominster,	Administration,	10439
1825	Mary	Millbury,	Guardianship,	10440
1846	Mary	Leominster,	Administration,	10441

YEAR.	NAME.	RESIDENCE.	NATURE.	CASE.
1826	CARTER, Mary A. A.	Lancaster,	Guardianship,	10442
1820	Mary E.	Leominster,	Guardianship,	10443
1848	Mary E.	Lancaster,	Guardianship,	10444
1850	Mary E.	Boylston,	Guardianship,	10445
1863	Mary E.	Sturbridge,	Guardianship,	10446
1865	Mary E.	Leominster,	Administration,	10447
1843	Mary W.	Berlin,	Guardianship,	10448
1877	Mary W.	Clinton,	Will,	10449
1869	Milton E.	Leominster,	Guardianship,	10450
1804	Nabby	Dudley,	Guardianship,	10451
1814	Nancy	Uxbridge,	Guardianship,	10452
1816	Nancy	Lancaster,	Guardianship,	10453
1825	Nancy	Sterling,	Guardianship,	10454
1851	Nancy	Berlin,	Will,	10455
1854	Nancy	Fitchburg,	Trustee,	10455½
1869	Nancy	Westborough,	Pension,	10456
1874	Nathan	Clinton,	Administration,	10457
1787	Nathaniel	Leominster,	Will,	10458
1812	Nathaniel	Leominster,	Will,	10459
1850	Nathaniel	Leominster,	Administration,	10460
1869	Nehemiah	Westborough,	Administration,	10461
1791	Oliver	Leominster,	Will,	10462
1871	Oliver	Berlin,	Will,	10463
1862	Oscar E.	Winchendon,	Administration,	10464
1869	Ossian A.	Leominster,	Guardianship,	10465
1852	Otis	Leominster,	Administration,	10466
1824	Peter	Sterling,	Administration,	10467
1874	Peter S.	Fitchburg,	Administration,	10468
1737	Phineas	Lancaster,	Guardianship,	10469
1809	Phineas	Leominster,	Guardianship,	10470
1810	Phineas	Leominster,	Will,	10470
1843	Phineas	Leominster,	Will,	10471
1872	Polly	Auburn,	Administration,	10472
1738	Prudence	Lancaster,	Guardianship,	10473
1762	Prudence	Lancaster,	Guardianship,	10474
1849	Prudence	Leominster,	Will,	10475
1816	Rebecca	Lancaster,	Guardianship,	10476
1785	Rhoda	Dudley,	Guardianship,	10477
1788	Rhoda	Dudley,	Administration,	10478
1807	Rhoda	Dudley,	Administration,	10479
1743	Roger	Dudley,	Guardianship,	10480
1824	Rufus	Millbury,	Administration,	10481
1825	Rufus	Millbury,	Guardianship,	10482
1842	Rufus	Berlin,	Administration,	10483
1739	Ruth	Lancaster,	Will,	10484

Year.	Name.	Residence.	Nature.	Case.
1815	CARTER, Sally	Berlin,	Guardianship,	10485
1821	Sally	Milford,	Guardianship,	10486
1838	Sally	Milford,	Administration,	10487
1804	Sally W.	Dudley,	Guardianship,	10488
1844	Salma	Millbury,	Will,	10489
1738	Samuel	Lancaster,	Administration,	10490
1761	Samuel	Lancaster,	Administration,	10491
1864	Samuel	Lancaster,	Administration,	10492
1876	Samuel	Fitchburg,	Guardianship,	10493
1876	Samuel	Fitchburg,	Will,	10493
1737	Sarah	Lancaster,	Guardianship,	10494
1741	Sarah	Dudley,	Guardianship,	10495
1826	Sarah	Lancaster,	Guardianship,	10496
1875	Sarah E.	Clinton,	Administration,	10497
1866	Sarah H.	Leominster,	Will,	10498
1868	Sarah W.	Petersham,	Administration,	10499
1841	Saunderson	Berlin,	Administration,	10500
1817	Sewell	Lancaster,	Guardianship,	10501
1820	Silas	Leominster,	Administration,	10502
1820	Silas, Jr.	Leominster,	Administration,	10503
1842	Silas J.	Hardwick,	Administration,	10504
1785	Silvia	Dudley,	Guardianship,	10505
1879	Solon	Leominster,	Administration,	10506
1864	Solon F.	Lancaster,	Guardianship,	10507
1825	Sophia	Sterling,	Guardianship,	10508
1853	Stedman T.	Berlin,	Guardianship,	10509
1741	Stephen	Dudley,	Guardianship,	10510
1879	Sumner L.	Leominster,	Administration,	10511
1852	Susan A.	Leominster,	Guardianship,	10512
1837	Susannah	Lancaster,	Will,	10513
1843	Sylvia A.	Leominster,	Guardianship,	10514
1737	Thomas	Lancaster,	Administration,	10515
1767	Thomas	Lancaster,	Guardianship,	10516
1773	Thomas	Leominster,	Administration,	10517
1802	Thomas	Lunenburg,	Will,	10518
1816	Thomas	Fitchburg,	Will,	10519
1823	Thomas	Lancaster,	Will,	10520
1832	Thomas	Fitchburg,	Guardianship,	10521
1863	Thomas	Lunenburg,	Will,	10522
1867	Thomas	Westminster,	Guardianship,	10523
1772	Timothy	Sutton,	Administration,	10524
1784	Timothy	Ward,	Administration,	10525
1863	Vilender	Westborough,	Will,	10526
1852	Wallace M.	Leominster,	Guardianship,	10527
1867	Wilder	Leominster,	Guardianship,	10528

YEAR.	NAME.	RESIDENCE.	NATURE.	CASE.
1741	CARTER, William	Dudley,	Administration,	10529
1741	William	Dudley,	Guardianship,	10530
1784	William	Dudley,	Will,	10531
1842	William	Grafton,	Guardianship,	10532
1845	William	Leominster,	Administration,	10533
1855	William	Fitchburg,	Administration,	10534
1863	William E.	Sturbridge,	Guardianship,	10535
1847	William S.	Leominster,	Administration,	10536
1874	CARTIER, Jacob	Worcester,	Guardianship,	10537
1796	CARVER, Sarah	Mendon,	Administration,	10538
1879	CASAVANT, Francis X.	Southbridge,	Administration,	10539
1796	CASE, Amos	Sutton,	Administration,	10540
1881	Clarissa	Charlton,	Will,	10541
1801	Edward	Mendon,	Guardianship,	10542
1822	Elijah	Grafton,	Administration,	10543
1822	Elijah A.	Grafton,	Guardianship,	10544
1827	John	Millbury,	Administration,	10545
1827	John	Millbury,	Guardianship,	10546
1822	John M.	Grafton,	Guardianship,	10547
1856	John R.	Charlton,	Will,	10548
1851	Lydia	Millbury,	Administration,	10549
1810	Mary	Sutton,	Will,	10550
1827	Mary	Millbury,	Guardianship,	10551
1877	CASEY, Annie	Milford,	Guardianship,	10552
1877	Delia	Milford,	Guardianship,	10553
1877	Honora	Milford,	Guardianship,	10554
1871	James	Worcester,	Administration,	10555
1876	John	Worcester,	Will,	10556
1853	John T.	Berlin,	Administration;	10557
1877	Margaret	Milford,	Guardianship,	10558
1877	Martin	Milford,	Guardianship,	10559
1877	Mary	Milford,	Guardianship,	10560
1867	Patrick	Westborough,	Will,	10561
1871	Patrick	Royalston,	Guardianship,	10562
1875	Patrick	Milford,	Administration,	10563
1877	Patrick	Milford,	Guardianship,	10564
1850	CASHMAN, Thomas	Worcester,	Guardianship,	10565
1837	CASS, Angelina	Mendon,	Guardianship,	10566
1879	Elbridge	Sturbridge,	Will,	10567
1837	Esther	Mendon,	Guardianship,	10568
1837	Gilbert	Mendon,	Guardianship,	10569
1837	Harriet	Mendon,	Guardianship,	10570
1844	Joanna	Mendon,	Will,	10571
1800	John	Mendon,	Guardianship,	10572
1837	Jonathan	Mendon,	Administration,	10573

YEAR.	NAME.	RESIDENCE.	NATURE.	CASE.
1837	CASS, Jonathan	Mendon,	Guardianship,	10574
1837	Mary	Mendon,	Guardianship,	10575
1837	Nancy	Mendon,	Guardianship,	10576
1879	Rhoda C.	Sturbridge,	Guardianship,	10577
	CASSADY AND CASSIDY,			
1876	Ellen	Worcester,	Guardianship,	10578
1875	John	Worcester,	Will,	10579
1875	Joseph	Uxbridge,	Guardianship,	10580
1875	Mary A.	Worcester,	Guardianship,	10581
1869	Mathew	Blackstone,	Guardianship,	10582
1871	Thomas	Milford,	Administration,	10583
1846	CASSUM, Michael	West Boylston,	Guardianship,	10584
	CASWELL AND CASWALL,			
1873	Chloe	Winchendon,	Will,	10585
1877	Cynthia	North Brookfield,	Will,	10586
1778	David	Douglas,	Will,	10587
1854	David	Winchendon,	Administration,	10588
1852	David A.	Winchendon,	Guardianship,	10589
1873	Edwin D.	Rockford, Mich.,	Guardianship,	10590
1867	Eunice	Fitchburg,	Will,	10591
1847	Eunice M.	Fitchburg,	Guardianship,	10592
1873	Hiram C.	Grand Rapids, Mich.,	Guardianship,	10593
1875	Hosea M.	Fitchburg,	Will,	10594
1847	Josiah	Fitchburg,	Will,	10595
1853	Josiah W.	Fitchburg,	Will,	10596
1852	Marietta	Winchendon,	Guardianship,	10597
1863	Mary C.	Keene, N. H.,	Guardianship,	10598
1863	Nathan	Douglas,	Administration,	10599
1851	Noah A.	Winchendon,	Administration,	10600
1819	Samuel	Fitchburg,	Will,	10601
1867	Stephen	Fitchburg,	Administration,	10602
1873	Wilder	North Brookfield,	Will,	10603
1871	CATIN, Martin	Lunenburg,	Will,	10604
1873	CATTARET, Anthony	Webster,	Guardianship,	10605
1873	Frederick	Webster,	Guardianship,	10606
1873	Henry	Webster,	Guardianship,	10607
1873	Louis	Webster,	Guardianship,	10608
1872	Theophilus	Webster,	Administration,	10609
1873	Theophilus	Webster,	Guardianship,	10610
1871	CATTRALL, Catharine C.	Leominster,	Will,	10611
	CAVANAGH AND CAVANAUGH,			
1880	Catherine	Worcester,	Administration,	10612
1879	William H.	Milford,	Administration,	10613
1859	CAVANEY, James	Athol,	Administration,	10614
1856	CAWTHORN, David	Northborough,	Administration,	10615

YEAR.	NAME.	RESIDENCE.	NATURE.	CASE.
1856	CAWTHORN, David F.	Northborough,	Guardianship,	10616
1856	Edwin H.	Northborough,	Guardianship,	10617
1879	CAY, Miranda	Milford,	Administration,	10618
1880	CAYA, Josephine E.	Southbridge,	Adoption, etc.,	10619
1876	CHABOT, Charles C.	Ashburnham,	Administration,	10620
1876	Charles S.	Ashburnham,	Guardianship,	10621
1876	Henrie	Ashburnham,	Guardianship,	10622
1876	Marie S.	Ashburnham,	Guardianship,	10623
1876	Philipe E.	Ashburnham,	Guardianship,	10624
1876	Selina	Ashburnham,	Guardianship,	10625
	CHACE see CHASE.			
1871	CHADBOURN, Joanna B.	Brookline,	Adoption, etc.,	10626
1767	CHADDICK, Anna	Worcester,	Administration,	10627
1765	Daniel	Worcester,	Guardianship,	10628
1794	David	Worcester,	Will,	10629
1765	Eunice	Worcester,	Guardianship,	10630
1765	Isaac	Worcester,	Guardianship,	10631
1768	John	Worcester,	Will,	10632
1763	John, Jr.	Worcester,	Administration,	10633
1769	Jonathan	Worcester,	Will,	10634
1770	Lucy	Worcester,	Guardianship,	10635
1765	Lydia	Worcester,	Guardianship,	10636
1770	Molly	Worcester,	Guardianship,	10637
1765	Sarah	Worcester,	Guardianship,	10638
1877	CHADDOCK, Moses G.	Los Angeles, Cal.,	Will,	10639
1865	CHADSEY, Euclid	Wickford, R. I.,	Administration,	10640
1867	Frances A.	Warren,	Administration,	10641
1861	Waite C.	Blackstone,	Administration,	10642
1864	William R.	Keene, N. H.,	Guardianship,	10643
1836	CHADWICK, Daniel	Worcester,	Administration,	10644
1803	David	Worcester,	Guardianship,	10645
1846	Emeline C.	Douglas,	Guardianship,	10646
1875	Hannah	Royalston,	Administration,	10647
1794	Isaac	Worcester,	Guardianship,	10648
1812	Isaac, 2nd	Worcester,	Administration,	10649
1836	Isaac	Worcester,	Pension,	10650
1836	Isaac	Worcester,	Administration,	10651
1830	Jerusha	Western,	Will,	10652
1836	John	Worcester,	Guardianship,	10653
1846	John U.	Douglas,	Administration,	10654
1846	John W.	Douglas,	Guardianship,	10655
1765	Joseph	Western,	Administration,	10656
1782	Joseph	Rutland,	Administration,	10657
1798	Joseph	Worcester,	Administration,	10658
1803	Lydia	Worcester,	Guardianship,	10659

Year.	Name.	Residence.	Nature.	Case.
1801	CHADWICK, Nathan	Western,	Administration,	10660
1871	Stephen	Holden,	Administration,	10661
	CHAFFEE AND CHAFEE,			
1749	Abigail	Woodstock,	Guardianship,	10662
1869	Alpheus C.	Oxford,	Administration,	10663
1863	Betsey	Woodstock, Conn.,	Administration,	10664
1867	Caroline	Thompson, Conn.,	Administration,	10665
1870	Frederick A.	Oxford,	Guardianship,	10666
1870	George B.	Oxford,	Guardianship,	10667
1745	Joel	Woodstock,	Administration,	10668
1747	Joel	Woodstock,	Guardianship,	10669
1858	John	Palmer,.	Guardianship,	10670
1745	Joshua	Woodstock,	Guardianship,	10671
1863	Levina M.	Oxford,	Will,	10672
1870	Marietta E.	Oxford,	Guardianship,	10673
1870	Martha A.	Oxford,	Guardianship,	10674
1863	Merrick	Dudley,	Administration,	10675
1822	Priscilla	Brookfield,	Administration,	10676
1876	Rufus	Gardner,	Will,	10677
1857	William	Palmer,	Guardianship,	10678
1826	CHAFFIN, Adelia	Princeton,	Guardianship,	10679
1829	Catherine	Holden,	Guardianship,	10680
1844	Catharine A.	Holden,	Guardianship,	10681
1876	Charles	Holden,	Guardianship,	10682
1860	Clara W.	Clinton,	Guardianship,	10683
1860	Clarissa	Holden,	Will,	10684
1826	Darwin	Princeton,	Guardianship,	10685
1829	David	Leominster,	Administration,	10686
1844	David F.	Leominster,	Guardianship,	10687
1826	Dorcas M.	Princeton,	Guardianship,	10688
1869	Edgar O.	Worcester,	Guardianship,	10689
1826	Edwin	Princeton,	Guardianship,	10690
1877	Elisha	Holden,	Guardianship,	10691
1879	Elisha	Holden,	Will,	10691
1829	Eliza	Holden,	Guardianship,	10692
1826	Elizabeth	Princeton,	Guardianship,	10693
1877	George M.	Phillipston,	Guardianship,	10694
1815	Gladwin	Harvard,	Administration,	10695
1856	Hannah	Holden,	Administration,	10696
1857	Hannah	Holden,	Pension,	10697
1865	Harry W.	West Boylston,	Guardianship,	10698
1865	Helen A.	West Boylston,	Guardianship,	10699
1844	Henry S.	Leominster,	Guardianship,	10700
1865	Hervey B.	Holden,	Guardianship,	10701
1815	John	Harvard,	Guardianship,	10702

YEAR.	NAME.	RESIDENCE.	NATURE.	CASE.
1827	CHAFFIN, John, 2nd	Holden,	Administration,	10703
1854	John	Holden,	Administration,	10704
1826	John C.	Princeton,	Guardianship,	10705
1847	Jonas	Holden,	Administration,	10706
1864	Jonas	West Boylston,	Administration,	10707
1829	Jonas, Jr.	Holden,	Guardianship,	10708
1861	Jonathan	Holden,	Will,	10709
1861	Jones	Worcester,	Administration,	10710
1815	Joseph	Harvard,	Guardianship,	10711
1874	Joseph	Worcester,	Adoption, etc.,	10712
1826	Leonard R.	Princeton,	Guardianship,	10713
1868	Lewis G.	Worcester,	Guardianship,	10714
1865	Louisa M.	West Boylston,	Guardianship,	10715
1829	Lucy	Holden,	Guardianship,	10716
1826	Maria	Princeton,	Guardianship,	10717
1826	Mary	Princeton,	Guardianship,	10718
1858	Mary W.	West Boylston,	Administration,	10719
1863	Mary W.	Holden,	Administration,	10720
1869	Moore M.	Worcester,	Will,	10721
1826	Moses A.	Princeton,	Guardianship,	10722
1815	Nancy	Harvard,	Guardianship,	10723
1830	Nathan, Jr.	Holden,	Administration,	10724
1838	Tilla	Holden,	Will,	10725
1838	Tilla	Holden,	Pension,	10726
1866	Tilla	Holden,	Will,	10727
1815	William	Harvard,	Guardianship,	10728
1844	William F.	Holden,	Guardianship,	10729
	CHAMBERLAIN and CHAMBER- LIN,			
1770	Abigail	Worcester,	Guardianship,	10730
1859	Abigail	Worcester,	Will,	10731
1881	Achsah	West Brookfield,	Administration,	10732
1848	Albert A.	Charlton,	Administration,	10733
1853	Andrew M.	Southbridge,	Change of Name,	10734
1840	Anna	Charlton,	Will,	10735
1827	Arathusa	Worcester,	Guardianship,	10736
1873	Arathusa H.	Worcester,	Will,	10737
1862	Arthur	Petersham,	Change of Name,	10738
1773	Asa	Dudley,	Guardianship,	10739
1841	Asahel, 2nd	Dudley,	Administration,	10740
1790	Augustus	Dudley,	Guardianship,	10741
1751	Benjamin	Dudley,	Guardianship,	10742
1768	Benjamin	Sutton,	Guardianship,	10743
1806	Benjamin	Westborough,	Will,	10744
1833	Benjamin S.	Charlton,	Guardianship,	10745

YEAR.	NAME.	RESIDENCE.	NATURE.	CASE.

CHAMBERLAIN AND CHAMBER-
LIN,

1783	Calvin	Douglas,	Guardianship,	10746
1856	Calvin	Dudley,	Administration,	10747
1869	Calvin	Auburn,	Administration,	10748
1878	Calvin A.	Westborough,	Guardianship,	10749
1827	Caroline	Worcester,	Guardianship,	10750
1846	Caroline	Ashburnham,	Guardianship,	10751
1878	Caroline C.	Westborough,	Guardianship,	10752
1857	Catherine S.	Sutton,	Guardianship,	10753
1791	Charles	Dudley,	Guardianship,	10754
1827	Charles C.	Worcester,	Guardianship,	10755
1852	Charles C.	Worcester,	Administration,	10756
1877	Charles E.	Oxford,	Adoption, etc.,	10757
1829	Charles E. P.	Beverly,	Guardianship,	10758
1791	Chester	Dudley,	Guardianship,	10759
1791	Chloe	Dudley,	Guardianship,	10760
1840	Chloe	Hardwick,	Will,	10761
1790	Clarrey	Dudley,	Guardianship,	10762
1872	Cordelia M.	Worcester,	Administration,	10763
1877	Cornelia A.	Southbridge,	Administration,	10764
1863	Curtis	Southborough,	Administration,	10765
1881	Cyrus L.	Winchendon,	Administration,	10766
1820	Daniel	Southborough,	Guardianship,	10767
1825	Daniel	Westborough,	Will,	10768
1840	Daniel	Westborough,	Administration,	10769
1860	Daniel	Westborough,	Will,	10770
1841	Deborah J.	Holden,	Guardianship,	10771
1854	Deborah J.	Leicester,	Administration,	10772
1863	Delia	Southbridge,	Administration,	10773
1820	Dennis	Southborough,	Guardianship,	10774
1872	Dora C.	Worcester,	Administration,	10775
1838	Dulcina	Charlton,	Guardianship,	10776
1850	Dwight	Southbridge,	Guardianship,	10777
1746	Ebenezer	Oxford,	Administration,	10778
1767	Ebenezer	Douglas,	Guardianship,	10779
1806	Ebenezer	Westborough,	Administration,	10780
1830	Ebenezer	Rutland,	Will,	10781
1819	Edmund	Southborough,	Will,	10782
1820	Edmund	Southborough,	Will,	10783
1876	Elbridge G.	Petersham,	Administration,	10784
1833	Eliakim	Charlton,	Will,	10785
1812	Elmira	Dudley,	Guardianship,	10786
1820	Esther	Southborough,	Guardianship,	10787
1879	Etta A.	Southbridge,	Adoption, etc.,	10788

	CHAMBERLAIN AND CHAMBER-LIN,			
1876	Eugene A.	Southborough,	Administration,	10789
1812	Evelina	Dudley,	Guardianship,	10790
1866	Franklin	Milford,	Will,	10791
1866	George A.	Worcester,	Will,	10792
1826	Hannah	Worcester,	Will,	10793
1873	Hannah B.	Worcester,	Will,	10794
1827	Hannah C.	Worcester,	Guardianship,	10795
1838	Harmon	Worcester,	Will,	10796
1853	Harriet E.	Oswego, N. Y.,	Guardianship,	10797
1862	Harriet M.	Petersham,	Change of Name,	10798
1872	Harriet N.	Millbury,	Administration,	10799
1790	Henry	Dudley,	Guardianship,	10800
1841	Henry	Holden,	Guardianship,	10801
1827	Henry H.	Worcester,	Guardianship,	10802
1790	Ichabod	Dudley,	Administration,	10803
1790	Ichabod	Dudley,	Guardianship,	10804
1763	Ithamer	Dudley,	Guardianship,	10805
1770	Jacob	Worcester,	Guardianship,	10806
1780	Jacob	Dudley,	Will,	10807
1790	Jacob	Worcester,	Administration,	10808
1791	Jacob	Dudley,	Administration,	10809
1791	Jacob	Dudley,	Guardianship,	10810
1812	Jacob	Dudley,	Guardianship,	10811
1834	Jacob	Millbury,	Will,	10812
1840	Jacob	Holden,	Administration,	10813
1841	Jacob	Holden,	Guardianship,	10814
1838	Jason	Charlton,	Administration,	10815
1743	John	Leicester,	Administration,	10816
1780	John	Dudley,	Guardianship,	10817
1782	John	Sutton,	Administration,	10818
1810	John	Worcester,	Guardianship,	10819
1813	John	Worcester,	Administration,	10819
1831	John	Royalston,	Will,	10820
1849	John	Southborough,	Will,	10821
1872	John	Southborough,	Will,	10822
1875	John C.	Southbridge,	Administration,	10823
1880	John H.	West Boylston,	Administration,	10824
1880	John N.	Sturbridge,	Administration,	10825
1878	Jonas H.	West Boylston,	Administration,	10826
1841	Jonathan	Holden,	Guardianship,	10827
1746	Joseph	Dudley,	Guardianship,	10828
1767	Joseph	Petersham,	Guardianship,	10829
1770	Joseph	Oxford,	Guardianship,	10830

CHAMBERLAIN AND CHAMBER-
LIN,

Year	Name	Residence	Nature	Case
1783	Joseph	Douglas,	Administration,	10831
1791	Joshua	Dudley,	Guardianship,	10832
1855	Laura M.	Southborough,	Adoption, etc.,	10833
1829	Lemuel	Southborough,	Administration,	10834
1841	Levi	Holden,	Guardianship,	10835
1864	Levi	Holden,	Administration,	10836
1811	Lincoln	Dudley,	Guardianship,	10837
1767	Lucy	Petersham,	Guardianship,	10838
1853	Lucy A.	Oswego, N. Y.,	Guardianship,	10839
1780	Luther	Dudley,	Guardianship,	10840
1782	Luther	Douglas,	Guardianship,	10841
1791	Luther	Oxford,	Administration,	10842
1811	Luther	Dudley,	Will,	10843
1812	Luther	Dudley,	Guardianship,	10844
1812	Luther	Westborough,	Guardianship,	10845
1849	Luther	Westborough,	Administration,	10846
1770	Lydia	Worcester,	Guardianship,	10847
1863	Lyman	Dana,	Will,	10848
1836	Lyscom	Upton,	Will,	10849
1850	Major	Southbridge,	Guardianship,	10850
1853	Major	Southbridge,	Change of Name,	10851
1770	Mary	Worcester,	Guardianship,	10852
1807	Mary	Sturbridge,	Administration,	10853
1871	Mary	Boston,	Adoption, etc.,	10854
1879	Mary C.	Southborough,	Guardianship,	10855
1820	Mehetable	Westborough,	Will,	10856
1814	Moses	Dudley,	Will,	10857
1880	Moses	Templeton,	Will,	10858
1869	Nahum W.	Millbury,	Will,	10859
1874	Nancy A.	Worcester,	Administration,	10860
1874	Nellie J.	West Brookfield,	Guardianship,	10861
1832	Olive	Royalston,	Guardianship,	10862
1857	Otis	Sutton,	Administration,	10863
1880	Otis	Winchendon,	Will,	10864
1820	Patty	Southborough,	Guardianship,	10865
1849	Percis	New Braintree,	Will,	10866
1840	Peter	Petersham,	Administration,	10867
1862	Peter W.	Petersham,	Change of Name,	10868
1812	Phebe	Dudley,	Guardianship,	10869
1748	Phillip	Dudley,	Guardianship,	10870
1790	Polly	Dudley,	Guardianship,	10871
1791	Polly	Dudley,	Guardianship,	10872
1863	Polly	Webster,	Guardianship,	10873

YEAR.	NAME.	RESIDENCE.	NATURE.	CASE.
	CHAMBERLAIN AND CHAMBER-			
	LIN,			
1868	Polly	Webster,	Administration,	10873
1790	Rebeccah	Dudley,	Guardianship,	10874
1783	Reubin	Douglas,	Guardianship,	10875
1791	Rhoda	Dudley,	Guardianship,	10876
1855	Robert H.	Worcester,	Guardianship,	10877
1790	Sabrey	Dudley,	Guardianship,	10878
1790	Sally	Dudley,	Guardianship,	10879
1758	Samuel	Petersham,	Administration,	10880
1772	Samuel	Dudley,	Guardianship,	10881
1825	Samuel	Petersham,	Administration,	10882
1838	Samuel	Charlton,	Guardianship,	10883
1858	Samuel	Westborough,	Will,	10884
1878	Samuel	Westborough,	Administration,	10885
1771	Samuel, Jr.	Dudley,	Administration,	10886
1812	Sarah	Dudley,	Guardianship,	10887
1818	Sarah	Dudley,	Administration,	10887
1873	Sarah	Woodstock, Conn.,	Administration,	10888
1870	Sarah B.	Bolton,	Administration,	10889
1878	Seth	Warren,	Will,	10890
1746	Simon	Douglas,	Administration,	10891
1806	Sophia	Westborough,	Guardianship,	10892
1848	Sophia	Sutton,	Administration,	10893
1829	Stephen	Beverly,	Guardianship,	10894
1853	Stephen	Oswego, N. Y.,	Guardianship,	10895
1767	Susannah	Petersham,	Guardianship,	10896
1770	Susannah	Worcester,	Guardianship,	10897
1850	Sylvanus	Southbridge,	Administration,	10898
1855	Thomas	Worcester,	Administration,	10899
1817	Timothy	Charlton,	Guardianship,	10900
1850	Truman	Southbridge,	Guardianship,	10901
1860	Tyler	Millbury,	Administration,	10902
1860	Wilber T.	Worcester,	Adoption, etc.,	10903
1767	William	Petersham,	Guardianship,	10904
1770	William	Worcester,	Guardianship,	10905
1825	CHAMBERS, David	Lancaster,	Will,	10906
1880	CHAMPAGNE, Louis	Millbury,	Will,	10907
1874	CHAMPIGNIE, Marie	Spencer,	Will,	10908
1865	CHAMPION, Jennie M.	Worcester,	Guardianship,	10909
1833	CHAMPNEY, Benjamin	Southborough,	Administration,	10910
1867	Eben F.	Grafton,	Guardianship,	10911
1881	Eben F.	Millbury,	Administration,	10912
1806	Jonathan	Southborough,	Administration,	10913
1806	Phebe	Southborough,	Guardianship,	10914

Year.	Name.	Residence.	Nature.	Case.
1866	CHAMPNEY, Samuel P.	Grafton,	Administration,	10915
1850	CHANDLER, Abby L.	Lancaster,	Guardianship,	10916
1826	Abel G.	Petersham,	Guardianship,	10917
1853	Abel G.	Ripton, Vt.,	Guardianship,	10918
1793	Anna	Worcester,	Administration,	10919
1826	Benjamin	Petersham,	Will,	10920
1798	Charles	Worcester,	Will,	10921
1830	Charles	Southbridge,	Administration,	10922
1875	Charles G.	Fitchburg,	Administration,	10923
1789	Clark	Petersham,	Guardianship,	10924
1804	Clark	Worcester,	Administration,	10925
1869	Dolly	Lancaster,	Will,	10926
1743	Elifalet	Lancaster,	Guardianship,	10927
1746	Eliphalet	Lancaster,	Administration,	10928
1783	Elizabeth	Worcester,	Guardianship,	10929
1856	Ephraim	Princeton,	Will,	10930
1866	Fanny	Worcester,	Guardianship,	10931
1777	Gardner	Hardwick,	Absentee,	10932
1782	Gardner	Worcester,	Administration,	10933
1783	Gardner L.	Worcester,	Guardianship,	10934
1878	George	Worcester,	Trustee,	10935
1826	Hannah B.	Petersham,	Sale Real Est.,	10936
1743	John	Woodstock,	Will,	10937
1778	John	Worcester,	Absentee,	10938
1782	John	Worcester,	Administration,	10939
1784	John	Petersham,	Administration,	10940
1829	John	Lancaster,	Guardianship,	10941
1866	Josephine	Worcester,	Will,	10942
1878	Josephine R.	Worcester,	Trustee,	10943
1853	Josiah S.	Ripton, Vt.,	Guardianship,	10944
1789	Lydia	Petersham,	Guardianship,	10945
1812	Martha	Petersham,	Administration,	10946
1826	Mary D.	Petersham,	Guardianship,	10947
1746	Moses	Lancaster,	Guardianship,	10948
1777	Nathaniel	Petersham,	Absentee,	10949
1801	Nathaniel	Worcester,	Will,	10950
1852	Nathaniel	Lancaster,	Will,	10951
1789	Nathaniel, Jr.	Petersham,	Guardianship,	10952
1777	Rufus	Worcester,	Absentee,	10953
1870	Sally B.	Charlton,	Administration,	10954
1791	Samuel	Thompson, Conn.,	Guardianship,	10955
1814	Samuel	Woodstock, Conn.,	Will,	10956
1743	Sanborn	Lancaster,	Guardianship,	10957
1778	Sarah	Worcester,	Will,	10958
1798	Sarah	Worcester,	Guardianship,	10959

YEAR.	NAME.	RESIDENCE.	NATURE.	CASE.
1801	CHANDLER, Sarah	Worcester,	Will,	10960
1866	Stephen	Pomfret, Conn.,	Foreign Will,	10961
1804	Thomas	Worcester,	Will,	10962
1793	William	Worcester,	Administration,	10963
1881	CHANEY, Daniel A.	Fitchburg,	Administration,	10964
	CHAPELL see CHAPPELL.			
1757	CHAPIN, Abigail	Mendon,	Guardianship,	10965
1876	Achsah	Worcester,	Will,	10966
1863	Adaline A.	Templeton,	Adoption,	10967
1844	Adams	Milford,	Pension,	10968
1875	Adolphus	Uxbridge,	Will,	10969
1820	Alace A.	Western,	Guardianship,	10970
1880	Aldus M.	Worcester,	Will,	10971
1833	Alexander	Milford,	Guardianship,	10972
1784	Amariah	Milford,	Guardianship,	10973
1840	Amariah	Uxbridge,	Will,	10974
1846	Amory	Providence, R. I.,	Foreign Will,	10975
1831	Amos	Milford,	Will,	10976
1879	Anna M.	Holden,	Guardianship,	10977
1856	Annie T.	Worcester,	Adoption, etc.,	10978
1861	Arthur T.	Portland, Me.,	Guardianship,	10979
1863	Asenath C.	Northbridge,	Administration,	10980
1869	Asenath E.	Milford,	Guardianship,	10981
1835	Benjamin	Worcester,	Administration,	10982
1777	Benjamin, Jr.	Worcester,	Administration,	10983
1844	Benjamin T.	New York, N. Y.,	Guardianship,	10984
1872	Beriah H.	Elmer, N. J.,	Administration,	10985
1868	Callie A.	Milford,	Guardianship,	10986
1835	Calvin L.	Worcester,	Guardianship,	10987
1835	Caroline	Worcester,	Guardianship,	10988
1878	Catharine F.	Worcester,	Administration,	10989
1860	Charles	Upton,	Administration,	10990
1848	Charles A.	Northbridge,	Guardianship,	10991
1851	Charles H.	Worcester,	Guardianship,	10992
1871	Charles J.	Milford,	Guardianship,	10993
1851	Charles P.	Worcester,	Will,	10994
1852	Charles P.	Worcester,	Guardianship,	10995
1879	Charles P.	Holden.	Guardianship,	10996
1872	Charles S.	Worcester,	Guardianship,	10997
1871	Charlotte L.	Phillipston,	Guardianship,	10998
1832	Clarissa	Sturbridge,	Guardianship,	10999
1841	Clarissa	Sturbridge,	Guardianship,	11000
1835	Comfort	Worcester,	Guardianship,	11001
1835	Cornelia	Worcester,	Guardianship,	11002
1838	Cyrus	Milford,	Guardianship,	11003

YEAR.	NAME.	RESIDENCE.	NATURE.	CASE.
1741	CHAPIN, Daniel	Mendon,	Guardianship,	11004
1775	Daniel	Mendon,	Administration,	11005
1871	Daniel E.	Worcester,	Will,	11006
1741	David	Mendon,	Guardianship,	11007
1814	David	Upton,	Will,	11008
1814	David	Upton,	Guardianship,	11009
1849	David N.	Westborough,	Guardianship,	11010
1753	Deborah	Uxbridge,	Guardianship,	11011
1757	Ebenezer	Mendon,	Guardianship,	11012
1867	Ede	Milford,	Will,	11013
1879	Ederetta	Holden,	Guardianship,	11014
1820	Edward	Western,	Guardianship,	11015
1848	Edward	Northbridge,	Guardianship,	11016
1879	Edward H.	Holden,	Guardianship,	11017
1851	Edward P.	Worcester,	Guardianship,	11018
1853	Edwin A.	Grafton,	Administration,	11019
1877	Edwin T.	Worcester,	Guardianship,	11020
1876	Effie L.	Worcester,	Guardianship,	11021
1832	Eleanor C.	Sturbridge,	Guardianship,	11022
1830	Eli	Worcester,	Will,	11023
1869	Eli	Milford,	Will,	11024
1863	Eli T.	Worcester,	Administration,	11025
1826	Elisha	Upton,	Administration,	11026
1783	Elizabeth	Mendon,	Guardianship,	11027
1837	Elizabeth	Western,	Will,	11028
1835	Elizabeth R.	Worcester,	Guardianship,	11029
1841	Emily	Sturbridge,	Guardianship,	11030
1812	Ephraim	Milford,	Will,	11031
1861	Eunice	Northbridge,	Will,	11032
1876	Fannie E.	Worcester,	Guardianship,	11033
1835	George E.	Worcester,	Guardianship,	11034
1873	George E.	Holden,	Will,	11035
1848	George W.	Northbridge,	Guardianship,	11036
1801	Gershom	Uxbridge,	Will,	11037
1877	Grace T.	Worcester,	Guardianship,	11038
1869	Hannah A.	Northbridge,	Administration,	11039
1835	Hannah F.	Worcester,	Guardianship,	11040
1868	Harriet	Milford,	Will,	11041
1820	Harriet A.	Western,	Guardianship,	11042
1856	Helen I.	Worcester,	Adoption, etc.,	11043
1871	Helen I.	Holden,	Guardianship,	11044
1827	Henry	Upton,	Guardianship,	11045
1867	Henry	Milford,	Guardianship,	11046
1876	Henry	Milford,	Will,	11047
1878	Henry	Worcester,	Will,	11048

YEAR.	NAME.	RESIDENCE.	NATURE.	CASE.
1861	CHAPIN, Henry D.	Portland, Me.,	Guardianship,	11049
1854	Henry L.	Milford,	Guardianship,	11050
1811	Hollis	Milford,	Guardianship,	11051
1838	Hollis	Milford,	Guardianship,	11052
1857	Hollis	Milford,	Administration,	11053
1876	Ida I.	Worcester,	Guardianship,	11054
1798	Jemima	Worcester,	Will,	11055
1880	Jennie F.	Northborough,	Adoption, etc.,	11056
1864	Joel	Milford,	Will,	11057
1770	John	Mendon,	Will,	11058
1879	John C.	Holden,	Guardianship,	11059
1835	John H.	Worcester,	Guardianship,	11060
1849	John S.	Uxbridge,	Administration,	11061
1788	Joseph	Milford,	Will,	11062
1809	Joseph	Uxbridge,	Will,	11063
1871	Joseph B.	Milford,	Administration,	11064
1869	Joseph J.	Milford,	Will,	11065
1839	Josiah S.	New York, N. Y.,	Guardianship,	11066
1832	Laurinda	Sturbridge,	Guardianship,	11067
1843	Lemuel P.	Milford,	Administration,	11068
1835	Leonard	Worcester,	Guardianship,	11069
1862	Leonard	Milford,	Will,	11070
1830	Levi	Milford,	Will,	11071
1874	Lewis	Worcester,	Will,	11072
1811	Linda	Milford,	Guardianship,	11073
1876	Lizzie E.	Worcester,	Guardianship,	11074
1783	Lois	Mendon,	Guardianship,	11075
1835	Lucy	Worcester,	Guardianship,	11076
1847	Lucy	Worcester,	Administration,	11077
1869	Lucy G.	Worcester,	Will,	11078
1741	Lydia	Mendon,	Guardianship,	11079
1813	Lydia	Milford,	Administration,	11080
1831	Margaret	Worcester,	Administration,	11081
1838	Maria	Milford,	Guardianship,	11082
1854	Marion	Milford,	Adoption, etc.,	11083
1846	Martha	Westborough,	Will,	11084
1811	Marvel	Milford,	Guardianship,	11085
1849	Marvel	Westborough,	Will,	11086
1838	Marvell	Milford	Will,	11087
1757	Mary	Mendon,	Guardianship,	11088
1783	Mary	Mendon,	Guardianship,	11089
1807	Mary	Milford,	Guardianship,	11090
1809	Mary	Milford,	Administration,	11090
1811	Mary N.	Milford,	Guardianship,	11091
1741	Moses	Mendon,	Guardianship,	11092

Year.	Name.	Residence.	Nature.	Case.
1802	CHAPIN, Moses	Milford,	Administration,	11093
1844	Moses	Grafton,	Will,	11094
1857	Moses T.	Mendon,	Will,	11095
1843	Moses W.	Uxbridge,	Guardianship,	11096
1851	Nathan	Milford,	Will,	11097
1835	Olive	Milford,	Will,	11098
1843	Oliver	Sturbridge,	Administration,	11099
1783	Perry	Mendon,	Guardianship,	11100
1867	Persis E.	Worcester,	Administration,	11101
1839	Phinehas	Uxbridge,	Will,	11102
1868	Priscilla	Milford,	Administration,	11103
1741	Rachell	Mendon,	Guardianship,	11104
1841	Rufus	Milford,	Administration,	11105
1753	Samuel	Uxbridge,	Administration,	11106
1828	Samuel	Bolton,	Administration,	11107
1877	Samuel B.	Worcester,	Guardianship,	11108
1848	Samuel F.	Northbridge,	Guardianship,	11109
1851	Sarah	Upton,	Administration,	11110
1827	Sarah A.	Upton,	Guardianship,	11111
1879	Sarah A.	Holden,	Guardianship,	11112
1871	Sarah P.	Milford,	Guardianship,	11113
1854	Sarah R.	Sturbridge,	Administration,	11114
1869	Sarah R.	Worcester,	Administration,	11115
1874	Semira	Milford,	Will,	11116
1740	Seth	Mendon,	Administration,	11117
1741	Seth	Mendon,	Guardianship,	11118
1757	Seth	Mendon,	Guardianship,	11119
1773	Seth	Mendon,	Guardianship,	11120
1833	Seth	Mendon,	Will,	11121
1816	Stephen	Milford,	Administration,	11122
1831	Thaddeus	Worcester,	Will,	11123
1741	Thomas	Mendon,	Guardianship,	11124
1835	William C. W.	Worcester,	Guardianship,	11125
1851	William P.	Worcester,	Guardianship,	11126
1811	William S.	Milford,	Guardianship,	11127
1855	Zebulon	Simsbury, Conn.,	Foreign Will,	11128
1842	CHAPLIN, Abby	Bolton,	Guardianship,	11129
1874	Abigail	Athol,	Guardianship,	11130
1878	Abigail	Athol,	Will,	11130
1866	Adeliza H.	Leominster,	Will,	11131
1853	Adolphus	Leominster,	Administration,	11132
1842	Charles F.	Bolton,	Guardianship,	11133
1775	David	Lunenburg,	Will,	11134
1822	Ebenezer	Hardwick,	Will,	11135
1844	Ebenezer	Athol,	Will,	11136

Year.	Name.	Residence.	Nature.	Case.
1842	CHAPLIN, Francena V.	Bolton,	Guardianship,	11137
1856	Jesse	Lunenburg,	Will,	11138
1792	Joseph	Leominster,	Will,	11139
1842	Martha M.	Bolton,	Guardianship,	11140
1842	Sarah L.	Bolton,	Guardianship,	11141
1842	William B.	Bolton,	Will,	11142
1861	CHAPMAN, Adam	Sterling,	Guardianship,	11143
1866	Alice B.	Milford,	Guardianship,	11144
1824	Angeline	Harvard,	Guardianship,	11145
1865	Calvin	Brookfield,	Guardianship,	11146
1785	Ebenezer	Barre,	Guardianship,	11147
1866	Eva L.	Milford,	Guardianship,	11148
1864	Ezra W.	Sterling,	Will,	11149
1866	Hannah	Milford,	Will,	11150
1866	Hannah A.	Milford,	Guardianship,	11151
1875	Henry	Uxbridge,	Will,	11152
1854	Henry K.	Belchertown,	Guardianship,	11153
1861	Isham S.	Worcester,	Will,	11154
1848	Joseph	Worcester,	Will,	11155
1868	Joseph W.	Southborough,	Administration,	11156
1824	Julianna	Harvard,	Guardianship,	11157
1824	Lowell	Harvard,	Guardianship,	11158
1861	Lucy C.	Sterling,	Guardianship,	11159
1824	Milly	Harvard,	Guardianship,	11160
1880	Moses C.	Leominster,	Administration,	11161
1866	Palmer	Charlton,	Will,	11162
1870	Phebe	Charlton,	Will,	11163
1880	Sarah L.	Leominster,	Guardianship,	11164
1857	Spencer	Worcester,	Will,	11165
1866	William A.	Worcester,	Guardianship,	11166
	CHAPPELL and CHAPELL,			
1849	Harriet A.	Providence, R. I.,	Foreign Sale,	11167
1849	John	Providence, R. I.,	Foreign Sale,	11168
1866	Lydia H.	Uxbridge,	Administration,	11169
1866	Naomi	Sutton,	Administration,	11170
1849	William T.	Providence, R. I.,	Foreign Sale,	11171
1868	CHARLES, Thena	Sturbridge,	Administration,	11172
	CHASE and CHACE,			
1778	Abel	Sutton,	Administration,	11173
1787	Abel	Sutton,	Administration,	11174
1794	Abel	Sutton,	Guardianship,	11175
1806	Abel	Sutton,	Guardianship,	11176
1828	Abel	Millbury,	Guardianship,	11177
1833	Abel	Millbury,	Will,	11178
1821	Abiel	North Brookfield,	Will,	11179

CHASE and CHACE,

Year	Name	Residence	Nature	Case
1783	Abigail	Sutton,	Guardianship,	11180
1792	Abigail	Bolton,	Guardianship,	11181
1792	Abigail	Petersham,	Administration,	11182
1806	Abigail	Leominster,	Guardianship,	11183
1825	Abigail A.	Leominster,	Guardianship,	11184
1825	Abner	Sutton,	Administration,	11185
1810	Abraham	Sutton,	Guardianship,	11186
1857	Abraham	Sutton,	Will,	11187
1875	Alanson	Clinton,	Administration,	11188
1876	Albert V. I.	Worcester,	Guardianship,	11189
1845	Albert W.	Worcester,	Guardianship,	11190
1850	Alonzo	Paxton,	Administration,	11191
1828	Alvin B.	Millbury,	Guardianship,	11192
1799	Ambrose	Sutton,	Administration,	11193
1850	Angeline I.	Grafton,	Guardianship,	11194
1839	Ann M.	Lancaster,	Guardianship,	11195
1821	Anna	North Brookfield,	Guardianship,	11196
1875	Anna L.	Northbridge,	Administration,	11197
1808	Anthony	Worcester,	Guardianship,	11198
1817	Anthony	Mendon,	Will,	11199
1879	Anthony	Worcester,	Will,	11200
1847	Asa	Douglas,	Will,	11201
1858	Asa	Douglas,	Pension,	11202
1835	Betsey S. M.	Millbury,	Guardianship,	11203
1867	Beulah C. R.	Grafton,	Administration,	11204
1783	Bradford	Sutton,	Administration,	11205
1808	Caleb	Sutton,	Will,	11206
1848	Caleb	Sutton,	Will,	11207
1827	Calvin	Royalston,	Administration,	11208
1849	Caroline N.	Southbridge,	Guardianship,	11209
1808	Catherine	Worcester,	Guardianship,	11210
1806	Cephas	Leominster,	Guardianship,	11211
1856	Cephas	Leominster,	Pension,	11212
1791	Charles	Royalston,	Guardianship,	11213
1806	Charles	Leominster,	Guardianship,	11214
1829	Charles	Millbury,	Administration,	11215
1844	Charles	Northbridge,	Will,	11216
1846	Charles	Baltimore, Md.,	Foreign Will,	11217
1852	Charles	Clinton,	Will,	11218
1871	Charles	Winchendon,	Will,	11219
1850	Charles A.	Grafton,	Administration,	11220
1857	Charles C.	Paxton,	Guardianship,	11221
1869	Charles F.	Royalston,	Guardianship,	11222
1839	Charles M.	Lancaster,	Guardianship,	11223

CHASE AND CHACE,

1850	Charles S.	Grafton,	Guardianship,	11224
1816	Chauncey	Royalston,	Guardianship,	11225
1878	Chauncey	Royalston,	Will,	11226
1834	Coggeshall	Mendon,	Administration,	11227
1791	Daniel	Royalston,	Guardianship,	11228
1793	Daniel	Sutton,	Administration,	11229
1874	Daniel	Sutton,	Administration,	11230
1836	Daniel N.	Mendon,	Guardianship,	11231
1791	David	Sutton,	Administration,	11232
1794	David	Sutton,	Guardianship,	11233
1816	David	Royalston,	Administration,	11234
1828	David P.	Millbury,	Will,	11235
1806	Deborah	Mendon,	Administration,	11236
1862	Deidamia	Royalston,	Will,	11237
1873	Diana	Harvard,	Administration,	11238
1794	Eber	Sutton,	Guardianship,	11239
1806	Eber	Sutton,	Administration,	11240
1876	Edward I.	Worcester,	Guardianship,	11241
1815	Elias	Barre,	Will,	11242
1835	Elisha	Mendon,	Administration,	11243
1836	Elisha	Mendon,	Guardianship,	11244
1866	Eliza A.	Brookfield,	Administration,	11245
1836	Elizabeth	Leicester,	Will,	11246
1871	Elizabeth	Springfield, Vt.,	Foreign Will,	11247
1878	Elizabeth N.	Smithfield, R. I.,	Administration,	11248
1792	Elizabeth W.	Bolton,	Guardianship,	11249
1869	Ella A.	Royalston,	Guardianship,	11250
1857	Ella M.	Paxton,	Guardianship,	11251
1857	Ellen	Westminster,	Administration,	11252
1857	Emma J.	Paxton,	Guardianship,	11253
1795	Esek	Charlton,	Administration,	11254
1869	Fannie R.	Royalston,	Guardianship,	11255
1869	Flora E.	Royalston,	Guardianship,	11256
1799	Follansbee	Sutton,	Will,	11257
1875	Frances M.	Milford,	Adoption, etc.,	11258
1791	Francis	Royalston,	Administration,	11259
1791	Francis	Royalston,	Guardianship,	11260
1877	Freeman	Athol,	Will,	11261
1877	Gardner	Douglas,	Will,	11262
1806	George	Leominster,	Guardianship,	11263
1824	George	Northborough	Administration,	11264
1841	George	Leominster,	Administration,	11265
1857	George B.	Northborough,	Administration,	11266
1865	George H.	Royalston,	Adoption,	11267

CHASE AND CHACE,

YEAR.	NAME.	RESIDENCE.	NATURE.	CASE.
1865	George H.	Royalston,	Guardianship,	11268
1864	George L.	Royalston,	Administration,	11269
1869	George W.	Royalston,	Guardianship,	11270
1791	Hannah	Royalston,	Guardianship,	11271
1842	Hannah	Auburn,	Will,	11272
1849	Hannah R.	Worcester,	Will,	11273
1849	Harriet N.	Southbridge,	Guardianship,	11274
1881	Harriet N.	Southbridge,	Will,	11275
1777	Henry	Petersham,	Will,	11276
1824	Henry	Leominster,	Guardianship,	11277
1839	Henry A.	Lancaster,	Guardianship,	11278
1857	Henry M.	Worcester,	Guardianship,	11279
1857	Henry P.	Boylston,	Administration,	11280
1844	Hiram	Eastpennsborough,Pa.,	Foreign Will,	11281
1843	Hiram W.	Sterling,	Guardianship,	11282
1845	Homer	Worcester,	Administration,	11283
1858	Horace L.	Brattleboro, Vt.,	Guardianship,	11284
1835	Horatio C.	Millbury,	Guardianship,	11285
1828	Ira	Millbury,	Guardianship,	11286
1854	Ira	Millbury,	Administration,	11287
1786	Isaac	Sutton,	Administration,	11288
1875	Isabel A.	Northbridge,	Administration,	11289
1797	Israel	Worcester,	Will,	11290
1835	James	Royalston,	Guardianship,	11291
1866	Joanna	Blackstone,	Guardianship,	11292
——	Joanna	North Brookfield,	Guardianship,	11293
1822	Joannah	New Braintree,	Will,	11294
1873	Job	Paxton,	Administration,	11295
1819	John	Leominster,	Administration,	11296
1833	John	Brookfield,	Administration,	11297
1869	John	Webster,	Will,	11298
1872	John	Dudley,	Administration,	11299
1824	Jonas	Millbury,	Administration,	11300
1808	Jonathan	Paxton,	Will,	11301
1857	Jonathan	Paxton,	Will,	11302
1847	Joseph H.	Leominster,	Guardianship,	11303
1869	Joseph H.	Royalston,	Guardianship,	11304
1792	Joseph W.	Bolton,	Guardianship,	11305
1859	Joseph W.	Fitchburg,	Guardianship,	11306
1740	Joshua	Harvard,	Administration,	11307
1842	Joshua	Millbury,	Administration,	11308
1794	Judith	Sutton,	Guardianship,	11309
1805	Judith	Sutton,	Will,	11310
1859	Lauretta R.	Fitchburg,	Guardianship,	11311

CHASE AND CHACE,

YEAR.	NAME.	RESIDENCE.	NATURE.	CASE.
1828	Leonard	Millbury,	Guardianship,	11312
1842	Leonard	Sterling,	Administration,	11313
1848	Loren R.	Douglas,	Guardianship,	11314
1875	Loring	Winchendon,	Administration,	11315
1806	Louisa	Leominster,	Guardianship,	11316
1862	Lucina	Worcester,	Administration,	11317
1783	Luke	Sutton,	Guardianship,	11318
1825	Luke	Leominster,	Guardianship,	11319
1859	Luraney	Fitchburg,	Administration,	11320
1836	Lydia P.	Mendon,	Guardianship,	11321
1846	Lydia S.	Stoddard, N. H.,	Guardianship,	11322
1808	Lyman	Worcester,	Guardianship,	11323
1821	Lyman	New Braintree,	Administration,	11324
1822	March	Sutton,	Administration,	11325
1841	Maria	Fitchburg,	Administration,	11326
1865	Marion E.	Royalston,	Adoption,	11327
1865	Marion E.	Royalston,	Guardianship,	11328
1825	Martha	Leominster,	Guardianship,	11329
1867	Martha A.	Worcester,	Guardianship,	11330
1761	Mary	Sutton,	Guardianship,	11331
1855	Mary	Sutton,	Administration,	11332
1825	Mary A.	Leominster,	Guardianship,	11333
1853	Mary A.	Sutton,	Guardianship,	11334
1878	Mary A.	Worcester,	Guardianship,	11335
1854	Mary E.	Millbury,	Guardianship,	11336
1878	Maud E.	Worcester,	Guardianship,	11337
1874	Melissa E.	Grafton,	Administration,	11338
1806	Metaphor	Leominster,	Administration,	11339
1848	Minor M.	Douglas,	Guardianship,	11340
1790	Moses	Sutton,	Administration,	11341
1849	Moses	Fitchburg,	Administration,	11342
1816	Nabby	Royalston,	Guardianship,	11343
1863	Nabby	Leominster,	Will,	11344
1816	Nancy	Royalston,	Guardianship,	11345
1840	Narcissa	Mendon,	Administration,	11346
1817	Nathan	Mendon,	Guardianship,	11347
1842	Nathan	Northbridge,	Guardianship,	11348
1743	Nehemiah	Sutton,	Administration,	11349
1808	Nehemiah	Sutton,	Administration,	11350
1810	Nehemiah	Sutton,	Guardianship,	11351
1834	Nehemiah	Sutton,	Will,	11352
1850	Olive	Winchendon,	Administration,	11353
1851	Olive	Douglas,	Pension,	11354
1855	Oliver	Worcester,	Administration,	11355

YEAR.	NAME.	RESIDENCE.	NATURE.	CASE.
	CHASE AND CHACE,			
1859	Onslow E.	Fitchburg,	Guardianship,	11356
1877	Oscar P.	Northbridge,	Adoption, etc.,	11357
1859	Pascal E.	Fitchburg,	Guardianship,	11358
1789	Paul	Sutton,	Administration,	11359
1871	Paul C.	Millbury,	Administration,	11360
1860	Paul C.	Westborough,	Trustee,	11360½
1780	Percis	Sutton,	Will,	11361
1835	Persis S. M.	Millbury,	Guardianship,	11362
1783	Peter	Sutton,	Guardianship,	11363
1858	Philip	Worcester,	Trustee,	11364
1764	Phillip	Sutton,	Will,	11365
1794	Polly	Sutton,	Guardianship,	11366
1816	Polly	Royalston,	Guardianship,	11367
1791	Rebecca	Royalston,	Guardianship,	11368
1833	Rebecca B.	Brookfield,	Guardianship,	11369
1859	Reuben F.	Sutton,	Will,	11370
1825	Rufus	Leominster,	Guardianship,	11371
1868	Rufus	Blackstone,	Will,	11372
1794	Ruth	Sutton,	Guardianship,	11373
1794	Sally	Sutton,	Guardianship,	11374
1842	Sally	Northbridge,	Guardianship,	11375
1783	Samuel	Sutton,	Guardianship,	11376
1865	Samuel	Blackstone,	Administration,	11377
1825	Sarah	Leominster,	Guardianship,	11378
1877	Sarah	Harvard,	Administration,	11379
1839	Sarah L.	Lancaster,	Guardianship,	11380
1869	Sarah M.	Royalston,	Guardianship,	11381
1833	Sarah P.	Brookfield,	Guardianship,	11382
1791	Seth	Sutton,	Will,	11383
1874	Silas R.	Royalston,	Will,	11384
1869	Sophia E.	Royalston,	Guardianship,	11385
1866	Sophia P.	Leominster,	Administration,	11386
1847	Sophronia A.	Leominster,	Guardianship,	11387
1781	Stephen	Unknown,	Guardianship,	11388
1819	Stephen	Leominster,	Will,	11389
1825	Summonsbe	Leominster,	Guardianship,	11390
1825	Sumonsbre, etc.	Leominster,	Administration,	11391
1845	Susan E.	Worcester,	Guardianship,	11392
1811	Susannah P.	Royalston,	Guardianship,	11393
1835	Thaddeus	Millbury,	Administration,	11394
1825	Thirza	Leominster,	Guardianship,	11395
1787	Thomas	Bolton,	Administration,	11396
1810	Vashti	Sutton,	Guardianship,	11397
1825	Vashti	Sutton,	Administration,	11398

YEAR.	NAME.	RESIDENCE.	NATURE.	CASE.
	CHASE and CHACE,			
1845	Victoria M.	Worcester,	Guardianship,	11399
1851	Warren	Fitchburg,	Will,	11400
1830	William	Douglas,	Will,	11401
1835	William	Royalston,	Administration,	11402
1863	William	Douglas,	Guardianship,	11403
1835	William C.	Sutton,	Guardianship,	11404
1821	Yetmercy	Mendon,	Administration,	11405
1867	CHEESEMAN, Josephine	Worcester,	Administration,	11406
1838	CHEEVER, Bartholomew	Princeton,	Pension,	11407
1846	Bartholomew	Princeton,	Administration,	11408
1866	Benjamin F.	Charlton,	Administration,	11409
1845	Betsey	Princeton,	Administration,	11410
1822	Daniel	Princeton,	Administration,	11411
1870	Daniel	Princeton,	Will,	11412
1823	David	Princeton,	Guardianship,	11413
1870	Dolly	Princeton,	Guardianship,	11414
1859	Emeline J.	Leominster,	Guardianship,	11415
1789	James	Barre,	Guardianship,	11416
1864	Joseph	Spencer,	Administration,	11417
1878	Lomira F.	Westborough,	Will,	11418
1859	Marion	Leominster,	Administration,	11419
1851	Moses G.	Princeton,	Will,	11420
1864	Nathaniel	Milford,	Administration,	11421
1872	Polly	Princeton,	Administration,	11422
1789	Richard	Princeton,	Will,	11423
1816	Samuel	North Brookfield,	Will,	11424
1872	William	Westborough,	Will,	11425
1832	CHENERY, Amanda	Holden,	Guardianship,	11426
1872	Cyrus	Holden,	Administration,	11427
1881	Harriet A.	Clinton,	Will,	11428
1863	Horace	Worcester,	Administration,	11429
1822	Isaac	Holden,	Will,	11430
1856	Thaddeus	Holden,	Administration,	11431
1832	Zillah	Holden,	Guardianship,	11432
	CHENEY, CHEENY and CHEENEY,			
1757	Abigail	Mendon,	Guardianship,	11433
1843	Alexander	Milford,	Will,	11434
1869	Almira O.	Milford,	Guardianship,	11435
1830	Andalusia N.	Southbridge,	Guardianship,	11436
1854	Ann	Milford,	Will,	11437
1862	Ardelia B.	Fitchburg,	Administration,	11438
1850	Arnold W.	Barre,	Administration,	11439
1798	Artemas	Milford,	Guardianship,	11440
1861	Artemas	Barre,	Administration,	11441

YEAR.	NAME.	RESIDENCE.	NATURE.	CASE.
	CHENEY, CHEENY AND CHEENEY,			
1853	Asa	Auburn,	Will,	11442
1835	Bathsheba	Oxford,	Administration,	11443
1862	Betsey	Hubbardston,	Administration,	11444
1757	Caleb	Mendon,	Guardianship,	11445
1800	Caleb	Milford,	Will,	11446
1830	Caleb	Milford,	Administration,	11447
1879	Caroline A.	Holden,	Will,	11448
1842	Celestany	Southbridge,	Guardianship,	11449
1842	Charles	Southbridge,	Administration,	11450
1865	Charlotte	Leicester,	Administration,	11451
1853	Charlotte P.	Leicester,	Will,	11452
1847	Cortes	Milford,	Guardianship,	11453
1847	Cynthia	Milford,	Guardianship,	11454
1857	Cyrus	Phillipston,	Will,	11455
1833	Cyrus, Jr.	Phillipston,	Guardianship,	11456
1878	Darwin C.	Milford,	Guardianship,	11457
1819	Delia	Holden,	Guardianship,	11458
1874	Dexter	Athol,	Will,	11459
1864	Eben D.	Worcester,	Will,	11460
1740	Ebenezer	Mendon,	Administration,	11461
1756	Ebenezer	Sturbridge,	Will,	11462
1757	Ebenezer	Mendon,	Guardianship,	11463
1798	Ebenezer	Milford,	Guardianship,	11464
1854	Ebenezer D.	Worcester,	Guardianship,	11465
1867	Edward C.	Gardner,	Guardianship,	11466
1843	Edward S.	Milford,	Guardianship,	11467
1847	Edwin	Milford,	Guardianship,	11468
1806	Elisha	Worcester,	Administration,	11469
1777	Elizabeth	Western,	Administration,	11470
1810	Elizabeth	Milford,	Administration,	11471
1838	Elizabeth	Holden,	Guardianship,	11472
1843	Elizabeth	Milford,	Guardianship,	11473
1850	Elizabeth	Milford,	Administration,	11474
1860	Ellen A.	Royalston,	Guardianship,	11475
1830	Emelia E.	Southbridge,	Guardianship,	11476
1867	Emily A.	Gardner,	Guardianship,	11477
1860	Emma E.	Royalston,	Guardianship,	11478
1849	Eunice	Holden,	Administration,	11479
1847	Everett	Milford,	Guardianship,	11480
1860	Ezra A.	Royalston,	Administration,	11481
1854	Frances M.	Philadelphia, Pa.,	Guardianship,	11482
1878	Frederick E.	Milford,	Guardianship,	11483
1849	George	Paxton,	Administration,	11484
1849	George F.	Paxton,	Guardianship,	11485

YEAR.	NAME.	RESIDENCE.	NATURE.	CASE.
	CHENEY, CHEENY AND CHEENEY,			
1875	George L.	Brookfield,	Administration,	11486
1770	Hannah	Western,	Guardianship,	11487
1852	Harriet E.	Leicester,	Will,	11488
1854	Harriet E.	Worcester,	Guardianship,	11489
1860	Henrietta F.	Royalston,	Guardianship,	11490
1878	Herbert I.	Milford,	Guardianship,	11491
1849	Herbert L.	Paxton,	Guardianship,	11492
1830	Hiram	Southbridge,	Administration,	11493
1869	Ina I.	Milford,	Guardianship,	11494
1818	James	Phillipston,	Administration,	11495
1819	James E.	Holden,	Guardianship,	11496
1869	James E.	Holden,	Will,	11497
1836	Jesse	Southborough,	Administration,	11498
1865	Joel	Southbridge,	Will,	11499
1770	John	Western,	Administration,	11500
1838	John	Holden,	Administration,	11501
1872	John	Milford,	Will,	11502
1773	John, Jr.	Sutton,	Will,	11503
1793	Joseph	Sturbridge,	Administration,	11504
1818	Joseph	Sturbridge,	Administration,	11505
1858	Joseph	Leicester,	Administration,	11506
1810	Josephus	Holden,	Administration,	11507
1830	Juliana S.	Southbridge,	Guardianship,	11508
1847	Laurinda	Milford,	Guardianship,	11509
1843	Lawrian	Milford,	Guardianship,	11510
1810	Letitia	Holden,	Guardianship,	11511
1757	Levi	Mendon,	Guardianship,	11512
1867	Lewis F.	Gardner,	Administration,	11513
1867	Lewis F.	Gardner,	Guardianship,	11514
1843	Lovice S.	Milford,	Guardianship,	11515
1866	Lucretia E.	Sterling,	Guardianship,	11516
1770	Lucy	Western,	Guardianship,	11517
1777	Lucy	Western,	Guardianship,	11518
1872	Lucy	Auburn,	Administration,	11519
1839	Lydia	Phillipston,	Will,	11520
1830	Lydia K.	Southbridge,	Guardianship,	11521
1770	Martha	Western,	Guardianship,	11522
1878	Marvin	Southbridge,	Will,	11523
1747	Mary	Roxbury,	Guardianship,	11524
1776	Mary	Western,	Administration,	11525
1809	Mary	Milford,	Guardianship,	11526
1814	Mary	Milford,	Will,	11527
1853	Mary D.	Holden,	Adoption, etc.,	11528

Year.	Name.	Residence.	Nature.	Case.
	CHENEY, CHEENY AND CHEENEY,			
1854	Mary E.	Philadelphia, Pa.,	Guardianship,	11529
1847	Milton	Milford,	Guardianship,	11530
1834	Nathan	Milford,	Administration,	11531
1759	Nathaniel	Mendon,	Administration,	11532
1816	Nathaniel	Sutton,	Administration,	11533
1867	Nathaniel	Sutton,	Administration,	11534
1878	Orray W.	Milford,	Guardianship,	11535
1840	Polly	Phillipston,	Guardianship,	11536
1869	Polly B.	Athol,	Will,	11537
1838	Polly P.	Holden,	Guardianship,	11538
1797	Priscilla	Dudley,	Will,	11539
1872	Rufus	Milford,	Administration,	11540
1847	Ruth	Milford,	Guardianship,	11541
1838	Sally C.	Holden,	Guardianship,	11542
1874	Samuel F.	Athol,	Will,	11543
1798	Sarah	Dudley,	Will,	11544
1839	Sarah	Milford,	Will,	11545
1843	Sarah	Milford,	Guardianship,	11546
1869	Sarah A.	Milford,	Guardianship,	11547
1798	Seth	Milford,	Guardianship,	11548
1814	Seth	Milford,	Administration,	11549
1743	Silence	Mendon,	Guardianship,	11550
1816	Simon	Holden,	Administration,	11551
1826	Solomon C.	Holden,	Will,	11552
1810	Tamar	Holden,	Guardianship,	11553
1747	Thomas	Brookfield,	Will,	11554
1776	Thomas	Western,	Will,	11555
1777	Thomas	Dudley,	Administration,	11556
1835	Thomas	Southbridge,	Administration,	11557
1825	Wales	Milford,	Will,	11558
1854	Willard, Jr.	Worcester,	Guardianship,	11559
1756	William	Mendon,	Administration,	11560
1757	William	Mendon,	Guardianship,	11561
1830	William	Milford,	Will,	11562
1869	Ziba	Milford,	Administration,	11563
1880	CHESLEY, Carrie E.	Blackstone,	Guardianship,	11564
1857	Hannah	Blackstone,	Administration,	11565
1880	Joseph	Blackstone,	Administration,	11566
1830	Joseph T.	Uxbridge,	Administration,	11567
1880	Mary M.	Blackstone,	Guardianship,	11568
1878	Moranda A.	Worcester,	Will,	11569
1855	CHESSMAN, Eliza	Milford,	Administration,	11570
1860	John	Randolph Co., Iowa,	Administration,	11571

YEAR.	NAME.	RESIDENCE.	NATURE.	CASE.
1857	CHESMORE, Wilber B.	Hopkinton,	Adoption, etc.,	11572
1758	CHESTNUTT, Molly	Shrewsbury,	Guardianship,	11573
1756	William	Shrewsbury,	Administration,	11574
1862	CHICK, Edson C.	Grafton,	Guardianship,	11575
1862	John S.	Grafton,	Guardianship,	11576
1844	CHICKERING, Benjamin	Phillipston,	Guardianship,	11577
1837	Calvin	Rutland,	Administration,	11578
1861	Caroline L.	Sturbridge,	Adoption, etc.,	11579
1860	Charles A.	Dudley,	Adoption, etc.,	11580
1879	Charles A.	Dudley,	Change of Name,	11581
1869	Charles H.	West Brookfield,	Guardianship,	11582
1861	Charles L.	Sturbridge,	Adoption, etc.,	11583
1816	Cyrus	Holden,	Guardianship,	11584
1831	Cyrus	Holden,	Administration,	11585
1869	Dwight	Spencer,	Administration,	11586
1873	Eliza A.	Brookfield,	Will,	11587
1869	Ezra H.	West Brookfield,	Guardianship,	11588
1867	George C.	Dudley,	Will,	11589
1869	George W.	West Brookfield,	Guardianship,	11590
1869	Henry G.	Spencer,	Administration,	11591
1869	John F.	West Brookfield,	Guardianship,	11592
1840	Joseph	Phillipston,	Guardianship,	11593
1844	Joseph	Phillipston,	Will,	11593
1874	Mary	Dudley,	Administration,	11594
1817	Nathan	Rutland,	Guardianship,	11595
1854	Nathaniel K.	Rutland,	Administration,	11596
1830	Oliver	Rutland,	Guardianship,	11597
1846	Oliver	Shrewsbury,	Administration,	11598
1854	Otis N.	Rutland,	Guardianship,	11599
1835	Rebekah	Holden,	Will,	11600
1849	Ruth	Warren,	Guardianship,	11601
1816	Samuel	Holden,	Administration,	11602
1870	Samuel	Rutland,	Will,	11603
1871	CHICOINE, John	Peru, Vt.,	Adoption, etc.,	11604
1879	Levi	Warren,	Will,	11605
	CHILDS AND CHILD,			
1830	Abijah	Sturbridge,	Guardianship,	11606
1830	Adaline	Sturbridge,	Guardianship,	11607
1830	Addison	Sturbridge,	Guardianship,	11608
1845	Almond	Upton,	Guardianship,	11609
1830	Amanda	Sturbridge,	Guardianship,	11610
1829	Amasa	Sturbridge,	Guardianship,	11611
1839	Amos	West Boylston,	Administration,	11612
1869	Amos	West Boylston,	Administration,	11613
1823	Amos, Jr.	West Boylston,	Guardianship,	11614

	CHILDS AND CHILD,			
1832	Anna	Mendon,	Administration,	11615
1832	Anna	Mendon,	Guardianship,	11616
1866	Benjamin N.	Worcester,	Will,	11617
1853	Benjamin S.	Worcester,	Administration,	11618
1869	Beulah	Westborough,	Will,	11619
1812	Chandler T.	Upton,	Guardianship,	11620
1865	Charles W.	Worcester,	Administration,	11621
1876	Chester E.	Woodstock, Conn.,	Guardianship,	11622
1830	Cynthia	Sturbridge,	Administration,	11623
1830	Cynthy	Sturbridge,	Guardianship,	11624
1824	Daniel	Millbury,	Administration,	11625
1825	Daniel	Mendon,	Will,	11626
1854	Daniel	Oxford,	Will,	11627
1758	Daniell	Grafton,	Guardianship,	11628
1803	David	Sterling,	Will,	11629
1812	David	Westminster,	Administration,	11630
1840	David	West Boylston,	Guardianship,	11631
1848	David E.	Rutland,	Guardianship,	11632
——	David L.	Boylston,	Guardianship,	11633
1789	Ebenezer	Barre,	Will,	11634
1809	Ebenezer	Hardwick,	Will,	11635
1843	Eli	Worcester,	Administration,	11636
1848	Eli I.	Rutland,	Guardianship,	11637
1881	Elisha	Royalston,	Administration,	11638
1859	Eliza C.	Millbury,	Administration,	11639
1747	Elizabeth	Worcester,	Guardianship,	11640
1806	Elizabeth	Upton,	Will,	11641
1808	Elizabeth	Sturbridge,	Administration,	11642
1840	Elizabeth F.	West Boylston,	Guardianship,	11643
1827	Elizabeth S.	Rutland,	Administration,	11644
1812	Emily	Upton,	Guardianship,	11645
1847	Ephraim	Rutland,	Administration,	11646
1848	Ephraim P.	Rutland,	Guardianship,	11647
1814	Eunice	Sutton,	Will,	11648
1872	Eunice G.	West Boylston,	Administration,	11649
1876	Ezra C.	Woodstock, Conn.,	Administration,	11650
1869	E. Prescott	Worcester,	Administration,	11651
1807	Fisher H.	Upton,	Guardianship,	11652
1845	Fisher H.	Upton,	Will,	11653
1843	Francis	Greenfield, O.,	Guardianship,	11654
1878	Frank S.	Oxford,	Guardianship,	11655
1840	George	Lancaster,	Guardianship,	11656
1843	George	Greenfield, O.,	Guardianship,	11657
1876	Grace A.	Woodstock, Conn.,	Guardianship,	11658

YEAR.	NAME.	RESIDENCE.	NATURE.	CASE.
	CHILDS AND CHILD,			
1758	Hanah	Grafton,	Guardianship,	11659
1876	Harriet	Upton,	Administration,	11660
1867	Harry D.	Charlton,	Guardianship,	11661
1848	Henry W.	Rutland,	Guardianship,	11662
1794	Isaac	Sturbridge,	Administration,	11663
1840	Isaac	Lancaster,	Administration,	11664
1840	James	Lancaster,	Guardianship,	11665
1858	James	Ashburnham,	Administration,	11666
1864	James	Lancaster,	Administration,	11667
1865	James M.	Worcester,	Will,	11668
1845	Jane	Upton,	Guardianship,	11669
1840	Jane A.	Lancaster,	Guardianship,	11670
1848	Jane A.	Lancaster,	Administration,	11671
1745	John	Worcester,	Administration,	11672
1834	John	Dudley,	Will,	11673
1837	John	Upton,	Administration,	11674
1840	John	West Boylston,	Guardianship,	11675
——	John	Boylston,	Guardianship,	11676
1864	John W.	Southborough,	Will,	11677
1750	Jonas	Westborough,	Administration,	11678
1760	Jonas	Westborough,	Guardianship,	11679
1817	Jonas	Westminster,	Guardianship,	11680
1819	Jonas	Westminster,	Administration,	11680
1747	Jonathan	Worcester,	Guardianship,	11681
1787	Jonathan	Grafton,	Will,	'11682
1808	Jonathan	Westborough,	Administration,	11683
1848	Jonathan	Rutland,	Guardianship,	11684
1789	Joshua	Grafton,	Guardianship,	11685
1781	Josiah	Upton,	Guardianship,	11686
1806	Josiah	Upton,	Will,	11687
1848	Juel	Rutland,	Guardianship,	11688
1874	J. Prentice	Woodstock, Conn.,	Foreign Will,	11689
——	Levi B.	Boylston,	Guardianship,	11690
1832	Liberty	Mendon,	Guardianship,	11691
1876	Lizzie C.	Woodstock, Conn.,	Guardianship,	11692
1866	Lucy	Woodstock, Conn.,	Foreign Will,	11693
1840	Lucy R.	West Boylston,	Guardianship,	11694
1814	Lydia	Westminster,	Administration,	11695
1878	Lydia B.	West Boylston,	Will,	11696
——	Marcus	Boylston,	Guardianship,	11697
1758	Mary	Grafton,	Guardianship,	11698
1783	Mary	Rutland,	Guardianship,	11699
1870	Mary	Worcester,	Administration,	11700
1878	Mary A.	Oxford,	Guardianship,	11701

Year.	Name.	Residence.	Nature.	Case.
	CHILD and CHILDS,			
1840	Mary B.	West Boylston,	Guardianship,	11702
1854	Mary D.	Webster,	Guardianship,	11703
1860	Mary E.	Worcester,	Guardianship,	11704
1805	Mehitable	Sterling,	Administration,	11705
1867	Melinda	West Boylston,	Will,	11706
1835	Molly	Dudley,	Guardianship,	11707
1826	Moses N.	Worcester,	Will,	11708
1830	Nancy	Sturbridge,	Guardianship,	11709
1840	Nancy A.	West Boylston,	Guardianship,	11710
1848	Nancy M.	Rutland,	Guardianship,	11711
1822	Nathan, Jr.	Dudley,	Guardianship,	11712
1757	Nathaniel	Grafton (Gore),	Administration,	11713
1807	Nathaniel T.	Upton,	Guardianship,	11714
1865	Norman P.	Worcester,	Administration,	11715
1843	Otis	Greenfield, O.,	Guardianship,	11716
1877	Polly	Lancaster,	Will,	11717
1864	Prudence M.	Woodstock, Conn.,	Administration,	11718
1816	Rufus	Lancaster,	Guardianship,	11719
1875	Sanford	Upton,	Will,	11720
1816	Sarah R.	Lancaster,	Guardianship,	11721
1859	Sarah S.	Woodstock, Conn.,	Foreign Will,	11722
1762	Silas	Westborough,	Guardianship,	11723
1867	Silence J.	Worcester,	Administration,	11724
1784	Susanna	Westminster,	Administration,	11725
1803	Susanna	Boylston,	Will,	11726
1805	Susanna	Sterling,	Guardianship,	11727
1843	Thomas	Greenfield, O.,	Guardianship,	11728
——	Walter	Boylston,	Guardianship,	11729
1777	William	Lincoln,	Guardianship,	11730
1846	Zachariah	West Boylston,	Administration,	11731
1846	Zachariah	West Boylston,	Pension,	11732
1865	CHILLER, Frank	Winchendon,	Guardianship,	11733
1847	CHILSON, Albert G.	Mendon,	Guardianship,	11734
1847	Annah E.	Mendon,	Guardianship,	11735
1846	Asa	Mendon,	Administration,	11736
1740	Benjamin	Uxbridge,	Guardianship,	11737
1866	Catharine	Leicester,	Administration,	11738
1826	Ebenezer	Spencer,	Administration,	11739
1871	Ellen T.	Milford,	Change of Name,	11740
1853	Evi	Leicester,	Administration,	11741
1855	George D.	Leicester,	Will,	11742
1871	Henry G.	Milford,	Change of Name,	11743
1740	Hepzibah	Uxbridge,	Guardianship,	11744
1871	Huldah J.	Milford,	Change of Name,	11745

YEAR.	NAME.	RESIDENCE.	NATURE.	CASE.
1740	CHILSON, Joseph	Uxbridge,	Administration,	11746
1872	Levi	Uxbridge,	Administration,	11747
1880	Levi	Uxbridge,	Administration,	11748
1847	Martha A.	Mendon,	Guardianship,	11749
1876	Willard	Milford,	Will,	11750
1786	CHIPMAN, Ebenezer	Barre,	Administration,	11751
1788	Ebenezer	Barre,	Guardianship,	11752
1788	Percis	Barre,	Guardianship,	11753
1788	Stephen	Barre,	Guardianship,	11754
1788	Susanna	Barre,	Guardianship,	11755
1832	CHITTENDON, Betsey	Princeton,	Guardianship,	11756
1832	Desire	Princeton,	Administration,	11757
1827	Isaac	Princeton,	Will,	11758
1832	Lucy	Princeton,	Administration,	11759
	CHOAT AND CHOATE,			
1800	Ebenezer	Lunenburg,	Will,	11760
1834	Ebenezer	Lunenburg,	Administration,	11761
1859	Hannah	Lunenburg,	Administration,	11762
1844	Mary	Fitchburg,	Administration,	11763
1830	Robert	Lunenburg,	Administration,	11764
1877	CHRISTLEY, John	Lancaster,	Will,	11765
1877	CHRISTMAS, Joseph E.	West Boylston,	Guardianship,	11766
1877	Louis	West Boylston,	Guardianship,	11767
1877	Louisa	West Boylston,	Guardianship,	11768
1877	Paul	West Boylston,	Guardianship,	11769
1877	Rosa	West Boylston,	Guardianship,	11770
1877	Samuel	West Boylston,	Administration,	11771
1877	Samuel	West Boylston,	Guardianship,	11772
1877	Sarah	West Boylston,	Guardianship,	11773
1877	Simon	West Boylston,	Guardianship,	11774
1839	CHUBB, Andrew S.	Royalston,	Guardianship,	11775
1739	Ebenezer	Westborough,	Guardianship,	11776
1823	Nahum	Athol,	Administration,	11777
1856	Prudence W.	Phillipston,	Administration,	11778
1840	Silas	Royalston,	Pension,	11779
1833	CHURCH, Adelphia E.	Hubbardston,	Guardianship,	11780
1816	Alexander	Holden,	Will,	11781
1809	Asa	Hubbardston,	Administration,	11782
1833	Asa H.	Hubbardston,	Guardianship,	11783
1806	Benjamin	Hubbardston,	Administration,	11784
1818	Benjamin	Hubbardston,	Administration,	11785
1876	Betsey W.	Templeton,	Administration,	11786
1876	Eliza	Hubbardston,	Will,	11787
1775	Ephraim	Holden,	Will,	11788
1816	Ephraim	Hubbardston,	Administration,	11789

YEAR.	NAME.	RESIDENCE.	NATURE.	CASE.
1833	CHURCH, Eunice A.	Hubbardston,	Guardianship,	11790
1810	Eunice D.	Hubbardston,	Guardianship,	11791
1863	Fanny	Worcester,	Will,	11792
1763	Hannah	Hardwick,	Guardianship,	11793
1851	Jane A.	Templeton,	Guardianship,	11794
1810	John	Hubbardston,	Guardianship,	11795
1833	John	Hubbardston,	Administration,	11796
1833	John B.	Hubbardston,	Guardianship,	11797
1864	Joseph	Templeton,	Administration,	11798
1766	Joshua	Templeton,	Administration,	11799
1851	Joshua	Templeton,	Administration,	11800
1810	Luke	Hubbardston,	Guardianship,	11801
1837	Luke	Hubbardston,	Administration,	11802
1867	Lydia	Templeton,	Administration,	11803
1810	Mary W.	Hubbardston,	Guardianship,	11804
1872	Nellie E.	Worcester,	Guardianship,	11805
1840	Patty	Hubbardston,	Will,	11806
1826	Paul	Royalston,	Will,	11807
1844	Rachel	Hubbardston,	Pension,	11808
1828	Rebecca	Holden,	Administration,	11809
1757	Samuell	Hardwick,	Administration,	11810
1845	Silas	Templeton,	Will,	11811
1846	Silas, Jr.	Templeton,	Will,	11812
1786	Stephen	Hubbardston,	Administration,	11813
1810	Stephen	Hubbardston,	Guardianship,	11814
1861	Stephen	Hubbardston,	Will,	11815
1799	Stephen P.	Hubbardston,	Guardianship,	11816
1763	Susannah	Hardwick,	Guardianship,	11817
1763	Ursula	Hardwick,	Guardianship,	11818
1864	CHURCHILL, Dolly	Clinton,	Will,	11819
1856	Hannah	Uxbridge,	Administration,	11820
1863	Horace M.	Fitchburg,	Administration,	11821
1876	Isabel M.	Millbury,	Administration,	11822
1834	Joseph	Douglas,	Pension,	11823
1876	Leslie S.	Millbury,	Guardianship,	11824
1871	CHUTE, Anna J.	Leominster,	Guardianship,	11825
1875	Homer H.	Leominster,	Guardianship,	11826
1876	John E.	Ashburnham,	Administration,	11827
1871	Joseph B.	Leominster,	Guardianship,	11828
1871	Mary J.	Leominster,	Guardianship,	11829
1871	Paul C.	Leominster,	Guardianship,	11830
1871	Willie A.	Leominster,	Guardianship,	11831
1856	CILLEY, Samuel	Barre,	Administration,	11832
1879	CLAFFEY, Patrick	North Brookfield,	Will,	11833
1853	CLAFLIN, Abby S.	Leominster,	Guardianship,	11834

YEAR.	NAME.	RESIDENCE.	NATURE.	CASE.
1848	CLAFLIN, Charlotte	Milford,	Guardianship,	11835
1761	Daniell	Brookfield,	Guardianship,	11836
1881	David	Westborough,	Administration,	11837
1851	Eliza A.	Milford,	Guardianship,	11838
1828	Elliot	Southborough,	Administration,	11839
1881	Emma I.	Worcester,	Administration,	11840
1851	Francis A.	Milford,	Guardianship,	11841
1870	Frank A.	Milford,	Will,	11842
1791	George	Petersham,	Guardianship,	11843
1761	James	Brookfield,	Guardianship,	11844
1848	John	Milford,	Will,	11845
1875	John	Worcester,	Administration,	11846
1851	John H.	Milford,	Guardianship,	11847
1869	John H.	Milford,	Administration,	11848
1841	Lucinda	Hubbardston,	Guardianship,	11849
1875	Luther	Upton,	Will,	11850
1876	Martin	Milford,	Administration,	11851
1841	Mary A.	Hubbardston,	Guardianship,	11852
1853	Mira E.	Leominster,	Guardianship,	11853
1826	Moses	Barre,	Administration,	11854
1761	Nathan	Brookfield,	Guardianship,	11855
1859	Otis	Westborough,	Will,	11856
1761	Robert	Brookfield,	Administration,	11857
1878	Rufus	Milford,	Administration,	11858
1829	Tamar T.	Northborough,	Administration,	11859
1746	Timothy	Hopkinton,	Guardianship,	11860
1826	Walter	Northborough,	Administration,	11861
	CLAIR see CLARE.			
1861	CLANCY, Catherine	Milford,	Guardianship,	11862
1861	Hannah	Milford,	Guardianship,	11863
1870	Hannah	Blackstone,	Administration,	11864
1861	Jeremiah	Milford,	Guardianship,	11865
1861	John	Milford,	Administration,	11866
	CLAPP AND CLAP,			
1880	Ada G.	Gardner,	Guardianship,	11867
1871	Albert	Grafton,	Will,	11868
1869	Albert B.	North Brookfield,	Administration,	11869
1880	Alice H.	Gardner,	Guardianship,	11870
1863	Asahel	Gardner,	Administration,	11871
1813	Caleb	Charlton,	Guardianship,	11872
1855	Charles C.	Worcester,	Administration,	11873
1864	Charles H.	Worcester,	Guardianship,	11874
1827	Daniel	Worcester,	Will,	11875
1878	Daniel	Shrewsbury,	Administration,	11876
1872	David	Holden,	Administration,	11877

YEAR.	NAME.	RESIDENCE.	NATURE.	CASE.
	CLAPP AND CLAP,			
1855	Dwight	Warren,	Guardianship,	11878
1855	Edward B.	Worcester,	Guardianship,	11879
1805	Eleazer	Uxbridge,	Administration,	11880
1817	Elijah	Brookfield,	Administration,	11881
1880	Eliza C.	Leicester,	Will,	11882
1867	Elizabeth	Leicester,	Will,	11883
1870	Elizabeth	Greenfield,	Trustee,	11884
1849	Ellen E.	West Brookfield,	Guardianship,	11885
1855	Emily J.	Worcester,	Guardianship,	11886
1872	Enos L.	Worcester,	Administration,	11887
1880	Eugene W.	Gardner,	Guardianship,	11888
1805	Ezra, Jr.	Lunenburg,	Administration,	11889
1868	Fannie	Leicester,	Guardianship,	11890
1864	Florence F.	Gardner,	Guardianship,	11891
1841	Francis B.	Mendon,	Guardianship,	11892
1861	George E.	Brookfield,	Will,	11893
1860	Hannah E.	Blackstone,	Administration,	11894
1863	Henry E.	Worcester,	Administration,	11895
1872	Henry J.	Shrewsbury,	Guardianship,	11896
1851	Jared P.	New Market, N. H.,	Guardianship,	11897
1850	Joel	Holden,	Will,	11898
1848	John	Leicester,	Guardianship,	11899
1852	John	Leicester,	Will,	11900
1829	Jonas, Jr.	Oakham,	Administration,	11901
1880	Joseph W.	Gardner,	Administration,	11902
1852	Laura F.	Leicester,	Guardianship,	11903
1855	Levi	Worcester,	Will,	11904
1844	Lucy	Grafton,	Guardianship,	11905
1875	Lucy A.	Worcester,	Guardianship,	11906
1871	Luther J.	Worcester,	Will,	11907
1855	Mary E.	Worcester,	Guardianship,	11908
1859	Mary E.	Worcester,	Change of Name,	11909
1873	Nancy	Holden,	Administration,	11910
1879	Nancy B.	Athol,	Will,	11911
1844	Oliver	Holden,	Guardianship,	11912
1859	Oliver	Blackstone,	Administration,	11913
1838	Patience	Holden,	Administration,	11914
1874	Rebecca	New Braintree,	Administration,	11915
1841	Sally	Oakham,	Will,	11916
1875	Samuel	Athol,	Will,	11917
1872	Silas	Oakham,	Will,	11918
1867	Simeon	Worcester,	Will,	11919
1846	William	Brookfield,	Administration,	11920
1864	**CLAPPER,** Ernest	Millbury,	Adoption, etc.,	11921

(274)

Year.	Name.	Residence.	Nature.	Case.
	CLARE AND CLAIR,			
1872	Abigail	Milford,	Will,	11922
1872	Jeremiah	Milford,	Guardianship,	11923
1872	John J.	Milford,	Guardianship,	11924
1747	Jonathan	Brookfield,	Administration,	11925
1880	Thomas	Holden,	Will,	11926
	CLARK AND CLARKE,			
1871	Aaron	Auburn,	Will,	11927
1867	Abel	Milford,	Will,	11928
1836	Abigail A.	Hubbardston,	Guardianship,	11929
1856	Abigail E.	Templeton,	Guardianship,	11930
1881	Abigail G.	Wayland,	Partition,	11931
1876	Abigail P.	Southbridge,	Will,	11932
1859	Abijah	Hubbardston,	Administration,	11933
1864	Abijah S.	Milford,	Will,	11934
1872	Abner C.	Sturbridge,	Guardianship,	11935
1880	Ada L.	Dudley,	Guardianship,	11936
1865	Addie E. M.	Milford,	Guardianship,	11937
1851	Addison L.	Worcester,	Guardianship,	11938
1857	Albert	Hubbardston,	Guardianship,	11939
1864	Albert	Leominster,	Will,	11940
1870	Alice N.	Westminster,	Guardianship,	11941
1815	Alma W.	Hardwick,	Guardianship,	11942
1856	Almon	Hubbardston,	Guardianship,	11943
1869	Almon	Petersham,	Administration,	11944
1862	Almon W.	Petersham,	Guardianship,	11945
1863	Almon W.	Hubbardston,	Administration,	11946
1876	Alonzo B.	Gardner,	Will,	11947
1857	Alson	Hubbardston,	Guardianship,	11948
1823	Amos	Oakham,	Administration,	11949
1860	Amos	Hubbardston,	Administration,	11950
1822	Amos F.	Hubbardston,	Guardianship,	11951
1839	Angelina M.	Hubbardston,	Guardianship,	11952
1857	Angenett	Exeter, N. H.,	Foreign Will,	11953
1838	Ann	Hubbardston,	Guardianship,	11954
1791	Anna	Sturbridge,	Guardianship,	11955
1799	Anna	Sturbridge,	Administration,	11955
1876	Anna E.	West Brookfield,	Guardianship,	11956
1851	Anna T.	Mendon,	Guardianship,	11957
1865	Ansel J.	Spencer,	Guardianship,	11958
1854	Anson	Rutland,	Administration,	11959
1836	Anson B.	Hubbardston,	Guardianship,	11960
1792	Anthony	Hubbardston,	Administration,	11961
1822	Anthony F.	Hubbardston,	Guardianship,	11962
1810	Asa	Dana,	Guardianship,	11963

CLARK AND CLARKE,

YEAR.	NAME.	RESIDENCE.	NATURE.	CASE.
1811	Asa	Princeton,	Guardianship,	11964
1826	Asa	Hubbardston,	Guardianship,	11965
1872	Asa	Hubbardston,	Administration,	11966
1881	Asa	Barre,	Administration,	11967
1870	Asa G.	Hubbardston,	Administration,	11968
1862	Asa W.	Petersham,	Guardianship,	11969
1835	Augustus D.	Grafton,	Guardianship,	11970
1814	Baxter,	Charlton,	Administration,	11971
1806	Benjamin	Pelham,	Guardianship,	11972
1810	Benjamin	Princeton,	Administration,	11973
1828	Benjamin	Gardner,	Will,	11974
1859	Benjamin	Lunenburg,	Administration,	11975
1864	Benjamin	Hubbardston,	Administration,	11976
1870	Benjamin	Upton,	Will,	11977
1860	Benjamin F.	Lunenburg,	Guardianship,	11978
1811	· Betsey	Princeton,	Guardianship,	11979
1859	Betsey	Rutland,	Administration,	11980
1872	Betsey	Hubbardston,	Administration,	11981
1877	Betsey	Southbridge,	Will,	11982
1846	Betsy	Petersham,	Will,	11983
1808	Bulah	Sturbridge,	Guardianship,	11984
1822	Caleb S.	Hubbardston,	Guardianship,	11985
1810	Caroline	Dana,	Guardianship,	11986
1853	Caroline L.	Hubbardston,	Guardianship,	11987
1866	Caroline M.	Rutland,	Guardianship,	11988
1876	Carpenter	Southbridge,	Administration,	11989
1871	Catharine S.	Northbridge,	Guardianship,	11990
1814	Charles	Sturbridge,	Guardianship,	11991
1851	Charles	Worcester,	Guardianship,	11992
1875	Charles	Milford,	Administration,	11993
1806	Charles F.	Sturbridge,	Guardianship,	11994
1826	Charles F.	Southbridge,	Administration,	11995
1857	Charles N.	Milford,	Guardianship,	11996
1876	Charles S.	Oakham,	Administration,	11997
1865	Charles W.	Milford,	Change of Name,	11998
1873	Charlotte	Hubbardston,	Will,	11999
1841	Chester	Milford,	Administration,	12000
1810	Chloe	Sturbridge,	Will,	12001
1847	Clara A.	Lowell,	Guardianship,	12002
1860	Clara J.	Lunenburg,	Guardianship,	12003
1853	Clara S.	Hubbardston,	Guardianship,	12004
1839	Clarissa M.	Hubbardston,	Guardianship,	12005
1876	Clayton A.	West Brookfield,	Guardianship,	12006
1867	Cora P.	Milford,	Guardianship,	12007

Year.	Name.	Residence.	Nature.	Case.
	CLARK and CLARKE,			
1810	Cyrus	Dana,	Guardianship,	12008
1836	Dana	Hubbardston,	Guardianship,	12009
1859	Dana	Barre,	Administration,	12010
1839	Danford	Hubbardston,	Guardianship,	12011
1768	Daniel	Lancaster,	Guardianship,	12012
1815	Daniel	Sturbridge,	Administration,	12013
1813	Daniel, Jr.	Sturbridge,	Guardianship,	12014
1810	David	Petersham,	Will,	12015
1828	David	Worcester,	Administration,	12016
1841	David	Ashburnham,	Administration,	12017
1841	David	Ashburnham,	Pension,	12018
1842	David	Princeton,	Administration,	12019
1842	David	Lunenburg,	Administration,	12020
1822	Deborah	North Brookfield,	Will,	12021
1857	Deliverance	Ashburnham,	Will,	12022
1806	Dexter	Sturbridge,	Guardianship,	12023
1826	Dexter	Southbridge,	Administration,	12024
1826	Diantha	Hubbardston,	Guardianship,	12025
1841	Diantha	Leominster,	Administration,	12026
1814	Dwight P.	Sturbridge,	Guardianship,	12027
1826	Dwight P.	Southbridge,	Will,	12028
1806	Ebenezer	Sturbridge,	Will,	12029
1809	Ebenezer	Sturbridge,	Administration,	12030
1820	Ebenezer	Sturbridge,	Administration,	12031
1847	Eber	Royalston,	Administration,	12032
1879	Edith B.	Oakham,	Administration,	12033
1794	Edward	Lancaster,	Administration,	12034
1815	Edward	Dana,	Guardianship,	12035
1821	Edward	Hardwick,	Administration,	12036
1849	Edward	Worcester,	Administration,	12037
1851	Edward C.	Mendon,	Guardianship,	12038
1871	Edward S.	Northbridge,	Guardianship,	12039
1836	Edwin H.	Hubbardston,	Guardianship,	12040
1838	Elbridge G.	Hubbardston,	Guardianship,	12041
1818	Eli	Hubbardston,	Administration,	12042
1826	Eli	Hubbardston,	Guardianship,	12043
1856	Eli	Hubbardston,	Administration,	12044
1866	Eli E.	Hubbardston,	Administration,	12045
1815	Elieutheria	Hardwick,	Guardianship,	12046
1815	Elisha W.	Hardwick,	Guardianship,	12047
1819	Eliza	Petersham,	Guardianship,	12048
1869	Eliza	Winchendon,	Administration,	12049
1851	Eliza A.	Hubbardston,	Guardianship,	12050

YEAR.	NAME.	RESIDENCE.	NATURE.	CASE.
	CLARK AND CLARKE,			
1734	Elizabeth	Rutland,	Guardianship,	12051
1767	Elizabeth	Mendon,	Guardianship,	12052
1786	Elizabeth	Lancaster,	Administration,	12053
1789	Elizabeth	Princeton,	Will,	12054
1815	Elizabeth	Hardwick,	Guardianship,	12055
1853	Elizabeth	North Brookfield,	Will,	12056
1854	Elizabeth	North Brookfield,	Pension,	12057
1876	Elizabeth D.	Bolton,	Will,	12058
1876	Elizabeth M.	Northborough,	Administration,	12059
1838	Ellen	Hubbardston,	Guardianship,	12060
1839	Ellen	Hubbardston,	Guardianship,	12061
1857	Ellen A.	Hubbardston,	Will,	12062
1872	Emeline E.	Southbridge,	Administration,	12063
1856	Emeline L.	Sturbridge,	Guardianship,	12064
1842	Emily	Milford,	Guardianship,	12065
1880	Emma H.	Worcester,	Administration,	12066
1854	Emory A.	Rutland,	Guardianship,	12067
1849	Erasmus	Sturbridge,	Will,	12068
1863	Erasmus	Southbridge,	Administration,	12069
1851	Etheridge	Foxborough,	Will,	12070
1872	Etta M.	Hubbardston,	Guardianship,	12071
1841	Eunice A.	Princeton,	Guardianship,	12072
1880	Eva E.	Auburn,	Guardianship,	12073
1814	Ezra	Hardwick,	Administration,	12074
1827	Ezra	Hubbardston	Administration,	12075
1871	Ezra	Barre,	Administration,	12076
1864	Ezra P.	Worcester,	Administration,	12077
1819	Fanny	Petersham,	Guardianship,	12078
1854	Fanny E.	Rutland,	Guardianship,	12079
1865	Fanny E.	Webster,	Guardianship,	12080
1839	Ferdinand	Hubbardston,	Guardianship,	12081
1880	Ferdinand N.	Hubbardston,	Administration,	12082
1870	Florence M.	Westminster,	Guardianship,	12083
1851	Frances J.	Hubbardston,	Guardianship,	12084
1844	Frances L.	Bath, Me.,	Guardianship,	12085
1838	Francis	Brookfield,	Administration,	12086
1857	Francis	Bolton,	Administration,	12087
1834	Francis O.	Brookfield,	Administration,	12088
1877	Frederick B.	Hubbardston,	Guardianship,	12089
1876	Frederick S.	Gardner,	Guardianship,	12090
1790	Freelove B.	New Braintree,	Guardianship,	12091
1873	Galen A.	Mendon,	Administration,	12092
1842	George	Ashburnham,	Administration,	12093
1864	George A.	Hubbardston,	Guardianship,	12094

Year.	Name.	Residence.	Nature.	Case.
	CLARK and CLARKE,			
1852	George D.	Gardner,	Administration,	12095
1844	George F.	Grafton,	Guardianship,	12096
1865	George F.	Athol,	Guardianship,	12097
1835	George I.	Grafton,	Guardianship,	12098
1862	George P.	Spencer,	Adoption, etc.,	12099
1834	Hammond	Oxford,	Will,	12100
1813	Hannah	Harvard,	Guardianship,	12101
1835	Hannah B. D.	Barre,	Guardianship,	12102
1818	Hardin	Petersham,	Administration,	12103
1839	Harriet	Hubbardston,	Guardianship,	12104
1877	Harriet	Hubbardston,	Administration,	12105
1848	Harriet E.	Camillas, N. Y.,	Guardianship,	12106
1879	Harriet M.	Dudley,	Will,	12107
1841	Harriet N.	Princeton,	Guardianship,	12108
1819	Harriot	Petersham,	Guardianship,	12109
1843	Harvey	Ashburnham,	Guardianship,	12110
1836	Helen M.	Berlin,	Guardianship,	12111
1880	Henry	Worcester,	Will,	12112
1854	Henry A.	Rutland,	Guardianship,	12113
1872	Henry A.	Millbury,	Administration,	12114
1880	Henry O.	Worcester,	Administration,	12115
1867	Henry S.	Worcester,	Administration,	12116
1858	Henry W.	Royalston,	Administration,	12117
1787	Hinsdell	Sturbridge,	Will,	12118
1826	Hiram	Hubbardston,	Guardianship,	12119
1855	Hiram	Northbridge,	Administration,	12120
1858	Hiram B.	Brookfield,	Administration,	12121
1819	Horace	Petersham,	Guardianship,	12122
1819	Hosea	Petersham,	Guardianship,	12123
1812	Hovey	Sterling,	Administration,	12124
1847	Idda F.	Lowell,	Guardianship,	12125
1845	Ira	Grafton,	Administration,	12126
1814	Isaac	Hardwick,	Will,	12127
1826	Isaac, 2nd	Hubbardston,	Guardianship,	12128
1836	Isaac	Hubbardston,	Will,	12129
1836	Isaac	Hubbardston,	Pension,	12130
1855	Isaac	Princeton,	Administration,	12131
1767	James	Mendon,	Guardianship,	12132
1824	James	North Brookfield,	Guardianship,	12133
1861	James K.	Oakham,	Guardianship,	12134
1847	James W.	Worcester,	Guardianship,	12135
1822	Jane	Hubbardston,	Guardianship,	12136
1855	Jemima	North Brookfield,	Administration,	12137
1859	Jessie W.	Worcester,	Adoption, etc.,	12138

CLARK AND CLARKE,

YEAR.	NAME.	RESIDENCE.	NATURE.	CASE.
1862	Joanna M.	Gardner,	Administration,	12139
1801	John	Spencer,	Administration,	12140
1808	John	Sturbridge,	Guardianship,	12141
1810	John	Hubbardston,	Administration,	12142
1838	John	Spencer,	Administration,	12143
1838	John	Spencer,	Pension,	12144
1847	John	Auburn,	Will,	12145
1874	John	Auburn,	Will,	12146
1860	John B.	Worcester,	Will,	12147
1854	John F.	Hubbardston,	Administration,	12148
1863	John F.	Worcester,	Administration,	12149
1869	John P.	Oakham,	Administration,	12150
1849	John Q.	Gardner,	Administration,	12151
1862	John W.	Petersham,	Guardianship,	12152
1864	John W.	Petersham,	Administration,	12153
1790	Jonah	Sturbridge,	Guardianship,	12154
1826	Jonah	Petersham,	Administration,	12155
1851	Jonas W.	Hubbardston,	Guardianship,	12156
1810	Jonathan	Harvard,	Will,	12157
1856	Jonathan	Sturbridge,	Guardianship,	12158
1766	Joseph	Mendon,	Administration,	12159
1772	Joseph	Worcester,	Administration,	12160
1808	Joseph	Ward,	Will,	12161
1829	Joseph	Hubbardston,	Administration,	12162
1837	Joseph	Gardner,	Pension,	12163
1839	Joseph	Gardner,	Will,	12164
1839	Joseph	Hubbardston,	Administration,	12165
1874	Joseph	Southbridge,	Administration,	12166
1865	Joseph B.	Webster,	Guardianship,	12167
1861	Joseph C.	Oakham,	Will,	12168
1868	Joseph G.	Worcester,	Administration,	12169
1852	Joseph P.	Hubbardston,	Guardianship,	12170
1767	Josiah	Mendon,	Guardianship,	12171
1845	Josiah	Rutland,	Will,	12172
1837	Julia	Southbridge,	Guardianship,	12173
1865	Justin	Spencer,	Administration,	12174
1865	Justina C.	Spencer,	Guardianship,	12175
1877	Justina C.	Spencer,	Administration,	12176
1855	Lathrop	Webster,	Administration,	12177
1850	Lemuel	Southbridge,	Administration,	12178
1839	Leonard	Hubbardston,	Administration,	12179
1839	Leonard	Hubbardston,	Guardianship,	12180
1877	Leonard	Hubbardston,	Administration,	12181
1839	Levina A.	Hubbardston,	Guardianship,	12182

YEAR.	NAME.	RESIDENCE.	NATURE.	CASE.
	CLARK and CLARKE,			
1861	Lewis C.	Oakham,	Guardianship,	12183
1870	Lewis F.	Northbridge,	Administration,	12184
1811	Livy	Dana,	Guardianship,	12185
1819	Livy	Hardwick,	Guardianship,	12186
1857	Lizzie	Hubbardston,	Guardianship,	12187
1876	Lizzie K.	West Brookfield,	Guardianship,	12188
1826	Lois	Hubbardston,	Guardianship,	12189
1837	Lois	Hubbardston,	Administration,	12190
1836	Louisa J.	Hubbardston,	Guardianship,	12191
1839	Lovell	Milford,	Administration,	12192
1867	Lovell W.	Milford,	Administration,	12193
1841	Lucinda	Worcester,	Administration,	12194
1839	Lucius	Hubbardston,	Guardianship,	12195
1813	Lucy	Harvard,	Guardianship,	12196
1839	Lucy	Hubbardston,	Guardianship,	12197
1880	Lucy M.	Worcester,	Guardianship,	12198
1855	Luther	Rutland,	Will,	12199
1864	Luther R.	Leominster,	Guardianship,	12200
1847	Lyman A.	Royalston,	Guardianship,	12201
1851	Lyman F.	Hubbardston,	Guardianship,	12202
1864	Lyman S.	Milford,	Administration,	12203
1844	Lysander C.	Worcester,	Administration,	12204
1845	Mahitable	Princeton,	Administration,	12205
1839	Makepeace	Hubbardston,	Administration,	12206
1847	Margaret	Petersham,	Will,	12207
1836	Maria A.	Berlin,	Guardianship,	12208
1853	Maria D.	Hubbardston,	Guardianship,	12209
1804	Martha	Sturbridge,	Will,	12210
1880	Martha M.	North Brookfield,	Administration,	12211
1877	Marvin S.	Southbridge,	Administration,	12212
1766	Mary	Lunenburg,	Guardianship,	12213
1768	Mary	Lancaster,	Guardianship,	12214
1819	Mary	Petersham,	Guardianship,	12215
1825	Mary	Southbridge,	Guardianship,	12216
1876	Mary C.	West Brookfield,	Guardianship,	12217
1841	Mary E.	Princeton,	Guardianship,	12218
1849	Mary E.	Southbridge,	Guardianship,	12219
1851	Mary E.	Mendon,	Guardianship,	12220
1878	Mary E.	Southbridge,	Guardianship,	12221
1870	Mary F.	Holden,	Guardianship,	12222
1761	Mathew	Lancaster,	Administration,	12223
1837	Mehitable	Southbridge,	Administration,	12224
1842	Mehitable	Royalston,	Pension,	12225
1859	Mehitable	Barre,	Will,	12226

CLARK AND CLARKE,

YEAR.	NAME.	RESIDENCE.	NATURE.	CASE.
1847	Merrick	Sturbridge,	Administration,	12227
1847	Merrick	Sturbridge,	Guardianship,	12228
1856	Minerva	Sturbridge,	Administration,	12229
1873	Miriam	Hubbardston,	Guardianship,	12230
1783	Moses	Sturbridge,	Will,	12231
1808	Moses	Sturbridge,	Will,	12232
1824	Moses	Hubbardston,	Administration,	12233
1838	Moses	Hubbardston,	Guardianship,	12234
1819	Moses E.	Hubbardston,	Administration,	12235
1847	Moses L.	Royalston,	Guardianship,	12236
1836	Nancy	Hubbardston,	Guardianship,	12237
1868	Nancy	Gloucester, R. I.,	Administration,	12238
1792	Nathan	Dudley,	Guardianship,	12239
1793	Nathan	Princeton,	Will,	12240
1813	Nathan	Paxton,	Guardianship,	12241
1825	Nathan	Hubbardston,	Administration,	12242
1826	Nathan	Hubbardston,	Guardianship,	12243
1836	Nathan	Hubbardston,	Administration,	12244
1819	Nathan B.	Southbridge,	Will,	12245
1789	Nathaniel	Dudley,	Administration,	12246
1854	Nathaniel	Northbridge,	Guardianship,	12247
1827	Nehemiah P.	Gibbonsville, N. Y.,	Administration,	12248
1853	Nehemiah P.	Hubbardston,	Guardianship,	12249
1819	Nelson	Petersham,	Guardianship,	12250
1868	Nelson F.	Southbridge,	Administration,	12251
1838	Nelson P.	Hubbardston,	Guardianship,	12252
1836	Noah A.	Hubbardston,	Guardianship,	12253
1839	Noel A.	Hubbardston,	Guardianship,	12254
1854	Olive	Norwich, Conn.,	Administration,	12255
1835	Oliver	Hubbardston,	Administration,	12256
1832	Oramel	Barre,	Guardianship,	12257
1806	Patty	Sturbridge,	Guardianship,	12258
1878	Permelia D.	Southbridge,	Administration,	12259
1792	Peter	Southborough,	Administration,	12260
1820	Peter	Hubbardston,	Administration,	12261
1848	Peter	Hubbardston,	Guardianship,	12262
1854	Peter	Hubbardston,	Will,	12262
1825	Philadelphus	Southbridge,	Guardianship,	12263
1811	Phineas	Princeton,	Guardianship,	12264
1816	Phinehas	Sturbridge,	Will,	12265
1838	Prudence	Sturbridge,	Administration,	12266
1843	Rachel	Petersham,	Will,	12267
1742	Robert	Lunenburg,	Guardianship,	12268
1767	Robert	Lunenburg,	Administration,	12268

YEAR.	NAME.	RESIDENCE.	NATURE.	CASE.
	CLARK AND CLARKE,			
1857	Rollin J. L. S.	Milford,	Administration,	12269
1861	Rufus	Brattleboro, Vt.,	Foreign Will,	12270
1819	Ruhamah	Petersham,	Guardianship,	12271
1826	Sally	Hubbardston,	Guardianship,	12272
1825	Sally M.	Southbridge,	Guardianship,	12273
1817	Samuel, 2nd	Hubbardston,	Guardianship,	12274
1837	Samuel	Hubbardston,	Administration,	12275
1838	Samuel	Hubbardston,	Guardianship,	12276
1842	Samuel	Auburn,	Will,	12277
1843	Samuel	Barre,	Will,	12278
1859	Samuel	Royalston,	Will,	12279
1859	Samuel	Uxbridge,	Will,	12280
1766	Sarah	Lunenburg,	Guardianship,	12281
1838	Sarah	Hubbardston,	Guardianship,	12282
1858	Sarah	Uxbridge,	Administration,	12283
1865	Sarah	Sterling,	Administration,	12284
1865	Sarah	Uxbridge,	Administration,	12285
1874	Sarah	Barre,	Will,	12286
1880	Sarah	Milford,	Administration,	12287
1857	Sarah A.	Hubbardston,	Guardianship,	12288
1870	Sarah A.	Worcester,	Administration,	12289
1871	Sarah H.	Leicester,	Administration,	12290
1851	Sarah L.	Mendon,	Guardianship,	12291
1826	Sarah M.	Hubbardston,	Guardianship,	12292
1859	Sarah M.	Ashburnham,	Guardianship,	12293
1835	Sarah P.	Grafton,	Guardianship,	12294
1856	Sarah P.	Northbridge,	Will,	12295
1839	Sewall	Hubbardston,	Guardianship,	12296
1852	Shepherd	Hubbardston,	Administration,	12297
1842	Silas N.	Charlton,	Guardianship,	12298
1790	Simeon	New Braintree,	Administration,	12299
1810	Simeon	Dana,	Administration,	12300
1813	Simeon	Paxton,	Will,	12301
1826	Simeon	Hubbardston,	Guardianship,	12302
1866	Simeon C.	Holden,	Administration,	12303
1833	Simpson, 2nd	Hubbardston,	Administration,	12304
1841	Simpson	Hubbardston,	Administration,	12305
1808	Solomon	Sturbridge,	Administration,	12306
1790	Stephen	Dudley,	Guardianship,	12307
1851	Stephen	Hubbardston,	Will,	12308
1852	Stillman	Southbridge,	Administration,	12309
1881	Stillman	Hardwick,	Will,	12310
1810	Stilman	Dana,	Guardianship,	12311
1815	Susan	Hardwick,	Guardianship,	12312

CLARK AND CLARKE,

YEAR.	NAME.	RESIDENCE.	NATURE.	CASE.
1880	Susan H.	Uxbridge,	Administration,	12313
1861	Susan J.	Worcester,	Administration,	12314
1779	Susanna	Shrewsbury,	Will,	12315
1824	Thirza A.	North Brookfield,	Guardianship,	12316
1831	Thomas	Barre,	Administration,	12317
1875	Thomas B.	Worcester,	Will,	12318
1879	Timothy P.	North Brookfield,	Administration,	12319
1844	Truman	Grafton,	Administration,	12320
1819	Tryphena	Petersham,	Guardianship,	12321
1825	Waldo	Southbridge,	Administration,	12322
1856	Walter	Sturbridge,	Guardianship,	12323
1862	Walter	Petersham,	Inventory,	12324
1871	Walter A.	Dana,	Guardianship,	12325
1862	Warren	Petersham,	Inventory,	12326
1856	Wealthy	Worcester,	Administration,	12327
1862	Wilber	Petersham,	Inventory,	12328
1842	Willard	Milford,	Guardianship,	12329
1865	Willard	Milford,	Change of Name,	12330
1764	William	Lancaster,	Guardianship,	12331
1782	William	Lunenburg,	Guardianship,	12332
1789	William	Dudley,	Administration,	12333
1810	William	Princeton,	Guardianship,	12334
1812	William	Hubbardston,	Administration,	12335
1834	William	Lunenburg,	Administration,	12336
1855	William	Petersham,	Administration,	12337
1836	William H.	Hubbardston,	Guardianship,	12338
1864	William H.	Sutton,	Guardianship,	12339
1869	William H.	Sutton,	Guardianship,	12340
1881	William H.	Wayland,	Partition,	12341
1877	William S.	Hubbardston,	Administration,	12342
1847	William T.	Lowell,	Guardianship,	12343
1872	Willie G.	Hubbardston,	Adoption, etc.,	12344
1797	Zeeb	Sturbridge,	Guardianship,	12345
1799	Zeeb	Sturbridge,	Administration,	12345
1860	CLARKIN, Catharine	Fall River,	Guardianship,	12346
1860	Hugh	Blackstone,	Administration,	12347

CLARY see CLEARY.

1873	CLAYTON, John	West Brookfield,	Will,	12348
1860	CLEARY, John	Leicester,	Administration,	12349
1875	John	Winchendon,	Will,	12350
1877	Maud	Dudley,	Adoption, etc.,	12351
1881	Patrick	Leominster,	Administration,	12352
1876	William H.	Leominster,	Administration,	12353

CLEAVELAND see CLEVELAND.

Year.	Name.	Residence.	Nature.	Case.
1870	CLEAVES, Abbie S.	Leominster,	Guardianship,	12354
1858	CLEGG, George	Fitchburg,	Guardianship,	12355
1858	Harriet	Fitchburg,	Guardianship,	12356
1857	Isaac	Fitchburg,	Administration,	12357
1859	Sarah	Westminster,	Will,	12358
1875	CLELAND, Margaret M.	Holden,	Administration,	12359
	CLEMANS, CLEMENCE, CLEM-			
	ENS, CLEMENT, CLEMENTS,			
	AND CLEMONS,			
1819	Aaron	Charlton,	Administration,	12360
1866	Agnes O.	Oxford,	Guardianship,	12361
1820	Asa	Charlton,	Will,	12362
1821	Asa	Charlton,	Guardianship,	12363
1831	Baruek	Sturbridge,	Administration,	12364
1828	Calvin	Southbridge,	Administration,	12365
1828	Calvin	Southbridge,	Guardianship,	12366
1821	Celesta	Charlton,	Guardianship,	12367
1868	Charles R.	Worcester,	Guardianship,	12368
1857	Chester	Webster,	Will,	12369
1877	Daniel D.	Southbridge,	Will,	12370
1866	DeWitt	Oxford,	Guardianship,	12371
1877	Edith J.	Royalston,	Guardianship,	12372
1821	Emily	Charlton,	Guardianship,	12373
1864	Eva M.	Worcester,	Adoption, etc.,	12374
1868	Eva M.	Worcester,	Guardianship,	12375
1868	George H.	Worcester,	Guardianship,	12376
1877	Hattie F.	Bolton,	Adoption, etc.,	12377
1868	Hattie P.	Worcester,	Guardianship,	12378
1863	Henry	Worcester,	Administration,	12379
1821	Isaac T.	Charlton,	Guardianship,	12380
1817	Jabez	Charlton,	Administration,	12381
1795	James	Petersham,	Administration,	12382
1838	Jerry	Dudley,	Administration,	12383
1838	Jerry D.	Dudley,	Guardianship,	12384
1854	Jerusha	Hubbardston,	Will,	12385
1838	John N.	Dudley,	Guardianship,	12386
1796	Jonathan	Petersham,	Guardianship,	12387
1879	Julia	Webster,	Will,	12388
1823	Lewis	Charlton,	Guardianship,	12389
1796	Lucretia	Petersham,	Guardianship,	12390
1828	Luther	Southbridge,	Guardianship,	12391
1859	Luther	Oxford,	Administration,	12392
1830	Margaret	Charlton,	Administration,	12393
1838	Mary A.	Dudley,	Guardianship,	12394
1875	Mary A.	Auburn,	Administration,	12395

**CLEMANS, CLEMENCE, CLEM-
ENS, CLEMENT, CLEMENTS
AND CLEMONS,**

1852	Merrick	Sturbridge,	Will,	12396
1835	Moses	Charlton,	Administration,	12397
1857	Moses	Worcester,	Administration,	12398
1807	Philip	Charlton,	Will,	12399
1828	Philipina	Southbridge,	Guardianship,	12400
1796	Polly	Petersham,	Guardianship,	12401
1821	Rachel	Charlton,	Guardianship,	12402
1851	Reuben	Charlton,	Will,	12403
1868	Richard H.	Worcester,	Administration,	12404
1838	Salem T.	Dudley,	Guardianship,	12405
1800	Samuel	Petersham,	Guardianship,	12406
1821	Synia	Charlton,	Guardianship,	12407
1796	Unice	Petersham,	Guardianship,	12408
1828	William H.	Southbridge,	Guardianship,	12409
1869	William P.	Milford,	Will,	12410
1876	William W.	Royalston,	Will,	12411

CLEVELAND AND CLEAVELAND,

1880	Alden B.	Uxbridge,	Will,	12412
1854	Alpheus A.	Barre,	Guardianship,	12413
1814	Alvan	Hardwick,	Guardianship,	12414
1879	Anthony W.	Winchendon,	Administration,	12415
1873	Arthur F.	Worcester,	Guardianship,	12416
1802	Asa	Hardwick,	Guardianship,	12417
1814	Calvin	Hardwick,	Guardianship,	12418
1880	Calvin	Fitchburg,	Administration,	12419
1841	Charles M.	West Boylston,	Guardianship,	12420
1855	Charles M.	Worcester,	Adoption, etc.,	12421
1873	Clarence E.	Worcester,	Guardianship,	12422
1881	Cornelia M.	Leominster,	Administration,	12423
1802	Ebenezer	Hardwick,	Administration,	12424
1870	Edward C.	Charlton,	Administration,	12425
1871	Edwin C.	Worcester,	Will,	12426
1812	Elijah	Hardwick,	Administration,	12427
1830	Eliza T., etc.	Grafton,	Guardianship,	12428
1866	Elizabeth	West Boylston,	Administration,	12429
1854	Elizabeth L. B.	Barre,	Guardianship,	12430
1861	Ella M.	Hardwick,	Adoption, etc.,	12431
1855	Ellen M.	Worcester,	Adoption, etc.,	12432
1851	Elmira	Charlton,	Guardianship,	12433
1876	Eva J.	Hardwick,	Guardianship,	12434
1877	Frederick M.	Hardwick,	Administration,	12435
1877	George	Northborough,	Administration,	12436

YEAR.	NAME.	RESIDENCE.	NATURE.	CASE.
	CLEVELAND and CLEAVELAND,			
1873	Grace G.	Worcester,	Guardianship,	12437
1830	Hannah S.	Grafton,	Guardianship,	12438
1877	Herbert W.	West Boylston,	Guardianship,	12439
1859	Ira	Milford,	Administration,	12440
1873	Jennie I.	Worcester,	Guardianship,	12441
1877	John M.	West Boylston,	Guardianship,	12442
1814	Joseph	Hardwick,	Guardianship,	12443
1854	Joseph G.	Barre,	Guardianship,	12444
1854	Julia A.	Barre,	Guardianship,	12445
1875	Lotan	West Boylston,	Will,	12446
1856	Luthera J.	Hardwick,	Guardianship,	12447
1830	Lydia M. A.	Grafton,	Guardianship,	12448
1802	Newcomb	Hardwick,	Guardianship,	12449
1853	Newcomb	Barre,	Administration,	12450
1842	Olive I.	Grafton,	Administration,	12451
1830	Olive J.	Grafton,	Guardianship,	12452
1814	Polley	Hardwick,	Guardianship,	12453
1802	Polly	Hardwick,	Guardianship,	12454
1875	Royal	Hardwick,	Will,	12455
1874	Sally	Hardwick,	Administration,	12456
1856	Sarah A.	Worcester,	Adoption, etc.,	12457
1879	Solomon	Union, Conn.,	Administration,	12458
1854	Thomas C.	Barre,	Guardianship,	12459
1802	William	Hardwick,	Guardianship,	12460
1854	William H.	Barre,	Guardianship,	12461
1862	William W.	Hardwick,	Administration,	12462
1801	CLEVERLY, John	Lancaster,	Administration,	12463
1871	Joseph	Lancaster,	Guardianship,	12464
1878	Joseph	Lancaster,	Administration,	12464
1779	Nathaniel	Harvard,	Guardianship,	12465
1851	Rachel	Harvard,	Administration,	12466
1807	Sarah	Lancaster,	Will,	12467
1852	CLIFFORD, Helen	West Boylston,	Guardianship,	12468
1878	Honora	Leominster,	Guardianship,	12469
1803	Jonathan	Hubbardston,	Administration,	12470
1803	Josephus	Hubbardston,	Guardianship,	12471
1873	Lucy B.	Fitchburg,	Sale Real Estate,	12472
1873	Mary P.	Worcester,	Will,	12473
1854	Mary S.	Worcester,	Will,	12474
1879	Myron A.	Worcester,	Administration,	12475
1803	Nelly	Hubbardston,	Guardianship,	12476
1803	Polly	Hubbardston,	Guardianship,	12477
1860	William J.	Fitchburg,	Administration,	12478
1872	Young S.	Worcester,	Will,	12479

Year.	Name.	Residence.	Nature.	Case.
1875	CLINTON, Emmie	Hartwick, N. Y.,	Adoption, etc.,	12480
1855	Henry	Hardwick,	Administration,	12481
1878	Henry S.	Worcester,	Guardianship,	12482
1878	Lewis P.	Worcester,	Guardianship,	12483
1873	CLOSSON, Ida B.	Westminster,	Guardianship,	12484
1873	John H.	Westminster,	Guardianship,	12485
1870	CLOUGH, Alexander A.	Worcester,	Guardianship,	12486
1870	A. Winslow	Worcester,	Guardianship,	12487
1870	Benjamin H.	Worcester,	Guardianship,	12488
1876	David	West Brookfield,	Administration,	12489
1870	Jennie	Worcester,	Guardianship,	12490
1852	Lewis	Winchendon,	Administration,	12491
1876	Mary M.	Worcester,	Administration,	12492
1803	Obadiah	Charlton,	Will,	12493
1868	Sarah M.	Winchendon,	Adoption, etc.,	12494
1792	CLOWES, Thomas	Grafton,	Administration,	12495
	CLOYES AND CLOYSE,			
1876	Carrie A.	Oakland, Cal.,	Guardianship,	12496
1874	Gardner	Westborough,	Will,	12497
1876	Hattie M.	Oakland, Cal.,	Guardianship,	12498
1876	Herbert P.	Oakland, Cal.,	Guardianship,	12499
1876	Ida	Oakland, Cal.,	Guardianship,	12500
1799	Joseph	Shrewsbury,	Administration,	12501
1833	Joseph	Grafton,	Administration,	12502
1855	Nathan	Worcester,	Administration,	12503
1856	Prudence	Rutland,	Will,	12504
1876	Walter G.	Oakland, Cal.,	Guardianship,	12505
1846	William	Spencer,	Administration,	12506
1873	COACHMAN, John C.	Charlton,	Will,	12507
1874	COAD, Joseph S.	Dudley,	Guardianship,	12508
1760	COATS, Cloe	Douglas,	Guardianship,	12509
1760	Esther	Douglas,	Guardianship,	12510
1760	Rhoda	Douglas,	Guardianship,	12511
1838	COBB, Calista R.	Groton,	Foreign Sale,	12512
1812	Charles	Princeton,	Guardianship,	12513
1867	Charles A.	Lancaster,	Will,	12514
1867	Clarissa	Barre,	Will,	12515
1816	Ebenezer	Hardwick,	Will,	12516
1835	Ebenezer	Hardwick,	Administration,	12517
1812	Elias H.	Princeton,	Guardianship,	12518
1812	Eliza	Princeton,	Guardianship,	12519
1869	Elmer	Milford,	Will,	12520
1812	Ezra	Princeton,	Guardianship,	12521
1831	Frederick	Hardwick,	Guardianship,	12522
1853	George N.	Worcester,	Administration,	12523

YEAR.	NAME.	RESIDENCE.	NATURE.	CASE.
1812	COBB, George W.	Princeton,	Guardianship,	12524
1814	Gersham	Hardwick,	Guardianship,	12525
1812	Gershom	Hardwick,	Administration,	12526
1815	Jacob	Phillipston,	Administration,	12527
1750	John	Leicester,	Will,	12528
1812	John	Princeton,	Guardianship,	12529
1859	Lewis	Woodstock, Conn.,	Foreign Will,	12530
1877	Louisa L.	Fitchburg,	Will,	12531
1881	Margaret	Millbury,	Will,	12532
1838	Mary A.	Groton,	Foreign Sale,	12533
1814	Miles	Hardwick,	Guardianship,	12534
1812	Nancy	Princeton,	Guardianship,	12535
1820	Perez	New Braintree,	Administration,	12536
1814	Prior	Hardwick,	Guardianship,	12537
1854	Salem	Shrewsbury,	Will,	12538
1812	Sally	Princeton,	Guardianship,	12539
1855	Sally	Hardwick,	Will,	12540
1810	Samuel	Princeton,	Administration,	12541
1813	Sherebiah	Hardwick,	Administration,	12542
1834	Sylvanus	Barre,	Will,	12543
1834	Sylvanus	Barre,	Pension,	12544
1879	Sylvia	Milford,	Will,	12545
1812	William	Princeton,	Guardianship,	12546
	COBBETT AND COBBITT see COR-			
	BETT.			
1871	COBLEIGH, Alice M.	Worcester,	Guardianship,	12547
1874	Anna	Templeton,	Will,	12548
1839	Anson	Templeton,	Administration,	12549
1871	Charles J.	Worcester,	Guardianship,	12550
1842	David	Templeton,	Administration,	12551
1873	David	Templeton,	Administration,	12552
1833	Dolly T.	Worcester,	Administration,	12553
1846	Elizabeth	Worcester,	Will,	12554
1825	Ephraim	Ashburnham,	Will,	12555
1871	Harriet M.	Worcester,	Guardianship,	12556
1871	Henry F.	Worcester,	Guardianship,	12557
1875	Irving V.	Hubbardston,	Guardianship,	12558
1805	John	Templeton,	Will,	12559
1870	John	Fitzwilliam, N. H.,	Foreign Will,	12560
1863	John R.	Barre,	Administration,	12561
1815	Jonathan	Worcester,	Administration,	12562
1880	Mehitable	Worcester,	Guardianship,	12563
1873	Nancy A.	Templeton,	Guardianship,	12564
1876	Nancy A.	Templeton,	Administration,	12564
1872	Ransom	Northbridge,	Will,	12565

YEAR.	NAME.	RESIDENCE.	NATURE.	CASE.
1871	COBLEIGH, Walter E.	Worcester,	Guardianship,	12566
1854	COBURN, Albert C.	Winchendon,	Guardianship,	12567
1851	Catharine E.	Sturbridge,	Guardianship,	12568
1817	Charles	Sturbridge,	Pension,	12569
1851	Charles C.	Sturbridge,	Administration,	12570
1854	Charles E.	Winchendon,	Guardianship,	12571
1870	Charles M.	Charlton,	Guardianship,	12572
1848	Clarence E.	Worcester,	Guardianship,	12573
1750	Daniel	Dudley,	Will,	12574
1848	Grovener C.	Worcester,	Administration,	12575
1878	Harry A.	Fitchburg,	Guardianship,	12576
1856	Henry	Southbridge,	Administration,	12577
1854	Henry F.	Winchendon,	Administration,	12578
1854	Henry H.	Winchendon,	Guardianship,	12579
1826	John	Charlton,	Administration,	12580
1825	John, Jr.	Charlton,	Administration,	12581
1854	Orlando L.	Winchendon,	Guardianship,	12582
1821	Sarah	Sturbridge,	Guardianship,	12583
1868	Stephen	Winchendon,	Will,	12584
1848	Stillman D.	Gardner,	Administration,	12585
1850	Stillman F.	Uxbridge,	Guardianship,	12586
1820	Sylvanus	Worcester,	Administration,	12587
1881	COCHRANE, Charles	Worcester,	Guardianship,	12588
1881	Patrick	Worcester,	Administration,	12589
1881	William	Worcester,	Guardianship,	12590
1845	COCKCROFT, Elizabeth H.	Leicester,	Guardianship,	12591
1845	Emily	Leicester,	Guardianship,	12592
1845	Hellen	Leicester,	Guardianship,	12593
1845	John	Leicester,	Will,	12594
1845	Thomas	Leicester,	Guardianship,	12595
1852	CODY, Nathan	Webster,	Administration,	12596
1853	Rhoda	Webster,	Guardianship,	12597
1858	Rhoda	Webster,	Administration,	12597
1744	William	Mendon,	Administration,	12598
	COE AND COES,			
1876	Aury G.	Worcester,	Administration,	12599
1851	Charlotte C.	Worcester,	Guardianship,	12600
1862	Deborah S.	Woodstock, Conn.,	Foreign Will,	12601
1876	Estella	Worcester,	Adoption,	12602
1876	Estella	Worcester,	Guardianship,	12603
1861	Frances H.	Worcester,	Guardianship,	12604
1860	Hannah	Worcester,	Will,	12605
1846	John	Worcester,	Will,	12606
1861	John	Worcester,	Guardianship,	12607
1867	Laura E.	Northbridge,	Guardianship,	12608

	COE and COES,			
1849	Levi C.	Worcester,	Administration,	12609
1876	Mary	Worcester,	Guardianship,	12610
1876	Mary	Worcester,	Adoption,	12611
1867	Mary A.	Northbridge,	Guardianship,	12612
1861	Sewall·H.	Worcester,	Guardianship,	12613
1829	William	Worcester,	Will,	12614
1850	William	Worcester,	Administration,	12615
1861	William	Worcester,	Guardianship,	12616
1870	William G.	Worcester,	Administration,	12617
	COFFEY, COFFY and COFFEE,			
1853	Dennis	Milford,	Administration,	12618
1855	Ellen	Worcester,	Guardianship,	12619
1871	Ellen	Worcester,	Guardianship,	12620
1837	Ishmael	Millbury,	Pension,	12621
1790·	John	Worcester,	Administration,	12622
1869	Mary E.	Harvard,	Administration,	12623
1862	Patrick	Worcester,	Pension,	12624
1867	Patrick	Milford,	Will,	12625
1855	Timothy	Worcester,	Will,	12626
1873	Timothy	Winchendon,	Will,	12627
1874	COFFIN, Charles H.	Westminster,	Guardianship,	12628
1857	Dolly	Templeton,	Will,	12629
1857	Dolly	Templeton,	Pension,	12630
1873	Edwin G.	Millbury,	Administration,	12631
1876	Etta	Unknown,	Adoption, etc.,	12632
1877	George S.	Winchendon,	Administration,	12633
1864	George W.	Southbridge,	Will,	12634
1829	John G.	Brookfield,	Will,	12635
1874	John H.	Hubbardston,	Guardianship,	12636
1872	Patience J.	Sturbridge,	Administration,	12637
1877	Tristram T.	Hubbardston,	Administration,	12638
1867	COFRAN, Joseph	Bolton,	Administration,	12639
	COFFY see COFFEY.			
	COFLIN see COUGHLIN.			
1870	COGANS, Sarah J.	Gardner,	Adoption, etc.,	12640
1878	COGGSHALL, Joseph H.	Sutton,	Will,	12641
1877	COGGSILL, Henry	Clinton,	Will,	12642
	COGGSWELL and COGSWELL,			
1827	Aaron	Spencer,	Administration,	12643
1851	Angelina E.	Leominster,	Guardianship,	12644
1805	Clarissa	Paxton,	Guardianship,	12645
1851	Francis R.	Leominster,	Guardianship,	12646
1851	George W.	Leominster,	Guardianship,	12647
1851	James D.	Leominster,	Guardianship,	12648

YEAR.	NAME.	RESIDENCE.	NATURE.	CASE.
	COGGSWELL AND COGSWELL,			
1838	Jemima	Lunenburg,	Will,	12649
1854	Lucy A.	Worcester,	Guardianship,	12650
1851	Martha C.	Leominster,	Guardianship,	12651
1880	Moses	Fitchburg,	Administration,	12652
1812	Polly	Spencer,	Administration,	12653
1828	Rufus	Leicester,	Administration,	12654
1877	Seth	Leominster,	Administration,	12655
1840	Susannah	Charlton,	Will,	12656
1836	William	Lunenburg,	Will,	12657
1860	COGOVAN, James	Milford,	Will,	12658
	COGSWELL see COGGSWELL.			
1866	COHEN, William	Worcester,	Administration,	12659
1780	COLBURN, Achsah	Sturbridge,	Guardianship,	12660
1867	Adelaide E.	Lunenburg,	Administration,	12661
1848	Almedia	Sturbridge,	Guardianship,	12662
1820	Alpheus	Holden,	Guardianship,	12663
1848	Amelia	Sturbridge,	Guardianship,	12664
1779	Benjamin	Sturbridge,	Administration,	12665
1780	Benjamin	Sturbridge,	Guardianship,	12666
1848	Betsey C.	Sturbridge,	Guardianship,	12667
1843	Betty	Leominster,	Administration,	12668
1843	Betty	Leominster,	Pension,	12669
1872	Charles	Clinton,	Administration,	12670
1843	Clarissa K.	Leominster,	Will,	12671
1865	David H.	Leominster,	Will,	12672
1793	Ebenezer	Leominster,	Administration,	12673
1848	Elbridge	Sturbridge,	Guardianship,	12674
1849	Elijah	Leominster,	Administration,	12675
1832	Elisha	Leominster,	Administration,	12676
1835	Ellen P.	Leominster,	Guardianship,	12677
1848	Ephraim	Sturbridge,	Administration,	12678
1780	Eunice	Sturbridge,	Guardianship,	12679
1861	Henrietta	Milwaukee, Wis.,	Foreign Will,	12680
1865	Jacob	Leominster,	Administration,	12681
1867	Jane W.	Lunenburg,	Administration,	12682
1791	Job	Holden,	Guardianship,	12683
1812	Job	Holden,	Administration,	12683
1879	John	Lunenburg,	Will,	12684
1873	Jonas	Leominster,	Will,	12685
1878	Matilda	Leominster,	Administration,	12686
1836	Nathan	Leominster,	Pension,	12687
1776	Nathaniel	Leominster,	Will,	12688
1798	Paul	Oxford,	Guardianship,	12689
1855	Smith	Leominster,	Administration,	12690

YEAR.	NAME.	RESIDENCE.	NATURE.	CASE.
1853	COLBURN, William G.	Leominster,	Administration,	12691
1843	William H.	Leominster,	Guardianship,	12692
1853	COLBY, Jonathan	Hardwick,	Administration,	12693
1868	Lydia	Pembroke, N. H.,	Administration,	12694
1802	COLE, Abel	Sutton,	Administration,	12695
1768	Abijah	Harvard,	Administration,	12696
1780	Abijah	Harvard,	Guardianship,	12697
1818	Alexander	Dudley,	Administration,	12698
1862	Alfred E.	Southbridge,	Guardianship,	12699
1814	Brookey	Sutton,	Guardianship,	12700
1814	Charlotte	Sutton,	Guardianship,	12701
1880	Charlotte	Sutton,	Will,	12702
1877	Daniel	Sutton,	Administration,	12703
1881	Daniel	Barre,	Will,	12704
1813	David	Sutton,	Will,	12705
1872	Edgar A.	Millbury,	Administration,	12706
1799	Elkanah	Gerry,	Guardianship,	12707
1862	Ella M.	Southbridge,	Guardianship,	12708
1874	Eva F.	Uxbridge,	Administration,	12709
1799	Ezekiel	Sutton,	Will,	12710
1862	George W.	Clinton,	Adoption, etc.,	12711
1826	Hannah	Ashford, Conn.,	Administration,	12712
1855	Hannah	Millbury,	Will,	12713
1846	Hiram	Leominster,	Will,	12714
1807	John	Sutton,	Will,	12715
1846	Josephine M.	Leominster,	Guardianship,	12716
1859	Lucretia	Sutton,	Will,	12717
1861	Nahum	Harvard,	Administration,	12718
1814	Peggy P.	Sutton,	Guardianship,	12719
1848	Phinney	Barre,	Will,	12720
1829	Polly	Sutton,	Guardianship,	12721
1858	Polly	Worcester,	Guardianship,	12722
1823	Potter	Leicester,	Administration,	12723
1862	Rachel S.	Cambridge,	Adoption, etc.,	12724
1822	Richard	Sturbridge,	Will,	12725
1880	Samuel D.	Brookfield,	Administration,	12726
1779	Sarah	Harvard,	Guardianship,	12727
1869	Stephen	Sutton,	Will,	12728
1814	Sumner	Sutton,	Guardianship,	12729
1877	Susan H.	Sutton,	Administration,	12730
1814	Susanna	Sutton,	Administration,	12731
1868	COLEARY, James	Westminster,	Will,	12732
	COLEMAN AND COLMAN,			
1819	Adeline L., etc.	Worcester,	Guardianship,	12733
1826	Amherst	Hubbardston,	Administration,	12734

YEAR.	NAME.	RESIDENCE.	NATURE.	CASE.
	COLEMAN and COLMAN,			
1861	Benjamin F., Jr.	Hubbardston,	Administration,	12735
1863	Charles C.	Worcester,	Will,	12736
1848	David C.	Hubbardston,	Guardianship,	12737
1861	David C.	Hubbardston,	Administration,	12738
1877	Ela S.	Gardner,	Administration,	12739
1840	Francis L.	Hubbardston,	Guardianship,	12740
1875	George B.	Worcester,	Administration,	12741
1840	Horace U.	Hubbardston,	Guardianship,	12742
1865	Horace U.	Milford,	Administration,	12743
1815	John	Templeton,	Will,	12744
1840	John	Hubbardston,	Administration,	12745
1879	John, etc.	Worcester,	Guardianship,	12746
1840	John W.	Hubbardston,	Guardianship,	12747
1840	Larkin	Hubbardston,	Guardianship,	12748
1876	Mary	Fitchburg,	Will,	12749
1864	Mary Z.	Worcester,	Guardianship,	12750
1869	Patrick	Fitchburg,	Adoption, etc.,	12751
1848	Perez	Hubbardston,	Administration,	12752
1864	Philander S.	Barre,	Administration,	12753
1854	Rebecca	Hubbardston,	Administration,	12754
1840	Reuben C.	Hubbardston,	Guardianship,	12755
1840	Samuel M.	Hubbardston,	Guardianship,	12756
1848	Samuel M.	Hubbardston,	Administration,	12757
1840	Sylvanus	Hubbardston,	Guardianship,	12758
1873	Tabitha P.	Templeton,	Administration,	12759
1881	Thomas J.	Templeton,	Will,	12760
1840	Washington	Hubbardston,	Guardianship,	12761
1864	Zurvillar	Worcester,	Will,	12762
1852	COLLAN, James	Barre,	Administration,	12763
	COLLAR and COLLER,			
1826	Charles	Grafton,	Guardianship,	12764
1868	Charles W.	Athol,	Administration,	12765
1826	Charlotte	Sutton,	Guardianship,	12766
1857	Hannah	Oxford,	Will,	12767
1749	James	Oxford,	Will,	12768
1840	Jason	Oxford,	Will,	12769
1754	John	Louisburg,	Administration,	12770
1768	John	Grafton,	Administration,	12771
1820	Jonathan	Oxford,	Administration,	12772
1757	Joseph	Worcester,	Administration,	12773
1881	Martha L.	Westborough,	Guardianship,	12774
1876	Sarah J.	Athol,	Administration,	12775
1819	William	Western,	Administration,	12776
1826	William	Springfield,	Guardianship,	12777

YEAR.	NAME.	RESIDENCE.	NATURE.	CASE.
	COLLESTER AND COLLISTER,			
1847	Candace	Warren,	Guardianship,	12778
1864	Eugene B.	Gardner,	Guardianship,	12779
1864	Frank M.	Gardner,	Guardianship,	12780
1845	Franklin	Warren,	Administration,	12781
1838	Horace	Warren,	Administration,	12782
1864	Laura M.	Gardner,	Guardianship,	12783
1838	Mary A.	Warren,	Guardianship,	12784
1873	Osgood	Fitchburg,	Administration,	12785
1845	Royal	Warren,	Administration,	12786
1864	Thorley	Gardner,	Administration,	12787
1868	COLLETT, Louis	Spencer,	Will,	12788
1850	COLLICOTT, Phillip	Milford,	Administration,	12789
1838	COLLIER, Alexander	Oxford,	Guardianship,	12790
1857	Alexander	Oxford,	Administration,	12791
1861	Edward	North Brookfield,	Will,	12792
1844	Ezra	Boylston,	Administration,	12793
1853	George W.	Grafton,	Administration,	12794
1858	Hannah	Oxford,	Pension,	12795
1842	Isanna M.	Grafton,	Guardianship,	12796
1857	James	Oxford,	Administration,	12797
1838	Jason	Oxford,	Guardianship,	12798
1847	Jason S.	Oxford,	Administration,	12799
1878	Margaret	North Brookfield,	Will,	12800
1863	Mary A.	Webster,	Will,	12801
1841	William B.	Grafton,	Administration,	12802
	COLLINS AND COLLINGS,			
1832	Aaron	Southborough,	Administration,	12803
1827	Abigail	Southborough,	Guardianship,	12804
1832	Abigail	Southborough,	Administration,	12805
1825	Abner P.	Southborough,	Guardianship,	12806
1863	Albert M.	Athol,	Guardianship,	12807
1826	Amos	Southborough,	Administration,	12808
1861	Ann	Hardwick,	Administration,	12809
1825	Ann P.	Southborough,	Guardianship,	12810
1872	Annie	Worcester,	Adoption, etc.,	12811
1873	Annie	Worcester,	Guardianship,	12812
1869	Annie B.	Fitchburg,	Guardianship,	12813
1826	Anthony S.	Hardwick,	Guardianship,	12814
1827	Benjamin	Southborough,	Administration,	12815
1880	Bernard	Milford,	Administration,	12816
1826	Betsey	Hardwick,	Guardianship,	12817
1825	Burleigh	Southborough,	Guardianship,	12818
1853	Burleigh	Westborough,	Will,	12819
1870	Charles A. F.	Milford,	Guardianship,	12820

Year.	Name.	Residence.	Nature.	Case.
	COLLINS and COLLINGS,			
1870	Charles M.	Bloomington, Ill.,	Guardianship,	12821
1872	Daniel	Winchendon,	Administration,	12822
1826	Daniel S.	Hardwick,	Guardianship,	12823
1870	Dolly	Southborough,	Guardianship,	12824
1870	Edgar E.	Bloomington, Ill.,	Guardianship,	12825
1845	Ellen E.	Northborough,	Guardianship,	12826
1869	Ellen P.	Killingly Conn.,	Guardianship,	12827
1827	Elmer	Southborough,	Guardianship,	12828
1870	Emma S.	Milford,	Guardianship,	12829
1787	Gamaliel	Hardwick,	Will,	12830
1825	Gamaliel	Hardwick,	Administration,	12831
1826	Gamaliel	Hardwick,	Guardianship,	12832
1866	George	Fitchburg,	Will,	12833
1827	Harriet	Southborough,	Guardianship,	12834
1845	Harriet N.	Northborough,	Guardianship,	12835
1843	Henry	Southborough,	Administration,	12836
1825	Hiram	Southborough,	Guardianship,	12837
1868	Hiram	Southborough,	Administration,	12838
1878	Hiram F.	Putnam, Conn.,	Administration,	12839
1870	Ida A.	Bloomington, Ill.,	Guardianship,	12840
1862	James	Holden,	Will,	12841
1791	Jedidiah	Leominster,	Will,	12842
1873	Jeremiah	Berlin,	Administration,	12843
1825	John	Southborough,	Administration,	12844
1860	John	Worcester,	Administration,	12845
1870	John	Webster,	Will,	12846
1878	John	Webster,	Guardianship,	12847
1825	Joseph	Southborough,	Guardianship,	12848
1872	Julia	Worcester,	Adoption, etc.,	12849
1873	Julia	Worcester,	Guardianship,	12850
1826	Julian	Hardwick,	Guardianship,	12851
1833	Lawson B.	Southborough,	Guardianship,	12852
1851	Levi	Ashburnham,	Administration,	12853
1866	Lillian G.	Milford,	Adoption, etc.,	12854
1827	Luke	Southborough,	Guardianship,	12855
1826	Marcy	Uxbridge,	Will,	12856
1875	Margaret E.	Milford,	Administration,	12857
1823	Mark	Southborough,	Will,	12858
1863	Marshall	Athol,	Administration,	12859
1845	Martha M.	Northborough,	Guardianship,	12860
1875	Mary	Southbridge,	Administration,	12861
1880	Mary A. B.	Fitchburg,	Will,	12862
1869	Mary A. J.	Killingly, Conn.,	Guardianship,	12863
1870	Mary C.	Bloomington, Ill.,	Guardianship,	12864

COLLINS AND COLLINGS,

YEAR.	NAME.	RESIDENCE.	NATURE.	CASE.
1879	Mary J.	Worcester,	Will,	12865
1874	Michael	Fitchburg,	Administration,	12866
1833	Nancy M.	Southborough,	Guardianship,	12867
1826	Patty	Hardwick,	Guardianship,	12868
1870	Polly	Southborough,	Administration,	12869
1839	Rebecca	Southborough,	Administration,	12870
1866	Sally	Southborough,	Administration,	12871
1825	Samuel	Southborough,	Guardianship,	12872
1832	Starry	Southbridge,	Administration,	12873
1857	Sylvanus	Athol,	Administration,	12874
1865	Thomas M.	Worcester,	Will,	12875
1870	Waldo A.	Milford,	Guardianship,	12876
1812	William	Southborough,	Will,	12877
1827	William	Southborough,	Guardianship,	12878
1863	William	Southbridge,	Guardianship,	12879

COLLIS see CORLISS.
COLLISTER see COLLESTER.

YEAR.	NAME.	RESIDENCE.	NATURE.	CASE.
1874	COLLITY, Bridget M.	Warren,	Will,	12880
1874	Daniel	Warren,	Guardianship,	12881
1874	Mary A.	Warren,	Guardianship,	12882
1859	COLON, Elizabeth	Phillipston,	Adoption, etc.,	12883
1873	Sanford	Phillipston,	Administration,	12884
1875	COLTON, Samuel H.	Worcester,	Will,	12885
1861	COLVILL, James	Worcester,	Administration,	12886
1861	COLVIN, Alvah P.	Holden,	Administration,	12887
1863	Benoni H.	West Boylston,	Administration,	12888
1863	Edgar C.	West Boylston,	Guardianship,	12889
1863	Flora A.	West Boylston,	Guardianship,	12890
1863	Josephine F.	West Boylston,	Guardianship,	12891
1872	Mark	Northbridge,	Will,	12892
1863	Sylvester	West Boylston,	Guardianship,	12893
1874	Zacheus	Blackstone,	Will,	12894
1792	COMAN, Benjamin	Dudley,	Guardianship,	12895
1861	Betsey	Thompson, Conn.,	Administration,	12896
1792	Samuel	Dudley,	Guardianship,	12897
1792	Sarah	Dudley,	Guardianship.	12898
1797	Sarah	Charlton,	Administration,	12899
1790	Stephen	Dudley,	Administration,	12900
1792	Winsor	Dudley,	Guardianship,	12901
1792	Ziba	Dudley,	Guardianship,	12902

COMB AND COMBS see COOMBS.

YEAR.	NAME.	RESIDENCE.	NATURE.	CASE.
1744	COMECHOR, Isaac	Worcester,	Administration,	12903
1832	COMEE, Abigail	Gardner,	Guardianship,	12904
1878	Charles H.	Fitchburg,	Will,	12905

Year.	Name.	Residence.	Nature.	Case.
1832	COMEE, Daniel W.	Gardner,	Guardianship,	12906
1848	David	Gardner,	Administration,	12907
1832	Eliza	Gardner,	Guardianship,	12908
1836	Eliza	Gardner,	Administration,	12909
1826	George W.	Gardner,	Guardianship,	12910
1832	James M.	Gardner,	Will,	12911
1832	Leander P.	Gardner,	Guardianship,	12912
1805	Otis	Dana,	Guardianship,	12913
1864	Sally	Gardner,	Administration,	12914
1832	William	Gardner,	Guardianship,	12915
	COMINS, COMMINGS and COM-INGS (see also CUMMINGS),			
1829	Barnabas	Charlton,	Administration,	12916
1870	Charles M.	Southbridge,	Administration,	12917
1879	Danforth B.	Worcester,	Will,	12918
1756	Elijah	Brookfield,	Guardianship,	12919
1837	Fanny L.	Charlton,	Guardianship,	12920
1832	Free	Charlton,	Will,	12921
1853	Free	Charlton,	Will,	12922
1840	Freeman	Charlton,	Administration,	12923
1837	George F.	Charlton,	Guardianship,	12924
1809	Isaac	Hardwick,	Administration,	12925
1862	Issacher	Charlton,	Administration,	12926
1762	Jacob	Oxford,	Will,	12927
1811	Jacob	Charlton,	Administration,	12928
1836	Jacob	Charlton,	Administration,	12929
1756	John	Southborough,	Will,	12930
1829	Julia A.	Charlton,	Guardianship,	12931
1829	Linus B.	Charlton,	Guardianship,	12932
1866	Lydia	Charlton,	Administration,	12933
1795	Margaret	Charlton,	Will,	12934
1829	Mary B.	Charlton,	Guardianship,	12935
1837	Mary B.	Charlton,	Guardianship,	12936
1847	Noah	Hardwick,	Administration,	12937
1829	Paschal B.	Charlton,	Administration,	12938
1808	Reuben	Charlton,	Will,	12939
1808	Reuben	Petersham,	Administration,	12940
1834	Reuben	Charlton,	Will,	12941
1760	Stehens	Sutton,	Will,	12942
1843	Stephen	Phillipston,	Guardianship,	12943
1844	Stephen	Phillipston,	Administration,	12943
1784	Thomas	Lancaster,	Will,	12944
1784	William	Charlton,	Will,	12945
1784	William	Charlton,	Guardianship,	12946

YEAR.	NAME.	RESIDENCE.	NATURE.	CASE.
1875	COMISKEY, John	Worcester,	Administration,	12947
1876	COMMEAN, Cora A., etc.	Winchendon,	Adoption, etc.,	12948
1822	COMSTOCK, Abner	Williamstown, Vt.,	Administration,	12949
1810	Anthony	Smithfield, R. I.,	Foreign Sale,	12950
1810	Anthony	Smithfield, R. I.,	Administration,	12951
1869	Charles	Winchendon,	Guardianship,	12952
1873	Chloe M.	Mendon,	Will,	12953
1832	Dan A.	Mendon,	Guardianship,	12954
1858	Dan A.	Blackstone,	Will,	12955
1834	Daniel	Thompson, Conn.,	Administration,	12956
1810	Elizabeth	Smithfield, R. I.,	Foreign Sale,	12957
1810	Ezra	Smithfield, R. I.,	Foreign Sale,	12958
1820	George	Mendon,	Will,	12959
1808	George, Jr.	Leicester,	Will,	12960
1832	Gilbert	Mendon,	Guardianship,	12961
1810	Hannah	Smithfield, R. I.,	Foreign Sale,	12962
1861	James	Blackstone,	Administration,	12963
1829	Laban	Uxbridge,	Will,	12964
1810	Martha	Smithfield, R. I.,	Foreign Sale,	12965
1832	Mercy H.	Mendon,	Guardianship,	12966
1810	Olive	Smithfield, R. I.,	Foreign Sale,	12967
1810	Phebe	Smithfield, R. I.,	Foreign Sale,	12968
1795	Polly	Uxbridge,	Guardianship,	12969
1863	Salmon	Westborough,	Administration,	12970
1857	Silas	Burrillville, R. I.,	Will,	12971
1810	William	Smithfield, R. I.,	Foreign Sale,	12972
1830	William	Mendon,	Administration,	12973
1832	William	Mendon,	Guardianship,	12974
1846	CONANT, Aaron	Gardner,	Administration,	12975
1836	Abel	Leominster,	Administration,	12976
1878	Abigail	Oakham,	Will,	12977
1807	Abner	Hardwick,	Administration,	12978
1844	Adelia M.	Charlton,	Guardianship,	12979
1876	Alice M.	Montague,	Adoption, etc.,	12980
1877	Andrew	Lunenburg,	Will,	12981
1845	Annes	Gardner,	Will,	12982
1837	Antoinette	Leominster,	Guardianship,	12983
1875	Artemas B.	Athol,	Will,	12984
1864	Arthur W.	Gardner,	Adoption, etc.,	12985
1801	Asa	Oxford,	Administration,	12986
1849	Augusta M.	Harvard,	Guardianship,	12987
1861	Benjamin H.	Worcester,	Administration,	12988
1819	Benjamin K.	Paxton,	Guardianship,	12989
1879	Benjamin P.	Hubbardston,	Administration,	12990
1867	Betsey P.	Sterling,	Will,	12991

YEAR.	NAME.	RESIDENCE.	NATURE.	CASE.
1843	CONANT, Caroline E.	Charlton,	Guardianship,	12992
1877	Charles	Oakham,	Will,	12993
1863	Charles A.	Barre,	Guardianship,	12994
1819	Cyrus W.	Paxton,	Guardianship,	12995
1874	Deborah M.	Athol,	Will,	12996
1783	Ebenezer	Ashburnham,	Will,	12997
1838	Elizabeth	Westminster,	Guardianship,	12998
1846	Elizabeth	Worcester,	Guardianship,	12999
1864	Ella I.	Gardner,	Guardianship,	13000
1880	Emily A.	Leominster,	Administration,	13001
1864	Erwin C.	Gardner,	Guardianship,	13002
1841	Eunice	Athol,	Administration,	13003
1789	Ezra	Oxford,	Administration,	13004
1819	Ezra S.	Paxton,	Guardianship,	13005
1864	Frank E.	Gardner,	Guardianship,	13006
1864	Fred H.	Gardner,	Guardianship,	13007
1862	Gaius	Paxton,	Will,	13008
1864	George F.	Gardner,	Administration,	13009
1861	George W.	Barre,	Administration,	13010
1864	Harriet	Northborough,	Guardianship,	13011
1844	Harriet P.	Charlton,	Guardianship,	13012
1859	Harrison C.	Leominster,	Guardianship,	13013
1816	Harvey	Dudley,	Guardianship,	13014
1879	Helen S.	Gardner,	Guardianship,	13015
1863	Henry E.	Barre,	Guardianship,	13016
1879	Herbert H.	Gardner,	Guardianship,	13017
1859	Herbert J.	Brookfield,	Guardianship,	13018
1846	Hezekiah	Worcester,	Guardianship,	13019
1843	Hosea	Charlton,	Administration,	13020
1819	Huldah	Harvard,	Will,	13021
1839	Jacob	Sterling,	Will,	13022
1867	James	Oakham,	Administration,	13023
1859	John	Brookfield,	Administration,	13024
1849	John O.	Harvard,	Guardianship,	13025
1859	Joseph	Leominster,	Will,	13026
1813	Josiah	Dudley,	Administration,	13027
1816	Josiah	Dudley,	Guardianship,	13028
1835	Josiah	Gardner,	Administration,	13029
1839	Josiah	Dudley,	Administration,	13030
1846	Josiah	Worcester,	Guardianship,	13031
1848	Josiah	Berlin,	Administration,	13032
1870	Josiah	Gardner,	Will,	13033
1863	Julius A.	Charlton,	Administration,	13034
1797	Learned	Oxford,	Guardianship,	13035
1825	Levi	Hubbardston,	Administration,	13036

YEAR.	NAME.	RESIDENCE.	NATURE.	CASE.
1878	CONANT, Levi	Hubbardston,	Will,	13037
1825	Lucy S.	Harvard,	Guardianship,	13038
1808	Lydia	Sterling,	Guardianship,	13039
1826	Lydia	Sterling,	Will,	13040
1825	Marion	Harvard,	Guardianship,	13041
1806	Mary	Oxford,	Guardianship,	13042
1847	Mary	Worcester,	Guardianship,	13043
1880	Mary	Royalston,	Will,	13044
1819	Mary A.	Paxton,	Guardianship,	13045
1843	Mary L.	Charlton,	Guardianship,	13046
1823	Matilda	Charlton,	Guardianship,	13047
1870	Milly	Northborough,	Administration,	13048
1865	Nancy	Barre,	Will,	13049
1873	Nancy	Leominster,	Administration,	13050
1839	Nancy P. H.	Sterling,	Guardianship,	13051
1862	Peter D.	Harvard,	Administration,	13052
1839	Pitt C.	Dudley,	Guardianship,	13053
1801	Polly	Oxford,	Guardianship,	13054
1808	Polly	Sterling,	Guardianship,	13055
1837	Rebecca M.	Leominster,	Guardianship,	13056
1823	Rufus	Charlton,	Administration,	13057
1823	Rufus	Charlton,	Guardianship,	13058
1877	Rufus	Southbridge,	Will,	13059
1843	Rufus L.	Charlton,	Guardianship,	13060
1797	Sally	Oxford,	Guardianship,	13061
1797	Samuel	Oxford,	Guardianship,	13062
1805	Samuel	Oxford,	Administration,	13063
1808	Samuel	Sterling,	Administration,	13064
1824	Samuel	Sterling,	Administration,	13065
1846	Samuel H.	Worcester,	Guardianship,	13066
1846	Sarah C.	Gardner,	Guardianship,	13067
1849	Sherman G.	Harvard,	Administration,	13068
1849	Sherman W.	Harvard,	Guardianship,	13069
1816	Silvia	Dudley,	Guardianship,	13070
1877	Susan	Oakham,	Administration,	13071
1840	Susannah	Oakham,	Will,	13072
1841	Susannah	Oakham,	Pension,	13073
1814	Thomas	Westminster,	Administration,	13074
1820	Thomas	Westminster,	Guardianship,	13075
1838	Thomas	Westminster,	Guardianship,	13076
	CONDON AND CONGDON,			
1864	Amy	Millbury,	Will,	13077
1868	Charles A.	Southbridge,	Guardianship,	13078
1867	Charles L.	Southbridge,	Guardianship,	13079
1781	David	Upton,	Administration,	13080

YEAR.	NAME.	RESIDENCE.	NATURE.	CASE.
	CONDON AND CONGDON,			
1866	Ellen	Leicester,	Guardianship,	13081
1867	James	Southbridge,	Administration,	13082
1838	John	Sturbridge,	Will,	13083
1849	John	Sturbridge,	Pension,	13084
1871	Martha B.	Southbridge,	Will,	13085
1852	Mary	Sturbridge,	Will,	13086
1866	Mary	Leicester,	Administration,	13087
1866	Mary	Leicester,	Guardianship,	13088
1864	Mary A.	Northbridge,	Administration,	13089
1864	Mary A.	Northbridge,	Guardianship,	13090
1870	Mary A.	Griswold, Conn.,	Administration,	13091
1784	Richard	Upton,	Guardianship,	13092
1811	Richard	Upton,	Administration,	13093
1784	Ruth	Upton,	Guardianship,	13094
1784	Samuel	Upton,	Guardianship,	13095
1811	Samuel	Upton,	Administration,	13096
1838	Samuel	Worcester,	Guardianship,	13097
1880	Samuel G.	Worcester,	Will,	13098
1864	Seneca	Grafton,	Administration,	13099
1784	Susanna	Upton,	Guardianship,	13100
1838	William	Upton,	Administration,	13101
1881	CONDY, Alexander	Worcester,	Sep. Support,	13102
1881	Eliza A.	Worcester,	Sep. Support,	13103
1870	CONE, Elizabeth	Shrewsbury,	Will,	13104
1874	CONERY, John	Worcester,	Will,	13105
1817	CONEY, Mary	Brookfield,	Administration,	13106
1805	William	Brookfield,	Will,	13107
1864	CONFIELD, Annie	Worcester,	Administration,	13108
	CONGDON see CONDON.			
1878	CONKEY, William	Worcester,	Administration,	13109
	CONKLIN AND CONKLING,			
1798	Benjamin	Leicester,	Will,	13110
1834	Benjamin, Jr.	Leicester,	Administration,	13111
1873	Sarah W.	Worcester,	Administration,	13112
1874	William E.	Providence, R. I.,	Adoption, etc.,	13113
	CONLIN, CONLON AND CONLAN,			
1863	Ann	Leicester,	Administration,	13114
1852	Hannah	Worcester,	Guardianship,	13115
1852	Hugh	Worcester,	Guardianship,	13116
1852	James	Worcester,	Guardianship,	13117
1870	James	Worcester,	Will,	13118
1852	John	Worcester,	Guardianship,	13119
1852	Martin	Worcester,	Guardianship,	13120
1871	Martin	Worcester,	Will,	13121

YEAR.	NAME.	RESIDENCE.	NATURE.	CASE.
	CONLAN, CONLIN AND CONLON,			
1852	Mary A.	Worcester,	Guardianship,	13122
1865	Mathew	Milford,	Will,	13123
1852	Michael	Worcester,	Will,	13124
1874	Michael	Southbridge,	Administration,	13125
1866	Patrick	Worcester,	Administration,	13126
1865	Peter	Worcester,	Administration,	13127
1874	Peter	Worcester,	Will,	13128
1866	Peter A.	Worcester,	Guardianship,	13129
1875	CONLEY, Ann	Worcester,	Will,	13130
1879	Catherine J.	Milford,	Guardianship,	13131
1864	George	Westborough,	Will,	13132
1871	Maria E.	Worcester,	Will,	13133
1864	William	Westborough,	Guardianship,	13134
1863	William C.	Worcester,	Administration,	13135
	CONLIN AND CONLON see CONLAN.			
1803	CONN, John	Ashburnham,	Guardianship,	13136
1803	John	Ashburnham,	Administration,	13137
1803	John, Jr.	Ashburnham,	Administration,	13138
1803	Lydia	Ashburnham,	Guardianship,	13139
1870	CONNELL, Barney	Leicester,	Administration,	13140
1870	Bridget	Leicester,	Guardianship,	13141
1870	Elizabeth	Leicester,	Guardianship,	13142
1873	Ellen	Fitchburg,	Will,	13143
1876	George F.	Fitchburg,	Guardianship,	13144
1875	Hugh	Worcester,	Administration,	13145
1870	Maria T.	Leicester,	Guardianship,	13146
1878	Mary E.	Worcester,	Will,	13147
1870	Peter	Fitchburg,	Administration,	13148
1870	Sarah J.	Leicester,	Guardianship,	13149
	CONNELLY AND CONNOLY,			
1865	James	Milford,	Will,	13150
1877	John B.	Fitchburg,	Guardianship,	13151
1877	William H.	Fitchburg,	Guardianship,	13152
	CONNER see CONNORS.			
1870	CONNEY, Thomas	Clinton,	Will,	13153
1881	CONNIHAN, Jeremiah	Holyoke,	Pension,	13154
	CONNORS, CONNOR, CONNER AND CORNER,			
1865	Ann	Clinton,	Guardianship,	13155
1876	Annie E.	Fitchburg,	Guardianship,	13156
1861	Barney	Worcester,	Will,	13157
1881	Bridget	Sterling,	Administration,	13158
1881	David	Northbridge,	Administration,	13159
1865	Edmund	Worcester,	Administration,	13160

CONNORS, CONNOR, CONNER,
AND CORNER,

1867	Eliza A.	Worcester,	Guardianship,	13161
1870	Ellen	Milford,	Guardianship,	13162
1866	Ellen M.	Worcester,	Guardianship,	13163
1866	Emma S.	Worcester,	Guardianship,	13164
1866	E. Chapin	Worcester,	Guardianship,	13165
1874	Frederic C.	Sterling,	Administration,	13166
1866	Frederic H.	Worcester,	Guardianship,	13167
1870	Frederick H.	Worcester,	Adoption, etc.,	13168
1866	George A.	Worcester,	Guardianship,	13169
1876	Hannah	Gardner,	Administration,	13170
1866	Henry	Millbury,	Administration,	13171
1870	James	Milford,	Guardianship,	13172
1876	Jennie M.	Fitchburg,	Guardianship,	13173
1850	John	Worcester,	Guardianship,	13174
1867	John	Milford,	Administration,	13175
1870	John	Milford,	Guardianship,	13176
1877	John	Rutland,	Will,	13177
1879	John	Templeton,	Administration,	13178
1805	Joseph	Petersham,	Administration,	13179
1858	Kyron	Petersham,	Administration,	13180
1870	Margaret	Milford,	Guardianship,	13181
1869	Mary	Worcester,	Will,	13182
1876	P. Charles	Fitchburg,	Administration,	13183
1805	Thomas	Charlton,	Guardianship,	13184
1870	Thomas	Milford,	Guardianship,	13185
1880	Thomas M.	Templeton,	Guardianship,	13186
1867	William J.	Worcester,	Guardianship,	13187
1872	CONROY, John	Worcester,	Administration,	13188
1858	Thomas	Worcester,	Adoption, etc.,	13189
1814	CONSTANTINE, Jacob	Ashburnham,	Administration,	13190
1823	Jacob	Ashburnham,	Guardianship,	13191
1814	Oliver	Ashburnham,	Guardianship,	13192

CONVERSE, CONVERS AND
CONVASS,

1811	Abigail	Leicester,	Administration,	13193
1864	Abigail	Thompson, Conn.,	Administration,	13194
1869	Alpheus T.	North Brookfield,	Administration,	13195
1790	Benjamin	Leicester,	Guardianship,	13196
1836	Benjamin G.	Princeton,	Guardianship,	13197
1814	Betsey	Charlton,	Administration,	13198
1870	Caroline S.	Webster,	Guardianship,	13199
1870	Charles C.	Webster,	Guardianship,	13200
1877	Charles C.	Philadelphia, Pa.,	Guardianship,	13201
1865	Charles T.	Brookfield,	Guardianship,	13202

YEAR.	NAME.	RESIDENCE.	NATURE.	CASE.
	CONVERSE, CONVERS AND CONVASS,			
1869	Chester	Webster,	Will,	13203
1811	Cinthia	Leicester,	Guardianship,	13204
1814	Daniel	Spencer,	Administration,	13205
1852	Daniel I.	Hardwick	Administration,	13206
1853	Elenor R.	New Braintree,	Guardianship,	13207
1846	Elijah	Dudley,	Administration,	13208
1843	Elisha	Brookfield,	Will,	13209
1843	Elisha	Brookfield,	Pension,	13210
1872	Eliza A.	Worcester,	Change of Name,	13211
1853	Eliza J.	New Braintree,	Guardianship,	13212
1845	Freeland	Charlton,	Administration,	13213
1872	George W.	Winchendon,	Will,	13214
1811	Harriot	Leicester,	Guardianship,	13215
1811	James	Brookfield,	Will,	13216
1849	Joseph	Worcester,	Will,	13217
1771	Josiah	Brookfield,	Administration,	13218
1853	Josiah C.	New Braintree,	Guardianship,	13219
1853	Lorenzo	New Braintree,	Will,	13220
1810	Luke	Leicester,	Administration,	13221
1811	Luke	Leicester,	Guardianship,	13222
1781	Mercy	Brookfield,	Will,	13223
1872	Mercy	Thompson, Conn.,	Administration,	13224
1864	Merrick B.	Worcester,	Administration,	13225
1811	Otis	Leicester,	Guardianship,	13226
1874	Otis	Worcester,	Administration,	13227
1811	Farmela	Leicester,	Guardianship,	13228
1864	Pliny M.	Worcester,	Guardianship,	13229
1812	Putnam	Mendon,	Guardianship,	13230
1809	Reuben	Leicester,	Administration,	13231
1877	Rhoda M.	New Braintree,	Administration,	13232
1870	Roswell	New Braintree,	Will,	13233
1850	Salem	Spencer,	Guardianship,	13234
1841	Samuel	Brookfield,	Administration,	13235
1868	Sibley	Leicester,	Administration,	13236
1811	Tamar W.	Leicester,	Guardianship,	13237
1811	Thomas W.	Leicester,	Guardianship,	13238
1865	Thomas W.	Brookfield,	Administration,	13239
1811	Tirzah	Leicester,	Guardianship,	13240
1850	Willard	Spencer,	Will,	13241
1850	Willard	Spencer,	Guardianship,	13242
1881	CONWAY, Charles	Shrewsbury,	Administration,	13243
1874	Mary	Clinton,	Will,	13244
1856	Sarah J.	Leicester,	Adoption, etc.,	13245

Year.	Name.	Residence.	Nature.
1826	CONWAY, Solomon	Western,	Guardianship,
1861	Solomon	Petersham,	Guardianship,
	COOK AND COOKE,		
1814	Aaron	Uxbridge,	Administration,
1846	Aaron	Lancaster,	Will,
1874	Aaron C.	Mendon,	Will,
1856	Abbie J.	Uxbridge,	Guardianship,
1852	Abby W.	Templeton,	Guardianship,
1770	Abigail	Mendon,	Will,
1772	Abigail	Mendon,	Guardianship,
1860	Abigail	Mendon,	Will,
1877	Abigail	Templeton,	Administration,
1873	Addie E.	Milford,	Guardianship,
1826	Adin	Sutton,	Administration,
1853	Adin A. B.	Milford,	Guardianship,
1880	Albert A.	Milford,	Will,
1849	Alice O.	Uxbridge,	Guardianship,
1813	Allen	Mendon,	Guardianship,
1869	Alson	Worcester,	Administration,
1872	Alvin	Uxbridge,	Administration,
1858	Amos	Milford,	Will,
1866	Andrew I.	Mendon,	Guardianship,
1853	Angelia	Milford,	Guardianship,
1880	Ann Jane	Uxbridge,	Will,
1847	Ariel	Mendon	Will,
1848	Ariel	Mendon,	Administration,
1772	Arthur	Mendon,	Guardianship,
1792	Asahel	Oxford (Gore),	Administration,
1833	Barton	Mendon,	Guardianship,
1849	Barton	Uxbridge,	Will,
1877	Barton B.	Milford,	Will,
1843	Benjamin	Athol,	Will,
1816	Benjamin, Jr.	Bellingham,	Guardianship,
1832	Catharine	Petersham,	Guardianship,
1844	Catharine	Worcester,	Guardianship,
1813	Celissa	Mendon,	Guardianship,
1866	Charles D.	West Brookfield,	Guardianship,
1867	Charles W.	Lunenburg,	Adoption, etc.,
1859	Charlotte	Unknown,	Trustee,
1853	Chloe H.	Milford,	Guardianship,
1864	Clarendon W.	Milford,	Guardianship,
1859	Clark	Mendon,	Administration,
1834	Daniel, 2d	Worcester,	Will,
1845	Daniel	Worcester,	Will,
1850	Daniel	Paxton,	Administration,

YEAR.	NAME.	RESIDENCE.	NATURE.	CASE.
	COOK and COOKE,			
1844	David	Royalston,	Will,	13290
1798	Ebenezer	Mendon,	Will,	13291
1848	Ebenezer	Douglas,	Will,	13292
1851	Edward H.	Blackstone,	Guardianship,	13293
1861	Edward O.	Winchendon,	Guardianship,	13294
1853	Edwin H.	Milford,	Guardianship,	13295
1875	Edwin H.	Milford,	Administration,	13296
1743	Elijah	Worcester,	Administration,	13297
1820	Elisha	Mendon,	Administration,	13298
1852	Elisha P.	Templeton,	Administration,	13299
1872	Eliza	Athol,	Administration,	13300
1851	Eliza A.	Paxton,	Guardianship,	13301
1880	Elizabeth	Mendon,	Administration,	13302
1832	Ellis	Petersham,	Guardianship,	13303
1862	Ellis	Uxbridge,	Administration,	13304
1871	Ellis	Petersham,	Administration,	13305
1880	Emeline	Charlton,	Will,	13306
1873	Ernest L.	Milford,	Guardianship,	13307
1772	Esock	Mendon,	Guardianship,	13308
1818	Ezekiel, Jr.	Mendon,	Administration,	13309
1864	Filora S.	Milford,	Guardianship,	13310
1866	Frederic D.	West Brookfield,	Guardianship,	13311
1870	Frederick	Petersham,	Administration,	13312
1857	George O.	West Brookfield,	Guardianship,	13313
1874	George T.	Bolton,	Guardianship,	13314
1848	George W.	Uxbridge,	Administration,	13315
1855	George W.	West Brookfield,	Will,	13316
1871	George W.	Petersham,	Guardianship,	13317
1853	Halsey L.	Milford,	Guardianship,	13318
1861	Hannah	Blackstone,	Will,	13319
1878	Hattie W.	Worcester,	Guardianship,	13320
1863	Henry A.	Lunenburg,	Guardianship,	13321
1866	Henry M.	Mendon,	Guardianship,	13322
1861	Hiram L.	Winchendon,	Guardianship,	13323
1838	Ichabod	Mendon,	Will,	13324
1851	Ichabod	Blackstone,	Administration,	13325
1880	Ichabod W.	Clinton,	Will,	13326
1865	Ira W.	Milford,	Administration,	13327
1838	Isaac B.	Providence, R. I.,	Administration,	13328
1866	Isabel C.	Mendon,	Guardianship,	13329
1876	Jacob S.	Athol,	Will,	13330
1765	Jane	Sudbury,	Guardianship,	13331
1844	Jane	Worcester,	Guardianship,	13332
1877	Jeanne H.	Blackstone,	Guardianship,	13333

COOK AND COOKE,

YEAR.	NAME.	RESIDENCE.	NATURE.	CASE.
1793	Jesse	Oxford,	Guardianship,	13334
1834	Jesse	Sterling,	Administration,	13335
1753	John	Uxbridge,	Administration,	13336
1848	John	Winchendon,	Administration,	13337
1877	John	Blackstone,	Will,	13338
1880	John	Uxbridge,	Will,	13339
1877	John G.	Blackstone,	Guardianship,	13340
1759	Jonathan	Uxbridge,	Administration,	13341
1824	Joseph	West Boylston,	Administration,	13342
1849	Joseph B.	Uxbridge,	Guardianship,	13343
1856	Joseph B.	Uxbridge,	Administration,	13344
1864	Joseph B.	Blackstone,	Administration,	13345
1772	Kesiah	Mendon,	Guardianship,	13346
1847	Laura	Worcester,	Guardianship,	13347
1877	Laura W.	Blackstone,	Guardianship,	13348
1877	Lenna B.	Blackstone,	Guardianship,	13349
1777	Lois	Tolland, Conn.,	Guardianship,	13350
1852	Louis	Blackstone,	Administration,	13351
1851	Louis A.	Blackstone,	Guardianship,	13352
1870	Louisa E.	Petersham,	Administration,	13353
1880	Lucy	Lunenburg,	Administration,	13354
1877	Lyman	Mendon,	Administration,	13355
1873	Lyman V. B.	Athol,	Will,	13356
1857	Maria C.	West Brookfield,	Guardianship,	13357
1859	Martin L.	Winchendon,	Administration,	13358
1765	Mary	Sudbury,	Guardianship,	13359
1841	Mary E.	Athol,	Guardianship,	13360
1865	Mary E.	Warren,	Guardianship,	13361
1866	Merit	Sutton,	Administration,	13362
1813	Milla	Mendon,	Guardianship,	13363
1875	Minerva	Blackstone,	Guardianship,	13364
1879	Myra	Templeton,	Administration,	13365
1750	Naomi	Uxbridge,	Guardianship,	13366
1870	Nathaniel	Petersham,	Administration,	13367
1868	Nellie	Athol,	Administration,	13368
1771	Noah	Mendon,	Administration,	13369
1772	Noah	Mendon,	Guardianship,	13370
1772	Olive	Mendon,	Guardianship,	13371
1857	Oliver S.	West Brookfield,	Will,	13372
1821	Paskco	Mendon,	Will,	13373
1835	Peter	Milford,	Guardianship,	13374
1856	Peter	Milford,	Administration,	13374
1846	Philadelphia	Uxbridge,	Will,	13375
1855	Philana	Blackstone,	Pension,	13376

COOK and COOKE,

YEAR.	NAME.	RESIDENCE.	NATURE.	CASE.
1851	Polly	Paxton,	Guardianship,	13377
1796	Robert	Worcester,	Administration,	13378
1855	Roger	Harvard,	Administration,	13379
1752	Samuel	Mendon,	Administration,	13380
1765	Samuel	Sudbury,	Guardianship,	13381
1767	Samuel	Mendon,	Administration,	13382
1808	Samuel	Templeton,	Will,	13383
1817	Samuel	Mendon,	Administration,	13384
1839	Samuel	Petersham,	Administration,	13385
1859	Samuel	Lunenburg,	Will,	13386
1874	Samuel	Leominster,	Administration,	13387
1878	Samuel J.	Lunenburg,	Will,	13388
1866	Sarah	Athol,	Will,	13389
1870	Sarah	Petersham,	Administration,	13390
1832	Sewall	Petersham,	Guardianship,	13391
1866	Silas D.	West Brookfield,	Administration,	13392
1853	Solon S.	Milford,	Guardianship,	13393
1831	Stephen	Mendon,	Will,	13394
1853	Stephen	Milwaukee, Wis.,	Administration,	13395
1853	Stephen A.	Milford,	Guardianship,	13396
1813	Sukey P.	Mendon,	Guardianship,	13397
1844	Susan	Lancaster,	Administration,	13398
1878	Sylvia	Lunenburg,	Administration,	13399
1813	Welcome	Mendon,	Guardianship,	13400
1849	Whitman V.	Milford,	Will,	13401
1866	William C.	Warren,	Guardianship,	13402
1881	William E.	Brookfield,	Administration,	13403
1866	William G.	West Brookfield,	Guardianship,	13404
1878	Ziba	Uxbridge,	Administration,	13405
1812	Zimri	Mendon,	Administration,	13406
1813	Zimri	Mendon,	Guardianship,	13407

COOLEDGE see COOLIDGE.

YEAR.	NAME.	RESIDENCE.	NATURE.	CASE.
1875	COOLEY, Alice	Brookfield,	Will,	13408
1873	Augusta	Sutton,	Guardianship,	13409
1755	Benjamin	Brookfield,	Guardianship,	13410
1805	Benjamin W.	Brookfield,	Administration,	13411
1873	George	Sutton,	Guardianship,	13412
1871	George D.	Sutton,	Guardianship,	13413
1877	Henry E.	Leominster,	Administration,	13414
1881	Mary B.	Leicester,	Will,	13415
1778	Obadiah	Brookfield,	Will,	13416
1829	Obadiah	Brookfield,	Administration,	13417
1870	Sarah A.	Webster,	Adoption, etc.,	13418
1866	Stella I.	Holden,	Adoption, etc.,	13419

YEAR.	NAME.	RESIDENCE.	NATURE.	CASE.
1858	COOLEY, Weston	Dana,	Will,	13420
1796	William	Brookfield,	Administration,	13421
1852	Zeruiah W.	Dana,	Will,	13422
	COOLIDGE AND COOLEDGE,			
1848	Abby A.	Bolton,	Guardianship,	13423
1878	Achsa	Gardner,	Administration,	13424
1825	Albert	Berlin,	Guardianship,	13425
1842	Albert	Bolton,	Guardianship,	13426
1855	Albert E.	Bolton,	Guardianship,	13427
1825	Amory	Berlin,	Guardianship,	13428
1851	Barak	Sterling,	Administration,	13429
1825	Caleb	Berlin,	Administration,	13430
1836	Caleb L.	Rutland,	Guardianship,	13431
1855	Charles	Worcester,	Administration,	13432
1862	Charles	Sterling,	Administration,	13433
1866	Charles	Westminster,	Administration,	13434
1848	Charles E.	Bolton,	Guardianship,	13435
1858	Charles M.	Gardner,	Administration,	13436
1866	Clinton W.	Westminster,	Guardianship,	13437
1841	Elisha	Leominster,	Will,	13438
1869	Emory	Northborough,	Administration,	13439
1867	Esther C.	Milford,	Administration,	13440
1866	Frank E.	Westminster,	Guardianship,	13441
1855	Frank O.	Bolton,	Guardianship,	13442
1870	George E.	Northborough,	Guardianship,	13443
1786	Hannah	Berlin,	Guardianship,	13444
1848	Hannah	Bolton,	Guardianship,	13445
1855	Harriet M.	Bolton,	Guardianship,	13446
1865	Hattie F.	Bolton,	Adoption, etc.,	13447
1866	Helen E.	Westminster,	Guardianship,	13448
1825	Henry	Berlin,	Guardianship,	13449
1851	Henry	Sterling,	Guardianship,	13450
1859	Henry A.	Gardner,	Guardianship,	13451
1861	Ira	Clinton,	Will,	13452
1786	Isaiah	Berlin,	Guardianship,	13453
1786	Isaiah	Berlin,	Administration,	13454
1846	James	Gardner,	Will,	13455
1852	James	Fitchburg,	Administration,	13456
1869	James	Athol,	Administration,	13457
1824	John	Worcester,	Administration,	13458
1841	John	Leominster,	Pension,	13459
1881	John N.	Leicester,	Guardianship,	13460
1865	John R.	Westminster,	Will,	13461
1851	Joseph	Gardner,	Administration,	13462
1848	Joseph H.	Bolton,	Guardianship,	13463

YEAR.	NAME.	RESIDENCE.	NATURE.	CASE.
	COOLIDGE AND COOLEDGE,			
1859	Joseph H.	Gardner,	Will,	13464
1858	Lelia L.	Gardner,	Guardianship,	13465
1836	Lemuel	Rutland,	Guardianship,	13466
1836	Lemuel	Rutland,	Administration,	13467
1874	Lucia A.	Westminster,	Administration,	13468
1859	Lucy A.	Gardner,	Guardianship,	13469
1848	Lucy J.	Bolton,	Guardianship,	13470
1870	Mary L.	Northborough,	Guardianship,	13471
1875	Mary W.	Harvard,	Administration,	13472
1825	Merick	Berlin,	Guardianship,	13473
1850	Moses A.	Boylston,	Will,	13474
1786	Obadiah	Berlin,	Guardianship,	13475
1804	Phillip	Bolton,	Will,	13476
1871	Ruggles S.	Worcester,	Administration,	13477
1881	Sarah B.	Leicester,	Guardianship,	13478
1848	Sarah H.	Bolton,	Guardianship,	13479
1873	Sarah S.	North Brookfield,	Administration,	13480
1786	Silas	Berlin,	Guardianship,	13481
1848	Silas	Bolton,	Will,	13482
1840	Silas, Jr.	Bolton,	Administration,	13483
1858	Sophia	Northborough,	Administration,	13484
1824	Stephen	Berlin,	Administration,	13485
1865	Theodate	Bolton,	Will,	13486
1826	William	Bolton,	Will,	13487
	COOMBS, COMBS AND COMB,			
1772	Anthony	Douglas,	Guardianship,	13488
1772	Barnabas	Douglas,	Guardianship,	13489
1877	Cyrus B.	Hubbardston,	Adoption, etc.,	13490
1772	Ethemore	Douglas,	Guardianship,	13491
1837	Ezra	Holden,	Guardianship,	13492
1848	George H.	Warren,	Guardianship,	13493
1880	George H.	Warren,	Administration,	13494
1852	Jacob	Brookfield,	Will,	13495
1851	John	Warren,	Administration,	13496
1862	John	Worcester,	Administration,	13497
1848	John T.	Warren,	Guardianship,	13498
1836	Joseph	Douglas,	Pension,	13499
1836	Joseph	Douglas,	Administration,	13500
1848	Levi	Warren,	Administration,	13501
1837	Nancy	Holden,	Guardianship,	13502
1772	Peter	Douglas,	Guardianship,	13503
1878	Rensalier C.	Woodstock, Conn.,	Administration,	13504
1837	Reuben	Holden,	Administration,	13505
1770	Reubin	Douglas,	Administration,	13506

YEAR.	NAME.	RESIDENCE.	NATURE.	CASE.
	COOMBS, COMBS AND COMB,			
1772	Reubin	Douglas,	Guardianship,	13507
1772	Rosillah	Douglas,	Guardianship,	13508
1837	Royal	Holden,	Guardianship,	13509
1845	Sarah A.	Bellingham,	Guardianship,	13510
1837	Simon E.	Holden,	Guardianship,	13511
1772	Susannah	Douglas,	Guardianship,	13512
1772	Thankful	Douglas,	Guardianship,	13513
1880	Waldo C.	Hardwick,	Guardianship,	13514
1876	COOMEY, Patrick, etc.	Worcester,	Administration,	13515
1867	COONEY, Andrew	Worcester,	Administration,	13516
1874	Bridget	Worcester,	Guardianship,	13517
1874	Elicia	Worcester,	Administration,	13518
1874	Francis	Worcester,	Guardianship,	13519
1864	James	Holden,	Guardianship,	13520
1864	John	Holden,	Guardianship,	13521
1864	Martin	Holden,	Guardianship,	13522
1864	Mary A.	Holden,	Guardianship,	13523
1864	Thomas H.	Holden,	Guardianship,	13524
1864	William	Holden,	Guardianship,	13525
1848	COOPER, Abner	Northbridge,	Will,	13526
1868	Elizabeth W.	Webster,	Administration,	13527
1838	George	Barre,	Guardianship,	13528
1850	George	Templeton,	Guardianship,	13529
1838	Jane	Barre,	Guardianship,	13530
1850	Jane	Templeton,	Guardianship,	13531
1832	Jedidiah	Westminster,	Will,	13532
1818	John	Northbridge,	Will,	13533
1828	John	West Boylston,	Administration,	13534
1838	John	Barre,	Guardianship,	13535
1803	John, Jr.	Northbridge,	Administration,	13536
1868	Mabel L.	Sturbridge,	Guardianship,	13537
1859	Mary	Westminster,	Will,	13538
1866	Mary	Auburn,	Administration,	13539
1838	Mary H.	Westminster,	Will,	13540
1863	Mary N.	Grafton,	Administration,	13541
1830	Moses	Fitchburg,	Administration,	13542
1821	Nathaniel	Northbridge,	Will,	13543
1851	Nathaniel	Northbridge,	Administration,	13544
1839	Phebe	Westminster,	Will,	13545
1870	Reuben S.	Worcester,	Guardianship,	13546
1838	Richard	Barre,	Guardianship,	13547
1749	Samuel	Grafton,	Will,	13548
1858	Samuel	Westminster,	Will,	13549
1838	Sarah	Barre,	Guardianship,	13550

YEAR.	NAME.	RESIDENCE.	NATURE.	CASE.
1864	COOPER, Sarah A.	Barre,	Administration,	13551
1877	Sarah A.	Northbridge,	Guardianship,	13552
1850	Sarah S.	Templeton,	Guardianship,	13553
1864	Warren	Royalston,	Administration,	13554
1831	Winsor	Fitchburg,	Guardianship,	13555
1865	COOTS, Anna F.	No. Bridgewater,	Adoption, etc.,	13556
1872	COPELAND, Ann	Westborough,	Administration,	13557
1853	Charles	Fitchburg,	Administration,	13558
1831	Ephraim	Leicester,	Guardianship,	13559
1842	Ephraim	Leicester,	Will,	13560
1816	Ephraim, Jr.	Leicester,	Administration,	13561
1818	Ephraim K.	Leicester,	Guardianship,	13562
1875	Ephraim K.	Douglas,	Administration,	13563
1880	Mary	Clinton,	Administration,	13564
1818	Tamesin	Leicester,	Guardianship,	13565
1854	Tamison	Leicester,	Will,	13566
1870	Thomas	Westborough,	Will,	13567
1862	COPELIN, Abiel	Dudley,	Administration,	13568
1859	Amasa	Thompson, Conn.,	Administration,	13569
1862	COPP, Andrew J.	Grafton,	Will,	13570
1862	A. James	Grafton,	Guardianship,	13571
1873	Clara J.	Brookfield,	Guardianship,	13572
1852	Cornelius	Worcester,	Guardianship,	13573
1873	Emma F.	Brookfield,	Guardianship,	13574
1842	Henry S.	Oxford,	Guardianship,	13575
1873	Ida L.	Brookfield,	Guardianship,	13576
1852	Julius	Worcester,	Guardianship,	13577
1873	Sarah L.	Brookfield,	Administration,	13578
1842	William	Oxford,	Administration,	13579
1862	William A.	Grafton,	Guardianship,	13580
1880	CORBEIL, Blanch	Webster,	Guardianship,	13581
1880	Leonadas	Webster,	Guardianship,	13582
1880	Louis	Webster,	Administration,	13583
	CORBEN see CORBIN.			
	CORBETT, CORBET, CORBITT,			
	CORBIT, COBBETT AND COB-			
	BITT,			
1752	Benjamin	Boston,	Guardianship,	13584
1796	Benoni	Milford,	Administration,	13585
1763	Bulah	Mendon,	Guardianship,	13586
1753	Daniel	Mendon,	Administration,	13587
1761	Daniel	Mendon,	Administration,	13588
1763	Daniel	Mendon,	Guardianship,	13589
1834	Edward	Douglas,	Pension,	13590
1878	Edward	Harvard,	Administration,	13591

CORBETT, CORBET, CORBITT,
CORBIT, COBBETT and COB-
BITT,

1763	Eldad	Mendon,	Guardianship,	13592
1824	Elijah, Jr.	Westborough,	Guardianship,	13593
1860	Ellen H.	Milford,	Guardianship,	13594
1763	Hepzibeth	Mendon,	Guardianship,	13595
1860	Hopestill	Milford,	Guardianship,	13596
1880	Hopestill	Milford,	Administration,	13596
1763	John	Mendon,	Guardianship,	13597
1834	John	Milford,	Administration,	13598
1834	John	Milford,	Pension,	13599
1864	John	Spencer,	Administration,	13600
1873	John	Milford,	Administration,	13601
1879	John H.	Harvard,	Guardianship,	13602
1763	Joseph	Mendon,	Guardianship,	13603
1771	Joseph, Jr.	Mendon,	Administration,	13604
1865	Lydia	Milford,	Administration,	13605
1763	Mary	Mendon,	Guardianship,	13606
1879	Mary E.	Harvard,	Guardianship,	13607
1839	Nathaniel	Franklin, O.,	Administration,	13608
1868	Otis	Worcester,	Will,	13609
1763	Peter	Mendon,	Guardianship,	13610
1858	Peter	Milford,	Administration,	13611
1763	Robert	Mendon,	Guardianship,	13612
1879	Thomas F.	Harvard,	Guardianship,	13613

CORBIN and CORBEN,

1874	Abial	Worcester,	Administration,	13614
1877	Alice	Dudley,	Guardianship,	13615
1844	Almira D.	Charlton,	Guardianship,	13616
1847	Amelia A.	Dudley,	Guardianship,	13617
1872	Amelia A.	Webster,	Will,	13618
1795	Alvin	Dudley,	Guardianship,	13619
1841	Artemas	Charlton,	Guardianship,	13620
1760	Asa	Dudley,	Guardianship,	13621
1880	Benjamin A.	Webster,	Will,	13622
1841	Calvin	Charlton,	Guardianship,	13623
1879	Carlton	Dudley,	Will,	13624
1880	Charles	Webster,	Adoption, etc.,	13625
1841	Clarissa L.	Charlton,	Guardianship,	13626
1843	Dexter	Charlton,	Administration,	13627
1795	Eastman	Dudley,	Guardianship,	13628
1833	Elbridge G.	Dudley,	Guardianship,	13629
1797	Elisha	Dudley,	Administration,	13630
1760	Elkanah	Dudley,	Guardianship,	13631
1865	Ellen	Webster,	Guardianship,	13632

YEAR.	NAME.	RESIDENCE.	NATURE.	CASE.
	CORBIN AND CORBEN,			
1760	Ephraim	Dudley,	Guardianship,	13633
1794	Ezra	Dudley,	Administration,	13634
1795	Ezra	Dudley,	Guardianship,	13635
1864	Francis B.	Worcester,	Guardianship,	13636
1877	Fred E.	Dudley,	Guardianship,	13637
1752	Hanah	. Dudley,	Administration,	13638
1853	Hannah	Charlton,	Administration,	13639
1865	Harrison G.	Webster,	Administration,	13640
1863	Ichabod	Woodstock, Conn.,	Foreign Will,	13641
1736	Jabez	Woodstock,	Will,	13642
1846	Jabez	Webster,	Will,	13643
1759	James	Dudley,	Administration,	13644
1841	Jedediah	Charlton,	Administration,	13645
1840	John	Dudley,	Guardianship,	13646
1849	John	Charlton,	Will,	13647
1873	John W.	Worcester,	Administration,	13648
1773	Joshua	Dudley,	Guardianship,	13649
1858	Josiah	Dudley,	Will,	13650
1833	Lament B.	Dudley,	Guardianship,	13651
1872	Lament B.	Oxford,	Administration,	13652
1818	Learned	Dudley,	Administration,	13653
1825	Lemuel	Dudley,	Administration,	13654
1856	Lemuel	Dudley,	Administration,	13655
1864	Levi G.	Worcester,	Guardianship,	13656
1840	Lewis	Dudley,	Administration,	13657
1840	Lewis	Dudley,	Guardianship,	13658
1847	Lucian B.	Dudley,	Guardianship,	13659
1865	Lucian B.	Dudley,	Administration,	13660
1856	Luther	Dudley,	Administration,	13661
1840	Maria	Dudley,	Guardianship,	13662
1840	Mary	Dudley,	Guardianship,	13663
1833	Mary A.	Dudley,	Guardianship,	13664
1852	Mary B.	Worcester,	Administration,	13665
1856	Martha E.	Webster,	Guardianship,	13666
1760	Moses	Dudley,	Guardianship,	13667
1773	Nathaniel	Dudley,	Guardianship,	13668
1816	Peleg	Oxford,	Will,	13669
1870	Penuel	Woodstock, Conn.,	Foreign Will,	13670
1857	Philena	Warren,	Administration,	13671
1847	Robert	Worcester,	Administration,	13672
1847	Roxalana	Dudley,	Guardianship,	13673
1847	Rufus	Webster,	Guardianship,	13674
1869	Rufus	Dudley,	Administration,	13675
1847	Rufus E.	Dudley,	Guardianship,	13676

YEAR.	NAME.	RESIDENCE.	NATURE.	CASE.
	CORBIN AND CORBEN,			
1857	Ruth A. G.	Warren,	Guardianship,	13677
1876	Sally	Webster,	Will,	13678
1872	Samuel	Union, Conn.,	Administration,	13679
1844	Schuyler D.	Charlton,	Guardianship,	13680
1880	Sophia	Woodstock, Conn.,	Foreign Will,	13681
1773	Stephen	Dudley,	Guardianship,	13682
1796	Susanna	Dudley,	Guardianship,	13683
1760	Tamer	Dudley,	Guardianship,	13684
1789	Tamer	Dudley,	Guardianship,	13685
1760	Timothy	Dudley,	Guardianship,	13686
1831	Timothy	Dudley,	Administration,	13687
1773	Zurvia	Dudley,	Guardianship,	13688
	CORBIT AND CORBITT see COR-BETT.			
1872	CORCORAN, Catherine	Clinton,	Will,	13689
1874	Catherine E.	Clinton,	Guardianship,	13690
1872	James	Clinton,	Administration,	13691
1879	James	Leicester,	Administration,	13692
1874	James P.	Leominster,	Guardianship,	13693
1857	John	Worcester,	Will,	13694
1874	Margaret J.	Clinton,	Guardianship,	13695
1874	Mary E.	Fitchburg,	Guardianship,	13696
1877	Michael	Brookfield,	Will,	13697
1874	Sarah A.	Leominster,	Guardianship,	13698
1871	William	Fitchburg,	Will,	13699
1869	CORDWELL, Asenath E.	Milford,	Guardianship,	13700
1869	Harriett C.	Milford,	Guardianship,	13701
1869	Josephine B.	Milford,	Guardianship,	13702
	COREY AND CORY,			
1852	Achsah	Ashburnham,	Will,	13703
1832	Almira	Sturbridge,	Administration,	13704
1863	Asahel	Ashburnham,	Will,	13705
1754	Benjamin	Lunenburg,	Administration,	13706
1755	Benjamin, Jr.	Lunenburg,	Administration,	13707
1826	Benjamin F.	Sturbridge,	Administration,	13708
1855	Clara A.	Worcester,	Adoption, etc.,	13709
1826	David	Sturbridge,	Administration,	13710
1823	David A.	Ashburnham,	Guardianship,	13711
1857	Eunice	Bolton,	Will,	13712
1756	Eunice R.	Lunenburg,	Guardianship,	13713
1818	Hezekiah	Ashburnham,	Will,	13714
1833	Hezekiah	Ashburnham,	Administration,	13715
1842	Hezekiah	Ashburnham,	Administration,	13716
1837	Jacob	Sturbridge,	Will,	13717

Year	Name.	Residence.	Nature.	Case.
	COREY and CORY,			
1853	John	Worcester,	Will,	13718
1826	Jonas	Ashburnham,	Guardianship,	13719
1878	Jonas	Fitchburg,	Administration,	13720
1823	Lucinda	Ashburnham,	Guardianship,	13721
1868	Lucy	Ashburnham,	Will,	13722
1823	Malinda	Ashburnham,	Guardianship,	13723
1874	Mary	Sturbridge,	Administration,	13724
1878	Peter	Millbury,	Administration,	13725
1865	Polly	Ashburnham,	Will,	13726
1820	Sarah	Gardner,	Administration,	13727
1789	Simeon	Ashburnham,	Will,	13728
1823	Stephen	Ashburnham,	Administration,	13729
1867	Stephen	Ashburnham,	Administration,	13730
1823	Walter	Ashburnham,	Guardianship,	13731
1862	Walter A.	Ashburnham,	Administration,	13732
1872	Walter G.	Fitchburg,	Guardianship,	13733
1878	CORKERY, Patrick	Uxbridge,	Will,	13734
1864	CORLEW, Joseph T.	Millbury,	Guardianship,	13735
1864	Mary J.	Millbury,	Guardianship,	13736
	CORLIS and COLLIS,			
1867	Ada F.	Brookfield,	Guardianship,	13737
1867	Frank F.	Brookfield,	Guardianship,	13738
1809	John	Western,	Administration,	13739
	CORLEY (see also CURLEY),			
1746	James	Bolton,	Administration,	13740
1746	Peter	Leicester,	Administration,	13741
1753	Samuel	Marlborough,	Guardianship,	13742
1873	CORMIER, Josephine	Southbridge,	Adoption, etc.,	13743
1828	CORNELL, Esther	Milford,	Will,	13744
1800	Ezekiel	Milford,	Will,	13745
	CORNER see CONNORS.			
1876	CORON, Frank S.	Brookfield,	Adoption, etc.,	13746
1881	Mary	Brookfield,	Adoption, etc.,	13747
1881	Octave	Brookfield,	Adoption, etc.,	13748
1881	Philomaine	Brookfield,	Adoption, etc.,	13749
1741	CORRARY, John	Woodstock, Conn.,	Administration,	13750
1870	CORSEN, Ezra A.	Sutton,	Administration,	13751
1849	CORSER, Friend	Fitchburg,	Administration,	13752
1880	George A.	Leicester,	Administration,	13753
1880	Georgianna M.	Leicester,	Guardianship,	13754
1880	Luella J.	Leicester,	Guardianship,	13755
	CORTIS and CORTTIS (see also CURTIS),			
1868	Clarissa	Thompson, Conn.,	Foreign Will,	13756

YEAR.	NAME.	RESIDENCE.	NATURE.	CASE.
	CORTIS AND CORTTIS (see also CURTIS),			
1748	Consider	Plympton,	Guardianship,	13757
1735	Edward	Dudley,	Administration,	13758
1753	Edward	Dudley,	Guardianship,	13759
1753	Francis	Dudley,	Administration,	13760
1769	Japheth,	Dudley,	Guardianship,	13761
1850	Japheth	Thompson, Conn.,	Foreign Will,	13762
1868	Ozias	Oxford,	Administration,	13763
1756	Sarah	Dudley,	Guardianship,	13764
1862	Susan	Dudley,	Administration,	13765
1877	COSAR, Josephine, etc.	Webster,	Guardianship,	13766
1877	Victoria, etc.	Webster,	Guardianship,	13767
1868	COSGROVE, Mary	Worcester,	Administration,	13768
1879	COSSEBOON, Etta	Nova Scotia,	Adoption, etc.,	13769
1879	COSSON, Julius	Spencer,	Will,	13770
1853	COSTELLO, Jaffrey	Fitchburg,	Administration,	13771
1874	James	Douglas,	Guardianship,	13772
1872	Martin	Clinton,	Guardianship,	13773
1852	COSTIGAN, Cornelius	Hollenferd, Ire.,	Guardianship,	13774
1852	Margaret	Hollenferd, Ire.,	Guardianship,	13775
1852	Mary	Hollenferd, Ire.,	Guardianship,	13776
1877	COTÉ, Godefroy	Worcester,	Will,	13777
1870	COTTER, Ellen	Millbury,	Administration,	13778
1880	Garret	Worcester,	Administration,	13779
1841	Jason	Oxford,	Pension,	13780
1855	COTTING, David S.	Southborough,	Administration,	13781
1855	Harriet F.	Southborough,	Guardianship,	13782
1797	Josiah	Southborough,	Administration,	13783
1798	Josiah	Southborough,	Guardianship,	13784
1798	Mira	Southborough,	Guardianship,	13785
1795	Samuel	Ashburnham,	Administration,	13786
1861	William	Fitchburg,	Will,	13787
1826	COTTON, Edward	Harvard,	Administration,	13788
1875	Elizabeth M.	Leominster,	Administration,	13789
1855	Rebekah	Boylston,	Administration,	13790
1844	Ward	Boylston,	Will,	13791
1875	Ward M.	Leominster,	Will,	13792
1865	COTTRELL, Alexander	Milford,	Guardianship,	13793
1865	Benjamin	Milford,	Guardianship,	13794
1865	Catharine	Milford,	Guardianship,	13795
1865	Robert	Milford,	Guardianship,	13796
1871	COUCH, Clara L.	Worcester,	Adoption,	13797
1871	John	Worcester,	Administration,	13798

YEAR.	NAME.	RESIDENCE.	NATURE.	CASE.
	COUGHLIN AND COFLIN,			
1869	Caroline	Milford,	Guardianship,	13799
1876	Etta	Springfield,	Adoption, etc.,	13800
1879	COUILLARD, J. B.	Douglas,	Will,	13801
1875	COULAHAN, Ella M.	Worcester,	Guardianship,	13802
1875	Henry M.	Worcester,	Guardianship,	13803
1874	Patrick	Worcester,	Will,	13804
1861	COUNTOIS, Ollille	Northborough,	Adoption,	13805
1854	COURTNEY, Daniel	Worcester,	Administration,	13806
1864	Patrick	Worcester,	Administration,	13807
1878	COVE, John	Worcester,	Administration,	13808
	COVELL AND COVILL,			
1860	Annette M.	Templeton,	Adoption, etc.,	13809
1866	Augustus L.	Gardner,	Administration,	13810
1876	Charles T.	Fitchburg,	Will,	13811
1840	Ephraim	Petersham,	Administration,	13812
1877	George E.	Fitchburg,	Guardianship,	13813
1877	Olin T.	Fitchburg,	Guardianship,	13814
1863	Phillip	Dana,	Administration,	13815
1877	Walter A.	Fitchburg,	Guardianship,	13816
	COWDEN AND COWDIN,			
1880	Alice E.	Rutland,	Guardianship,	13817
1856	Asa P.	Fitchburg,	Will,	13818
1880	Charlotte	Fitchburg,	Will,	13819
1827	Craige	Fitchburg,	Guardianship,	13820
1833	Craigue	Bolton,	Administration,	13821
1827	Daniel	Fitchburg,	Guardianship,	13822
1876	Deborah	Ashburnham,	Will,	13823
1863	Dorinda D.	Princeton,	Will,	13824
1827	Eliza A.	Fitchburg,	Guardianship,	13825
1819	Elizabeth	Princeton,	Will,	13826
1880	Fred F.	Rutland,	Guardianship,	13827
1822	Hannah	Fitchburg,	Administration,	13828
1837	Harriet	Rutland,	Guardianship,	13829
1748	James	Holden,	Administration,	13830
1748	James	Holden,	Guardianship,	13831
1848	James	Rutland,	Pension,	13832
1854	James D.	Fitchburg,	Will,	13833
1748	John	Holden,	Guardianship,	13834
1847	John	Rutland,	Administration,	13835
1848	Jonas	Rutland,	Administration,	13836
1872	Jonas	Rutland,	Will,	13837
1837	Jonas, Jr.	Rutland,	Guardianship,	13838
1826	Joseph	Fitchburg,	Guardianship,	13839
1836	Joseph	Worcester,	Will,	13840

YEAR.	NAME.	RESIDENCE.	NATURE.	CASE.
	COWDEN and COWDIN,			
1849	Josephine	Fitchburg,	Guardianship,	13841
1808	Mary	Fitchburg,	Will,	13842
1826	Mary	Fitchburg,	Guardianship,	13843
1847	Mirick H.	Rutland,	Guardianship,	13844
1837	Persis	Rutland,	Guardianship,	13845
1847	Philena M.	Rutland,	Guardianship,	13846
1748	Robert	Holden,	Guardianship,	13847
1785	Robert	Princeton,	Administration,	13848
1827	Robert	Fitchburg,	Guardianship,	13849
1796	Samuel	Fitchburg,	Guardianship,	13850
1812	Samuel	Rutland,	Will,	13851
1820	Samuel	Fitchburg,	Administration,	13852
1827	Samuel L.	Fitchburg,	Guardianship,	13853
1849	Samuel L.	Fitchburg,	Administration,	13854
1847	Sarah A.	Rutland,	Guardianship,	13855
1792	Thomas	Fitchburg,	Will,	13856
1778	William	Worcester,	Administration,	13857
1796	William	Fitchburg,	Guardianship,	13858
1800	William	Fitchburg,	Will,	13859
1849	COWDREY, Adeline E. L.	Leominster,	Guardianship,	13860
1839	Andrew W.	Lunenburg,	Guardianship,	13861
1834	Ezra	Lunenburg,	Administration,	13862
1872	Frederick A.	Leominster,	Guardianship,	13863
1862	Lizzie A.	Leominster,	Adoption, etc.,	13864
1849	Luther J.	Leominster,	Guardianship,	13865
1839	Mary A.	Lunenburg,	Guardianship,	13866
1839	Sarah J.	Lunenburg,	Guardianship,	13867
1849	Timothy	Leominster,	Will,	13868
1839	William	Lunenburg,	Administration,	13869
1843	COWEE, Aaron	Gardner,	Guardianship,	13870
1843	Addeline	Gardner,	Guardianship,	13871
1843	Alvin G.	Gardner,	Guardianship,	13872
1775	Andrew	Western,	Will,	13873
1864	Catharine	Gardner,	Administration,	13874
1865	Ellen E.	Gardner,	Guardianship,	13875
1858	Florence M.	Westminster,	Guardianship,	13876
1865	Frank	Gardner,	Guardianship,	13877
1865	Fred	Gardner,	Guardianship,	13878
1843	George L.	Gardner,	Guardianship,	13879
1865	George L.	Athol,	Guardianship,	13880
1865	George W.	Gardner,	Administration,	13881
1865	Hattie J.	Gardner,	Guardianship,	13882
1801	James	Westminster,	Will,	13883
1864	Joel	Gardner,	Will,	13884

YEAR.	NAME.	RESIDENCE.	NATURE.	CASE.
1863	COWEE, John	Gardner,	Administration,	13885
1843	Mary	Gardner,	Guardianship,	13886
1852	Mary C.	Westminster,	Administration,	13887
1872	Myra	Westminster,	Will,	13888
1858	Orange G.	Westminster,	Administration,	13889
1850	Pearson	Westminster,	Will,	13890
1876	Person	Gardner,	Will,	13891
1843	Sibel C.	Gardner,	Guardianship,	13892
1860	Susan	Fitchburg,	Will,	13893
1837	William	Warren,	Will,	13894
1865	William N.	Athol,	Guardianship,	13895
1838	William P.	Warren,	Guardianship,	13896
1771	COWEN, Thomas	Brookfield,	Administration,	13897
	COWL, COWLES AND COWLS,			
1798	Cyrus	Belchertown,	Guardianship,	13898
1864	Cyrus	Leicester,	Administration,	13899
1852	Lewis	Warren,	Administration,	13900
1852	William L.	Warren,	Guardianship,	13901
1849	COX, Charles E.	Cambridge,	Guardianship,	13902
1768	Ebenezer	Hardwick,	Will,	13903
1797	Ebenezer	Hardwick,	Guardianship,	13904
1851	Elisha	Bolton,	Administration,	13905
1877	Frederick S.	Milford,	Will,	13906
1782	Hannah	Hardwick,	Guardianship,	13907
1782	Jemima	Hardwick,	Guardianship,	13908
1782	John D.	Hardwick,	Guardianship,	13909
1795	John D.	Hardwick,	Will,	13910
1797	Marcia	Hardwick,	Guardianship,	13911
1866	Mary	Bolton,	Will,	13912
1797	Pamela	Hardwick,	Guardianship,	13913
1856	Samuel	Worcester,	Administration,	13914
1782	Thankful	Hardwick,	Guardianship,	13915
1854	COYLE, Edward	Blackstone,	Administration,	13916
1860	COZZENS, Charles	Southbridge,	Will,	13917
1880	Charles B.	Southbridge,	Administration,	13918
1870	Clarietta	Webster,	Guardianship,	13919
1870	Henry S.	Webster,	Guardianship,	13920
1849	Leonard	Leominster,	Administration,	13921
1849	Leonard E.	Leominster,	Guardianship,	13922
1816	CRABTREE, Calvin	Brookfield,	Will,	13923
1809	John	Brookfield,	Guardianship,	13924
1821	Seth	Brookfield,	Guardianship,	13925
1876	Seth	West Brookfield,	Administration,	13926
1821	Susannah	Brookfield,	Guardianship,	13927
	CRAGE see CRAIG.			

YEAR.	NAME.	RESIDENCE.	NATURE.	CASE.
	CRAGGIN AND CRAGIN,			
1777	Amos	Mendon,	Administration,	13928
1788	Benjamin	Mendon,	Will,	13929
	CRAIG, CRAIGE AND CRAGE,			
1844	Abijah	Auburn,	Pension,	13930
1852	Amos	Leicester,	Will,	13931
1877	Belcarras	Templeton,	Will,	13932
1848	Daniel A.	Leicester,	Guardianship,	13933
1870	Esther	Charlton,	Administration,	13934
1779	James	Oakham,	Absentee,	13935
1781	Joseph	Oakham,	Will,	13936
1848	Leonard	Leicester,	Administration,	13937
1848	Mary E.	Leicester,	Guardianship,	13938
1852	Nathan	Spencer,	Will,	13939
1852	Nathan	Spencer,	Pension,	13940
1862	Nathan	Leicester,	Administration,	13941
1814	Robert	Leicester,	Administration,	13942
1847	Sukey	Auburn,	Pension,	13943
1871	William	Auburn,	Will,	13944
	CRAIN see CRANE.			
1863	CRAM, Charles A.	Fitchburg,	Change of Name,	13945
1863	George L.	Fitchburg,	Change of Name,	13946
1863	Luke	Fitchburg,	Change of Name,	13947
1871	Pamelia W.	Gorham, Me.,	Guardianship,	13948
1859	Sarah	Milford,	Administration,	13949
1863	Sarah A.	Fitchburg,	Change of Name,	13950
1863	Walter D.	Fitchburg,	Change of Name,	13951
1864	CRANDALL, Hattie M.	Southbridge,	Guardianship,	13952
	CRANE AND CRAIN,			
1863	Albert	Leominster,	Administration,	13953
1857	Andrew	Milford,	Administration,	13954
1874	B. T. (Mrs.)	Worcester,	Administration,	13955
1862	Calvin	Grafton,	Administration,	13956
1857	Dominick	Milford,	Guardianship,	13957
1857	Hannah	Milford,	Administration,	13958
1879	Hosea	Millbury,	Will,	13959
1872	Hugh	Leominster,	Administration,	13960
1876	Jared	Athol,	Will,	13961
1872	John H.	Leominster,	Guardianship,	13962
1872	Kate	Leominster,	Guardianship,	13963
1863	Katie E.	Leominster,	Guardianship,	13964
1814	Lemuel	Oxford,	Will,	13965
1846	Lemuel	Oxford,	Administration,	13966
1872	Lizzie	Leominster,	Guardianship,	13967
1866	Margery	Oxford,	Guardianship,	13968

YEAR.	NAME.	RESIDENCE.	NATURE.	CASE.
	CRANE AND CRAIN,			
1779	Martha	Uxbridge,	Will,	13969
1872	Mary A.	Leominster,	Guardianship,	13970
1860	Origin	Grafton,	Administration,	13971
1862	Thomas O.	Leicester,	Administration,	13972
1847	CRANNELL, John T.	Worcester,	Guardianship,	13973
1872	CRAPO, Emma	Unknown,	Adoption, etc.,	13974
1738	CRARY, John	Mendon,	Guardianship,	13975
1863	CRAUGH, Julia	Rutland,	Administration,	13976
1871	CRAVEN, John	Worcester,	Will,	13977
1872	Mary A.	Worcester,	Guardianship,	13978
1872	Willie	Worcester,	Guardianship,	13979
	CRAWFORD AND CROFORD,			
1754	Aaron	Rutland,	Will,	13980
1873	Alexander	Oakham,	Administration,	13981
1858	Alfred G.	Oakham,	Guardianship,	13982
1868	Almira	Barre,	Administration,	13983
1848	Ann M.	Worcester,	Guardianship,	13984
1858	Cora J.	Oakham,	Guardianship,	13985
1827	Elias B.	Oakham,	Guardianship,	13986
1858	Ellen A.	Barre,	Guardianship,	13987
1839	Emily A.	Oakham,	Guardianship,	13988
1859	Frederick B.	Barre,	Guardianship,	13989
1857	Galen A.	Oakham,	Will,	13990
1781	Grace	Western,	Guardianship,	13991
1858	Henry	Milford,	Will,	13992
1858	Hugh	Milford,	Guardianship,	13993
1861	Isabella	Oakham,	Administration,	13994
1785	James	Carleton, N. B.,	Guardianship,	13995
1814	James	Oakham,	Administration,	13996
1858	James	Milford,	Guardianship,	13997
1785	Jenny	Carleton, N. B.,	Guardianship,	13998
1780	John	Western,	Administration,	13999
1785	John	Carleton, N. B.,	Guardianship,	14000
1793	John	Boylston,	Will,	14001
1824	John	Oakham,	Will,	14002
1829	John	Northborough,	Will,	14003
1830	John B.	Northborough,	Guardianship,	14004
1782	Joseph	Western,	Guardianship,	14005
1858	Joseph B.	Milford,	Guardianship,	14006
1839	Laureston F.	Oakham,	Will,	14007
1857	Lemira	Upton,	Administration,	14008
1785	Levi	Carleton, N. B.,	Guardianship,	14009
1785	Lewis	Carleton, N. B.,	Guardianship,	14010
1851	Lucy	Northborough,	Will,	14011

YEAR.	NAME.	RESIDENCE.	NATURE.	CASE.
	CRAWFORD AND CROFORD,			
1774	Margarett	Rutland,	Administration,	14012
1768	Martha	Worcester,	Will,	14013
1785	Mary	Carleton, N. B.,	Guardianship,	14014
1825	Mary	Oakham,	Administration,	14015
1829	Mary	Oakham,	Will,	14016
1842	Mary A.	Princeton,	Guardianship,	14017
1868	Mary A.	Oakham,	Will,	14018
1839	Mary E.	Oakham,	Guardianship,	14019
1840	Mary E.	Oakham,	Guardianship,	14020
1858	Mary E.	Oakham,	Guardianship,	14021
1848	Mary J.	Worcester,	Guardianship,	14022
1746	Mathew	Worcester,	Guardianship,	14023
1840	Nathan W.	Oakham,	Guardianship,	14024
1785	Robert	Royalston,	Will,	14025
1785	Robert	Fallom, Vt.,	Guardianship,	14026
1847	Rufus	Oakham,	Guardianship,	14027
1875	Rufus	Oakham,	Administration,	14028
1760	Samuel	Rutland,	Will,	14029
1771	Samuel	Rutland,	Administration,	14030
1841	Samuel	Oakham,	Administration,	14031
1858	Samuel	Milford,	Guardianship,	14032
1874	Samuel	Oakham,	Administration,	14033
1858	Sarah C.	Barre,	Guardianship,	14034
1858	Sidney	Barre,	Guardianship,	14035
1761	William	Worcester,	Will,	14036
1769	William	Boston,	Guardianship,	14037
1779	William	Shrewsbury,	Absentee,	14038
1833	William	Oakham,	Will,	14039
1864	William	Oakham,	Administration,	14040
1874	William I.	Douglas,	Guardianship,	14041
1827	William T.	Oakham,	Guardianship,	14042
1858	William T.	Barre,	Administration,	14043
	CRAYTON see CREIGHTON.			
1854	CREED, Albert F.	Leominster,	Guardianship,	14044
1854	Edmund W.	Leominster,	Guardianship,	14045
1847	Elizabeth	Millbury,	Guardianship,	14046
1854	Helen A.	Leominster,	Guardianship,	14047
1854	Milton A.	Leominster,	Guardianship,	14048
1854	Moses E.	Leominster,	Guardianship,	14049
1870	Patrick	Leicester,	Will,	14050
1848	Thomas G.	Leominster,	Administration,	14051
	CREIGHTON AND CRAYTON,			
1857	Anne	Southbridge,	Will,	14052
1855	William	Winchendon,	Administration,	14053
1839	CRESSEY, Timothy E.	Columbus, O.,	Guardianship,	14054

YEAR.	NAME.	RESIDENCE.	NATURE.	CASE.
1779	CRISTERT, Timothy	Newton,	Guardianship,	14055
1876	CRITTENDEN, Mary C.	New Sharon, Iowa,	Guardianship,	14056
	CROAKE AND CROAK,			
1850	James	Leominster,	Administration,	14057
1867	James	Worcester,	Will,	14058
1877	Mary	Worcester,	Will,	14059
1870	William	Worcester,	Administration,	14060
1837	CROCKER, Abigail W.	Oakham,	Guardianship,	14061
1870	Abraham	Uxbridge,	Administration,	14062
1826	Allen	Boston,	Guardianship,	14063
1849	Allen	Douglas,	Administration,	14064
1875	Alvah	Fitchburg,	Administration,	14065
1837	Caroline	Oakham,	Guardianship,	14066
1862	Cora A.	Templeton,	Adoption, etc.,	14067
1856	Elvira K.	Fitchburg,	Will,	14068
1857	Ephraim	Fitchburg,	Administration,	14069
1878	Helen E.	Fitchburg,	Administration,	14070
1855	James	Templeton,	Administration,	14071
1855	James	Templeton,	Pension,	14072
1826	Joseph	Boston,	Guardianship,	14073
1849	Josephine	Douglas,	Guardianship,	14074
1838	Julia N.	Fitchburg,	Guardianship,	14075
1872	Lucy A.	Fitchburg,	Will,	14076
1831	Mary C.	Taunton,	Foreign Sale,	14077
1837	Mary L.	Oakham,	Guardianship,	14078
1814	Paul	Lunenburg,	Administration,	14079
1861	Phineas A.	Fitchburg,	Administration,	14080
1837	Reliance	Oakham,	Guardianship,	14081
1838	Samuel E.	Fitchburg,	Guardianship,	14082
1826	Samuel M., Jr.	Boston,	Guardianship,	14083
1835	Solomon	Oakham,	Will,	14084
1837	Solomon	Oakham,	Guardianship,	14085
1838	Varanus E.	Fitchburg,	Administration,	14086
1880	CROCKETT, Nathaniel W.	Milford,	Administration,	14087
1853	CROFOOT, Athlin S.	Douglas,	Guardianship,	14088
1853	Charles L.	Douglas,	Guardianship,	14089
1853	Edwin S.	Douglas,	Guardianship,	14090
	CROFORD see CRAWFORD.			
1881	CROGAN, Betsey	Leicester,	Administration,	14091
1862	CROMPTON, William	Millbury,	Administration,	14092
	CRONAN AND CRONIN,			
1875	Elizabeth	Fitchburg,	Guardianship,	14093
1871	Ellen	Millbury,	Guardianship,	14094
1871	Henry	Millbury,	Guardianship,	14095
1871	James	Millbury,	Guardianship,	14096

	CRONAN AND CRONIN.			
1878	Jeremiah J.	Worcester,	Administration,	14097
1865	John	West Brookfield,	Administration,	14098
1871	John	Millbury,	Guardianship,	14099
1875	Joseph	Fitchburg,	Guardianship,	14100
1875	Mary E.	Fitchburg,	Guardianship,	14101
1876	Michael	Milford,	Administration,	14102
1872	Patrick	Fitchburg,	Administration,	14103
1871	Thomas	Millbury,	Guardianship,	14104
1869	William	Worcester,	Guardianship,	14105
1804	CRONEY, John	Northbridge,	Will,	14106
	CRONIN see CRONAN.			
1784	CROOKER, Betsy	Harvard,	Guardianship,	14107
1784	Nancy	Harvard,	Guardianship,	14108
1784	Patty	Harvard,	Guardianship,	14109
1783	Peleg	Harvard,	Administration,	14110
1784	Polly	Harvard,	Guardianship,	14111
1784	Sally	Harvard,	Guardianship,	14112
1749	CROSBY, Aaron	Shrewsbury,	Guardianship,	14113
1874	Abby W.	Worcester,	Guardianship,	14114
1749	Abigail	Shrewsbury,	Guardianship,	14115
1777	Abigail	Bedford,	Guardianship,	14116
1850	Amelia	Brookfield,	Guardianship,	14117
1836	Amos	Brookfield,	Administration,	14118
1873	Aurelius	Grafton,	Administration,	14119
1789	Benjamin	Worcester,	Administration,	14120
1850	Caroline H.	Brookfield,	Guardianship,	14121
1746	Catharine	Worcester,	Guardianship,	14122
1854	Catharine V.	Brookfield,	Will,	14123
1871	Charles G.	Leominster,	Will,	14124
1841	David	Worcester,	Guardianship,	14125
1749	Elisha	Shrewsbury,	Guardianship,	14126
1793	Elisha	Shrewsbury,	Administration,	14127
1821	Eliza	Brookfield,	Guardianship,	14128
1841	Elizabeth S.	Worcester,	Guardianship,	14129
1868	Elizabeth S.	Shrewsbury,	Administration,	14130
1817	Emery	Athol,	Guardianship,	14131
1793	Fanny	Shrewsbury,	Guardianship,	14132
1852	Fitch	Ashburnham,	Will,	14133
1840	Frederick	Ashburnham,	Administration,	14134
1793	Gardner	Shrewsbury,	Guardianship,	14135
1749	Hanah	Shrewsbury,	Guardianship,	14136
1846	Hannah	Leominster,	Will,	14137
1865	Hannah	Sterling,	Administration,	14138
1850	Harriet R.	Brookfield,	Guardianship,	14139

Year.	Name.	Residence.	Nature.	Case.
1793	CROSBY, Henrietta	Shrewsbury,	Guardianship,	14140
1841	Henry S.	Worcester,	Guardianship,	14141
1850	Henry V.	Brookfield,	Guardianship,	14142
1842	Hiram W.	Northborough,	Guardianship,	14143
1825	Isaac	Milford,	Administration,	14144
1840	Isaiah	Worcester,	Administration,	14145
1841	Isaiah	Worcester,	Guardianship,	14146
1873	Isaiah	Worcester,	Administration,	14147
1749	Jabez	Shrewsbury,	Guardianship,	14148
1803	Jabez	Brookfield,	Will,	14149
1785	Jeremiah	Charlton,	Guardianship,	14150
1833	Joel	Leominster,	Will,	14151
1738	John	Shrewsbury,	Will,	14152
1880	John Q.	Westborough,	Administration,	14153
1822	Jonathan	Athol,	Administration,	14154
1863	Jonathan	Holden,	Will,	14155
1744	Joseph	Worcester,	Administration,	14156
1746	Joseph	Worcester,	Guardianship,	14157
1867	Josiah	Berlin,	Administration,	14158
1841	Laura C.	Worcester,	Guardianship,	14159
1850	Lucia A.	Brookfield,	Guardianship,	14160
1821	Lucia M.	Brookfield,	Guardianship,	14161
1817	Lucy	Athol,	Guardianship,	14162
1866	Martha	Gardner,	Administration,	14163
1817	Mary	Brookfield,	Administration,	14164
1841	Mary A.	Worcester,	Guardianship,	14165
1835	Mary E.	Holden,	Administration,	14166
1856	Maverett E.	Clinton,	Guardianship,	14167
1850	Moses	Holden,	Administration,	14168
1817	Nancy	Athol,	Guardianship,	14169
1818	Oliver	Brookfield,	Will,	14170
1817	Phillip	Shrewsbury,	Administration,	14171
1864	Polly	Northborough,	Will,	14172
1785	Prince	Charlton,	Guardianship,	14173
1857	Rebekah D.	Ashburnham,	Will,	14174
1821	Sally	Brookfield,	Guardianship,	14175
1849	Sally	Brookfield,	Will,	14176
1749	Samuel	Shrewsbury,	Guardianship,	14177
1777	Samuel	Bedford,	Guardianship,	14178
1748	Samuell	Shrewsbury,	Administration,	14179
1749	Sarah	Shrewsbury,	Guardianship,	14180
1749	Silas	Shrewsbury,	Guardianship,	14181
1862	Simeon	Barre,	Administration,	14182
1833	Simeon, Jr.	Hardwick,	Guardianship,	14183
1844	Sparron	Holden,	Administration,	14184

YEAR.	NAME.	RESIDENCE.	NATURE.	CASE.
1850	CROSBY, Theodotia D.	Brookfield,	Guardianship,	14185
1872	Uberto C.	Worcester,	Will,	14186
1793	Walter	Shrewsbury,	Guardianship,	14187
1859	William	Brookfield,	Guardianship,	14188
1848	William O.	Brookfield,	Pension,	14189
1842	Zacheus	Northborough,	Will,	14190
	CROSMAN see CROSSMAN.			
1874	CROSS, Charles E. L.	Royalston,	Guardianship,	14191
1866	Charlie E. L.	Royalston,	Adoption, etc.,	14192
1868	Fanny H. T.	Worcester,	Adoption,	14193
1873	Fanny H. T.	Worcester,	Change of Name,	14193
1874	Fred W.	Royalston,	Guardianship,	14194
1853	Martha	Aurora, Ill.,	Guardianship,	14195
1873	Parker	Clinton,	Administration,	14196
1866	Rosilla G.	Salamanca, N. Y.,	Guardianship,	14197
1874	Wilder	Royalston,	Administration,	14198
1880	William	Worcester,	Will,	14199
	CROSSETT AND CROSSET,			
1873	Archibald	Holden,	Will,	14200
1804	David	Sturbridge,	Administration,	14201
1769	James	Shrewsbury,	Administration,	14202
1877	Roxa	Holden,	Will,	14203
1801	William	Petersham,	Administration,	14204
	CROSSMAN AND CROSMAN,			
1875	Ann	Brookfield,	Will,	14205
1849	Daniel	Blackstone,	Will,	14206
1819	Electa	Spencer,	Will,	14207
1804	Ezra	Sutton,	Administration,	14208
1819	Fanny	Spencer,	Guardianship,	14209
1851	Ferdinand J. F.	Hindsburg, Vt.,	Guardianship,	14210
1865	Ferdinand J. F.	Sutton,	Administration,	14211
1866	George M.	Sutton,	Guardianship,	14212
1796	John M.	Douglas,	Guardianship,	14213
1778	Joshua	Leicester,	Administration,	14214
1866	Lucy	Augusta, Me.,	Administration,	14215
1811	Otis	Spencer,	Administration,	14216
1819	Otis	Spencer,	Guardianship,	14217
1790	Peter	Berlin,	Administration,	14218
1857	Samuel	Sutton,	Pension,	14219
1866	Sarah A.	Sutton	Guardianship,	14220
1851	Stephen	Sutton,	Will,	14221
1856	Sukey	Sutton,	Will,	14222
1873	William	Sutton,	Will,	14223
1878	CROUCH, Arvilla	Warren,	Administration,	14224
1859	Elijah	Southborough,	Administration,	14225

Year.	Name.	Residence.	Nature.	Case.
1855	CROUCH, Enoch	Harvard,	Will,	14226
1857	Harriet C.	Harvard,	Will,	14227
1868	Joel	Petersham,	Administration,	14228
1880	Levi S.	Warren,	Will,	14229
1881	Martha	Southborough,	Will,	14230
1876	CROUGH, William	Dudley,	Administration,	14231
1847	CROVER, Charles C.	Southbridge,	Administration,	14232
1865	Eunice	Southbridge,	Administration,	14233
1861	CROWD, Eleanor	Woodstock, Conn.,	Foreign Will,	14234
1880	CROWE, Catharine	Worcester,	Guardianship,	14235
1868	James	Worcester,	Administration,	14236
	CROWELL, CROWEL AND CROWL,			
1843	Artemas	Petersham,	Administration,	14237
1881	Carrie E.	West Brookfield,	Guardianship,	14238
1812	Cyrus	Petersham,	Administration,	14239
1794	David	Brookfield,	Guardianship,	14240
1814	David	Brookfield,	Guardianship,	14241
1794	Ebenezer	Brookfield,	Guardianship,	14242
1839	Eliza	Brookfield,	Guardianship,	14243
1865	Emma J.	Freeport, Ill.,	Guardianship,	14244
1839	George	Brookfield,	Guardianship,	14245
1870	George	West Brookfield,	Administration,	14246
1794	Hannah	Brookfield,	Guardianship,	14247
1794	Jared	Brookfield,	Guardianship,	14248
1848	Jared	West Brookfield,	Guardianship,	14249
1794	Joseph	Brookfield,	Guardianship,	14250
1804	Joseph	Hardwick,	Guardianship,	14251
1793	Joshua	Brookfield,	Administration,	14252
1794	Joshua	Brookfield,	Guardianship,	14253
1813	Joshua	Hardwick,	Will,	14254
1794	Nathaniel	Brookfield,	Guardianship,	14255
1812	Nathaniel	Brookfield,	Will,	14256
1865	Nathaniel S.	New Braintree,	Administration,	14257
1830	Paul	Brookfield,	Will,	14258
1880	Sally	West Brookfield,	Will,	14259
1839	Stephen	Brookfield,	Will,	14260
1796	Thomas	Hardwick,	Guardianship,	14261
1812	Thomas	Hardwick,	Administration,	14262
1865	William	Freeport, Ill.,	Guardianship,	14263
1869	CROWLEY, Edmund	Worcester,	Guardianship,	14264
1869	Honora	Worcester,	Guardianship,	14265
1869	Joanna	Worcester,	Guardianship,	14266
1874	Johanna	Worcester,	Adoption, etc.,	14267
1870	John	Worcester,	Administration,	14268
1857	Mary	Worcester,	Administration,	14269

| --- | --- | --- | --- | --- |
1864	CROWLEY, Thomas P.	Templeton,	Guardianship,	14270
1858	CROXFORD, Patty	Holden,	Will,	14271
1870	CRUICKSHANKS, Anna M.	Spencer,	Administration,	14272
1870	John DeW.	Spencer,	Guardianship,	14273
1870	Mary S.	Spencer,	Guardianship,	14274
1865	CRYNE, Tearney	Milford,	Adoption,	14275
1867	Tearney	Milford,	Change of Name,	14275
1868	CUDDY, Edward F.	Grafton,	Guardianship,	14276
1868	Eliza	Grafton,	Guardianship,	14277
1868	James W.	Grafton,	Guardianship,	14278
1878	Mary	Worcester,	Will,	14279
1868	Mary A.	Grafton,	Guardianship,	14280
1868	Nicholas	Grafton,	Guardianship,	14281
1790	CUDWORTH, Edward	Ward,	Administration,	14282
1803	Edward	Ward,	Administration,	14283
1846	Jonathan	Oxford,	Administration,	14284
1870	Turner	Webster,	Administration,	14285
	CULLAN AND CULLEN,			
1852	James	Barre,	Administration,	14286
1875	John	Fitchburg,	Will,	14287
1875	John P.	Charlton,	Guardianship,	14288
1875	Margaret	Charlton,	Guardianship,	14289
1875	Matthew	Charlton,	Guardianship,	14290
1874	Thomas	Charlton,	Will,	14291
1875	Thomas P.	Charlton,	Guardianship,	14292
1868	CULVER, Elizabeth T.	Upton,	Administration,	14293
1858	Frank J.	Worcester,	Guardianship,	14294
1875	Frank J.	Upton,	Administration,	14295
1857	Jesse S.	Worcester,	Administration,	14296
1864	Joshua	Worcester,	Will,	14297
	CUMMINGS, CUMINGS AND CUMMINS,			
1840	Abel	Douglas,	Will,	14298
1800	Abner	Sutton,	Administration,	14299
1858	Almirah B.	Mendon,	Change of Name,	14300
1876	Anastatia	Clinton,	Guardianship,	14301
1815	Asa	Ward,	Will,	14302
1837	Asa	Sutton,	Guardianship,	14303
1841	Asa	Sutton,	Administration,	14303
1831	Asa, Jr.	Sutton,	Administration,	14304
1837	Asa W.	Sutton,	Guardianship,	14305
1876	Benjamin	West Brookfield,	Will,	14306
1855	Catharine	Lancaster,	Will,	14307
1876	Catharine	Clinton,	Guardianship,	14308
1865	Catharine H.	Oxford,	Administration,	14309

Year.	Name.	Residence.	Nature.	Case.
	CUMMINGS, CUMINGS and CUMMINS,			
1870	Celestina D.	Worcester,	Administration,	14310
1812	Charles	Uxbridge,	Guardianship,	14311
1846	Charles	Uxbridge,	Administration,	14312
1870	Charles	Worcester,	Administration,	14313
1870	Charles	Worcester,	Guardianship,	14314
1863	Charles B.	Shrewsbury,	Guardianship,	14315
1846	Charles F.	Douglas,	Guardianship,	14316
1846	Charles H.	Uxbridge,	Guardianship,	14317
1879	Chester	Worcester,	Administration,	14318
1846	Chloris C.	Douglas,	Guardianship,	14319
1801	Clarissa	Sutton,	Guardianship,	14320
1792	Daniel	Ward,	Administration,	14321
1808	Daniel	Ward,	Administration,	14322
1875	Daniel	Barre,	Will,	14323
1862	Daniel W.	Paxton,	Administration,	14324
1834	David	Sterling,	Administration,	14325
1834	David	Sterling,	Pension,	14326
1836	Davis W.	Sutton,	Administration,	14327
1872	Deborah	Worcester,	Will,	14328
1872	Diadama	Auburn,	Administration,	14329
1873	Edward	Southbridge,	Administration,	14330
1877	Effie	Athol,	Guardianship,	14331
1865	Elizabeth	Millbury,	Guardianship,	14332
1877	Emma	Athol,	Guardianship,	14333
1865	Fanny M.	Millbury,	Guardianship,	14334
1870	Francis	Worcester,	Guardianship,	14335
1839	George	Grafton,	Will,	14336
1870	George	Worcester,	Guardianship,	14337
1865	George C.	Fitchburg,	Guardianship,	14338
1812	Gerry W.	Uxbridge,	Guardianship,	14339
1751	Gershom	Brookfield,	Guardianship,	14340
1880	Harriet E.	Shrewsbury,	Administration,	14341
1863	Hepzibah	Westminster,	Administration,	14342
1870	Hester	Millbury,	Administration,	14343
1874	Ida A.	Shrewsbury,	Guardianship,	14344
1864	Israel	Fitchburg,	Administration,	14345
1762	Jacob	Oxford,	Guardianship,	14346
1814	Jacob	Sutton,	Administration,	14347
1876	James A.	Athol,	Administration,	14348
1858	James P. C.	Fitchburg,	Administration,	14349
1869	Jason G.	Phillipston,	Pension,	14350
1879	Jennette E.	Grafton,	Guardianship,	14351
1865	Joanna	Anoka, Minn.,	Administration,	14352

YEAR.	NAME.	RESIDENCE.	NATURE.	CASE.
	CUMMINGS, CUMINGS AND CUMMINS,			
1748	John	Brookfield,	Guardianship,	14353
1793	John	Lancaster,	Guardianship,	14354
1832	John	Ward,	Administration,	14355
1876	John	Clinton,	Administration,	14356
1878	John	Worcester,	Administration,	14357
1853	John B.	Shrewsbury,	Administration,	14358
1876	John E.	Clinton,	Guardianship,	14359
1812	John N.	Uxbridge,	Guardianship,	14360
1875	John S.	Auburn,	Administration,	14361
1873	Jonas	Shrewsbury,	Administration,	14362
1822	Jonathan, Jr.	Leominster,	Will,	14363
1788	Joseph	Douglas,	Administration,	14364
1815	Joseph	Hardwick,	Administration,	14365
1841	Joseph	Harvard,	Will,	14366
1862	Joseph	Shrewsbury,	Administration,	14367
1863	Joseph B.	Templeton,	Administration,	14368
1861	Joshua	Westminster,	Administration,	14369
1812	Josiah	Uxbridge,	Guardianship,	14370
1867	Josiah	Uxbridge,	Administration,	14371
1846	Julius A.	Uxbridge,	Guardianship,	14372
1793	Katherine	Lancaster,	Guardianship,	14373
1762	Lemuel	Oxford,	Guardianship,	14374
1860	Lois	Uxbridge,	Will,	14375
1860	Lorinda M.	Paxton,	Will,	14376
1837	Mary	Auburn,	Guardianship,	14377
1873	Mary A.	Blackstone,	Guardianship,	14378
1876	Mary A.	Clinton,	Guardianship,	14379
1879	Mary A.	Worcester,	Guardianship,	14380
1874	Mary J.	Shrewsbury,	Guardianship,	14381
1881	Mercy L.	Templeton,	Administration,	14382
1880	Moses	Leominster,	Administration,	14383
1801	Nancy	Sutton,	Guardianship,	14384
1776	Nathaniel	Douglas,	Administration,	14385
1865	Nellie Etta	Fitchburg,	Guardianship,	14386
1876	Patrick	Worcester,	Administration,	14387
1875	Preston	Holden,	Will,	14388
1879	Relief	Webster,	Will,	14389
1812	Reuben	Uxbridge,	Administration,	14390
1812	Reuben	Uxbridge,	Guardianship,	14391
1846	Reuben	Uxbridge,	Guardianship,	14392
1878	Right	Lancaster,	Guardianship,	14393
1871	Royal	Milford,	Will,	14394
1846	Ruth E.	Douglas,	Guardianship,	14395

	CUMMINGS, CUMINGS AND CUMMINS,			
1876	R. Eliza	Milford,	Administration,	14396
1841	Salley	Sutton,	Administration,	14397
1758	Samuel	Uxbridge,	Will,	14398
1812	Samuel	Uxbridge,	Guardianship,	14399
1837	Sarah	Auburn,	Guardianship,	14400
1847	Silas	Douglas,	Administration,	14401
1876	Stephen	Sutton,	Administration,	14402
1870	Thomas	Worcester,	Guardianship,	14403
1879	Thomas	Worcester,	Guardianship,	14404
1864	William A.	Uxbridge,	Adoption, etc.,	14405
1881	William T.	Winchendon,	Guardianship,	14406
1854	CUNDALL, Betsey	Pomfret, Conn.,	Administration,	14407
1874	Sarah D.	Worcester,	Partition,	14408
1858	CUNLIFFE, Mary F.	Worcester,	Adoption, etc.,	14409
1869	CUNNEEN, James S.	Southborough,	Guardianship,	14410
1865	Michael	Southborough,	Administration,	14411
1869	Thomas J.	Southborough,	Guardianship,	14412
1831	CUNNINGHAM, Abigail	Lunenburg,	Will,	14413
1853	Abigail D.	Worcester,	Administration,	14414
1843	Ann	Spencer,	Guardianship,	14415
1781	Anna	Spencer,	Guardianship,	14416
1824	Asenath	Spencer,	Guardianship,	14417
1871	Catharine	Millbury,	Administration,	14418
1867	Curtis	Northbridge,	Will,	14419
1852	Eli A.	Marlborough,	Guardianship,	14420
1869	Eliza	Worcester,	Will,	14421
1800	Elizabeth	Spencer,	Will,	14422
1879	Frederick H.	Bolton,	Guardianship,	14423
1805	George	Boston,	Guardianship,	14424
1796	Harry	Unknown,	Guardianship,	14425
1754	Hugh	Spencer,	Will,	14426
1760	Hugh	Brookfield,	Will,	14427
1802	Hugh	Brookfield,	Will,	14428
1786	James	Rutland,	Will,	14429
1822	James	Lunenburg,	Will,	14430
1843	Jane	Spencer,	Guardianship,	14431
1789	John	Spencer,	Administration,	14432
1847	John	Westminster,	Administration,	14433
1879	John A.	Bolton,	Guardianship,	14434
1843	Joseph	Spencer,	Guardianship,	14435
1852	Levi E.	Worcester,	Will,	14436
1852	Lucy A.	Marlborough,	Guardianship,	14437
1856	Margaret	Ireland,	Guardianship,	14438

Year.	Name.	Residence.	Nature.	Case.
1861	CUNNINGHAM, Margaret	Worcester,	Administration,	14439
1869	Margaret	Worcester,	Guardianship,	14440
1793	Martha	Barre,	Guardianship,	14441
1880	Martha	Lunenburg,	Will,	14442
1824	Martha B.	Boston,	Guardianship,	14443
1825	Mary	Rutland,	Will,	14444
1831	Mary C. A.	Lunenburg,	Guardianship,	14445
1766	Nathaniel	Spencer,	Guardianship,	14446
1829	Nathaniel	Spencer,	Will,	14447
1836	Nathaniel	Spencer,	Will,	14448
1841	Nathaniel F.	Lunenburg,	Will,	14449
1879	Paul	Bolton,	Guardianship,	14450
1824	Phebe A.	Boston,	Guardianship,	14451
1879	Rachel	Bolton,	Guardianship,	14452
1823	Reuben	Spencer,	Will,	14453
1824	Reuben	Spencer,	Guardianship,	14454
1843	Reuben	Spencer,	Guardianship,	14455
1843	Reuben	Spencer,	Administration,	14456
1869	Richard	Worcester,	Guardianship,	14457
1766	Robert	Spencer,	Administration,	14458
1785	Robert	Barre,	Administration,	14459
1793	Robert	Barre,	Guardianship,	14460
1843	Robert	Spencer,	Guardianship,	14461
1839	Ruth	Paxton,	Administration,	14462
1843	Ruth	Spencer,	Guardianship,	14463
1847	Sally	Spencer,	Administration,	14464
1856	Sally	Pomfret, Conn.,	Administration,	14465
1824	Samuel	Spencer,	Guardianship,	14466
1825	Sarah B.	Fitchburg,	Guardianship,	14467
1824	Simon D.	Boston,	Guardianship,	14468
1880	Thomas	Clinton,	Will,	14469
1779	William	Spencer,	Will,	14470
1816	William	Lunenburg,	Will,	14471
1823	William	Fitchburg,	Will,	14472
1879	William L.	Bolton,	Guardianship,	14473
1830	Zabdiel A.	Lunenburg,	Administration,	14474
1869	CURBOY, Patrick	Sturbridge,	Administration,	14475
	CURLEY, CURLYS and KERLEY			
	(see also CORLY),			
1864	John	Milford,	Guardianship,	14476
1869	Mary	Upton,	Administration,	14477
1880	Mary	Clinton,	Administration,	14478
1872	Ralph	Southbridge,	Guardianship,	14479
1864	Thomas	Upton,	Will,	14480

Year.	Name.	Residence.	Nature.	Case.
	CURRAN and CURRIN,			
1873	Johanna	Worcester,	Guardianship,	14481
1865	Mary	Worcester,	Guardianship,	14482
1873	Mary	Worcester,	Guardianship,	14483
1881	Patrick	Worcester,	Will,	14484
	CURRAY and CURRIE,			
1787	Archibald	Barre,	Guardianship,	14485
1868	Mary A.	Milford,	Will,	14486
1875	CURRIER, Augustus N.	Worcester,	Trustee,	14487
1866	Bart O.	Worcester,	Guardianship,	14488
1860	George I.	Sterling,	Guardianship,	14489
1881	Isaac H.	Sterling	Will,	14490
1866	Jess A. O.	Worcester,	Guardianship,	14491
1860	Maria L.	Sterling,	Guardianship,	14492
	CURRIN see CURRAN.			
	CURTAIN and CURTIN,			
1848	Daniel	Fitchburg,	Will,	14493
1866	Martin	Westborough,	Will,	14494
1874	Mary	Westborough,	Will,	14495
1861	Mary A.	Worcester,	Guardianship,	14496
1861	Patrick	Worcester,	Will,	14497
1869	Patrick	Westborough,	Will,	14498
	CURTIS, CURTISS and CURTICE,			
1828	Abel	Dana,	Administration,	14499
1747	Abigail	Worcester,	Guardianship,	14500
1802	Abner	Winchendon,	Will,	14501
1812	Albert	Worcester,	Guardianship,	14502
1860	Albert W.	Worcester,	Guardianship,	14503
1879	Annie G.	Worcester,	Guardianship,	14504
1880	Arthur N.	Brookfield,	Guardianship,	14505
1809	Asa	Dudley,	Will,	14506
1791	Azubah	Princeton,	Guardianship,	14507
1858	Azubah	Worcester,	Will,	14508
1858	Benjamin F.	Worcester,	Administration,	14509
1819	Bethiah	Dudley,	Administration,	14510
1802	Caleb	Charlton,	Will,	14511
1862	Caroline A.	Leominster,	Guardianship,	14512
1871	Caroline E.	Worcester,	Administration,	14513
1792	Catharine	Worcester,	Guardianship,	14514
1862	Charles	Leominster,	Guardianship,	14515
1870	Charles	Winchendon,	Guardianship,	14516
1860	Charles F.	Worcester,	Guardianship,	14517
1872	Charles F.	Worcester,	Administration,	14518
1878	Chester	Southbridge,	Will,	14519
1862	Clara A.	Leominster,	Guardianship,	14520

(335—SERIES A.)

CURTIS, CURTISS and CURTICE,

YEAR.	NAME.	RESIDENCE.	NATURE.	CASE.
1839	Clark	Dana,	Guardianship,	14521
1800	Daniel	Sturbridge,	Guardianship,	14522
1770	David	Worcester,	Guardianship,	14523
1806	David	Petersham,	Will,	14524
1813	David	Worcester,	Administration,	14525
1815	David	Sturbridge,	Administration,	14526
1816	David	Sturbridge,	Guardianship,	14527
1854	David R.	Worcester,	Administration,	14528
1816	Dolly F.	Worcester,	Guardianship,	14529
1770	Dorothy	Worcester,	Guardianship,	14530
1871	Eben R.	Worcester,	Guardianship,	14531
1796	Ebenezer	Winchendon,	Will,	14532
1840	Ebenezer	Douglas,	Administration,	14533
1841	Ebenezer	Douglas,	Pension,	14534
1879	Edgar L.	Worcester,	Guardianship,	14535
1877	Edith J.	Worcester,	Guardianship,	14536
1816	Edward	Dudley,	Administration,	14537
1869	Edward	Worcester,	Will,	14538
1816	Edward W.	Worcester,	Guardianship,	14539
1880	Elbert A.	Brookfield,	Guardianship,	14540
1770	Elizabeth	Worcester,	Guardianship,	14541
1777	Elizabeth	Shrewsbury,	Administration,	14542
1791	Elizabeth	Princeton,	Guardianship,	14543
1855	Elizabeth	Worcester,	Will,	14544
1870	Elizabeth	Winchendon,	Guardianship,	14545
1808	Elizabeth P.	Worcester,	Guardianship,	14546
1856	Ellen M.	West Boylston,	Guardianship,	14547
1862	Ellen M.	Leominster,	Guardianship,	14548
1747	Ephraim	Worcester,	Guardianship,	14549
1747	Ephraim	Worcester,	Administration,	14550
1812	Ephraim	Worcester,	Guardianship,	14551
1824	Ephraim, 2d	Worcester,	Administration,	14552
1839	Ephraim	Worcester,	Administration,	14553
1812	Eunice	Worcester,	Guardianship,	14554
1871	Eunice	Worcester,	Administration,	14555
1839	Eunice M.	Boylston,	Guardianship,	14556
1862	Ezra	Leominster,	Will,	14557
1828	Francis	Westminster,	Will,	14558
1819	Francis C.	Dudley,	Guardianship,	14559
1812	Franklin	Worcester,	Guardianship,	14560
1816	George	Worcester,	Guardianship,	14561
1870	George A.	Worcester,	Guardianship,	14562
1827	George F. S.	Worcester,	Guardianship,	14563
1800	Hannah	Sturbridge,	Guardianship,	14564

CURTIS, CURTISS AND CURTICE,

YEAR.	NAME.	RESIDENCE.	NATURE.	CASE.
1828	Hannah	Dudley,	Will,	14565
1858	Hannah C.	Worcester,	Administration,	14566
1871	Harriet	Worcester,	Will,	14567
1858	Harriet V.	West Boylston,	Guardianship,	14568
1870	Helen R.	Worcester,	Guardianship,	14569
1849	Henry C.	Dudley,	Guardianship,	14570
1862	Herbert A.	Leominster,	Guardianship,	14571
1860	Huldah	Worcester,	Administration,	14572
1831	Humphrey	Gardner,	Administration,	14573
1789	James	Princeton,	Administration,	14574
1791	James	Princeton,	Guardianship,	14575
1769	Japheth	Dudley,	Guardianship,	14576
1872	Jared	Worcester,	Administration,	14577
1856	Jesse	West Boylston,	Will,	14578
1867	Jessie G.	Webster,	Guardianship,	14579
1770	John	Worcester,	Guardianship,	14580
1797	John	Worcester,	Will,	14581
1801	John	Dudley,	Will,	14582
1812	John	Worcester,	Guardianship,	14583
1826	John	Worcester,	Administration,	14584
1838	John	Dudley,	Will,	14585
1768	John, Jr.,	Worcester,	Administration,	14586
1823	John B.	Worcester,	Administration,	14587
1827	John E.	Worcester,	Guardianship,	14588
1849	John E.	Dudley,	Guardianship,	14589
1747	Jonathan	Dedham,	Will,	14590
1800	Jonathan	Sturbridge,	Guardianship,	14591
1849	Jonathan P.	Sturbridge,	Administration,	14592
1864	Jonathan P.	Westborough,	Will,	14593
1824	Joseph	Lunenburg,	Administration,	14594
1857	Joseph,	Barre,	Administration,	14595
1858	Joseph,	West Boylston,	Guardianship,	14596
1868	Joseph,	Worcester,	Administration,	14597
1800	Joshua B.	Sturbridge,	Guardianship,	14598
1747	Judith,	Worcester,	Guardianship,	14599
1867	Lavina,	Oxford,	Administration,	14600
1791	Leonard E.	Princeton,	Guardianship,	14601
1816	Louisa,	Sturbridge,	Guardianship,	14602
1862	Lucy,	Westborough,	Administration,	14603
1812	Lydia,	Worcester,	Guardianship,	14604
1842	Lydia,	Worcester,	Will,	14605
1862	Lydia,	Leominster,	Guardianship,	14606
1816	Maria,	Sturbridge,	Guardianship,	14607
1834	Maria,	Southbridge,	Will,	14608

YEAR.	NAME.	RESIDENCE.	NATURE.	CASE.
	CURTIS, CURTISS, AND CURTICE,			
1881	Maria R.	Worcester,	Administration,	14609
1747	Mary	Worcester,	Guardianship,	14610
1792	Mary	Worcester,	Guardianship,	14611
1802	Mary	Charlton,	Administration,	14612
1839	Mary	Worcester,	Administration,	14613
1849	Mary	Dudley,	Guardianship,	14614
1854	Mary	Petersham,	Administration,	14615
1834	Mary M.	Sturbridge,	Guardianship,	14616
1831	Moses	Winchendon,	Guardianship,	14617
1770	Nathaniel	Worcester,	Guardianship,	14618
1808	Nathaniel	Worcester,	Guardianship,	14619
1818	Nathaniel	Worcester,	Administration,	14620
1818	Nathaniel, 2d	Worcester,	Administration,	14621
1747	Oliver	Worcester,	Guardianship,	14622
1837	Oliver	Worcester,	Will,	14623
1866	Oliver	Worcester,	Administration,	14624
1839	Perry	Sutton,	Guardianship,	14625
1770	Rebecca	Worcester,	Guardianship,	14626
1816	Rebecca J.	Worcester,	Guardianship,	14627
1877	Rosaline	Clinton,	Administration,	14628
1870	Roxana	Winchendon,	Guardianship,	14629
1791	Sally	Princeton,	Guardianship,	14630
1872	Salmon	Barre,	Administration,	14631
1747	Samuel	Worcester,	Guardianship,	14632
1777	Samuel	Charlton,	Will,	14633
1808	Samuel	Worcester,	Guardianship,	14634
1815	Samuel	Worcester,	Will,	14635
1811	Samuel, Jr.	Worcester,	Administration,	14636
1862	Samuel H.	Leominster,	Guardianship,	14637
1793	Sarah	Worcester,	Administration,	14638
1827	Sarah A.	Worcester,	Guardianship,	14639
1800	Silvanus	Sturbridge,	Will,	14640
1800	Silvanus	Sturbridge,	Guardianship,	14641
1821	Solomon	Western,	Administration,	14642
1791	Sophia	Princeton,	Guardianship,	14643
1839	Sophronia	Dana,	Guardianship,	14644
1816	Susanna	Worcester,	Guardianship,	14645
1879	S. Addie	Southbridge,	Administration,	14646
1880	S. Louisa	Brookfield,	Administration,	14647
1800	Theodora	Sturbridge,	Guardianship,	14648
1839	Thomas	Petersham,	Administration,	14649
1791	Tyler	Princeton,	Guardianship,	14650
1807	Tyler	Worcester,	Administration,	14651
1808	Tyler	Worcester,	Guardianship,	14652

YEAR.	NAME.	RESIDENCE.	NATURE.	CASE.
	CURTIS, CURTISS AND CURTICE,			
1824	Tyler	Worcester,	Guardianship,	14653
1842	Tyler	Worcester,	Will,	14654
1827	Tyler P.	Worcester,	Guardianship,	14655
1812	William	Worcester,	Guardianship,	14656
1876	William	Winchendon,	Guardianship,	14657
1876	Willie O.	Winchendon,	Guardianship,	14657
1877	Willie O.	Winchendon,	Partition,	14658
1879	CUSHING, Anna W.	Fitchburg,	Guardianship,	14659
1868	Annie P.	Milford,	Guardianship,	14660
1760	Bridget	Shrewsbury,	Guardianship,	14661
1880	Caroline R.	Fitchburg,	Guardianship,	14662
1809	Charles	Lunenburg,	Will,	14663
1827	David	Ashburnham,	Administration,	14664
1851	Edmund	Lunenburg,	Will,	14665
1836	Elizabeth S.	Fitchburg,	Guardianship,	14666
1879	Ellen M.	Fitchburg,	Guardianship,	14667
1851	George R.	Ashburnham,	Will,	14668
1856	George W.	Ashburnham,	Will,	14669
1837	Hannah	Lunenburg,	Pension,	14670
1868	Hannah R. H.	Ashburnham,	Administration,	14671
1836	Isaac	Fitchburg,	Administration,	14672
1760	Job	Shrewsbury,	Administration,	14673
1808	Job	Shrewsbury,	Administration,	14674
1760	John	Shrewsbury,	Guardianship,	14675
1823	John	Ashburnham,	Will,	14676
1879	Joseph	Fitchburg,	Guardianship,	14677
1880	Julina G.	Ashburnham,	Will,	14678
1860	Katie W.	Ashburnham,	Guardianship,	14679
1848	Laban	Ashburnham,	Administration,	14680
1760	Mary	Shrewsbury,	Guardianship,	14681
1867	Mary	Lunenburg,	Will,	14682
1879	Mathew M.	Fitchburg,	Guardianship,	14683
1879	Milton L.	Fitchburg,	Guardianship,	14684
1879	Milton M.	Fitchburg,	Administration,	14685
1874	Nancy W.	Fitchburg,	Administration,	14686
1880	Nellie M.	Buffalo, N. Y.,	Foreign Sale,	14687
1814	Sarah	Grafton,	Administration,	14688
1859	Sarah	Lunenburg,	Administration,	14689
1872	Stephen	Ashburnham,	Will,	14690
1836	William	Fitchburg,	Guardianship,	14691
1863	CUSHMAN, Apollos	Oakham,	Administration,	14692
1830	Elizabeth	Homer, N. Y.,	Foreign Guard.,	14693
1830	Harriet S.	Buffalo, N. Y.,	Foreign Guard.,	14694
1830	Henry I.	Buffalo, N. Y.,	Foreign Guard.,	14695
1865	Izennst P.	Willimantic, Conn.,	Administration,	14696

Year.	Name.	Residence.	Nature.	Case.
1873	CUSHMAN, Martin G.	Smithfield, R. I.,	Administration,	14697
1830	Mathew J.	Buffalo, N. Y.,	Foreign Guard.,	14698
1873	Thankful H.	Worcester,	Administration,	14699
1867	CUSICK, John	Westborough,	Guardianship,	14700
1881	CUSSON, Joseph A.	Worcester,	Will,	14701
1881	CUTHBERT, Estella J.	Fitchburg,	Adoption, etc.,	14702
1817	CUTLER, Abby	Western,	Guardianship,	14703
1760	Abigail	Rutland,	Guardianship,	14704
1772	Abigail	Brookfield,	Guardianship,	14705
1783	Abigail	Templeton,	Administration,	14706
1787	Abigail	Grafton,	Administration,	14707
1805	Abigail	Grafton,	Will,	14708
1795	Abijah	Brookfield,	Will,	14709
1873	Abijah	West Brookfield,	Will,	14710
1750	Abner	Rutland,	Administration,	14711
1760	Abner	Rutland,	Guardianship,	14712
1852	Albert J.	Shrewsbury,	Guardianship,	14713
1785	Allis	Lexington,	Guardianship,	14714
1817	Almira	Western,	Guardianship,	14715
1819	Amos	Grafton,	Guardianship,	14716
1834	Amos	Grafton,	Guardianship,	14717
1834	Amos	Grafton,	Administration,	14717
1830	Amos M.	Westminster,	Guardianship,	14718
1760	Anna	Rutland	Guardianship,	14719
1777	Anthony	Brookfield,	Guardianship,	14720
1779	Arathusa	Northborough,	Guardianship,	14721
1859	Asa	Putnam, Conn.,	Administration,	14722
1829	Asher	Westminster,	Administration,	14723
1871	Augustus	Warren,	Will,	14724
1852	Austin	Shrewsbury,	Guardianship,	14725
1761	Bethiah	Western,	Guardianship,	14726
1840	Betsey	Grafton,	Administration,	14727
1868	Betsey	Warren,	Will,	14728
1786	Caleb	Milford,	Guardianship,	14729
1864	Caleb W.	Westminster,	Administration,	14730
1840	Caroline E.	Grafton,	Guardianship,	14731
1840	Charles	Grafton,	Administration,	14732
1855	Charles	Holden,	Administration,	14733
1856	Charles	Holden,	Guardianship,	14734
1869	Charles	West Brookfield,	Administration,	14735
1866	Charles F.	Warren,	Administration,	14736
1841	Charles R.	Ashburnham,	Guardianship,	14737
1816	Converse F.	Hardwick,	Administration,	14738
1846	Daniel L.	Grafton,	Administration,	14739
1779	David	Grafton,	Administration,	14740

YEAR.	NAME.	RESIDENCE.	NATURE.	CASE.
1783	CUTLER, David	Milford,	Will,	14741
1841	Denny	Millbury,	Administration,	14742
1761	Ebenezer	Western,	Guardianship,	14743
1779	Ebenezer	Grafton,	Will,	14744
1779	Ebenezer	Northborough,	Absentee,	14745
1779	Ebenezer	Northborough,	Guardianship,	14746
1814	Ebenezer	Western,	Administration,	14747
1819	Ebenezer	Grafton,	Administration,	14748
1852	Ebenezer	Shrewsbury,	Will,	14749
1858	Edward N,	Warren,	Guardianship,	14750
1869	Edward N.	Warren,	Administration,	14751
1852	Eleanor	Shrewsbury,	Guardianship,	14752
1863	Elias H.	Warren,	Administration,	14753
1826	Elijah	Hardwick,	Administration,	14754
1856	Eliza A.	Warren,	Guardianship,	14755
1740	Elizabeth	Grafton,	Guardianship,	14756
1830	Elizabeth	Shrewsbury,	Will,	14757
1849	Elizabeth	Grafton,	Administration,	14758
1849	Elizabeth	Grafton,	Pension,	14759
1863	Elvira A.	Lancaster,	Guardianship,	14760
1796	Enos	Brookfield,	Guardianship,	14761
1764	Ephraim	Brookfield,	Complaint,	14762
1849	Eunice	Grafton,	Will,	14763
1800	Ezekiel	Royalston,	Will,	14764
1853	Fanny O.	Warren,	Guardianship,	14765
1841	Frances J.	Millbury,	Guardianship,	14766
1856	George E.	Holden,	Guardianship,	14767
1857	George R.	Worcester,	Guardianship,	14768
1856	Hannah A.	Grafton,	Adoption, etc.,	14769
1779	Hasadiah E.	Northborough,	Guardianship,	14770
1853	Holton O.	Warren,	Guardianship,	14771
1878	Holton O.	Warren,	Guardianship,	14772
1872	Ira E.	Fitchburg,	Will,	14773
1772	Isaac	Brookfield,	Guardianship,	14774
1785	Isaac	Lexington,	Guardianship,	14775
1827	Isaac	Ashburnham,	Administration,	14776
1839	Isaac	Shrewsbury,	Will,	14777
1834	Isaac B.	Grafton,	Guardianship,	14778
1740	James	Grafton,	Administration,	14779
1740	James	Grafton,	Guardianship,	14780
1757	James	Rutland,	Guardianship,	14781
1843	James	Warren,	Will,	14782
1863	James B.	Lancaster,	Administration,	14783
1871	James M.	Fitchburg,	Administration,	14784
1841	Jesse	Spencer,	Administration,	14785

YEAR.	NAME.	RESIDENCE.	NATURE.	CASE.
1786	CUTLER, Joanna	Milford,	Guardianship,	14786
1858	Joanna K.	Warren,	Guardianship,	14787
1752	Joel	Rutland,	Guardianship,	14788
1759	John	Brookfield,	Administration,	14789
1785	John	Lexington,	Guardianship,	14790
1857	John C.	Worcester,	Guardianship,	14791
1779	Jonas	Northborough,	Guardianship,	14792
1785	Jonas	Lexington,	Guardianship,	14793
1830	Jonas	Westminster,	Guardianship,	14794
1830	Jonas	Westminster,	Administration,	14795
1757	Jonathan	Oxford,	Administration,	14796
1759	Joseph	Brookfield,	Guardianship,	14797
1809	Joseph	Brookfield,	Guardianship,	14798
1816	Joseph	Western,	Will,	14799
1825	Joseph	Brookfield,	Will,	14800
1837	Joseph	Western,	Will,	14801
1876	Joseph	Warren,	Administration,	14802
1853	Joseph, Jr.	Warren,	Guardianship,	14803
1776	Josiah	Brookfield,	Guardianship,	14804
1840	Josiah	Grafton,	Will,	14805
1856	Julia M.	Holden,	Guardianship,	14806
1772	Kathron	Brookfield,	Guardianship,	14807
1873	Lucia	Thompson, Conn.,	Administration,	14808
1781	Lydia	Brookfield,	Guardianship,	14809
1740	Marah	Grafton,	Guardianship,	14810
1830	Martha	Westminster,	Guardianship,	14811
1809	Mary	Brookfield,	Guardianship,	14812
1853	Mary A.	Warren,	Guardianship,	14813
1877	Mary J.	Northborough,	Will,	14814
1740	Mehetabell	Grafton,	Guardianship,	14815
1779	Meriam	Northborough,	Administration,	14816
1784	Meriam	Northborough,	Administration,	14817
1876	Millie	Worcester,	Will,	14818
1785	Molly	Lexington,	Guardianship,	14819
1854	Moses	Westminster,	Administration,	14820
1785	Nabby	Lexington,	Guardianship,	14821
1863	Nancy H.	Worcester,	Administration,	14822
1744	Nathan	Concord,	Guardianship,	14823
1785	Nathaniel	Lexington,	Guardianship,	14824
1877	Nettie	Worcester,	Guardianship,	14825
1855	Newell	Warren,	Will,	14826
1761	Oliver	Western,	Guardianship,	14827
1876	Orsamus	West Brookfield,	Administration,	14828
1809	Otis	Brookfield,	Guardianship,	14829
1781	Parthenia	Brookfield,	Guardianship,	14830

YEAR.	NAME.	RESIDENCE.	NATURE.	CASE.
1809	CUTLER, Pliny	Brookfield,	Guardianship,	14831
1867	Pliny	West Brookfield,	Will,	14832
1833	Reuben	Western,	Administration,	14833
1872	Rhoda G.	Petersham,	Administration,	14834
1761	Robert	Brookfield,	Administration,	14835
1809	Robert	Brookfield,	Administration,	14836
1819	Robert	Brookfield,	Guardianship,	14837
1869	Robert	Petersham,	Will,	14838
1817	Royal	Western,	Guardianship,	14839
1779	Rufus	Northborough,	Guardianship,	14840
1772	Ruth	Brookfield,	Guardianship,	14841
1860	Ruth	Shrewsbury,	Will,	14842
1875	Sally D.	Leicester,	Administration,	14843
1759	Samuel	Brookfield,	Guardianship,	14844
1819	Samuel	Brookfield,	Guardianship,	14845
1819	Samuel	Grafton,	Guardianship,	14846
1832	Samuel	Grafton,	Administration,	14847
1834	Samuel M.	Grafton,	Guardianship,	14848
1852	Samuel W.	Shrewsbury,	Guardianship,	14849
1761	Sarah	Western,	Guardianship,	14850
1841	Sarah C.	Millbury,	Guardianship,	14851
1779	Serafina	Northborough,	Guardianship,	14852
1760	Silas	Rutland,	Guardianship,	14853
1812	Silas	Templeton,	Administration,	14854
1848	Silas	Paxton,	Guardianship,	14855
1872	Silas B.	Paxton,	Administration,	14856
1861	Stephen	Grafton,	Administration,	14857
1853	Susan J.	Warren,	Guardianship,	14858
1740	Tabitha	Grafton,	Guardianship,	14859
1768	Thaddeus	Brookfield,	Will,	14860
1753	Thomas	Rutland,	Guardianship,	14861
1760	Thomas	Western,	Will,	14862
1761	Thomas	Western,	Guardianship,	14863
1761	Thomas	Western,	Administration,	14864
1785	Thomas	Lexington,	Guardianship,	14865
1853	Thomas	Warren,	Will,	14866
1826	Thomas B.	Brookfield,	Administration,	14867
1832	William	Hardwick,	Will,	14868
1841	William D.	Millbury,	Guardianship,	14869
1857	William N.	Warren,	Administration,	14870
1872	CUTTER, Calvin	Warren,	Administration,	14871
1866	Calvin C.	Westminster,	Administration,	14872
1848	Charles	Spencer	Will,	14873
1864	Charles S.	Southborough,	Will,	14874
1796	Ephraim	Brookfield,	Will,	14875

Year.	Name.	Residence.	Nature.	Case.
1800	CUTTER, Isaac	Spencer,	Will,	14876
1852	James M.	Fitchburg,	Administration,	14877
1813	Jedediah	Spencer,	Administration,	14878
1876	John	Winchendon,	Will,	14879
1845	John W.	Spencer,	Guardianship,	14880
1813	Lucy	Spencer,	Guardianship,	14881
1847	Marcus	Fitchburg,	Will,	14882
1844	Mehetable	Spencer,	Will,	14883
1787	Nathaniel	Athol,	Will,	14884
1840	Rebekah P.	Malden,	Will,	14885
1804	Robert	Unknown,	Guardianship,	14886
1848	Sarah C.	Spencer,	Guardianship,	14887
1768	CUTTING, Abigail	Rutland,	Guardianship,	14888
1779	Abigail	Royalston,	Guardianship,	14889
1777	Abraham	Westminster,	Guardianship,	14890
1811	Abraham	Princeton,	Administration,	14891
1813	Abraham	Princeton,	Guardianship,	14892
1860	Abraham	Worcester,	Administration,	14893
1767	Absalom	Rutland,	Administration,	14894
1878	Absalom	Worcester,	Will,	14895
1855	Almeda	Templeton,	Will,	14896
1778	Alpheus	Shrewsbury,	Guardianship,	14897
1777	Asa	Westminster,	Guardianship,	14898
1813	Asa	Princeton,	Guardianship,	14899
1828	Benjamin R.	Templeton,	Guardianship,	14900
1879	Caleb	Worcester,	Will,	14901
1847	Charles	Leicester,	Guardianship,	14902
1858	Charles	Leicester,	Administration,	14902
1874	Charles A.	Templeton,	Will,	14903
1878	Charles M.	West Boylston,	Administration,	14904
1768	Darius	Rutland,	Guardianship,	14905
1830	Darius	Leicester,	Administration,	14906
1854	David P.	Worcester,	Administration,	14907
1778	Dolley	Athol,	Guardianship,	14908
1769	Earl	Athol,	Guardianship,	14909
1847	Earl	Phillipston,	Will,	14910
1842	Earl, Jr.	Phillipston,	Will,	14911
1768	Easther	Rutland,	Guardianship,	14912
1779	Ebenezer	Shrewsbury,	Guardianship,	14913
1825	Ebenezer	Sturbridge,	Will,	14914
1870	Edwin A.	Lancaster,	Guardianship,	14915
1752	Eliphalett	Shrewsbury,	Guardianship,	14916
1876	Eliza	Sutton,	Guardianship,	14917
1829	Elizabeth	Templeton,	Guardianship,	14918
1843	Elizabeth	Templeton,	Administration,	14919

YEAR.	NAME.	RESIDENCE.	NATURE.	CASE.
1851	CUTTING, Elizabeth	Webster,	Will,	14920
1879	Elizabeth	Harvard,	Administration,	14921
1863	Emily T.	Clinton,	Guardianship,	14922
1875	Emma S.	Templeton,	Partition,	14923
1803	Ephraim	Princeton,	Guardianship,	14924
1866	Eugenia M.	Worcester,	Guardianship,	14925
1829	Eunice	Ashburnham,	Will,	14926
1813	Flavel	Princeton,	Guardianship,	14927
1853	Flavel	Westminster,	Will,	14928
1748	Francis	Shrewsbury,	Guardianship,	14929
1847	Francis M.	Southbridge,	Guardianship,	14930
1863	Frank L.	Worcester,	Guardianship,	14931
1863	Frederic	West Boylston,	Administration,	14932
1863	Frederick A.	Worcester,	Guardianship,	14933
1766	George	Athol,	Guardianship,	14934
1766	George	Athol,	Administration,	14935
1778	George	Athol,	Guardianship,	14936
1778	George	Athol,	Administration,	14937
1818	George	Unknown,	Pension,	14938
1768	Gershom	Rutland,	Guardianship,	14939
1769	Hannah	Athol,	Guardianship,	14940
1863	Hannah L.	Clinton,	Guardianship,	14941
1869	Henry	Southbridge,	Administration,	14942
1865	Horatio A.	Shrewsbury,	Administration,	14943
1777	Isaac	Paxton,	Administration,	14944
1751	James	Shrewsbury,	Administration,	14945
1853	James K.	Phillipston,	Administration,	14946
1869	Jennie A.	Westminster,	Guardianship,	14947
1766	John	Athol,	Guardianship,	14948
1777	John	Westminster,	Guardianship,	14949
1803	John	Princeton,	Guardianship,	14950
1835	John	Phillipston,	Will,	14951
1840	John	West Boylston,	Administration,	14952
1865	John A.	Shrewsbury,	Guardianship,	14953
1768	Jonah	Rutland,	Guardianship,	14954
1748	Jonas	Shrewsbury,	Will,	14955
1813	Jonas	Princeton	Guardianship,	14956
1866	Jonas	Westminster,	Administration,	14957
1778	Jonathan	Shrewsbury,	Administration,	14958
1779	Jonathan	Shrewsbury,	Guardianship,	14959
1834	Jonathan	Templeton,	Will,	14960
1834	Jonathan	Templeton,	Pension,	14961
1854	Jonathan	Templeton,	Will,	14962
1775	Josiah	Westminster,	Administration,	14963
1777	Josiah	Westminster,	Guardianship,	14964

YEAR.	NAME.	RESIDENCE.	NATURE.	CASE.
1790	CUTTING, Josiah	Boylston,	Administration,	14965
1803	Josiah	Princeton,	Administration,	14966
1803	Josiah	Princeton,	Guardianship,	14967
1829	Josiah	Templeton,	Guardianship,	14968
1847	Josiah	Princeton,	Administration,	14969
1863	Josiah	Templeton,	Administration,	14970
1859	Josiah A.	Hubbardston,	Administration,	14971
1870	Josiah C.	Lancaster,	Guardianship,	14972
1769	Judith	Athol,	Guardianship,	14973
1871	Laphira B.	Southbridge,	Administration,	14974
1860	Leonard	Clinton,	Administration,	14975
1848	Levi B.	Princeton,	Guardianship,	14976
1875	Levina S.	Templeton,	Partition,	14977
1877	Lois	Phillipston,	Will,	14978
1848	Lucretia D.	Princeton,	Guardianship,	14979
1766	Lucy	Leicester,	Guardianship,	14980
1803	Lydia	Princeton,	Guardianship,	14981
1813	Lydia L.	Princeton,	Guardianship,	14982
1861	Lydia M.	Princeton,	Administration,	14983
1769	Mary	Athol,	Guardianship,	14984
1803	Mary	Princeton,	Guardianship,	14985
1813	Mary A.	Princeton,	Guardianship,	14986
1847	Mary P.	Southbridge,	Guardianship,	14987
1777	Merriam	Westminster,	Guardianship,	14988
1777	Nathan	Westminster,	Guardianship,	14989
1803	Nathan	Hubbardston,	Administration,	14990
1844	Nathan	Lancaster,	Administration,	14991
1813	Nathan H.	Princeton,	Guardianship,	14992
1864	Olive R.	Templeton,	Will,	14993
1769	Oliver	Athol,	Guardianship,	14994
1778	Oliver	Athol,	Guardianship,	14995
1863	Oliver B.	Berlin,	Guardianship,	14996
1830	Otis	Leicester,	Guardianship,	14997
1841	Otis	Worcester,	Administration,	14998
1860	Otis S.	Leicester,	Guardianship,	14999
1813	Phebe	Princeton,	Guardianship,	15000
1778	Polley	Athol,	Guardianship,	15001
1857	Priscilla	Boylston,	Administration,	15002
1779	Rhoda	Royalston,	Guardianship,	15003
1803	Ruth	Princeton,	Guardianship,	15004
1835	Ruth	Princeton,	Administration,	15005
1846	Sally	Leicester,	Administration,	15006
1760	Salmon	Shrewsbury,	Administration,	15007
1769	Samuel	Athol,	Guardianship,	15008
1828	Samuel	Templeton,	Will,	15009

YEAR.	NAME.	RESIDENCE.	NATURE.	CASE.
1779	CUTTING, Sarah	Royalston,	Guardianship,	15010
1783	Sarah	Shrewsbury,	Administration,	15011
1789	Sarah	Royalston,	Will,	15012
1875	Sarah B.	Templeton,	Partition,	15013
1867	Sarah E.	Millbury,	Guardianship,	15014
1848	Sarah M.	Princeton,	Guardianship,	15015
1860	Sarah S.	Leicester,	Guardianship,	15016
1863	Sarepta	Bolton,	Administration,	15017
1778	Silas	Royalston,	Administration,	15018
1826	Silas	Holden,	Administration,	15019
1791	Thaniel	Shrewsbury,	Guardianship,	15020
1867	Thaniel	Millbury,	Administration,	15021
1803	Thomas U.	Princeton,	Guardianship,	15022
1831	Thomas U.	Princeton,	Administration,	15023
1830	Wealthy	Leicester,	Guardianship,	15024
1769	William	Athol,	Guardianship,	15025
1847	William	Leicester,	Guardianship,	15026
1869	Willie H.	Westminster,	Guardianship,	15027
1782	DABY, Asa	Harvard,	Guardianship,	15028
1813	Asa	Harvard,	Administration,	15029
1813	Asa	Harvard,	Guardianship,	15030
1800	Betsy	Waterford,	Guardianship,	15031
1813	Elizabeth	Harvard,	Guardianship,	15032
1813	Ethan	Harvard,	Guardianship,	15033
1876	Ethan	Harvard,	Will,	15034
1760	Hannah	Harvard,	Guardianship,	15035
1760	John	Harvard,	Guardianship,	15036
1769	John	Harvard,	Will,	15037
1781	John	Harvard,	Administration,	15038
1809	John	Harvard,	Administration,	15039
1760	Mercy	Harvard,	Guardianship,	15040
1800	Olive	Waterford,	Guardianship,	15041
1845	Sarah J.	Harvard,	Guardianship,	15042
1782	Simon	Harvard,	Guardianship,	15043
	DADMAN AND DADMUN,			
1869	Appleton	Worcester,	Will,	15044
1860	Charles A.	Fitchburg,	Adoption,	15045
1880	Charles E.	Fitchburg,	Administration,	15046
1843	Charles R.	Harvard,	Guardianship,	15047
1865	Fannie M.	Fitchburg,	Adoption, etc.,	15048
1864	Frances M.	Fitchburg,	Guardianship,	15049
1843	Francis W.	Harvard,	Guardianship,	15050
1864	Jennie A.	Fitchburg,	Guardianship,	15051
1880	Mary E.	Worcester,	Administration,	15052
1880	Mary F.	Millbury,	Guardianship,	15053

YEAR.	NAME.	RESIDENCE.	NATURE.	CASE.
	DADMAN AND DADMUN,			
1843	Mary H.	Harvard,	Guardianship,	15054
1870	Mary L.	Worcester,	Guardianship,	15055
1822	Samuel	Templeton,	Administration,	15056
1865	Samuel	Fitchburg,	Will,	15057
1841	Willard	Harvard,	Administration,	15058
1843	William Henry	Harvard,	Guardianship,	15059
1872	DADY, Ellen M.	Uxbridge,	Administration,	15060
1765	DAGGER, Richard	Holden,	Guardianship,	15061
	DAGGET AND DAGGETT,			
1872	Albert	Spencer,	Administration,	15062
1749	Arthur	Sutton,	Guardianship,	15063
1775	Arthur	Sutton,	Administration,	15064
1778	Betty	Sutton,	Guardianship,	15065
1841	Charity W.	Millbury,	Administration,	15066
1765	David	New Salem,	Guardianship,	15067
1793	David	Charlton,	Guardianship,	15068
1761	Ebenezer	Mendon,	Administration,	15069
1762	Ebenezer	Sutton,	Will,	15070
1778	Gideon	Sutton,	Guardianship,	15071
1763	John	Petersham,	Guardianship,	15072
1756	Samuel	Sutton,	Will,	15073
1783	Samuel	Sutton,	Administration,	15074
1805	Samuel	Sutton,	Administration,	15075
1839	Samuel W., Jr.	Mendon,	Guardianship,	15076
1778	Tamer	Sutton,	Guardianship,	15077
1758	Thomas	Petersham,	Administration,	15078
1870	DAHLMAN, Josephine	Worcester,	Guardianship,	15079
1870	Lizzie	Worcester,	Adoption, etc.,	15080
1877	DAIGLE, Catharine	Worcester,	Guardianship,	15081
1876	Kain	Worcester,	Administration,	15082
1876	Margaret	Worcester,	Guardianship,	15083
1877	Mary A.	Worcester,	Guardianship,	15084
	DAILEY AND DALEY,			
1868	Ann	Milford,	Guardianship,	15085
1874	Annie G.	Worcester,	Guardianship,	15086
1881	Aurelia	Lunenburg,	Guardianship,	15087
1868	Catharine	Milford,	Guardianship,	15088
1875	Catharine	Uxbridge,	Guardianship,	15089
1868	Charles	Milford,	Guardianship,	15090
1864	Dennis	Uxbridge,	Guardianship,	15091
1855	Edmund	Templeton,	Administration,	15092
1875	Jeremiah	Uxbridge,	Guardianship,	15093
1868	John	Milford,	Guardianship,	15094
1875	John A.	Uxbridge,	Guardianship,	15095

YEAR.	NAME.	RESIDENCE.	NATURE.	CASE.
	DAILEY and DALEY,			
1864	John F.	Worcester,	Adoption,	15096
1872	John F.	Worcester,	Guardianship,	15097
1875	Julia	Uxbridge,	Guardianship,	15098
1874	Katie E.	Worcester,	Guardianship,	15099
1868	Mary	Milford,	Guardianship,	15100
1875	Mary	Uxbridge,	Guardianship,	15101
1881	Mary	West Boylston,	Administration,	15102
1874	Nellie G.	Worcester,	Guardianship,	15103
1868	Patrick	Milford,	Administration,	15104
1875	Rose	Leicester,	Guardianship,	15105
1874	Timothy	Worcester,	Guardianship,	15106
1864	William	Worcester,	Will,	15107
1837	DAKIN, Ann M.	Boylston,	Guardianship,	15108
1874	Betsey	Bolton,	Will,	15109
1837	David	Worcester,	Will,	15110
1861	Henry J.	Millbury,	Administration,	15111
1868	James H.	Worcester,	Administration,	15112
1745	John	Lancaster,	Administration,	15113
1869	Luke	Worcester,	Administration,	15114
1837	Luther	Worcester,	Administration,	15115
1805	Oliver	Boylston,	Will,	15116
1812	Oliver	Boylston,	Will,	15117
1870	DALE, John	Rutland,	Will,	15118
1762	DALRYMPLE, Andrew	Uxbridge,	Will,	15119
1788	Andrew	Dudley,	Guardianship,	15120
1788	Barbary	Dudley,	Guardianship,	15121
1819	Betsy	Southbridge,	Administration,	15122
1844	Caleb W.	Hubbardston,	Guardianship,	15123
1855	Caleb W.	Shrewsbury,	Change of Name,	15124
1844	Charles H.	Hubbardston,	Guardianship,	15125
1873	Charlotte	Grafton,	Guardianship,	15126
1873	Ellen J.	Grafton,	Guardianship,	15127
1787	George	Dudley,	Guardianship,	15128
1844	Hannah E.	Hubbardston,	Guardianship,	15129
1784	John	Dudley,	Administration,	15130
1788	John	Dudley,	Guardianship,	15131
1860	John	Ashburnham,	Administration,	15132
1843	Jonathan B.	Hubbardston,	Administration,	15133
1845	Otis	Northborough,	Administration,	15134
1845	Phineas H.	Northborough,	Guardianship,	15135
1785	Robert	Dudley,	Guardianship,	15136
1796	Sally	Dudley,	Guardianship,	15137
1844	Samuel A.	Hubbardston,	Guardianship,	15138
1788	Sarah	Dudley,	Guardianship,	15139

YEAR.	NAME.	RESIDENCE.	NATURE.	CASE.
1844	DALRYMPLE, Sarah S.	Hubbardston,	Guardianship,	15140
1844	Sewall D.	Hubbardston,	Guardianship,	15141
1785	Thomas	Dudley,	Guardianship,	15142
1844	William E.	Hubbardston,	Guardianship,	15143
1745	DALSTON, Samuel	Worcester,	Will,	15144
1879	DALTON, Albert	Fitchburg,	Guardianship,	15145
	DALEY see DAILEY.			
	DAMAN see DAMON.			
1869	DAME, Soulonge	Ashburnham,	Administration,	15146
	DAMON AND DAMAN,			
1826	Abraham P.	Lancaster,	Administration,	15147
1880	Albert B.	Fitchburg,	Change of Name,	15148
1880	Albert B.	Fitchburg,	Will,	15149
1880	Alfred H.	Fitchburg,	Change of Name,	15150
1864	Alony C.	Holden,	Administration,	15151
1879	Angeline M.	Worcester,	Guardianship,	15152
1861	Augustus F.	Holden,	Administration,	15153
1854	Charles A.	Holden,	Guardianship,	15154
1860	Charles F.	Holden,	Administration,	15155
1873	Chloe F.	Winchendon,	Will,	15156
1874	Cornelius J.	Leominster,	Guardianship,	15157
1740	Daniel	Leicester,	Administration,	15158
1748	Daniel	Leicester,	Guardianship,	15159
1763	Ebenezer	Uxbridge,	Guardianship,	15160
1748	Elijah	Leicester,	Guardianship,	15161
1874	Ellsworth E.	Leominster,	Guardianship,	15162
1874	Ernest	Leominster,	Guardianship,	15163
1875	Eugene A.	Leominster,	Administration,	15164
1853	George F.	Leominster,	Guardianship,	15165
1824	George H.	Barre,	Guardianship,	15166
1877	Hannah W.	Princeton,	Will,	15167
1851	Harriet A.	Holden,	Guardianship,	15168
1865	Harriet A.	Holden,	Administration,	15168
1839	Horace	Fitchburg,	Guardianship,	15169
1794	John	Western,	Administration,	15170
1823	John	Western,	Will,	15171
1873	John	Leominster,	Administration,	15172
1761	Joseph	Uxbridge,	Administration,	15173
1854	Joseph	Barre,	Administration,	15174
1880	J. Marshall	Lancaster,	Administration,	15175
1875	Lester F.	Milford,	Administration,	15176
1820	Lucinda	Westminster,	Guardianship,	15177
1856	Lucy	Gardner,	Will,	15178
1750	Mary	Leicester,	Guardianship,	15179
1820	Mary	Westminster,	Guardianship,	15180
1854	Mary	Holden,	Guardianship,	15181

YEAR.	NAME.	RESIDENCE.	NATURE.	CASE.
	DAMON AND DAMAN,			
1839	Mary E.	Fitchburg,	Guardianship,	15182
1871	Michael	Leominster,	Will,	15183
1874	Milton O.	Leominster,	Guardianship,	15184
1823	Patty	Western,	Guardianship,	15185
1867	Penniman	Holden,	Administration,	15186
1844	Rebecca	Lancaster,	Will,	15187
1813	Samuel	Holden,	Will,	15188
1845	Samuel	Lancaster,	Will,	15189
1851	Samuel	Holden,	Administration,	15190
1853	Samuel	Holden,	Administration,	15191
1879	Sarah A.	Westminster,	Will,	15192
1805	Stephen, Jr.	Holden,	Guardianship,	15193
1851	Susan A.	Holden,	Guardianship,	15194
1864	Susan E.	Gardner,	Guardianship,	15195
1820	Thomas	Westminster,	Guardianship,	15196
1839	Thomas	Fitchburg,	Administration,	15197
1848	Thomas	Lunenburg,	Guardianship,	15198
1864	Thomas	Warren,	Will,	15199
1820	Timothy	Westminster,	Will,	15200
1880	William	Fitchburg,	Administration,	15201
1872	DANA, Alfred W.	Worcester,	Change of Name,	15202
1871	Caleb	Worcester,	Will,	15203
1855	Caroline J.	Lancaster,	Guardianship,	15204
1872	Charles Henshaw	Worcester,	Change of Name,	15205
1854	Delos L.	Oxford,	Guardianship,	15206
1789	Edmond	Ashburnham,	Guardianship,	15207
1819	Eleanor B.	Princeton,	Guardianship,	15208
1855	Eliza A. M.	Lancaster,	Guardianship,	15209
1881	E. Beaman	Worcester,	Administration,	15210
1787	George	Ashburnham,	Administration,	15211
1813	Hannah	Oxford,	Administration,	15212
1855	Henrietta E.	Lancaster,	Guardianship,	15213
1851	Jeremiah	Killingly, Conn.,	Foreign Will,	15214
1831	Jesse	Sterling,	Administration,	15215
1879	Jesse D.	Worcester,	Administration,	15216
1819	Jessie D.	West Boylston,	Guardianship,	15217
1754	John	Oxford,	Guardianship,	15218
1818	John	Princeton,	Administration,	15219
1818	John, Jr.	Princeton,	Administration,	15220
1802	John T.	Princeton,	Administration,	15221
1801	Josiah	Barre,	Administration,	15222
1826	Lucinda	Princeton,	Will,	15223
1835	Lucinda	Princeton,	Administration,	15224
1866	Lucy	Oxford,	Administration,	15225

Year.	Name.	Residence.	Nature.	Case.
1855	DANA, Mary F.	Lancaster,	Guardianship,	15226
1739	Phineas	Oxford,	Administration,	15227
1835	Phineas B.	Sterling,	Administration,	15228
1819	Sally	Princeton,	Guardianship,	15229
1864	Sally	Sutton,	Administration,	15230
1805	Sarah	Barre,	Administration,	15231
1819	Sarah E.	West Boylston,	Guardianship,	15232
1875	Sarah H.	Oxford,	Administration,	15233
1806	Sarah S.	Boston,	Guardianship,	15234
1855	Stephen	Lancaster,	Will,	15235
1869	Sylvanus	Millbury,	Administration,	15236
1880	DANE, Addie O.	North Brookfield,	Guardianship,	15237
1851	Daniel	West Brookfield,	Administration,	15238
1880	Daniel	West Brookfield,	Will,	15239
1876	Emerson	North Brookfield,	Administration,	15240
1838	John	Brookfield,	Administration,	15241
1814	Joseph	Brookfield,	Will,	15242
1876	Mary D.	North Brookfield,	Guardianship,	15243
1870	Sumner E.	West Brookfield,	Administration,	15244
1825	William	North Brookfield,	Administration,	15245
1844	William	Brookfield,	Will,	15246
1825	William, Jr.	North Brookfield,	Will,	15247
1874	DANFORTH, Ann R.	Hardwick,	Administration,	15248
1846	Anna	Harvard,	Administration,	15249
1806	Benjamin	Harvard,	Administration,	15250
1785	Dorothy	Montague,	Guardianship,	15251
1866	Edwin I.	Milford,	Guardianship,	15252
1868	Elias	Lancaster,	Will,	15253
1866	Harriet C.	Milford,	Guardianship,	15254
1814	Huldah	Templeton,	Will,	15255
1737	John	Westborough,	Will,	15256
1803	John	Athol,	Administration,	15257
1834	Jonathan	Hardwick,	Administration,	15258
1859	Sarah P.	Bolton,	Guardianship,	15259
	DANIELS, DANIELL AND DANIELLS,			
1811	Abigail	Grafton,	Will,	15260
1753	Abraham	Uxbridge,	Administration,	15261
1854	Absalom	Blackstone,	Will,	15262
1804	Adams	Milford,	Administration,	15263
1804	Alanson S.	Milford,	Guardianship,	15264
1868	Alice M.	Milford,	Guardianship,	15265
1779	Anna	Mendon,	Guardianship,	15266
1767	Antipas	Mendon,	Guardianship,	15267
1752	Asa	Mendon,	Guardianship,	15268

Year.	Name.	Residence.	Nature.	Case.
	DANIELS, DANIELL AND DANIELLS,			
1868	Austin	Chicago, Ill.,	Administration,	15269
1806	Betsey	Brookfield,	Guardianship,	15270
1875	Carrie E.	Blackstone,	Guardianship,	15271
1853	Catharine	Milford,	Will,	15272
1804	Charles	Brookfield,	Guardianship,	15273
1856	Charles	Westborough,	Guardianship,	15274
1867	Charles	Westborough,	Will,	15274
1874	Charles	Grafton,	Administration,	15275
1823	Charlotte T.	Mendon,	Guardianship,	15276
1861	Christopher C.	Milford,	Will,	15277
1857	Cyrus	Leicester,	Will,	15278
1804	Dan A.	Milford,	Guardianship,	15279
1832	Darius	Mendon,	Administration,	15280
1778	David	Mendon,	Will,	15281
1811	David	Mendon,	Will,	15282
1850	David	Smithfield, R. I.,	Administration,	15283
1876	David	Fitchburg,	Will,	15284
1821	Dexter	Milford,	Guardianship,	15285
1859	Elbridge G.	Blackstone,	Will,	15286
1772	Eleazer	Mendon,	Administration,	15287
1779	Eleazer	Mendon,	Guardianship,	15288
1821	Elisha	Milford,	Administration,	15289
1872	Elmer E.	Grafton,	Guardianship,	15290
1747	Ephraim	Mendon,	Administration,	15291
1873	Fred H.	Worcester,	Guardianship,	15292
1873	Fred J.	Oxford,	Guardianship,	15293
1849	George S.	Blackstone,	Administration,	15294
1872	Georgie D.	Grafton,	Guardianship,	15295
1873	Georgie D.	Cambridge,	Adoption, etc.,	15296
1839	Gilbert E.	Milford,	Guardianship,	15297
1839	Hastings	Milford,	Administration,	15298
1839	Hiram	Mendon,	Guardianship,	15299
1875	Hiram	Blackstone,	Administration,	15300
1875	Hiram T.	Blackstone,	Guardianship,	15301
1841	Horace	Mendon,	Guardianship,	15302
1799	Huldah	Mendon,	Will,	15303
1767	Increase	Mendon,	Guardianship,	15304
1875	James M.	Worcester,	Administration,	15305
1877	James W.	Oxford,	Guardianship,	15306
1733	John	Mendon,	Administration,	15307
1735	John	Mendon,	Guardianship,	15308
1767	John	Mendon,	Administration,	15309
1767	John	Mendon,	Guardianship,	15310

YEAR.	NAME.	RESIDENCE.	NATURE.	CASE.
	DANIELS, DANIELL AND DANIELLS,			
1825	John	Grafton,	Guardianship,	15311
1823	John M.	Mendon,	Guardianship,	15312
1779	Joseph	Mendon,	Administration,	15313
1826	Joseph	Worcester,	Will,	15314
1842	Joseph	Worcester,	Administration,	15315
1757	Joshua	Mendon,	Guardianship,	15316
1868	Laura A.	Milford,	Guardianship,	15317
1844	Lawson	North Brookfield,	Guardianship,	15318
1804	Levi	Brookfield,	Administration,	15319
1840	Louis R.	Mendon,	Guardianship,	15320
1851	Marcena	Mendon,	Guardianship,	15321
1877	Martha A.	Hubbardston,	Will,	15322
1735	Mary	Mendon,	Guardianship,	15323
1842	Mary	Uxbridge,	Will,	15324
1842	Mary	Uxbridge,	Pension,	15325
1844	Mary A. P.	North Brookfield,	Guardianship,	15326
1831	Moses	Mendon,	Will,	15327
1862	Moses	Blackstone,	Will,	15328
1780	Nahum	Mendon,	Guardianship,	15329
1811	Nancy	Mendon,	Guardianship,	15330
1839	Nathan	Mendon,	Will,	15331
1849	Nathan	Leicester,	Administration,	15332
1832	Olive	Mendon,	Will,	15333
1875	Olive P.	Milford,	Administration,	15334
1831	Oliver	Milford,	Will,	15335
1844	Otis	North Brookfield,	Administration,	15336
1815	Peninnah	Brookfield,	Administration,	15337
1811	Polly	Mendon,	Guardianship,	15338
1767	Rachel	Mendon,	Guardianship,	15339
1872	Rachel A.	Grafton,	Guardianship,	15340
1839	Rachel M.	Mendon,	Guardianship,	15341
1735	Rachell	Mendon,	Guardianship,	15342
1750	Rachell	Grafton,	Administration,	15343
1840	Riley	Mendon,	Administration,	15344
1861	Riley	Mendon,	Administration,	15345
1754	Robert	Sturbridge,	Administration,	15346
1841	Royal	Mendon,	Guardianship,	15347
1871	Sally P.	Westborough,	Will,	15348
1747	Samuel	Mendon,	Guardianship,	15349
1798	Samuel	Milford,	Will,	15350
1746	Samuell	Mendon,	Administration,	15351
1757	Sarah	Mendon,	Guardianship,	15352
1879	Sarah G.	Uxbridge,	Administration,	15353

YEAR.	NAME.	RESIDENCE.	NATURE.	CASE.
	DANIELS, DANIELL AND DANIELLS,			
1839	Sebrina T.	Milford,	Guardianship,	15354
1779	Sem	Mendon,	Guardianship,	15355
1878	Seth	Oxford,	Will,	15356
1767	Silence	Mendon,	Guardianship,	15357
1864	Simeon	Brookfield,	Will,	15358
1811	Smith	Mendon,	Guardianship,	15359
1857	Susannah	Gardner,	Will,	15360
1735	Sylome	Mendon,	Guardianship,	15361
1852	Thankful	Worcester,	Administration,	15362
1872	Walter H.	Sutton,	Guardiauship,	15363
1767	William	Mendon,	Guardianship,	15364
1873	William P.	Worcester,	Will,	15365
1825	Zebulon	Grafton,	Administration,	15366
1880	DANUE, Margaret	Worcester,	Administration,	15367
	DARBY (see also DERBY),			
1870	Aaron	Westminster,	Will,	15368
1785	Amos	Fitchburg,	Administration,	15369
1783	Andrew	Westminster,	Will,	15370
1806	Andrew	Westminster,	Will,	15371
1841	Calvin	Worcester,	Will,	15372
1835	Charles	Leominster,	Administration,	15373
1872	David	Webster,	Administration,	15374
1824	Deliverance	Leominster,	Administration,	15375
1822	Joseph	Westminster,	Administration,	15376
1805	Moses	Westminster,	Administration,	15377
1830	Reuben	Leominster,	Administration,	15378
1855	Walter	Westminster,	Administration,	15379
1878	DARCY, John	Fitchburg,	Administration,	15380
1857	Mary A.	Lancaster,	Guardianship,	15381
1766	DARLING, Aaron	Mendon,	Guardianship,	15382
1864	Abigail	Charlton,	Administration,	15383
1878	Adaline D., etc.	Rutland,	Guardianship,	15384
1870	Albert W.	Worcester,	Guardianship,	15385
1778	Alpheus	Mendon,	Guardianship,	15386
1867	Amasa	Charlton,	Will,	15387
1778	Anna	Mendon,	Guardianship,	15388
1848	Anna M.	Rutland,	Guardianship,	15389
1813	Arnold	Mendon,	Guardianship,	15390
1772	Benjamin	Mendon,	Will,	15391
1783	Benjamin	Lunenburg,	Administration,	15392
1783	Benjamin	Lunenburg,	Guardianship,	15393
1842	Benson	Mendon,	Administration,	15394
1764	Caleb	Mendon,	Guardianship,	15395

YEAR.	NAME.	RESIDENCE.	NATURE.	CASE.
1862	DARLING, Calvin J.	Charlton,	Administration,	15396
1808	Cassius	Leominster,	Guardianship,	15397
1808	Charles B.	Leominster,	Guardianship,	15398
1864	Charles F.	Charlton,	Administration,	15399
1868	Cyrus	Worcester,	Administration,	15400
1745	Daniel	Mendon,	Will,	15401
1778	Daniel	Mendon,	Will,	15402
1808	Daniel	Unknown,	Guardianship,	15403
1877	Daniel	Blackstone,	Administration,	15404
1877	Daniel	Rutland,	Will,	15405
1835	Daniel F.	Mendon,	Guardianship,	15406
1769	Deborah	Mendon,	Guardianship,	15407
1766	Dennis	Mendon,	Guardianship,	15408
1800	Elizabeth	Mendon,	Guardianship,	15409
1783	Eunice	Lunenburg,	Guardianship,	15410
1848	Franklin L.	Rutland,	Guardianship,	15411
1870	Frederick A.	Worcester,	Guardianship,	15412
1766	Henry	Mendon,	Guardianship,	15413
1810	Isaac	Mendon,	Administration,	15414
1783	James	Lunenburg,	Guardianship,	15415
1842	James	Mendon,	Administration,	15416
1813	Jesse	Mendon,	Administration,	15417
1813	Jesse	Mendon,	Guardianship,	15418
1881	Jesse Gertrude	Douglas,	Adoption,	15419
1830	Jewett B.	Winchendon,	Administration,	15420
1837	Job	Sutton,	Administration,	15421
1837	Job	Sutton,	Pension,	15422
1778	John	Mendon,	Guardianship,	15423
1800	John	Mendon,	Will,	15424
1831	John	Mendon,	Guardianship,	15425
1879	John W.	Milford,	Administration,	15426
1808	Joseph	Leominster,	Administration,	15427
1808	Joseph S.	Leominster,	Guardianship,	15428
1856	Josephine C.	Blackstone,	Guardianship,	15429
1835	Joshua	Mendon,	Administration,	15430
1844	Judson	Sutton,	Guardianship,	15431
1804	Leonard W.	Mendon,	Guardianship,	15432
1783	Levi	Lunenburg,	Guardianship,	15433
1867	Lewis	Blackstone,	Administration,	15434
1783	Lois	Lunenburg,	Guardianship,	15435
1848	Lucy	Rutland,	Guardianship,	15436
1872	Lucy	Uxbridge,	Will,	15437
1867	Margaret	Thompson, Conn.,	Administration,	15438
1812	Maria I.	Mendon,	Guardianship,	15439
1814	Mary	Mendon,	Administration,	15440

YEAR.	NAME.	RESIDENCE.	NATURE.	CASE.
1848	DARLING, Mary B.	Rutland,	Guardianship,	15441
1842	Mary G.	Mendon,	Guardianship,	15442
1783	Molley	Lunenburg,	Guardianship,	15443
1847	Moses L.	Worcester,	Administration,	15444
1853	Mowry	Mendon,	Guardianship,	15445
1863	Mowry	Mendon,	Administration,	15446
1870	Myron J.	Leicester,	Guardianship,	15447
1778	Nathan	Mendon,	Guardianship,	15448
1856	Newton	Blackstone,	Administration,	15449
1870	Newton	Worcester,	Guardianship,	15450
1864	Olive	Mendon,	Will,	15451
1844	Palmer	Sutton,	Guardianship,	15452
1869	Palmer	Worcester,	Administration,	15453
1783	Patience	Lunenburg,	Guardianship,	15454
1800	Patience	Mendon,	Guardianship,	15455
1798	Pelatiah	Mendon,	Administration,	15456
1848	Permelia	Douglas,	Administration,	15457
1767	Peter	Mendon,	Guardianship,	15458
1797	Peter	Mendon,	Will,	15459
1861	Peter	Charlton,	Administration,	15460
1870	Polly	Uxbridge,	Will,	15461
1877	Relief	Blackstone,	Administration,	15462
1847	Ruth	Blackstone,	Will,	15463
1795	Samuel	Mendon,	Will,	15464
1857	Samuel	Millbury,	Administration,	15465
1763	Samuel, Jr.	Mendon,	Administration,	15466
1806	Sarah	Mendon,	Will,	15467
1842	Sarah E.	Mendon,	Guardianship,	15468
1778	Seth	Mendon,	Guardianship,	15469
1778	Simeon	Mendon,	Guardianship,	15470
1876	Sylvia	Blackstone,	Will,	15471
1777	Thomas	Mendon,	Administration,	15472
1788	Thomas	Oakham,	Administration,	15473
1784	Timothy	Grafton,	Administration,	15474
1766	Tryall	Mendon,	Guardianship,	15475
1881	Walter E.	Douglas,	Adoption,	15476
1746	William	Mendon,	Guardianship,	15477
1808	William A.	Leominster,	Guardianship,	15478
1844	Zelek	Sutton,	Will,	15479
1844	Zelek	Sutton,	Pension,	15480
1864	Zelek	Milford,	Administration,	15481
1864	DARNEY, Mary A.	Worcester,	Adoption, etc.,	15482
1843	DAVENPORT, Aaron	Sutton,	Will,	15483
1842	Abel	Petersham,	Administration,	15484
1858	Adaline A.	Mendon,	Guardianship,	15485

YEAR.	NAME.	RESIDENCE.	NATURE.	CASE.
1877	DAVENPORT, Adelia E. F.	Mendon,	Will,	15486
1858	Almirah B.	Mendon,	Change of Name,	15487
1804	Amasa	Charlton,	Guardianship,	15488
1803	Amy P.	Boston,	Guardianship,	15489
1847	Ann P.	Mendon,	Guardianship,	15490
1843	Augustus	Petersham,	Guardianship,	15491
1858	Austin D.	Mendon,	Guardianship,	15492
1862	Benjamin	Mendon,	Will,	15493
1854	Betsey	Mendon,	Will,	15494
1813	Charles A.	Mendon,	Guardianship,	15495
1823	Chloe	Mendon,	Will,	15496
1803	Daniel P.	Boston,	Guardianship,	15497
1812	David	Mendon,	Will,	15498
1813	David	Mendon,	Guardianship,	15499
1855	David	Mendon,	Will,	15500
1847	David D.	Mendon,	Guardianship,	15501
1747	Eleazer	Woodstock,	Administration,	15502
1863	Ellen F.	Mendon,	Guardianship,	15503
1826	Emily	West Boylston,	Guardianship,	15504
1815	Emily B.	Boylston,	Guardianship,	15505
1847	George L.	Mendon,	Administration,	15506
1847	Harriett B.	Mendon,	Guardianship,	15507
1859	Hattie R.	Boylston,	Guardianship,	15508
1847	Henry	Mendon,	Guardianship,	15509
1875	Ida M.	Boston,	Adoption, etc.,	15510
1851	Isaac	Milford,	Administration,	15511
1838	Jerome	Petersham,	Administration,	15512
1843	Joel	Petersham,	Will,	15513
1813	John	Williamstown, Vt.,	Administration,	15514
1814	John	Boylston,	Administration,	15515
1858	John L.	Mendon,	Guardianship,	15516
1815	John W.	Boylston,	Guardianship,	15517
1862	Joseph G.	Mendon,	Will,	15518
1874	Julia A. R.	Worcester,	Administration,	15519
1843	Latica	Petersham,	Guardianship,	15520
1843	Lucretia	Petersham,	Guardianship,	15521
1820	Lucy	Boylston,	Guardianship,	15522
1815	Lucy B.	Boylston,	Guardianship,	15523
1875	Lydia H.	Leominster,	Administration,	15524
1879	Marguerite	Worcester,	Guardianship,	15525
1858	Marshall E.	Mendon,	Guardianship,	15526
1842	Martha A.	Athol,	Trustee,	15527
1843	Martha A.	Petersham,	Guardianship,	15528
1859	Martha L.	Boylston,	Guardianship,	15529
1875	Mary H.	Mendon,	Will,	15530

Year.	Name.	Residence.	Nature.	Case.
1815	DAVENPORT, Mary M.	Boylston,	Guardianship,	15531
1814	Matthew	Boylston,	Administration,	15532
1813	Moses	Mendon,	Guardianship,	15533
1851	Nathan W.	Milford,	Guardianship,	15534
1793	Nathaniel	Boylston,	Will,	15535
1859	Nathaniel	Boylston,	Administration,	15536
1876	Palmer	Holden,	Administration,	15537
1815	Percis R.	Boylston,	Guardianship,	15538
1749	Persis	Woodstock,	Guardianship,	15539
1847	Rebecca	Mendon,	Guardianship,	15540
1749	Richard	Woodstock,	Guardianship,	15541
1761	Richard	Sutton,	Will,	15542
1773	Samuel	Mendon,	Will,	15543
1813	Seth	Mendon,	Will,	15544
1843	Seth	Mendon,	Will,	15545
1858	Seth	Mendon,	Will,	15546
1858	Seth T.	Mendon,	Guardianship,	15547
1859	Silas	Upton,	Administration,	15548
1854	Sophia F.	Mendon,	Guardianship,	15549
1854	Stearns G.	Mendon,	Guardianship,	15550
1816	Tamar	Boylston,	Will,	15551
1831	Tamasin	Petersham,	Administration,	15552
1877	Tryphosa	Woodstock, Conn.,	Administration,	15553
1836	Watee	Mendon,	Will,	15554
1796	William	Sutton,	Will,	15555
1808	William	Petersham,	Administration,	15556
1815	William	Boylston,	Guardianship,	15557
1847	William H.	Mendon,	Guardianship,	15558
1858	William J.	Boylston,	Administration,	15559
1859	William N.	Boylston,	Guardianship,	15560
1864	DAVID, Catharine	Grafton,	Will,	15561
	DAVIDSON and DAVISON,			
1779	Abigail	Mendon,	Guardianship,	15562
1848	Almira E.	Auburn,	Guardianship,	15563
1868	Amory	Clinton,	Administration,	15564
1865	Caroline A.	Clinton,	Guardianship,	15565
1865	Charles M.	Clinton,	Administration,	15566
1860	Charlotte M.	Boylston,	Guardianship,	15567
1865	Emma L.	Clinton,	Guardianship,	15568
1858	Frances I.	Lancaster,	Guardianship,	15569
1868	Georgiana H.	Clinton,	Administration,	15570
1875	Henry H.	Sterling,	Administration,	15571
1791	Jedediah	Charlton,	Will,	15572
1777	John	Charlton,	Administration,	15573
1860	John	Boylston,	Administration,	15574

YEAR.	NAME.	RESIDENCE.	NATURE.	CASE.
	DAVIDSON AND DAVISON,			
1880	Mabel M.	Millbury,	Guardianship,	15575
1779	Margret	Mendon,	Guardianship,	15576
1865	Martha E.	Clinton,	Guardianship,	15577
1855	Mary	Charlton,	Administration,	15578
1880	Mary E.	Millbury,	Guardianship,	15579
1860	Merion M.	Boylston,	Guardianship,	15580
1855	Molly	Charlton,	Pension,	15581
1858	Peter E.	Lancaster,	Administration,	15582
1840	Samuel	Douglas,	Pension,	15583
1860	Sarah J.	Boylston,	Guardianship,	15584
1816	Thomas	Grafton,	Administration,	15585
1847	William F.	Stafford, Conn.,	Administration,	15586
1880	William G.	Millbury,	Guardianship,	15587
1770	DAVIS, Aaron	Brookfield,	Guardianship,	15588
1804	Aaron	Harvard,	Administration,	15589
1848	Aaron W.	Oxford,	Guardianship,	15590
1865	Aaron W.	Templeton,	Administration,	15591
1844	Abby P.	Hubbardston,	Guardianship,	15592
1858	Abel	Templeton,	Administration,	15593
1762	Abigail	Harvard,	Administration,	15594
1805	Abigail	Oxford,	Will,	15595
1833	Abigail	Oxford,	Guardianship,	15596
1841	Abigail	Holden,	Will,	15597
1847	Abigail	Templeton,	Guardianship,	15598
1874	Abigail S.	Westborough,	Administration,	15599
1814	Abijah	Oxford,	Guardianship,	15600
1833	Abijah	Oxford,	Will,	15601
1810	Abraham	Leverett,	Guardianship,	15602
1827	Adaline	Princeton,	Guardianship,	15603
1833	Adaline	Oxford,	Guardianship,	15604
1840	Adaline	Hubbardston,	Sale Real Estate,	15605
1865	Adaline M.	Charlton,	Guardianship,	15606
1814	Adams	Boylston,	Guardianship,	15607
1840	Addison	West Boylston,	Administration,	15608
1881	Adin B.	Millbury,	Administration,	15609
1856	Albert	Upton,	Guardianship,	15610
1819	Alexander P.	Royalston,	Guardianship,	15611
1812	Alfred	Brookfield,	Guardianship,	15612
1846	Alfred	Leominster,	Will,	15613
1864	Alfred W.	Millbury,	Guardianship,	15614
1865	Alice	Charlton,	Guardianship,	15615
1881	Alice J.	Worcester,	Guardianship,	15616
1830	Alonzo	Gardner,	Guardianship,	15617
1877	Alpheus	Charlton,	Will,	15618

YEAR.	NAME.	RESIDENCE.	NATURE.	CASE.
1864	DAVIS, Alsia A., etc.	Southbridge,	Guardianship,	15619
1832	Alvin	Hubbardston,	Guardianship,	15620
1815	Ama D.	Holden	Guardianship,	15621
1802	Amasa	Charlton,	Will,	15622
1804	Amasa	Charlton,	Guardianship,	15623
1757	Amos	Grafton,	Guardianship,	15624
1757	Amos	Grafton,	Administration,	15625
1806	Amos	Grafton,	Will,	15626
1854	Andrew M.	Worcester,	Guardianship,	15627
1857	Angelina	Bolton,	Guardianship,	15628
1856	Angeline L.	Upton,	Guardianship,	15629
1803	Anna	Oxford,	Guardianship,	15630
1859	Anna E.	Northborough,	Guardianship,	15631
1878	Anna M.	Westport, N. Y.,	Trustee,	15631½
1854	Arthur P.	Rochester, N. Y.,	Guardianship,	15632
1798	Asa	Rutland,	Will,	15633
1813	Asa	Oxford,	Guardianship,	15634
1824	Asa	Charlton,	Administration,	15635
1840	Asa	Charlton,	Administration,	15636
1859	Asahel	Royalston,	Will,	15637
1824	Augustus	Oxford,	Guardianship,	15638
1846	Augustus	Ashburnham,	Guardianship,	15639
1857	Austin	Oxford,	Change of Name,	15640
1871	Austin	Lancaster,	Administration,	15641
1851	Barnabas	Paxton,	Administration,	15642
1850	Barzillai	Brookfield,	Administration,	15643
1759	Benjamin	Western,	Administration,	15644
1803	Benjamin	Oxford,	Administration,	15645
1844	Benjamin L.	Templeton,	Administration,	15646
1838	Bennett	Ashburnham,	Pension,	15647
1798	Betsey	Templeton,	Guardianship,	15648
1830	Betsey	Gardner,	Guardianship,	15649
1833	Betsey	Western,	Guardianship,	15650
1833	Betsey	Oxford,	Guardianship,	15651
1849	Betsey	Worcester,	Guardianship,	15652
1850	Betsey	Worcester,	Will,	15652
1876	Betsey	Douglas,	Administration,	15653
1798	Betsy	Princeton,	Guardianship,	15654
1800	Betsy	Rutland,	Guardianship,	15655
1803	Betsy	Oxford,	Guardianship,	15656
1810	Betsy	Templeton,	Guardianship,	15657
1863	Betsy	Warren,	Administration,	15658
1838	Blydenburg W.	West Boylston,	Guardianship,	15659
1844	Brigham	Hubbardston,	Administration,	15660
1877	Calvin A.	Brookfield,	Will,	15661

YEAR.	NAME.	RESIDENCE.	NATURE.	CASE.
1866	DAVIS, Calvin B.	Princeton,	Will,	15662
1815	Calvin D.	Holden,	Guardianship,	15663
1855	Calvin D.	Phillipston,	Administration,	15664
1844	Carlo B.	Hubbardston,	Guardianship,	15665
1826	Caroline	Princeton,	Guardianship,	15666
1837	Caroline B.	Templeton,	Guardianship,	15667
1840	Catharine	Charlton,	Guardianship,	15668
1870	Catharine	Rutland,	Guardianship,	15669
1825	Charles	Rutland,	Guardianship,	15670
1832	Charles	Hubbardston,	Guardianship,	15671
1834	Charles	Oxford,	Guardianship,	15672
1837	Charles	Ashburnham,	Administration,	15673
1843	Charles	Oxford,	Guardianship,	15674
1844	Charles	Philadelphia, Pa.,	Guardianship,	15675
1856	Charles	Oxford,	Administration,	15674
1862	Charles	Worcester,	Will,	15676
1816	Charles A.	Princeton,	Guardianship,	15677
1853	Charles A.	Upton,	Guardianship,	15678
1855	Charles A.	Upton,	Adoption,	15679
1877	Charles A.	Hubbardston,	Guardianship,	15680
1843	Charles D.	Northborough,	Guardianship,	15681
1837	Charles E.	Ashburnham,	Guardianship,	15682
1863	Charles E.	Ashburnham,	Administration,	15683
1843	Charles F.	Holden,	Guardianship,	15684
1856	Charles F.	Holden,	Guardianship,	15685
1877	Charles F.	Paxton,	Guardianship,	15686
1859	Charles II.	Sterling,	Guardianship,	15687
1874	Charles M.	Worcester,	Administration,	15688
1863	Charles O.	Ashburnham,	Guardianship,	15689
1871	Charles S.	Oxford,	Guardianship,	15690
1874	Charles W.	Fitchburg,	Administration,	15691
1877	Charles W.	Templeton,	Administration,	15692
1846	Charlotte E.	Lowell,	Guardianship,	15693
1844	Chester	Webster,	Administration,	15694
1844	Chester T.	Webster,	Guardianship,	15695
1870	Clara B.	Fitchburg,	Adoption, etc.,	15696
1871	Clara S.	Princeton,	Guardianship,	15697
1869	Clarissa	Leicester,	Administration,	15698
1873	Clinton	Northborough,	Guardianship,	15699
1874	Cora A.	Athol,	Guardianship,	15700
1875	Cora A.	Winchendon,	Adoption, etc.,	15701
1841	Craft	Oxford,	Administration,	15702
1871	Craft	Oxford,	Administration,	15703
1833	Cynthia	Princeton,	Will,	15704
1868	Cyrus	Royalston,	Administration,	15705

YEAR.	NAME.	RESIDENCE.	NATURE.	CASE.
1820	DAVIS, Dana	Templeton,	Guardianship,	15706
1800	Danforth	Rutland,	Guardianship,	15707
1837	Danforth	Rutland,	Guardianship,	15708
1764	Daniel	Rutland,	Will,	15709
1783	Daniel	Rutland,	Will,	15710
1815	Daniel	Holden,	Administration,	15711
1848	Daniel	Princeton,	Will,	15712
1856	Daniel	Upton,	Administration,	15713
1782	David	Rutland,	Guardianship,	15714
1806	David	Holden,	Guardianship,	15715
1824	David	Paxton,	Will,	15716
1852	David	Paxton,	Will,	15717
1857	David	Holden,	Administration,	15718
1863	David	Holden,	Guardianship,	15719
1831	Deborah	Oxford,	Administration,	15720
1836	Deborah	Fitchburg,	Administration,	15721
1789	Deliverance	Ashburnham,	Will,	15722
1790	Deliverance	Ashburnham,	Guardianship,	15723
1863	Dennis	Holden,	Administration,	15724
1829	Diana	Upton,	Guardianship,	15725
1839	Dorcas	Princeton,	Pension,	15726
1840	Dorcas	Princeton,	Administration,	15727
1840	Dresser L.	Charlton,	Guardianship,	15728
1850	Drusilla	Harvard,	Will,	15729
1821	Dulceny	Templeton,	Guardianship,	15730
1844	Dyer	Dudley,	Administration,	15731
1844	Dyer	Dudley,	Guardianship,	15732
1753	Ebenezer	Brookfield,	Guardianship,	15733
1770	Ebenezer	Mendon,	Guardianship,	15734
1792	Ebenezer	Oxford,	Will,	15735
1792	Ebenezer	Harvard,	Will,	15736
1794	Ebenezer	Oxford,	Administration,	15737
1808	Ebenezer	Oxford,	Guardianship,	15738
1808	Ebenezer	Royalston,	Administration,	15739
1816	Ebenezer	Charlton,	Will,	15740
1838	Ebenezer B.	Ashburnham,	Administration,	15741
1808	Eden	Dudley,	Guardianship,	15742
1822	Eden	Dudley,	Administration,	15742
1784	Edward	Oxford,	Will,	15743
1796	Edward	Dudley,	Will,	15744
1834	Edward	Dudley.	Will,	15745
1864	Edwin	Southbridge,	Adoption, etc.,	15746
1875	Edwin	Fitchburg,	Guardianship,	15747
1838	Edwin A.	Northborough,	Guardianship,	15748
1878	Eleazer	Fitchburg,	Will,	15749

YEAR.	NAME.	RESIDENCE.	NATURE.	CASE.
1762	DAVIS, Eleazer	Harvard,	Administration,	15750
1784	Eleazer	Templeton,	Administration,	15751
1797	Eleazer	Holden,	Administration,	15752
1800	Eleazer	Holden,	Guardianship,	15753
1842	Elijah	Oxford,	Administration,	15754
1796	Elisha	Oxford,	Will,	15755
1806	Elisha	Grafton,	Guardianship,	15756
1816	Elisha	Lancaster,	Will,	15757
1839	Elisha	Sutton,	Will,	15758
1808	Eliza	Royalston,	Administration,	15759
1812	Eliza	Royalston,	Guardianship,	15760
1825	Eliza	Rutland,	Guardianship,	15761
1828	Eliza	Princeton,	Administration,	15762
1838	Eliza A.	West Boylston,	Guardianship,	15763
1868	Eliza A.	Dana,	Guardianship,	15764
1851	Eliza J.	Princeton,	Guardianship,	15765
1767	Elizabeth	Harvard,	Guardianship,	15766
1775	Elizabeth	Oxford,	Guardianship,	15767
1800	Elizabeth	Harvard,	Guardianship,	15768
1811	Elizabeth	Princeton,	Guardianship,	15769
1815	Elizabeth	Rutland,	Guardianship,	15770
1844	Elizabeth	Philadelphia, Pa.,	Guardianship,	15771
1849	Elizabeth	Hardwick,	Will,	15772
1862	Elizabeth	Shrewsbury,	Will,	15773
1865	Elizabeth	Holden,	Administration,	15774
1873	Elizabeth B.	Northborough,	Guardianship,	15775
1827	Elizabeth E.	Leominster,	Guardianship,	15776
1870	Elizabeth W.	Northborough,	Will,	15777
1847	Ella F.	Charlton,	Guardianship,	15778
1845	Ellen	Templeton,	Guardianship,	15779
1847	Ellen M.	Worcester,	Guardianship,	15780
1844	Ellen P.	Webster,	Guardianship,	15781
1871	Ellen S.	Princeton,	Guardianship,	15782
1805	Elnathan	Holden,	Will,	15783
1827	Elnathan	Holden,	Guardianship,	15784
1881	Elnathan	Auburn,	Will,	15785
1856	Elsey A., etc.	Southbridge,	Guardianship,	15786
1824	Elsy	Oxford,	Guardianship,	15787
1826	Emeline	Princeton,	Guardianship,	15788
1826	Emily	Princeton,	Guardianship,	15789
1861	Emma F.	Dudley,	Guardianship,	15790
1877	Emma M.	Paxton,	Guardianship,	15791
1881	Emma M.	Paxton,	Administration,	15791
1867	Emma P.	Athol,	Guardianship,	14792
1767	Ephraim	Petersham,	Administration,	15793

YEAR.	NAME.	RESIDENCE.	NATURE.	CASE.
1814	DAVIS, Erastus	Oxford,	Guardianship,	15794
1834	Erastus	Oxford,	Guardianship,	15795
1835	Erastus	Millbury,	Guardianship,	15796
1875	Erastus	Millbury,	Administration,	15797
1877	Esther E.	Oxford,	Administration,	15798
1824	Estus	Oxford,	Guardianship,	15799
1837	Ethan	Holden,	Will,	15800
1827	Ethan, Jr.	Holden,	Guardianship,	15801
1876	Ethel F.	Fitchburg,	Adoption, etc.,	15802
1816	Eunice	Lancaster,	Guardianship,	15803
1826	Eunice	Princeton,	Guardianship,	15804
1830	Eunice	Holden,	Will,	15805
1806	Ezekiel	Wendell,	Guardianship,	15806
1817	Ezekiel, 2d	Oxford,	Guardianship,	15807
1783	Ezra	Charlton,	Guardianship,	15808
1833	Ezra	Oxford,	Administration,	15809
1833	Ezra	Oxford,	Guardianship,	15810
1862	Ezra	Oxford,	Administration,	15811
1812	Flint	Harvard,	Administration,	15812
1812	Foster	Brookfield,	Guardianship,	15813
1812	Francis	Brookfield,	Guardianship,	15814
1838	Francis	West Boylston,	Administration,	15815
1863	Francis	Holden,	Will,	15816
1881	Francis A.	Millbury,	Guardianship,	15817
1872	Francis H.	Southborough,	Administration,	15818
1870	Francis N.	Oxford,	Guardianship,	15819
1838	Francis W.	West Boylston,	Guardianship,	15820
1875	Frank	Lunenburg,	Will,	15821
1833	Franklin	Oxford,	Guardianship,	15822
1827	Frederick	Dudley,	Guardianship,	15823
1847	Frederick	Charlton,	Administration,	15824
1862	Frederick	Webster,	Guardianship,	15825
1869	Frederick H.	Bolton,	Guardianship,	15826
1847	Frederick V. A.	Charlton,	Guardianship,	15827
1824	Freeman	Oxford,	Guardianship,	15828
1806	Gardner	Holden,	Guardianship,	15829
1825	George	Rutland,	Guardianship,	15830
1830	George	Gardner,	Guardianship,	15831
1837	George	Rutland,	Guardianship,	15832
1843	George	Sterling,	Guardianship,	15833
1845	George	Templeton,	Guardianship,	15834
1862	George	Sterling,	Will,	15835
1863	George	Sturbridge,	Administration,	15836
1875	George	Fitchburg,	Administration,	15837
1844	George A.	Lancaster,	Guardianship,	15838

Year.	Name.	Residence.	Nature.	Case.
1851	DAVIS, George A.	Princeton,	Guardianship,	15839
1873	George C.	Northborough,	Will,	15840
1854	George F.	Rutland,	Guardianship,	15841
1881	George P.	Charlton,	Administration,	15842
1798	George W.	Templeton,	Guardianship,	15843
1805	George W.	Templeton,	Guardianship,	15844
1857	George W.	Gardner,	Administration,	15845
1878	George W.	Worcester,	Will,	15846
1877	Gertrude E.	Worcester,	Guardianship,	15847
1840	Grace	Phillipston,	Pension,	15848
1869	Hall	Bolton,	Administration,	15849
1861	Halsey	Charlton,	Will,	15850
1815	Hamlin	Harvard,	Guardianship,	15851
1761	Hannah	Rutland,	Administration,	15852
1794	Hannah	Oxford,	Guardianship,	15853
1804	Hannah	Charlton,	Guardianship,	15854
1817	Hannah	Dudley,	Administration,	15855
1833	Hannah, etc.	Oxford,	Guardianship,	15856
1879	Hannah	Millbury,	Will,	15857
1869	Harrie W.	Bolton,	Guardianship,	15858
1843	Harriet	Calais, Vt.,	Guardianship,	15859
1851	Harriet	Princeton,	Guardianship,	15860
1847	Harriet A.	Templeton,	Guardianship,	15861
1881	Harriet E.	Worcester,	Administration,	15862
1869	Harriet N.	Rochester, N. Y.,	Foreign Will,	15863
1881	Harry E.	Blackstone,	Guardianship,	15864
1881	Hattie J.	Blackstone,	Guardianship,	15865
1863	Helen H.	Templeton,	Adoption, etc.,	15866
1802	Henry	Charlton,	Guardianship,	15867
1868	Henry	Dudley,	Administration,	15868
1843	Henry C.	Northborough,	Guardianship,	15869
1840	Henry P.	Charlton,	Guardianship,	15870
1778	Hezekiah	Dudley,	Guardianship,	15871
1804	Hezekiah	Charlton,	Guardianship,	15872
1844	Hezekiah	Dudley,	Guardianship,	15873
1844	Hezekiah H.	Dudley,	Administration,	15874
1825	Hiram	Rutland,	Guardianship,	15875
1846	Hiram	Worcester,	Will,	15876
1874	Hiram	Fitchburg,	Administration,	15877
1849	Hiram K.	West Boylston,	Administration,	15878
1797	Hovey	Oxford,	Administration,	15879
1868	Ida E.	Worcester,	Guardianship,	15880
1827	Ira	Princeton,	Administration,	15881
1761	Isaac	Rutland,	Guardianship,	15882
1805	Isaac	Oxford,	Guardianship,	15883

YEAR.	NAME.	RESIDENCE.	NATURE.	CASE.
1813	DAVIS, Isaac	Leverett,	Guardianship,	15884
1826	Isaac	Princeton,	Guardianship,	15885
1826	Isaac	Northborough,	Will,	15886
1833	Isaac	Rutland,	Administration,	15887
1858	Isaac	Northborough,	Will,	15888
1864	Isaac	North Brookfield,	Will,	15889
1838	Isaac E.	West Boylston,	Guardianship,	15890
1813	Isaiah	Harvard,	Administration,	15891
1791	Israel	Holden,	Will,	15892
1811	Israel	Holden,	Will,	15893
1872	Israel	Hubbardston,	Will,	15894
1794	Jacob	Harvard,	Guardianship,	15895
1798	James	Princeton,	Guardianship,	15896
1814	James	Princeton,	Administration,	15897
1821	James	Holden,	Will,	15898
1822	James	Holden,	Guardianship,	15899
1825	James	Rutland,	Guardianship,	15900
1843	James	Douglas,	Administration,	15901
1865	James	Worcester,	Administration,	15902
1797	James H.	Oxford,	Administration,	15903
1868	James H.	Worcester,	Guardianship,	15904
1869	James R.	Fitchburg,	Will,	15905
1869	James S. M.	Rutland,	Administration,	15906
1875	Jane E.	Oxford,	Administration,	15907
1881	Jennie L.	Blackstone,	Guardianship,	15908
1822	Jeremiah	Oxford,	Will,	15909
1865	Jerusha	North Brookfield,	Administration,	15910
1832	Joanna	Royalston,	Will,	15911
1867	Joanna J.	Dudley,	Administration,	15912
1782	Joel	Rutland,	Guardianship,	15913
1837	Joel	Rutland,	Administration,	15914
1837	Joel	Westminster,	Administration,	15915
1874	Joel	Worcester,	Administration,	15916
1761	John	Rutland,	Guardianship,	15917
1768	John	Harvard,	Will,	15918
1769	John	Brookfield,	Administration,	15919
1795	John	Royalston,	Will,	15920
1800	John	Rutland,	Guardianship,	15921
1801	John	Oxford,	Administration,	15922
1824	John	Princeton,	Will,	15923
1825	John	Rutland,	Guardianship,	15924
1826	John	Paxton,	Will,	15925
1827	John	Lunenburg,	Administration,	15926
1832	John	Hubbardston,	Guardianship,	15927
1834	John	Oxford,	Guardianship,	15928

(367—SERIES A.)

YEAR.	NAME.	RESIDENCE.	NATURE.	CASE.
1840	DAVIS, John	Charlton,	Administration,	15929
1843	John	Sterling,	Administration,	15930
1843	John	Princeton,	Guardianship,	15931
1844	John	Philadelphia, Pa.,	Guardianship,	15932
1850	John	Webster,	Guardianship,	15933
1854	John	Worcester,	Will,	15934
1857	John	Bolton,	Guardianship,	15935
1870	John	Rutland,	Administration,	15936
1871	John	Holden,	Will,	15937
1871	John	Rutland,	Will,	15938
1876	John	Hubbardston,	Administration,	15939
1838	John A.	West Boylston,	Administration,	15940
1847	John B.	Templeton,	Guardianship,	15941
1840	John E.	Charlton,	Guardianship,	15942
1842	John G.	Princeton,	Administration,	15943
1820	John H.	Sturbridge,	Administration,	15944
1867	John H.	Athol,	Guardianship,	15945
1875	John H.	Athol,	Guardianship,	15946
1832	John L.	Holden,	Guardianship,	15947
1857	John M.	Warren,	Guardianship,	15948
1862	John M.	Webster,	Administration,	15949
1845	John W.	Hubbardston,	Guardianship,	15950
1845	John W.	Hubbardston,	Will,	15951
1764	Jonas	Harvard,	Administration,	15952
1767	Jonas	Harvard,	Guardianship,	15953
1794	Jonas	Oxford,	Guardianship,	15954
1814	Jonas	Harvard,	Guardianship,	15955
1842	Jonathan	Fitchburg,	Administration,	15956
1868	Jonathan	Oxford,	Will,	15957
1857	Jonathan A.	Oxford,	Change of Name,	15958
1880	Jonathan P.	Fitchburg,	Will,	15959
1732	Joseph	Brookfield,	Administration,	15960
1777	Joseph	Western,	Guardianship,	15961
1799	Joseph	Holden,	Will,	15962
1800	Joseph	Shrewsbury,	Administration,	15963
1800	Joseph	Rutland,	Guardianship,	15964
1813	Joseph	Oxford,	Administration,	15965
1839	Joseph	Royalston,	Will,	15966
1843	Joseph	Northborough,	Will,	15967
1849	Joseph	Lancaster,	Administration,	15968
1853	Joseph	Rutland,	Administration,	15969
1855	Joseph	Dudley,	Administration,	15970
1868	Joseph	Templeton,	Will,	15971
1868	Joseph	Royalston,	Will,	15972
1873	Joseph H.	Southbridge,	Will,	15973

YEAR.	NAME.	RESIDENCE.	NATURE.	CASE.
1831	DAVIS, Joseph J.	Shrewsbury,	Administration,	15974
1838	Joseph P.	Northborough,	Guardianship,	15975
1827	Joshua	Dudley,	Guardianship,	15976
1827	Joshua	Dudley,	Will,	15977
1877	Joshua	Oxford,	Will,	15978
1846	Josiah	Ashburnham,	Will,	15979
1804	Josiah, Jr.	Princeton,	Will,	15980
1873	Julia G.	Northborough,	Guardianship,	15981
1841	Julius	Charlton,	Guardianship,	15982
1875	Kendall	Templeton,	Will,	15983
1811	Larned	Oxford,	Administration,	15984
1870	Larned	Oxford,	Administration,	15985
1837	Laura A.	Ashburnham,	Guardianship,	15986
1843	Leander	Calais, Vt.,	Guardianship,	15987
1772	Learned	Oxford,	Guardianship,	15988
1828	Lemuel	Holden,	Administration,	15989
1876	Lena E.	Worcester,	Guardianship,	15990
1877	Leonard W.	Auburn,	Administration,	15991
1847	Lettice	Princeton,	Will,	15992
1847	Lettice	Princeton,	Pension,	15993
1807	Levi	Charlton,	Will,	15994
1817	Levi	Fitchburg,	Will,	15995
1818	Levi	Fitchburg,	Guardianship,	15996
1866	Lorenzo D.	Worcester,	Will,	15997
1814	Loring	Oxford,	Guardianship,	15998
1820	Loring	Templeton,	Guardianship,	15999
1842	Loring	Oxford,	Administration,	16000
1871	Louisa T.	Worcester,	Guardianship,	16001
1848	Lucius F.	Worcester,	Administration,	16002
1816	Lucretia	Princeton,	Guardianship,	16003
1757	Lucy	Grafton,	Guardianship,	16004
1790	Lucy	Ashburnham,	Guardianship,	16005
1801	Lucy	Princeton,	Guardianship,	16006
1806	Lucy	Grafton,	Guardianship,	16007
1806	Lucy	Holden,	Guardianship,	16008
1825	Lucy	Rutland,	Guardianship,	16009
1829	Lucy	Paxton,	Administration,	16010
1870	Lucy	Fitchburg,	Will,	16011
1844	Lucy A.	Dudley,	Guardianship,	16012
1858	Lucy A.	Gardner,	Administration,	16013
1869	Lucy C.	Ashburnham,	Will,	16014
1877	Lucy C.	Worcester,	Administration,	16015
1801	Luther	Oxford,	Guardianship,	16016
1795	Lydia	Rutland,	Guardianship,	16017
1806	Lydia	Grafton,	Guardianship,	16018

Year.	Name.	Residence.	Nature.	Case.
1807	DAVIS, Lydia	Charlton,	Guardianship,	16019
1850	Lydia	Webster,	Guardianship,	16020
1853	Lydia	Harvard,	Will,	16021
1880	Lydia	Templeton,	Administration,	16022
1851	Lydia A.	Princeton,	Guardianship,	16023
1825	Lyman	Rutland,	Guardianship,	16024
1834	Lyman	Rutland,	Administration,	16025
1865	Malinda R.	Athol,	Will,	16026
1854	Marcia A.	Upton,	Administration,	16027
1761	Marcy	Rutland,	Guardianship,	16028
1855	Marcy	Paxton,	Will,	16029
1816	Maria	Princeton,	Guardianship,	16030
1878	Maria	Fitchburg,	Administration,	16031
1864	Maria L.	Oxford,	Guardianship,	16032
1841	Martha	Charlton,	Guardianship,	16033
1854	Martha	Northborough,	Will,	16034
1832	Martha A.	Hubbardston,	Guardianship,	16035
1851	Martha P.	Princeton,	Guardianship,	16036
1872	Martin	Sterling,	Will,	16037
1832	Marvin A.	Hubbardston,	Guardianship,	16038
1757	Mary	Grafton,	Guardianship,	16039
1800	Mary	Harvard,	Guardianship,	16040
1806	Mary	Holden,	Guardianship,	16041
1814	Mary	Oxford,	Guardianship,	16042
1825	Mary	Rutland,	Will,	16043
1826	Mary	Princeton,	Guardianship,	16044
1829	Mary	Upton,	Guardianship,	16045
1834	Mary	Oakham,	Will,	16046
1834	Mary	Oxford,	Guardianship,	16047
1853	Mary	Holden,	Adoption, etc.,	16048
1867	Mary	Oxford,	Will,	16049
1869	Mary	Templeton,	Administration,	16050
1869	Mary	Lancaster,	Will,	16051
1876	Mary	Milford,	Will,	16052
1880	Mary	Westborough,	Will,	16053
1822	Mary A.	Sturbridge,	Guardianship,	16054
1843	Mary A.	Holden,	Guardianship,	16055
1844	Mary A.	Webster,	Guardianship,	16056
1851	Mary A.	Princeton,	Guardianship,	16057
1875	Mary A.	Holden,	Will,	16058
1837	Mary E.	Ashburnham,	Guardianship,	16059
1843	Mary E.	Sterling,	Guardianship,	16060
1871	Mary E.	Lancaster,	Administration,	16061
1878	Mary F.	Paxton,	Administration,	16062
1875	Mary H. E.	Worcester,	Will,	16063

YEAR.	NAME.	RESIDENCE.	NATURE.	CASE.
1833	DAVIS, Mary J.	Oxford,	Guardianship,	16064
1875	Mary J.	Worcester,	Guardianship,	16065
1873	Mary L.	Northborough,	Guardianship,	16066
1838	Mary R.	West Boylston,	Guardianship,	16067
1842	Mary S.	West Boylston,	Guardianship,	16068
1783	Matilda	Charlton,	Guardianship,	16069
1811	Matilda	Falmouth,	Guardianship,	16070
1872	May Louise	Leominster,	Adoption, etc.,	16071
1847	Mehetable L.	Holden,	Will,	16072
1767	Mercy	Harvard,	Guardianship,	16073
1785	Micah	Princeton,	Administration,	16074
1790	Milley	Ashburnham,	Guardianship,	16075
1870	Miriam E.	Clinton,	Administration,	16076
1832	Moses	Hubbardston,	Guardianship,	16077
1871	Nabby	Ashburnham,	Will,	16078
1844	Nahum	Oxford,	Guardianship,	16079
1801	Nancy	Princeton,	Guardianship,	16080
1829	Nancy	Upton,	Guardianship,	16081
1869	Nancy A.	Brattleborough, Vt.,	Foreign Will,	16082
1811	Nathan	Brookfield,	Administration,	16083
1773	Nathaniel	Dudley,	Will,	16084
1784	Nathaniel	Dudley,	Guardianship,	16085
1801	Nathaniel	Oxford,	Guardianship,	16086
1850	Nathaniel	Oxford,	Administration,	16087
1821	Nehemiah	Oxford,	Administration,	16088
1822	Nehemiah	Oxford,	Guardianship,	16089
1868	Nelly V.	Worcester,	Guardianship,	16090
1767	Olive	Harvard,	Guardianship,	16091
1807	Olive	Princeton,	Administration,	16092
1873	Olive G.	Holden,	Will,	16093
1762	Oliver	Harvard,	Guardianship,	16094
1784	Oliver	Templeton,	Guardianship,	16095
1803	Oliver	Princeton,	Administration,	16096
1837	Oliver	Ashburnham,	Guardianship,	16097
1857	Oliver	Hubbardston,	Administration,	16098
1863	Orrin L.	Grafton,	Will,	16099
1822	Otis	Sturbridge,	Guardianship,	16100
1829	Otis	Upton,	Guardianship,	16101
1852	Otis	Upton,	Administration,	16102
1859	Otis	Lunenburg,	Will,	16103
1878	Otis	Sturbridge,	Administration,	16104
1880	Otis G.	Templeton,	Administration,	16105
1782	Parley	Dudley,	Guardianship,	16106
1789	Patience	Ashburnham,	Will,	16107
1835	Paul	Holden,	Will,	16108

YEAR.	NAME.	RESIDENCE.	NATURE.	CASE.
1864	DAVIS, Paul	Holden,	Administration,	16109
1735	Peter	Brookfield,	Guardianship,	16110
1767	Peter	Harvard,	Guardianship,	16111
1781	Peter	Rutland,	Administration,	16112
1782	Peter	Rutland,	Guardianship,	16113
1800	Peter	Rutland,	Guardianship,	16114
1800	Peter	Royalston,	Guardianship,	16115
1802	Peter	Rutland,	Administration,	16116
1855	Phebe	Holden,	Administration,	16117
1851	Philo F.	Princeton,	Guardianship,	16118
1762	Phineas	Mendon,	Administration,	16119
1822	Phineas	Milford,	Administration,	16120
1828	Phineas	Upton,	Administration,	16121
1838	Phineas A.	West Boylston,	Guardianship,	16122
1831	Phinehas	Harvard,	Will,	16123
1834	Phinehas	Northborough,	Will,	16124
1800	Polly	Rutland,	Guardianship,	16125
1803	Polly	Oxford,	Guardianship,	16126
1819	Polly	Milford,	Will,	16127
1827	Prince	Dudley,	Guardianship,	16128
1857	Prince	Webster,	Administration,	16129
1860	Rachel	Webster,	Administration,	16130
1757	Rebecca	Grafton,	Guardianship,	16131
1800	Rebecca	Rutland,	Guardianship,	16132
1843	Rebecca	Calais, Vt.,	Guardianship,	16133
1861	Rebecca	Harvard,	Administration,	16134
1861	Rebecca	Harvard,	Pension,	16135
1827	Relief	Holden,	Guardianship,	16136
1868	Relief	Paxton,	Administration,	16137
1857	Reuben	Bolton,	Administration,	16138
1860	Reuben	Dudley,	Administration,	16139
1863	Reuben	Oxford,	Administration,	16140
1781	Reubin	Charlton,	Administration,	16141
1783	Reubin	Charlton,	Guardianship,	16142
1876	Rhoda	Worcester,	Administration,	16143
1836	Richard T.	Leicester,	Guardianship,	16144
1849	Robert	Grafton,	Will,	16145
1869	Robert H.	Uxbridge,	Administration,	16146
1806	Roxana	Holden,	Guardianship,	16147
1877	Roxana	Worcester,	Administration,	16148
1833	Rufus	Dudley,	Administration,	16149
1879	Rufus	Princeton,	Administration,	16150
1865	Ruhamah	Holden,	Administration,	16151
1837	Ruhamy W.	Ashburnham,	Guardianship,	16152
1772	Ruth	Oxford,	Guardianship,	16153

Year.	Name.	Residence.	Nature.	Case.
1822	DAVIS, Ruth	Sturbridge,	Guardianship,	16154
1837	Ruth	Douglas,	Will,	16155
1876	Ruth	Princeton,	Administration,	16156
1855	Ruth M.	Douglas,	Guardianship,	16157
1838	Salem	Sutton,	Guardianship,	16158
1859	Salem	Charlton,	Administration,	16159
1871	Salem	Oxford,	Guardianship,	16160
1878	Salem	Oxford,	Administration,	16160
1860	Salem W.	Charlton,	Guardianship,	16161
1878	Sallie	Sterling,	Will,	16162
1783	Sally	Charlton,	Guardianship,	16163
1801	Sally	Princeton,	Guardianship,	16164
1815	Sally	Harvard,	Guardianship,	16165
1821	Sally	Templeton,	Guardianship,	16166
1826	Sally	Princeton,	Guardianship,	16167
1857	Sally	Worcester,	Administration,	16168
1844	Sally M.	Dudley,	Guardianship,	16169
1806	Salmon	Leverett,	Guardianship,	16170
1734	Samuel	Rutland,	Will,	16171
1760	Samuel	Oxford,	Administration,	16172
1760	Samuel	Brookfield,	Administration,	16173
1761	Samuel	Rutland,	Guardianship,	16174
1775	Samuel	Lunenburg,	Will,	16175
1800	Samuel	Princeton,	Administration,	16176
1800	Samuel	Rutland,	Administration,	16177
1817	Samuel	Oakham,	Will,	16178
1822	Samuel	Oxford,	Guardianship,	16179
1856	Samuel	Southbridge,	Administration,	16180
1881	Samuel	Oxford,	Administration,	16181
1845	Samuel G.	Templeton,	Will,	16182
1879	Samuel N.	Sturbridge,	Administration,	16183
1789	Sarah	Ward,	Administration,	16184
1825	Sarah	Rutland,	Guardianship,	16185
1829	Sarah	Upton,	Guardianship,	16186
1837	Sarah	Ashburnham,	Guardianship,	16187
1846	Sarah	Templeton,	Will,	16188
1843	Sarah A.	Princeton,	Guardianship,	16189
1879	Sarah M. G.	Rutland,	Administration,	16190
1861	Sarah U.	Dudley,	Guardianship,	16191
1785	Silas	Lunenburg,	Administration,	16192
1795	Silas	Templeton,	Administration,	16193
1798	Silas	Templeton,	Guardianship,	16194
1832	Silas	Hubbardston,	Administration,	16195
1837	Silas	Rutland,	Will,	16196
1880	Silas	Princeton,	Will,	16197

YEAR.	NAME.	RESIDENCE.	NATURE.	CASE.
1832	DAVIS, Silas S.	Hubbardston,	Guardianship,	16198
1754	Simon	Rutland,	Administration,	16199
1765	Simon	Rutland,	Guardianship,	16200
1828	Simon	Princeton,	Will,	16201
1843	Simon C.	Princeton,	Guardianship,	16202
1820	Solomon	Templeton,	Administration,	16203
1830	Solomon	Princeton,	Will,	16204
1867	Solomon	Spencer,	Will,	16205
1821	Solomon N.	Upton,	Guardianship,	16206
1846	Solomon W.	New Braintree,	Administration,	16207
1804	Sophia	Charlton,	Guardianship,	16208
1878	Sophronia G.	Princeton,	Will,	16209
1854	Squier	Royalston,	Pension,	16210
1876	Stella	Fitchburg,	Administration,	16211
1875	Stephen	Fitchburg,	Administration,	16212
1856	Stephen E.	Oxford,	Administration,	16213
1838	Stephen W.	West Boylston,	Guardianship,	16214
1847	Sumner	Templeton,	Administration,	16215
1847	Susan	Templeton,	Guardianship,	16216
1857	Susan E.	Southbridge,	Guardianship,	16217
1864	Susan L.	Phillipston,	Guardianship,	16218
1848	Susan P.	Oxford,	Guardianship,	16219
1790	Susanah	Ashburnham,	Guardianship,	16220
1813	Susanna	Oxford,	Administration,	16221
1851	Susanna	Athol,	Will,	16222
1801	Susannah	Oxford,	Guardianship,	16223
1827	Susannah	Dudley,	Guardianship,	16224
1843	Sylvanus	Douglas,	Guardianship,	16225
1879	Tamma	Royalston,	Administration,	16226
1857	Theodotia	Brookfield,	Will,	16227
1778	Thomas	Oxford,	Administration,	16228
1800	Thomas	Harvard,	Administration,	16229
1806	Thomas	Wendell,	Guardianship,	16230
1832	Thomas	Sutton,	Administration,	16231
1834	Thomas, 2d	Oxford,	Guardianship,	16232
1843	Thomas	Sterling,	Guardianship,	16233
1844	Thomas	Lancaster,	Pension,	16234
1854	Thomas	Templeton,	Change of Name,	16235
1838	Thomas B.	West Boylston,	Administration,	16236
1842	Thomas B.	West Boylston,	Guardianship,	16237
1857	Thomas J.	Holden,	Will,	16238
1854	Thomas W.	Templeton,	Change of Name,	16239
1821	Timothy	Oxford,	Administration,	16240
1847	Tryphosa	Templeton,	Guardianship,	16241
1862	Viola	Webster,	Guardianship,	16242

YEAR.	NAME.	RESIDENCE.	NATURE.	CASE.
1830	DAVIS, Walter	Gardner,	Guardianship,	16243
1847	Walter A.	Fitchburg,	Guardianship,	16244
1877	Walter W.	Rutland,	Administration,	16245
1863	Ward	Worcester,	Will,	16246
1843	Warren	Sterling,	Guardianship,	16247
1879	Washburn	Harvard,	Will,	16248
1821	Washington	Templeton,	Guardianship,	16249
1834	Willard	Oxford,	Administration,	16250
1774	William	Oxford,	Guardianship,	16251
1777	William	Oxford,	Will,	16251
1833	William	Harvard,	Pension,	16252
1842	William	Holden,	Administration,	16253
1843	William	Sterling,	Guardianship,	16254
1875	William	Fitchburg,	Guardianship,	16255
1837	William E.	Northborough,	Will,	16256
1854	William F.	Rutland,	Administration,	16257
1871	William F.	Oxford,	Guardianship,	16258
1881	William L.	Millbury,	Guardianship,	16259
1849	William R.	Leicester,	Administration,	16260
1838	William S.	Northborough,	Guardianship,	16261
1852	William W.	Warren,	Will,	16262
1877	William W.	Rutland,	Will,	16263
1842	Winslow	Gardner,	Administration,	16264
1771	Zadock	Harvard,	Administration,	16265
1790	Zadock	Ashburnham,	Guardianship,	16266
1843	Zillah	Holden,	Will,	16267
	DAVISON see DAVIDSON.			
	DAW see DORR.			
1873	DAWES, Ellen E.	Nashua,	Guardianship,	16268
1853	DAWLESS, George Y.	Sterling,	Guardianship,	16269
1881	Maria S.	Worcester,	Will,	16270
1853	William H.	Sterling,	Guardianship,	16271
1856	DAWLEY, Daniel W.	Grafton,	Guardianship,	16272
1864	John O.	Northbridge,	Guardianship,	16273
1858	Mary A.	Grafton,	Administration,	16274
1854	William P.	Grafton,	Administration,	16275
1881	DAWSON, John	Worcester,	Will,	16276
1829	DAY, Aaron	Sutton,	Administration,	16277
1880	Abba	Uxbridge,	Will,	16278
1867	Abbie W.	Royalston,	Guardianship,	16279
1781	Abigail	Mendon,	Guardianship,	16280
1881	Abigail	Gardner,	Administration,	16281
1867	Alice	Royalston,	Guardianship,	16282
1878	Alice	Fitchburg,	Administration,	16283
1865	Almira	Templeton,	Sale Real Estate,	16284

YEAR.	NAME.	RESIDENCE.	NATURE.	CASE.
1858	DAY, Almira A.	Royalston,	Guardianship,	16285
1853	Ambrey	Templeton,	Pension,	16286
1877	Amelia J.	Royalston,	Guardianship,	16287
1837	Ann E.	Dudley,	Guardianship,	16288
1848	Asa	Leominster,	Will,	16289
1872	Benjamin F.	Winchendon,	Administration,	16290
1864	Catharine	Milford,	Guardianship,	16291
1852	Chauncey N.	Winchendon,	Will,	16292
1869	Cromwell	Fitchburg,	Administration,	16293
1781	Daniel	Mendon,	Guardianship,	16294
1782	Daniel	Winchendon,	Guardianship,	16295
1850	Daniel	Uxbridge,	Administration,	16296
1851	Daniel	Winchendon,	Administration,	16297
1852	Daniel	Northbridge,	Administration,	16298
1853	Daniel P.	Northbridge,	Guardianship,	16299
1792	David	Oxford,	Guardianship,	16300
1792	David	Oxford,	Will,	16301
1876	David	Oxford,	Trustee,	16302
1841	David W.	Gardner,	Administration,	16303
1877	David W.	Royalston,	Administration,	16304
1792	Ebenezer	Oxford,	Guardianship,	16305
1872	Ebenezer A.	Webster,	Administration,	16306
1874	Edwin H.	Winchendon,	Guardianship,	16307
1782	Elizabeth	Winchendon,	Guardianship,	16308
1848	Ellen M.	Leominster,	Guardianship,	16309
1857	Emily A.	Paxton,	Guardianship,	16310
1828	Eunice	Worcester,	Will,	16311
1852	Eunice	Paxton,	Administration,	16312
1880	Eva L.	Berlin,	Adoption, etc.,	16313
1781	Ezekiel	Mendon,	Guardianship,	16314
1852	Ezekiel	Winchendon,	Administration,	16315
1792	Fisher	Oxford,	Guardianship,	16316
1855	Frances E.	Millbury,	Adoption, etc.,	16317
1880	Fred W.	Templeton,	Guardianship,	16318
1875	Frederick L.	Dudley,	Guardianship,	16319
1862	George	Worcester,	Administration,	16320
1875	George	Dudley,	Guardianship,	16321
1836	George A.	Worcester,	Administration,	16322
1864	George F. P.	Fitchburg,	Guardianship,	16323
1877	George L.	Royalston,	Guardianship,	16324
1877	Gilman	Templeton,	Will,	16325
1857	Harriet M. W.	Paxton,	Guardianship,	16326
1873	Hiel	Oxford,	Will,	16327
1781	Hopestill	Mendon,	Guardianship,	16328
1857	Ira	Royalston,	Administration,	16329

Year.	Name.	Residence.	Nature.	Case.
1870	DAY, Isaac	Southborough,	Will,	16330
1847.	Jabez	Webster,	Will,	16331
1854	James	Paxton,	Administration,	16332
1878	James W.	Uxbridge,	Administration,	16333
1780	Jane	Dudley,	Administration,	16334
1781	Joanna	Mendon,	Guardianship,	16335
1821	John	Templeton,	Administration,	16336
1864	John	Milford,	Guardianship,	16337
1870	John	Barre,	Guardianship,	16338
1836	John E.	Dudley,	Administration,	16339
1837	John E. P.	Dudley,	Guardianship,	16340
1849	John J.	Worcester,	Administration,	16341
1792	Jonathan	Oxford,	Guardianship,	16342
1802	Jonathan	Oxford,	Will,	16343
1809	Jonathan	Oxford,	Administration,	16344
1819	Jonathan	Dudley,	Administration,	16345
1777	Joseph	Mendon,	Administration,	16346
1817	Joseph	Paxton,	Will,	16347
1853	Joseph	Winchendon,	Administration,	16348
1866	Joseph	Uxbridge,	Will,	16349
1864	Leonard	Fitchburg,	Administration,	16350
1863	Leonard S.	Hubbardston,	Administration,	16351
1853	Lewis P.	Northbridge,	Guardianship,	16352
1875	Lucien H.	Dudley,	Administration,	16353
1782	Lydia	Winchendon,	Guardianship,	16354
1867	Lyman	Warren,	Administration,	16355
1857	Marion E.	Paxton,	Guardianship,	16356
1760	Mary	Dudley,	Guardianship,	16357
1830	Mary	Paxton,	Administration,	16358
1841	Mary A.	Gardner,	Guardianship,	16359
1858	Mary A.	Royalston,	Guardianship,	16360
1864	Mary A.	Sutton,	Administration,	16361
1837	Mary J.	Dudley,	Guardianship,	16362
1869	Michael	Westminster,	Administration,	16363
1870	Michael D.	Worcester,	Guardianship,	16364
1877	Minnie E.	Royalston,	Guardianship,	16365
1865	Moses	Upton,	Administration,	16366
1874	Nabby T.	Hubbardston,	Administration,	16367
1850	Nathan	Warren,	Will,	16368
1872	Nettie E.	Worcester,	Guardianship,	16369
1811	Orrin E.	Oxford,	Guardianship,	16370
1877	Preston	Oakham,	Will,	16371
1876	Rebecca	Oxford,	Will,	16372
1876	Rebecca	Oxford,	Trustee,	16373
1774	Richard	Winchendon,	Administration,	16374

(377)

YEAR.	NAME.	RESIDENCE.	NATURE.	CASE.
1864	DAY, Richard	Milford,	Guardianship,	16375
1877	Sally	Millbury,	Will,	16376
1864	Sarah C.	Ashburnham,	Administration,	16377
1880	Sewell	Lancaster,	Will,	16378
1853	Susan F.	Northbridge,	Guardianship,	16379
1848	Susan P.	Fitchburg,	Guardianship,	16380
1782	Susannah	Winchendon,	Guardianship,	16381
1872	Thankful	Charlton,	Will,	16382
1867	Uri	Royalston,	Administration,	16383
1863	Uri C.	Royalston,	Guardianship,	16384
1874	Walter E.	Winchendon,	Guardianship,	16385
1880	Walter L.	Templeton,	Guardianship,	16386
1859	William F.	Templeton,	Will,	16387
1879	William F.	Fitchburg,	Will,	16388
1852	Zebina	Sutton,	Will,	16389
1873	DAYTON, Emma	New Lisbon, Wis.,	Guardianship,	16390
1873	(Name not given)	Fitchburg,	Adoption, etc.,	16391
1845	DEALING, Henry S.	Southbridge,	Guardianship,	16392
1850	Sarah	Southbridge,	Administration,	16393
	DEAN AND DEANE,			
1861	Abbie	Oakham,	Guardianship,	16394
1830	Abiel	North Brookfield,	Will,	16395
1863	Abigail	Rutland,	Guardianship,	16396
1845	Alpheus	Sutton,	Administration,	16397
1862	Andrew J.	Fitchburg,	Guardianship,	16398
1774	Asa	Hardwick,	Guardianship,	16399
1851	Asahel B.	Oakham,	Guardianship,	16400
1856	Baloh	Worcester,	Will,	16401
1857	Blake	Oakham,	Will,	16402
1803	Calvin	Brookfield,	Guardianship,	16403
1812	Calvin	Uxbridge,	Administration,	16404
1844	Calvin	North Brookfield,	Administration,	16405
1868	Charles	New York, N. Y.,	Administration,	16406
1848	Charles B.	Hardwick,	Guardianship,	16407
1880	Charles B.	Worcester,	Administration,	16408
1844	Charles I.	Sutton,	Administration,	16409
1864	Charles S.	Oakham,	Guardianship,	16410
1880	Charlotte C.	Milford,	Administration,	16411
1861	Daniel	Oakham,	Guardianship,	16412
1848	David A.	Hardwick,	Administration,	16413
1866	David B.	Coventry, Conn.,	Administration,	16414
1868	Delia M.	Milford,	Administration,	16415
1865	Edmund	Oakham,	Administration,	16416
1858	Edward S.	Rutland,	Administration,	16417
1851	Elijah C.	Oakham,	Guardianship,	16418

Year.	Name.	Residence.	Nature.	Case.
	DEAN and DEANE,			
1872	Etta L.	Worcester,	Guardianship,	16419
1874	Etta L.	Worcester,	Administration,	16420
1851	Fanny C.	Oakham,	Guardianship,	16421
1851	Francis	Fitchburg,	Will,	16422
1851	George W.	Oakham,	Guardianship,	16423
1851	Hannah R.	Oakham,	Guardianship,	16424
1855	Hiram	Rutland,	Guardianship,	16425
1857	Horatio	Warren,	Will,	16426
1802	Isaiah	Spencer,	Administration,	16427
1861	Isaiah	Oakham,	Guardianship,	16428
1812	James	Oakham,	Will,	16429
1868	James	Oakham,	Will,	16430
1881	Jeremiah	Worcester,	Will,	16431
1851	John, 2d	Oakham,	Administration,	16432
1868	John	Warren,	Will,	16433
1861	John L.	Oakham,	Guardianship,	16434
1814	Lucy	Oakham,	Guardianship,	16435
1854	Lurana	Oakham,	Guardianship,	16436
1867	Martha	Worcester,	Administration,	16437
1867	Martin	Worcester,	Administration,	16438
1862	Mary A.	Fitchburg,	Guardianship,	16439
1872	Mary E.	Worcester,	Administration,	16440
1854	Merrick S. P.	Rutland,	Administration,	16441
1774	Molly	Hardwick,	Guardianship,	16442
1774	Nathaniel	Hardwick,	Guardianship,	16443
1822	Nathaniel	Shrewsbury,	Will,	16444
1874	Nellie D.	Dudley,	Adoption, etc.,	16445
1844	Olive M.	Sutton,	Guardianship,	16446
1875	Oliver	Milford,	Administration,	16447
1767	Paul	Hardwick,	Administration,	16448
1828	Paul	Hardwick,	Will,	16449
1855	Perrin	Rutland,	Guardianship,	16450
1774	Phebe	Hardwick,	Guardianship,	16451
1835	Rebeccah	Warren,	Administration,	16452
1774	Robert	Hardwick,	Guardianship,	16453
1810	Salmon	Brookfield,	Administration,	16454
1861	Samuel R.	Oakham,	Guardianship,	16455
1774	Sarah	Hardwick,	Guardianship,	16456
1774	Seth	Hardwick,	Guardianship,	16457
1833	Stephen	Barre,	Administration,	16458
1862	Sullivan	Oakham,	Administration,	16459
1855	William	Rutland,	Guardianship,	16460
1881	DEARTH, Luther S.	Boylston,	Administration,	16461
1786	DEATH, Asa	Templeton,	Guardianship,	16462

YEAR.	NAME.	RESIDENCE.	NATURE.	CASE.
1777	DEATH, John	Templeton,	Administration,	16463
1788	John	Gerry,	Guardianship,	16464
	DeBLOIS AND DEBLOIS,			
1875	Marie	West Brookfield,	Will,	16465
1880	Oliver	Southbridge,	Will,	16466
1878	Petronille	Southbridge,	Will,	16467
1873	DECELLES, Paul	Sturbridge,	Administration,	16468
1875	DEE, Alice R.	Westborough,	Guardianship,	16469
1870	Ellen S.	West Boylston,	Administration,	16470
1875	Honora	Westborough,	Guardianship,	16471
1875	Katie	Westborough,	Guardianship,	16472
1875	Mary A.	Westborough,	Guardianship,	16473
1875	Matthew S.	Westborough,	Guardianship,	16474
1875	William	Westborough,	Administration,	16475
1874	DEERY, Catharine	Worcester,	Guardianship,	16476
1874	James	Worcester,	Guardianship,	16477
1874	James	Worcester,	Administration,	16478
1874	John	Worcester,	Guardianship,	16479
1881	Mary	Worcester,	Will,	16480
1874	Mary E.	Worcester,	Guardianship,	16481
1874	Peter	Worcester,	Guardianship,	16482
1851	DEETS, Lucretia S.	Douglas,	Guardianship,	16483
1870	DEFOE, Almira	Shrewsbury,	Adoption, etc.,	16484
1870	Charles	Shrewsbury,	Adoption, etc.,	16485
1873	DEGAN, Ann	Blackstone,	Guardianship,	16486
1873	Charles E.	Blackstone,	Guardianship,	16487
1873	Ellen	Blackstone,	Guardianship,	16488
1873	Fred	Blackstone,	Guardianship,	16489
1873	James	Blackstone,	Guardianship,	16490
1873	John	Blackstone,	Guardianship,	16491
1873	John	Blackstone,	Administration,	16492
1873	Mary J.	Blackstone,	Guardianship,	16493
1873	Thomas	Blackstone,	Guardianship,	16494
1873	William	Blackstone,	Guardianship,	16495
1862	DELAHANTY, John	Templeton,	Will,	16496
1880	Mary A.	Worcester,	Administration,	16497
	DeLAND AND DELAND,			
1881	Armit B.	Warren,	Administration,	16498
1881	Carrie E.	Warren,	Guardianship,	16499
1851	Charles M.	Worcester,	Administration,	16500
1799	Daniel	Brookfield,	Guardianship,	16501
1873	Esther B.	Worcester,	Will,	16502
1853	George W.	Worcester,	Guardianship,	16503
1879	Henry	North Brookfield,	Will,	16504
1827	Jedediah	North Brookfield,	Administration,	16505

Year.	Name.	Residence.	Nature.	Case.
	DeLAND and DELAND,			
1870	John	North Brookfield,	Administration,	16506
1865	John H.	North Brookfield,	Administration,	16507
1853	Miriam	North Brookfield,	Will,	16508
1834	Persis	North Brookfield,	Will,	16509
1847	Philip	North Brookfield,	Will,	16510
	DELANEY and DELANY,			
1873	Bridget	Worcester,	Administration,	16511
1824	Cyrus	Shrewsbury,	Guardianship,	16512
1850	Cyrus	Worcester,	Administration,	16513
1863	Cyrus E.	Worcester,	Administration,	16514
1865	Dennis	Worcester,	Administration,	16515
1872	Michael	Worcester,	Will,	16516
1879	Patrick	Putnam, Conn.,	Administration,	16517
1867	DELANO, Chancey O.	Hubbardston,	Administration,	16518
1861	Henry A.	New Braintree,	Will,	16519
1757	Jonathan	New Braintree,	Will,	16520
1881	Louisa W.	New Braintree,	Will,	16521
1834	Philip	New Braintree,	Administration,	16522
1835	Philip	New Braintree,	Pension,	16523
	DELANY see DELANEY.			
1872	DELAY, Margaret	Gardner,	Will,	16524
1855	DELON, Mary A.	Boston,	Adoption, etc.,	16525
1872	DELVEY, Arthur N.	Spencer,	Guardianship,	16526
1872	Chester W.	Spencer,	Guardianship,	16527
1872	Ruth E.	Spencer,	Guardianship,	16528
1873	DEMARY, Mary A.	Lunenburg,	Administration,	16529
1828	DEMOND, Asa	Rutland,	Administration,	16530
1849	Daniel	Rutland,	Administration,	16531
1824	Elijah	Rutland,	Will,	16532
1877	Elijah	Westborough,	Will,	16533
1826	Harriet S.	Rutland,	Guardianship,	16534
1864	Lucy B.	Westborough,	Administration,	16535
1866	Miles	Rutland,	Administration,	16536
1847	Minerva	Worcester,	Guardianship,	16537
1828	Nathaniel L.	Rutland,	Guardianship,	16538
1847	Philinda	Worcester,	Guardianship,	16539
1828	Sullivan	Rutland,	Guardianship,	16540
1785	DENESON, James	Sturbridge,	Will,	16541
1880	DENETTE, Margaret	Webster,	Will,	16542
1763	DENING, George	Mendon,	Administration,	16543
1873	DENNEHEY, Mary	Worcester,	Administration,	16544
	DENNIE see DENNY.			
1845	DENNIS, Adonijah	Hardwick,	Will,	16545
1881	Adonijah	Hardwick,	Will,	16546

Year.	Name.	Residence.	Nature.	Case.
1787	DENNIS, Benjamin,	Charlton,	Administration,	16547
1838	Charlotte M.	Barre,	Guardianship,	16548
1785	David	Hardwick,	Guardianship,	16549
1796	David	Hardwick,	Administration,	16550
1860	David N.	Grafton,	Guardianship,	16551
1827	Dorothy	Barre,	Will,	16552
1838	Dorothy	Petersham,	Guardianship,	16553
1839	Ebenezer	Barre,	Administration,	16554
1837	Ebenezer R.	Petersham,	Administration,	16555
1867	Edward P.	Grafton,	Will,	16556
1845	Edward S.	Millbury,	Administration,	16557
1841	Elliot	Barre,	Administration,	16558
1860	Emma E.	Petersham,	Guardianship,	16559
1870	Emma E.	Petersham,	Administration,	16560
1878	Erasmus	Worcester,	Administration,	16561
1875	Eunice S.	Hardwick,	Administration,	16562
1838	Harriet H.	Petersham,	Guardianship,	16563
1860	Hattie E.	Petersham,	Guardianship,	16564
1870	Hattie E.	Petersham,	Administration,	16565
1866	Holmes	Marlborough, N. J.,	Guardianship,	16566
1838	Huldah A.	Petersham,	Guardianship,	16567
1785	Isaac	Hardwick,	Guardianship,	16568
1845	James T.	Millbury,	Adoption, ship,	16569
1816	Jonah	Charlton,	Administration,	16570
1802	Jonathan	Charlton,	Will,	16571
1816	Jonathan	Charlton,	Administration,	16572
1871	Joseph H.	Worcester,	Administration,	16573
1869	Julia M.	Barre,	Guardianship,	16574
1869	Keziah	Barre,	Administration,	16575
1860	Lot	Petersham,	Administration,	16576
1860	Lot	Petersham,	Guardianship,	16577
1866	Margaret	Marlborough, N. J.,	Guardianship,	16578
1877	Martha E.	Westborough,	Will,	16579
1807	Mehitable	Charlton,	Administration,	16580
1788	Nathan	Dudley,	Administration,	16581
1785	Patience	Hardwick,	Guardianship,	16582
1785	Polly	Hardwick,	Guardianship,	16583
1839	Reuben	Charlton,	Administration,	16584
1865	Rodney G.	Southborough,	Will,	16585
1783	Samuel	Hardwick,	Administration,	16586
1785	Samuel	Hardwick,	Guardianship,	16587
1809	Thomas	Barre,	Administration,	16588
1838	Thomas	Barre,	Administration,	16589
1838	Willard	Barre,	Guardianship,	16590

YEAR.	NAME.	RESIDENCE.	NATURE.	CASE.
	DENNY AND DENNIE,			
1816	Adeline	Leicester,	Guardianship,	16591
1833	Amelia	Worcester,	Trustee,	16592
1830	Austin	Worcester,	Administration,	16593
1831	Austin G.	Worcester,	Guardianship,	16594
1859	Caroline	Worcester,	Will,	16595
1831	Caroline A.	Worcester,	Guardianship,	16596
1864	Caroline F.	Holden,	Administration,	16597
1825	Catharine	Leicester,	Guardianship,	16598
1810	Charles	Leicester,	Guardianship,	16599
1829	Charles	Leicester,	Administration,	16600
1856	Charles E.	Spencer,	Will,	16601
1823	Christopher C.	Leicester,	Guardianship,	16602
1760	Daniel	Leicester,	Will,	16603
1822	Daniel	Worcester,	Administration,	16604
1833	Daniel	Boston,	Trustee,	16605
1831	Daniel B.	Worcester,	Guardianship,	16606
1851	Desire B.	Oakham,	Will,	16607
1874	Edward	Barre,	Administration,	16608
1819	Edward W.	Leicester,	Guardianship,	16609
1852	Edward W.	Westborough,	Guardianship,	16610
1865	E. Y., M. W.	Worcester,	Will,	16611
1819	ON, Mar.	Leicester,	Guardianship,	16612
1823	Elizabeth H.	Leicester,	Guardianship,	16613
1852	George	Westborough,	Will,	16614
1831	George E.	Worcester,	Guardianship,	16615
1823	Harriet	Worcester,	Guardianship,	16616
1823	Harriet F.	Leicester,	Guardianship,	16617
1823	Henry A.	Leicester,	Guardianship,	16618
1819	Isaac	North Brookfield,	Guardianship,	16619
1852	James H.	Westborough,	Guardianship,	16620
1802	John	Worcester,	Administration,	16621
1862	John	Southborough,	Guardianship,	16622
1810	John A.	Leicester,	Guardianship,	16623
1865	John A.	Leicester,	Administration,	16624
1822	Joseph	Leicester,	Administration,	16625
1823	Joseph A.	Leicester,	Guardianship,	16626
1875	Joseph A.	Leicester,	Will,	16627
1862	Josephine J.	Southborough,	Guardianship,	16628
1825	Julian	Leicester,	Guardianship,	16629
1819	Laura A.	Leicester,	Guardianship,	16630
1823	Lucinda II.	Leicester,	Guardianship,	16631
1858	Lucretia	Leicester,	Will,	16632
1776	Mary	Leicester,	Guardianship,	16633
1810	Mary	Leicester,	Guardianship,	16634

DENNY and DENNIE,

Year	Name	Residence	Nature	Case
1811	Mary	Leicester,	Will,	16635
1852	Mary H.	Westborough,	Guardianship,	16636
1864	Nancy	Lunenburg,	Will,	16637
1857	Nathaniel P.	Barre,	Will,	16638
1879	Nellie M.	Worcester,	Guardianship,	16639
1823	Phebe H.	Leicester,	Guardianship,	16640
1816	Phineas S.	Leicester,	Guardianship,	16641
1825	Rachel	Leicester,	Guardianship,	16642
1878	Reubin S.	Leicester,	Administration,	16643
1852	Robert B.	Westborough,	Guardianship,	16644
1816	Sally	Leicester,	Guardianship,	16645
1803	Samuel	Worcester,	Guardianship,	16646
1817	Samuel	Leicester,	Will,	16647
1832	Samuel	Oakham,	Will,	16648
1816	Sarah	Leicester,	Will,	16649
1823	Sarah H.	Leicester,	Guardianship,	16650
1776	Tamesin	Leicester,	Guardianship,	16651
1774	Thomas	Leicester,	Administration,	16652
1776	Thomas	Leicester,	Guardianship,	16653
1814	Thomas	Leicester,	Will,	16654
1851	Thomas	Barre,	Administration,	16655
1825	William	Leicester,	Guardianship,	16656
1851	William	North Brookfield,	Will,	16657

DENSMORE see DINSMORE.

Year	Name	Residence	Nature	Case
1868	DENTON, Eugene C.	Fitchburg,	Guardianship,	16658
1868	Stephen E.	Fitchburg,	Administration,	16659
1856	DEPUTRIN, Rebecca	Fitchburg,	Will,	16660

DERBY (see also DARBY),

Year	Name	Residence	Nature	Case
1880	Abigail K.	Westminster,	Will,	16661
1852	Alden W.	Leominster,	Guardianship,	16662
1865	Almond	Westminster,	Will,	16663
1869	Augusta	Leominster,	Guardianship,	16664
1870	A. Sidney	Leominster,	Guardianship,	16665
1823	Ezra	Westminster,	Administration,	16666
1880	Gilbert	Leominster,	Will,	16667
1877	Haskell	Leominster,	Will,	16668
1870	Henry	Leominster,	Administration,	16669
1827	John	Westminster,	Administration,	16670
1852	Josiah	Leominster,	Administration,	16671
1876	Josiah	Ashburnham,	Administration,	16672
1852	Julia A.	Leominster,	Guardianship,	16673
1874	Julia A.	Leominster,	Administration,	16674
1851	Leander	Leominster,	Administration,	16675
1869	Lizzie C.	Leominster,	Guardianship,	16676

YEAR.	NAME.	RESIDENCE.	NATURE.	CASE.
	DERBY (see also DARBY),			
1869	Mary L.	Leominster,	Guardianship,	16677
1851	Milo	Ashburnham,	Administration,	16678
1823	Nathan	Westminster,	Guardianship,	16679
1823	Orrin	Westminster,	Guardianship,	16680
1851	Phebe G.	Westminster,	Administration,	16681
1866	Polly	Leominster,	Administration,	16682
1845	Reuben A.	Leominster,	Guardianship,	16683
1872	Sally H.	Leominster,	Administration,	16684
1870	Sarah E.	Leominster,	Guardianship,	16685
1873	DERMODY, Martin	Spencer,	Will,	16686
1872	DERNIER, Martha A.	Worcester,	Administration,	16687
1873	DESAUTELL, Simeon	Milford,	Will,	16688
1863	DESMOND, Timothy	Milford,	Will,	16689
	DESPEAU AND DISPEAU,			
1834	Joseph	Grafton,	Will,	16690
1855	Mary	Grafton,	Will,	16691
1867	DEVERAUX, Anthony	Worcester,	Will,	16692
1877	Margaret	Worcester,	Will,	16693
1877	Margaret	Worcester,	Guardianship,	16694
1868	DEVERE, Emma J.	Moline, Ill.,	Guardianship,	16695
1881	DEVINE, Daniel T.	Milford,	Guardianship,	16696
1875	James	Fitchburg,	Administration,	16697
1877	James	Westborough,	Administration,	16698
1877	James W.	Westborough,	Guardianship,	16699
1881	Jane L.	Milford,	Guardianship,	16700
1877	John	Westborough,	Guardianship,	16701
1877	Lizzie	Westborough,	Guardianship,	16702
1877	Margaret A.	Westborough,	Guardianship,	16703
1877	Mary	Westborough,	Guardianship,	16704
1877	Patrick J.	Worcester,	Administration,	16705
1877	Thomas P.	Westborough,	Guardianship,	16706
1873	DEVITT, Michael	Worcester,	Administration,	16707
1875	DEVLIN, Patrick	Northbridge,	Will,	16708
1760	DEW, Thomas	Brookfield,	Administration,	16709
1840	DEWEY, Amasa	Petersham,	Administration,	16710
1861	Charles	Millbury,	Administration,	16711
1874	Franklin	Worcester,	Guardianship,	16712
1853	Marcia	Worcester,	Will,	16713
1840	Mary E.	Petersham,	Guardianship,	16714
1878	DEWHURST, William	Winchendon,	Administration,	16715
1852	DEWING, Abby A.	Worcester,	Guardianship,	16716
1852	Alonzo F.	Worcester,	Guardianship,	16717
1852	Charles P.	Worcester,	Guardianship,	16718
1871	Cheney	North Brookfield,	Will,	16719

YEAR.	NAME.	RESIDENCE.	NATURE.	CASE.
1865	DEWING, Clara A.	North Brookfield,	Guardianship,	16720
1880	Ebenezer	Revere,	Partition,	16721
1864	Elijah	Mendon,	Will,	16722
1865	Emma A.	North Brookfield,	Guardianship,	16723
1875	Emma A.	North Brookfield,	Will,	16724
1829	Eunice B.	North Brookfield,	Administration,	16725
1865	Gideon B.	North Brookfield,	Administration,	16726
1873	Harriet N.	North Brookfield,	Will,	16727
1876	Jeremiah	North Brookfield,	Administration,	16728
1863	John F.	North Brookfield,	Administration,	16729
1812	Samuel	North Brookfield,	Administration,	16730
1859	DeWITT, Alexander	Oxford,	Guardianship,	16731
1879	Alexander	Oxford,	Will,	16732
1875	Asenath F.	Shrewsbury,	Administration,	16733
1871	Hannah	Oxford,	Administration,	16734
1853	Hollis	Oxford,	Will,	16735
1852	Horace S.	Oxford,	Change of Name,	16736
1859	Horace S.	Oxford,	Administration,	16737
1869	Mary M.	Oxford,	Guardianship,	16738
1848	Stearns	Oxford,	Administration,	16739
	DeWOLF and D'WOLF,			
1879	Ellen C.	Spencer,	Will,	16740
1865	Henrietta M.	Upton,	Will,	16741
1828	DEXTER, Abigail	Hardwick,	Will,	16742
1863	Albert H.	Hardwick,	Guardianship,	16743
1817	Arathusa	Hardwick,	Guardianship,	16744
1792	Benjamin	Hardwick,	Administration,	16745
1797	Betsey	Hardwick,	Guardianship,	16746
1881	Calvin M.	West Boylston,	Guardianship,	16747
1838	Charity	Hardwick,	Will,	16748
1863	Charles E.	Hardwick,	Guardianship,	16749
1863	Clara L.	Hardwick,	Guardianship,	16750
1773	Daniel	Athol,	Guardianship,	16751
1850	Ebenezer	Leominster,	Will,	16752
1862	Edward	Hardwick,	Will,	16753
1817	Eleazer	Hardwick,	Guardianship,	16754
1817	Eleazer	————	Pension,	16755
1860	E. Wheeler	Royalston,	Administration,	16756
1855	George A.	Bolton,	Guardianship,	16757
1851	George T.	Hardwick,	Guardianship,	16758
1851	Harriet J.	Hardwick,	Guardianship,	16759
1849	Henry H.	Barre,	Guardianship,	16760
1880	Henry H.	West Boylston,	Administration,	16761
1836	Henry W.	Hardwick,	Guardianship,	16762
1836	Horace	Hardwick,	Guardianship,	16763

YEAR.	NAME.	RESIDENCE.	NATURE.	CASE.
1797	DEXTER, Ichabod	Hardwick,	Administration,	16764
1851	Ichabod	Hardwick,	Will,	16765
1854	James M.	Bolton,	Administration,	16766
1827	Jedediah	Hardwick,	Administration,	16767
1811	Jesse	Upton,	Will,	16768
1849	Job	Barre,	Administration,	16769
1836	John	Hardwick,	Will,	16770
1837	John	Leominster,	Administration,	16771
1867	John B.	Worcester,	Will,	16772
1864	John B., Jr.	Worcester,	Administration,	16773
1817	Joseph D.	Hardwick,	Guardianship,	16774
1868	Lewis	Smithfield, R. I.,	Foreign Will,	16775
1837	Lucy	Hardwick,	Guardianship,	16776
1828	Luthera	Hardwick,	Guardianship,	16777
1797	Lydia	Hardwick,	Guardianship,	16778
1881	Minnie E.	West Boylston,	Guardianship,	16779
1846	Nathan	Charlton,	Administration,	16780
1846	Nathan	Charlton,	Pension,	16781
1820	Peter	Worcester,	Will,	16782
1844	Richard	Malden,	Guardianship,	16783
1798	Sally	Marlborough,	Guardianship,	16784
1828	Sally	Hardwick,	Guardianship,	16785
1811	Samuel	Mendon,	Will,	16786
1828	Samuel, 2d	Hardwick,	Guardianship,	16787
1861	Samuel	Hardwick,	Will,	16788
1844	Samuel G.	Malden,	Guardianship,	16789
1855	Sarah E.	Bolton,	Guardianship,	16790
1810	Simeon	Royalston,	Will,	16791
1817	Thankful	Hardwick,	Guardianship,	16792
1817	Willard	Hardwick,	Guardianship.	16793
1798	William	Marlborough,	Guardianship,	16794
1804	William	Leominster,	Administration,	16795
1836	William	Hardwick,	Administration,	16796
1863	Willie H.	Hardwick,	Guardianship,	16797
1851	Zenas H.	Hardwick,	Will,	16798
1851	Zenas H.	Hardwick,	Guardianship,	16799
1879	DICKENS, Charles H.	Worcester,	Guardianship,	16800
	DICKENSON see DICKINSON.			
	DICKEY AND DICKY,			
1769	David	Rutland,	Administration,	16801
1850	James	Sterling,	Pension,	16802
1857	Lydia	Webster,	Guardianship,	16803
1875	Sarah H.	Worcester,	Administration,	16804
	DICKINSON AND DICKENSON,			
1871	Adeline B.	Providence, R. I.,	Administration,	16805

Year.	Name.	Residence.	Nature.	Case.
	DICKINSON and DICKENSON,			
1788	Amos	Ashburnham,	Administration,	16806
1873	Betsey S.	Gardner,	Administration,	16807
1875	Caroline	Templeton,	Will,	16808
1865	Charles L.	Spencer,	Guardianship,	16809
1852	Daniel H.	Harvard,	Guardianship,	16810
1822	David	Petersham,	Administration,	16811
1851	Edward T.	Deerfield,	Guardianship,	16812
1813	Elizabeth	West Boylston,	Guardianship,	16813
1839	Elizabeth	Worcester,	Guardianship,	16814
1874	Ella E.	Fitchburg,	Guardianship,	16815
1873	Esther	Barre,	Will,	16816
1863	Eudora A.	Gardner,	Guardianship,	16817
1823	Francis	Harvard,	Will,	16918
1839	Frederick	Worcester,	Guardianship,	16819
1851	Frederick	Deerfield,	Guardianship,	16820
1865	George S.	Spencer,	Guardianship,	16821
1861	Harriet E.	Leicester,	Administration,	16822
1852	James G.	Harvard,	Guardianship,	16823
1852	John W.	Harvard,	Guardianship,	16824
1826	Lemuel	Lancaster,	Will,	16825
1875	Lois	Harvard,	Administration,	16826
1875	Lois E.	Harvard,	Administration,	16827
1870	Loyal G.	Leicester,	Administration,	16828
1854	Mary A.	Petersham,	Guardianship,	16829
1813	Phebe	West Boylston,	Guardianship,	16830
1841	Samuel	Harvard,	Administration,	16831
1881	Samuel B.	Shrewsbury,	Will,	16832
1867	Sarah A.	Leicester,	Administration,	16833
1825	Sarah W.	Petersham,	Guardianship,	16834
1873	Ursula M.	Worcester,	Partition,	16835
1852	Willard	Harvard,	Administration,	16836
1819	DICKMAN, Elbridge	Unknown,	Sale of Real Est.,	16837
1845	Nancy	Southborough,	Guardianship,	16838
1845	Nancy	Southborough,	Administration,	16838
1819	Samuel	Unknown,	Sale of Real Est.,	16839
	DICKY see DICKEY.			
1867	DIERSCH, Agnes	Clinton,	Guardianship,	16840
1867	Laura	Clinton,	Guardianship,	16841
1867	Paulina	Clinton,	Guardianship,	16842
1867	Wilhelmina	Clinton,	Guardianship,	16843
1867	William	Clinton,	Guardianship,	16844
	DIKE and DYKE,			
1849	Amadeus	Sutton,	Administration,	16845
1873	Amos	Lunenburg,	Administration,	16846

YEAR.	NAME.	RESIDENCE.	NATURE.	CASE.
	DIKE AND DYKE,			
1849	Artemas	Sutton,	Guardianship,	16847
1856	Artemas	Sutton,	Administration,	16847
1874	Benjamin	Holden,	Administration,	16848
1878	Benjamin	Holden,	Administration,	16849
1777	Daniel	Sutton,	Will,	16850
1821	David	Athol,	Guardianship,	16851
1880	George	Thompson, Conn.,	Administration,	16852
1806	James	Sutton,	Administration,	16853
1760	John	Sutton,	Guardianship,	16854
1875	Joseph	Fitchburg,	Will,	16855
1746	Nathaniell	Dudley,	Will,	16856
1825	Nicholas	Westminster,	Guardianship,	16857
1833	Nicholas	Westminster,	Administration,	16857
1838	Nicholas	Westminster,	Pension,	16858
1849	Rufus	Sutton,	Administration,	16859
1864	Sarah B.	Sterling,	Will,	16860
1862	DILLABER, Elizabeth Y.	Sutton,	Administration,	16861
1879	Priscilla	Southbridge,	Administration,	16862
1860	DILLINGHAM, Abby	Southborough,	Guardianship,	16863
1859	Benjamin C.	Southborough,	Administration,	16864
1860	Benjamin F.	Southborough,	Guardianship,	16865
1860	Charles T.	Southborough,	Guardianship,	16866
1854	John	Southborough,	Guardianship,	16867
1879	Lucy A.	Worcester,	Administration,	16868
1873	Marcellus P.	Hubbardston,	Administration,	16869
1854	Thomas R.	Southborough,	Administration,	16870
1868	DILLON, Ann	West Brookfield,	Guardianship,	16871
1868	Eliza	West Brookfield,	Guardianship,	16872
1862	James	West Brookfield,	Guardianship,	16873
1863	John	West Brookfield,	Guardianship,	16874
1807	DIMICK, Jesse	Petersham,	Administration,	16875
1868	DINGWELL, Julia T.	Worcester,	Adoption, etc.,	16876
1881	DINNEEN, John	Templeton,	Administration,	16877
	DINSMORE AND DENSMORE,			
1859	Andrew	Leominster,	Guardianship,	16878
1859	Andrew	Leominster,	Adoption, etc.,	16879
1871	David	Northborough,	Administration,	16880
1872	Florence A.	New York, N. Y.,	Guardianship,	16881
1840	George W.	Holden,	Administration,	16882
1878	John	Westborough,	Change of Name,	16883
1878	John W.	Westborough,	Change of Name,	16884
1874	DION, Sophie	Worcester,	Will,	16885
	DISPEAU see DESPEAU.			
1838	DISPER, Jesse	Milford,	Administration,	16886

(389)

Year.	Name.	Residence.	Nature.	Case.
1839	DISPER, Jesse	Milford,	Guardianship,	16887
1839	Sally	Milford,	Guardianship,	16888
1839	Samuel	Milford,	Guardianship,	16889
	DIVOLL AND DIVOL,			
1827	Abigail	Leominster,	Administration,	16890
1849	Abigail H.	Leominster,	Guardianship,	16891
1852	Abigail H.	Leominster,	Will,	16892
1823	Bryant	Leominster,	Guardianship,	16893
1867	Bryant	Leominster,	Will,	16894
1850	Caroline	Lancaster,	Guardianship,	16895
1770	Elizabeth	Lunenburg,	Guardianship,	16896
1866	Ella C. G.	Lancaster,	Guardianship,	16897
1850	Ellen M.	Lancaster,	Guardianship,	16898
1850	Emily	Lancaster,	Guardianship,	16899
1849	Emma J.	Leominster,	Guardianship,	16900
1816	Emmons	Fitchburg,	Administration,	16901
1876	Francis	Leominster,	Administration,	16902
1850	Francis A.	Lancaster,	Guardianship,	16903
1843	George	Lancaster,	Guardianship,	16904
1864	George W.	Lancaster,	Administration,	16905
1849	James	Leominster,	Administration,	16906
1761	John	Lunenburg,	Will,	16907
1843	John	Leominster,	Administration,	16908
1874	John	Leominster,	Administration,	16909
1828	Judith	Lunenburg,	Guardianship,	16910
1850	Julia	Lancaster,	Guardianship,	16911
1824	Levi	Leominster,	Administration,	16912
1835	Levi	Winchendon,	Administration,	16913
1862	Levi	Winchendon,	Administration,	16914
1867	Louis	Leominster,	Guardianship,	16915
1826	Luke	Leominster,	Administration,	16916
1788	Manassah	Lunenburg,	Administration,	16917
1798	Manassah	Lancaster,	Administration,	16918
1770	Manasseh	Lunenburg,	Guardianship,	16919
1791	Manasseh	Lunenburg,	Guardianship,	16920
1833	Manasseh	Lancaster,	Administration,	16921
1823	Mary	Leominster,	Guardianship,	16922
1864	Mary	Lunenburg,	Will,	16923
1870	Mary	Lunenburg,	Administration,	16924
1849	Mary M.	Leominster,	Guardianship,	16925
1828	Nancy	Leominster,	Guardianship,	16926
1828	Nathaniel B.	Leominster,	Guardianship,	16927
1822	Oliver	Leominster,	Will,	16928
1812	Peter	Lancaster,	Guardianship,	16929
1812	Peter	Lancaster,	Administration,	16930

YEAR.	NAME.	RESIDENCE.	NATURE.	CASE.
	DIVOLL AND DIVOL,			
1770	Phebe	Lunenburg,	Guardianship,	16931
1811	Phineas	Lunenburg,	Will,	16932
1820	Phinehas	Lunenburg,	Administration,	16933
1828	Phinehas	Lunenburg,	Guardianship,	16934
1828	Roxa A.	Leominster,	Guardianship,	16935
1754	Ruth	Lancaster,	Administration,	16936
1836	Sarah	Lunenburg,	Administration,	16937
1812	Susan	Lancaster,	Guardianship,	16938
1828	Susan	Lunenburg,	Guardianship,	19939
1849	Susan P.	Leominster,	Guardianship,	16940
1770	Susannah	Lunenburg,	Guardianship,	16941
1791	Susannah	Lunenburg,	Guardianship,	16942
1843	Thomas	Lancaster,	Administration,	16943
1874	Thomas H.	Leominster,	Will,	16944
1731	William	Lancaster,	Administration,	16945
1785	William	Leominster,	Will,	16946
1801	William	Leominster,	Administration,	16947
1849	William	Lancaster,	Administration,	16948
1850	William C.	Lancaster,	Guardianship,	16949
1818	DIX, David	Southbridge,	Will,	16950
1821	Elizabeth	Southbridge,	Will,	16951
1867	Seth A.	Westborough,	Administration,	16952
1852	DIXEY, Edmund F.	Unknown,	Guardianship,	16953
1869	DIXON, Ann L.	Webster,	Change of Name,	16954
1859	Anna L.	Webster,	Guardianship,	16955
1849	Charles W.	Webster,	Guardianship,	16956
1858	George	Webster,	Will,	16957
1849	John	Webster,	Administration,	16958
1880	Joseph	Clinton,	Administration,	16959
1871	Mary	Webster,	Administration,	16960
1854	Robert	Webster,	Will,	16961
1849	Sarah A. E.	Webster,	Guardianship,	16962
1849	William H.	Webster,	Guardianship,	16963
	DOANE AND DOAN,			
1877	Achsah	Brookfield,	Administration,	16964
1853	Adah	Dana,	Administration,	16965
1838	Amos	Brookfield,	Guardianship,	16966
1844	Amos	Charlton,	Administration,	16967
1878	Amos	Royalston,	Administration,	16968
1869	Anna M.	North Brookfield,	Administration,	16969
1857	Asa	Charlton,	Guardianship,	16970
1824	Benjamin	North Brookfield,	Administration,	16971
1830	Benjamin	North Brookfield,	Guardianship,	16972
1865	Benjamin	North Brookfield,	Administration,	16973

YEAR.	NAME.	RESIDENCE.	NATURE.	CASE.
	DOANE AND DOAN,			
1849	Caroline O.	Brookfield,	Guardianship,	16974
1839	Charles P.	Phillipston,	Guardianship,	16975
1859	Daniel M.	Phillipston,	Guardianship,	16976
1812	David	North Brookfield,	Will,	16977
1869	Ebenezer	Phillipston,	Will,	16978
1852	Edward M.	North Brookfield,	Guardianship,	16979
1810	Elisha	Brookfield,	Will,	16980
1838	Elisha	Brookfield,	Will,	16981
1853	Elkanah	Dana,	Administration,	16982
1859	Ella Z.	North Brookfield,	Guardianship,	16983
1853	Ellen	Dana,	Guardianship,	16984
1853	Ellen	Charlton,	Guardianship,	16985
1830	Eunice	North Brookfield,	Guardianship,	16986
1865	Eunice	North Brookfield,	Administration,	16987
1853	Frances A.	Charlton,	Guardianship,	16988
1878	Frances L.	Warren,	Adoption, etc.,	16989
1877	Francis C.	Athol,	Administration,	16990
1844	George W.	Charlton,	Guardianship,	16991
1855	Hammond	Dana,	Administration,	16992
1829	Hannah	North Brookfield,	Administration,	16993
1878	Isaac	Dana,	Will,	16994
1840	Isaac Y.	Phillipston,	Administration,	16995
1827	Jesse	North Brookfield,	Administration,	16996
1859	Joel	Phillipston,	Administration,	16997
1852	John N.	North Brookfield,	Will,	16998
1829	Joseph	North Brookfield,	Will,	16999
1847	Joseph	North Brookfield,	Administration,	17000
1865	Joseph	North Brookfield,	Administration,	17001
1830	Josiah M.	North Brookfield,	Guardianship,	17002
1852	Josiah M.	North Brookfield,	Administration,	17003
1855	Julia E. H.	Dana,	Guardianship,	17004
1859	J. Roderick	Phillipston,	Guardianship,	17005
1838	Laura A.	Brookfield,	Guardianship,	17006
1879	Leon W.	Warren,	Adoption, etc.,	17007
1868	Leonard	Dana,	Will,	17008
1844	Levi	Charlton,	Guardianship,	17009
1857	Lott	Athol,	Will,	17010
1852	Louisa	Charlton,	Will,	17011
1839	Lucy A.	Phillipston,	Guardianship,	17012
1844	Lyman	Charlton,	Guardianship,	17013
1797	Marcy	Brookfield,	Guardianship,	17014
1849	Marshall	Brookfield,	Will,	17015
1868	Marshall	Worcester,	Administration,	17016
1837	Martha	Spencer,	Will,	17017

Year.	Name.	Residence.	Nature.	Case.
	DOANE AND DOAN,			
1838	Martha	Spencer,	Pension,	17018
1825	Mary	North Brookfield	Guardianship,	17019
1839	Mary J.	Phillipston,	Guardianship,	17020
1865	Mercy	North Brookfield,	Will,	17021
1841	Mercy S.	Phillipston,	Guardianship,	17022
1797	Nathan	Brookfield,	Will,	17023
1838	Randall R.	Phillipston,	Administration,	17024
1859	Randall R.	Phillipston,	Guardianship,	17025
1859	Roswell L.	Phillipston,	Guardianship,	17026
1844	Roxanna	Charlton,	Guardianship,	17027
1839	William W.	Phillipston,	Guardianship,	17028
1827	DODD, Betsy	Holden,	Guardianship,	17029
1827	Caroline	Holden,	Guardianship,	17030
1873	Carrie E.	Paxton,	Guardianship,	17031
1827	Charles	Holden,	Guardianship,	17032
1827	Elisha	Holden,	Guardianship,	17033
1873	Eliza H.	Paxton,	Guardianship,	17034
1827	George	Holden,	Guardianship,	17035
1873	George B.	Paxton,	Guardianship,	17036
1827	James	Holden,	Guardianship,	17037
1827	James	Holden,	Will,	17038
1810	John	Rutland,	Administration,	17039
1829	John	Princeton,	Guardianship,	17040
1857	John	Princeton,	Administration,	17041
1857	John M.	Princeton,	Guardianship,	17042
1823	Joseph	Holden,	Administration,	17043
1827	Joseph	Holden,	Guardianship,	17044
1811	Julia Ann S.	Princeton,	Guardianship,	17045
1810	Rufus	Westminster,	Administration,	17046
1811	Sally M.	Princeton,	Guardianship,	17047
1827	Silas	Holden,	Guardianship,	17048
1877	Susan A.	Paxton,	Guardianship,	17049
1864	Susie A.	Paxton,	Adoption, etc.,	17050
1811	Theodore S.	Princeton,	Guardianship,	17051
1814	William	Holden,	Administration,	17052
1877	William W.	Paxton,	Administration,	17053
1774	DODGE, Abner	Dudley,	Guardianship,	17054
1881	Abner H.	Northbridge,	Administration,	17055
1878	Adeline D.	Sutton,	Administration,	17056
1843	Ann M.	Charlton,	Guardianship,	17057
1860	Annetta E.	Upton,	Guardianship,	17058
1861	Annetta E.	Unknown,	Adoption, etc.,	17059
1778	Asa	Worcester,	Guardianship,	17060
1816	Asahel	Charlton,	Guardianship,	17061

YEAR.	NAME.	RESIDENCE.	NATURE.	CASE.
1843	DODGE, Asahel	Charlton,	Administration,	17062
1834	Benjamin M.	Sutton,	Administration,	17063
1873	Carrie M.	Sutton,	Adoption, etc.,	17064
1774	Daniel	Dudley,	Guardianship,	17065
1787	Daniel	Dudley,	Will,	17066
1827	Daniel	Ward,	Administration,	17067
1820	Darius	West Brookfield,	Guardianship,	17068
1815	David	Charlton,	Administration,	17069
1816	David	Charlton,	Guardianship,	17070
1866	Edward H.	Worcester,	Guardianship,	17071
1843	Elijah	Lunenburg,	Will,	17072
1770	Elizabeth	Brookfield,	Guardianship,	17073
1861	Elizabeth	Leicester,	Will,	17074
1866	Ellen A.	Blackstone,	Guardianship,	17075
1799	Elnathan	Brookfield,	Guardianship,	17076
1766	Francis	Brookfield,	Administration,	17077
1864	Frank P.	Worcester,	Guardianship,	17078
1867	Frederic E.	Northbridge,	Guardianship,	17079
1865	George	Lancaster,	Will,	17080
1856	George W.	Sutton,	Guardianship,	17081
1863	Gibbs	Charlton,	Will,	17082
1770	Hannah	Brookfield,	Guardianship,	17083
1877	Harriet A.	Westborough,	Guardianship,	17084
1850	Harvey	Dudley,	Guardianship,	17085
1766	Hepzibah	Brookfield,	Guardianship,	17086
1790	Isaac	Sutton,	Will,	17087
1834	Isaac	Sutton,	Will,	17088
1770	Jabez	Shrewsbury,	Guardianship,	17089
1774	Jabez	Shrewsbury,	Administration,	17090
1764	Jesse	Lunenburg,	Guardianship,	17091
1778	John	Worcester,	Guardianship,	17092
1782	John	Brookfield,	Administration,	17093
1866	John	Sutton,	Administration,	17094
1872	John	New Braintree,	Will,	17095
1770	John, Jr.	Brookfield,	Guardianship,	17096
1799	Jonah	Brookfield,	Guardianship,	17097
1793	Joshua	Brookfield,	Will,	17098
1796	Joshua	Brookfield,	Will,	17099
1848	Josiah	Sutton,	Administration,	17100
1844	Julina	Charlton,	Guardianship,	17101
1827	Lucy	Brookfield,	Will,	17102
1845	Lucy	Leominster,	Administration,	17103
1844	Lucy A.	Charlton,	Guardianship,	17104
1778	Lydia	Worcester,	Guardianship,	17105
1861	Lydia A.	Upton,	Administration,	17106

YEAR.	NAME.	RESIDENCE.	NATURE.	CASE.
1879	DODGE, Lydia C.	North Brookfield,	Will,	17107
1824	Mark	Dudley,	Will,	17108
1797	Martha	Sutton,	Will,	17109
1844	Mary A.	Charlton,	Guardianship,	17110
1843	Mary E.	Charlton,	Guardianship,	17111
1816	Maynard	Charlton,	Guardianship,	17112
1826	Moses	Charlton,	Will,	17113
1816	Nancy	Charlton,	Guardianship,	17114
1813	Nathaniel	North Brookfield,	Will,	17115
1843	Nathaniel	North Brookfield,	Administration,	17116
1862	Nathaniel	Sutton,	Will,	17117
1876	Nathaniel B.	Westborough,	Administration,	17118
1867	Nelson G.	Northbridge,	Guardianship,	17119
1871	Olney	Uxbridge,	Administration,	17120
1773	Paul	Dudley,	Administration,	17121
1853	Paul	Dudley,	Will,	17122
1864	Pickering	Worcester,	Will,	17123
1799	Polly	Brookfield,	Guardianship,	17124
1816	Polly	Charlton,	Guardianship,	17125
1864	Rebecca G.	Worcester,	Guardianship,	17126
1762	Reuben	Lunenburg,	Administration,	17127
1792	Reuben	Westminster,	Guardianship,	17128
1844	Rhoda	Charlton,	Guardianship,	17129
1815	Richard H.	Sutton,	Will,	17130
1844	Robert	Charlton,	Administration,	17131
1859	Rufus	North Brookfield,	Will,	17132
1791	Ruth	Harvard,	Guardianship,	17133
1860	Sally W.	Ovid, Mich.,	Administration,	17134
1791	Sarah	Harvard,	Guardianship,	17135
1827	Sarah	North Brookfield,	Administration,	17136
1830	Sarah	North Brookfield,	Administration,	17137
1869	Sarah	Sutton,	Administration,	17138
1860	Sereno P.	Northbridge,	Administration,	17139
1867	Sheldon A.	Northbridge,	Guardianship,	17140
1855	Stephen	Leominster,	Administration,	17141
1876	Stillman	North Brookfield,	Administration,	17142
1791	Susannah	Harvard,	Guardianship,	17143
1837	Thadeus	Brookfield,	Pension,	17144
1862	Thankful	North Brookfield,	Administration,	17145
1840	Thomas	Leominster,	Will,	17146
1867	Willard	Sutton,	Will,	17147
1874	DODWELL, John	Gardner,	Administration,	17148
1857	DOE, Alfred	Worcester,	Administration,	17149
	DOHERTY see DOUGHERTY.			

YEAR.	NAME.	RESIDENCE.	NATURE.	CASE.
	DOLAN AND DOLEN,			
1875	Mary S.	Worcester,	Will,	17150
1862	Thomas	Blackstone,	Will,	17151
1880	William, etc.	Worcester,	Administration,	17152
1864	DOLBEAR, Benjamin	Templeton,	Administration,	17153
1845	Joel	Templeton,	Administration,	17154
1870	Laurinda E.	Templeton,	Will,	17155
1850	Mary	Templeton,	Pension,	17156
1855	DOLBY, Sherman W.	Harvard,	Administration,	17157
1818	DOLE, Abigail	Lunenburg,	Guardianship,	17158
1845	Artemas W.	Fitchburg,	Guardianship,	17159
1845	Catharine W.	Fitchburg,	Guardianship,	17160
1845	Clarrissa H.	Fitchburg,	Guardianship,	17161
1818	Elam	Lunenburg,	Guardianship,	17162
1778	Elijah	Lancaster,	Will,	17163
1776	Enoch	Lancaster,	Administration,	17164
1845	George R.	Fitchburg,	Guardianship,	17165
1818	John	Lunenburg,	Guardianship,	17166
1825	John	Fitchburg,	Administration,	17167
1845	John	Fitchburg,	Administration,	17168
1817	John, Jr.	Lunenburg,	Administration,	17169
1845	Mary E.	Fitchburg,	Guardianship,	17170
1867	Patience	Fitchburg,	Administration,	17171
1818	Stephen, 2d	Lunenburg,	Guardianship,	17172
1848	Stephen	Fitchburg,	Will,	17173
1770	Thomas	Westminster,	Administration,	17174
	DOLEN see DOLAN.			
1872	DOLLARD, Ann	Blackstone,	Will,	17175
1865	James	Blackstone,	Will,	17176
1875	DOLLEN, Moses	Worcester,	Will,	17177
1859	DOLLIVER, Ann E.	Worcester,	Guardianship,	17178
1863	Delia E.	Grafton,	Administration,	17179
1833	Horatio	Worcester,	Guardianship,	17180
1863	John	Grafton,	Will,	17181
1859	John B.	Worcester,	Administration,	17182
1833	Joseph	Worcester,	Guardianship,	17183
1881	Joseph	Shrewsbury,	Administration,	17184
1833	Martha	Worcester,	Guardianship,	17185
1859	Mary E.	Worcester,	Guardianship,	17186
1880	Samuel B.	Grafton,	Will,	17187
1877	DOLOFF, John,	Fitchburg,	Will,	17188
1880	Mary A.	Fitchburg,	Will,	17189
1880	DOLPHIN, Martin	Clinton,	Will,	17190
	DONAHOE AND DONAHUE,			
1880	Ann	Worcester,	Administration,	17191

YEAR.	NAME.	RESIDENCE.	NATURE.	CASE.
	DONAHOE AND DONAHUE,			
1878	Annie	Worcester,	Will,	17192
1876	Charles	Woonsocket, R. I.,	Administration,	17193
1878	Cornelius	Worcester,	Administration,	17194
1874	Daniel A.	Worcester,	Guardianship,	17195
1867	Ellen	Worcester,	Guardianship,	17196
1867	James	Worcester,	Guardianship,	17197
1867	Maria	Worcester,	Guardianship,	17198
1874	Mary	Worcester,	Administration,	17199
1876	Mary J.	Southborough,	Guardianship,	17200
1872	Michael	Worcester,	Will,	17201
1876	Stephen	Brookfield,	Administration,	17202
1876	Thomas	Southborough,	Guardianship,	17203
1869	Thomas D.	Worcester,	Will,	17204
	DONALLON see DONLAN.			
	DONALLY see DONNELLY.			
	DONAVON see DONOVAN.			
1877	DONDAY, Frank	Templeton,	Administration,	17205
1873	DONEGAN, Michael	Northbridge,	Will,	17206
1852	DONKERSLEY, George	Thompson, Conn.,	Administration,	17207
1852	John	Thompson, Conn.,	Administration,	17208
	DONLAN, DONLON, DONNAL-LON AND DONELLAN,			
1876	Ann	Millbury,	Will,	17209
1867	Ellen	Oxford,	Guardianship,	17210
1871	Ellen A.	Gardner,	Guardianship,	17211
1862	John	Oxford,	Will,	17112
1867	Mallick	Oxford,	Guardianship,	17213
1859	Martin, etc.	Gardner,	Administration,	17214
1871	Mary	Gardner,	Guardianship,	17215
1867	Mary A.	Oxford,	Guardianship,	17216
1865	Nancy	Upton,	Administration,	17217
	DONNELLY, DONELLY AND DONALLY,			
1878	Ann	Worcester,	Administration,	17218
1875	Annie	Milford,	Guardianship,	17219
1875	Edward	Milford,	Guardianship,	17220
1875	Elizabeth	Milford,	Guardianship,	17221
1875	John	Milford,	Administration,	17222
1881	John	Worcester,	Guardianship,	17223
1870	John B.	Fitchburg,	Guardianship,	17224
1859	Martin	Gardner,	Guardianship,	17225
1870	Patrick	Westminster,	Administration,	17226
1870	Patrick H.	Fitchburg,	Guardianship,	17227
1870	Thomas F.	Fitchburg,	Guardianship,	17228

YEAR.	NAME.	RESIDENCE.	NATURE.	CASE.
	DONNELLY, DONELLY AND DONALLY,			
1875	William	Milford,	Guardianship,	17229
	DONOVAN, DONNOVAN, DONNI- VAN AND DONAVAN,			
1860	Byron	Westborough,	Guardianship,	17230
1865	Catharine	Royalston,	Administration,	17231
1878	Charles	Fitchburg,	Guardianship,	17232
1860	Charlotte M.	Westborough,	Guardianship,	17233
1874	Cornelius	Worcester,	Administration,	17234
1880	Elizabeth	Milford,	Will,	17235
1860	Ellen	Westborough,	Guardianship,	17236
1860	James	Westborough,	Guardianship,	17237
1878	James	Fitchburg,	Administration,	17238
1880	James	Milford,	Guardianship,	17239
1871	Jeremiah	Worcester,	Guardianship,	17240
1858	John	Millbury,	Administration,	17241
1860	Patrick	North Brookfield,	Administration,	17242
1880	Thomas	Milford,	Guardianship,	17243
1870	DOOLAN, David	Ashburnham,	Guardianship,	17244
1870	Ella	Ashburnham,	Guardianship,	17245
1870	Hannah	Ashburnham,	Guardianship,	17246
1870	John	Ashburnham,	Guardianship,	17247
1870	Josie	Ashburnham,	Guardianship,	17248
1870	Margaret	Ashburnham,	Guardianship,	17249
1870	Mary	Ashburnham,	Guardianship,	17250
1876	Mary	Ashburnham,	Will,	17251
1870	William	Ashburnham,	Guardianship,	17252
1879	DOOLEY, Annie	Milford,	Guardianship,	17253
1879	Bernard	Milford,	Guardianship,	17254
1879	Francis	Milford,	Guardianship,	17255
1849	Joseph L.	Holden,	Guardianship,	17256
1849	Mary J.	Holden,	Guardianship,	17257
1879	Patrick H.	Milford,	Guardianship,	17258
1879	William J.	Milford,	Guardianship,	17259
1868	DOOLING, Ellen	Fitchburg,	Guardianship,	17260
1868	William	Fitchburg,	Guardianship,	17261
1880	William, etc.	Worcester,	Administration,	17262
1785	DOOLITTLE, Charles	Hardwick,	Will,	17263
1869	Cyrenus	Athol,	Administration,	17264
1831	DORAN, Cornelius	Dudley,	Will,	17265
	DORCEY see DORSEY.			
1808	DORCHESTER, Ishmael	Sterling,	Guardianship,	17266
1853	DORE, James L.	Holden,	Administration,	17267
1875	John	Leicester,	Administration,	17268

YEAR.	NAME.	RESIDENCE.	NATURE.	CASE.
1764	DORETY, Charles	Brookfield,	Guardianship,	17269
1761	Samuel	Brookfield,	Administration,	17270
1862	DORGAN, John	Blackstone,	Administration,	17271
1863	DORMAN, James A.	Worcester,	Administration,	17272
1880	DORNAN, Andrew	Oxford,	Administration,	17273
	DORR AND DAW,			
1828	Catherine	Fitchburg,	Administration,	17274
1864	Enos	Worcester,	Will,	17275
1867	Henry	Sutton,	Administration,	17276
1768	Joseph	Mendon,	Will,	17277
1809	Joseph	Brookfield,	Administration,	17278
1780	Mary	Worcester,	Will,	17279
1865	Patrick	Worcester,	Will,	17280
1816	Thomas S.	Brookfield,	Administration,	17281
1871	DORRANCE, Alexander	Chaplin, Conn.,	Foreign Will,	17282
	DORSEY AND DORCEY,			
1879	Anastasia	Worcester,	Administration,	17283
1871	Bridget	Worcester,	Will,	17284
1870	Ellen	Oxford,	Administration,	17285
	DOTY, DOUGHTY AND DOUTY,			
1842	Bainbridge	Charlton,	Guardianship,	17286
1818	Benjamin	Charlton,	Will,	17287
1837	Benjamin	Charlton,	Administration,	17288
1840	Betsey	Charlton,	Administration,	17289
1874	Clara H.	Shrewsbury,	Will,	17290
1830	John	Westminster,	Will,	17291
1842	Martha L.	Charlton,	Guardianship,	17292
1841	Mary	Westminster,	Will,	17293
1842	Mary E.	Charlton,	Guardianship,	17294
1835	Pearson C.	Westminster,	Guardianship,	17295
1842	Salem	Charlton,	Administration,	17296
1881	Stilman	Charlton,	Will,	17297
1835	Timothy	Westminster,	Administration,	17298
1859	DOUBLEDAY, Eliza	Dana,	Guardianship,	17299
1858	Jason	Dana,	Administration,	17300
1859	Jason W.	Dana,	Guardianship,	17301
1838	Joseph	Dana,	Pension,	17302
1854	Lucy	Dana,	Pension,	17303
1859	Lucy A.	Dana,	Guardianship,	17304
1875	Mary J.	Dana,	Administration,	17305
	DOUGHERTY, DOUGHARTY AND DOHERTY,			
1867	Ann	Milford,	Guardianship,	17306
1873	Ann	Worcester,	Will,	17307
1748	Charles	Brookfield,	Administration,	17308

YEAR.	NAME.	RESIDENCE.	NATURE.	CASE.
	DOUGHERTY, DOUGHARTY AND DOHERTY,			
1777	Charles	Brookfield,	Administration,	17309
1870	Garret	Holden,	Administration,	17310
1871	Garret	Worcester,	Guardianship,	17311
1867	James	Milford,	Guardianship,	17312
1870	James	Worcester,	Administration,	17313
1763	Jane	Brookfield,	Will,	17314
1867	John	Milford,	Guardianship,	17315
1871	Mary A.	Worcester,	Guardianship,	17316
1867	Mary J.	Milford,	Guardianship,	17317
1764	Micah	Brookfield,	Guardianship,	17318
1877	Patrick	Worcester,	Administration,	17319
1867	Peter	Milford,	Guardianship,	17320
1877	Samuel W.	Worcester,	Partition,	17321
	DOUGHNEY see DOWNEY.			
	DOUGHTY see DOTY.			
1880	DOUGLAS, Bridget C.	Southbridge,	Will,	17322
1878	Francis	Worcester,	Will,	17323
1872	George R.	Westborough,	Administration,	17324
1879	John, etc.	Worcester,	Administration,	17325
	DOUTY see DOTY.			
1868	DOVE, Elizabeth	Milford,	Administration,	17326
1867	DOVER, Albert	Douglas,	Guardianship,	17327
1867	Amili	Douglas,	Guardianship,	17328
1867	John B.	Douglas,	Guardianship,	17329
1867	Mary J.	Douglas,	Guardianship,	17330
	DOW, DOWE AND DOWS (see also DOWSE),			
1816	Amasa	Trenton, N. Y.,	Guardianship,	17331
1815	Anna	Ward,	Administration,	17332
1816	Daniel	Trenton, N. Y.,	Guardianship,	17333
1875	Edith M.	Worcester,	Guardianship,	17334
1878	Edward S.	Fitchburg,	Guardianship,	17335
1846	Elbridge	Worcester,	Will,	17336
1816	Emeline	Trenton, N. Y.,	Guardianship,	17337
1854	Gardner W.	Rutland,	Guardianship,	17338
1880	George G.	Shrewsbury,	Trustee,	17339
1878	Harriet A.	Fitchburg,	Administration,	17340
1773	James	New Braintree,	Will,	17341
1880	Jane E.	Shrewsbury,	Trustee,	17342
1878	Jonathan R.	Holden,	Will,	17343
1814	Joseph	New Braintree,	Will,	17344
1880	Joseph H.	Charlton,	Will,	17345
1818	Sarah	New Braintree,	Administration,	17346
1854	William H.	Rutland,	Guardianship,	17347

YEAR.	NAME.	RESIDENCE.	NATURE.	CASE.
	DOW, DOWE AND DOWS (see also DOWSE),			
1868	William H.	Westminster,	Change of Name,	17348
1875	William H.	Worcester,	Will,	17349
1854	Zebulon	Rutland,	Administration,	17350
1880	Zylpha E.	Shrewsbury,	Trustee,	17351
1864	DOWD, Abby	Worcester,	Administration,	17352
1881	Andrew	Worcester,	Administration,	17353
1864	Annie	Worcester,	Adoption, etc.,	17354
1864	Catherine	Worcester,	Adoption, etc.,	17355
1864	Mary A.	Worcester,	Adoption, etc.,	17356
1870	DOWDING, Ann	Blackstone,	Will,	17357
	DOWE see DOW.			
1827	DOWELL, William	Southborough,	Administration,	17358
1866	DOWLING, Michael	West Brookfield,	Administration,	17359
1872	Richard	Uxbridge,	Will,	17360
	DOWNE AND DOWNES,			
1849	Frances L.	Leicester,	Guardianship,	17361
1828	Joseph	Fitchburg,	Will,	17362
1853	Joseph	Fitchburg,	Will,	17363
1866	Levi	Fitchburg,	Administration,	17364
1859	Louisa F.	Fitchburg,	Guardianship,	17365
1859	Mary E.	Fitchburg,	Guardianship,	17366
1861	Timothy F.	Fitchburg,	Administration,	17367
1849	Sidney	Leicester,	Administration,	17368
1859	William S.	Fitchburg,	Administration,	17369
	DOWNEY AND DOUGHNEY,			
1877	Ann	Bolton,	Will,	17370
1875	James	Worcester,	Administration,	17371
1875	William	Worcester,	Guardianship,	17372
1879	William	Brookfield,	Will,	17373
	DOWS see DOW.			
	DOWSE (see also DOW),			
1844	Elizabeth D.	Oxford,	Guardianship,	17374
1844	Martha S.	Oxford,	Guardianship,	17375
1844	Mary B.	Oxford,	Guardianship,	17376
1844	Samuel	Oxford,	Will,	17377
1844	Thomas	Oxford,	Guardianship,	17378
1870	DOYLE, Andrew	North Brookfield,	Guardianship,	17379
1879	Andrew H.	Southborough,	Guardianship,	17380
1877	Annie	North Brookfield,	Partition,	17381
1878	Dennis	Hardwick,	Administration,	17382
1867	James	Worcester,	Administration,	17383
1869	James	Worcester,	Will,	17384
1875	John	North Brookfield,	Guardianship,	17385
1877	John	North Brookfield,	Partition,	17386

Year.	Name.	Residence.	Nature.	Case.
1879	DOYLE, John	Gardner,	Administration,	17387
1870	John, Jr.	North Brookfield,	Guardianship,	17388
1875	Joseph	North Brookfield,	Guardianship,	17389
1877	Joseph	North Brookfield,	Partition,	17390
1881	Julia H.	Hardwick,	Guardianship,	17391
1870	Lizzie	Worcester,	Adoption, etc.,	17392
1871	Margaret M.	Worcester,	Guardianship,	17393
1877	Mary	North Brookfield,	Partition,	17394
1870	Mary A.	North Brookfield,	Guardianship,	17395
1873	Mary A.	Worcester,	Administration,	17396
1881	Mary A.	Hardwick,	Guardianship,	17397
1854	Michael	Leominster,	Administration,	17398
1871	Michael J.	Worcester,	Guardianship,	17399
1867	Owen	Milford,	Will,	17400
1875	Patrick	North Brookfield,	Guardianship,	17401
1877	Patrick	North Brookfield,	Partition,	17402
1881	Patrick F.	Hardwick,	Guardianship,	17403
1866	Rose	Oxford,	Administration,	17404
1870	Teresa	North Brookfield,	Guardianship,	17405
1870	Timothy C.	North Brookfield,	Guardianship,	17406
1875	William	North Brookfield,	Guardianship,	17407
1875	William	North Brookfield,	Administration,	17408
1877	William	North Brookfield,	Partition,	17409
1868	DRAGAN, Francis	Webster,	Adoption, etc.,	17410
1809	DRAKE, Albee	Douglas,	Guardianship,	17411
1876	Albert S.	Milford,	Will,	17412
1880	Annie B.	Milford,	Guardianship,	17413
1880	Bradley M.	Athol,	Guardianship,	17414
1814	Daniel	North Brookfield,	Guardianship,	17415
1817	Daniel	North Brookfield,	Administration,	17416
1879	Daniel	North Brookfield,	Administration,	17417
1841	Elizabeth	Spencer,	Will,	17418
1814	Francis	North Brookfield,	Guardianship,	17419
1880	Hattie C.	Athol,	Guardianship,	17420
1855	Horatio N.	Sturbridge,	Administration,	17421
1848	Joel	Grafton,	Will,	17422
1843	Jonathan	Grafton,	Administration,	17423
1871	Joseph	Winchendon,	Guardianship,	17424
1880	Lottie L.	Milford,	Guardianship,	17425
1814	Lucinda	North Brookfield,	Guardianship,	17426
1819	Lucinda	North Brookfield,	Administration,	17427
1877	Lucy	Grafton,	Administration,	17428
1814	Mary	North Brookfield,	Guardianship,	17429
1860	Mary E.	Worcester,	Guardianship,	17430
1814	Reuben	North Brookfield,	Guardianship,	17431
1879	Rosa A.	Athol,	Guardianship,	17432

YEAR.	NAME.	RESIDENCE.	NATURE.	CASE.
1860	DRAKE, Samuel	Worcester,	Administration,	17433
1863	Simeon A.	Sturbridge,	Will,	17434
1809	Stephen	Douglas,	Administration,	17435
1809	Stephen	Douglas,	Guardianship,	17436
1860	Susan	Worcester,	Guardianship,	17437
1868	William	Spencer,	Will,	17438
1860	William E.	Worcester,	Guardianship,	17439
1846	DRAPER, Alpha	Spencer,	Administration,	17440
1856	Ann E.	Worcester,	Guardianship,	17441
1810	Arnold	Spencer,	Guardianship,	17442
1875	Calista A.	Worcester,	Will,	17443
1866	Catherine C.	Brookfield,	Will,	17444
1866	Celestia	Sturbridge,	Administration,	17445
1854	Charles H.	Spencer,	Guardianship,	17446
1880	Clarence P.	North Brookfield,	Guardianship,	17447
1867	Clarinda W.	Spencer,	Will,	17448
1787	David	Uxbridge,	Administration,	17449
1845	David	Leicester,	Will,	17450
1861	Deborah	Douglas,	Administration,	17451
1866	Edwin	Worcester,	Will,	17452
1849	Eleazer B.	Spencer,	Administration,	17453
1844	Eliza	Leicester,	Will,	17454
1866	Eliza H.	Worcester,	Guardianship,	17455
1880	Emma L.	Milford,	Administration,	17456
1857	Frost	Douglas,	Administration,	17457
1846	George	Spencer,	Guardianship,	17458
1848	George	Sturbridge,	Administration,	17459
1854	George L.	Spencer,	Guardianship,	17460
1846	Henry	Spencer,	Guardianship,	17461
1880	Hiram E.	North Brookfield,	Guardianship,	17462
1781	James	Spencer,	Will,	17463
1825	James	Spencer,	Will,	17464
1856	James	Worcester,	Guardianship,	17465
1868	James	Spencer,	Will,	17466
1853	John B.	Spencer,	Administration,	17467
1793	Joshua	Spencer,	Administration,	17468
1859	Joshua	Worcester,	Guardianship,	17469
1867	Julia	Douglas,	Administration,	17470
1827	Julia A.	Spencer,	Guardianship,	17471
1880	Laura A.	North Brookfield,	Guardianship,	17472
1856	Lizzie F.	Worcester,	Guardianship,	17473
1854	Lorenzo	Spencer,	Guardianship,	17474
1813	Luke	Brookfield,	Administration,	17475
1834	Luke T.	Brookfield,	Guardianship,	17476
1856	Maria C.	Worcester,	Guardianship,	17477
1791	Martha	Spencer,	Will,	17478

Year.	Name.	Residence.	Nature.	Case.
1874	DRAPER, Miriam	Sturbridge,	Agreement,	17479
1744	Samuel	Sutton,	Will,	17480
1849	Simeon	Brookfield,	Administration,	17481
1849	Simeon	Brookfield,	Pension,	17482
1856	Sophia A.	Worcester,	Guardianship,	17483
1856	Sylvia C.	Worcester,	Guardianship,	17484
1777	Thomas	New Braintree,	Will,	17485
1855	William A.	Worcester,	Administration,	17486
1871	DRENNING, Mary A.	Greenfield,	Adoption, etc.,	17487
1813	DRESSER, Aaron	Charlton,	Administration,	17488
1847	Aaron A.	Worcester,	Guardianship,	17489
1857	Aaron P.	Charlton,	Administration,	17490
1821	Abigail	Charlton,	Administration,	17491
1830	Amos	Lunenburg,	Will,	17492
1777	Anna	Charlton,	Guardianship,	17493
1809	Anne	Sturbridge,	Will,	17494
1799	Artemas	Partridgefield,	Guardianship,	17495
1816	Asa	Charlton,	Will,	17496
1863	Asa	Southbridge,	Will,	17497
1777	Caleb	Charlton,	Guardianship,	17498
1854	Charles C.	Southbridge,	Guardianship,	17499
1826	Chester A.	Southbridge,	Guardianship,	17500
1828	Deborah	Southbridge,	Administration,	17501
1843	Edwin	Sterling,	Guardianship,	17502
1799	Elijah	Partridgefield,	Guardianship,	17503
1840	Galon	Sterling,	Guardianship,	17504
1826	George	Southbridge,	Guardianship,	17505
1854	George	Southbridge,	Guardianship,	17506
1849	George G.	Worcester,	Administration,	17507
1866	George L.	Charlton,	Sale Real Estate,	17508
1835	Harvey	Charlton,	Will,	17509
1801	Henry	Partridgefield,	Guardianship,	17510
1836	Henry	Charlton,	Guardianship,	17511
1841	Henry	Charlton,	Administration,	17512
1866	Herbert A.	Charlton,	Sale Real Estate,	17513
1836	Jerome	Charlton,	Guardianship,	17514
1851	Jerome	Charlton,	Will,	17515
1789	John	Charlton,	Administration,	17516
1814	John	Charlton,	Guardianship,	17517
1776	John, Jr.	Charlton,	Administration,	17518
1847	John P.	Worcester,	Guardianship,	17519
1847	John S.	Worcester,	Administration,	17520
1803	Joseph	Partridgefield,	Guardianship,	17521
1777	Joshua	Charlton,	Guardianship,	17522
1854	Julia E.	Southbridge,	Guardianship,	17523
1854	Martha C.	Southbridge,	Guardianship,	17524

(404)

YEAR.	NAME.	RESIDENCE.	NATURE.	CASE.
1862	DRESSER, Mary	Charlton,	Will,	17525
1836	Mercy	Charlton,	Guardianship,	17526
1808	Meriam	Charlton,	Guardianship,	17527
1854	Miriam	Southbridge,	Guardianship,	17528
1813	Moses	Charlton,	Will,	17529
1820	Moses	Charlton,	Administration,	17530
1814	Pamela	Charlton,	Guardianship,	17531
1814	Pamela	Charlton,	Administration,	17532
1836	Pamela	Charlton,	Guardianship,	17533
1826	Pamelia	Southbridge,	Guardianship,	17534
1854	Persis	Southbridge,	Guardianship,	17535
1789	Priscilla	Sturbridge,	Partition,	17535 ½
1799	Rebecca	Partridgefield,	Guardianship,	17536
1827	Richard	Charlton,	Will,	17537
1807	Rowland	Sturbridge,	Will,	17538
1854	Samuel	Southbridge,	Guardianship,	17539
1868	Samuel S.	Southbridge,	Administration,	17540
1847	Sarah E.	Worcester,	Guardianship,	17541
1854	Silas	Southbridge,	Administration,	17542
1866	Susanna	Charlton,	Administration,	17543
1868	Zilpha	Charlton,	Administration,	17544
1877	DREW, Mary H.	Worcester,	Administration,	17545
1870	DRISCOLL, Daniel	Worcester,	Administration,	17546
1871	Dennis	Worcester,	Administration,	17547
1873	Henry	Worcester,	Guardianship,	17548
1873	John	Worcester,	Guardianship,	17549
1872	Nancy	Worcester,	Will,	17550
1873	Nellie	Worcester,	Guardianship,	17551
1873	Patrick	Worcester,	Will,	17552
1873	William	Worcester,	Guardianship,	17553
1878	DROHAN, Mary A.	Worcester,	Guardianship,	17554
1878	Nicholas	Worcester,	Will,	17555
1878	Nicholas J.	Worcester,	Guardianship,	17556
1807	DROWNE, Katherine	Worcester,	Will,	17557
1760	DRUCE, Daniel	Grafton,	Guardianship,	17558
1760	Elizabeth	Grafton,	Guardianship,	17559
1758	Ichabod	Grafton,	Administration,	17560
1760	John	Grafton,	Guardianship,	17561
1760	Lois	Grafton,	Guardianship,	17562
1760	Mary	Grafton,	Guardianship,	17563
1760	Nathan	Grafton,	Guardianship,	17564
1758	William	Grafton,	Guardianship,	17565
1872	DRURY, Abbie B.	Spencer,	Adoption, etc.,	17566
1873	Abbie B.	Spencer,	Guardianship,	17567
1834	Abel	Worcester,	Will,	17568

Year.	Name.	Residence.	Nature.	Case.
1784	DRURY, Abraham	Temple, N. H.,	Guardianship,	17569
1862	Adams	Spencer,	Administration,	17570
1839	Almira	Auburn,	Guardianship,	17571
1861	Alpheus	Charlton,	Administration,	17572
1839	Alvah	Auburn,	Administration,	17573
1819	Amos	Athol,	Guardianship,	17574
1822	Amos	Athol,	Will,	17575
1784	Anna	Temple, N. H.,	Guardianship,	17576
1827	Arethusa	Spencer,	Guardianship,	17577
1870	Artemas H.	Gardner,	Administration,	17578
1861	Arthur H.	Worcester,	Guardianship,	17579
1863	Betsey	Worcester,	Administration,	17580
1805	Caleb	Shrewsbury,	Will,	17581
1858	Calvin A.	Royalston,	Will,	17582
1860	Calvin A.	Royalston,	Guardianship,	17583
1847	Cornelius H.	Leicester,	Guardianship,	17584
1827	Cylena	Spencer,	Guardianship,	18585
1786	Damaris	Athol,	Guardianship,	17586
1863	David	Athol,	Administration,	17587
1868	David	Grafton,	Administration,	17588
1827	David A.	Spencer,	Guardianship,	17589
1827	Dexter	Spencer,	Guardianship,	17590
1815	Ebenezer	Spencer,	Will,	17591
1841	Ebenezer	Charlton,	Will,	17592
1786	Edward	Athol,	Administration,	17593
1881	Edward	Athol,	Will,	17594
1845	Eleazer	Westminster,	Will,	17595
1844	Eleazer, Jr.	Rutland,	Administration,	17596
1797	Elijah	Grafton,	Administration,	17597
1846	Elijah	Grafton,	Administration,	17598
1841	Elisha	Winchendon,	Guardianship,	17599
1841	Elisha	Winchendon,	Administration,	17600
1855	Elizabeth	Westminster,	Will,	17601
1856	Elizabeth	Westminster,	Pension,	17602
1847	Emory	Leicester,	Administration,	17603
1839	Enoch P.	Auburn,	Guardianship,	17604
1863	Ephraim	Worcester,	Administration,	17605
1856	Eunice A.	Holden,	Adoption, etc.,	17606
1871	Frederic L.	Royalston,	Guardianship,	17607
1872	George A.	Spencer,	Adoption, etc.,	17608
1750	Gershom	Grafton,	Guardianship,	17609
1856	Hannah	Holden,	Will,	17610
1878	Harriet T.	Athol,	Administration,	17611
1874	Henry G.	Oakham,	Will,	17612
1861	Hiram E.	Worcester,	Guardianship,	17613

YEAR.	NAME.	RESIDENCE.	NATURE.	CASE.
1859	DRURY, Horace	Royalston,	Guardianship,	17614
1784	Isaac	Temple, N. H.,	Guardianship,	17615
1810	Isaac	Shrewsbury,	Will,	17616
1842	Isaac	Charlton,	Administration,	17617
1861	Jennie E.	Worcester,	Guardianship,	17618
1791	Joel	Gerry,	Guardianship,	17619
1865	Joel	Athol,	Will,	17620
1850	John	Shrewsbury,	Administration,	17621
1861	John	Charlton,	Administration,	17622
1851	John E.	Westminster,	Guardianship,	17623
1868	John E.	West Boylston,	Administration,	17624
1878	John S.	Athol,	Will,	17625
1786	Jonathan	Athol,	Guardianship,	17626
1864	Jonathan	Royalston,	Administration,	17627
1836	Laura	Shrewsbury,	Administration,	17628
1871	Leander M.	Royalston,	Guardianship,	17629
1851	Levi A.	Westminster,	Guardianship,	17630
1787	Lois	Shrewsbury,	Administration,	17631
1836	Lorenzo C.	Holden,	Guardianship,	17632
1841	Lovina	Winchendon,	Guardianship,	17633
1836	Luke	Shrewsbury,	Will,	17634
1766	Lydia	Spencer,	Guardianship,	17635
1797	Lydia	Grafton,	Guardianship,	17636
1860	Lyman M.	Westminster,	Guardianship,	17637
1847	Maria H.	Leicester,	Guardianship,	17638
1876	Martha C.	Worcester,	Administration,	17639
1792	Mary	Shrewsbury,	Will,	17640
1869	Mary	Leicester,	Administration,	17641
1839	Mary A.	Auburn,	Guardianship,	17642
1827	Melissa W.	Spencer,	Guardianship,	17643
1786	Olive	Athol,	Guardianship,	17644
1845	Persis	Grafton,	Will,	17645
1860	Pinkney	Holden,	Administration,	17646
1861	Polly	Charlton,	Administration,	17647
1864	Ruth	Grafton,	Administration,	17648
1786	Samuel	Athol,	Guardianship,	17649
1819	Samuel	Athol,	Administration,	17650
1767	Sarah	Spencer,	Guardianship,	17651
1860	Sarah A.	Royalston,	Guardianship,	17652
1873	Sarah W.	Gardner,	Administration,	17653
1873	Simeon S.	Athol,	Administration,	17654
1860	Susan F.	Royalston,	Guardianship,	17655
1767	Susanah	Spencer,	Guardianship,	17656
1786	Susannah	Athol,	Guardianship,	17657
1779	Thomas	Ward,	Administration,	17658

YEAR.	NAME.	RESIDENCE.	NATURE.	CASE.
1784	DRURY, Thomas	Grafton,	Administration,	17659
1791	Thomas	Gerry,	Guardianship,	17660
1791	Thomas	Gerry,	Administration,	17661
1829	Thomas	Phillipston,	Administration,	17662
1860	Thomas	Westminster,	Administration,	17663
1839	Thomas A.	Auburn,	Guardianship,	17664
1828	Varney	Spencer,	Administration,	17665
1839	Wealthy H.	Auburn,	Guardianship,	17666
1764	William	Spencer,	Administration,	17667
1815	William	Brookfield,	Guardianship,	17668
1815	William	Brookfield,	Will,	17668
1816	William	Brookfield,	Administration,	17669
1850	William	Holden,	Will,	17670
1850	William	Holden,	Pension,	17671
1860	William E.	Worcester,	Administration,	17672
1839	William H.	Auburn,	Guardianship,	17673
1861	William H.	Worcester,	Guardianship,	17674
1856	William W.	Holden,	Adoption, etc.,	17675
1785	Winsor	Shrewsbury,	Guardianship,	17676
1840	DRYDEN, Artemas	Holden,	Will,	17677
1840	Artemas	Holden,	Pension,	17678
1851	Artemas	Holden,	Will,	17679
1861	Harriet W.	Worcester,	Administration,	17680
1782	Thomas	Holden,	Administration,	17681
1878	DRYSDALE, Henry	Clinton,	Will,	17682
1869	DUBOIS, Rachel	Worcester,	Administration,	17683
1868	DUBORD, Charles F.	North Brookfield,	Administration,	17684
1860	DUCKWORTH, Lawrence	Southbridge,	Administration,	17685
1832	DUDLEY, Abba W., etc.	Harvard,	Guardianship,	17686
1842	Abby G.	Sutton,	Guardianship,	17687
1854	Abby W.	Harvard,	Administration,	17688
1813	Abel	Sutton,	Will,	17689
1870	Alice L.	Douglas,	Guardianship,	17690
1846	Amasa	Uxbridge,	Will,	17691
1874	Ann	Northbridge,	Will,	17692
1845	Ann A. T.	Sutton,	Guardianship,	17693
1829	Anna	Douglas,	Guardianship,	17694
1870	Anna E.	Lunenburg,	Guardianship,	17695
1847	Asa T.	Douglas,	Guardianship,	17696
1855	Asa T.	Douglas,	Administration,	17697
1825	Azubah	Douglas,	Guardianship,	17698
1825	Benjamin	Douglas,	Guardianship,	17699
1831	Benjamin	Douglas,	Will,	17700
1870	Benjamin	Douglas,	Administration,	17701
1828	Benjamin, Jr.	Douglas,	Administration,	17702

YEAR.	NAME.	RESIDENCE.	NATURE.	CASE.
1830	DUDLEY, Caleb	Sutton,	Administration,	17703
1840	Caleb F.	Sutton,	Guardianship,	17704
1829	Caroline E.	Douglas,	Guardianship,	17705
1835	Caroline M.	Lancaster,	Guardianship,	17706
1866	Carrie M.	Hardwick,	Guardianship,	17707
1747	Charles	Sutton,	Administration,	17708
1835	Charles H.	Lancaster,	Guardianship,	17709
1840	Charles H.	Sutton,	Guardianship,	17710
1870	Charles S.	Douglas,	Guardianship,	17711
1872	Charles T.	Douglas,	Guardianship,	17712
1764	David	Sutton,	Guardianship,	17713
1814	David	Millbury,	Will,	17714
1829	David	Douglas,	Administration,	17715
1836	David	Sutton,	Administration,	17716
1837	David T.	Sutton,	Guardianship,	17717
1830	David W.	Douglas,	Guardianship,	17718
1880	Dennis	Grafton,	Will,	17719
1865	Dolly T.	Sutton,	Administration,	17720
1844	Edward T.	Worcester,	Guardianship,	17721
1877	Edwin	Petersham,	Guardianship,	17722
1809	Elias	Northbridge,	Guardianship,	17723
1835	Eliza	Lancaster,	Guardianship,	17724
1830	Eliza J.	Douglas,	Guardianship,	17725
1837	Elizabeth	Petersham,	Administration,	17726
1848	Elizabeth	Petersham,	Will,	17727
1846	Elmira	Sutton,	Will,	17728
1832	Emilia, etc.	Harvard,	Guardianship,	17729
1860	Emma J.	Southborough,	Guardianship,	17730
1860	Estella L.	Southborough,	Guardianship,	17731
1870	Estes M.	Lunenburg,	Guardianship,	17732
1760	Francis	Sutton,	Will,	17733
1870	Francis A.	Douglas,	Guardianship,	17734
1865	Frederick A.	Worcester,	Guardianship,	17735
1875	Frederick A.	Gardner,	Administration,	17736
1863	Frederick N.	Shrewsbury,	Guardianship,	17737
1873	Frederick N.	Shrewsbury,	Administration,	17738
1866	George F.	Hardwick,	Guardianship,	17739
1830	George R.	Douglas,	Guardianship,	17740
1870	George W.	Lunenburg,	Guardianship,	17741
1835	Gerry	Shrewsbury,	Administration,	17742
1828	Guilford	Harvard,	Administration,	17743
1801	Hannah	Sutton,	Administration,	17744
1809	Hannah	Northbridge,	Guardianship,	17745
1865	Hannah M.	Blackstone,	Administration,	17746
1875	Harriet A.	Harvard,	Guardianship,	17747

Year.	Name.	Residence.	Nature.	Case.
1872	DUDLEY, Herbert H.	Northbridge,	Guardianship,	17748
1790	James	Sutton,	Guardianship,	17749
1845	James	Sutton,	Administration,	17750
1866	James E.	Northbridge,	Will,	17751
1845	James M.	Sutton,	Guardianship,	17752
1845	Jane L.	Sutton,	Guardianship,	17753
1870	Jason	Sutton,	Administration,	17754
1797	Jemima	Sutton,	Guardianship,	17755
1786	John	Sutton,	Administration,	17756
1790	John	Sutton,	Guardianship,	17757
1814	John	Petersham,	Administration,	17758
1843	John	Worcester,	Administration,	17759
1859	John	Sutton,	Administration,	17760
1861	John	Harvard,	Administration,	17761
1880	John	Sutton,	Administration,	17762
1835	John E.	Lancaster,	Guardianship,	17763
1845	John L.	Sutton,	Guardianship,	17764
1809	John S.	Northbridge,	Guardianship,	17765
1789	Jonathan	Sutton,	Administration,	17766
1795	Jonathan	Sutton,	Administration,	17767
1846	Jonathan	Sutton,	Administration,	17768
1848	Jonathan	Sutton,	Administration,	17769
1790	Joseph	Sutton,	Guardianship,	17770
1799	Joseph	Sutton,	Administration,	17771
1800	Joseph	Sutton,	Guardianship,	17772
1865	Joseph	Petersham,	Will,	17773
1866	Joseph	Northbridge,	Administration,	17774
1800	Juda	Sutton,	Guardianship,	17775
1866	Julia E.	Hardwick,	Guardianship,	17776
1834	Lemuel	Douglas,	Administration,	17777
1842	Leonard	Sutton,	Administration,	17778
1842	Leonard F.	Sutton,	Guardianship,	17779
1797	Lucy	Sutton,	Guardianship,	17780
1874	Lucy	Sutton,	Will,	17781
1830	Luia M.	Douglas,	Guardianship,	17782
1866	Lydia	Petersham,	Administration,	17783
1860	L. Edna	Southborough,	Guardianship,	17784
1840	Marcus M.	Sutton,	Guardianship,	17785
1843	Marcy	Douglas,	Guardianship,	17786
1871	Marcy	Douglas,	Administration,	17786
1871	Martha	Douglas,	Administration,	17787
1835	Martha A.	Lancaster,	Guardianship,	17788
1857	Martha E.	Worcester,	Administration,	17789
1809	Mary	Northbridge,	Guardianship,	17790
1855	Mary A.	Douglas,	Guardianship,	17791

YEAR.	NAME.	RESIDENCE.	NATURE.	CASE.
1840	DUDLEY, Mary C.	Sutton,	Guardianship,	17792
1866	Mary J.	Hardwick,	Guardianship,	17793
1870	Mary K.	Lunenburg,	Guardianship,	17794
1788	Molly	Douglas,	Guardianship,	17795
1870	Nancy	Petersham,	Administration,	17796
1835	Nathan A. M.	Lancaster,	Guardianship,	17797
1866	Nellie A.	Hardwick,	Guardianship,	17798
1825	Nelson	Douglas,	Guardianship,	17799
1788	Olive	Douglas,	Guardianship,	17800
1829	Olive	Douglas,	Guardianship,	17801
1870	Oliver W.	Lunenburg,	Administration,	17802
1809	Otis	Northbridge,	Guardianship,	17803
1843	Patience	Harvard,	Will,	17804
1837	Paul	Douglas,	Pension,	17805
1872	Paul W.	Northbridge,	Administration,	17806
1836	Peter	Sutton,	Will,	17807
1840	Peter	Sutton,	Will,	17808
1829	Phebe	Douglas,	Guardianship,	17809
1851	Phebe	Sutton,	Administration,	17810
1829	Polly	Douglas,	Guardianship,	17811
1797	Prudence	Sutton,	Guardianship,	17812
1867	Reuben A.	Worcester,	Administration,	17813
1855	Ruth	Holden,	Pension,	17814
1797	Sally	Sutton,	Guardianship,	17815
1825	Sally	Douglas,	Guardianship,	17816
1847	Sally	Douglas,	Guardianship,	17817
1778	Samuel	Douglas,	Administration,	17818
1832	Samuel	Harvard,	Will,	17819
1847	Samuel	Douglas,	Will,	17820
1848	Samuel	Petersham,	Administration,	17821
1825	Samuel, Jr.	Douglas,	Guardianship,	17822
1790	Sarah	Sutton,	Guardianship,	17823
1875	Sarah E.	Harvard,	Guardianship,	17824
1872	Sarah J.	Northbridge,	Guardianship,	17825
1835	Sarah L.	Lancaster,	Guardianship,	17826
1840	Sarah P.	Sutton,	Guardianship,	17827
1876	Sarah R.	Webster,	Administration,	17828
1830	Sherman	Harvard,	Administration,	17829
1800	Silas	Sutton,	Guardianship,	17830
1870	Silas	Harvard,	Will,	17831
1857	Simon	Petersham,	Will,	17832
1875	Simon	Millbury,	Administration,	17833
1865	Sumner F.	Worcester,	Guardianship,	17834
1872	Walter W.	Northbridge,	Guardianship,	17835
1786	William	Douglas,	Administration,	17836

Year.	Name.	Residence.	Nature.	Case.
1811	DUDLEY, William	Dudley,	Administration,	17837
1861	William	Shrewsbury,	Administration,	17838
1863	William	Worcester,	Will,	17839
1879	William	Douglas,	Will,	17840
1819	Zacheus	Harvard,	Will,	17841
1855	DUEQUETTE, David	Webster,	Administration,	17842
	DUFFY, DUFFEY AND DUFFEE,			
1873	Bernard	Millbury,	Administration,	17843
1863	Eliza A.	Fitchburg,	Guardianship,	17844
1859	John	Northborough,	Change of Name,	17845
1863	John	Fitchburg,	Guardianship,	17846
1878	Mary	Millbury,	Will,	17847
1863	Mary J.	Fitchburg,	Guardianship,	17848
1859	Patrick	Northborough,	Change of Name,	17849
1863	Sarah A.	Fitchburg,	Guardianship,	17850
1861	Timothy	Fitchburg	Will,	17851
1879	William	Milford,	Administration,	17852
1879	DUFOE, Peter	Douglas,	Administration,	17853
	DUGAN see DUGGAN.			
1817	DUGAR, Charles	Southbridge,	Will,	17854
1873	Charles	Charlton,	Will,	17855
1863	Peter	Charlton,	Administration,	17856
	DUGGAN AND DUGAN,			
1874	Bedelia	Bolton,	Guardianship,	17857
1874	Bridget	Worcester,	Administration,	17858
1876	Bridget	Uxbridge,	Administration,	17859
1876	Bridget	Danielsonville, Conn.,	Guardianship,	17860
1876	Catherine	New Britain, Conn.,	Guardianship,	17861
1876	Catherine J.	Danielsonville, Conn.,	Guardianship,	17862
1857	Cornelius	Millbury,	Guardianship,	17863
1868	Cornelius	Millbury,	Will,	17864
1876	Cornelius	Webster,	Will,	17865
1778	Daniel	Charlton,	Administration,	17866
1872	David	Milford,	Guardianship,	17867
1877	Ellen	Webster,	Guardianship,	17868
1857	Johana	Millbury,	Guardianship,	17869
1876	Johanna	New Britain, Conn.,	Guardianship,	17870
1857	John	Millbury,	Will,	17871
1874	John	Bolton,	Administration,	17872
1874	John	Bolton,	Guardianship,	17873
1873	Leona I.	Charlton,	Adoption, etc.,	17874
1874	Margaret	Bolton,	Guardianship,	17875
1875	Mary	Webster,	Will,	17876
1874	Mary A.	Bolton,	Guardianship,	17877
1876	Mary E.	Danielsonville, Conn.,	Guardianship,	17878
1866	Michael	Bolton,	Administration,	17879

YEAR.	NAME.	RESIDENCE.	NATURE.	CASE.
	DUGGAN AND DUGAN,			
1877	Michael	Webster,	Guardianship,	17880
1874	Rosa	Bolton,	Guardianship,	17881
1847	William	Worcester,	Administration,	17882
1871	William	Webster,	Will,	17883
1877	William	Webster,	Guardianship,	17884
1818	DUICK, Benjamin	Pomfret, Conn.,	Foreign Will,	17885
1880	DUMAS, Francis	Spencer,	Guardianship,	17886
1880	Francis	Spencer,	Guardianship,	17887
1874	Joseph	Gardner,	Administration,	17888
1880	Louis	Templeton,	Will,	17889
1880	Mary	Spencer,	Guardianship,	17890
1880	Paul J.	Spencer,	Guardianship,	17891
1880	Pierre	Spencer,	Guardianship,	17892
1873	Virginia	Webster,	Adoption, etc.,	17893
	DUMPHY AND DUMPHE,			
1868	Bridget	North Brookfield,	Guardianship,	17894
1878	Charles H.	Worcester,	Guardianship,	17895
1868	Edward	North Brookfield,	Guardianship,	17896
1878	Grace A.	Worcester,	Guardianship,	17897
1868	James	North Brookfield,	Guardianship,	17898
1868	John	North Brookfield,	Guardianship,	17899
1868	John	North Brookfield,	Administration,	17900
1868	Thomas	North Brookfield,	Adoption, etc.,	17901
1868	Thomas	North Brookfield,	Guardianship,	17902
1868	Thomas M.	Sturbridge,	Adoption, etc.,	17903
1878	William E.	Worcester,	Guardianship,	17904
1855	DUNBAR, Catherine D.	Southbridge,	Guardianship,	17905
1846	Charles C.	Charlton,	Guardianship,	17906
1796	Chloe	Leicester,	Guardianship,	17907
1828	David	Charlton,	Will,	17908
1818	Dorothy	Charlton,	Guardianship,	17909
1880	Dorothy	Worcester,	Will,	17910
1877	Ebenezer	Leicester,	Will,	17911
1847	James D.	Brookfield,	Administration,	17912
1818	Joanna	Charlton,	Guardianship,	17913
1796	John	Leicester,	Guardianship,	17914
1796	Lucretia	Leicester,	Guardianship,	17915
1796	Lucy	Leicester,	Guardianship,	17916
1818	Patience	Charlton,	Guardianship,	17917
1818	Rufus D.	Charlton,	Guardianship,	17918
1817	Samuel	Charlton,	Administration,	17919
1846	Samuel	Charlton,	Guardianship,	17920
1846	Samuel	Charlton,	Administration,	17921
1838	Sarah	Charlton,	Administration,	17922

Year.	Name.	Residence.	Nature.	Case.
1865	DUNBAR, Sarah	Leicester,	Will,	17923
1876	Susan	Worcester,	Administration,	17924
1796	Thomas	Leicester,	Administration,	17925
	DUNCAN AND DUNKIN,			
1787	Andrew	Worcester,	Administration,	17926
1805	Clark	Dudley,	Guardianship,	17927
1735	John	Chelmsford,	Administration,	17928
1739	John	Worcester,	Will,	17929
1773	Jonas	Rutland,	Administration,	17930
1877	Joseph	Worcester,	Administration,	17931
1771	Samuel	Rutland,	Will,	17932
1773	Samuel	Rutland,	Administration,	17933
1835	Sarah	Worcester,	Will,	17934
1739	Simeon	Worcester,	Guardianship,	17935
1782	Simeon	Worcester,	Administration,	17936
1836	Simeon	Worcester,	Pension,	17937
1875	Tryphosa L.	North Brookfield,	Administration,	17938
1801	William	Dudley,	Will,	17939
1858	William	Brookfield,	Administration,	17940
1873	William	North Brookfield,	Will,	17941
1852	DUNHAM, Elizabeth	Blackstone,	Will,	17942
1854	Elizabeth	Harvard,	Administration,	17943
1859	Jerusha	Winchendon,	Guardianship,	17944
1851	Mary	Blackstone,	Administration,	17945
	DUNKIN see DUNCAN.			
1877	DUNLAP, Amelia F.	Fitchburg,	Administration,	17946
1764	Andrew	Westborough,	Guardianship,	17947
1778	DUNN, Agnes	Oakham,	Guardianship,	17948
1864	Albert M.	Northbridge,	Guardianship,	17949
1778	Alexander	Oakham,	Guardianship,	17950
1869	Alice	Athol,	Administration,	17951
1869	Alice	Athol,	Pension,	17952
1864	Alice A.	Northbridge,	Guardianship,	17953
1864	Augustus B.	Northbridge,	Guardianship,	17954
1795	David	Northbridge,	Will,	17955
1796	David	Northbridge,	Guardianship,	17956
1848	David, Jr.	Upton,	Administration,	17957
1871	Edward B.	Fitchburg,	Will,	17958
1796	Elizabeth	Northbridge,	Guardianship,	17959
1864	Emma I.	Northbridge,	Guardianship,	17960
1864	Emory	Northbridge,	Administration,	17961
1796	Ezra	Northbridge,	Guardianship,	17962
1843	Ezra	Spencer,	Administration,	17963
1845	Ezra E.	Spencer,	Guardianship,	17964
1864	Francis D.	Northbridge,	Guardianship,	17965

YEAR.	NAME.	RESIDENCE.	NATURE.	CASE.
1852	DUNN, Franklin	Holden,	Administration,	17966
1778	George	Oakham,	Guardianship,	17967
1835	George E.	Bolton,	Guardianship,	17968
1871	George E.	Fitchburg,	Guardianship,	17969
1820	Henry	Northbridge,	Will,	17970
1867	Henry	Auburn,	Will,	17971
1852	Irving A.	Holden,	Guardianship,	17972
1778	James	Oakham,	Guardianship,	17973
1873	James	Worcester,	Will,	17974
1778	Jane	Oakham,	Guardianship,	17975
1860	Jeremiah	West Brookfield,	Administration,	17976
1778	Joel	Oakham,	Guardianship,	17977
1845	Joel W.	Spencer,	Guardianship,	17978
1879	Joel W.	Spencer,	Administration,	17979
1778	John	Oakham,	Guardianship,	17980
1796	John	Northbridge,	Guardianship,	17981
1851	John	Grafton,	Administration,	17982
1875	John	Worcester,	Guardianship,	17983
1878	John	Gardner,	Will,	17984
1796	John, Jr.	Brookfield,	Will,	17985
1866	John B.	Millbury,	Guardianship,	17986
1835	John L.	Bolton,	Guardianship,	17987
1778	Joseph	Oakham,	Guardianship,	17988
1868	Joseph	West Brookfield,	Will,	17989
1865	Julia	Milford,	Guardianship,	17990
1834	Lucas	Bolton,	Administration,	17991
1852	Lydia A.	Holden,	Guardianship,	17992
1870	Mary	Worcester,	Administration,	17993
1865	Mary A.	Milford,	Guardianship,	17994
1864	Mary C.	Northbridge,	Guardianship,	17995
1868	Mary E.	Fitchburg,	Guardianship,	17996
1865	Michael	Milford,	Guardianship,	17997
1875	Nicholas	Worcester,	Administration,	17998
1879	Patrick	Hardwick,	Administration,	17999
1778	Rachel	Oakham,	Guardianship,	18000
1849	Rachel	Auburn,	Will,	18001
1778	William	Oakham,	Administration,	18002
1826	William	Petersham,	Administration,	18003
1878	DUNNAWIN, Edmund	Worcester,	Administration,	18004
	DUNNELL AND DUNNEL,			
1841	Franklin	Millbury,	Guardianship,	18005
1758	Jonathan, Jr.	Sutton,	Administration,	18006
1841	Remark	Millbury,	Administration,	18007
1841	Sarah	Millbury,	Guardianship,	18008

YEAR.	NAME.	RESIDENCE.	NATURE.	CASE.
	DUNSMOOR AND DUNSMORE,			
1748	Catherine	Lancaster,	Guardianship,	18009
1827	Ebenezer	Lunenburg,	Administration,	18010
1838	Elizabeth J.	Lunenburg,	Guardianship,	18011
1836	Henry	Lunenburg,	Administration,	18012
1838	Henry LaF.	Lunenburg,	Guardianship,	18013
1828	Isaac	New York,	Administration,	18014
1838	James N.	Lunenburg,	Guardianship,	18015
1747	John	Lancaster,	Will,	18016
1794	John	Lunenburg,	Will,	18017
1839	Joseph	Lunenburg,	Guardianship,	18018
1838	Luther G.	Lunenburg,	Guardianship,	18019
1838	Morton S.	Lunenburg,	Guardianship,	18020
1773	Oliver	New Braintree,	Will,	18021
1852	Polly	West Boylston,	Guardianship,	18022
1821	Reuben	Princeton,	Administration,	18023
1847	Samuel	Lunenburg,	Guardianship,	18024
1837	Sarah	West Boylston,	Pension,	18025
1824	Silas	West Boylston,	Administration,	18026
1753	Thomas	Brookfield,	Will,	18027
1804	Thomas	Groton,	Guardianship,	18028
1839	Thomas	Lunenburg,	Guardianship,	18029
1854	Thomas	Lunenburg,	Administration,	18030
1748	William	Lancaster,	Guardianship,	18031
1783	William	Shrewsbury,	Administration,	18032
1784	William	Lancaster,	Administration,	18033
1836	William	Lunenburg,	Will,	18034
1839	William	Lunenburg,	Guardianship,	18035
1758	DUNSTER, David	Narragansett, No. 2,	Will,	18036
1806	David	Westminster,	Guardianship,	18037
1805	Ephraim	Westminster,	Guardianship,	18038
1819	Hubbard	Gardner,	Administration,	18039
1805	Hubbard R.	Westminster,	Administration,	18040
1850	Jason	Westminster,	Will,	18041
1850	Jason A.	Westminster,	Guardianship,	18042
1850	Mary C.	Westminster,	Guardianship,	18043
1812	Nathan	Westminster,	Guardianship,	18044
1839	Samuel	Ashburnham,	Will,	18045
1850	Sarah A.	Westminster,	Guardianship,	18046
1789	DUNTON, Abner	Sturbridge,	Administration,	18047
1790	Abner	Sturbridge,	Guardianship,	18048
1824	Abner	Brookfield,	Administration,	18049
1865	Anna M.	Boylston,	Guardianship,	18050
1811	Benjamin	Barre,	Administration,	18051
1830	Benjamin	Phillipston,	Will,	18052

YEAR.	NAME.	RESIDENCE.	NATURE.	CASE.
1854	DUNTON, Benjamin A.	Phillipston,	Guardianship,	18053
1843	Bulah	Holden,	Administration,	18054
1856	Calvin	Boylston,	Administration,	18055
1771	Ebenezer	Southborough,	Administration,	18056
1820	Ebenezer	Phillipston,	Will,	18057
1821	Ebenezer	Sturbridge,	Will,	18058
1854	Frank E.	Spencer,	Guardianship,	18059
1796	Hitty	Holden,	Guardianship,	18060
1792	Isaac	Holden,	Administration,	18061
1852	James	Southborough,	Pension,	18062
1788	Jedidiah	Athol,	Guardianship,	18063
1811	John	Sturbridge,	Will,	18064
1814	Levi	Leicester,	Administration,	18065
1827	Levi	Leicester,	Guardianship,	18066
1866	Lizzie C.	Moorse, N. Y.,	Adoption, etc.,	18067
1874	Luther M.	Templeton,	Will,	18068
1855	Lydia J.	Holden,	Guardianship,	18069
1853	Mary	Phillipston,	Administration,	18070
1872	Mary H.	Sturbridge	Administration,	18071
1854	Mary L.	Spencer,	Guardianship,	18072
1854	Mary M.	Phillipston,	Guardianship,	18073
1790	Molly	Sturbridge,	Guardianship,	18074
1870	Moses	Millbury,	Administration,	18075
1866	Nellie J.	Phillipston,	Adoption, etc.,	18076
1878	Newton	Brookfield,	Administration,	18077
1842	Persis	Phillipston,	Will,	18078
1815	Reuben	Boylston,	Administration,	18079
1865	Reuben	Boylston,	Will,	18080
1821	Robert B.	Northborough,	Guardianship,	18081
1855	Royal S.	Holden,	Administration,	18082
1796	Sally	Holden,	Guardianship,	18083
1852	Sally	Southborough,	Guardianship,	18084
1855	Sally	Southborough,	Administration,	18084
1857	Sally	Sturbridge,	Will,	18085
1857	Sally	Southborough,	Pension,	18086
1796	Samuel	Holden,	Guardianship,	18087
1790	Sarah	Sturbridge,	Guardianship,	18088
1873	Susan N.	Millbury,	Administration,	18089
1823	Sylvanus	Barre,	Guardianship,	18090
1863	Sylvanus	Hubbardston,	Will,	18091
1758	Thomas	Western,	Will,	18092
1853	Warren H.	Spencer,	Administration,	18093
1849	Zenas	Sturbridge,	Will,	18094
1787	DUPEE, Elias	Westminster,	Guardianship,	18095
1745	Isaac	Leominster,	Guardianship,	18096

YEAR.	NAME.	RESIDENCE.	NATURE.	CASE.
1785	DUPEE, Isaac	Westminster,	Administration,	18097
1787	Isaac	Templeton,	Administration,	18098
1744	John	Leominster,	Administration,	18099
1744	John	Leominster,	Guardianship,	18100
1838	John	Westminster,	Will,	18101
1841	John	Westminster,	Pension,	18102
1808	Jonas	Westminster,	Guardianship,	18103
1787	Joshua	Westminster,	Guardianship,	18104
1791	Thomas	Westminster,	Guardianship,	18105
	DUPREE, DUPREY AND DUPREZ,			
1877	Ada F.	Westborough,	Guardianship,	18106
1864	George F.	Spencer,	Adoption, etc.,	18107
1869	Oliver	Webster,	Will,	18108
1864	DURANT, Amos	Fitchburg,	Administration,	18109
1872	Sarah B.	Warren,	Administration,	18110
1879	William	Leominster,	Will,	18111
1864	William H.	Warren,	Administration,	18112
1859	DURFEE, Dexter H.	Southbridge,	Guardianship,	18113
1859	Henry E.	Southbridge,	Administration,	18114
1854	Joseph	Southbridge,	Will,	18115
1877	Mary A.	No. Livermore, Me.,	*Administration.*	18116
1859	Susan M.	Southbridge,	Guardianship,	18117
1880	DURKEE, Clarence E.	Dudley,	Guardianship,	18118
1880	Clement E.	Dudley,	Guardianship,	18119
1874	Erastus	Dudley,	Administration,	18120
1880	Florence E.	Dudley,	Guardianship,	18121
1880	Lyman P.	Dudley,	Administration,	18122
1837	DUSTIN, Alexander	Sterling,	Will,	18123
1879	DUTCHER, Warren W.	Milford,	Will,	18124
1880	DUTTON, Betsey B.	Fitchburg,	Administration,	18125
1816	Laura A.	Ashburnham,	Guardianship,	18126
1839	Polly	Worcester,	Administration,	18127
1815	Samuel, Jr.	Ashburnham,	Will,	18128
1816	Samuel S.	Ashburnham,	Guardianship,	18129
1816	Solomon L.	Ashburnham,	Guardianship,	18130
1839	DWELLY, Joseph	Oakham,	Will,	18131
1840	Joseph	Oakham,	Pension,	18132
1840	Joseph B.	Oakham,	Guardianship,	18133
1855	Ruth	Holden,	Will,	18134
1855	Ruth	Holden,	Pension,	18135
1833	DWIGHT, Anna	Western,	Will,	18136
1817	Caroline A.	Western,	Guardianship,	18137
1865	Daniel	Dudley,	Will,	18138
1866	Daniel H.	Dudley,	Guardianship,	18139
1779	Elihu	Western,	Guardianship,	18140

YEAR.	NAME.	RESIDENCE.	NATURE.	CASE.
1879	DWIGHT, Louisa L.	Oakham,	Will,	18141
1874	Mary, etc.	Dudley,	Will,	18142
1866	Mary A.	Dudley,	Guardianship,	18143
1874	Mary A.	Dudley,	Will,	18142
1773	Mehetable	Ashburnham,	Guardianship,	18144
1779	Samuel	Western,	Guardianship,	18145
1773	Sarah	Ashburnham,	Guardianship,	18146
1778	Simeon	Western,	Administration,	18147
1816	Simeon	Western,	Administration,	18148
1866	Susan E.	Dudley,	Guardianship,	18149
1769	Timothy	Ashburnham,	Administration,	18150
1848	William	Detroit, Mich.,	Administration,	18151
	DWINELL, DWINEL AND DWINNELL,			
1871	Abby J.	Upton,	Guardianship,	18152
1814	Abraham	Millbury,	Administration,	18153
1815	Alice	Millbury,	Guardianship,	18154
1866	Ann E.	Millbury,	Guardianship,	18155
1818	Candace	Harvard,	Guardianship,	18156
1815	Cyrus	Millbury,	Guardianship,	18157
1818	Edwin	Harvard,	Guardianship,	18158
1818	Elijah	Harvard,	Administration,	18159
1815	Eliza	Millbury,	Guardianship,	18160
1854	Eliza	Ashburnham,	Guardianship,	18161
1816	Ellis	Millbury,	Guardianship,	18162
1871	Frederic J.	Upton,	Guardianship,	18163
1871	George W.	Upton,	Guardianship,	18164
1842	Hannah	Millbury,	Administration,	18165
1843	Hannah	Millbury,	Pension,	18166
1818	Harriet	Harvard,	Guardianship,	18167
1814	Henry	Sutton,	Administration,	18168
1871	Henry E.	Upton,	Guardianship,	18169
1871	Herbert R.	Upton,	Guardianship,	18170
1815	Hiram	Millbury,	Guardianship,	18171
1874	Hiram	Ashburnham,	Administration,	18172
1818	Jared	Harvard,	Guardianship,	18173
1860	Jared	Bolton,	Administration,	18174
1818	Jerome	Harvard,	Guardianship,	18175
1819	John	Millbury,	Administration,	18176
1854	Jonas W.	Ashburnham,	Guardianship,	18177
1771	Jonathan	Sutton,	Will,	18178
1870	Leonard	Millbury,	Will,	18179
1818	Lovisa	Harvard,	Guardianship,	18180
1815	Lucy	Millbury,	Guardianship,	18181
1854	Marius M.	Ashburnham,	Guardianship,	18182

Year.	Name.	Residence.	Nature.	Case.
	DWINELL, DWINEL AND DWINNELL,			
1818	Mary	Harvard,	Guardianship,	18183
1786	Mehitable	Sutton,	Will,	18184
1854	Minerva	Ashburnham,	Guardianship,	18185
1818	Pliny	Harvard,	Guardianship,	18186
1815	Polly	Millbury,	Guardianship,	18187
1870	Richard	Upton,	Administration,	18188
1818	Sally	Harvard,	Guardianship,	18189
1858	Sally	Millbury,	Administration,	18190
1858	Sarah, etc.	Millbury,	Administration,	18190
1818	Silvia	Harvard,	Guardianship,	18191
1830	Solomon	Millbury,	Administration,	18192
1867	Solomon	Millbury,	Will,	18193
1854	Waldo W.	Ashburnham,	Guardianship,	18194
	DWYER AND DWYRE,			
1868	Arthur W.	Paxton,	Guardianship,	18195
1873	Edward	Blackstone,	Will,	18196
1881	James	New Zealand,	Will,	18197
1865	Jane	Webster,	Administration,	18198
1869	John	Milford,	Guardianship,	18199
1869	Mary A.	Milford,	Guardianship,	18200
1861	Patrick	Hardwick,	Will,	18201
1869	Patrick J.	Milford,	Guardianship,	18202
1869	Thomas	Webster,	Guardianship,	18203
1869	Thomas H.	Milford,	Guardianship,	18204
1867	William	Paxton,	Administration,	18205
1869	William E.	Milford,	Guardianship,	18206
	DYER AND DYAR,			
1864	Ai O.	Gardner,	Administration,	18207
1869	Benjamin	Oxford,	Administration,	18208
1875	Calvin	Worcester,	Trustee,	18209
1865	Carrie	Spencer,	Guardianship,	18210
1865	Charles E.	Spencer,	Guardianship,	18211
1828	Dyson	Worcester,	Guardianship,	18212
1865	Edward C.	Spencer,	Will,	18213
1796	Enoch	Princeton,	Guardianship,	18214
1852	George W.	Gardner,	Guardianship,	18215
1829	Harriet A.	Harvard,	Guardianship,	18216
1870	Henry	Sturbridge,	Will,	18217
1835	Hiram	Union, O.,	Guardianship,	18218
1880	Horatio N.	Templeton,	Administration,	18219
1795	Jacob	Princeton,	Guardianship,	18220
1877	Jennie M.	Templeton,	Guardianship,	18221
1829	Jeremiah	Harvard,	Will,	18222

(420)

YEAR.	NAME.	RESIDENCE.	NATURE.	CASE.
	DYER and DYAR,			
1784	John	Dudley,	Administration,	18223
1852	John	Gardner,	Administration,	18224
1870	John	Leominster,	Will,	18225
1852	John A.	Gardner,	Guardianship,	18226
1872	Martha E.	Clinton,	Change of Name,	18227
1873	Mary	Leominster,	Guardianship,	18228
1876	Mary	Leominster,	Administration,	18229
1829	Mary A.	Harvard,	Guardianship,	18230
1860	Mary J.	Berlin,	Guardianship,	18231
1879	Moses	Northbridge,	Administration,	18232
1852	Oscar	Gardner,	Guardianship,	18233
1873	Peter	Leominster,	Guardianship,	18234
1808	Samuel	Athol,	Administration,	18235
1873	Sarah O.	Worcester,	Will,	18236
1865	Sarah W.	Spencer,	Guardianship,	18237
1817	Shebna	Athol,	Administration,	18238
1865	Theodore J.	Templeton,	Administration,	18239
1852	Thomas L.	Gardner,	Guardianship,	18240
1818	Thomson	New Braintree,	Guardianship,	18241
1873	William	Leominster,	Guardianship,	18242
1877	William	Leominster,	Adoption, etc.,	18243
1871	William B.	Milford,	Will,	18244
	DYKE see DIKE.			
1857	DYSON, Alice A.	Millbury,	Guardianship,	18245
1857	Edwin	Millbury,	Guardianship,	18246
1857	Eli	Millbury,	Will,	18247
1868	James	Millbury,	Will,	18248
1857	James E.	Millbury,	Guardianship,	18249
1857	John T.	Millbury,	Guardianship,	18250
1857	Lydia	Millbury,	Guardianship,	18251
1857	Mary J.	Millbury,	Guardianship,	18252
1734	EAGER, Abraham	Shrewsbury,	Will,	18253
1778	Abraham	Shrewsbury,	Will,	18254
1875	Adeline	Westminster,	Guardianship,	18255
1828	Anna	Boylston,	Administration,	18256
1761	Ashbell	Shrewsbury,	Guardianship,	18257
1831	Augustus	Westminster,	Guardianship,	18258
1871	Augustus	Westminster,	Will,	18259
1734	Benjamin	Shrewsbury,	Guardianship,	18260
1759	Benjamin	Shrewsbury,	Will,	18261
1787	Bezaleel	Northborough,	Will,	18262
1837	Charles D.	Northborough,	Guardianship,	18263
1871	Charles D.	Westminster,	Guardianship,	18264
1881	Denna	Northborough,	Will,	18265

Year.	Name.	Residence.	Nature.	Case.
1788	EAGER, Dinah	Shrewsbury,	Will,	18266
1759	Dorothy	Shrewsbury,	Guardianship,	18267
1825	Dwight F.	Sterling,	Guardianship,	18268
1804	Ephraim	Sterling,	Administration,	18269
1866	Ephraim	West Boylston,	Administration,	18270
1880	Ernest W.	Fitchburg	Guardianship,	18271
1821	Fanny	Northborough,	Guardianship,	18272
1839	Farwell	Lancaster,	Administration,	18273
1802	Fortunatus	Sterling,	Will,	18274
1819	Fortunatus	West Boylston,	Administration,	18275
1810	Francis	Northborough,	Will,	18276
1871	George A.	Westminster,	Guardianship,	18277
1872	George A.	Clinton,	Administration,	18278
1837	George H.	Northborough,	Guardianship,	18279
1859	Harriet L.	Westminster,	Administration,	18280
1762	Hazadiah	Westborough,	Guardianship,	18281
1875	Horatio	Westminster,	Will,	18282
1773	Jacob	Grafton,	Administration,	18283
1755	James	Westborough,	Will,	18284
1761	James	Westborough,	Administration,	18285
1762	James	Westborough,	Guardianship,	18286
1779	James	Northborough,	Absentee,	18287
1829	James	Boylston,	Administration,	18288
1815	Jasper	Millbury,	Guardianship,	18289
1762	John	Westborough,	Guardianship,	18290
1779	John	Northborough,	Absentee,	18291
1820	John	Northborough,	Will,	18292
1837	John D.	Northborough,	Guardianship,	18293
1830	Jonathan	Westminster,	Will,	18294
1814	Joseph	Boylston,	Administration,	18295
1837	Joseph	Boylston,	Administration,	18296
1837	Laura W.	Northborough,	Guardianship,	18297
1822	Lewis	Shrewsbury,	Will,	18298
1844	Lois	Royalston,	Guardianship,	18299
1762	Mary	Westborough,	Guardianship,	18300
1809	Mary	Boylston,	Guardianship,	18301
1837	Mary A.	Northborough,	Guardianship,	18302
1777	Moses	Northborough,	Administration,	18303
1871	Myra A.	Westminster,	Guardianship,	18304
1829	Nahum	Leicester,	Administration,	18305
1858	Nahum	Northborough,	Administration,	18306
1781	Noah	Shrewsbury,	Administration,	18307
1836	Oliver	Northborough,	Pension,	18308
1820	Paul	Dana,	Will,	18309
1841	Sally	Shrewsbury,	Will,	18310

YEAR.	NAME.	RESIDENCE.	NATURE.	CASE.
1872	EAGER, Sally	Northborough,	Will,	18311
1821	Sarah F.	Northborough,	Guardianship,	18312
1849	Seraphina	Northborough,	Pension,	18313
1808	Solomon	Royalston,	Guardianship,	18314
1810	Solomon	Royalston,	Administration,	18315
1810	Stephen	Sutton,	Will,	18316
1865	Stephen	Oxford,	Administration,	18317
1802	Uriah	Sterling,	Guardianship,	18318
1861	Uriah	Sterling,	Administration,	18319
1837	William	Northborough,	Will,	18320
1864	William A.	Leominster,	Adoption, etc.,	18321
1880	William A.	Fitchburg,	Guardianship,	18322
1876	William L.	Fitchburg,	Administration,	18323
1871	William S.	Westminster,	Guardianship,	18324
1759	Windsor,	Shrewsbury,	Guardianship,	18325
1781	Zachariah	Lancaster,	Will,	18326
1762	Zilpha	Westborough,	Guardianship,	18327
1855	EAMES, Aaron A.	Milford,	Guardianship,	18328
1848	Abba	Milford,	Guardianship,	18329
1848	Alonzo	Milford,	Guardianship,	18330
1848	Amelia C.	Milford,	Guardianship,	18331
1862	Anna E.	Milford,	Guardianship,	18332
1864	Anna E.	Milford,	Guardianship,	18333
1762	Annis	Sutton,	Guardianship,	18334
1854	Appleton P.	Milford,	Administration,	18335
1790	Charles	Leominster,	Administration,	18336
1822	Charles	Barre,	Guardianship,	18337
1854	Charles P.	Milford,	Guardianship,	18338
1875	Charles T.	Milford,	Will,	18339
1853	Charles W.	Milford,	Guardianship,	18340
1876	Charles W.	Grafton,	Will,	18341
1865	Clara E.	Upton,	Guardianship,	18342
1853	Clarisa F.	West Brookfield,	Guardianship,	18343
1864	Dennis	Milford,	Will,	18344
1853	Dexter M.	Milford,	Guardianship,	18345
1848	Edward E. M.	Milford,	Guardianship,	18346
1864	Emma E.	Milford,	Guardianship,	18347
1845	George L.	New Orleans, La.,	Guardianship,	18348
1838	Gershom	Boylston,	Will,	18349
1865	Harrison	Upton,	Administration,	18350
1865	Helen M.	Upton,	Guardianship,	18351
1848	Helen S.	Milford,	Guardianship,	18352
1865	Henry	Spencer,	Will,	18353
1864	Herbert E.	Milford,	Guardianship,	18354
1854	Izanna J.	Milford,	Guardianship,	18355

Year.	Name.	Residence.	Nature.	Case.
1864	EAMES, Jackson T.	Westborough,	Guardianship,	18356
1762	Jacob	Sutton,	Guardianship,	18357
1762	Jemima	Sutton,	Guardianship,	18358
1821	John	Barre,	Administration,	18359
1874	Judson	Mendon,	Administration,	18360
1879	Justin E.	Milford,	Will,	18361
1854	Laura A.	Milford,	Guardianship,	18362
1862	Leonard	Milford,	Administration,	18363
1870	Levi L.	Worcester,	Administration,	18364
1869	Lucy	Barre,	Will,	18365
1762	Mary	Sutton,	Guardianship,	18366
1828	Moses	Upton,	Will,	18367
1762	Nathaniel	Sutton,	Guardianship,	18368
1873	Nathaniel	Westminster,	Will,	18369
1854	Persis	Worcester,	Administration,	18370
1816	Peter	Petersham,	Administration,	18371
1845	Phinehas	Milford,	Guardianship,	18372
1845	Phinehas	Milford,	Will,	18372
1862	Russell	Grafton,	Will,	18373
1842	Simpson	Barre,	Administration,	18374
1867	Thomas J.	Westborough,	Guardianship,	18375
1874	Walter D.	Mendon,	Guardianship,	18376
1850	Warren F.	Northborough,	Guardianship,	18377
1815	William	West Boylston,	Administration,	18378
1835	William	Worcester,	Administration,	18379
	EARLE and EARL,			
1846	Aaron	Leicester,	Administration,	18380
1768	Abigail	Leicester,	Guardianship,	18381
1829	Abigail R.	Leicester,	Guardianship,	18382
1864	Alfred C.	Worcester,	Guardianship,	18383
1869	Alfred C.	Worcester,	Administration,	18384
1858	Alice C.	Worcester,	Trustee,	18385
1781	Alpheus	Templeton,	Guardianship,	18386
1849	Alpheus	Hubbardston,	Administration,	18387
1816	Amarilla	Paxton,	Pension,	18388
1818	Amarilla	Paxton,	Guardianship,	18389
1818	Amasa	Paxton,	Administration,	18390
1843	Amos R.	Sutton,	Guardianship,	18391
1824	Anna	Leicester,	Guardianship,	18392
1770	Annah	Paxton,	Administration,	18393
1859	Anthony	Worcester,	Guardianship,	18394
1814	Antipas, 2d	Leicester,	Guardianship,	18395
1817	Antipas	Leicester,	Administration,	18396
1828	Antipas, 2d	Leicester,	Administration,	18395
1837	Asabel	Leicester,	Administration,	18397

YEAR.	NAME.	RESIDENCE.	NATURE.	CASE.
	EARLE AND EARL,			
1761	Benjamin	Leicester,	Will,	18398
1875	Benjamin	Leicester,	Administration,	18399
1781	Calvin	Templeton,	Guardianship,	18400
1818	Camilla H.	Paxton,	Guardianship,	18401
1829	Caroline M.	Leicester,	Guardianship,	18402
1851	Charles N.	Worcester,	Guardianship,	18403
1814	Clark	Worcester,	Will,	18404
1859	Clark	Worcester,	Guardianship,	18405
1854	Cyrus E.	Boylston,	Administration,	18406
1767	David	Leicester,	Will,	18407
1767	David	Leicester,	Guardianship,	18408
1824	Edward	Leicester,	Guardianship,	18409
1877	Edward	Worcester,	Will,	18410
1878	Edward	Worcester,	Trustee,	18411
1832	Eliza	Worcester,	Guardianship,	18412
1846	Elizabeth	Leicester,	Guardianship,	18413
1855	Elizabeth	Leicester,	Administration,	18414
1869	Elizabeth	Worcester,	Administration,	18415
1829	Elizabeth C.	Leicester,	Guardianship,	18416
1859	Elizabeth C.	North Brookfield,	Administration,	18417
1869	Elmer	Worcester,	Administration,	18418
1810	Elmira	Leicester,	Guardianship,	18419
1850	Emeline A.	Worcester,	Guardianship,	18420
1850	Enoch	Worcester,	Guardianship,	18421
1850	Enoch	Worcester,	Will,	18421
1850	Enoch	Worcester,	Guardianship,	18422
1860	Freelove	Leicester,	Administration,	18423
1761	Gardiner	Leicester,	Guardianship,	18424
1827	George	Leicester,	Administration,	18425
1833	George C.	Sutton,	Administration,	18426
1843	George R.	Sutton,	Guardianship,	18427
1858	Henry	Worcester,	Administration,	18428
1872	Henry	Worcester,	Administration,	18429
1843	Henry C.	Sutton,	Guardianship,	18430
1881	Henry H.	Athol,	Administration,	18431
1818	Henry W.	Leicester,	Guardianship,	18432
1837	Henry W.	Worcester,	Guardianship,	18433
1815	Horace	Leicester,	Guardianship,	18434
1832	Horace	Worcester,	Will,	18435
1881	Ira	Worcester,	Administration,	18436
1875	Iris B.	Leicester,	Administration,	18437
1829	Israel C.	Leicester,	Guardianship,	18438
1768	Jacob	Leicester,	Guardianship,	18439
1829	James	Leicester,	Administration,	18440

Year.	Name.	Residence.	Nature.	Case.
	EARLE and EARL,			
1768	John	Leicester,	Guardianship,	18441
1833	John	Hardwick,	Administration,	18442
1833	John	Hardwick,	Pension,	18443
1856	John	Worcester,	Will,	18444
1860	John E.	Hardwick,	Administration,	18445
1874	John M.	Worcester,	Will,	18446
1799	John P.	Leicester,	Guardianship,	18447
1846	Jonah	Leicester,	Administration,	18448
1813	Jonathan	Leicester,	Will,	18449
1829	Joseph L.	Leicester,	Guardianship,	18450
1818	Julia M.	Paxton,	Guardianship,	18451
1829	Leander M.	Leicester,	Guardianship,	18452
1864	Lloyd M.	Worcester,	Guardianship,	18453
1851	Louisa S.	Worcester,	Guardianship,	18454
1864	Margaret C.	Worcester,	Guardianship,	18455
1864	Marianna M.	Worcester,	Guardianship,	18456
1768	Martha	Leicester,	Guardianship,	18457
1843	Martha A.	Sutton,	Guardianship,	18458
1859	Mary A.	Worcester,	Guardianship,	18459
1824	Mary B.	Leicester,	Guardianship,	18460
1818	Melissa	Leicester,	Guardianship,	18461
1864	Morris	Worcester,	Guardianship,	18462
1864	Nancy H.	Worcester,	Guardianship,	18463
1859	Nathaniel	Leicester,	Will,	18464
1799	Nathaniel P.	Leicester,	Guardianship,	18465
1853	Nathaniel P.	Leicester,	Administration,	18466
1868	Oliver K.	Worcester,	Administration,	18467
1878	Oliver K.	Worcester,	Trustee,	18468
1864	Oliver K., Jr.	Worcester,	Guardianship,	18469
1839	Ormacinda	Leicester,	Administration,	18470
1810	Otis D.	Leicester,	Guardianship,	18471
1831	Otis D.	New Haven, Conn.,	Will,	18472
1855	Ozella H.	Leicester,	Guardianship,	18473
1849	Patience	Leicester,	Administration,	18474
1781	Phebe	Templeton,	Guardianship,	18475
1834	Pliny	Leicester,	Administration,	18476
1850	Rachel	Leicester,	Guardianship,	18477
1851	Rachel	Leicester,	Will,	18478
1757	Ralph	Leicester,	Will,	18479
1860	Ralph	Charleston, S. C.,	Administration,	18480
1875	Rhoda A.	Hubbardston,	Administration,	18481
1821	Richard	Leicester,	Guardianship,	18482
1820	Robert	Leicester,	Administration,	18483
1855	Ruth	Worcester,	Will,	18484

Year.	Name.	Residence.	Nature.	Case.
	EARLE AND EARL,			
1818	Sarah	Leicester,	Guardianship,	18485
1820	Sarah	Ashburnham,	Administration,	18486
1824	Sarah	Leicester,	Guardianship,	18487
1849	Sarah B.	Worcester,	Administration,	18488
1869	Sarah H.	Worcester,	Administration,	18489
1843	Sarah J.	Sutton,	Guardianship,	18490
1842	Silas	Leicester,	Administration,	18491
1829	Slade A.	Leicester,	Guardianship,	18492
1800	Slead	Leicester,	Will,	18493
1827	Sophia	Phillipston,	Guardianship,	18494
1825	Stephen	Phillipston,	Will,	18495
1856	Stephen	Leicester,	Administration,	18496
1825	Stephen, Jr.	Princeton,	Administration,	18497
1878	Stephen C.	Worcester,	Trustee,	18498
1841	Susan A.	Leicester,	Guardianship,	18499
1768	Thaddeus	Leicester,	Guardianship,	18500
1779	Thaddeus	Templeton,	Administration,	18501
1810	Theodore	Leicester,	Guardianship,	18502
1819	Thomas	Leicester,	Administration,	18503
1858	Thomas, etc.	Worcester,	Trustee,	18504
1871	Thomas	Worcester,	Administration,	18505
1879	Thomas H.	Worcester,	Guardianship,	18506
1819	Timothy	Leicester,	Administration,	18507
1881	Timothy K.	Worcester,	Will,	18508
1813	Waldo	Leicester,	Guardianship,	18509
1851	Willard	Worcester,	Administration,	18510
1769	William	Paxton,	Will,	18511
1800	William	Worcester,	Will,	18512
1805	William	Leicester,	Will,	18513
1849	William H.	Hubbardston,	Guardianship,	18514
1807	Winthrop	Leicester,	Administration,	18515
1810	Winthrop	Leicester,	Guardianship,	18516
1828	Winthrop	Leicester,	Will,	18517
	EARLY AND EARLEY,			
1872	Annie J.	Spencer,	Guardianship,	18518
1876	Charles	Worcester,	Administration,	18519
1856	James	Worcester,	Guardianship,	18520
1872	James W.	Spencer,	Guardianship,	18521
1871	Jeremiah	Spencer,	Administration,	18522
1872	Jeremiah E.	Spencer,	Guardianship,	18523
1880	Maggie	Worcester,	Administration,	18524
1880	Margaret, etc.	Worcester,	Administration,	18524
1872	Maria	Spencer,	Guardianship,	18525
1856	Mary	Worcester,	Guardianship,	18526

EARLY AND EARLEY,

YEAR.	NAME.	RESIDENCE.	NATURE.	CASE.
1861	Mary E.	Spencer,	Guardianship,	18527
1861	Michael	Spencer,	Guardianship,	18528
1881	Michael	Worcester,	Guardianship,	18529
1872	Michael F.	Spencer,	Guardianship,	18530
1860	Patrick	Spencer,	Administration,	18531
1861	Sarah	Spencer,	Guardianship,	18532
1872	Sarah E.	Spencer,	Guardianship,	18533
1875	EASLER, William A.	Leominster,	Will,	18534
1822	EASTMAN, Caroline	Amherst,	Guardianship,	18535
1859	Craft	Douglas,	Change of Name,	18536
1859	Edward C.	Douglas,	Change of Name,	18537
1873	Samuel	Southbridge,	Guardianship,	18538
1802	EATON, Aaron	Fitchburg,	Administration,	18539
1877	Aaron	Fitchburg,	Will,	18540
1863	Abigail B.	Worcester,	Administration,	18541
1879	Addie L.	Westminster,	Guardianship,	18542
1877	Adelina P.	Leominster,	Administration,	18543
1848	Alonzo	Fitchburg,	Guardianship,	18544
1832	Alpheus	Worcester,	Will,	18545
1881	Amasa F.	Gardner,	Guardianship,	18546
1862	Amos	Lunenburg,	Administration,	18547
1851	Betsey	Worcester,	Administration,	18548
1872	Betsey	Royalston,	Guardianship,	18549
1872	Betsey	Royalston,	Administration,	18549
1876	Betsey	Gardner,	Administration,	18550
1846	Catherine C.	Worcester,	Guardianship,	18551
1835	Charles	Worcester,	Guardianship,	18552
1852	Charles	Gardner,	Guardianship,	18553
1855	Charles	Lancaster,	Will,	18554
1867	Charles	Worcester,	Guardianship,	18555
1848	Charles I.	Providence, R. I.,	Guardianship,	18556
1851	Charlotte	Worcester,	Guardianship,	18557
1868	Charlotte	Worcester,	Administration,	18558
1801	Collins	Leominster,	Will,	18559
1859	Daniel S.	New Bedford,	Guardianship,	18560
1879	Della A.	Westminster,	Guardianship,	18561
1800	Ebenezer	Gardner,	Administration,	18562
1869	Edwin B.	Worcester,	Guardianship,	18563
1864	Eleanor	Westminster,	Administration,	18564
1879	Elias B.	Oxford,	Guardianship,	18565
1810	Eliza	Barre,	Guardianship,	18566
1813	Eliza	Fitchburg,	Guardianship,	18567
1855	Emily P.	Auburn,	Guardianship,	18568
1881	Emma F.	Gardner,	Guardianship,	18569

YEAR.	NAME.	RESIDENCE.	NATURE.	CASE.
1813	EATON, Esther P.	Fitchburg,	Guardianship,	18570
1879	Esther P.	Fitchburg,	Administration,	18571
1765	Eunice	Worcester,	Guardianship,	18572
1877	Eunice, etc.	Rutland,	Administration,	18573
1859	Eunice A.	New Bedford,	Guardianship,	18574
1877	Eunice I.	Rutland,	Administration,	18575
1875	Frances M.	Everett,	Adoption, etc.,	18576
1855	Francis	Westminster,	Guardianship,	18577
1835	Frederick	Worcester,	Guardianship,	18578
1875	Frederick	Worcester,	Will,	18579
1800	George	Gardner,	Guardianship,	18580
1802	George	Barre,	Guardianship,	18581
1861	Henry A.	Worcester,	Will,	18582
1853	Henry B.	Worcester,	Guardianship,	18583
1848	Henry R.	Providence, R. I.,	Guardianship,	18584
1853	Henry T.	Worcester,	Administration,	18585
1840	Horace H.	Brookfield,	Guardianship,	18586
1844	Huldah	Phillipston,	Guardianship,	18587
1800	Humphrey	Gardner,	Guardianship,	18588
1810	Isabella A.	Barre,	Guardianship,	18589
1835	James	Worcester,	Guardianship,	18590
1853	Jefferson	Westminster,	Guardianship,	18591
1859	Jennie R.	Barre,	Adoption, etc.,	18592
1877	Jennie R.	Barre,	Guardianship,	18593
1880	Jeremiah	Worcester,	Will,	18594
1809	John	Fitchburg,	Guardianship,	18595
1827	John	Worcester,	Administration,	18596
1844	John	Westminster,	Administration,	18597
1865	John	Gardner,	Administration,	18598
1772	John E.	Spencer,	Guardianship,	18599
1812	John E.	Dudley,	Will,	18600
1851	John F.	Worcester,	Guardianship,	18601
1810	Jonas	Barre,	Guardianship,	18602
1813	Jonas	Gerry,	Administration,	18603
1843	Jonas	Auburn,	Will,	18604
1810	Jonas, Jr.	Barre,	Administration,	18605
1759	Jonathan	Worcester,	Administration,	18606
1819	Jonathan	Gardner,	Will,	18607
1823	Joseph	Royalston,	Administration,	18608
1868	Joseph M.	Leominster,	Will,	18609
1863	Josiah	Ashburnham,	Administration,	18610
1772	Joshua	Spencer,	Administration,	18611
1827	Lovina	Ashby,	Guardianship,	18612
1846	Lucy	Millbury,	Guardianship,	18613
1847	Lucy	Millbury,	Will,	18613

(429)

YEAR.	NAME.	RESIDENCE.	NATURE.	CASE.
1847	EATON, Lucy	Lancaster,	Will,	18614
1813	Lucy D.	Fitchburg,	Guardianship,	18615
1873	Lucy E.	Westborough,	Administration,	18616
1850	Lydia	Worcester,	Administration,	18617
1810	Lydia A.	Barre,	Guardianship,	18618
1831	Maltiah	Phillipston,	Will,	18619
1880	Maria L.	San Jose, Cal.,	Administration,	18620
1840	Marian C.	Brookfield,	Guardianship,	18621
1881	Marshall	Westminster,	Administration,	18622
1873	Marson	Shrewsbury,	Administration,	18623
1865	Martha W.	Fitchburg,	Will,	18624
1813	Mary	Fitchburg,	Guardianship,	18625
1852	Mary A.	Gardner,	Guardianship,	18626
1813	Mehitable	Fitchburg,	Guardianship,	18627
1875	Merrick	Hollis, N. H.,	Administration,	18628
1810	Nabby	Barre,	Guardianship,	18629
1861	Nathan	Westminster,	Will,	18630
1826	Nathaniel	Lancaster,	Administration,	18631
1833	Nathaniel	Worcester,	Administration,	18632
1881	Nellie F.	Gardner,	Guardianship,	18633
1881	Oliver K.	Fitchburg,	Administration,	18634
1802	Parker	Fitchburg,	Guardianship,	18635
1816	Person	New Ipswich, N. H.,	Administration,	18636
1873	Peter	Gardner,	Administration,	18637
1879	Polly	Gardner,	Administration,	18638
1819	Rebecca	Gardner,	Guardianship,	18639
1763	Reuben	Worcester,	Guardianship,	18640
1815	Reuben	Fitchburg,	Administration,	18641
1817	Reuben	Sutton,	Administration,	18642
1813	Reuben, Jr.	Sutton,	Administration,	18643
1809	Sally	Fitchburg,	Guardianship,	18644
1810	Sally	Barre,	Guardianship,	18645
1768	Samuel	Worcester,	Will,	18646
1769	Samuel	Worcester,	Guardianship,	18647
1856	Sarah	Fitchburg,	Will,	18648
1856	Sarah	Fitchburg,	Pension,	18649
1835	Sarah D.	Worcester,	Guardianship,	18650
1840	Sarah E.	Brookfield,	Guardianship,	18651
1851	Simeon	Westminster,	Guardianship,	18652
1879	Stillman	Westminster,	Administration,	18653
1859	Sumner	Shrewsbury,	Administration,	18654
1835	Susan R.	Worcester,	Guardianship,	18655
1788	Thomas	Worcester,	Administration,	18656
1809	Thomas, 3d	Fitchburg,	Administration,	18657
1813	Thomas	Fitchburg,	Administration,	18658

YEAR.	NAME.	RESIDENCE.	NATURE.	CASE.
1876	EATON, Thomas	Auburn,	Will,	18659
1850	Thomas B.	Worcester,	Administration,	18660
1851	Thomas B.	Worcester,	Guardianship,	18661
1855	Thomas B.	Auburn,	Guardianship,	18662
1859	Thomas C.	New Bedford,	Guardianship,	18663
1820	Uriah	Holden,	Guardianship,	18664
1840	William	Brookfield,	Will,	18665
1859	William	Worcester,	Will,	18666
1861	William	Worcester,	Administration,	18667
1876	William	Auburn,	Will,	18668
1848	William H.	Providence, R. I.,	Guardianship,	18669
1840	William S.	Brookfield,	Guardianship,	18670
1859	William S.	New Bedford,	Guardianship,	18671
1810	Zebediah A.	Barre,	Guardianship,	18672
	EAVES see EVES.			
1860	EBIT, Rosannah	Worcester,	Will,	18673
1860	Rosannah	Worcester,	Pension,	18674
1822	William	Petersham,	Administration,	18675
1830	ECCLES, John	Dudley,	Administration,	18676
1865	Roger	Clinton,	Administration,	18677
1824	EDDY, Abiel	Brookfield,	Guardianship,	18678
1878	Abigail	Sterling,	Administration,	18679
1832	Abraham	Royalston,	Will,	18680
1832	Alexander H.	Oxford,	Guardianship,	18681
1787	Amasa	Orange,	Guardianship,	18682
1870	Amasa	Auburn,	Will,	18683
1830	Amos	Millbury,	Administration,	18684
1875	Amy A.	Auburn,	Will,	18685
1857	Anna	Millbury,	Will,	18686
1849	Anna E.	Oxford,	Guardianship,	18687
1862	Anna M.	Royalston,	Guardianship,	18688
1834	Arnold	Uxbridge,	Administration,	18689
1787	Asa	Orange,	Guardianship,	18690
1855	Augustus	Webster,	Will,	18691
1820	Azariah	Leicester,	Will,	18692
1828	Barnet W.	Sterling,	Administration,	18693
1746	Benjamin	Oxford,	Receipt,	18694
1826	Benjamin	Oxford,	Administration,	18695
1871	Benjamin	Dudley,	Will,	18696
1846	Benjamin F.	Winchendon,	Will,	18697
1846	Benjamin W.	Winchendon,	Guardianship,	18698
1865	Betsey	Webster,	Administration,	18699
1874	Charles E.	Oxford,	Guardianship,	18700
1862	Charles H.	Royalston,	Guardianship,	18701
1847	Daniel B.	Douglas,	Administration,	18702

YEAR.	NAME.	RESIDENCE.	NATURE.	CASE.
1858	EDDY, Daniel F.	Oxford,	Administration,	18703
1826	David	Ward,	Administration,	18704
1769	Ebenezer	Oxford,	Administration,	18705
1864	Edgar W.	Templeton,	Guardianship,	18706
1765	Edmund	Oxford,	Guardianship,	18707
1839	Edmund	Charlton,	Will,	18708
1875	Eliphalet	Saratoga Sp'ngs N.Y.,	Administration,	18709
1784	Elizabeth	Ward,	Administration,	18710
1849	Emeline	Oxford,	Guardianship,	18711
1836	Emerson	Millbury,	Guardianship,	18712
1851	Emerson	Millbury,	Administration,	18712
1849	Emory	Oxford,	Administration,	18713
1863	Erastus O.	Templeton,	Administration,	18714
1867	Eunice	West Brookfield,	Will,	18715
1868	Finetta	Royalston,	Administration,	18716
1865	Franklin A.	Royalston,	Will,	18717
1853	Garrison	Fitchburg,	Guardianship,	18718
1874	George S.	Oxford,	Guardianship,	18719
1864	George T.	Templeton,	Guardianship,	18720
1866	Hannah	Webster,	Will,	18721
1856	Hannah N.	Oxford,	Will,	18722
1874	Helen L.	Oxford,	Guardianship,	18723
1849	Henry	Oxford,	Guardianship,	18724
1850	James	Auburn,	Will,	18725
1769	Jemima	Oxford,	Guardianship,	18726
1866	Jesse	Auburn,	Administration,	18727
1846	Joel W.	Oxford,	Guardianship,	18728
1762	John	Oxford,	Will,	18729
1819	John	Brookfield,	Will,	18730
1821	John	Dudley,	Will,	18731
1823	John	Northbridge,	Will,	18732
1867	John	Dudley,	Will,	18733
1863	John M.	Royalston,	Administration,	18734
1825	Jonas	Oxford,	Will,	18735
1832	Jonas	Worcester,	Administration,	18736
1854	Jonas	Oxford,	Guardianship,	18737
1819	Joshua	Sterling,	Will,	18738
1765	Josiah	Oxford,	Guardianship,	18739
1824	Josiah	Southbridge,	Administration,	18740
1873	Jotham	Webster,	Will,	18741
1880	Justus	Millbury,	Administration,	18742
1857	Laura	Oxford,	Will,	18743
1814	Leonard	Oxford,	Guardianship,	18744
1816	Leonard	Ward,	Guardianship,	18745
1825	Leonard	Oxford,	Administration,	18746

YEAR.	NAME.	RESIDENCE.	NATURE.	CASE.
1762	EDDY, Levi	Oxford,	Guardianship,	18747
1821	Levi	Ward,	Will,	18748
1845	Levi	Burrillville, R. I.,	Foreign Will,	18749
1871	Levi	Worcester,	Administration,	18750
1816	Lewis	Ward,	Guardianship,	18751
1875	Lewis	Worcester,	Administration,	18752
1864	Lizzie L.	Templeton,	Guardianship,	18753
1877	Lydia	Oxford,	Guardianship,	18754
1878	Lydia	Oxford,	Will,	18754
1871	Maria M.	Worcester,	Will,	18755
1858	Marion	Worcester,	Administration,	18756
1816	Mary	Ward,	Guardianship,	18757
1824	Mary	Brookfield,	Guardianship,	18758
1827	Mary	Oxford,	Guardianship,	18759
1839	Mary	Sutton,	Administration,	18759
1867	Mary A.	Thompson, Conn.,	Administration,	18760
1868	Mary A.	Grafton,	Guardianship,	18761
1879	Mary A.	Leicester,	Will,	18762
1846	Mary A. E.	Winchendon,	Guardianship,	18763
1874	Mary E.	Oxford,	Guardianship,	18764
1874	Nathaniel	Oxford,	Will,	18765
1832	Parley,	Oxford (Gore),	Administration,	18766
1767	Patience	Oxford,	Will,	18767
1841	Perley	Charlton,	Administration,	18768
1838	Polly	Oxford,	Administration,	18769
1814	Rachel	Oxford,	Guardianship,	18770
1828	Randall	Douglas,	Guardianship,	18771
1813	Reuben	Oxford,	Administration,	18772
1876	Reuben T.	Webster,	Administration,	18773
1880	Rufus	Oxford,	Administration,	18774
1875	Rufus M.	Charlton,	Will,	18775
1769	Ruth	Oxford,	Guardianship,	18776
1816	Sally	Ward,	Guardianship,	18777
1846	Sally T.	Oxford,	Guardianship,	18778
1762	Samuel	Oxford,	Administration,	18779
1798	Samuel	Ward,	Will,	18780
1813	Samuel	Ward,	Administration,	18781
1816	Samuel	Ward,	Guardianship,	18782
1830	Samuel	Charlton,	Administration,	18783
1868	Sarah A.	Grafton,	Guardianship,	18784
1876	Sarah E.	Southbridge,	Administration,	18785
1823	Seth	Brookfield,	Administration,	18786
1807	Silas	Oxford,	Will,	18787
1879	Sophia	Grafton,	Administration,	18788
1877	Susan	Auburn,	Administration,	18789

YEAR.	NAME.	RESIDENCE.	NATURE.	CASE.
1816	EDDY, Susanna	Ward,	Guardianship,	18790
1832	Thomas F.	Oxford,	Guardianship,	18791
1805	William	Oxford,	Will,	18792
1868	William	Royalston,	Administration,	18793
1859	William H.	Royalston,	Administration,	18794
1874	William H.	Oxford,	Administration,	18795
1851	EDES, Henry	Worcester,	Administration,	18796
1787	Peter	Harvard,	Will,	18797
1877	EDGAR, George	Southbridge,	Adoption, etc.,	18798
1806	EDGARTON, Benjamin	Lancaster,	Administration,	18799
1855	Leonard	Harvard,	Will,	18800
1856	Leonard J.	Oriskany Falls, N.Y.,	Sale Real Estate,	18801
1856	Susan E.	Oriskany Falls, N.Y.,	Sale Real Estate,	18802
1878	EDGECOMB, Scott	Leominster,	Administration,	18803
1817	EDGELL, Benjamin	Gardner,	Administration,	18804
1876	Farwell	Gardner,	Administration,	18805
1847	Louisa	Gardner,	Will,	18806
1809	William	Westminster,	Will,	18807
1831	William	Westminster,	Administration,	18808
1865	William	Westminster,	Administration,	18809
1879	EDGERLEY, Mary	Harvard,	Will,	18810
	EDMANDS AND EDMUNDS,			
1793	Aaron	Brookfield,	Guardianship,	18811
1817	Amos	Winchendon,	Will,	18812
1817	Anna	Winchendon,	Guardianship,	18813
1793	Anne	Brookfield,	Guardianship,	18814
1858	Artemas	Winchendon,	Will,	18815
1852	Charles O.	Poughkeepsie, N. Y.,	Guardianship,	18816
1851	Chauncy	Poughkeepsie, N. Y.,	Administration,	18817
1772	Ebenezer	Dudley,	Administration,	18818
1773	Ebenezer	Dudley,	Guardianship,	18819
1834	Ebenezer	Dudley,	Pension,	18820
1773	Elizabeth	Dudley,	Guardianship,	18821
1860	Experience	Dudley,	Administration,	18822
1773	Hannah	Dudley,	Guardianship,	18823
1793	Hannah	Brookfield,	Guardianship,	18824
1852	Helen	Poughkeepsie, N. Y.,	Guardianship,	18825
1773	Jemima	Dudley,	Guardianship,	18826
1773	John	Dudley,	Guardianship,	18827
1838	John	North Brookfield,	Will,	18828
1768	Joseph	Dudley,	Will,	18829
1877	Luther	Southbridge,	Administration,	18830
1773	Moses	Dudley,	Guardianship,	18831
1880	Sally D.	North Brookfield,	Administration,	18832
1792	Samuel	Brookfield,	Administration,	18833

EDMANDS AND EDMUNDS,

YEAR.	NAME.	RESIDENCE.	NATURE.	CASE.
1842	Samuel	North Brookfield,	Will,	18834
1866	Sophronia	Thompson, Conn.,	Administration,	18835
1773	Stephen	Dudley,	Guardianship,	18836
1853	Thomas	Leominster,	Guardianship,	18837
1870	Thomas	Leominster,	Administration,	18837
1750	William	Halifax, N. S.,	Assignment,	18837½
1847	EDSON, Calvin	North Brookfield,	Administration,	18838
1849	Elijah	Berlin,	Administration,	18839
1851	Ephraim	Oxford,	Administration,	18840
1857	Joseph W.	New Braintree,	Will,	18841
1833	Rodolphus	Oxford,	Administration,	18842
1778	Silvester	Brookfield,	Guardianship,	18843
1826	EDWARDS, Abigail H.	Holden,	Guardianship,	18844
1777	Andrew	Douglas,	Administration,	18845
1843	Benjamin	Leicester,	Administration,	18846
1879	Benjamin A.	Bolton,	Will,	18847
1779	Edward	Charlton,	Guardianship,	18848
1867	Ella S.	Worcester,	Adoption, etc.,	18849
1860	Experience	Dudley,	Pension,	18850
1867	Fidelle A.	Worcester,	Adoption, etc.,	18851
1837	George	Southbridge,	Guardianship,	18852
1802	Hannah	Charlton,	Guardianship,	18853
1862	Henry H.	Barre,	Guardianship,	18854
1872	Ida F.	Southbridge,	Guardianship,	18855
1802	Jacob	Charlton,	Guardianship,	18856
1867	Jacob	Dudley,	Administration,	18857
1862	James W.	Harmony, Ind.,	Guardianship,	18858
1826	John	Charlton,	Guardianship,	18859
1837	John	Southbridge,	Guardianship,	18860
1872	John	Southbridge,	Will,	18861
1826	Jonathan C.	Holden,	Guardianship,	18862
1803	Josiah	Charlton,	Guardianship,	18863
1857	Martha B.	West Brookfield,	Change of Name,	18864
1815	Mary A.	Sturbridge,	Guardianship,	18865
1828	Mary A.	Charlton,	Guardianship,	18866
1835	Mary A.	Southbridge,	Administration,	18866
1802	Mehitable	Charlton,	Administration,	18867
1878	Michael R.	Worcester,	Administration,	18868
1826	Parnal M.	Holden,	Guardianship,	18869
1802	Patty	Charlton,	Guardianship,	18870
1806	Peter	Oxford,	Guardianship,	18871
1838	Philip	Holden,	Administration,	18872
1837	Pierpont	Southbridge,	Guardianship,	18873
1801	Robert	Charlton,	Administration,	18874

1763	EDWARDS, Samuel	Douglas,	Will,	18875
1828	Samuel C.	Charlton,	Guardianship,	18876
1881	Samuel F.	Bolton,	Administration,	18877
1814	Samuel T.	Charlton,	Guardianship,	18878
1763	Sarah	Douglas,	Guardianship,	18879
1867	Sarah R.	Petersham,	Will,	18880
1826	Silence H.	Holden,	Guardianship,	18881
1826	Submit S.	Holden,	Guardianship,	18882
1859	Susan S.	Westborough,	Will,	18883
1802	Thomas	Charlton,	Administration,	18884
1807	Thomas	Charlton,	Guardianship,	18885
1826	William P.	Holden,	Guardianship,	18886
1826	Zilpah	Oxford,	Administration,	18887
1801	EGERY, Daniel	Hardwick,	Will,	18888
1879	Ebenezer H.	Barre,	Administration,	18889
1876	Mary L.	Barre,	Administration,	18890
	EGGLESTON AND EGLESTON,			
1874	Alden B.	Athol,	Will,	18891
1874	Catherine	Worcester,	Guardianship,	18892
1880	Cordelia C.	Harvard,	Administration,	18893
1874	John	Worcester,	Administration,	18894
1874	Mary	Worcester,	Guardianship,	18895
1873	EHEHALT, Albert	Worcester,	Administration,	18896
1792	EHLICK, Christian	Grafton,	Administration,	18897
1796	Jacob	Grafton,	Guardianship,	18898
1796	Nathan	Grafton,	Guardianship,	18899
1796	Sarah	Grafton,	Guardianship,	18900
1849	ELAM, Emily C.	Worcester,	Guardianship,	18901
1856	Emily C.	Worcester,	Will,	18902
1849	ELDER, Clark	Worcester,	Administration,	18903
1876	Harriet N.	Worcester,	Guardianship,	18904
1820	James	Lancaster,	Administration,	18905
1876	James	Worcester,	Will,	18906
1841	John	Worcester,	Will,	18907
1855	Lydia	Worcester,	Will,	18908
1849	Maria	Worcester,	Guardianship,	18909
1848	Nathaniel	Worcester,	Guardianship,	18910
1785	William	Worcester,	Will,	18911
1874	ELDRED, Frederick A.	Worcester,	Will,	18912
1874	Jennie L.	Worcester,	Guardianship,	18913
	ELDRIDGE AND ELDREDGE,			
1865	Abner E.	Worcester,	Administration,	18914
1858	Adalaide	Spencer,	Guardianship,	18915
1858	Caroline B.	Spencer,	Guardianship,	18916

YEAR.	NAME.	RESIDENCE.	NATURE.	CASE.
	ELDRIDGE AND ELDREDGE,			
1859	Emma	Milford,	Adoption, etc.,	18917
1858	Nathaniel W.	Spencer,	Guardianship,	18918
1857	Silas	Spencer,	Will,	18919
1869	Storrs	Worcester,	Will,	18920
1876	Walter N.	Spencer,	Administration,	18921
	ELIOT see ELLIOTT.			
1878	ELLECK, William C.	Leominster,	Administration,	18922
	ELLENWOOD, ELLINWOOD AND ELLINGWOOD,			
1797	Abigail	Athol,	Guardianship,	18923
1831	Abigail	Athol,	Guardianship,	18924
1843	Addison	Hubbardston,	Administration,	18925
1848	Arah	Fitchburg,	Will,	18926
1848	Artemas W.	Fitchburg,	Guardianship,	18927
1870	Austin F.	Athol,	Administration,	18928
1831	Benjamin	Athol,	Guardianship,	18929
1844	Charles	Hubbardston,	Guardianship,	18930
1794	Daniel	Athol,	Administration,	18931
1831	Daniel	Athol,	Administration,	18932
1877	Daniel	Athol,	Administration,	18933
1879	Daniel (Estate of)	Athol,	Partition,	18934
1831	Daniel A.	Athol,	Guardianship,	18935
1848	Eliza A.	Fitchburg,	Guardianship,	18936
1854	Eliza M.	Athol,	Guardianship,	18937
1868	Elvira	Leominster,	Administration,	18938
1848	Emily M.	Fitchburg,	Guardianship,	18939
1746	Ephraim	Woodstock,	Guardianship,	18940
1840	Frederic T.	Athol,	Guardianship,	18941
1840	George B.	Athol,	Guardianship,	18942
1797	James	Athol,	Guardianship,	18943
1745	Jonathan	Woodstock,	Administration,	18944
1746	Johannah	Woodstock,	Guardianship,	18945
1797	Justus	Athol,	Guardianship,	18946
1844	Justus	Hubbardston,	Will,	18947
1848	Lucretia T.	Fitchburg,	Guardianship,	18948
1797	Lucy	Athol,	Guardianship,	18949
1844	Lucy	Hubbardston,	Guardianship,	18950
1837	Lucy A.	Athol,	Guardianship,	18951
1746	Mary	Woodstock,	Guardianship,	18952
1848	Mary	Fitchburg,	Guardianship,	18953
1847	Nathan	Fitchburg,	Administration,	18954
1870	Rebecca F.	Athol,	Guardianship,	18955
1848	Sarah M.	Fitchburg,	Guardianship,	18956
1797	Seneca	Athol,	Guardianship,	18957
1851	Sophia	Hubbardston,	Administration,	18958

YEAR.	NAME.	RESIDENCE.	NATURE.	CASE.
	ELLENWOOD, ELLINWOOD AND ELLINGWOOD,			
1840	Thomas	Athol,	Will,	18959
1837	Tilden B.	Athol,	Guardianship,	18960
	ELLIOTT, ELIOT AND ELLIOT,			
1829	Aaron	Sutton,	Will,	18961
1831	Aaron	Sutton,	Administration,	18962
1833	Aarou	Oxford,	Administration,	18963
1816	Andrew	Millbury,	Guardianship,	18964
1817	Andrew	Millbury,	Will,	18964
1816	Andrew, Jr.	Millbury,	Administration,	18965
1817	Andrew W.	Millbury,	Guardianship,	18966
1821	Asahel	Uxbridge,	Administration,	18967
1817	Caleb B.	Millbury,	Guardianship,	18968
1846	Caleb B.	Millbury,	Will,	18969
1828	Carter	Worcester,	Administration,	18970
1831	Cynthia G.	Sutton,	Guardianship,	18971
1763	David	Sutton,	Administration,	18972
1836	David	Ward,	Administration,	18973
1795	Ebenezer	Royalston,	Administration,	18974
1831	George	Sutton,	Guardianship,	18975
1782	Hannah	Spencer,	Administration,	18976
1853	James T.	Sutton,	Administration,	18977
1788	John	Sutton,	Administration,	18978
1800	. John	Boston,	Guardianship,	18979
1814	Jonathan	Sutton,	Administration,	18980
1821	Joseph	Leicester,	Will,	18981
1831	Joseph	Sutton,	Guardianship,	18982
1832	Julia A.	Sutton,	Guardianship,	18983
1846	Levi	Sutton,	Administration,	18984
1832	Luriaann	Sutton,	Guardianship,	18985
1817	Mary	Millbury,	Guardianship,	18986
1842	Mary	Circleville, O.,	Administration,	18987
1872	Mary J.	Millbury,	Will,	18988
1831	Nancy	Sutton,	Guardianship,	18989
1877	Rosa E.	Thompson, Conn.,	Adoption, etc.,	18990
1787	Samuel	Sutton,	Administration,	18991
1817	Sarah W.	Millbury,	Guardianship,	18992
1822	Simeon	Sutton,	Guardianship,	18993
1791	Stephen	Sutton,	Guardianship,	18994
1850	Stephen D.	Grafton,	Administration,	18995
1863	Submit B.	Sutton,	Administration,	18996
1845	Susannah	Oxford,	Guardianship,	18997
1845	Susannah	Oxford,	Will,	18997
1796	William	Brimfield,	Guardianship,	18998

YEAR.	NAME.	RESIDENCE.	NATURE.	CASE.
1843	ELLIS, Abel	Sutton,	Will,	18999
1858	Abigail	Warren,	Will,	19000
1827	Augustus	Barre,	Guardianship,	19001
1881	Azubah B.	Warren,	Administration,	19002
1866	Baxter	West Brookfield,	Will,	19003
1814	Bethuel	Barre,	Administration,	19004
1881	Bethuel	Winchendon,	Will,	19005
1866	Charles	Uxbridge,	Will,	19006
1871	Charles H.	Worcester,	Adoption, etc.,	19007
1854	Charlotte	Berlin,	Guardianship,	19008
1873	Clark	Milford,	Administration,	19009
1864	Cora B.	Leominster,	Guardianship,	19010
1804	Dorothy	Sturbridge,	Guardianship,	19011
1881	Eben B.	Winchendon,	Guardianship,	19012
1861	Eliza	Woodstock, Conn.,	Administration,	19013
1847	Elizabeth	Brookfield,	Will,	19014
1839	Ezekiel	Royalston,	Will,	19015
1841	Ezekiel	Royalston,	Pension,	19016
1863	Freeborn	Milford,	Administration,	19017
1804	Freeman	Sturbridge,	Guardianship,	19018
1842	George	Sturbridge,	Guardianship,	19019
1854	George	Berlin,	Guardianship,	19020
1827	Hannah	Barre,	Guardianship,	19021
1878	Harriet H.	Worcester,	Administration,	19022
1813	James	Royalston,	Administration,	19023
1804	Jedediah	Sturbridge,	Guardianship,	19024
1804	Jedediah	Sturbridge,	Will,	19025
1864	John	Hardwick,	Will,	19026
1856	John A.	Southbridge,	Guardianship,	19027
1846	Joseph	Bolton,	Guardianship,	19028
1860	Laura A.	Milford,	Guardianship,	19029
1827	Levi	Hardwick,	Guardianship,	19030
1862	Lizzie H.	Milford,	Adoption, etc.,	19031
1864	Lizzie H.	Milford,	Adoption, etc.,	19031
1874	Lizzie H.	Milford,	Guardianship,	19032
1804	Lucretia	Sturbridge,	Guardianship,	19033
1827	Margaret	Barre,	Administration,	19034
1860	Mary A.	Milford,	Guardianship,	19035
1869	Mary A.	Fitchburg,	Administration,	19036
1819	Nathan B.	Brookfield,	Will,	19037
1874	Nettie M.	Hammonton, N. J.,	Guardianship,	19038
1804	Oliver	Sturbridge,	Guardianship,	19039
1819	Oliver	Southbridge,	Guardianship,	19040
1848	Oliver	Southbridge,	Administration,	19040
1849	Rachel	Sutton,	Will,	19041

Year.	Name.	Residence.	Nature.	Case.
1839	ELLIS, Royal	Charlton,	Will,	19042
1840	Royal L.	New Albany, Ind.,	Guardianship,	19043
1803	Samuel	Sturbridge,	Will,	19044
1822	Samuel	Southbridge,	Administration,	19045
1844	Sarah	Charlton,	Will,	19046
1863	Sarah	Grafton,	Will,	19047
1843	Seth	Hardwick,	Administration,	19048
1843	Shepard	Warren,	Will,	19049
1804	Silas	Sturbridge,	Guardianship,	19050
1839	Smith	Southbridge	Administration,	19051
1760	Stephen	Mendon,	Guardianship,	19052
1879	Stillman	Warren,	Will,	19053
1858	Susan	West Brookfield,	Will,	19054
1865	Susan B.	Southbridge,	Administration,	19055
1814	Thankful	Brookfield,	Will,	19056
1873	Thomas L.	Paxton,	Will,	19057
1747	Turner	Uxbridge,	Guardianship,	19058
1874	Walter H.	Hammonton, N. J.,	Guardianship,	19059
1790	ELLISON, Hannah	Northbridge,	Guardianship,	19060
1772	John	Uxbridge,	Administration,	19061
1877	Oscar P.	Uxbridge,	Adoption, etc.,	19062
1773	Sarah	Uxbridge,	Guardianship,	19063
1870	ELLS, Elizabeth W. Davis	Northborough,	Will,	19064
1871	ELLSWORTH, Albert	Worcester,	Guardianship,	19065
1857	Alexander W.	Barre,	Administration,	19066
1876	Catharine T.	Milford,	Guardianship,	19067
1865	Ellen A.	Barre,	Guardianship,	19068
1874	Emma A.	Gardner,	Adoption, etc.,	19069
1871	Hattie L.	Worcester,	Guardianship,	19070
1865	Henry	Barre,	Administration,	19071
1859	Henry L.	New Haven, Conn.,	Will,	19072
1832	John	Hardwick,	Guardianship,	19073
1857	Maria R.	Barre,	Guardianship,	19074
1865	Mary C.	Barre,	Guardianship,	19075
1871	Samuel	Worcester,	Will,	19076
1865	ELMER, Joseph	Worcester,	Administration,	19077
1865	ELWELL, Abiel	Dudley,	Will,	19078
1853	Albert H.	Hardwick,	Guardianship,	19079
1800	Benjamin	Dudley,	Guardianship,	19080
1878	Charles B.	Dudley,	Administration,	19081
1849	David	Hardwick,	Will,	19082
1840	Emerson	Hardwick,	Guardianship,	19083
1853	Henry B.	Hardwick,	Guardianship,	19084
1859	Jonathan F.	Worcester,	Administration,	19085
1756	Joshua	Sturbridge,	Will,	19086

YEAR.	NAME.	RESIDENCE.	NATURE.	CASE.
1798	ELWELL, Lucy	Hardwick,	Guardianship,	19087
1799	Mark	Dudley,	Will,	19088
1857	Mark	Dudley,	Will,	19089
1798	Polly	Hardwick,	Guardianship,	19090
1798	Roxanna	Hardwick,	Guardianship,	19091
1798	Ruth	Hardwick,	Guardianship,	19092
1798	Thomas	Hardwick,	Will,	19093
1840	Thomas	Hardwick,	Administration,	19094
1840	Thomas G.	Hardwick,	Guardianship,	19095
1839	ELY, William N.	Brimfield,	Guardianship,	19096
1830	EMERSON, Aaron	Douglas,	Guardianship,	19097
1846	Alfred B.	Harvard,	Guardianship,	19098
1862	Amos B.	Tolland, Conn.,	Foreign Will,	19099
1834	Caleb	Douglas,	Guardianship,	19100
1823	Charles	Lancaster,	Guardianship,	19101
1855	Charles W.	Millbury,	Adoption,	19102
1834	Darling	Douglas,	Guardianship,	19103
1873	Elihu	Leicester,	Will,	19104
1823	Elijah C.	Lancaster,	Guardianship,	19105
1881	Eliza	Auburn,	Will,	19106
1867	Flora E.	Royalston,	Guardianship,	19107
1823	Francis B.	Lancaster,	Guardianship,	19108
1850	Frank S.	Worcester,	Guardianship,	19109
1841	George	Webster,	Will,	19110
1852	George O.	Webster,	Guardianship,	19111
1864	Helen M.	Reading,	Guardianship,	19112
1823	Hiram	Lancaster,	Guardianship,	19113
1872	Horace	Douglas,	Will,	19114
1750	Jacob	Harvard,	Guardianship,	19115
1850	Jacob	Harvard,	Will,	19116
1878	Jason	Millbury,	Administration,	19117
1780	John	Uxbridge,	Will,	19118
1781	John	Uxbridge,	Guardianship,	19119
1826	John	Oxford,	Administration,	19120
1881	John	Holden,	Administration,	19121
1757	Jonathan	Uxbridge,	Administration,	19122
1766	Jonathan	Uxbridge,	Guardianship,	19123
1745	Joseph	Falmouth,	Administration,	19124
1803	Joseph	Lancaster,	Administration,	19125
1830	Joseph	Douglas,	Will,	19126
1830	Joseph	Douglas,	Guardianship,	19127
1837	Joseph	Royalston,	Administration,	19128
1837	Joseph	Royalston,	Pension,	19129
1844	Joseph	Douglas,	Administration,	19130
1834	Levi	Webster,	Will,	19131

YEAR.	NAME.	RESIDENCE.	NATURE.	CASE.
1857	EMERSON, Lilla J.	Worcester,	Guardianship,	19132
1766	Lucy	Uxbridge,	Guardianship,	19133
1859	Lucy	Lancaster,	Administration,	19134
1774	Luke	Uxbridge,	Will,	19135
1801	Marcy	Douglas,	Will,	19136
1858	Martha	Thompson, Conn.,	Administration,	19137
1852	Mary	Webster,	Guardianship,	19138
1879	Mary R.	Auburn,	Will,	19139
1844	Mercy	Douglas,	Guardianship,	19140
1847	Merey	Douglas,	Administration,	19140
1880	Millen	Uxbridge,	Partition,	19141
1822	Moses	Lancaster,	Will,	19142
1758	Nathaniel	Douglas,	Guardianship,	19143
1759	Nathaniel	Douglas,	Administration,	19144
1841	Newman	Webster,	Administration,	19145
1875	Oliver	Northbridge,	Administration,	19146
1820	Peter	Harvard,	Will,	19147
1861	Polly	Webster,	Administration,	19148
1816	Putnam	Douglas,	Guardianship,	19149
1758	Reuben	Douglas,	Administration,	19150
1861	Samuel	Uxbridge,	Administration,	19151
1737	Sarah	Mendon,	Administration,	19152
1757	Sarah	Uxbridge,	Guardianship,	19153
1821	Smith	Oxford,	Administration,	19154
1851	Stephen H.	Norridgewock, Me.,	Guardianship,	19155
1876	Susan J.	Thompson, Conn.,	Foreign Will,	19156
1781	Thomas	Uxbridge,	Guardianship,	19157
1851	Thomas	Auburn,	Administration,	19158
1858	Willard	Thompson, Conn.,	Foreign Will,	19159
1861	Willard G.	Upton,	Administration,	19160
1873	William	Auburn,	Will,	19161
1851	William H.	Auburn,	Guardianship,	19162
1867	William H.	Royalston,	Administration,	19163
1876	William H.	Auburn,	Guardianship,	19164
	EMERY AND EMORY,			
1858	Daniel	Fitchburg,	Administration,	19165
1872	Harriet L. P.	Southborough,	Guardianship,	19166
1867	John W.	Winchendon,	Administration,	19167
1873	Moses	Southborough,	Will,	19168
1811	Oliver	Winchendon,	Administration,	19169
1877	Seth	Allenstown, N. H.,	Administration,	19170
1874	EMMONS, Elijah	Brookfield,	Administration,	19171
1856	Lucy	Dana,	Guardianship,	19172
1872	Nellie J.	Douglas,	Adoption, etc.,	19173
1814	Robert	Dana,	Guardianship,	19174
	EMORY see EMERY.			

YEAR.	NAME.	RESIDENCE.	NATURE.	CASE.
1854	ENCHES, Jesse F.	Blackstone,	Administration,	19175
1871	ENDICOTT, Harriett	Sterling,	Will,	19176
1865	Timothy	Sterling,	Will,	19177
1861	ENGLEY, Abbie M.	Uxbridge,	Guardianship,	19178
1861	Albert	Uxbridge,	Administration,	19179
1837	Charles W.	Mendon,	Guardianship,	19180
1837	Davis B.	Mendon,	Guardianship,	19181
1836	James	Mendon,	Administration,	19182
1837	James N.	Mendon,	Guardianship,	19183
1870	Joseph	Uxbridge,	Will,	19184
1844	Levina	Mendon,	Administration,	19185
1861	Melissa A.	Uxbridge,	Guardianship,	19186
1837	Nancy M.	Mendon,	Guardianship,	19187
1837	Timothy	Mendon,	Administration,	19188
1837	Timothy	Mendon,	Pension,	19189
1870	William D.	Blackstone,	Administration,	19190
1837	William G.	Mendon,	Guardianship,	19191
1857	ENNIS, Patrick	Oxford,	Administration,	19192
1862	ENTWISLE, Sally	Sturbridge,	Administration,	19193
1875	ENWRIGHT, Honorah	Worcester,	Will,	19194
1875	Mary A.	Worcester,	Guardianship,	19195
1861	Michael	Worcester,	Administration,	19196
1777	EPHRAIM, Ebenezer	Worcester,	Administration,	19197
1861	ERSKINE, John	Milford,	Will,	19198
1879	ERWIN, Ann	Worcester,	Administration,	19199
1872	Catherine	Clinton,	Will,	19200
1876	Edward	Worcester,	Will,	19201
1879	Edward	Worcester,	Guardianship,	19202
1872	John	Clinton,	Will,	19203
1879	Mary	Worcester,	Guardianship,	19204
1879	Nellie	Worcester,	Guardianship,	19205
1860	ESTABROOK, Abigail	Rutland,	Administration,	19206
1865	Alfred H.	Grafton,	Guardianship,	19207
1877	Alfred H.	Marlborough,	Partition,	19208
1829	Alona	Holden,	Guardianship,	19209
1859	Alphonzo D.	Paxton,	Guardianship,	19210
1880	Amanda	Fitchburg,	Administration,	19211
1832	Arethusa	Hardwick,	Guardianship,	19212
1859	Arthur F.	Paxton,	Guardianship,	19213
1864	Austin	New York, N. Y.,	Administration,	19214
1827	Benjamin	Hardwick,	Guardianship,	19215
1828	Benjamin	Hardwick,	Will,	19215
1872	Benjamin	Athol,	Will,	19216
1865	Charles A.	Grafton,	Guardianship,	19217
1877	Charles A.	Newton,	Partition,	19218

Year.	Name.	Residence.	Nature.	Case.
1877	ESTABROOK, Charles W.	Worcester,	Partition,	19219
1832	Cyrus M.	Westminster,	Guardianship,	19220
1798	Daniel	Rutland,	Will,	19221
1816	Daniel	Rutland,	Will,	19222
1819	Daniel	Rutland,	Guardianship,	19223
1810	Daniel, Jr.	Oakham,	Administration,	19224
1842	Daniel F.	Paxton,	Guardianship,	19225
1842	Dennis F.	Paxton,	Guardianship,	19226
1842	Dwight	Paxton,	Guardianship,	19227
1842	Dwight	Paxton,	Administration,	19228
1811	Ebenezer	Holden,	Administration,	19229
1829	Ebenezer	Holden,	Guardianship,	19230
1831	Ebenezer	Holden,	Administration,	19231
1872	Ebenezer R.	Worcester,	Administration,	19232
1859	Edson F.	Paxton,	Guardianship,	19233
1877	Edward	Marlborough,	Partition,	19234
1856	Edward A.	New York, N. Y.,	Guardianship,	19235
1865	Edward M.	Grafton,	Guardianship,	19236
1832	Edward W.	Westminster,	Guardianship,	19237
1826	Eliza B.	Holden,	Guardianship,	19238
1837	Ellen A.	Holden,	Guardianship,	19239
1865	Emma E.	Grafton,	Guardianship,	19240
1825	Eunice	Holden,	Will,	19241
1854	Eunice	Holden,	Guardianship,	19242
1855	Eunice	Holden,	Administration,	19242
1842	Fanny B.	Paxton,	Guardianship,	19243
1869	Frances E.	Grafton,	Guardianship,	19244
1877	Fred W.	Nashua, N. H.,	Partition,	19245
1865	Frederick W.	Grafton,	Guardianship,	19246
1846	George	Rutland,	Administration,	19247
1845	George A.	Rutland,	Administration,	19248
1877	George W.	Grafton,	Partition,	19249
1863	Hannah	Royalston,	Will,	19250
1847	Hannah A.	Holden,	Guardianship,	19251
1865	Hattie J.	Grafton,	Guardianship,	19252
1865	Henry T.	Grafton,	Guardianship,	19253
1877	Henry T.	Marlborough,	Partition,	19254
1865	Hervey W.	Grafton,	Guardianship,	19255
1877	Jacob W.	Grafton,	Partition,	19256
1825	James	Holden,	Administration,	19257
1874	James	Worcester,	Will,	19258
1869	James W.	Grafton,	Guardianship,	19259
1877	James W.	Grafton,	Partition,	19260
1782	Jedediah	Lunenburg	Will,	16261
1845	Jedediah	Rutland,	Will,	19262

YEAR.	NAME.	RESIDENCE.	NATURE.	CASE.
1804	ESTABROOK, John	Westminster,	Will,	19263
1847	John	Holden,	Administration,	19264
1877	John	Marlborough,	Partition,	19265
1847	John D.	Holden,	Guardianship,	19266
1865	John W.	Grafton,	Administration,	19267
1866	John W.	Grafton,	Guardianship,	19268
1818	Jonah	Rutland,	Administration,	19269
1829	Jonathan	Holden,	Administration,	19270
1836	Jones	Holden,	Administration,	19271
1837	Jones D.	Holden,	Guardianship,	19272
1878	Jones E.	Worcester,	Will,	19273
1826	Joseph	Westminster,	Administration,	19274
1829	Joseph	Royalston,	Will,	19275
1829	Joseph	Royalston,	Guardianship,	19276
1830	Joseph	Athol,	Will,	19277
1832	Joseph	Holden,	Guardianship,	19278
1846	Joseph	Holden,	Administration,	19278
1847	Joseph D.	Holden,	Guardianship,	19279
1846	Joseph M.	Holden,	Guardianship,	19280
1832	Joseph W.	Westminster,	Guardianship,	19281
1846	Josiah S.	Holden,	Guardianship,	19282
1846	Julia M.	Holden,	Guardianship,	19283
1869	Louisa	Union, Conn.,	Administration,	19284
1844	Lydia	Southbridge,	Will,	19285
1847	Lydia E.	Holden,	Guardianship,	19286
1829	Maria	Royalston,	Guardianship,	19287
1837	Marion M.	Holden,	Guardianship,	19288
1846	Martha J.	Holden,	Guardianship,	19289
1868	Mary	Westminster,	Administration,	19290
1832	Mary A.	Westminster,	Guardianship,	19291
1842	Mary A.	Paxton,	Guardianship,	19292
1861	Mary A.	Leominster,	Administration,	19293
1863	Mary A.	Leominster,	Guardianship,	19294
1865	Mary L.	Grafton,	Guardianship,	19295
1859	Mehitable M.	Holden,	Administration,	19296
1867	Millisent	Westminster,	Will,	19297
1875	Nathaniel C.	Leominster,	Will,	19298
1863	Nathaniel C., Jr.	Leominster,	Administration,	19299
1873	Pauline	Milford,	Adoption, etc.,	19300
1825	Persis	Rutland,	Guardianship,	19301
1816	Polly H.	Templeton,	Guardianship,	19302
1832	Ruth R.	Westminster,	Guardianship,	19303
1784	Samuel	Holden,	Administration,	19304
1832	Samuel	Rutland,	Guardianship,	19305
1858	Sarah A.	Worcester,	Guardianship,	19306

YEAR.	NAME.	RESIDENCE.	NATURE.	CASE.
1858	ESTABROOK, Sarah A.	Worcester,	Administration,	19307
1837	Sarah J.	Holden,	Guardianship,	19308
1875	Sophia	Rutland,	Administration,	19309
1852	Stillman	Worcester,	Administration,	19310
1859	Sylvester B.	Paxton,	Guardianship,	19311
1871	Taylor	Rutland,	Administration,	19312
1818	Thaddeus	Paxton,	Administration,	19313
1876	Washington	Grafton,	Administration,	19314
1846	William F.	Holden,	Guardianship,	19315
1865	William F.	Worcester,	Guardianship,	19316
1877	William H.	Marlborough,	Partition,	19317
	ESTE see ESTEY.			
1871	ESTEN, Daniel	Douglas,	Will,	19318
1880	Mary	Blackstone,	Will,	19319
1868	Mary E.	Douglas,	Guardianship,	19320
	ESTEY, ESTY AND ESTE,			
1848	Abijah	Blackstone,	Administration,	19321
1858	Ann J.	Worcester,	Adoption, etc.,	19322
1854	Eliza A.	Westminster,	Guardianship,	19323
1854	Emma A.	Westminster,	Guardianship,	19324
1876	Fannie E.	Westminster,	Guardianship,	19325
1854	Francis	Westminster,	Guardianship,	19326
1865	Francis	Westminster,	Will,	16327
1853	Henry	Southborough,	Administration,	19328
1855	James R.	Worcester,	Guardianship,	19329
1850	John	Winchendon	Administration,	19330
1864	Lemuel I.	Dana,	Administration,	19331
1881	Mary	Princeton,	Administration,	19332
1854	Mary A.	Westminster,	Guardianship,	19333
1858	Nancy	Southborough,	Will,	19334
1854	Oliver	Westminster,	Administration,	19335
1839	Solomon	Southborough,	Administration,	19336
1868	Solomon	Southborough,	Will,	19337
1879	Warren	Mendon,	Will,	19338
1862	William W.	Westminster,	Administration,	19339
1845	ETLEY, Sophia A.	Mendon,	Guardianship,	19340
1792	EUFRS, Charlotte	Sterling,	Guardianship,	19341
1791	John	Sterling,	Administration,	19342
1792	John F.	Sterling,	Guardianship,	19343
1792	Joseph	Sterling,	Guardianship,	19344
1792	Patty	Sterling,	Guardianship,	19345
1792	Samuel	Sterling,	Guardianship,	19346
1792	Sukey	Sterling,	Guardianship,	19347
1835	EUSTIS, Benjamin	Rutland,	Administration,	19348
1801	Chamberlain	Rutland,	Administration,	19349
1801	Elizabeth	Rutland,	Guardianship,	19350

YEAR.	NAME.	RESIDENCE.	NATURE.	CASE.
1801	EUSTIS, John	Rutland,	Guardianship,	19351
1776	Nathaniel	Charlton,	Will,	19352
1879	EVANS, Abbie	Worcester,	Guardianship,	19353
1856	Alden	Royalston,	Administration,	19354
1844	Benjamin F.	Milford,	Guardianship,	19355
1820	Erastus	Worcester,	Guardianship,	19356
1804	George	Winchendon,	Guardianship,	19357
1867	George	Winchendon,	Will,	19358
1804	Jonathan	Winchendon,	Administration,	19359
1860	Jonathan	Winchendon,	Will,	19360
1804	Josiah	Winchendon,	Guardianship,	19361
1810	Josiah	Winchendon,	Guardianship,	19362
1867	Keziah	Winchendon,	Administration,	19363
1879	Lillian M.	Worcester,	Guardianship,	19364
1873	Lucy A.	Fitchburg,	Administration,	19365
1867	Martha E.	Winchendon,	Guardianship,	19366
1844	Mary E.	Milford,	Guardianship,	19367
1879	Maud	Worcester,	Guardianship,	19368
1814	Mehitable	Winchendon,	Administration,	19369
1804	Polly	Winchendon,	Guardianship,	19370
1871	Rebecca B.	Spencer,	Will,	19371
1804	Resign	Winchendon,	Guardianship,	19372
1879	Robert E.	Worcester,	Guardianship,	19373
1861	Rowland G.	Litchfield, Me.,	Foreign Sale,	19374
1812	Samuel	Leominster,	Will,	19375
1844	Samuel	Milford,	Administration,	19376
1844	Samuel J.	Milford,	Guardianship,	19377
1837	Thankful	Oakham,	Will,	19378
1804	Washington	Winchendon,	Guardianship,	19379
1871	Zula E.	Oxford,	Adoption, etc.,	19380
1850	EVELETH, Abigail	Princeton,	Administration,	19381
1791	Amariah	Princeton,	Guardianship,	19382
1756	Anna	Sudbury,	Guardianship,	19383
1797	Asa	Hadley,	Guardianship,	19384
1791	Asahel	Princeton,	Guardianship,	19385
1797	Betsey	Hadley,	Guardianship,	19386
1833	Charles H.	Worcester,	Guardianship,	19387
1756	David	Rutland,	Administration,	19388
1797	David	Hadley,	Guardianship,	19389
1845	Edwin F.	Princeton,	Administration,	19390
1848	Edwin F.	Princeton,	Guardianship,	19391
1861	Eliza A.	Princeton,	Administration,	19392
1833	Ellen M.	Worcester,	Guardianship,	19393
1829	Ephraim	Princeton,	Administration,	19394
1845	Frances	Princeton,	Guardianship,	19395

Year.	Name.	Residence.	Nature.	Case.
1791	EVELETH, Francis	Princeton,	Guardianship,	19396
1797	John, Jr.	Hadley,	Guardianship,	19397
1790	Joseph	Princeton,	Administration,	19398
1867	Joseph G.	Princeton,	Guardianship,	19399
1829	Joshua	Worcester,	Administration,	19400
1845	Joshua	Princeton,	Will,	19401
1872	Lucretia	Princeton,	Will,	19402
1797	Lucy	Hadley,	Guardianship,	19403
1845	Mary A. G. C.	Princeton,	Guardianship,	19404
1791	Nabby	Princeton,	Guardianship,	19405
1854	Patience	Worcester,	Pension,	19406
1797	Polly	Hadley,	Guardianship,	19407
1810	Ruth	Princeton,	Will,	19408
1791	Sukey	Princeton,	Guardianship,	19409
1791	Theophilus	Princeton,	Guardianship,	19410
1762	EVERDEEN, John	Douglas,	Guardianship,	19411
1762	Walter	Douglas,	Guardianship,	19412
1854	EVERDON, Susan S.	Southbridge,	Guardianship,	19413
	EVERET and EVERETT,			
1839	Abram	Princeton,	Guardianship,	19414
1839	Alexander H.	Lancaster,	Guardianship,	19415
1839	Ann V.	Lancaster,	Guardianship,	19416
1803	Asa C.	Westminster,	Guardianship,	19417
1775	David	Princeton,	Administration,	19418
1803	David	Westminster,	Guardianship,	19419
1850	David	Templeton,	Will,	19420
1840	Dorcas	Westminster,	Administration,	19421
1864	Edward A.	Princeton,	Guardianship,	19422
1856	Eleanor M.	Sturbridge,	Guardianship,	19423
1856	Elizabeth M.	Sturbridge,	Guardianship,	19424
1858	Elizabeth M.	Brookfield,	Adoption,	19425
1871	Elizabeth M.	Brookfield,	Change of Name,	19426
1879	Ida	Lancaster,	Guardianship,	19427
1803	Joel	Westminster,	Guardianship,	19428
1859	John	Templeton,	Administration,	19429
1803	John C.	Westminster,	Guardianship,	19430
1879	John C.	Lunenburg,	Administration,	19431
1825	Joshua	Princeton,	Will,	19432
1803	Meletiah	Westminster,	Guardianship,	19433
1864	Mendall G.	Princeton,	Administration,	19434
1864	Mendall H.	Princeton,	Guardianship,	19435
1803	Milla	Westminster,	Guardianship,	19436
1803	Pelatiah	Westminster,	Guardianship,	19437
1821	Pelatiah	Westminster,	Administration,	19438
1803	Polly	Westminster,	Guardianship,	19439

	EVERET AND EVERETT,			
1870	Richard	Paxton,	Guardianship,	19440
1839	Rosamond	Lancaster,	Guardianship,	19441
1856	Sumner H.	Sturbridge,	Guardianship,	19442
1858	Sumner H.	Brookfield,	Adoption,	19443
1871	Sumner H.	Brookfield,	Change of Name,	19444
1856	Susan M.	Sturbridge,	Guardianship,	19445
1824	William S.	Princeton,	Guardianship,	19446
1866	EVERTON, Olive H. M.	Mendon,	Guardianship,	19447
1866	Samuel E.	Mendon,	Guardianship,	19448
	EVES AND EAVES,			
1797	Joseph	Royalston,	Guardianship,	19449
1810	Joseph	Royalston,	Guardianship,	19450
1859	EWER, Hannah J.	Fitchburg,	Administration,	19451
1880	EXLEY, Joseph	Worcester,	Administration,	19452
1880	FABERY, Adrian, etc.	Worcester,	Administration,	19453
1881	Leopoldina	Worcester,	Administration,	19454
1880	Lilly	Worcester,	Guardianship,	19455
1821	FACUNDAS, Abraham	Shrewsbury,	Administration,	19456
	FAHAY AND FAHY,			
1863	Bartley	Lancaster,	Guardianship,	19457
1873	Delia	Milford,	Guardianship,	19458
1873	James	Milford,	Guardianship,	19459
1863	John P.	Lancaster,	Guardianship,	19460
1873	Katie	Milford,	Guardianship,	19461
1873	Maggie	Milford,	Guardianship,	19462
1863	Maria	Lancaster,	Guardianship,	19463
1873	Mary	Milford,	Guardianship,	19464
1873	Michael	Milford,	Guardianship,	19465
1863	Patrick	Lancaster,	Guardianship,	19466
1862	Peter	Lancaster,	Administration,	19467
1859	Thomas	Lancaster,	Administration,	19468
1863	Thomas	Lancaster,	Guardianship,	19469
1880	FAHRING, Anna M. C. K.	Clinton,	Adoption, etc.,	19470
1880	Gerhard H.	Clinton,	Adoption, etc.,	19471
1880	Sophie M.	Clinton,	Adoption, etc.,	19472
	FAHY see FAHAY.			
	FAIRBANK AND FAIRBANKS,			
1874	Abbie N.	West Boylston,	Guardianship,	19473
1770	Abel	Lancaster,	Guardianship,	19474
1801	Abel	Lancaster,	Guardianship,	19475
1809	Abel	Sterling,	Administration,	19476
1778	Abigail	Lancaster,	Guardianship,	19477
1801	Abigail	Lancaster,	Guardianship,	19478
1826	Abigail	Harvard,	Guardianship,	19479

YEAR.	NAME.	RESIDENCE.	NATURE.	CASE.
	FAIRBANK AND FAIRBANKS,			
1826	Abigail	Ashburnham,	Guardianship,	19480
1816	Abigail W.	Machias, Me.,	Guardianship,	19481
1818	Abijah	Sterling,	Will,	19482
1806	Achsah	Berlin,	Administration,	19483
1849	Adaline	Worcester,	Guardianship,	19484
1858	Albert	Blackstone,	Administration,	19485
1851	Albert P.	Ashburnham,	Administration,	19486
1867	Alfred N.	Sterling,	Guardianship,	19487
1832	Alpheus	West Boylston,	Administration,	19488
1861	Alton W.	Grafton,	Guardianship,	19489
1809	Amos	Harvard,	Will,	19490
1821	Amos	Douglas,	Will,	19491
1837	Amos	Harvard,	Administration,	19492
1858	Amos	Douglas,	Will,	19493
1824	Amos L.	West Boylston,	Guardianship,	19494
1821	Ann	Sterling,	Will,	19495
1850	Aratus	West Boylston,	Will,	19496
1859	Archibald T.	Grafton,	Administration,	19497
1836	Artemas	West Boylston,	Administration,	19498
1871	Arthur W.	Ashburnham,	Guardianship,	19499
1797	Asa	Leominster (Gore),	Guardianship,	19500
1825	Asa	Templeton,	Guardianship,	19501
1842	Asa	Templeton,	Administration,	19502
1827	Asahel	Sutton,	Administration,	19503
1846	Asahel	Warren,	Will,	19504
1858	Asaph W.	Hardin Co., Iowa,	Sale Real Estate,	19505
1791	Asenath	Harvard,	Guardianship,	19506
1829	Asenath	Athol,	Guardianship,	19507
1834	Asenath	West Boylston,	Will,	19508
1856	Augustus	Busti, N. Y.,	Guardianship,	19509
1840	Avesta W.	Leicester,	Guardianship,	19510
1824	Baruck B.	West Boylston,	Administration,	19511
1824	Baruck B.	West Boylston,	Guardianship,	19512
1849	Benjamin	Sterling,	Will,	19513
1801	Betsey	Lancaster,	Guardianship,	19514
1797	Betsy	Leominster (Gore),	Guardianship,	19515
1778	Bulah	Lancaster,	Guardianship,	19516
1770	Calvin	Lancaster,	Guardianship,	19517
1837	Catharine M.	West Boylston,	Guardianship,	19518
1824	Charles	West Boylston,	Guardianship,	19519
1842	Charles	West Boylston,	Guardianship,	19520
1844	Charles	Grafton,	Guardianship,	19521
1853	Charles A.	Fitchburg,	Administration,	19522
1874	Charles S.	West Boylston,	Guardianship,	19523

YEAR.	NAME.	RESIDENCE.	NATURE.	CASE.
	FAIRBANK AND FAIRBANKS,			
1855	Charlotte	Milford,	Will,	19524
1785	Chloe	Charlestown, N. H.,	Guardianship,	19525
1799	Clarissa	Mendon,	Guardianship,	19526
1837	Clarissa A.	West Boylston,	Guardianship,	19527
1816	Clark	Harvard,	Guardianship,	19528
1801	Cyrus	Lancaster,	Administration,	19529
1835	Cyrus	Lancaster,	Will,	19530
1852	Cyrus	Ashburnham,	Pension,	19531
1839	Daniel	Holden,	Guardianship,	19532
1857	Daniel	Grafton,	Administration,	19533
1840	David	Douglas,	Will,	19534
1844	Drury	Grafton,	Administration,	19535
1785	Ebenezer	Charlestown, N. H.,	Guardianship,	19536
1797	Eli	Leominster (Gore),	Guardianship,	19537
1849	Eli	Worcester,	Administration,	19538
1849	Eli	Worcester,	Guardianship,	19539
1803	Elijah	Leominster,	Administration,	19540
1811	Elijah	Lunenburg,	Will,	19541
1811	Elijah	Lunenburg,	Guardianship,	19542
1770	Elizabeth	Lancaster,	Guardianship,	19543
1826	Elizabeth	Harvard,	Guardianship,	19544
1837	Elizabeth S.	West Boylston,	Guardianship,	19545
1825	Ellis	Douglas,	Guardianship,	19546
1799	Elmira	Mendon,	Guardianship,	19547
1849	Emma	Milford,	Guardianship,	19548
1871	Emory	Ashburnham,	Administration,	19549
1774	Ephraim	Harvard,	Guardianship,	19550
1778	Ephraim	Lancaster,	Guardianship,	19551
1799	Ephraim	Berlin,	Will,	19552
1826	Ephraim	Lunenburg,	Administration,	19553
1845	Ephraim	Athol,	Will,	19554
1864	Ephraim	Winchendon,	Will,	19555
1871	Esther	West Boylston,	Will,	19556
1771	Eunice	Lancaster,	Administration,	19557
1852	Eunice	Gardner,	Pension,	19558
1869	Francis P.	Grafton,	Administration,	19559
1867	Frank P.	Winchendon,	Guardianship,	19560
1861	Frederick W.	Worcester,	Guardianship,	19561
1834	Freeman	Westborough,	Guardianship,	19562
1874	George F.	West Boylston,	Guardianship,	19563
1867	George H.	Sterling,	Guardianship,	19564
1829	George W.	Athol,	Guardianship,	19565
1841	George W.	West Boylston,	Administration,	19566
1826	Gideon	Milford,	Administration,	19567

YEAR.	NAME.	RESIDENCE.	NATURE.	CASE.
	FAIRBANK and FAIRBANKS,			
1867	Grace E.	Winchendon,	Guardianship,	19568
1785	Hannah	Charlestown, N. H.,	Guardianship,	19569
1825	Hannah	Douglas,	Guardianship,	19570
1826	Hannah	Harvard,	Guardianship,	19571
1849	Hannah	Harvard,	Will,	19572
1857	Hannah	Gardner,	Administration,	19573
1880	Hannah G.	Sutton,	Administration,	19574
1829	Harriet	Athol,	Guardianship,	19575
1869	Harriet	Worcester,	Guardianship,	19576
1837	Harriet F.	West Boylston,	Guardianship,	19577
1873	Harrison	West Boylston,	Will,	19578
1864	Henry B.	Grafton,	Administration,	19579
1865	Henry G.	Westborough,	Administration,	19580
1874	Henry H.	West Boylston,	Guardianship,	19581
1861	Henry M.	Worcester,	Will,	19582
1857	Herbert G.	Westborough,	Adoption, etc.,	19583
1861	Herbert H.	Worcester,	Guardianship,	19584
1811	Horace	Douglas,	Guardianship,	19585
1841	Isaac	Sterling,	Administration,	19586
1832	Isaiah	Grafton,	Will,	19587
1832	Isaiah, Jr.	Westborough,	Administration,	19588
1774	Jabez	Harvard,	Will,	19589
1774	Jabez	Harvard,	Guardianship,	19590
1789	Jabez	Bolton,	Administration,	19591
1795	Jabez	Leominster (Gore),	Will,	19592
1797	Jabez	Leominster (Gore),	Guardianship,	19593
1813	Jabez	Harvard,	Administration,	19594
1822	Jabez	West Boylston,	Will,	19595
1824	Jabez	Gardner,	Guardianship,	19596
1831	Jabez	Gardner,	Will,	19597
1841	Jabez	Fitchburg,	Will,	19598
1816	Jacob	Harvard,	Guardianship,	19599
1831	Jacob	Harvard,	Administration,	19600
1850	Jacob	Ashburnham,	Will,	19601
1778	James	Lancaster,	Guardianship,	19602
1834	James H.	Gardner,	Guardianship,	19603
1837	Jane A.	West Boylston,	Guardianship,	19604
1874	Jane S.	Harvard,	Administration,	19605
1856	Jenet	Busti, N. Y.,	Guardianship,	19606
1847	Jerusha	Fitchburg,	Administration,	19607
1816	Joel W.	Harvard,	Guardianship,	19608
1858	Joel W.	Hardin Co., Iowa,	Sale Real Estate,	19609
1784	John	Douglas,	Guardianship,	19610
1813	John	Harvard,	Guardianship,	19611

YEAR.	NAME.	RESIDENCE.	NATURE.	CASE.
	FAIRBANK AND FAIRBANKS,			
1820	John	West Boylston,	Administration,	19612
1875	John	Harvard,	Will,	19613
1829	Jonas	Lancaster,	Will,	19614
1798	Jonathan	Sterling,	Administration,	19615
1823	Jonathan	Athol,	Administration,	19616
1840	Jonathan	Harvard,	Will,	19617
1843	Jonathan	Warren,	Administration,	19618
1850	Jonathan	Holden,	Will,	19619
1772	Joseph	Harvard,	Will,	19620
1791	Joseph	Harvard,	Guardianship,	19621
1802	Joseph	Harvard,	Will,	19622
1813	Joseph	Sterling,	Will,	19623
1826	Joseph	Harvard,	Administration,	19624
1826	Joseph	Harvard,	Guardianship,	19625
1784	Joseph, Jr.	Harvard,	Will,	19626
1875	Joseph H.	Westborough,	Will,	19627
1852	Joseph K.	Sterling,	Administration,	19628
1811	Joseph S.	Lunenburg,	Guardianship,	19629
1769	Joshua	Lancaster,	Administration,	19630
1781	Joshua	Douglas,	Will,	19631
1825	Joshua	Douglas,	Administration,	19632
1839	Joshua	Holden,	Guardianship,	19633
1839	Joshua	Holden,	Will,	19634
1777	Josiah	Lancaster,	Administration,	19635
1778	Josiah	Lancaster,	Guardianship,	19636
1795	Josiah	Northborough,	Administration,	19637
1796	Josiah	Northborough,	Guardianship,	19638
1801	Josiah	Lancaster,	Guardianship,	19639
1826	Josiah	Harvard,	Guardianship,	19640
1852	Josiah	Leicester,	Administration,	19641
1840	Josiah M.	Leicester,	Guardianship,	19642
1853	Josiah M.	Leicester,	Guardianship,	19643
1837	Julia A.	West Boylston,	Guardianship,	19644
1799	Laban	Mendon,	Administration,	19645
1799	Laban	Mendon,	Guardianship,	19646
1845	Laban	Georgia, Vt.,	Administration,	19647
1819	Lemuel	West Boylston,	Administration,	19648
1876	Letha M.	Grafton,	Administration,	19649
1778	Levi	Lancaster,	Guardianship,	19650
1845	Levi	Gardner,	Will,	19651
1846	Levi	Unknown,	Pension,	19652
1864	Levi	Gardner,	Will,	19653
1867	Levi N.	Winchendon,	Administration,	19654
1799	Lewis	Mendon,	Guardianship,	19655

YEAR.	NAME.	RESIDENCE.	NATURE.	CASE.
	FAIRBANK AND FAIRBANKS,			
1811	Lincoln	Douglas,	Administration,	19656
1811	Lincoln	Douglas,	Guardianship,	19657
1826	Louisa	Ashburnham,	Guardianship,	19658
1829	Louisa	Athol,	Guardianship,	19659
1849	Louisa	Milford,	Guardianship,	19660
1816	Lucenia	Harvard,	Guardianship,	19661
1797	Lucy	Leominster (Gore),	Guardianship,	19662
1770	Luther	Lancaster,	Guardianship,	19663
1811	Luther	Lunenburg,	Guardianship,	19664
1852	Lydia	Ashburnham,	Administration,	19665
1863	Lydia	Harvard,	Will,	19666
1876	Lydia	Harvard,	Will,	19667
1879	Lydia	Northborough,	Administration,	19668
1856	Lydia C.	Busti, N. Y.,	Guardianship,	19669
1842	Lyman	West Boylston,	Guardianship,	19670
1806	Manassah	Berlin,	Will,	19671
1778	Manassah	Lancaster,	Guardianship,	19672
1880	Maria P.	Blackstone,	Administration,	19673
1770	Martha	Lancaster,	Guardianship,	19674
1777	Martha	Lancaster,	Administration,	19675
1838	Martha	Mendon,	Administration,	19676
1849	Martha A.	Milford,	Guardianship,	19677
1858	Martha M.	Hardin Co., Iowa,	Sale Real Estate,	19678
1774	Mary	Harvard,	Guardianship,	19679
1811	Mary	Lunenburg,	Guardianship,	19680
1816	Mary	Harvard,	Guardianship,	19681
1834	Mary	Westborough,	Guardianship,	19682
1867	Mary E.	Winchendon,	Guardianship,	19683
1874	Mary L.	West Boylston,	Guardianship,	19684
1843	Maryett A.	West Boylston,	Guardianship,	19685
1848	Matilda	Athol,	Will,	19686
1829	Meriam	Athol,	Guardianship,	19687
1873	Millie	Uxbridge,	Administration,	19688
1874	Moses	Fitchburg,	Will,	19689
1849	Nahum	Milford,	Administration,	19690
1849	Nahum	Milford,	Guardianship,	19691
1799	Nancy	Mendon,	Guardianship,	19692
1839	Nancy	Holden,	Guardianship,	19693
1849	Nancy	Worcester,	Guardianship,	19694
1880	Nancy	Westborough,	Administration,	19695
1852	Noah	Gardner,	Will,	19696
1829	Oliver	Sterling,	Administration,	19697
1858	Oliver	Holden,	Administration,	19698
1824	Orin	West Boylston,	Guardianship,	19699

YEAR.	NAME.	RESIDENCE.	NATURE.	CASE.
	FAIRBANK AND FAIRBANKS,			
1778	Patty	Lancaster,	Guardianship,	19700
1824	Percis B.	West Boylston,	Guardianship,	19701
1837	Persis	Berlin,	Will,	19702
1824	Phebe	West Boylston,	Administration,	19703
1783	Philemon	Athol,	Will,	19704
1783	Philemon	Athol,	Guardianship,	19705
1870	Philena	Grafton,	Guardianship,	19706
1800	Phineas	Harvard,	Will,	19707
1843	Phineas	Bolton,	Administration,	19708
1876	Phineas J.	Bolton,	Guardianship,	19709
1879	Phineas J.	Bolton,	Will,	19709
1783	Polly	Athol,	Guardianship,	19710
1797	Polly	Leominster (Gore),	Guardianship,	19711
1842	Polly	West Boylston,	Guardianship,	19712
1856	Polly	Sterling,	Administration,	19712
1874	Prudence	West Boylston,.	Administration,	19713
1806	Rachel	Mendon,	Administration,	19714
1842	Rebeckah	West Boylston,	Guardianship,	19715
1879	Robert F.	Fitchburg,	Adoption, etc.,	19716
1865	Ruth A.	Douglas,	Will,	19717
1877	Sallie A.	Sterling,	Administration,	19718
1803	Sally	Leominster,	Guardianship,	19719
1813	Sally	Harvard,	Guardianship,	19720
1872	Samantha B.	Worcester,	Administration,	19721
1790	Samuel	Mendon,	Will,	19722
1797	Samuel	Leominster (Gore),	Guardianship,	19723
1799	Samuel	Mendon,	Guardianship,	19724
1825	Samuel	Mendon,	Will,	19725
1774	Sarah	Harvard,	Guardianship,	19726
1801	Sarah	Lancaster,	Guardianship,	19727
1864	Sarah	Milford,	Administration,	19728
1876	Sarah A.	Grafton,	Guardianship,	19729
1849	Sarah J.	Milford,	Guardianship,	19730
1831	Sardis	Gardner,	Guardianship,	19731
1843	Sawyer	West Boylston,	Guardianship,	19732
1834	Seth	West Boylston,	Administration,	19733
1834	Sewell	Gardner,	Administration,	19734
1834	Sewell W.	Gardner,	Guardianship,	19735
1796	Silas	Fitchburg,	Guardianship,	19736
1847	Silas	Lancaster,	Administration,	19737
1816	Sophia	Harvard,	Guardianship,	19738
1801	Stephen	Lancaster,	Guardianship,	19739
1852	Stephen	Gardner,	Administration,	19740
1867	Sukey	Winchendon,	Administration,	19741

YEAR.	NAME.	RESIDENCE.	NATURE.	CASE.
	FAIRBANK AND FAIRBANKS,			
1849	Sumner	Milford,	Guardianship,	19742
1874	Sumner	Leominster,	Administration,	19743
1791	Susa	Harvard,	Guardianship,	19744
1875	Susan	Sterling,	Will,	19745
1813	Thomas	Harvard,	Administration,	19746
1816	Thomas	Athol,	Administration,	19747
1879	Timothy J.	Lancaster,	Will,	19748
1872	Uriah	West Boylston,	Administration,	19749
1785	Ury	Charlestown, N. H.,	Guardianship,	19750
1881	Walter	Gardner,	Will,	19751
1857	Walter H.	Harvard,	Administration,	19752
1843	Willard A.	West Boylston,	Guardianship,	19753
1840	William	West Boylston,	Administration,	19754
1834	William N.	Grafton,	Administration,	19755
1867	Willie H.	Sterling,	Guardianship,	19756
1848	FAIRFIELD, Albert	Douglas,	Guardianship,	19757
1848	Asa	Douglas,	Guardianship,	19758
1848	Clark	Douglas,	Guardianship,	19759
1848	John N.	Douglas,	Guardianship,	19760
1829	Reuben	Douglas,	Guardianship,	19761
1868	Reuben	Douglas,	Will,	19762
1848	Simon	Douglas,	Will,	19763
1825	FALES, Abiather	Templeton,	Administration,	19764
1855	Abigail	Worcester,	Administration,	19765
1836	Abner	Templeton,	Administration,	19766
1877	Alpha	Milford,	Will,	19767
1833	Amos	Dana,	Administration,	19768
1868	Amy	Worcester,	Administration,	19769
1866	Andrew	Worcester,	Administration,	19770
1849	Anna	Lancaster,	Administration,	19771
1874	Charles	Brookfield,	Administration,	19772
1845	Charles H.	Shrewsbury,	Guardianship,	19773
1836	Copeland	Templeton,	Sale Real Estate,	19774
1866	Edward H.	Templeton,	Guardianship,	19775
1862	Ellen M.	Holden,	Guardianship,	19776
1867	Emerson	Uxbridge,	Will,	19777
1867	Emmons	Templeton,	Administration,	19778
1836	Eunice	Dana	Guardianship,	19779
1877	Francis L.	Milford,	Adoption,	19780
1862	Frederick H.	Holden,	Guardianship,	19781
1864	Hannah	Upton,	Administration,	19782
1836	Harvey	Oakham,	Will,	19783
1810	James	Spencer,	Will,	19784
1821	Jeremiah	Lancaster,	Administration,	19785

Year.	Name.	Residence.	Nature.	Case.
1848	FALES, Jeremiah	Lancaster,	Will,	19786
1866	Joel	Templeton,	Administration,	19787
1867	John M.	West Brookfield,	Administration,	19788
1878	John M.	West Brookfield,	Guardianship,	19789
1836	Joseph	Dana,	Guardianship,	19790
1851	Kesiah	Oakham,	Pension,	19791
1872	Leander	Shrewsbury,	Will,	19792
1826	Lemuel	Holden,	Will,	19793
1821	Lewis	North Brookfield,	Administration,	19794
1845	Lewis B.	Shrewsbury,	Guardianship,	19795
1875	Lowell	Milford,	Will,	19796
1863	Marshall N.	Westbrook, Me.,	Administration,	19797
1838	Myra	Templeton,	Administration,	19798
1881	Nancy	Holden,	Administration,	19799
1880	Otis P.	Templeton,	Administration,	19800
1862	Samuel D.	Holden,	Administration,	19801
1845	Susan C.	Shrewsbury,	Guardianship,	19802
1848	Warren	Lancaster,	Administration,	19803
1877	Willard L.	Milford,	Adoption,	19804
1866	William E.	Templeton,	Guardianship,	19805
1866	FALIS, Henry	Hubbardston,	Administration,	19806
1868	Henry	Milford,	Guardianship,	19807
1842	James	Hubbardston,	Will,	19808
1817	John H.	Hubbardston,	Will,	19809
1843	Malissa	Hubbardston,	Guardianship,	19810
1868	Mary E.	Royalston,	Guardianship,	19811
1801	FALLASS, William	Bolton,	Will,	19812
1880	FALLON, Ellen,	Clinton,	Will,	19813
1872	FANNING, David	Milford,	Will,	19814
1869	Ellen	Sutton,	Guardianship,	19815
1869	James	Sutton,	Guardianship,	19816
1869	John	Sutton,	Guardianship,	19817
1869	Katy	Sutton,	Guardianship,	19818
1869	Margaret	Sutton,	Guardianship,	19819
1869	Mary	Sutton,	Guardianship,	19820
1869	Peter	Sutton,	Administration,	19821
	FARLEY AND FARLY,			
1821	Benjamin M., Jr.	Hollis, N. H.,	Guardianship,	19822
1852	Christopher P.	Hollis, N. H.,	Administration,	19823
1872	Dennis	West Brookfield,	Administration,	19824
1864	Edward	Worcester,	Guardianship,	19825
1873	Elizabeth F.	West Brookfield,	Guardianship,	19826
1879	George F.	Worcester,	Will,	19827
1873	James D.	West Brookfield,	Guardianship,	19828
1870	James G.	North Brookfield,	Will,	19829

YEAR.	NAME.	RESIDENCE.	NATURE.	CASE.
	FARLEY AND FARLY,			
1879	John A.	Worcester,	Will,	19830
1821	Lucretia G.	Hollis, N. H.,	Guardianship,	19831
1821	Lucy	Hollis, N. H.,	Guardianship,	19832
1864	Mary A.	Worcester,	Guardianship,	19833
1821	Sally	Hollis, N. H.,	Guardianship,	19834
1873	Sarah C.	West Brookfield,	Guardianship,	19835
1870	Sarah M.	North Brookfield,	Guardianship,	19836
1809	FARMER, Abigail	Princeton,	Administration,	19837
1829	Ezra	Lunenburg,	Administration,	19838
1842	Hannah	Hubbardston,	Administration,	19839
1735	John	Lunenburg,	Administration,	19840
1873	John	Lunenburg,	Administration,	19841
1878	Peter	Clinton,	Will,	19842
1736	Rachell	Lunenburg,	Guardianship,	19843
1736	Rebecca	Lunenburg,	Guardianship,	19844
1737	Rebecca	Lunenburg,	Administration,	19845
1776	Simon	Lancaster,	Guardianship,	19846
1862	William	Lunenburg,	Administration,	19847
	FARNAM AND FARNHAM see FARNUM.			
1813	FARNSWORTH, Abigail	Harvard,	Guardianship,	19848
1830	Abigail	Harvard,	Guardianship,	19849
1850	Abigail	Bolton,	Administration,	19850
1870	Abijah	Unknown,	Sale Real Estate,	19851
1870	Abilena S.	Millbury,	Sale Real Estate,	19852
1873	Alice P.	Lancaster,	Guardianship,	19853
1873	Andrew J.	Harvard,	Administration,	19854
1764	Asa	Harvard,	Guardianship,	19855
1830	Asa	Westminster,	Will,	19856
1831	Asa	Leominster,	Administration,	19857
1867	Asa	Athol,	Will,	19858
1866	Asahel	Fitchburg,	Will,	19859
1813	Benjamin S.	Harvard,	Guardianship,	19860
1864	Betsey	Harvard,	Will,	19861
1849	Calvin	Lunenburg,	Administration,	19862
1878	Charles H.	Leominster,	Guardianship,	19863
1869	Charles R.	Mattoon, Ill.,	Administration,	19864
1738	Deborah	Harvard,	Guardianship,	19865
1764	Elias	Harvard,	Guardianship,	19866
1872	Elmira	Millbury,	Will,	19867
1878	Emily M.	Fitchburg,	Will,	19868
1737	Ephraim	Harvard,	Administration,	19869
1738	Ephraim	Harvard,	Guardianship,	19870
1756	Ephraim	Bolton,	Administration,	19871
1813	Ephraim	Petersham,	Guardianship,	19872

YEAR.	NAME.	RESIDENCE.	NATURE.	CASE.
1814	FARNSWORTH, Ephraim	Petersham,	Administration,	19872
1850	Esther	Fitchburg,	Guardianship,	19873
1879	Fannie G.	Fitchburg,	Administration,	19874
1873	Fanny G.	Fitchburg,	Guardianship,	19875
1744	Hannah	Harvard,	Guardianship,	19876
1855	Henry	Harvard,	Administration,	19877
1850	Henry G.	Fitchburg,	Will,	19878
1859	Ira	Harvard,	Will,	19879
1830	Jerome	Harvard,	Guardianship,	19880
1757	John	Harvard,	Will,	19881
1767	John	Harvard,	Guardianship,	19882
1759	Jonathan	Harvard,	Administration,	19883
1764	Jonathan	Harvard,	Guardianship,	19884
1863	Jonathan	Fitchburg,	Will,	19885
1811	Joseph	Harvard,	Administration,	19886
1850	Joseph	Fitchburg,	Guardianship,	19887
1851	Joseph	Fitchburg,	Will,	19888
1731	Joshua	Lunenburg,	Guardianship,	19889
1747	Joshua	Lunenburg,	Will,	19890
1830	Julia	Harvard,	Guardianship,	19891
1851	Laura A.	Fitchburg,	Guardianship,	19892
1873	Leonard	Fitchburg,	Will,	19893
1873	Levi	Fitchburg,	Administration,	19894
1873	Lucius B.	Fitchburg,	Administration,	19895
1863	Lydia	Harvard,	Will,	19896
1764	Mary	Harvard,	Guardianship,	19897
1851	Mary S.	Fitchburg,	Guardianship,	19898
1811	Nathaniel	Harvard,	Will,	19899
1833	Obediah	Bolton,	Administration,	19900
1835	Oliver	Templeton,	Will,	19901
1752	Phinehas	Harvard,	Will,	19902
1746	Samuel	Lunenburg,	Administration,	19903
1819	Sarah	Petersham,	Guardianship,	19904
1831	Sarah	Westminster,	Will,	19905
1833	Sarah	Petersham,	Administration,	19906
1872	Sarah W.	Fitchburg,	Will,	19907
1869	Simon	Millbury,	Will,	19908
1764	Thomas	Harvard,	Guardianship,	19909
1828	William	Harvard,	Will,	19910
	FARNUM, FARNHAM AND FARNAM,			
1773	Abigail	Uxbridge,	Will,	19911
1844	Alexander	Mendon,	Foreign Sale,	19912
1825	Caleb	Uxbridge,	Guardianship,	19913
1829	Caleb	Uxbridge,	Administration,	19913
1838	Caleb	Worcester,	Administration,	19914

Year.	Name.	Residence.	Nature.	Case.
	FARNUM, FARNHAM AND FARNAM,			
1823	Calista	Charlton,	Guardianship,	19915
1814	Chamberlain	Calais, Vt.,	Guardianship,	19916
1780	Daniel	Uxbridge,	Guardianship,	19917
1833	Daniel	Uxbridge,	Will,	19918
1879	Daniel	Northbridge,	Administration,	19919
1844	Darius D.	Mendon,	Administration,	19920
1788	David	Uxbridge,	Will,	19921
1844	Easman	Mendon,	Administration,	19922
1846	Elizabeth B.	Providence, R. I.,	Foreign Sale,	19923
1846	Ellis A.	Providence, R. I.,	Foreign Sale,	19924
1844	Emily	Mendon,	Foreign Sale,	19925
1823	Franklin M.	Charlton,	Guardianship,	19926
1869	Franklin M.	Charlton,	Administration,	19927
1846	Frederick L.	Providence, R. I.,	Foreign Sale,	19928
1814	Hannah	Calais, Vt.,	Guardianship,	19929
1846	Henry A.	Providence, R. I.,	Foreign Sale,	19930
1877	Jesse	Grafton,	Will,	19931
1749	John	Uxbridge,	Will,	19932
1781	John	Uxbridge,	Will,	19933
1778	Jonathan	Uxbridge,	Will,	19934
1870	Jonathan	Uxbridge,	Will,	19935
1873	Joseph S.	Worcester,	Will,	19936
1828	Joshua	Southbridge,	Administration,	19937
1780	Lydia	Uxbridge,	Guardianship,	19938
1848	Marcus	Uxbridge,	Guardianship,	19939
1832	Mary	Charlton,	Administration,	19940
1858	Mary	Uxbridge,	Will,	19941
1873	Mary	Uxbridge,	Will,	19942
1823	Miranda	Charlton,	Guardianship,	19943
1770	Moses	Uxbridge,	Will,	19944
1780	Moses	Uxbridge,	Will,	19945
1844	Moses	Mendon,	Foreign Sale,	19946
1855	Moses	Blackstone,	Administration,	19947
1821	Otis	Charlton,	Administration,	19948
1823	Otis	Charlton,	Guardianship,	19949
1832	Peter	Grafton,	Will,	19950
1780	Phebe	Uxbridge,	Guardianship,	19951
1853	Phebe	Worcester,	Administration,	19952
1823	Roxalana	Charlton,	Guardianship,	19953
1874	Roxalana	Charlton,	Will,	19954
1823	Saloma	Charlton,	Guardianship,	19955
1783	Sarah	Uxbridge,	Guardianship,	19956
1864	Sarah M.	Uxbridge,	Change of Name,	19957

YEAR.	NAME.	RESIDENCE.	NATURE.	CASE.
	FARNUM, FARNHAM and FARNAM,			
1854	Sylvester D.	Worcester,	Administration,	19958
1766	Thomas	Uxbridge,	Will,	19959
1814	Thomas	Charlton,	Administration,	19960
1779	Urana	Uxbridge,	Will,	19961
1877	Whipple	Uxbridge,	Will,	19962
1878	FARON, Michael	Millbury,	Will,	19963
1881	FARQUHAR, William R.	Sturbridge,	Will,	19964
1871	FARR, Charles	Athol,	Will,	19965
1774	Daniel	Shrewsbury,	Administration,	19966
1845	Edwards D.	Harvard,	Guardianship,	19967
1845	Esther	Harvard,	Guardianship,	19968
1819	Francis	Harvard,	Administration,	19969
1766	Jonathan	Hardwick,	Guardianship,	19970
1844	Jonathan	Harvard,	Administration,	19971
1755	Joseph	Southborough,	Will,	19972
1849	Laurinda S.	Leicester,	Administration,	19973
1863	Louisa M.	Worcester,	Administration,	19974
1847	Maria	Leominster,	Guardianship,	19975
1845	Mary U.	Harvard,	Guardianship,	19976
1845	Ruth	Harvard,	Guardianship,	19977
1859	Sarah	Harvard,	Administration,	19978
1845	Stephen B.	Harvard,	Guardianship,	19979
1840	Thomas	Harvard,	Administration,	19980
1766	William	Hardwick,	Guardianship,	19981
1834	William	Fitchburg,	Administration,	19982
1834	William	Fitchburg,	Pension,	19983
1847	William	Leominster,	Administration,	19984
1847	William	Leominster,	Guardianship,	19985
1869	William T.	Worcester,	Will,	19986
1758	FARRAR, Adam H.	Lancaster,	Guardianship,	19987
1857	Albert A.	Fitchburg,	Guardianship,	19988
1831	Amiel T.	Upton,	Guardianship,	19989
1856	Austin	Fitchburg,	Administration,	19990
1807	Benjamin	Upton,	Will,	19991
1866	Clark	Keene, N. H.,	Will,	19992
1863	Cornelia S.	Princeton,	Administration,	19993
1758	Daniel	Lancaster,	Guardianship,	19994
1862	Daniel	Winchendon,	Will,	19995
1875	Daniel	Leominster,	Administration,	19996
1742	David	Lancaster,	Will,	19997
1811	Deborah	Upton,	Will,	19998
1878	Edward B.	Leominster,	Guardianship,	19999
1874	Elbridge G.	Upton,	Administration,	20000

YEAR.	NAME.	RESIDENCE.	NATURE.	CASE.
1832	FARRAR, George W.	Upton,	Guardianship,	20001
1878	Gertrude E.	Leominster,	Guardianship,	20002
1877	Gertrude M.	Ashland,	Adoption, etc.,	20003
1758	Hannah	Lancaster,	Guardianship,	20004
1795	Hannah	Shrewsbury,	Guardianship,	20005
1878	Humphrey	Winchester, N. H.,	Foreign Sale,	20006
1856	James W.	Holden,	Administration,	20007
1864	Jane R.	Grafton,	Administration,	20008
1862	Joel	Fitchburg,	Administration,	20009
1756	John	Lancaster,	Administration,	20010
1793	John	Shrewsbury,	Administration,	20011
1864	John	Ashburnham,	Administration,	20012
1785	Joseph	Barre,	Guardianship,	20013
1812	Joseph	Barre,	Administration,	20013
1862	Lucy	Ashburnham,	Administration,	20014
1862	Morris	Fitchburg,	Guardianship,	20015
1742	Nathan	Road Town,	Will,	20016
1758	Nathan	Lancaster,	Guardianship,	20017
1758	Nathaniel	Lancaster,	Guardianship,	20018
1852	Polly	Northborough,	Administration,	20019
1852	Polly	Northborough,	Pension,	20020
1853	Reuel	Petersham,	Will,	20021
1854	Susanna	Barre,	Administration,	20022
1758	Tabitha	Lancaster,	Guardianship,	20023
	FARRELL AND FARROLL,			
1861	Ann	Worcester,	Administration,	20024
1868	Bridget	Fitchburg,	Guardianship,	20025
1861	Catharine B.	Webster,	Administration,	20026
1862	John	Webster,	Guardianship,	20027
1870	Joseph H.	Fitchburg,	Guardianship,	20028
1870	Julia A.	Fitchburg,	Guardianship,	20029
1870	Julia B.	Fitchburg,	Administration,	20030
1870	Martin E.	Fitchburg,	Guardianship,	20031
1862	Michael	Webster,	Guardianship,	20032
1879	Michael	Auburn,	Will,	20033
1858	Patrick	Worcester,	Will,	20034
1861	Rosanna	Dudley,	Guardianship,	20035
1861	Valentine	Webster,	Administration,	20036
1857	FARRELLY, Edward	Milford,	Will,	20037
	FARRIGAN see FERRIGAN.			
1878	FARRINGTON, Abigail A.	Upton,	Administration,	20038
1806	Asahel	Sturbridge,	Guardianship,	20039
1806	Josiah	Sturbridge,	Administration,	20040
1806	Nancy	Sturbridge,	Guardianship,	20041
1806	Nathan	Sturbridge,	Guardianship,	20042

Year.	Name.	Residence.	Nature.	Case.
1864	FARRY, Fanny J.	Grafton,	Guardianship,	20043
1864	Matilda	Grafton,	Guardianship,	20044
1864	William	Grafton,	Guardianship,	20045
1854	FARWELL, Abel	Fitchburg,	Will,	20046
1854	Abel S.	Fitchburg,	Guardianship,	20047
1816	Abel W.	Fitchburg,	Guardianship,	20048
1831	Abel W.	Pinckneyville, Miss.,	Administration,	20049
1829	Abraham	Fitchburg,	Will,	20050
1825	Alfred	Harvard,	Guardianship,	20051
1825	Andrew	Harvard,	Guardianship,	20052
1873	Andrew	Harvard,	Administration,	20053
1825	Arathusa	Harvard,	Guardianship,	20054
1836	Arathusa	Harvard,	Administration,	20055
1851	Artemas	Fitchburg,	Administration,	20056
1863	Artemas S.	Leominster,	Administration,	20057
1843	Asa	Fitchburg,	Will,	20058
1851	Augusta M.	Lancaster,	Guardianship,	20059
1856	Austin P.	Fitchburg,	Administration,	20060
1809	Benjamin	Fitchburg,	Guardianship,	20061
1862	Benjamin	Lancaster,	Will,	20062
1873	Bethiah	Harvard,	Guardianship,	20063
1874	Bethiah W.	Harvard,	Administration,	20064
1868	Charles	Fitchburg,	Administration,	20065
1858	Clara A.	Fitchburg,	Guardianship,	20066
1808	Daniel	Fitchburg,	Administration,	20067
1816	Daniel	Fitchburg,	Administration,	20068
1817	Daniel	Fitchburg,	Administration,	20069
1816	Dorcas	Fitchburg,	Guardianship,	20070
1859	Edward S.	Fitchburg,	Guardianship,	20071
1838	Eliza J.	Fitchburg,	Guardianship,	20072
1828	Elvira K.	Fitchburg,	Guardianship,	20073
1865	Emeretta F.	Boylston,	Adoption, etc.,	20074
1857	Emily J.	Fitchburg,	Change of Name,	20075
1877	Emma L.	Ashby,	Adoption, etc.,	20076
1851	Frederic E.	Lancaster,	Guardianship,	20077
1816	George	Fitchburg,	Guardianship,	20078
1825	George	Harvard,	Guardianship,	20079
1850	George W.	Leominster,	Guardianship,	20080
1862	Grata	Lancaster,	Administration,	20081
1873	Harriet N.	Harvard,	Guardianship,	20082
1809	Harry	Fitchburg,	Guardianship,	20083
1851	Henry A.	Fitchburg,	Guardianship,	20084
1840	Henry N.	Fitchburg,	Guardianship,	20085
1809	Hepzibah	Fitchburg,	Guardianship,	20086
1811	Hepzibah	Fitchburg,	Will,	20087

YEAR.	NAME.	RESIDENCE.	NATURE.	CASE.
1772	FARWELL, Isaac	Harvard,	Guardianship,	20088
1811	Isaac	Fitchburg,	Guardianship,	20089
1871	Isabella	Boylston,	Administration,	20090
1811	Jacob	Fitchburg,	Guardianship,	20091
1828	James	Fitchburg,	Guardianship,	20092
1867	James	Lancaster,	Administration,	20093
1806	John	Fitchburg,	Will,	20094
1814	John	Harvard,	Will,	20095
1824	John	Harvard,	Administration,	20096
1825	John	Harvard,	Guardianship,	20097
1856	John	Fitchburg,	Administration,	20098
1878	John	Hubbardston,	Will,	20099
1880	John	Harvard,	Administration,	20100
1859	John E.	Fitchburg,	Will,	20101
1866	John T.	Fitchburg,	Administration,	20102
1772	Joseph	Harvard,	Guardianship,	20103
1828	Joseph	Fitchburg,	Administration,	20104
1828	Joseph	Fitchburg,	Guardianship,	20105
1834	Joseph	Lancaster,	Will,	20106
1838	Joseph	Fitchburg,	Administration,	20107
1838	Joseph J.	Fitchburg,	Guardianship,	20108
1825	Joseph L.	Fitchburg,	Guardianship,	20109
1872	Lena E.	Fitchburg,	Adoption, etc.,	20110
1840	Levi	Fitchburg,	Administration,	20111
1840	Levi	Fitchburg,	Guardianship,	20112
1862	Levi	Fitchburg,	Will,	20113
1858	Levi A.	Fitchburg,	Guardianship,	20114
1851	Levi D.	Lancaster,	Guardianship,	20115
1851	Lovey M.	Lancaster,	Guardianship,	20116
1846	Lucius A.	Lancaster,	Guardianship,	20117
1811	Lucy	Fitchburg,	Guardianship,	20118
1825	Lucy	Harvard,	Guardianship,	20119
1856	Luther	Lunenburg,	Will,	20120
1873	Luther	Harvard,	Will,	20121
1816	Lyman	Fitchburg,	Guardianship,	20122
1809	Mary	Fitchburg,	Guardianship,	20123
1811	Mary A.	Fitchburg,	Guardianship,	20124
1850	Mary A.	Leominster,	Guardianship,	20125
1851	Mary A.	Leominster,	Administration,	20126
1851	Mary A. R.	Lancaster,	Guardianship,	20127
1811	Melinda	Fitchburg,	Guardianship,	20128
1809	Meriam T.	Fitchburg,	Guardianship,	20129
1863	Nancy B.	Fitchburg,	Administration,	20130
1859	Paris T.	Fitchburg,	Guardianship,	20131
1809	Peter	Fitchburg,	Guardianship,	20132

YEAR.	NAME.	RESIDENCE.	NATURE.	CASE.
1816	FARWELL, Ruth	Fitchburg,	Administration,	20133
1808	Simeon	Fitchburg,	Administration,	20134
1809	Simeon	Fitchburg,	Guardianship,	20135
1825	Sophia	Harvard,	Guardianship,	20136
1849	Susan E.	Worcester,	Guardianship,	20137
1850	William	Leominster,	Administration,	20138
1811	Zaccheus	Fitchburg,	Guardianship,	20139
	FASSETT see FAWCETT.			
1845	FAULKNER, Annie	Millbury,	Will,	20140
1846	Eunice	Lancaster,	Will,	20141
1872	Martha	Oxford,	Administration,	20142
1804	William E.	Brookfield,	Administration,	20143
	FAUSSAT see FAWCETT.			
1880	FAVOR, John	Worcester,	Administration,	20144
	FAWCETT, FASSETT, FOSSETT,			
	FAUSSAT AND FAWCETTE,			
1874	Abel	Boylston,	Administration,	20145
1843	Benjamin	Boylston,	Will,	20146
1857	Benjamin C.	Boylston,	Guardianship,	20147
1846	Benjamin F.	Northborough,	Guardianship,	20148
1875	Betsey	Boylston,	Administration,	20149
1869	Carrie F.	Winchendon,	Guardianship,	20150
1844	Dexter H.	Boylston,	Guardianship,	20151
1867	John	Grafton,	Administration,	20152
1834	Jonathan	Boylston,	Will,	20153
1834	Jonathan	Boylston,	Pension,	20154
1846	Jonathan	Northborough,	Administration,	20155
1843	Joseph	Boylston,	Guardianship,	20156
1858	Joseph et als.	Boylston,	Trustee,	20157
1828	Lincoln	Boylston,	Guardianship,	20158
1856	Lucinda	Northborough,	Will,	20159
1857	Lucy C.	Boylston,	Guardianship,	20160
1836	Lydia A.	Boylston,	Guardianship,	20161
1828	Martin	Boylston,	Guardianship,	20162
1875	Martin	Grafton,	Administration,	20163
1868	Persis	Boylston,	Administration,	20164
1778	FAY, Aaron	Southbridge,	Administration,	20165
1840	Aaron	Grafton,	Administration,	20166
1875	Abby C.	Lancaster,	Administration,	20167
1794	Abraham	Northborough,	Administration,	20168
1873	Abraham	Northborough,	Administration,	20169
1880	Adaline A.	Fitchburg,	Administration,	20170
1843	Adam	Barre,	Administration,	20171
1864	Adam H.	Fitchburg,	Administration,	20172
1860	Alfred E.	Westborough,	Guardianship,	20173
1880	Allen C.	Milford,	Administration,	20174

Year.	Name.	Residence.	Nature.	Case.
1779	FAY, Alpheus	Southborough,	Guardianship,	20175
1830	Alpheus	Southborough,	Will,	20176
1829	Altha R.	Charlton,	Will,	20177
1866	Angelina M.	Shrewsbury,	Administration,	20178
1811	Anna	Southborough,	Guardianship,	20179
1817	Annis	Southborough,	Guardianship,	20180
1864	Apollos	Hardwick,	Administration,	20181
1851	Appleton C.	Worcester,	Guardianship,	20182
1794	Arathusa	Northborough,	Guardianship,	20183
1811	Artemas	Southborough,	Guardianship,	20184
1851	Arvilla E.	Southborough,	Guardianship,	20185
1837	Asa	Northborough,	Administration,	20186
1843	Asa W.	Barre,	Guardianship,	20187
1777	Benjamin	Westborough,	Administration,	20188
1834	Benjamin	Westborough,	Administration,	20189
1851	Benjamin	Westborough,	Will,	20190
1858	Benjamin B.	Westborough,	Guardianship,	20191
1876	Benjamin W.	Grafton,	Administration,	20192
1833	Bethiah	Southborough,	Will,	20193
1855	Betsey C.	Southborough,	Will,	20194
1870	Betsey M.	Northborough,	Will,	20195
1794	Betsy	Northborough,	Guardianship,	20196
1854	Brigham	Southborough,	Will,	20197
1875	Caroline B.	Lancaster,	Guardianship,	20198
1852	Caroline E.	Westborough,	Guardianship,	20199
1843	Caroline M.	Grafton,	Guardianship,	20200
1814	Catharine	Westborough,	Administration,	20201
1875	Chandler	Webster,	Will,	20202
1777	Charles	Westborough,	Guardianship,	20203
1818	Charles	Shrewsbury,	Administration,	20204
1860	Charles D.	Williamsburg, N. Y.,	Guardianship,	20205
1871	Charles D.	Upton,	Administration,	20206
1860	Charles E.	Westborough,	Guardianship,	20207
1872	Charles H.	Northbridge,	Administration,	20208
1851	Charles L.	Southborough,	Administration,	20209
1868	Charles M.	Charlton,	Will,	20210
1843	Charles T.	Grafton,	Guardianship,	20211
1854	Charles T.	Grafton,	Administration,	20212
1845	Charlotte	Northbridge,	Guardianship,	20213
1869	Clara A.	Athol,	Guardianship,	20214
1874	Clara A.	Barre,	Will,	20215
1794	Clarissa	Northborough,	Guardianship,	20216
1811	Clarissa	Southborough,	Guardianship,	20217
1875	Cora L.	Worcester,	Guardianship,	20218
1836	Cyrus	Sturbridge,	Will,	20219
1876	Cyrus	Sturbridge,	Will,	20220

YEAR.	NAME.	RESIDENCE.	NATURE.	CASE.
1843	FAY, Daniel	Westborough,	Administration,	20221
1878	Darius	Southborough,	Administration,	20222
1754	David	Leicester,	Administration,	20223
1806	David	Southborough,	Will,	20224
1806	David	Southborough,	Guardianship,	20225
1810	David	Northborough,	Will,	20226
1818	David	Shrewsbury,	Guardianship,	20227
1828	David	Westborough,	Administration,	20228
1839	David	Westborough,	Guardianship,	20229
1855	David	Worcester,	Will,	20230
1877	David	Barre,	Will,	20231
1877	David	Grafton,	Administration,	20232
1779	Deborah	Southborough,	Guardianship,	20233
1844	Dexter	Berlin,	Guardianship,	20234
1811	Dolly	Southborough,	Guardianship,	20235
1862	Dorinda E.	Southborough,	Administration,	20236
1827	Edmund	Southborough,	Will,	20237
1869	Eleanor E.	Worcester,	Administration,	20238
1826	Eli	Southborough,	Administration,	20239
1852	Elihu	Westborough,	Administration,	20240
1811	Elijah	Southborough,	Guardianship,	20241
1815	Elipas	Westborough,	Guardianship,	20242
1851	Eliphalet L.	Southborough,	Guardianship,	20243
1819	Elisha	Southborough,	Will,	20244
1874	Eliza	Worcester,	Administration,	20245
1845	Eliza B.	Northbridge,	Guardianship,	20246
1843	Eliza O.	Barre,	Guardianship,	20247
1733	Elizabeth	Westborough,	Guardianship,	20248
1779	Elizabeth	Southborough,	Guardianship,	20249
1784	Elizabeth	Grafton,	Will,	20250
1864	Elizabeth	Southborough,	Will,	20251
1818	Elizabeth L.	Shrewsbury,	Guardianship,	20252
1853	Ella E.	Shutesbury,	Adoption, etc.,	20253
1870	Ella L.	Worcester,	Guardianship,	20254
1856	Emily A.	Hardwick,	Guardianship,	20255
1860	Emma C.	Westborough,	Guardianship,	20256
1840	Emory	Grafton,	Guardianship,	20257
1828	Esther	Southborough,	Guardianship,	20258
1853	Estus S.	Shutesbury,	Adoption, etc.,	20259
1855	Eugene A.	Westborough,	Guardianship,	20260
1778	Eunice	Southborough,	Guardianship,	20261
1872	Eunice A.	Worcester,	Will,	20262
1848	Fanny	Worcester,	Will,	20263
1872	Frances A.	Charlton,	Administration,	20264
1778	Francis	Southborough,	Guardianship,	20265

YEAR.	NAME.	RESIDENCE.	NATURE.	CASE.
1876	FAY, Francis B.	Lancaster,	Will,	20266
1871	Frank	Worcester,	Guardianship,	20267
1875	Frank T.	Lancaster,	Guardianship,	20268
1856	Franklin H.	Hardwick,	Guardianship,	20269
1855	George	Barre,	Will,	20270
1845	George E.	Troy, N. Y.,	Guardianship,	20271
1878	George I.	Westborough,	Guardianship,	20272
1861	George N.	Grafton,	Administration,	20273
1845	George O.	Westborough,	Guardianship,	20274
1877	George T.	Warren,	Will,	20275
1853	Gilbert O.	Westborough,	Sale Real Estate,	20276
1854	Gilman	Southborough,	Guardianship,	20277
1868	Grant	Southborough,	Will,	20278
1733	Hannah	Westborough,	Guardianship,	20279
1767	Hannah	Leicester,	Guardianship,	20280
1828	Hannah	Southborough,	Guardianship,	20281
1874	Hannah D.	Southborough,	Will,	20282
1871	Harriet	Southborough,	Administration,	20283
1817	Harrison	Southborough,	Guardianship,	20284
1811	Harrison K.	Southborough,	Guardianship,	20285
1863	Harrison P.	Southborough,	Guardianship,	20286
1867	Helen A.	Athol,	Guardianship,	20287
1816	Heman	Southborough,	Administration,	20288
1805	Henry	Charlton,	Guardianship,	20289
1810	Henry	Charlton,	Guardianship,	20290
1857	Henry L.	Southborough,	Guardianship,	20291
1800	Hezekiah	Southborough,	Will,	20292
1832	Hezekiah	Southborough,	Administration,	20293
1880	Isabella U.	Barre,	Will,	20294
1828	Isaiah	Southborough,	Guardianship,	20295
1777	James	Hardwick,	Will,	20296
1777	James	Westborough,	Guardianship,	20297
1778	James	Westborough,	Administration,	20298
1857	James	Westborough,	Administration,	20299
1857	James H.	Athol,	Guardianship,	20300
1857	James S.	Athol,	Will,	20301
1845	Jane M.	Westborough,	Guardianship,	20302
1783	Jason	Charlton,	Administration,	20303
1830	Jason	Barre,	Guardianship,	20304
1843	Jason	Barre,	Administration,	20305
1733	Jedediah	Westborough,	Guardianship,	20306
1839	Jedediah	Royalston,	Will,	20307
1786	Jeduthan	Westborough,	Will,	20308
1767	Jemima	Leicester,	Guardianship,	20309
1868	Jennie B.	Charlton,	Guardianship,	20310

YEAR.	NAME.	RESIDENCE.	NATURE.	CASE.
1778	FAY, Jeremiah	Southborough,	Guardianship,	20311
1826	Joanna	Southborough,	Will,	20312
1777	Joel	Westborough,	Guardianship,	20313
1830	Joel	Westborough,	Will,	20314
1843	Joel	Grafton,	Administration,	20315
1860	Joel B.	Shrewsbury,	Administration,	20316
1843	Joel H.	Grafton,	Guardianship,	20317
1857	Joel W.	Westborough,	Administration,	20318
1747	John	Westborough,	Administration,	20319
1789	John	Southborough,	Will,	20320
1837	John	Westborough,	Will,	20321
1845	John	Leominster,	Will,	20322
1863	John	Harvard,	Administration,	20323
1864	John	Sturbridge,	Will,	20324
1732	John, Jr.	Westborough,	Administration,	20325
1756	John, Jr.	Southborough,	Administration,	20326
1863	John F.	Northborough,	Will,	20327
1849	Jonas	Athol,	Administration,	20328
1733	Jonathan	Westborough,	Guardianship,	20329
1800	Jonathan	Westborough,	Will,	20330
1852	Jonathan	Brookfield,	Administration,	20331
1818	Jonathan P.	Shrewsbury,	Guardianship,	20332
1852	Joseph	Southborough,	Will,	20333
1733	Josiah	Westborough,	Guardianship,	20334
1777	Josiah	Southborough,	Administration,	20335
1834	Josiah	Athol,	Will,	20336
1869	Josiah	Westborough,	Administration,	20337
1869	Julia	Grafton,	Administration,	20338
1856	Larissa L.	Hardwick,	Guardianship,	20339
1879	Lavana	Westborough,	Guardianship,	20340
1865	Leander	Shrewsbury,	Administration,	20341
1867	Leona M.	Athol,	Guardianship,	20342
1840	Lewis	Grafton,	Guardianship,	20343
1880	Lewis	Northborough,	Will,	20344
1806	Lincoln	Southborough,	Guardianship,	20345
1873	Lizzie E.	Worcester,	Guardianship,	20346
1815	Lomira	Westborough,	Guardianship,	20347
1880	Lorana	Southborough,	Guardianship,	20348
1857	Lovett	Southborough,	Administration,	20349
1859	Lovina	Southborough,	Will,	20350
1811	Lovisa	Southborough,	Guardianship,	20351
1828	Lucy	Southborough,	Guardianship,	20352
1865	Luther	Westborough,	Administration,	20353
1828	Lydia	Southborough,	Guardianship,	20354
1879	Lyman	Princeton,	Administration,	20355

YEAR.	NAME.	RESIDENCE.	NATURE.	CASE.
1880	FAY, Lyman	Providence, R. I.,	Guardianship,	20356
1846	Manasseh	Southborough,	Administration,	20357
1863	Margaret	Upton,	Administration,	20358
1860	Margaret M.	Williamsburg, N. Y.,	Guardianship,	20359
1844	Martha	Southborough,	Administration,	20360
1844	Martha	Southborough,	Pension,	20361
1845	Martha A.	Westborough,	Guardianship,	20362
1877	Martha P.	Worcester,	Will,	20363
1860	Martha W.	Williamsburg, N. Y.,	Guardianship,	20364
1804	Mary	Charlton,	Guardianship,	20365
1833	Mary	Southborough,	Administration,	20366
1855	Mary	Hardwick,	Will,	20367
1858	Mary	Westborough,	Will,	20368
1873	Mary	Southborough,	Will,	20369
1858	Mary A.	Athol,	Guardianship,	20370
1862	Mary J.	Worcester,	Will,	20371
1853	Mehetabel B.	Westborough,	Will,	20372
1777	Mehitable	Westborough,	Guardianship,	20373
1856	Mercy A.	Hardwick,	Guardianship,	20374
1876	Merena	Upton,	Administration,	20375
1843	Merriam	Grafton,	Guardianship,	20376
1855	Moses	Southborough,	Will,	20377
1865	Moses C.	Southborough,	Administration,	20378
1817	Nahum	Southborough,	Guardianship,	20379
1841	Nahum	Northborough,	Will,	20380
1806	Nancy	Southborough,	Guardianship,	20381
1865	Nancy	Westborough,	Will,	20382
1831	Nathan	Southborough,	Guardianship,	20383
1831	Nathan	Southborough,	Will,	20384
1854	Nathan	Southborough,	Will,	20385
1812	Nathaniel	Southborough,	Will,	20386
1863	Orlando W.	Southborough,	Guardianship,	20387
1844	Otis	Southborough,	Will,	20388
1853	Otis	Westborough,	Administration,	20389
1841	Patience	Westborough,	Will,	20390
1861	Patty	Thompson, Conn.,	Administration,	20391
1779	Peter	Southborough,	Guardianship,	20392
1833	Peter	Southborough,	Will,	20393
1806	Polly	Southborough,	Guardianship,	20394
1873	Rebecca L.	Athol,	Administration,	20395
1880	Rebecca R.	Worcester,	Administration,	20396
1861	Relief	Grafton,	Administration,	20397
1811	Reuben	Southborough,	Will,	20398
1778	Rhoda	Southborough,	Guardianship,	20399
1811	Rice	Southborough,	Guardianship,	20400

(470)

Year.	Name.	Residence.	Nature.	Case.
1810	FAY, Robert	Southborough,	Administration,	20401
1815	Russell	Southborough,	Guardianship,	20402
1843	Sabinus	Westborough,	Guardianship,	20403
1794	Sally	Northborough,	Guardianship,	20404
1761	Samuel	Westborough,	Will,	20405
1793	Samuel	Westborough,	Will,	20406
1827	Samuel	Oxford,	Administration,	20407
1855	Samuel	Southborough,	Administration,	20408
1804	Sarah	Westborough,	Will,	20409
1856	Sarah	Westborough,	Will,	20410
1858	Sarah A.	Athol,	Guardianship,	20411
1869	Sarah A.	Winchendon,	Change of Name,	20412
1872	Sarah A.	Athol,	Administration,	20413
1856	Sarah E.	Hardwick,	Guardianship,	20414
1847	Silas	Princeton,	Administration,	20415
1815	Solomon	Westborough,	Administration,	20416
1815	Solomon T.	Westborough,	Guardianship,	20417
1871	Solomon T.	Westborough,	Administration,	20418
1794	Sophia	Northborough,	Guardianship,	20419
1867	Sophia	Fitchburg,	Will,	20420
1804	Stephen	Charlton,	Administration,	20421
1828	Stephen	New Braintree,	Will,	20422
1859	Stephen	New Braintree,	Will,	20423
1850	Sukey	Southborough,	Administration,	20424
1866	Sullivan	Southborough,	Will,	20425
1813	Susan	Charlton,	Will,	20426
1866	Susan	Princeton,	Will,	20427
1815	Susan M.	Westborough,	Guardianship,	20428
1850	Sylvester	Southborough,	Will,	20429
1794	Thaddeus	Northborough,	Guardianship,	20430
1845	Thomas M.	Westborough,	Administration,	20431
1802	Timothy	Northborough,	Will,	20432
1831	Timothy	Hardwick,	Administration,	20433
1872	Timothy	Hardwick,	Will,	20434
1828	Tryphosa	Southborough,	Guardianship,	20435
1851	Visa	Southborough,	Will,	20436
1867	Waldo E.	Athol,	Guardianship,	20437
1863	Warren	Southborough,	Administration,	20438
1864	Warren	Northborough,	Will,	20439
1877	Willard W.	Brookfield,	Will,	20440
1781	William	Barre,	Will,	20441
1797	William	Barre,	Guardianship,	20442
1816	William	Barre,	Guardianship,	20443
1871	William	Shrewsbury,	Administration,	20444
1840	William N.	Grafton,	Guardianship,	20445

YEAR.	NAME.	RESIDENCE.	NATURE.	CASE.
1844	FAY, Zilpah E.	Berlin,	Guardianship,	20446
1829	FAYERWEATHER, George J.	Westborough,	Guardianship,	20447
1826	John	Westborough,	Will,	20448
1829	Sarah H.	Westborough,	Guardianship,	20449
1828	Thomas H.	Westborough,	Guardianship,	20450
	FEARIN AND FEARING,			
1856	Alice	Holden,	Guardianship,	20451
1864	John	Holden,	Administration,	20452
1865	FEARNLEY, Edwin B.	Leicester,	Guardianship,	20453
1865	Sarah J.	Leicester,	Guardianship,	20454
1865	William	Leicester,	Administration,	20455
1865	William	Leicester,	Guardianship,	20456
1864	FEELEY, Albert B.	Fitchburg,	Guardianship,	20457
1861	John	Clinton,	Administration,	20458
1880	Mary	Clinton,	Will,	20459
1864	Thomas A.	Fitchburg,	Guardianship,	20460
1864	William H.	Fitchburg,	Guardianship,	20461
1873	FEENEY, Catherine	Worcester,	Guardianship,	20462
1873	Daniel	Worcester,	Guardianship,	20463
1873	Margaret	Worcester,	Guardianship,	20464
1873	Patrick	Worcester,	Administration,	20465
1873	Patrick	Worcester,	Guardianship,	20466
1863	FEGAN, John	Webster,	Will,	20467
1861	FELCH, Levi	Grafton,	Administration,	20468
1841	Mary	Royalston,	Guardianship,	20469
1875	Sally	Rutland,	Will,	20470
1803	Samuel	Royalston,	Administration,	20471
1840	Samuel	Royalston,	Administration,	20472
1872	Walton	Oakham,	Will,	20473
1761	FELLOWS, Jacob	Oxford,	Guardianship,	20474
1816	John	Barre,	Will,	20475
1866	Joseph E.	Oxford,	Administration,	20476
1876	Joseph H.	Rutland,	Administration,	20477
1852	FELT, Charlotte F.	Athol,	Guardianship,	20478
1849	Elijah	Athol,	Administration,	20479
1852	Hannah M.	Athol,	Guardianship,	20480
1852	Mary A.	Athol,	Guardianship,	20481
1880	FELTON, Abigail H.	Barre,	Will,	20482
1777	Amos	Petersham,	Guardianship,	20483
1820	Benjamin	Brookfield,	Administration,	20484
1823	Cordelia	Dana,	Guardianship,	20485
1776	David	Petersham,	Will,	20486
1819	David H.	Athol,	Administration,	20487
1876	Edward B.	Boston,	Trustee,	20488
1876	George	Marlborough,	Trustee,	20489

YEAR.	NAME.	RESIDENCE.	NATURE.	CASE.
1777	FELTON, George W.	Petersham,	Guardianship,	20490
1817	George W.	Petersham,	Administration,	20491
1876	John	Boston,	Trustee,	20492
1835	Joseph	Barre,	Inventory,	20493
1817	Josiah	Dana,	Administration,	20494
1880	Landsford B.	Milford,	Will,	20495
1777	Lydia	Petersham,	Guardianship,	20496
1876	Martha B.	Swampscott,	Trustee,	20497
1872	Martha E.	Clinton,	Change of Name,	20498
1870	Matthias	Millbury,	Guardianship,	20499
1863	Moses H.	Barre,	Administration,	20500
1777	Nabby	Petersham,	Guardianship,	20501
1875	Nathaniel	Barre,	Will,	20502
1841	Newell	Cincinnati, O.,	Pension,	20503
1875	Oliver C.	Brookfield,	Will,	20504
1777	Phebe	Petersham,	Guardianship,	20505
1876	Reuben H.	Warren,	Administration,	20506
1830	Silence	Barre,	Will,	20507
1749	Skelton	Rutland,	Will,	20508
1822	Skelton	Barre,	Administration,	20509
1835	Skelton	Oakham,	Will,	20510
1851	Sylvester	Berlin,	Administration,	20511
1858	FENDER, Jane, etc.	Berlin,	Administration,	20512
1875	FENNELL, John	North Brookfield,	Will,	20513
1824	FENNO, Almira	Gardner,	Guardianship,	20514
1876	Charles W.	Worcester,	Guardianship,	20515
1846	Ebenezer	Templeton,	Administration,	20516
1876	Edgar E.	Westminster,	Guardianship,	20517
1876	Frances E.	Worcester,	Guardianship,	20518
1875	Franklin B.	Westminster,	Administration,	20519
1876	Franklin W.	Westminster,	Guardianship,	20520
1822	Joseph	Fitchburg,	Administration,	20521
1824	Lucinda	Gardner,	Guardianship,	20522
1824	Lyman	Gardner,	Guardianship,	20523
1861	Martha	Westminster,	Administration,	20524
1880	Martha	Templeton,	Administration,	20525
1871	Reuben	Westminster,	Administration,	20526
1863	Sally	Worcester,	Will,	20527
1824	William	Gardner,	Administration,	20528
1870	William D.	Worcester,	Administration,	20529
1761	FENTON, Joseph	Rutland,	Guardianship,	20530
1874	Mary	Milford,	Pension,	20531
1754	Samuel	Rutland,	Will,	20532
1857	FENWICK, Benedict	Boston,	Trustee,	20533
1875	FERGUSON, Frank	Milford,	Guardianship,	20534

Year.	Name.	Residence.	Nature.	Case.
1875	FERGUSON, George H.	Milford,	Guardianship,	20535
1876	James	Fitchburg,	Administration,	20536
1866	Lydia S.	Belfast, Me.,	Guardianship,	20537
1876	Margaret	Clinton,	Administration,	20538
1875	Mary J.	Milford,	Guardianship,	20539
1879	Patrick	Millbury,	Will,	20540
1880	Peter	New Braintree,	Guardianship,	20541
1861	Robert	Uxbridge,	Administration,	20542
1871	FERNALD, Alice A.	Grafton,	Guardianship,	20543
1865	Betsey	Mendon,	Administration,	20544
1871	Emma L.	Grafton,	Guardianship,	20545
1871	Hiram	Grafton,	Administration,	20546
	FERRIGAN AND FARRIGAN,			
1876	James E.	Barre,	Guardianship,	20547
1876	John	Barre,	Administration,	20548
1876	Katy A.	Barre,	Guardianship,	20549
1880	Mary J.	Barre,	Guardianship,	20550
1880	FERRIN, Harry M.	Westborough,	Guardianship,	20551
1880	John G.	Westborough,	Administration,	20552
1862	FERRY, Nolson	Grafton,	Administration,	20553
1874	William A.	Grafton,	Administration,	20554
1808	FESSENDEN, Abigail	Westborough,	Guardianship,	20555
1821	Abraham	Shrewsbury,	Administration,	20556
1857	Amanda S.	Westminster,	Guardianship,	20557
1808	Asa	Westminster,	Guardianship,	20558
1849	Charles O.	Shrewsbury,	Guardianship,	20559
1794	Elizabeth	Rutland,	Guardianship,	20560
1840	Eunice	Westminster,	Will,	20561
1840	Eunice	Westminster,	Pension,	20562
1848	Frances A.	Worcester,	Guardianship,	20563
1855	Frances A.	Worcester,	Administration,	20564
1857	Frances A.	Westminster,	Guardianship,	20565
1868	Franklin G.	Fitchburg,	Guardianship,	20566
1857	George T.	Westminster,	Guardianship,	20567
1843	Hannah	Gardner,	Guardianship,	20568
1825	Isaac	Gardner,	Administration,	20569
1754	John	Dudley,	Administration,	20570
1793	John	Rutland,	Administration,	20571
1808	John	Westborough,	Will,	20572
1810	John	Winchendon,	Administration,	20573
1836	John	Westminster,	Will,	20574
1848	John	Worcester,	Administration,	20575
1857	John	Westminster,	Administration,	20576
1848	John M.	Worcester,	Guardianship,	20577
1843	John S.	Shrewsbury,	Administration,	20578

YEAR.	NAME.	RESIDENCE.	NATURE.	CASE.
1808	FESSENDEN, Jonas	Westminster,	Administration,	20579
1820	Lucy	Westborough,	Administration,	20580
1837	Lucy	Westminster,	Administration,	20581
1848	Lucy A.	Worcester,	Guardianship,	20582
1879	Mabel	Templeton,	Adoption, etc.,	20583
1822	Mary	Barre,	Administration,	20584
1881	Nancy B.	Templeton,	Will,	20585
1789	Peter	Barre,	Administration,	20586
1845	Peter	Barre,	Administration,	20587
1840	Sarah	Barre,	Administration,	20588
1794	Sarah W.	Rutland,	Guardianship,	20589
1871	Seth W.	Shrewsbury,	Will,	20590
1748	Stephen	Worcester,	Administration,	20591
1794	Stephen	Rutland,	Guardianship,	20592
1859	Tabitha	Barre,	Pension,	20593
1794	Thomas	Rutland,	Guardianship,	20594
1834	Timothy	Westminster,	Administration,	20595
1818	William	Barre,	Administration,	20596
1848	Willie W.	Worcester,	Guardianship,	20597
1849	Wyman	Shrewsbury,	Administration,	20598
1860	FIELD, Ann S.	Leominster,	Administration,	20599
1804	Asa K.	Western,	Administration,	20600
1881	Caleb C.	Leominster,	Will,	20601
1819	Charles	New Braintree,	Guardianship,	20602
1865	Charlotte P.	Milford,	Will,	20603
1880	Charlotte T.	Milford,	Guardianship,	20604
1833	David H.	Brookfield,	Administration,	20605
1783	Ebenezer	Western,	Administration,	20606
1813	Ebenezer	Western,	Guardianship,	20607
1825	Erasmus D.	New Braintree,	Guardianship,	20608
1880	Eunice W.	Worcester,	Will,	20609
1880	Frank D.	Milford,	Guardianship,	20610
1826	George	Hardwick,	Will,	20611
1854	George A.	Grafton,	Administration,	20612
1880	Grace P.	Milford,	Guardianship,	20613
1815	John	New Braintree,	Administration,	20614
1823	John	New Braintree,	Guardianship,	20615
1813	Joseph	Western,	Guardianship,	20616
1815	Joseph	Western,	Will,	20617
1855	Joseph F.	Warren,	Guardianship,	20618
1873	Katie A.	Worcester,	Guardianship,	20619
1860	Martha	West Brookfield,	Administration,	20620
1832	Mary	Western,	Will,	20621
1792	Nathan	Oakham,	Administration,	20622
1879	Oliver L.	Fitchburg,	Will,	20623

YEAR.	NAME.	RESIDENCE.	NATURE.	CASE.
1876	FIELD, Patrick	Milford,	Administration,	20624
1799	Roubin	Oakham,	Guardianship,	20625
1761	Robert	Western,	Administration,	20626
1843	Robert	Hardwick,	Will,	20627
1873	Samuel T.	Worcester,	Guardianship,	20628
1874	Samuel T.	Worcester,	Administration,	20628
1851	Seth	West Brookfield,	Administration,	20629
1851	Seth	West Brookfield,	Pension,	20630
1801	Spencer	Oakham,	Will,	20631
1819	Spencer	New Braintree,	Guardianship,	20632
1872	Thomas	Petersham,	Administration,	20633
1874	William N.	Worcester,	Guardianship,	20634
1829	FIELDING, Grace	Leicester,	Will,	20635
1780	FIFE, Deliverance	Bolton,	Guardianship,	20636
1791	Hannah	Berlin,	Guardianship,	20637
1791	Hepzibah	Berlin,	Guardianship,	20638
1779	James	Bolton,	Administration,	20639
1779	James	Bolton,	Guardianship,	20640
1791	James	Bolton,	Administration,	20641
1791	Jesse	Berlin,	Guardianship,	20642
1791	Lucy	Berlin,	Guardianship,	20643
1779	Martha	Bolton,	Guardianship,	20644
1787	Robert	Berlin,	Administration,	20645
1791	Robert	Berlin,	Guardianship,	20646
1779	Sarah	Bolton,	Guardianship,	20647
1791	Sarah	Berlin,	Guardianship,	20648
1835	William	Bolton,	Administration,	20649
1854	William	Berlin,	Administration,	20650
1862	FILDIN, Ann	Worcester,	Administration,	20651
1826	FILMORE, Francis H.	Shrewsbury,	Guardianship,	20652
1822	George	Shrewsbury,	Guardianship,	20653
1832	George	Shrewsbury,	Will,	20653
1826	John W.	Shrewsbury,	Guardianship,	20654
1842	Sarah	Petersham,	Administration,	20655
1826	William	Shrewsbury,	Guardianship,	20656
1876	FINAN, (No name given)	Ashburnham,	Adoption, etc.,	20657
	FINDALL AND FINDELL,			
1865	Alice E.	Westminster,	Adoption, etc.,	20658
1865	George A.	Westminster,	Guardianship,	20659
	FINEY see FINNEY.			
1877	FINN, Bridget	Milford,	Will,	20660
1880	Mary A.	Milford,	Guardianship,	20661
1880	Michael H.	Milford,	Guardianship,	20662
1877	William	Milford,	Guardianship,	20663
1878	William	Milford,	Will,	20664
1869	FINNEGAN, Patrick	Worcester,	Administration,	20665

YEAR.	NAME.	RESIDENCE.	NATURE.	CASE.
1876	FINNERAN, Bryan	Worcester,	Paym't of Dep.,	20666
1873	Ellen	Worcester,	Administration,	20667
1876	James W.	Worcester,	Administration,	20668
1865	John	Worcester,	Administration,	20669
1872	John	Worcester,	Will,	20670
1879	FINNERTY, Michael	Clinton,	Will,	20671
1864	Stephen E. McG.	Milford,	Adoption, etc.,	20672
	FINNEY AND FINEY,			
1877	Edgar W.	Grafton,	Guardianship,	20673
1770	Joel	Easton, Conn.,	Guardianship,	20674
1861	FIRTH, Augusta K.	Worcester,	Administration,	20675
1865	Elizabeth	Worcester,	Will,	20676
1865	John	Worcester,	Will,	20677
	FISCHER see FISHER.			
1790	FISH, Abigail	Uxbridge,	Will,	20678
1773	Benjamin	Uxbridge,	Will,	20679
1863	Carrie A.	Hardwick,	Guardianship,	20680
1866	Delia A.	Worcester,	Will,	20681
1795	Elisha	Upton,	Will,	20682
1846	Ezra W.	Athol,	Guardianship,	20683
1837	Hannah	Westborough,	Will,	20684
1859	Hellen B.	Milford,	Adoption, etc.,	20685
1846	Henry	Athol,	Administration,	20686
1850	Henry	Hardwick,	Will,	20687
1865	Henry	Hardwick,	Will,	20688
1863	Henry S.	Hardwick,	Guardianship,	20689
1848	Horatio K.	Athol,	Administration,	20690
1877	Jason	Athol,	Administration,	20691
1857	John R.	Hardwick,	Administration,	20692
1865	Laura E.	Hardwick,	Guardianship,	20693
1875	Lucy H.	Worcester,	Will,	20694
1764	Mary	Mendon,	Administration,	20695
1765	Nathan	Uxbridge,	Guardianship,	20696
1779	Nathaniel	Uxbridge,	Will,	20697
1843	Orrison E.	Worcester,	Administration,	20698
1773	Rhoda	Uxbridge,	Guardianship,	20699
1768	Ruth	Uxbridge,	Administration,	20700
1846	Samuel	Athol,	Guardianship,	20701
1863	Samuel	Athol,	Will,	20702
1825	Simeon	Athol,	Administration,	20703
1766	Stephen	Uxbridge,	Will,	20704
1782	Thomas	Oxford,	Will,	20705
	FISHER AND FISCHER,			
1861	Abby L.	Worcester,	Adoption,	20706
1840	Abby V.	Wrentham,	Guardianship,	20707
1865	Adelaide L.	Milford,	Guardianship,	20708

(477)

Year.	Name.	Residence.	Nature.	Case.
	FISHER and FISCHER,			
1824	Albert	Bolton,	Guardianship,	20709
1874	Alice L.	Royalston,	Adoption, etc.,	20710
1875	Alma M.	Uxbridge,	Will,	20711
1851	Alpheus	West Boylston,	Administration,	20712
1862	Amasa H.	Milford,	Will,	20713
1878	Amelia	Templeton,	Guardianship,	20714
1824	Amory	Bolton,	Guardianship,	20715
1813	Betsy	Lancaster,	Guardianship,	20716
1872	Caroline M.	Uxbridge,	Will,	20717
1864	Charles	Southborough,	Will,	20718
1864	Charles F.	Southborough,	Will,	20719
1823	Charles T.	Templeton,	Guardianship,	20720
1878	Christian	Templeton,	Administration,	20721
1835	Cinthia A.	Harvard,	Guardianship,	20722
1850	David	Royalston,	Administration,	20723
1849	David H.	Royalston,	Guardianship,	20724
1872	Dennis	Millbury,	Guardianship,	20725
1873	Dennis	Millbury,	Will,	20725
1854	Dexter K.	Clinton,	Administration,	20726
1852	Edgar E.	Winchendon,	Guardianship,	20727
1846	Edwin S.	Warren,	Guardianship,	20728
1858	Ellen S.	Northborough,	Guardianship,	20729
1870	Emma E.	Worcester,	Guardianship,	20730
1862	Emma F.	Milford,	Guardianship,	20731
1856	Emmons N.	Sterling,	Administration,	20732
1880	Erastus	Worcester,	Administration,	20733
1846	Esther M.	Warren,	Guardianship,	20734
1867	Frederic	Leicester,	Guardianship,	20735
1853	George	Harvard,	Administration,	20736
1852	George E.	Westborough,	Change of Name,	20737
1852	George W. E.	Westborough,	Change of Name,	20738
1813	Harmon	Lancaster,	Guardianship,	20739
1822	Haskol	Bolton,	Guardianship,	20740
1854	Henry M.	Harvard,	Guardianship,	20741
1835	Horace	Harvard,	Guardianship,	20742
1878	Ida	Templeton,	Guardianship,	20743
1870	Ida E.	Worcester,	Guardianship,	20744
1869	Israel	Barre,	Administration,	20745
1880	Israel	Barre,	Administration,	20746
1878	Jabez G.	Westborough,	Will,	20747
1761	Jacob	Holden,	Administration,	20748
1820	Jacob	Bolton,	Administration,	20749
1843	Jacob	Lancaster,	Will,	20750
1877	Jacob	Lancaster,	Will,	20751

YEAR.	NAME.	RESIDENCE.	NATURE.	CASE.
	FISHER AND FISCHER,			
1868	Jane	Worcester,	Guardianship,	20752
1849	Jane L.	Royalston,	Guardianship,	20753
1879	Jason	Royalston,	Will,	20754
1813	Joshua	Lancaster,	Administration,	20755
1869	Josiah S.	Uxbridge,	Administration,	20756
1877	Julia	Westborough,	Will,	20757
1864	Julia C.	Southborough,	Guardianship,	20758
1835	Levi W.	Grafton,	Guardianship,	20759
1850	Lois	Hubbardston,	Will,	20760
1879	Louisa C.	Southborough,	Guardianship,	20761
1880	Louisa C.	Westborough,	Administration,	20761
1870	Louisa G.	Millbury,	Administration,	20762
1846	Lowell	Warren,	Administration,	20763
1840	Luther S.	Wrentham,	Guardianship,	20764
1848	Lydia M.	Holden,	Guardianship,	20765
1864	Margaret N.	Southborough,	Guardianship,	20766
1866	Mary	Milford,	Guardianship,	20767
1872	Mary	Northborough,	Will,	20768
1835	Mary A.	Harvard,	Guardianship,	20769
1876	Mary B.	Northborough,	Administration,	20770
1865	Mary D.	Milford,	Guardianship,	20771
1864	Mary E.	Southborough,	Guardianship,	20772
1868	Mary E.	Worcester,	Guardianship,	20773
1874	Minnie G.	Royalston,	Adoption, etc.,	25774
1823	Mira	Templeton,	Guardianship,	20775
1865	Nahum	Westborough,	Will,	20766
1881	Nahum	Westborough,	Will,	20777
1828	Nathan	Westborough,	Administration,	20778
1875	Nathan	Uxbridge,	Administration,	20779
1848	Nathaniel, Jr.	Northborough,	Guardianship,	20780
1859	Nathaniel, Jr.	Northborough,	Guardianship,	20781
1879	Nathaniel E.	Westborough,	Will,	20782
1866	Nellie	Milford,	Adoption, etc.,	20783
1865	Nellie F.	Milford,	Guardianship,	20784
1813	Orrin	Lancaster,	Guardianship,	20785
1841	Paul A.	Winchendon,	Administration,	20786
1873	Philena	Barre,	Will,	20787
1813	Pitts	Lancaster,	Guardianship,	20788
1868	Robert	Worcester,	Guardianship,	20789
1868	Robert D.	Worcester,	Guardianship,	20790
1824	Sally	Bolton,	Guardianship,	20791
1824	Samuel	Bolton,	Guardianship,	20792
1830	Samuel	Westborough,	Will,	20793
1849	Samuel	Royalston,	Administration,	20794

YEAR.	NAME.	RESIDENCE.	NATURE.	CASE.
	FISHER AND FISCHER,			
1854	Samuel	Northborough,	Administration,	20795
1762	Sarah	Holden,	Guardianship,	20796
1869	Sarah Ann	Winchendon,	Change of Name,	20797
1848	Sarah J.	Holden,	Guardianship,	20798
1868	Sarah M.	Millbury,	Administration,	20799
1863	Seth	Shrewsbury,	Administration,	20800
1848	Sophronia S.	Northborough,	Guardianship,	20801
1865	Susanna C.	West Boylston,	Administration,	20802
1822	Thomas	Templeton,	Administration,	20803
1860	Thomas	Templeton,	Administration,	20804
1832	Timothy	Grafton,	Will,	20805
1870	Walter T.	Worcester,	Guardianship,	20806
1835	Warren	Harvard,	Guardianship,	20807
1875	Washington F.	Worcester,	Will,	20808
1881	Waterman A.	Worcester,	Will,	20809
1835	Willard	Harvard,	Guardianship,	20810
1760	William	Holden,	Administration,	20811
	FISK AND FISKE,			
1790	Aaron	Petersham	Administration,	20812
1856	Abbie F.	Webster,	Adoption,	20813
1791	Abigail	Petersham,	Guardianship,	20814
1856	Abigail A.	Northborough,	Administration,	20815
1807	Abijah	Upton	Will,	20816
1804	Abner	Holden,	Guardianship,	20817
1865	Abner	Hubbardston,	Administration,	20818
1844	Alice	Oxford,	Administration,	20819
1841	Alonzo H.	Holden,	Guardianship,	20820
1813	Amasa	Sturbridge,	Administration,	20821
1800	Amos	Fitchburg,	Guardianship,	20822
1860	Amy	Sturbridge,	Will,	20823
1790	Anna	Petersham,	Guardianship,	20824
1801	Anna	Upton,	Guardianship,	20825
1786	Azubah	Worcester,	Guardianship,	20826
1805	Benjamin	Upton,	Will,	20827
1820	Benjamin	Upton,	Will,	20828
1857	Benjamin	Millbury,	Administration,	20829
1803	Betsey	Upton,	Guardianship,	20830
1804	Betsey	Holden,	Guardianship,	20831
1816	Betsey	Upton,	Administration,	20832
1804	Bezaleel	Holden,	Guardianship,	20833
1850	Bezaleel	Worcester,	Will,	20834
1840	Charles	Hardwick,	Guardianship,	20835
1823	Charles W.	Hardwick,	Administration,	20836
1866	Charles W.	Worcester,	Guardianship,	20837

YEAR.	NAME.	RESIDENCE.	NATURE.	CASE.
	FISK AND FISKE,			
1862	Clara	Petersham,	Will,	20838
1868	Clara L.	West Boylston,	Guardianship,	20839
1801	Clarissa	Upton,	Guardianship,	20840
1835	Clark	Upton,	Administration,	20841
1754	Daniel	Upton,	Will,	20842
1758	Daniel	Upton,	Administration,	20843
1778	Daniel	Sturbridge,	Will,	20844
1815	Daniel	Oxford,	Administration,	20845
1840	Daniel	Upton,	Will,	20846
1841	Daniel	Upton,	Pension,	20847
1860	Daniel	Sturbridge,	Will,	20848
1840	Daniel E.	Upton,	Guardianship,	20849
1878	Daniel S.	Brookfield,	Will,	20850
1755	David	Sutton,	Guardianship,	20851
1778	David	Worcester,	Will,	20852
1794	David	Holden,	Administration,	20853
1794	David	Holden,	Guardianship,	20854
1809	David	Barre,	Guardianship,	20855
1811	David	Barre,	Administration,	20856
1817	David	Sturbridge,	Will,	20857
1830	Ebenezer	West Boylston,	Administration,	20858
1881	Edgar E.	Gardner,	Adoption, etc.,	20859
1866	Edward S.	Worcester,	Guardianship,	20860
1843	Edwards W.	Milford,	Guardianship,	20861
1880	Edwin	Brookfield,	Will,	20862
1879	Edwin W.	Upton,	Administration,	20863
1801	Elias	Upton,	Guardianship,	20864
1870	Elisha B.	Upton,	Will,	20865
1847	Eliza	Southbridge,	Will,	20866
1807	Elizabeth	Upton,	Guardianship,	20867
1881	Elizabeth L.	Templeton,	Administration,	20868
1843	Elizabeth R.	Milford,	Guardianship,	20869
1850	Elizabeth W.	Worcester,	Guardianship,	20870
1866	Ella M.	Worcester,	Guardianship,	20871
1801	Emeline	Upton,	Guardianship,	20872
1801	Emmons II.	Upton,	Guardianship,	20873
1831	Eran A.	Upton,	Guardianship,	20874
1875	Eugene W.	Grafton,	Guardianship,	20875
1812	Eunice	Harvard,	Will,	20876
1840	Frances	Worcester,	Administration,	20877
1869	Frank N.	Leominster,	Guardianship,	20878
1760	Hannah	Upton,	Guardianship,	20879
1875	Harry E.	Grafton,	Guardianship,	20880
1861	Harvey	Barre,	Will,	20881

YEAR.	NAME.	RESIDENCE.	NATURE.	CASE.
	FISK and FISKE,			
1790	Henry	Sturbridge,	Will,	20882
1815	Henry	Sturbridge,	Administration,	20883
1820	Hepsibeth	Barre,	Guardianship,	20884
1839	Hepzibah	Barre,	Will,	20885
1807	Horace	Upton,	Guardianship,	20886
1867	Horace S.	Northborough,	Will,	20887
1804	Isaac	Holden,	Guardianship,	20888
1809	Isaac	Barre,	Guardianship,	20889
1820	Isaac	Holden,	Will,	20890
1848	Isaac	Holden,	Administration,	20891
1848	Jacob	Rutland,	Pension,	20892
1843	James	Milford,	Administration,	20893
1868	James	West Boylston,	Will,	20894
1788	Joel	Northborough,	Guardianship,	20895
1758	John	Worcester,	Will,	20896
1763	John	Worcester,	Administration,	20897
1772	John	Lunenburg,	Will,	20898
1785	John	Worcester,	Administration,	20899
1791	John	Templeton,	Guardianship,	20900
1794	John	Holden,	Guardianship,	20901
1828	John	Barre,	Administration,	20902
1836	John	Worcester,	Administration,	20903
1855	John	New Braintree,	Will,	20904
1875	John C.	Brookfield,	Administration,	20905
1855	John M.	West Brookfield,	Will,	20906
1869	John M.	Leominster,	Guardianship,	20907
1799	Jonas	Leominster,	Will,	20908
1755	Jonathan	Sutton,	Guardianship,	20909
1781	Jonathan	Worcester,	Administration,	20910
1808	Jonathan	Barre,	Administration,	20911
1822	Jonathan	Holden,	Administration,	20912
1862	Jonathan O.	Upton,	Guardianship,	20913
1872	Jonathan S.	Grafton,	Will,	20914
1836	Joseph A.	Worcester,	Guardianship,	20915
1869	Joseph A.	Leominster,	Administration,	20916
1836	Joshua	Sturbridge,	Will,	20917
1866	Laura W.	Sturbridge,	Administration,	20918
1852	Lemuel	Holden,	Will,	20919
1804	Leonard	Holden,	Guardianship,	20920
1879	Levens M.	Sturbridge,	Will,	20921
1803	Levi	Upton,	Administration,	20922
1866	Lizzie G.	Worcester,	Guardianship,	20923
1801	Lucinda	Upton,	Guardianship,	20924
1843	Lucy	Petersham,	Administration,	20925

YEAR.	NAME.	RESIDENCE.	NATURE.	CASE.
	FISK AND FISKE,			
1785	Luther	Worcester,	Administration,	20926
1817	Luther	Leicester,	Administration,	20927
1778	Lydia	Sturbridge,	Guardianship,	20928
1863	Lydia	Barre,	Will,	20929
1863	Lydia	Worcester,	Guardianship,	20930
1844	Margery	Upton,	Administration,	20931
1800	Mary	Brookfield,	Guardianship,	20932
1850	Mary J.	Worcester,	Guardianship,	20933
1881	Matilda	Sturbridge,	Will,	20934
1876	Miriam L.	Upton,	Administration,	20935
1857	Moses	Sturbridge,	Will,	20936
1803	Nahum	Holden,	Will,	20937
1804	Nancy	Holden,	Guardianship,	20938
1778	Nathan	Sturbridge,	Guardianship,	20939
1799	Nathan	Brookfield,	Administration,	20940
1824	Nathan	Sturbridge,	Guardianship,	20941
1829	Nathan	Sturbridge,	Administration,	20941
1791	Olive	Petersham,	Guardianship,	20942
1837	Oliver	Worcester,	Administration,	20943
1879	Philo W.	Upton,	Administration,	20944
1803	Rebecca	Upton,	Guardianship,	20945
1864	Richard	Worcester,	Administration,	20946
1869	Richard	Blackstone,	Administration,	20947
1760	Robert	Upton,	Guardianship,	20948
1854	Roxana	Worcester,	Administration,	20949
1794	Ruth	Holden,	Guardianship,	20950
1804	Sally	Holden,	Guardianship,	20951
1850	Sally	Southbridge,	Administration,	20952
1852	Sally	Petersham,	Administration,	20953
1880	Sally	Upton,	Administration,	20954
1735	Samuel	Southborough,	Administration,	20955
1778	Samuel	Sturbridge,	Guardianship,	20956
1790	Samuel	Petersham,	Guardianship,	20957
1794	Samuel	Holden,	Guardianship,	20958
1818	Samuel	Hardwick,	Administration,	20959
1832	Samuel	Barre,	Administration,	20960
1834	Samuel	Southbridge,	Administration,	20961
1834	Samuel	Southbridge,	Guardianship,	20962
1878	Samuel	Holden,	Administration,	20963
1870	Samuel L.	Philadelphia, Pa.,	Administration,	20964
1814	Samuel P.	Claremont, N. H.,	Foreign Guard.,	20965
1881	Sanford	Webster,	Administration,	20966
1755	Sarah	Sutton,	Guardianship,	20967
1840	Sarah	Hardwick,	Administration,	20968

FISK AND FISKE,

YEAR.	NAME.	RESIDENCE.	NATURE.	CASE.
1804	Simeon	Templeton,	Administration,	20969
1840	Simeon	Sturbridge,	Will,	20970
1760	Submit	Upton,	Guardianship,	20971
1778	Susan	Sturbridge,	Guardianship,	20972
1790	Thomas	Petersham,	Guardianship,	20973
1850	Walter L.	Worcester,	Guardianship,	20974
1859	Wilbur	Winchendon,	Adoption, etc.,	20975
1753	William	Sutton,	Administration,	20976
1800	William	Brookfield,	Administration,	20977
1800	William	Brookfield,	Guardianship,	20978
1872	William A.	Grafton,	Guardianship,	20979
1875	William A.	Grafton,	Administration,	20979
1760	Zilpha	Upton,	Guardianship,	20980
1880	FITCH, Albert E.	Westborough,	Guardianship,	20981
1855	Andrew L. H.	Lancaster,	Guardianship,	20982
1820	Austin G.	Leominster,	Guardianship,	20983
1826	Charles B.	Sterling,	Guardianship,	20984
1843	Charles F.	Lancaster,	Guardianship,	20985
1834	Charles H.	Shrewsbury,	Will,	20986
1820	Channey F.	Leominster,	Guardianship,	20987
1872	C. Edward	Sterling,	Administration,	20988
1820	Dana H.	Leominster,	Guardianship,	20989
1877	Dana H.	Worcester,	Will,	20990
1826	Ebenezer	Sterling,	Will,	20991
1825	Edward R.	Sterling,	Administration,	20992
1843	Edwin R.	Lancaster,	Guardianship,	20993
1880	Emma A.	Westborough,	Guardianship,	20994
1819	Ezra	Leominster,	Administration,	20995
1820	Ezra	Leominster,	Guardianship,	20996
1864	Ezra	Worcester,	Administration,	20997
1855	George	Lancaster,	Will,	20998
1845	George E.	Westborough,	Guardianship,	20999
1877	Harriet	Worcester,	Administration,	21000
1845	Harriette M.	Westborough,	Guardianship,	21001
1872	James A.	Sterling,	Guardianship,	21002
1876	James H.	Worcester,	Will,	21003
1861	James T.	Sterling,	Administration,	21004
1826	James W.	Sterling,	Guardianship,	21005
1845	John B.	Westborough,	Guardianship,	21006
1820	Mary	Leominster,	Guardianship,	21007
1849	Mary E.	Lancaster,	Guardianship,	21008
1875	Minna S.	Worcester,	Administration,	21009
1777	Miriam	Mendon,	Guardianship,	21010
1820	Pamela	Leominster,	Guardianship,	21011

YEAR.	NAME.	RESIDENCE.	NATURE.	CASE.
1820	FITCH, Sarah	Leominster,	Guardianship,	21012
1843	Stillman	Westborough	Administration,	21013
1850	Susan	Shrewsbury,	Will,	21014
1862	Susan	Sterling,	Will,	21015
1826	Susan K.	Sterling,	Guardianship,	21016
1836	Susan K.	Sterling,	Will,	21017
1826	Timothy E.	Sterling,	Guardianship,	21018
1840	Timothy E.	Sterling,	Administration,	21019
1843	Torrey	Lancaster,	Administration,	21020
1827	William	Sterling,	Administration,	21021
1876	FITTON, Abby A.	Worcester,	Guardianship,	21022
1857	James	Worcester,	Trustee,	21023
	FITTS AND FITZ,			
1864	Abigail L.	Oxford,	Will,	21024
1853	Albert L.	Oxford,	Guardianship,	21025
1880	Alvin	Oxford,	Administration,	21026
1849	Andrew	Oxford,	Administration,	21027
1851	Andrew P.	Leicester,	Administration,	21028
1817	Anna	Charlton,	Guardianship,	21029
1818	Anna	Charlton,	Administration,	21030
1825	Anna	Charlton,	Guardianship,	21031
1877	Anna L.	Douglas,	Guardianship,	21032
1807	Annah	Oakham,	Will,	21033
1816	Asel	Charlton,	Administration,	21034
1817	Asel E.	Charlton,	Guardianship,	21035
1858	Benjamin	Oxford,	Administration,	21036
1853	Caleb	Charlton,	Administration,	21037
1877	Camilla	Douglas,	Guardianship,	21038
1817	Caroline	Charlton,	Guardianship,	21039
1852	Catharine	Worcester,	Administration,	21040
1853	Charles H.	Charlton,	Guardianship,	21041
1877	Charles H.	Douglas,	Guardianship,	21042
1837	Daniel	Oxford,	Will,	21043
1790	Ebenezer	Dudley,	Administration,	21044
1840	Ebenezer	Charlton,	Administration,	21045
1853	Emeline	Oxford,	Guardianship,	21046
1877	Emma S.	Douglas,	Guardianship,	21047
1817	Francis D.	Charlton,	Guardianship,	21048
1865	Freddie J.	Northborough,	Guardianship,	21049
1804	George	Royalston,	Guardianship,	21050
1839	George A.	Worcester,	Guardianship,	21051
1865	James B.	Northborough,	Administration,	21052
1853	Jerome	Charlton,	Guardianship,	21053
1853	Jesse	Oakham,	Administration,	21054
1865	John	Winchendon,	Administration,	21055

(485)

YEAR.	NAME.	RESIDENCE.	NATURE.	CASE.
	FITTS AND FITZ,			
1839	John A.	Worcester,	Guardianship,	21056
1876	John W.	Brookfield,	Will,	21057
1793	Jonathan	Oakham,	Will,	21058
1853	Leonard	Charlton,	Guardianship,	21059
1853	Lewis	Oxford,	Administration,	21060
1877	Lillian G.	Douglas,	Guardianship,	21061
1856	Lubin	Charlton,	Administration,	21062
1853	Lucinda	Charlton,	Guardianship,	21063
1852	Lyman	West Brookfield,	Guardianship,	21064
1853	Olive J.	Charlton,	Guardianship,	21065
1817	Pascal	Charlton,	Guardianship,	21066
1877	Paschal D.	Douglas,	Administration,	21067
1839	Peter	Oakham,	Will,	21068
1753	Robert	Sutton,	Will,	21069
1754	Robert	Sutton,	Will,	21070
1803	Robert	Royalston,	Administration,	21071
1804	Robert	Royalston,	Guardianship,	21072
1832	Robert	Ward,	Will,	21073
1817	Roswell	Charlton,	Guardianship,	21074
1853	Russell	Charlton,	Guardianship,	21075
1879	Russell	Charlton,	Will,	21076
1790	Ruth	Dudley,	Administration,	21077
1853	Sarah A.	Charlton,	Guardianship,	21078
1868	Sarah B.	Leicester,	Will,	21079
1853	Sarah M.	Oxford,	Guardianship,	21080
1867	Silas	Oxford,	Will,	21081
1825	Walter	Oxford,	Administration,	21082
1852	Winfield S.	Oxford,	Guardianship,	21083
1859	FITZGERALD, Catharine	Worcester,	Will,	21084
1833	Elizabeth	Fitchburg,	Administration,	21085
1861	Hattie	Boston,	Adoption, etc.,	21086
1868	Mary	Worcester,	Will,	21087
1880	Patrick C.	Fitchburg,	Administration,	21088
1880	FITZMAURICE, Thomas	Milford,	Will,	21089
1875	FITZPATRICK, Annie H.	Worcester,	Guardianship,	21090
1875	Bridget A.	Milford,	Will,	21091
1869	James R.	Worcester,	Guardianship,	21092
1865	John	Oxford,	Administration,	21093
1878	John	Grafton,	Administration,	21094
1875	John B.	Worcester,	Guardianship,	21095
1870	John C. S.	Baltimore, Md.,	Foreign Will,	21096
1869	John T.	Worcester,	Guardianship,	21097
1875	Matthew G.	Worcester.	Guardianship,	21098
1865	FITZSIMMONS, Ann	Milford,	Administration,	21099

YEAR.	NAME.	RESIDENCE.	NATURE.	CASE.
1865	FITZSIMMONS, Nancy A.	Milford,	Administration,	21100
1836	FLAGG, Aaron	Worcester,	Will,	21101
1832	Aaron L.	Boylston,	Administration,	21102
1798	Abel	Worcester,	Guardianship,	21103
1865	Abel	Worcester,	Administration,	21104
1851	Abijah	Boylston,	Will,	21105
1874	Adaline	Brookfield,	Administration,	21106
1850	Adaline P.	Boylston,	Guardianship,	21107
1847	Albert F.	Milford,	Guardianship,	21108
1852	Allah E.	Worcester,	Guardianship,	21109
1845	Alony A.	Rutland,	Guardianship,	21110
1842	Alpheus	Winchendon,	Will,	21111
1777	Amos	Worcester,	Guardianship,	21112
1803	Amos	Worcester,	Administration,	21113
1818	Amos	Worcester,	·Will,	21114
1846	Antoinette M.	Southborough,	Guardianship,	21115
1875	Antoinette M.	Southborough,	Will,	21116
1861	Arathusa	Petersham,	Guardianship,	21117
1869	Arathusa	Petersham,	Administration,	21117
1768	Asa	Worcester,	Guardianship,	21118
1768	Asa	Worcester,	Administration,	21119
1803	Asa	Worcester,	Guardianship,	21120
1805	Asa	Worcester,	Administration,	21121
1825	Asa	Boylston,	Administration,	21122
1827	Augusta	Holden,	Guardianship,	21123
1837	Augustus	Boylston,	Guardianship,	21124
1876	Austin	Worcester,	Administration,	21125
1852	Avah S.	Worcester,	Guardianship,	21126
1741	Benjamin	Worcester,	Administration,	21127
1751	Benjamin	Worcester,	Will,	21128
1768	Benjamin	Worcester,	Guardianship,	21129
1798	Benjamin	Worcester,	Guardianship,	21130
1803	Benjamin	Worcester,	Guardianship,	21131
1805	Benjamin	Worcester,	Administration,	21132
1813	Benjamin	Boylston,	Will,	21133
1813	Benjamin	Boylston,	Guardianship,	21134
1818	Benjamin	Worcester,	Will,	21135
1819	Benjamin	Worcester,	Administration,	21136
1832	Benjamin	Holden,	Will,	21137
1858	Benjamin	Boylston,	Will,	21138
1871	Benjamin	Northborough,	Administration,	21139
1869	Berthier	Brookfield,	Administration,	21140
1827	Betsey	Boylston,	Will,	21141
1870	Betsey	Southborough,	Administration,	21142
1777	Betty	Worcester,	Guardianship,	21143

YEAR.	NAME.	RESIDENCE.	NATURE.	CASE.
1806	FLAGG, Bliss	Upton,	Guardianship,	21144
1816	Caleb	Worcester,	Guardianship,	21145
1876	Calvin	Worcester,	Will,	21146
1843	Caroline L.	Worcester,	Guardianship,	21147
1830	Catharine	Worcester,	Administration,	21148
1824	Charles	Boylston,	Guardianship,	21149
1827	Charles	Holden,	Guardianship,	21150
1841	Charles	Southborough,	Administration,	21151
1846	Charles	Worcester,	Will,	21152
1826	Charles H.	Sterling,	Guardianship,	21153
1846	Charles II.	Southborough,	Guardianship,	21154
1859	Charles H.	Southborough,	Administration,	21155
1859	Charles H.	West Boylston,	Administration,	21156
1876	Charles M.	Royalston,	Will,	21157
1837	Clarissa	Holden,	Guardianship,	21158
1811	Clark	Worcester,	Guardianship,	21159
1861	Cynthia	Worcester,	Guardianship,	21160
1798	Daniel	Worcester,	Guardianship,	21161
1810	Daniel	Worcester,	Will,	21162
1876	Darius S.	Milford,	Will,	21163
1769	David	Worcester,	Guardianship,	21164
1803	David	Worcester,	Administration,	21165
1820	David	Worcester,	Guardianship,	21166
1852	David	Worcester,	Will,	21167
1869	David W.	Worcester,	Will,	21168
1806	Deborah	Upton,	Guardianship,	21169
1810	Deborah	Upton,	Administration,	21170
1806	Delphia	Upton,	Guardianship,	21171
1870	Dexter	Holden,	Administration,	21172
1777	Dolly	Worcester,	Guardianship,	21173
1824	Dolly	Worcester,	Will,	21174
1825	Dolly	Worcester,	Guardianship,	21175
1835	Dolly	Worcester,	Trustee,	21176
1836	Earle	Barre,	Administration,	21177
1759	Ebenezer	Lancaster,	Guardianship,	21178
1772	Ebenezer	Worcester,	Administration,	21179
1796	Ebenezer	Shrewsbury,	Administration,	21180
1844	Eleanor P.	Southborough,	Guardianship,	21181
1771	Eleazer	Grafton,	Will,	21182
1772	Eleazer	Grafton,	Guardianship,	21183
1823	Eleazer	Northbridge,	Guardianship,	21184
1836	Eleazer	Northbridge,	Pension,	21185
1767	Eleazer, Jr.	Grafton,	Administration,	21186
1769	Eli	Worcester,	Guardianship,	21187
1814	Eli	Worcester,	Guardianship,	21188

(488)

YEAR.	NAME.	RESIDENCE.	NATURE.	CASE.
1813	FLAGG, Elijah	Worcester,	Administration,	21189
1842	Elijah	Southborough,	Will,	21190
1865	Elijah	Worcester,	Will,	21191
1804	Elisha	Petersham,	Will,	21192
1854	Elisha	Worcester,	Administration,	21193
1876	Eliza A. B.	Worcester,	Administration,	21194
1769	Elizabeth	Worcester,	Administration,	21195
1866	Elizabeth L.	Royalston,	Adoption, etc.,	21196
1853	Elliott A.	Worcester,	Guardianship,	21197
1881	Elmira	Worcester,	Will,	21198
1876	Emma J.	Worcester,	Guardianship,	21199
1856	Enoch	Worcester,	Will,	21200
1777	Esther	Grafton,	Guardianship,	21201
1817	Eunice	Worcester,	Guardianship,	21202
1861	Eunice E.	Rutland,	Administration,	21203
1873	Francis	Boylston,	Will,	21204
1871	Frederic O.	Holden,	Guardianship,	21205
1864	Frederick W.	Worcester,	Guardianship,	21206
1870	George	Holden,	Will,	21207
1845	George A.	Holden,	Guardianship,	21208
1852	George E.	Worcester,	Guardianship,	21209
1871	George E.	Worcester,	Will,	21210
1859	George W.	Southborough,	Guardianship,	21211
1742	Gershom	Shrewsbury,	Administration,	21212
1743	Gershom	Shrewsbury,	Guardianship,	21213
1759	Gershom	Lancaster,	Administration,	21214
1759	Gershom	Lancaster,	Guardianship,	21215
1771	Gershom	Harvard,	Administration,	21216
1773	Gershom	Lancaster,	Guardianship,	21217
1780	Gershom	Shrewsbury,	Guardianship,	21218
1823	Gershom	Boylston,	Administration,	21219
1772	Griswell	Harvard,	Guardianship,	21220
1843	Hannah	Worcester,	Will,	21221
1843	Hannah	Worcester,	Pension,	21222
1860	Hannah	Worcester,	Administration,	21223
1877	Hannah W.	Lunenburg,	Administration,	21224
1806	Harvy	Upton,	Guardianship,	21225
1845	Henry C.	Worcester,	Guardianship,	21226
1854	Horace L.	Southborough,	Administration,	21227
1850	Isabella P.	Boylston,	Guardianship,	21228
1864	James E.	Worcester,	Guardianship,	21229
1817	James F.	Worcester,	Guardianship,	21230
1864	James F.	Worcester,	Will,	21231
1842	Jane A.	Grafton,	Guardianship,	21232
1843	Jeremiah	Grafton,	Administration,	21233

YEAR.	NAME.	RESIDENCE.	NATURE.	CASE.
1777	FLAGG, Joel	Worcester,	Guardianship,	21234
1793	Joel	Holden,	Administration,	21235
1794	Joel	Holden,	Guardianship,	21236
1853	Joel	Worcester,	Administration,	21237
1824	Joel T.	Boylston,	Guardianship,	21238
1798	John	Worcester,	Guardianship,	21239
1803	John	Worcester,	Guardianship,	21240
1814	John	Worcester,	Guardianship,	21241
1843	John	Templeton,	Administration,	21242
1868	John	Worcester,	Administration,	21243
1875	John	Lunenburg,	Administration,	21244
1844	John L.	Grafton,	Guardianship,	21245
1852	John O.	Worcester,	Guardianship,	21246
1794	Jonathan	Holden,	Guardianship,	21247
1844	Jonathan	Holden,	Will,	21248
1844	Jonathan	Worcester,	Will,	21249
1847	Jonathan	Boylston,	Administration,	21250
1837	Joseph	Boylston,	Guardianship,	21251
1842	Joseph	Grafton,	Administration,	21252
1848	Joseph	Royalston,	Guardianship,	21253
1864	Joseph	Fitzwilliam, N. H.,	Administration,	21253
1867	Joseph	Berlin,	Will,	21254
1842	Joseph C.	Grafton,	Guardianship,	21255
1873	Joseph W.	Worcester,	Administration,	21256
1777	Joshua	Worcester,	Guardianship,	21257
1859	Joshua	Dana,	Will,	21258
1871	Joshua	Dana,	Administration,	21259
1873	Joshua	Hubbardston,	Administration,	21260
1774	Josiah	Worcester,	Will,	21261
1841	Josiah	Brookfield,	Administration,	21262
1860	Josiah	Brookfield,	Administration,	21263
1868	Josiah	Hubbardston,	Will,	21264
1743	Jotham	Shrewsbury,	Guardianship,	21265
1777	Jotham	Shrewsbury,	Administration,	21266
1778	Jotham	Shrewsbury,	Guardianship,	21267
1826	Jotham	Boylston,	Will,	21268
1834	Kezia	Holden,	Administration,	21269
1845	Leland	Southborough,	Administration,	21270
1844	Leonard	Worcester,	Administration,	21271
1769	Levi	Worcester,	Guardianship,	21272
1777	Levi	Worcester,	Guardianship,	21273
1802	Levi	Worcester,	Administration,	21274
1803	Levi	Worcester,	Guardianship,	21275
1813	Levi	Boylston,	Guardianship,	21276
1847	Levi	Lunenburg,	Will,	21277

YEAR.	NAME.	RESIDENCE.	NATURE.	CASE.
1868	FLAGG, Levi	Boylston,	Will,	21278
1852	Levi B.	Worcester,	Administration,	21279
1846	Lucinda S.	Southborough,	Guardianship,	21280
1836	Lucretia	Boylston,	Will,	21281
1874	Lucretia D.	Boylston,	Administration,	21282
1850	Lucretia O.	Boylston,	Guardianship,	21283
1870	Lucy A.	Worcester,	Guardianship,	21284
1837	Lucy F.	Holden,	Guardianship,	21285
1801	Lydia	Grafton,	Administration,	21286
1824	Lydia	Grafton,	Will,	21287
1846	Lydia A.	Southborough,	Guardianship,	21288
1836	Lyman	Holden,	Administration,	21289
1858	Lyman	Dana,	Will,	21290
1850	Lysander	Boylston,	Guardianship,	21291
1824	Maria S.	Boylston,	Guardianship,	21292
1874	Marietta	Worcester,	Will,	21293
1870	Marshall	Worcester,	Administration,	21294
1875	Martha	Shrewsbury,	Administration,	21295
1871	Martha E.	Worcester,	Administration,	21296
1859	Martha M.	Southborough,	Guardianship,	21297
1751	Mary	Worcester,	Guardianship,	21298
1759	Mary	Lancaster,	Guardianship,	21299
1816	Mary	Worcester,	Guardianship,	21300
1856	Mary	Brookfield,	Will,	21301
1863	Mary	Boylston,	Will,	21302
1881	Mary	Shrewsbury,	Administration,	21303
1872	Mary A.	Worcester,	Will,	21304
1850	Mary A. H.	Boylston,	Guardianship,	21305
1855	Mary A. S.	Upton,	Guardianship,	21306
1859	Mary B.	Worcester,	Will,	21307
1864	Mary E.'	Worcester,	Guardianship,	21308
1845	Mary J.	Worcester,	Guardianship,	21309
1853	Mary J.	Worcester,	Administration,	21310
1869	Mary J.	Brookfield,	Guardianship,	21311
1848	Mary M.	Boylston,	Guardianship,	21312
1870	Mary P.	Boylston,	Will,	21313
1806	Mehitabel	Upton,	Guardianship,	21314
1811	Mehitable	Upton,	Will,	21315
1862	Nahum	Boylston,	Administration,	21316
1827	Nancy	Holden,	Guardianship,	21317
1819	Nancy R.	West Boylston,	Guardianship,	21318
1756	Nathan	Grafton,	Administration,	21319
1777	Nathan	Grafton,	Administration,	21320
1769	Nathaniel	Worcester,	Guardianship,	21321
1786	Nathaniel	Upton,	Administration,	21322

Year.	Name.	Residence.	Nature.	Case.
1805	FLAGG, Nathaniel	Upton,	Administration,	21323
1806	Nathaniel	Upton,	Guardianship,	21324
1810	Nathaniel	Worcester,	Will,	21325
1876	Nathaniel B.	Shrewsbury,	Will,	21326
1816	Nathaniel C.	Worcester,	Administration,	21327
1841	Patty	Northbridge,	Administration,	21328
1841	Patty	Northbridge,	Pension,	21329
1873	Patty	Berlin,	Administration,	21330
1743	Persis	Shrewsbury,	Guardianship,	21331
1848	Persis	Boylston,	Will,	21332
1832	Phebe A.	Holden,	Guardianship,	21333
1806	Phila	Upton,	Guardianship,	21334
1791	Phineas	Worcester,	Administration,	21335
1778	Pliny	Shrewsbury,	Guardianship,	21336
1798	Polly	Worcester,	Guardianship,	21337
1777	Rachel	Grafton,	Guardianship,	21338
1778	Rebecca	Shrewsbury,	Guardianship,	21339
1807	Rebecca	Lancaster,	Will,	21340
1845	Rebecca	Sterling,	Administration,	21341
1817	Rebecca J.	Worcester,	Guardianship,	21342
1845	Rebeckah B.	Southborough,	Will,	21343
1800	Richard	Holden,	Will,	21344
1825	Richard	Worcester,	Guardianship,	21345
1806	Roxella	Upton,	Guardianship,	21346
1805	Rufus	Boylston,	Administration,	21347
1863	Russell S.	Winchendon,	Administration,	21348
1848	Ruth	Lunenburg,	Will,	21349
1837	Sabrina	Holden,	Guardianship,	21350
1813	Sally	Boylston,	Guardianship,	21351
1844	Sally	Boylston,	Will,	21352
1849	Sally	Worcester,	Will,	21353
1778	Samuel	Shrewsbury,	Guardianship,	21354
1815	Samuel	Brookfield,	Will,	21355
1819	Samuel	Worcester,	Will,	21356
1822	Samuel	Grafton,	Will,	21357
1825	Samuel	Worcester,	Will,	21358
1825	Samuel	Worcester,	Guardianship,	21359
1842	Samuel B.	Grafton,	Guardianship,	21360
1855	Samuel C.	Upton,	Will,	21361
1871	Samuel W.	Lancaster,	Will,	21362
1772	Sarah	Grafton,	Guardianship,	21363
1798	Sarah	Worcester,	Guardianship,	21364
1803	Sarah	Worcester,	Guardianship,	21365
1837	Sarah	Holden,	Guardianship,	21366
1870	Sarah	Grafton,	Will,	21367

YEAR.	NAME.	RESIDENCE.	NATURE.	CASE.
1832	FLAGG, Sarah A.	Grafton,	Administration,	21368
1865	Sarah A.	Northborough,	Administration,	21369
1860	Sarah S.	Worcester,	Administration,	21370
1813	Seth	Boylston,	Guardianship,	21371
1777	Silas	Worcester,	Guardianship,	21372
1818	Silas	West Boylston,	Administration,	21373
1845	Silas H.	Worcester,	Administration,	21374
1777	Silus	Mendon,	Administration,	21375
1743	Solomon	Shrewsbury,	Guardianship,	21376
1767	Solomon	Shrewsbury,	Guardianship,	21377
1778	Solomon	Shrewsbury,	Guardianship,	21378
1796	Solomon	Boylston,	Guardianship,	21379
1848	Solon	Boylston,	Guardianship,	21380
1867	Solon G.	Boylston,	Will,	21381
1743	Stephen	Shrewsbury,	Guardianship,	21382
1815	Stephen	Boylston,	Will,	21383
1849	Stephen	Boylston,	Administration,	21384
1849	Sullivan F.	Southborough,	Guardianship,	21385
1842	Susan C.	Grafton,	Guardianship,	21386
1873	Susan W.	Worcester,	Guardianship,	21387
1860	Sylvanus	Waterbury, Vt.,	Administration,	21388
1778	Thankful	Shrewsbury,	Guardianship,	21389
1844	Thomas J.	Grafton,	Guardianship,	21390
1845	Thomas M.	Worcester,	Guardianship,	21391
1878	Walter C.	Worcester,	Administration,	21392
1873	Ward C.	Worcester,	Guardianship,	21393
1849	Warren	Rutland,	Administration,	21394
1762	William	Holden,	Guardianship,	21395
1816	William	Worcester,	Guardianship,	21396
1843	William	Worcester,	Administration,	21397
1844	William	Worcester,	Guardianship,	21398
1849	William	Southborough,	Will,	21399
1849	William	Boylston,	Administration,	21400
1856	William	Holden,	Administration,	21401
1842	William B.	Holden,	Will,	21402
1859	William D.	Boylston,	Administration,	21403
1845	William H.	Holden,	Guardianship,	21404
1846	William H.	Southborough,	Guardianship,	21405
1873	Willie L.	Worcester,	Guardianship,	21406
1847	Zebediah	Milford,	Will,	21407
1778	Zenobia	Shrewsbury,	Guardianship,	21408
1870	FLAHERTY, Catharine F.	Milford,	Guardianship,	21409
1870	Elizabeth	Milford,	Guardianship,	21410
1870	Ellen M.	Milford,	Guardianship,	21411
1870	John J.	Milford,	Guardianship,	21412

YEAR.	NAME.	RESIDENCE.	NATURE.	CASE.
1877	FLAHERTY, Margaret	Worcester,	Guardianship,.	21413
1877	Martin	Worcester,	Will,	21414
1877	Martin	Worcester,	Guardianship,	21415
1870	Mary A.	Milford,	Guardianship,	21416
1877	Patrick	Worcester,	Guardianship,	21417
1870	Sarah J.	Milford,	Guardianship,	21418
1871	FLAHM, Bridget, etc.	Worcester,	Administration,	21419
	FLANAGAN see FLANIGAN.			
1867	FLANDERS, Charles W.	Petersham,	Guardianship,	21420
	FLANIGAN AND FLANAGAN,			
1876	John	Milford,	Will,	21421
1880	Mary	Milford,	Administration,	21422
1866	Nicholas	Milford,	Will,	21423
1873	Thomas	Milford,	Administration,	21424
1873	Thomas	Milford,	Guardianship,	21425
1857	FLASHMAN, Samuel	Webster,	Administration,	21426
1875	FLEECKER, Fraziska	Webster,	Administration,	21427
1871	FLEHIVE, Bridget	Worcester,	Administration,	21428
	FLEMMING AND FLEMING,			
1874	James	Dublin, Ire.,	Guardianship,	21429
1874	Mary J.	Worcester,	Guardianship,	21430
1864	Michael	Worcester,	Guardianship,	21431
1869	Thomas	Worcester,	Guardianship,	21432
1860	FLETCHER, Aaron V.	Worcester,	Administration,	21433
1851	Abby E.	Northbridge,	Guardianship,	21434
1826	Abigail	Ashburnham,	Guardianship,	21435
1762	Abraham	Mendon,	Administration,	21436
1848	Abraham	Mendon,	Administration,	21437
1847	Alanson	Blackstone,	Will,	21438
1857	Allen F.	Athol,	Guardianship,	21439
1766	Alpheus	Rutland,	Administration,	21440
1789	Alpheus	Barre,	Guardianship,	21441
1789	Anna	Barre,	Guardianship,	21442
1822	Asa	Mendon,	Will,	21443
1789	Barna	Barre,	Administration,	21444
1849	Benjamin F.	Mendon,	Guardianship,	21445
1870	Betsey	Lunenburg,	Will,	21446
1785	Caleb	Templeton,	Guardianship,	21447
1807	Caleb	Templeton,	Administration,	21447
1805	Calvin	Bolton,	Guardianship,	21448
1812	Carshena	Gerry,	Guardianship,	21449
1847	Charles H.	Blackstone,	Guardianship,	21450
1812	Cinthia	Gerry,	Guardianship,	21451
1869	Clara A.	Northbridge,	Guardianship,	21452
1812	Dix	Gerry,	Guardianship,	21453
1815	Ebenezer	Worcester,	Guardianship,	21454

YEAR.	NAME.	RESIDENCE.	NATURE.	CASE.
1770	FLETCHER, Eleazer	Sutton,	Administration,	21455
1770	Eleazer	Grafton,	Will,	21456
1833	Eliza	Uxbridge,	Guardianship,	21457
1852	Eliza A.	Boston,	Guardianship,	21458
1771	Elizabeth	Rutland,	Guardianship,	21459
1864	Elizabeth	Lancaster,	Administration,	21460
1871	Ellen M.	Clinton,	Guardianship,	21461
1851	Emily M.	Northbridge,	Guardianship,	21462
1857	Emma C.	Milford,	Guardianship,	21463
1869	Ephraim S.	Northbridge,	Administration,	21464
1858	Ezra W.	Northbridge,	Will,	21465
1871	Frances L.	Clinton,	Guardianship,	21466
1822	Francis	Templeton,	Administration,	21467
1812	Frederick	Gerry,	Guardianship,	21468
1856	George E. W.	Lancaster,	Guardianship,	21469
1851	George F.	Northbridge,	Guardianship,	21470
1877	Gertrude M.	Lancaster,	Adoption, etc.,	21471
1871	Gilbert H.	Northbridge,	Will,	21472
1849	Harriet E.	Mendon,	Guardianship,	21473
1854	Harriet E.	Uxbridge,	Administration,	21474
1868	Henry	Louisville, Ky.,	Administration,	21475
1878	Herbert B.	West Boylston,	Administration,	21476
1754	Hezekiah	Rutland,	Administration,	21477
1777	Hezekiah	Mendon,	Will,	21478
1860	Hezekiah	Mendon,	Will,	21479
1835	James	Northbridge,	Will,	21480
1851	James B,	Northbridge,	Guardianship,	21481
1825	Joel	Templeton,	Will,	21482
1760	John	Lancaster,	Administration,	21483
1792	John	Rutland,	Will,	21484
1812	John	Gerry,	Guardianship,	21485
1788	Jonathan	Barre,	Will,	21486
1789	Jonathan	Barre,	Guardianship,	21487
1797	Jonathan	Barre,	Administration,	21488
1805	Joseph	Bolton,	Administration,	21489
1862	Joseph	Ashburnham,	Administration,	21490
1861	Joseph P. L.	Worcester,	Guardianship,	21491
1772	Joshua	Grafton,	Administration,	21492
1815	Joshua	Lancaster,	Administration,	21493
1843	Joshua	Ashburnham,	Pension,	21494
1844	Joshua	Lancaster,	Administration,	21495
1851	Josiah S.	Northbridge,	Guardianship,	21496
1867	Laurinda C.	Northbridge,	Administration,	21497
1851	Lewis C.	Northbridge,	Guardianship,	21498
1869	Lewis C.	Northbridge,	Guardianship,	21499

(495—SERIES A.)

Year.	Name.	Residence.	Nature.	Case.
1877	FLETCHER, Loring	Warren,	Will,	21500
1812	Lucy	Gerry,	Guardianship,	21501
1871	Lucy	Clinton,	Will,	21502
1812	Martha	Gerry,	Guardianship,	21503
1857	Martin	Milford,	Will,	21504
1812	Martin W.	Gerry,	Guardianship,	21505
1789	Mary	Barre,	Guardianship,	21506
1855	Mary	Charlton,	Guardianship,	21507
1857	Mary	Winchendon,	Pension,	21508
1857	Mary	Winchendon,	Will,	21509
1864	Mary	Lancaster,	Administration,	21510
1859	Mary A.	Leominster,	Administration,	21511
1867	Mary A.	Lancaster,	Foreign Will,	21512
1864	Mary C.	Worcester,	Administration,	21513
1875	Mary H.	Grafton,	Will,	21514
1833	Nathan	Charlton,	Pension,	21515
1807	Oliver	Templeton,	Guardianship,	21516
1859	Peleg A.	Northbridge,	Guardianship,	21517
1859	Perley	Charlton,	Will,	21518
1812	Peter	Gerry,	Administration,	21519
1812	Peter	Gerry,	Guardianship,	21520
1843	Rachel	Uxbridge,	Will,	21521
1867	Samuel	Northbridge,	Will,	21522
1851	Samuel J.	Northbridge,	Guardianship,	21523
1771	Sarah	Rutland,	Guardianship,	21524
1812	Sarah	Gerry,	Guardianship,	21525
1840	Sarah	Northbridge,	Will,	21526
1831	Stacy	Uxbridge,	Will,	21527
1763	Susanna	Rutland,	Guardianship,	21528
1763	Thomas	Rutland,	Guardianship,	21529
1823	Timothy	Lancaster,	Administration,	21530
1851	William W.	Northbridge,	Guardianship,	21531
1859	Zebina	Southbridge,	Administration,	21532
1754	FLING, Joseph	Sutton,	Guardianship,	21533
1860	FLINT, Ada T.	Milford,	Guardianship,	21534
1858	Addie E.	Winchendon,	Guardianship,	21535
1837	Alsada E.	Oakham,	Guardianship,	21536
1858	Asa M.	Winchendon,	Guardianship,	21537
1850	Austin	Leicester,	Will,	21538
1850	Austin	Leicester,	Pension,	21539
1858	Austin	Worcester,	Administration,	21540
1830	Benjamin	Fitchburg,	Administration,	21541
1877	Carrie	Spencer,	Guardianship,	21542
1858	Charles D.	Winchendon,	Guardianship,	21543

YEAR.	NAME.	RESIDENCE.	NATURE.	CASE.
1879	FLINT, Charles E.	Ashby,	Adoption, etc.,	21544
1837	Daniel	Oakham,	Administration,	21545
1849	Daniel	Fitchburg,	Will,	21546
1837	Daniel W.	Oakham,	Guardianship,	21547
1877	Daniel W.	Spencer,	Administration,	21548
1858	David	Winchendon,	Administration,	21549
1872	David B.	Winchendon,	Will,	21550
1835	Ebenezer	Ashburnham,	Administration,	21551
1842	Edmond	Fitchburg,	Administration,	21552
1840	Edmund	Fitchburg,	Pension,	21553
1818	Edward	Shrewsbury,	Will,	21554
1880	Edward	Leicester,	Will,	21555
1878	Ellen	Leicester,	Will,	21556
1858	Emma M.	Winchendon,	Guardianship,	21557
1828	Ezekiel	Westminster,	Will,	21558
1867	Fanny M.	Phillipston,	Guardianship,	21559
1874	Fanny M.	Phillipston,	Change of Name,	21560
1877	Frank S.	Spencer,	Guardianship,	21561
1876	Franklin C.	Auburn,	Will,	21562
1873	Frederick A.	Worcester,	Guardianship,	21563
1868	George A.	Gardner,	Administration,	21564
1858	George H.	Winchendon,	Guardianship,	21565
1874	George I.	Athol,	Administration,	21566
1864	George S.	Rutland,	Will,	21567
1871	Harriet M.	Shrewsbury,	Will,	21568
1877	Harry H.	Spencer,	Guardianship,	21569
1867	Helen E.	Ashburnham,	Adoption, etc.,	21570
1859	Helen M.	Fitchburg,	Will,	21571
1870	Herbert L.	Fitchburg,	Adoption,	21572
1859	Jabez	Fitchburg,	Administration,	21573
1860	Jerusha	Worcester,	Administration,	21574
1810	John	Petersham,	Administration,	21575
1810	John	Petersham,	Guardianship,	21576
1822	John	Winchendon,	Will,	21577
1847	John	Winchendon,	Administration,	21578
1865	John	Templeton,	Administration,	21579
1747	Joseph	Leicester,	Administration,	21580
1795	Joseph II.	Shrewsbury,	Guardianship,	21581
1857	Josiah	Shrewsbury,	Administration,	21582
1871	Josiah	Athol,	Will,	21583
1851	Josiah D.	Leicester,	Guardianship,	21584
1857	Julia D.	Southborough,	Change of Name,	21585
1867	Laura	Leicester,	Will,	21586
1851	Laura A.	Leicester,	Guardianship,	21587
1881	Louise M.	Auburn,	Administration,	21588

YEAR.	NAME.	RESIDENCE.	NATURE.	CASE.
1866	FLINT, Maria E.	Templeton,	Administration,	21589
1837	Mary A.	Oakham,	Guardianship,	21590
1857	Mary L.	Southborough,	Change of Name,	21591
1825	Nathan	Winchendon,	Administration,	21592
1858	Philemon C.	Winchendon,	Guardianship,	21593
1803	Rebecca	Fitchburg,	Will,	21594
1851	Robert O.	Leicester,	Guardianship,	21595
1860	Rufus H.	Milford,	Administration,	21596
1859	Samuel W.	Fitchburg,	Guardianship,	21597
1828	Thomas	Rutland,	Administration,	21598
1880	Thomas G.	. Ashburnham,	Will,	21599
1842	Tilly	Rutland,	Pension,	21600
1840	Willard	Royalston,	Administration,	21601
1867	William T.	Phillipston,	Guardianship,	21602
1871	William T.	Winchendon,	Guardianship,	21603
1874	William T.	Phillipston,	Change of Name,	21604
1879	FLOOD, Bessie W.	Clinton,	Administration,	21605
1839	Martin	Millbury,	Guardianship,	21606
1857	FLOYD, Emma E. R.	Harvard,	Guardianship,	21607
1821	William	Lancaster,	Administration,	21608
1878	FLYER, Mary M.	Millbury,	Will,	21609
1865	FLYNN, Abby	Milford,	Guardianship,	21610
1880	Alice	Worcester,	Guardianship,	21611
1859	Ann	Southbridge,	Guardianship,	21612
1873	Annie	Worcester,	Guardianship,	21613
1873	Bridget	Worcester,	Guardianship,	21614
1880	Bridget	Worcester,	Guardianship,	21615
1877	Cornelius	Worcester,	Administration,	21616
1870	David A.	Douglas,	Guardianship,	21617
1870	Edmund B.	Douglas,	Guardianship,	21618
1878	Emily	Worcester,	Guardianship,	21619
1875	Garrett	Milford,	Administration,	21620
1873	James	Worcester,	Guardianship,	21621
1874	James	Millbury,	Will,	21622
1880	James	Worcester,	Guardianship,	21623
1859	John	Southbridge,	Administration,	21624
1859	John	Southbridge,	Guardianship,	21625
1863	John	Clinton,	Guardianship,	21626
1868	John	Worcester,	Administration,	21627
1873	John	Worcester,	Guardianship,	21628
1880	John	Worcester,	Administration,	21629
1880	John J.	Worcester,	Administration,	21630
1880	John J.	Worcester,	Guardianship,	21631
1873	Kate	Worcester,	Guardianship,	21632
1870	Lizzie A.	Douglas,	Guardianship,	21633

YEAR.	NAME.	RESIDENCE.	NATURE.	CASE.
1863	FLYNN, Margaret	Worcester,	Administration,	21634
1878	Margaret	Worcester,	M't'g Real Estate,	21635
1859	Mary	Southbridge,	Guardianship,	21636
1880	Mary A.	Worcester,	Guardianship,	21637
1873	Mary E.	Worcester,	Guardianship,	21638
1873	Mary E.	Fitchburg,	Guardianship,	21639
1857	Michael	Grafton,	Adoption,	21640
1864	Michael	Worcester,	Administration,	21641
1880	Nicholas	Worcester,	Guardianship,	21642
1873	Owen	Worcester,	Administration,	21643
1873	Owen	Worcester,	Guardianship,	21644
1859	Patrick	Southbridge,	Guardianship,	21645
1865	Patrick	Milford,	Administration,	21646
1866	Patrick	Worcester,	Will,	21647
1874	Patrick	Worcester,	Will,	21648
1880	Richard	Worcester,	Guardianship,	21649
1870	Robert W.	Douglas,	Guardianship,	21650
1859	Thomas	Southbridge,	Guardianship,	21651
1870	Thomas F.	Douglas,	Administration,	21652
1870	Thomas F.	Douglas,	Guardianship,	21653
1767	FOBES, Abner	Uxbridge,	Administration,	21654
1783	Abner	Upton,	Guardianship,	21655
1767	Absalom	Uxbridge,	Guardianship,	21656
1778	Absalom	Upton,	Administration,	21657
1783	Absalom	Upton,	Guardianship,	21658
1867	Charles A.	Petersham,	Guardianship,	21659
1767	Charlotte	Uxbridge,	Guardianship,	21660
1767	Edward	Uxbridge,	Guardianship,	21661
1767	Hannah	Uxbridge,	Guardianship,	21662
1846	John	Petersham,	Administration,	21663
1848	John	Petersham,	Guardianship,	21664
1827	Joseph	Oakham,	Will,	21665
1877	Joseph	Oakham,	Will,	21666
1767	Jotham	Uxbridge,	Guardianship,	21667
1783	Jotham	Upton,	Guardianship,	21668
1783	Libeus	Upton,	Guardianship,	21669
1767	Molly	Uxbridge,	Guardianship,	21670
1852	Peres	Oakham,	Will,	21671
1866	P. Ames	Oakham,	Will,	21672
1816	Seth	Oakham,	Administration,	21673
	FOGARTY AND FOGERTY,			
1853	Ellen	Worcester,	Guardianship,	21674
1852	Michael	Worcester,	Will,	21675
1853	Michael	Worcester,	Guardianship,	21676
1860	Michael	Worcester,	Guardianship,	21677

YEAR.	NAME.	RESIDENCE.	NATURE.	CASE.
	FOGARTY AND FOGERTY,			
1872	Michael	Worcester,	Administration,	21678
1879	Michael	Leicester,	Administration,	21679
1861	FOGG, Charles H.	Winchendon,	Guardianship,	21680
1865	Elbridge G.	Northbridge,	Administration,	21681
1861	Heman J.	Winchendon,	Administration,	21682
1872	Martha A.	Northbridge,	Will,	21683
1861	FOLEY, Ann A.	Moretown, Vt.,	Guardianship,	21684
1876	Catherine	Southbridge,	Administration,	21685
1876	Daniel	Worcester,	Will,	21686
1880	Daniel	Worcester,	Guardianship,	21687
1866	Ellen M.	Grafton,	Guardianship,	21688
1861	James	Moretown, Vt.,	Guardianship,	21689
1879	James	Worcester,	Administration,	21690
1871	John	Worcester,	Guardianship,	21691
1866	John F.	Grafton,	Guardianship,	21692
1866	Mary A.	Grafton,	Guardianship,	21693
1861	Mary J.	Moretown, Vt.,	Guardianship,	21694
1866	Michael	Grafton,	Guardianship,	21695
1872	Patrick	Worcester,	Will,	21696
1866	Simon	Savanna, Ill.,	Administration,	21697
1861	Thomas	Moretown, Vt.,	Guardianship,	21698
1864	William	Warren,	Administration,	21699
1866	William	Grafton,	Guardianship,	21700
1878	William H.	Worcester,	Administration,	21701
1862	FOLGER, Albert H.	Worcester,	Guardianship,	21702
1858	Minnie I.	Milford,	Adoption, etc.,	21703
1862	William H.	Worcester,	Administration,	21704
	FOLLANSBY, FOLLANSBEE AND FOLLINSBEE,			
1875	Cutting	Barre,	Administration,	21705
1830	Edward	Leominster,	Administration,	21706
1797	Francis	Leominster,	Will,	21707
1849	FOLLET, Aaron	Hubbardston,	Administration,	21708
1848	Curtis M.	Uxbridge,	Guardianship,	21709
1848	Helen L.	Uxbridge,	Guardianship,	21710
1788	Isaac	Hubbardston,	Guardianship,	21711
1844	Isaac	Hubbardston,	Administration,	21712
1788	John	Hubbardston,	Guardianship,	21713
1804	John	Hubbardston,	Administration,	21714
1844	John	Hubbardston,	Guardianship,	21715
1869	Jonas	Hubbardston,	Administration,	21716
1865	Jonathan M.	Hubbardston,	Administration,	21717
1788	Katy	Hubbardston,	Guardianship,	21718
1844	Mary A. S.	Hubbardston,	Guardianship,	21719

YEAR.	NAME.	RESIDENCE.	NATURE.	CASE.
1804	FOLLET, Metcalf	Hubbardston,	Guardianship,	21720
1804	Rhoda	Hubbardston,	Guardianship,	21721
1788	Sally	Hubbardston,	Guardianship,	21722
1788	Samuel	Hubbardston,	Guardianship,	21723
1804	Samuel	Hubbardston,	Administration,	21724
1848	Samuel D.	Uxbridge,	Guardianship,	21725
1848	Samuel W.	Uxbridge,	Will,	21726
	FOLLINSBEE see FOLLANSBY.			
1845	FOOT, Joseph I.	Brookfield,	Will,	21727
	FORBES (see also FORBUSH),			
1847	Abigail	North Brookfield,	Will,	21728
1805	Achsah	Westborough,	Guardianship,	21729
1810	Adah	Brookfield,	Guardianship,	21730
1773	Ann	Oakham,	Guardianship,	21731
1771	Archibald	Oakham,	Guardianship,	21732
1790	Archibald	Oakham,	Guardianship,	21733
1847	Archibald	Barre,	Administration,	21734
1768	Arther	Oakham,	Administration,	21735
1854	Arthur P.	Worcester,	Guardianship,	21736
1871	Baxter	Westborough,	Will,	21737
1791	Benjamin M.	Barre,	Guardianship,	21738
1819	Betsey	Royalston,	Guardianship,	21739
1773	Charles	Oakham,	Guardianship,	21740
1842	Charles B.	Westborough,	Guardianship,	21741
1780	Daniel	Westborough,	Will,	21742
1808	Daniel	Brookfield,	Administration,	21743
1868	Daniel	Upton,	Will,	21744
1854	Daniel H.	Westborough,	Will,	21745
1854	Daniel H.	Westborough,	Guardianship,	21746
1838	Daniel W.	Westborough,	Guardianship,	21747
1814	David	Keene, N. H.,	Foreign Will,	21748
1847	David	Royalston,	Will,	21749
1810	Dexter	Brookfield,	Guardianship,	21750
1867	Dexter	North Brookfield,	Administration,	21751
1847	Eli	North Brookfield,	Will,	21752
1805	Elias	Westborough,	Guardianship,	21753
1862	Elias	Millbury,	Will,	21754
1848	Elijah	Westborough,	Will,	21755
1808	Elisha	Westborough,	Administration,	21756
1854	Eliza F.	Worcester,	Guardianship,	21757
1880	Eliza S.	Westborough,	Guardianship,	21758
1773	Elizabeth	Oakham,	Guardianship,	21759
1839	Elizabeth	Rutland,	Guardianship,	21760
1863	Ellen M.	Millbury,	Guardianship,	21761
1863	Ephraim T.	Westborough,	Will,	21762
1867	Esther	Westborough,	Administration,	21763

Year.	Name.	Residence.	Nature.	Case.
	FORBES (see also FORBUSH),			
1867	Esther L.	Westborough,	Guardianship,	21764
1878	Evelyn D.	Clinton,	Guardianship,	21765
1867	Francis W.	Westborough,	Guardianship,	21766
1878	Franklin	Clinton,	Will,	21767
1874	George	Brookfield,	Will,	21768
1810	Hannah	Upton,	Guardianship,	21769
1863	Harriet E.	Millbury,	Guardianship,	21770
1838	Henry E.	Westborough,	Guardianship,	21771
1842	Henry E.	Westborough,	Guardianship,	21772
1873	Hiram	North Brookfield,	Will,	21773
1805	Jacob	Oakham,	Guardianship,	21774
1773	James	Oakham,	Guardianship,	21775
1797	James	Oakham,	Administration,	21776
1805	James	Oakham,	Guardianship,	21777
1819	James	Royalston,	Will,	21778
1852	Jane	Dana,	Guardianship,	21779
1854	Jane	Dana,	Will,	21779
1810	John	Upton,	Guardianship,	21780
1866	John M.	Boylston,	Administration,	21781
1864	John W.	Worcester,	Will,	21782
1773	Jonathan	Oakham,	Guardianship,	21783
1805	Jonathan	Westborough,	Will,	21784
1834	Jonathan	Dana,	Pension,	21785
1834	Jonathan	Dana,	Administration,	21786
1861	Jonathan	Westborough,	Will,	21787
1854	Jonathan E.	Westborough,	Guardianship,	21788
1876	Joseph W.	Westborough,	Will,	21789
1805	Lammon	Oakham,	Guardianship,	21790
1810	Levi	Brookfield,	Guardianship,	21791
1810	Margaret	Upton,	Guardianship,	21792
1773	Margaret	Oakham,	Guardianship,	21793
1879	Marian	Royalston,	Will,	21794
1773	Martha	Oakham,	Guardianship,	21795
1820	Martha	Barre,	Administration,	21796
1879	Martha	Brookfield,	Will,	21797
1859	Mary A.	Westborough,	Administration,	21798
1862	Mary E.	Millbury,	Guardianship,	21799
1854	Mary J.	Westborough,	Guardianship,	21800
1842	Mary M.	Westborough,	Guardianship,	21801
1861	Mary W.	Millbury,	Administration,	21802
1810	Moses	Brookfield,	Guardianship,	21803
1854	Moses S.	Worcester,	Guardianship,	21804
1838	Nahum	Westborough,	Administration,	21805
1842	Nahum	Westborough,	Administration,	21806

YEAR.	NAME.	RESIDENCE.	NATURE.	CASE.
	FORBES (see also FORBUSH),			
1805	Nancy	Westborough,	Guardianship,	21807
1819	Olive	Royalston,	Guardianship,	21808
1819	Phineas	Westborough,	Administration,	21809
1763	Phineas	Westborough,	Guardianship,	21810
1804	Polly	Westborough,	Guardianship,	21811
1802	Rebecca	Westborough,	Will,	21812
1790	Ruth	Oakham,	Administration,	21813
1838	Samuel B.	Westborough,	Guardianship,	21814
1824	Sarah	Westborough,	Will,	21815
1829	Sarah	Westborough,	Administration,	21816
1800	Simon	Upton,	Administration,	21817
1816	Stephen	Oakham,	Guardianship,	21818
1862	Stephen	Leicester,	Will,	21819
1838	Susan E.	Westborough,	Guardianship,	21820
1855	Susannah	Barre,	Administration,	21821
1810	Talvin	Brookfield,	Guardianship,	21822
1788	William	Barre,	Will,	21823
1790	William	Oakham,	Guardianship,	21824
1791	William	Barre,	Administration,	21825
1808	William	Oxford,	Administration,	21826
1819	William	Royalston,	Guardianship,	21827
1863	William H.	Millbury,	Guardianship,	21828
1879	William H.	Worcester,	Administration,	21829
1867	William T.	Westborough,	Guardianship,	21830
	FORBUSH, FURBUSH and FOR-BUS (see also FORBES),			
1752	Aaron	Brookfield,	Will,	21831
1855	Adaline M.	Upton,	Guardianship,	21832
1850	Adelia M.	Upton,	Guardianship,	21833
1846	Andrew P.	Westborough,	Guardianship,	21834
1762	Anna	Worcester,	Guardianship,	21835
1854	Anna	Rutland,	Administration,	21836
1856	Anna	Upton,	Administration,	21837
1821	Anna M.	Upton,	Guardianship,	21838
1768	Arther	Oakham,	Administration,	21839
1877	Arthur D.	Upton,	Guardianship,	21840
1818	Asa	Westborough,	Administration,	21841
1813	Benjamin	Brookfield,	Administration,	21842
1818	Benjamin F.	Westborough,	Guardianship,	21843
1876	Benjamin F.	Westborough,	Will,	21844
1811	Betsey	Brookfield,	Will,	21845
1813	Betsey	Grafton,	Administration,	21846
1798	Betsy	Grafton,	Guardianship,	21847
1821	Brigham H.	Upton,	Guardianship,	21848

YEAR.	NAME.	RESIDENCE.	NATURE.	CASE.
	FORBUSH, FURBUSH AND FORBUS (see also FORBES),			
1838	Caleb W.	Westborough,	Administration,	21849
1839	Calista M.	Upton,	Guardianship,	21850
1855	Calvin A.	Upton,	Guardianship,	21851
1847	Catharine	Brookfield,	Will,	21852
1825	Charles C.	Westborough,	Guardianship,	21853
1845	Charles C.	Grafton,	Administration,	21854
1850	Charlotte L.	Grafton,	Guardianship,	21855
1798	Cinthia	Grafton,	Guardianship,	21856
1850	Clarissa M.	Grafton,	Guardianship,	21857
1832	Coolidge	Westborough,	Will,	21858
1778	Daniel	Harvard,	Administration,	21859
1834	Daniel	Harvard,	Administration,	21860
1788	David	Grafton,	Will,	21861
1827	David	Royalston,	Administration,	21862
1844	David	Westminster,	Will,	21863
1862	Dolly W.	Worcester,	Administration,	21864
1850	Elbridge	Grafton,	Administration,	21865
1821	Elijah	Upton,	Guardianship,	21866
1821	Elijah	Upton,	Administration,	21867
1876	Emeline	Upton,	Administration,	21868
1869	Emma J.	Grafton,	Guardianship,	21869
1864	Enoch	Grafton,	Administration,	21870
1798	Eri	Grafton,	Guardianship,	21871
1825	George	Westborough,	Guardianship,	21872
1821	Halford	Upton,	Guardianship,	21873
1839	Halford	Upton,	Administration,	21874
1821	Hannah	Upton,	Guardianship,	21875
1870	Harvey	Minnesota,	Administration,	21876
1877	Horace	Upton,	Administration,	21877
1809	Isaac	Westborough,	Administration,	21878
1825	Isaac	Westborough,	Guardianship,	21879
1762	James	Worcester,	Guardianship,	21880
1763	James	Rutland,	Will,	21881
1762	James, Jr.	Worcester,	Administration,	21882
1798	Joel	Westborough,	Administration,	21883
1863	Joel	Westborough,	Will,	21884
1760	John	Westborough,	Guardianship,	21885
1762	John	Worcester,	Guardianship,	21886
1776	John	Harvard,	Administration,	21887
1776	John	Harvard,	Guardianship,	21888
1793	John	Upton,	Administration,	21889
1794	John	Upton,	Guardianship,	21890
1849	John	Harvard,	Will,	21891

(504)

FORBUSH, FURBUSH AND.
FORBUS (see also FORBES),

1809	Jonah	Westborough,	Will,	21892
1825	Jonah	Westborough,	Guardianship,	21893
1761	Jonathan	Westborough,	Guardianship,	21894
1776	Jonathan	Harvard,	Guardianship,	21895
1798	Jonathan	Grafton,	Administration,	21896
1756	Jonathan, Jr.	Westborough,	Will,	21897
1878	Joseph	Upton,	Administration,	21898
1824	Lambert	Westborough,	Administration,	21899
1813	Levi	Upton,	Administration,	21900
1798	Levina	Grafton,	Guardianship,	21901
1817	Lois	Grafton,	Will,	21902
1835	Lomira C.	Westborough,	Guardianship,	21903
1880	Lowell	Worcester,	Administration,	21904
1747	Lucy	Westborough,	Guardianship,	21905
1822	Lucy	Harvard,	Will,	21906
1832	Lucy	Westborough,	Will,	21907
1798	Lurinda	Grafton,	Guardianship,	21908
1762	Lydia	Worcester,	Guardianship,	21909
1869	Manasseh S.	Westminster,	Will,	21910
1763	Mary	Worcester,	Guardianship,	21911
1788	Mary	Grafton,	Guardianship,	21912
1825	Mary M.	Westborough,	Guardianship,	21913
1846	Mary S.	Westborough,	Guardianship,	21914
1822	Molly	Harvard,	Will,	21915
1821	Newell	Upton,	Guardianship,	21916
1850	Newell	Upton,	Administration,	21917
1846	Orestes	Westborough,	Administration,	21918
1747	Phineas	Westborough,	Administration,	21919
1808	Rachel	Harvard,	Will,	21920
1875	Rachel	Westborough,	Administration,	21921
1879	Rhoda G.	Grafton,	Will,	21922
1799	Robert	Rutland,	Will,	21923
1882	Russell O.	Westborough,	Guardianship,	21924
1767	Samuel	Westborough,	Will,	21925
1818	Samuel	Westborough,	Will,	21926
1827	Samuel	Westborough,	Administration,	21927
1827	Samuel	Harvard,	Administration,	21928
1762	Sarah	Worcester,	Guardianship,	21929
1835	Sarah F.	Westborough,	Guardianship,	21930
1840	Silas	Grafton,	Administration,	21931
1841	Silas	Rutland,	Administration,	21932
1870	Sophia	Shrewsbury,	Will,	21933
1747	Submit	Westborough,	Guardianship,	21934

YEAR.	NAME.	RESIDENCE.	NATURE.	CASE.
	FORBUSH, FURBUSH AND FORBUS (see also FORBES),			
1854	Susan B.	Westborough,	Will,	21935
1835	Susan S.	Worcester,	Guardianship,	21936
1869	Susan S.	Grafton,	Guardianship,	21937
1798	Sybel	Grafton,	Guardianship,	21938
1738	Thomas	Westborough,	Will,	21939
1757	Thomas	Hardwick,	Administration,	21940
1783	Thomas	Westborough,	Administration,	21941
1855	Thomas S.	Upton,	Will,	21942
1877	Waldo W.	Upton,	Guardianship,	21943
1855	Wendell H.	Upton,	Guardianship,	21944
1778	William	Worcester,	Guardianship,	21945
1846	William H.	Westborough,	Guardianship,	21946
1881	William H.	Westborough,	Will,	21947
1880	FORCE, Lillian	Milford,	Adoption, etc.,	21948
1848	Lucinda	Mendon,	Will,	21949
	FORD AND FORDE,			
1866	Absalom P.	Leominster,	Will,	21950
1870	Addie S.	Worcester,	Guardianship,	21951
1881	Caroline A. R.	Mendon,	Guardianship,	21952
1856	George O.	Gardner,	Adoption, etc.,	21953
1870	George O.	Gardner,	Change of Name,	21953
1881	George R.	Mendon,	Guardianship,	21954
1873	Georgie D.	Grafton,	Adoption, etc.,	21955
1851	John	Milford,	Administration,	21956
1881	Lewis S.	Mendon,	Guardianship,	21957
1880	Margaret	Worcester,	Administration,	21958
1877	Mary	Worcester,	Administration,	21959
1880	Mary H.	Mendon,	Will,	21960
1868	Miranda P.	Leominster,	Will,	21961
1878	Orville D.	West Boylston,	Will,	21962
1874	Richard A.	Worcester,	Adoption, etc.,	21963
1864	Thomas K.	Athol,	Administration,	21964
1870	Thomas S.	Worcester,	Will,	21965
1870	Walter F.	Worcester,	Guardianship,	21966
1879	FOREHAND, Annie J.	Worcester,	Guardianship,	21967
1879	Nettie A.	Worcester,	Guardianship,	21968
1879	Walter	Worcester,	Administration,	21969
	FORREST AND FOREST,			
1863	Michael	Spencer,	Guardianship,	21970
1875	Richard, Jr.	Spencer,	Administration,	21971
1860	William	Brookfield,	Will,	21972
	FORRISTALL AND FORRESTAL,			
1872	Charles E.	Winchendon,	Administration,	21973

	FORRISTALL AND FORRESTAL,			
1872	Charles W.	Winchendon,	Guardianship,	21974
1850	Dexter	Winchendon,	Guardianship,	21975
1868	Edward	North Brookfield,	Will,	21976
1873	John	Winchendon,	Administration,	21977
1879	FORTIER, Zephirin	Fitchburg,	Administration,	21978
1881	FORTIN, Andrew	Spencer,	Will,	21979
1874	FOSDICK, Robert F.	Sutton,	Will,	21980
1864	Samuel W.	Clinton,	Administration,	21981
1869	FOSGATE, Harriet N. P.	Fitchburg,	Administration,	21982
1824	Joel	Berlin,	Will,	21983
1870	Oliver	Berlin,	Will,	21984
1866	FOSHAY, Ella M.	Spencer,	Adoption, etc.,	21985
1867	Sarah L.	Grafton,	Administration,	21986
	FOSKETT, FOSKET, FOSKIT AND FOSKITT,			
1875	Anna	Charlton,	Administration,	21987
1850	Asa	Charlton,	Will,	21988
1868	Carrie A.	Gardner,	Guardianship,	21989
1864	Celia E.	Winchendon,	Administration,	21990
1855	Daniel	Westminster,	Will,	21991
1878	Daniel	Westminster,	Administration,	21992
1879	Darius	Athol,	Administration,	21993
1781	Ebenezer	Charlton,	Administration,	21994
1860	Ebenezer	Charlton,	Administration,	21995
1849	Edward L.	Warren,	Guardianship,	21996
1856	George F.	Gardner,	Adoption, etc.,	21997
1870	George F.	Gardner,	Change of Name,	21997
1796	John	Westminster,	Will,	21998
1764	Jonathan	Sturbridge,	Will,	21999
1876	Levi	Winchendon,	Will,	22000
1849	Loren F.	Warren,	Administration,	22001
1844	Lucy A.	Winchendon,	Guardianship,	22002
1844	Mary E.	Winchendon,	Guardianship,	22003
1874	Moses	Winchendon,	Will,	22004
1857	Ruth	Charlton,	Will,	22005
1814	Thomas	Charlton,	Will,	22006
1868	Willard	Gardner,	Will,	22007
1863	William	Charlton,	Will,	22008
	FOSSETT see FAWCETT.			
1777	FOSTER, Aaron	Bolton,	Administration,	22009
1866	Abbie	Warren,	Guardianship,	22010
1745	Abigail	Hardwick,	Guardianship,	22011
1837	Abigail	Warren,	Guardianship,	22012
1877	Abigail F.	Worcester,	Administration,	22013

Year.	Name.	Residence.	Nature.	Case.
1881	FOSTER, Abigail G.	Warren,	Guardianship,	22014
1852	Abner	Phillipston,	Administration,	22015
1827	Adaline	Ashburnham,	Guardianship,	22016
1873	Adams	Holden,	Will,	22017
1878	Addie L.	Ashburnham,	Adoption, etc.,	22018
1863	Addison	Gardner,	Administration,	22019
1832	Albert	Worcester,	Guardianship,	22020
1852	Alfred D.	Worcester,	Administration,	22021
1823	Algernon S.	Brookfield,	Administration,	22022
1869	Alvah A.	Worcester, ·	Guardianship,	22023
1793	Amos	Ashburnham,	Guardianship,	22024
1872	Ann M.	Milford,	Guardianship,	22025
1792	Arminda	Dudley,	Guardianship,	22026
1823	Augustus	Millbury,	Guardianship,	22027
1826	Benjamin H.	Lancaster,	Administration,	22028
1800	Benoni	Royalston,	Guardianship,	22029
1820	Benoni	Royalston,	Guardianship,	22030
1792	Betsey	Dudley,	Guardianship,	22031
1799	Betsey	Holden,	Guardianship,	22032
1801	Betsey	Paxton,	Guardianship,	22033
1810	Betsey	Dana,	Guardianship,	22034
1873	Betsey	Oakham,	Will,	22035
1804	Caty	Ashburnham,	Guardianship,	22036
1853	Charles	Rutland,	Guardianship,	22037
1869	Charles	Athol,	Will,	22038
1852	Charles A.	Worcester,	Guardianship,	22039
1855	Charles A.	Charlestown,	Guardianship,	22040
1864	Charles G.	Webster,	Administration,	22041
1880	Charles J.	Worcester,	Change of Name,	22042
1869	Charles O.	Worcester,	Guardianship,	22043
1798	Charlotte	New Braintree,	Guardianship,	22044
1862	Christopher C. W.	Barre,	Administration,	22045
1752	Daniel	Harvard,	Will,	22046
1795	Daniel	New Braintree,	Administration,	22047
1798	Daniel	New Braintree,	Guardianship,	22048
1866	Daniel	Athol,	Will,	22049
1837	Daniel O.	Warren,	Guardianship,	22050
1863	Daniel W.	Athol,	Administration,	22051
1815	David	Gardner,	Administration,	22052
1854	David O.	Leominster,	Guardianship,	22053
1810	Deborah	Dana,	Guardianship,	22054
1832	Demarens	Worcester,	Guardianship,	22055
1804	Dorothy	Ashburnham,	Guardianship,	22056
1818	Dorothy	Brookfield,	Will,	22057
1823	Dwight	Brookfield,	Will,	22058

YEAR.	NAME.	RESIDENCE.	NATURE.	CASE.
1811	FOSTER, Ebenezer	Oakham,	Will,	22059
1775	Edward	Sturbridge,	Will,	22060
1823	Elias	Southbridge,	Guardianship,	22061
1798	Elisha	Holden,	Will,	22062
1799	Elisha	Holden,	Guardianship,	22063
1810	Elisha	Dana,	Guardianship,	22064
1852	Elisha	Dana,	Will,	22065
1818	Eliza R.	Brookfield,	Guardianship,	22066
1798	Elizabeth	New Braintree,	Guardianship,	22067
1831	Elizabeth E.	Petersham,	Guardianship,	22068
1869	Elizabeth S.	Worcester,	Guardianship,	22069
1827	Elvira	Ashburnham,	Guardianship,	22070
1823	Emily	Millbury,	Guardianship,	22071
1831	Emily L.	Petersham,	Guardianship,	22072
1865	Emma L.	Westminster,	Guardianship,	22073
1799	Eunice	Holden,	Guardianship,	22074
1822	Eunice	Western,	Inventory,	22075
1860	Fanny	Dana,	Administration,	22076
1798	Fordyce	New Braintree,	Guardianship,	22077
1852	Franklin E.	Dana,	Guardianship,	22078
1877	Frederick	Hardwick,	Administration,	22079
1878	George	Lunenburg,	Will,	22080
1874	George P.	Leicester,	Will,	22081
1799	Hannah	Holden,	Guardianship,	22082
1810	Hannah	Dana,	Guardianship,	22083
1823	Hannah	Millbury,	Guardianship,	22084
1831	Harriet A.	Petersham,	Guardianship,	22085
1851	Harriet E.	Oxford,	Guardianship,	22086
1865	Harriet E., etc.	Holden,	Guardianship,	22087
1797	Heman	Oakham,	Guardianship,	22088
1819	Heman	Rutland,	Administration,	22089
1879	Henry R.	Winchendon,	Guardianship,	22090
1854	Henry S.	Leominster,	Guardianship,	22091
1879	Herbert D.	Winchendon,	Guardianship,	22092
1865	Herbert L.	Westminster,	Guardianship,	22093
1867	Hiram W.	Athol,	Administration,	22094
1800	Hugh	Royalston,	Guardianship,	22095
1875	Ida L.	New Braintree,	Administration,	22096
1863	Ira B.	Leominster,	Administration,	22097
1823	Isaac	Lunenburg,	Will,	22098
1865	Isaac	Lunenburg,	Will,	22099
1837	Isabella F.	Warren,	Guardianship,	22100
1798	Isabinda	New Braintree,	Guardianship,	22101
1810	Italy	Dana,	Guardianship,	22102
1741	Jacob	Woodstock,	Administration,	22103

YEAR.	NAME.	RESIDENCE.	NATURE.	CASE.
1745	FOSTER, Jacob	Hardwick,	Guardianship,	22104
1787	James	Athol,	Will,	22105
1855	James M.	Charlestown,	Guardianship,	22106
1779	Jedediah	Brookfield,	Administration,	22107
1880	Jennie W.	Chelsea,	Adoption, etc.,	22108
1875	Jerome B.	North Brookfield,	Guardianship,	22109
1871	Jerome W.	Ashburnham,	Will,	22110
1799	Jerusha	Holden,	Guardianship,	22111
1796	Jesse	Gardner,	Guardianship,	22112
1793	Joel	Ashburnham,	Guardianship,	22113
1804	Joel	Ashburnham,	Guardianship,	22114
1745	John	Hardwick,	Guardianship,	22115
1745	John	Hardwick,	Administration,	22116
1755	John	Rutland,	Administration,	22117
1800	John	Royalston,	Guardianship,	22118
1828	John	Petersham,	Administration,	22119
1831	John B.	Petersham,	Guardianship,	22120
1851	John P.	Oxford,	Will,	22121
1849	John W.	Athol,	Administration,	22122
1745	Jonathan	Hardwick,	Guardianship,	22123
1745	Jonathan	Shrewsbury	Will,	22124
1745	Joseph	Hardwick,	Guardianship,	22125
1837	Joseph B.	Warren,	Guardianship,	22126
1801	Josiah	Gardner,	Guardianship,	22127
1864	Josiah	Westminster,	Administration,	22128
1789	Jude	Paxton,	Administration,	22129
1801	Judith	Paxton,	Guardianship,	22130
1865	Judson	Westminster,	Guardianship,	22131
1800	Katharine	Royalston,	Guardianship,	22132
1801	Lemuel	Barre,	Administration,	22133
1827	Leonard	Ashburnham,	Guardianship,	22134
1834	Lewis R.	Warren,	Guardianship,	22135
1818	Loisa	Brookfield,	Guardianship,	22136
1832	Lorean	Dudley,	Guardianship,	22137
1865	Lowell	Westminster,	Guardianship,	22138
1810	Lucena	Dana,	Guardianship,	22139
1804	Lucy	Ashburnham,	Guardianship,	22140
1865	Lucy A.	Lunenburg,	Guardianship,	22141
1831	Lucy L.	Petersham,	Guardianship,	22142
1798	Luke	New Braintree,	Guardianship,	22143
1800	Luke	Royalston,	Guardianship,	22144
1817	Luke B.	Rutland,	Administration,	22145
1745	Lydia	Hardwick,	Guardianship,	22146
1801	Lydia	Paxton,	Guardianship,	22147
1851	Maria J.	Oxford,	Guardianship,	22148

Year.	Name.	Residence.	Nature.	Case.
1849	FOSTER, Mark P.	Templeton,	Administration,	22149
1800	Mary	Royalston,	Guardianship,	22150
1804	Mary	Ashburnham,	Guardianship,	22151
1832	Mary	Worcester,	Guardianship,	22152
1864	Mary	Worcester,	Administration,	22153
1853	Mary E.	Rutland,	Guardianship,	22154
1876	Mercy C.	Worcester,	Administration,	22155
1839	Molly	Oakham,	Administration,	22156
1811	Nancy	Western,	Guardianship,	22157
1827	Nancy	Ashburnham,	Guardianship,	22158
1832	Nancy	Worcester,	Guardianship,	22159
1809	Nathan	Western,	Administration,	22160
1852	Nathan F.	Worcester,	Guardianship,	22161
1804	Nathaniel	Ashburnham,	Guardianship,	22162
1804	Nathaniel	Ashburnham,	Will,	22163
1823	Nathaniel	New Braintree,	Will,	22164
1826	Nathaniel	Ashburnham,	Administration,	22165
1867	Nellie	Ashburnham,	Guardianship,	22166
1793	Obadiah	Ashburnham,	Guardianship,	22167
1793	Obed	Ashburnham,	Guardianship,	22167
1792	Pearly	Dudley,	Guardianship,	22168
1830	Pearly	Dudley,	Guardianship,	22169
1831	Pearly	Dudley,	Administration,	22169
1802	Perley	Dudley,	Guardianship,	22170
1795	Peter	Gardner,	Guardianship,	22171
1829	Peter	Worcester,	Administration,	22172
1818	Phebe	Brookfield,	Guardianship,	22173
1801	Polly	Paxton,	Guardianship,	22174
1852	Polly	Sterling,	Will,	22175
1811	Priscilla E.	Western,	Guardianship,	22176
1803	Rachel	Sturbridge,	Will,	22177
1839	Rachel	Dudley,	Will,	22178
1804	Rebecca	Ashburnham,	Guardianship,	22179
1875	Reuben	Webster,	Will,	22180
1800	Rhoda	Royalston,	Guardianship,	22181
1804	Rufus	Gardner,	Guardianship,	22182
1780	Ruth	Brookfield,	Guardianship,	22183
1850	Ruth	Ashburnham,	Will,	22184
1799	Sally	Holden,	Guardianship,	22185
1804	Sally	Ashburnham,	Guardianship,	22186
1771	Samuel	Douglas,	Administration,	22187
1793	Samuel	Ashburnham,	Will,	22188
1799	Samuel	Holden,	Guardianship,	22189
1847	Samuel	Gardner,	Administration,	22190
1864	Samuel	Worcester,	Will,	22191

YEAR.	NAME.	RESIDENCE.	NATURE.	CASE.
1878	FOSTER, Samuel	Fitchburg,	Will,	22192
1850	Samuel B.	Worcester,	Will,	22193
1873	Samuel E.	Fitchburg,	Administration,	22194
1822	Samuel K.	Rutland,	Guardianship,	22195
1852	Sarah A.	Worcester,	Guardianship,	22196
1836	Sherlock	Warren,	Administration,	22197
1800	Silas	Royalston,	Administration,	22198
1800	Silas	Royalston,	Guardianship,	22199
1832	Silvy	Dudley,	Guardianship,	22200
1824	Smith	Sturbridge,	Administration,	22201
1825	Smith W.	Southbridge,	Guardianship,	22202
1794	Solomon	Brookfield,	Will,	22203
1811	Sophia	Western,	Guardianship,	22204
1800	Sukey	Royalston,	Guardianship,	22205
1875	Susan	Northbridge,	Will,	22206
1793	Susanna	Ashburnham,	Guardianship,	22207
1830	Susannah	Southbridge,	Administration,	22208
1852	Taft	Worcester,	Administration,	22209
1837	Tammy	Warren,	Guardianship,	22210
1810	Tilly	Dana,	Administration,	22211
1795	Timothy	Dudley,	Will,	22212
1874	Tryphena	Gardner,	Administration,	22213
1866	Uriah H.	Barre,	Administration,	22214
1879	Walter R.	Worcester,	Administration,	22215
1878	Willard	Gardner,	Administration,	22216
1791	William	Dudley,	Administration,	22217
1817	William	Brookfield,	Administration,	22218
1818	William	Brookfield,	Guardianship,	22219
1832	William E.	Dudley,	Guardianship,	22220
1880	FOULDS, Clara	Worcester,	Administration,	22221
1879	FOVAND, Delia	Dudley,	Adoption, etc.,	22222
	FOWLE AND FOWLES,			
1825	Curtis	Worcester,	Will,	22223
1774	Jacob	Lancaster,	Will,	22224
1799	John	Barre,	Administration,	22225
1803	Rebecca	Worcester,	Administration,	22226
1757	Ruth	Lancaster,	Guardianship,	22227
1825	Susanna	Worcester,	Will,	22228
1860	Susanna	Westminster,	Will,	22229
1854	William	Athol,	Will,	22230
1873	William	Burrillville, R. I.,	Administration,	22231
1857	FOWLER, Adolphus	Grafton,	Will,	22232
1863	Austin	Providence, R. I.,	Administration,	22233
1842	Austin H.	Sutton,	Guardianship,	22234
1842	Bernard	Sutton,	Guardianship,	22235

Name.	Residence.	Nature.	Case.
FOWLER, Bernard	Northbridge,	Will,	22236
Caleb	Northbridge,	Guardianship,	22237
Edward	Grafton,	Guardianship,	22238
Ezekiel	Lunenburg,	Administration,	22239
Ezekiel	Worcester,	Will,	22240
Ezekiel	Grafton,	Guardianship,	22241
Franklin	Grafton,	Guardianship,	22242
George D.	Northbridge,	Guardianship,	22243
Hannah	Worcester,	Will,	22244
Henry	Bolton,	Guardianship,	22245
Huldah	Northbridge,	Will,	22246
Jane	Dana,	Pension,	22247
John	Northbridge,	Will,	22248
John	Grafton,	Guardianship,	22249
John	Grafton,	Administration,	22250
Mary	Bolton,	Guardianship,	22251
Mary E.	Grafton,	Guardianship,	22252
Oscar A.	Gardner,	Administration,	22253
Richard	Lunenburg,	Administration,	22254
Richard	Lunenburg,	Administration,	22255
Robert	Sutton,	Administration,	22256
Ruth D.	Northbridge,	Administration,	22257
Samuel	Northbridge,	Will,	22258
Sophia M.	Sutton,	Guardianship,	22259
Willis	Northbridge,	Guardianship,	22260
FOWLES see FOWLE.			
FOX, Abel	Fitchburg,	Guardianship,	22261
Abel	Fitchburg,	Administration,	22262
Abel A.	Fitchburg,	Guardianship,	22263
Alfred	Fitchburg,	Guardianship,	22264
Annie R. S.	Worcester,	Will,	22265
Arthur L.	Worcester,	Administration,	22266
Charles H.	Fitchburg,	Administration,	22267
Edward	Fitchburg,	Guardianship,	22268
Edward H.	Fitchburg,	Guardianship,	22269
George	Milford,	Will,	22270
George J.	Fitchburg,	Guardianship,	22271
Joseph	Fitchburg,	Will,	22272
Joseph	Fitchburg,	Guardianship,	22273
Joseph, Jr.	St. Croix,	Foreign Will,	22274
Joseph D.	Fitchburg,	Guardianship,	22275
Joseph D.	Assyria, Mich.,	Administration,	22275
Lemuel J.	Worcester,	Administration,	22276
Marcus	Fitchburg,	Guardianship,	22277
Margaret	Blackstone,	Will,	22278
Maria	Worcester,	Guardianship,	22279

| --- | --- | --- | --- | --- |
1849	FOX, Martha A.	Fitchburg,	Guardianship,	22280
1832	Mary	Fitchburg,	Administration,	22281
1833	Mary A.	Fitchburg,	Guardianship,	22282
1832	Oliver	Fitchburg,	Will,	22283
1785	Sarah	Dracut,	Guardianship,	22284
1860	William B.	Worcester,	Administration,	22285
1824	FOXCROFT, Charlotte	Worcester,	Guardianship,	22286
1824	Elizabeth H.	Worcester,	Guardianship,	22287
1824	George	Worcester,	Guardianship,	22288
1824	John	Worcester,	Will,	22289
1824	Mary	Worcester,	Guardianship,	22290
1878	FRAIL, Abby B.	Southborough,	Will,	22291
	FRAIZER see FRASER.			
1876	FRANCIS, Harry B.	Lunenburg,	Guardianship,	22292
1828	Lucy	Lunenburg,	Administration,	22293
1876	Lucy	Worcester,	Administration,	22294
1828	Philemon B.	Lunenburg,	Guardianship,	22295
1828	Samuel	Lunenburg,	Guardianship,	22296
1876	Sidney P.	Lunenburg,	Will,	22297
1816	Simon	Lunenburg,	Guardianship,	22298
1819	Simon	Lunenburg,	Administration,	22298
1828	Sullivan R.	Lunenburg,	Guardianship,	22299
1828	Tryphena	Lunenburg,	Guardianship,	22300
1858	FRANKLIN, Benjamin	Southbridge,	Administration,	22301
1880	Edward A.	Worcester,	Administration,	22302
1878	John	Gardner,	Will,	22303
1878	John P.	Gardner,	Guardianship,	22304
1850	Levi	Brookfield,	Administration,	22305
1808	Record	Hardwick,	Will,	22306
1874	Sarah S.	Worcester,	Administration,	22307
1878	William T.	Gardner,	Guardianship,	22308
1865	FRARY, Emma F.	Holden,	Adoption, etc.,	22309
1868	Emma F.	Holden,	Adoption, etc.,	22309
1866	William H.	Holden,	Adoption, etc.,	22310
	FRASER AND FRAIZER,			
1875	Agnes	Milford,	Guardianship,	22311
1880	Alexander	Worcester,	Guardianship,	22312
1842	Felice	Uxbridge,	Will,	22313
1822	Henry	Uxbridge,	Guardianship,	22314
1875	James	Milford,	Administration,	22315
1875	Joanna	Milford,	Guardianship,	22316
1852	John J. B.	Royalston,	Guardianship,	22317
1875	Margaret E.	Milford,	Guardianship,	22318
1842	Ruth	Uxbridge,	Guardianship,	22319
1852	William	Leominster,	Administration,	22320
1782	FREDRICK, Prince	Athol,	Administration,	22321

Year.	Name.	Residence.	Nature.	Case.
1807	FREEBORN, Esther	Paxton,	Will,	22322
1796	Sharp	Paxton,	Dower,	22323
1879	FREELAND, Adaline	Sutton,	Guardianship,	22324
1859	Frances J. W.	Sutton,	Administration,	22325
1860	Frances J. W.	Sutton,	Guardianship,	22326
1862	Freeman	Sutton,	Guardianship,	22327
1875	Freeman	Sutton,	Administration,	22327
1800	Hitty	Sutton,	Guardianship,	22328
1796	James	Sutton,	Administration,	22329
1832	James	Sutton,	Guardianship,	22330
1871	James C.	Fitchburg,	Will,	22331
1800	Sally	Sutton,	Guardianship,	22332
1875	FREEMAN, Alanson S.	Mendon,	Will,	22333
1795	Alpheus	Mendon,	Guardianship,	22334
1825	Alpheus	Mendon,	Administration,	22335
1852	Andrew S.	Millbury,	Change of Name,	22336
1838	Ann, etc.	Worcester,	Guardianship,	22337
1838	Anne	Worcester,	Guardianship,	22337
1853	Arminda	Webster,	Administration,	22338
1807	Augusta	Sturbridge.	Guardianship,	22339
1806	Benjamin	Sturbridge,	Will,	22340
1873	Betsey H.	Brookfield,	Will, ·	22341
1831	Caroline	Dudley,	Guardianship,	22342
1831	Charles	Dudley,	Guardianship,	22343
1854	Charles	Webster,	Guardianship,	22344
1772	Chester	Sturbridge,	Guardianship,	22345
1835	Chester	Brookfield,	Administration,	22346
1831	Chloe	Dudley,	Guardianship,	22347
1825	Chloe A.	Mendon,	Guardianship,	22348
1867	Clarissa D.	Webster,	Administration,	22349
1806	Comfort	Sturbridge,	Administration,	22350
1807	Comfort	Sturbridge,	Guardianship,	22351
1772	Deliverance	Hardwick,	Guardianship,	22352
1877	Dyer	Webster,	Will,	22353
1795	Ebenezer	Mendon,	Guardianship,	22354
1769	Edmund	Hardwick,	Guardianship,	22355
1795	Edward	Mendon,	Guardianship,	22356
1866	Edward D.	Webster,	Guardianship,	22357
1816	Eli	Hardwick,	Will,	22358
1816	Elijah	Oakham,	Administration,	22359
1821	Elijah	Oakham,	Guardianship,	22360
1859	Ellen B. H.	West Brookfield,	Administration,	22361
1863	Ernest E.	Worcester,	Guardianship,	22362
1831	Frederick	Dudley,	Guardianship,	22363
1867	George E.	Lunenburg,	Guardianship,	22364

Year.	Name.	Residence.	Nature.	Case.
1866	FREEMAN, Harriet E.	Webster,	Guardianship,	22365
1821	Harvey	Sturbridge,	Guardianship,	22366
1821	Haskell	Barre,	Will,	22367
1835	Hatch	Barre,	Administration,	22368
1872	Hattie L.	Blackstone,	Guardianship,	22369
1821	Horace	Sturbridge,	Guardianship,	22370
1821	Hoyt	Sturbridge,	Guardianship,	22371
1776	Isaac	Brookfield,	Administration,	22372
1880	James L.	Gardner,	Guardianship,	22373
1825	James M.	Mendon,	Guardianship,	22374
1772	Jane	Hardwick,	Guardianship,	22375
1773	Jared	Sturbridge,	Guardianship,	22376
1872	Jessie W.	Westborough,	Adoption, etc.,	22377
1839	John W.	Worcester,	Guardianship,	22378
1772	Joseph	Hardwick,	Guardianship,	22379
1816	Joseph	Sturbridge,	Will,	22380
1839	Joshua	Worcester,	Will,	22381
1839	Joshua	Worcester,	Guardianship,	22382
1839	Josiah G.	Worcester,	Guardianship,	22383
1821	Julia A.	Oakham,	Guardianship,	22384
1866	Lizzie F.	Webster,	Guardianship,	22385
1825	Lucy	Mendon,	Guardianship,	22386
1831	Lucy	Sturbridge,	Administration,	22387
1773	Martha	Sturbridge,	Guardianship,	22388
1773	Mary	Sturbridge,	Guardianship,	22389
1881	Mary	Lunenburg,	Administration,	22390
1825	Mary A.	Mendon,	Guardianship,	22391
1839	Mary A.	Worcester,	Guardianship,	22392
1876	Nancy	Shrewsbury,	Administration,	22393
1769	Nathan	Hardwick,	Administration,	22394
1772	Nathan	Hardwick,	Guardianship,	22395
1795	Phebe	Mendon,	Guardianship,	22396
1867	Philip H.	Lunenburg,	Guardianship,	22397
1855	Pliny	Webster,	Administration,	22398
1825	Rachel	Mendon,	Guardianship,	22399
1794	Ralph	Mendon,	Administration,	22400
1807	Ralph	Mendon,	Administration,	22401
1772	Rany	Sturbridge,	Guardianship,	22402
1831	Rufus	Dudley,	Guardianship,	22403
1865	Rufus	Webster,	Administration,	22404
1845	Rufus G. A.	Westborough,	Guardianship,	22405
1870	Sally	Dana,	Administration,	22406
1772	Samuel	Sturbridge,	Administration,	22407
1772	Samuel	Sturbridge,	Guardianship,	22408
1825	Samuel	Hardwick,	Administration,	22409

YEAR.	NAME.	RESIDENCE.	NATURE.	CASE.
1831	FREEMAN, Samuel	Dudley,	Administration,	22410
1772	Samuel, Jr.	Sturbridge,	Administration,	22411
1831	Samuel, Jr.	Dudley,	Guardianship,	22412
1772	Sarah	Hardwick,	Guardianship,	22413
1852	Sarah	Brookfield,	Will,	22414
1852	Silas A.	Millbury,	Change of Name,	22415
1880	Silas M.	Millbury,	Will,	22416
1821	Susan	Oakham,	Guardianship,	22417
1843	Susan A.	Southbridge,	Guardianship,	22418
1773	Walter	Sturbridge,	Guardianship,	22419
1831	Wealthy	Dudley,	Guardianship,	22420
1831	William	Dudley,	Guardianship,	22421
1872	William F.	Blackstone,	Administration,	22422
1845	William H.	Westborough,	Administration,	22423
1845	William H.	Westborough,	Guardianship,	22424
1839	William T.	Worcester,	Guardianship,	22425
1824	FRENCH, Abel	Fitchburg,	Administration,	22426
1789	Abial	Mendon,	Will,	22427
1786	Abijah	Milford,	Administration,	22428
1793	Abijah	Milford,	Guardianship,	22429
1792	Adam	Milford,	Guardianship,	22430
1864	Adams E.	Winchendon,	Administration,	22431
1793	Amme	Milford,	Guardianship,	22432
1877	Asaph	Templeton,	Will,	22433
1837	Catharine D.	Oakham,	Guardianship,	22434
1841	Catherine D.	Oakham,	Will,	22435
1844	Cyrus	Brookfield,	Administration,	22436
1793	Delpha	Milford,	Guardianship,	22437
1772	Desire	Templeton,	Administration,	22438
1837	Edwin	Oakham,	Guardianship,	22439
1838	Elizabeth	Ashburnham,	Administration,	22440
1864	Elvirus F.	Winchendon,	Guardianship,	22441
1792	Ezra	Douglas,	Administration,	22442
1845	Fisher	Templeton,	Administration,	22443
1864	Flora G.	Winchendon,	Guardianship,	22444
1872	Hiram	Worcester,	Administration,	22445
1826	Isaac	Oakham,	Will,	22446
1793	Joanna	Milford,	Guardianship,	22447
1829	Joel	Ashburnham,	Administration,	22448
1776	John	Mendon,	Will,	22449
1823	John	Oakham,	Will,	22450
1762	Joseph	Holden,	Administration,	22451
1843	Leavit	Ashburnham,	Guardianship,	22452
1835	Levi	Fitchburg,	Guardianship,	22453
1845	Lipha	Templeton,	Will,	22454

YEAR.	NAME.	RESIDENCE.	NATURE.	CASE.
1809	FRENCH, Lois	Royalston,	Guardianship,	22455
1847	Loresta	Weirs, N. H.,	Guardianship,	22456
1847	Lyceria L.	Weirs, N. H.,	Guardianship,	22457
1868	Mary	Athol,	Will,	22458
1844	Mehetable	Templeton,	Will,	22459
1869	Melinda K.	Grafton,	Administration,	22460
1874	Mercy W.	Harvard,	Administration,	22461
1799	Micah	Royalston,	Will,	22462
1841	Perez D.	Ashburnham,	Administration,	22463
1793	Perley	Milford,	Guardianship,	22464
1875	Philemon	Clinton,	Administration,	22465
1845	Ruth	Fitchburg,	Administration,	22466
1791	Samuel	Milford,	Will,	22467
1798	Samuel	Fitchburg,	Guardianship,	22468
1813	Sarah	Mendon,	Administration,	22469
1839	Sarah	Upton,	Will,	22470
1802	William	Mendon,	Will,	22471
1837	William W.	Grafton,	Guardianship,	22472
1809	Zeba	Royalston,	Guardianship,	22473
1816	Ziba	Royalston,	Guardianship,	22474
1881	FRENIER, Charles	Winchendon,	Administration,	22475
1876	FRENNEY, Charles E.	Gardner,	Adoption, etc.,	22476
1866	FRETTS, Anna	Milford,	Guardianship,	22477
1813	FRINK, Elizabeth	Rutland,	Administration,	22478
1878	George W.	Milford,	Administration,	22479
1866	Hiram E.	Oakham,	Guardianship,	22480
1805	John	Rutland,	Will,	22481
1838	John	Rutland,	Will,	22482
1876	John A.	Paxton,	Administration,	22483
1839	Josiah C.	Rutland,	Guardianship,	22484
1866	Lillie B.	Oakham,	Guardianship,	22485
1853	Medora I.	Milford,	Guardianship,	22486
1819	Samuel	Rutland,	Guardianship,	22487
1846	Samuel	Paxton,	Pension,	22488
1859	William A.	Oakham,	Change of Name,	22489
1801	FRIZZELL, Earl	Harvard,	Administration,	22490
1776	FROBISH, James	Worcester,	Guardianship,	22491
1792	FROST, Amariah	Milford,	Will,	22492
1877	Ann C.	Grafton,	Administration,	22493
1846	Artemas	Harvard,	Administration,	22494
1866	Bradford	New York, N. Y.,	Administration,	22495
1825	Clarissa	Harvard,	Guardianship,	22496
1789	Dana	Rutland,	Guardianship,	22497
1849	Dana	Rutland,	Will,	22498
1860	David	Fitchburg,	Guardianship,	22499

YEAR.	NAME.	RESIDENCE.	NATURE.	CASE.
1792	FROST, Deborah	Rutland,	Administration,	22500
1865	Eben H.	Fitchburg,	Will,	22501
1787	Ebenezer	Rutland,	Will,	22502
1877	Ebenezer	Ashburnham,	Will,	22503
1792	Elias	Milford,	Guardianship,	22504
1752	George	Portsmouth, N. H.,	Guardianship,	22505
1873	George W.	Lancaster,	Will,	22506
1828	Hermon	Hubbardston,	Guardianship,	22507
1789	James	Rutland,	Guardianship,	22508
1783	John	Princeton,	Administration,	22509
1878	John W.	Lancaster,	Administration,	22510
1824	Jonathan	Paxton,	Will,	22511
1874	Joseph	Lunenburg,	Administration,	22512
1868	J. Milton	Ashburnham,	Will,	22513
1881	Mabel M.	Worcester,	Adoption, etc.,	22514
1846	Mary A. R.	Harvard,	Guardianship,	22515
1869	Moses B.	Grafton,	Administration,	22516
1824	Polly	Paxton,	Guardianship,	22517
1821	Ruth	Holden,	Administration,	22518
1825	Sally	Harvard,	Guardianship,	22519
1875	Sally S.	Ashburnham,	Administration,	22520
1787	Samuel	Princeton,	Guardianship,	22521
1841	Sarah	Harvard,	Administration,	22522
1824	Scripture	Harvard,	Will,	22523
1858	Selim	Athol,	Will,	22524
1838	Seth	New Braintree,	Will,	22525
1859	Sophia	New Braintree,	Administration,	22526
1789	Stephen	Princeton,	Guardianship,	22527
1789	Stephen	Rutland,	Guardianship,	22528
1828	Stephen	Hubbardston,	Will,	22529
1865	Sumner	Hubbardston,	Administration,	22530
1861	Sylvester	Fitchburg,	Will,	22531
1867	William	Hardwick,	Administration,	22532
1819	FROTHINGHAM, Daniel	Lancaster,	Pension,	22533
1819	Lydia	Lancaster,	Guardianship,	22534
1819	Rebecca	Lancaster,	Guardianship,	22535
	FRY AND FRYE,			
1851	Benjamin	Hardwick,	Administration,	22536
1861	Benjamin	Royalston,	Administration,	22537
1871	Charles A.	Berlin,	Guardianship,	22538
1871	Chester J.	Berlin,	Guardianship,	22539
1868	Cora B.	Berlin,	Guardianship,	22540
1828	Cynthia	Brookfield,	Guardianship,	22541
1855	David A.	Northbridge,	Administration,	22542
1832	Ebenezer	Royalston,	Will,	22543

Year.	Name.	Residence.	Nature.	Case.
	FRY and FRYE,			
1871	George E.	Berlin,	Guardianship,	22544
1876	George F.	Berlin,	Administration,	22545
1869	James N.	Bolton,	Will,	22546
1868	Job	Athol,	Administration,	22547
1767	John	Reading,	Guardianship,	22548
1817	John	Bolton,	Will,	22549
1866	John	Royalston,	Will,	22550
1813	John, Jr.	Bolton,	Administration,	22551
1839	John E.	Bolton,	Guardianship,	22552
1844	Jonathan	Bolton,	Administration,	22553
1767	Joseph	Reading,	Guardianship,	22554
1779	Joseph	Harvard,	Administration,	22555
1871	Leslie M.	Berlin,	Guardianship,	22556
1839	Mary A.	Bolton,	Guardianship,	22557
1860	Pernal	Winchendon,	Administration,	22558
1875	Ruth	Bolton,	Will,	22559
1839	Thomas	Bolton,	Will,	22560
1839	Thomas E.	Bolton,	Guardianship,	22561
1877	William	Berlin,	Administration,	22562
1866	FRYER, Rosa	Boston,	Adoption, etc.,	22563
	FULLAM and FULLUM,			
1868	Belinda S.	Leominster,	Administration,	22564
1852	Betsey	Fitchburg,	Pension,	22565
1852	Betsey	Fitchburg,	Administration,	22566
1834	Charles E.	Leominster,	Guardianship,	22567
1833	Jacob	Leominster,	Will,	22568
1861	Jacob	Leominster,	Administration,	22569
1834	Mary E.	Leominster,	Guardianship,	22570
1837	Oliver	Fitchburg,	Pension,	22571
1842	Rebecca	Leominster,	Guardianship,	22572
1834	Timothy S.	Leominster,	Guardianship,	22573
1829	Warren	Fitchburg,	Administration,	22574
1809	FULLER, Abigail	Lunenburg,	Guardianship,	22575
1839	Adaline A. C.	Worcester,	Guardianship,	22576
1861	Adaline V.	Thompson, Conn.,	Administration,	22577
1863	Alfred N.	Harvard,	Guardianship,	22578
1842	Almira H.	Holden,	Guardianship,	22579
1824	Ambrose	Royalston,	Guardianship,	22580
1830	Ambrose	Topsham, Vt.,	Administration,	22581
1801	Amos	Boylston,	Will,	22582
1840	Amos	Sutton,	Guardianship,	22583
1849	Amos	Sutton,	Administration,	22584
1867	Andrew L.	Clinton,	Will,	22585
1849	Ann	Sutton,	Guardianship,	22586

YEAR.	NAME.	RESIDENCE.	NATURE.	CASE.
1840	FULLER, Ann J.	Sutton,	Guardianship,	22587
1853	Ann W.	Sutton,	Administration,	22588
1880	Arthur W.	Worcester,	Guardianship,	22589
1844	Austin B.	Northbridge,	Guardianship,	22590
1868	Austin F.	Millbury,	Administration,	22591
1860	Augustus F.	Worcester,	Administration,	22592
1838	Benjamin	Ashburnham,	Will,	22593
1873	Benjamin F.	Fitchburg,	Will,	22594
1878	Betsey C.	Millbury,	Will,	22595
1780	Beulah	Holden,	Guardianship,	22596
1863	Brigham	Sutton,	Administration,	22597
1859	Caleb S.	Worcester,	Will,	22598
1868	Catharine	Ashburnham,	Will,	22599
1863	Charles B.	Worcester,	Guardianship,	22600
1820	Charles T.	Leominster,	Guardianship,	22601
1834	Charles T.	Leominster,	Administration,	22602
1844	Daniel	Northbridge,	Guardianship,	22603
1839	Daniel D.	Worcester,	Administration,	22604
1839	Daniel D.	Worcester,	Guardianship,	22605
1861	David T.	Oakham,	Guardianship,	22606
1869	Ebenezer	Worcester,	Administration,	22607
1811	Ebenezer S.	Paxton,	Guardianship,	22608
1874	Edith A.	Webster,	Adoption, etc.,	22609
1877	Edith R.	Milford,	Administration,	22610
1783	Edward	Leominster,	Will,	22611
1803	Edward	Lancaster,	Will,	22612
1834	Edward	Leominster,	Will,	22613
1874	Edward L.	Millbury,	Guardianship,	22614
1834	Elisha	Phillipston,	Pension,	22615
1855	Elisha	Worcester,	Administration,	22616
1859	Elisha	Sutton,	Will,	22617
1879	Emeline G.	Phillipston,	Administration,	22618
1840	Emerson	Sutton,	Guardianship,	22619
1873	Emily	Oakham,	Administration,	22620
1876	Ephraim	Lancaster,	Will,	22621
1853	Eugene B.	Oakham,	Adoption, etc.,	22622
1860	Eugene B.	Oakham,	Change of Name,	22622
1878	Eugene B.	Worcester,	Guardianship,	22623
1855	Eunice	Millbury,	Pension,	22624
1855	Eunice	Millbury,	Administration,	22625
1840	Eustis	Sutton,	Guardianship,	22626
1878	Evelyn A.	Phillipston,	Guardianship,	22627
1847	Freeman	Worcester,	Administration,	22628
1847	Freeman W.	Worcester,	Guardianship,	22629
1850	George	Sutton,	Guardianship,	22630

YEAR.	NAME.	RESIDENCE.	NATURE.	CASE.
1866	FULLER, George A.	Fitchburg,	Administration,	22631
1820	George E.	Leominster,	Guardianship,	22632
1880	George H.	Worcester,	Guardianship,	22633
1780	Hannah	Holden,	Guardianship,	22634
1822	Hannah F.	Holden,	Guardianship,	22635
1860	Henry H.	Worcester,	Guardianship,	22636
1844	Henry M.	Northbridge,	Guardianship,	22637
1865	Herbert N.	Charlton,	Administration,	22638
1778	Jabez	Oakham,	Administration,	22639
1800	Jacob	Athol,	Administration,	22640
1831	James	Lancaster,	Will,	22641
1879	James	Worcester,	Will,	22642
1878	Jennie	Alameda Co., Cal.,	Will,	22643
1778	Jeremiah	Holden,	Administration,	22644
1878	Joel B.	Worcester,	Administration,	22645
1801	John	Lunenburg,	Will,	22646
1808	John	Lunenburg,	Administration,	22647
1822	John	Lancaster,	Guardianship,	22648
1820	John A.	Leominster,	Guardianship,	22649
1809	John E.	Lunenburg,	Guardianship,	22650
1818	John T.	Leominster,	Administration,	22651
1758	Jonathan	Sutton,	Will,	22652
1769	Jonathan	Oxford,	Administration,	22653
1770	Jonathan	Oxford,	Guardianship,	22654
1840	Jonathan	Charlton,	Pension,	22655
1840	Jonathan	Charlton,	Administration,	22656
1847	Jonathan	Sutton,	Administration,	22657
1769	Joseph	Lunenburg,	Administration,	22658
1819	Joseph	Holden,	Administration,	22659
1838	Joseph	Holden,	Pension,	22660
1838	Joseph	Holden,	Administration,	22661
1865	Joseph	Clinton,	Will,	22662
1864	Julia A.	Sutton,	Administration,	22663
1872	Keziah B.	Southbridge,	Administration,	22664
1807	Lemuel	Worcester,	Administration,	22665
1861	Leonard	Oakham,	Administration,	22666
1877	Leonard C.	Petersham,	Guardianship,	22667
1814	Levi	Sutton,	Will,	22668
1844	Levi	Northbridge,	Administration,	22669
1876	Levi	Sutton,	Guardianship,	22670
1844	Levi A.	Northbridge,	Guardianship,	22671
1840	Louisa	Sutton,	Guardianship,	22672
1879	Lucy	Northbridge,	Administration,	22673
1844	Lucy M. B.	Northbridge,	Guardianship,	22674
1844	Lydia M.	Northbridge,	Guardianship,	22675

YEAR.	NAME.	RESIDENCE.	NATURE.	CASE.
1861	FULLER, Manson	Worcester,	Will,	22676
1880	Marshall	Worcester,	Administration,	22677
1829	Martha E.	Leominster,	Guardianship,	22678
1809	Mary	Lunenburg,	Guardianship,	22679
1825	Mary	Leominster,	Administration,	22680
1836	Mary	Holden,	Administration,	22681
1820	Mary A.	Leominster,	Guardianship,	22682
1878	Mary E.	Phillipston,	Guardianship,	22683
1861	Mary J.	Oakham,	Guardianship,	22684
1840	Munroe	Sutton,	Guardianship,	22685
1780	Natban	Holden,	Guardianship,	22686
1807	Nehemiah	Fitchburg,	Will,	22687
1876	Nellie M.	Shirley,	Guardianship,	22688
1863	Newell	Harvard,	Administration,	22689
1876	Phebe	Northbridge,	Will,	22690
1869	Phebe M.	New Braintree,	Guardianship,	22691
1848	Pliny F.	Phillipston,	Guardianship,	22692
1878	Pliny F.	Phillipston,	Administration,	22693
1802	Prudence	Lunenburg,	Administration,	22694
1780	Rachel	Holden,	Guardianship,	22695
1861	Reuben	Worcester,	Trustee,	22696
1840	Rufus	Sutton,	Administration,	22697
1847	Rufus P.	Phillipston,	Administration,	22698
1760	Sarah	Leominster,	Will,	22699
1861	Sarah E.	Oakham,	Guardianship,	22700
1811	Silas	Boylston,	Guardianship,	22701
1827	Silas	Boylston,	Administration,	22701
1778	Simeon	Sutton,	Guardianship,	22702
1850	Simeon	Sutton,	Administration,	22703
1844	Sophrona P.	Holden,	Administration,	22704
1780	Thomas	Holden,	Guardianship,	22705
1829	Turner	Sutton,	Administration,	22706
1854	Warren	Hamilton, Can.,	Administration,	22707
1875	Willard	Sutton,	Will,	22708
1778	William	Sutton,	Will,	22709
1829	William	Leominster,	Administration,	22710
1872	William	Athol,	Administration,	22711
1829	William S.	Leominster,	Guardianship,	22712
1873	William S.	Millbury,	Will,	22713
1849	William W.	Oregon, Ill.,	Will,	22714
1776	FULLERTON, Nathaniel	Worcester,	Administration,	22715
1811	Samuel	Worcester,	Will,	22716
	FULLUM see FULLAM.			
1880	FURNESS, John	Worcester,	Administration,	22717
1860	FURY, Lawrence	Clinton,	Guardianship,	22718
1860	Mary	Clinton,	Guardianship,	22719

(523)

YEAR.	NAME.	RESIDENCE.	NATURE.	CASE.
1878	FURY, Mary	Clinton,	Will,	22720
1859	Michael	Clinton,	Administration,	22721
1860	Michael	Clinton,	Guardianship,	22722
1860	William	Clinton,	Guardianship,	22723
1863	GAEDE, Louisa	Clinton,	Adoption, etc.,	22724
	GAFFIELD see GARFIELD.			
1877	GAFFNEY, Isabella	Worcester,	Will,	22725
1881	James	Millbury,	Will,	22726
1881	Mary	Milford,	Administration,	22727
1856	GAFFY, Sarah J.	Worcester,	Adoption, etc.,	22728
1865	GAGE, Alonzo F.	Harvard,	Guardianship,	22729
1865	Caroline F.	Harvard,	Guardianship,	22730
1858	Charles E.	Gardner,	Guardianship,	22731
1860	George J.	Leominster,	Adoption, etc.,	22732
1862	George M.	Fitchburg,	Administration,	22733
1865	George T.	Harvard,	Guardianship,	22734
1862	Ida S.	Fitchburg,	Guardianship,	22735
1871	John	Phillipston,	Administration,	22736
1865	Lewis P.	Harvard,	Guardianship,	22737
1877	Mary A.	Athol,	Guardianship,	22738
1858	Mary E.	Gardner,	Guardianship,	22739
1866	Merrill	Athol,	Will,	22740
1849	Minot G.	Lancaster,	Guardianship,	22741
1802	Moses	Milford,	Will,	22742
1863	Moses M.	Fitchburg,	Will,	22743
1858	Nancy B.	Templeton,	Administration,	22744
1858	Nelson M.	Gardner,	Guardianship,	22745
1852	Orrison	Gardner,	Administration,	22746
1880	Rebecca J.	Fitchburg,	Administration,	22747
1877	Reuben P.	Athol,	Will,	22748
1866	Robert M.	Athol,	Guardianship,	22749
1851	Samuel	Templeton,	Will,	22750
1868	GAHEGAN, Edward J.	Milford,	Guardianship,	22751
1868	John	Milford,	Guardianship,	22752
1868	Mary A.	Milford,	Guardianship,	22753
1868	Thomas T.	Milford,	Guardianship,	22754
1801	GALE, Abel	Holden,	Will,	22755
1804	Abijah	Westborough,	Will,	22756
1857	Ada I.	Worcester,	Adoption, etc.,	22757
1857	Ada I.	Millbury,	Guardianship,	22758
1765	Amsden	Westborough,	Guardianship,	22759
1862	Arthur F.	Charlton,	Guardianship,	22760
1829	Betsy	Boylston,	Will,	22761
1774	Calvin	Princeton,	Guardianship,	22762
1787	Calvin	Worcester,	Miscellaneous,	22763

Year.	Name.	Residence.	Nature.	Case.
1805	GALE, Cyrus	Westborough,	Guardianship,	22764
1880	Cyrus	Northborough,	Will,	22765
1781	David	Royalston,	Guardianship,	22766
1805	David	Westborough,	Guardianship,	22767
1781	Dilly	Royalston,	Guardianship,	22768
1798	Elijah	Oxford,	Administration,	22769
1774	Elisha	Princeton,	Will,	22770
1815	Elizabeth	Millbury,	Guardianship,	22771
1850	Enoch	Charlton,	Will,	22772
1815	Esther	Boylston,	Will,	22773
1849	Esther	Petersham,	Administration,	22774
1849	Esther	Petersham,	Pension,	22775
1854	Frederick W.	Worcester,	Will,	22776
1856	George A.	Northborough,	Administration,	22777
1852	Horace H.	Petersham,	Guardianship,	22778
1779	Isaac	Royalston,	Administration,	22779
1793	Isaac	Sutton,	Will,	22780
1826	Isaac	Royalston,	Administration,	22781
1761	Jacob	Westborough,	Guardianship,	22782
1814	Jacob A.	Westborough,	Administration,	22783
1781	James	Royalston,	Guardianship,	22784
1798	Jesse	Oxford,	Administration,	22785
1869	Jesse	Petersham,	Will,	22786
1819	John G.	Boylston,	Pension,	22787
1781	Jonas	Royalston,	Guardianship,	22788
1784	Jonas	Holden,	Will,	22789
1806	Jonas	Holden,	Administration,	22790
1814	Jonas, Jr.	Millbury,	Will,	22791
1815	Jonas R.	Millbury,	Guardianship,	22792
1781	Jonathan	Royalston,	Guardianship,	22793
1833	Jonathan	Royalston,	Administration,	22794
1833	Jonathan	Royalston,	Pension,	22795
1867	Jonathan D.	Royalston,	Will,	22796
1781	Judith	Royalston,	Guardianship,	22797
1866	Leander	Millbury,	Administration,	22798
1815	Leonard	Millbury,	Guardianship,	22799
1829	Lewis	Westborough,	Guardianship,	22800
1852	Lewis	Petersham,	Administration,	22801
1874	Lewis H.	Worcester,	Adoption, etc.,	22802
1815	Lucy	Millbury,	Guardianship,	22803
1774	Luther	Princeton,	Guardianship,	22804
1742	Lydia	Waltham,	Guardianship,	22805
1795	Lydia	Westborough,	Will,	22806
1850	Lyman	Worcester,	Administration,	22807
1847	Mary S.	Worcester,	Administration,	22808

(525)

YEAR.	NAME.	RESIDENCE.	NATURE.	CASE.
1824	GALE, Oliver	West Boylston,	Will,	22809
1865	Otis	Royalston,	Will,	22810
1854	Sarah W.	Worcester,	Administration,	22811
1831	Susanna	Westborough,	Administration,	22812
1756	Thadeus	Westborough,	Administration,	22813
1851	Walter	Northborough,	Guardianship,	22814
1852	William W.	Petersham,	Guardianship,	22815
1869	GALLAGHER, Bridget	Milford,	Guardianship,	22816
1867	Catharine	Clinton,	Administration,	22817
1869	John	Milford,	Guardianship,	22818
1869	Mary	Milford,	Administration,	22819
1872	Mary	Clinton,	Guardianship,	22820
1864	Michael	Clinton,	Administration,	22821
1867	Sarah	Clinton,	Administration,	22822
1869	William	Milford,	Guardianship,	22823
1809	GALLOND, Aurelia G.	Petersham,	Guardianship,	22824
1850	Irana	Petersham,	Will,	22825
1803	Jeremiah	Petersham,	Administration,	22826
1851	Jeremiah	Petersham,	Will,	22827
1807	John	Petersham,	Administration,	22828
1849	John H.	Petersham,	Guardianship,	22829
1809	John L.	Petersham,	Guardianship,	22830
1853	John L.	Petersham,	Will,	22831
1832	Joseph	Petersham,	Administration,	22832
1849	Sarah A.	Petersham,	Guardianship,	22833
1754	GALLOWAY, William	Hopkinton,	Guardianship,	22834
1847	GALLUP, Asa	Brookfield,	Administration,	22835
1838	Benjamin	Plainfield, Conn.,	Foreign Will,	22836
1875	Dorothy	Leominster,	Administration,	22837
1854	George M.	Brookfield,	Change of Name,	22838
1845	Joseph	Sterling,	Administration,	22839
1855	Prudence	Brookfield,	Administration,	22840
1870	Silas	Brookfield,	Administration,	22841
1854	Thomas	Brookfield,	Will,	22842
1877	GALVIN, Michael	Uxbridge,	Will,	22843
1875	Patrick	Dudley,	Will,	22844
1880	GAMAGE, Sarah R.	Southborough,	Will,	22845
1847	GAMBLE, George	Sutton,	Guardianship,	22846
1847	John W.	Sutton,	Administration,	22847
1875	GAMMELL, Francis	Templeton,	Administration,	22848
1881	Nora	Templeton,	Administration,	22849
1878	GANNON, Margaret	Fitchburg,	Administration,	22850
1880	Mary	Westborough,	Administration,	22851
1770	GANSON, Abigail	Petersham,	Guardianship,	22852
1769	John	Petersham,	Administration,	22853

(526)

YEAR.	NAME.	RESIDENCE.	NATURE.	CASE.
1770	GANSON, John	Petersham,	Guardianship,	22854
1770	Joseph	Petersham,	Guardianship,	22855
1770	Nathan	Petersham,	Guardianship,	22856
1868	GARDEM, James B.	Winchendon,	Administration,	22857
1825	GARDNER, Agatha H.	Harvard,	Guardianship,	22858
1814	Andrew	Harvard,	Guardianship,	22859
1843	Ann E.	Fitchburg,	Administration,	22860
1843	Ann S.	Mendon,	Guardianship,	22861
1864	Betsey	Southborough,	Guardianship,	22862
1870	Betsey	Southborough,	Will,	22862
1868	Bridget	Worcester,	Guardianship,	22863
1861	Catharine	Leominster,	Guardianship,	22864
1863	Catharine	Leominster,	Will,	22864
1848	Charles	Brookfield,	Will,	22865
1830	David	Southborough,	Will,	22866
1873	Edward E.	Worcester,	Guardianship,	22867
1854	Electa	Leominster,	Will,	22868
1871	Eliza, etc.	Worcester,	Guardianship,	22869
1873	Eliza, etc.	Worcester,	Will,	22869
1849	Elizabeth	Leominster,	Will,	22870
1838	Elizabeth G.	Fitchburg,	Guardianship,	22871
1866	Elizabeth G.	Fitchburg,	Will,	22872
1877	Emily	Fitchburg,	Will,	22873
1855	Emma	Worcester,	Guardianship,	22874
1814	Francis	Leominster,	Administration,	22875
1876	George B.	Charlton,	Administration,	22876
1873	George E.	Worcester,	Guardianship,	22877
1848	Jack, etc.	Worcester,	Pension,	22878
1858	Jerome	Harvard,	Administration,	22879
1868	John	Worcester,	Guardianship,	22880
1837	Joseph C.	Fitchburg,	Administration,	22881
1854	Mary	Worcester,	Pension,	22882
1868	Mary	Worcester,	Guardianship,	22883
1813	Moses	Harvard,	Will,	22884
1758	Peter	Uxbridge,	Administration,	22885
1790	Peter	Uxbridge,	Guardianship,	22886
1843	Rollin	Mendon,	Guardianship,	22887
1843	Samuel	Mendon,	Guardianship,	22888
1841	Stephen P.	Bolton,	Will,	22889
1852	Susanna	Worcester,	Will,	22890
1868	Thomas	Worcester,	Guardianship,	22891
1872	Thomas	Mendon,	Will,	22892
1843	Thomas, Jr.	Mendon,	Guardianship,	22893
1861	William H.	Worcester,	Change of Name,	22894
1875	Zebulon N.	Leicester,	Administration,	22895

(527—SERIES A.)

YEAR.	NAME.	RESIDENCE.	NATURE.	CASE.
	GARFIELD AND GAFFIELD,			
1831	Abigail	Royalston,	Will,	22896
1866	Alona V.	Princeton,	Guardianship,	22897
1831	Ann S.	Shrewsbury,	Guardianship,	22898
1857	Ansel H.	Royalston,	Administration,	22899
1857	Ansel U.	Royalston,	Guardianship,	22900
1871	Arnold M.	Worcester,	Guardianship,	22901
1777	Asa	Spencer,	Guardianship,	22902
1756	Benjamin	Fort Dumoner, N. H.,	Guardianship,	22903
1865	Charles E.	Shrewsbury,	Guardianship,	22904
1871	Charles E.	Shrewsbury,	Administration,	22905
1871	Charles L.	Worcester,	Guardianship,	22906
1871	Charlotte E.	Worcester,	Guardianship,	22907
1757	Daniell	Shrewsbury,	Will,	22908
1866	Delia A.	Princeton,	Guardianship,	22909
1799	Ebenezer	Shrewsbury,	Will,	22910
1833	Ebenezer	Shrewsbury,	Will,	22911
1861	Edwin M.	Shrewsbury,	Guardianship,	22912
1865	Edwin M.	Shrewsbury,	Administration,	22912
1756	Elijah	Fort Dumoner, N. H.,	Guardianship,	22913
1794	Elijah	Fitchburg,	Will,	22914
1830	Elisha	Ashburnham,	Administration,	22915
1831	Emily A.	Shrewsbury,	Guardianship,	22916
1867	Esther W.	Royalston,	Will,	22917
1837	George	Athol,	Will,	22918
1837	George R.	Athol,	Guardianship,	22919
1837	Joel	Petersham,	Administration,	22920
1865	John	Worcester,	Will,	22921
1838	Joseph	Spencer,	Administration,	22922
1876	Joseph	Spencer,	Will,	22923
1828	Joshua	Royalston,	Administration,	22924
1843	Moses	Athol,	Will,	22925
1871	Moses	Princeton,	Will,	22926
1841	Nancy A.	Worcester,	Guardianship,	22927
1831	Nathan	Shrewsbury,	Administration,	22928
1756	Nathaniel	Fort Dumoner, N. H.,	Guardianship,	22929
1803	Nathaniel	Royalston,	Guardianship,	22930
1866	Paul	Princeton,	Will,	22931
1837	Reuben	Athol,	Guardianship,	22932
1841	Russell	Worcester,	Administration,	22933
1834	Ruth	Westminster,	Administration,	22934
1863	Sally	Shrewsbury,	Administration,	22935
1756	Samuel	Fort Dumoner, N. H.,	Guardianship,	22936
1764	Samuel	Spencer,	Guardianship,	22937
1776	Samuel	Spencer,	Administration,	22938

NAME.	RESIDENCE.	NATURE.	CASE.
GARFIELD and GAFFIELD,			
Samuel, Jr.	Spencer,	Administration,	22939
Sarah M.	Worcester,	Guardianship,	22940
Silas	Spencer,	Guardianship,	22941
Susan W.	Worcester,	Guardianship,	22942
William	Waltham,	Guardianship,	22943
GARLINGTON, Thomas	Sturbridge,	Administration,	22944
GARRAHAN, William	Southborough,	Will,	22945
GARRITY, Patrick	Blackstone,	Will,	22946
GARSIDE, Joshua	Uxbridge,	Administration,	22947
GARVEY, Ellen	Worcester,	Guardianship,	22948
William	Worcester,	Will,	22949
GARY (see also GEARY),			
Benjamin, Jr.	Lunenburg,	Will,	22950
Elihu	Sterling,	Administration,	22951
Hannah	Leominster,	Guardianship,	22952
Jane	Leominster,	Guardianship,	22953
Jonas	Leominster,	Guardianship,	22954
Jonathan	Lancaster,	Guardianship,	22955
Joseph	Lancaster,	Will,	22956
Moses	Sterling,	Administration,	22957
Nathan	Lancaster,	Guardianship,	22958
Nathan	Sterling,	Will,	22959
Perney W.	Sterling,	Guardianship,	22960
Reuben	Sterling,	Will,	22961
Thomas	Sterling,	Will,	22962
GASCHETT, Daniel	Providence, R. I.,	Administration,	22963
Isaac	Westborough,	Guardianship,	22964
John	Providence, R. I.,	Guardianship,	22965
Levi	Providence, R. I.,	Guardianship,	22966
Reuben	Providence, R. I.,	Guardianship,	22967
GASKILL and GASKELL,			
Alice R.	Blackstone,	Guardianship,	22968
Anna E.	Uxbridge,	Guardianship,	22969
Anna J.	Uxbridge,	Guardianship,	22970
Arminda T.	Blackstone,	Guardianship,	22971
Asa B.	Uxbridge,	Guardianship,	22972
Asa B.	Uxbridge,	Administration,	22973
Benjamin	Uxbridge,	Will,	22974
Charles F.	Uxbridge,	Guardianship,	22975
Ebenezer	Mendon,	Administration,	22976
Elisha	Woonsocket, R. I.,	Foreign Will,	22977
Esther	Blackstone,	Administration,	22978
Eunice	Uxbridge,	Guardianship,	22979
Ezekiel	Uxbridge,	Administration,	22980

YEAR.	NAME.	RESIDENCE.	NATURE.	CASE.
	GASKILL AND GASKELL,			
1848	George	Blackstone,	Will,	22981
1863	George H.	Uxbridge,	Guardianship,	22982
1868	George O.	Uxbridge,	Guardianship,	22983
1867	Gilbert	Blackstone,	Administration,	22984
1862	Hannah	Blackstone,	Will,	22985
1868	Jane M.	Uxbridge,	Guardianship,	22986
1785	Joseph	Berlin,	Will,	22987
1815	Joseph	Uxbridge,	Guardianship,	22988
1857	Joseph	Uxbridge,	Administration,	22989
1863	Lebbeus	Cumberland, R. I.,	Foreign Will,	22990
1815	Levina	Uxbridge,	Guardianship,	22991
1858	Lindley M.	Uxbridge,	Guardianship,	22992
1860	Naum	Mendon,	Will,	22993
1846	Peter	Blackstone,	Will,	22994
1846	Peter	Mendon,	Will,	22995
1847	Samuel	Mendon,	Will,	22996
1761	Samuell	Mendon,	Will,	22997
1868	Susan	Smithfield, R. I.,	Foreign Will,	22998
1815	Verney	Uxbridge,	Guardianship,	22999
	GASSETT AND GASSET,			
1846	Anna	Bolton,	Will,	23000
1866	Charles W.	Shrewsbury,	Guardianship,	23001
1875	Frederick D.	Milford,	Adoption, etc.,	23002
1814	Henry	Northborough,	Will,	23003
1854	Henry A.	Westborough,	Administration,	23004
1814	Joel	Northborough,	Guardianship,	23005
1834	John	Northborough,	Administration,	23006
1834	John	Northborough,	Pension,	23007
1768	Reuben	Hopkinton,	Guardianship,	23008
1832	Winslow	Northborough,	Administration,	23009
	GATCHELL see GETCHELL.			
1869	**GATELY,** Mary	Clinton,	Will,	23010
1873	Thomas	Clinton,	Will,	23011
1760	**GATES,** Aaron	Rutland,	Guardianship,	23012
1816	Aaron	Barre,	Administration,	23013
1849	Aaron	Hubbardston,	Will,	23014
1837	Abel E.	Ashburnham,	Guardianship,	23015
1877	Addie J.	Shrewsbury,	Guardianship,	23016
1865	Adelaide A.	Barre,	Guardianship,	23017
1782	Alford	Rutland,	Guardianship,	23018
1873	Alice L.	Worcester,	Guardianship,	23019
1824	Alice P.	Rutland,	Guardianship,	23020
1824	Amelia	Rutland,	Guardianship,	23021
1842	Amory	Barre,	Guardianship,	23022
1804	Amos	Westminster,	Will,	23023

(530)

Year.	Name.	Residence.	Nature.	Case.
1845	GATES, Ann M.	Leominster,	Guardianship,	23024
1838	Anna	Hubbardston,	Administration,	23025
1852	Anna	Leominster,	Administration,	23026
1872	Anna E. E.	Worcester,	Will,	23027
1812	Artemas	Leominster,	Guardianship,	23028
1815	Artemas	Worcester,	Administration,	23029
1860	Artemas	Leominster,	Will,	23030
1860	Artemas F.	Leominster,	Guardianship,	23031
1779	Asa	Worcester,	Guardianship,	23032
1877	Asaph	Westminster,	Administration,	23033
1839	Augustus	Leominster,	Guardianship,	23034
1758	Benjamin	Rutland District,	Administration,	23035
1797	Benjamin	Barre,	Administration,	23036
1850	Benjamin	Templeton,	Administration,	23037
1854	Benjamin A.	Gardner,	Administration,	23038
1848	Betsey	Worcester,	Administration,	23039
1811	Betsy	Hubbardston,	Guardianship,	23040
1861	Caroline	Petersham,	Guardianship,	23041
1877	Carrie L.	Shrewsbury,	Guardianship,	23042
1812	Carter	Leominster,	Guardianship,	23043
1846	Carter	Leominster,	Will,	23044
1820	Catharine	Barre,	Administration,	23045
1823	Charles	Leominster,	Guardianship,	23046
1825	Charles	Petersham,	Guardianship,	23047
1827	Charles	Hubbardston,	Administration,	23048
1842	Charles	Barre,	Guardianship,	23049
1872	Charles	Petersham,	Administration,	23050
1845	Charles E.	Leominster,	Guardianship,	23051
1864	Charles E.	Leominster,	Will,	23052
1864	Charles E.	Leominster,	Guardianship,	23053
1856	Charles F.	Worcester,	Guardianship,	23054
1824	Charlotte	Rutland,	Guardianship,	23055
1837	Charlotte	Ashburnham,	Guardianship,	23056
1865	Clara W.	Fitchburg,	Adoption, etc.,	23057
1864	Clovis M.	Oxford,	Administration,	23058
1812	Daniel	Leominster,	Guardianship,	23059
1834	Daniel	Petersham,	Pension,	23060
1837	Daniel	Ashburnham,	Administration,	23061
1847	Daniel	Westminster,	Will,	23062
1861	Daniel M.	Northborough,	Administration,	23063
1872	Daniel M.	Barre,	Administration,	23064
1837	Daniel W.	Ashburnham,	Guardianship,	23065
1829	Darwin	Gardner,	Guardianship,	23066
1839	David	Bolton,	Administration,	23067
1872	David R.	Worcester,	Administration,	23068

Year.	Name.	Residence.	Nature.	Case.
1864	GATES, Delia	Worcester,	Administration,	23069
1837	Delphos	Hubbardston,	Administration,	23070
1871	Dennis	Gardner,	Will,	23071
1824	Dolly S.	Boylston,	Guardianship,	23072
1866	Edmond	Petersham,	Administration,	23073
1868	Edward A.	Worcester,	Adoption, etc.,	23074
1839	Edwin	Leominster,	Guardianship,	23075
1854	Edwin	Grafton,	Guardianship,	23076
1812	Elias	Leominster,	Guardianship,	23077
1824	Elias	Leominster,	Administration,	23078
1854	Eliza	Gardner,	Guardianship,	23079
1848	Eliza W.	Barre,	Guardianship,	23080
1837	Elizabeth	Petersham,	Guardianship,	23081
1866	Ella M.	Ware,	Adoption, etc.,	23082
1867	Elsie A.	Westminster,	Guardianship,	23083
1856	Emma L.	Worcester,	Guardianship,	23084
1881	Emory W.	Worcester,	Administration,	23085
1869	Ephraim, Jr.	Bolton,	Administration,	23086
1867	Eunice M.	Worcester,	Guardianship,	23087
1827	Experience	Barre,	Administration,	23088
1803	Ezekiel	Gardner,	Guardianship,	23089
1872	Florence M.	Worcester,	Adoption, etc.,	23090
1826	Francis	Hubbardston,	Guardianship,	23091
1846	Francis	Hubbardston,	Administration,	23092
1854	Francis	Gardner,	Guardianship,	23093
1879	Frank F.	Worcester,	Adoption, etc.,	23094
1877	Fred K.	Shrewsbury,	Guardianship,	23095
1875	Frederick G.	Worcester,	Guardianship,	23096
1855	Frederick S.	Petersham,	Guardianship,	23097
1839	Gardner R.	Leominster,	Guardianship,	23098
1848	Gardner R.	Leominster,	Administration,	23099
1845	George	Leominster,	Guardianship,	23100
1866	George	Petersham,	Administration,	23101
1874	George	Bolton,	Administration,	23102
1824	George A.	Rutland,	Guardianship,	23103
1856	George H.	Worcester,	Guardianship,	23104
1848	George S.	Barre,	Guardianship,	23105
1860	George W.	Leominster,	Guardianship,	23106
1871	Gilbert H.	Petersham,	Guardianship,	23107
1839	Hannah	Westminster,	Pension,	23108
1850	Hannah	Templeton,	Administration,	23109
1831	Harriet	Westminster,	Guardianship,	23110
1877	Hattie E.	Shrewsbury,	Guardianship,	23111
1854	Helen	Gardner,	Guardianship,	23112
1873	Helen M.	Worcester,	Guardianship,	23113

YEAR.	NAME.	RESIDENCE.	NATURE.	CASE.
1838	GATES, Henry	Hubbardston,	Administration,	23114
1855	Henry	Worcester,	Administration,	23115
1870	Henry	Leominster,	Will,	23116
1879	Henry F.	Westborough,	Will,	23117
1875	Herbert L.	Worcester,	Guardianship,	23118
1839	Hesseltine	Ashburnham,	Administration,	23119
1777	Hezekiah	Lancaster,	Will,	23120
1854	Hiram	Gardner,	Guardianship,	23121
1865	Hiram	Gardner,	Administration,	23122
1826	Horace	Hubbardston,	Guardianship,	23123
1797	Horatio	Barre,	Guardianship,	23124
1811	Horatio	Hubbardston,	Guardianship,	23125
1837	Horatio N.	Hubbardston,	Guardianship,	23126
1875	Howard	Worcester,	Guardianship,	23127
1870	Ida D.	Bolton,	Adoption, etc.,	23128
1869	Ida D. F.	Bolton,	Guardianship,	23129
1853	Irving C.	Hubbardston,	Guardianship,	23130
1796	Isaac	Harvard,	Administration,	23131
1796	Isaac	Harvard,	Guardianship,	23132
1854	Isaac	Gardner,	Guardianship,	23133
1880	Jaalam	Worcester,	Administration,	23134
1773	James	Worcester,	Guardianship,	23135
1820	James	Petersham,	Administration,	23136
1852	James C.	Leominster,	Administration,	23137
1845	Jeremiah K.	Westminster,	Will,	23138
1828	Joanna	Worcester,	Will,	23139
1847	Joel H.	Royalston,	Guardianship,	23140
1763	John, 2d	Worcester,	Will,	23141
1779	John	Worcester,	Guardianship,	23142
1824	John	Petersham,	Will,	23143
1840	John	Worcester,	Administration,	23144
1870	John	Oxford,	Administration,	23145
1878	John	Worcester,	Administration,	23146
1839	John D.	Leominster,	Guardianship,	23147
1797	John M.	Barre,	Guardianship,	23148
1863	John M.	Barre,	Administration,	23149
1826	John N.	Hubbardston,	Guardianship,	23150
1837	John N.	Hubbardston,	Administration,	23151
1839	Jonas	Leominster,	Will,	23152
1756	Jonathan	Worcester,	Will,	23153
1758	Jonathan	Rutland District,	Guardianship,	23154
1803	Jonathan	Worcester,	Will,	23155
1808	Jonathan	Hubbardston,	Will,	23156
1814	Jonathan	Worcester,	Administration,	23157
1827	Jonathan	Westminster,	Administration,	23158

(533)

YEAR.	NAME.	RESIDENCE.	NATURE.	CASE.
1830	GATES, Joseph	Rutland,	Administration,	23159
1848	Joseph	Barre,	Administration,	23160
1829	Joshua	Worcester,	Administration,	23161
1848	Josiah R.	Barre,	Guardianship,	23162
1840	Julia M.	Worcester,	Guardianship,	23163
1877	J. Newell	Shrewsbury,	Administration,	23164
1881	Larkin N.	Worcester,	Guardianship,	23165
1847	Laura	Royalston,	Guardianship,	23166
1818	Lavinia E.	Barre,	Guardianship,	23167
1875	Leon	Worcester,	Guardianship,	23168
1779	Levi	Worcester,	Guardianship,	23169
1827	Levi	Sterling,	Administration,	23170
1878	Levi	Worcester,	Administration,	23171
1773	Levina	Rutland,	Guardianship,	23172
1880	Lewis	Worcester,	Will,	23173
1877	Lewis E.	Shrewsbury,	Guardianship,	23174
1848	Lewis W.	Barre,	Guardianship,	23175
1875	Lewis W.	Rutland,	Administration,	23176
1864	Lizzie M.	Leominster,	Guardianship,	23177
1847	Lodema	Royalston,	Guardianship,	23178
1805	Lois	Westminster,	Guardianship,	23179
1848	Lois	Leominster,	Will,	23180
1871	Lorinda	Leominster,	Will,	23181
1877	Lottie P.	Shrewsbury,	Guardianship,	23182
1837	Louisa	Ashburnham,	Guardianship,	23183
1864	Louisa	Gardner,	Will,	23184
1879	Lovina A.	Westborough,	Guardianship,	23185
1823	Lucinda	Petersham,	Guardianship,	23186
1773	Lucretia	Rutland,	Guardianship,	23187
1829	Lucy	Lancaster,	Administration,	23188
1855	Lucy	Worcester,	Administration,	23189
1879	Lucy A.	Leominster,	Will,	23190
1823	Luke, 2d	Leominster,	Guardianship,	23191
1831	Luke	Leominster,	Administration,	23192
1847	Luther	Sterling,	Administration,	23193
1855	Lyman E.	Petersham,	Guardianship,	23194
1817	Makepeace	Barre,	Will,	23195
1756	Marcy	Lancaster,	Will,	23196
1824	Maria P.	Rutland,	Guardianship,	23197
1862	Martha	Leominster,	Will,	23198
1848	Martha J.	Barre,	Guardianship,	23199
1856	Martha J.	Rutland,	Administration,	23200
1779	Mary	Worcester,	Guardianship,	23201
1797	Mary	Barre,	Guardianship,	23202
1823	Mary	Leominster,	Guardianship,	23203

YEAR.	NAME.	RESIDENCE.	NATURE.	CASE.
1823	GATES, Mary	Petersham,	Guardianship,	23204
1854	Mary	Gardner,	Guardianship,	23205
1825	Mary A.	Leominster,	Guardianship,	23206
1877	Mary H.	Oxford,	Administration,	23207
1782	Matilda	Rutland,	Guardianship,	23208
1873	Maud M.	Worcester,	Guardianship,	23209
1876	Milo H.	Gardner,	Guardianship,	23210
1826	Minerva	Hubbardston,	Guardianship,	23211
1813	Molly	Leominster,	Will,	23212
1797	Nabby	Harvard,	Guardianship,	23213
1811	Nabby	Harvard,	Administration,	23214
1864	Nancy	Barre,	Will,	23215
1867	Nancy	Petersham,	Will,	23216
1865	Nathan	Gardner,	Administration,	23217
1825	Nathaniel	Worcester,	Administration,	23218
1832	Nathaniel	Worcester,	Administration,	23219
1854	Newball	Gardner,	Guardianship,	23220
1841	Oliver C.	Petersham	Administration,	23221
1845	Parker	Westminster,	Guardianship,	23222
1769	Paul	Worcester,	Guardianship,	23223
1843	Paul	Worcester,	Administration,	23224
1843	Paul	Worcester,	Pension,	23225
1805	Phineas	Westminster,	Administration,	23226
1855	Reuben	Templeton,	Administration,	23227
1874	Reuben	Fitchburg,	Administration,	23228
1788	Reubin	Leominster,	Will,	23229
1803	Reubin	Gardner,	Guardianship,	23230
1822	Reubin	Gardner,	Guardianship,	23231
1830	Ruth	Barre,	Administration,	23232
1811	Sally A.	Hubbardston,	Guardianship,	23233
1824	Sally M.	Rutland,	Guardianship,	23234
1765	Samuel	Worcester,	Guardianship,	23235
1790	Samuel	Petersham,	Will,	23236
1822	Samuel	Petersham,	Administration,	23237
1853	Samuel	Worcester,	Will,	23238
1867	Samuel F.	Worcester,	Administration,	23239
1876	Samuel G.	Gardner,	Will,	23240
1797	Samuel S.	Barre,	Guardianship,	23241
1856	Samuel S.	Barre,	Will,	23242
1779	Sarah	Worcester,	Guardianship,	23243
1863	Sarah	Gardner,	Administration,	23244
1840	Sarah A.	Worcester,	Guardianship,	23245
1850	Sarah E.	Leominster,	Will,	23246
1840	Sarah R.	Worcester,	Guardianship,	23247
1852	Sarah R.	Barre,	Guardianship,	23248

YEAR.	NAME.	RESIDENCE.	NATURE.	CASE.
1771	GATES, Silas	Worcester,	Guardianship,	23249
1823	Silas, Jr.	Leominster,	Guardianship,	23250
1777	Simon	Worcester,	Will,	23251
1803	Simon	Gardner,	Administration,	23252
1849	Simon	Worcester,	Will,	23253
1849	Simon	Worcester,	Pension,	23254
1852	Simon	Gardner,	Administration,	23255
1840	Simon D.	Worcester,	Guardianship,	23256
1877	Simon S.	Crystal Lake, Ill.,	Foreign Will,	23257
1761	Solomon	Worcester,	Will,	23258
1812	Sophia	Leominster,	Guardianship,	23259
1822	Sophia	Leominster,	Will,	23259
1773	Stephen	Rutland,	Will,	23260
1823	Stephen	Petersham,	Guardianship,	23261
1847	Stephen	Royalston,	Administration,	23262
1813	Submit	Harvard,	Administration,	23263
1867	Susan F.	Worcester,	Guardianship,	23264
1826	Sylvia	Hubbardston,	Guardianship,	23265
1815	Thomas	Lancaster,	Will,	23266
1876	Thomas	Worcester,	Guardianship,	23267
1876	Thomas	Worcester,	Administration,	23267
1823	Vashti	Leominster,	Guardianship,	23268
1863	Walter	Gardner,	Administration,	23269
1877	Walter H.	Shrewsbury,	Guardianship,	23270
1784	William	Worcester,	Administration,	23271
1811	William	Worcester,	Will,	23272
1831	William	Westminster,	Guardianship,	23273
1836	William	Barre,	Administration,	23274
1838	William	Leominster,	Guardianship,	23275
1843	William H.	Barre,	Administration,	23276
1789	Zacheus	Barre,	Will,	23277
1797	Zacheus	Harvard,	Guardianship,	23278
1822	Zadock	Rutland,	Will,	23279
1824	Zadock W.	Rutland,	Guardianship,	23280
1863	Zadock W.	Rutland,	Will,	23281
1773	Zelotes	Rutland,	Guardianship,	23282
1850	GAUGHAN, Ann	Lancaster,	Guardianship,	23283
1862	GAUGHERY, Michael	Clinton,	Guardianship,	23284
1865	GAULT, Caroline	North Brookfield,	Administration,	23285
1865	Charles	North Brookfield,	Guardianship,	23286
1842	Isaac	North Brookfield,	Guardianship,	23287
1848	James	Oakham,	Guardianship,	23288
1807	Mathew	Oakham,	Will,	23289
1848	William	Oakham,	Administration,	23290

YEAR.	NAME.	RESIDENCE.	NATURE.	CASE.
	GAUT (see also GOTT),			
1832	Caroline	Westminster,	Guardianship,	23291
1832	Harriet	Westminster,	Guardianship,	23292
1832	Joseph R.	Westminster,	Guardianship,	23293
1832	Lucy Ann	Westminster,	Guardianship,	23294
1830	Thomas	Westminster,	Administration,	23295
1864	William	Barre,	Administration,	23296
1879	GAVIN, Catherine A.	Worcester,	Guardianship,	23297
1849	GAVNEY, Mary	Blackstone,	Administration,	23298
1878	GAY, Abbie M.	Fitchburg,	Administration,	23299
1852	Abby J.	Brookfield,	Guardianship,	23300
1835	Artemas H.	Templeton,	Administration,	23301
1826	Benjamin	Charlton,	Administration,	23302
1852	Benjamin O.	Brookfield,	Guardianship,	23303
1862	Caty	Hubbardston,	Administration,	23304
1852	Charles P.	Brookfield,	Guardianship,	23305
1863	Elizabeth C.	Hubbardston,	Will,	23306
1869	Emma L.	Worcester,	Guardianship,	23307
1763	Francis	Hopkinton,	Guardianship,	23308
1832	George	Leominster,	Will,	23309
1848	George	Hubbardston,	Guardianship,	23310
1853	George	Brookfield,	Will,	23311
1851	Hamilton	Bennington, Vt.,	Administration,	23312
1853	Helen A.	Brookfield,	Guardianship,	23313
1844	Isaac	Brookfield,	Administration,	23314
1880	Jennie L.	Hopkinton,	Adoption, etc.,	23315
1769	Jonathan	Hopkinton,	Guardianship,	23316
1868	Louisa M.	Webster,	Administration,	23317
1852	Mary E.	Brookfield,	Guardianship,	23318
1879	Mary P.	Brookfield,	Administration,	23319
1859	Matilda A.	Sturbridge,	Guardianship,	23320
1880	Nancy	Templeton,	Will,	23321
1859	Otis	Sturbridge,	Administration,	23322
1859	Otis N.	Sturbridge,	Guardianship,	23323
1840	Phineas	Brookfield,	Administration,	23324
1848	Samuel	Hubbardston,	Administration,	23325
1840	Sarah A.	Brookfield,	Guardianship,	23326
1848	Seth	Hartford, Conn.,	Administration,	23327
1869	Susan E.	Worcester,	Guardianship,	23328
1747	Thomas	Mendon,	Administration,	23329
1852	William	Brookfield,	Administration,	23330
1852	William A.	Brookfield,	Guardianship,	23331
1872	GAYLORD, William	Clinton,	Administration,	23332
	GEANDREAU (see also GEN-DREAU),			
1878	Mitchell	Sutton,	Will,	23333

YEAR.	NAME.	RESIDENCE.	NATURE.	CASE.
1876	GEARAN, Michael	Worcester,	Administration,	23334
	GEARY (see also GARY),			
1758	Jonathan	Lancaster,	Administration,	23335
1791	Nathaniel	Harvard,	Will,	23336
1814	Thomas	Sterling,	Administration,	23337
1819	Thomas	Sterling,	Guardianship,	23338
1814	William	Sterling,	Guardianship,	23339
1869	GEBHARD, Louis	Milford,	Administration,	23340
1864	GEDDES, Peter S. W.	Winchendon,	Administration,	23341
	GERELDS see GEROULD.			
	GEER AND GERE,			
1863	Catherine	Westborough,	Pension,	23342
1818	Ebenezer	Worcester,	Will,	23343
1845	Ebenezer S.	Worcester,	Will,	23344
1880	George	Worcester,	Administration,	23345
1838	Henry F.	Worcester,	Guardianship,	23346
1875	Henry F.	Worcester,	Will,	23347
1813	Isaac	Northampton,	Will,	23348
1852	John M.	Worcester,	Guardianship,	23349
1878	Mary M. F.	Millbury,	Will,	23350
1838	Sarah J.	Worcester,	Guardianship,	23351
1871	GEESE, Caroline	Worcester,	Administration,	23352
1878	Charles	Worcester,	Will,	23353
1880	GENDILESCO, Vicenzo, etc.	Worcester,	Administration,	23354
	GENDREAU (see also GEAN-DREAU),			
1876	Hurbert, Jr.	North Brookfield,	Guardianship,	23355
1876	Lawrence	North Brookfield,	Guardianship,	23356
1876	Mary	North Brookfield,	Guardianship,	23357
1876	Rose	North Brookfield,	Guardianship,	23358
1880	GENTILENA, Vicenzo, etc.	Worcester,	Administration,	23359
1877	GEORGE, Andrew L.	Worcester,	Administration,	23360
1868	Edgar	Worcester,	Administration,	23361
1865	Frank	Leominster,	Administration,	23362
1827	Nathan	Mendon,	Guardianship,	33363
1872	Nathan	Mendon,	Administration,	23364
1827	Richard	Mendon,	Administration,	23365
1878	Samuel S.	Fitchburg,	Guardianship,	23366
	GERE see GEER.			
1872	GERMAIN, Paul	West Brookfield,	Will,	23367
1864	GERNHARD, Catherine	Worcester,	Adoption, etc.,	23368
	GEROULD, GERELDS, GER-ROULD, JERAULD AND JERAULT,			
1878	Albert A.	Clinton,	Will,	23369

(538)

YEAR.	NAME.	RESIDENCE.	NATURE.	CASE.
	GEROULD, GERELDS, GER-ROULD, JERAULD AND JERAULT,			
1835	Allyn	Stafford, Conn.,	Foreign Sale,	23370
1777	Asahel	Sturbridge,	Guardianship,	23371
1785	Asahel	Sturbridge,	Guardianship,	23372
1835	Bathsheba	Sturbridge,	Administration,	23373
1835	Elizabeth	Stafford, Conn.,	Foreign Sale,	23374
1867	Elizabeth	Worcester,	Administration,	23375
1835	Henry	Stafford, Conn.,	Foreign Sale,	23376
1809	Jacob	Sturbridge,	Guardianship,	23377
1871	James H.	Worcester,	Will,	23378
1777	Joshua	Sturbridge,	Administration,	23379
1809	Joshua	Sturbridge,	Guardianship,	23380
1835	Lois	Sturbridge,	Administration,	23381
1809	Lucy	Sturbridge,	Guardianship,	23382
1777	Mary	Sturbridge,	Guardianship,	23383
1835	Mary	Stafford, Conn.,	Foreign Sale,	23384
1879	Minnie E.	Clinton,	Guardianship,	23385
1809	Persis	Sturbridge,	Guardianship,	23386
1869	Sela W.	Worcester,	Will,	23387
1785	Stephen	Sturbridge,	Will,	23388
1808	Stephen	Sturbridge,	Administration,	23389
1809	Stephen	Sturbridge,	Guardianship,	23390
1853	Stephen	Northborough,	Pension,	23391
1857	Stephen	Northborough,	Will,	23392
1851	Stephen, Jr.	Northborough,	Administration,	23393
1879	William E.	Clinton,	Guardianship,	23394
1822	GERRISH, Ruth	Westminster,	Will,	23395
1797	Samuel	Westminster,	Administration,	23396
	GERROULD see GEROULD.			
1856	GERRY, Adeline	Harvard,	Guardianship,	23397
1843	Elizabeth R.	Harvard,	Will,	23398
1754	George	Harvard,	Administration,	23399
1877	George	Athol,	Administration,	23400
1856	Helen R.	Harvard,	Guardianship,	23401
1839	Hepsibah	Sterling,	Guardianship,	23402
1843	Hepsibah	Princeton,	Will,	23403
1844	Hepsibah	Princeton,	Pension,	23404
1829	Ichabod	Sterling,	Administration,	23405
1835	John	Grafton,	Administration,	23406
1847	John	Harvard,	Administration,	23407
1856	John	Harvard,	Administration,	23408
1851	Jonathan	Sterling,	Administration,	23409
1857	Sally	Grafton,	Will,	23410

YEAR.	NAME.	RESIDENCE.	NATURE.	CASE.
1825	GERRY, Solomon	Sterling,	Administration,	23411
1852	Thomas	Fitchburg,	Administration,	23412
1855	Thomas	Sterling,	Administration,	23413
1881	Ward S.	Harvard,	Will,	23414
	GETCHELL AND GATCHELL,			
1863	Harlow D.	Worcester,	Administration,	23415
1861	Moses W.	Blackstone,	Administration,	23416
1848	William	Northborough,	Will,	23417
1874	GETTINGS, Frank	Worcester,	Guardianship,	23418
1846	GETTY, Lydia	Oxford,	Will,	23419
1871	GEUTCH, Frederick	Clinton,	Administration,	23420
1844	GHERARDI, Aaron B.	Worcester,	Guardianship,	23421
1844	Clara J.	Worcester,	Guardianship,	23422
	GIBBONS AND GIBBENS,			
1873	Ann	Milford,	Will,	23423
1878	Patrick D.	Clinton,	Will,	23424
1747	Peter	Hardwick,	Guardianship,	23425
1874	Richard	Clinton,	Administration,	23426
1774	GIBBS, Abigail F.	Westminster,	Guardianship,	23427
1774	Achsah W.	Westminster,	Guardianship,	23428
1782	Alpheus	Princeton,	Guardianship,	23429
1774	Asa	Princeton,	Guardianship,	23430
1865	Benjamin F. D.	Fitchburg,	Administration,	23431
1866	Carrie A.	Westminster,	Guardianship,	23432
1813	Catharine	Sturbridge,	Will,	23433
1878	Charles N.	Petersham,	Administration,	23434
1823	Cyrus	Ashburnham,	Guardianship,	23435
1881	Daniel L.	Spencer,	Will,	23436
1824	Dolly S.	Boylston,	Guardianship,	23437
1774	Edmund	Westminster,	Guardianship,	23438
1774	Elijah	Westminster,	Administration,	23439
1774	Elijah	Westminster,	Guardianship,	23440
1823	Elizabeth	Westminster,	Administration,	23441
1824	Elizabeth	Boylston,	Guardianship,	23442
1866	Ella F.	Westminster,	Guardianship,	23443
1778	Ezra	Princeton,	Guardianship,	23444
1862	George E.	Rutland,	Guardianship,	23445
1774	Hannah	Princeton, .	Guardianship,	23446
1867	Hannah H.	Grafton,	Will,	23447
1785	Hezekiah	Berlin,	Guardianship,	23448
1793	Hezekiah	Berlin,	Will,	23449
1855	Hezekiah	Boylston,	Will,	23450
1824	Hezekiah, Jr.	Boylston,	Guardianship,	23451
1872	Horace M.	Boylston,	Administration,	23452
1833	Isaac	Dana,	Administration,	23453

YEAR.	NAME.	RESIDENCE.	NATURE.	CASE.
1777	GIBBS, Jacob	Sutton,	Will,	23454
1797	James	Sturbridge,	Will,	23455
1841	James	Westminster,	Guardianship,	23456
1760	John	Sutton,	Will,	23457
1780	John	Lancaster,	Will,	23458
1824	John	Boylston,	Guardianship,	23459
1825	John	Charlton,	Administration,	23460
1834	John	Charlton,	Administration,	23461
1848	Jonathan	Sturbridge,	Will,	23462
1748	Joseph	Boston,	Guardianship,	23463
1774	Joseph	Princeton,	Administration,	23464
1774	Joseph	Princeton,	Guardianship,	23465
1805	Joseph	Milford,	Will,	23466
1829	Joseph	Ashburnham,	Administration,	23467
1862	Joseph S.	Rutland,	Will,	23468
1752	Katherine	Boston,	Administration,	23469
1824	Keziah R.	Boylston,	Guardianship,	23470
1823	Leonard	Ashburnham,	Guardianship,	23471
1866	Lina W.	Westminster,	Guardianship,	23472
1874	Lucy	Sturbridge,	Will,	23473
1774	Mary	Princeton,	Guardianship,	23474
1824	Merriam	Boylston,	Guardianship,	23475
1827	Merriam	Rutland,	Guardianship,	23476
1829	Merrick H.	Ashburnham,	Guardianship,	23477
1866	Nettie A.	Westminster,	Guardianship,	23478
1874	Roxy	Sturbridge,	Will,	23479
1758	Samuel	Narragansett, No. 2,	Administration,	23480
1774	Samuel	Westminster,	Guardianship,	23481
1857	Sarah B.	Spencer,	Will,	23482
1774	Susanna	Westminster,	Guardianship,	23483
1793	Willard	Spencer,	Guardianship,	23484
1770	William	Princeton,	Administration,	23485
1782	William	Princeton,	Guardianship,	23486
1826	Zephaniah	Sturbridge,	Administration,	23487
1873	GIBLIN, Ann M.	Sutton,	Guardianship,	23488
1852	GIBSON, Aaron B.	Fitchburg,	Guardianship,	23489
1855	Alonzo E.	Barre,	Change of Name,	23490
1865	Amasa	Barre,	Will,	23491
1855	Anna A.	Rockingham, Vt.,	Guardianship,	23492
1756	Arrington	Lunenburg,	Administration,	23493
1820	Arrington	Fitchburg,	Guardianship,	23494
1864	Arrington	Fitchburg,	Will,	23495
1870	Arrington	Fitchburg,	Sale Real Estate,	23496
1845	Barker	Fitchburg,	Will,	23497
1841	Bezaleel	Leominster,	Guardianship,	23498

Year.	Name.	Residence.	Nature.	Case.
1855	GIBSON, Bezaleel	Leominster,	Administration,	23498
1858	Charles O.	Leominster,	Guardianship,	23499
1858	Diantha L.	Leominster,	Guardianship,	23500
1875	Effie	Fitchburg,	Adoption, etc.,	23501
1858	Ella S.	Leominster,	Guardianship,	23502
1854	Ellen C.	Leominster,	Guardianship,	23503
1841	Elnathan	Fitchburg,	Administration,	23504
1841	Elnathan C.	Fitchburg,	Guardianship,	23505
1757	Ephraim	Stow,	Guardianship,	23506
1844	Ephraim	Fitchburg,	Administration,	23507
1821	Evelina J.	Fitchburg,	Guardianship,	23508
1859	Frank W.	Fitchburg,	Adoption, etc.,	23509
1852	George W.	Fitchburg,	Guardianship,	23510
1854	Henry	Fitchburg,	Guardianship,	23511
1818	Israel	Fitchburg,	Will,	23512
1820	Israel	Fitchburg,	Guardianship,	23513
1835	James	Fitzwilliam, N. H.,	Administration,	23514
1854	James	Leominster,	Will,	23515
1872	James R. W.	Fitchburg,	Guardianship,	23516
1761	John	Lunenburg,	Administration,	23517
1784	John	Fitchburg,	Administration,	23518
1856	John	Templeton,	Will,	23519
1854	John A.	Leominster,	Guardianship,	23520
1826	Joseph	Fitchburg,	Will,	23521
1820	Lemuel W.	Fitchburg,	Guardianship,	23522
1821	Leonard L.	Fitchburg,	Guardianship,	23523
1860	Lizzie A.	Barre,	Adoption, etc.,	23524
1865	Lizzie A.	Barre,	Guardianship,	23525
1876	Loenza C.	Fitchburg,	Will,	23526
1865	Lois H.	Barre,	Will,	23527
1820	Lucinda W.	Fitchburg,	Guardianship,	23528
1878	Lucinda W.	Fitchburg,	Guardianship, ·	23529
1880	Lucinda W.	Fitchburg,	Will,	23529
1870	Lucy C.	Fitchburg,	Sale Real Estate,	23530
1820	Margaret	Fitchburg,	Guardianship,	23531
1821	Mary A.	Fitchburg,	Guardianship,	23532
1852	Mary A.	Millbury,	Administration,	23533
1877	Nancy W.	Northborough,	Will,	23534
1869	Nettie	Marlborough,	Adoption, etc.,	23535
1800	Reuben	Fitchburg,	Will,	23536
1820	Reuben	Fitchburg,	Guardianship,	23537
1836	Reuben	Fitchburg,	Will,	23538
1824	Samuel	Fitchburg,	Administration,	23539
1871	Samuel	Northborough,	Will,	23540
1877	Sarah	Oxford,	Administration,	23541

YEAR.	NAME.	RESIDENCE.	NATURE.	CASE.
1841	GIBSON, Sarah A.	Fitchburg,	Guardianship,	23542
1856	Sarah F.	Leominster,	Guardianship,	23543
1835	Simeon	Fitchburg,	Guardianship,	23544
1852	Simeon	Fitchburg,	Will,	23545
1820	Solomon	Fitchburg,	Administration,	23546
1864	Stephen	Lunenburg,	Administration,	23547
1821	Susanna	Fitchburg,	Guardianship,	23548
1841	Thomas	Ashburnham,	Pension,	23549
1769	Timothy	Lunenburg,	Guardianship,	23550
1832	Timothy	Lunenburg,	Will,	23551
1866	William F.	Clinton,	Guardianship,	23552
1866	William H.	Clinton,	Administration,	23553
1865	GIDDINGS, Alice W.	West Brookfield,	Guardianship,	23554
1838	Alonzo	Dana,	Guardianship,	23555
1838	Aurilla	Dana,	Guardianship,	23556
1864	Chandler	West Brookfield,	Will,	23557
1865	Clara C.	West Brookfield,	Guardianship,	23558
1865	Ida R.	West Brookfield,	Guardianship,	23559
1865	Isaac W.	West Brookfield,	Guardianship,	22560
1786	Job	Lunenburg,	Administration,	23561
1837	Joseph	Dana,	Administration,	23562
1810	Lucy	Lunenburg,	Administration,	23563
1838	Lyman	Dana,	Guardianship,	23564
1865	Mary P.	West Brookfield,	Guardianship,	23565
1838	Warren	Dana,	Guardianship,	23566
	GIFFIN AND GIFFEN,			
1837	Abner	Hardwick,	Administration,	23567
1770	David	Spencer,	Administration,	23568
1861	Erastus P.	North Brookfield,	Will,	23569
1770	Isabel	Spencer,	Will,	23570
1770	Robert	Spencer,	Will,	23571
1833	GIFFORD, Ann	Uxbridge,	Will,	23572
1776	Annanias	Uxbridge,	Will,	23573
1862	Annanias	Uxbridge,	Will,	23574
1865	Charles B.	Uxbridge,	Guardianship,	23575
1872	Daniel	Uxbridge,	Will,	23576
1876	Edwin E.	Sturbridge,	Guardianship,	23577
1870	Fanny	Sturbridge,	Will,	23578
1876	Harry S.	Sturbridge,	Guardianship,	23579
1866	Herbert C.	Uxbridge,	Guardianship,	23580
1869	Joanna	Uxbridge,	Will,	23581
1878	Joseph	Uxbridge,	Administration,	23582
1876	Leonore C.	Sturbridge,	Guardianship,	23583
1875	Mary E.	Sturbridge,	Will,	23584
1876	Minnie E.	Sturbridge,	Guardianship,	23585

Year.	Name.	Residence.	Nature.	Case.
1863	GIFFORD, Sarah	Uxbridge,	Will,	23586
1824	Seth	Uxbridge,	Administration,	23587
1837	Seth	Uxbridge,	Administration,	23588
	GILBERT AND GILBURT,			
1808	Aaron	Brookfield,	Administration,	23589
1809	Aaron	Brookfield,	Guardianship,	23590
1873	Abby F.	West Brookfield,	Guardianship,	23591
1756	Abigail	Brookfield,	Guardianship,	23592
1761	Abigail	Brookfield,	Administration,	23593
1840	Abigail F.	North Brookfield,	Guardianship,	23594
1864	Addie J.	Walpole, N. H.,	Foreign Sale,	23595
1827	Alanson A.	Hardwick,	Administration,	23596
1838	Alanson A. C.	Hardwick,	Guardianship,	23597
1877	Albert A.	North Brookfield,	Administration,	23598
1846	Almira J.	Brookfield,	Guardianship,	23599
1837	Alpheus	New Braintree,	Will,	23600
1838	Alvah L.	North Brookfield,	Administration,	23601
1797	Amaryllis	Brookfield,	Guardianship,	23602
1845	Amelia A.	Brookfield,	Guardianship,	23603
1867	Amelia A.	West Brookfield,	Administration,	23604
1816	Amos	North Brookfield,	Guardianship,	23605
1852	Amos	West Brookfield,	Will,	23606
1801	Anna	Brookfield,	Guardianship,	23607
1816	Austin	North Brookfield,	Guardianship,	23608
1846	Austin S.	Brookfield,	Guardianship,	23609
1837	Avery W.	New Braintree,	Guardianship,	23610
1785	Benjamin	Brookfield,	Guardianship,	23611
1843	Calvin	Brookfield,	Will,	23612
1797	Charles	Brookfield,	Guardianship,	23613
1840	Charlotte D.	North Brookfield,	Guardianship,	23614
1851	Charlotte W.	North Brookfield,	Guardianship,	23615
1873	Coleman W.	West Brookfield,	Will,	23616
1780	Cornelius	Brookfield,	Guardianship,	23617
1766	Damarus	Brookfield,	Guardianship,	23618
1839	Danforth	North Brookfield,	Administration,	23619
1785	Daniel	Brookfield,	Guardianship,	23620
1824	Daniel	North Brookfield,	Will,	23621
1851	Daniel	North Brookfield,	Administration,	23622
1876	Dexter	Templeton,	Guardianship,	23623
1844	Dolly B.	Brookfield,	Will,	23624
1840	Edward H.	North Brookfield,	Guardianship,	23625
1847	Edward P.	Brookfield,	Guardianship,	23626
1846	Edwin T.	Brookfield,	Guardianship,	23627
1774	Elam	Brookfield,	Guardianship,	23628
1836	Elbridge G.	Brookfield,	Guardianship,	23629

NAME.	RESIDENCE.	NATURE.	CASE.
GILBERT AND GILBURT,			
Elizabeth	Brookfield,	Guardianship,	23630
Elizabeth	Brookfield,	Guardianship,	23631
Elizabeth	New Braintree,	Guardianship,	23632
Elvira A.	New Braintree,	Guardianship,	23633
Elvira P.	West Brookfield,	Administration,	23634
Emily A.	Brookfield,	Guardianship,	23635
Emily M.	Warren,	Guardianship,	23636
Emma H.	Walpole, N. H.,	Foreign Sale,	23637
Estes	Brookfield,	Will,	23638
Esther	Brookfield,	Guardianship,	23639
Esther	North Brookfield,	Will,	23640
Eunice	Brookfield,	Guardianship,	23641
Ezekiel	Brookfield,	Guardianship,	23642
Ezra	West Brookfield,	Will,	23643
Ezra	West Brookfield,	Administration,	23644
Fanny	Templeton,	Will,	23645
George H.	Ware,	Trustee,	23646
Gershom	Brookfield,	Will,	23647
Harvey	Brookfield,	Guardianship,	23648
Harvey	Brookfield,	Will,	23649
Harvey	Brookfield,	Guardianship,	23650
Henrietta A.	West Brookfield,	Will,	23651
Henry	Brookfield,	Administration,	23652
Henry D.	Brookfield,	Guardianship,	23653
Henry D.	New Braintree,	Administration,	23654
Hiram	Hardwick,	Guardianship,	23655
Humphrey	North Brookfield,	Will,	23656
Jacob	Brookfield,	Guardianship,	23657
Jedediah	Brookfield,	Administration,	23658
Jerusha M.	Brookfield,	Guardianship,	23659
Joel	Brookfield,	Pension,	23660
Joel	Brookfield,	Will,	23661
John	Brookfield,	Administration,	23662
John	West Brookfield,	Will,	23663
Jonas	Brookfield,	Administration,	23664
Jonas	Brookfield,	Pension,	23665
Jonathan	Brookfield,	Administration,	23666
Jonathan	Brookfield,	Guardianship,	23667
Jonathan	New Braintree,	Will,	23668
Jonathan	New Braintree,	Guardianship,	23669
Joseph	Brookfield,	Guardianship,	23670
Joseph	Brookfield,	Administration,	23671
Joseph	Brookfield,	Guardianship,	23672
Joseph	Hardwick,	Administration,	23673

(545)

Year.	Name.	Residence.	Nature.	Case.
	GILBERT and GILBURT,			
1846	Joseph	Brookfield,	Will,	23674
1756	Josiah	Brookfield,	Administration,	23675
1756	Josiah	Brookfield,	Guardianship,	23676
1781	Josiah	New Braintree,	Guardianship,	23677
1811	Josiah	New Braintree,	Will,	23678
1756	Jude	Brookfield,	Guardianship,	23679
1873	Julia M.	West Brookfield,	Guardianship,	23680
1835	Justin W.	Brookfield,	Administration,	23681
1880	Kate S.	New Braintree,	Guardianship,	23682
1817	Lemuel	Hardwick,	Administration,	23683
1865	Lemuel	West Brookfield,	Administration,	23684
1816	Levi	Brookfield,	Will,	23685
1816	Liberty	North Brookfield,	Guardianship,	23686
1836	Lucian M.	Brookfield,	Guardianship,	23687
1756	Lucy	Brookfield,	Guardianship,	23688
1779	Lucy	Brookfield,	Administration,	23689
1856	Lucy	New Braintree,	Will,	23690
1865	Lucy	North Brookfield,	Administration,	23691
1771	Luke	Brookfield,	Will,	23692
1774	Luke	Brookfield,	Guardianship,	23693
1756	Lydia	Brookfield,	Guardianship,	23694
1774	Lydia	Brookfield,	Guardianship,	23695
1816	Lydia	North Brookfield,	Guardianship,	23696
1845	Lyman H.	Brookfield,	Guardianship,	23697
1864	Lyman H.	North Brookfield,	Will,	23698
1776	Martha	Brookfield,	Guardianship,	23699
1756	Mary	Brookfield,	Guardianship,	23700
1881	Mary B.	Worcester,	Will,	23701
1862	Mary L.	Warren,	Guardianship,	23702
1867	Mary S.	West Brookfield,	Administration,	23703
1756	Merriam	Brookfield,	Guardianship,	23704
1774	Merriam	Brookfield,	Guardianship,	23705
1756	Moses	Brookfield,	Guardianship,	23706
1780	Moses	Brookfield,	Guardianship,	23707
1774	Naomi	Brookfield,	Guardianship,	23708
1826	Nathan	Brookfield,	Will,	23709
1788	Nathaniel	Brookfield,	Administration,	23710
1796	Nathaniel	Brookfield,	Administration,	23711
1797	Nathaniel	Brookfield,	Guardianship,	23712
1816	Newton	North Brookfield,	Guardianship,	23713
1780	Olive	Brookfield,	Guardianship,	23714
1859	Orrin P.	Worcester,	Administration,	23715
1826	Pamela	Hardwick,	Guardianship,	23716
1777	Parmelia	Brookfield,	Guardianship,	23717

NAME.	RESIDENCE.	NATURE.	CASE.
GILBERT AND GILBURT,			
Pelatiah	Brookfield,	Will,	23718
Phineas	Brookfield,	Administration,	23719
Pitt	Brookfield,	Guardianship,	23720
Rachael	West Brookfield,	Administration,	23721
Reuben	North Brookfield,	Administration,	23722
Ruth	Brookfield,	Will,	23723
Ruth	Brookfield,	Pension,	23724
Ruth	Brookfield,	Will,	23725
Sally	West Brookfield,	Will,	23726
Samuel	Brookfield,	Guardianship,	23727
Samuel	Brookfield,	Guardianship,	23728
Samuel	Brookfield,	Will,	23729
Samuel	Brookfield,	Administration,	23730
Samuel A.	New Braintree,	Guardianship,	23731
Samuel P.	Northborough,	Will,	23732
Simeon	New Braintree,	Guardianship,	23733
Solomon	Brookfield,	Guardianship,	23734
Solomon	Brookfield,	Will,	23735
Sophia	Brookfield,	Guardianship,	23736
Susan E.	Brookfield,	Guardianship,	23737
Tamison	Brookfield,	Guardianship,	23738
Thaddeus	Brookfield,	Guardianship,	23739
Thomas	Brookfield,	Will,	23740
Thomas	Brookfield,	Will,	23741
Thomas	Brookfield,	Administration,	23742
Thomas	North Brookfield,	Guardianship,	23743
Thomas	North Brookfield,	Administration,	23744
Timothy	Hardwick,	Will,	23745
Timothy W.	Warren,	Guardianship,	23746
Uriah	Brookfield,	Administration,	23747
Walter	North Brookfield,	Administration,	23748
Walter H.	Sutton,	Guardianship,	23749
Willard	Warren,	Will,	23750
William E.	West Brookfield,	Change of Name,	23751
William M.	Sutton,	Administration,	23752
("Negro boy")	Barre,	Guardianship,	23753
GILCHRIST, GILCHREST AND			
GILLCHREST,			
Charles	Lunenburg,	Administration,	23754
Charles S.	Lunenburg,	Will,	23755
Charles W.	Lunenburg,	Guardianship,	23756
Elbridge H.	Lunenburg,	Guardianship,	23757
Elizabeth	Lunenburg,	Will,	23758
Florence A.	Lunenburg,	Guardianship,	23759

7)

|---|---|---|---|---|

GILCHRIST, GILCHREST AND GILLCHREST,

Year	Name	Residence	Nature	Case
1878	Isabel	Fitchburg,	Will,	23760
1838	James	Lunenburg,	Will,	23761
1839	James	Lunenburg,	Guardianship,	23762
1876	James	Lunenburg,	Will,	23763
1824	James R.	Lunenburg,	Guardianship,	23764
1824	John	Lunenburg,	Administration,	23765
1880	John F.	Lunenburg,	Administration,	23766
1880	John P.	Lunenburg,	Guardianship,	23767
1859	Margaret E.	Lunenburg,	Guardianship,	23768
1820	Mary	Fitchburg,	Will,	23769
1862	Mary E.	Lunenburg,	Guardianship,	23770
1876	Mary E.	Lunenburg,	Administration,	23771
1824	Ruth A.	Lunenburg,	Guardianship,	23772
1877	Sally	Lunenburg,	Administration,	23773
1796	William	Lunenburg,	Will,	23774
1858	William	Lunenburg,	Will,	23775
1862	William A.	Lunenburg,	Guardianship,	23776
1876	William A.	Lunenburg,	Administration,	23777
1869	GILDAY, Annie	Worcester,	Guardianship,	23778
1869	John	Worcester,	Administration,	23779

GILE AND GILES,

Year	Name	Residence	Nature	Case
1847	Andrew J.	Lunenburg,	Guardianship,	23780
1875	Fanny L.	Worcester,	Guardianship,	23781
1804	James	Sutton,	Administration,	23782
1847	John S.	Lunenburg,	Guardianship,	23783
1847	Judith M.	Lunenburg,	Guardianship,	23784
1847	Thomas W.	Lunenburg,	Will,	23785
1847	Wilber F.	Lunenburg,	Guardianship,	23786

GILFORD see GUILFORD.

Year	Name	Residence	Nature	Case
1760	GILL, Anna	Westminster,	Guardianship,	23787
1843	Augustus C.	Fitchburg,	Guardianship,	23788
1843	Caleb B.	Fitchburg,	Guardianship,	23789
1843	Catherine B.	Fitchburg,	Guardianship,	23790
1880	Charles S.	Shrewsbury,	Guardianship,	23791
1843	Clara J.	Fitchburg,	Guardianship,	23792
1843	Dixon L., Jr.	Fitchburg,	Guardianship,	23793
1760	Eleonar	Westminster,	Guardianship,	23794
1843	Eliza A.	Fitchburg,	Guardianship,	23795
1760	Elizabeth	Westminster,	Guardianship,	23796
1758	Fanny	Sturbridge,	Guardianship,	23797
1801	Fanny	Princeton,	Guardianship,	23798
1758	Gils	Brookfield,	Guardianship,	23799
1863	Hannah F. M.	Worcester,	Change of Name,	23800

YEAR.	NAME.	RESIDENCE.	NATURE.	CASE.
1880	GILL, Henry B.	Shrewsbury,	Administration,	23801
1801	Hull A.	Princeton,	Guardianship,	23802
1758	John	Sturbridge,	Guardianship,	23803
1759	John	Narragansett, No. 2,	Administration,	23804
1760	John	Westminster,	Guardianship,	23805
1804	John	Princeton,	Will,	23806
1810	John	Winchendon,	Guardianship,	23807
1856	Joshua	Winchendon,	Administration,	23808
1866	Lizzie L.	Blackstone,	Guardianship,	23809
1801	Marcy	Princeton,	Guardianship,	23810
1880	Mark	Worcester,	Administration,	23811
1801	Mary A.	Princeton,	Guardianship,	23812
1801	Michael	Princeton,	Guardianship,	23813
1849	Michael	Westminster,	Pension,	23814
1800	Moses	Princeton,	Will,	23815
1801	Moses	Princeton,	Guardianship,	23816
1801	Moses	Princeton,	Guardianship,	23817
1818	Moses	Princeton,	Guardianship,	23818
1839	Moses	Princeton,	Administration,	23819
1801	Nancy B.	Princeton,	Guardianship,	23820
1801	Nancy K.	Princeton,	Guardianship,	23821
1801	Sarah P.	Princeton,	Guardianship,	23822
1818	Susanna	Princeton,	Guardianship,	23823
1801	Thomas B.	Princeton,	Guardianship,	23824
1758	William	Sturbridge,	Administration,	23825
1758	William	Sturbridge,	Guardianship,	23826
	GILLCHREST see GILCHRIST.			
	GILLEN see GILLON.			
1876	GILLERAN, Owen	Blackstone,	Will,	23827
1871	GILLMARTIN, Catharine	Worcester,	Will,	23828
	GILLON AND GILLEN,			
1867	Catherine	Blackstone,	Will,	23829
1864	Charles	Milford,	Administration,	23830
1865	Charles	Milford,	Guardianship,	23831
1865	Ellen	Milford,	Guardianship,	23832
1865	George	Worcester,	Will,	23833
1865	Hugh	Milford,	Guardianship,	23834
1853	John	Blackstone,	Administration,	23835
1865	Mary	Milford,	Guardianship,	23836
1853	GILMAN, Betsey	Clinton,	Will,	23837
1868	Ella F.	Milford,	Guardianship,	23838
1866	Franklin	Worcester,	Will,	23839
1857	George A.	Westborough,	Guardianship,	23840
1857	John C.	Westborough,	Will,	23841
1857	John E.	Westborough,	Guardianship,	23842

YEAR.	NAME.	RESIDENCE.	NATURE.	CASE.
1871	GILMAN, Lewis H.	Worcester,	Guardianship,	23843
1874	Lewis H.	Worcester,	Adoption, etc.,	23844
1868	Mary L.	Milford,	Guardianship,	23845
1870	Roswell M.	Auburn,	Administration,	23846
1857	William L.	Westborough,	Guardianship,	23847
1866	GILMORE, Betsey	Westborough,	Will,	23848
1866	Charles A.	Westborough,	Will,	23849
1875	David	Northbridge,	Administration,	23850
1871	David H.	Fitchburg,	Administration,	23851
1872	Ede M.	Southborough,	Guardianship,	23852
1876	Eliza A.	Westborough,	Will,	23853
1834	George	Douglas,	Administration,	23854
1872	George N.	Southborough,	Guardianship,	23855
1862	Henry	Brookfield,	Administration,	23856
1866	Henry A.	Westborough,	Guardianship,	23857
1866	Hervey A.	Westborough,	Guardianship,	23858
1755	Isabell	Rutland,	Will,	23859
1809	James	Sutton,	Guardianship,	23860
1855	Martha A. F.	Westborough,	Guardianship,	23861
1861	Moses	Southborough,	Will,	23862
1866	Myron W.	Westborough,	Guardianship,	23863
1873	Nancy	North Brookfield,	Will,	23864
1872	Nelson	Southborough,	Administration,	23865
1861	Sarah J.	Southborough,	Guardianship,	23866
1872	Sarah S.	Southborough,	Guardianship,	23867
1739	GILSON, Jonas	Lunenburg,	Administration,	23868
1743	Jonas	Lunenburg,	Guardianship,	23869
1759	Jonas	Lunenburg,	Administration,	23870
1750	Joseph	Lunenburg,	Guardianship,	23871
1878	Merrick L.	Westminster,	Will,	23872
1749	Prudence	Lunenburg,	Guardianship,	23873
1795	GIMBEE, Cezar	Grafton,	Administration,	23874
1796	Cezar	Grafton,	Guardianship,	23875
1796	Moses	Grafton,	Guardianship,	23876
1844	Moses L.	Grafton,	Trustee,	23877
1844	Zona	Grafton,	Trustee,	23878
1839	GIPSON, Ann M.	Ashburnham,	Guardianship,	23879
1839	Caroline C.	Ashburnham,	Guardianship,	23880
1868	Dolly	Ashburnham,	Guardianship,	23881
1861	Henry	Ashburnham,	Will,	23882
1866	Henry	Lunenburg,	Will,	23883
1839	Irene A.	Ashburnham,	Guardianship,	23884
1839	Lucinda A.	Ashburnham,	Guardianship,	23885
1839	Mary H.	Ashburnham,	Guardianship,	23886
1839	William	Ashburnham,	Administration,	23887

Year.	Name.	Residence.	Nature.	Case.
1855	GIRD, Joseph W.	Worcester,	Guardianship,	23888
1864	Joseph W.	Worcester,	Will,	23888
1865	Josephine W.	Worcester,	Guardianship,	23889
	GITTIM see JITTIM.			
1877	GLADWIN, Emma H.	Worcester,	Adoption, etc.,	23890
1763	GLASFORD, James	Worcester,	Administration,	23891
1757	Jennett	Worcester,	Will,	23892
1877	GLASHEEN, Hanora	Gardner,	Administration,	23893
1875	Michael T.	Phillipston,	Administration,	23894
1839	GLASS, John	North Brookfield,	Administration,	23895
1840	John	North Brookfield,	Pension,	23896
1870	GLASSETT, Honora	Ashburnham,	Guardianship,	23897
1870	Mary	Ashburnham,	Guardianship,	23898
1870	Thomas	Ashburnham,	Guardianship,	23899
1873	GLAZIER, Abram F.	Gardner,	Administration,	23900
1864	Annie L.	Ashburnham,	Guardianship,	23901
1756	Benjamin	Lancaster,	Administration,	23902
1760	Benjamin	Lancaster,	Guardianship,	23903
1869	Charles A.	Boylston,	Guardianship,	23904
1864	Corisander S.	Ashburnham,	Guardianship,	23905
1760	Ebenezer	Lancaster,	Guardianship,	23906
1866	Elizabeth J.	Ashburnham,	Administration,	23907
1869	Ezra A.	Boylston,	Administration,	23908
1869	George E.	Boylston,	Guardianship,	23909
1869	Henry E.	Boylston,	Guardianship,	23910
1873	John	Worcester,	Will,	23911
1875	John	Worcester,	Administration,	23912
1861	John C.	Ashburnham,	Will,	23913
1765	Jonathan	Hardwick,	Guardianship,	23914
1760	Jotham	Lancaster,	Guardianship,	23915
1861	Jotham	West Boylston,	Will,	23916
1858	Lewis	Gardner,	Will,	23917
1864	Lewis	Ashburnham,	Administration,	23918
1873	Lucy K.	Gardner,	Will,	23919
1876	Mary K.	Gardner,	Will,	23920
1856	Oliver	Northborough,	Pension,	23921
1856	Oliver	Northborough,	Administration,	23922
1851	Olivia	Sturbridge,	Guardianship,	23923
1852	Orange	Fitchburg,	Administration,	23924
1851	Sewell	Sturbridge,	Administration,	23925
1869	Sherman A.	Boylston,	Guardianship,	23926
1847	Smyrna, 2d	Gardner,	Administration,	23927
1864	Sophia B.	Ashburnham,	Administration,	23928
1869	Walter H.	Boylston,	Guardianship,	23929

GLEASON, GLEESON, GLESEN, GLEZEN AND GLEAZON.

YEAR.	NAME.	RESIDENCE.	NATURE.	CASE.
1732	Aaron	Oxford,	Guardianship,	23930
1755	Abigail	Worcester,	Guardianship,	23931
1810	Abigail	Dana,	Guardianship,	23932
1841	Abigail	Princeton,	Administration,	23933
1824	Abigail H.	Worcester,	Guardianship,	23934
1818	Abijah	Oxford,	Guardianship,	23935
1855	Abijah	Millbury,	Will,	23936
1858	Ada F.	Providence, R. I.,	Guardianship,	23937
1829	Almira	Petersham,	Guardianship,	23938
1875	Ama D.	Worcester,	Will,	23939
1770	Anna	Princeton,	Guardianship,	23940
1849	Augusta	Warren,	Guardianship,	23941
1876	Austin	Worcester,	Administration,	23942
1746	Benjamin	Worcester,	Administration,	23943
1761	Benjamin	Worcester,	Guardianship,	23944
1818	Benjamin	Spencer,	Will,	23945
1869	Benjamin F.	Worcester,	Administration,	23946
1813	Benjamin W.	Petersham,	Guardianship,	23947
1807	Bourne	Worcester,	Guardianship,	23948
1870	Bourne	Worcester,	Administration,	23949
1747	Caleb	Upton,	Guardianship,	23950
1872	Caroline C.	West Brookfield,	Administration,	23951
1860	Caroline M.	West Brookfield,	Guardianship,	23952
1874	Carroll L.	Westborough,	Partition,	23953
1790	Charles	Dudley,	Will,	23954
1840	Charles	Worcester,	Guardianship,	23955
1863	Charles A.	New Braintree,	Guardianship,	23956
1819	Charles E.	Brookfield,	Guardianship,	23957
1846	Charles S.	Oxford,	Guardianship,	23958
1840	Curtis	Petersham,	Administration,	23959
1732	Daniel	Oxford,	Guardianship,	23960
1756	Daniel	Worcester,	Guardianship,	23961
1806	Daniel	Worcester,	Administration,	23962
1844	Daniel	Sutton,	Guardianship,	23963
1759	David	Oxford,	Guardianship,	23964
1762	David	Worcester,	Guardianship,	23965
1833	David	Ward,	Will,	23966
1816	David, Jr.	Ward,	Will,	23967
1860	David B.	West Brookfield,	Will,	23968
1770	Deborah	Princeton,	Guardianship,	23969
1835	Ebenezer W.	Hardwick,	Guardianship,	23970
1848	Edward	Worcester,	Guardianship,	23971
1862	Edward C.	Millbury,	Will,	23972

YEAR.	NAME.	RESIDENCE.	NATURE.	CASE.

GLEASON, GLEESON, GLESEN, GLEZEN AND GLEAZON,

YEAR.	NAME.	RESIDENCE.	NATURE.	CASE.
1839	Edwin	Worcester,	Guardianship,	23973
1776	Elijah	Oxford,	Administration,	23974
1786	Elijah	Oxford,	Guardianship,	23975
1850	Elijah	Westborough,	Will,	23976
1854	Elijah	Worcester,	Administration,	23977
1838	Elijah D.	Sutton,	Guardianship,	23978
1848	Eliphalet G.	Worcester,	Administration,	23979
1813	Eliza, etc.	Petersham,	Guardianship,	23980
1826	Eliza A.	Western,	Guardianship,	23981
1829	Eliza F.	Petersham,	Guardianship,	23982
1858	Eliza M.	Providence, R. I.,	Guardianship,	23983
1732	Elizabeth	Oxford,	Guardianship,	23984
1777	Elizabeth	Oxford,	Guardianship,	23985
1824	Elizabeth	Worcester,	Guardianship,	23986
1849	Elizabeth	Warren,	Guardianship,	23987
1861	Ella A.	Worcester,	Guardianship,	23988
1877	Ellen C.	Sturbridge,	Change of Name,	23989
1871	Ellen E.	Brookfield,	Administration,	23990
1859	Ellen F.	Shrewsbury,	Guardianship,	23991
1855	Ellen M.	Holden,	Adoption, etc.,	23992
1868	Elmira S.	Hardwick,	Guardianship,	23993
1875	Elsie H.	Princeton,	Administration,	23994
1839	Emeline	Worcester,	Guardianship,	23995
1876	Emeline	New Braintree,	Administration,	23996
1867	Esther	Worcester,	Will,	23997
1868	Eugene C.	Westborough,	Guardianship,	23998
1874	Eugene C.	Westborough,	Partition,	23999
1812	Eunice	Ward,	Guardianship,	24000
1759	Ezra	Oxford,	Guardianship,	24001
1760	Ezra	Princeton,	Administration,	24002
1763	Ezra	Oxford,	Guardianship,	24003
1811	Ezra	Ward,	Will,	24004
1847	Ezra	Princeton,	Administration,	24005
1812	Florinda	Ward,	Guardianship,	24006
1869	Francis W.	Dana,	Guardianship,	24007
1868	Frank L.	Hardwick,	Guardianship,	24008
1869	Franklin C.	Worcester,	Guardianship,	24009
1856	Frederick L.	Worcester,	Guardianship,	24010
1846	George H.	Oxford,	Guardianship,	24011
1863	George S.	West Brookfield,	Administration,	24012
1844	George W.	Worcester,	Guardianship,	24013
1866	Grace L.	Worcester,	Adoption, etc.,	24014
1876	Hale C.	Lunenburg,	Administration,	24015

YEAR.	NAME.	RESIDENCE.	NATURE.	CASE.

GLEASON, GLEESON, GLESEN, GLEZEN AND GLEAZON,

YEAR.	NAME.	RESIDENCE.	NATURE.	CASE.
1747	Hannah	Upton,	Guardianship,	24016
1856	Hannah H.	Worcester,	Guardianship,	24017
1813	Harriet	Petersham,	Guardianship,	24018
1843	Harriet	Warren,	Guardianship,	24019
1848	Harriet	Worcester,	Guardianship,	24020
1864	Helen E.	West Brookfield,	Guardianship,	24021
1856	Henry H.	Worcester,	Guardianship,	24022
1868	Herbert N.	Westborough,	Guardianship,	24023
1874	Herbert N.	Newton,	Partition,	24024
1848	Hiram	Warren,	Administration,	24025
1856	Hiram	Worcester,	Administration,	24026
1826	Huldah	Western,	Guardianship,	24027
1869	Huldah C.	Millbury,	Will,	24028
1807	Ira	Worcester,	Guardianship,	24029
1829	Ira	Worcester,	Administration,	24030
1835	Ira T.	Sutton,	Guardianship,	24031
1759	Isaac	Oxford,	Guardianship,	24032
1768	Isaac	Holden,	Administration,	24033
1776	Isaac	Worcester,	Administration,	24034
1779	Isaac	Worcester,	Will,	24035
1780	Isaac	Worcester,	Guardianship,	24036
1807	Isaac	Worcester,	Guardianship,	24037
1821	Isaac	Western,	Administration,	24038
1850	Isaac	West Brookfield,	Will,	24039
1860	Isaac	West Brookfield,	Administration,	24040
1751	Isaac, Jr.	Western,	Administration,	24041
1844	James	Worcester,	Will,	24042
1878	James	Southbridge,	Administration,	24043
1821	James F.	Worcester,	Guardianship,	24044
1868	James H.	Hardwick,	Guardianship,	24045
1817	Jason	Holden,	Guardianship,	24046
1823	Jason	Holden,	Guardianship,	24047
1765	Jesse	Princeton,	Guardianship,	24048
1819	Joel	Holden,	Administration,	24049
1843	Joel	Rutland,	Will,	24050
1817	Joel, Jr.	Holden,	Guardianship,	24051
1759	John	Rutland,	Guardianship,	24052
1779	John	Charlton,	Guardianship,	24053
1787	John	Worcester,	Administration,	24054
1818	John	Ward,	Administration,	24055
1819	John	Princeton,	Administration,	24056
1823	John	Worcester,	Administration,	24057
1824	John	Worcester,	Guardianship,	24058

YEAR.	NAME.	RESIDENCE.	NATURE.	CASE.
	GLEASON, GLEESON, GLESEN, GLEZEN AND GLEAZON.			
1825	John	Brookfield,	Will,	24059
1829	John	Petersham,	Guardianship,	24060
1840	John	Worcester,	Pension,	24061
1845	John	Dana,	Will,	24062
1819	John, Jr.	Brookfield,	Administration,	24063
1837	John, Jr.	Worcester,	Administration,	24064
1825	John B.	Western,	Administration,	24065
1856	John B.	Worcester,	Guardianship,	24066
1864	John B.	Worcester,	Administration,	24067
1874	John F.	Worcester,	Administration,	24068
1745	Jonas	Oxford,	Administration,	24069
1810	Jonathan	Dana,	Guardianship,	24070
1815	Jonathan	Western,	Administration,	24071
1819	Jonathan, 2d	Worcester,	Administration,	24072
1827	Jonathan	Worcester,	Will,	24073
1838	Jonathan	Worcester,	Will,	24074
1841	Jonathan	Worcester,	Administration,	24075
1860	Jonathan A.	Worcester,	Will,	24076
1824	Jonathan E.	Worcester,	Guardianship,	24077
1732	Joseph	Oxford,	Guardianship,	24078
1747	Joseph	Upton,	Administration,	24079
1747	Joseph	Upton,	Guardianship,	24080
1767	Joseph	Worcester,	Guardianship,	24081
1810	Joseph	Dana,	Guardianship,	24082
1814	Joseph	Petersham,	Will,	24083
1829	Joseph	Petersham,	Guardianship,	24084
1808	Joseph, Jr.	Petersham,	Administration,	24085
1819	Joseph H.	Hubbardston,	Guardianship,	24086
1817	Josiah	Oxford,	Administration,	24087
1853	Josiah	New Braintree,	Administration,	24088
1826	Julia	Western,	Guardianship,	24089
1810	Lauriston	Dana,	Guardianship,	24090
1818	Leander	Ward,	Guardianship,	24091
1868	Leslie C.	Westborough,	Guardianship,	24092
1848	Lorenzo	Worcester,	Guardianship,	24093
1813	Louisa, etc.	Petersham,	Guardianship,	24094
1817	Louisa	Holden,	Guardianship,	24095
1817	Lucy	Spencer,	Guardianship,	24096
1842	Lucy	Spencer,	Will,	24097
1817	Luthera	Holden,	Guardianship,	24098
1777	Lydia	Worcester,	Guardianship,	24099
1839	Lydia	Auburn,	Administration,	24100
1846	Lydia	Oxford,	Will,	24101

**GLEASON, GLEESON, GLESEN,
GLEZEN AND GLEAZEN.**

Year	Name	Residence	Nature	Case
1761	Marcy	Oxford,	Guardianship,	24102
1840	Maria E.	Worcester,	Guardianship,	24103
1822	Martha	Princeton,	Guardianship,	24104
1841	Martha A.	Sutton,	Guardianship,	24105
1877	Martin	Fitchburg,	Will,	24106
1759	Mary	Oxford,	Guardianship,	24107
1820	Mary	Holden,	Administration,	24108
1863	Mary	New Braintree,	Will,	24109
1867	Mary	Holden,	Administration,	24110
1807	Mary A.	Worcester,	Guardianship,	24111
1855	Mary E.	Worcester,	Adoption, etc.,	24112
1861	Mary E.	Worcester,	Guardianship,	24113
1868	Mary H.	Westborough,	Guardianship,	24114
1874	Mary H.	Westborough,	Partition,	24115
1809	Mercy	Ward,	Will,	24116
1824	Meriam	Western,	Administration,	24117
1812	Naomi	Ward,	Guardianship,	24118
1758	Nathaniel	Oxford,	Will,	24119
1806	Nathaniel	Hardwick,	Will,	24120
1817	Nathaniel C.	Spencer,	Guardianship,	24121
1870	Nelly	Webster,	Adoption, etc.,	24122
1843	Orrill	Warren,	Guardianship,	24123
1776	Persis	Worcester,	Guardianship,	24124
1856	Phebe M.	Worcester,	Guardianship,	24125
1857	Phebe T.	Dana,	Guardianship,	24126
1870	Phebe T.	Dana,	Will,	24127
1855	Philander	Worcester,	Administration,	24128
1807	Phineas	Worcester,	Guardianship,	24129
1808	Phineas	Westborough,	Will,	24130
1810	Phineas	Worcester,	Administration,	24131
1758	Phinehas	Rutland,	Will,	24132
1761	Phinehas	Worcester,	Administration,	24133
1762	Phinehas	Worcester,	Guardianship,	24134
1834	Phinehas	Princeton,	Will,	24135
1849	Phinehas	Westborough,	Administration,	24136
1849	Phinehas M.	Princeton,	Guardianship,	24137
1874	Phinehas M.	Princeton,	Will,	24137
1815	Polly	Western,	Guardianship,	24138
1829	Polly	Worcester,	Will,	24139
1732	Priscilla	Oxford,	Guardianship,	24140
1755	Priscilla	Worcester,	Guardianship,	24141
1777	Priscilla	Worcester,	Guardianship,	24142
1777	Priscilla	Worcester,	Administration,	24142

GLEASON, GLEESON, GLESEN,
GLEZEN AND GLEAZON,

Year.	Name.	Residence.	Nature.	Case.
1777	Prudence	Worcester,	Guardianship,	24143
1777	Reuben	Worcester,	Administration,	24144
1832	Reuben	Worcester,	Administration,	24145
1870	Robert S.	Worcester,	Will,	24146
1873	Rufus	Princeton,	Will,	24147
1759	Ruth	Oxford,	Guardianship,	24148
1869	Ruth	West Brookfield,	Administration,	24149
1807	Sally	Worcester,	Guardianship,	24150
1844	Samuel	Worcester,	Guardianship,	24151
1864	Samuel	Spencer,	Will,	24152
1867	Samuel	Worcester,	Administration,	24153
1879	Samuel B.	Princeton,	Will,	24154
1824	Samuel S.	Worcester,	Guardianship,	24155
1825	Sarah	Princeton,	Administration,	24156
1827	Sarah	Petersham,	Will,	24157
1776	Silas	Worcester,	Guardianship,	24158
1806	Silas	Worcester,	Administration,	24159
1807	Silas	Worcester,	Guardianship,	24160
1872	Silas	Leicester,	Will,	24161
1810	Simeon	Dana,	Administration,	24162
1839	Simeon	Worcester,	Administration,	24163
1732	Simon	Oxford,	Guardianship,	24164
1776	Solomon	Worcester,	Guardianship,	24165
1859	Sophia B.	Worcester,	Will,	24166
1843	Stephen	Warren,	Administration,	24167
1817	Sukey	Spencer,	Guardianship,	24168
1825	Sukey	Worcester,	Guardianship,	24169
1868	Theodore C.	Westborough,	Guardianship,	24170
1874	Theodore C.	Westborough,	Partition,	24171
1731	Thomas	Oxford,	Administration,	24172
1755	Thomas	Worcester,	Administration,	24173
1756	Thomas	Worcester,	Guardianship,	24174
1759	Thomas	Rutland,	Guardianship,	24175
1777	Thomas	Oxford,	Guardianship,	24176
1817	Thomas	Hubbardston,	Will,	24177
1757	Thomas, Jr.	Oxford,	Administration,	24178
1780	Timothy	Worcester,	Guardianship,	25179
1841	Timothy	Sutton,	Will,	24180
1776	Uriah	Charlton,	Administration,	24181
1869	Walter F.	Worcester,	Guardianship,	24182
1826	Wealthy	Western,	Guardianship,	24183
1819	Wealthy J.	Brookfield,	Guardianship,	24184
1857	Williams A.	Dana,	Guardianship,	24185

GLEASON, GLEESON, GLESEN,
GLEZEN AND GLEAZON,

YEAR.	NAME.	RESIDENCE.	NATURE.	CASE.
1867	Williams A.	Dana,	Administration,	24186
1819	William L.	Brookfield,	Guardianship,	24187
1863	William P.	New Braintree,	Guardianship,	24188
1868	Zebina	Westborough,	Administration,	24189
1868	Zebina A.	Westborough,	Guardianship,	24190
1874	Zebina A.	Westborough,	Partition,	24191
1777	Zuba	Worcester,	Guardianship,	24192
1872	GLENNEN, Bernard	Worcester,	Administration,	24193
1873	Catharine E.	Worcester,	Guardianship,	24194
1873	Ellen	Worcester,	Guardianship,	24195
1873	Hannah	Worcester,	Guardianship,	24196
1873	Mary T.	Worcester,	Guardianship,	24197
1873	Thomas	Worcester,	Guardianship,	24198

GLESEN AND GLEZEN see
GLEASON.

YEAR.	NAME.	RESIDENCE.	NATURE.	CASE.
1875	GLORY, Edward	Webster,	Administration,	24199
1869	GLOUCESTER, William	Milford,	Guardianship,	24200
1814	GLOVER, Henry	Westborough,	Guardianship,	24201
1864	Henry	Oxford,	Will,	24202
1813	Lewis	Westborough,	Guardianship,	24203
1825	Lowel	Grafton,	Administration,	24204
1817	Lowell	Grafton,	Guardianship,	24205
1860	Mary	Waterbury, Vt.,	Administration,	24206
1842	Mary A.	Leominster,	Administration,	24207
1814	Moses M.	Grafton,	Guardianship,	24208
1867	GLUFLING, James, Jr.	Templeton,	Guardianship,	24209

GODDARD AND GODARD,

YEAR.	NAME.	RESIDENCE.	NATURE.	CASE.
1856	Abby A.	Worcester,	Guardianship,	24210
1802	Abiel	Athol,	Guardianship,	24211
1762	Abigail	Athol,	Guardianship,	24212
1880	Ada L.	Charlton,	Guardianship,	24213
1864	Alice R.	Athol,	Guardianship,	24214
1817	Anna S.	Petersham,	Guardianship,	24215
1880	Artemas	Charlton,	Guardianship,	24216
1880	Asa	Charlton,	Guardianship,	24217
1849	Asahel	Millbury,	Administration,	24218
1856	Asenath	Paxton,	Will,	24219
1855	Ashbel	Petersham,	Will,	24220
1803	Asbbell	Athol,	Guardianship,	24221
1829	Augustus N.	Brookfield,	Guardianship,	24222
1754	Benjamin	Shrewsbury,	Will,	24223
1759	Benjamin	Grafton,	Administration,	24224
1762	Benjamin	Athol,	Guardianship,	24225

YEAR.	NAME.	RESIDENCE.	NATURE.	CASE.
	GODDARD and GODARD,			
1806	Benjamin	Grafton,	Will,	24226
1807	Benjamin	Royalston,	Guardianship,	24227
1835	Benjamin	Shrewsbury,	Administration,	24228
1842	Benjamin	Holden,	Administration,	24229
1870	Benjamin	Worcester,	Will,	24230
1857	Betsey	Northborough,	Administration,	24231
1877	Betsey	Royalston,	Will,	24232
1762	Bette	Athol,	Guardianship,	24233
1839	Calvin	Petersham,	Will,	24234
1865	Charles	Grafton,	Will,	24235
1858	Czarina W.	Royalston,	Will,	24236
1807	Danforth	Royalston,	Guardianship,	24237
1789	Daniel	Petersham,	Guardianship,	24238
1803	Daniel	Athol,	Guardianship,	24239
1807	Daniel	Shrewsbury,	Will,	24240
1795	Daniel, Jr.	Shrewsbury,	Will,	24241
1754	David	Leicester,	Guardianship,	24242
1754	David	Leicester,	Will,	24243
1778	David	Athol,	Administration,	24244
1847	David	Petersham,	Will,	24245
1874	David	Athol,	Administration,	24246
1835	Eben	Lancaster,	Pension,	24247
1754	Ebenezer	Leicester,	Guardianship,	24248
1762	Ebenezer	Athol,	Will,	24249
1762	Ebenezer	Athol,	Guardianship,	24250
1803	Eber	Athol,	Guardianship,	24251
1754	Edward	Leicester,	Guardianship,	24252
1758	Edward	Shrewsbury,	Guardianship,	24253
1762	Edward	Athol,	Guardianship,	24254
1777	Edward	Shrewsbury,	Will,	24255
1782	Edward	Shrewsbury,	Will,	24256
1837	Edward P.	Worcester,	Guardianship,	24257
1862	Edward P.	Hawkesbury, Can.,	Foreign Will,	24258
1854	Elijah	Athol,	Will,	24259
1784	Elisha	Sutton,	Will,	24260
1856	Eliza J.	Worcester,	Guardianship,	24261
1863	Elizabeth	Paxton,	Administration,	24262
1808	Elmira K.	Sutton,	Guardianship,	24263
1762	Esther	Athol,	Guardianship,	24264
1854	Eunice	Worcester,	Will,	24265
1868	Ezra	Worcester,	Will,	24266
1867	Fanny A.	Shrewsbury,	Will,	24267
1866	Fanny B.	Landis, N. J.,	Guardianship,	24268
1845	Frances C.	Worcester,	Guardianship,	24269

Year.	Name.	Residence.	Nature.	Case.
	GODDARD and GODARD,			
1869	Francis	Athol,	Will,	24270
1851	Frederick B.	Millbury,	Guardianship,	24271
1832	Gardner,	Shrewsbury,	Guardianship,	24272
1864	George	Westminster,	Administration,	24273
1878	George	Upton,	Will,	24274
1845	George II.	Worcester,	Guardianship,	24275
1855	George S.	Charlton,	Guardianship,	24276
1877	Goodell	Athol,	Will,	24277
1759	Hanah	Grafton,	Guardianship,	24278
1817	Hannah	Petersham,	Guardianship,	24279
1855	Harlan P.	Leominster,	Guardianship,	24280
1863	Harriet B.	Grafton,	Administration,	24281
1797	Harriot M.	Shrewsbury,	Guardianship,	24282
1848	Henry	Royalston,	Administration,	24283
1845	Henry H.	Worcester,	Guardianship,	24284
1781	Hepzibah	Shrewsbury,	Will,	24285
1860	Herman P.	Templeton,	Administration,	24286
1863	Hollis	Athol,	Administration,	24287
1735	Hugh	Boston,	Guardianship,	24288
1792	Huldah	Sutton,	Administration,	24289
1793	Huldah	Sutton,	Guardianship,	24290
1855	Huldah	Grafton,	Administration,	24291
1874	Ira T.	Athol,	Guardianship,	24292
1862	Isaac	Worcester,	Will,	24293
1761	James	Grafton,	Guardianship,	24294
1815	James	Berlin,	Will,	24295
1842	James	Berlin,	Will,	24296
1854	James	Berlin,	Guardianship,	24297
1870	Joel	Fitchburg,	Will,	24298
1880	Joel	Webster,	Administration,	24299
1785	John	Worcester,	Will,	24300
1807	John	Sutton,	Will,	24301
1817	John B.	Petersham,	Guardianship,	24302
1867	John D.	Shrewsbury,	Inventory,	24303
1836	Joseph	Worcester,	Administration,	24304
1879	Joseph	New Braintree,	Administration,	24305
1837	Joseph C.	Worcester,	Guardianship,	24306
1784	Josiah	Sutton,	Administration,	24307
1801	Josiah	Athol,	Administration,	24308
1873	J. Williams	Athol,	Administration,	24309
1848	Keziah	Berlin,	Will,	24310
1852	Lucretia	Worcester,	Will,	24311
1852	Lucy	Lancaster,	Will,	24312
1852	Lucy	Lancaster,	Pension,	24313

YEAR.	NAME.	RESIDENCE.	NATURE.	CASE.
	GODDARD AND GODARD,			
1855	Lucy	Royalston,	Guardianship,	24314
1855	Lucy	Worcester,	Will,	24315
1869	Lucy S.	Westborough,	Adoption, etc.,	24316
1814	Luther	Leicester,	Administration,	24317
1842	Luther	Worcester,	Will,	24318
1796	Lydia	Westminster,	Will,	24319
1846	Martha	Holden,	Administration,	24320
1754	Mary	Leicester,	Guardianship,	24321
1759	Mary	Grafton,	Guardianship,	24322
1762	Mary	Athol,	Guardianship,	24323
1817	Mary	Petersham,	Guardianship,	24324
1817	Mary	Worcester,	Will,	24325
. 1859	Mary A.	Worcester,	Administration,	24326
1855	Mary C.	Leominster,	Guardianship,	24327
1849	Mary E.	Millbury,	Guardianship,	24328
1873	Mary F.	Charlton,	Administration,	24329
1855	Mary T.	Royalston,	Guardianship,	24330
1797	Mary W.	Shrewsbury,	Guardianship,	24331
1874	Mary W.	Sterling,	Will,	24332
1851	Mehetabel	Worcester,	Will,	24333
1872	Mehitable	Athol,	Will,	24334
1754	Mercy	Leicester,	Guardianship,	24335
1878	Minnie A.	Worcester,	Guardianship,	24336
1864	Moses E.	Athol,	Guardianship,	24337
1803	Nabby	Athol,	Guardianship,	24338
1802	Nahum	Athol,	Guardianship,	24339
1858	Nahum	Royalston,	Will,	24340
1807	Nathaniel	Royalston,	Guardianship,	24341
1817	Nathaniel	Petersham,	Administration,	24342
1888	Nathaniel	Millbury,	Releases,	24343
1855	Obadiah W.	Royalston,	Will,	24344
1856	Orlando J.	Worcester,	Guardianship,	24345
1878	Orlando J.	Worcester,	Administration,	24346
1870	Parley	Worcester,	Will,	24347
1856	Patty	Holden,	Administration,	24348
1778	Phebe	Athol,	Guardianship,	24349
1859	Pliny M.	Berlin,	Guardianship,	24350
1793	Polly	Sutton,	Guardianship,	24351
1867	Priscilla	Grafton,	Administration,	24352
1856	Rebecca N.	Worcester,	Guardianship,	24353
1865	Rebecca W.	Royalston,	Guardianship,	24354
1862	Rebekah	Shrewsbury,	Administration,	24355
1803	Rhoda	Athol,	Guardianship,	24356
1785	Robert	Sutton,	Will,	24357

GODDARD AND GODARD,

YEAR.	NAME.	RESIDENCE.	NATURE.	CASE.
1807	Robert	Petersham,	Administration,	24358
1802	Sally	Athol,	Guardianship,	24359
1847	Sally	Holden,	Administration,	24360
1841	Salmon	Royalston,	Will,	24361
1762	Samuel	Athol,	Guardianship,	24362
1803	Samuel	Worcester,	Will,	24363
1806	Samuel	Royalston,	Administration,	24364
1856	Samuel	Shrewsbury,	Administration,	24365
1859	Samuel	Worcester,	Administration,	24366
1846	Samuel G.	Fitchburg,	Administration,	24367
1760	Samuell	Grafton,	Guardianship,	24368
1778	Sarah	Athol,	Guardianship,	24369
1865	Sarah H.	Barre,	Adoption, etc.,	24370
1872	Sarah H.	Barre,	Guardianship,	24371
1809	Silas	Gerry,	Administration,	24372
1758	Simon	Shrewsbury,	Will,	24373
1806	Simon, Jr.	Gerry,	Will,	24374
1762	Sophia	Athol,	Guardianship,	24375
1854	Sophia	Shrewsbury,	Administration,	24376
1854	Sophia	Shrewsbury,	Pension,	24377
1856	Stephen	Petersham,	Administration,	24378
1867	Stephen	Boylston,	Will,	24379
1754	Susanna	Leicester,	Guardianship,	24380
1853	Sylvia	Lancaster,	Will,	24381
1856	Sylvia S.	Worcester,	Guardianship,	24382
1807	Tamar	Royalston,	Guardianship,	24383
1808	Tamar H.	Sutton,	Guardianship,	24384
1880	Tamar H.	Sutton,	Administration,	24385
1859	Virgil	Berlin,	Guardianship,	24386
1864	Wesley D.	Royalston,	Administration,	24387
1754	William	Leicester,	Guardianship,	24388
1786	William	Berlin,	Guardianship,	24389
1788	William	Petersham,	Administration,	24390
1850	William	Fitchburg,	Administration,	24391
1845	William E.	Worcester,	Guardianship,	24392
1875	GODDING, Alvah	Winchendon,	Will,	24393
1871	Ellen R.	Taunton,	Partition,	24394
1862	GODFREY, Anna R.	Milford,	Guardianship,	24395
1796	Asa	Westborough,	Guardianship,	24396
1822	Benjamin	Milford,	Will,	24397
1806	Benjamin, Jr.	Milford,	Guardianship,	24398
1862	Charles B.	Milford,	Guardianship,	24399
1806	Charlotte F.	Milford,	Guardianship,	24400
1853	David S.	Milford,	Will,	24401

YEAR.	NAME.	RESIDENCE.	NATURE.	CASE.
1855	GODFREY, David S.	Milford,	Guardianship,	24402
1806	Hopestill	Milford,	Guardianship,	24403
1794	James	Westborough,	Administration,	24404
1862	Lydia B.	Milford,	Guardianship,	24405
1806	Mary	Milford,	Guardianship,	24406
1861	Nancy	Milford,	Will,	24407
1796	Salmon	Westborough,	Guardianship,	24408
1817	Samuel A.	Barre,	Administration,	24409
1806	Samuel W.	Milford,	Guardianship,	24410
1827	Sarah	Milford,	Guardianship,	24411
1862	Stearns	Milford,	Guardianship,	24412
1796	Sullivan	Westborough,	Guardianship,	24413
1806	William	Milford,	Guardianship,	24414
1839	William	Milford,	Administration,	24415
1817	William B.	Barre,	Guardianship,	24416
1880	GODINSKI, Isaac	Worcester,	Guardianship,	24417
1866	GODMAN, Anna F.	Delaware, O.,	Guardianship,	24418
1752	Comfort	Mendon,	Guardianship,	24419
1751	James	Mendon,	Administration,	24420
1752	John	Mendon,	Guardianship,	24421
1867	GOEN, Mary	Templeton,	Administration,	24422
	GOFFE see GOUGH.			
1864	GOHERY, Catharine	Clinton,	Guardianship,	24423
1864	Ellen	Clinton,	Guardianship,	24424
1864	John	Clinton,	Guardianship,	24425
1863	Michael	Clinton,	Administration,	24426
1873	GOLDEN, Barney	Worcester,	Administration,	24427
1868	Peter	Leominster,	Administration,	24428
1873	GOLDSMITH, Jonathan G.	Templeton,	Will,	24429
1824	Richard	Harvard,	Will,	24430
1859	Theodore	Harvard,	Will,	24431
	GOLDTHWAITE AND GOLD-THWAIT,			
1854	Alery	Uxbridge,	Guardianship,	24432
1804	Betsey	Northbridge,	Guardianship,	24433
1879	Charles	Northbridge,	Will,	24434
1843	Chloe	Northbridge,	Administration,	24435
1860	Constantine	Northbridge,	Administration,	24436
1876	Cynthia	Northbridge,	Administration,	24437
1832	Gershom C.	Northbridge,	Guardianship,	24438
1804	Jacob	Northbridge,	Administration,	24439
1846	James	Uxbridge,	Administration,	24440
1870	Josiah	Northbridge,	Administration,	24441
1853	Mary	Northbridge,	Will,	24442
1877	Mary D.	Uxbridge,	Administration,	24443

YEAR.	NAME.	RESIDENCE.	NATURE.	CASE.
	GOLDTHWAITE AND GOLD-THWAIT,			
1847	Mercy T.	Worcester,	Administration,	24444
1858	Nancy	Northbridge,	Administration,	24445
1842	Nathan	Worcester,	Administration,	24446
1858	Obed	Northbridge,	Administration,	24447
1826	Patience	Northbridge,	Administration,	24448
1860	Persis	Worcester,	Administration,	24449
1871	Peter	Northbridge,	Guardianship,	24450
1878	Peter	Uxbridge,	Will,	24451
1804	Rachel	Northbridge,	Guardianship,	24452
1788	Samuel	Northbridge,	Guardianship,	24453
1794	Stephen	Sutton,	Guardianship,	24454
1812	Stephen	Northbridge,	Administration,	24455
1817	Stephen	Northbridge,	Guardianship,	24456
1832	Stephen	Northbridge,	Administration,	24456
1880	Stephen	Uxbridge,	Administration,	24457
1846	Thomas	Northbridge,	Will,	24458
1814	Verry	Northbridge,	Guardianship,	24459
	GOODELL, GOODALE AND GOODALL,			
1757	Aaron	Shrewsbury,	Guardianship,	24460
1817	Aaron	West Boylston,	Will,	24461
1818	Aaron	West Boylston,	Guardianship,	24462
1840	Aaron	West Boylston,	Will,	24463
1840	Aaron	West Boylston,	Guardianship,	24464
1853	Abel	West Boylston,	Will,	24465
1835	Abraham	Charlton,	Will,	24466
1872	Aggie M.	Johnstown, N. Y.,	Guardianship,	24467
1821	Almira N.	West Boylston,	Guardianship,	24468
1829	Almira P.	Spencer,	Guardianship,	24469
1829	Alvira	Rutland,	Guardianship,	24470
1747	Amos	Sutton,	Administration,	24471
1748	Amos	Sutton,	Guardianship,	24472
1757	Anna	Brookfield,	Guardianship,	24473
1770	Asa	Sutton,	Guardianship,	24474
1833	Asa	Millbury,	Will,	24475
1876	Asa	Woodstock, Conn.,	Administration,	24476
1824	Asa, Jr.	Millbury,	Administration,	24477
1853	Austin	Millbury,	Guardianship,	24478
1872	Austin	Millbury,	Administration,	24479
1801	Benjamin	Sturbridge,	Administration,	24480
1872	Betsey D.	Clinton,	Will,	24481
1821	Betsey T.	West Boylston,	Guardianship,	24482
1770	Bettee	Sutton,	Guardianship,	24483

YEAR.	NAME.	RESIDENCE.	NATURE.	CASE.
	GOODELL, GOODALE AND GOODALL,			
1837	Betty	West Boylston,	Will,	24484
1841	Caroline	West Boylston,	Guardianship,	24485
1873	Caroline H.	Worcester,	Adoption, etc.,	24486
1858	Catherine S.	Saco, Me.,	Foreign Will,	24487
1863	Charles F.	North Brookfield,	Guardianship,	24488
1802	Chester K.	Sturbridge,	Guardianship,	24489
1757	David	Shrewsbury,	Guardianship,	24490
1833	David	Oakham,	Will,	24491
1826	David, Jr.	Oakham,	Will,	24492
1802	Ebenezer W.	Sutton,	Guardianship,	24493
1846	Ebenezer W.	Millbury,	Administration,	24494
1756	Edward	Shrewsbury,	Administration,	24495
1818	Edward	West Boylston,	Guardianship,	24496
1853	Edwin	Millbury,	Guardianship,	24497
1740	Eleazer	Sutton,	Will,	24498
1745	Eleazer	Sutton,	Guardianship,	24499
1769	Eleazer	Sutton,	Administration,	24500
1757	Elizabeth	Shrewsbury,	Guardianship,	24501
1826	Elvira	Rutland,	Guardianship,	24502
1821	Eunice B.	West Boylston,	Guardianship,	24503
1830	Eunice B.	West Boylston,	Guardianship,	24504
1835	Ezra	Boylston,	Guardianship,	24505
1874	George F.	Clinton,	Will,	24506
1830	George W.	West Boylston,	Guardianship,	24507
1795	Hannah	Pomfret, Conn.,	Foreign Will,	24508
1818	Hannah	West Boylston,	Guardianship,	24509
1858	Hannah L.	Millbury,	Will,	24510
1830	Harriet	West Boylston,	Guardianship,	24511
1863	Harriet E.	North Brookfield,	Guardianship,	24512
1802	Harriot	Sturbridge,	Guardianship,	24513
1877	Hosea B.	North Brookfield,	Administration,	24514
1868	Ida M. W.	Worcester,	Guardianship,	24515
1880	Isaac N.	Southbridge,	Administration,	24516
1852	Jason	Winchendon,	Administration,	24517
1849	Jeduthan	Dudley,	Will,	24518
1765	Joel	Lancaster,	Guardianship,	24519
1747	John	Sutton,	Guardianship,	24520
1770	John	Sutton,	Guardianship,	24521
1818	John	Millbury,	Will,	24522
1823	John	Westminster,	Will,	24523
1824	John	Rutland,	Administration,	24524
1827	John	Worcester,	Will,	24525
1820	John A.	Millbury,	Guardianship,	24526

	GOODELL, GOODALE AND GOODALL,			
1863	John H.	North Brookfield,	Guardianship,	24527
1826	John M.	Rutland,	Guardianship,	24528
1873	John W.	Southbridge,	Administration,	24529
1849	Jonathan	Athol,	Administration,	24530
1830	Jonathan M.	West Boylston,	Guardianship,	24531
1849	Jonathan W., etc.	Athol,	Guardianship,	24532
1790	Joseph	Athol,	Administration,	24533
1770	Joshua	Sutton,	Guardianship,	24534
1807	Joshua	Rutland,	Administration,	24535
1812	Joshua E.	Rutland,	Guardianship,	24536
1857	Laura	Sturbridge,	Administration,	24537
1854	Levi	West Boylston,	Will,	24538
1830	Levi, Jr.	West Boylston,	Guardianship,	24539
1830	Louisa M.	West Boylston,	Guardianship,	24540
1836	Lucy H. P.	Sutton,	Will,	24541
1853	Lydia A.	Millbury,	Guardianship,	24542
1870	Lyman	Millbury,	Will,	24543
1747	Mary	Sutton,	Guardianship,	24544
1770	Mary	Sutton,	Guardianship,	24545
1825	Mary	Westminster,	Will,	24546
1864	Mary J.	Barre,	Administration,	24547
1821	Mary M.	West Boylston,	Guardianship,	24548
1858	Mehitable	West Boylston,	Will,	24549
1757	Moses	Shrewsbury,	Guardianship,	24550
1815	Moses	West Boylston,	Will,	24551
1757	Nathan	Brookfield,	Guardianship,	24552
1762	Nathan	Lancaster,	Will,	24553
1765	Nathan	Lancaster,	Guardianship,	24554
1814	Nathaniel	Charlton,	Administration,	24555
1818	Norman H.	West Boylston,	Guardianship,	24556
1879	Norman H., Jr.	Worcester,	Administration,	24557
1818	Normas	West Boylston,	Guardianship,	24558
1826	Orra	Millbury,	Will,	24559
1757	Paul	Shrewsbury,	Guardianship,	24560
1829	Paul	West Boylston,	Will,	24561
1830	Paul	West Boylston,	Guardianship,	24562
1847	Paul	Worcester,	Administration,	24563
1839	Persis	Athol,	Will,	24564
1757	Peter	Shrewsbury,	Guardianship,	24565
1834	Peter	West Boylston,	Administration,	24566
1802	Polly	Sutton,	Guardianship,	24567
1802	Ralph	Sturbridge,	Guardianship,	24568
1877	Raymond D.	North Brookfield,	Guardianship,	24569

YEAR.	NAME.	RESIDENCE.	NATURE.	CASE.
	GOODELL, GOODALE AND **GOODALL,**			
1741	Rebecca	Sutton,	Guardianship,	24570
1858	Releaf	Millbury,	Will,	24571
1802	Relief	Sutton,	Guardianship,	24572
1880	Robert B. T.	Boylston,	Will,	24573
1802	Roxalana	Sturbridge,	Guardianship,	24574
1818	Sally	West Boylston,	Guardianship,	24575
1873	Sally	Westminster,	Will,	24576
1734	Samuel	Woodstock,	Guardianship,	24577
1769	Samuel	Sutton,	Administration,	24578
1770	Samuel	Sutton,	Guardianship,	24579
1800	Samuel	Sutton,	Will,	24580
1802	Samuel	Sutton,	Guardianship,	24581
1853	Samuel	Millbury,	Guardianship,	24582
1879	Samuel A.	Oakham,	Guardianship,	24583
1879	Samuel A.	Oakham,	Administration,	24583
1830	Samuel D.	West Boylston,	Guardianship,	24584
1812	Sarah L.	Rutland,	Guardianship,	24585
1858	Sarah W.	Millbury,	Will,	24586
1796	Silence	Sutton,	Administration,	24587
1832	Silence	West Boylston,	Guardianship,	24588
1830	Simon	West Boylston,	Guardianship,	24589
1853	Simon	Millbury,	Guardianship,	54590
1744	Solomon	Brookfield,	Will,	24591
1757	Solomon	Brookfield,	Guardianship,	24592
1853	Susan E.	Millbury,	Guardianship,	24593
1818	Susana	West Boylston,	Guardianship,	24594
1821	Susanna P.	West Boylston,	Guardianship,	24595
1788	Timothy	Athol,	Guardianship,	24596
1880	Ulysses A.	Southbridge,	Guardianship,	24597
1802	Ward	Sturbridge,	Guardianship,	24598
1765	William	Lancaster,	Guardianship,	24599
1880	William	Clinton,	Will,	24600
1853	William A.	Millbury,	Guardianship,	24601
1879	William D.	Fitchburg,	Will,	24602
1863	William F.	North Brookfield,	Guardianship,	24603
1849	Wyman, etc.	Athol,	Guardianship,	24604
1808	Zachariah	Charlton,	Administration,	24605
	GOODENOW see **GOODNOW.**			
1858	**GOODHUE,** Anna	Lancaster,	Administration,	24606
1814	Anna W.	Salem,	Guardianship,	24607
1881	Benjamin W., Jr.	Chicago, Ill.,	Foreign Sale,	24608
1871	Elizabeth S.	Beloit, Wis.,	Foreign Sale,	24609
1871	Elizabeth S.	Beloit, Wis.,	Foreign Will,	24609

YEAR.	NAME.	RESIDENCE.	NATURE.	CASE.
1881	GOODHUE, Gilbert H.	Chicago, Ill.,	Foreign Sale,	24610
1879	GOODIER, Samuel	Southbridge,	Will,	24611
1874	GOODMAN, Allen	Dana,	Guardianship,	24612
1874	Allen	Dana,	Administration,	24612
1879	Dora M.	Dana,	Guardianship,	24613
	GOODNOW, GOODENOW AND GOODENOUGH,			
1858	Abbie L.	Fitchburg,	Guardianship,	24614
1848	Abby C.	Sterling,	Guardianship,	24615
1805	Abel M.	Boylston,	Administration,	24616
1806	Abel M.	Boylston,	Guardianship,	24617
1839	Abigail	Paxton,	Guardianship,	24618
1845	Abigail	Leicester,	Administration,	24618
1806	Amettai	Boylston,	Guardianship,	24619
1807	Amittai	Boylston	Administration,	24620
1783	Anne	Hubbardston,	Guardianship,	24621
1798	Artemas	Princeton,	Guardianship,	24622
1798	Asa	Princeton,	Guardianship,	24623
1814	Asa	Northborough,	Will,	24624
1834	Asa	Bucksport, Me.,	Administration,	24625
1845	Augusta R.	Grafton,	Guardianship,	24626
1845	Augustus	Grafton,	Administration,	24627
1793	Beulah	Paxton,	Administration,	24628
1798	Calvin	Princeton,	Guardianship,	24629
1801	Daniel	Petersham,	Guardianship,	24630
1778	David	Lancaster,	Will,	24631
1839	David T.	Southborough,	Guardianship,	24632
1798	Edward	Princeton,	Administration,	24633
1855	Edward	Princeton,	Will,	24634
1821	Eli	Northborough,	Guardianship,	24635
1821	Elijah	West Boylston,	Administration,	24636
1759	Elizabeth	Hardwick,	Guardianship,	24637
1802	Elizabeth	Petersham,	Guardianship,	24638
1835	Emeline	Templeton,	Guardianship,	24639
1789	Ephraim	Boylston,	Guardianship,	24640
1828	Eunice	West Boylston,	Administration,	24641
1835	George H.	Templeton,	Guardianship,	24642
1813	George W.	Paxton,	Guardianship,	24643
1759	Hannah	Hardwick,	Guardianship,	24644
1848	Harriet E.	Sterling,	Guardianship,	24645
1806	Harrison D.	Boylston,	Guardianship,	24646
1806	Henry	Boylston,	Guardianship,	24647
1835	Hepsey	Templeton,	Guardianship,	24648
1845	Hull	Rutland,	Administration,	24649
1865	James O.	Rutland,	Guardianship,	24650

GOODNOW, GOODENOW AND GOODENOUGH,

YEAR.	NAME.	RESIDENCE.	NATURE.	CASE.
1828	Jerusha H.	Princeton,	Guardianship,	24651
1801	Jesse	Petersham,	Administration,	24652
1822	Joel	Westminster,	Guardianship,	24653
1798	John	Princeton,	Guardianship,	24654
1802	John	Petersham,	Guardianship,	24655
1870	John, etc.	Worcester,	Will,	24656
1811	Jonas	Boylston,	Will,	24657
1828	Jonas	Southborough,	Administration,	24658
1835	Jonas	Southborough,	Guardianship,	24659
1844	Jonas	Southborough,	Guardianship,	24660
1848	Jonas	Shrewsbury,	Guardianship,	24661
1848	Jonas B.	Sterling,	Administration,	24662
1750	Jonathan	Hardwick,	Administration,	24663
1828	Jones	West Boylston,	Guardianship,	24664
1801	Joseph	Petersham,	Guardianship,	24665
1815	Joseph	Boylston,	Guardianship,	24666
1821	Josiah W.	Petersham,	Will,	24667
1783	Jotham	Hubbardston,	Guardianship,	24668
1835	Jotham	Templeton,	Guardianship,	24669
1789	Levi	Boylston,	Guardianship,	24670
1858	Lizzie L.	Fitchburg,	Guardianship,	24671
1842	Lois	Princeton,	Will,	24672
1865	Lucretia P.	Rutland,	Guardianship,	24673
1808	Lucy	Petersham,	Guardianship,	24674
1858	Lyman H.	Fitchburg,	Guardianship,	24675
1866	Lyman H.	Ashburnham,	Administration,	24676
1835	Martha	Southborough,	Guardianship,	24677
1826	Mary	Boylston,	Administration,	24678
1835	Mary A.	Templeton,	Guardianship,	24679
1869	Mary A.	Arlington, Vt.,	Adoption, etc.,	24680
1822	Mary B.	Petersham,	Guardianship,	24681
1872	Merance	Spencer,	Will,	24682
1881	Minnie M.	Clinton,	Administration,	24683
1848	Nathaniel	Shrewsbury,	Administration,	24684
1861	Nellie P.	Upton,	Adoption, etc.,	24685
1782	Peter	Hubbardston,	Administration,	24686
1783	Peter	Hubbardston,	Guardianship,	24687
1798	Peter	Princeton,	Guardianship,	24688
1806	Polly	Boylston,	Guardianship,	24689
1831	Rebecca	Southborough,	Administration,	24690
1878	Roxselana	Athol,	Will,	24691
1806	Sally	Boylston,	Guardianship,	24692
1801	Samuel	Petersham,	Guardianship,	24693

GOODNOW, GOODENOW AND GOODENOUGH,

1822	Sarah S.	Petersham,	Guardianship,	24694
1828	Silas H.	West Boylston,	Guardianship,	24695
1858	Silas H.	Fitchburg,	Administration,	24696
1789	Stephen	Boylston,	Guardianship,	24697
1798	Sukey	Princeton,	Guardianship,	24698
1835	Susan	Templeton,	Guardianship,	24699
1799	Thomas	Northborough,	Will,	24700
1798	William	Princeton,	Guardianship,	24701
1801	William	Petersham,	Guardianship,	24702
1828	William E.	Princeton,	Guardianship,	24703
1865	Windsor W.	Bolton,	Guardianship,	24704

GOODRICH AND GOODRIDGE,

1847	Abby F.	Fitchburg,	Guardianship,	24705
1842	Abijah	Fitchburg,	Will,	24706
1842	Abijah	Fitchburg,	Pension,	24707
1828	Albert	Fitchburg,	Guardianship,	24708
1881	Alice J.	Grafton,	Adoption, etc.,	24709
1855	Amelia F.	Worcester,	Administration,	24710
1773	Benjamin	Lunenburg,	Administration,	24711
1824	Benjamin	Winchendon,	Administration,	24712
1834	Benjamin	Lunenburg,	Administration,	24713
1868	Benjamin	Lunenburg,	Administration,	24714
1877	Betsey	Lunenburg,	Administration,	24715
1820	Betsy B.	Winchendon,	Guardianship,	24716
1814	Butler	Rutland,	Guardianship,	24717
1814	Calvin	Winchendon,	Administration,	24718
1820	Calvin G.	Winchendon,	Guardianship,	24719
1847	Charles A.	Fitchburg,	Guardianship,	24720
1814	Charles B.	Rutland,	Guardianship,	24721
1869	Daniel	Lunenburg,	Will,	24722
1734	David	Lunenburg,	Guardianship,	24723
1786	David	Fitchburg,	Will,	24724
1813	David	Winchendon,	Will,	24725
1819	David	Winchendon,	Administration,	24726
1820	David J.	Winchendon,	Guardianship,	24727
1863	Edmund	West Brookfield,	Will,	24728
1814	Eli R.	Rutland,	Guardianship,	24729
1818	Eliphalet	Winchendon,	Partition,	24730
1879	Elizabeth D.	Worcester,	Will,	24731
1777	Ezekiel	Lunenburg,	Administration,	24732
1778	Francis	Lunenburg,	Guardianship,	24733
1869	George D.	Worcester,	Guardianship,	24734
1870	George D.	Worcester,	Administration,	24734

NAME.	RESIDENCE.	NATURE.	CASE.
GOODRICH and GOODRIDGE,			
Gideon	Winchendon,	Guardianship,	24735
Hannah	Fitchburg,	Administration,	24736
Hezekiah	Rutland,	Will,	24737
Jefferson A.	Fitchburg,	Administration,	24738
Jesse W.	Worcester,	Administration,	24739
Joseph	Lunenburg,	Guardianship,	24740
Joseph	Lunenburg,	Administration,	24741
Joseph P.	Lunenburg,	Guardianship,	24742
Joshua	Lunenburg,	Will,	24743
Joshua	Lunenburg,	Will,	24744
Joshua '	Fitchburg,	Will,	24745
Laura A.	Lunenburg,	Guardianship,	24746
Levi	Lunenburg,	Will,	24747
Lewis A.	Lunenburg,	Administration,	24748
Lucy M.	Northborough,	Guardianship,	24749
Luther	Fitchburg,	Administration,	24750
Maria	Lunenburg,	Guardianship,	24751
Mary	Rutland,	Administration,	24752
Mary	Lunenburg,	Administration,	24753
Mary A.	Winchendon,	Guardianship,	24754
Mary A.	Fitchburg,	Guardianship,	24755
Mary A.	Lunenburg,	Guardianship,	24756
Melia	Worcester,	Administration,	24757
Nancy B.	Fitchburg,	Guardianship,	24758
Naomi A.	Lunenburg,	Guardianship,	24759
Orilla	Lunenburg,	Guardianship,	24760
Phillip	Lunenburg,	Administration,	24761
Phillip, Jr.	Lunenburg,	Administration,	24762
Phinehas	Lunenburg,	Will,	24763
Samuel P.	Winchendon,	Administration,	24764
Sewall	Leicester,	Administration,	24765
Simon	Lunenburg,	Will,	24766
Susanna H.	Winchendon,	Guardianship,	24767
Walter E.	Leicester,	Guardianship,	24768
Zabdiel	Lunenburg,	Administration,	24769
GOODSPEED, Amelia	Leominster,	Will,	24770
Betsy	Hubbardston,	Administration,	24771
Charles	Worcester,	Administration,	24772
Charles E.	Gardner,	Guardianship,	24773
Daniel J.	Gardner,	Administration,	24774
Elizabeth	Hubbardston,	Guardianship,	24775
Frank H.	Gardner,	Guardianship,	24776
Harriet G.	Hubbardston,	Guardianship,	24777
Heman	Hubbardston,	Will,	24778

YEAR.	NAME.	RESIDENCE.	NATURE.	CASE.
1851	GOODSPEED, Henry C.	Winchendon,	Guardianship,	24779
1800	Isaac	Hubbardston,	Will,	24780
1851	Isaac	Winchendon,	Will,	24781
1863	James F.	Gardner,	Guardianship,	24782
1863	Lucy A.	Gardner,	Guardianship,	24783
1875	Lucy W.	Winchendon,	Administration,	24784
1832	Luther	Hubbardston,	Administration,	24785
1840	Mary A.	Hubbardston,	Guardianship,	24786
1863	Mary A.	Gardner,	Guardianship,	24787
1840	Philander P.	Hubbardston,	Guardianship,	24788
1873	Sophila A.	Worcester,	Administration,	24789
1839	Thomas	Hubbardston,	Administration,	24790
1840	Thomas H.	Hubbardston,	Guardianship,	24791
1863	William W.	Gardner,	Guardianship,	24792
1866	GOODWIN, Alice I.	Webster,	Guardianship,	24793
1866	Clara V.	Worcester,	Guardianship,	24794
1871	Elizabeth A.	Westminster,	Guardianship,	24795
1867	Elvira M.	Westminster,	Guardianship,	24796
1870	Emma G.	Worcester,	Guardianship,	24797
1866	Frank W.	Worcester,	Guardianship,	24798
1867	George A.	Westminster,	Guardianship,	24799
1849	George G.	Worcester,	Miscellaneous,	24800
1810	Harriet	Worcester,	Guardianship,	24801
1867	Herbert	Westminster,	Guardianship,	24802
1876	Ida E.	Leicester,	Guardianship,	24803
1832	Isaac	Worcester,	Will,	24804
1808	James	Worcester,	Will,	24805
1810	James	Worcester,	Guardianship,	24806
1831	James	Lancaster,	Will,	24807
1856	James S.	Worcester,	Administration,	24808
1830	Jesse H.	Templeton,	Guardianship,	24809
1810	Leander	Worcester,	Guardianship,	24810
1867	Lizzie A.	Westminster,	Guardianship,	24811
1810	Loring	Worcester,	Guardianship,	24812
1785	Margaret	Grafton,	Administration,	24813
1866	Martin	Worcester,	Will,	24814
1750	Mary	Sutton,	Guardianship,	24815
1745	Nathaniel	Sutton,	Administration,	24816
1867	Sylvia	Worcester,	Administration,	24817
1866	Sylvia E.	Webster,	Guardianship,	24818
1834	William S.	Lancaster,	Guardianship,	24819
1870	William S.	Worcester,	Administration,	24820
	GOOGIN AND GOOGINS,			
1832	Elizabeth	Oxford,	Will,	24821
1833	George	Oxford,	Guardianship,	24822

YEAR.	NAME.	RESIDENCE.	NATURE.	CASE.
	GOOGIN AND GOOGINS,			
1832	William,	Oxford,	Will,	24823
1743	GOOKIN, Daniel	Worcester,	Administration,	24824
1870	GORDON, Edwin A.	Lancaster,	Guardianship,	24825
1864	Emma	Sacramento, Cal.,	Guardianship,	24826
1870	Emma L.	Lancaster,	Guardianship,	24827
1824	James	Douglas,	Guardianship,	24828
1869	Jonathan S.	Lancaster,	Administration,	24829
1824	Sarah M.	Douglas,	Guardianship,	24830
1824	Thomas P.	Douglas,	Guardianship,	24831
1824	Thomas P.	Douglas,	Administration,	24832
1811	William	Southborough,	Will,	24833
1824	William	Douglas,	Guardianship,	24834
1777	GORE, Alexander	Upton,	Administration,	24835
1842	Alvan B.	Sturbridge,	Guardianship,	24836
1779	Betty	Upton,	Guardianship,	24837
1873	Darius	La Harpe, Ill.,	Administration,	24838
1779	Ebenezer	Upton,	Guardianship,	24839
1876	Ebenezer	Upton,	Administration,	24840
1795	Elijah	Dudley,	Will,	24841
1834	Ellison	Upton,	Administration,	24842
1842	Emeline E.	Sturbridge,	Guardianship,	24843
1833	Hannah	Dudley,	Administration,	24844
1842	Henry H.	Sturbridge,	Guardianship,	24845
1816	John	Dudley,	Will,	24846
1842	John	Sturbridge,	Will,	24847
1859	John (L.)	Hardwick,	Guardianship,	24848
1842	John LaF.	Sturbridge,	Guardianship,	24849
1842	Julia A.	Sturbridge,	Guardianship,	24850
1854	Lewis	Upton,	Administration,	24851
1779	Militia	Upton,	Guardianship,	24852
1853	Sally	Dudley,	Will,	24853
1854	Sarah L.	Upton,	Guardianship,	24854
1868	Sylvia	Dudley,	Will,	24855
1842	William N.	Sturbridge,	Guardianship,	24856
1870	GOREY, Bridget	Sterling,	Guardianship,	24857
1848	John	Lancaster,	Administration,	24858
1880	GORHAM, Alfred	Ellington, Minn.,	Foreign Guard.,	24859
1870	Caroline A.	Blackstone,	Will,	24860
1870	Charles C.	Blackstone,	Guardianship,	24861
1875	Chester	Worcester,	Will,	24862
1879	James A.	Dana,	Will,	24863
1881	Jason	Barre,	Will,	24864
1847	John	Barre,	Will,	24865
1847	John	Barre,	Pension,	24866

Year.	Name.	Residence.	Nature.	Case.
1819	GORHAM, Joseph	Barre,	Will,	24867
1879	Marion G. D.	Barre,	Guardianship,	24868
1835	Mary A.	Barre,	Guardianship,	24869
1881	Sarah R.	Worcester,	Will,	24870
1825	Stephen	Hardwick,	Administration,	24871
1843	Susan B.	Barre,	Guardianship,	24872
1831	William O.	Hardwick,	Guardianship,	24873
1879	GORMAN, Arthur	Leominster,	Guardianship,	24874
1879	James	Upton,	Guardianship,	24875
1879	John	Upton,	Guardianship,	24876
1858	Margaret	Worcester,	Administration,	24877
1867	Mary A.	Fitchburg,	Adoption, etc.,	24878
1879	Nellie	Upton,	Guardianship,	24879
1878	Richard	Upton,	Will,	24880
1879	Thomas	Upton,	Guardianship,	24881
1874	GORTON, Charlotte H.	North Brookfield,	Administration,	24882
1838	John	Charlton,	Will,	24883
1857	Thomas	Grafton,	Administration,	24884
1843	GOSS, Asa	Sterling,	Administration,	24885
1760	Comfort	Brookfield,	Guardianship,	24886
1879	Cynthia A.	Lancaster,	Guardianship,	24887
1810	Daniel	Lancaster,	Will,	24888
1841	Daniel	Lancaster,	Administration,	24889
1879	Daniel	Lancaster,	Will,	24890
1856	Henry	Mendon,	Will,	24891
1870	Hepsibeth	Sterling,	Administration,	24892
1747	John	Lancaster,	Administration,	24893
1759	John	Brookfield,	Administration,	24894
1847	John	Lancaster,	Administration,	24895
1821	Joseph	Sterling,	Administration,	24896
1858	Josiah	Bolton,	Will,	24897
1745	Judith	Brookfield,	Guardianship,	24898
1748	Judith	Brookfield,	Administration,	24899
1851	Lucy	Sterling,	Administration,	24900
1881	Martha A.	Sterling,	Administration,	24901
1834	Mary	West Boylston,	Will,	24902
1842	Pearly	Mendon,	Administration,	24903
1843	Peter	Sterling,	Administration,	24904
1747	Phillip	Brookfield,	Administration,	24905
1742	Phillip, Jr.	Brookfield,	Administration,	24906
1878	Samuel A.	Worcester,	Administration,	24907
1843	Sarah	Sterling,	Will,	24908
1845	Sarah W.	Lancaster,	Guardianship,	24909
1745	Thomas	Brookfield,	Guardianship,	24910
1780	Thomas	Bolton,	Will,	24911

YEAR.	NAME.	RESIDENCE.	NATURE.	CASE.
1864	GOSS, William	Worcester,	Will,	24912
1821	Zebulon	Mendon,	Will,	24913
	GOTT (see also GAUT),			
1761	Benjamin	Brookfield,	Administration,	24914
1864	Lemuel, Jr.	Berlin,	Administration,	24915
	GOUGII AND GOFFE,			
1871	Ann	Uxbridge,	Administration,	24916
1871	Betsey	Lunenburg,	Administration,	24917
1853	Charles	Blackstone,	Guardianship,	24918
1872	Ebenezer W.	Millbury,	Administration,	24919
1859	Eliza	Millbury,	Will,	24920
1853	Emma	Blackstone,	Guardianship,	24921
1853	James	Blackstone,	Guardianship,	24922
1853	James	Blackstone,	Administration,	24923
1846	Joseph	Millbury,	Administration,	24924
1869	Rosena	Blackstone,	Administration,	24925
1859	GOULD, Aaron	Douglas,	Will,	24926
1873	Achsah	Westborough,	Administration,	24927
1864	Ada L.	Leicester,	Adoption,	24928
1864	Ada L.	Leicester,	Guardianship,	24929
1872	Albert	Worcester,	Administration,	24930
1828	Amos	Charlton,	Administration,	24931
1811	Amos C.	Douglas,	Guardianship,	24932
1765	Anna	Sutton,	Guardianship,	24933
1844	Augustin	Milford,	Guardianship,	24934
1811	Beersheba	Douglas,	Guardianship,	24935
1746	Benjamin	Lunenburg,	Administration,	24936
1852	Benjamin	Douglas,	Administration,	24937
1758	Caleb	Sutton,	Administration,	24938
1861	Carrie M.	Oxford,	Adoption, etc.,	24939
1869	Catherine W.	Vassalborough, Me.,	Foreign Will,	24940
1872	Charles	Leominster,	Will,	24941
1852	Chester C.	Templeton,	Administration,	24942
1864	Clara E.	Leicester,	Adoption, etc.,	24943
1864	Clara E.	Leicester,	Guardianship,	24944
1811	Comfort	Douglas,	Guardianship,	24945
1864	Cora M.	Leicester,	Adoption, etc.,	24946
1864	Cora M.	Leicester,	Guardianship,	24947
1864	Curtis	Athol,	Will,	24948
1837	Davis	Leicester,	Guardianship,	24949
1765	Ebenezer	Sutton,	Administration,	24950
1810	Ebenezer	Douglas,	Administration,	24951
1811	Ebenezer	Douglas,	Guardianship,	24952
1805	Eliezer	Douglas,	Will,	24953
1832	Elijah	Phillipston,	Will,	24954

(575—SERIES A.)

YEAR.	NAME.	RESIDENCE.	NATURE.	CASE.
1815	GOULD, Elizabeth	Worcester,	Guardianship,	24955
1878	Elsy	Charlton,	Administration,	24956
1860	Elvira O.	Worcester,	Guardianship,	24957
1852	Emma M.	Worcester,	Change of Name,	24958
1860	Erving A.	Worcester,	Guardianship,	24959
1859	Eugene E.	Douglas,	Guardianship,	24960
1880	Florence E.	Ashburnham,	Administration,	24961
1847	Franklin	Charlton,	Guardianship,	24962
1871	George	Worcester,	Administration,	24963
1870	George G.	Leominster,	Administration,	24964
1864	George W.	Leicester,	Administration,	24965
1879	Gertrude T.	Westborough,	Adoption, etc.,	24966
1783	Haffield	Sutton,	Guardianship,	24967
1856	Haffield	Hardwick,	Will,	24968
1765	Hannah	Sutton,	Guardianship,	24969
1783	Hannah	Sutton,	Guardianship,	24970
1818	Harriet	Charlton,	Guardianship,	24971
1847	Harvey	Charlton,	Guardianship,	24972
1863	Henry B.	Hardwick,	Administration,	24973
1864	Henry M.	Phillipston,	Guardianship,	24974
1847	Hollis	Charlton,	Guardianship,	24975
1864	Hollis	Douglas,	Administration,	24976
1876	Irving H.	Templeton,	Administration,	24977
1878	Isaac	Westborough,	Administration,	24978
1878	Isabella	Boston,	Adoption, etc.,	24979
1846	James, Jr.	Nashville, Tenn.,	Administration,	24980
1826	Jason	Douglas,	Will,	24981
1825	Jedediah	Douglas,	Will,	24982
1831	Jedediah	New Braintree,	Administration,	24983
1847	Joanna H.	Douglas,	Administration,	24984
1745	John	Southborough,	Administration,	24985
1765	John	Sutton,	Guardianship,	24986
1783	John	Sutton,	Guardianship,	24987
1811	John	Douglas,	Guardianship,	24988
1818	John	Charlton,	Pension,	24989
1859	Jonas	New Braintree,	Administration,	24990
1765	Jonathan	Sutton,	Guardianship,	24991
1768	Jonathan	Sutton,	Guardianship,	24992
1782	Jonathan	Sutton,	Administration,	24993
1783	Jonathan	Sutton,	Guardianship,	24994
1809	Jonathan	New Braintree,	Administration,	24995
1836	Jonathan	Charlton,	Administration,	24996
1841	Jonathan	Millbury,	Will,	24997
1785	Joseph	Sutton,	Will,	24998
1833	Joseph	Dudley,	Guardianship,	24999

Year.	Name.	Residence.	Nature.	Case.
1860	GOULD, Joseph H.	Worcester,	Administration,	25000
1879	Judson	Douglas,	Will,	25001
1847	Julia A.	Charlton,	Guardianship,	25002
1859	Julian H.	Douglas,	Guardianship,	23003
1874	Laura	Fitchburg,	Administration,	25004
1860	Lavina A.	Worcester,	Guardianship,	25005
1876	Lawson	Charlton,	Administration,	25006
1880	Leonia I.	Fitchburg,	Adoption, etc.,	25007
1860	Levander M.	Worcester,	Guardianship,	25008
1855	Levi L.	Millbury,	Administration,	25009
1837	Lewis	Sutton,	Administration,	25010
1844	Lucinda	Phillpston,	Pension,	25011
1868	Lucinda J.	Phillipston,	Will,	25012
1844	Luthera	Milford,	Guardianship,	25013
1853	Lydia	Millbury,	Administration,	25014
1847	Manson	Charlton,	Guardianship,	25015
1847	Martha C.	Worcester,	Guardianship,	25016
1880	Martin C.	Gardner,	Will,	25017
1827	Marvel	Douglas,	Guardianship,	25018
1847	Mary E.	Douglas,	Guardianship,	25019
1874	Mary E.	Webster,	Trustee,	25020
1871	Metty, etc.	Worcester,	Administration,	25021
1845	Moses	Milford,	Guardianship,	25022
1811	Nancy	Douglas,	Guardianship,	25023
1869	Nancy E.	Charlton,	Guardianship,	25024
1748	Nathaniel	Lunenburg,	Administration,	25025
1845	Olive	Milford,	Guardianship,	25026
1864	Olive	Douglas,	Will,	25027
1877	Parley	Douglas,	Will,	25028
1834	Perley I.	Milford,	Administration,	25029
1872	Pliny P.	Phillipston,	Administration,	25030
1878	Ransom M.	Worcester,	Will,	25031
1807	Rebecca	Salem,	Receipt,	25032
1860	Revia A.	Worcester,	Guardianship,	25033
1849	Rhoda	Grafton,	Administration,	25034
1873	Robert S.	Sterling,	Will,	25035
1860	Rovena S.	Worcester,	Guardianship,	25036
1850	Rufus	Uxbridge,	Administration,	25037
1811	Sally	Douglas,	Guardianship,	25038
1827	Sally	Douglas,	Guardianship,	25039
1758	Samuel	Hopkinton,	Guardianship,	25040
1828	Samuel	Worcester,	Will,	25041
1847	Sarah G.	Worcester,	Guardianship,	25042
1764	Simeon	Sutton,	Guardianship,	25043
1763	Stephen	Sutton,	Guardianship,	25044

YEAR.	NAME.	RESIDENCE.	NATURE.	CASE.
1831	GOULD, Stephen	Millbury,	Administration,	25045
1871	Submit	Worcester,	Administration,	25046
1811	Susanna	Douglas,	Guardianship,	25047
1871	Susannah	Charlton,	Administration,	25048
1844	Sylvanus S.	Charlton,	Guardianship,	24049
1768	Thomas	Sutton,	Will,	25050
1866	Thomas	Lunenburg,	Will,	25051
1879	Thomas	Lunenburg,	Administration,	25052
1756	Thomas, Jr.	Sutton,	Will,	25053
1847	Tirzah	Charlton,	Guardianship,	25054
1851	Willard	Westborough,	Administration,	25055
——	Willard	Douglas,	Will,	25056
1811	William	Douglas,	Guardianship,	25057
1818	William	Charlton,	Guardianship,	25058
1834	William	Lancaster,	Will,	25059
1839	William	Lancaster,	Guardianship,	25060
1839	William	Athol,	Will,	25061
1830	William S.	Charlton,	Guardianship,	25062
1836	William T.	Sturbridge,	Administration,	25063
1859	Willie V.	Douglas,	Guardianship,	25064
1745	Zacheus	Lunenburg,	Will,	25065
1796	GOULDING, Abigail	Worcester,	Administration,	25066
1845	Abigail C. D.	Phillipston,	Guardianship,	25067
1812	Adeline L., etc.	Worcester,	Guardianship,	25068
1845	Agnes S.	Phillipston,	Guardianship,	25069
1797	Azubah	Worcester,	Guardianship,	25070
1873	Barney, etc.	Worcester,	Administration,	25071
1872	Caro F.	Worcester,	Adoption, etc.,	25072
1875	Caro F.	Worcester,	Adoption, etc.,	25072
1829	Clark	Worcester,	Administration,	25073
1851	Cornelius D.	Northborough,	Guardianship,	25074
1796	Curtis	Western,	Guardianship,	25075
1845	Cynthia K.	Phillipston,	Guardianship,	25076
1854	Eli	Worcester,	Trustee,	25077
1880	Eli	Worcester,	Administration,	25078
1852	Ellen	Westborough,	Administration,	25079
1838	Ephraim	Grafton,	Will,	25080
1869	Ephraim	Millbury,	Administration,	25081
1796	Fanny	Worcester,	Guardianship,	25082
1830	Fanny	Worcester,	Guardianship,	25083
1850	Fanny A.	Grafton,	Guardianship,	25084
1850	Francis P.	Grafton,	Guardianship,	25085
1864	Freddie L.	Worcester,	Guardianship,	25086
1830	Frederic	Worcester,	Guardianship,	25087
1827	Grace	Ward,	Guardianship,	25088

YEAR.	NAME.	RESIDENCE.	NATURE.	CASE.
1774	GOULDING, Hannah	Worcester,	Guardianship,	25089
1796	Hannah	Western,	Guardianship,	25090
1830	Hannah	Worcester,	Guardianship,	25091
1857	Harriet	Sterling,	Administration,	25092
1864	Henry, 2d	Worcester,	Administration,	25093
1866	Henry	Worcester,	Will,	25094
1841	Ignatius	Phillipston,	Will,	25095
1791	James	Worcester,	Administration,	25096
1873	Jane L.	Worcester,	Administration,	25097
1810	Joel R.	Hubbardston,	Guardianship,	25098
1829	Joel R.	Hubbardston,	Guardianship,	25099
1791	John	Grafton,	Administration,	25100
1873	John	Worcester,	Guardianship,	25101
1877	John	Worcester,	Administration,	25102
1814	John R.	Winchendon,	Administration,	25103
1826	Jonah	Ward,	Will,	25104
1799	Joshua	Grafton,	Administration,	25105
1790	Levi	Worcester,	Guardianship,	25106
1810	Levi	Worcester,	Administration,	25107
1822	Levi	Worcester,	Guardianship,	25108
1790	Lucinda	Worcester,	Guardianship,	25109
1851	Lucretia	Worcester,	Administration,	25110
1796	Luther	Western,	Guardianship,	25111
1790	Nabby	Worcester,	Guardianship,	25112
1800	Nabby	Worcester,	Administration,	25113
1796	Otis	Western,	Guardianship,	25114
1792	Palmer	Worcester,	Administration,	25115
1790	Patty	Worcester,	Guardianship,	25116
1792	Patty	Grafton,	Guardianship,	25117
1796	Perciss	Western,	Guardianship,	25118
1790	Peter	Worcester,	Administration,	25119
1790	Peter	Worcester,	Guardianship,	25120
1830	Peter	Worcester,	Guardianship,	25121
1830	Phineas	Paxton,	Administration,	25122
1797	Polly P.	Worcester,	Guardianship,	25123
1849	Prudence	Worcester,	Administration,	25124
1816	Ruth	Phillipston,	Administration,	25125
1790	Sally	Worcester,	Guardianship,	25126
1827	Sally	Ward,	Guardianship,	25127
1880	Sally	Grafton,	Will,	25128
1797	Samuel	Holden,	Administration,	25129
1774	Sarah	Worcester,	Guardianship,	25130
1796	Sibble	Western,	Guardianship,	25131
1850	Susan E.	Grafton,	Guardianship,	25132
1796	Timothy	Western,	Guardianship,	25133

YEAR.	NAME.	RESIDENCE.	NATURE.	CASE.
1827	GOULDING, Valorus	Ward,	Guardianship,	25134
1828	William	Hubbardston,	Will,	25135
1829	William J.	Hubbardston,	Guardianship,	25136
1799	Windsor	Holden,	Guardianship,	25137
1802	Windsor	Holden,	Administration,	25137
1861	Windsor	Shrewsbury,	Will,	25138
1790	Zervilla	Worcester,	Guardianship,	25139
1853	GOURLEY, Jane	Leicester,	Administration,	25140
1881	GOUTOSKY, Elizabeth	Harvard,	Guardianship,	25141
1781	GOWIN, Ebenezer	Lunenburg,	Will,	25142
1851	GOWING, Lucy	Keene, N. H.,	Administration,	25143
1800	Thomas	Leominster,	Administration,	25144
1873	GRACE, John D.	Charlton,	Guardianship,	25145
1877	Patrick	Worcester,	Guardianship,	25146
1873	GRACEAN, Josephine	Southbridge,	Adoption, etc.,	25147
1880	GRADY, Austin	Clinton,	Guardianship,	25148
1880	Catharine A.	Clinton,	Guardianship,	25149
1873	Catherine	Clinton,	Will,	25150
1875	Ellen	Worcester,	Administration,	25151
1880	Honora	Clinton,	Guardianship,	25152
1880	John W.	Clinton,	Guardianship,	25153
1880	Malachi	Clinton,	Administration,	25154
1880	Michael J.	Clinton,	Guardianship,	25155
1872	William	Dudley,	Will,	25156
1881	GRAFTON, Lula	Unknown,	Adoption, etc.,	25157
1828	GRAFTON INDIANS	Grafton,	Trustee,	25158
	GRAHAM AND GRAYHAM,			
1776	Alexander	Rutland,	Will,	25159
1814	Alexander	Rutland,	Guardianship,	25160
1777	Andrew	Rutland,	Guardianship,	25161
1784	Andrew	Spencer,	Administration,	25162
1850	Ann	Willington, Conn.,	Administration,	25163
1814	Asa D.	Rutland,	Guardianship,	25164
1875	Benjamin	Lunenburg,	Administration,	25165
1777	Dolly	Rutland,	Guardianship,	25166
1777	Hannah	Rutland,	Guardianship,	25167
1777	James	Rutland,	Guardianship,	25168
1870	James	Fitchburg,	Administration,	25169
1808	Jane	Spencer,	Administration,	25170
1777	Jesse	Spencer,	Guardianship,	25171
1776	John	Spencer,	Administration,	25172
1777	John	Spencer,	Guardianship,	25173
1814	John	Rutland,	Guardianship,	25174
1861	John	Leicester,	Will,	25175
1872	Juliette	North Brookfield,	Guardianship,	25176

YEAR.	NAME.	RESIDENCE.	NATURE.	CASE.
	GRAHAM AND GRAYHAM,			
1777	Lucy	Rutland,	Guardianship,	25177
1777	Margaret	Rutland,	Guardianship,	25178
1767	Martha	Rutland,	Guardianship,	25179
1767	Mary	Rutland,	Guardianship,	25180
1777	Mary	Spencer,	Guardianship,	25181
1814	Mary	Rutland,	Guardianship,	25182
1879	Mary	Leominster,	Will,	25183
1814	Pamela	Rutland,	Guardianship,	25184
1777	Samuel	Spencer,	Guardianship,	25185
1874	Samuel	Holden,	Will,	25186
1767	Sarah	Rutland,	Guardianship,	25187
1764	William	Rutland,	Will,	25188
1767	William	Rutland,	Guardianship,	25189
1777	William	Rutland,	Guardianship,	25190
1813	William	Rutland,	Administration,	25191
1814	William	Rutland,	Guardianship,	25192
1825	William	Spencer,	Guardianship,	25193
1853	William	New Braintree,	Administration,	25193
	GRAINGER see GRANGER.			
1880	GRANDFIELD, Delia A.	Northbridge,	Will,	25194
	GRANGER AND GRAINGER,			
1865	Carrie L.	Morrison, Ill.,	Guardianship,	25195
1838	Charles	New Braintree,	Guardianship,	25196
1785	Daniel	New Braintree,	Guardianship,	25197
1817	Daniel	New Braintree,	Guardianship,	25198
1849	Daniel	Hardwick,	Administration,	25199
1860	Daniel N.	Hardwick,	Guardianship,	25200
1817	David	New Braintree,	Guardianship,	25201
1785	Hannah	New Braintree,	Guardianship,	25202
1864	Henry H.	Hardwick,	Will,	25203
1838	Henry M.	New Braintree,	Guardianship,	25204
1783	John	New Braintree,	Administration,	25205
1817	Lucy	New Braintree,	Guardianship,	25206
1876	Lucy	New Braintree,	Will,	25207
1869	Maria	Auburn,	Administration,	25208
1872	Martin	New Braintree,	Will,	25209
1785	Mehitable	New Braintree,	Guardianship,	25210
1817	Mehitable	New Braintree,	Guardianship,	25211
1816	Noah	New Braintree,	Administration,	25212
1831	Parley	Petersham,	Administration,	25213
1817	Patty	New Braintree,	Guardianship,	25214
1868	Patty	New Braintree,	Administration,	25215
1785	Rebecca	New Braintree,	Guardianship,	25216
1841	Rebeccah	New Braintree,	Administration,	25217

YEAR.	NAME.	RESIDENCE.	NATURE.	CASE.
	GRANGER AND GRAINGER,			
1841	Rebeccah	New Braintree,	Pension,	25218
1785	Rhoda	New Braintree,	Guardianship,	25219
1817	Rhoda	New Braintree,	Guardianship,	25220
1785	Roger	New Braintree,	Guardianship,	25221
1817	Sally	New Braintree,	Guardianship,	25222
1785	Samuel	New Braintree,	Will,	25223
1785	Submit	New Braintree,	Guardianship,	25224
1817	Sumner	New Braintree,	Guardianship,	25225
1817	Varnum	New Braintree,	Guardianship,	25226
1785	Washington	New Braintree,	Guardianship,	25227
1864	William F.	Hardwick,	Administration,	25228
1829	**GRANT, Aaron**	Royalston,	Will,	25229
1846	Aaron	Royalston,	Will,	25230
1846	Aaron A.	Royalston,	Guardianship,	25231
1862	Billings	Ellington, Conn.,	Foreign Will,	25232
1858	James	Blackstone,	Will,	25233
1850	Levi M.	Winchendon,	Administration,	25234
1856	Lucy	Royalston,	Guardianship,	25235
1859	Mary	Blackstone,	Will,	25236
1812	Philip R.	Hardwick,	Administration,	25237
1811	Samuel	Worcester,	Administration,	25238
1874	Stillman B.	Fitchburg,	Will,	25239
1864	William	Barre,	Administration,	25240
	GRATON AND GREATON,			
1861	Abigail	Worcester,	Will,	25241
1857	Becca	Winchendon,	Will,	25242
1843	Edward	Southbridge,	Administration,	25243
1843	Edward R.	Southbridge,	Guardianship,	25244
1737	Hannah	Leicester,	Guardianship,	25245
1737	James	Leicester,	Guardianship,	25246
1737	John	Leicester,	Administration,	25247
1827	John	Leicester,	Will,	25248
1737	Joseph	Leicester,	Guardianship,	25249
1753	Joseph	Leicester,	Guardianship,	25250
1810	LaFayette	Winchendon,	Guardianship,	25251
1850	Laura	Leicester,	Administration,	25252
1810	Leona	Winchendon,	Guardianship,	25253
1846	Lucy	Winchendon,	Administration,	25254
1867	Lucy L.	Worcester,	Administration,	25255
1810	Marsena	Winchendon,	Guardianship,	25256
1737	Martha	Leicester,	Guardianship,	25257
1737	Mary	Leicester,	Guardianship,	25258
1810	Sally P.	Winchendon,	Guardianship,	25259
1869	Sally P.	Winchendon,	Administration,	25260

YEAR.	NAME.	RESIDENCE.	NATURE.	CASE.
	GRATON AND GREATON,			
1810	Smyrna	Winchendon,	Guardianship,	25261
1865	Smyrna	Winchendon,	Will,	25262
1810	Tamar	Winchendon,	Guardianship,	25263
1737	Thomas	Leicester,	Guardianship,	25264
1746	Thomas	Leicester,	Administration,	25265
1809	Thomas	Winchendon,	Administration,	25266
1869	Thomas	Paxton,	Administration,	25267
1810	Thomas A.	Winchendon,	Guardianship,	25268
1834	Tryphena	Leicester,	Will,	25269
1783	GRAVES, Abigail	Westminster,	Guardianship,	25270
1830	Abner	Athol,	Will,	25271
1849	Abner	Athol,	Will,	25272
1841	Alvin	Southborough,	Guardianship,	25273
1878	Augustus H.	West Boylston,	Administration,	25274
1841	Caroline M.	Southborough,	Guardianship,	25275
1865	Charles B.	Sutton,	Administration,	25276
1841	Dexter	Southborough,	Administration,	25277
1871	Dolly	Athol,	Guardianship,	25278
1875	Dolly	Athol,	Will,	25278
1867	Dolly B.	Worcester,	Administration,	25279
1795	Eleazer	Athol,	Administration,	25280
1822	Eleazer	Athol,	Administration,	25281
1881	Electa	Hardwick,	Administration,	25282
1865	Elijah	Royalston,	Will,	25283
1862	Fanny C.	Lunenburg,	Guardianship,	25284
1873	Frank A.	North Brookfield,	Guardianship,	25285
1847	Frederick S.	Worcester,	Guardianship,	25286
1865	Henry	North Brookfield,	Will,	25287
1873	Ira	Millbury,	Administration,	25288
1875	Jane	Worcester,	Administration,	25289
1817	Jonathan	Westminster,	Administration,	25290
1826	Jonathan	Westminster,	Guardianship,	25291
1757	Katherine	Sudbury,	Guardianship,	25292
1873	Leonard, Jr.	North Brookfield,	Administration,	25293
1835	Levi	Westminster,	Administration,	25294
1835	Levi	Westminster,	Pension,	25295
1783	Lucy	Westminster,	Guardianship,	25296
1862	Luther M.	Lunenburg,	Administration,	25297
1855	Lydia	Westminster,	Administration,	25298
1873	Mabel A.	North Brookfield,	Guardianship,	25299
1863	Mary J.	Worcester,	Administration,	25300
1841	Mary M.	Southborough,	Guardianship,	25301
1801	Nathaniel	Athol,	Administration,	25302
1862	Nelson B.	Lunenburg,	Guardianship,	25303

Year.	Name.	Residence.	Nature.	Case.
1800	GRAVES, Patience	Westminster,	Will,	25304
1783	Peter	Westminster,	Guardianship,	25305
1783	Priscilla	Westminster,	Guardianship,	25306
1798	Richard	Westminster,	Administration,	25307
1826	Richard	Ashburnham,	Administration,	25308
1800	Sally	Shrewsbury,	Administration,	25309
1835	Samuel	Royalston,	Administration,	25310
1757	Sarah	Sudbury,	Guardianship,	25311
1800	Sarah, etc.	Shrewsbury,	Administration,	25312
1783	Susanna	Westminster,	Guardianship,	25313
1756	Thomas	Southborough,	Will,	25314
1875	Watson	Southborough,	Will,	25315
	GRAY AND GREY,			
1804	Abel	Fitchburg,	Guardianship,	25316
1876	Alexander	Athol,	Will,	25317
1852	Anthony	Oxford,	Guardianship,	25318
1871	Anthony	Oxford,	Administration,	25318
1857	Arthur	Paxton,	Guardianship,	25319
1829	Austin	Southborough,	Administration,	25320
1804	Betsey	Fitchburg,	Guardianship,	25321
1859	Catherine S.	Worcester,	Guardianship,	25322
1838	Charles A.	Paxton,	Guardianship,	25323
1822	Daniel W.	New York, N. Y.,	Foreign Guard.,	25324
1804	Dorothy	Fitchburg,	Guardianship,	25325
1823	Elizabeth	Western,	Will,	25326
1859	Fannie	Worcester,	Guardianship,	25327
1864	Freddie S.	Brookfield,	Guardianship,	25328
1851	George	Northborough,	Administration,	25329
1857	George	Paxton,	Guardianship,	25330
1864	George E.	Sterling,	Guardianship,	25331
1880	George F.	Warren,	Adoption, etc.,	25332
1874	George G.	Leominster,	Will,	25333
1876	George M.	Oakham,	Guardianship,	25334
1857	George W.	Warren,	Guardianship,	25335
1864	Hattie L.	Grafton,	Guardianship,	25336
1864	Howland W.	Grafton, N. H.,	Guardianship,	25337
1783	Isaac	Worcester,	Guardianship,	25338
1785	Jacob	Worcester,	Guardianship,	25339
1816	John	Charlton,	Guardianship,	25340
1859	John	Worcester,	Administration,	25341
1822	John D.	New York, N. Y.,	Foreign Guard.,	25342
1880	John M.	Templeton,	Will,	25343
1856	John W. W.	Sterling,	Guardianship,	25344
1804	Joseph	Fitchburg,	Administration,	25345
1865	Lilla A.	Kennebunk, Me.,	Administration,	25346

YEAR.	NAME.	RESIDENCE.	NATURE.	CASE.
	GRAY AND GREY,			
1804	Lydia	Fitchburg,	Guardianship,	25347
1804	Mary	Fitchburg,	Guardianship,	25348
1874	Mary C.	Worcester,	Guardianship,	25349
1851	Mary E.	Northborough,	Guardianship,	25350
1783	Mathew	Worcester,	Will,	25351
1876	Mattie M.	Oakham,	Guardianship,	25352
1832	Moses	Worcester,	Administration,	25353
1824	Nathaniel	Worcester,	Administration,	25354
1834	Nehemiah H.	Westborough,	Administration,	25355
1867	Patty	Worcester,	Administration,	25356
1814	Reuben	Worcester,	Will,	25357
1766	Robert	Worcester,	Will,	25358
1786	Robert	Western,	Will,	25359
1799	Robert	Worcester,	Will,	25360
1766	Samuel	Worcester,	Guardianship,	25361
1802	Samuel	Western,	Guardianship,	25362
1840	Samuel	Paxton,	Administration,	25363
1853	Sanford K.	Upton,	Administration,	25364
1822	Sarah	New York, N. Y.,	Foreign Guard.,	25365
1857	Sibyl	Paxton,	Guardianship,	25366
1864	Stephen W.	West Boylston,	Administration,	25367
1852	Susan E.	Worcester,	Guardianship,	25368
1822	Thomas	New York, N. Y.,	Foreign Guard.,	25369
1849	Thomas	Athol,	Administration,	25370
1857	William	Paxton,	Administration,	25371
1875	William L.	Worcester,	Administration,	25372
1859	William S.	Worcester,	Guardianship,	25373
	GRAYHAM see GRAHAM.			
1867	GRAYSON, Caroline A.	Worcester,	Adoption, etc.,	25374
1880	GREANY, Charles W.	Worcester,	Guardianship,	25375
1880	Harry A.	Worcester,	Guardianship,	25376
1880	Henry	Worcester,	Will,	25377
	GREATON see GRATON.			
	GREELY AND GREELEY,			
1872	Dillie	Royalston,	Guardianship,	25378
1871	Nathaniel	Royalston,	Administration,	25379
	GREEN AND GREENE,			
1866	Aaron	Brookfield,	Will,	25380
1864	Abbie F.	Lancaster,	Guardianship,	25381
1864	Abbie R.	Shrewsbury,	Guardianship,	25382
1843	Abel	Leicester,	Will,	25383
1846	Abigail	Westborough,	Will,	25384
1867	Abigail	Templeton,	Administration,	25385
1855	Adelaide A.	Leominster,	Guardianship,	25386

GREEN and GREENE,

YEAR.	NAME.	RESIDENCE.	NATURE.	CASE.
1866	Albert T.	Spencer,	Guardianship,	25387
1877	Alice A.	Warwick, R. I.,	Foreign Will,	25388
1837	Andrew	Worcester,	Administration,	25389
1856	Andrew A.	Northbridge,	Guardianship,	25390
1834	Andrew H.	Worcester,	Guardianship,	25391
1842	Ann	Lunenburg,	Guardianship,	25392
1829	Ann E.	Spencer,	Guardianship,	25393
1847	Ann M.	Grafton,	Guardianship,	25394
1843	Anson	Lunenburg,	Guardianship,	25395
1800	Ardin	Westminster,	Administration,	25396
1846	Asa W.	Lancaster,	Guardianship,	25397
1788	Barnard	Brookfield,	Guardianship,	25398
1858	Benedict A.	Grafton,	Will,	25399
1753	Benjamin	Mendon,	Will,	25400
1753	Benjamin	Mendon,	Guardianship,	25401
1797	Benjamin	Uxbridge,	Will,	25402
1825	Benjamin	Uxbridge,	Administration,	25403
1836	Benjamin	Spencer,	Administration,	25404
1837	Benjamin	Uxbridge,	Administration,	25405
1845	Benjamin	Douglas,	Pension,	25406
1872	Benjamin	Worcester,	Will,	25407
1847	Benjamin F.	Grafton,	Administration,	25408
1838	Benjamin H.	Fitchburg,	Guardianship,	25409
1864	Bernard R.	Lancaster,	Guardianship,	25410
1823	Betsey	Spencer,	Administration,	25411
1788	Betsy	Brookfield,	Guardianship,	25412
1843	Calvin	Lunenburg,	Guardianship,	25413
1880	Charity	North Brookfield,	Guardianship,	25414
1814	Charles	Ward,	Guardianship,	25415
1835	Charles	Spencer,	Guardianship,	25416
1842	Charles	Lunenburg,	Guardianship,	25417
1862	Charles	Gardner,	Will,	25418
1880	Charles	Spencer,	Administration,	25419
1858	Charles A.	Westborough,	Guardianship,	25420
1847	Charles E.	Grafton,	Guardianship,	25421
1855	Charles E.	Leominster,	Guardianship,	25422
1871	Charles F.	Clinton,	Administration,	25423
1875	Charles H.	Princeton,	Guardianship,	25424
1865	Charles J.	Leicester,	Guardianship,	25425
1880	Charles N.	Spencer,	Guardianship,	25426
1857	Charles P.	Westborough,	Administration,	25427
1852	Charles S.	Oakham,	Guardianship,	25428
1794	Clarinda	Paxton,	Guardianship,	25429
1870	Cora E.	Milford,	Guardianship,	25430

YEAR.	NAME.	RESIDENCE.	NATURE.	CASE.
	GREEN AND GREENE,			
1800	Cromwell	Spencer,	Guardianship,	25431
1811	Daniel	Leicester,	Guardianship,	25432
1828	Daniel	Leicester,	Guardianship,	25433
1838	Daniel	Barre,	Administration,	25434
1861	Daniel	Auburn,	Administration,	25435
1876	Daniel	Spencer,	Guardianship,	25436
1846	Daniel W.	Lancaster,	Guardianship,	25437
1868	Daniel W.	Spencer,	Guardianship,	25438
1749	David	Woodstock,	Administration,	25439
1749	David	Woodstock,	Guardianship,	25440
1866	David	Westborough,	Administration,	25441
1858	Delia W.	Westborough,	Guardianship,	25442
1748	Edward	Mendon,	Guardianship,	25443
1869	Edward	Warren Co., Ill.,	Foreign Will,	25444
1872	Edward E.	De Ruyter, N. Y.,	Guardianship,	25445
1871	Edward L.	Clinton,	Guardianship,	25446
1868	Edwards W.	Worcester,	Administration,	25447
1880	Effie G.	Spencer,	Adoption, etc.,	25448
1815	Elbridge	Spencer,	Guardianship,	25449
1838	Elijah	Westborough,	Guardianship,	25450
1749	Eliphalet	Woodstock,	Guardianship,	25451
1817	Eliza	Spencer,	Guardianship,	25452
1846	Eliza A. H.	Lancaster,	Guardianship,	25453
1872	Eliza G.	Barre,	Guardianship,	25454
1857	Eliza J.	Oakham,	Guardianship,	25455
1786	Elizabeth	Leicester,	Guardianship,	25456
1797	Elizabeth	Oakham,	Guardianship,	25457
1810	Elizabeth	Worcester,	Guardianship,	25458
1854	Elizabeth	Worcester,	Will,	25459
1873	Elizabeth	Auburn,	Will,	25460
1847	Ellen S.	Grafton,	Guardianship,	25461
1864	Elmina M.	Lancaster,	Guardianship,	25462
1864	Emilie A.	Lancaster,	Guardianship,	25463
1863	Emma A.	Gardner,	Guardianship,	25464
1833	Esek	Milford,	Will,	25465
1870	Etta M.	Milford,	Guardianship,	25466
1788	Ezra	Brookfield,	Guardianship,	25467
1817	Ezra	Spencer,	Guardianship,	25468
1817	Ezra	Spencer,	Will,	25469
1845	Ezra	North Brookfield,	Will,	25470
1863	Ezra	Lancaster,	Administration,	25471
1845	Fanny	Gardner,	Administration,	25472
1872	Frances J.	De Ruyter, N. Y.,	Guardianship,	25473
1837	Francis	Northborough,	Administration,	25474

YEAR.	NAME.	RESIDENCE.	NATURE.	CASE.
	GREEN AND GREENE,			
1875	Frank E.	Worcester,	Adoption,	25475
1857	Franklin P.	Oakham,	Guardianship,	25476
1846	Franklin W.	Lancaster,	Guardianship,	25477
1810	Frederic W.	Worcester,	Guardianship,	25478
1873	George	Fitchburg,	Administration,	25479
1855	George A.	Leominster,	Guardianship,	25480
1864	George E.	Lancaster,	Guardianship,	25481
1847	George F.	Grafton,	Guardianship,	25482
1858	George F.	Shrewsbury,	Will,	25483
1846	George M.	Lancaster,	Guardianship,	25484
1856	George S.	Oakham,	Administration,	25485
1839	George W.	Spencer,	Guardianship,	25486
1857	George W.	Oakham,	Guardianship,	25487
1860	George W.	Oakham,	Adoption, etc.,	25488
1863	George W.	Royalston,	Administration,	25489
1875	Gilbert	Clinton,	Administration,	25490
1864	Gilbert (S.)	Warren,	Guardianship,	25491
1855	Gilbert W.	Leominster,	Guardianship,	25492
1821	Hannah	Uxbridge,	Will,	25493
1842	Hannah	Lunenburg,	Guardianship,	25494
1852	Hannah	Shrewsbury,	Guardianship,	25495
1863	Hannah	Spencer,	Will,	25496
1858	Hannah L.	Westborough,	Guardianship,	25497
1856	Hannah S.	Northbridge,	Administration,	25498
1846	Harriet S.	North Brookfield,	Guardianship,	25499
1865	Harry	Hubbardston,	Will,	25500
1874	Hattie S.	North Brookfield,	Will,	25501
1855	Henry	Leominster,	Will,	25502
1861	Henry	Newport, Vt.,	Guardianship,	25503
1858	Henry G.	Westborough,	Guardianship,	25504
1867	Henry H.	Chicago, Ill.,	Guardianship,	25505
1871	Henry H.	Clinton,	Guardianship,	25506
1855	Henry I.	Leominster,	Guardianship,	25507
1807	Henry P.	Mendon,	Guardianship,	25508
1866	Hiram M.	Brookfield,	Guardianship,	25509
1835	Horace	Spencer,	Guardianship,	25510
1878	Horace	North Brookfield,	Administration,	25511
1812	Isaac	Leicester,	Administration,	25512
1835	Isaac	Ashburnham,	Pension,	25513
1811	Jabez	Leicester,	Guardianship,	25514
1811	Jabez	Leicester,	Administration,	25515
1793	James	Paxton,	Administration,	25516
1810	James	Worcester,	Guardianship,	25517
1828	James	Spencer,	Administration,	25518

YEAR.	NAME.	RESIDENCE.	NATURE.	CASE.
	GREEN and GREENE,			
1874	James	Worcester,	Will,	25519
1864	James D.	Lancaster,	Guardianship,	25520
1866	James P.	Brookfield,	Guardianship,	25521
1838	James S.	Fitchburg,	Guardianship,	25522
1844	James S.	Millbury,	Administration,	25523
1819	Jeduthan	Rutland,	Will,	25524
1871	Jeduthan	Rutland,	Will,	25525
1870	Joel	Oakham,	Administration,	25526
1872	Joey L.	De Ruyter, N. Y.,	Guardianship,	25527
1742	John	Mendon,	Will,	25528
1744	John, 3d	Brookfield,	Will,	25529
1748	John	Mendon,	Will,	25530
1751	John	Brookfield,	Will,	25531
1755	John	Hardwick,	Will,	25532
1758	John	Hardwick,	Guardianship,	25533
1799	John	Worcester,	Will,	25534
1804	John	Ward,	Administration,	25535
1808	John	Worcester,	Will,	25536
1828	John	Northborough,	Guardianship,	25537
1843	John	Northborough,	Administration,	25537
1829	John	Spencer,	Guardianship,	25538
1865	John	Worcester,	Will,	25539
1868	John	Spencer,	Guardianship,	25540
1872	John C.	Hubbardston,	Will,	25541
1846	John D.	Lancaster,	Guardianship,	25542
1858	John D.	Rutland,	Will,	25543
1880	John H.	Spencer,	Guardianship,	25544
1834	John P.	Worcester,	Guardianship,	25545
1873	John R.	Worcester,	Will,	25546
1781	Joktan	Leicester,	Administration,	25547
1794	Jonathan	Berlin,	Administration,	25548
1794	Joseph	Westborough,	Will,	25549
1808	Joseph	Westborough,	Administration,	25550
1811	Joseph	Leicester,	Guardianship,	25551
1844	Joseph	Hubbardston,	Will,	25552
1853	Joseph	Hubbardston,	Administration,	25553
1858	Joseph J.	Thompson, Conn.,	Will,	25554
1869	Joseph M.	New Braintree,	Administration,	25555
1745	Joshua	Mendon,	Administration,	25556
1746	Joshua	Mendon,	Guardianship,	25557
1811	Josiah	Leicester,	Guardianship,	25558
1877	Josiah	Spencer,	Will,	25559
1834	Julia	Worcester,	Will,	25560
1834	Julia E.	Worcester,	Guardianship,	25561

GREEN and GREENE,

YEAR.	NAME.	RESIDENCE.	NATURE.	CASE.
1854	Julia F.	Templeton,	Guardianship,	25562
1855	Justus	New Braintree,	Administration,	25563
1861	Lambert	Northborough,	Guardianship,	25564
1749	Larkin	Worcester,	Guardianship,	25565
1818	Lemuel	Spencer,	Will,	25566
1872	Levi	Clinton,	Administration,	25567
1794	Lewis H.	Paxton,	Guardianship,	25568
1875	Lillian F.	Princeton,	Guardianship,	25569
1748	Linsford	Mendon,	Guardianship,	25570
1815	Lorinda	Spencer,	Guardianship,	25571
1786	Lucretia	Leicester,	Guardianship,	25572
1872	Lucretia	Spencer,	Administration,	25573
1786	Lucy	Leicester,	Guardianship,	25574
1837	Lucy	Westborough,	Will,	25575
1867	Lucy	Shrewsbury,	Administration,	25576
1879	Lucy	Millbury,	Will,	25577
1865	Lucy A.	Leicester,	Guardianship,	25578
1871	Lucy A.	Leicester,	Will,	25579
1847	Lucy B.	Grafton,	Guardianship,	25580
1814	Lucy M.	Grafton,	Guardianship,	25581
1880	Luther	Shrewsbury,	Administration,	25582
1746	Lydia	Mendon,	Guardianship,	25583
1749	Lydia	Woodstock,	Guardianship,	25584
1756	Lydia	Mendon,	Guardianship,	25585
1804	Lydia	Spencer,	Will,	25586
1834	Lydia P.	Worcester,	Guardianship,	25587
1852	Lyman S.	Oakham,	Guardianship,	25588
1824	Margaret	Gardner,	Will,	25589
1864	Marian A.	Lancaster,	Guardianship,	25590
1866	Martha S.	Rutland,	Will,	25591
1834	Martin	Worcester,	Guardianship,	25592
1811	Mary	Leicester,	Guardianship,	25593
1832	Mary	Uxbridge,	Guardianship,	25594
1838	Mary C.	Fitchburg,	Guardianship,	25595
1861	Mary E.	Worcester,	Guardianship,	25596
1854	Mary J.	Templeton,	Guardianship,	25597
1834	Mary R.	Worcester,	Guardianship,	25598
1810	Meltiah B.	Worcester,	Guardianship,	25599
1858	Moses	Northborough,	Guardianship,	25600
1860	Moses	Northborough,	Administration,	25600
1858	Myron D.	Westborough,	Guardianship,	25301
1776	Nahum	Royalston,	Administration,	25602
1810	Nancy	Worcester,	Guardianship,	25603
1873	Nancy	Millbury,	Will,	25604

YEAR.	NAME.	RESIDENCE.	NATURE.	CASE.
	GREEN AND GREENE,			
1877	Nancy	Leominster,	Guardianship,	25605
1786	Nathan	Leicester,	Guardianship,	25606
1822	Nathan	Gardner,	Will,	25607
1822	Nathan	Northborough,	Administration,	25608
1840	Nathan	Gardner,	Administration,	25609
1788	Nathaniel	Brookfield,	Guardianship,	25610
1791	Nathaniel	Charlton,	Will,	25611
1852	Nathaniel	Shrewsbury,	Will,	25612
1863	Nathaniel	Spencer,	Will,	25613
1867	Nathaniel	Shrewsbury,	Administration,	25614
1874	Nathaniel	North Brookfield,	Administration,	25615
1878	Nathaniel	Leicester,	Guardianship,	25616
1868	Nellie L.	Spencer,	Guardianship,	25617
1842	Olive	Lunenburg,	Guardianship,	25618
1834	Oliver	Ashburnham,	Will,	25619
1834	Oliver B.	Worcester,	Guardianship,	25620
1834	Orville E.	Shrewsbury,	Guardianship,	25621
1795	Peter	Lancaster,	Administration,	25622
1872	Phebe	Spencer,	Administration,	25623
1866	Phebe A.	Spencer,	Guardianship,	25624
1776	Phinehas	Leicester,	Administration,	25625
1862	Polly	Webster,	Administration,	25626
1862	Prudence	Douglas,	Will,	25627
1862	Prudence	Douglas,	Pension,	25628
1756	Rachell	Mendon,	Guardianship,	25629
1794	Relief	Paxton,	Guardianship,	25630
1791	Robert	Oakham,	Guardianship,	25631
1858	Robert E.	Grafton,	Guardianship,	25632
1786	Ruth	Leicester,	Guardianship,	25633
1832	Ruth	Rutland,	Will,	25634
1850	Ruth	Mendon,	Will,	25635
1788	Sally	Brookfield,	Guardianship,	25636
1858	Sally	Grafton,	Administration,	25637
1865	Sally M.	Barre,	Administration,	25638
1736	Samuel	Leicester,	Will,	25639
1779	Samuel	Mendon,	Will,	25640
1808	Samuel	Westborough,	Guardianship,	25641
1810	Samuel	Worcester,	Guardianship,	25642
1811	Samuel	Leicester,	Administration,	25643
1834	Samuel F.	Worcester,	Guardianship,	25644
1748	Sarah	Worcester,	Guardianship,	25645
1786	Sarah	Leicester,	Guardianship,	25646
1825	Sarah	Spencer,	Administration,	25647
1842	Sarah	North Brookfield,	Will,	25648

	GREEN and GREENE,			
1842	Sarah	North Brookfield,	Pension,	25649
1842	Sarah	Lunenburg,	Guardianship,	25650
1864	Sarah E.	Lancaster,	Guardianship,	25651
1858	Sarah M.	Lancaster,	Administration,	25652
1864	Schuyler	Warren,	Administration,	25653
1781	Silas	Leicester,	Guardianship,	25654
1842	Simeon	Lunenburg,	Administration,	25655
1842	Simeon	Lunenburg,	Guardianship,	25656
1840	Solomon	Lancaster,	Administration,	25657
1872	Stella A.	Barre,	Guardianship,	25658
1786	Stephen	Leicester,	Guardianship,	25659
1787	Stephen	Brookfield,	Administration,	25660
1858	Stephen	Grafton,	Administration,	25661
1832	Stephen C.	Uxbridge,	Will,	25662
1832	Stephen C.	Uxbridge,	Guardianship,	25663
1861	Stephen E.	Worcester,	Guardianship,	25664
1843	Sullivan	Lunenburg,	Guardianship,	25665
1845	Susan	Mendon,	Will,	25666
1832	Susan B.	Uxbridge,	Guardianship,	25667
1855	Susan J.	Brookfield,	Will,	25668
1864	Susannah A.	Shrewsbury,	Guardianship,	25669
1873	Sybil	Spencer,	Administration,	25670
1738	Thomas	Worcester,	Guardianship,	25671
1738	Thomas	Worcester,	Administration,	25672
1746	Thomas	Brookfield,	Administration,	25673
1773	Thomas	Leicester,	Administration,	25674
1812	Thomas	Ward,	Will,	25675
1815	Thomas	Ward,	Administration,	25676
1825	Thomas	Providence, R. I.,	Sale Real Estate,	25677
1813	Thomas P.	Ward,	Guardianship,	25678
1794	Timothy	Brookfield,	Will,	25679
1794	Timothy	Brookfield,	Administration,	25680
1835	Timothy	Spencer,	Guardianship,	25681
1866	Timothy	Spencer,	Will,	25682
1788	Timothy, Jr.	Brookfield,	Administration,	25683
1858	Walter E.	Grafton,	Guardianship,	25684
1745	William	Upton,	Will,	25685
1758	William	Hardwick,	Guardianship,	25686
1799	William	Spencer,	Will,	25687
1800	William	Spencer,	Administration,	25688
1805	William	Spencer,	Administration,	25689
1812	William	New Braintree,	Administration,	25690
1828	William	Rutland,	Administration,	25691
1853	William	Templeton,	Administration,	25692

GREEN AND GREENE,

William H.	Brookfield,	Guardianship,	25693
William H.	De Ruyter, N. Y.,	Guardianship,	25694
William N.	Worcester,	Guardianship,	25695
William N.	Worcester,	Administration,	25696
William S.	Milford,	Administration,	25697
Williams	Lancaster,	Administration,	25698
Willie E.	Milford,	Guardianship,	25699
Zalmon	Mendon,	Will,	25700
Zolva	Leicester,	Guardianship,	25701
Zolvia	Leicester,	Administration,	25702

GREENHELGH, Ann — Worcester, Administration, 25703

GREENLEAF AND GREENLIEF,

Almira L.	Templeton,	Guardianship,	25704
Betsey S.	Bolton,	Guardianship,	25705
Calvin	Bolton,	Administration,	25706
Daniel	Bolton,	Will,	25707
Daniel	Bolton,	Guardianship,	25708
Daniel	Worcester,	Administration,	25709
Daniel, Jr.	Bolton,	Will,	25710
Edmund Q.	Western,	Guardianship,	25711
Elizabeth P.	Templeton,	Guardianship,	25712
Frederic	Athol,	Guardianship,	25713
Frederick W.	Worcester,	Will,	25714
Gertrude	Athol,	Guardianship,	25715
Harriet E.	Worcester,	Administration,	25716
James L.	Mendon,	Administration,	25717
John, Jr.	Templeton,	Administration,	25718
John R.	Athol,	Guardianship,	25719
Josephine A.	Athol,	Guardianship,	25720
Loring	Bolton,	Guardianship,	25721
Lucy	Berlin,	Administration,	25722
Myra J.	Worcester,	Administration,	25723
Nancy	Templeton,	Guardianship,	25724
Samuel	Boston,	Guardianship,	25725
Samuel	Templeton,	Guardianship,	25726
Sarah	Templeton,	Guardianship,	25727
Sophia H.	Worcester,	Administration,	25728
Thomas	Medford,	Guardianship,	25729
Thorn	Bolton,	Guardianship,	25730
William	Bolton,	Administration,	25731
William	Worcester,	Will,	25732
William J.	Western,	Guardianship,	25733

GREENMAN, Adelade V. — Blackstone, Administration, 25734

GREENOUGH, D. Florence — Clinton, Guardianship, 25735

Year.	Name.	Residence.	Nature.	Case.
1854	GREENOUGH, Helen E.	Clinton,	Guardianship,	25736
1854	Howard D.	Clinton,	Guardianship,	25737
1854	Ira V. B.	Clinton,	Guardianship,	25738
1844	Lydia	Oxford,	Administration,	25739
1854	Marcia E.	Clinton,	Guardianship,	25740
1871	GREENWAY, Betsey	Lancaster,	Will,	25741
1824	GREENWOOD, Aaron	Gardner,	Will,	25742
1878	Aaron	Worcester,	Will,	25743
1863	Abby	Worcester,	Administration,	25744
1814	Abijah	Hubbardston,	Will,	25745
1864	Abijah H.	Hubbardston,	Administration,	25746
1872	Abner P.	Holden,	Administration,	25747
1862	Addie M.	Westborough,	Guardianship,	25748
1821	Alvan	Gardner,	Will,	25749
1840	Alvan M.	Gardner,	Will,	25750
1822	Alvin M.	Gardner,	Guardianship,	25751
1870	Angeline	Templeton,	Administration,	25752
1879	Ann	Clinton,	Administration,	25753
1816	Augusta	Hubbardston,	Guardianship,	25754
1822	Calvin S.	Gardner,	Guardianship,	25755
1873	,Calvin S.	Gardner,	Will,	25756
1875	Caroline	Hubbardston,	Administration,	25757
1822	Charles	Gardner,	Guardianship,	25758
1844	Charles, 2d	Gardner,	Administration,	25759
1851	Charles	Gardner,	Administration,	25760
1828	Cynthia	Hubbardston,	Guardianship,	25761
1834	Daniel	Webster,	Will,	25762
1816	Edmund R.	Hubbardston,	Guardianship,	25763
1859	Elizabeth	Templeton,	Adoption, etc.,	25764
1852	Esther	Grafton,	Administration,	25765
1824	Ethan A.	Princeton,	Guardianship,	25766
1856	Ethan A.	Hubbardston,	Will,	25767
1859	Fidelia	West Boylston,	Will,	25768
1873	Frederick C.	Holden,	Guardianship,	25769
1844	Gilbert H.	Gardner,	Guardianship,	25770
1873	Helen E.	Holden,	Guardianship,	25771
1865	Henry	Winchendon,	Will,	25772
1877	Henry K.	Millbury	Administration,	25773
1852	Holland	Grafton,	Will,	25774
1816	Horace	Hubbardston,	Guardianship,	25775
1863	Horace	Hubbardston,	Will,	25776
1809	James	Sutton,	Will,	25777
1857	James	Blackstone,	Will,	25778
1822	James H.	Gardner,	Guardianship,	25779
1853	Joel C.	Templeton,	Will,	25780

YEAR.	NAME.	RESIDENCE.	NATURE.	CASE.
1850	GREENWOOD, John	Templeton,	Administration,	25781
1871	John L.	Templeton,	Will,	25782
1852	Jonas	Worcester,	Administration,	25783
1822	Jonathan	Gardner,	Will,	25784
1846	Jonathan	Templeton,	Administration,	25785
1776	Joseph	Holden,	Will,	25786
1872	Joseph E.	Hubbardston,	Will,	25787
1826	Levi	Hubbardston,	Administration,	25788
1866	Levi	Templeton,	Administration,	25789
1858	Lucy N.	Worcester,	Administration,	25790
1880	Lyman	Hubbardston,	Administration,	25791
1862	Marcus	Westborough,	Administration,	25792
1822	Maria	Gardner,	Guardianship,	25793
1875	Mark T.	Fitchburg,	Will,	25794
1844	Marstin D.	Gardner,	Guardianship,	25795
1822	Mary	Gardner,	Guardianship,	25796
1827	Moses	Hubbardston,	Administration,	25797
1828	Moses	Hubbardston,	Administration,	25798
1861	Nellie E.	Ashburnham,	Guardianship,	25799
1849	Oliver	Templeton,	Will,	25800
1814	Otis	Hubbardston,	Will,	25801
1850	Phebe	Templeton,	Guardianship,	25802
1857	Phebe	Templeton,	Administration,	$25802\frac{1}{2}$
1859	Polly	Hubbardston,	Administration,	25803
1826	Reuben	Southborough,	Administration,	25804
1805	Samuel	Leicester,	Administration,	25805
1855	Samuel D.	Holden,	Administration,	25806
1879	Sarah G.	Gardner,	Administration,	25807
1842	Sibbel	Gardner,	Administration,	25808
1857	Silas	Hubbardston,	Administration,	25809
1868	Simeon A.	Worcester,	Administration,	25810
1822	Sophia	Gardner,	Guardianship,	25811
1840	Theodore	Gardner,	Guardianship,	25812
1826	Thomas	Winchendon,	Will,	25813
1861	Walter	Gardner,	Administration,	25814
1880	Walter	Templeton,	Administration,	25815
1822	William	Gardner,	Guardianship,	25816
1878	GREGORY, Abby M.	Winchendon,	Administration,	25817
1870	Betsey A.	Princeton,	Administration,	25818
1836	Caroline	Winchendon,	Guardianship,	25819
1837	Charles A.	Royalston,	Guardianship,	25820
1780	Daniel	Framingham,	Guardianship,	25821
1822	Daniel	Westborough,	Will,	25822
1849	Daniel	Uxbridge,	Guardianship,	25823
1876	Edward	Burrillville, R. I.,	Administration,	25824

(595)

Year.	Name.	Residence.	Nature.	Case.
1777	GREGORY, Elijah	Barre,	Administration,	25825
1778	Elijah	Barre,	Guardianship,	25826
1823	Elisha	Princeton,	Will,	25827
1853	Elisha	Winchendon,	Will,	25828
1880	Elisha	Princeton,	Administration,	25829
1835	Elisha, Jr.	Winchendon,	Administration,	25830
1849	Eunice	Templeton,	Will,	25831
1808	Franklin	Royalston,	Guardianship,	25832
1836	Franklin	Royalston,	Administration,	25833
1837	Franklin E.	Royalston,	Guardianship,	25834
1837	Frederick W.	Royalston,	Guardianship,	25835
1837	George H.	Royalston,	Guardianship,	25836
1778	Hannah	Barre,	Guardianship,	25837
1848	Harriet	Princeton,	Guardianship,	25838
1808	Isaac	Royalston,	Administration,	25839
1837	Isaac H.	Royalston,	Guardianship,	25840
1852	Jeremiah	Uxbridge,	Administration,	25841
1876	John H.	Princeton,	Administration,	25842
1836	John M.	Winchendon,	Guardianship,	25843
1837	John P.	Royalston,	Guardianship,	25844
1837	Martha A.	Royalston,	Guardianship,	25845
1848	Phineas	Princeton,	Administration,	25846
1821	Phinehas	Princeton,	Will,	25847
1778	Rachel	Barre,	Guardianship,	25848
1827	Samuel	Templeton,	Will,	25849
1780	Sarah	Framingham,	Guardianship,	25850
1837	Sarah W.	Royalston,	Guardianship,	25851
1808	Tille	Royalston,	Guardianship,	25852
1870	GRENON, Jean B., etc.	Worcester,	Will,	25853
1870	John	Worcester,	Will,	25853
	GREY see GRAY.			
1864	GRIFFEY, James	Fitchburg,	Administration,	25854
1874	GRIFFIN, Ada O.	Westminster,	Guardianship,	25855
1865	Agnes	Milford,	Guardianship,	25856
1871	Anson	West Brookfield,	Administration,	25857
1874	Carlos G.	Westminster,	Administration,	25858
1869	Catherine	Spencer,	Adoption, etc.,	25859
1830	Charles	Worcester,	Administration,	25860
1879	Daniel	North Brookfield,	Will,	25861
1824	David	Hardwick,	Administration,	25862
1865	Delia	Milford,	Guardianship,	25863
1865	Ellen	Milford,	Guardianship,	25864
1874	Frances	North Brookfield,	Guardianship,	25865
1865	Francis	Milford,	Administration,	25866
1769	James	Oxford,	Will,	25867

YEAR.	NAME.	RESIDENCE.	NATURE.	CASE.
1862	GRIFFIN, James	Fitchburg,	Administration,	25868
1846	Jane M.	Worcester,	Guardianship,	25869
1761	John	Lunenburg,	Will,	25870
1874	Lillian W.	Westminster,	Guardianship,	25871
1865	Mary A.	Milford,	Guardianship,	25872
1865	Thomas H.	Milford,	Guardianship,	25873
1841	GRIGGS, Almira T.	Millbury,	Guardianship,	25874
1809	David	Worcester,	Administration,	25875
1851	Frances H.	Sutton,	Guardianship,	25876
1862	Frances H.	Grafton,	Adoption, etc.,	25877
1871	George A.	Worcester,	Guardianship,	25878
1799	John	Worcester,	Administration,	25879
1850	John	Sutton,	Administration,	25880
1851	John	Sutton,	Guardianship,	25881
1806	Joseph	Sutton,	Guardianship,	25882
1853	Joseph	Worcester,	Administration,	25883
1841	Joseph T.	Millbury,	Guardianship,	25884
1851	Margaret L.	Sutton,	Guardianship,	25885
1841	Mary G.	Millbury,	Guardianship,	25886
1871	Oscar L.	Worcester,	Guardianship,	25887
1791	Samuel	Worcester,	Administration,	25888
1879	Samuel	Westborough,	Administration,	25889
1868	Sarah	Union, Conn.,	Administration,	25890
1871	Susie S.	Worcester,	Guardianship,	25891
1800	Thomas	Sutton,	Administration,	25892
1868	GRIMES, Aaron	Hubbardston,	Will,	25893
1855	Bill	Hubbardston,	Will,	25894
1845	Charles	Hubbardston,	Administration,	25895
1846	Charles	Hubbardston,	Guardianship,	25896
1876	Hiram	Hubbardston,	Guardianship,	25897
1795	John	Hubbardston,	Guardianship,	25898
1790	Joseph	Hubbardston,	Guardianship,	25899
1794	Joseph	Hubbardston,	Will,	25900
1834	Joseph	Hubbardston,	Will,	25901
1846	Mary V.	Hubbardston,	Guardianship,	25902
1845	Porter	Hubbardston,	Guardianship,	25903
1846	Thomas B.	Hubbardston,	Guardianship,	25904
1874	GRISWOLD, Addie M.	Holden,	Guardianship,	25905
1869	Charles E.	Oakham,	Guardianship,	25906
1874	Hermon A.	Holden,	Guardianship,	25907
1853	Jeremiah	Fitchburg,	Administration,	25908
1864	John W.	Ashburnham,	Guardianship,	25909
1876	John W.	Ashburnham,	Adoption, etc.,	25910
1879	Jonah B.	Sturbridge,	Administration,	25911
1865	Lucius D.	Londonderry, Vt.,	Administration,	25912

Year.	Name.	Residence.	Nature.	Case.
1866	GRISWOLD, Sarah W.	Templeton,	Will,	25913
1844	William H.	Dudley,	Administration,	25914
1876	GROGAN, Edward	Worcester,	Guardianship,	25915
1876	George	Worcester,	Guardianship,	25916
1857	James	Southbridge,	Administration,	25917
1876	James	Worcester,	Guardianship,	25918
1870	James W.	Webster,	Guardianship,	25919
1870	Mary	Charlton,	Guardianship,	25920
1876	Mary A.	Worcester,	Guardianship,	25921
1878	Mary A.	Charlton,	Will,	25922
1876	Michael	Worcester,	Administration,	25923
1876	Thomas	Worcester,	Guardianship,	25924
1777	GROO, Peter	Douglas,	Guardianship,	25925
	GROSS and GROSE,			
1791	Daniel	Petersham,	Administration,	25926
1761	Obadiah	Lancaster,	Guardianship,	25927
1760	Thomas	Leicester,	Guardianship,	25928
1821	GROSVENOR, Caroline H.	Brookfield,	Guardianship,	25929
1842	Charles W.	Paxton,	Guardianship,	25930
1849	Cyrus P. D.	Southbridge,	Administration,	25931
1834	Daniel	Petersham,	Will,	25932
1821	Daniel B.	Brookfield,	Administration,	25933
1845	Daniel P., Jr.	Salem,	Guardianship,	25934
1842	David H.	Petersham,	Administration,	25935
1841	Deborah	Petersham,	Will,	25936
1789	Ebenezer	Harvard,	Administration,	25937
1845	Edward P.	Salem,	Guardianship,	25938
1866	Eliza	Petersham,	Administration,	25939
1792	Elizabeth	Harvard,	Guardianship,	25940
1838	Francis L.	Brookfield,	Guardianship,	25941
1845	Harriet E.	Salem,	Guardianship,	25942
1813	John	Worcester,	Guardianship,	25943
1842	Jonathan B.	Paxton,	Guardianship,	25944
1854	Jonathan P.	Paxton,	Will,	25945
1821	Joseph W.	Brookfield,	Guardianship,	25946
1838	Joseph W.	Brookfield,	Guardianship,	25947
1838	Joseph W.	Brookfield,	Will,	25948
1850	Lois P.	Paxton,	Guardianship,	25949
1799	Lucy	Harvard,	Administration,	25050
1842	Lucy	Brookfield,	Will,	25951
1821	Lucy W. A.	Brookfield,	Guardianship,	25952
1792	Mary	Harvard,	Guardianship,	25953
1813	Mary	Worcester,	Guardianship,	25954
1879	Moses G.	Worcester,	Will,	25955
1792	Sally	Harvard,	Guardianship,	25956

Year.	Name.	Residence.	Nature.	Case.
1850	GROSVENOR, Samuel A.	Paxton,	Administration,	25957
1842	Sarah T.	Paxton,	Guardianship,	25958
1876	GROUT, Abby R.	Uxbridge,	Will,	25959
1789	Abigail	Westminster,	Will,	25960
1840	Ann	Winchendon,	Guardianship,	25961
1877	Anna E.	Leominster,	Guardianship,	25962
1828	Benjamin B.	Westborough,	Guardianship,	25993
1808	Betsey	Westborough,	Guardianship,	25964
1874	Carrie A.	Worcester,	Guardianship,	25965
1828	Catharine E.	Westborough,	Guardianship,	25966
1876	Charles	Leominster,	Administration,	25967
1874	Clara A.	Worcester,	Guardianship,	25968
1877	Clara L.	Leominster,	Guardianship,	25969
1802	Cyrus	Uxbridge,	Guardianship,	25970
1813	Cyrus	Uxbridge,	Administration,	25971
1852	Cyrus	Winchendon,	Administration,	25972
1852	Cyrus A.	Winchendon,	Administration,	25973
1790	Daniel	Worcester,	Guardianship,	25974
1813	Dorinda W.	Uxbridge,	Guardianship,	25975
1846	Edwin	Worcester,	Will,	25976
1824	Eliza	Northborough,	Guardianship,	25977
1866	Eliza	Spencer,	Guardianship,	25978
1862	Emma J.	Westborough,	Guardianship,	25979
1874	Emma L.	Worcester,	Guardianship,	25980
1840	Eunice	Winchendon,	Guardianship,	25981
1864	Francis	Worcester,	Will,	25982
1877	George H.	Leominster,	Administration,	25983
1862	George M.	Westborough,	Guardianship,	25984
1878	Grace N.	Leominster,	Administration,	25985
1835	Hannah	Winchendon,	Guardianship,	26986
1837	Hannah	Worcester,	Administration,	25987
1870	Hannah	Worcester,	Will,	25988
1862	Harriet M.	Westborough,	Guardianship,	25989
1852	Hellen E.	Winchendon,	Guardianship,	25990
1870	Henry M.	Spencer,	Administration,	25991
1862	Henry S.	Westborough,	Guardianship,	25992
1835	Isaac	Winchendon,	Administration,	25993
1832	Isaac, Jr.	Winchendon,	Administration,	25994
1869	Jeremiah	Spencer,	Will,	25995
1781	John	Jaffrey, N. H.,	Administration,	25996
1798	John	Uxbridge,	Administration,	25997
1807	John	Petersham,	Administration,	25998
1809	John	Petersham,	Guardianship,	25999
1822	John	Uxbridge,	Administration,	26000
1748	Jonathan	Worcester,	Administration,	26001

YEAR.	NAME.	RESIDENCE.	NATURE.	CASE.
1751	GROUT, Jonathan	Worcester,	Guardianship,	26002
1801	Jonathan	Westborough,	Will,	26003
1807	Jonathan	Petersham,	Will,	26004
1828	Jonathan	Worcester,	Will,	26005
1849	Jonathan	Millbury,	Will,	26006
1878	Jonathan D.	Worcester,	Administration,	26007
1759	Joseph	Westborough,	Administration,	26008
1775	Joseph	Spencer,	Administration,	26009
1870	Joseph	Rutland,	Guardianship,	26010
1852	Joseph L.	Winchendon,	Guardianship,	26011
1828	Joseph P.	Westborough,	Guardianship,	26012
1776	Josiah	Petersham,	Administration,	26013
1757	Keziah	Sutton,	Guardianship,	26014
1839	Lewis	Winchendon,	Administration,	26015
1846	Lydia A. B.	Worcester,	Guardianship,	26016
1862	Marcus	Westborough,	Will,	26017
1870	Martha	Rutland,	Guardianship,	26018
1844	Mary	Worcester,	Will,	26019
1862	Mary E.	Westborough,	Guardianship,	26020
1852	Mary P.	Winchendon,	Guardianship,	26021
1808	Melinda	Westborough,	Guardianship,	26022
1808	Mindwell	Westborough,	Guardianship,	26023
1850	Moses	Westborough,	Will,	26024
1836	Moses W.	Worcester,	Administration,	26025
1862	Myra L.	Westborough,	Guardianship,	26026
1822	Nabby R.	Uxbridge,	Guardianship,	26027
1808	Nancy	Westborough,	Guardianship,	26028
1825	Otis	Spencer,	Guardianship,	26029
1809	Paul	Petersham,	Guardianship,	26030
1751	Priscilla	Worcester,	Guardianship,	26031
1773	Priscilla	Worcester,	Will,	26032
1852	Rachell M.	Winchendon,	Guardianship,	26033
1837	Relief O.	Holden,	Guardianship,	26034
1837	Rhoda	Uxbridge,	Will,	26035
1808	Sally R.	Westborough,	Guardianship,	26036
1808	Samuel	Westborough,	Guardianship,	26037
1826	Samuel	Westborough,	Guardianship,	26038
1827	Samuel	Westborough,	Administration,	26038
1827	Samuel, Jr.	Westborough,	Guardianship,	26039
1835	Samuel B.	Winchendon,	Guardianship,	26040
1870	Samuel R.	Rutland,	Guardianship,	26041
1866	Sarah	Millbury,	Administration,	26042
1812	Sarah	Petersham,	Guardianship,	26043
1823	Seth	Northborough,	Administration,	26044
1751	Silence	Worcester,	Guardianship,	26045

Year.	Name.	Residence.	Nature.	Case.
1809	GROUT, Sophia	Petersham,	Guardianship,	26046
1824	Susan	Petersham,	Will,	26047
1870	Susan	Rutland,	Guardianship,	26048
1822	Susan A.	Uxbridge,	Guardianship,	26049
1828	Susan B.	Westborough,	Guardianship,	26050
1804	Thomas	Spencer,	Will,	26051
1809	Thomas	Petersham,	Guardianship,	26052
1840	William	Winchendon,	Guardianship,	26053
1780	GROVE, Jacob	Douglas,	Guardianship,	26054
1828	GROVER, Benjamin	Grafton,	Guardianship,	26055
1845	Benjamin	Grafton,	Administration,	26055
1853	Elijah	Dana	Administration,	26056
1877	H. Norman	Akron, O.,	Adoption, etc.,	26057
1865	John	Worcester,	Will,	26058
1879	Margaret	Boston,	Adoption, etc.,	26059
1865	Martha L.	Harvard,	Guardianship,	26060
1850	Mary	Lancaster,	Administration,	26061
1865	Olive M.	Harvard,	Guardianship,	26062
1867	Sarah	Oxford,	Administration,	26063
1815	GROVES, Perley F.	Charlton,	Administration,	26064
1872	Pliny	Hamlin, N. Y.,	Foreign Will,	26065
1863	GROW, Betsey	Philadelphia, Pa.,	Administration,	26066
1765	Samuel	Westborough,	Will,	26067
1870	Wilkes S.	Westborough,	Administration,	26068
1876	GUERIN, Eustache C.	Dudley,	Will,	26069
1876	GUERTIN, Prosper	Worcester,	Administration,	26070
1874	GUILD, Charles J.	Worcester,	Administration,	26071
1864	Hannah F.	Milford,	Guardianship,	26072
1879	Joseph W.	Gardner,	Administration,	26073
1869	Marson A.	Worcester,	Guardianship,	26074
1864	Walter O.	Milford,	Guardianship,	26075
1874	Willard G.	Gardner,	Administration,	26076
	GUILFORD AND GILFORD,			
1808	Arnold	Brookfield,	Guardianship,	26077
1877	Arnold	Brookfield,	Administration,	26078
1814	Asa	Spencer,	Guardianship,	26079
1808	Catharine	Brookfield,	Guardianship,	26080
1809	Eliza	Brookfield,	Guardianship,	26081
1874	Eliza C.	Spencer,	Administration,	26082
1814	George	Spencer,	Guardianship,	26083
1880	Hattie B.	Hardwick,	Adoption, etc.,	26084
1809	John	Spencer,	Guardianship,	26085
1814	John	Spencer,	Will,	26085
1828	John	Spencer,	Administration,	26086
1863	John F.	Spencer,	Administration,	26087

Year.	Name.	Residence.	Nature.	Case.
	GUILFORD AND GILFORD,			
1809	Jonas	Spencer,	Administration,	26088
1866	Jonas	Spencer,	Will,	26089
1867	Jonas	Spencer,	Administration,	26090
1809	Lucy	Brookfield,	Guardianship,	26091
1814	Lydia	Spencer,	Guardianship,	26092
1850	Lydia	Spencer,	Guardianship,	26093
1809	Nabby	Brookfield,	Guardianship,	26094
1808	Nancy	Brookfield,	Guardianship,	26095
1809	Orlo	Brookfield,	Guardianship,	26096
1814	Sally	Spencer,	Guardianship,	26097
1838	Sally	Sturbridge,	Administration,	26098
1808	Susanna	Brookfield,	Guardianship,	26099
1808	William	Brookfield,	Will,	26100
1871	William	Brookfield,	Administration,	26101
1865	GUILFOYLE, Daniel	Holden,	Guardianship,	26102
1874	Daniel	Holden,	Administration,	26103
1875	Daniel F.	Worcester,	Guardianship,	26104
1875	John	Holden,	Guardianship,	26105
1875	John E.	Worcester,	Guardianship,	26106
1875	Joseph	Holden,	Guardianship,	26107
1875	Julia E.	Worcester,	Guardianship,	26108
1875	Louis D.	Holden,	Guardianship,	26109
1875	Margaret E.	Holden,	Guardianship,	26110
1875	Margaret M.	Worcester,	Guardianship,	26111
1875	Mary E.	Holden,	Guardianship,	26112
1875	Patrick	Worcester,	Will,	26113
1875	Sarah	Holden,	Guardianship,	26114
1875	Timothy T.	Worcester,	Guardianship,	26115
1875	William R.	Worcester,	Guardianship,	26116
1876	GUINEY, Bridget	Worcester,	Guardianship,	26117
1876	Catherine	Worcester,	Guardianship,	26118
1873	Daniel	Worcester,	Administration,	26119
1876	David	Worcester,	Guardianship,	26120
1876	Patrick	Worcester,	Guardianship,	26121
1878	GULLIVER, Edgar S.	Worcester,	Guardianship,	26122
1873	GUNDERSON, Carl G.	Worcester,	Guardianship,	26123
1872	Christopher	Worcester,	Will,	26124
1873	Gustavus A.	Worcester,	Guardianship,	26125
1873	G. Matilda	Worcester,	Guardianship,	26126
1873	M. Louisa	Worcester,	Guardianship,	26127
1873	Norman	Worcester,	Guardianship,	26128
1856	GUNN, Ellen M.	Uxbridge,	Guardianship,	26129
1854	George	Uxbridge,	Administration,	26130
1856	Horace E.	Uxbridge,	Guardianship,	26131

Year.	Name.	Residence.	Nature.	Case.
1832	GUNN, Justin	Mendon,	Administration,	26132
1855	Lydia	Westminster,	Pension,	26133
1869	GUNNO, Alexander	Worcester,	Administration,	26134
1880	GUNTHER, Otto R.	Worcester,	Administration,	26135
1799	GURNEY, Hannah	Worcester,	Will,	26136
1863	Waldo	Grafton,	Adoption,	26137
1864	William W.	Spencer,	Administration,	26138
1879	GURRY, Ann	Upton,	Will,	26139
1860	HAAS, Ferdinand	Worcester,	Guardianship,	26140
1860	John	Worcester,	Guardianship,	26141
1860	Sebastian	Worcester,	Guardianship,	26142
1865	HABERTHIER, Bernhart	Shrewsbury,	Administration,	26143
1865	Charles	Shrewsbury,	Guardianship,	26144
1865	Elizabeth	Shrewsbury,	Guardianship,	26145
1865	Joseph W.	Shrewsbury,	Guardianship,	26146
1865	Louisa	Shrewsbury,	Guardianship,	26147
1858	HACKER, William E.	Philadelphia, Pa.,	Foreign Will,	26148
1871	HACKETT, Harvelin T.	Hartland, Vt.,	Guardianship,	26149
	HADLEY, HEADLEY and HEADLE,			
1815	Aaron	Sterling,	Guardianship,	26150
1809	Abel	Sterling,	Guardianship,	26151
1827	Abel	Sterling,	Administration,	26152
1843	Abigail	Ashburnham,	Guardianship,	26153
1814	Abraham	Sterling,	Administration,	26154
1843	Almira	Ashburnham,	Guardianship,	26155
1855	Amanda M.	Lunenburg,	Guardianship,	26156
1857	Arvilla A.	Ashburnham,	Guardianship,	26157
1843	Cummings	Ashburnham,	Administration,	26158
1857	David	Ashburnham,	Administration,	26159
1855	Edmund P.	Lunenburg,	Guardianship,	26160
1881	Edmund P.	Leominster,	Administration,	26161
1881	Elizabeth E.	Rutland,	Administration,	26162
1843	Emeline	Ashburnham,	Guardianship,	26163
1814	Ephraim	West Boylston,	Administration,	26164
1869	Frank A.	Ashburnham,	Adoption, etc.,	26165
1855	Frederick R.	Lunenburg,	Guardianship,	26166
1843	Harriet	Ashburnham,	Guardianship,	26167
1818	Isaac	Sterling,	Pension,	26168
1761	John	Lancaster,	Guardianship,	26169
1812	John, 2d	Sterling,	Administration,	26170
1815	John	Sterling,	Guardianship,	26171
1809	Josiah	Sterling,	Will,	26172
1843	Levi	Ashburnham,	Guardianship,	26173
1852	Levi	Princeton,	Will,	26174

YEAR.	NAME.	RESIDENCE.	NATURE.	CASE.
	HADLEY, HEADLEY AND HEADLE,			
1857	Louisa J.	Ashburnham,	Guardianship,	26175
1809	Manassah	Sterling,	Guardianship,	26176
1809	Martha	Sterling,	Guardianship,	26177
1855	Mary F.	Lunenburg,	Guardianship,	26178
1868	Mary J.	Leominster,	Administration,	26179
1815	Peter	Sterling,	Guardianship,	26180
1809	Samuel	Sterling,	Guardianship,	26181
1847	Samuel	Sterling,	Administration,	26182
1828	Sarah M.	Sterling,	Guardianship,	26183
1833	William	Mendon,	Administration,	26184
1860	William	Westminster,	Administration,	26185
1855	William G.	Lunenburg,	Guardianship,	26186
1855	William R.	Lunenburg,	Administration,	26187
1760	HADLOCK, Deborah	Ipswich,	Guardianship,	26188
1881	HADWEN, Charles	Worcester,	Trustee,	26189
1881	Charles	Worcester,	Will,	26190
1881	William	Nantucket,	Trustee,	26191
1853	HAGAN, James W.	Upton,	Adoption, etc.,	26192
1871	Michael	Sturbridge,	Guardianship,	26193
1878	Owen	Worcester,	Administration,	26194
	HAGAR AND HAGER,			
1846	Aaron	Athol,	Pension,	26195
1873	Abigail	Barre,	Will,	26196
1772	Abraham	Western,	Guardianship,	26197
1834	Abraham	West Boylston,	Administration,	26198
1867	Alice M.	Sutton,	Adoption, etc.,	26199
1863	Almira T.	Dudley,	Administration,	26200
1880	Amelia E.	Athol,	Administration,	26201
1869	Charles S.	Athol,	Guardianship,	26202
1873	Charles W.	Athol,	Guardianship,	26203
1869	Clara J.	Athol,	Guardianship,	26204
1830	David	Oakham,	Will,	26205
1846	David	Oakham,	Guardianship,	26206
1846	Dolly	Oakham,	Guardianship,	26207
1774	Elijah	Westminster,	Guardianship,	26208
1841	Elijah	Westminster,	Administration,	26209
1849	George W.	Fitchburg,	Administration,	26210
1869	Henry S.	Athol,	Administration,	26211
1869	Henry W.	Athol,	Guardianship,	26212
1846	James	Oakham,	Administration,	26213
1867	James L.	Petersham,	Will,	26214
1842	John	Phillipston,	Pension,	26215
1842	Joseph	Westminster,	Guardianship,	26216
1872	Joseph E.	Athol,	Administration,	26217

YEAR.	NAME.	RESIDENCE.	NATURE.	CASE.
	HAGAR AND HAGER,			
1823	Jonathan,	Westminster,	Will,	26218
1842	Laura	Westminster,	Administration,	26219
1824	Lois	Bolton,	Administration,	26220
1845	Lucy L.	Oakham,	Administration,	26221
1782	Mary	Westminster,	Will,	26222
1865	Mary	Westminster,	Administration,	26223
1815	Moses	Westminster,	Administration,	26224
1854	Rachel	Athol,	Administration,	26225
1854	Rachel	Athol,	Pension,	26226
1774	Samuel	Westminster,	Will,	26227
1826	Samuel	Westminster,	Guardianship,	26228
1762	Susannah	Worcester,	Guardianship,	26229
1872	Washington	Phillipston,	Will,	26230
	HAGARTY, HAGERTY AND HAGGERTY,			
1851	Edward	Milford,	Administration,	26231
1852	Edward	Milford,	Guardianship,	26232
1868	Grace M.	Lowell,	Adoption, etc.,	26233
1878	Johanna	Worcester,	Administration,	26234
1867	John	Worcester,	Guardianship,	26235
1865	HAGENKOTTER, Joseph E.	Clinton,	Guardianship,	26236
	HAGER see HAGAR.			
	HAGERTY AND HAGGERTY, see HAGARTY.			
	HAGGET AND HAGGETT,			
1854	Joel	Paxton,	Change of Name,	26237
1771	William	Brookfield,	Guardianship,	26238
	HAIL AND HAILD see HALE.			
	HAINES see HAYNES.			
	HAIR, HAIRE AND HARE,			
1765	Abraham	Brookfield,	Guardianship,	26239
1777	Abraham	Brookfield,	Will,	26239
1846	Addison S.	North Brookfield,	Guardianship,	26240
1872	Catherine	Templeton,	Guardianship,	26241
1865	Charles H.	North Brookfield,	Guardianship,	26242
1872	Daniel	Templeton,	Guardianship,	26243
1759	Edward	Worcester,	Guardianship,	26244
1796	Frances	Brookfield,	Guardianship,	26245
1858	Francis	North Brookfield,	Will,	26246
1863	Henry F.	North Brookfield,	Administration,	26247
1771	John	Worcester,	Guardianship,	26248
1843	John	Worcester,	Administration,	26249
1843	John	Worcester,	Pension,	26250
1876	Lucy	Sturbridge,	Administration,	26251
1846	Lydia S.	North Brookfield,	Guardianship,	26252

YEAR.	NAME.	RESIDENCE.	NATURE.	CASE.
	HAIR, HAIRE AND HARE,			
1872	Margaret	Templeton,	Guardianship,	26253
1796	Moses W.	Brookfield,	Guardianship,	26254
1846	Phebe A.	North Brookfield,	Guardianship,	26255
1796	Reed	Brookfield,	Guardianship,	26256
1796	Sally	Brookfield,	Guardianship,	26257
1796	Samuel	Brookfield,	Guardianship,	26258
1796	Samuel	Brookfield,	Administration,	26259
1866	Samuel	North Brookfield,	Administration,	26260
1818	Thomas	Worcester,	Pension,	26261
1872	Thomas	Templeton,	Guardianship,	26262
1865	William F.	North Brookfield,	Guardianship,	26263
	HALE, HAIL, HAILD AND HALES,			
1874	Abby C.	Hubbardston,	Guardianship,	26264
1809	Abigail	Leominster,	Guardianship,	26265
1777	Abner	Harvard,	Guardianship,	26266
1873	Alice E.	Templeton,	Guardianship,	26267
1878	Amos H.	Winchendon,	Will,	26268
1767	Ambrose	Harvard,	Will,	26269
1872	Annie M.	New York, N. Y.,	Guardianship,	26270
1809	Annis	Templeton,	Guardianship,	26271
1853	Asa	Winchendon,	Will,	26272
1870	Austin	Winchendon,	Administration,	26273
1771	Benjamin	Harvard,	Administration,	26274
1779	Benjamin	Harvard,	Guardianship,	26275
1876	Benjamin W.	Hanover, N. H.,	Foreign Will,	26276
1791	Betsy,	Dummerston, Vt.,	Guardianship,	26277
1873	Burritt A.	Templeton,	Guardianship,	26278
1842	Calvin	Leominster,	Will,	26279
1842	Calvin	Leominster,	Pension,	26280
1809	Catharine	Leominster,	Guardianship,	26281
1854	Catharine S.	Hubbardston,	Guardianship,	26282
1852	Charles	Leominster,	Will,	26283
1860	Charles	Millbury,	Administration,	26284
1872	Charles E.	Millbury,	Administration,	26285
1869	Clara	Worcester,	Adoption, etc.,	26286
1854	Clara S.	Hubbardston,	Guardianship,	26287
1850	Cunningham	Hulmeville, Pa.,	Guardianship,	26288
1864	Daniel	Winchendon,	Will,	26289
1867	Daniel	Brookfield,	Will,	26290
1781	David	Harvard,	Guardianship,	26291
1834	David K.	Worcester,	Guardianship,	26292
1791	Dorcas	Dummerston, Vt.,	Guardianship,	26293
1797	Edward	Athol,	Guardianship,	26294
1856	Eldora C.	Sutton,	Guardianship,	26295

YEAR.	NAME.	RESIDENCE.	NATURE.	CASE.
	HALE, HAIL, HAILD AND HALES,			
1873	Eldora M.	Templeton,	Guardianship,	26296
1809	Elisha	Douglas,	Will,	26297
1865	Elisha	Sutton,	Will,	26298
1820	Elizabeth	Leominster,	Administration,	26299
1875	Ella F.	Leominster,	Adoption, etc.,	26300
1873	Ellsworth E.	Templeton,	Guardianship,	26301
1853	Elvira	Fitchburg,	Administration,	26302
1863	Elvira M.	Orange,	Guardianship,	26303
1799	Ephraim	Athol,	Guardianship,	26304
1802	Ezra	Leominster,	Will,	26305
1876	Frances C.	Fitchburg,	Will,	26306
1878	Freddie G.	Royalston,	Adoption, etc.,	26307
1843	Freeman S.	Winchendon,	Guardianship,	26308
1880	George W.	Grafton,	Will,	26309
1756	Gershom	Harvard,	Administration,	26310
1843	Hannah	Leominster,	Administration,	26311
1860	Hannah	Templeton,	Will,	26312
1850	Harriet H.	Fitchburg,	Guardianship,	26313
1848	Hellen M.	Phillipston,	Guardianship,	26314
1872	Henrietta	Sutton,	Guardianship,	26315
1863	Hobert L.	Hubbardston,	Will,	26316
1858	Hopa	Royalston,	Will,	26317
1862	Hoyt	Petersham,	Administration,	26318
1776	Isaac	Harvard,	Administration,	26319
1777	Isaac	Harvard,	Guardianship,	26320
1774	Israel	Harvard,	Guardianship,	26321
1794	Israel	Petersham	Administration,	26322
1832	Jacob	Winchendon,	Will,	26323
1843	Jacob	Winchendon,	Will,	26324
1863	Jacob C.	Weston, Vt.,	Foreign Sale,	26325
1877	Jasper	Leominster,	Administration,	26326
1879	Jennie L.	Fitchburg,	Guardianship,	26327
1781	Joanna	Harvard,	Guardianship,	26328
1799	Joel	Athol,	Guardianship,	26329
1799	John	Athol,	Guardianship,	26330
1874	John O.	Hubbardston,	Guardianship,	26331
1878	John W.	Royalston,	Administration,	26332
1846	Jonas	Berlin,	Administration,	26333
1768	Jonathan	Sutton,	Will,	26334
1827	Jonathan	Royalston,	Guardianship,	26335
1834	Joseph	Templeton,	Guardianship,	26336
1817	Joshua	Worcester,	Administration,	26337
1874	J. Browning	Hubbardston,	Guardianship,	26338

Year.	Name.	Residence.	Nature.	Case.
	HALE, HAIL, HAILD AND HALES,			
1873	J. Otis	Hubbardston,	Administration,	26339
1809	Katharine	Leominster,	Guardianship,	26340
1874	Lucinda	Burrillville, R. I.,	Administration,	26341
1777	Lucy	Harvard,	Guardianship,	26342
1809	Lucy	Leominster,	Guardianship,	26343
1824	Lucy	Leominster,	Administration,	26344
1878	Lucy B.	Hubbardston,	Administration,	26345
1874	Lucy D.	Hubbardston,	Guardianship,	26346
1862	Luke	Hubbardston,	Guardianship,	26347
1864	Luke	Hubbardston,	Administration,	26348
1845	Luther	Hubbardston,	Administration,	26349
1869	Lydia D.	Grafton,	Administration,	26350
1860	Malora H.	Winchendon,	Guardianship,	26351
1868	Maria F.	Fitchburg,	Administration,	26352
1872	Marian E.	New York, N. Y.,	Guardianship,	26353
1863	Martha M.	Chelmsford,	Foreign Sale,	26354
1779	Mary	Harvard,	Guardianship,	26355
1800	Mary	Harvard,	Administration,	26356
1876	Mary	Leominster,	Administration,	26357
1874	Mary G.	Royalston,	Administration,	26358
1857	Mary W.	Leominster,	Administration,	26359
1862	Merrill	Hubbardston,	Guardianship,	26360
1873	Merritt	Winchendon,	Will,	26361
1854	Minerva F.	Hubbardston,	Guardianship,	26362
1844	Miriam	Winchendon,	Will,	26363
1848	Mortimer T.	Phillipston,	Guardianship,	26364
1863	Mortimer T.	Holden,	Administration,	26365
1826	Moses	Winchendon,	Will,	26366
1854	Moses	Fitchburg,	Administration,	26367
1869	Nancy H.	Millbury,	Administration,	26368
1867	Nathaniel W.	Winchendon,	Will,	26369
1866	Nettie H.	Fitchburg,	Adoption, etc.,	26370
1879	Nettie H.	Fitchburg,	Guardianship,	26371
1876	N. Russell T.	New Braintree,	Administration,	26372
1777	Oliver	Harvard,	Guardianship,	26373
1799	Oliver	Leominster,	Will,	26374
1809	Oliver	Templeton,	Administration,	26375
1853	Oliver	Hubbardston,	Administration,	26376
1874	Oliver	Hubbardston,	Guardianship,	26377
1860	Orrelba E.	Winchendon,	Guardianship,	26378
1848	Othniel T.	Phillipston,	Administration,	26379
1810	Polly	Templeton,	Guardianship,	26380
1779	Rachel	Harvard,	Guardianship,	26381

	HALE, HAIL, HAILD AND HALES,			
1828	Reuhiu	Princeton,	Will,	26382
1807	Robert	Douglas,	Administration,	26383
1861	Rowland	Hubbardston,	Administration,	26384
1856	Saladin	Sutton,	Administration,	26385
1791	Sally	Dummerston, Vt.,	Guardianship,	26386
1799	Samuel	Athol,	Will,	26387
1799	Samuel	Athol,	Guardianship,	26388
1813	Samuel	Dana,	Will,	26389
1834	Samuel	Leominster,	Administration,	26390
1880	Samuel	Fitchburg,	Will,	26391
1864	Samuel B.	Winchendon,	Will,	26392
1781	Sarah	Harvard,	Guardianship,	26393
1872	Seth F.	Dana,	Administration,	26394
1854	Seth P. H.	Hubbardston,	Guardianship,	26395
1832	Silas	Phillipston,	Will,	26396
1809	Silvia	Leominster,	Guardianship,	26397
1808	Solon	Leominster,	Guardianship,	26398
1855	Stephen	Royalston,	Will,	26399
1860	Stillman	Winchendon,	Administration,	26400
1796	Thomas	Brookfield,	Will,	26401
1808	Thomas	Leominster,	Administration,	26402
1809	Thomas	Leominster,	Guardianship,	26403
1834	Thomas	North Brookfield,	Will,	26404
1861	Thomas	Hubbardston,	Administration,	26405
1874	Thomas	Fitchburg,	Administration,	26406
1872	Thomas T.	Fort Ruby, Nev.,	Administration,	26407
1872	William	Upton,	Will,	26408
1853	William C.	Worcester,	Will,	26409
1861	William C.	Hubbardston,	Guardianship,	26410
1871	William S.	Leominster,	Will,	26411
1876	HALEY, Bridget	Clinton,	Guardianship,	26412
1867	Hugh	Clinton,	Administration,	26413
1863	George B.	West Boylston,	Guardianship,	26414
1876	John	Clinton,	Guardianship,	26415
1873	John B.	Worcester,	Guardianship,	26416
1876	Mary	Clinton,	Guardianship,	26417
1876	Michael	Clinton,	Guardianship,	26418
1863	Sarah E.	West Boylston,	Guardianship,	26419
1781	HALL, Aaron	Grafton,	Guardianship,	26420
1853	Abby S.	Spencer,	Guardianship,	26421
1824	Acosta	Sutton,	Guardianship,	26422
1833	Albert F.	Oxford,	Guardianship,	26423
1864	Albert F.	Millbury,	Administration,	26424

YEAR.	NAME.	RESIDENCE.	NATURE.	CASE.
1866	HALL, Albert F.	Millbury,	Pension,	26425
1870	Alice M.	Dudley,	Guardianship,	26426
1870	Alvah	Uxbridge,	Will,	26427
1824	Amanda	Sutton,	Guardianship,	26428
1848	Andrew	Uxbridge,	Will,	26429
1858	Angeline D.	Upton,	Administration,	26430
1863	Ann E.	Worcester,	Guardianship,	26431
1876	Ann E.	Worcester,	Administration,	26432
1847	Ann J.	Worcester,	Guardianship,	26433
1871	Anna	Millbury,	Administration,	26434
1880	Asa	Millbury,	Administration,	26435
1839	Bailey	Leominster,	Administration,	26436
1842	Baxter	Uxbridge,	Administration,	26437
1842	Baxter	Uxbridge,	Pension,	26438
1859	Bethiah	Richmond, Vt.,	Administration,	26439
1870	Caleb S.	Dudley,	Administration,	26440
1855	Calvin	Sutton,	Administration,	26441
1871	Calvin	Oxford,	Will,	26442
1841	Caroline C.	Worcester,	Guardianship,	26443
1860	Catharine B.	Sutton,	Administration,	26444
1864	Charles	Fitchburg,	Will,	26445
1841	Charles A.	Worcester,	Guardianship,	26446
1859	Charles R.	Upton,	Will,	26447
1863	Charles S.	Worcester,	Guardianship,	26448
1800	Chloe	Uxbridge,	Guardianship,	26449
1800	Clarissa	Uxbridge,	Guardianship,	26450
1868	Daniel S.	Charlton,	Will,	26451
1789	David	Sutton,	Will,	26452
1798	David	Uxbridge,	Administration,	26453
1833	David	Oxford,	Guardianship,	26454
1847	David	Worcester,	Will,	26455
1815	David E.	Sutton,	Administration,	26456
1872	David E.	Sutton,	Will,	26457
1827	Dolly	Sutton,	Administration,	26458
1858	Edmund T.	Holden,	Administration,	26459
1765	Edward	Uxbridge,	Will,	26460
1852	Edward	Spencer,	Administration,	26461
1857	Edward	Millbury,	Guardianship,	26462
1853	Edward H.	Spencer,	Guardianship,	26463
1862	Elbridge G.	Worcester,	Administration,	26464
1781	Elijah	Grafton,	Guardianship,	26465
1754	Elizabeth	Grafton,	Guardianship,	26466
1867	Ella E.	Holden,	Guardianship,	26467
1881	Ellen M.	Fitchburg,	Will,	26468
1824	Eltheda	Sutton,	Guardianship,	26469
1858	Emma A.	Holden,	Guardianship,	26470

Year.	Name.	Residence.	Nature.	Case.
1848	HALL, Eunice	Uxbridge,	Guardianship,	26471
1870	Everett C.	Dudley,	Guardianship,	26472
1868	Francis A.	Millbury,	Administration,	26473
1871	Frank B.	Worcester,	Administration,	26474
1872	Gaius A.	Winchendon,	Guardianship,	26475
1874	George	Boylston,	Administration,	26476
1858	George W.	Holden,	Guardianship,	26477
1865	Georgianna F.	Millbury,	Guardianship,	26478
1866	Georgianna F.	Millbury,	Pension,	26479
1801	Gordies	Brookfield,	Guardianship,	26480
1754	Hannah	Grafton,	Guardianship,	26481
1806	Hannah	Sutton,	Guardianship,	26482
1833	Hannah W.	Oxford,	Guardianship,	26483
1806	Harriet	Sutton,	Guardianship,	26484
1833	Harriet N.	Oxford,	Guardianship,	26485
1841	Harriet W.	Worcester,	Guardianship,	26486
1863	Henrietta E.	Douglas,	Guardianship,	26487
1858	Henrietta E. M.	Worcester,	Adoption, etc.,	26488
1795	Henry	Ashburnham,	Administration,	26489
1761	Hepzibeth	Petersham,	Guardianship,	26490
1839	Hermon	Douglas,	Will,	26491
1806	Increase S.	Sutton,	Guardianship,	26492
1864	Isaac	Fitchburg,	Administration,	26493
1841	James	Northborough,	Administration,	26494
1871	James	Worcester,	Will,	26495
1807	James	Northbridge,	Administration,	26496
1826	James	Leominster,	Will,	26497
1853	James E.	Spencer	Guardianship,	26498
1853	Jane F.	Spencer,	Guardianship,	26499
1757	Jean	Sutton,	Will,	26500
1871	Jennie	New Orleans, La.,	Guardianship,	26501
1806	John	Sutton,	Guardianship,	26502
1806	John	Sutton,	Administration,	26503
1834	John	Ashburnham,	Pension,	26504
1854	John	Worcester,	Guardianship,	26505
1858	John	Holden,	Will,	26506
1869	John	Worcester,	Administration,	26507
1874	John	Millbury,	Will,	26508
1854	John, Jr.	Worcester,	Guardianship,	26509
1872	John B.	Leominster,	Will,	26510
1841	John C.	Worcester,	Will,	26511
1851	John P.	Uxbridge,	Administration,	26512
1841	John W.	Worcester,	Guardianship,	26513
1747	Jonathan	Grafton,	Administration,	26514
1777	Jonathan	Grafton,	Will,	26515

Year.	Name.	Residence.	Nature.	Case.
1840	HALL, Joseph	Sutton,	Administration,	26516
1877	Joseph E.	Clinton,	Administration,	26517
1855	Joshua	Lunenburg,	Will,	26518
1839	Josiah	Sutton,	Will,	26519
1841	Josiah	Sutton,	Pension,	26520
1847	Judson W.	Worcester,	Guardianship,	26521
1847	Julia E.	Worcester,	Guardianship,	26522
1848	Laura J.	Uxbridge	Guardianship,	26523
1871	Lee	New Orleans, La.,	Guardianship,	26524
1875	Lefe M.	Webster,	Adoption, etc.,	26525
1795	Levi	Providence, R. I.,	Sale Real Estate,	26526
1880	Louisa F.	Upton,	Administration,	26527
1876	Luasenath	Sutton,	Will,	26528
1858	Luther	Sutton,	Will,	26529
1848	Marcus M.	Millbury,	Will,	26530
1855	Mary	Sutton,	Pension,	26531
1860	Mary	Sutton,	Administration,	26532
1862	Mary	Spencer,	Administration,	26533
1878	Mary D.	Milford,	Will,	26534
1852	Mary J.	Upton,	Guardianship,	26535
1855	Mary J.	Millbury,	Guardianship,	26536
1858	Mary M.	Fitchburg,	Will,	26537
1853	Mary N.	Spencer,	Guardianship,	26538
1849	Mercy	Holden,	Administration,	26539
1848	Merrick E.	Uxbridge,	Guardianship,	26540
1848	Minerva	Uxbridge,	Guardianship,	26541
1869	Minnie A.	Sutton,	Guardianship,	26542
1867	Minny A.	Sutton,	Adoption, etc.,	26543
1824	Miranda	Sutton,	Guardianship,	26544
1835	Moses	Spencer,	Administration,	26545
1836	Moses	Spencer,	Guardianship,	26546
1853	Nancy	Worcester,	Administration,	26547
1833	Nancy C.	Oxford,	Guardianship,	26548
1878	Nancy W.	Worcester,	Will,	26549
1835	Nathan	Oxford,	Administration,	26550
1858	Nathan	Holden,	Administration,	26551
1856	Nathan W.	Southbridge,	Administration,	26552
1843	Nehemiah	Uxbridge,	Will,	26553
1865	Nellie V.	Millbury,	Guardianship,	26554
1842	Oliver, Jr.	Worcester,	Guardianship,	26555
1869	Otis	Sutton,	Administration,	26556
1801	Paola	Brookfield,	Guardianship,	26557
1753	Parcival	Sutton,	Will,	26558
1832	Parris	Oxford,	Administration,	26559
1801	Pasuel	Brookfield,	Guardianship,	26560

YEAR.	NAME.	RESIDENCE.	NATURE.	CASE.
1824	HALL, Pelthira	Sutton,	Guardianship,	26561
1772	Percival	New Braintree,	Guardianship,	26562
1875	Percival	New Braintree,	Will,	26563
1842	Phineas	Stoddard, N. H.,	Administration,	26564
1863	Polly	Charlton,	Will,	26565
1848	Rexvilla	Uxbridge,	Guardianship,	26566
1878	Richardson	Worcester,	Administration,	26567
1867	Rodney	Fitchburg,	Administration,	26568
1801	Ruth	Brookfield,	Guardianship,	26569
1800	Sally	Uxbridge,	Guardianship,	26570
1809	Sally	Westminster,	Guardianship,	26571
1754	Samuel	Grafton,	Guardianship,	26572
1761	Samuel	Petersham,	Guardianship,	26573
1781	Samuel	Grafton,	Guardianship,	26574
1799	Samuel	Brookfield,	Administration,	26575
1801	Samuel	Brookfield,	Guardianship,	26576
1815	Samuel	Spencer,	Administration,	26577
1861	Samuel	Charlton,	Will,	26578
1841	Samuel B.	Worcester,	Guardianship,	26579
1842	Samuel S.	Worcester,	Guardianship,	26580
1754	Sarah	Grafton,	Guardianship,	26581
1784	Sarah	Windsor, Vt.,	Guardianship,	26582
1875	Sarah	Upton,	Will,	26583
1869	Selissa	Cumberland, R. I.,	Foreign Will,	26584
1871	Sidney	New Orleans, La.,	Guardianship,	26585
1842	Silence M.	Northborough,	Guardianship,	26586
1826	Simeon	Sutton,	Administration,	26587
1824	Stephen	Sutton,	Will,	26588
1800	Submit	Uxbridge,	Guardianship,	26589
1880	Susan	Southbridge,	Administration,	26590
1852	Thaddeus	Millbury,	Will,	26591
1794	Thankfull	Grafton,	Will,	26592
1853	Therel L.	Millbury,	Guardianship,	26593
1756	Thomas	Dudley,	Will,	26594
1798	Thomas	Charlton,	Administration,	26595
1751	Timothy	Harvard,	Administration,	26596
1785	Timothy	Brookfield,	Will,	26597
1867	Willard	Sutton,	Administration,	26598
1860	William	Sutton,	Administration,	26599
1852	William B.	Upton,	Will,	26600
1841	William H.	Worcester,	Guardianship,	26601
1800	Willis	Uxbridge,	Guardianship,	26602
1800	Willis	Sutton,	Administration,	26603
1854	Willis J.	Millbury,	Administration,	26604
1772	Zacheus	New Braintree,	Will,	26605

YEAR.	NAME.	RESIDENCE.	NATURE.	CASE.
1824	HALL, Zarah	Sutton,	Guardianship,	26606
1870	HALLOCK, Charlotte	Templeton,	Administration,	26607
1875	Elizabeth	Westborough,	Administration,	26608
1875	HALLORAN, Johana	Worcester,	Will,	26609
1812	HALLOWELL, Abner	Spencer,	Administration,	26610
1873	Calvin	Gardner,	Will,	26611
1824	David	Spencer,	Guardianship,	26612
1868	David R.	Spencer,	Administration,	26613
1874	Dorothy W.	Gardner,	Administration,	26614
1801	Joseph	Spencer,	Administration,	26615
1874	HALLOWS, James	Dudley,	Will,	26616
1856	HAM, Andrew H.	Worcester,	Change of Name,	26617

HAMANT, HAMENT AND HAM-
MANT (see also HAMMOND),

1872	Annie L.	Worcester,	Guardianship,	26618
1880	Charles F.	North Brookfield,	Guardianship,	26619
1812	David	Sturbridge,	Guardianship,	26620
1841	Franklin	Sturbridge,	Guardianship,	26621
1881	Horace	North Brookfield,	Administration,	26622
1812	Isaac	Sturbridge,	Guardianship,	26623
1877	Isaac	Brookfield,	Will,	26624
1810	Job	Sturbridge,	Will,	26625
1880	Katie M.	North Brookfield,	Guardianship,	26626
1872	Lotson S.	Worcester,	Administration,	26627
1860	Louisa	Brookfield,	Administration,	26628
1880	Lucius F.	North Brookfield,	Administration,	26629
1878	Luther	Sturbridge,	Administration,	26630
1812	Sally	Sturbridge,	Guardianship,	26631
1804	Samuel	Sturbridge,	Administration,	26632
1812	Seth	Sturbridge,	Administration,	26633
1784	Timothy	Medfield,	Distribution,	26634
1805	William	Sturbridge,	Guardianship,	26635

HAMBLETON see HAMILTON.

1870	HAMBURY, Edwin	Leicester,	Administration,	26636

HAMENT see HAMANT.

HAMILTON AND HAMBLETON,

1811	Adolphus	Brookfield,	Guardianship,	26637
1875	Alanson	West Brookfield,	Will,	26638
1844	Albert	Brookfield,	Guardianship,	26639
1871	Alice F.	Brookfield,	Guardianship,	26640
1791	Amos	Brookfield,	Administration,	26641
1778	Anne	Brookfield,	Guardianship,	26642
1875	Arthur W.	Brookfield,	Guardianship,	26643
1799	Asa	Brookfield,	Guardianship,	26644
1831	Asa	Worcester,	Administration,	26645
1856	Austin	Barre,	Administration,	26646

YEAR.	NAME.	RESIDENCE.	NATURE.	CASE.

HAMILTON AND HAMBLETON,

YEAR.	NAME.	RESIDENCE.	NATURE.	CASE.
1824	Benjamin F.	Barre,	Guardianship,	26647
1839	Bulah	Brookfield,	Pension,	26648
1798	Calvin	Brookfield,	Guardianship,	26649
1811	Calvin	Brookfield,	Guardianship,	26650
1856	Calvin L.	Barre,	Guardianship,	26651
1811	Caroline	Brookfield,	Guardianship,	26652
1817	Celestia	Brookfield,	Guardianship,	26653
1879	Charles A.	Worcester,	Will,	26654
1798	Charlotte	Brookfield,	Guardianship,	26655
1817	Charlotte	Brookfield,	Guardianship,	26656
1856	Charlotte S.	Barre,	Guardianship,	26657
1797	Chauncy	Brookfield,	Administration,	26658
1807	Cheney	Brookfield,	Guardianship,	26659
1813	Cheney	Brookfield,	Administration,	26660
1820	Edward	North Brookfield,	Guardianship,	26661
1870	Edward	Worcester,	Will,	26662
1749	Eliphalet	Brookfield,	Guardianship,	26663
1762	Eliphalet	Brookfield,	Will,	26664
1838	Eliphalet	Brookfield,	Pension,	26665
1834	Elizabeth	Worcester,	Will,	26666
1798	Fanny	Brookfield,	Guardianship,	26667
1817	Fidelia	Brookfield,	Guardianship,	26668
1842	Frederick	Sackett's Harbor, N.Y.,	Administration,	26669
1881	George	Templeton,	Will,	26670
1870	George H.	Worcester,	Guardianship,	26671
1849	George W.	Hubbardston,	Guardianship,	26672
1811	Hanson	Brookfield,	Guardianship,	26673
1798	Harriot	Brookfield,	Guardianship,	26674
1824	Henry	Brookfield,	Guardianship,	26675
1817	Henry D.	Brookfield,	Guardianship,	26676
1821	Henry H.	Brookfield,	Guardianship,	26677
1820	Hiram	North Brookfield,	Guardianship,	26678
1809	Israel	Brookfield,	Administration,	26679
1811	Israel	Brookfield,	Guardianship,	26680
1735	James	Worcester,	Will,	26681
1817	James	Barre,	Administration,	26682
1854	Jane E.	Brookfield,	Guardianship,	26683
1796	Jason	Brookfield,	Administration,	26684
1820	Joel	North Brookfield,	Guardianship,	26685
1739	John	Westborough,	Guardianship,	26686
1746	John	Brookfield,	Administration,	26687
1833	John A.	Barre,	Administration,	26688
1771	Jonah	Brookfield,	Administration,	26689
1773	Jonah	New Braintree,	Administration,	26690

YEAR.	NAME.	RESIDENCE.	NATURE.	CASE.

HAMILTON AND HAMBLETON,

YEAR.	NAME.	RESIDENCE.	NATURE.	CASE.
1778	Jonah	New Braintree,	Guardianship,	26691
1777	Jonas	New Braintree,	Guardianship,	26692
1747	Joseph	Brookfield,	Will,	26693
1827	Joseph	Brookfield,	Administration,	26694
1820	Joseph, Jr.	Brookfield,	Administration,	26695
1856	Joseph A.	Barre,	Guardianship,	26696
1820	Joseph P.	Brookfield,	Guardianship,	26697
1834	Joseph W.	Brookfield,	Administration,	26698
1792	Josiah	Brookfield,	Administration,	26699
1809	Josiah	Brookfield,	Will,	26700
1819	Josiah	Brookfield,	Administration,	26701
1798	Jude	Brookfield,	Will,	26702
1799	Leonard	Brookfield,	Guardianship,	26703
1761	Levi	Brookfield,	Administration,	26704
1819	Margaret	Hardwick,	Will,	26705
1855	Margaret	Charlton,	Pension,	26706
1863	Mary D.	Worcester,	Administration,	26707
1871	Merritt	Petersham,	Will,	26708
1802	Michael	Barre,	Will,	26709
1798	Nancy	Brookfield,	Guardianship,	26710
1819	Nathan	Brookfield,	Administration,	26711
1847	Nathan	Brookfield,	Pension,	26712
1771	Obed	Brookfield,	Guardianship,	26713
1774	Obed	Brookfield,	Administration,	26714
1811	Olive	Brookfield,	Guardianship,	26715
1820	Otis	North Brookfield,	Guardianship,	26716
1790	Reuben	Worcester,	Administration,	26717
1814	Rhoda	Brookfield,	Administration,	26718
1862	Robert	Blackstone,	Administration,	26719
1817	Rufus	North Brookfield,	Will,	26720
1798	Sally	Brookfield,	Guardianship,	26721
1837	Sally	Brookfield,	Will,	26722
1778	Samuel	Worcester,	Guardianship,	26723
1854	Seraph M.	Brookfield,	Guardianship,	26724
1748	Seth	Brookfield,	Guardianship,	26725
1762	Seth	Brookfield,	Will,	26726
1813	Seth	Brookfield,	Administration,	26727
1817	Seth	Brookfield,	Pension,	26728
1824	Sewall	Worcester,	Administration,	26729
1799	Silas	Brookfield,	Guardianship,	26730
1860	Squier	Brookfield,	Will,	26731
1817	Susan	Brookfield,	Guardianship,	26732
1852	Susan S.	Barre,	Administration,	26733
1834	Susanna	Barre,	Will,	26734

	HAMILTON AND HAMBLETON,			
1777	Thomas	Brookfield,	Administration,	26735
1778	Thomas	Brookfield,	Guardianship,	26736
1772	Timothy	Brookfield,	Will,	26737
1798	Walter	Brookfield,	Guardianship,	26738
1798	Washington	Brookfield,	Guardianship,	26739
1816	William	Barre,	Guardianship,	26740
1832	William	Brookfield,	Administration,	26741
1874	William	Clinton,	Will,	26742
1824	HAMLIN, Africa	Harvard,	Administration,	26743
1871	Lavinia S.	Boston,	Sale Real Estate,	26744
1871	William H.	Kansas,	Sale Real Estate,	26745
	HAMMANT see HAMANT.			
1868	HAMMERBACKER, John C.	Worcester,	Will,	26746
	HAMMOND, HAMMON AND HAM-			
	OND (see also HAMANT),			
1843	Aaron	Charlton,	Will,	26747
1856	Andrew H.	Worcester,	Change of Name,	26748
1760	Anna	Lunenburg,	Guardianship,	26749
1760	Avis	Lunenburg,	Guardianship,	26750
1809	Benjamin	Rutland,	Administration,	26751
1801	Bulah	Spencer,	Administration,	26752
1831	Charles	Petersham,	Administration,	26753
1790	David	Petersham,	Administration,	26754
1813	David	Charlton,	Will,	26755
1783	Ebenezer	Charlton,	Administration,	26756
1784	Ebenezer	Charlton,	Guardianship,	26757
1821	Ebenezer	Petersham,	Will,	26758
1862	Ebenezer	Charlton,	Administration,	26759
1813	Elias H.	Oakham,	Guardianship,	26760
1815	Elijah	Oakham,	Will,	26761
1875	Elijah	Oxford,	Administration,	26762
1879	Elijah	Worcester,	Partition,	26763
1851	Elisha	West Brookfield,	Administration,	26764
1840	Elisha G.	Brookfield,	Guardianship,	26765
1818	Enoch, Jr.	Petersham,	Administration,	26766
1843	Enock	Douglas,	Guardianship,	26767
1783	Esther	Charlton,	Guardianship,	26768
1830	Eunice	Oakham,	Administration,	26769
1845	Eveline A.	Barre,	Guardianship,	26770
1878	Frederick H.	Fitchburg,	Administration,	26771
1879	Frederick H.	Worcester,	Partition,	26772
1771	Hinsdell	Sturbridge,	Guardianship,	26773
1862	James	Worcester,	Will,	26774
1876	Jeduthan	Brookfield,	Will,	26775

HAMMOND, HAMMON AND HAM-
OND (see also HAMANT),

YEAR.	NAME.	RESIDENCE.	NATURE.	CASE.
1875	Jennie A.	Worcester,	Guardianship,	26776
1771	Joel	Sturbridge,	Guardianship,	26777
1843	John	Douglas,	Administration,	26778
1871	John	Worcester,	Administration,	26779
1843	John C.	Douglas,	Guardianship,	26780
1791	Jonas	Charlton,	Will,	26781
1879	Joseph P.	Worcester,	Partition,	26782
1860	Josiah H.	Grafton,	Administration,	26783
1843	Lemuel H.	Douglas,	Guardianship,	26784
1817	Levi	Lancaster,	Administration,	27785
1871	Levi	Charlton,	Will,	26786
1843	Louisa	Douglas,	Guardianship,	26787
1843	Lucy	Douglas,	Guardianship,	26788
1859	Lucy	Petersham,	Administration,	26789
1824	Luke	Petersham,	Guardianship,	26790
1807	Mary	Uxbridge,	Administration,	26791
1828	Moses,	Charlton,	Administration,	26792
1843	Nancy E.	Douglas,	Guardianship,	26793
1824	Nathan	Petersham,	Guardianship,	26794
1851	Nathan	Petersham,	Will,	26795
1879	Otis S.	Worcester,	Partition,	26796
1880	Otis S.	Worcester,	Will,	26797
1805	Parley	Lancaster,	Guardianship,	26798
1827	Parley	Lancaster,	Will,	26799
1824	Perley	Petersham,	Guardianship,	26800
1760	Phineas	Lunenburg,	Guardianship,	26801
1791	Polly	Petersham,	Guardianship,	26802
1879	Rebecca	Fon-du-lac, Wis.,	Partition,	26803
1881	Ruhamah	Charlton,	Administration,	26804
1760	Samuel	Lunenburg,	Guardianship,	26805
1760	Samuel	Lunenburg,	Will,	26806
1845	Samuel	Barre,	Administration,	26807
1869	Samuel	Southbridge,	Will,	26808
1843	Samuel A.	Douglas,	Guardianship,	26809
1783	Sarah	Charlton,	Guardianship,	26810
1791	Sarah	Petersham,	Guardianship,	26811
1771	Seth	Sturbridge,	Administration,	26812
1771	Simeon	Sturbridge,	Guardianship,	26813
1880	Susan M.	Worcester,	Will,	26814
1815	Susanna	Oxford,	Administration,	26815
1847	Thomas	Fitchburg,	Administration,	26816
1748	Timothy	Hardwick,	Administration,	26817
1824	Timothy	Petersham,	Guardianship,	26818

	HAMMOND, HAMMON AND HAM-OND (see also HAMANT),			
1845	Timothy C.	Barre,	Guardianship,	26819
1825	William H.	Rutland,	Administration,	26820
1771	Zillah	Sturbridge,	Guardianship,	26821
1864	HAMPSON, Henry F.	Worcester,	Administration,	26822
1854	Martha E.	Worcester,	Adoption,	26823
1864	Martha E.	Worcester,	Change of Name,	26823
1854	HANCHETT, Ephraim	Douglas,	Administration,	26824
1855	Nancy S.	Douglas,	Guardianship,	26825
1855	Thatcher S.	Douglas,	Guardianship,	26826
1853	HANCOCK, Anson	Grafton,	Will,	26827
1810	Augustus	Unknown,	Sale Real Estate,	26828
1868	Augustus	Barre,	Administration,	26829
1800	Betsy	Winchendon,	Guardianship,	26830
1793	Bill	Winchendon,	Administration,	26831
1864	Catharine W.	Barre,	Administration,	26832
1848	Charles	Buffalo, N. Y.,	Guardianship,	26833
1853	Charles N.	Grafton,	Guardianship,	26834
1871	Charlotte M.	Lincoln, R. I.,	Guardianship,	26835
1803	David	Winchendon,	Guardianship,	26836
1848	George L.	Buffalo, N. Y.,	Guardianship,	26837
1800	Joel	Winchendon,	Guardianship,	26838
1835	John	Templeton,	Administration,	26839
1849	John D.	Blackstone,	Guardianship,	26840
1800	Joseph	Winchendon,	Guardianship,	26841
1810	Josiah	Unknown,	Sale Real Estate,	26842
1800	Lucy	Winchendon,	Guardianship,	26843
1853	Maria J.	Grafton,	Guardianship,	26844
1810	Nathan	Unknown,	Sale Real Estate,	26845
1857	Nathan	Barre,	Administration,	26846
1866	Nathan	Grafton,	Will,	26847
1843	Nathan S.	Barre,	Administration,	26848
1848	Robert T.	Buffalo, N. Y.,	Guardianship,	26849
1880	Robert T.	Royalston,	Will,	26850
1821	Rufus	Templeton,	Administration,	26851
1800	Samuel	Winchendon,	Guardianship,	26852
1779	Thomas	Lancaster,	Guardianship,	26853
1848	William	Blackstone,	Will,	26854
1868	William	Dudley,	Will,	26855
1849	William T.	Blackstone,	Guardianship,	26856
1849	HAND, William	Grafton,	Administration,	26857
1847	HANDLEY, George W.	Ashburnham,	Guardianship,	26858
1847	Martha A.	Ashburnham,	Guardianship,	26859
1858	Nathan	Ashburnham,	Administration,	26860

Year.	Name.	Residence.	Nature.	Case.
1847	HANDLEY, Sally W.	Ashburnham,	Guardianship,	26861
1817	HANDY, Benjamin	Uxbridge,	Will,	26862
1818	David	Mendon,	Guardianship,	26863
1880	Thomas H.	Worcester,	Administration,	26864
1869	HANLON, Hugh	Auburn,	Administration,	26865
1858	Mary A.	Worcester,	Guardianship,	26866
1858	Patrick	Worcester,	Will,	26867
1880	Thomas	Worcester,	Will,	26868
1796	HANMER, Zenus	Hardwick,	Administration,	26869
1861	HANNA, Henrietta	Northbridge,	Guardianship,	26870
1878	Maria H.	Westborough,	Will,	26871
1861	Mary	Northbridge,	Guardianship,	26872
1852	Thomas	Westborough,	Will,	26873
1862	HANNAFORD, Charles H.	Auburn,	Guardianship,	26874
1861	HANNAHAN, Johanna	Millbury,	Administration,	26875
1863	HANNAN, Betsey	Milford,	Will,	26876
1871	Eliza	Southbridge,	Guardianship,	26877
	HANNEGAN AND HANNIGAN,			
1878	Catherine O.	Worcester,	Will,	26878
1873	David	Worcester,	Will,	26879
1878	Mary A.	Gardner,	Administration,	26880
1859	Richard	Fitchburg,	Administration,	26881
1859	HANNUM, Charles, Jr.	Petersham	Administration,	26882
1854	Eldora R.	Douglas,	Adoption, etc.,	26883
1865	Josiah	Douglas,	Administration,	26884
1873	HANSON, George	Southbridge,	Will,	26885
1849	HANYBERRY, James	West Boylston,	Guardianship,	26886
1860	HAPGOOD, Alfred W.	Harvard,	Guardianship,	26887
1832	Andrew	Harvard,	Administration,	26888
1822	Ann H.	Petersham,	Guardianship,	26889
1846	Artemas	Barre,	Will,	26890
1791	Asa	Barre,	Will,	26891
1868	Asa	Worcester,	Administration,	26892
1876	Charles B.	Harvard,	Guardianship,	26893
1750	Damaris	Shrewsbury,	Guardianship,	29894
1847	Daniel	Templeton,	Administration,	26895
1829	David	Shrewsbury,	Will,	26896
1843	David T.	Shrewsbury,	Will,	26897
1853	Elijah	Shrewsbury,	Will,	26898
1876	Ella M.	Harvard,	Guardianship,	26899
1844	Ephraim	Shrewsbury,	Administration,	26900
1847	Euthera	Templeton,	Guardianship,	26901
1873	Francis	Holden,	Will,	26902
1878	George	Harvard,	Administration,	26903
1876	Hannah G.	Harvard,	Guardianship,	26904

YEAR.	NAME.	RESIDENCE.	NATURE.	CASE.
1874	HAPGOOD, Hattie M.	Oakham,	Adoption,	26905
1877	Horace	Athol,	Will,	26906
1837	Hutchins	Petersham,	Will,	26907
1874	Ida L.	Oakham,	Adoption, etc.,	26908
1860	Jabez	Harvard,	Administration,	26909
1865	Jennie M.	Winchendon,	Guardianship,	26910
1847	Jerusha	Templeton,	Guardianship,	26911
1750	Joab	Shrewsbury,	Guardianship,	26912
1855	Joel	Harvard,	Will,	26913
1750	John	Shrewsbury,	Guardianship,	26914
1761	John	Shrewsbury,	Administration,	26915
1859	John	Harvard,	Will,	26916
1847	John D.	Templeton,	Guardianship,	26917
1877	John H.	Leominster,	Adoption, etc.,	26918
1830	Jonathan	Princeton,	Administration,	26919
1876	Jonathan F.	Harvard,	Administration,	26920
1818	Joseph	Princeton,	Administration,	26921
1866	Laura	Holden,	Administration,	26922
1831	Levi	Petersham,	Guardianship,	26923
1851	Lucy	Shrewsbury,	Will,	26924
1871	Lyman W.	Petersham,	Administration,	26925
1874	Lyman W.	Athol,	Will,	26926
1837	Marcus M.	Templeton,	Guardianship,	26927
1774	Marcy	Bolton,	Will,	26928
1866	Mary	Harvard,	Will,	26929
1872	Mary A.	Harvard,	Administration,	26930
1847	Mary E. M.	Templeton,	Guardianship,	26931
1831	Mary F.	Petersham,	Guardianship,	26932
1758	Nathaniel	Bolton,	Will,	26933
1847	Newell	Hubbardston,	Administration,	26934
1863	Otis W.	Winchendon,	Will,	26935
1750	Seth	Shrewsbury,	Guardianship,	26936
1804	Seth	Petersham,	Will,	26937
1864	Seth	Petersham,	Will,	26938
1782	Shadrach	Harvard,	Will,	26939
1818	Shadrach	Harvard,	Will,	26940
1853	Shadrach	Harvard,	Administration,	26941
1831	Susan E.	Petersham,	Guardianship,	26942
1876	Theodore G.	Harvard,	Guardianship,	26943
1745	Thomas	Shrewsbury,	Administration,	26944
1820	Thomas	Petersham,	Administration,	26945
1750	Unis	Shrewsbury,	Guardianship,	26946
1872	William F.	Worcester,	Guardianship,	26947
1830	Windsor	Hubbardston,	Administration,	26948
1839	HARBACK, Daniel	Sutton,	Administration,	26949

(621)

YEAR.	NAME.	RESIDENCE.	NATURE.	CASE.
1804	HARBACK, David	Sutton,	Guardianship,	26950
1880	Elizabeth	Sterling,	Will,	26951
1844	George R.	Sutton,	Guardianship,	26952
1851	George R.	Sutton,	Administration,	26953
1812	Hiram R.	Worcester,	Guardianship,	26954
1801	John	Sutton,	Administration,	26955
1849	Mary	Sutton,	Administration,	26956
1849	Origen	Sutton,	Administration,	26957
1844	Persia M.	Sutton,	Guardianship,	26958
1878	Rufus H.	Sutton,	Administration,	26959
1791	Thomas	Sutton,	Will,	26960
1854	HARD, Harriet N.	Milford,	Will,	26961
1854	Josephine E. N.	New York, N. Y.,	Guardianship,	26962
1854	Lawrence M.	New York, N. Y.,	Guardianship,	26963
1829	HARDING, Abigail	Southbridge,	Guardianship,	26964
1826	Abijah	Barre,	Will,	26965
1816	Abijah, Jr.	Barre,	Administration,	26966
1816	Abijah S.	Barre,	Guardianship,	26967
1859	Ann B.	New Ipswich, N. H.,	Guardianship,	26968
1880	Augusta	Sturbridge,	Will,	26969
1766	Caleb	Sturbridge,	Guardianship,	26970
1880	Charles H.	Bradford, Vt.,	Foreign Will,	26971
1863	Darius H.	Winchendon,	Will,	26972
1829	Deborah A.	Southbridge,	Guardianship,	26973
1872	Elbridge G.	Southbridge,	Administration,	26974
1790	Elijah	Sturbridge,	Administration,	26975
1826	Eliza	Medfield,	Guardianship,	26976
1829	Elizabeth	Southbridge,	Guardianship,	26977
1857	Ellen L.	Barre,	Guardianship,	26978
1769	Esther	Sturbridge,	Guardianship,	26979
1863	Florence E.	Winchendon,	Guardianship,	26980
1778	Hannah	Sturbridge,	Guardianship,	26981
1865	Henry A.	Worcester,	Administration,	26982
1800	Jabez	Sturbridge,	Will,	26983
1839	Jabez	Sturbridge,	Will,	26984
1769	Jerusha	Sturbridge,	Guardianship,	26985
1769	John	Sturbridge,	Guardianship,	26986
1780	John	Sturbridge,	Administration,	26987
1859	John H.	New Ipswich, N. H.,	Guardianship,	26988
1807	John W.	Sturbridge,	Guardianship,	26989
1796	Joshua	Sturbridge,	Will,	26990
1836	Joshua	Woodstock, Conn.,	Pension,	26991
1816	Leander	Barre,	Guardianship,	26992
1862	Lewis	Worcester,	Will,	26993
1816	Lorenzo	Barre,	Guardianship,	26994

YEAR.	NAME.	RESIDENCE.	NATURE.	CASE.
1807	HARDING, Lucy	Sturbridge,	Guardianship,	26995
1873	Lucy A.	Southbridge,	Guardianship,	26996
1790	Lyman	Sturbridge,	Guardianship,	26997
1857	Lysander	Barre,	Guardianship,	26998
1807	Martha	Sturbridge,	Guardianship,	26999
1857	Martha E.	Barre,	Guardianship,	27000
1769	Mary	Sturbridge,	Guardianship,	27001
1829	Matilda	Southbridge,	Guardianship,	27002
1853	Matilda F.	Southbridge,	Administration,	27003
1829	Melinda	Southbridge,	Guardianship,	27004
1823	Meriam	Sturbridge,	Administration,	27005
1846	Miriam	Sturbridge,	Guardianship,	27006
1826	Moses	Sturbridge,	Administration,	27007
1790	Nathan N.	Sturbridge,	Guardianship,	27008
1826	Nathan N.	Southbridge,	Administration,	27009
1844	Oliver	Barre,	Administration,	27010
1880	Palmer	Southbridge,	Will,	27011
1854	Ralph	Southbridge,	Will,	27012
1831	Ruth	Barre,	Administration,	27013
1816	Samuel L.	Barre,	Guardianship,	27014
1841	Sarah	Sturbridge,	Will,	27015
1842	Sarah	Sturbridge,	Guardianship,	27016
1859	Sarah	New Ipswich, N. H.,	Guardianship,	27017
1829	Serepta	Southbridge,	Guardianship,	27018
1807	Stephen	Sturbridge,	Guardianship,	27019
1807	Stephen	Sturbridge,	Administration,	27020
1845	Stephen	Sturbridge,	Administration,	27021
1769	Thankfull	Sturbridge,	Guardianship,	27022
1826	Thomas	Barre,	Guardianship,	27023
1769	Vashty	Sturbridge,	Guardianship,	27024
1857	HARDY, Abner H.	Westborough,	Will,	27025
1843	Asenath M.	Westborough,	Guardianship,	27026
1879	Bertha M.	Worcester,	Guardianship,	27027
1881	Carrie F.	Fitchburg,	Guardianship,	27028
1866	Charles O.	Harvard,	Administration,	27029
1777	Constantine	Westborough,	Administration,	27030
1777	Constantine	Westborough,	Guardianship,	27031
1781	Eli	Westborough,	Guardianship,	27032
1872	Emerson C.	Harvard,	Will,	27033
1864	Ephraim B.	Westborough,	Will,	27034
1781	Esther	Westborough,	Guardianship,	27035
1881	Frank O.	Fitchburg,	Guardianship,	27036
1848	George H.	Boston,	Guardianship,	27037
1784	Jemima	Westborough,	Guardianship,	27038
1781	Josiah	Westborough,	Guardianship,	27039

YEAR.	NAME.	RESIDENCE.	NATURE.	CASE.
1859	HARDY, Lucy B.	Westborough,	Will,	27040
1843	Martha	Westborough,	Administration,	27041
1777	Mary	Westborough,	Guardianship,	27042
1777	Mindwell	Westborough,	Guardianship,	27043
1879	Minnie D.	Worcester,	Guardianship,	27044
1879	Nellie M.	Worcester,	Guardianship,	27045
1781	Noah	Westborough,	Administration,	27046
1874	Philip	Gardner,	Will,	27047
1776	Phineas	Westborough,	Administration,	27048
1778	Prudence	Westborough,	Guardianship,	27049
1842	Prudence	Westborough,	Will,	27050
1777	Rachel	Westborough,	Guardianship,	27051
1770	Samuel	Newburyport,	Guardianship,	27052
1870	Sarah	Leicester,	Administration,	27053
1777	Silas	Westborough,	Guardianship,	27054
1777	Tabitha	Westborough,	Guardianship,	27055
1842	Tabitha	Westborough,	Will,	27056
1881	Walter A.	Fitchburg,	Guardianship,	27057
1865	Warren C.	Worcester,	Administration,	27058
	HARE see HAIR.			
1869	HARGREAVES, William	Leicester,	Administration,	27059
1863	HARKNESS, Albert L.	Fitzwilliam, N. H.,	Foreign Sale,	27060
1863	Charles F.	Fitzwilliam, N. H.,	Foreign Sale,	27061
1812	Elijah	Uxbridge,	Guardianship,	27062
1836	Elijah	Millbury,	Administration,	27063
1853	Elijah A.	Worcester,	Guardianship,	27064
1850	Elijah E.	Blackstone,	Guardianship,	27065
1845	Elisha	Worcester,	Will,	27066
1875	Ella M.	Chicago, Ill.,	Guardianship,	27067
1839	Hannah	Mendon,	Will,	27068
1806	James	Uxbridge,	Administration,	27069
1856	James	Smithfield, R. I.,	Foreign Will,	27070
1850	James E.	Blackstone,	Guardianship,	27071
1762	John	Lunenburg,	Guardianship,	27072
1863	John E.	Fitzwilliam, N. H.,	Foreign Sale,	27073
1874	Lucy	Worcester,	Administration,	27074
1820	Mary M.	Mendon,	Guardianship,	27075
1812	Moses	Uxbridge,	Guardianship,	27076
1812	Nathan	Uxbridge,	Guardianship,	27077
1873	Nathan	Worcester,	Administration,	27078
1820	Prushapine	Mendon,	Guardianship,	27079
1762	Robert	Lunenburg,	Guardianship,	27080
1817	Samuel	Mendon,	Will,	27081
1820	Sophia A.	Mendon,	Guardianship,	27082
1875	Southwick	Blackstone,	Will,	27083

YEAR.	NAME.	RESIDENCE.	NATURE.	CASE.
1818	HARKNESS, Sullivan	Mendon,	Guardianship,	27084
1872	Sullivan	No. Smithfield, R. I.,	Foreign Will,	27085
1753	Thomas	Lunenburg,	Administration,	27086
1819	Thomas	Lunenburg,	Will,	27087
1850	HARLOW, Abner	Grafton,	Will,	27088
1843	Abner, Jr.	Shrewsbury,	Administration,	27089
1849	Arunah	Shrewsbury,	Will,	27090
1858	Edward E.	Clinton,	Administration,	27091
1851	Ellen J.	Marquette Co., Mich.,	Guardianship,	27092
1828	Ellis	Harvard,	Administration,	27093
1878	George C.	Southborough,	Will,	27094
1851	George P.	Marquette Co., Mich.,	Guardianship,	27095
1833	George V.	Oakham,	Administration,	27096
1877	Gideon	Shrewsbury,	Will,	27097
1868	Hezekiah J.	Lunenburg,	Administration,	27098
1877	Matthew	Westborough,	Will,	27099
1865	Thomas	Shrewsbury,	Will,	27100
1812	William	Lunenburg,	Will,	27101
1851	William	Lunenburg,	Will,	27102
1855	HARMON, George M.	North Brookfield,	Guardianship,	27103
1854	Marvin	North Brookfield,	Administration,	27104
1774	Thomas	Hutchinson,	Administration,	27105
1854	HAROD, Samuel J.	Worcester,	Administration,	27106
1868	HARPER, Alonzo D.	Worcester,	Administration,	27107
1755	Andrew	Harvard,	Administration,	27108
1788	Benjamin	Oakham,	Administration,	27109
1878	Edmund C.	Worcester,	Guardianship,	27110
1877	Emily L.	Dudley,	Adoption, etc.,	27111
1872	Frances	Worcester,	Will,	27112
1878	Francis B.	Worcester,	Guardianship,	27113
1776	George	Oakham,	Will,	27114
1761	Jane	Unknown,	Inventory,	27115
1755	John	Harvard,	Guardianship,	27116
1878	Joseph A.	Worcester,	Guardianship,	27117
1880	Joseph C.	Worcester,	Administration,	27118
1878	Louis B.	Worcester,	Administration,	27119
1875	Lydia	West Boylston,	Will,	27120
1761	Moses	Unknown,	Inventory,	27121
1878	Omer L.	Worcester,	Guardianship,	27122
1876	Paul	Millbury,	Will,	27123
1876	Paulina	Millbury,	Will,	27124
1757	William	Harvard,	Administration,	27125
1774	William	Oakham,	Will,	27126
1866	HARRADIN, Anna E.	Boston,	Guardianship,	27127
1866	John H.	Westborough,	Guardianship,	27128

YEAR.	NAME.	RESIDENCE.	NATURE.	CASE.
1872	HARRIGAN, James	West Boylston,	Change of Name,	27129
1878	Michael	Warren,	Change of Name,	27130
1874	Paul	Gardner,	Administration,	27131
1862	HARRIGIDON, Anne	Worcester,	Adoption, etc.,	27132
	HARRIMAN AND HERIMAN,			
1878	Bridget	Winchendon,	Administration,	27133
1756	John	Lunenburg,	Administration,	27134
1856	Lucy A.	Gardner,	Administration,	27135
1843	HARRINGTON, Aaron G.	Shrewsbury,	Guardianship,	27136
1791	Abel	Hubbardston,	Administration,	27137
1764	Abigail	Westminster,	Guardianship,	27138
1869	Abigail	Shrewsbury,	Will,	27139
1821	Abijah	Princeton,	Will,	27140
1792	Adam	Shrewsbury,	Administration,	27141
1869	Adam	Worcester,	Will,	27142
1855	Addison D.	Paxton,	Guardianship,	27143
1865	Alice J.	Worcester,	Guardianship,	27144
1828	Allen	North Brookfield,	Guardianship,	27145
1842	Allen	Brookfield,	Administration,	27146
1793	Amasa	Brookfield,	Guardianship,	27147
1856	Amos	Brookfield,	Will,	27148
1847	Andrew	Worcester,	Guardianship,	27149
1852	Andrew J.	Grafton,	Guardianship,	27150
1843	Angeline A.	Shrewsbury,	Guardianship,	27151
1782	Anna	Grafton,	Guardianship,	27152
1796	Anna	Hubbardston,	Guardianship,	27153
1848	Anner	Southbridge,	Will,	27154
1829	Antipas	Westborough,	Administration,	27155
1865	Apphia	North Brookfield,	Will,	27156
1800	Artemas	Worcester,	Guardianship,	27157
1848	Artemas	Boylston,	Administration,	27158
1866	Arthur F.	Worcester,	Guardianship,	27159
1861	Augusta A.	Grafton,	Guardianship,	27160
1870	Austin	Oakham,	Will,	27161
1820	Barnard	Northborough,	Guardianship,	27162
1813	Benjamin	Westminster,	Administration,	27163
1813	Benjamin	Westminster,	Guardianship,	27164
1820	Benjamin	Westborough,	Administration,	27165
1852	Benjamin	Princeton,	Will,	27166
1873	Benjamin	Worcester,	Will,	27167
1817	Betsey	Spencer,	Guardianship,	27168
1839	Betsey	Spencer,	Pension,	27169
1855	Betsey	Worcester,	Administration,	27170
1859	Betsey	Worcester,	Guardianship,	27171
1859	Betsey	Worcester,	Will,	27171

YEAR.	NAME.	RESIDENCE.	NATURE.	CASE.
1783	HARRINGTON, Betty	Brookfield,	Guardianship,	27172
1823	Caleb	Northborough,	Will,	27173
1825	Caleb	Hubbardston,	Administration,	27174
1841	Calvin	Shrewsbury,	Administration,	27175
1828	Caroline	North Brookfield,	Guardianship,	27176
1878	Caroline A.	Grafton,	Administration,	27177
1854	Caroline D.	Westborough,	Guardianship,	27178
1860	Charlena C.	Worcester,	Guardianship,	27179
1839	Charles	Grafton,	Guardianship,	27180
1857	Charles	Oakham,	Administration,	27181
1875	Charles	Brookfield,	Will,	27182
1825	Charles A.	Worcester,	Guardianship,	27183
1855	Charles A.	Paxton,	Guardianship,	27184
1864	Charles A.	Worcester,	Will,	27185
1850	Charles D.	Worcester,	Guardianship,	27186
1860	Charles L.	Worcester,	Guardianship,	27187
1863	Charles L.	Eureka, Cal.,	Administration,	27188
1864	Charles W.	Barre,	Guardianship,	27189
1866	Charley D.	Charlton,	Guardianship,	27190
1838	Charlotte	Lunenburg,	Guardianship,	27191
1864	Charlotte E.	Barre,	Guardianship,	27192
1875	Christine I.	Worcester,	Administration,	27193
1875	Clarissa	Royalston,	Administration,	27194
1875	Content	North Brookfield,	Will,	27195
1821	Curtis	Westborough,	Guardianship,	27196
1840	Cyrus P.	Grafton,	Guardianship,	27197
1813	Daniel	Westminster,	Guardianship,	27198
1823	Daniel	Shrewsbury,	Administration,	27199
1843	Daniel	Shrewsbury,	Administration,	27200
1845	Daniel	Carlyle, Ill.,	Foreign Will,	27201
1860	Daniel	Worcester,	Guardianship,	27202
1863	Daniel	Worcester,	Will,	27202
1878	Daniel	Shrewsbury,	Will,	27203
1843	Daniel S.	Shrewsbury,	Guardianship,	27204
1815	David	Westborough,	Guardianship,	27205
1823	Dexter	Shrewsbury,	Guardianship,	27206
1828	Dexter	Shrewsbury,	Administration,	27207
1863	Dolly F.	New Braintree,	Administration,	27208
1866	Eben	Worcester,	Guardianship,	27209
1822	Ebenezer	Worcester,	Will,	27210
1825	Ebenezer	Worcester,	Guardianship,	27211
1839	Ebenezer	Worcester,	Guardianship,	27212
1851	Ebenezer	Worcester,	Will,	27213
1847	Edmund	Westborough,	Administration,	27214
1847	Edward	Worcester,	Guardianship,	27215

Year.	Name.	Residence.	Nature.	Case.
1863	HARRINGTON, Elbridge G.	Grafton,	Administration,	27216
1846	Eleanor	Hardwick,	Will,	27217
1847	Eleanor	Hardwick,	Pension,	27218
1793	Eli	Brookfield,	Guardianship,	27219
1853	Eli	Westborough,	Guardianship,	27220
1847	Eli F.	Brookfield,	Guardianship,	27221
1793	Elias	Brookfield,	Guardianship,	27222
1828	Elias	North Brookfield,	Administration,	27223
1811	Elijah	Worcester,	Will,	27224
1818	Elijah	Shrewsbury,	Will,	27225
1857	Elijah	Shrewsbury,	Will,	27226
1817	Elisha	Spencer,	Guardianship,	27227
1817	Elisha	Spencer,	Administration,	27228
1854	Elisha R.	Westborough,	Guardianship,	27229
1878	Eliza W.	Worcester,	Administration,	27230
1841	Elizabeth	Mendon,	Administration,	27231
1878	Ellen	North Brookfield,	Administration,	27232
1842	Ellen L.	Southborough,	Guardianship,	27233
1876	Elsie A.	Worcester,	Administration,	27234
1842	Elvira	Brookfield,	Guardianship,	27235
1852	Emery	Grafton,	Administration,	27236
1840	Emily E.	Grafton,	Guardianship,	27237
1871	Emma I.	Fitchburg,	Guardianship,	27238
1793	Ephraim	Brookfield,	Guardianship,	27239
1793	Ephraim	Brookfield,	Will,	27240
1815	Ephraim	Paxton,	Guardianship,	27241
1816	Ephraim	Grafton,	Administration,	27242
1849	Esther	Worcester,	Will,	27243
1864	Esther	Worcester,	Guardianship,	27244
1865	Esther	Oxford,	Administration,	27244
1873	Eva H.	Shrewsbury,	Guardianship,	27245
1865	Fanny	Auburn,	Will,	27246
1841	Fortunatus	Shrewsbury,	Will,	27247
1839	Franklin	Grafton,	Administration,	27248
1863	Franklin B.	Lunenburg,	Will,	27249
1855	Frederic O.	Worcester,	Guardianship,	27250
1850	Frederick L.	Worcester,	Guardianship,	27251
1760	George	Brookfield,	Will,	27252
1783	George	Brookfield,	Administration,	27253
1849	George	Westborough,	Guardianship,	27254
1847	George A.	Brookfield,	Guardianship,	27255
1849	George A.	Worcester,	Administration,	27256
1871	George E.	Fitchburg,	Guardianship,	27257
1850	George G.	Worcester,	Guardianship,	27258
1871	George G.	Worcester,	Administration,	27259

YEAR.	NAME.	RESIDENCE.	NATURE.	CASE.
1840	HARRINGTON, George W.	Grafton,	Guardianship,	27260
1794	Hannah	Shrewsbury,	Guardianship,	27261
1821	Hannah	Westborough,	Guardianship,	27262
1849	Hannah	Grafton,	Guardianship,	27263
1851	Hannah	Grafton,	Will,	27263
1867	Hannah	Berlin,	Will,	27264
1842	Henry	Worcester,	Guardianship,	27265
1881	Henry	Royalston,	Will,	27266
1879	Henry H.	Worcester,	Administration,	27267
1853	Henry N.	Worcester,	Guardianship,	27268
1840	Henry W.	Grafton,	Will,	27269
1864	Holloway	Shrewsbury,	Administration,	27270
1866	Ida F.	Worcester,	Guardianship,	27271
1794	Isaac	Shrewsbury,	Guardianship,	27272
1805	Isaac	Shrewsbury,	Will,	27273
1843	Isaac	Shrewsbury,	Administration,	27274
1868	Isaac	Rutland,	Administration,	27275
1862	Isaac E.	Grafton,	Guardianship,	27276
1827	Jackson	Shrewsbury,	Guardianship,	27277
1842	James	Worcester,	Guardianship,	27278
1847	James	Worcester,	Will,	27279
1847	James	Worcester,	Guardianship,	27280
1872	James	West Boylston,	Change of Name,	27281
1876	James H.	Worcester,	Partition,	27282
1842	Jane	Worcester,	Guardianship,	27283
1840	Jane L.	Grafton,	Guardianship,	27284
1791	Jason	Hubbardston,	Guardianship,	27285
1834	Jeremiah	Worcester,	Will,	27286
1813	John	Westminster,	Guardianship,	27287
1825	John	Petersham,	Administration,	27288
1829	John	Westborough,	Administration,	27289
1845	John	Westborough,	Administration,	27290
1857	John	Fitchburg,	Guardianship,	27291
1847	John C.	Brookfield,	Guardianship,	27292
1829	John E.	Westborough,	Guardianship,	27293
1847	John E.	Worcester,	Guardianship,	27294
1858	Jonathan	Worcester,	Administration,	27295
1816	Joseph	Westborough,	Will,	27296
1875	Joseph A.	Worcester,	Will,	27297
1782	Joshua	Grafton,	Guardianship,	27298
1791	Joshua	Western,	Administration,	27299
1844	Joshua	Grafton,	Administration,	27300
1840	Joshua P.	Grafton,	Guardianship,	27301
1861	Joshua W.	Grafton,	Administration,	27302
1779	Josiah	Worcester,	Will,	27303

YEAR.	NAME.	RESIDENCE.	NATURE.	CASE.
1786	HARRINGTON, Josiah	Worcester,	Administration,	27304
1803	Josiah	Hubbardston,	Administration,	27305
1805	Josiah	Shrewsbury,	Guardianship,	27306
1818	Josiah	Hubbardston,	Guardianship,	27307
1874	Lawson	Westborough,	Administration,	27308
1830	Lemuel	Paxton,	Administration,	27309
1833	Lemuel	Hardwick,	Pension,	27310
1833	Lemuel	Hardwick,	Will,	27311
1834	Levi	Oakham,	Administration,	27312
1842	Levi	Southborough,	Administration,	27313
1793	Loami	Brookfield,	Guardianship,	27314
1841	Loammi	Paxton,	Will,	27315
1864	Lois A.	Worcester,	Administration,	27316
1852	Louesa F.	Worcester,	Will,	27317
1828	Louisa	North Brookfield,	Guardianship,	27318
1876	Lucian	New Braintree,	Administration,	27319
1848	Lucien	Worcester,	Guardianship,	27320
1793	Lucinda	Brookfield,	Guardianship,	27321
1828	Lucinda	North Brookfield,	Guardianship,	27322
1854	Lucinda	Brookfield,	Administration,	27223
1871	Lucinda	Grafton,	Will,	27324
1794	Lucretia	Shrewsbury,	Guardianship,	27325
1843	Lucretia	Worcester,	Will,	27326
1782	Lucy	Grafton,	Guardianship,	27327
1817	Lucy	Spencer,	Guardianship,	27328
1855	Lucy A.	Paxton,	Guardianship,	27329
1829	Lucy L.	Westborough,	Guardianship,	27330
1855	Luke	Millbury,	Administration,	27331
1862	Luke	Shrewsbury,	Administration,	27332
1828	Luther	Royalston,	Guardianship,	27333
1791	Lydia	Hubbardston,	Guardianship,	27334
1866	Lyman	Winchendon,	Will,	27335
1842	Marcella L.	Southborough,	Guardianship,	27336
1817	Maria	Spencer,	Guardianship,	27337
1842	Maria	Worcester,	Guardianship,	27338
1851	Martin	Grafton,	Will,	27339
1782	Mary	Grafton,	Guardianship,	27340
1834	Mary	Princeton,	Administration,	27341
1850	Mary A.	Worcester,	Guardianship,	27342
1853	Mary B.	Worcester,	Will,	27343
1864	Mary E.	Barre,	Guardianship,	27344
1869	Mary F.	Westborough,	Will,	27345
1829	Mary S.	Westborough,	Guardianship,	27346
1841	Micah	Paxton,	Pension,	27347
1874	Michael	Clinton,	Will,	27348

Year.	Name.	Residence.	Nature.	Case.
1784	HARRINGTON, Moses	Grafton,	Will,	27349
1818	Moses	Grafton,	Will,	27350
1849	Nahum	Westborough,	Will,	27351
1820	Nancy	Grafton,	Guardianship,	27352
1864	Nancy	Princeton,	Will,	27353
1852	Nancy A.	Worcester,	Adoption, etc.,	27354
1817	Nathan	Paxton,	Will,	27355
1845	Nathaniel	New Braintree,	Administration,	27356
1827	Nehemiah	Hubbardston,	Will,	27357
1845	Noah	Barre,	Pension,	27358
1852	Obadiah K.	Leominster,	Administration,	27359
1855	Oliver	Worcester,	Will,	27360
1864	Patty	Grafton,	Administration,	27361
1881	Phebe A.	West Brookfield,	Administration,	27362
1783	Polly	Brookfield,	Guardianship,	27363
1791	Polly	Hubbardston,	Guardianship,	27364
1845	Rachel	Millbury,	Guardianship,	27365
1879	Rebecca C.	Worcester,	Will,	27366
1844	Relief	Shrewsbury,	Pension,	27367
1877	Relief	Shrewsbury,	Will,	27368
1842	Reuben	Southbridge,	Will,	27369
1783	Rice	Brookfield,	Guardianship,	27370
1847	Rufus	Brookfield,	Will,	27371
1855	Rufus	Sycamore, Ill.,	Foreign Will,	27372
1827	Salem	Shrewsbury,	Guardianship,	27373
1853	Sally	Charlton,	Will,	27374
1743	Samuel	Grafton,	Administration,	27375
1744	Samuel	Grafton,	Guardianship,	27376
1773	Samuel	Grafton,	Administration,	27377
1782	Samuel	Grafton,	Guardianship,	27378
1802	Samuel	Grafton,	Administration,	27379
1803	Samuel	New Braintree,	Will,	27380
1825	Samuel	Westminster,	Administration,	27381
1835	Samuel	Paxton,	Will,	27382
1837	Samuel	Worcester,	Guardianship,	27383
1837	Samuel	Worcester,	Will,	27383
1842	Samuel	Worcester,	Will,	27384
1849	Samuel	Westborough,	Will,	27385
1871	Samuel	Worcester,	Will,	27386
1880	Samuel	Sturbridge,	Will,	27387
1821	Samuel A.	Westborough,	Guardianship,	27388
1828	Samuel D.	North Brookfield,	Guardianship,	27389
1854	Samuel D.	Westborough,	Guardianship,	27390
1875	Samuel D.	Toledo, O.,	Administration,	27391
1880	Samuel S.	Shrewsbury,	Will,	27392

YEAR.	NAME.	RESIDENCE.	NATURE.	CASE.
1813	HARRINGTON, Sarah	Westminster,	Guardianship,	27393
1838	Sarah	Northborough,	Will,	27394
1839	Sarah	Northborough,	Pension,	27395
1881	Sarah	Shrewsbury,	Will,	27396
1828	Sarah A.	North Brookfield,	Guardianship,	27397
1853	Sarah A.	Worcester,	Guardianship,	27398
1860	Sarah F.	So. Woodstock,Conn.,	Administration,	27399
1864	Sarah F.	Barre,	Guardianship,	27400
1865	Sarah F.	Barre,	Adoption, etc.,	27401
1854	Sarah M.	Westborough,	Guardianship,	27402
1863	Sarah M.	Shrewsbury,	Will,	27403
1863	Sarah P.	Clinton,	Administration,	27404
1847	Sarah T.	Brookfield,	Guardianship,	27405
1842	Sarah W.	Worcester,	Guardianship,	27406
1881	Sarah W.	Millbury,	Administration,	27407
1874	Schuyler	Shrewsbury,	Will,	27408
1815	Seth	Westminster,	Will,	27409
1877	Silas D.	Paxton,	Will,	27410
1808	Solomon W.	Grafton,	Administration,	27411
1817	Sophia	Spencer,	Guardianship,	27412
1806	Stephen	Westborough,	Administration,	27413
1880	Sumner	Upton,	Will,	27414
1862	Susan H.	Grafton,	Guardianship,	27415
1866	Theodore	Worcester,	Guardianship,	27416
1791	Thomas	Shrewsbury,	Will,	27417
1835	Thomas	Shrewsbury,	Administration,	27418
1849	Thomas	Shrewsbury,	Administration,	27419
1873	Thomas	Shrewsbury,	Guardianship,	27420
1826	Thomas G.	Hubbardston,	Guardianship,	27421
1880	Thomas R.	Millbury,	Will,	27422
1829	Thomas R.	Westborough,	Guardianship,	27423
1796	Timothy	Lancaster,	Will,	27424
1833	Waitte C.	Westborough,	Will,	27425
1842	Waldo M.	Southborough,	Guardianship,	27426
1880	Waldo M.	Worcester,	Administration,	27427
1808	Wentworth	Northborough,	Administration,	27428
1831	Wentworth	Westborough,	Administration,	27429
1814	William	Westborough,	Guardianship,	27430
1831	William	Westborough,	Administration,	27431
1839	William	Upton,	Will,	27432
1839	William	Lunenburg,	Guardianship,	27433
1839	William	Upton,	Pension,	27434
1863	William	Millbury,	Guardianship,	27435
1871	William	Worcester,	Administration,	27436
1839	William B.	Grafton,	Administration,	27437

YEAR.	NAME.	RESIDENCE	NATURE.	CASE.
1843	HARRINGTON, William D.	Shrewsbury,	Administration,	27438
1865	William H.	Worcester,	Guardianship,	27439
1881	William H.	Worcester,	Administration,	27440
1794	Zillah	Shrewsbury,	Guardianship,	27441
1839	HARRIS, Aaron	Lunenburg,	Guardianship,	27442
1843	Aaron	Lunenburg,	Administration,	27443
1838	Abigail R.	Lancaster,	Guardianship,	27444
1810	Abijah	Oxford,	Administration,	27445
1840	Adeline	Grafton,	Guardianship,	27446
1838	Alfred	Lancaster,	Guardianship,	27447
1876	Alfred	Worcester,	Administration,	27448
1875	Alice B.	Phillipston,	Guardianship,	27449
1864	Allen	Worcester,	Will,	27450
1847	Amaziah	Sterling,	Will,	27451
1849	Arad	Worcester,	Will,	27452
1833	Archibald C.	Oxford,	Guardianship,	27453
1869	Arthur E.	Ashburnham,	Guardianship,	27454
1819	Asa	Oxford,	Administration,	27455
1844	Asahel	Lancaster,	Administration,	27456
1785	Calvin	Worcester,	Guardianship,	27457
1829	Catharine	Petersham,	Guardianship,	27458
1874	Charles	Worcester,	Adoption, etc.,	27459
1861	Charles B.	Clinton,	Guardianship,	27460
1874	Charles H.	Millbury,	Guardianship,	27461
1863	Charles T.	Gardner,	Administration,	27462
1864	Charles W.	Keene, N. H.,	Guardianship,	27463
1768	Daniel	Shrewsbury,	Administration,	27464
1785	Daniel	Worcester,	Administration,	27465
1820	Daniel	Fitchburg,	Administration,	27466
1838	Daniel	Lancaster,	Will,	27467
1839	Daniel	Bolton,	Pension,	27468
1819	Day	Oxford,	Guardianship,	27469
1870	Diantha	Milford,	Guardianship,	27470
1770	Ebenezer	Lancaster,	Will,	27471
1861	Edmund	Clinton,	Administration,	27472
1873	Edward	Woonsocket, R. I.,	Foreign Will,	27473
1861	Edwin A.	Clinton,	Guardianship,	27474
1875	Edwin A.	Clinton,	Will,	27475
1785	Elisha	Worcester,	Guardianship,	27476
1819	Eliza	Oxford,	Guardianship,	27477
1838	Eliza H.	Lancaster,	Guardianship,	27478
1834	Elizabeth	Princeton,	Will,	27479
1864	Elizabeth	Westminster,	Administration,	27480
1864	Ellen E.	Keene, N. H.,	Guardianship,	27481
1870	Ellen M.	Clinton,	Will,	27482

YEAR.	NAME.	RESIDENCE.	NATURE.	CASE.
1839	HARRIS, Emory	Lancaster,	Will,	27483
1879	Emory	Clinton,	Administration,	27484
1838	Emory, Jr.	Lancaster,	Guardianship,	27485
1868	Estella A.	Millbury,	Guardianship,	27486
1875	Flora K.	Clinton,	Guardianship,	27487
1869	Flora M.	Worcester,	Guardianship,	27488
1875	Foster	Sterling,	Will,	27489
1855	Frances L.	Oxford,	Guardianship,	27490
1838	Francis	Lancaster,	Guardianship,	27491
1869	Franklin N.	Ashburnham,	Administration,	27492
1864	Freddie	Keene, N. H.,	Guardianship,	27493
1838	Frederick W.	Lancaster,	Guardianship,	27494
1833	General L.	Shrewsbury,	Administration,	27495
1867	George S.	Clinton,	Will,	27496
1870	George S.	Clinton,	Guardianship,	27497
1861	George W.	Clinton,	Guardianship,	27498
1856	Hannah	Leominster,	Administration,	27499
1876	Harriet M.	Rutland,	Will,	27500
1868	Harry W.	Millbury,	Administration,	27501
1879	Hattie E.	Clinton,	Guardianship,	27502
1870	Helen J.	Clinton,	Guardianship,	27503
1839	Henry L.	Millbury,	Guardianship,	27504
1845	Henry L.	Worcester,	Administration,	27505
1757	Hepzibah	Road Town,	Guardianship,	27506
1773	Hepzibah	Holden,	Will,	27507
1840	Hopestill	Webster,	Administration,	27508
1840	Isaac	Grafton,	Guardianship,	27509
1840	Isaac	Grafton,	Will,	27510
1811	Israel	Uxbridge,	Will,	27511
1863	James	Lunenburg,	Will,	27512
1839	Jane E.	Millbury,	Guardianship,	27513
1863	Jerome	Lunenburg,	Guardianship,	27514
1877	Jerome G.	Lunenburg,	Administration,	27515
1817	Joel	Harvard,	Administration,	27516
1739	John	Lancaster,	Will,	27517
1807	John	Petersham,	Will,	27518
1868	John	Millbury,	Guardianship,	27519
1880	John J.	Worcester,	Administration,	27520
1874	John L.	Worcester,	Change of Name,	27521
1877	John M.	Fitchburg,	Administration,	27522
1863	Jonas	Lunenburg,	Guardianship,	27523
1788	Jonathan	Leominster,	Administration,	27524
1838	Julia	Lancaster,	Guardianship,	27525
1785	Lemuel	Worcester,	Guardianship,	27526
1861	Lilla J.	Clinton,	Guardianship,	27527

Year.	Name.	Residence.	Nature.	Case.
1872	HARRIS, Louella M.	Dudley,	Guardianship,	27528
1840	Lucia	Grafton,	Guardianship,	27529
1819	Lucien	Oxford,	Guardianship,	27530
1857	Lucy	Blackstone,	Will,	27531
1833	Lucy A.	Oxford,	Guardianship,	27532
1879	Lucy G.	Winchendon,	Guardianship,	27533
1881	Lucy G.	Winchendon,	Will,	27533
1855	Maria P.	Oxford,	Administration,	27534
1839	Martha A.	Millbury,	Guardianship,	27535
1839	Martin	Worcester,	Guardianship,	27536
1785	Mary	Worcester,	Guardianship,	27537
1872	Mary	Sterling,	Administration,	27538
1878	Mary B.	Worcester,	Adoption, etc.,	27539
1873	Mary D.	Millbury,	Will,	27540
1870	Mary E.	Worcester,	Guardianship,	27541
1880	Mary F.	Leominster,	Administration,	27542
1850	Nathan	Milford,	Will,	27543
1785	Noah	Worcester,	Guardianship,	27544
1804	Noah	Worcester,	Will,	27545
1822	Noah	Sturbridge,	Will,	27546
1853	Orange S.	Winchendon,	Guardianship,	27547
1795	Phebe	Harvard,	Administration,	27548
1810	Polly	Royalston,	Guardianship,	27549
1875	Reuben	Winchendon,	Administration,	27550
1798	Richard	Harvard,	Will,	27551
1833	Rufus	Oxford.	Will,	27552
1872	Sally K.	Clinton,	Will,	27553
1864	Sally W.	Clinton,	Will,	27554
1798	Samuel	Oxford,	Will,	27555
1809	Samuel	Royalston,	Administration,	27556
1810	Samuel	Royalston,	Guardianship,	27557
1827	Samuel	Petersham,	Administration,	27558
1829	Samuel	Petersham,	Guardianship,	27559
1841	Samuel	Fitchburg,	Will,	27560
1863	Samuel W.	Fitchburg,	Will,	27561
1824	Sarah	Oxford,	Will,	27562
1839	Sarah A.	Worcester,	Guardianship,	27563
1839	Sarah H.	Lunenburg,	Guardianship,	27564
1838	Sidney	Lancaster,	Guardianship,	27565
1862	Sidney	Clinton,	Will,	27566
1880	Solomon H.	Winchendon,	Administration,	27567
1829	Sophronia	Petersham,	Guardianship,	27568
1829	Stephen	Petersham,	Guardianship,	27569
1874	Stephen	Phillipston,	Administration,	27570
1833	Sterns De W.	Oxford,	Guardianship,	27571

YEAR.	NAME.	RESIDENCE.	NATURE.	CASE.
1866	HARRIS, Submit	Fitchburg,	Guardianship,	27572
1870	Submit	Fitchburg,	Will,	27572
1880	Sylvanus	Oxford,	Will,	27573
1866	Thomas	Fitchburg,	Will,	27574
1777	Timothy	Oxford,	Will,	27575
1868	Walter	Millbury,	Guardianship,	27576
1878	Waty	West Boylston,	Administration,	27577
1778	William	Lancaster,	Administration,	27578
1837	William	Winchendon,	Will,	27579
1839	William	Lunenburg,	Will,	27580
1867	William	Ashburnham,	Will,	27581
1878	William	Lunenburg,	Administration,	27582
1792	William A.	Hardwick,	Administration,	27583
1876	HARRISON, Frances A.	Millbury,	Will,	27584
1878	Mary A.	Millbury,	Will,	27585
1820	HARROD, Noah	Lunenburg,	Administration,	27586
1880	William K.	Harvard,	Administration,	27587
	HART AND HARTT,			
1859	Abby	Worcester,	Administration,	27588
1817	Amasa	Ward,	Guardianship,	27589
1819	Betsey	Ward,	Guardianship,	27590
1859	Betsey	Auburn,	Will,	27591
1863	Charles E.	Auburn,	Guardianship,	27592
1817	Comfort B.	Ward,	Guardianship,	27593
1859	Cora E.	New Orleans, La.,	Guardianship,	27594
1817	Edward R.	Ward,	Guardianship,	27595
1863	Ellen	Auburn,	Guardianship,	27596
1875	Frank F.	Worcester,	Guardianship,	27597
1867	Frederick G.	Webster,	Guardianship,	27598
1846	Henry	Worcester,	Guardianship,	27599
1867	Henry L.	Lunenburg,	Guardianship,	27600
1826	James	Ward,	Will,	27601
1861	James	Auburn,	Administration,	27602
1807	John	Ward,	Will,	27603
1867	John G.	Webster,	Administration,	27604
1879	Joseph	Sutton,	Guardianship,	27605
1817	Lewis	Ward,	Guardianship,	27606
1817	Loring	Ward,	Guardianship,	27607
1854	Louisa W.	Portsmouth, Va.,	Guardianship,	27608
1817	Mary	Ward,	Guardianship,	27609
1861	Mary A.	Auburn,	Administration,	27610
1854	Mary F.	Portsmouth, Va.,	Guardianship,	27611
1816	Patty	Ward,	Guardianship,	27612
1819	Peter	Ward,	Guardianship,	27613
1758	Samuel	Lunenburg,	Administration,	27614

Year.	Name.	Residence.	Nature.	Case.
	HART and HARTT,			
1770	Samuel	Lunenburg,	Will,	27615
1817	Sarah E.	Ward,	Guardianship,	27616
1817	Thomas	Ward,	Will,	27617
1866	William	Worcester,	Administration,	27618
1863	William H.	Auburn,	Guardianship,	27619
1874	HARTFORD, Ellen B.	Worcester,	Partition,	27620
1815	HARTHAN, Antipas S.	West Boylston,	Will,	27621
1823	David	West Boylston,	Administration,	27622
1876	Dennis	West Boylston,	Administration,	27623
1856	Dennis I.	West Boylston,	Guardianship,	27624
1803	Micah	Boylston,	Administration,	27625
1840	Prudence	West Boylston,	Administration,	27626
1824	Prudence M.	West Boylston,	Guardianship,	27627
1824	Silas S.	West Boylston,	Guardianship,	27628
1824	Ward B.	West Boylston,	Guardianship,	27629
1875	HARTNETT, Maurice	Warren,	Administration,	27630
1815	HARTSHORN, Betty	Boylston,	Administration,	27631
1813	Calvin	Boylston,	Guardianship,	27632
1837	Calvin L.	Worcester,	Guardianship,	27633
1855	Daniel	Boylston,	Guardianship,	27634
1856	Daniel	Boylston,	Administration,	27634
1813	Ebenezer	Boylston,	Administration,	27635
1829	Eunice S.	Boylston,	Guardianship,	27636
1814	Grata	Boylston,	Guardianship,	27637
1863	Hannah L.	Boylston,	Administration,	27638
1866	Harvey	Southbridge,	Will,	27639
1813	Jonas	Boylston,	Guardianship,	27640
1880	Jonas	Worcester,	Will,	27641
1873	Levi	Amherst, N. H.,	Administration,	27642
1813	Mary G.	Boylston,	Guardianship,	27643
1813	Sarah G.	Boylston,	Guardianship,	27643
1829	Stephen H.	Boylston,	Guardianship,	27644
1813	Susan	Boylston,	Guardianship,	27645
	HARTT see HART.			
1877	HARTWELL, Abigail	Berlin,	Administration,	27646
1820	Abijah	Fitchburg,	Administration,	27647
1853	Abijah	Fitchburg,	Will,	27648
1854	Abijah	Fitchburg,	Trustee,	27649
1866	Abijah	Fitchburg,	Trustee,	27650
1848	Alonzo	Fitchburg,	Guardianship,	27651
1804	Asahel	Lunenburg,	Will,	27652
1813	Benjamin	Fitchburg,	Administration,	27653
1847	Benjamin	Fitchburg,	Guardianship,	27654
1847	Benjamin	Fitchburg,	Administration,	27655
1868	Betsey	Leominster,	Will,	27656

YEAR.	NAME.	RESIDENCE.	NATURE.	CASE.
1848	HARTWELL, Caroline	Fitchburg,	Guardianship,	27657
1854	Caroline	Winchendon,	Will,	27658
1873	Caroline M.	Worcester,	Adoption, etc.,	27659
1878	David	Fitchburg,	Administration,	27660
1878	David A.	Fitchburg,	Guardianship,	27661
1856	Edmund	West Boylston,	Will,	27662
1865	Edwin	Fitchburg,	Administration,	27663
1878	Edwin E.	Fitchburg,	Guardianship,	27664
1826	Eliab G.	West Boylston,	Administration,	27665
1838	Ephraim	Fitchburg,	Pension,	27666
1845	Ephraim	Fitchburg,	Administration,	27667
1873	Eugene A.	Fitchburg,	Guardianship,	27668
1868	George	West Boylston,	Guardianship,	27669
1881	George H.	Southbridge,	Administration,	27670
1881	George H.	Southbridge,	Guardianship,	27671
1873	Herbert W.	Fitchburg,	Guardianship,	27672
1787	Isaac	Oxford,	Will,	27673
1831	Isaac	Princeton,	Will,	27674
1845	Isaac W.	Princeton,	Guardianship,	27675
1864	James	Fitchburg,	Will,	27676
1875	James A.	Berlin,	Guardianship,	27677
1881	Jane	Lunenburg,	Administration,	27678
1872	Joel W.	Fitchburg,	Administration,	27679
1817	John	Lunenburg,	Administration,	27680
1820	Jonas .	Princeton,	Will,	27681
1821	Jonas H.	Princeton,	Guardianship,	27682
1807	Joseph	Lunenburg,	Will,	27683
1817	Joseph	Lunenburg,	Guardianship,	27684
1845	Joseph	Princeton,	Administration,	27685
1872	Joseph	Leominster,	Will,	27686
1848	Josiah	Fitchburg,	Administration,	27687
1821	Julia A.	Princeton,	Guardianship,	27688
1870	Leonard	Berlin,	Will,	27689
1849	Leonard B.	Fitchburg,	Will,	27690
1859	Lizzie F.	Lunenburg,	Guardianship,	27691
1878	Lucie S.	Brooklyn, N. Y.,	Administration,	27692
1875	Lydia L.	Southbridge,	Guardianship,	27693
1821	Lydia M.	Princeton,	Guardianship,	27694
1868	Mae	West Boylston,	Guardianship,	27695
1868	Margie	West Boylston,	Guardianship,	27696
1819	Mary	Fitchburg,	Will,	27697
1821	Mary A.	Princeton,	Guardianship,	27698
1858	Mary D.	Fitchburg,	Administration,	27699
1855	Mary E.	Fitchburg,	Guardianship,	27700
1877	Mary P.	Fitchburg,	Administration,	27701

Year.	Name.	Residence.	Nature.	Case.
1847	HARTWELL, Milo	Fitchburg,	Guardianship,	27702
1769	Nathan	Harvard,	Administration,	27703
1864	Olive	West Boylston,	Will,	27704
1803	Phineas	Fitchburg,	Will,	27705
1820	Porter	Fitchburg,	Guardianship,	27706
1820	Sally	Fitchburg,	Guardianship,	27707
1806	Samuel	Winchendon,	Administration,	27708
1826	Samuel	Oxford,	Administration,	27709
1834	Samuel	Winchendon,	Administration,	27710
1874	Samuel	Southbridge,	Will,	27711
1820	Sarah	Fitchburg,	Guardianship,	27712
1840	Sarah	Fitchburg,	Administration,	27713
1881	Sarah	Lunenburg,	Administration,	27714
1878	Sarah J.	Fitchburg,	Guardianship,	27715
1845	Sarah L.	Princeton,	Guardianship,	27716
1871	Seth	Oxford,	Administration,	27717
1868	Stedman W.	Fitzwilliam, N. H.,	Administration,	27718
1820	Susan	Fitchburg,	Guardianship,	27719
1881	Susan	Harvard,	Administration,	27720
1845	Susan A.	Princeton,	Guardianship,	27721
1834	Susannah	Oxford,	Administration,	27722
1875	Thomas E.	Clinton,	Administration,	27723
1817	William B.	Lunenburg,	Guardianship,	27724
1858	William E.	Fitchburg,	Administration,	27725
1821	William W.	Princeton,	Guardianship,	27726
1879	HARTY, Edward	Phillipston,	Guardianship,	27727
1879	Katie	Phillipston,	Guardianship,	27728
1879	Patrick	Phillipston,	Guardianship,	27729
1878	Thomas	Phillipston,	Will,	27730
1858	William	Worcester,	Will,	27731
1871	William H.	Templeton,	Administration,	27732
1767	HARVEY, Benjamin	Mendon,	Guardianship,	27733
1817	Benjamin	Mendon,	Will,	27734
1860	Catherine B. T.	Upton,	Will,	27735
1865	Edwin B.	Providence, R. I.,	Administration,	27736
1766	Jacob	Mendon,	Administration,	27737
1850	Jonah	Southborough,	Will,	27738
1764	Jonathan	Mendon,	Will,	27739
1767	Lucy	Mendon,	Guardianship,	27740
1767	Mercy	Mendon,	Guardianship,	27741
1850	Samuel	Sturbridge,	Guardianship,	27742
1852	William	Mendon,	Guardianship,	27743
1871	HARWOOD, Abby C.	Barre,	Guardianship,	27744
1756	Abel	Worcester,	Guardianship,	27745
1770	Abel	Hardwick,	Administration,	27746

YEAR.	NAME.	RESIDENCE.	NATURE.	CASE.
1814	HARWOOD, Abel	North Brookfield,	Administration,	27747
1815	Abel	North Brookfield,	Guardianship,	27748
1879	Angeline	Barre, Vt.,	Administration,	27749
1854	Asa	Sturbridge,	Will,	27750
1850	A. Franklin	Sturbridge,	Administration,	27751
1821	Caleb	Barre,	Administration,	27752
1881	Caleb	Barre,	Administration,	27753
1842	Catharine	Oxford,	Guardianship,	27754
1866	Catharine	Charlton,	Administration,	27755
1843	Charles H.	Barre,	Guardianship,	27756
1875	Charles W.	Worcester,	Guardianship,	27757
1867	Cora L.	Barre,	Adoption, etc.,	27758
1823	Daniel	Barre,	Administration,	27759
1752	David	Sutton,	Administration,	27760
1782	David	Sutton,	Will,	27761
1808	David	Oxford,	Will,	27762
1853	David	Oxford,	Will,	27763
1853	David	Barre,	Pension,	27764
1746	Ebenezer	Worcester,	Administration,	27765
1759	Ebenezer	Sutton,	Will,	27766
1769	Ebenezer	Sutton,	Guardianship,	27767
1799	Ebenezer	Brookfield,	Administration,	27768
1801	Ebenezer	Brookfield,	Guardianship,	27769
1871	Edward W.	Barre,	Guardianship,	27770
1865	Elihu	Oxford,	Administration,	27771
1820	Eliphalet	Leicester,	Guardianship,	27772
1815	Eliza	North Brookfield,	Guardianship,	27773
1757	Elizabeth	Sutton,	Guardianship,	27774
1871	Elizabeth	Barre,	Guardianship,	27775
1803	Ezra, Jr.	Charlton,	Administration,	27776
1875	Francis E.	Barre,	Administration,	27777
1873	George A.	Fitchburg,	Administration,	27778
1815	George W.	North Brookfield,	Guardianship,	27779
1866	George W.	Charlton,	Guardianship,	27780
1826	Gershom	Charlton,	Will,	27781
1769	Hannah	Sutton,	Guardianship,	27782
1810	Hannah	Charlton,	Guardianship,	27783
1818	Hannah	Leicester,	Administration,	27784
1843	Harrison	Barre,	Administration,	27785
1803	James	Leicester,	Will,	27786
1765	Jesse	Leicester,	Guardianship,	27787
1788	John	Uxbridge,	Will,	27788
1872	Jonas	North Brookfield,	Will,	27789
1764	Jonathan	Sutton,	Guardianship,	27790
1802	Jonathan	Charlton,	Guardianship,	27791

YEAR.	NAME.	RESIDENCE.	NATURE.	CASE.
1816	HARWOOD, Jonathan	Charlton,	Administration,	27792
1842	Jonathan	Oxford,	Administration,	27793
1810	Lewis	Charlton,	Guardianship,	27794
1878	Lucetta	Oxford,	Administration,	27795
1843	Lucy H.	Barre,	Guardianship,	27796
1822	Lydia G.	Barre,	Guardianship,	27797
1876	Lysander	Athol,	Will,	27798
1809	Martha	Leicester,	Guardianship,	27799
1801	Mary	Brookfield,	Guardianship,	27800
1825	Mary	Sutton,	Administration,	27801
1850	Mary	Barre,	Will,	27802
1871	Mary E.	Charlton,	Guardianship,	27803
1843	Mary R.	Barre,	Guardianship,	27804
1765	Nathaniel	Leicester,	Administration,	27805
1801	Nathaniel	Brookfield,	Administration,	27806
1856	Nathaniel	Brookfield,	Administration,	27807
1756	Peter	Worcester,	Guardianship,	27808
1838	Peter	Spencer,	Pension,	27809
1847	Peter	Barre,	Will,	27810
1876	Peter	Barre,	Will,	27811
1810	Polly	Charlton,	Guardianship,	27812
1815	Rasellas	North Brookfield,	Guardianship,	27813
1832	Rasellas	North Brookfield,	Administration,	27814
1815	Rebecca	North Brookfield,	Guardianship,	27815
1826	Rhoda	Oxford,	Guardianship,	27816
1842	Sarah E.	Oxford,	Guardianship,	27817
1851	Simeon	Barre,	Will,	27818
1798	Solomon	Charlton,	Administration,	27819
1826	Solomon	Oxford,	Administration,	27820
1804	Stephen	Oxford,	Administration,	27821
1835	Stephen	Athol,	Will,	27822
1876	Sumner	Hubbardston,	Administration,	27823
1839	Susannah	Charlton,	Will,	27824
1843	Sylvester	Charlton,	Administration,	27825
1880	Thomas A.	North Brookfield,	Will,	27826
1822	Tirzah	Barre,	Guardianship,	27827
1871	Walter H.	Barre,	Guardianship,	27828
1866	Wilcut	Barre,	Administration,	27829
1857	(No name given)	Sturbridge,	Adoption,	27830
1758	HASEY, Esther	Leicester,	Guardianship,	27831
1758	Jerusha	Leicester,	Guardianship,	27832
1753	John	Leicester,	Administration,	27833
1770	John	Leicester,	Guardianship,	27834
1758	Mary	Leicester,	Guardianship,	27835
1758	Phebe	Leicester,	Guardianship,	27836

YEAR.	NAME.	RESIDENCE.	NATURE.	CASE.
1758	HASEY, Samuel	Leicester,	Guardianship,	27837
1758	Sarah	Leicester,	Guardianship,	27838
1758	Zacheus	Leicester,	Guardianship,	27839
1785	HASHAM, Mayhew	Grafton,	Guardianship,	27840
1823	HASKELL, Abigail	Lunenburg,	Guardianship,	27841
1796	Abraham	Lunenburg,	Guardianship,	27842
1817	Abraham B.	Lunenburg,	Guardianship,	27843
1827	Adaline M.	Sutton,	Guardianship,	27844
1873	Alanson	North Brookfield,	Will,	27845
1838	Albert H.	Lunenburg,	Guardianship,	27846
1759	Allice	New Braintree,	Administration,	27847
1869	Amasa	Dudley,	Will,	27848
1774	Ame	Brookfield,	Administration,	27849
1793	Ame	Fitchburg,	Guardianship,	27850
1861	Amey	Northbridge,	Administration,	27851
1774	Ami	Harvard,	Guardianship,	27852
1796	Andrew	Western,	Will,	27853
1869	Ann L.	Webster,	Change of Name,	27854
1803	Asa	Westborough,	Administration,	27855
1804	Asa	Westborough,	Guardianship,	27856
1824	Asa	Westborough,	Guardianship,	27857
1858	Asa	Harvard,	Will,	27858
1778	Benjamin	Bolton,	Guardianship,	27859
1870	Betsey B.	Petersham,	Will,	27860
1864	Brigham E.	Dudley,	Guardianship,	27861
1851	Calvin	Worcester,	Administration,	27862
1864	Calvin	Harvard,	Administration,	27863
1827	Caroline M.	Sutton,	Guardianship,	27864
1865	Charles F.	Harvard,	Guardianship,	27865
1869	Charles H.	Dana,	Administration,	27866
1822	Charles L.	Fitchburg,	Guardianship,	27867
1865	Charles L.	Oakham,	Administration,	27868
1838	Charlotte M. C.	Lunenburg,	Guardianship,	27869
1804	Clarendia	Westborough,	Guardianship,	27870
1827	Clementina S.	Sutton,	Guardianship,	27871
1867	Cora N.	Dudley,	Guardianship,	27872
1854	David	Clinton,	Administration,	27873
1867	Dudley R.	Dudley,	Administration,	27874
1825	Ebenezer	Holden,	Administration,	27875
1863	Edward	Harvard,	Administration,	27876
1811	Elias	Lancaster,	Will,	27877
1804	Elijah	Westborough,	Guardianship,	27878
1865	Eliza	Harvard,	Administration,	27879
1827	Eliza A. D.	Sutton,	Guardianship,	27880
1822	Eliza D.	Fitchburg,	Guardianship,	27881

YEAR.	NAME.	RESIDENCE.	NATURE.	CASE.
1817	HASKELL, Eliza G.	Lunenburg,	Guardianship,	27882
1778	Elizabeth	Bolton,	Guardianship,	27883
1838	Elizabeth	Dudley,	Guardianship,	27884
1838	Elizabeth	Southbridge,	Partition,	27885
1867	Ella J.	Harvard,	Adoption, etc.,	27886
1868	Ellen L.	Oakham,	Adoption, etc.,	27887
1874	Elvira	Harvard,	Will,	27888
1850	Emily J.	Rochester, N. Y.,	Guardianship,	27889
1861	Emma C.	North Brookfield,	Guardianship,	27890
1863	Ephraim	Petersham,	Will,	27891
1879	Ernest A.	Athol,	Guardianship,	27892
1769	Eunice	Harvard,	Guardianship,	27893
1784	Eunice	Harvard,	Will,	27894
1854	Eunice H.	Clinton,	Guardianship,	27895
1778	Ezekiel	Bolton,	Will,	27896
1778	Ezekiel	Bolton,	Guardianship,	27897
1847	Francis E.	Rochester, N. Y.,	Guardianship,	27898
1838	Franklin L.	Lunenburg,	Guardianship,	27899
1854	George F.	Clinton,	Guardianship,	27900
1864	George W.	Worcester,	Administration,	27901
1759	Hannah	New Braintree,	Guardianship,	27902
1838	Hannah	Dudley,	Guardianship,	27903
1838	Hannah	Southbridge,	Partition,	27904
1878	Harriet M.	Clinton,	Guardianship,	27905
1739	Henry	Harvard,	Will,	27906
1796	Henry	Lunenburg,	Guardianship,	27907
1807	Henry	Lancaster,	Administration,	27908
1850	Henry C.	North Brookfield,	Guardianship,	27909
1822	Henry W.	Fitchburg,	Guardianship,	27910
1867	Ida	Dudley,	Guardianship,	27911
1853	Jacob	Harvard,	Will,	27912
1796	James	Lunenburg,	Guardianship,	27913
1827	James	Harvard,	Will,	27914
1828	James	Dudley,	Administration,	27915
1786	Jeremiah	Lancaster,	Administration,	27916
1759	John	Hardwick,	Guardianship,	27917
1778	John	Bolton,	Guardianship,	27918
1805	John	Dudley,	Administration,	27919
1828	John	Harvard,	Guardianship,	27920
1852	John	Lancaster,	Will,	27921
1863	John	Dudley,	Administration,	27922
1860	John A.	Lancaster,	Will,	27923
1838	John P.	Lunenburg,	Guardianship,	27924
1827	John S.	Sutton,	Guardianship,	27925
1868	Jonathan	Fitchburg,	Administration,	27926

Year.	Name.	Residence.	Nature.	Case.
1879	HASKELL, Jonathan R.	Hardwick,	Administration,	27927
1774	Joseph	Harvard,	Guardianship,	27928
1793	Joseph	Fitchburg,	Guardianship,	27929
1819	Joseph	Fitchburg,	Administration,	27930
1823	Joseph	Lunenburg,	Guardianship,	27931
1834	Joseph	Templeton,	Pension,	27932
1870	Joseph	Leominster,	Will,	27933
1819	Josiah	Harvard,	Will,	27934
1843	Josiah	Templeton,	Pension,	27935
1838	Juliette	Dudley,	Guardianship,	27936
1838	Juliette	Southbridge,	Partition,	27937
1759	Kezia	Hardwick,	Guardianship,	27938
1838	Laura A. C.	Lunenburg,	Guardianship,	27939
1793	Lemuel	Fitchburg,	Administration,	27940
1793	Lemuel	Fitchburg,	Guardianship,	27941
1861	Leonard	North Brookfield,	Administration,	27942
1863	Levi B.	Harvard,	Will,	27943
1873	Loring	Oakham,	Administration,	27944
1804	Lydia	Westborough,	Guardianship,	27945
1876	Lydia	Westborough,	Will,	27946
1850	Lydia N.	North Brookfield,	Administration,	27947
1875	Maria	Barre,	Will,	27948
1783	Martha	Lunenburg,	Guardianship,	27949
1778	Mary	Bolton,	Guardianship,	27950
1823	Mary A.	Lunenburg,	Guardianship,	27951
1861	Medora E.	Shrewsbury,	Guardianship,	27952
1760	Moses	Harvard,	Administration,	27953
1778	Moses	Bolton,	Guardianship,	27954
1864	Moses	Templeton,	Will,	27955
1877	Nancy	Woodstock, Conn.,	Administration,	27956
1769	Olive	Harvard,	Guardianship,	27957
1773	Oliver	Harvard,	Guardianship,	27958
1816	Oliver	Templeton,	Guardianship,	27959
1802	Peter	Fitchburg,	Administration,	27960
1796	Peter N.	Lunenburg,	Guardianship,	27961
1817	Peter N.	Lunenburg,	Guardianship,	27962
1823	Phebe	Lunenburg,	Guardianship,	27963
1823	Phebe	Lunenburg,	Sale Real Estate,	27964
1860	Phebe	Petersham,	Administration,	27965
1759	Philip	Hardwick,	Guardianship,	27966
1823	Phineas	Westhorough,	Will,	27967
1804	Polly	Westborough,	Guardianship,	27968
1778	Rebecca	Bolton,	Guardianship,	27969
1858	Rebecca	Lancaster,	Administration,	27970
1875	Rebecca	Dudley,	Administration,	27971

YEAR.	NAME.	RESIDENCE.	NATURE.	CASE.
1750	HASKELL, Roger	Hardwick,	Administration,	27972
1759	Roger	New Braintree,	Guardianship,	27973
1813	Roger	Oakham,	Will,	27974
1759	Rogers	Hardwick,	Guardianship,	27975
1793	Sally	Fitchburg,	Guardianship,	27976
1770	Samuel	Harvard,	Administration,	27977
1778	Samuel	Bolton,	Guardianship,	27978
1820	Samuel	North Brookfield,	Will,	27979
1850	Samuel	North Brookfield,	Will,	27980
1876	Samuel	Webster,	Will,	27981
1850	Samuel C.	North Brookfield,	Guardianship,	27982
1759	Sarah	Hardwick,	Guardianship,	27983
1774	Sarah	Harvard,	Guardianship,	27984
1823	Sarah G.	Lunenburg,	Guardianship,	27985
1773	Sibell	Harvard,	Guardianship,	27986
1759	Simeon	Hardwick,	Guardianship,	27987
1847	Simeon	Oakham,	Will,	27988
1822	Solomon S.	Fitchburg,	Guardianship,	27989
1796	Sophia	Lunenburg,	Guardianship,	27990
1817	Sophia	Lunenburg,	Guardianship,	27991
1811	Stephen	Templeton,	Guardianship,	27992
1816	Stephen	Templeton,	Administration,	27992
1830	Stephen	Petersham,	Administration,	27993
1847	Stephen	Dudley,	Will,	27994
1807	Susanna	Dudley,	Administration,	27995
1799	Sybel	Harvard,	Administration,	27996
1852	Sylvania	Southbridge,	Administration,	27997
1787	Thankful	Lancaster,	Guardianship,	27998
1788	Thankful	Lancaster,	Will,	27998
1868	Thomas	Oakham,	Administration,	27999
1823	Thurlow	Lunenburg,	Guardianship,	28000
1847	William	Southbridge,	Administration,	28001
1860	William	Uxbridge,	Administration,	28002
1838	William A.	Lunenburg,	Guardianship,	28003
1880	William C.	North Brookfield,	Administration,	28004
1878	William D.	Clinton,	Guardianship,	28005
1878	William H.	Clinton,	Administration,	28006
1759	Zachariah	Hardwick,	Administration,	28007
1868	HASKINS, Annie B.	Worcester,	Administration,	28008
1840	Celia	Hardwick,	Guardianship,	28009
1866	Cora F.	Worcester,	Adoption, etc.,	28010
1843	George T.	West Boylston,	Guardianship,	28011
1848	Helen F.	Worcester,	Guardianship,	28012
1848	Jason	Worcester,	Administration,	28013
1848	Joel	Hardwick,	Administration,	28014

YEAR.	NAME.	RESIDENCE.	NATURE.	CASE.
1878	HASKINS, Lillian M.	Athol,	Administration,	28015
1853	Susan A.	Worcester,	Administration,	28016
1843	William L. G.	West Boylston,	Guardianship,	28017
	HASLA AND HASLER,			
1869	Martin	Leominster,	Administration,	28018
1878	John B.	Webster,	Will,	28019
1873	HASLEY, Grace	Fitchburg,	Adoption, etc.,	28020
1828	HASSANAMISCO INDIANS,	Grafton,	Trustee,	28021
1854	HASTINGS, Abby C.	West Boylston,	Adoption, etc.,	28022
1855	Abby C.	West Boylston,	Guardianship,	28023
1824	Abel	Boylston,	Guardianship,	28024
1846	Abel	Boylston,	Administration,	28025
1873	Addie J.	Milford,	Guardianship,	28026
1824	Albert	Fitchburg,	Guardianship,	28027
1866	Albert E.	Hardwick,	Guardianship,	28028
1873	Alfred H.	Milford,	Administration,	28029
1824	Allice	Boylston,	Administration,	28030
1879	Almyra P.	Berlin,	Will,	28031
1862	Alonzo	Bolton,	Guardianship,	28032
1827	Amanda	Sterling,	Sale Real Estate,	28033
1808	Amherst	Petersham,	Guardianship,	28034
1815	Amos	Ashburnham,	Guardianship,	28035
1821	Anna	West Boylston,	Guardianship,	28036
1849	Anna W.	Mendon,	Guardianship,	28037
1880	Anna W.	Mendon,	Guardianship,	28038
1813	Benjamin	Boylston,	Administration,	28039
1836	Benjamin	Boylston,	Guardianship,	28040
1813	Betsey	Boylston,	Administration,	28041
1877	Betsey	Boylston,	Administration,	28042
1871	Betsey M.	Lunenburg,	Will,	28043
1826	Caleb	Lunenburg,	Will,	28044
1857	Calvin	Northborough,	Will,	28045
1851	Charles	Ashburnham,	Will,	28046
1851	Charles	Southborough,	Administration,	28047
1848	Charles C. P.	Mendon,	Administration,	28048
1849	Charles C. P.	Mendon,	Guardianship,	28049
1874	Charles C. P.	Mendon,	Will,	28050
1840	Charles D.	Worcester,	Guardianship,	28051
1870	Charles W.	Oakham,	Guardianship,	28052
1863	Christopher S.	Berlin,	Administration,	28053
1808	Dan	Petersham,	Guardianship,	28054
1777	Daniel	Shrewsbury,	Will,	28055
1806	Daniel	Petersham,	Will,	28056
1823	David	Boylston,	Will,	28057
1836	David	Boylston,	Administration,	28058

YEAR.	NAME.	RESIDENCE.	NATURE.	CASE.
1849	HASTINGS, David B.	Boylston,	Guardianship,	28059
1860	David P.	Lunenburg,	Will,	28060
1849	David W.	Boylston,	Administration,	28061
1863	Deborah A.	Bolton,	Will,	28062
1875	Dorinda C.	Hubbardston,	Administration,	28063
1807	Ebenezer	Worcester,	Administration,	28064
1839	Ebenezer S.	Worcester,	Guardianship,	28065
1873	Edgar H.	Lunenburg,	Guardianship,	28066
1873	Edwin C.	Milford,	Guardianship,	28067
1811	Eliakim	Boylston,	Administration,	28068
1878	Elijah S.	Northborough,	Will,	28069
1808	Eliza	Petersham,	Guardianship,	28070
1846	Elizabeth	Shrewsbury,	Administration,	28071
1851	Ellen A.	Southborough,	Guardianship,	28072
1813	Emery	Petersham,	Guardianship,	28073
1846	Emily E.	Boylston,	Guardianship,	28074
1877	Emma E.	West Meriden, Conn.,	Adoption, etc.,	28075
1855	Ephraim	Berlin,	Administration,	28076
1797	Esther	Boylston,	Will,	28077
1846	Eunice	Holden,	Administration,	28078
1809	Ezra	Boylston,	Guardianship,	28079
1815	Ezra	Ashburnham,	Administration,	28080
1829	Ezra	West Boylston,	Administration,	28081
1840	Frances L.	Worcester,	Guardianship,	28082
1873	Frank M.	Lunenburg,	Guardianship,	28083
1880	George	Sutton,	Administration,	28084
1809	Hannah	Boylston,	Guardianship,	28085
1871	Hannah	Boylston,	Administration,	28086
1871	Henry	Berlin,	Administration,	28087
1836	Henry C.	Boylston,	Guardianship,	28088
1851	Henry W.	Southborough,	Guardianship,	28089
1811	Hezekiah H.	Boylston,	Guardianship,	28090
1873	Irvin E.	Milford,	Guardianship,	28091
1876	Isabella	Sterling,	Will,	28092
1870	James	Boylston,	Administration,	28093
1815	James M.	Ashburnham,	Guardianship,	28094
1873	Joanna N.	Shrewsbury,	Administration,	28095
1742	John	Lunenburg,	Will,	28096
1802	John	Boylston,	Administration,	28097
1825	John	Bolton,	Administration,	28098
1829	John	Hardwick,	Will,	28099
1836	John	Boylston,	Guardianship,	28100
1840	John	Worcester,	Guardianship,	28101
1849	John A.	Boylston,	Guardianship,	28102
1835	John N.	Ashburnham,	Guardianship,	28103

YEAR.	NAME.	RESIDENCE.	NATURE.	CASE.
1844	HASTINGS, John T.	Boylston,	Guardianship,	28104
1846	Jonas	Shrewsbnry,	Administration,	28105
1857	Jonas	Millbury,	Will,	28106
1823	Jonathan	Lunenburg,	Guardianship,	28107
1825	Jonathan	Lunenburg,	Administration,	28107
1833	Jonathan	Boylston,	Will,	28108
1835	Jonathan	Boylston,	Will,	28109
1805	Joseph	Shrewsbury,	Will,	28110
1811	Joseph	Boylston,	Guardianship,	28111
1832	Joseph	Millbury,	Administration,	28112
1867	Joseph	Shrewsbury,	Will,	28113
1796	Joseph, Jr.	Shrewsbury,	Will,	28114
1868	Jotham	Shrewsbury,	Administration,	28115
1827	Julia	Sterling,	Sale Real Estate,	28116
1851	Leander A.	Southborough,	Guardianship,	28117
1872	Leonard	Ashburnham,	Administration,	28118
1811	Levi M.	Boylston,	Guardianship,	28119
1854	Lilla M.	Hubbardston,	Adoption, etc.,	28120
1808	Lois	Petersham,	Guardianship,	28121
1832	Lois	Barre,	Will,	28122
1815	Louisa	Ashburnham,	Guardianship,	28123
1874	Louisa S.	Berlin,	Guardianship,	28124
1842	Lucretia	Brookfield,	Will,	28125
1871	Lucy	Shrewsbury,	Administration,	28126
1848	Lucy P.	Worcester,	Will,	28127
1811	Luke	Boylston,	Guardianship,	28128
1869	Lydia S.	Worcester,	Will,	28129
1824	Marshall	Fitchburg,	Administration,	28130
1792	Martha	Boylston,	Guardianship,	28131
1824	Martha	Fitchburg,	Guardianship,	28132
1868	Martha	Clinton,	Administration,	28133
1876	Martha C.	Sterling,	Administration,	28134
1815	Mary	Ashburnham,	Guardianship,	28135
1866	Mary	Barre,	Administration,	28136
1874	Mary	Sterling,	Administration,	28137
1824	Mary C.	Fitchburg,	Guardianship,	28138
1835	Mary C.	Ashburnham,	Guardianship,	28139
1874	Mary F.	Westborough,	Administration,	28140
1862	Mary M.	Bolton,	Guardianship,	28141
1849	Mary M. H.	Mendon,	Guardianship,	28142
1767	Moses	Shrewsbury,	Will,	28143
1767	Moses	Shrewsbury,	Guardianship,	28144
1821	Moses	Brookfield,	Administration,	28145
1849	Nahum	West Boylston,	Administration,	28146
1761	Nathan	Watertown,	Guardianship,	28147

Year.	Name.	Residence.	Nature.	Case.
1789	HASTINGS, Nathaniel	Boylston,	Administration,	28148
1809	Nathaniel	Boylston,	Guardianship,	28149
1820	Nathaniel	Berlin,	Will,	28150
1854	Nathaniel	Boylston,	Administration,	28151
1767	Nevenson	Shrewsbury,	Guardianship,	28152
1835	Nevenson	Brookfield,	Administration,	28153
1835	Nevenson	Brookfield,	Pension,	28154
1816	Patience	Boylston,	Administration,	28155
1809	Patty	Boylston,	Guardianship,	28156
1875	Polly	Millbury,	Will,	28157
1845	Rebecca	Brookfield,	Administration,	28158
1803	Reuben	Boylston,	Guardianship,	28159
1827	Reuben	Sterling,	Sale Real Estate,	28160
1873	Reuben	Berlin,	Will,	28161
1837	Robert	Mendon,	Will,	28162
1874	Rufus S.	Berlin,	Administration,	28163
1809	Sally	Boylston,	Guardianship,	28164
1823	Samuel	Princeton,	Will,	28165
1842	Samuel	Princeton,	Will,	28166
1863	Samuel H.	Hubbardston,	Administration,	28167
1813	Sarah	Boylston,	Guardianship,	28168
1849	Sarah	Boylston,	Guardianship,	28169
1836	Sarah H.	Ashburnham,	Guardianship,	28170
1874	Sarah I.	Berlin,	Guardianship,	28171
1839	Sarah O.	Worcester,	Guardianship,	28172
1827	Seth	Mendon,	Guardianship,	28173
1831	Seth	Mendon,	Administration,	28174
1809	Silas	Boylston,	Administration,	28175
1833	Silas	Boylston,	Administration,	28176
1862	Silence	Sterling,	Will,	28177
1839	Simeon	Worcester,	Administration,	28178
1792	Stephen	Boylston,	Administration,	28179
1815	Stephen	Ashburnham,	Guardianship,	28180
1840	Stephen	Sterling,	Administration,	28181
1871	Susan W.	Ashburnham,	Will,	28182
1854	Tamar S.	Boylston,	Guardianship,	28183
1843	Theophilus	Hardwick,	Pension,	28184
1843	Theophilus	Hardwick,	Administration,	28185
1813	Thomas	Berlin,	Administration,	28186
1824	Timothy	Boylston,	Guardianship,	28187
1878	Timothy, 1st	Westborough,	Administration,	28188
1824	Timothy F.	Boylston,	Administration,	28189
1835	Walter	Barre,	Administration,	28190
1811	Washington	Boylston,	Guardianship,	28191
1827	Washington	Sterling,	Sale Real Estate,	28192

YEAR.	NAME.	RESIDENCE.	NATURE.	CASE.
1863	HASTINGS, Washington	Worcester,	Will,	28193
1811	William	Worcester,	Guardianship,	28194
1837	William	Bolton,	Will,	28195
1842	William S.	Mendon,	Administration,	28196
1849	William S.	Mendon,	Guardianship,	28197
1779	Zaccheus	Brookfield,	Guardianship,	28198
1854	HASWELL, Florence	Burlington, Vt.,	Foreign Sale,	28199
1838	HATCH, Alfred E.	Spencer,	Guardianship,	28200
1864	Benjamin F.	Brookfield,	Guardianship,	28201
1838	Caroline	Spencer,	Guardianship,	28202
1878	Cheney	Leicester,	Will,	28203
1836	Eli	Spencer,	Administration,	28204
1868	Frank J.	Fitchburg,	Administration,	28205
1867	Hannah	Rutland,	Administration,	28206
1864	Hiram	Brookfield,	Guardianship,	28207
1845	John P.	Bolton,	Administration,	28208
1820	Joshua	Leicester,	Will,	28209
1784	Micah	Spencer,	Administration,	28210
1864	Nellie E.	Leicester,	Adoption, etc.,	28211
1850	Nymphus	Leominster,	Administration,	28212
1827	Olive	Brookfield,	Guardianship,	28213
1824	Ruth	Brookfield,	Administration,	28214
1811	Stevens	Brookfield,	Administration,	28215
1842	Thomas	Brookfield,	Will,	28216
1867	William	Worcester,	Administration,	28217
1838	William D.	Spencer,	Guardianship,	28218
1786	HATFIELD, Dolly	Brookfield,	Guardianship,	28219
1786	Jonathan	Brookfield,	Guardianship,	28220
1786	Silas W.	Brookfield,	Guardianship,	28221
1786	Zebadiah	Brookfield,	Guardianship,	28222
1817	HATHAWAY, Betsey	Sutton,	Guardianship,	28223
1835	Charles	Hardwick,	Guardianship,	28224
1864	Charles S.	Athol,	Will,	28225
1867	Clara M.	Warren, R. I.,	Guardianship,	28226
1861	Daniel	Charlton,	Will,	28227
1817	Dexter	Sutton,	Guardianship,	28228
1871	Dorothy P.	Warren,	Administration,	28229
1843	Edwin	Warren,	Administration,	28230
1828	Elizabeth B.	Northbridge,	Guardianship,	28231
1867	Emily R.	Warren, R. I.,	Guardianship,	28232
1835	Ezra	Warren,	Administration,	28233
1831	Fanny C.	Worcester,	Guardianship,	28234
1831	Henry	Worcester,	Guardianship,	28235
1831	Hiram H.	Worcester,	Guardianship,	28236
1831	Isabel	Worcester,	Guardianship,	28237

YEAR.	NAME.	RESIDENCE.	NATURE.	CASE.
1837	HATHAWAY, James E.	Hardwick,	Guardianship,	28238
1835	Jeremiah	Hardwick,	Will,	28239
1853	Joel	Barre,	Pension,	28240
1853	Joel	Barre,	Administration,	28241
1818	John	Sutton,	Administration,	28242
1831	John E.	Worcester,	Guardianship,	28243
1862	John E.	Shrewsbury,	Administration,	28244
1857	John H.	Millbury,	Administration,	28245
1863	Joseph G.	Millbury,	Administration,	28246
1863	Joseph R.	Millbury,	Administration,	28247
1870	Lawson B.	Sutton,	Will,	28248
1817	Leonard	Sutton,	Guardianship,	28249
1841	Levi	North Brookfield,	Pension,	28250
1841	Levi	North Brookfield,	Administration,	28251
1826	Mercy	Willington, R. I.,	Guardianship,	28252
1878	Mercy A.	Northbridge,	Administration,	28253
1831	Nancy A.	Northbridge,	Guardianship,	28254
1865	Nancy M.	Grafton,	Administration,	28255
1869	Osman	Milford,	Administration,	28256
1869	Richmond	Warren,	Will,	28257
1852	Robert	Warren,	Pension,	28258
1852	Robert	Warren,	Administration,	28259
1859	Ruth	Worcester,	Will,	28260
1831	Ruth H.	Worcester,	Guardianship,	28261
1853	Sally	Barre,	Administration,	28262
1831	Sally E.	Worcester,	Guardianship,	28263
1831	Samuel	Worcester,	Will,	28264
1831	Samuel	Worcester,	Guardianship,	28265
1831	Sarah A.	Northbridge,	Guardianship,	28266
1825	Simeon	Sutton,	Administration,	28267
1866	Sophia	Sutton,	Will,	28268
1822	Thomas	North Brookfield,	Guardianship,	28269
1824	Thomas	North Brookfield,	Administration,	28270
1831	Thomas S.	Northbridge,	Guardianship,	28271
1849	Timothy	Hardwick,	Will,	28272
1850	Timothy	Hardwick,	Pension,	28273
1836	Timothy, Jr.	Hardwick,	Administration,	28274
1817	Warren	Sutton,	Guardianship,	28275
1817	Warren	Sutton,	Administration,	28276
1825	Wesson	Northbridge,	Administration,	28277
1831	William	Northbridge,	Guardianship,	28278
1833	HATHERLY, Hester	West Boylston,	Will,	28279
1828	Thomas	West Boylston,	Will,	28280
1871	HATHORNE, Ophelia B.	Worcester,	Will,	28281
1811	HAVEN, Aaron	Dana,	Administration,	28282

Year.	Name.	Residence.	Nature.	Case.
1840	HAVEN, Abraham	Woodstock, Conn.,	Foreign Will,	28283
1796	Anna	Leicester,	Guardianship,	28284
1815	Caroline P.	Shrewsbury,	Guardianship,	28285
1824	Comfort	Hopkinton,	Guardianship,	28286
1775	Daniel	Worcester,	Administration,	28287
1807	Daniel	Athol,	Administration,	28288
1842	Ebenezer	Lancaster,	Will,	28289
1868	Effie	Milford,	Guardianship,	28290
1829	Elijah	Ashburnham,	Guardianship,	28291
1796	Elkanah	Leicester,	Administration,	28292
1846	Elkanah	Leicester,	Will,	28293
1851	Erastus U.	Dudley,	Guardianship,	28294
1846	Esther	Worcester,	Administration,	28295
1851	Ezra	Athol,	Guardianship,	28296
1772	Hannah	Athol,	Guardianship,	28297
1824	Hannah A.	Hopkinton,	Guardianship,	28298
1855	Hannah G.	Worcester,	Administration,	28299
1868	Harry W.	Milford,	Guardianship,	28300
1881	Hollis J.	Worcester,	Sep. Support,	28301
1881	Ida M.	Worcester,	Custody Minor,	28302
1851	James	Dudley,	Administration,	28303
1784	John	Sutton,	Will,	28304
1815	John	Sutton,	Administration,	28305
1827	John	Ashburnham,	Guardianship,	28306
1831	John	Ashburnham,	Administration,	28306
1831	John	Athol,	Administration,	28307
1849	John	Athol,	Will,	28308
1839	John E.	York, Me.,	Foreign Sale,	28309
1823	John W.	Dana,	Guardianship,	28310
1877	John W.	Athol,	Guardianship,	28311
1770	Jonathan	Athol,	Administration,	28312
1791	Jonathan	Ashburnham,	Administration,	28313
1875	Jubal H.	Worcester,	Will,	28314
1868	Lillian G.	Milford,	Guardianship,	28315
1772	Lois	Athol,	Guardianship,	28316
1820	Lois	Ashburnham,	Administration,	28317
1815	Lorenzo G.	Shrewsbury,	Guardianship,	28318
1828	Lorenzo G.	Shrewsbury,	Guardianship,	28319
1835	Luther	Milford,	Will,	28320
1852	Luther D.	Milford,	Guardianship,	28321
1868	Luther D.	Milford,	Administration,	28322
1772	Lydia	Athol,	Guardianship,	28323
1861	Mary A. M.	Leicester,	Adoption,	28324
1881	Mary J.	Worcester,	Sep. Support,	28325
1815	Montgomery	Shrewsbury,	Guardianship,	28326
1818	Montgomery	Shrewsbury,	Guardianship,	28327

Year.	Name.	Residence.	Nature.	Case.
1828	HAVEN, Montgomery	Shrewsbury,	Administration,	28327
1788	Patty	Hopkinton,	Guardianship,	28328
1855	Richard	Bolton,	Will,	28329
1815	Samuel, Jr.	Shrewsbury,	Administration,	28330
1815	Samuel A.	Shrewsbury,	Guardianship,	28331
1827	Samuel A.	Shrewsbury,	Guardianship,	28332
1829	Samuel A.	Shrewsbury.	Administration,	28332
1839	Samuel F., Jr.	Worcester,	Guardianship,	28333
1843	Sarah	Hopkinton,	Guardianship,	28334
1826	Susan	Hopkinton,	Guardianship,	28335
1791	Susanna	Spencer,	Will,	28336
1841	Susanna	Oxford,	Administration,	28337
1823	Thomas B.	Shrewsbury,	Administration,	28338
1852	Willard	Milford,	Administration,	28339
1851	William H.	Dudley,	Guardianship,	28340
1871	HAVERSICK, Dorothea	Webster,	Administration,	28341
1867	William	Oxford,	Administration,	28342
1871	William	Webster,	Guardianship,	28343
1856	HAVERSTOCK, Charles A.	Worcester,	Guardianship,	28344
1856	Frances A.	Worcester,	Guardianship,	28345
1857	Frances A.	Worcester,	Adoption, etc.,	28346
1856	James A.	Worcester,	Administration,	28347
1856	Mary E.	Worcester,	Guardianship,	28348
1856	William E.	Worcester,	Guardianship,	28349
	HAWES and HAWS,			
1864	Albert P.	Worcester,	Guardianship,	28350
1865	Amos	Leominster,	Will,	28351
1816	Amy E.	Westborough,	Guardianship,	28352
1868	Angelina	Mendon,	Guardianship,	28353
1820	Artemas	Petersham,	Administration,	28354
1876	Artemas	Worcester,	Will,	28355
1874	Arthur W.	West Boylston,	Guardianship,	28356
1861	Ashbell M.	Oxford,	Administration,	28357
1832	Benjamin	Leominster,	Pension,	28358
1844	Benjamin	Leominster,	Will,	28359
1799	Beriah	New Braintree,	Will,	28360
1865	Charles H.	Oxford,	Adoption, etc.,	28361
1832	Charles M.	Petersham,	Guardianship,	28362
1864	Charlotte L. J.	Worcester,	Administration,	28363
1866	Charlotte P.	Worcester,	Will,	28364
1848	Clarinda A.	Brookfield,	Guardianship,	28365
1870	Cynthia	Worcester,	Administration,	28366
1815	Dan	Barre,	Will,	28367
1874	Daniel	Barre,	Administration,	28368
1780	David	Worcester,	Guardianship,	28369

Year.	Name.	Residence.	Nature.	Case.
	HAWES and HAWS,			
1842	David	Worcester,	Administration,	28370
1787	Ebenezer	Worcester,	Guardianship,	28371
1778	Eleazer	Worcester,	Will,	28372
1832	Eliza R.	Petersham,	Guardianship,	28373
1868	Emilie	Oxford,	Will,	28374
1869	Fanny	Brookfield,	Will,	28375
1867	Fanny R.	Worcester,	Guardianship,	28376
1880	Flora L.	Barre,	Guardianship,	28377
1874	Freddie A.	West Boylston,	Guardianship,	28378
1881	Frederick A.	Milford,	Guardianship,	28379
1845	Hannah	Westborough,	Administration,	28380
1879	Hiram	Barre,	Will,	28381
1821	James	Westborough,	Will,	28382
1813	James, Jr.	Westborough,	Will,	28383
1843	Jason	Barre,	Pension,	28384
1843	Jason	Barre,	Will,	28385
1839	Joel	Brookfield,	Administration,	28386
1876	John	Barre,	Will,	28387
1867	John W.	Worcester,	Guardianship,	28388
1848	Kirkland A.	Brookfield,	Guardianship,	28389
1874	Lafayette	West Boylston,	Administration,	28390
1869	Lottie	Worcester,	Adoption, etc.,	28391
1871	Lura R.	Barre,	Administration,	28392
1869	Mabel A.	North Wrentham,	Adoption, etc.,	28393
1865	Mary	Leominster,	Administration,	28394
1869	Mary J. H.	Worcester,	Guardianship,	28395
1816	Mary L.	Westborough,	Guardianship,	28396
1816	Nancy M.	Westborough,	Guardianship,	28397
1869	Olive W.	Worcester,	Administration,	28398
1876	Polly	Oxford,	Administration,	28399
1848	Preston	Brookfield,	Administration,	28400
1864	Preston W.	Brookfield,	Will,	28401
1821	Robert	Fitchburg,	Administration,	28402
1829	Roswell	Petersham,	Administration,	28403
1867	Russell L.	Worcester,	Will,	28404
1880	Sally	Barre,	Administration,	28405
1816	Sally L.	Westborough,	Guardianship,	28406
1873	Samuel	Fitchburg,	Will,	28407
1850	Sarah	Leominster,	Pension,	28408
1832	Seth	Petersham,	Guardianship,	28409
1844	Seth	Rutland,	Administration,	28410
1860	Sewall	Leicester,	Will,	28411
1847	William	Worcester,	Administration,	28412
1852	William	Worcester,	Change of Name,	28413
1881	William A.	Milford,	Guardianship,	28414

YEAR.	NAME.	RESIDENCE.	NATURE.	CASE.
	HAWES AND HAWS,			
1852	Wolf	Worcester,	Change of Name,	28415
1870	Zilla	Leicester,	Guardianship,	28416
	HAWKES AND HAWKS,			
1874	Achsah	Westminster,	Will,	28417
1856	Alice	Lancaster,	Administration,	28418
1839	Benjamin	Ashburnham,	Will,	28419
1860	Benjamin	Templeton,	Will,	28420
1877	Caroline E.	Petersham,	Guardianship,	28421
1880	Celia	Northbridge,	Will,	28422
1837	Daniel	Southbridge,	Guardianship,	28423
1847	John	Lancaster,	Will,	28424
1869	Laura A.	Templeton,	Administration,	28425
1846	Phebe	Ashburnham,	Guardianship,	28426
1848	Phebe	Ashburnham,	Administration,	28426
1848	Phebe	Ashburnham,	Pension,	28427
1878	HAWKINS, Gertrude	Lunenburg,	Guardianship,	28428
1847	Hannah	Northborough,	Will,	28429
1848	Hannah	Northborough,	Pension,	28430
1796	Samuel	Williamstown,	Guardianship,	28431
	HAWKS see HAWKES.			
1872	HAWORTH, Mary R.	Leominster,	Adoption, etc.,	28432
1877	HAY, George W.	Ashburnham,	Administration,	28433
1858	HAYDEN, Abby A.	Harvard,	Guardianship,	28434
1858	Anna	Millbury,	Pension,	28435
1858	Anne	Millbury,	Administration,	28436
1806	Asa	Sutton,	Guardianship,	28437
1808	Asa	Sutton,	Administration,	28437
1811	Asa	Sutton,	Guardianship,	28438
1880	Asa	Millbury,	Will,	28439
1851	Benjamin	Harvard,	Will,	28440
1811	Betsey	Sutton,	Guardianship,	28441
1880	Celia, etc.	Grafton,	Will,	28442
1858	Clara A.	Harvard,	Guardianship,	28443
1823	Daniel	Leominster,	Administration,	28444
1870	Dennis A.	Fitzwilliam, N. H.,	Guardianship,	28445
1879	Ebenezer C.	Fitchburg,	Administration,	28446
1858	Ela	Harvard,	Guardianship,	28447
1805	Elias	Sutton,	Guardianship,	28448
1806	Elias	Sutton,	Will,	28448
1871	Emily G.	Millbury,	Administration,	28449
1860	Fanny	Harvard,	Will,	28450
1858	George W.	Harvard,	Guardianship,	28451
1831	Hannah C.	Grafton,	Guardianship,	28452
1831	Henry B.	Grafton,	Guardianship,	28453
1819	Joanna	Upton,	Will,	28454

YEAR.	NAME.	RESIDENCE.	NATURE.	CASE.
1811	HAYDEN, Joel	Sutton,	Guardianship,	28455
1848	Joel	Sutton,	Administration,	28456
1811	Jonathan	Grafton,	Will,	28457
1851	Jonathan	Grafton,	Administration,	28458
1865	Joseph	Lunenburg,	Administration,	28459
1849	Julian Ann	Amherst,	Foreign Sale,	28460
1853	Lewis T.	Harvard,	Administration,	28461
1811	Lydia	Sutton,	Guardianship,	28462
1879	Mary B.	Fitchburg,	Administration,	28463
1849	Mary J.	Amherst,	Foreign Sale,	28464
1854	Mercy	Grafton,	Will,	28465
1781	Molly	Unknown,	Receipt,	28466
1829	Moses	Grafton,	Administration,	28467
1856	Moses	Westborough,	Administration,	28468
1830	Moses C.	Grafton,	Administration,	28469
1831	Moses C.	Grafton,	Guardianship,	28470
1873	Otis	Sudbury,	Trustee,	28471
1862	Sally	Grafton,	Will,	28472
1879	Sarah E.	Fitchburg,	Administration,	28473
1849	Sarah F.	Amherst,	Foreign Sale,	28474
1866	Sarah W.	Uxbridge,	Administration,	28475
1810	Solomon	Grafton,	Administration,	28476
1849	Susan E.	Amherst,	Foreign Sale,	28477
1877	Sylvia E.	Oxford,	Administration,	28478
1849	Thomas W.	Amherst,	Foreign Sale,	28479
1858	Warren	Harvard,	Administration,	28480
1866	William H.	Fitchburg,	Administration,	28481
1870	Willie	Fitzwilliam, N. H.,	Guardianship,	28482
1835	Zebudah	Grafton,	Guardianship,	28483
1874	HAYES, Annie L.	Worcester,	Guardianship,	28484
1869	Charles H.	Charlton,	Guardianship,	28485
1869	Edward	Worcester,	Guardianship,	28486
1869	Emma	Charlton,	Guardianship,	28487
1869	Frederick	Charlton,	Guardianship,	28488
1869	George	Charlton,	Guardianship,	28489
1869	James A.	Charlton,	Guardianship,	28490
1865	Margaret	Winchendon,	Guardianship,	28491
1869	Margaret	Charlton,	Guardianship,	28492
1881	Margaret	Milford,	Will,	28493
1869	Mary	Worcester,	Guardianship,	28494
1869	Mary A.	Charlton,	Guardianship,	28495
1856	Mary E.	Worcester,	Administration,	28496
1869	Michael B.	Charlton,	Will,	28497
1864	Patrick	Worcester,	Administration,	28498
1874	Thomas	Worcester,	Administration,	28499
1865	Timothy	Winchendon,	Administration,	28500

YEAR.	NAME.	RESIDENCE	NATURE.	CASE.
1869	HAYES, Willie	Charlton,	Guardianship,	28501
1871	HAYFORD, Ernest L.	Worcester,	Guardianship,	28502
1871	Ira	Worcester,	Administration,	28503
1784	Samuel	Hardwick,	Administration,	28504
1842	HAYNES, Aaron	Princeton,	Pension,	28505
1870	Achsah	Sturbridge,	Will,	28506
1870	Alfred A.	Clinton,	Administration,	28507
1871	Asenath	Leominster,	Will,	28508
1866	Augusta	Princeton,	Guardianship,	28509
1878	Candace A.	Hubbardston,	Will,	28510
1787	Charles	Winchendon,	Will,	28511
1865	Daniel R.	Leominster,	Will,	28512
1849	Desire	Princeton,	Will,	28513
1855	Edward C.	Leominster,	Adoption, etc.,	28514
.1863	Elnathan	Lunenburg,	Will,	28515
1817	Ezra W.	Gardner,	Administration,	28516
1863	Francis W.	Hopkinton,	Adoption, etc.,	28517
1866	George A.	Princeton,	Guardianship,	28518
1863	Henry	Sturbridge,	Administration,	28519
1849	Henry D.	Sturbridge,	Guardianship,	28520
1829	James	Westminster,	Administration,	28521
1849	John P.	Sturbridge,	Guardianship,	28522
1867	Joshua A.	Princeton,	Administration,	28523
1817	Martha W.	Gardner,	Guardianship,	28524
1877	Martha W.	Leominster,	Administration,	28525
1817	Mary	Gardner,	Guardianship,	28526
1866	Mary E.	Princeton,	Guardianship,	28527
1877	Melvina	Worcester,	Will,	28528
1856	Rebekah	Gardner,	Will,	28529
1817	Reuben	Gardner,	Guardianship,	28530
1841	Reuben	Gardner,	Will,	28531
1842	Reuben	Gardner,	Pension,	28532
1871	Reuben	Barre,	Will,	28533
1863	Ruth	Gardner,	Will,	28534
1829	Samuel	Bolton,	Will,	28535
1829	Samuel B.	Bolton,	Guardianship,	28536
1878	Sarah L., etc.	Charlton,	Administration,	28537
1840	Silas	Bolton,	Will,	28538
1875	Silas B.	Princeton,	Guardianship,	28539
1857	Thaddeus	Rutland,	Will,	28540
1849	HAYTHORN, Rosina C.	Blackstone,	Guardianship,	28541
	HAYWARD, HAYWOOD AND HEYWOOD,			
1866	Abbott R.	Grafton,	Guardianship,	28542
1769	Abel	Worcester,	Administration,	28543

HAYWARD, HAYWOOD AND HEYWOOD,

YEAR.	NAME.	RESIDENCE.	NATURE.	CASE.
1771	Abel	Worcester,	Guardianship,	28544
1821	Abel	Worcester,	Will,	28545
1794	Abigail	Brookfield,	Will,	28546
1835	Abigail	Milford,	Guardianship,	28547
1794	Ahaz	Milford,	Guardianship,	28548
1852	Alonzo P.	Princeton,	Guardianship,	28549
1871	Alonzo P.	Princeton,	Administration,	28550
1801	Alpheus	Holden,	Will,	28551
1855	Alpheus	Athol,	Administration,	28552
1778	Amasiah	Douglas,	Guardianship,	28553
1792	Amos	Holden,	Will,	28554
1800	Amos	Winchendon,	Guardianship,	28555
1833	Amos	Winchendon,	Administration,	28556
1869	Ann J.	Milford,	Administration,	28557
1778	Antipas	Douglas,	Guardianship,	28558
1814	Asahel	Oxford,	Administration,	28559
1868	Asahel	Oxford,	Will,	28560
1877	Austin	Millbury,	Administration,	28561
1825	Bainbridge	Upton,	Guardianship,	28562
1828	Barzillai	Oakham,	Administration,	28563
1746	Benjamin	Worcester,	Administration,	28564
1784	Benjamin	Mendon,	Administration,	28565
1797	Benjamin	Brookfield,	Administration,	28566
1799	Benjamin	Brookfield,	Guardianship,	28567
1816	Benjamin	Worcester,	Administration,	28568
1849	Benjamin	Gardner,	Administration,	28569
1860	Benjamin	Worcester,	Administration,	28570
1875	Benjamin	Grafton,	Administration,	28571
1843	Benjamin F.	Gardner,	Will,	28572
1870	Benjamin F.	Worcester,	Administration,	28573
1831	Benoni	Mendon,	Will,	28574
1872	Betsey E.	Westminster,	Administration,	28575
1800	Beulah	Winchendon,	Guardianship,	28576
1826	Billings	Oxford,	Administration,	28577
1832	Caleb	Mendon,	Administration,	28578
1832	Caleb M. T.	Mendon,	Guardianship,	28579
1861	Calvin	Fitchburg,	Administration,	28580
1845	Caroline R.	Sutton,	Guardianship,	28581
1794	Cephas	Milford,	Guardianship,	28582
1808	Charles	Grafton,	Guardianship,	28583
1857	Charles H.	Athol,	Guardianship,	28584
1845	Charles R.	Sutton,	Guardianship,	28585
1861	Charles R.	Rutland,	Administration,	28586

YEAR.	NAME.	RESIDENCE.	NATURE.	CASE.
	HAYWARD, HAYWOOD AND HEYWOOD,			
1832	Chloe D. H.	Mendon,	Guardianship,	28587
1815	Clarissa	Oxford,	Guardianship,	28588
1771	Daniel	Worcester,	Guardianship,	28589
1773	Daniel	Worcester,	Will,	28590
1773	Daniel	Worcester,	Guardianship,	28591
1810	Daniel	Worcester,	Administration,	28592
1810	Daniel	Winchendon,	Will,	28593
1817	Daniel	Worcester,	Will,	28594
1819	Daniel	Royalston,	Guardianship,	28595
1875	Daniel	Shrewsbury,	Will,	28596
1802	David	Milford,	Administration,	28597
1757	Deborah	Western,	Guardianship,	28598
1774	Ebenezer,	Brookfield,	Administration,	28599
1875	Ebenezer W.	Uxbridge,	Will,	28600
1866	Edward W.	Grafton,	Guardianship,	28601
1746	Eleazer	Brookfield,	Administration,	28602
1808	Elijah	Mendon,	Administration,	28603
1838	Elisha	Mendon,	Administration,	28604
1857	Elisha	Blackstone,	Administration,	28605
1825	Eliza A.	Upton,	Guardianship,	28606
1843	Eliza M.	Gardner,	Guardianship,	28607
1740	Elizabeth	Westborough,	Administration,	28608
1764	Elizabeth	Dorchester, Can.,	Guardianship,	28609
1773	Elizabeth	Brookfield,	Guardianship,	28610
1774	Elizabeth	Brookfield,	Guardianship,	28611
1802	Ephraim	Milford,	Guardianship,	28612
1837	Ephraim C.	Spencer,	Administration,	28613
1872	Esther	Worcester,	Sale Real Estate,	28614
1823	Ezra	New York, N. Y.,	Administration,	28615
1845	Frederick E.	Sutton,	Guardianship,	28616
1857	George	Athol,	Guardianship,	28617
1845	George E.	Sutton,	Guardianship,	28618
1851	George L.	Lincoln,	Guardianship,	28619
1825	Gordon N.	Upton,	Guardianship,	28620
1779	Grace	Worcester,	Administration,	28621
1805	Grata	Templeton,	Guardianship,	28622
1757	Hannah	Western,	Guardianship,	28623
1771	Hannah	Worcester,	Guardianship,	28624
1784	Hannah	Brookfield,	Guardianship,	28625
1794	Hannah	Brookfield,	Will,	28626
1873	Hannah	Barre,	Administration,	28627
1819	Hannah G.	Royalston,	Guardianship,	28628
1832	Hannah H. H.	Mendon,	Guardianship,	28629

Year.	Name.	Residence.	Nature.	Case.
	HAYWARD, HAYWOOD AND HEYWOOD,			
1866	Harry A.	Grafton,	Guardianship,	28630
1880	Harry T.	Uxbridge,	Guardianship,	28631
1872	Hartley	Worcester,	Sale Real Estate,	28632
1858	Hartwell	Millbury,	Will,	28633
1869	Helen E.	Sterling,	Guardianship,	28634
1872	Henry	Worcester,	Will,	28635
1735	Hezekiah	Mendon,	Guardianship,	28636
1850	Hiram	Sturbridge,	Administration,	28637
1839	Hitty	Worcester,	Will,	28638
1804	Huldah	Templeton,	Administration,	28639
1807	Ichabod	Mendon,	Administration,	28640
1764	Jacob	Mendon,	Guardianship,	28641
1822	Jacob	Milford,	Will,	28642
1778	James	Douglas,	Administration,	28643
1852	James	Worcester,	Administration,	28644
1879	James T.	Oldham, Eng.,	Adoption, etc.,	28645
1850	Jane E.	Sturbridge,	Guardianship,	28646
1859	Jerusha	Fitchburg,	Will,	28647
1794	Jesse	Milford,	Administration,	28648
1735	John	Mendon,	Administration,	28649
1736	John	Mendon,	Guardianship,	28650
1779	John	Lunenburg,	Will,	28651
1816	John	Shrewsbury,	Guardianship,	28652
1830	John	Mendon,	Will,	28653
1868	John	Westminster,	Administration,	28654
1774	John, Jr.	Mendon,	Administration,	28655
1839	John A.	Milford,	Guardianship,	28656
1862	John A.	Upton,	Administration,	28657
1756	Jonah	Western,	Administration,	28658
1756	Jonas	Western,	Administration,	28658
1751	Jonathan	Mendon,	Guardianship,	28659
1751	Jonathan	Mendon,	Administration,	28660
1760	Jonathan	Mendon,	Administration,	28661
1816	Jonathan	Upton,	Will,	28662
1802	Jonathan, Jr.	Upton,	Administration,	28663
1778	Joseph	Douglas,	Guardianship,	28664
1795	Joseph	Brookfield,	Administration,	28665
1799	Joseph	Brookfield,	Guardianship,	28666
1817	Joseph	Worcester,	Guardianship,	28667
1834	Joseph	Brookfield,	Administration,	28668
1836	Joseph	Millbury,	Will,	28669
1869	Joseph P.	Sterling,	Will,	28670
1806	Josiah	Sturbridge,	Will,	28671

YEAR.	NAME.	RESIDENCE.	NATURE.	CASE.
	HAYWARD, HAYWOOD AND HEYWOOD,			
1845	Josiah	Sturbridge,	Will,	28672
1794	Jotham	Milford,	Guardianship,	28673
1854	Jotham	Mendon,	Will,	28674
1852	Kezia	Worcester,	Will,	28675
1841	Lemuel	Winchendon,	Administration,	28676
1841	Lemuel	Winchendon,	Pension,	28677
1799	Levi	Winchendon,	Will,	28678
1800	Levi	Winchendon,	Guardianship,	28679
1804	Levi	Grafton,	Administration,	28680
1808	Levi C.	Grafton,	Guardianship,	28681
1873	Levi C.	Grafton,	Will,	28682
1816	Levi F.	Upton,	Guardianship,	28683
1811	Levina	Grafton,	Administration,	28684
1835	Lewis	Milford,	Administration,	28685
1839	Lewis P.	Milford,	Guardianship,	28686
1867	Lincoln	Lunenburg,	Will,	28687
1794	Lucinda	Milford,	Guardianship,	28688
1764	Lucretia	Dorchester, Can.,	Guardianship,	28689
1794	Lucretia	Milford,	Guardianship,	28690
1843	Lucy A.	Gardner,	Guardianship,	28691
1865	Lucy P.	Millbury,	Will,	28692
1757	Lydia	Mendon,	Guardianship,	28693
1799	Lydia	Brookfield,	Guardianship,	28694
1815	Lydia	Upton,	Guardianship,	28695
1824	Lydia	Upton,	Will,	28696
1852	Lydia	Brookfield,	Administration,	28697
1852	Lyman B.	Princeton,	Guardianship,	28698
1862	Lysander A.	Upton,	Guardianship,	28699
1757	Marcy	Western,	Guardianship,	28700
1757	Mary	Western,	Guardianship,	28701
1773	Mary	Brookfield,	Guardianship,	28702
1800	Mary	Winchendon,	Guardianship,	28703
1831	Mary	Mendon,	Guardianship,	28704
1837	Mary	Mendon,	Will,	28705
1880	Mary	Mendon,	Guardianship,	28706
1850	Mary A.	Sturbridge,	Guardianship,	28707
1866	Mary A.	Grafton,	Guardianship,	28708
1879	Mary A.	Oldham, Eng.,	Adoption, etc.,	28709
1880	Mary B.	Uxbridge,	Guardianship,	28710
1843	Mary F.	Gardner,	Guardianship,	28711
1861	Mary M.	Mendon,	Will,	28712
1832	Mary M. H.	Mendon,	Guardianship,	28713
1875	Mary P.	Sutton,	Will,	28714

YEAR.	NAME.	RESIDENCE.	NATURE.	CASE.
	HAYWARD, HAYWOOD AND HEYWOOD,			
1851	Mary S.	Lincoln,	Guardianship,	28715
1867	Mary S.	Holden,	Guardianship,	28716
1839	Mehitable	Worcester,	Will,	28717
1844	Mehitable	Worcester,	Pension,	28718
1801	Meletiah	Upton,	Administration,	28719
1843	Melissa M.	Gardner,	Guardianship,	28720
1755	Moses	Mendon,	Guardianship,	28721
1757	Moses	Western,	Guardianship,	28722
1841	Nancy	Worcester,	Administration,	28723
1781	Nathan	Lunenburg,	Will,	28724
1858	Nathan	Mendon,	Will,	28725
1834	Nathaniel	Shrewsbury,	Will,	28726
1822	Nathaniel, Jr.	Worcester,	Guardianship,	28727
1874	Nellie M.	Milford,	Guardianship,	28728
1869	Nettie I. L.	Sterling,	Guardianship,	28729
1880	Olive	Mendon,	Guardianship,	28730
1879	Orelia	Westminster,	Guardianship,	28731
1805	Patty	Holden,	Will,	28732
1877	Persis W.	Dana,	Guardianship,	28733
1786	Phineas	Mendon,	Guardianship,	28734
1850	Pliny	Sturbridge,	Guardianship,	28735
1877	Priscilla E.	Barre,	Administration,	28736
1778	Rachael	Douglas,	Guardianship,	28737
1881	Ralph	Millbury,	Administration,	28738
1751	Rebecca	Mendon,	Guardianship,	28739
1778	Rebecca	Douglas,	Guardianship,	28740
1799	Rebecca	Brookfield,	Guardianship,	28741
1840	Rebecca	Millbury,	Administration,	28742
1852	Rebecca	Brookfield,	Administration,	28743
1868	Rebecca C.	Winchendon,	Administration,	28744
1873	Roena	Gardner,	Administration,	28745
1815	Rufus	Oxford,	Guardianship,	28746
1873	Rufus	Oxford,	Will,	28747
1858	Ruth E.	Mendon,	Guardianship,	28748
1794	Sally	Milford,	Guardianship,	28749
1865	Sally H.	Rutland,	Administration,	28750
1735	Samuel	Mendon,	Guardianship,	28751
1741	Samuel	Mendon,	Distribution,	28752
1766	Samuel	Mendon,	Guardianship,	28753
1768	Samuel	Mendon,	Will,	28754
1774	Samuel	Brookfield,	Guardianship,	28755
1792	Samuel	Holden,	Will,	28756
1804	Samuel	Templeton,	Administration,	28757

YEAR.	NAME.	RESIDENCE.	NATURE.	CASE.
	HAYWARD, HAYWOOD AND HEYWOOD,			
1841	' Samuel	Leominster,	Will,	28758
1841	Samuel	Rutland,	Pension,	28759
1859	Samuel C.	Fitchburg,	Administration,	28760
1736	Sarah	Mendon,	Guardianship,	28761
1757	Sarah	Western,	Guardianship,	28762
1834	Sarah	Worcester,	Administration,	28763
1870	Sarah	Bolton,	Will,	28764
1843	Sarah I.	Gardner,	Guardianship,	28765
1826	Seth	Gardner,	Will,	28766
1803	Seth, Jr.	Gardner,	Administration,	28767
1832	Seth H.	Mendon,	Guardianship,	28768
1868	Sidney L.	Sterling,	Adoption, etc.,	28769
1825	Silas	Royalston,	Will,	28770
1819	Silas, Jr.	Royalston,	Administration,	28771
1819	Silas N.	Royalston,	Guardianship,	28772
1774	Simeon	Charlton,	Will,	28773
1797	Simeon	Sutton,	Will,	28774
1798	Simeon	Gerry,	Administration,	28775
1857	Simon	Rutland,	Guardianship,	28776
1857	Simon	Rutland,	Administration,	28776
1757	Solomon	Western,	Guardianship,	28777
1862	Sophia D.	Mendon,	Guardianship,	28778
1813	Stephen	Worcester,	Administration,	28779
1836	Stephen	Sutton,	Administration,	28780
1860	Susan	Fitchburg,	Administration,	28781
1871	Susan B.	Uxbridge,	Will,	28782
1878	Susan H.	Uxbridge,	Administration,	28783
1880	Sylvia W.	Uxbridge,	Guardianship,	28784
1807	Thaddeus	Holden,	Will,	28785
1761	Thomas	Dorchester, Can.,	Will,	28786
1794	Thomas	Templeton,	Administration,	28787
1878	Tilly B.	Sterling,	Will,	28788
1846	Timothy	Gardner,	Will,	28789
1868	Timothy	North Brookfield,	Administration,	28790
1848	Trueworthy	Athol,	Guardianship,	28791
1778	Urial	Douglas,	Guardianship,	28792
1881	Walter	Fitchburg,	Will,	28793
1859	Walter C.	Fitchburg,	Guardianship,	28794
1825	William A.	Upton,	Guardianship,	28795
1757	Zerviah	Western,	Guardianship,	28796
	HAZARD AND HAZZARD,			
1865	Dolly	Brookfield,	Sale Real Estate,	28797
1864	Henry	Boylston,	Guardianship,	28798

YEAR.	NAME.	RESIDENCE.	NATURE.	CASE.
	HAZARD AND HAZZARD,			
1876	Henry	Lancaster,	Guardianship,	28799
1865	Joel	Brookfield,	Sale Real Estate,	28800
1864	Lorenzo T.	Brookfield,	Guardianship,	28801
	HAZEL AND HAZZELL,			
1876	Honorah	Worcester,	Will,	28802
1875	James	Worcester,	Will,	28803
1864	HAZELHURST, Henry	Webster,	Administration,	28804
1745	HAZELTINE, Abner	Mendon,	Guardianship,	28805
1777	Anna	Sutton,	Guardianship,	28806
1777	Benjamin	Sutton,	Guardianship,	28807
1809	Betty	West Boylston,	Administration,	28808
1844	Charles B. R.	Worcester,	Guardianship,	28809
1747	Daniel	Mendon,	Will,	28810
1777	David	Sutton,	Guardianship,	28811
1777	Hannah	Sutton,	Guardianship,	28812
1844	Harriet S.	Worcester,	Guardianship,	28813
1777	John	Sutton,	Guardianship,	28814
1777	John	Upton,	Administration,	28815
1777	Judith	Sutton,	Guardianship,	28816
1777	Mary	Sutton,	Guardianship,	28817
1824	Mary A.	Unknown,	Sale Real Estate,	28818
1764	Nathaniel	Harvard,	Administration,	28819
1784	Nathaniel	Harvard,	Guardianship,	28820
1844	Pardon	Worcester,	Will,	28821
1773	Silas	Sutton,	Administration,	28822
1777	Silas	Sutton,	Guardianship,	28823
1777	Stephen	Sutton,	Guardianship,	28824
1852	HAZEN, Norman	Royalston,	Administration,	28825
	HAZZARD see HAZARD.			
	HAZZELL see HAZEL.			
1867	HEAD, James	Clinton,	Guardianship,	28826
1853	Jane	Clinton,	Adoption, etc.,	28827
1822	HEALD, Anna D.	Hubbardston,	Guardianship,	28828
1869	Calvin	Hubbardston,	Administration,	28829
1874	Charles L.	Worcester,	Guardianship,	28830
1814	Ebenezer	Rutland,	Administration,	28831
1865	Emmeline H.	Winchendon,	Guardianship,	28832
1877	George E.	Southbridge,	Adoption, etc.,	28833
1860	George N.	Ashburnham.	Guardianship,	28834
1872	Harriet P.	Hubbardston,	Guardianship,	28835
1867	Harvey	Ashburnham,	Administration,	28836
1874	Herbert C.	Worcester,	Guardianship,	28837
1822	James F.	Hubbardston,	Guardianship,	28838
1870	John	Barre,	Administration,	28839

Year.	Name.	Residence.	Nature.	Case.
1822	HEALD, John W.	Hubbardston,	Guardianship,	28840
1769	Jonathan	Harvard,	Will,	28841
1758	Josiah	Rutland,	Administration,	28842
1872	Lucy R.	Hubbardston,	Guardianship,	28843
1860	Newton	Ashburnham,	Administration,	28844
1815	Sally	Hubbardston,	Guardianship,	28845
1800	Simon	Rutland,	Will,	28846
1880	Simpson C.	Worcester,	Administration,	28847
1815	Stephen	Hubbardston,	Guardianship,	28848
1870	Tamar	Barre,	Will,	28849
1814	Timothy	Hubbardston,	Administration,	28850
	HEALEY and HEALY,			
1813	Abigail	Dudley,	Guardianship,	28851
1829	Abigail	Dudley,	Will,	28852
1869	Alice	Grand Rapids, Mich.,	Will,	28853
1874	Ann	Worcester,	Will,	28854
1863	Arethusa W.	Dudley,	Guardianship,	28855
1820	Becca D.	Dudley,	Guardianship,	28856
1813	Caleb	Dudley,	Guardianship,	28857
1821	Chandler	Dudley,	Guardianship,	28858
1852	Charles	Dudley,	Will,	28859
1820	Clarinda	Dudley,	Guardianship,	28860
1868	Daniel	Millbury,	Administration,	28861
1820	David	Dudley,	Administration,	28862
1821	David L.	Dudley,	Guardianship,	28863
1863	Davis	Dudley,	Administration,	28864
1813	Deborah	Dudley,	Guardianship,	28865
1843	Dolly	Dudley,	Pension,	28866
1874	Eliza	Worcester,	Will,	28867
1793	Elizabeth	Worcester,	Administration,	28868
1863	Ellen L.	Dudley,	Guardianship,	28869
1813	Enoch	Dudley,	Guardianship,	28870
1866	Hammond	Dudley,	Will,	28871
1780	Hannah	Dudley,	Will,	28872
1863	Harriet M.	Dudley,	Guardianship,	28873
1867	Henry D.	Dudley,	Administration,	28874
1818	Hezekiah	Dudley,	Administration,	28875
1820	Hezekiah	Dudley,	Guardianship,	28876
1821	Jedediah	Worcester,	Administration,	28877
1872	John	Worcester,	Will,	28878
1797	Joseph	Oxford,	Administration,	28879
1806	Joseph	Oxford,	Guardianship,	28880
1813	Joseph	Dudley,	Administration,	28881
1838	Joseph	Oxford,	Administration,	28882
1772	Joshua	Dudley,	Will,	28883

Year.	Name.	Residence.	Nature.	Case.
	HEALEY and HEALY,			
1837	Lemuel	Dudley,	Administration,	28884
1866	Lemuel	Dudley,	Administration,	28885
1821	Luther	Dudley,	Guardianship,	28886
1828	Luther	Dudley,	Guardianship,	28887
1833	Luther	Dudley,	Administration,	28888
1813	Lydia	Dudley,	Guardianship,	28889
1872	Margaret	Worcester,	Guardianship,	28890
1877	Margaret	Worcester,	Will,	28891
1813	Mary	Dudley,	Guardianship,	28892
1834	Moses	Dudley,	Administration,	28893
1871	Moses	Dudley,	Will,	28894
1795	Nathaniel	Worcester,	Administration,	28895
1817	Nathaniel	Dudley,	Will,	28896
1821	Nathaniel	Dudley,	Guardianship,	28897
1812	Nathaniel, Jr.	Dudley,	Administration,	28898
1833	Pearly	Dudley,	Administration,	28899
1806	Ruth	Oxford,	Guardianship,	28900
1823	Ruth	Oxford,	Administration,	28901
1848	Ruth	Southbridge,	Will,	28902
1817	Samuel	Dudley,	Will,	28903
1837	Seraph	Dudley,	Guardianship,	28904
1869	Thomas	Worcester,	Will,	28905
1872	Thomas	Worcester,	Guardianship,	28906
1850	William	Dudley,	Administration,	28907
1864	William	Southbridge,	Administration,	28908
1865	HEAP, James	Millbury,	Administration,	28909
	HEARD see HURD.			
	HEARSEY see HERSEY.			
1785	HEATH, Daniel	Milford,	Guardianship,	28910
1861	Emma F.	Worcester,	Guardianship,	28911
1862	Jerome A.	Worcester,	Will,	28912
1860	John W.	Worcester,	Administration,	28913
1845	Jonathan	Northborough,	Will,	28914
1881	Nathan W.	Milford,	Will,	28915
1868	Samuel	Lunenburg,	Administration,	28916
1785	Samuel W.	Milford,	Guardianship,	28917
1785	Samuel W.	Milford,	Administration,	28918
1874	Samuel W.	Douglas,	Partition,	28919
1877	Samuel W.	Douglas,	Administration,	28920
	HEBARD, HEBBARD and			
	HIBBARD,			
1832	Adrian	Sturbridge,	Guardianship,	28921
1856	Anna V.	Worcester,	Guardianship,	28922
1777	Daniel	Dudley,	Administration,	28923

(666)

YEAR.	NAME.	RESIDENCE.	NATURE.	CASE.
	HEBARD, HEBBARD AND HIBBARD,			
1831	Eleazer	Sturbridge,	Will,	28924
1842	Eleazer	Brookfield,	Administration,	28925
1822	Eleazer, Jr.,	Sturbridge,	Guardianship,	28926
1832	Elizabeth	Sturbridge,	Guardianship,	28927
1856	Ida F.	Worcester,	Guardianship,	28928
1832	Jerusha	Sturbridge,	Guardianship,	28929
1753	Jonathan	Dudley,	Will,	28930
1832	Josiah F.	Sturbridge,	Guardianship,	28931
1787	Levi	Sturbridge,	Administration,	28932
1832	Lucius	Sturbridge,	Guardianship,	28933
1855	Lucius	Worcester,	Administration,	28934
1861	Mary	Douglas,	Adoption,	28935
1834	Merril L.	Sturbridge,	Administration,	28936
1832	Merrill	Sturbridge,	Guardianship,	28937
1874	HECTOR, Augustus	Worcester,	Adoption, etc.,	28938
1872	HEDDEN, Freddie M.	Worcester,	Adoption, etc.,	28939
1789	HEDGE, Elisha	Barre,	Administration,	28940
1881	Washington L.	Worcester,	Will,	28941
1873	HEFFERAN, John	Charlton,	Will,	28942
1872	HEHIR, Thomas	Templeton,	Administration,	28943
1876	HEINRICKS, Adolph	Worcester,	Administration,	28944
1874	HELF, Peter	Leicester,	Will,	28945
	HELLYAR, HELLYER AND HILLYER,			
1864	Charles E.	Warren,	Guardianship,	28946
1869	George	Worcester,	Administration,	28947
1862	Jane A.	Warren,	Guardianship,	28948
1862	John	Warren,	Administration,	28949
1862	Mary E.	Warren,	Guardianship,	28950
1864	Samuel	Warren,	Will,	28951
1864	Samuel H.	Warren,	Guardianship,	28952
1864	William H.	Warren,	Guardianship,	28953
	HEMENWAY, HEMINWAY AND HEMINGWAY,			
1845	Amos	Barre,	Will,	28954
1880	Artemas P.	Douglas,	Will,	28955
1815	Cyrena	Worcester,	Guardianship,	28956
1794	Daniel	Shrewsbury,	Administration,	28957
1838	Daniel	Barre,	Administration,	28958
1871	Daniel	Barre,	Administration,	28959
1876	Daniel M.	Westborough,	Administration,	28960
1805	David	Heath,	Guardianship,	28961
1777	Ebenezer	Ashburnham,	Administration,	28962

Year.	Name.	Residence.	Nature.	Case.
	HEMENWAY, HEMINWAY AND **HEMINGWAY,**			
1859	Edward H.	Worcester,	Will,	28963
1805	Elbridge G.	Heath,	Guardianship,	28964
1847	Emmons	Blackstone,	Administration,	28965
1822	Ephraim	Worcester,	Guardianship,	28966
1879	Ethan	Barre,	Administration,	28967
1802	Francis	Worcester,	Guardianship,	28968
1825	Francis	Northbridge,	Will,	28969
1849	Frederick A.	Shrewsbury,	Guardianship,	28970
1855	George E.	Northborough,	Change of Name,	28971
1847	Hepsebeth	Worcester,	Administration,	28972
1848	Hepzibeth	Worcester,	Pension,	28973
1732	Isaac	Woodstock,	Guardianship,	28974
1739	Isaac	Woodstock,	Will,	28975
1866	Israel	Buffalo, N. Y.,	Administration,	28976
1830	Ivory	Petersham,	Guardianship,	28977
1801	Jacob	Worcester,	Will,	28978
1819	Jeffrey	Worcester,	Will,	28979
1815	John	Worcester,	Guardianship,	28980
1828	Jonas	Shrewsbury,	Administration,	28981
1850	Josiah	Shrewsbury,	Guardianship,	28982
1873	Leslie	Worcester,	Adoption, etc.,	28983
1805	Lucy	Heath,	Guardianship,	28984
1849	Lucy M.	Shrewsbury,	Guardianship,	28985
1743	Margarett	Woodstock,	Will,	28986
1744	Margarett	Woodstock,	Guardianship,	28987
1802	Mary	Worcester,	Will,	28988
1802	Mary R.	Worcester,	Guardianship,	28989
1795	Phillip	Shrewsbury,	Guardianship,	28990
1793	Phineas	Worcester,	Guardianship,	28991
1854	Polly	Templeton,	Pension,	28992
1855	Rachel	Barre,	Will,	28993
1880	Sally	Shrewsbury,	Will,	28994
1821	Sally P.	Shrewsbury,	Guardianship,	28995
1847	Sarah	Worcester,	Administration,	28996
1863	Seth	Shrewsbury,	Administration,	28997
1830	Silas	Shrewsbury,	Administration,	28998
1803	Timothy	Uxbridge,	Guardianship,	28999
1821	Vashni	Shrewsbury,	Administration,	29000
1855	Warren	Northborough,	Change of Name,	29001
1867	HEMPHILL, Jane	West Boylston,	Administration,	29002
1867	William J.	West Boylston,	Guardianship,	29003
1877	HENCHION, Patrick	Worcester,	Will,	29004
1777	HENDERSON, Abner	Rutland,	Guardianship,	29005

(668)

Year.	Name.	Residence.	Nature.	Case.
1776	HENDERSON, David	Rutland,	Guardianship,	29006
1776	Edward	Rutland,	Guardianship,	29007
1842	Elizabeth	Oakham,	Administration,	29008
1842	Elizabeth	Oakham,	Pension,	29009
1776	James	Rutland,	Will,	29010
1863	James G.	Worcester,	Administration,	29011
1742	John	Lancaster,	Guardianship,	29012
1821	John	Leominster,	Will,	29013
1776	Jonathan	Rutland,	Guardianship,	29014
1777	Joseph	Rutland,	Guardianship,	29015
1777	Josiah	Rutland,	Guardianship,	29016
1777	Martha	Rutland,	Guardianship,	29017
1783	Martha	Rutland,	Administration,	29018
1852	Samuel	Webster,	Will,	29019
1777	Sarah	Rutland,	Guardianship,	29020
1777	Susannah	Rutland,	Guardianship,	29021
1826	William	Oakham,	Administration,	29022
1874	HENDRICK, Horace S.	Worcester,	Administration,	29023
1876	Maria H.	Worcester,	Guardianship,	29024
1876	Stillman	Southbridge,	Administration,	29025
	HENNESSEY AND HENNESSY,			
1879	Bridget	Northbridge,	Administration,	29026
1872	Charles J.	Warren,	Sale Real Estate,	29027
1878	Hannah	North Brookfield,	Guardianship,	29028
1872	James	Warren,	Sale Real Estate,	29029
1877	James	North Brookfield,	Administration,	29030
1878	James	North Brookfield,	Guardianship,	29031
1872	John	Warren,	Sale Real Estate,	29032
1872	Kate	Warren,	Sale Real Estate,	29033
1878	Kate	North Brookfield,	Guardianship,	29034
1872	Margaret	Warren,	Sale Real Estate,	29035
1872	Michael	Warren,	Sale Real Estate,	29036
1871	Richard	Warren,	Administration,	29037
1872	Richard	Warren,	Sale Real Estate,	29038
1858	HENRY, Aaron	Charlton,	Will,	29039
1864	Agnes	Leicester,	Guardianship,	29040
1843	Alanson J.	Rutland,	Administration,	29041
1855	Alvin P.	Grafton,	Guardianship,	29042
1869	Carrie E.	Leominster,	Guardianship,	29043
1861	Charles A.	Rutland,	Guardianship,	29044
1752	David	Leicester,	Guardianship,	29045
1810	David	Rutland,	Will,	29046
1853	David	Rutland,	Administration,	29047
1879	Deborah	Holden,	Will,	29048
1875	Ebenezer	Holden,	Administration,	29049

YEAR	NAME.	RESIDENCE.	NATURE.	CASE.
1864	HENRY, Eliza	Woodstock, Conn.,	Administration,	29050
1864	Ellen	Worcester,	Guardianship,	29051
1861	Francis	Rutland,	Will,	29052
1880	Franklin	Charlton,	Will,	29053
1880	Frederic A.	Holden,	Guardianship,	29054
1869	George O.	Leominster,	Guardianship,	29055
1871	Harlan F.	Shrewsbury,	Administration,	29056
1878	Harlan F.	Shrewsbury,	Guardianship,	29057
1861	Helen M.	Rutland,	Guardianship,	29058
1880	Jane	Charlton,	Will,	29059
1792	John	Barre,	Will,	29060
1864	John	Worcester,	Guardianship,	29061
1827	John Q.	Rutland,	Guardianship,	29062
1826	Johnson	Rutland,	Will,	29063
1869	Lewis	Spencer,	Guardianship,	29064
1867	Lucy M.	Uxbridge,	Guardianship,	29065
1864	Margaret	Worcester,	Guardianship,	29066
1855	Martha A. T.	Grafton,	Guardianship,	29067
1864	Mary	Worcester,	Guardianship,	29068
1868	Mary E.	Holden,	Adoption, etc.,	29069
1868	Mary E.	Leominster,	Administration,	29070
1816	Miletus	Barre,	Guardianship,	29071
1849	Patrick	Worcester,	Administration,	29072
1864	Paul	Leicester,	Guardianship,	29073
1869	Paulina W.	Spencer,	Administration,	29074
1864	Peter	Leicester,	Guardianship,	29075
1864	Peter	Worcester,	Will,	29076
1855	Phebe E.	Grafton,	Guardianship,	29077
1864	Richard	Uxbridge,	Administration,	29078
1749	Robert	Leicester,	Administration,	29079
1825	Robert	Barre,	Administration,	29080
1862	Robert	Spencer,	Administration,	29081
1877	Samuel G.	Westborough,	Administration,	29082
1859	Sanford	Topeka, Kan.,	Administration,	29083
1861	Sarah A.	Rutland,	Guardianship,	29084
1769	Silas	Shirley,	Guardianship,	29085
1855	Susan A.	Grafton,	Guardianship,	29086
1827	Susan P.	Rutland,	Guardianship,	29087
1881	Walter	Worcester,	Administration,	29088
1752	William	Leicester,	Guardianship,	29089
1812	William	Westford, Vt.,	Administration,	29090
1814	William	Rutland,	Administration,	29091
1814	William	Barre,	Will,	.29092
1827	William	Rutland,	Administration,	29093
1859	William	Spencer,	Guardianship,	29094

YEAR.	NAME.	RESIDENCE.	NATURE.	CASE.
1864	HENRY, William	Leicester,	Will,	29095
1869	William	Spencer,	Administration,	29094
	HENSHAW AND HINSHAW,			
1831	Almira	Leicester,	Will,	29096
1872	Alvin	Brookfield,	Will,	29097
1854	Anna	Leicester,	Administration,	29098
1877	Austin F.	Worcester,	Administration,	29099
1871	Baxter	Brookfield,	Will,	29100
1809	Charles	Leicester,	Guardianship,	29101
1872	Charlotte	Fitchburg,	Will,	29102
1781	Daniel	Leicester,	Will,	29103
1792	Daniel	Worcester,	Will,	29104
1808	David	Leicester,	Will,	29105
1809	David	Leicester,	Guardianship,	29106
1852	David	Leicester,	Will,	29107
1770	Dorothy	Brookfield,	Will,	29108
1853	Eliza A. P.	Leicester,	Guardianship,	29109
1808	Elizabeth	Gardner,	Will,	29110
1866	Elizabeth	Leicester,	Will,	29111
1871	George B.	Brookfield,	Administration,	29112
1860	Horatio G.	Leicester,	Will,	29113
1809	John	Leicester,	Guardianship,	29114
1825	John P.	Athol,	Administration,	29115
1794	Joseph	Shrewsbury,	Will,	29116
1828	Joseph	Ward,	Guardianship,	29117
1823	Joshua	Shrewsbury,	Will,	29118
1854	Joshua	Leicester,	Will,	29119
1855	Joshua	Brookfield,	Will,	29120
1829	Josiah	Brookfield,	Administration,	29121
1834	Josiah	Brookfield,	Pension,	29122
1871	Josiah	West Brookfield,	Will,	29123
1856	Justus G.	Worcester,	Administration,	29124
1809	Laura	Leicester,	Guardianship,	29125
1868	Leonard	Brookfield,	Will,	29126
1834	Lewis	Brookfield,	Guardianship,	29127
1834	Loring	Brookfield,	Guardianship,	29128
1842	Marcia J.	Charlton,	Guardianship,	29129
1872	Mary A.	Leicester,	Guardianship,	29130
1842	Mary C.	Charlton,	Guardianship,	29131
1834	Melinda A.	Brookfield,	Guardianship,	29132
1851	Royal	Brookfield,	Administration,	29133
1822	Sarah	Shrewsbury,	Will,	29134
1848	Thomas	Brookfield,	Will,	29135
1849	Thomas	Brookfield,	Pension,	29136
1820	William	Leicester,	Will,	29137

	HENSHAW AND HINSHAW,			
1842	William	Charlton,	Administration,	29138
1877	William	Spencer,	Will,	29139
1842	William A.	Charlton,	Guardianship,	29140
1870	HENTZ, Jacob	Worcester,	Administration,	29141
1857	HERBERT, Charles H.	Grafton,	Guardianship,	29142
1742	Joseph	Lancaster,	Will,	29143
1857	Mary A.	Grafton,	Guardianship,	29144
1857	Sarah F.	Grafton,	Guardianship,	29145
1866	HEREDEEN, Ida E.	Charlton	Adoption, etc.,	29146
1866	Levi	Charlton,	Will,	29147
1825	HERENDEEN, Anna	Douglas,	Administration,	29148
1820	David	Douglas,	Guardianship,	29149
1833	Joseph	Douglas,	Administration,	29150
1839	Ruth	Douglas,	Will,	29151
1820	Simeon	Douglas,	Administration,	29152
1820	Simon	Douglas,	Guardianship,	29153
1854	Simon	Douglas,	Will,	29154
	HERIMAN see HARRIMAN.			
1864	HERLIHY, Jeremiah	Grafton,	Administration,	29155
1881	Michael, etc.	Worcester,	Administration,	29156
	HERN AND HERNE,			
1861	Margaret A.	Milford,	Adoption,	29157
1842	Thomas	Sutton,	Guardianship,	29158
1871	HERRICK, Charles F.	Worcester,	Administration,	29159
1872	Edwin A.	Brookfield, Vt.,	Adoption, etc.,	29160
1877	Eliza J.	Ashburnham,	Will,	29161
1871	Ella S.	Athol,	Guardianship,	29162
1869	Ira	Royalston,	Administration,	29163
1878	Mary E.	Millbury,	Partition,	29164
1871	Mary J.	Worcester,	Guardianship,	29165
1837	Osgood	Millbury,	Will,	29166
1807	Samuel	Barre,	Administration,	29167
1875	William A.	Worcester,	Guardianship,	29168
	HERSEY AND HEARSEY,			
1856	Albert	Spencer,	Guardianship,	29169
1874	Albert O.	Milford,	Guardianship,	29170
1840	Alonzo	Spencer,	Guardianship,	29171
1862	Charles	Harvard,	Will,	29172
1865	Charles	Hawkesbury, Can.,	Foreign Will,	29173
1869	Charles	Worcester,	Administration,	29174
1819	David	Worcester,	Will,	29175
1826	Deborah	Worcester,	Administration,	29176
1859	Elizabeth H.	Harvard,	Guardianship,	29177
1863	Elizabeth H.	Harvard,	Administration,	29177

	HERSEY AND HEARSEY,			
1874	Ellen A.	Harvard,	Administration,	29178
1851	Eugene C.	Sterling,	Guardianship,	29179
1859	Hannah	Harvard,	Administration,	29180
1880	Martin	Spencer,	Will,	29181
1877	Mary	Harvard,	Will,	29182
1855	Mary J.	Worcester,	Guardianship,	29183
1855	Nancy C.	Worcester,	Guardianship,	29184
1839	Thomas	Harvard,	Administration,	29185
1855	Thomas	Spencer,	Administration,	29186
1831	HERVEY, Byram	New Braintree,	Administration,	29187
1832	Byram H.	New Braintree,	Guardianship,	29188
1847	Elizabeth A.	Leominster,	Guardianship,	29189
1879	Hannah R.	Hardwick,	Will,	29190
1832	Henry	New Braintree,	Guardianship,	29191
1857	James M.	Worcester,	Guardianship,	29192
1866	Mary H.	Milford,	Administration,	29193
1856	Nathaniel	Worcester,	Will,	29194
1850	Parnel	New Braintree,	Will,	29195
1832	Parnel K.	New Braintree,	Guardianship,	29196
1877	Sarah T.	Petersham,	Guardianship,	29197
1873	Spaulding	Southborough,	Administration,	29198
1832	Willard	New Braintree,	Guardianship,	29199
1877	William F.	Oxford,	Guardianship,	29200
	HESSIAN, HESSION AND HESSIONS,			
1861	Jeffrey C.	Fitchburg,	Guardianship,	29201
1868	John B.	Fitchburg,	Administration,	29202
1873	Patrick	Worcester,	Will,	29203
1864	HETHERINGTON, Anna W.	Webster,	Guardianship,	29204
1864	Cara M.	Webster,	Guardianship,	29205
1864	Wendell P.	Webster,	Guardianship,	29206
1862	William	Webster,	Administration,	29207
1864	William R.	Webster,	Guardianship,	29208
1870	HEVEY, Sophronie	Southbridge,	Adoption,	29209
1870	Sufranie	Southbridge,	Guardianship,	29210
	HEWETT, HEWITT AND HEWIT,			
1866	Adelia	Northbridge,	Guardianship,	29211
1876	Alfred F.	Providence, R. I.,	Administration,	29212
1862	Betsey	Northbridge,	Will,	29213
1880	Brooksey	Uxbridge,	Administration,	29214
1855	Clara M.	Northbridge,	Guardianship,	29215
1877	Daniel	Auburn,	Will,	29216
1877	Elbridge	Worcester,	Administration,	29217
1854	Eli	Northbridge,	Administration,	29218

HEWETT, HEWITT and HEWIT,

YEAR.	NAME.	RESIDENCE.	NATURE.	CASE.
1855	Eliza J.	Sutton,	Guardianship,	29219
1855	Elvira L.	Northbridge,	Guardianship,	29220
1879	Emily I.	Auburn,	Administration,	29221
1855	George F. B.	Northbridge,	Guardianship,	29222
1868	Hammond	Sutton,	Will,	29223
1866	Harriet	Northbridge,	Guardianship,	29224
1872	Jesse P.	Sutton,	Administration,	29225
1866	John	Northbridge,	Guardianship,	29226
1855	Lowell E.	Blackstone,	Guardianship,	29227
1869	Lydia	Sutton,	Administration,	29228
1855	L. Cornelia	Northbridge,	Guardianship,	29229
1866	Mary	Northbridge,	Guardianship,	29230
1880	Nancy M.	Auburn,	Will,	29231
1819	Nathan	Dudley,	Administration,	29232
1855	Nathaniel M.	Northbridge,	Guardianship,	29233
1855	Olivia E.	Northbridge,	Guardianship,	29234
1866	Orrin	Northbridge,	Guardianship,	29235
1855	Orrin L.	Northbridge,	Administration,	29236
1854	Richard L.	Blackstone,	Administration,	29237
1833	Timothy	Sutton,	Administration,	29238
1876	Valentine G.	West Brookfield,	Will,	29239
1855	Warren	Sutton,	Guardianship,	29240
1841	William	Sutton,	Will,	29241
1860	HEWINS, William T.	Worcester,	Administration,	29242

HEWIT and HEWITT see HEWETT.

HEYWOOD see HAYWARD.

HIBBERD see HEBARD.

YEAR	NAME	RESIDENCE	NATURE	CASE
1879	HIBBERT, Elizabeth	Worcester,	Guardianship,	29243
1879	Etta	Worcester,	Guardianship,	29244
1879	Louis	Worcester,	Guardianship,	29245
1870	HIBRA, Azubath	Winchendon,	Administration,	29246
1861	HICKEY, Emily A.	Worcester,	Administration,	29247
1878	John T.	Milford,	Guardianship,	29248
1866	Mary	Worcester,	Guardianship,	29249
1875	Simon	Milford,	Administration,	29250
1878	Simon P.	Milford,	Guardianship,	29251
1881	Thomas	Upton,	Will,	29252
1853	HICKMORE, James	Shrewsbury,	Administration,	29253

HICKS and HIX,

YEAR	NAME	RESIDENCE	NATURE	CASE
1759	Barney	Douglas,	Administration,	29254
1827	Benjamin	Sutton,	Administration,	29255
1827	David	Weathersfield, Vt.,	Administration,	29256
1857	Elijah	Worcester,	Will,	29257
1815	Fanny	Sutton,	Guardianship,	29258

YEAR.	NAME.	RESIDENCE.	NATURE.	CASE.
	HICKS and HIX,			
1870	Frederick J.	Phillipston,	Adoption, etc.,	29259
1816	Hiram	Sutton,	Guardianship,	29260
1820	Jemima	Sutton,	Guardianship,	29261
1815	Joseph	Sutton,	Administration,	29262
1826	Josiah	Royalston,	Will,	29263
1816	Lucinda	Sutton,	Guardianship,	29264
1816	Polly	Sutton,	Guardianship,	29265
1857	Serepta	Athol,	Guardianship,	29266
1861	Serepta	Athol,	Administration,	29266
1849	Solomon	Charlton,	Administration,	29267
1813	Sumner	Sutton,	Guardianship,	29268
1871	HIGGINS, Bridget	Worcester,	Will,	29269
1874	Elizabeth	Worcester,	Guardianship,	29270
1870	Frederick A. J.	Worcester,	Change of Name,	29271
1863	George S.	Milford,	Administration,	29272
1881	Hattie E.	Worcester,	Guardianship,	29273
1874	James	Worcester,	Guardianship,	29274
1866	Jennie L.	Worcester,	Guardianship,	29275
1874	Jeremiah	Worcester,	Guardianship,	29276
1879	John	Barre,	Will,	29277
1856	Kate	Milford,	Guardianship,	29278
1871	Lawrence	Worcester,	Will,	29279
1847	Lucy A.	Southborough,	Will,	29280
1874	Mary A.	Worcester,	Guardianship,	29281
1874	Nellie	Worcester,	Guardianship,	29282
1874	Patrick	Worcester,	Will,	29283
1858	Rachel	Hardwick,	Will,	29284
1862	Thomas	Worcester,	Administration,	29285
1862	Thomas	Worcester,	Guardianship,	29286
1848	HIGLEY, Daniel W.	Templeton,	Guardianship,	29287
1848	Edson	Templeton,	Administration,	29288
1848	Levi H.	Templeton,	Guardianship,	29289
1871	HIGNEY, Cyrene N.	Worcester,	Administration,	29290
1856	HILBERT, William H.	Lunenburg,	Guardianship,	29291
1872	HILDRETH, Amos	Harvard,	Administration,	29292
1847	Clark	Petersham,	Administration,	29293
1823	Elijah	Petersham,	Will,	29294
1824	Elijah	Petersham,	Guardianship,	29295
1875	Frederick	Milford,	Adoption, etc.,	29296
1856	George	Lunenburg,	Will,	29297
1863	Hezekiah	Grafton,	Will,	29298
1848	Horatio N.	Bolton,	Guardianship,	29299
1856	Horatio N.	Bolton,	Guardianship,	29300
1839	Hosea	Sterling,	Administration,	29301
1764	Isaac	Petersham,	Will,	29302

YEAR.	NAME.	RESIDENCE.	NATURE.	CASE.
1856	HILDRETH, James	Lunenburg,	Guardianship,	29303
1857	James E.	Ashburnham,	Administration,	29304
1856	Joseph S.	Bolton,	Guardianship,	29305
1869	Joseph S.	Bolton,	Administration,	29306
1869	Lillian M.	West Boylston,	Adoption, etc.,	29307
1856	Lucy A. F.	Lunenburg,	Guardianship,	29308
1873	Lucy J.	Sterling,	Administration,	29309
1875	Melinda	Petersham,	Administration,	29310
1811	Oliver	Petersham,	Administration,	29311
1824	Polly	Petersham,	Administration,	29312
1808	Ralph	Rutland,	Guardianship,	29313
1846	Richard	Sterling,	Guardianship,	29314
1811	Sally	Petersham,	Guardianship,	29315
1875	Samuel	Barre,	Administration,	29316
1856	Sophia A.	Lunenburg,	Guardianship,	29317
1817	Timothy	Sterling,	Will,	29318
1856	Willard P.	Lunenburg,	Guardianship,	29319
	HILL AND HILLS,			
1781	Aaron	Lancaster,	Guardianship,	29320
1852	Aaron	Athol,	Will,	29321
1874	Aaron M.	Douglas,	Partition,	29322
1868	Abby A.	Gardner,	Guardianship,	29323
1781	Abigail	Lancaster,	Guardianship,	29324
1815	Abigail	Gardner,	Administration,	29325
1838	Abijah	Athol,	Will,	29326
1788	Abraham	Oxford,	Will,	29327
1846	Adams S.	Boston,	Guardianship,	29328
1865	Albert	Shrewsbury,	Administration,	29329
1857	Alfred H.	Sterling,	Guardianship,	29330
1871	Alonzo	Worcester,	Administration,	29331
1862	Andrew J.	Athol,	Guardianship,	29332
1877	Angeline	Oxford,	Administration,	29333
1761	Anna	Lancaster,	Guardianship,	29334
1834	Anna	Grafton,	Will,	29335
1844	Anna	Mendon,	Pension,	29336
1861	Annie	Sutton,	Guardianship,	29337
1773	Asa	Sutton,	Guardianship,	29338
1828	Asa	Gardner,	Will,	29339
1838	Asa	Sterling,	Administration,	29340
1850	Asa	Douglas,	Will,	29341
1873	Asa	Harvard,	Will,	29342
1807	Barnabas	Dudley,	Guardianship,	29343
1827	Barnabas	Dudley,	Administration,	29344
1780	Barzilla	Ashburnham,	Guardianship,	29345
1766	Benjamin	Grafton,	Administration,	29346

HILL AND HILLS,

YEAR.	NAME.	RESIDENCE.	NATURE.	CASE.
1768	Benjamin	Grafton,	Guardianship,	29347
1862	Benjamin	Douglas,	Guardianship,	29348
1801	Benjamin C.	Douglas,	Guardianship,	29349
1851	Benjamin C.	Sutton,	Administration,	29350
1853	Betsey	Leominster,	Administration,	29351
1828	Betty	Leominster,	Administration,	29352
1778	Caleb	Lancaster,	Administration,	29353
1788	Caleb	Douglas,	Will,	29354
1793	Caleb	Douglas,	Guardianship,	29355
1796	Caleb	Uxbridge,	Administration,	29355
1802	Caleb	Douglas,	Guardianship,	29356
1851	Caleb	Douglas,	Administration,	29357
1836	Calvin	Douglas,	Guardianship,	29358
1853	Carlos	Oakham,	Guardianship,	29359
1861	Catherine M.	Athol,	Will,	29360
1845	Charles	Brookfield,	Will,	29361
1851	Charles	Leominster,	Administration,	29362
1872	Charles	Royalston,	Administration,	29363
1868	Charles B.	Gardner,	Guardianship,	29364
1859	Charles P.	Royalston,	Guardianship,	29365
1851	Charles W.	Leominster,	Guardianship,	29366
1838	Charlotte	Sterling,	Guardianship,	29367
1874	Charlotte	Douglas,	Partition,	29368
1877	Charlotte	Clinton,	Guardianship,	29369
1866	Charlotte S.	Holden,	Administration,	29370
1795	Chloe	Shrewsbury,	Guardianship,	29371
1815	Dan	Mendon,	Guardianship,	29372
1864	Dan	Mendon,	Will,	29373
1849	Danford	Athol,	Administration,	29374
1814	Daniel	Mendon,	Will,	29375
1814	Daniel	Mendon,	Administration,	29376
1853	Daniel	Spencer,	Will,	29377
1781	David	Lancaster,	Guardianship,	29378
1852	David A.	Leominster,	Administration,	29379
1830	David W.	Royalston,	Guardianship,	29380
1819	Dennis	Leominster,	Guardianship,	29381
1880	Dennis P.	Columbus, Ark.,	Guardianship,	29382
1853	Dexter	Oakham,	Administration,	29383
1847	Edmund	Upton,	Administration,	29384
1858	Edmund	Upton,	Administration,	29385
1857	Edward B.	Sterling,	Guardianship,	29386
1879	Edwards	Charlton,	Administration,	29387
1827	Edwin	Gardner,	Guardianship,	29388
1851	Edwin D.	Sutton,	Guardianship,	29389

Year.	Name.	Residence.	Nature.	Case.
	HILL and HILLS,			
1842	Edwin L.	Providence, R. I.,	Guardianship,	29390
1838	Eli	Sterling,	Guardianship,	29391
1827	Eliza	Gardner,	Guardianship,	29392
1851	Eliza A.	Sutton,	Guardianship,	29393
1862	Eliza A.	Athol,	Guardianship,	29394
1854	Elizabeth A.	Fitchburg,	Guardianship,	29395
1842	Ellen J.	Providence, R. 1.,	Guardianship,	29396
1854	Emma C.	Fitchburg,	Guardianship,	29397
1870	Enoch	Charlton,	Guardianship,	29398
1870	Enoch	Charlton,	Administration,	29398
1753	Enock	Lancaster,	Administration,	29399
1795	Ephraim	Douglas,	Will,	29400
1826	Ephraim	Royalston,	Administration,	29401
1877	Erastus	North Brookfield,	Administration,	29402
1857	Eugene H.	Sterling,	Guardianship,	29403
1853	Eva A.	Oakham,	Guardianship,	29404
1799	Ezra	Uxbridge,	Guardianship,	29405
1863	Feverlean E.	Winchendon,	Guardianship,	29406
1862	Frances A.	Athol,	Guardianship,	29407
1854	Francis D.	Fitchburg,	Guardianship,	29408
1833	Francis L.	Gardner,	Administration,	29409
1875	Franklin	Templeton,	Guardianship,	29410
1845	George	Blackstone,	Administration,	29411
1835	George H.	Leominster,	Guardianship,	29412
1868	Grace F.	Douglas,	Will,	29413
1848	Hamilton A.	Worcester,	Guardianship,	29414
1806	Hannah	Sterling,	Will,	29415
1870	Hannah	Charlton,	Administration,	29416
1838	Hannah E.	Sterling,	Guardianship,	29417
1826	Hanson	Charlton,	Guardianship,	29418
1840	Henry	Spencer,	Administration,	29419
1878	Henry C.	Gardner,	Administration,	29420
1850	Huldah	Royalston,	Administration,	29421
1839	Huldah M.	Athol,	Guardianship,	29422
1797	Irena	Uxbridge,	Guardianship,	29423
1852	Isaac	Concord,	Administration,	29424
1853	Isabella	Oakham,	Guardianship,	29425
1777	Israel	Oakham,	Administration,	29426
1801	James	Douglas,	Guardianship,	29427
1807	James	Dudley,	Administration,	29428
1874	James	Auburn,	Administration,	29429
1827	Jesse	Gardner,	Will,	29430
1823	Jesse, Jr.	Gardner,	Administration,	29431
1870	Jessie L.	Westminster,	Guardianship,	29432

Year.	Name.	Residence.	Nature.	Case.
	HILL and HILLS,			
1793	Joel	Grafton,	Guardianship,	29433
1814	Joel	Upton,	Administration,	29434
1764	John	Harvard,	Administration,	29435
1766	John	Lunenburg,	Will,	29436
1775	John	Brookfield,	Will,	29437
1781	John	Lancaster,	Guardianship,	29438
1784	John	Leominster,	Administration,	29439
1789	John	Spencer,	Will,	29440
1790	John	Sterling,	Guardianship,	29441
1793	John	Leominster,	Administration,	29442
1808	John	Mendon,	Guardianship,	29443
1814	John	Mendon,	Will,	29444
1832	John	Harvard,	Administration,	29445
1835	John	Harvard,	Administration,	29446
1839	John	Warren,	Will,	29447
1868	John	Charlton,	Will,	29448
1806	Jonah	Royalston,	Will,	29449
1829	Jonas	Royalston,	Administration,	29450
1787	Joseph	Grafton,	Will,	29451
1878	Joseph S.	Worcester,	Administration,	29452
1851	Josephine A.	Leominster,	Guardianship,	29453
1758	Joshua	Sutton,	Administration,	29454
1759	Joshua	Sutton,	Guardianship,	29455
1862	Joshua	Spencer,	Will,	29456
1863	Josiah	Winchendon,	Administration,	29457
1819	Josiah J.	Leominster,	Guardianship,	29458
1879	Josiah J.	Leominster,	Will,	29459
1793	Julia	Grafton,	Guardianship,	29460
1853	Julius	Oakham,	Guardianship,	29461
1860	Kittredge	North Brookfield,	Will,	29462
1858	Levi	Royalston,	Guardianship,	29463
1814	Levi	Templeton,	Administration,	29464
1781	Levina	Lancaster,	Guardianship,	29465
1790	Levina	Sterling,	Guardianship,	29466
1870	Lucia M. B.	Westminster,	Will,	29467
1801	Lucinda	Douglas,	Guardianship,	29468
1861	Lucy	Gardner,	Adoption, etc.,	29469
1836	Luther	Douglas,	Guardianship,	29470
1875	Lydia	Douglas,	Administration,	29471
1870	Marion	Douglas,	Guardianship,	29472
1874	Marion E.	Douglas,	Partition,	29473
1841	Martha	Royalston,	Will,	29474
1793	Mary	Grafton,	Guardianship,	29475
1849	Mary, etc.	Sutton,	Administration,	29476

(679)

YEAR.	NAME.	RESIDENCE.	NATURE.	CASE.
	HILL AND HILLS,			
1873	Mary A.	Sutton,	Adoption, etc.,	29477
1868	Mary B.	North Brookfield,	Administration,	29478
1852	Mary F.	Leominster,	Guardianship,	29479
1868	Mary L.	Gardner,	Guardianship,	29480
1840	Mary P.	Westminster,	Will,	29481
1787	Mathew	Dudley,	Administration,	29482
1822	Mercy	Mendon,	Administration,	29483
1797	Micah	Uxbridge,	Guardianship,	29484
1801	Micah	Douglas,	Guardianship,	29485
1836	Micah	Douglas,	Will,	29486
1827	Milton	Gardner,	Guardianship,	29487
1819	Miranda	Leominster,	Guardianship,	29488
1768	Molly	Grafton,	Guardianship,	29489
1780	Moses	Ashburnham,	Administration,	29490
1797	Moses	Uxbridge,	Guardianship,	29491
1800	Moses	Douglas,	Administration,	29492
1821	Moses	Athol,	Administration,	29493
1852	Moses	North Brookfield,	Guardianship,	29494
1862	Moses	Douglas,	Guardianship,	29495
1869	Moses B.	Douglas,	Administration,	29496
1867	Moses S.	Douglas,	Administration,	29497
1793	Nancy	Grafton,	Guardianship,	29498
1877	Nancy B.	Mendon,	Administration,	29499
1818	Nathan	Dana,	Will,	29500
1822	Nathaniel	No town,	Administration,	29501
1840	Noah	Douglas,	Pension,	29502
1795	Oliver	Shrewsbury,	Guardianship,	29503
1830	Oliver	Royalston,	Will,	29504
1847	Oliver	Harvard,	Administration,	29505
1871	Oliver V.	Leominster,	Administration,	29506
1853	Oscar	Oakham,	Guardianship,	29507
1801	Paris	Douglas,	Guardianship,	29508
1836	Paris	Douglas,	Guardianship,	29509
1819	Peter	North Brookfield,	Guardianship,	29510
1792	Phebe	Uxbridge,	Will,	29511
1795	Polly	Shrewsbury,	Guardianship,	29512
1852	Polly	Webster,	Administration,	29513
1854	Richard	Fitchburg,	Administration,	29514
1769	Robert	Lunenburg,	Guardianship,	29515
1868	Salem	Royalston,	Administration,	29516
1873	Sally	Douglas,	Guardianship,	29517
1768	Samuel	Mendon,	Guardianship,	29518
1797	Samuel	Harvard,	Will,	29519
1836	Samuel	Mendon,	Pension,	29520

YEAR.	NAME.	RESIDENCE.	NATURE.	CASE.
	HILL AND HILLS,			
1827	Sarah	Gardner,	Guardianship,	29521
1829	Sarah	Harvard,	Will,	29522
1830	Sarah	Royalston,	Guardianship,	29523
1849	Sarah	Gardner,	Pension,	29524
1849	Sarah	Gardner,	Will,	29525
1857	Sarah	Ashburnham,	Will,	29526
1867	Sarah	North Brookfield,	Administration,	29527
1880	Sarah H.	Dudley,	Will,	29528
1851	Sarah J.	Leominster,	Guardianship,	29529
1875	Sarah J.	Milford,	Will,	29530
1759	Silas	Sutton,	Guardianship,	29531
1776	Silas	Oakham,	Administration,	29532
1858	Silas	Canaan, N. H.,	Foreign Sale,	29533
1816	Smith	Leominster,	Administration,	29534
1819	Smith	Leominster,	Guardianship,	29535
1801	Submit	Douglas,	Guardianship,	29536
1780	Sylvanus	Ashburnham,	Guardianship,	29537
1863	Theodore J.	Winchendon,	Administration,	29538
1766	Thomas	Lunenburg,	Guardianship,	29539
1851	Thomas	Leominster,	Administration,	29540
1851	Thomas A.	Leominster,	Guardianship,	29541
1781	Timothy	Lancaster,	Guardianship,	29542
1790	Timothy	Sterling,	Guardianship,	29543
1823	Tristram A.	Leominster,	Guardianship,	29544
1815	Uranah	Mendon,	Guardianship,	29545
1831	Valentine	Spencer,	Administration,	29546
1819	Volney	Leominster,	Guardianship,	29547
1867	Washington	Spencer,	Administration,	29548
1872	Washington	Warren,	Will,	29549
1797	William	Western,	Administration,	29550
1862	William	Athol,	Administration,	29551
1869	William B.	Douglas,	Guardianship,	29552
1874	William B.	Douglas,	Partition,	29553
1857	William L.	Athol,	Administration,	29554
1868	Willie H.	Gardner,	Guardianship,	29555
1865	Willington	Spencer,	Will,	29556
1814	HILLER, Joseph	Lancaster,	Will,	29557
1792	HILLHOUSE, Moida	Barre,	Administration,	29558
1878	HILLIARD, Francis	Worcester,	Administration,	29559
1867	Samuel	Milford,	Will,	29560
1853	HILLMAN, Alfred C.	West Boylston,	Will,	29561
	HILLS see HILL.			
	HILLYER see HELLYAR.			
1767	HILT, Katharine	Unknown,	Guardianship,	29562

YEAR.	NAME.	RESIDENCE.	NATURE.	CASE.
1837	HILTON, Almer C.	Fitchburg,	Guardianship,	29563
1837	Amos S.	Fitchburg,	Guardianship,	29564
1834	Clark	Fitchburg,	Administration,	29565
1761	David	Lunenburg,	Guardianship,	29566
1869	David	Blackstone,	Will,	29567
1879	Edward	Oxford,	Will,	29568
1812	Mary	Lunenburg,	Guardianship,	29569
1812	Nancy	Lunenburg,	Guardianship,	29570
1871	Rebecca	Fitchburg,	Will,	29571
1756	Samuel	Lunenburg,	Will,	29572
1812	Samuel	Lunenburg,	Guardianship,	29573
1876	Sarah	Blackstone,	Will,	29574
1812	Sophia	Lunenburg,	Guardianship,	29575
1761	Thomas	Lunenburg,	Guardianship,	29576
1835	Thomas	Fitchburg,	Administration,	29577
1761	William	Lunenburg,	Guardianship,	29578
1841	HIMES, Stephen W.	Petersham,	Guardianship,	29579
1864	HINCHCLIFFE, Elizabeth K.	Barre,	Guardianship,	29580
1877	George	Millbury,	Administration,	29581
1876	Mary A.	Oxford,	Administration,	29582
1864	Rebecca J.	Barre,	Guardianship,	29583
1864	Sarah E.	Barre,	Guardianship,	29584
1767	HINCHER, Josiah	Brookfield,	Guardianship,	29585
1769	Priscilla	Brookfield,	Guardianship,	29586
1813	Ruth	Brookfield,	Will,	29587
1801	William	Brookfield,	Will,	29588
	HINCKLEY AND HINKLEY,			
1864	Alma M.	Barre,	Guardianship,	29589
1807	Barnabas	Hardwick,	Will,	29590
1837	Barnabas	Hardwick,	Guardianship,	29591
1852	Charlotte C.	Athol,	Administration,	29592
1837	Daniel B.	Hardwick,	Guardianship,	29593
1756	David	Brookfield,	Administration,	29594
1864	Eliza R.	Barre,	Guardianship,	29595
1872	George H.	Barre,	Guardianship,	29596
1872	Herbert R.	Barre,	Guardianship,	29597
1753	Job	Brookfield,	Will,	29598
1783	Job	Brookfield,	Administration,	29599
1819	Judah	Barre,	Will,	29600
1753	Marcy	Brookfield,	Guardianship,	29601
1827	Martha	Barre,	Guardianship,	29602
1872	Martha G.	Barre,	Guardianship,	29603
1864	Mary L.	Barre,	Guardianship,	29604
1819	Patty	Barre,	Guardianship,	29605
1799	Samuel	Brookfield,	Will,	29606

YEAR.	NAME.	RESIDENCE.	NATURE.	CASE.
	HINCKLEY AND HINKLEY,			
1849	Samuel	Hardwick,	Pension,	29607
1831	Samuel A.	Hardwick,	Guardianship,	29608
1841	Samuel A.	Hardwick,	Guardianship,	29609
1872	Sarah E.	Barre,	Guardianship,	29610
1797	Seth	Hardwick,	Will,	29611
1837	Seth	Hardwick,	Administration,	29612
1872	Timothy R.	Barre,	Administration,	29613
1879	Timothy R.	Barre,	Will,	29614
1864	William W.	North Brookfield,	Administration,	29615
	HINDS, HINES AND HYNES,			
1875	Abbie F.	North Brookfield,	Guardianship,	29616
1877	Abbie F.	Concord, N. H.,	Foreign Will,	29617
1868	Abijah	Gardner,	Will,	29618
1795	Abraham	Boylston,	Guardianship,	29619
1835	Abraham	Hinsdale, N. H.,	Foreign Will,	29620
1874	Albert	West Boylston,	Administration,	29621
1877	Albert W.	West Boylston,	Guardianship,	29622
1853	Amanda C.	Holden,	Guardianship,	29623
1794	Benjamin	Boylston,	Administration,	29624
1838	Bertrand	West Boylston,	Guardianship,	29625
1856	Cicero	West Boylston,	Administration,	29626
1875	Cora L., etc.	Worcester,	Guardianship,	29627
1800	Cornelius	Barre,	Guardianship,	29628
1864	Eli	Spencer,	Will,	29629
1795	Elisha	Boylston,	Guardianship,	29630
1813	Elizabeth	Harvard,	Guardianship,	29631
1861	Ellen R.	Ashburnham,	Guardianship,	29632
1795	Ephraim	Boylston,	Guardianship,	29633
1858	Ephraim	West Boylston,	Administration,	29634
1819	Forbes, Jr.	Barre,	Guardianship,	29635
1861	Francis	Ashburnham,	Administration,	29636
1761	Grace	Western,	Guardianship,	29637
1880	Harriet E.	Worcester,	Administration,	29638
1870	Harriet L.	West Boylston,	Will,	29639
1751	Jacob	Shrewsbury,	Administration,	29640
1751	Jacob	Shrewsbury,	Guardianship,	29641
1761	Jacob	Western,	Administration,	29642
1756	Jasou	Western,	Administration,	29643
1748	John	Brookfield,	Will,	29644
1756	John	Brookfield,	Administration,	29645
1757	John	Brookfield,	Guardianship,	29646
1811	John	Hubbardston,	Administration,	29647
1813	John	North Brookfield,	Administration,	29648
1813	John	Harvard,	Administration,	29649

YEAR.	NAME.	RESIDENCE.	NATURE.	CASE.
	HINDS, HINES AND HYNES,			
1849	John	Millbury,	Administration,	29650
1871	John	Worcester,	Guardianship,	29651
1806	Joseph	Petersham,	Guardianship,	29652
1835	Joseph	West Boylston,	Will,	29653
1853	Joseph	Holden	Will,	29654
1856	Joseph	Petersham,	Administration,	29655
1853	Joseph S.	Holden,	Guardianship,	29656
1875	Joseph S.	Holden,	Administration,	29657
1879	Lewis L.	Warren,	Administration,	29658
1757	Martha	Brookfield,	Guardianship,	29659
1861	Martha E.	Ashburnham,	Guardianship,	29660
1757	Mary	Brookfield,	Guardianship,	29661
1807	Mary	Brookfield,	Guardianship,	29662
1813	Mary	Harvard,	Guardianship,	29663
1817	Mary	North Brookfield,	Administration,	29664
1871	Mary	Holden,	Will,	29665
1813	Nancy	Harvard,	Guardianship,	29666
1791	Nimrod	Brooksettlement, Me.,	Power of Att'y,	29667
1757	Oliver	Brookfield,	Guardianship,	29668
1875	Oliver	North Brookfield,	Will,	29669
1876	Patty	Brookfield,	Administration,	29670
1862	Persis	Gardner,	Administration,	29671
1761	Phena	Western,	Guardianship,	29672
1859	Rebekah	West Boylston,	Will,	29673
1817	Rhoda	North Brookfield,	Guardianship,	29674
1871	Richard	Worcester,	Guardianship,	29675
1813	Sally	Harvard,	Guardianship,	29676
1851	Samuel M.	Lancaster,	Administration,	29677
1877	Susan	Petersham,	Will,	29678
1795	Tabitha	Boylston,	Guardianship,	29679
1826	Tabitha	West Boylston,	Administration,	29680
1871	Thomas F.	Worcester,	Guardianship,	29681
1825	William	Barre,	Will,	29682
	HISCOX AND HISCOCK,			
1867	Caroline A.	Warren,	Adoption, etc.,	29683
1769	David	Sutton,	Guardianship,	29684
1868	Luther R.	Charlton,	Administration,	29685
1769	Nathan	Sutton,	Guardianship,	29686
1769	Sarah	Sutton,	Guardianship,	29687
1769	Stephen	Sutton,	Guardianship,	29688
1815	HITCHCOCK, Abigail W.	Brookfield,	Guardianship,	29689
1874	Alfred	Fitchburg,	Will,	29690
1862	Alfred A.	Fitchburg,	Change of Name,	29691
1862	Alfred O.	Fitchburg,	Change of Name,	29692

YEAR.	NAME.	RESIDENCE.	NATURE.	CASE.
1854	HITCHCOCK, Alice M.	Leicester,	Guardianship,	29693
1854	Ann E.	West Brookfield,	Guardianship,	29694
1866	Anna	Millbury,	Administration,	29695
1863	Aurilla P.	Fitchburg,	Administration,	29696
1814	Caleb	Brookfield,	Will,	29697
1874	Caleb S.	Warren,	Administration,	29698
1784	Daniel	Brookfield,	Guardianship,	29699
1819	Daniel	Brookfield,	Guardianship,	29700
1837	Daniel	Brookfield,	Will,	29701
1860	Daniel T.	Warren,	Will,	29702
1814	David	Brookfield,	Will,	29703
1874	David	Worcester,	Will,	29704
1797	David, Jr.	Brookfield,	Administration,	29705
1815	David K.	Brookfield,	Guardianship,	29706
1872	Eaton	Sturbridge,	Administration,	29707
1862	Edward W.	Fitchburg,	Change of Name,	29708
1854	Edwin F.	West Brookfield,	Guardianship,	29709
1781	Enoch	Western,	Guardianship,	29710
1861	Frederick S.	Warren,	Guardianship,	29711
1853	George D.	Worcester,	Administration,	29712
1800	Hannah	Brookfield,	Guardianship,	29713
1824	Hannah	New Braintree,	Will,	29714
1840	Harriet K.	Homer, N. Y.,	Guardianship,	29715
1862	Hiland C.	Fitchburg,	Guardianship,	29716
1815	Hollis	Brookfield,	Administration,	29717
1862	James R. W.	Fitchburg,	Change of Name,	29718
1874	James R. W.	Fitchburg,	Guardianship,	29719
1862	James W.	Fitchburg,	Change of Name,	29720
1777	John	Western,	Will,	29721
1784	John	Brookfield,	Guardianship,	29722
1820	John	Brookfield,	Guardianship,	29723
1831	John	Brookfield,	Will,	29724
1777	Jonathan	Western,	Guardianship,	29725
1881	Joseph F.	Warren,	Will,	29726
1781	Levi	Western,	Guardianship,	29727
1876	Levi	Millbury,	Administration,	29728
1821	Martha	Brookfield,	Administration,	29729
1800	Mary	Brookfield,	Guardianship,	29730
1861	Mary S.	Warren,	Guardianship,	29731
1800	Moses	Brookfield,	Will,	29732
1854	Rebecca	West Brookfield,	Administration,	29733
1800	Sophia	Brookfield,	Guardianship,	29734
1840	Sophronia	Arkansas Ter.,	Guardianship,	29735
1800	William	Brookfield,	Guardianship,	29736
1854	William H.	West Brookfield,	Guardianship,	29737

YEAR.	NAME.	RESIDENCE.	NATURE.	CASE.
	HIX see HICKS.			
	HOAR AND HORE,			
1830	Abigail	Westminster,	Will,	29738
1845	Alonzo P.	Princeton,	Guardianship,	29739
1849	Charles	New Braintree,	Will,	29740
1849	Charles S.	New Braintree,	Guardianship,	29741
1859	Charles S.	New Braintree,	Change of Name,	29742
1782	Daniel	Westminster,	Administration,	29743
1794	David	Brimfield,	Guardianship,	29744
1845	Dwight	Princeton,	Guardianship,	29745
1810	Ezra	Westminster,	Guardianship,	29746
1845	Ezra	Princeton,	Administration,	29747
1845	Ezra H.	Princeton,	Guardianship,	29748
1845	Fidelia M.	Princeton,	Guardianship,	29749
1810	Hannah	Westminster,	Guardianship,	29750
1794	Isaac	Winchendon,	Administration,	29751
1809	Isaac	Brookfield,	Guardianship,	29752
1812	John	Westminster,	Administration,	29753
1845	Lyman B.	Princeton,	Guardianship,	29754
1862	Mary	Worcester,	Guardianship,	29755
1845	Mary R.	Princeton,	Guardianship,	29756
1849	Nancy	New Braintree,	Guardianship,	29757
1809	Nathan	Brookfield,	Guardianship,	29758
1862	Rockwood	Worcester,	Guardianship,	29759
1820	Sally	North Brookfield,	Guardianship,	29760
1783	Samuel	Westminster,	Guardianship,	29761
1817	Samuel	North Brookfield,	Administration,	29762
1810	Stephen	Westminster,	Administration,	29763
1832	Timothy	Westminster,	Administration,	29764
1873	HOBAN, James	Southbridge,	Will,	29765
1863	HOBART, Charlotte	Leicester,	Will,	29766
1835	John	Leicester,	Will,	29767
1813	Shebelel	Ashburnham,	Will,	29768
1844	Simon	Grafton,	Administration,	29769
1843	Susanna	Ashburnham,	Will,	29770
1840	Thomas	Ashburnham,	Will,	29771
1859	HOBBS, Altha J.	Charlton,	Guardianship,	29772
1779	Anna	Brookfield,	Guardianship,	29773
1813	Anna	Spencer,	Administration,	29774
1849	Asa	Sturbridge,	Administration,	29775
1854	Asenath	Brookfield,	Administration,	29776
1827	Benjamin	Sturbridge,	Administration,	29777
1873	Caroline	Worcester,	Administration,	29778
1850	Charles F.	Brookfield,	Guardianship,	29779
1866	Charles F.	Brookfield,	Will,	29780

YEAR.	NAME.	RESIDENCE.	NATURE.	CASE.
1869	HOBBS, Cora L.	Worcester,	Guardianship,	29781
1778	Daniel	Brookfield,	Guardianship,	29782
1846	Daniel	Spencer,	Administration,	29783
1852	Dolly	Worcester,	Administration,	29784
1845	Elvira L.	Sturbridge,	Guardianship,	29785
1849	Emily F.	Sturbridge,	Guardianship,	29786
1849	Fanny M.	Sturbridge,	Guardianship,	29787
1872	George	Worcester,	Administration,	29788
1845	George J.	Sturbridge,	Guardianship,	29789
1876	George T.	Uxbridge,	Guardianship,	29790
1856	Hannah	Sturbridge,	Will,	29791
1840	Hartwell	Sturbridge,	Guardianship,	29792
1837	Henry	Worcester,	Administration,	29793
1847	Isaac	Sturbridge,	Administration,	29794
1778	Jesse	Brookfield,	Guardianship,	29795
1841	Jesse	Brookfield,	Administration,	29796
1778	John	Brookfield,	Will,	29797
1850	John	Brookfield,	Will,	29798
1850	John F.	Brookfield,	Guardianship,	29799
1862	John F.	Union, Conn.,	Administration,	29800
1828	John G.	Princeton,	Guardianship,	29801
1840	Josiah, 2d	Sturbridge,	Administration,	29802
1845	Josiah	Sturbridge,	Administration,	29803
1828	Lois	Princeton,	Guardianship,	29804
1833	Lois	Princeton,	Will,	29805
1871	Louisa	Worcester,	Will,	29806
1817	Lydia	Sturbridge,	Will,	29807
1840	Lyman	Sturbridge,	Guardianship,	29808
1837	Marcy.	Princeton,	Administration,	29809
1849	Mary A.	Sturbridge,	Guardianship,	29810
1850	Mary A.	Brookfield,	Guardianship,	29811
1811	Meriam	Brookfield,	Guardianship,	29812
1823	Moses	Princeton,	Administration,	29813
1843	Moses	Brookfield,	Will,	29814
1873	Moses	Brookfield,	Administration,	29815
1865	Nancy B.	Worcester,	Guardianship,	29816
1868	Nancy B.	Worcester,	Will,	29816
1813	Nathan	Sturbridge,	Will,	29817
1811	Philita	Brookfield,	Guardianship,	29818
1779	Ruth	Brookfield,	Guardianship,	29819
1801	Ruth	Brookfield,	Will,	29820
1823	Samuel	Sturbridge,	Will,	29821
1855	Samuel	Sturbridge,	Administration,	29822
1849	Samuel D.	Sturbridge,	Guardianship,	29823
1811	Samuel M.	Brookfield,	Guardianship,	29824

YEAR.	NAME.	RESIDENCE.	NATURE.	CASE.
1864	HOBBS, Samuel M.	Worcester,	Will,	29825
1840	Selina	Sturbridge,	Guardianship,	29826
1802	Silas	Brookfield,	Administration,	29827
1840	Thankful	Sturbridge,	Guardianship,	29828
1844	Thomas J.	Hubbardston,	Administration,	29829
1830	William	Hubbardston,	Administration,	29830
1854	William	Worcester,	Will,	29831
1850	William E.	Brookfield,	Guardianship,	29832
1869	William H.	Worcester,	Guardianship,	29833
1869	HOBSON, Lillian M.	West Boylston,	Adoption, etc.,	29834
1879	Lillie M.	West Boylston,	Guardianship,	29835
1869	Mary	West Boylston,	Administration,	29836
	HODGDON AND HODGDEN,			
1874	Josiah R.	Westborough,	Administration,	29837
1866	Sarah N.	Walden, Vt.,	Adoption, etc.,	29838
	HODGE AND HODGES,			
1881	Adelaide M.	Webster,	Will,	29839
1845	Adolphus	Warren,	Will,	29840
1864	Alice, etc.	Barre,	Guardianship,	29841
1827	Barnum,	Rutland,	Guardianship,	29842
1868	Bradford	Petersham,	Administration,	29843
1832	Brutus	Brookfield,	Administration,	29844
1864	Celia	Barre,	Guardianship,	29845
1789	Daniel	Hardwick,	Administration,	29846
1830	Daniel	Western,	Will,	29847
1829	Daniel M.	Western,	Guardianship,	29848
1875	Emily F.	Templeton,	Will,	29849
1817	Erastus D.	Phillipston,	Guardianship,	29850
1829	George	Western,	Guardianship,	29851
1864	George F.	Barre,	Guardianship,	29852
1816	Guilford	Phillipston,	Administration,	29853
1876	Henry A.	Petersham,	Will,	29854
1864	Henry H.	Barre,	Guardianship,	29855
1874	Henry H.	Barre,	Administration,	29856
1822	Jeremy	Rutland,	Guardianship,	29857
1825	Jeremy	Rutland,	Administration,	29857
1863	Joel	Barre,	Administration,	29858
1829	John	Western,	Guardianship,	29859
1859	Lemuel	Petersham,	Will,	29860
1829	Lewis	Western,	Guardianship,	29861
1879	Lilla M.	Royalston,	Guardianship,	29862
1864	Lydia	Petersham,	Administration,	29863
1829	Maria L.	Western,	Guardianship,	29864
1872	Mary A.	Barre,	Administration,	29865
1818	Phebe	Phillipston,	Administration,	29866

YEAR	NAME.	RESIDENCE.	NATURE.	CASE.
	HODGE AND HODGES,			
1844	Rachael	Warren,	Will,	29867
1832	Sarah M.	Brookfield,	Guardianship,	29868
1811	Tisdale	Petersham,	Administration,	29869
1817	Tisdale	Phillipston,	Guardianship,	29870
1829	William	Western,	Guardianship,	29871
1846	William A.	Warren,	Guardianship,	29872
1802	HODGKINS, Asa	Fitchburg,	Guardianship,	29873
1847	Daniel	Leicester	Guardianship,	29874
1805	Hezekiah	Fitchburg,	Will,	29875
1802	Ira	Fitchburg,	Guardianship,	29876
1763	Jonas	Billerica,	Guardianship,	29877
1763	Molly	Billerica,	Guardianship,	29878
1866	Orlando	Worcester,	Administration,	29879
1763	Sarah	Billerica,	Guardianship,	29880
1864	HODGMAN, George	Gardner,	Administration,	29881
1847	Otis	New Braintree,	Guardianship,	29882
1859	Rosalie W.	Millbury,	Adoption, etc.,	29883
1781	Samuel	Brookfield,	Administration,	29884
1782	Samuel	Brookfield,	Guardianship,	29885
1873	HODGSON, William	Southbridge,	Will,	29886
	HODSKIN AND HODSKING,			
1856	Anna	Athol,	Administration,	29887
1856	Anna	Athol,	Pension,	29888
1800	David	Fitchburg,	Administration,	29889
1867	HOFFMAN, Elizabeth	Worcester,	Administration,	29890
1875	George F.	Fitchburg,	Guardianship,	29891
1880	William	Worcester,	Administration,	29892
1874	HOGAN, Ellen	Webster,	Guardianship,	29893
1874	James	Webster,	Guardianship,	29894
1878	Jeremiah M.	Spencer,	Administration,	29895
1864	John	Southbridge,	Administration,	29896
1868	John	Dudley,	Will,	29897
1874	John	Webster,	Guardianship,	29898
1874	Margaret	Webster,	Guardianship,	29899
1881	Margaret	Worcester,	Will,	29900
1873	Mary	Webster,	Administration,	29901
1873	Michael	Webster,	Administration,	29902
1874	Patrick	Webster,	Guardianship,	29903
1874	Patrick	Worcester,	Administration,	29904
1873	Thomas	Webster,	Will,	29905
1863	William	Gardner,	Will,	29906
	HOIT see HOYT.			
1825	HOLBROOK, Aaron	Holden,	Administration,	29907
1777	Abel	Worcester,	Administration,	29908
1778	Abel	Worcester,	Guardianship,	29909

YEAR.	NAME.	RESIDENCE.	NATURE.	CASE.
1768	HOLBROOK, Abial	Mendon,	Guardianship,	29910
1782	Abigail	Uxbridge,	Guardianship,	29911
1843	Albert	Worcester,	Guardianship,	29912
1845	Alfred B.	Charlton,	Guardianship,	29913
1849	Alvan B.	Sturbridge,	Guardianship,	29914
1789	Amariah	Sturbridge,	Partition,	29915
1799	Amariah	Sturbridge,	Administration,	29916
1800	Amariah	Sturbridge,	Guardianship,	29917
1777	Amos	Worcester,	Administration,	29918
1873	Ann B.	Sterling,	Will,	29919
1766	Anna	Mendon,	Guardianship,	29920
1842	Anna	Mendon,	Will,	29921
1874	Anna	Oxford,	Administration,	29922
1856	Anna F.	Milford,	Guardianship,	29923
1864	Annah	Upton,	Will,	29924
1778	Asa	Worcester,	Guardianship,	29925
1874	Asa	Oxford,	Will,	29926
1880	Asa	Holden,	Administration,	29927
1825	Asenath	Grafton,	Guardianship,	29928
1838	Asenath	Sturbridge,	Guardianship,	29929
1808	Austin	Grafton,	Guardianship,	29930
1861	Austin	Grafton,	Administration,	29931
1767	Benjamin	Mendon,	Administration,	29932
1865	Benjamin	Milford,	Administration,	29933
1803	Betsey	Charlton,	Guardianship,	29934
1825	Calvin	Milford,	Administration,	29935
1808	Candace	Grafton,	Guardianship,	29936
1863	Cephas	New Braintree,	Will,	29937
1876	Charles A.	Worcester,	Administration,	29938
1876	Charles E.	Worcester,	Guardianship,	29939
1835	Charles G.	Westborough,	Guardianship,	29940
1875	Charlotte G.	New Braintree,	Administration,	29941
1779	Chloe	Uxbridge,	Guardianship,	29942
1867	Cora E.	Milford,	Adoption, etc.,	29943
1854	Cyrus	Sterling,	Will,	29944
1879	Cyrus	Northborough,	Guardianship,	29945
1765	Daniel	Mendon,	Administration,	29946
1766	Daniel	Mendon,	Guardianship,	29947
1779	Daniel	Uxbridge,	Guardianship,	29948
1782	Daniel	Upton,	Guardianship,	29949
1800	Daniel	Sturbridge,	Guardianship,	29950
1827	Daniel	Upton,	Will,	29951
1828	Daniel	Upton,	Guardianship,	29952
1841	Daniel	Berlin,	Administration,	29953
1860	Daniel	Milford,	Will,	29954

YEAR.	NAME.	RESIDENCE.	NATURE.	CASE.
1835	HOLBROOK, Daniel, Jr.	Westborough,	Will,	29955
1834	Darius	Brookfield,	Pension,	29956
1782	David	Upton,	Guardianship,	29957
1787	David	Douglas,	Guardianship,	29958
1828	David	Holden,	Will,	29959
1838	David	Holden,	Administration,	29960
1856	David F.	Milford,	Guardianship,	29961
1778	Deborah	Worcester,	Guardianship,	29962
1821	Delia M.	Sutton,	Guardianship,	29963
1860	Dexter	Northborough,	Administration,	29964
1805	Ebenezer	Milford,	Will,	29965
1849	Edward	Sturbridge,	Guardianship,	29966
1776	Eleazer	Worcester,	Administration,	29967
1778	Eleazer	Worcester,	Guardianship,	29968
1761	Eli	Brimfield,	Guardianship,	29969
1764	Elias	Brimfield,	Guardianship,	29970
1870	Elias	Sturbridge,	Will,	29971
1807	Elisha S.	Sturbridge,	Administration,	29972
1857	Elizabeth	Grafton,	Will,	29973
1855	Ellen S.	Northbridge,	Guardianship,	29974
1854	Emory	Grafton,	Change of Name,	29975
1787	Enos	Douglas,	Guardianship,	29976
1849	Erasmus	Sturbridge,	Will,	29977
1869	Eugene C.	Milford,	Guardianship,	29978
1778	Eunice	Worcester,	Guardianship,	29979
1860	Eva E.	Milford,	Guardianship,	29980
1828	Ezra W.	Upton,	Guardianship,	29981
1858	Ezra W.	Milford,	Administration,	29982
1854	Ferdinand	Grafton,	Change of Name,	29983
1873	Frank E.	Ashland,	Adoption, etc.,	29984
1853	Franklin	Barre,	Administration,	29985
1868	George	Sturbridge,	Will,	29986
1871	George	Westborough,	Will,	29987
1842	George C.	Holden,	Guardianship,	29988
1778	Hannah	Worcester,	Guardianship,	29989
1800	Hannah	Sturbridge,	Guardianship,	29990
1843	Hannah	Berlin,	Will,	29991
1866	Hannah C.	Blackstone,	Change of Name,	29992
1825	Hannah G.	Grafton,	Guardianship,	29993
1782	Henry	Uxbridge,	Guardianship,	29994
1829	Henry	Mendon,	Administration,	29995
1874	Henry	Barre,	Administration,	29996
1856	Henry A.	Milford,	Guardianship,	29997
1869	Henry C.	Upton,	Guardianship,	29998
1850	Horatio	Petersham,	Guardianship,	29999

YEAR.	NAME.	RESIDENCE.	NATURE.	CASE.
1757	HOLBROOK, Isaac	Uxbridge,	Administration,	30000
1809	James, Jr.	Sturbridge,	Administration,	30001
1795	Jemima	Upton,	Guardianship,	30002
1766	Job	Mendon,	Guardianship,	30003
1756	John	Grafton,	Will,	30004
1774	John	Uxbridge,	Will,	30005
1789	John	Sturbridge,	Partition,	30006
1839	John	Sturbridge,	Will,	30007
1839	John	Sturbridge,	Pension,	30008
1851	John	Sturbridge,	Will,	30009
1778	Jonathan	Worcester,	Guardianship,	30010
1828	Jonathan D.	Upton,	Guardianship,	30011
1817	Joseph	Worcester,	Administration,	30012
1823	Joseph	Worcester,	Guardianship,	30013
1809	Joseph F.	Worcester,	Guardianship,	30014
1802	Josiah	Charlton,	Administration,	30015
1849	Julia	Sturbridge,	Guardianship,	30016
1828	Julianna	Upton,	Guardianship,	30017
1741	Katherine	Uxbridge,	Guardianship,	30018
1766	Katherine	Mendon,	Guardianship,	30019
1778	Keziah	Worcester,	Guardianship,	30020
1871	Keziah	Sutton,	Administration,	30021
1845	Laura J.	Charlton,	Guardianship,	30022
1809	Lewis	Worcester,	Guardianship,	30023
1814	Lewis, 2d	Worcester,	Guardianship,	30024
1821	Lewis	Sutton,	Guardianship,	30025
1823	Lewis	Worcester,	Administration,	30026
1862	Lowell	Northborough,	Will,	30027
1845	Lucinda M.	Charlton,	Guardianship,	30028
1782	Lucy	Uxbridge,	Guardianship,	30029
1849	Lucy	Sturbridge,	Guardianship,	30030
1823	Lucy E.	Worcester,	Guardianship,	30031
1856	Luther	Milford,	Administration,	30032
1778	Lydia	Worcester,	Guardianship,	30033
1778	Lydia	Worcester,	Guardianship,	30034
1781	Lydia	Worcester,	Administration,	30035
1831	Lyman	Mendon,	Guardianship,	30036
1877	Lyman	Blackstone,	Administration,	30037
1819	Mahala	Upton,	Guardianship,	30038
1770	Margery	Mendon,	Guardianship,	30039
1782	Margery	Upton,	Guardianship,	30040
1778	Martha	Worcester,	Guardianship,	30041
1791	Martha	Worcester,	Administration,	30042
1825	Martha P.	Grafton,	Guardianship,	30043
1855	Mary	Sutton,	Trustee,	30044

| --- | --- | --- | --- | --- |
1860	HOLBROOK, Mary F.	Milford,	Guardianship,	30045
1808	Mary W.	Grafton,	Guardianship,	30046
1823	Melia F.	Worcester,	Guardianship,	30047
1828	Melita	Upton,	Guardianship,	30048
1829	Melita	Upton,	Will,	30049
1880	Micah	Worcester,	Will,	30050
1756	Moses	Grafton,	Guardianship,	30051
1807	Moses	Templeton,	Guardianship,	30052
1808	Moses	Grafton,	Administration,	30053
1869	Nahum A.	Upton,	Guardianship,	30054
1869	Nahum W.	Upton,	Administration,	30055
1803	Nancy	Charlton,	Guardianship,	30056
1872	Nancy	Milford,	Will,	30057
1782	Nathan	Upton,	Guardianship,	30058
1816	Nathan	Upton,	Will,	30059
1819	Nathan	Upton,	Guardianship,	30060
1832	Nathan	Croyden, N. H.,	Guardianship,	30061
1839	Nathan	Barre,	Administration,	30062
1850	Nathan	Milford,	Administration,	30063
1867	Nella	Blackstone,	Will,	30064
1831	Nelson	Mendon,	Guardianship,	30065
1855	Nelson	Blackstone,	Administration,	30066
1843	Olive	Warren,	Pension,	30067
1825	Orace	Milford,	Guardianship,	30068
1838	Otis	Uxbridge,	Administration,	30069
1825	Partridge	Milford,	Guardianship,	30070
1800	Patience	Sturbridge,	Guardianship,	30071
1793	Patty	Grafton,	Guardianship,	30072
1808	Patty	Grafton,	Guardianship,	30073
1766	Paul	Mendon,	Guardianship,	30074
1770	Peter	Mendon,	Guardianship,	30075
1781	Peter, Jr.	Upton,	Will,	30076
1867	Phila	Uxbridge,	Administration,	30077
1808	Phineas	Worcester,	Administration,	30078
1823	Phineas	Worcester,	Guardianship,	30079
1809	Phineas E.	Worcester,	Guardianship,	30080
1766	Phinehas	Mendon,	Guardianship,	30081
1873	Pliny	Worcester,	Administration,	30082
1803	Polly	Charlton,	Guardianship,	30083
1789	Priscilla	Sturbridge,	Partition,	30084
1808	Puah	Grafton,	Guardianship,	30085
1753	Rachell	Mendon,	Guardianship,	30086
1768	Reubin	Mendon,	Guardianship,	30087
1823	Rhoda B.	Worcester,	Guardianship,	30088
1808	Robert M.	Grafton,	Guardianship,	30089

YEAR.	NAME.	RESIDENCE.	NATURE.	CASE.
1829	HOLBROOK, Sabrina	Upton,	Administration,	30090
1808	Sally	Grafton,	Guardianship,	30091
1825	Sally B.	Grafton,	Guardianship,	30092
1848	Samuel	Douglas,	Administration,	30093
1768	Samuel, Jr.	Uxbridge,	Will,	30094
1771	Sarah	Mendon,	Guardianship,	30095
1778	Sarah	Worcester,	Guardianship,	30096
1800	Sarah	Sturbridge,	Guardianship,	30097
1805	Sarah	Grafton,	Administration,	30098
1876	Sarah F.	Worcester,	Guardianship,	30099
1866	Sarah N.	Leicester,	Adoption, etc.,	30100
1819	Serepta	Upton,	Guardianship,	30101
1759	Seth	Uxbridge,	Guardianship,	30102
1766	Silas	Mendon,	Guardianship,	30103
1759	Silence	Uxbridge,	Guardianship,	30104
1822	Silvester	Sturbridge,	Guardianship,	30105
1814	Simeon	Upton,	Will,	30106
1826	Simeon	Northbridge,	Administration,	30107
1852	Simeon	Upton,	Administration,	30108
1803	Sina	Charlton,	Guardianship,	30109
1782	Stephen	Uxbridge,	Guardianship,	30110
1820	Stephen	Sutton,	Administration,	30111
1830	Stephen	Uxbridge,	Will,	30112
1850	Stephen	Grafton,	Will,	30113
1825	Stephen E.	Grafton,	Guardianship,	30114
1740	Sylvanus	Uxbridge,	Administration,	30115
1741	Sylvanus	Uxbridge,	Guardianship,	30116
1781	Sylvanus	Uxbridge,	Administration,	30117
1828	Sylvanus	Douglas,	Administration,	30118
1856	Sylvanus	Northbridge,	Administration,	30119
1855	Sylvanus, Jr.	Northbridge,	Guardianship,	30120
1815	Sylvester	Sturbridge,	Will,	30121
1822	Sylvester	Sturbridge,	Guardianship,	30122
1845	Sylvester	Charlton,	Administration,	30123
1880	Sylvia	Worcester,	Will,	30124
1861	Theron	Milford,	Will,	30125
1800	Tirza	Sturbridge,	Guardianship,	30126
1822	Vialia	Sturbridge,	Guardianship,	30127
1831	Willard	Mendon,	Guardianship,	30128
1775	William	Mendon,	Will,	30129
1792	William	Grafton,	Administration,	30130
1825	William	Grafton,	Guardianship,	30131
1856	William	Leicester,	Administration,	30132
1829	Ziba	Milford,	Administration,	30133
1830	HOLCOMB, Abigail	Sterling,	Will,	30134

(694)

YEAR.	NAME.	RESIDENCE.	NATURE.	CASE.
1837	HOLCOMB, Augustine	Sterling,	Will,	30135
1860	Ella F.	Worcester,	Guardianship,	30136
1860	Emerson L.	Worcester,	Administration,	30137
1826	Reubén	Sterling,	Will,	30138
1837	Susan H.	Sterling,	Guardianship,	30139
1837	William F.	Sterling,	Guardianship,	30140
	HOLDEN AND HOLDIN,			
1836	Abby P.	Barre,	Guardianship,	30141
1757	Abigail	Harvard,	Guardianship,	30142
1777	Abigail	Barre,	Guardianship,	30143
1804	Abigail	Westminster,	Guardianship,	30144
1805	Abner	Westminster,	Will,	30145
1824	Abner	Westminster,	Will,	30146
1857	Achsah	Rutland,	Administration,	30147
1873	Alice M.	Westminster,	Guardianship,	30148
1852	Amasa	Barre,	Administration,	30149
1854	Anna	Barre,	Administration,	30150
1863	Anna P.	Charlton,	Guardianship,	30151
1873	Annie B.	Westminster,	Guardianship,	30152
1869	Asa	Westminster,	Will,	30153
1784	Benjamin	Barre,	Administration,	30154
1820	Benjamin	Princeton,	Administration,	30155
1832	Benjamin	Princeton,	Administration,	30156
1799	Caleb M.	Rutland,	Guardianship,	30157
1874	Caleb M.	Barre,	Will,	30158
1865	Calvin N.	Grafton,	Administration,	30159
1854	Caroline	Barre,	Administration,	30160
1873	Caroline	Worcester,	Will,	30161
1842	Caroline V.	Templeton,	Guardianship,	30162
1838	Celia H.	Barre,	Guardianship,	30163
1873	Charles E.	Westminster,	Guardianship,	30164
1873	Charles H.	Worcester,	Guardianship,	30165
1836	Charles W.	Barre,	Guardianship,	30166
1849	Charles W.	New York, N. Y.,	Administration,	30167
1755	Daniel	Rutland District,	Administration,	30168
1761	Daniel	Rutland,	Guardianship,	30169
1811	Daniel	Charlton,	Administration,	30170
1818	Daniel	Charlton,	Pension,	30171
1863	Daniel F.	Charlton,	Guardianship,	30172
1842	David	Barre,	Guardianship,	30173
1863	Eathan	Barre,	Will,	30174
1864	Edward J.	Shrewsbury,	Guardianship,	30175
1866	Electa A.	Athol,	Guardianship,	30176
1827	Eli	Templeton,	Guardianship,	30177
1838	Elias	Westminster,	Will,	30178

Year.	Name.	Residence.	Nature.	Case.
	HOLDEN and HOLDIN,			
1804	Elizabeth	Westminster,	Guardianship,	30179
1828	Elizabeth	Westminster,	Administration,	30180
1863	Elizabeth A.	Charlton,	Guardianship,	30181
1868	Ella M.	Gardner,	Guardianship,	30182
1804	Elmira	Westminster,	Guardianship,	30183
1804	Esther	Westminster,	Guardianship,	30184
1799	Fidelia	Rutland,	Guardianship,	30185
1873	Frank S.	Westminster,	Guardianship,	30186
1880	Frederick A.	Holden,	Guardianship,	30187
1873	George	Westminster,	Administration,	30188
1880	George	Barre,	Guardianship,	30189
1769	Hannah	Rutland,	Administration,	30190
1804	Hannah	Westminster,	Guardianship,	30191
1836	Hannah	Barre,	Administration,	30192
1836	Harriet	Barre,	Guardianship,	30193
1838	Harriet S.	Barre,	Guardianship,	30194
1866	Harrison A.	Athol,	Guardianship,	30195
1825	Harvey	Winchendon,	Administration,	30196
1838	Hiram	Barre,	Guardianship,	30197
1855	Hollis	Gardner,	Adoption,	30198
1862	Hollis	Shrewsbury,	Administration,	30199
1864	Hollis D.	Shrewsbury,	Guardianship,	30200
1741	James	Sutton,	Administration,	30201
1766	James	Rutland District,	Will,	30202
1771	James	Rutland,	Guardianship,	30203
1815	James	Westminster,	Guardianship,	30204
1827	James	Barre,	Administration,	30205
1856	James	Barre,	Administration,	30206
1756	Jeduthun	Rutland,	Guardianship,	30207
1856	Joel	Rutland,	Administration,	30208
1741	John	Sutton,	Guardianship,	30209
1828	John	Leicester,	Administration,	30210
1863	John	Holden,	Will,	30211
1863	John S.	Charlton,	Guardianship,	30212
1858	Jonah	Barre,	Will,	30213
1878	Jonas	Fitchburg,	Will,	30214
1826	Jonathan	Templeton,	Administration,	30215
1827	Jonathan	Templeton,	Guardianship,	30216
1769	Joseph	Westminster,	Administration,	30217
1774	Joseph	Westminster,	Administration,	30218
1797	Joseph	Westminster,	Will,	30219
1798	Joseph	Rutland,	Administration,	30220
1799	Joseph B.	Rutland,	Guardianship,	30221
1828	Joseph B.	Rutland,	Guardianship,	30222

YEAR.	NAME.	RESIDENCE.	NATURE.	CASE.
	HOLDEN AND HOLDIN,			
1868	Joshua H.	Gardner,	Administration,	30223
1777	Josiah	Barre,	Administration,	30224
1835	Josiah D.	Barre,	Administration,	30225
1857	Josiah F.	Shrewsbury,	Will,	30226
1756	Justinian	Harvard,	Administration,	30227
1828	Justus	Barre,	Administration,	30228
1804	Levi	Westminster,	Guardianship,	30229
1854	Levi	Gardner,	Administration,	20230
1836	Lewis	Barre,	Guardianship,	30231
1863	Lewis	Charlton,	Administration,	30232
1779	Lucy	Westminster,	Guardianship,	30233
1827	Lucy	Westminster,	Guardianship,	30234
1872	Lydia B.	Fitchburg,	Will,	30235
1852	Lyman G.	Barre,	Guardianship,	30236
1874	Mabel H.	Barre,	Adoption, etc.,	30237
1815	Malyndia	Lunenburg,	Guardianship,	30238
1836	Martha	Barre,	Guardianship,	30239
1843	Martha W.	Barre,	Will,	30240
1836	Mary A. J.	Winchendon,	Guardianship,	30241
1838	Mary C.	Barre,	Guardianship,	30242
1881	Mary H.	Shrewsbury,	Will,	30243
1873	Mary J.	Westminster,	Guardianship,	30244
1865	Molly	Gardner,	Will,	30245
1831	Moses	Barre,	Will,	30246
1874	Moses G.	Rutland,	Administration,	30247
1766	Nathan	Rutland,	Guardianship,	30248
1777	Nathan	Barre,	Guardianship,	30249
1806	Nathan	Hubbardston,	Administration,	30250
1838	Nathan	Barre,	Administration,	30251
1838	Parker	Barre,	Guardianship,	30252
1804	Polly	Westminster,	Guardianship,	30253
1799	Reubin	Ashburnham,	Administration,	30254
1826	Robert	Templeton,	Administration,	30255
1841	Robert	Templeton,	Will,	30256
1831	Rufus	Winchendon,	Administration,	30257
1842	Rufus	Barre,	Administration,	30258
1816	Rufus J.	Charlton,	Administration,	30259
1778	Samuel	Westminster,	Administration,	30260
1804	Sarah	Westminster,	Guardianship,	30261
1865	Sarah C.	Paxton,	Guardianship,	30262
1794	Stephen	Westminster,	Will,	30263
1803	Stephen	Westminster,	Administration,	30264
1827	Susan	Templeton,	Guardianship,	30265
1879	Willard	Barre,	Administration,	30266

YEAR.	NAME.	RESIDENCE.	NATURE.	CASE.
	HOLDEN AND HOLDIN,			
1741	William	Sutton,	Guardianship,	30267
1865	William	Athol,	Administration,	30268
1873	William S.	Westminster,	Guardianship,	30269
1850	HOLDER, Anna F.	Bolton,	Guardianship,	30270
1845	Charles A.	Bolton,	Guardianship,	30271
1863	Daniel	Berlin,	Will,	30272
1864	David	Clinton,	Administration,	30273
1838	David G.	Bolton,	Guardianship,	30274
1852	George W.	Clinton,	Administration,	30275
1852	Isaac B.	Clinton,	Administration,	30276
1857	Joseph	Bolton,	Administration,	30277
1845	Josiah B.	Bolton,	Guardianship,	30278
1839	Lydia B.	Bolton,	Guardianship,	30279
1850	Mary G.	Bolton,	Guardianship,	30280
1845	Nathan B.	Bolton,	Guardianship,	30281
1850	Rachel S.	Bolton,	Guardianship,	30282
1839	Sarah	Bolton,	Guardianship,	30283
1856	Sarah G.	Clinton,	Guardianship,	30284
1856	Susan	Clinton,	Guardianship,	30285
1830	Thomas	Berlin,	Will,	30286
1856	Thomas	Clinton,	Administration,	30287
	HOLDIN see HOLDEN.			
1863	HOLDSWORTH, David	Northbridge,	Will,	30288
1765	HOLLAND, Abigail	Shrewsbury,	Guardianship,	30289
1765	Abigail	Sutton,	Guardianship,	30290
1794	Abigail	Sutton,	Administration,	30291
1811	Abraham	Western,	Guardianship,	30292
1880	Addison II.	Barre,	Administration,	30293
1764	Anna	Harvard,	Guardianship,	30294
1764	Antipas	Sutton,	Administration,	30295
1765	Antipas	Sutton,	Guardianship,	30296
1836	Eliza A.	Waterville, Me.,	Foreign Sale,	30297
1765	Elizabeth	Sutton,	Guardianship,	30298
1786	Ephraim	Boylston,	Will,	30299
1860	Ephraim	Barre,	Administration,	30300
1756	Experience	Harvard,	Administration,	30301
1878	Frances	Westborough,	Administration,	30302
1810	George	Western,	Administration,	30303
1825	George	Petersham,	Administration,	30304
1827	George F.	Petersham,	Guardianship,	30305
1871	George F.	Milford,	Guardianship,	30306
1836	George P.	Waterville, Me.,	Foreign Sale,	30307
1834	Hepsibah	Petersham,	Will,	30308
1871	Hooper	Barre,	Guardianship,	30309

YEAR.	NAME.	RESIDENCE.	NATURE.	CASE.
1834	HOLLAND, James	Barre,	Administration,	30310
1880	James	North Brookfield,	Will,	30311
1858	James F.	Southborough,	Will,	30312
1858	James H.	Southborough,	Guardianship,	30313
1875	James H.	Westborough,	Will,	30313
1765	Joab	Shrewsbury,	Guardianship,	30314
1832	Joab	Barre,	Administration,	30315
1761	John	Harvard,	Guardianship,	30316
1765	John	Sutton,	Guardianship,	30317
1765	John	Shrewsbury,	Guardianship,	30318
1794	John	Sutton,	Will,	30319
1829	John	Petersham,	Administration,	30320
1856	John	Barre,	Administration,	30321
1824	John, Jr.	Petersham,	Administration,	30322
1765	Jonah	Shrewsbury,	Guardianship,	30323
1771	Jonas	Petersham,	Will,	30324
1765	Joseph	Sutton,	Guardianship,	30325
1811	Louisa	Western,	Guardianship,	30326
1821	Luther	Petersham,	Will,	30327
1836	Maria J.	Waterville, Mo.,	Foreign Sale,	30328
1765	Mary	Shrewsbury,	Guardianship,	30329
1811	Mary	Western,	Guardianship,	30330
1872	Mary	Leominster,	Administration,	30331
1836	Mary A.	Waterville, Mo.,	Foreign Sale,	30332
1871	Mary M.	Milford,	Guardianship,	30333
1791	Nathan	Worcester,	Guardianship,	30334
1863	Nelson J.	Newfane, Vt.,	Administration,	30335
1771	Park	Petersham,	Guardianship,	30336
1765	Paul	Shrewsbury,	Guardianship,	30337
1835	Prescot	Petersham,	Administration,	30338
1765	Reubin	Shrewsbury,	Guardianship,	30339
1755	Robert	Harvard,	Administration,	30340
1764	Samuel	Shrewsbury,	Administration,	30341
1827	Samuel	Petersham,	Guardianship,	30342
1850	Samuel	Barre,	Administration,	30343
1855	Samuel	Leominster,	Administration,	30344
1765	Sarah	Shrewsbury,	Guardianship,	30345
1829	Sarah S.	Petersham,	Guardianship,	30346
1771	Vashty	Petersham,	Guardianship,	30347
1794	Wilder	Petersham,	Guardianship,	30348
1877	HOLLANDER, Gasper	Worcester,	Administration,	30349
1880	HOLLEY, Agnes	Dudley,	Administration,	30350
1839	Ann E.	Lancaster,	Guardianship,	30351
1875	John M.	Dudley,	Administration,	30352
1877	HOLLINGSWORTH, Ethel	Fitchburg,	Guardianship,	30353

YEAR.	NAME.	RESIDENCE.	NATURE.	CASE.
1877	HOLLINGSWORTH, Helen E.	Fitchburg,	Guardianship,	30353
1877	Herbert C.	Fitchburg,	Guardianship,	30354
1873	HOLLIS, Barnabas	Fitchburg,	Administration,	30355
1863	Dorcas	Worcester,	Administration,	30356
1868	George H.	Boston,	Adoption,	30357
1868	John E.	Boston,	Adoption,	30358
1733	HOLLOWAY, Adam	Westborough,	Will,	30359
1789	Mary	Northborough,	Will,	30360
1760	William	Westborough,	Will,	30361
1836	HOLMAN, Aaron	Millbury,	Guardianship,	30362
1856	Abby T.	Harvard,	Guardianship,	30363
1804	Abel	Ward,	Guardianship,	30364
1816	Abel	Ward,	Will,	30365
1862	Abel	Auburn,	Administration,	30366
1804	Abigail	Ward,	Guardianship,	30367
1805	Abigail	Bolton,	Guardianship,	30368
1815	Abigail	Bolton,	Guardianship,	30369
1845	Abigail	Bolton,	Administration,	30370
1784	Abraham	Bolton,	Administration,	30371
1805	Abraham	Bolton,	Administration,	30372
1815	Abraham	Bolton,	Administration,	30373
1815	Abraham	Bolton,	Guardianship,	30374
1848	Albert G.	Winchendon,	Guardianship,	30375
1858	Albert P.	Leicester,	Guardianship,	30376
1834	Alexander	Millbury,	Administration,	30377
1877	Alice M.	Westborough,	Adoption, etc.,	30378
1806	Amory	Bolton,	Guardianship,	30379
1847	Amory	Berlin,	Administration,	30380
1848	Andrew M.	Winchendon,	Guardianship,	30381
1878	Angie R.	Leicester,	Guardianship,	30382
1879	Annie H.	Worcester,	Guardianship,	30383
1785	Asa	Bolton,	Guardianship,	30384
1856	Asa	Clinton,	Administration,	30385
1823	Augustus	Charlton,	Guardianship,	30386
1790	Betsy	Templeton,	Guardianship,	30387
1849	Betsy	Millbury,	Administration,	30388
1785	Betty	Bolton,	Guardianship,	30389
1861	Candace	Auburn,	Administration,	30390
1839	Candice S.	Ward,	Guardianship,	30391
1826	Charles	Templeton,	Administration,	30392
1834	Charles	Royalston,	Sale Real Estate,	30393
1833	Charles A.	Templeton,	Guardianship,	30394
1865	Charles L.	Lunenburg,	Guardianship,	30395
1863	Charles S.	Auburn,	Guardianship,	30396
1826	Christopher G.	Northbridge,	Guardianship,	30397

Year.	Name.	Residence.	Nature.	Case.
1878	HOLMAN, Clara E.	Leicester,	Guardianship,	30398
1867	Clara P.	Douglas,	Will,	30399
1846	Clark	Millbury,	Administration,	30400
1828	Cyrus	Royalston,	Administration,	30401
1871	Cyrus W.	Worcester,	Administration,	30402
1852	Daniel	Worcester,	Administration,	30403
1742	David	Sutton,	Guardianship,	30404
1812	David	Sutton,	Guardianship,	30405
1813	David	Millbury,	Will,	30406
1866	David	Douglas,	Will,	30407
1881	David	Oxford	Will,	30408
1872	David C.	Millbury,	Administration,	30409
1843	David W.	Mendon,	Administration,	30410
1742	Edward	Sutton,	Guardianship,	30411
1742	Edward	Sutton,	Will,	30412
1869	Eliakim A.	Harvard,	Will,	30413
1857	Elijah	Millbury,	Will,	30414
1855	Elijah R.	Sterling,	Administration,	30415
1765	Eliphalet	Sutton,	Guardianship,	30416
1838	Eliphalet	Auburn,	Pension,	30417
1862	Eliza	Athol,	Will,	30418
1833	Elizabeth	Lancaster,	Guardianship,	30419
1877	Elizabeth	Worcester,	Administration,	30420
1858	Elizabeth A.	Millbury,	Administration,	30421
1865	Elmer E.	Lunenburg,	Guardianship,	30422
1806	Elsa	Bolton,	Guardianship,	30423
1847	Emeline	Berlin,	Guardianship,	30424
1879	Emeline D.	Leicester,	Administration,	30425
1852	Emma J.	Worcester,	Guardianship,	30426
1864	Ephraim T.	Millbury,	Administration,	30427
1823	Esther	Charlton,	Guardianship,	30428
1850	Esther A.	Leicester,	Guardianship,	30429
1803	Francis	Ward,	Administration,	30430
1804	Francis	Ward,	Guardianship,	30431
1842	Francis	Auburn,	Will,	30432
1863	Francis H.	Auburn,	Administration,	30433
1847	Franklin	Berlin,	Guardianship,	30434
1858	George O.	Leicester,	Guardianship,	30435
1870	Grant D.	Oxford,	Guardianship,	30436
1813	Hannah	Millbury,	Will,	30437
1847	Harriot	Berlin,	Guardianship,	30438
1834	Harvey	Royalston,	Sale Real Estate,	30439
1834	Henry	Royalston,	Sale Real Estate,	30440
1833	Hervey	Templeton,	Administration,	30441
1825	Ira	Lunenburg,	Administration,	30442

Year.	Name.	Residence.	Nature.	Case.
1862	HOLMAN, James G.	Millbury,	Administration,	30443
1829	Jane B.	Royalston	Guardianship,	30444
1835	Jane E.	Millbury,	Guardianship,	30445
1739	Jeremiah	Bolton,	Administration,	30446
1823	Jeremiah	Charlton,	Administration,	30447
1742	John	Sutton,	Guardianship,	30448
1785	John	Bolton,	Guardianship,	30449
1827	John	Lancaster,	Administration,	30450
1846	John	Royalston,	Administration,	30451
1853	John	Auburn,	Will,	30452
1859	John	Royalston,	Will,	30453
1864	John	Fitchburg,	Administration,	30454
1756	John, Jr.	Sutton,	Will,	30455
1878	John E.	Worcester,	Administration,	30456
1833	John H.	Templeton,	Guardianship,	30457
1806	Jonas	Bolton,	Guardianship,	30458
1785	Jonathan	Bolton,	Guardianship,	30459
1790	Jonathan	Templeton,	Administration,	30460
1814	Jonathan	Millbury,	Will,	30461
1742	Joshua	Sutton,	Guardianship,	30462
1765	Judah	Sutton,	Guardianship,	30463
1878	Laura E.	Leicester,	Guardianship,	30464
1850	Leonard	Leicester,	Guardianship,	30465
1878	Lucy	Berlin,	Administration,	30466
1833	Luke H.	Templeton,	Guardianship,	30467
1878	Lyman R.	Leicester,	Guardianship,	30468
1759	Mary	Sutton,	Administration,	30469
1844	Mary A.	Mendon,	Guardianship,	30470
1829	Mary B.	Royalston,	Guardianship,	30471
1835	Mary L.	Millbury,	Guardianship,	30472
1847	Mary L.	Berlin,	Guardianship,	30473
1855	Mary L.	Millbury,	Administration,	30474
1823	Morris	Charlton,	Guardianship,	30475
1866	Nathan	Leicester,	Administration,	30476
1785	Nathaniel	Bolton,	Guardianship,	30477
1805	Nathaniel	Bolton,	Administration,	30478
1806	Nathaniel	Bolton,	Guardianship,	30479
1865	Olin S.	Lunenburg,	Guardianship,	30480
1785	Oliver	Bolton,	Guardianship,	30481
1805	Oliver	Petersham,	Guardianship,	30482
1815	Oracy	Bolton,	Guardianship,	30483
1868	Orion	Lancaster,	Administration,	30484
1864	Orlando	Lunenburg,	Administration,	30485
1849	Parley	Leicester,	Administration,	30486
1879	Parley	Leicester,	Will,	30487

Year.	Name.	Residence.	Nature.	Case.
1790	HOLMAN, Polly	Templeton,	Guardianship,	30488
1858	Porter,	Sterling,	Administration,	30489
1857	Presson	Leicester,	Administration,	30490
1879	Ralph H.	Worcester,	Guardianship,	30491
1863	Rhoda	Leicester,	Administration,	30492
1848	Richard H.	Winchendon,	Guardianship,	30493
1853	Rufus	Sterling,	Will,	30494
1765	Ruth	Sutton,	Guardianship,	30495
1790	Sally	Templeton,	Guardianship,	30496
1825	Sally	Millbury,	Will,	30497
1842	Sally	Charlton,	Administration,	30498
1841	Samuel	Auburn,	Will,	30499
1848	Samuel	Winchendon,	Will,	30500
1742	Sarah	Sutton,	Guardianship,	30501
1839	Sarah	Ward,	Guardianship,	30502
1858	Sarah	Auburn,	Will,	30503
1829	Sarah R.	Royalston,	Guardianship,	30504
1860	Seth	Royalston,	Will,	30505
1855	Silas W.	Harvard,	Will,	30506
1856	Silas W.	Harvard,	Guardianship,	30507
1859	Silence	Douglas,	Will,	30508
1829	Simeon	Ward,	Will,	30509
1839	Simeon D.	Ward,	Guardianship,	30510
1826	Simeon G.	Northbridge,	Guardianship,	30511
1742	Solomon	Sutton,	Guardianship,	30512
1785	Solomon	Sutton,	Will,	30513
1804	Solomon	Petersham,	Will,	30514
1804	Solomon	Ward,	Guardianship,	30515
1872	Solomon O.	Athol,	Will,	30516
1806	Sophia	Bolton,	Guardianship,	30517
1849	Sophronia	Leicester,	Administration,	30518
1762	Stephen	Sutton,	Administration,	30519
1765	Stephen	Sutton,	Guardianship,	30520
1833	Stephen	Royalston,	Guardianship,	30521
1833	Stephen	Royalston,	Administration,	30522
1839	Sumner	Ward,	Guardianship,	30523
1863	Susan C.	Auburn,	Guardianship,	30524
1869	Susan C.	Harvard,	Will,	30525
1849	Susanna	Millbury,	Will,	30526
1849	Susannah	Millbury,	Pension,	30527
1791	Thomas	Sutton,	Guardianship,	30528
1794	Thomas	Sutton,	Will,	30528
1778	William	Athol,	Administration,	30529
1863	William F.	Auburn,	Guardianship,	30530
1848	William W.	Winchendon,	Guardianship,	30531

YEAR.	NAME.	RESIDENCE.	NATURE.	CASE.
1878	HOLMAN, William Y.	Worcester,	Will,	30532
1863	HOLMES, Abby A.	Southbridge,	Guardianship,	30533
1875	Ada M.	West Brookfield,	Guardianship,	30534
1789	Adam	New Braintree,	Will,	30535
1853	Amelia U.	Westborough,	Guardianship,	30536
1872	Aurilla	Charlton,	Will,	30537
1858	Azotus	North Brookfield,	Administration,	30538
1844	Burton	Grafton,	Guardianship,	30539
1803	Catharine	Worcester,	Guardianship,	30540
1834	Charles T.	New Braintree,	Administration,	30541
1857	Charlotte L.	New Braintree,	Guardianship,	30542
1865	Charlotte L.	West Brookfield,	Administration,	30543
1867	Chester D.	Blackstone,	Will,	30544
1872	Clara M.	Worcester,	Guardianship,	30545
1844	Clementine W.	Grafton,	Guardianship,	30546
1854	Daniel F.	Sturbridge,	Administration,	30547
1854	Daniel H.	Sturbridge,	Guardianship,	30548
1745	David	Woodstock,	Administration,	30549
1872	Edwin A.	Worcester,	Guardianship,	30550
1844	Edwin H.	Grafton,	Guardianship,	30551
1865	Eliza	Fitchburg,	Will,	30552
1857	Eliza J.	New Braintree,	Guardianship,	30553
1857	Emily A.	New Braintree,	Guardianship,	30554
1874	Emily A.	North Brookfield,	Administration,	30555
1829	Ezra	Dudley,	Guardianship,	30556
1869	Fanny C.	Ashburnham,	Administration,	30557
1873	Francis G.	Worcester,	Administration,	30558
1870	Frederick	Charlton,	Administration,	30559
1875	Frederick B.	West Brookfield,	Guardianship,	30560
1872	Frederick P.	Worcester,	Guardianship,	30561
1850	George	North Brookfield,	Guardianship,	30562
1859	George	Sturbridge,	Administration,	30563
1863	George	Southbridge,	Administration,	30564
1855	George W.	Southbridge,	Will,	30565
1863	Hamilton G.	Southbridge,	Guardianship,	30566
1879	Hannah	New Braintree,	Guardianship,	30567
1832	Hannah P.	Westborough,	Guardianship,	30568
1857	Harriot E.	New Braintree,	Guardianship,	30569
1863	Hartwell	North Brookfield,	Administration,	30570
1863	Helen E.	Southbridge,	Guardianship,	30571
1779	Jacob	Worcester,	Will,	30572
1803	Jacob	Worcester,	Administration,	30573
1848	Jacob	Leicester,	Administration,	30574
1823	James	New Braintree,	Will,	30575
1832	Jasper D.	Westborough,	Guardianship,	30576

YEAR.	NAME.	RESIDENCE.	NATURE.	CASE.
1853	HOLMES, John	Westborough,	Administration,	30577
1857	John L.	New Braintree,	Guardianship,	30578
1869	John P.	Milford,	Guardianship,	30579
1832	Julia M.	Westborough,	Guardianship,	30580
1863	Lena A.	Southbridge,	Guardianship,	30581
1874	Lottie L.	North Brookfield,	Guardianship,	30582
1849	Luther	North Brookfield,	Will,	30583
1857	Lyman A.	New Braintree,	Guardianship,	30584
1871	Lyman A.	North Brookfield,	Administration,	30585
1844	Marion E.	Grafton,	Guardianship,	30586
1863	Mary A.	Southbridge,	Guardianship,	30587
1832	Mary L.	Westborough,	Guardianship,	30588
1746	Moses	Woodstock,	Guardianship,	30589
1832	Nancy P.	Westborough,	Guardianship,	30590
1851	Nathaniel	Leicester,	Administration,	30591
1854	Perley A.	Sturbridge,	Guardianship,	30592
1876	Perley A.	Sturbridge,	Administration,	30593
1854	Persis	Sturbridge,	Guardianship,	30594
1860	Peter	Paxton,	Administration,	30595
1878	Pitt	Worcester,	Will,	30596
1857	Samuel H.	New Braintree,	Guardianship,	30597
1857	Samuel W.	New Braintree,	Administration,	30598
1854	Sanford	Sturbridge,	Guardianship,	30599
1832	Sarah J.	Westborough,	Guardianship,	30600
1803	Sophia	Worcester,	Guardianship,	30601
1746	Stephen	Woodstock,	Guardianship,	30602
1862	Thankful	Leicester,	Will,	30603
1848	Thomas	West Boylston,	Administration,	30604
1807	William	Sterling,	Will,	30605
1834	William H.	New Braintree,	Administration,	30606
1872	William W.	Webster,	Administration,	30607
1815	HOLT, Abel	West Boylston,	Will,	30608
1802	Abel, Jr.	Holden,	Administration,	30609
1774	Abiel	Lancaster,	Guardianship,	30610
1865	Abiel	Ashburnham,	Will,	30611
1744	Abiell	Lunenburg,	Administration,	30612
1811	Abigail	Bolton,	Administration,	30613
1805	Adaline	Berlin,	Guardianship,	30614
1815	Amasa	Berlin,	Administration,	30615
1851	Amos J.	Sterling,	Administration,	30616
1869	Anna T.	Athol,	Will,	30617
1847	Asa	West Boylston,	Administration,	30618
1774	Barzilla	Lancaster,	Will,	30619
1861	Benjamin	Lancaster,	Will,	30620
1857	Betsey C.	Hubbardston,	Administration,	30621

YEAR.	NAME.	RESIDENCE.	NATURE.	CASE.
1789	HOLT, Betsy	Shrewsbury,	Guardianship,	30622
1841	Catharine	Fitchburg,	Will,	30623
1876	Cynthia M.	Leominster,	Administration,	30624
1830	Daniel	Fitchburg,	Administration,	30625
1838	Davis	Hubbardston,	Guardianship,	30626
1804	Dolly	Fitchburg,	Guardianship,	30627
1865	Edah	Ashburnham,	Administration,	30628
1851	Elias	Hubbardston,	Administration,	30629
1805	Eliza	Berlin,	Guardianship,	30630
1854	Ella M.	Fitchburg,	Guardianship,	30631
1851	Emeline	West Boylston,	Will,	30632
1845	Ephraim	Holden,	Pension,	30633
1838	Ephraim M.	North Brookfield,	Administration,	30634
1867	Eva E.	Barre,	Guardianship,	30635
1878	Frederick	West Brookfield,	Administration,	30636
1862	George C.	Royalston,	Adoption, etc.,	30637
1840	George F.	Sterling,	Guardianship,	30638
1869	Hamilton	Worcester,	Will,	30639
1826	Harriet B.	Brookfield,	Guardianship,	30640
1840	Harriet K.	Sterling,	Guardianship,	30641
1849	Harriet O.	Leominster,	Administration,	30642
1871	Henry	West Boylston,	Will,	30643
1828	Henry K.	West Boylston,	Administration,	30644
1821	Jacob	Brookfield,	Administration,	30645
1826	Jacob	Brookfield,	Guardianship,	30646
1870	Joab S.	Holden,	Will,	30647
1860	John	Worcester,	Administration,	30648
1865	John H.	Fitchburg,	Administration,	30649
1872	John T.	Fitchburg,	Administration,	30650
1853	Jonas	West Boylston,	Will,	30651
1805	Jonathan	Lunenburg,	Will,	30652
1754	Joseph	Lunenburg,	Will,	30653
1803	Joseph	Fitchburg,	Administration,	30654
1873	Joseph E.	Hubbardston,	Guardianship,	30655
1840	Joseph W.	Dudley,	Guardianship,	30656
1774	Jotham	Lancaster,	Guardianship,	30657
1805	Laura, etc.	Berlin,	Guardianship,	30658
1753	Lemuel	Lancaster,	Guardianship,	30659
1774	Levi	Lancaster,	Guardianship,	30660
1828	Liberty	Fitchburg,	Guardianship,	30661
1829	Louisa S.	Holden,	Guardianship,	30662
1854	Martha E.	Worcester,	Adoption,	30663
1864	Martha E.	Worcester,	Change of Name,	30663
1841	Martha J.	West Boylston,	Guardianship,	30664
1875	Mary A.	Worcester,	Administration,	30665

Year	Name	Residence	Nature	Case
1879	HOLT, Mary J.	West Brookfield,	Guardianship,	30666
1841	Parkman	West Boylston,	Administration,	30667
1875	Russell	West Boylston,	Administration,	30668
1804	Sally	Fitchburg,	Guardianship,	30669
1854	Sarah	Hardwick,	Will,	30670
1848	Sarah C.	Hardwick,	Will,	30671
1846	Sarah E.	Worcester,	Guardianship,	30672
1794	Silas	Westminster,	Guardianship,	30673
1812	Silas	West Boylston,	Administration,	30674
1856	Silas	Hubbardston,	Adoption, etc.,	30675
1833	Simeon K.	Hubbardston,	Administration,	30676
1808	Thomas	Bolton,	Will,	30677
1836	Thomas	Hardwick,	Administration,	30678
1843	Thomas R.	Hardwick,	Administration,	30679
1741	Uriah	Lancaster,	Administration,	30680
1745	Uriah	Lancaster,	Guardianship,	30681
1877	Ward E.	West Boylston,	Administration,	30682
1760	William	Lunenburg,	Administration,	30683
1867	Willie C.	Barre,	Guardianship,	30684
	HOLTEN AND HOLTON,			
1853	David M.	Westminster, Vt.,	Foreign Sale,	30685
1740	Ebenezer	Sutton,	Guardianship,	30686
1765	Ebenezer	Worcester,	Will,	30687
1853	Edward A.	Westminster, Vt.,	Foreign Sale,	30688
1766	Elisha	Sutton,	Guardianship,	30689
1866	Emily A.	Millbury,	Guardianship,	30690
1866	Freeland	Millbury,	Guardianship,	30691
1866	George A.	Millbury,	Guardianship,	30692
1783	Isabilla	Charlton,	Guardianship,	30693
1782	Israel	Charlton,	Administration,	30694
1744	James	Salem,	Guardianship,	30695
1853	Joel H.	Westminster, Vt.,	Foreign Sale,	30696
1760	John	Sutton,	Administration,	30697
1740	Keziah	Sutton,	Guardianship,	30698
1741	Mary	Worcester,	Administration,	30699
1740	Nathan	Sutton,	Guardianship,	30700
1773	Nathan	Worcester,	Guardianship,	30701
1783	Polly	Charlton,	Guardianship,	30702
1783	Relief	Charlton,	Guardianship,	30703
1783	Sewell	Charlton,	Guardianship,	30704
1739	Timothy	Sutton,	Administration,	30705
1875	HOLYOKE, Lydia H.	Northborough,	Will,	30706
1841	HOMER, Amasa	Rutland,	Guardianship,	30707
1870	Edward	Milford,	Will,	30708
1841	Elizabeth	Rutland,	Guardianship,	30709

YEAR.	NAME.	RESIDENCE	NATURE.	CASE.
1841	HOMER, Eunice P.	Rutland,	Guardianship,	30710
1841	George W.	Rutland,	Guardianship,	30711
1863	Henrietta E.	Worcester,	Guardianship,	30712
1773	John	Winchendon,	Administration,	30713
1869	Lottie J.	Brookfield,	Guardianship,	30714
1871	Lottie J.	Worcester,	Administration,	30714
1841	Mary	Rutland,	Guardianship,	30715
1852	Samuel R.	Rutland,	Administration,	30716
1841	Sarah M.	Rutland,	Guardianship,	30717
1841	Sophrona R.	Rutland,	Guardianship,	30718
1812	Thomas	Rutland,	Will,	30719
1841	Thomas	Rutland,	Guardianship,	30720
1773	William	Winchendon,	Guardianship,	30721
1841	William	Rutland,	Administration,	30722
1746	HOMONY, Cuffee	Woodstock,	Administration,	30723
1880	HOOD, Alonzo D.	Phillipston,	Administration,	30724
1875	Charles E.	Southbridge,	Administration,	30725
1878	Sarah A.	Lancaster,	Administration,	30726
1860	HOOKER, Abigail	Fitchburg,	Administration,	30727
1876	Abigail J.	Sutton,	Administration,	30728
1866	Alonzo S.	New Braintree,	Guardianship,	30729
1880	Alonzo S.	New Braintree,	Administration,	30729
1776	Amos	Dudley,	Administration,	30730
1873	Charles A.	Brookfield,	Administration,	30731
1861	Clarinda F.	Southbridge,	Administration,	30732
1866	Daniel W.	New Braintree,	Will,	30733
1844	Francis S.	Rutland,	Administration,	30734
1848	Francis S.	Rutland,	Administration,	30735
1848	George	Rutland,	Guardianship,	30736
1841	Hannah	Dudley,	Will,	30737
1848	Harriet	Rutland,	Guardianship,	30738
1850	Harriet	Sturbridge,	Will,	30739
1789	Henry	Sturbridge,	Administration,	30740
1776	Hollowell	Dudley,	Guardianship,	30741
1777	Jacob	Uxbridge,	Administration,	30742
1848	James	Rutland,	Guardianship,	30743
1849	John	Rutland,	Guardianship,	30744
1852	John	Rutland,	Administration,	30744
1855	Lemuel	Sturbridge,	Will,	30745
1869	Mary E.	Sturbridge,	Guardianship,	30746
1853	Oliver	Southbridge,	Administration,	30747
1776	Parker	Dudley,	Guardianship,	30748
1776	Samuel	Dudley,	Guardianship,	30749
1852	Samuel	Sturbridge,	Administration,	30750
1861	Simeon	Sturbridge,	Will,	30751

YEAR.	NAME.	RESIDENCE.	NATURE.	CASE.
1876	HOOKER, Veranes C.	Sutton,	Will,	30752
1850	Walter	North Brookfield,	Administration,	30753
1879	Whitney C.	New Braintree,	Administration,	30754
1874	HOOLEY, Daniel	Worcester,	Guardianship,	30755
1874	Ellen	Worcester,	Guardianship,	30756
1855	HOOPER, C. Frederick	New Ipswich, N. H.,	Guardianship,	30757
1855	Elizabeth S.	New Ipswich, N. H.,	Guardianship,	30758
1855	Emily R.	New Ipswich, N. H.,	Guardianship,	30759
1879	Frank G.	Woburn,	Adoption, etc.,	30760
1855	William H.	New Ipswich, N. H.,	Guardianship,	30761
1857	William R., Jr.	Worcester,	Guardianship,	30762
1872	HOPKINS, Bertha J.	Worcester,	Adoption, etc.,	30763
1841	Charles	Petersham,	Guardianship,	30764
1848	Edward P.	Northbridge,	Guardianship,	30765
1872	Elizabeth M.	Worcester,	Guardianship,	30766
1874	James	Leicester,	Administration,	30767
1836	James P.	Petersham,	Guardianship,	30768
1783	John	Northbridge,	Will,	30769
1872	John T.	Worcester,	Guardianship,	30770
1848	Josiah	Northbridge,	Administration,	30771
1834	Samuel	Petersham,	Will,	30772
1811	Susanna	Worcester,	Guardianship,	30773
1738	Thomas	Leicester,	Administration,	30774
1872	Thomas	Worcester,	Will,	30775
1836	Warren	Petersham,	Guardianship,	30776
1880	Willard	Northbridge,	Will,	30777
1848	Willis C.	Northbridge,	Guardianship,	30778
1876	HOPPIN, George W.	Worcester,	Guardianship,	30779
1860	Ida M.	Worcester,	Adoption, etc.,	30780
1876	Susan E.	Worcester,	Will,	30781
1865	HOPWOOD, Sally	Worcester,	Will,	30782
1874	HORAN, John	Fitchburg,	Administration,	30783
1874	John	Fitchburg,	Guardianship,	30784
1863	John H.	West Boylston,	Administration,	30785
1881	Margaret	Fitchburg,	Administration,	30786
1874	Mary E.	Fitchburg,	Guardianship,	30787
1880	Patrick	Worcester,	Administration,	30788
	HORE see HOAR.			
	HORNE AND HORN,			
1769	Elizabeth	Southborough,	Guardianship,	30789
1789	Elizabeth	Southborough,	Guardianship,	30790
1800	John	Southborough,	Guardianship,	30791
1862	John H.	West Boylston,	Administration,	30792
1871	Jonathan F.	Southborough,	Administration,	30793
1769	Katharine	Southborough,	Guardianship,	30794

YEAR.	NAME.	RESIDENCE.	NATURE.	CASE.
	HORNE AND HORN,			
1763	Robert	Southborough,	Administration,	30795
1769	Robert	Southborough,	Guardianship,	30796
1800	Robert	Southborough,	Administration,	30797
1800	Robert	Southborough,	Guardianship,	30798
1769	Samuel	Southborough,	Guardianship,	30799
1789	Samuel	Southborough,	Will,	30800
1789	Samuel	Southborough,	Guardianship,	30801
1789	William	Southborough,	Guardianship,	30802
1800	Winsor	Southborough,	Guardianship,	30803
1855	HORR, Abba	Oxford,	Guardianship,	30804
1863	Calvin	Dana,	Guardianship,	30805
1863	Calvin	Dana,	Administration,	30805
1864	Edwin	Dana,	Guardianship,	30806
1868	Frederick E.	Worcester,	Guardianship,	30807
1855	Huldah	Oxford,	Guardianship,	30808
1833	Isaac	North Brookfield,	Administration,	30809
1864	Leander	Dana,	Guardianship,	30810
1857	Lydia	Athol,	Administration,	30811
1843	Sally	North Brookfield,	Administration,	30812
1844	Sarah	North Brookfield,	Will,	30813
1868	Sarah P.	Athol,	Will,	30814
1868	Timothy	Worcester,	Administration,	30815
1880	HORRIGAN, Mary	Clinton,	Partition,	30816
1853	HORTON, Alexander	Templeton,	Administration,	30817
1876	Annie L.	Brattleborough, Vt.,	Guardianship,	30818
1866	Arathusia	Templeton,	Administration,	30819
1813	Artemas	Templeton,	Will,	30820
1866	Charles E.	Douglas,	Guardianship,	30821
1866	Clarissa B.	Douglas,	Partition,	30822
1876	Edward G.	Brattleborough, Vt.,	Guardianship,	30823
1864	Edward S.	Uxbridge,	Administration,	30824
1876	George H.	Brattleborough, Vt.,	Guardianship,	30825
1795	Gideon	Royalston,	Guardianship,	30826
1841	Hannah M.	Templeton,	Guardianship,	30827
1876	Harry R.	Brattleborough, Vt.,	Guardianship,	30828
1874	Henry R.	Fitchburg,	Administration,	30829
1841	James	Templeton,	Guardianship,	30830
1809	Jonathan	Templeton,	Will,	30831
1818	Joseph	Templeton,	Guardianship,	30832
1811	Levi	Templeton,	Guardianship,	30833
1840	Levi	Templeton,	Will,	30834
1792	Lewis	Royalston,	Will,	30835
1794	Lewis	Royalston,	Guardianship,	30836
1794	Lucy	Royalston,	Guardianship,	30837

YEAR.	NAME.	RESIDENCE.	NATURE.	CASE.
1799	HORTON, Lucy	Royalston,	Administration,	30838
1841	Lucy	Templeton,	Guardianship,	30839
1876	Minnie E.	Brattleborough, Vt.,	Guardianship,	30840
1808	Stephen	Templeton,	Guardianship,	30841
1812	Stephen	Templeton,	Administration,	30842
1866	William	Douglas,	Administration,	30843
1866	William	Douglas,	Partition,	30844
1866	William	Douglas,	Guardianship,	30845
1871	HOSEMAN, George	Unknown,	Adoption, etc.,	30846
1802	HOSLEY, David	Lancaster,	Administration,	30847
1849	Samuel	Gardner,	Administration,	30848
1868	HOSMER, Allen C.	Leominster,	Guardianship,	30849
1846	Asa	Templeton,	Administration,	30850
1869	Asa	Templeton,	Administration,	30851
1859	Clara D.	Fitchburg,	Guardianship,	30852
1830	Daniel	West Boylston,	Administration,	30853
1842	David	Auburn,	Administration,	30854
1842	David	Auburn,	Pension,	30855
1877	David W.	Harvard,	Administration,	30856
1878	Ebenezer M.	West Boylston,	Administration,	30857
1855	Edward	Templeton,	Administration,	30858
1876	Eli	Harvard,	Will,	30859
1870	Flora	Templeton,	Guardianship,	30860
1870	Frank	Templeton,	Guardianship,	30861
1877	Frank L.	Harvard,	Guardianship,	30862
1876	George F.	Worcester,	Administration,	30863
1877	George L.	Harvard,	Guardianship,	30864
1860	Jerusha G.	Templeton,	Will,	30865
1858	John	Templeton,	Will,	30866
1855	John E.	Templeton,	Guardianship,	30867
1867	Joshua	Templeton,	Administration,	30868
1846	Josiah	Templeton,	Guardianship,	30869
1868	Josiah	Leominster,	Will,	30870
1877	Laura J.	Harvard,	Guardianship,	30871
1795	Lucinda	Templeton,	Guardianship,	30872
1855	Lucy E.	Templeton,	Guardianship,	30873
1880	Lucy P.	Templeton,	Administration,	30874
1867	Mary	Templeton,	Guardianship,	30875
1859	Mary F.	Fitchburg,	Guardianship,	30876
1877	Nathan	Templeton,	Administration,	30877
1857	Sarah	Auburn,	Administration,	30878
1857	Sarah	Auburn,	Pension,	30879
1823	Susan C.	Sterling,	Guardianship,	30880
1880	Susie M.	Templeton,	Guardianship,	30881
1852	HOUCK, Miles W.	Worcester,	Change of Name,	30882

YEAR.	NAME.	RESIDENCE.	NATURE.	CASE.
1838	HOUGH, Samuel A.	Sutton,	Administration,	30883
1865	HOUGHTON, Abby A.	Leominster,	Guardianship,	30884
1834	Abel	Grafton,	Administration,	30885
1777	Abiather	Leominster,	Administration,	30886
1766	Abigail	Bolton,	Guardianship,	30887
1820	Abigail	Bolton,	Administration,	30888
1876	Abigail	Leominster,	Administration,	30889
1855	Abigail J.	Winchendon,	Administration,	30890
1823	Abigail M.	Berlin,	Guardianship,	30891
1833	Alfred	Bolton,	Guardianship,	30892
1863	Alfred S.	Lunenburg,	Guardianship,	30893
1879	Alice	Lancaster,	Will,	30894
1780	Allice	Leominster,	Guardianship,	30895
1834	Amory	Bolton,	Guardianship,	30896
1838	Amory	Berlin,	Guardianship,	30897
1850	Amory	Boylston,	Administration,	30898
1821	Amory J.	Berlin,	Guardianship,	30899
1846	Andrew	Ashburnham,	Guardianship,	30900
1800	Ann	Bolton,	Guardianship,	30901
1868	Anna	Lancaster,	Administration,	30902
1860	Apollos	Lancaster,	Will,	30903
1847	Arabella A.	Bolton,	Guardianship,	30904
1759	Arctus	Harvard,	Administration,	30905
1843	Asa	Harvard,	Administration,	30906
1807	Asahel	Lunenburg,	Administration,	30907
1739	Axa	Lancaster,	Guardianship,	30908
1759	Benjamin	Lancaster,	Administration,	30909
1764	Benjamin	Bolton,	Administration,	30910
1764	Benjamin	Lancaster,	Administration,	30911
1766	Benjamin	Bolton,	Guardianship,	30912
1801	Benjamin	Princeton,	Guardianship,	30913
1803	Benjamin	Bolton,	Administration,	30914
1805	Benjamin	Princeton,	Administration,	30915
1819	Benjamin	Sterling,	Administration,	30916
1837	Benjamin	Lancaster,	Will,	30917
1837	Benjamin	Boylston,	Administration,	30918
1860	Benjamin	Harvard,	Administration,	30919
1875	Bessie M.	Sterling,	Guardianship,	30920
1876	Betsey	Princeton,	Will,	30921
1768	Betty	Bolton,	Guardianship,	30922
1823	Caleb	Berlin,	Administration,	30923
1802	Carolina	Petersham,	Guardianship,	30924
1865	Cephas	Bolton,	Administration,	30925
1871	Charles	Worcester,	Will,	30926
1871	Charles E.	Barre,	Administration,	30927

YEAR.	NAME.	RESIDENCE.	NATURE.	CASE.
1833	HOUGHTON, Charles S.	Bolton,	Guardianship,	30928
1865	Charles S.	Leominster,	Guardianship,	30929
1863	Charlotte E.	Lunenburg,	Guardianship,	30930
1854	Clara S.	Leominster,	Adoption, etc.,	30931
1877	Cora A.	Spencer,	Guardianship,	30932
1819	Cyrene	Bolton,	Guardianship,	30933
1819	Cyrus	Bolton,	Administration,	30934
1823	Cyrus	Berlin,	Guardianship,	30935
1834	Cyrus	Berlin,	Will,	30936
1846	Cyrus	Winchendon,	Administration,	30937
1859	Daniel	Harvard,	Guardianship,	30938
1866	Daniel	Harvard,	Administration,	30938
1835	Danjel W.	Lunenburg,	Guardianship,	30939
1880	Daniel W.	Athol,	Will,	30940
1867	David	Leominster,	Will,	30941
1820	Delia	Sterling,	Guardianship,	30942
1741	Ebenezer	Bolton,	Guardianship,	30943
1755	Ebenezer	Bolton,	Administration,	30944
1790	Ebenezer	Leominster,	Will,	30945
1826	Ebenezer	Leominster,	Will,	30946
1826	Edmund	Lunenburg,	Guardianship,	30947
1876	Edmund	Lunenburg,	Administration,	30948
1856	Edward E.	Bolton,	Administration,	30949
1865	Edward E.	Bolton,	Guardianship,	30950
1855	Eleanor	Petersham,	Will,	30951
1790	Eleazer	Lunenburg,	Will,	30952
1814	Eleazer	Bolton,	Administration,	30953
1827	Eleazer	Lunenburg,	Will,	30954
1821	Eleazer J.	Berlin,	Guardianship,	30955
1846	Eli	Sterling,	Administration,	30956
1778	Elijah	Lancaster,	Guardianship,	30957
1819	Elijah	Harvard,	Administration,	30958
1833	Elijah	Sterling,	Will,	30959
1762	Elisha	Harvard,	Guardianship,	30960
1778	Elizabeth	Leominster,	Guardianship,	30961
1875	Ella E.	Sterling,	Guardianship,	30962
1858	Ella G.	Harvard,	Adoption, etc.,	30963
1813	Emery	Harvard,	Administration,	30964
1821	Emily	Berlin,	Guardianship,	30965
1865	Emma M.	Leominster,	Guardianship,	30966
1739	Epha	Lancaster,	Guardianship,	30967
1762	Ephraim	Harvard,	Guardianship,	30968
1777	Ephraim	Lancaster,	Will,	30969
1851	Ephraim W.	Harvard,	Guardianship,	30970
1802	Esther	Petersham,	Guardianship,	30971

| --- | --- | --- | --- | --- |
1843	HOUGHTON, Esther	Barre,	Administration,	30972
1869	Esther	Barre,	Will,	30973
1765	Eunice	Bolton,	Guardianship,	30974
1778	Eunice	Lancaster,	Guardianship,	30975
1801	Eunice	Princeton,	Guardianship,	30976
1789	Ezra	Sterling,	Administration,	30977
1783	Ezra, Jr.	Sterling,	Administration,	30978
1837	Fisk	Sterling,	Will,	30979
1858	Francis A.	Leominster,	Guardianship,	30980
1823	George	Berlin,	Guardianship,	30981
1875	George	Sterling,	Administration,	30982
1841	George A.	Worcester,	Guardianship,	30983
1875	George K., etc.	Sterling,	Administration,	30984
1849	George W.	Worcester,	Administration,	30985
1757	Gershom	Leominster,	Will,	30986
1878	Harriet	Barre,	Will,	30987
1879	Helen M.	Fitchburg,	Administration,	30988
1778	Henry	Harvard,	Will,	30989
1789	Henry	Bolton,	Guardianship,	30990
1838	Henry	Bolton,	Will,	30991
1846	Henry	Ashburnham,	Guardianship,	30992
1847	Henry E.	Sterling,	Guardianship,	30993
1857	Henry H.	Petersham,	Guardianship,	30994
1865	Henry H.	Leominster,	Guardianship,	30995
1880	Henry H.	Leominster,	Administration,	30996
1838	Henry T.	Berlin,	Guardianship,	30997
1807	Hepzibah	Bolton,	Will,	30998
1853	Hiram	Harvard,	Will,	30999
1838	Horace	Berlin,	Guardianship,	31000
1777	Israel	Lancaster,	Will,	31001
1852	Israel, 2d	Petersham,	Administration,	31002
1856	Israel	Petersham,	Administration,	31003
1841	Israel N.	Petersham,	Administration,	31004
1828	Jaazaniah	Bolton,	Will,	31005
1750	Jacob	Bolton,	Administration,	31006
1802	Jacob	Bolton,	Administration,	31007
1772	Jacob, Jr.	Bolton,	Guardianship,	31008
1811	James	Bolton,	Administration,	31009
1870	James	Sterling,	Administration,	31010
1771	James, Jr.	Lancaster,	Will,	31011
1857	James A.	Petersham,	Guardianship,	31012
1863	James E.	Sterling,	Guardianship,	31013
1827	Jane	Leominster,	Guardianship,	31014
1846	Jane L.	Ashburnham,	Guardianship,	31015
1777	Jemima	Leominster,	Guardianship,	31016

1816	HOUGHTON, Joel	Sterling,	Administration,	31017
1820	Joel	Sterling,	Guardianship,	31018
1737	John	Lancaster,	Administration,	31019
1743	John	Bolton,	Guardianship,	31020
1777	John	Leominster,	Guardianship,	31021
1781	John	Leominster,	Guardianship,	31022
1796	John	Leominster,	Administration,	31023
1769	John, Jr.	Bolton,	Administration,	31024
1838	Jonah	Berlin,	Administration,	31025
1739	Jonas	Bolton,	Administration,	31026
1743	Jonas	Bolton,	Guardianship,	31027
1801	Jonas	Bolton,	Will,	31028
1817	Jonas	Sterling,	Administration,	31029
1821	Jonas	Berlin,	Guardianship,	31030
1847	Jonas	Bolton,	Will,	31031
1848	Jonas	Bolton,	Pension,	31032
1819	Jonas S.	Sterling,	Guardianship,	31033
1864	Jonas S.	Sterling,	Administration,	31034
1737	Jonathan	Lancaster,	Will,	31035
1744	Jonathan	Bolton,	Administration,	31036
1781	Jonathan	Leominster,	Guardianship,	31037
1829	Jonathan	Bolton,	Administration,	31038
1819	Jonathan P.	Bolton,	Dower,	31039
1821	Jonathan P.	Bolton,	Guardianship,	31040
1764	Joseph	Bolton,	Guardianship,	31041
1785	Joseph	Lancaster,	Administration,	31042
1789	Joseph	Bolton,	Guardianship,	31043
1789	Joseph	Bolton,	Administration,	31044
1833	Joseph, 2d	Bolton,	Administration,	31045
1847	Joseph	Bolton,	Will,	31046
1779	Joshua	Lancaster,	Will,	31047
1841	Josiah P.	Worcester,	Guardianship,	31048
1843	Judith	Berlin,	Will,	31049
1770	Kezia	Lancaster,	Guardianship,	31050
1771	Keziah	Bolton,	Guardianship,	31051
1801	Levi	Bolton,	Guardianship,	31052
1818	Levi	Lunenburg,	Administration,	31053
1821	Levi	Berlin,	Guardianship,	31054
1837	Levi	Petersham,	Administration,	31055
1847	Levi, 2d	Lunenburg,	Administration,	31056
1851	Levi	Berlin,	Administration,	31057
1852	Levi	Lancaster,	Administration,	31058
1866	Levi	Lunenburg,	Will,	31059
1880	Levi	Shrewsbury,	Will,	31060
1834	Levina B.	Bolton,	Will,	31061

(715)

YEAR.	NAME.	RESIDENCE.	NATURE.	CASE.
1833	HOUGHTON, Lewis B.	Bolton,	Guardianship,	31062
1823	Lewis N.	Berlin,	Guardianship,	31063
1772	Lieutenant	Bolton,	Guardianship,	31064
1869	Lilla B.	Worcester,	Adoption, etc.,	31065
1871	Loenza	Leominster,	Will,	31066
1827	Louisa	Leominster,	Guardianship,	31067
1862	Louisa	Bolton,	Guardianship,	31068
1827	Louvina	Leominster,	Guardianship,	31069
1844	Lucia	Barre,	Administration,	31070
1847	Lucinda	Sterling,	Guardianship,	31071
1869	Lucinda H.	Berlin,	Adoption, etc.,	31072
1802	Lucretia	Petersham,	Guardianship,	31073
1836	Lucretia S.	Petersham,	Guardianship,	31074
1804	Lucy	Bolton,	Will,	31075
1820	Lucy	Sterling,	Guardianship,	31076
1821	Lucy	Berlin,	Guardianship,	31077
1827	Lucy	Sterling,	Administration,	31078
1841	Lucy J.	Worcester,	Guardianship,	31079
1877	Luke	Barre,	Administration,	31080
1838	Luther	Barre,	Administration,	31081
1875	Luther W.	Bolton,	Administration,	31082
1853	Lydia	Petersham,	Administration,	31083
1841	Lydia A.	Worcester,	Guardianship,	31084
1826	Lyman	Lunenburg,	Guardianship,	31085
1841	Lyman J.	Worcester,	Guardianship,	31086
1827	Manassah	Sterling,	Administration,	31087
1877	Manasseh	Sterling,	Administration,	31088
1778	Marcy	Lancaster,	Guardianship,	31089
1789	Marcy	Bolton,	Guardianship,	31090
1844	Maria	Petersham,	Administration,	31091
1778	Martha	Lancaster,	Guardianship,	31092
1823	Martha	Bolton,	Will,	31093
1841	Martha E.	Worcester,	Guardianship,	31094
1847	Martha J.	Sterling,	Guardianship,	31095
1833	Martin	Bolton,	Administration,	31096
1859	Martin A.	Leominster,	Guardianship,	31097
1746	Mary	Bolton,	Guardianship,	31098
1748	Mary	Bolton,	Administration,	31099
1791	Mary	Bolton,	Administration,	31100
1827	Mary	Leominster,	Guardianship,	31101
1866	Mary	Bolton,	Will,	31102
1878	Mary	Lunenburg,	Administration,	31103
1838	Mary A.	Berlin,	Guardianship,	31104
1866	Mary A.	Holden,	Will,	31105
1847	Mary E.	Sterling,	Guardianship,	31106

YEAR.	NAME.	RESIDENCE.	NATURE.	CASE.
1859	HOUGHTON, Mary H.	Worcester,	Administration,	31107
1858	Mary M.	Barre,	Guardianship,	31108
1819	Mary P.	Sterling,	Guardianship,	31109
1802	Matilda	Petersham,	Guardianship,	31110
1823	Merrick	Bolton,	Administration,	31111
1836	Miranda	Petersham,	Guardianship,	31112
1839	Nathaniel	Sterling,	Administration,	31113
1839	Nathaniel	Sterling,	Pension,	31114
1841	Nathaniel	Barre,	Administration,	31115
1858	Nathaniel	Sterling,	Guardianship,	31116
1858	Nathaniel T.	Leominster,	Guardianship,	31117
1866	Nettie	Winchendon,	Adoption, etc.,	31118
1790	Oliver	Leominster,	Administration,	31119
1790	Oliver	Leominster,	Guardianship,	31120
1845	Ostrander	Holden,	Administration,	31121
1819	Parkman	Bolton,	Guardianship,	31122
1801	Peabody	Princeton,	Guardianship,	31123
1830	Peabody	Princeton,	Administration,	31124
1743	Persis	Bolton,	Guardianship,	31125
1823	Persis	Berlin,	Guardianship,	31126
1777	Peter	Leominster,	Guardianship,	31127
1830	Peter	Harvard,	Will,	31128
1790	Pharez	Petersham,	Administration,	31129
1765	Phineas	Bolton,	Administration,	31130
1797	Phineas	Lancaster,	Administration,	31131
1831	Phineas W.	Harvard,	Guardianship,	31132
1843	Polly	Berlin,	Will,	31133
1857	Polly	Leominster,	Administration,	31134
1858	Polly	Lancaster,	Pension,	31135
1760	Priscilla	Lancaster,	Guardianship,	31136
1784	Priscilla	Westminster,	Administration,	31136
1743	Prudence	Bolton,	Guardianship,	31137
1769	Rachel	Lancaster,	Administration,	31138
1770	Rachel	Lancaster,	Guardianship,	31139
1830	Rebecca	Berlin,	Will,	31140
1863	Richard N.	Holden,	Guardianship,	31141
1879	Richard N.	Princeton,	Guardianship,	31142
1846	Richard W.	Ashburnham,	Will,	31143
1844	Robert	Winchendon,	Pension,	31144
1847	Robert C.	Lancaster,	Administration,	31145
1739	Rufus	Lancaster,	Guardianship,	31146
1759	Rufus	Leominster,	Administration,	31147
1761	Rufus	Leominster,	Guardianship,	31148
1777	Rufus	Leominster,	Administration,	31149
1781	Rufus	Leominster,	Guardianship,	31150

YEAR.	NAME.	RESIDENCE.	NATURE.	CASE.
1853	HOUGHTON, Rufus	Bolton,	Will,	31151
1875	Rufus	Rutland,	Will,	31152
1857	Ruth, 2d	Sterling,	Administration,	31153
1861	Ruth	Sterling,	Administration,	31154
1801	Sabra	Bolton,	Guardianship,	31155
1821	Sabra	Berlin,	Guardianship,	31156
1872	Sally	Leominster,	Will,	31157
1856	Sally B.	Lunenburg,	Administration,	31158
1820	Sally K.	Sterling,	Guardianship,	31159
1820	Salmon	Sterling,	Guardianship,	31160
1825	Salmon	West Boylston,	Administration,	31161
1844	Salmon	Lancaster,	Administration,	31162
1778	Samuel	Leominster,	Guardianship,	31163
1819	Samuel	Sterling,	Guardianship,	31164
1845	Samuel	Fitchburg,	Administration,	31165
1867	Samuel	Sterling,	Will,	31166
1869	Samuel H.	Worcester,	Administration,	31167
1799	Sanderson	Bolton,	Administration,	31168
1833	Sanderson	Bolton,	Administration,	31169
1876	Sanford	Harvard,	Administration,	31170
1770	Sarah	Lancaster,	Guardianship,	31171
1801	Sarah	Princeton,	Guardianship,	31172
1851	Sarah	Harvard,	Will,	31173
1876	Sarah	Petersham,	Will,	31174
1847	Sarah L.	Sterling,	Guardianship,	31175
1814	Saul	Sterling,	Administration,	31176
1797	Silas	Princeton,	Will,	31177
1820	Silas, 2d	Berlin,	Administration,	31178
1821	Silas	Berlin,	Guardianship,	31179
1830	Silas	Berlin,	Administration,	31180
1787	Silas, Jr.	Princeton,	Guardianship,	31181
1814	Simon	Bolton,	Administration,	31182
1781	Solomon	Lancaster,	Administration,	31183
1783	Solomon	Shrewsbury,	Absentee,	31184
1825	Stephen	Lunenburg,	Administration,	31185
1841	Stephen	Lancaster,	Administration,	31186
1861	Stephen	Bolton,	Administration,	31187
1863	Stephen	Lunenburg,	Administration,	31188
1823	Susan S.	Berlin,	Guardianship,	31189
1778	Thaddeus	Petersham,	Administration,	31190
1778	Thankful	Lancaster,	Guardianship,	31191
1833	Thankful	Princeton,	Administration,	31192
1863	Theodore W.	Holden,	Guardianship,	31193
1756	Thomas	Leominster,	Administration,	31194
1764	Thomas	Harvard,	Will,	31195

Year.	Name.	Residence.	Nature.	Case.
1778	HOUGHTON, Thomas	Leominster,	Administration,	31196
1778	Thomas	Leominster,	Guardianship,	31197
1801	Thomas	Princeton,	Guardianship,	31198
1862	Thomas	Harvard,	Will,	31199
1863	Thomas	Bolton,	Administration,	31200
1863	Thomas D.	Petersham,	Will,	31201
1846	Torrey	Sterling,	Administration,	31202
1761	Tyrus	Lancaster,	Administration,	31203
1856	Vesta B.	Sutton,	Will,	31204
1743	William	Lancaster,	Administration,	31205
1823	William	Berlin,	Guardianship,	31206
1853	William	Harvard,	Administration,	31207
1857	William	Bolton,	Administration,	31208
1858	William H.	Barre,	Guardianship,	31209
1829	Zarah	Petersham,	Will,	31210
1739	Zerish	Lancaster,	Guardianship,	31211
1868	HOULIHAN, Ann	Worcester,	Guardianship,	31212
1880	Daniel M.	Worcester,	Will,	31213
1756	HOUSE, Joseph	Lancaster,	Administration,	31214
1802	Prudence	Sterling,	Administration,	31215
1843	HOUSEN, Sarah	Westborough,	Administration,	31216
1850	HOVEY, Abigail	Dana,	Guardianship,	31217
1795	Abijah	Lunenburg,	Will,	31218
1813	Benjamin	Sutton,	Guardianship,	31219
1778	Content	Oxford,	Guardianship,	31220
1758	Daniel	Oxford,	Will,	31221
1774	Daniel	Leicester,	Administration,	31222
1777	Daniel	Oxford,	Administration,	31223
1805	Daniel	Oxford,	Guardianship,	31224
1839	Daniel	Sutton,	Administration,	31225
1819	Darius	Brookfield,	Administration,	31226
1839	Elizabeth	Sutton,	Guardianship,	31227
1839	Erastus F.	Sutton,	Guardianship,	31228
1791	Ezekiel	Charlton,	Administration,	31229
1866	Flora I.	Worcester,	Guardianship,	31230
1859	George A.	Millbury,	Guardianship,	31231
1777	Gideon	Oxford,	Guardianship,	31232
1801	Gideon	Oxford,	Administration,	31233
1805	Hannah	Oxford,	Guardianship,	31234
1859	Harriet F.	Millbury,	Guardianship,	31235
1859	Hiram F.	Millbury,	Guardianship,	31236
1752	James	Oxford,	Will,	31237
1858	James	Worcester,	Guardianship,	31238
1842	Joseph F.	Fitchburg,	Will,	31239
1778	Lyda	Oxford,	Guardianship,	31240

YEAR.	NAME.	RESIDENCE.	NATURE.	CASE.
1778	HOVEY, Mary	Oxford,	Guardianship,	31241
1778	Meriam	Oxford,	Guardianship,	31242
1805	Perez G.	Oxford,	Guardianship,	31243
1820	Phineas	Sutton,	Administration,	31244
1872	Prudence A.	Worcester,	Will,	31245
1783	Ruth	Leicester,	Guardianship,	31246
1814	Ruth	Sutton,	Guardianship,	31247
1778	Sarah	Oxford,	Guardianship,	31248
1872	Sarah A.	New York, N. Y.,	Guardianship,	31249
1870	Silas	Leicester,	Administration,	31250
1814	Simon	Sutton,	Guardianship,	31251
1814	William	Sutton,	Guardianship,	31252
1855	William	Worcester,	Administration,	31253
1859	William A.	Millbury,	Guardianship,	31254
1839	William H.	Sutton,	Guardianship,	31255
1871	William H.	Millbury,	Guardianship,	31256
1872	Zeruah	Sturbridge,	Guardianship,	31257
1872	Zeruah	Sturbridge,	Administration,	31257
	HOW see HOWE.			
1777	HOWARD, Abel	Sturbridge,	Guardianship,	31258
1803	Abigail	Holden,	Administration,	31259
1866	Abijah	Milford,	Will,	31260
1844	Abishai	Sturbridge,	Will,	31261
1876	Alden E.	Milford,	Administration,	31262
1852	Alice A.	Northbridge,	Guardianship,	31263
1876	Alice M.	Milford,	Guardianship,	31264
1862	Almira	Leicester,	Administration,	31265
1852	Amasa	Northbridge,	Administration,	31266
1829	Amos	Milford,	Administration,	31267
1849	Amos	Princeton,	Administration,	31268
1859	Amos	Holden,	Administration,	31269
1851	Amos E.	Westminster,	Administration,	31270
1849	Amos L.	Princeton,	Guardianship,	31271
1830	Andrew J.	Milford,	Guardianship,	31272
1765	Anna	Holden,	Guardianship,	31273
1876	Anna P.	Westminster,	Administration,	31274
1864	Apollos	Royalston,	Administration,	31275
1879	Arthur C.	Hardwick,	Guardianship,	31276
1859	Arthur N.	Blackstone,	Guardianship,	31277
1867	Asa L.	Fitchburg,	Will,	31278
1833	Asa W.	Princeton,	Will,	31279
1834	Asa W.	Lancaster,	Guardianship,	31280
1816	Barnard	Bolton,	Administration,	31281
1763	Benjamin	Holden,	Administration,	31282
1881	Benjamin	Blackstone,	Will,	31283

YEAR.	NAME.	RESIDENCE.	NATURE.	CASE.
1877	HOWARD, Bridget	Worcester,	Will,	31284
1873	Caleb	Lancaster,	Will,	31285
1873	Carrie E.	Clinton,	Guardianship,	31286
1823	Cary	Hardwick,	Administration,	31287
1859	Catharine C.	Holden,	Guardianship,	31288
1825	Catherine	Hardwick,	Guardianship,	31289
1881	Cecil J.	Westborough,	Will,	31290
1847	Charles	Fitchburg,	Will,	31291
1841	Charles G.	Worcester,	Guardianship,	31292
1836	Charles L.	Ashburnham,	Guardianship,	31293
1876	Clinton	Hardwick,	Will,	31294
1831	Cynthia P.	Athol,	Guardianship,	31295
1834	Daniel M.	Lancaster,	Guardianship,	31296
1862	Dolly	Holden,	Administration,	31297
1813	Dorcas	Sutton,	Guardianship,	31298
1836	Dorothy H.	Ashburnham,	Guardianship,	31299
1876	Earnest G.	Milford,	Guardianship,	31300
1854	Ebenezer	Sturbridge,	Will,	31301
1795	Ebenezer, Jr.	Sturbridge,	Guardianship,	31302
1863	Edgar E.	Milford,	Guardianship,	31303
1859	Edwin C.	Holden,	Guardianship,	31304
1867	Edwin C.	Worcester,	Administration,	31305
1807	Elihu	Northbridge,	Will,	31306
1797	Elizabeth	Brookfield,	Guardianship,	31307
1876	Ella F.	Worcester,	Guardianship,	31308
1876	Ella J.	Milford,	Guardianship,	31309
1825	Elutheria F.	Hardwick,	Guardianship,	31310
1872	Elvira	Milford,	Administration,	31311
1831	Emily M.	Athol,	Guardianship,	31312
1876	Emma R.	Boston,	Adoption, etc.,	31313
1765	Eunice	Holden,	Guardianship,	31314
1852	Eustus I.	Northbridge,	Guardianship,	31315
1833	Fanny	Brookfield,	Guardianship,	31316
1877	Francis P.	Worcester,	Guardianship,	31317
1863	Frank D.	Milford,	Guardianship,	31318
1873	Frank E.	Clinton,	Guardianship,	31319
1834	Franklin	Lancaster,	Guardianship,	31320
1876	Frederick A.	Milford,	Guardianship,	31321
1833	George	North Brookfield,	Guardianship,	31322
1860	George	Lancaster,	Will,	31323
1863	George	Lunenburg,	Administration,	31324
1817	George B.	Bolton,	Guardianship,	31325
1876	George B.	Milford,	Guardianship,	31326
1825	George C.	Hardwick,	Guardianship,	31327
1873	George F.	Clinton,	Administration,	31328

YEAR.	NAME.	RESIDENCE.	NATURE.	CASE.
1868	HOWARD, George S.	Sutton,	Administration,	31329
1841	Gilbert	Worcester,	Administration,	31330
1806	Grace	Holden,	Guardianship,	31331
1806	Hannah	Holden,	Guardianship,	31332
1817	Hannah	Bolton,	Guardianship,	31333
1848	Hannah	Bolton,	Will,	31334
1831	Harriet P.	Athol,	Guardianship,	31335
1862	Harrison	Leicester,	Administration,	31336
1834	Henry A.	Lancaster,	Guardianship,	31337
1879	Horace	Holden,	Administration,	31338
1879	Huldah	Royalston,	Will,	31339
1879	Isabel A.	Cumberland, R. I.,	Guardianship,	31340
1867	Jacob	Holden,	Will,	31341
1836	James	Sutton,	Guardianship,	31342
1839	James	Sutton,	Will,	31343
1880	James H.	Lunenburg,	Guardianship,	31344
1842	Jane R.	Sutton,	Guardianship,	31345
1866	Jesse	Milford,	Administration,	31346
1844	Job	Bolton,	Will,	31347
1829	Joel	Milford,	Will,	31348
1835	Joel	Milford,	Guardianship,	31349
1858	Joel	Milford,	Administration,	31350
1875	Joel R.	Templetou,	Will,	31351
1814	John	Oxford,	Will,	31352
1826	John	Leicester,	Administration,	31353
1880	John	Lunenburg,	Will,	31354
1871	John F.	Oakham,	Administration,	31355
1881	John W.	Templeton,	Administration,	31356
1813	Jonathan	Sutton,	Guardianship,	31357
1836	Joseph	Holden,	Will,	31358
1866	Joseph	Holden,	Will,	31359
1881	Joseph	Westminster,	Administration,	31360
1850	Josiah	Royalston,	Administration,	31361
1795	♦ Jotham	Sturbridge,	Guardianship,	31362
1859	Julia A.	Westminster,	Guardianship,	31363
1866	Julia A.	Fitchburg,	Guardianship,	31364
1833	Justin	North Brookfield,	Guardianship,	31365
1875	Justin	Worcester,	Administration,	31366
1859	Larkin N.	Sturbridge,	Will,	31367
1777	Leonard	Sturbridge,	Guardianship,	31368
1873	Lester H.	Clinton,	Guardianship,	31369
1875	Levi	Bolton,	Will,	31370
1879	Lillian F.	Cumberland, R. I.,	Guardianship,	31371
1879	Lorenzo D.	Millbury,	Will,	31372
1806	Lovina	Upton,	Guardianship,	31373

YEAR.	NAME.	RESIDENCE.	NATURE.	CASE.
1863	HOWARD, Lucretia	Westminster,	Guardianship,	31374
1867	Lucretia	Princeton,	Administration,	31374
1875	Lucy	Worcester,	Administration,	31375
1831	Lucy A.	Athol,	Guardianship,	31376
1836	Lucy E.	Ashburnham,	Guardianship,	31377
1765	Lydia	Holden,	Guardianship,	31378
1806	Lydia	Upton,	Guardianship,	31379
1864	Lyman	Winchendon,	Will,	31380
1876	Martha A.	Holden,	Administration,	31381
1765	Mary	Holden,	Guardianship,	31382
1818	Mary	Dudley,	Administration,	31383
1874	Mary	Athol,	Administration,	31384
1834	Mary A.	Lancaster,	Guardianship,	31385
1877	Mary A.	North Brookfield,	Administration,	31386
1877	Mary E.	Worcester,	Guardianship,	31387
1871	Mary F.	Worcester,	Guardianship,	31388
1878	Merrill J.	Fitchburg,	Will,	31389
1828	Micah	No town,	Administration,	31390
1806	Minerva	Upton,	Guardianship,	31391
1831	Miranda M.	Athol,	Guardianship,	31392
1777	Moses	Sturbridge,	Guardianship,	31393
1836	Moses	Brookfield,	Administration,	31394
1878	Nancy	Westminster,	Administration,	31395
1879	Nathan	Westminster,	Administration,	31396
1876	Nathaniel A.	Clinton,	Administration,	31397
1856	Nicholas P.	Leominster,	Change of Name,	31398
1874	N. Porter	Westminster,	Guardianship,	31399
1834	Olive	Lancaster,	Guardianship,	31400
1833	Pardon B.	Mendon,	Administration,	31401
1825	Prudence W.	Hardwick,	Guardianship,	31402
1879	Prusia J.	Cumberland, R. I.,	Guardianship,	31403
1819	Rebecca	Westminster,	Administration,	31404
1830	Rebecca	Milford,	Guardianship,	31405
1841	Rebecca J.	Worcester,	Guardianship,	31406
1852	Sally	Blackstone,	Administration,	31407
1878	Sally	Clinton,	Administration,	31408
1862	Sally B.	Sturbridge,	Will,	31409
1880	Sally L.	Templeton,	Administration,	31410
1797	Samuel	Brookfield,	Guardianship,	31411
1863	Samuel J.	Milford,	Administration,	31412
1860	Sidney	Clinton,	Will,	31413
1830	Simeon	Athol,	Administration,	31414
1866	Simeon	Athol,	Will,	31415
1878	Simeon	Smithfield, R. I.,	Administration,	31416
1879	Spaulding	Webster,	Administration,	31417

YEAR.	NAME.	RESIDENCE.	NATURE.	CASE.
1831	HOWARD, Stillman	Athol,	Guardianship,	31418
1871	Sylvia	Winchendon,	Will,	31419
1861	Thomas	Ashburnham,	Will,	31420
1806	Timothy	Upton,	Guardianship,	31421
1846	Timothy	Lunenburg,	Will,	31422
1836	Timothy, Jr.	Lunenburg,	Administration,	31423
1825	Tryal	Northbridge,	Will,	31424
1852	Tyler	Northbridge,	Administration,	31425
1881	Vida E.	Westborough,	Guardianship,	31426
1873	Walter F.	Clinton,	Guardianship,	31427
1859	Warren	Holden,	Guardianship,	31428
1856	Warren H.	Leominster,	Change of Name,	31429
1765	William	Holden,	Guardianship,	31430
1777	William	Sturbridge,	Administration,	31431
1841	William	Brookfield,	Will,	31432
1869	William	Hardwick,	Will,	31433
1851	Zuriel	Milford,	Will,	31434
1864	HOWARTH, John	Grafton,	Will,	31435
	HOWE, HOWES AND HOW,			
1762	Aaron	Leicester,	Guardianship,	31436
1826	Aaron	Shrewsbury,	Guardianship,	31437
1852	Abby	Auburn,	Guardianship,	31438
1843	Abby M.	Westborough,	Guardianship,	31439
1756	Abel	Worcester,	Guardianship,	31440
1836	Abel	Holden,	Administration,	31441
1843	Abel	Northborough,	Administration,	31442
1844	Abel E.	Berlin,	Guardianship,	31443
1858	Abel P.	Rutland,	Administration,	31444
1756	Abigail	Worcester,	Guardianship,	31445
1778	Abigail	Lancaster,	Guardianship,	31446
1801	Abigail	Barre,	Guardianship,	31447
1824	Abigail	Rutland,	Guardianship,	31448
1826	Abigail	Barre,	Will,	31449
1826	Abigail	Rutland,	Will,	31450
1877	Abigail W.	Leicester,	Will,	31451
1756	Abisha	Worcester,	Guardianship,	31452
1777	Abner	Brookfield,	Guardianship,	31453
1777	Abner	Brookfield,	Administration,	31454
1779	Abraham	Shrewsbury,	Administration,	31455
1790	Abraham	Brookfield,	Will,	31456
1809	Abraham	Brookfield,	Guardianship,	31457
1810	Abraham	Princeton,	Will,	31458
1861	Abraham	Holden,	Administration,	31459
1831	Abram S.	Paxton,	Guardianship,	31460
1872	Ada F., etc.	Grafton,	Guardianship,	31461

HOWE, HOWES AND HOW,

YEAR.	NAME.	RESIDENCE.	NATURE.	CASE.
1869	Adolphus	Westborough,	Administration,	31462
1777	Adonijah	Brookfield,	Guardianship,	31463
1800	Adonijah	Princeton,	Will,	31464
1834	Adonijah	Princeton,	Administration,	31465
1827	Adonijah C.	Princeton,	Guardianship,	31466
1827	Albert Carlton	Princeton,	Guardianship,	31467
1836	Albert Carr	Princeton,	Guardianship,	31468
1855	Albert J.	Worcester,	Will,	31469
1847	Albert S.	Brookfield,	Guardianship,	31470
1863	Albion S.	West Boylston,	Guardianship,	31471
1851	Alfred	Auburn,	Guardianship,	31472
1862	Alfred F.	Worcester,	Administration,	31473
1806	Alice	Rutland,	Guardianship,	31474
1876	Almira L.	Brookfield,	Administration,	31475
1864	Alonzo F.	Berlin,	Administration,	31476
1816	Alphonso	Spencer,	Guardianship,	31477
1877	Alvah	Woonsocket, R. I.,	Administration,	31478
1877	Alvah S.	Woonsocket, R. I.,	Administration,	31479
1875	Alvin W.	Bolton,	Guardianship,	31480
1768	Amariah	Brookfield,	Guardianship,	31481
1781	Amasa	Shrewsbury,	Guardianship,	31482
1876	Amasa	Holden,	Will,	31483
1828	Amos	Brookfield,	Will,	31484
1836	Amos	Gardner,	Administration,	31485
1827	Andrew	Boston,	Guardianship,	31486
1855	Angeline A.	Mendon,	Guardianship,	31487
1875	Angeline D.	North Brookfield,	Administration,	31488
1847	Angenette C.	Brookfield,	Guardianship,	31489
1842	Ann E.	Gardner,	Guardianship,	31490
1813	Anna	Petersham,	Administration,	31491
1819	Anna	Princeton,	Guardianship,	31492
1865	Anna F.	Leominster,	Adoption, etc.,	31493
1866	Ansel L.	Auburn,	Administration,	31494
1755	Antipas	Leicester,	Guardianship,	31495
1827	Antipas	Princeton,	Will,	31496
1806	Arnold	Barre	Administration,	31497
1800	Artemas	Oakham,	Will,	31498
1811	Artemas	Templeton,	Will,	31499
1819	Artemas	Princeton,	Administration,	31500
1854	Artemas	Paxton,	Will,	31501
1826	Artemas W.	Templeton,	Administration,	31502
1875	Arzubah	Oxford,	Administration,	31503
1800	Asa	Petersham,	Administration,	31504
1857	Augustus E.	Barre,	Guardianship,	31505

Year.	Name.	Residence.	Nature.	Case.
	HOWE, HOWES and HOW,			
1860	Barney	West Boylston,	Will,	31506
1827	Barzillai M.	Boston,	Guardianship,	31507
1880	Belle A.	Brookfield,	Guardianship,	31508
1753	Benjamin	Brookfield,	Guardianship,	31509
1768	Benjamin	Leicester,	Guardianship,	31510
1788	Benjamin	Westborough,	Will,	31511
1833	Benjamin	Petersham,	Will,	31512
1835	Benjamin	Gardner,	Administration,	31513
1866	Benjamin B.	Petersham,	Guardianship,	31514
1871	Benjamin G.	Worcester,	Administration,	31515
1826	Benjamin L.	Shrewsbury,	Administration,	31516
1826	Benjamin L.	Shrewsbury,	Guardianship,	31517
1829	Benjamin S.	Templeton,	. Administration,	31518
1842	Betsey	Gardner,	Guardianship,	31519
1881	Betsey K.	Leominster,	Will,	31520
1807	Betsy	Brookfield,	Guardianship,	31521
1751	Bezaleel	Leicester,	Administration,	31522
1778	Bezaleel	Lancaster,	Will,	31523
1789	Buckley	Hubbardston,	Administration,	31524
1790	Buckley	Hubbardston,	Guardianship,	31525
1800	Buckley, Jr.	Hubbardston,	Administration,	31526
1824	Caleb C.	Rutland,	Guardianship,	31527
1849	Calvin	Rutland,	Will,	31528
1863	Calvin	Dana,	Guardianship,	31529
1868	Calvin	Shrewsbury,	Administration,	31530
1868	Calvin G.	Rutland,	Will,	31531
1750	Caroline	Rutland,	Guardianship,	31532
1842	Caroline	Templeton,	Guardianship,	31533
1826	Caroline A.	Shrewsbury,	Guardianship,	31534
1866	Carrie E.	Worcester,	Guardianship,	31535
1871	Carrie E.	Worcester,	Adoption,	31536
1753	Charles	Brookfield,	Guardianship,	31537
1850	Charles	Leominster,	Administration,	31538
1860	Charles	Westminster,	Administration,	31539
1848	Charles D.	Worcester,	Administration,	31540
1844	Charles E.	Berlin,	Guardianship,	31541
1862	Charles F.	Westminster,	Guardianship,	31542
1855	Charles H.	Mendon,	Guardianship,	31543
1819	Charlotte	Brookfield,	Guardianship,	31544
1825	Charlotte A.	Brookfield,	Guardianship,	31545
1875	Charlotte B.	Spencer,	Will,	31546
1857	Christiana B.	Barre,	Guardianship,	31547
1858	Cora L.	Clinton,	Guardianship,	31548
1836	Curtis	Northborough,	Guardianship,	31549

Year.	Name.	Residence.	Nature.	Case.
	HOWE, HOWES and HOW,			
1854	Curtis	Northborough,	Will,	31550
1829	Cutler	Spencer,	Administration,	31551
1762	Damaris	Leicester,	Guardianship,	31552
1739	Daniel	Shrewsbury,	Administration,	31553
1768	Daniel	Shrewsbury,	Will,	31554
1777	Daniel	Hubbardston,	Administration,	31555
1777	Daniel	Hubbardston,	Guardianship,	31556
1810	Daniel	Hubbardston,	Will,	31557
1857	Daniel	Princeton,	Administration,	31558
1750	Daniel, Jr.	Shrewsbury,	Administration,	31559
1877	Daniel A.	Westborough,	Guardianship,	31560
1848	Daniel M.	Westminster,	Administration,	31561
1849	Daniel M.	Westminster,	Guardianship,	31562
1746	David	Bolton,	Administration,	31563
1746	David	Bolton,	Administration,	31564
1802	David	Rutland,	Will,	31565
1826	David	Lancaster,	Administration,	31566
1827	David	Lancaster,	Guardianship,	31567
1842	David	Templeton,	Guardianship,	31568
1868	David	Leominster,	Will,	21569
1869	David, 2d	Leominster,	Will,	31570
1807	Dennis	Shrewsbury,	Will,	31571
1828	Dexter	Hubbardston,	Guardianship,	31572
1761	Dorothy	New Braintree,	Guardianship,	31573
1753	Ebenezer	Brookfield,	Will,	31574
1753	Ebenezer	Brookfield,	Guardianship,	31575
1809	Ebenezer	Gardner,	Will,	31576
1876	Ebenezer	Gardner,	Will,	31577
1837	Ebenezer D.	Gardner,	Will,	31578
1874	Edith W.	Petersham,	Change of Name,	31579
1801	Edmund	Barre,	Will,	31580
1801	Edmund	Barre,	Guardianship,	31581
1864	Edson H.	Rutland,	Will,	31582
1842	Edward	Templeton,	Guardianship,	31583
1860	Edward	West Boylston,	Guardianship,	31584
1871	Edward	West Boylston,	Will,	31584
1855	Edward A.	Barre,	Change of Name,	31585
1856	Edward E.	West Boylston,	Guardianship,	31586
1826	Edward K.	Shrewsbury,	Guardianship,	31587
1847	Edwin A.	Brookfield,	Guardianship,	31588
1880	Edwin F.	Bolton,	Administration,	31589
1816	Elbridge	Spencer,	Guardianship,	31590
1847	Elbridge	Brookfield,	Guardianship,	31591
1851	Elbridge	Oxford,	Administration,	31592

(727)

Year.	Name.	Residence.	Nature.	Case.

HOWE, HOWES and HOW,

Year.	Name.	Residence.	Nature.	Case.
1812	Elbridge G.	Paxton,	Guardianship,	31593
1872	Eleanor	Holden,	Administration,	31594
1852	Eleanor L.	Auburn,	Administration,	31595
1804	Eli	Brookfield,	Will,	31596
1750	Elijah	Rutland,	Guardianship,	31597
1761·	Elijah	New Braintree,	Guardianship,	31598
1808	Elijah	Spencer,	Will,	31599
1816	Elijah	Spencer,	Administration,	31600
1845	Elijah	Spencer,	Administration,	31601
1785	Eliphalet	Princeton,	Administration,	31602
1806	Eliphalet	Rutland,	Guardianship,	31603
1857	Eliphalet	Barre,	Will,	31604
1876	Eliza	Brookfield,	Will,	31605
1827	Eliza D.	Rutland,	Guardianship,	31606
1748	Elizabeth	Rutland,	Guardianship,	31607
1748	Elizabeth	Bolton,	Guardianship,	31608
1777	Elizabeth	Hubbardston,	Guardianship,	31609
1825	Elizabeth	Brookfield,	Will,	31610
1870	Elizabeth	Rutland,	Will,	31611
1824	Elizabeth C.	Rutland,	Guardianship,	31612
1832	Elizabeth D.	Spencer,	Administration,	31613
1880	Elizabeth H.	Webster,	Will,	31614
1855	Elizabeth S.	Boylston,	Guardianship,	31615
1874	Elizabeth S.	Webster,	Trustee,	31616
1858	Ella F.	Clinton,	Guardianship,	31617
1859	Ella J.	Lancaster,	Adoption,	31618
1877	Ella J.	Westborough,	Guardianship,	31619
1848	Ellen E.	Worcester,	Guardianship,	31620
1852	Ellen E.	Auburn,	Guardianship,	31621
1843	Ellen F. G.	Northborough,	Guardianship,	31622
1871	Ellis D.	Worcester,	Guardianship,	31623
1846	Elmer B.	Boylston,	Guardianship,	31624
1866	Elsie M.	Hardwick,	Guardianship,	31625
1870	Emeline	Southbridge,	Change of Name,	31626
1819	Emily	Princeton,	Guardianship,	31627
1839	Emily	Gardner,	Guardianship,	31628
1869	Emilyett	Leicester,	Guardianship,	31629
1795	Ephraim	Brookfield,	Will,	31630
1843	Ephraim, Jr.	Berlin,	Administration,	31631
1827	Ephraim M.	Princeton,	Guardianship,	31632
1877	Ernest W.	West Boylston,	Adoption, etc.,	31633
1768	Esther	Leicester,	Guardianship,	31634
1811	Esther	Hubbardston,	Guardianship,	31635
1865	Esther	Spencer,	Will,	31636

Year.	Name.	Residence.	Nature.	Case.
	HOWE, HOWES and HOW,			
1866	Esther	Spencer,	Will,	31637
1866	Esther	Spencer,	Pension,	31638
1811	Eunice	Princeton,	Administration,	31639
1861	Eunice	Holden,	Administration,	31640
1800	Ezekiel	Shrewsbury,	Will,	31641
1842	Ezekiel	Gardner,	Will,	31642
1853	E. Henry	Barre,	Administration,	31643
1865	Fanny B.	Paxton,	Will,	31644
1870	Fanny W.	Charlton,	Administration,	31645
1807	Fisk	Templeton,	Will,	31646
1862	Florence I.	Westminster,	Guardianship,	31647
1847	Frances A.	Brookfield,	Guardianship,	31648
1864	Frances E.	Worcester,	Guardianship,	31649
1758	Francis	Rutland,	Will,	31650
1819	Francis	Brookfield,	Guardianship,	31651
1827	Francis	Boston,	Guardianship,	31652
1852	Francis	Barre,	Pension,	31653
1873	Francis	Spencer,	Administration,	31654
1879	Francis	Brookfield,	Will,	31655
1857	Francis E.	Barre,	Guardianship,	31656
1863	Frank H.	West Boylston,	Guardianship,	31657
1874	Frank W.	Templeton,	Guardianship,	31658
1862	Franklin	Westminster,	Administration,	31659
1753	Frederick	Rutland,	Guardianship,	31660
1754	Frederick	Leicester,	Guardianship,	31661
1764	Frederick	Leicester,	Administration,	31662
1827	Frederick	Lancaster,	Guardianship,	31663
1848	Frederick	Spencer,	Will,	31664
1855	Frederick	Leominster,	Will,	31665
1880	Frederick A.	Princeton,	Administration,	31666
1845	George	Milford,	Will,	31667
1857	George	Gardner,	Administration,	31668
1874	George	Boston,	Trustee,	31669
1855	George A.	Boylston,	Guardianship,	31670
1859	George B.	Millbury,	Guardianship,	31671
1877	George B.	West Boylston,	Administration,	31672
1846	George E.	Milford,	Guardianship,	31673
1873	George F.	Milford,	Guardianship,	31674
1879	George H.	Princeton,	Administration,	31675
1842	George L.	Worcester,	Guardianship,	31676
1849	George M.	Westminster,	Guardianship,	31677
1860	George P.	Boylston,	Administration,	31678
1876	George S.	Worcester,	Will,	31679
1815	Gideon	Shrewsbury,	Will,	31680

YEAR.	NAME.	RESIDENCE.	NATURE.	CASE.
	HOWE, HOWES AND HOW,			
1867	Gilman A.	Sterling,	Administration,	31681
1746	Hannah	Worcester,	Guardianship,	31682
1768	Hannah	Leicester,	Guardianship,	31683
1790	Hannah	Rutland,	Guardianship,	31684
1790	Hannah	Spencer,	Guardianship,	31685
1874	Hannah	Northborough,	Will,	31686
1830	Harriet	West Boylston,	Guardianship,	31687
1861	Harriet	Holden,	Guardianship,	31688
1853	Harriet M.	Auburn, N. H.,	Guardianship,	31689
1872	Harriet M.	Bolton,	Will,	31690
1852	Harriot L.	Northborough,	Guardianship,	31691
1835	Harrison	Gardner,	Guardianship,	31692
1852	Harrison A.	Warren,	Administration,	31693
1880	Harry E.	Brookfield,	Guardianship,	31694
1853	Harvey O.	Auburn, N. H.,	Guardianship,	31695
1873	Hattie E.	Milford,	Guardianship,	31696
1853	Helen V.	Auburn, N. H.,	Guardianship,	31697
1862	Henry	Lunenburg,	Administration,	31698
1871	Henry	Shrewsbury,	Administration,	31699
1853	Henry N.	Auburn, N. H.,	Guardianship,	31700
1823	Henry P.	Worcester,	Guardianship,	31701
1827	Henry P.	Lancaster,	Guardianship,	31702
1847	Henry P.	Worcester,	Administration,	31703
1852	Henry S.	Warren,	Guardianship,	31704
1816	Hiram	Spencer,	Guardianship,	31705
1829	Hiram	West Boylston,	Administration,	31706
1842	Hiram F.	West Boylston,	Guardianship,	31707
1854	Hollis S.	Holden,	Administration,	31708
1857	Horace G.	Gardner,	Guardianship,	31709
1858	Hubert N.	Holden,	Guardianship,	31710
1766	Ichabod	Brookfield,	Will,	31711
1877	Ida E.	Worcester,	Guardianship,	31712
1872	Ida F.	Grafton,	Guardianship,	31713
1751	Isaac	Leicester,	Administration,	31714
1768	Isaac	Leicester,	Guardianship,	31715
1839	Isaac	Northborough,	Administration,	31716
1843	Isaac	Leominster,	Administration,	31717
1871	Isaac II.	Fitchburg,	Administration,	31718
1803	Isabel	Oakham,	Guardianship,	31719
1748	Israel	Rutland,	Administration,	31720
1859	Israel	Princeton,	Will,	31721
1832	Israel G.	Westborough,	Guardianship,	31722
1762	Jaazaniah	Leicester,	Will,	31723
1850	Jacob	Worcester,	Administration,	31724

YEAR.	NAME.	RESIDENCE.	NATURE.	CASE.
	HOWE, HOWES AND HOW,			
1755	James	Worcester,	Administration,	31725
1756	James	Worcester,	Guardianship,	31726
1777	James	Brookfield,	Guardianship,	31727
1801	James	Shrewsbury,	Administration,	31728
1874	James H.	Webster,	Trustee,	31729
1877	James W.	Westborough,	Guardianship,	31730
1881	Jane	Athol,	Administration,	31731
1831	Jarvis	Paxton,	Guardianship,	31732
1879	Jarvis	North Brookfield,	Administration,	31733
1827	Jasper	Holden,	Administration,	31734
1761	Jedediah	New Braintree,	Administration,	31735
1842	Jedediah B.	Worcester,	Administration,	31736
1766	Jedidiah	Brookfield,	Will,	31737
1777	Job L.	Brookfield,	Guardianship,	31738
1802	Joel	Petersham,	Will,	31739
1830	Joel	West Boylston,	Guardianship,	31740
1842	Joel	West Boylston,	Administration,	31741
1854	Joel	Spencer,	Pension,	31742
1867	Joel	Keene, N. H.,	Administration,	31743
1863	Joel II.	West Boylston,	Will,	31744
1756	John	Rutland,	Administration,	31745
1757	John	Grafton,	Administration,	31746
1768	John	Leicester,	Guardianship,	31747
1776	John	Spencer,	Guardianship,	31748
1785	John	Templeton,	Guardianship,	31749
1831	John	Paxton,	Administration,	31750
1834	John	Phillipston,	Administration,	31751
1842	John	Boylston,	Administration,	31752
1846	John	Boylston,	Administration,	31753
1855	John	Boylston,	Administration,	31754
1866	John	Mendon,	Will,	31755
1866	John	Petersham,	Administration,	31756
1873	John	Worcester,	Will,	31757
1826	John D.	Shrewsbury,	Guardianship,	31758
1860	John F.	Boston,	Adoption, etc.,	31759
1844	John H.	Berlin,	Guardianship,	31760
1847	John M.	Brookfield,	Guardianship,	31761
1838	John R.	Petersham,	Guardianship,	31762
1855	John W.	Boylston,	Guardianship,	31763
1751	Jonah	Shrewsbury,	Guardianship,	31764
1825	Jonah	Rutland,	Administration,	31765
1826	Jonah	Shrewsbury,	Will,	31766
1811	Jonah, Jr.	Paxton,	Administration,	31767
1813	Jonas	Rutland,	Will,	31768

Year.	Name.	Residence.	Nature.	Case.
	HOWE, HOWES and HOW,			
1822	Jonas	Rutland,	Administration,	31769
1857	Jonas	Bolton,	Administration,	31770
1865	Jonas	Petersham,	Administration,	31771
1824	Jonas H.	Rutland,	Guardianship,	31772
1826	Jonas H.	Rutland,	Administration,	31773
1755	Jonathan	Leicester,	Guardianship,	31774
1788	Jonathan	Rutland,	Will,	31775
1790	Jonathan	Rutland,	Guardianship,	31776
1821	Jonathan	Holden,	Will,	31777
1835	Jonathan	Paxton,	Will,	31778
1835	Jonathan	Paxton,	Pension,	31779
1852	Jonathan	Rutland,	Administration,	31780
1753	Joseph	Brookfield,	Guardianship,	31781
1864	Joseph	Warren,	Will,	31782
1849	Joseph G.	Westminster,	Guardianship,	31783
1852	Joseph J.	Northborough,	Guardianship,	31784
1858	Joseph M.	Princeton,	Guardianship,	31785
1864	Joseph M.	Princeton,	Administration,	31785
1761	Josiah	New Braintree,	Guardianship,	31786
1767	Josiah	Charlton,	Administration,	31787
1843	Josiah	Westminster,	Will,	31788
1805	Jotham	Holden,	Will,	31789
1809	Jotham	Barre,	Administration,	31790
1861	Jotham	Clinton,	Will,	31791
1866	Jotham	Holden,	Will,	31792
1880	Julia S.	Brookfield,	Guardianship,	31793
1807	Katy	Templeton,	Guardianship,	31794
1856	Keziah	Gardner,	Administration,	31795
1778	King	Lancaster,	Guardianship,	31796
1807	Lambert	Templeton,	Guardianship,	31797
1826	Laura	Shrewsbury,	Guardianship,	31798
1880	Laura	Southborough,	Will,	31799
1862	Laura E.	Westminster,	Guardianship,	31800
1848	Lauretter M.	Worcester,	Guardianship,	31801
1863	Lemuel	Grafton,	Will,	31802
1823	Leonard	Worcester,	Guardianship,	31803
1871	Leonard W.	Worcester,	Guardianship,	31804
1826	Levi	Boylston,	Administration,	31805
1840	Levi	Bolton,	Will,	31806
1863	Levi	Sterling,	Administration,	31807
1865	Levi	Worcester,	Administration,	31808
1814	Lewis	Hardwick,	Administration,	31809
1843	Lewis	Worcester,	Guardianship,	31810
1842	Lewis S.	West Boylston,	Guardianship,	31811

YEAR.	NAME.	RESIDENCE.	NATURE.	CASE.
	HOWE, HOWES and HOW,			
1816	Liberty	Spencer,	Guardianship,	31812
1805	Lois	Boylston,	Administration,	31813
1847	Lorinda S.	Brookfield,	Guardianship,	31814
1823	Louisa	Worcester,	Guardianship,	31815
1830	Lovewell	Southborough,	Administration,	31816
1826	Lovisa	Northborough,	Will, .	31817
1819	Lucinda	Princeton,	Guardianship,	31818
1821	Lucinda	Princeton,	Will,	31819
1748	Lucy	Rutland,	Guardianship,	31820
1768	Lucy	Leicester,	Guardianship,	31821
1814	Lucy	Rutland,	Administration,	31822
1831	Lucy	Paxton,	Guardianship,	31823
1835	Lucy	Gardner,	Guardianship,	31824
1833	Lucy E.	Berlin,	Guardianship,	31825
1874	Lucy E.	Petersham,	Change of Name,	31826
1815	Lucy R.	Hardwick,	Guardianship,	31827
1768	Lydia	Leicester,	Guardianship,	31828
1839	Lydia	Phillipston,	Will,	31829
1843	Lydia	Oakham,	Will,	31830
1873	Lydia G.	Leominster,	Will,	31831
1853	Lyman	Shrewsbury,	Will,	31832
1833	Lyman B.	Worcester,	Will,	31833
1756	Mansfield	Worcester,	Guardianship,	31834
1770	Mansfield	Shrewsbury,	Administration,	31835
1872	Margaret R.	Spencer,	Adoption, etc.,	31836
1756	Margarett	Worcester,	Guardianship,	31837
1857	Maria	Barre,	Guardianship,	31838
1880	Maria H.	Gardner,	Administration,	31839
1861	Martha	Holden,	Guardianship,	31840
1859	Martha A.	Millbury,	Guardianship,	31841
1862	Martha L.	Westminster,	Guardianship,	31842
1855	Martin S.	Mendon,	Guardianship,	31843
1755	Martyn	Brookfield,	Administration,	31844
1766	Mary	Brookfield,	Guardianship,	31845
1769	Mary	Westborough,	Guardianship,	31846
1803	Mary	Oakham,	Guardianship,	31847
1835	Mary	Gardner,	Guardianship,	31848
1846	Mary	Boylston,	Guardianship,	31849
1852	Mary	Rutland,	Will,	31850
1871	Mary	Rutland,	Administration,	31851
1858	Mary A.	Clinton,	Guardianship,	31852
1874	Mary A.	Petersham,	Will,	31853
1855	Mary F.	Boylston,	Guardianship,	31854
1833	Mary G.	Berlin,	Guardianship,	31855

Year	Name.	Residence.	Nature.	Case.
	HOWE, HOWES and HOW,			
1862	Mary L.	Worcester,	Will,	31856
1862	Mary L.	Westminster,	Guardianship,	31857
1878	Mary M.	Berlin,	Will,	31858
1844	Mary S.	Berlin,	Guardianship,	31859
1872	Matilda C.	Holden,	Administration,	31860
1837	Mercy	Gardner,	Will,	31861
1826	Merriam	Shrewsbury,	Guardianship,	31862
1749	Micajah	Rutland,	Guardianship,	31863
1877	Minnie E.	Millbury,	Guardianship,	31864
1842	Molly	Boylston,	Administration,	31865
1842	Molly	Boylston,	Pension,	31866
1851	Molly	West Boylston,	Will,	31867
1749	Moses	Rutland,	Will,	31868
1846	Moses	Rutland,	Administration,	31869
1857	Myron W.	Gardner,	Guardianship,	31870
1790	Nabby	Hubbardston,	Guardianship,	31871
1807	Nancy	Brookfield,	Guardianship,	31872
1844	Nancy	Brookfield,	Guardianship,	31873
1879	Nancy M.	Worcester,	Will,	31874
1781	Nathan	Shrewsbury,	Will,	31875
1798	Nathan	Gerry,	Guardianship,	31876
1851	Nathan	Shrewsbury,	Will,	31877
1851	Nathan	Shrewsbury,	Pension,	31878
1873	Nathan	Holden,	Will,	31879
1861	Nathan, Jr.	Holden,	Guardianship,	31880
1857	Nathaniel L.	Clinton,	Administration,	31881
1858	Nathaniel L.	Clinton,	Guardianship,	31882
1753	Nehemiah	Brookfield,	Guardianship,	31883
1760	Noah	Westborough,	Will,	31884
1830	Olive	West Boylston,	Guardianship,	31885
1866	Olive E.	Hardwick,	Guardianship,	31886
1774	Oliver	Brookfield,	Guardianship,	31887
1819	Oliver C.	Brookfield,	Guardianship,	31888
1872	Oliver C.	Brookfield,	Will,	31889
1819	Orange F.	Westminster,	Guardianship,	31890
1859	Orilla A.	Millbury,	Guardianship,	31891
1845	Patty	Templeton,	Administration,	31892
1806	Peabody	Princeton,	Administration,	31893
1777	Percis	Brookfield,	Guardianship,	31894
1790	Percis	Hubbardston,	Guardianship,	31895
1839	Perley	Gardner,	Administration,	31896
1755	Persis	Leicester,	Guardianship,	31897
1807	Persis	Brookfield,	Guardianship,	31898
1872	Persis	North Brookfield,	Will,	31899

Year.	Name.	Residence.	Nature.	Case.
	HOWE, HOWES and HOW,			
1880	Persis	Berlin,	Administration,	31900
1790	Peter	Hubbardston,	Guardianship,	31901
1806	Peter	Rutland,	Guardianship,	31902
1870	Peter P.	Southborough,	Will,	31903
1878	Phebe B.	Paxton,	Administration,	31904
1838	Philip R.	Spencer,	Administration,	31905
1778	Phineas	Lancaster,	Guardianship,	31906
1811	Phineas	Worcester,	Administration,	31907
1881	Phineas M.	Paxton,	Administration,	31908
1801	Phinehas	Boylston,	Will,	31909
1812	Rachel W.	Paxton,	Guardianship,	31910
1756	Rachell	Worcester,	Guardianship,	31911
1790	Rebecah	Hubbardston,	Guardianship,	31912
1748	Rebecca	Rutland,	Guardianship,	31913
1764	Rebecca	Leicester,	Guardianship,	31914
1777	Rebecca	Brookfield,	Guardianship,	31915
1864	Rebecca	Fitchburg,	Administration,	31916
1864	Rebecca	Fitchburg,	Pension,	31917
1877	Ruhamah H	Millbury,	Administration,	31918
1748	Ruth	Rutland,	Guardianship,	31919
1790	Ruth	Spencer,	Guardianship,	31920
1828	Ruth	Hubbardston,	Guardianship,	31921
1877	Ruth A.	Templeton,	Will,	31922
1875	Ruth P. M.	West Brookfield,	Will,	31923
1826	Sally	Rutland,	Will,	31924
1862	Sally	Princeton,	Will,	31925
1878	Sally	Sterling,	Guardianship,	31926
1834	Samuel	Grafton,	Administration,	31927
1865	Samuel	Southborough,	Administration,	31928
1879	Samuel	Sterling,	Will,	31929
1858	Samuel N.	Holden,	Administration,	31930
1864	Samuel S.	Worcester,	Administration,	31931
1814	Samuel W.	Holden,	Guardianship,	31932
1857	Samuel W.	Gardner,	Guardianship,	31933
1753	Sarah	Brookfield,	Guardianship,	31934
1756	Sarah	Worcester,	Guardianship,	31935
1777	Sarah	Brookfield,	Guardianship,	31936
1778	Sarah	Lancaster,	Guardianship,	31937
1790	Sarah	Rutland,	Guardianship,	31938
1801	Sarah	Brookfield,	Administration,	31939
1806	Sarah	Rutland,	Guardianship,	31940
1827	Sarah	Princeton,	Will,	31941
1850	Sarah	Petersham,	Administration,	31942
1875	Sarah	Worcester,	Will,	31943

YEAR.	NAME.	RESIDENCE.	NATURE.	CASE.
	HOWE, HOWES AND HOW,			
1816	Sarah A.	Spencer,	Guardianship,	31944
1827	Sarah A.	Princeton,	Guardianship,	31945
1844	Sarah A.	Berlin,	Guardianship,	31946
1848	Sarah A.	Phillipston,	Guardianship,	31947
1859	Sarah A. L.	Holden,	Adoption, etc.,	31948
1863	Sarah F.	West Boylston,	Guardianship,	31949
1855	Sarah H.	Mendon,	Guardianship,	31950
1847	Sarah J.	Brookfield,	Guardianship,	31951
1828	Sarah L.	Princeton,	Guardianship,	31952
1858	Sarah M.	Clinton,	Guardianship,	31953
1858	Sarah M.	Princeton,	Guardianship,	31954
1872	Sarah R.	Worcester,	Will,	31955
1876	Sarah T.	Worcester,	Administration,	31956
1803	Seraph	Oakham,	Guardianship,	31957
1852	Sereno	Auburn,	Guardianship,	31958
1761	Silas	New Braintree,	Guardianship,	31959
1768	Silas	Leicester,	Administration,	31960
1817	Silas	Boylston,	Will,	31961
1832	Silas	Westborough,	Guardianship,	31962
1867	Silas	Sterling,	Will,	31963
1761	Silas, Jr.	Brookfield,	Guardianship,	31964
1864	Silas, Jr.	Sterling,	Will,	31965
1761	Solomon	New Braintree,	Guardianship,	31966
1830	Solomon	Berlin,	Will,	31967
1833	Solomon II.	Berlin,	Guardianship,	31968
1831	Stephen	Petersham,	Will,	31969
1874	Stephen	Templeton,	Administration,	31970
1877	Stephen	Northborough,	Will,	31971
1838	Stilman	Winchendon,	Administration,	31972
1790	Sukey	Hubbardston,	Guardianship,	31973
1879	Susan B.	Burlington, Vt.,	Administration,	31974
1857	Susan J.	Gardner,	Guardianship,	31975
1864	Susan S.	Grafton,	Administration,	31976
1852	Susanna	Gardner,	Will,	31977
1803	Susanna R.	Oakham,	Guardianship,	31978
1864	Susannah	Rutland,	Will,	31979
1802	Sylvanus	Petersham,	Will,	31980
1849	Sylvanus	Petersham,	Administration,	31981
1856	Sylvia S.	Shrewsbury,	Administration,	31982
1858	Tamar	Boylston,	Administration,	31983
1855	Tamer E.	Boylston,	Guardianship	31984
1777	Thankfull	Brookfield,	Guardianship,	31985
1790	Thomas	Rutland,	Guardianship,	31986
1827	Thomas	Boston,	Guardianship,	31987

Year.	Name.	Residence.	Nature.	Case.
	HOWE, HOWES and HOW,			
1876	Thomas	Princeton,	Administration,	31988
1839	Thomas S.	Winchendon,	Guardianship,	31989
1769	Timothy	Brookfield,	Guardianship,	31990
1844	Timothy L.	Berlin,	Guardianship,	31991
1812	Tirzah	Paxton,	Guardianship,	31992
1816	Tylor	Spencer,	Guardianship,	31993
1777	Unis	Brookfield,	Guardianship,	31994
1866	Ursula W.	Worcester,	Will,	31995
1839	Vashti	Petersham,	Administration,	31996
1853	Vilette B.	Warren,	Will,	31997
1862	Volney W.	Westminster,	Guardianship,	31998
1877	Vorena P.	Millbury,	Guardianship,	31999
1877	Walter E.	Westborough,	Guardianship,	32000
1858	Walter G.	Clinton,	Guardianship,	32001
1855	Washington	Petersham,	Will,	32002
1812	Willard	Paxton,	Guardianship,	32003
1813	William	Shrewsbury,	Administration,	32004
1816	William	Spencer,	Guardianship,	32005
1823	William	Worcester,	Guardianship,	32006
1827	William	Boston,	Guardianship,	32007
1828	William	Hubbardston,	Guardianship,	32008
1844	William	Brookfield,	Administration,	32009
1859	William	Petersham,	Administration,	32010
1865	William	Brookfield,	Will,	32011
1866	William	Leominster,	Administration,	32012
1870	William	Sterling,	Guardianship,	32013
1863	William A.	Berlin,	Administration,	32014
1875	William B.	Worcester,	Will,	32015
1866	William H.	Worcester,	Guardianship,	32016
1875	William H.	Shrewsbury,	Administration,	32017
1867	William P.	West Boylston,	Administration,	32018
1858	William R.	Princeton,	Guardianship,	32019
1842	Winslow	Templeton,	Administration,	32020
1778	Winsor	Lancaster,	Guardianship,	32021
1875	Zara	Sterling,	Will,	32022
1756	Zurviah	Worcester,	Guardianship,	32023
1821	HOWELL, Barnabas F.	Douglas,	Administration,	32024
1876	Barnabas F.	Clinton,	Administration,	32025
1822	James	Douglas,	Guardianship,	32026
1873	James	Douglas,	Administration,	32027
1846	John F.	Douglas,	Guardianship,	32028
1820	Richard	Douglas,	Will,	32029
1794	HOWLAND, Abiah	Spencer,	Guardianship,	32030
1794	Abigail	Spencer,	Guardianship,	32031

(737)

Year.	Name.	Residence.	Nature.	Case.
1859	HOWLAND, Abner	Spencer,	Administration,	32032
1860	Alice S.	Worcester,	Adoption, etc.,	32033
1865	Frederick P.	Barre,	Guardianship,	32034
1817	Harriet	Brookfield,	Guardianship,	32035
1817	Harrison O.	Brookfield,	Guardianship,	32036
1856	Helen I.	Worcester,	Adoption, etc.,	32037
1817	Henry J.	Brookfield,	Guardianship,	32038
1794	James	Spencer,	Guardianship,	32039
1810	John	Brookfield,	Will,	32040
1854	John	Worcester,	Administration,	32041
1839	Joseph	Douglas,	Administration,	32042
1863	Joseph	Douglas,	Guardianship,	32043
1825	Josiah P.	Barre,	Guardianship,	32044
1817	Louisa	Brookfield,	Guardianship,	32045
1817	Maria	Brookfield,	Guardianship,	32046
1876	Marvin	Blackstone,	Will,	32047
1879	Mattie P.	Spencer,	Administration,	32048
1878	Otis	Spencer,	Will,	32049
1863	Paul W.	Douglas,	Administration,	32050
1794	Polly	Spencer,	Guardianship,	32051
1829	Rachel	Spencer,	Will,	32052
1825	Rufus	Barre,	Guardianship,	32053
1881	Seraph M.	Fitchburg,	Administration,	32054
1863	Seth	Douglas,	Administration,	32055
1833	Shove	Hardwick,	Administration,	32056
1833	Shove	Hardwick,	Pension,	32057
1817	Southwick A.	Brookfield,	Guardianship,	32058
1868	Southworth	Worcester,	Administration,	32059
1794	Susannah	Spencer,	Guardianship,	32060
1816	Thomas	Douglas,	Will,	32061
1824	Timothy	Barre,	Administration,	32062
1825	Timothy J.	Barre,	Guardianship,	32063
1881	Wilber	Spencer,	Will,	32064
1794	Willard	Spencer,	Guardianship,	32065
1825	William L.	Barre,	Guardianship,	32066
1874	William M.	Leominster,	Will,	32067
1878	HOXIE, Edward	Boston,	Adoption, etc.,	32068
1879	HOYE, Alexander	Dudley,	Administration,	32069
1860	HOYLE, Alfred R.	Millbury,	Guardianship,	32070
1874	Alice	Dudley,	Sale Real Estate,	32071
1859	Almira	Northbridge,	Guardianship,	32072
1859	Andrew	Northbridge,	Guardianship,	32073
1859	Artemas	Oxford,	Guardianship,	32074
1874	Arthur	Dudley,	Sale Real Estate,	32075
1859	Charles	Northbridge,	Guardianship,	32076

YEAR.	NAME.	RESIDENCE.	NATURE.	CASE.
1859	HOYLE, Emma W.	Northbridge,	Guardianship,	32077
1859	Francis	Northbridge,	Guardianship,	32078
1872	George	Worcester,	Administration,	32079
1860	Henry	Millbury,	Guardianship,	32080
1874	Lilly	Dudley,	Sale Real Estate,	32081
1858	Susan	Dudley,	Administration,	32082
1859	Susan	Northbridge,	Guardianship,	32083
1871	William E.	Webster,	Administration,	32084
	HOYT AND HOIT,			
1851	Asa	Dana,	Pension,	32085
1856	Betsey	Dana,	Guardianship,	32086
1805	David	Princeton,	Administration,	32087
1806	David	Princeton,	Guardianship,	32088
1824	Elizabeth A.	New Braintree,	Guardianship,	32089
1871	Ella V.	Worcester,	Guardianship,	32090
1866	George	Athol,	Will,	32091
1824	Gustavus	New Braintree,	Guardianship,	32092
1806	Hannah	Princeton,	Guardianship,	32093
1824	Henry A.	New Braintree,	Guardianship,	32094
1806	Joel	Princeton,	Guardianship,	32095
1761	John	Shrewsbury,	Guardianship,	32096
1823	John F.	New Braintree,	Administration,	32097
1790	Joseph	Northbridge,	Sale Real Estate,	32098
1834	Margaret	Rutland,	Will,	32099
1806	Maria	Princeton,	Guardianship,	32100
1761	Reuben	Shrewsbury,	Guardianship,	32101
1767	Sarah	Shrewsbury,	Guardianship,	32102
1760	Weyman	Shrewsbury,	Guardianship,	32103
1778	HUBBARD, Abel	Worcester,	Guardianship,	32104
1879	Adam	Webster,	Will,	32105
1850	Albert H.	Worcester,	Guardianship,	32106
1838	Alvira	Worcester,	Guardianship,	32107
1819	Amos	Holden,	Administration,	32108
1867	Anna F.	Holden,	Adoption, etc.,	32109
1844	Appleton B.	Southborough,	Guardianship,	32110
1778	Artemas	Worcester,	Guardianship,	32111
1802	Benjamin	Winchendon,	Will,	32112
1836	Benjamin	Holden,	Administration,	32113
1836	Benjamin	Holden,	Guardianship,	32114
1863	Billa	Holden,	Will,	32115
1852	Browning	Paxton,	Administration,	32116
1833	Calvin	Paxton,	Administration,	32117
1865	Calvin	Holden,	Administration,	32118
1847	Chloe B.	Holden,	Will,	32119
1861	Clara E.	Holden,	Adoption, etc.,	32120

Year.	Name.	Residence.	Nature.	Case.
1865	HUBBARD, Clara E.	Holden,	Guardianship,	32121
1783	Clark	Holden,	Guardianship,	32122
1837	Cooledge	Rutland,	Guardianship,	32123
1842	Cooledge	Rutland,	Administration,	32123
1790	Daniel	Brookfield,	Guardianship,	32124
1805	Daniel	Leicester,	Administration,	32125
1880	Daniel	Oxford,	Administration,	32126
1838	David B.	Worcester,	Guardianship,	32127
1874	Edward B. B.	Worcester,	Adoption,	32128
1836	Eli	Holden,	Guardianship,	32129
1814	Elisha	Holden,	Will,	32130
1863	Elisha M.	Holden,	Administration,	32131
1852	Eliza M.	Paxton,	Guardianship,	32132
1857	Eliza W.	Holden,	Will,	32133
1860	Elizabeth	Paxton,	Will,	32134
1820	Elizabeth L. W.	Worcester,	Guardianship,	32135
1819	Elizabeth T.	Worcester,	Administration,	32136
1791	Ephraim	Rutland,	Will,	32137
1825	Ethan D.	Hinsdale,	Guardianship,	32138
1878	Felix	Harvard,	Will,	32139
1852	Frances A.	Paxton,	Guardianship,	32140
1858	Francis H.	Leominster,	Guardianship,	32141
1864	Fred M.	Holden,	Guardianship,	32142
1850	Frederick W.	Worcester,	Guardianship,	32143
1850	George	Worcester,	Administration,	32144
1850	George M.	Worcester,	Guardianship,	32145
1837	George R.	Paxton,	Guardianship,	32146
1864	George R.	Paxton,	Administration,	32147
1865	Gilbert E.	Holden,	Guardianship,	32148
1837	Harriet E.	Paxton,	Guardianship,	32149
1872	Harry	Shrewsbury,	Will,	32150
1865	Hattie S.	Holden,	Guardianship,	32151
1844	Henry B.	Southborough,	Guardianship,	32152
1875	Henry B.	Worcester,	Will,	32153
1825	Hiram	Hinsdale,	Guardianship,	32154
1872	James	Royalston,	Will,	32155
1870	James D.	Milford,	Will,	32156
1814	Jane M.	Rutland,	Guardianship,	32157
1853	Jane M.	Rutland,	Guardianship,	32158
1853	Joel	Rutland,	Pension,	32159
1853	Joel	Rutland,	Will,	32160
1761	John	Holden,	Will,	32161
1790	John	Brookfield,	Guardianship,	32162
1838	John	Worcester,	Administration,	32163
1855	John M.	Holden,	Administration,	32164

YEAR.	NAME.	SIDENCE.	NATURE.	CASE.
1838	HUBBARD AND HUTSON,	ester,	Guardianship,	32165
1825	John	Wes ester,	Will,	32166
1777	Jonas r	Lec cester,	Administration,	32167
1778	Jonas n	Ur cester,	Guardianship,	32168
1851	Jonas iel	G den,	Administration,	32169
1832	Jonathan	Cixton,	Will,	32170
1837	Jonathan	Rutland,	Will,	32171
1878	Jonathan	Winchendon,	Administration,	32172
1832	Joseph	Holden,	Administration,	32173
1850	Joseph	Holden,	Administration,	32174
1875	Joseph	Rutland,	Administration,	32175
1837	Joseph L.	Paxton,	Guardianship,	32176
1765	Josiah	Lunenburg,	Guardianship,	32177
1778	Levi	Worcester,	Guardianship,	32178
1783	Levi	Holden,	Guardianship,	32179
1862	Lizzie E.	Milford,	Adoption, etc.,	32180
1864	Lizzie E.	Bellingham,	Adoption, etc.,	32180
1825	Lucy	Hinsdale,	Guardianship,	32181
1825	Lucy	Holden,	Administration,	32182
1852	Lucy	Hubbardston,	Administration,	32183
1872	Lucy A.	Worcester,	Guardianship,	32184
1814	Lucy M.	Rutland,	Guardianship,	32185
1838	Marcus D.	Worcester,	Guardianship,	32186
1838	Martha	Worcester,	Guardianship,	32187
1858	Martha G.	Leominster,	Guardianship,	32188
1873	Martha R.	Webster,	Administration,	32189
1790	Mary	Brookfield,	Guardianship,	32190
1838	Mary	Rutland,	Guardianship,	32191
1836	Mary A.	Holden,	Guardianship,	32192
1872	Mary W.	Holden,	Administration,	32193
1838	Melinda	Worcester,	Guardianship,	32194
1863	Olive	Rutland,	Will,	32195
1864	Orville D.	Holden,	Guardianship,	32196
1836	Percis W.	Holden,	Guardianship,	32197
1826	Peter	Holden,	Administration,	32198
1874	Peter W.	Royalston,	Guardianship,	32199
1839	Polly	Rutland,	Administration,	32200
1765	Rebecca	Lunenburg,	Guardianship,	32201
1778	Reuben	Worcester,	Guardianship,	32202
1778	Sally	Worcester,	Guardianship,	32203
1825	Sally	Hinsdale,	Guardianship,	32204
1835	Sally	Worcester,	Administration,	32205
1860	Sally	Worcester,	Administration,	32206
1783	Samuel	Holden,	Will,	32207
1823	Samuel	Holden,	Will,	32208

YEAR.	NAME.	RESIDENCE.	NATE.	CASE.
1825	HUBBARD, Samuel	Holden,	Gua~nistration,	32209
1836	Samuel	Holden,	Gus,	32210
1850	Samuel W.	Rutland,	Gu:l,	32211
1864	Silas M.	Rutland,	Ad.l,	32212
1841	Simon	Brookfield,	G.ll,	32213
1875	Simon	Leicester,	Will,	32214
1874	Sophia	Oxford,	Will,	32215
1866	Stillman	Worcester,	Will,	32216
1778	Thaddeus	Worcester,	Guardianship,	32217
1863	Timothy F.	Winche..	Administration,	32218
1839	Willard M.	Holden,	Will,	32219
1837	William	Rutland,	Administration,	32220
1859	William A.	Leominster,	Guardianship,	32221
1853	William H.	Rutland,	Administration,	32222
1857	Willie F.	Holden,	Adoption, etc.,	32223
1857	Willie F.	Holden,	Guardianship,	32224
1866	Willie H.	Princeton,	Guardianship,	32225
1869	HUBBELL, Lyman M.	Fitchburg,	Administration,	32226
1873	HUBER, Charles	Worcester,	Will,	32227
1873	Emilie	Worcester,	Guardianship,	32228
1880	HUBON, Peter E.	Worcester,	Will,	32229
1865	HUCKINS, George H.	Grafton,	Guardianship,	32230
1881	HUDLIN, Clara B.	Milford,	Guardianship,	32231
1881	Gracie E.	Milford,	Guardianship,	32232
1881	Henry	Milford,	Administration,	32233
1881	Herman J.	Milford,	Guardianship,	32234
	HUDSON AND HUTSON,			
1791	Adin	Oakham,	Administration,	32235
1791	Alice	Oakham,	Guardianship,	32236
1881	Archibald B.	Grafton,	Guardianship,	32237
1858	Arvilla S.	Templeton,	Administration,	32238
1868	Betsey	Boylston,	Will,	32239
1755	Darius	Grafton,	Guardianship,	32240
1853	Ella J.	Boylston,	Adoption,	32241
1774	Enos	Hancock,	Guardianship,	32242
1755	Ezekiel	Grafton,	Guardianship,	32243
1873	Ezra	Templeton,	Administration,	32244
1854	Joel	Paxton,	Change of Name,	32245
1765	John	Oxford,	Will,	32246
1855	John	Millbury,	Administration,	32247
1864	John A.	Worcester,	Guardianship,	32248
1791	Joseph	Oakham,	Administration,	32249
1792	Joseph	Oxford,	Administration,	32250
1866	Lycia L.	Worcester,	Guardianship,	32251
1850	Marie L.	Sturbridge,	Administration,	32252

YEAR.	NAME.	RESIDENCE.	NATURE.	CASE.
	HUDSON AND HUTSON,			
1853	Mary	West Boylston,	Will,	32253
1825	Melzar	Leominster,	Administration,	32254
1835	Natban	Upton,	Guardianship,	32255
1753	Nathaniel	Grafton,	Administration,	32256
1862	Oliver B.	Grafton,	Guardianship,	32257
1855	Ozias	Worcester,	Administration,	32258
1857	Reuben M.	Worcester,	Administration,	32259
1859	Robert	Boylston,	Administration,	32260
1821	Samuel	Westborough,	Will,	32261
1845	Sarah	Hardwick,	Administration,	32262
1772	Seth	Pownall, N. Y.,	Guardianship,	32263
1821	Silas B.	Westborough,	Guardianship,	32264
1778	Thomas	Templeton,	Administration,	32265
1784	Thomas	Southborough,	Will,	32266
1757	William	Lancaster,	Administration,	32267
1862	William	Worcester,	Administration,	32268
1864	William F.	Worcester,	Guardianship,	32269
1862	William W.	Grafton,	Guardianship,	32270
1881	HUGGINS, Fanny T.	Boston,	Adoption, etc.,	32271
	HUGHES AND HUSE,			
1864	Andrew J.	Worcester,	Administration,	32272
1846	Charles W.	Leominster,	Guardianship,	32273
1851	Dennison	Leominster,	Administration,	32274
1813	Enoch, Jr.	Harvard,	Will,	32275
1840	John D.	Harvard,	Will,	32276
1866	Mary	Blackstone,	Guardianship,	32277
1846	Mary E.	Leominster,	Guardianship,	32278
1881	Michael	Worcester,	Will,	32279
1871	Mira A.	Worcester,	Administration,	32280
1867	Patrick	Smithfield, R. I.,	Administration,	32281
1866	Patrick F.	Blackstone,	Guardianship,	32282
1874	Patrick F.	Blackstone,	Will,	32283
1869	Rebecca	Harvard,	Administration,	32284
1870	Robert	Douglas,	Administration,	32285
1846	Roxana M.	Leominster,	Guardianship,	32286
1811	Sally	Uxbridge,	Guardianship,	32287
1866	Sarah	Blackstone,	Guardianship,	32288
1880	Thomas	Winchendon,	Will,	32289
1851	HULBURD, Dwight K.	Sturbridge,	Guardianship,	32290
1826	HULL, Aratius B.	Worcester,	Will,	32291
1772	Asa	Sutton,	Guardianship,	32292
1871	Elias	Millbury,	Guardianship,	32293
1871	Elias	Millbury,	Will,	32293
1854	Elizabeth	Shrewsbury,	Administration,	32294

YEAR.	NAME.	RESIDENCE.	NATURE.	CASE.
1854	HULL, Elizabeth	Shrewsbury,	Pension,	32295
1852	Ellen R.	Millbury,	Guardianship,	32296
1871	George	Leominster,	Will,	32297
1875	Hannah LeB.	Sutton,	Will,	32298
1844	Jabez	Millbury,	Administration,	32299
1759	James	Sutton,	Will,	32300
1762	James	Sutton,	Guardianship,	32301
1823	James W.	Millbury,	Administration,	32302
1787	Jesse	Uxbridge,	Guardianship,	32303
1787	Joel	Uxbridge,	Guardianship,	32304
1787	Mary	Uxbridge,	Guardianship,	32305
1852	Samuel E.	Millbury,	Guardianship,	32306
1787	William	Uxbridge,	Guardianship,	32307
1829	William, Jr.	Millbury,	Administration,	32308
1784	HUMES, Amos	Douglas,	Guardianship,	32309
1861	Amos	Douglas,	Administration,	32310
1865	Betsey	Millbury,	Administration,	32311
1855	Caroline A.	Fitchburg,	Guardianship,	32312
1855	Clara A.	Holden,	Guardianship,	32313
1871	Clarence A.	Worcester,	Adoption, etc.,	32314
1768	David	Douglas,	Guardianship,	32315
1777	David	Sutton,	Guardianship,	32316
1784	David	Douglas,	Guardianship,	32317
1849	David	Douglas,	Administration,	32318
1768	Experience	Uxbridge,	Guardianship,	32319
1855	Francis B.	Holden,	Guardianship,	32320
1863	George W.	Douglas,	Administration,	32321
1863	Georgia E.	Douglas,	Guardianship,	32322
1855	Herbert M.	Holden,	Guardianship,	32323
1855	Jonas W.	Holden,	Guardianship,	32324
1822	Josiah	Douglas,	Administration,	32325
1822	Josiah	Douglas,	Pension,	32326
1864	Juliaett	Douglas,	Guardianship,	32327
1768	Kesiah	Douglas,	Guardianship,	32328
1771	Kesiah	Douglas,	Administration,	32329
1760	Margaret	Douglas,	Guardianship,	32330
1858	Mary F.	Northbridge,	Administration,	32331
1784	Molley	Douglas,	Guardianship,	32332
1784	Moses	Douglas,	Guardianship,	32333
1784	Nahum	Douglas,	Guardianship,	32334
1846	Nancy	Dudley,	Guardianship,	32335
1762	Nicholas	Uxbridge,	Will,	32336
1865	Phebe	Douglas,	Administration,	32337
1878	Reuben	Leicester,	Administration,	32338
1765	Richard	Douglas,	Administration,	32339

YEAR.	NAME.	RESIDENCE.	NATURE.	CASE.
1782	HUMES, Robert	Douglas,	Will,	32340
1760	Ruth	Douglas,	Guardianship,	32341
1768	Sarah	Douglas,	Guardianship,	32342
1760	Stephen	Douglas,	Guardianship,	32343
1762	Thomas	Uxbridge,	Guardianship,	32344
1864	Warren	Douglas,	Guardianship,	32345
1877	Warren	Douglas,	Administration,	32345
1825	HUMPHREY, Asa	North Brookfield,	Administration,	32346
1828	Benjamin	Sturbridge,	Administration,	32347
1860	Betsey	Athol,	Will,	32348
1835	Caroline	Athol,	Guardianship,	32349
1860	Charles	Lancaster,	Administration,	32350
1862	Clara	Lancaster,	Guardianship,	32351
1868	Cora F.	Millbury,	Guardianship,	32352
1870	Daniel H.	Oxford,	Will,	32353
1761	Ebenezer	Oxford,	Will,	32354
1836	Ebenezer	Oxford,	Will,	32355
1836	Ebenezer	Oxford,	Pension,	32356
1877	Edward,	Lunenburg,	Administration,	32357
1868	Edward P.	Appleton, Wis.,	Guardianship,	32358
1837	Elizabeth	Southbridge,	Administration,	32359
1824	Hannah	Sturbridge,	Administration,	32360
1793	Isaac	Dudley,	Administration,	32361
1796	James	Athol,	Will,	32362
1836	James	Athol,	Will,	32363
1862	Jane M.	Lancaster,	Guardianship,	32364
1837	John	Athol,	Will,	32365
1837	John	Athol,	Pension,	32366
1862	John	Athol,	Administration,	32367
1829	John F.	Athol,	Administration,	32368
1835	John F.	Athol,	Guardianship,	32369
1870	John H.	Philadelphia, Pa.,	Foreign Will,	32370
1829	John W.	Dudley,	Will,	32371
1845	John W.	Athol,	Will,	32372
1829	Laura A.	Dudley,	Guardianship,	32373
1865	Lawson	Oxford,	Will,	32374
1787	Lois	Athol,	Guardianship,	32375
1869	Louisa	Milford,	Administration,	32376
1865	Luman W.	Oxford,	Guardianship,	32377
1864	Margaret L.	Milford,	Adoption, etc.,	32378
1868	Maria L.	Millbury,	Guardianship,	32379
1787	Martha	Athol,	Guardianship,	32380
1878	Ono E.	Oxford,	Will,	32381
1871	Phebe G.	Oxford,	Administration,	32382
1830	Polly	Dudley,	Guardianship,	32383

YEAR.	NAME.	RESIDENCE.	NATURE.	CASE.
1835	HUMPHREY, Rebecca	Athol,	Guardianship,	32384
1848	Royal	Athol,	Will,	32385
1787	Samuel	Athol,	Administration,	32386
1787	Samuel	Athol,	Guardianship,	32387
1787	Sarah	Athol,	Guardianship,	32388
1865	Sophia	Oxford,	Administration,	32389
1761	HUNKINS, Thomas	Oxford,	Guardianship,	32390
1762	Thomas	Oxford,	Will,	32390
1737	HUNSTABLE, Samuel L.	Worcester,	Will,	32391
1876	HUNT, Aaron	Templeton,	Administration,	32392
1782	Abel	Templeton,	Administration,	32393
1786	Abel	Templeton,	Guardianship,	32394
1868	Adam	Milford,	Will,	32395
1846	Albert	Milford,	Administration,	32396
1879	Albert, etc.	Decatur, Mich.,	Guardianship,	32397
1879	Albert J., etc.	Decatur, Mich.,	Guardianship,	32397
1854	Alfred E.	Southborough,	Guardianship,	32398
1854	Alfred M.	Southborough,	Administration,	32399
1865	Alice S.	Worcester,	Guardianship,	32400
1865	Amey E.	Worcester,	Guardianship,	32401
1877	Andrew J.	Clinton,	Administration,	32402
1839	Ann M.	Upton,	Guardianship,	32403
1869	Anna W.	Warren,	Guardianship,	32404
1875	Annie F.	Winchendon,	Guardianship,	32405
1835	Austin	Douglas,	Guardianship,	32406
1783	Betty	Templeton,	Guardianship,	32407
1857	Caroline E.	Barre,	Guardianship,	32408
1865	Charles W.	Milford,	Guardianship,	32409
1879	Charlotte, etc.	Decatur, Mich.,	Guardianship,	32410
1867	Cora E.	Milford,	Adoption, etc.,	32411
1876	Cora E.	Milford,	Guardianship,	32412
1868	Cotton	West Brookfield,	Administration,	32413
1879	Daisy D.	Decatur, Mich.,	Guardianship,	32414
1801	Daniel	Milford,	Will,	32415
1811	Daniel	Providence, R. I.,	Foreign Will,	32416
1875	Daniel	Winchendon,	Guardianship,	32417
1867	Daniel S.	Hardwick,	Guardianship,	32418
1875	David	Clinton,	Administration,	32419
1777	Deborah	Lancaster,	Guardianship,	32420
1777	Deliverance	Paxton,	Guardianship,	32421
1778	Deliverance	Paxton,	Administration,	32422
1866	Dolly	Leominster,	Administration,	32423
1777	Dorothy	Paxton,	Guardianship,	32424
1780	Dorothy	Paxton,	Will,	32425
1846	Dorothy	Ashburnham,	Will,	32426

YEAR.	NAME.	RESIDENCE.	NATURE.	CASE.
1774	HUNT, Ebenezer	Paxton,	Administration,	32427
1777	Ebenezer	Paxton,	Administration,	32428
1836	Ebenezer	Milford,	Administration,	32429
1857	Edgar A.	Douglas,	Guardianship,	32430
1857	Edwin A.	Douglas,	Administration,	32431
1857	Edwin A.	Douglas,	Guardianship,	32432
1880	Edwin O.	Milford,	Administration,	32433
1786	Elihu	Templeton,	Guardianship,	32434
1867	Eliza A.	Hardwick,	Guardianship,	32435
1846	Elizabeth M.	Milford,	Guardianship,	32436
1840	Elona	Douglas,	Guardianship,	32437
1854	Emma S.	Milford,	Guardianship,	32438
1860	Evelyn M.	Grafton,	Guardianship,	32439
1803	Ezekiel	Douglas,	Will,	32440
1802	Ezra	Milford,	Guardianship,	32441
1867	Fannie M.	Hardwick,	Guardianship,	32442
1875	Francis P.	Winchendon,	Guardianship,	32443
1864	Frederick S.	Worcester,	Will,	32444
1865	Frederick S.	Worcester,	Guardianship,	32445
1857	George	Barre,	Administration,	32446
1867	George	Hardwick,	Guardianship,	32447
1865	George E.	Worcester,	Guardianship,	32448
1811	Hannah	Providence, R. I.,	Guardianship,	32449
1864	Harriet N.	Worcester,	Guardianship,	32450
1880	Harry E.	Milford,	Guardianship,	32451
1867	Henry	Hardwick,	Administration,	32452
1867	Hiram	Hardwick,	Guardianship,	32453
1873	Hiram	Milford,	Guardianship,	32454
1880	Hiram	Milford,	Administration,	32454
1845	Hulda	Sutton,	Guardianship,	32455
1783	Jaazaniah	Paxton,	Guardianship,	32456
1874	James C.	Paxton,	Administration,	32457
1875	James J.	Winchendon,	Guardianship,	32458
1879	Jennie, etc.	Decatur, Mich.,	Guardianship,	32459
1879	Jennie A.	Decatur, Mich.,	Guardianship,	32459
1815	Jeremiah	Northborough,	Administration,	32460
1876	Jeremiah	Northborough,	Will,	32461
1777	Jesse	Paxton,	Guardianship,	32462
1802	Joel	Milford,	Guardianship,	32463
1858	Joel M.	Worcester,	Guardianship,	32464
1778	John	Hardwick,	Administration,	32465
1811	John	Providence, R. I.,	Guardianship,	32466
1845	John	Sutton,	Administration,	32467
1867	John	Hardwick,	Guardianship,	32468
1879	John	Upton,	Will,	32469

Year.	Name.	Residence.	Nature.	Case.
1864	HUNT, John A.	Worcester,	Guardianship,	32470
1881	John A.	Southborough,	Guardianship,	32471
1777	Jonathan	Paxton,	Guardianship,	32472
1777	Joseph	Paxton,	Guardianship,	32473
1778	Joseph	Hardwick,	Guardianship,	32474
1839	Joseph	Upton,	Will,	32475
1864	Joseph	Milford,	Will,	32476
1839	Joseph D.	Upton,	Guardianship,	32477
1860	Joseph T.	Grafton,	Guardianship,	32478
1875	Katie A.	Winchendon,	Guardianship,	32479
1880	Lanelen E.	Milford,	Guardianship,	32480
1854	Lucy M.	Southborough,	Guardianship,	32481
1857	Luther M.	Worcester,	Administration,	32482
1879	Lydia F.	Harvard,	Will,	32483
1854	Lydia S.	Southborough,	Guardianship,	32484
1871	Martin	Winchendon,	Administration,	32485
1854	Martin L.	Southborough,	Guardianship,	32486
1875	Martin M.	Winchendon,	Guardianship,	32487
1845	Mary	Sutton,	Guardianship,	32488
1860	Mary	Worcester,	Will,	32489
1871	Mary	Worcester,	Will,	32490
1875	Mary E.	Winchendon,	Guardianship,	32491
1881	Mary E.	Southborough,	Guardianship,	32492
1866	Mary L.	Ashburnham,	Will,	32493
1867	Mary W.	Hardwick,	Guardianship,	32494
1828	Merrick	Douglas,	Administration,	32495
1839	Milow	Upton,	Guardianship,	32496
1854	Morton P.	Milford,	Guardianship,	32497
1802	Moses	Milford,	Guardianship,	32498
1833	Moses	Hardwick,	Administration,	32499
1864	Nancy	Boylston,	Administration,	32500
1880	Nancy	Blackstone,	Will,	32501
1867	Nathaniel	Webster,	Will,	32502
1783	Oliver	Templeton,	Guardianship,	32503
1826	Oliver	Templeton,	Administration,	32504
1835	Oliver	Douglas,	Administration,	32505
1855	Oliver	Templeton,	Administration,	32506
1864	Orsamus	Shrewsbury,	Will,	32507
1861	Otis	Leominster,	Will,	32508
1858	Otis W.	Douglas,	Administration,	32509
1859	Otis W.	Douglas,	Guardianship,	32510
1783	Patience	Hardwick,	Will,	32511
1859	Patty	Northborough,	Administration,	32512
1844	Pearley	Milford,	Administration,	32513
1777	Peter	Lancaster,	Guardianship,	32514

YEAR.	NAME.	RESIDENCE.	NATURE.	CASE.
1834	HUNT, Peter	Ashburnham,	Administration,	32515
1860	Peter	Grafton,	Will,	32516
1835	Peter T.	Ashburnham,	Guardianship,	32517
1811	Phebe	Providence, R. I.,	Guardianship,	32518
1845	Phebe	Sutton,	Guardianship,	32519
1802	Philip	Milford,	Guardianship,	32520
1839	Philo	Upton,	Guardianship,	32521
1854	Philo	Milford,	Will,	32522
1857	Rachel A.	Southborough,	Administration,	32523
1804	Rebecca	Templeton,	Administration,	32524
1840	Samuel	Oakham,	Pension,	32525
1777	Sherebiah	Lancaster,	Guardianship,	32526
1794	Shrimpton	Bolton,	Administration,	32527
1741	Silence	Sudbury,	Guardianship,	32528
1869	Stephen	Northborough,	Will,	32529
1835	Tamison	Ashburnham,	Guardianship,	32530
1880	Timothy	Rutland,	Administration,	32531
1845	Vilura A.	Sutton,	Guardianship,	32532
1858	Walter E.	Worcester,	Guardianship,	32533
1867	Warren	Douglas,	Will,	32534
1857	Washington	Cumberland, R. I.,	Administration,	32535
1866	Willard W.	Douglas,	Guardianship,	32536
1777	William	Lancaster,	Guardianship,	32537
1867	William H.	Hardwick,	Guardianship,	32538
1865	William J.	Worcester,	Guardianship,	32539
1869	William T. W.	Arica, Pa.,	Administration,	32540
1854	Winthrop A.	Northborough,	Administration,	32541
1821	Zachariah	Brookfield,	Will,	32542
1856	Zephaniah	Barre,	Administration,	32543
1855	HUNTER, Abigail H.	Worcester,	Will,	32544
1786	Abraham	New Braintree,	Will,	32545
1808	Abraham	Brookfield,	Will,	32546
1826	Abraham	Oakham,	Administration,	32547
1846	Abraham	North Brookfield,	Administration,	32548
1848	Charles H.	New Braintree,	Guardianship,	32549
1848	Daniel	New Braintree,	Will,	32550
1848	Daniel F.	New Braintree,	Guardianship,	32551
1805	Eli	Brookfield,	Guardianship,	32552
1862	Hannah	North Brookfield,	Will,	32553
1804	Ira	Brookfield,	Guardianship,	32554
1819	Isaac	New Braintree,	Administration,	32555
1841	Isaac, Jr.	North Brookfield,	Administration,	32556
1816	John	New Braintree,	Will,	32557
1837	Lucy R.	Oakham,	Guardianship,	32558
1847	Luther	New York, N. Y.,	Administration,	32559

YEAR.	NAME.	RESIDENCE.	NATURE.	CASE.
1848	HUNTER, Mary A.	New Braintree,	Guardianship,	32560
1855	Mary A.	New Braintree,	Administration,	32561
1849	Orrel	New Braintree,	Guardianship,	32562
1837	Sarah H.	Oakham,	Guardianship,	32563
1804	William	Brookfield,	Administration,	32564
1859	William	Hardwick,	Will,	32565
1848	William H.	New Braintree,	Guardianship,	32566
1849	(Infant)	New Braintree,	Administration,	32567
	HUNTING AND HUNTTING,			
1864	Aaron	Hubbardston,	Will,	32568
1823	Alexander	Hubbardston,	Administration,	32569
1861	Charles	Hubbardston,	Administration,	32570
1881	Charles A.	Hubbardston,	Guardianship,	32571
1851	Converse	Hubbardston,	Will,	32572
1872	Daniel	Hubbardston,	Administration,	32573
1881	Gill W.	Hubbardston,	Guardianship,	32574
1871	Henry N.	Gardner,	Adoption, etc.,	32575
1881	Henry R.	Hubbardston,	Guardianship,	32576
1881	John W.	Gardner,	Guardianship,	32577
1821	Joseph	Milford,	Will,	32578
1826	Joseph	Milford,	Will,	32579
1881	Julianna	Hubbardston,	Administration,	32580
1881	Kate J.	Hubbardston,	Guardianship,	32581
1820	Mary	Milford,	Administration,	32582
1849	Moses	Westminster,	Administration,	32583
1849	Moses	Westminster,	Pension,	32584
1836	Stephen	Hubbardston,	Will,	32585
1881	Willie G.	Hubbardston,	Guardianship,	32586
1839	HUNTINGTON, Azel	Spencer,	Administration,	32587
1840	Emmeline	Spencer,	Guardianship,	32588
1881	Francis C.	Worcester,	Guardianship,	32589
1881	Margaret W.	Worcester,	Guardianship,	32590
1881	Mary H.	Worcester,	Guardianship,	32591
1881	Theresa	Worcester,	Guardianship,	32592
1838	Waldo	Douglas,	Administration,	32593
1873	HUNTLEY, Isaiah	Spencer,	Administration,	32594
1856	Osmon L.	Fitchburg,	Will,	32595
1857	HUNTOON, Emma L.	Milford,	Adoption,	32596
	HUNTTING see HUNTING.			
	HURD AND HEARD,			
1848	Dinah	Worcester,	Will,	32597
1769	Edmund	Holden,	Will,	32598
1778	Eunice	Holden,	Guardianship,	32599
1783	Eunice	Lancaster,	Will,	32600
1866	John	Oxford.	Will,	32601

YEAR.	NAME.	RESIDENCE.	NATURE.	CASE.
	HURD AND HEARD,			
1820	Joseph	Oxford,	Will,	32602
1860	Joseph H.	Hubbardston,	Guardianship,	32603
1866	Mary B.	Oxford,	Will,	32604
1825	Nathan	Leicester,	Will,	32605
1862	Permela	Newport, N. H.,	Administration,	32606
1750	Peter	Oxford,	Administration,	32607
1783	Priscilla	Holden,	Will,	32608
1791	Sarah	Rutland,	Administration,	32609
1778	Thomas	Holden,	Administration,	32610
1841	William	Oxford,	Administration,	32611
1861	Winthrop	Grafton,	Administration,	32612
	HURLBERT AND HURLBURD,			
1875	Elizabeth	Worcester,	Administration,	32613
1851	Horace	Sturbridge,	Administration,	32614
1862	Isabella M.	Worcester,	Guardianship,	32615
1870	Mary E.	Bolton,	Administration,	32616
1860	Thomas N.	Worcester,	Administration,	32617
1866	**HURLEY,** Daniel	Worcester,	Guardianship,	32618
1872	Ellen	West Brookfield,	Guardianship,	32619
1853	Jeremiah	Fitchburg,	Administration,	32620
1866	John	Worcester,	Guardianship,	32621
1866	Margaret	Worcester,	Guardianship,	32622
1866	Mary A.	Worcester,	Guardianship,	32623
1878	Michael	Millbury,	Administration,	32624
1881	Michael, etc.	Worcester,	Administration,	32625
1870	Thomas, Jr.	Clinton,	Guardianship,	32626
1862	**HURST,** Thomas	Leicester,	Administration,	32627
	HUSE see HUGHES.			
1871	**HUSSEY,** Alice	Athol,	Adoption, etc.,	32628
1873	Maud	Milford,	Adoption, etc.,	32629
	HUTCHINS AND HUCHINS,			
1845	Caroline F.	Abington, Conn.,	Foreign Sale,	32630
1867	Charles	Douglas,	Administration,	32631
1847	Cyrus	Sturbridge,	Dower,	32632
1749	Edward	Dudley,	Guardianship,	32633
1757	Elizabeth	Harvard,	Will,	32634
1873	Harriet N.	Douglas,	Administration,	32635
1870	Jessie G.	Douglas,	Guardianship,	32636
1757	Joseph	Harvard,	Will,	32637
1771	Joshua	Lunenburg,	Will,	32638
1845	Mary E.	Abington, Conn.,	Foreign Sale,	32639
1870	Oliver C.	Douglas,	Guardianship,	32640
1747	Thomas	Dudley,	Will,	32641
1772	William	Harvard,	Will,	32642

YEAR.	NAME.	RESIDENCE.	NATURE.	CASE.
1851	HUTCHINSON, Abby A.	Oxford,	Guardianship,	32643
1872	Andrew	Worcester,	Administration,	32644
1844	Ann J.	Worcester,	Guardianship,	32645
1820	.Bartholomew	Sutton,	Will,	32646
1840	Benjamin	Royalston,	Will,	32647
1851	Daniel	Oxford,	Guardianship,	32648
1861	Ebenezer	Fitchburg,	Will,	32649
1861	Ebenezer, Jr.	Leominster,	Administration,	32650
1840	Edwin H.	Sutton,	Guardianship,	32651
1830	Elizabeth	Mendon,	Administration,	32652
1854	Elizabeth M.	Sutton,	Guardianship,	32653
1840	Emeline B.	Sutton,	Guardianship,	32654
1851	Emily	Oxford,	Guardianship,	32655
1879	Frank	Athol,	Administration,	32656
1877	Gracie E.	Fitchburg,	Adoption, etc.,	32657
1851	Jesse	Oxford,	Guardianship,	32658
1851	John	Oxford,	Guardianship,	32659
1857	John	Sutton,	Administration,	32660
1854	Joshua	Sutton,	Will,	32661
1880	Leonia I.	Fitchburg,	Adoption, etc.,	32662
1851	Louisa	Oxford,	Guardianship,	32663
1869	Mary A.	Fitchburg,	Adoption, etc.,	32664
1840	Mary L.	Sutton,	Guardianship,	32665
1757	Nathaniel	Sutton,	Will,	32666
1851	Samuel	Oxford,	Guardianship,	32667
1875	Samuel	Philadelphia, Pa.,	Administration,	32668
1865	Simon	Sutton,	Will,	32669
1851	Stephen	Oxford,	Will,	32670
	HUTSON see HUDSON.			
1879	HUTT, William R.	Lancaster,	Administration,	32671
1872	HYATT, George W.	Leominster,	Administration,	32672
1813	HYDE, Abigail	Sutton,	Guardianship,	32673
1828	Abigail	Sutton,	Will,	32674
1880	Albert F.	Southborough,	Guardianship,	32675
1842	Alpheus	Sturbridge,	Administration,	32676
1797	Benjanin	Sturbridge,	Will,	32677
1869	Benjanin D.	Sturbridge,	Administration,	32678
1862	Beriah W.	Worcester,	Administration,	32679
1813	Daniel	Sutton,	Guardianship,	32680
1821	Daniel	Sutton,	Administration,	32681
1813	David	Sutton,	Guardianship,	32682
1880	Dwight	Brookfield,	Will,	32683
1813	Ebenezer	Sutton,	Administration,	32684
1854	Emily E.	Hubbardston,	Adoption, etc.,	32685
1830	Emory	Sturbridge,	Administration,	32686

YEAR.	NAME.	RESIDENCE.	NATURE.	CASE.
1860	HYDE, Eunice	Hubbardston,	Will,	32687
1837	Ezra	Winchendon,	Will,	32688
1834	Gardner	Leominster,	Guardianship,	32689
1871	George F.	Southbridge,	Administration,	32690
1867	Jemima	Upton,	Administration,	32691
1824	Job	Winchendon,	Will,	32692
1877	Job	Keene, N. H.,	Foreign Will,	32693
1866	Joel	Winchendon,	Will,	32694
1826	John	Winchendon,	Will,	32695
1870	John	Southbridge,	Administration,	32696
1838	Joshua	Sturbridge,	Will,	32697
1840	Joshua	Sturbridge,	Pension,	32698
1813	Lydia	Sutton,	Guardianship,	32699
1870	Mary E.	Worcester,	Adoption, etc.,	32700
1870	Reuben	Winchendon,	Will,	32701
1875	Sarah T.	Winchendon,	Will,	32702
1853	Warren	Worcester,	Change of Name,	32703
1851	William	Hubbardston,	Administration,	32704
1866	William DeW.	Winchendon,	Guardianship,	32705
1879	HYLAND, Annie	Northbridge,	Guardianship,	32706
1879	Jane	Northbridge,	Guardianship,	32707
1879	John	Northbridge,	Guardianship,	32708
1879	Mary	Northbridge,	Guardianship,	32709
1872	Peter	Hardwick,	Administration,	32710
1879	Stephen	Northbridge,	Guardianship,	32711
1875	William	Hardwick,	Pension,	32712
1866	HYMES, Mary L.	Petersham,	Adoption, etc.,	32713
1867	Minnietta M.	Petersham,	Adoption, etc.,	32714
1875	IDE, Adda M.	Ashford, Conn.,	Foreign Guard.,	32715
1875	Charles F.	Ashford, Conn.,	Foreign Guard.,	32716
1852	Emma H.	Unknown,	Change of Name,	32717
1867	Eunice	Uxbridge,	Administration,	32718
1864	George	Webster,	Will,	32719
1865	Lucretia A.	Webster,	Guardianship,	32720
1799	Lute	Medway,	Guardianship,	32721
1878	Mary	Charlton,	Administration,	32722
1862	Nellie F.	Milford,	Adoption, etc.,	32723
1864	Patience G.	Webster,	Administration,	32724
1838	Reuben,	Douglas,	Pension,	32725
1864	Sylvania	Webster,	Guardianship,	32726
1857	Timothy N.	Milford,	Change of Name,	32727
1831	ILSLEY, Robert	Portland, Me.,	Foreign Will,	32728
1828	INDIANS, Hassanamisco	Grafton,	Trustee,	32729
1861	INGERSOLL, Richard	Petersham,	Will,	32730
1744	INGOLSBY, Ebenezer	Boston,	Guardianship,	32731

Year.	Name.	Residence.	Nature.	Case.
1880	INGRAHAM, Louis H.	Oxford,	Guardianship,	32732
1878	Nellie L.	Worcester,	Guardianship,	32733
1866	Sarah E.	Oxford,	Administration,	32734
1880	Walter H.	Oxford, -	Guardianship,	32735
1880	William H.	Brookfield,	Will,	32736
1864	INMAN, Delia	Northbridge,	Administration,	32737
1778	Edward	Dudley,	Will,	32738
1836	Martin V. B.	Mendon,	Guardianship,	32739
1860	Mary	Burrillville, R. I.,	Administration,	32740
1836	Nathaniel	Mendon,	Will,	32741
1837	Nathaniel	Smithfield, R. I.,	Foreign Sale,	32742
1837	Willard A.	Smithfield, R. I.,	Foreign Sale,	32743
1799	IRELAND, Abraham	Lunenburg,	Administration,	32744
1869	IRONS, Edwin B.	Webster,	Guardianship,	32745
1869	Mowry B.	Webster,	Administration,	32746
1860	IVES, Jesse B.	North Brookfield,	Guardianship,	32747
1875	JACKMAN, Noah	Westborough,	Administration,	32748
1858	Sarah B.	Warren,	Change of Name,	32749
1853	William A.	Lancaster,	Administration,	32750
1876	JACKSON, Aaron B.	Gardner,	Administration,	32751
1826	Abel	Gardner,	Administration,	32752
1827	Abel	Gardner,	Guardianship,	32753
1875	Abraham B.	Sturbridge,	Administration,	32754
1877	Adaline S. P.	Worcester,	Administration,	32755
1827	Betsey	Gardner,	Administration,	32756
1841	Betsey T.	Gardner,	Guardianship,	32757
1869	Charles W.	North Brookfield,	Guardianship,	32758
1873	Chloe	Winchendon,	Guardianship,	32759
1756	Daniel	Rutland,	Administration,	32760
1790	David	Spencer,	Administration,	32761
1827	David F.	Gardner,	Guardianship,	32762
1844	Edward A.	Gardner,	Guardianship,	32763
1868	Edward A.	Petersham,	Administration,	32764
1814	Elisha	Gardner,	Will,	32765
1855	Elisha	Gardner,	Will,	32766
1863	Elisha S.	Gardner,	Will,	32767
1827	Elizabeth	Gardner,	Guardianship,	32768
1850	Elizabeth	Leicester,	Will,	32769
1816	Elvira	Westminster,	Guardianship,	32770
1862	Eri	Sutton,	Administration,	32771
1779	Eunice	Westminster,	Guardianship,	32772
1872	Gertrude A.	Southbridge,	Adoption, etc.,	32773
1872	Hannah	Worcester,	Administration,	32774
1827	Harriet	Gardner,	Guardianship,	32775
1873	Henry W.	Southbridge,	Administration,	32776

Year.	Name.	Residence.	Nature.	Case.
1852	JACKSON, Hittie E. M.	Westminster,	Will,	32777
1816	Horace	Westminster,	Guardianship,	32778
1779	Isaac	Westminster,	Guardianship,	32779
1844	Isaac	Gardner,	Administration,	32780
1865	James A.	Petersham,	Will,	32781
1871	Jane L.	Leominster,	Guardianship,	32782
1878	Jennie E.	Westborough,	Administration,	32783
1869	Jesse	Sutton,	Administration,	32784
1768	Jonathan	Rutland,	Will,	32785
1768	Jonathan	Rutland,	Guardianship,	32786
1776	Jonathan	Templeton,	Administration,	32787
1800	Jonathan	Templeton,	Administration,	32788
1837	Joseph	Templeton,	Administration,	32789
1863	Joseph M.	Petersham,	Will,	32790
1778	Josiah	Westminster,	Administration,	32791
1842	Josiah	Gardner,	Administration,	32792
1871	Josiah	Gardner,	Administration,	32793
1880	Josiah A.	Gardner,	Administration,	32794
1869	Laura E.	North Brookfield,	Guardianship,	32795
1865	Laura J.	Westminster,	Guardianship,	32796
1861	Levi	Worcester,	Administration,	32797
1865	Levi	Westminster,	Administration,	32798
1843	Lucy	Petersham,	Administration,	32799
1779	Lydia	Westminster,	Guardianship,	32800
1844	Maria	Gardner,	Guardianship,	32801
1865	Martha C.	Westminster,	Guardianship,	32802
1769	Mary	Rutland District,	Guardianship,	32803
1847	Mary E.	Southbridge,	Guardianship,	33804
1759	Mathew	Rutland District,	Guardianship,	32805
1829	Matthew	Leicester,	Will,	32806
1811	Nathan	Fitchburg,	Will,	32807
1862	Nathaniel	Lunenburg,	Will,	32808
1772	Oliver	Westborough,	Guardianship,	32809
1816	Oliver	Westminster,	Administration,	32810
1844	Rockwell	Gardner,	Guardianship,	32811
1808	Samuel	Hubbardston,	Guardianship,	32812
1779	Sarah	Westminster,	Guardianship,	32813
1847	Sarah	Southbridge,	Guardianship,	32814
1818	Sarah G. B.	Mendon,	Guardianship,	32815
1803	Sebes	Westminster,	Will,	32816
1838	Sophronia	Templeton,	Guardianship,	32817
1841	Susan E.	Gardner,	Guardianship,	32818
1827	Susanna	Gardner,	Guardianship,	32819
1807	William	Westminster,	Guardianship,	32820
1856	William	Templeton,	Administration,	32821

YEAR.	NAME.	RESIDENCE.	NATURE.	CASE.
1877	JACKSON, William H.	Lunenburg,	Will,	32822
1881	(No name given)	Paxton,	Adoption, etc.,	32823
1862	JACOBS, Adaline	Millbury,	Administration,	32824
1805	Adolphus	Uxbridge,	Guardianship,	32825
1859	Alvah G.	Royalston,	Administration,	32826
1860	Anna	Auburn,	Administration,	32827
1852	Anna M. R.	Millbury,	Guardianship,	32828
1830	Benjamin	Uxbridge,	Administration,	32829
1873	Charles	West Boylston,	Guardianship,	32830
1819	Comfort	Uxbridge,	Will,	32831
1870	Elmer S.	Webster,	Guardianship,	32832
1826	Enoch	Royalston,	Guardianship,	32833
1848	Eunice	Thompson, Conn.,	Foreign Sale,	32834
1867	Ezra	Thompson, Conn.,	Administration,	32835
1873	Frederick	West Boylston,	Guardianship,	32836
1870	George A.	Webster,	Administration,	32837
1848	Hannah	Thompson, Conn.,	Foreign Sale,	32838
1871	Harriet J.	Worcester,	Will,	32839
1826	Horrace	Royalston,	Guardianship,	32840
1826	Ira	Royalston,	Guardianship,	32841
1826	Isaac	Royalston,	Guardianship,	32842
1824	Israel	Ward,	Guardianship,	32843
1830	Israel	Ward,	Administration,	32843
1859	Israel	Millbury,	Administration,	32844
1808	James B.	Sturbridge,	Guardianship,	32845
1814	John	Ward,	Will,	32846
1841	John	Millbury,	Will,	32847
1739	Joseph	Woodstock,	Administration,	32848
1805	Joseph	Uxbridge,	Guardianship,	32849
1850	Joseph	Royalston,	Will,	32850
1870	Lillian B.	Webster,	Guardianship,	32851
1805	Martha	Uxbridge,	Guardianship,	32852
1866	Mary A.	Dudley,	Will,	32853
1826	Moses	Royalston,	Guardianship,	32854
1826	Philander S.	Royalston,	Guardianship,	32855
1825	Polly	Royalston,	Administration,	32856
1873	Selinda	West Boylston,	Guardianship,	32857
1824	Simeon	Royalston,	Administration,	32858
1826	Simeon	Royalston,	Guardianship,	32859
1824	Simon	Oakham,	Administration,	32860
1855	Simon T.	Worcester,	Administration,	32861
1826	Sumner	Royalston,	Guardianship,	32862
1845	Sumner	Auburn,	Guardianship,	32863
1819	Vernon	Royalston,	Guardianship,	32864
1801	Whitman	Royalston,	Will,	32865

Year.	Name.	Residence	Nature.	Case.
1805	JACOBS, William	Uxbridge,	Will,	32866
1805	William	Uxbridge,	Guardianship,	32867
1853	JAMES, Alonzo R.	Worcester,	Guardianship,	32868
1875	Corinna L.	Boylston,	Guardianship,	32869
1843	Eleazer	Worcester,	Administration,	32870
1871	George	New York, N. Y.,	Guardianship,	32871
1871	Henry	New York, N. Y.,	Guardianship,	32872
1875	Horace	Boylston,	Will,	32873
1871	Isabella	New York, N. Y.,	Guardianship,	32874
1782	John	Southborough,	Will,	32875
1870	John	Hardwick,	Administration,	32876
1758	Joseph	Lancaster,	Will,	32877
1776	Lydia	Lancaster,	Will,	32878
1853	Polly A.	Worcester,	Guardianship,	32879
1853	Remington K.	Worcester,	Will,	32880
1871	Reuben L.	Worcester,	Will,	32881
1844	Thomas	Lunenburg,	Administration,	32882
1872	JAMESON, Lydia	Hardwick,	Administration,	32883
1760	William	Rutland,	Administration,	32884
1852	JANES, Alanson	Worcester,	Administration,	32885
1869	Asa A.	Worcester,	Guardianship,	32886
1856	Dexter	Sturbridge,	Will,	32887
1869	Eddy	Worcester,	Guardianship,	32888
1869	George	Worcester,	Guardianship,	32889
1857	George A.	Sturbridge,	Guardianship,	32890
1869	Joseph	Worcester,	Administration,	32891
1875	Mary	Worcester,	Will,	32892
1857	Mary M.	Sturbridge,	Guardianship,	32893
1877	Timothy	Warren,	Will,	32894
1833	JAPSON, William	Lunenburg,	Pension,	32895
1853	JAQUES, Abiel	Worcester,	Administration,	32896
1872	George	Worcester,	Will,	32897
1862	John C.	Worcester,	Administration,	32898
1878	Sarah	Milford,	Adoption, etc.,	32899
1851	JAQUITH, Abby M.	Fitchburg,	Guardianship,	32900
1860	Abigail	Templeton,	Will,	32901
1851	Abraham	Fitchburg,	Will,	32902
1839	Francis F.	Fitchburg,	Guardianship,	32903
1837	Isaac P.	Gardner,	Guardianship,	32904
1839	John P.	Fitchburg,	Administration,	32905
1873	Lysander B.	Fitchburg,	Will,	32906
1881	Maria C.	Gardner,	Will,	32907
1866	Mary L.	Ashburnham,	Adoption, etc.,	32908
1869	Sarah	Uxbridge,	Will,	32909
1786	JARHA, Zippio	Dudley,	Administration,	32910

YEAR	NAME.	RESIDENCE.	NATURE.	CASE.
1876	JARVIE, Peter	Southbridge,	Will,	32911
1851	JASEPH, Albert B.	Boston,	Guardianship,	32912
	JEFFERDS, JEFFORD,			
	JEFFORDS AND JEFFERS,			
1877	Arlon J.	Northbridge,	Adoption, etc.,	32913
1877	Harriet L. L.	Milford,	Adoption, etc.,	32914
1760	John	Dudley,	Guardianship,	32915
1802	Mary	Dudley,	Will,	32916
1797	Nathan	Dudley,	Will,	32917
	JEFFERSON, JEPHERSON AND			
	JEFFERSON,			
1798	Aaron	Douglas,	Guardianship,	32918
1876	Aaron	Douglas,	Administration,	32919
1841	Adolphus	Uxbridge,	Administration,	32920
1845	Alice M.	Douglas,	Guardianship,	32921
1845	Caroline M.	Douglas,	Guardianship,	32922
1858	Deborah	Douglas,	Administration,	32923
1858	Deborah	Douglas,	Pension,	32924
1767	Ezekiel	Douglas,	Guardianship,	32925
1841	George	Uxbridge,	Guardianship,	32926
1845	Jedediah	Douglas,	Pension,	32927
1760	John	Douglas,	Administration,	32928
1798	John	Uxbridge,	Guardianship,	32929
1849	John	Uxbridge,	Pension,	32930
1878	John	West Boylston,	Will,	32931
1827	Martha	Douglas,	Guardianship,	32932
1841	Martin V. B.	Uxbridge,	Guardianship,	32933
1863	Mary	Uxbridge,	Administration,	32934
1863	Mary	Uxbridge,	Pension,	32935
1841	Mary A.	Uxbridge,	Guardianship,	32936
1845	Nelson	Douglas,	Guardianship,	32937
1859	Otis	Douglas,	Will,	32938
1843	Pamelia	Uxbridge,	Administration,	32939
1863	Peter	Milford,	Administration,	32940
1808	Reuben	Oxford,	Administration,	32941
1774	Reubin	Douglas,	Guardianship,	32942
1868	Royal	Uxbridge,	Administration,	32943
1864	Royal L.	San Francisco, Cal.,	Administration,	32944
1844	Sarah M.	Douglas,	Guardianship,	32945
1844	Waterman	Douglas,	Administration,	32946
1867	Welcome	Uxbridge,	Administration,	32947
1802	William	Douglas,	Will,	32948
1857	William	Douglas,	Administration,	32949
1844	William A.	Douglas,	Guardianship,	32950
1857	Willis	Douglas,	Administration,	32951

YEAR.	NAME.	RESIDENCE.	NATURE.	CASE.
1817	JEFFREY, George C.	Northborough,	Guardianship,	32952
1817	Nancy T.	Northborough,	Guardianship,	32953
1817	Rebecca J.	Northborough,	Guardianship,	32954
1817	Stephen W.	Northborough,	Guardianship,	32955
1879	JEFTS, Anna L.	Fitchburg,	Guardianship,	32956
1879	Bessie	Fitchburg,	Guardianship,	32957
1879	Ruth M.	Fitchburg,	Guardianship,	32958
	JENCKES see JENKS.			
1874	JENICE, Frank	Worcester,	Adoption, etc.,	32959
1818	JENKINS, Abigail	Barre,	Guardianship,	32960
1824	Albert	Hardwick,	Guardianship,	32961
1824	Atwood B.	Hardwick,	Guardianship,	32962
1869	Aura	Barre,	Administration,	32963
1788	Benjamin	Barre,	Will,	32964
1808	Benjamin	Barre,	Will,	32965
1814	Benjamin	Hardwick,	Administration,	32966
1824	Benjamin F.	Hardwick,	Guardianship,	32967
1785	Hannah	Barre,	Guardianship,	32968
1841	Hannah	Barre,	Will,	32969
1824	Jason	Hardwick,	Guardianship,	32970
1878	Joseph H.	Worcester,	Administration,	32971
1875	Louisa W.	Barre,	Administration,	32972
1785	Mary	Barre,	Guardianship,	32973
1881	Nellie M.	Westborough,	Guardianship,	32974
1881	Priscilla	Barre,	Will,	32975
1785	Robert	Barre,	Guardianship,	32976
1785	Sarah	Barre,	Guardianship,	32977
1821	Southworth	Barre,	Will,	32978
1881	Susan M.	Westborough,	Administration,	32979
1817	Timothy	Barre,	Will,	32980
1818	Timothy	Barre,	Guardianship,	32981
	JENKS, JENCKS, JENCKES AND JINKS,			
1843	Abby	Brookfield,	Guardianship,	32982
1872	Addie L.	Pawtucket, R. I.,	Guardianship,	32983
1843	Alfred H.	Brookfield,	Administration,	32984
1865	Ann E.	Grafton,	Will,	32985
1793	Benjamin	Brookfield,	Guardianship,	32986
1858	Charles	North Brookfield,	Administration,	32987
1861	Charles B.	Grafton,	Administration,	32988
1843	Charles II.	Brookfield,	Guardianship,	32989
1863	Charles H.	Worcester,	Administration,	32990
1793	Daniel	Brookfield,	Guardianship,	32991
1877	Deborah	North Brookfield,	Will,	32992
1823	Edward	Spencer,	Guardianship,	32993

(759)

JENKS, JENCKS, JENCKES
AND JINKS,

YEAR.	NAME.	RESIDENCE.	NATURE.	CASE.
1793	Eli	Brookfield,	Guardianship,	32994
1851	Eli	North Brookfield,	Will,	32995
1833	Ezra	Worcester,	Guardianship,	32996
1866	Flora A.	Oakham,	Guardianship,	32997
1846	Francis E.	North Brookfield,	Guardianship,	32998
1781	Freelove	Brookfield,	Guardianship,	32999
1823	George	Spencer,	Guardianship,	33000
1790	Gideon	Brookfield,	Administration,	33001
1824	Gideon B.	Brookfield,	Guardianship,	33002
1877	Gideon B.	North Brookfield,	Administration,	33003
1845	Hannah	Mendon,	Will,	33004
1849	Hannah	Spencer,	Guardianship,	33005
1872	Hattie M.	Pawtucket, R. I.,	Guardianship,	33006
1843	Helen	Brookfield,	Guardianship,	33007
1866	Henry C.	Oakham,	Guardianship,	33008
1818	Isaac	Spencer,	Will,	33009
1879	Jennette E.	Westborough,	Guardianship,	33010
1823	John	Spencer,	Guardianship,	33011
1823	John	Spencer,	Administration,	33012
1781	Jonathan	Brookfield,	Will,	33013
1793	Jonathan	Brookfield,	Guardianship,	33014
1864	Joseph E.	Blackstone,	Guardianship,	33015
1843	Julia A.	Brookfield,	Guardianship,	33016
1865	J. Henry	Keene, N. H.,	Administration,	33017
1872	Latimer B.	Pawtucket, R. I.,	Guardianship,	33018
1846	Lavinia E.	North Brookfield,	Guardianship,	33019
1843	Leroy S.	Brookfield,	Guardianship,	33020
1793	Lydia	Brookfield,	Guardianship,	33021
1781	Marcy	Brookfield,	Guardianship,	33022
1793	Mary	Brookfield,	Guardianship,	33023
1843	Mary	Brookfield,	Guardianship,	33024
1817	Molly	Lancaster,	Will,	33025
1859	Nancy B.	North Brookfield,	Will,	33026
1837	Nicholas	North Brookfield,	Will,	33027
1823	Olive	Spencer,	Guardianship,	33028
1833	Olive D.	Worcester,	Guardianship,	33029
1878	Olive W.	Worcester,	Guardianship,	33030
1864	Patty	North Brookfield,	Administration,	33031
1788	Rachel	Spencer,	Will,	33032
1859	Rebecca	Burrillville, R. I.,	Administration,	33033
1843	Sarah J.	Brookfield,	Guardianship,	33034
1793	Thankfull	Brookfield,	Guardianship,	33035
1793	William	Brookfield,	Guardianship,	33036

	JENKS, JENCKS, JENCKES AND JINKS,			
1843	William G.	Brookfield,	Guardianship,	33037
1876	William N.	Worcester,	Administration,	33038
1831	JENNEY, Abigail	Douglas,	Will,	33039
1874	Chiron	Hardwick,	Administration,	33040
1796	John	Hardwick,	Will,	33041
1814	John	Hardwick,	Will,	33042
1836	John	Northborough,	Administration,	33043
1870	Jonathan	Douglas,	Will,	33044
1783	Thomas	New Braintree,	Will,	33045
	JENNINGS AND JENINGS,			
1797	Benjamin	Brookfield,	Administration,	33046
1836	Benjamin	Brookfield,	Administration,	33047
1814	Charles	Brookfield,	Guardianship,	33048
1836	Chloe	Brookfield,	Will,	33049
1770	Ebenezer	Brookfield,	Administration,	33050
1876	George B.	Leominster,	Administration,	33051
1819	Gershom	Brookfield,	Administration,	33052
1810	Hannah	Brookfield,	Administration,	33053
1813	Joel	Brookfield,	Will,	33054
1798	John, Jr.	Brookfield,	Administration,	33055
1754	Jonathan	Brookfield,	Will,	33056
1839	Jonathan	Brookfield,	Miscellaneous,	33057
1746	Joseph, Jr.	Brookfield,	Administration,	33058
1842	Mary	Brookfield,	Guardianship,	33059
1850	Mary	Warren,	Pension,	33060
1819	Moses	Brookfield,	Administration,	33061
1865	Polly B.	Warren,	Will,	33062
1760	Ruth	Brookfield,	Administration,	33063
1764	Solomon	Western,	Guardianship,	33064
1746	Stephen	Brookfield,	Administration,	33065
1769	Stephen	Brookfield,	Administration,	33066
1753	Thankfull	Brookfield,	Guardianship,	33067
1879	Wealthy	Webster,	Administration,	33068
	JENNISON AND JENISON,			
1761	Abigail	Sutton,	Guardianship,	33069
1859	Abigail L.	Uxbridge,	Will,	33070
1863	Abigail R.	Templeton,	Guardianship,	33071
1871	Alice	Philadelphia, Pa.,	Guardianship,	33072
1783	Betty	Worcester,	Guardianship,	33073
1835	Charles	Southborough,	Guardianship,	33074
1834	Dana	Southborough,	Guardianship,	33075
1835	Dana	Southborough,	Administration,	33075
1839	Daniel	Auburn,	Will,	33076

Year.	Name.	Residence.	Nature.	Case.
	JENNISON and JENISON,			
1852	Dolly	Hubbardston,	Will,	33077
1879	Edwin	Charlton,	Will,	33078
1760	Elias	Sutton,	Administration,	33079
1761	Elias	Sutton,	Guardianship,	33080
1757	Elizabeth	Worcester,	Will,	33081
1784	Faith	Worcester,	Administration,	33082
1813	Gardner	Ward,	Guardianship,	33083
1830	George	Southborough,	Guardianship,	33084
1841	George	Worcester,	Administration,	33085
1842	George	Worcester,	Guardianship,	33086
1835	George H.	Southborough,	Guardianship,	33087
1841	Hannah J.	Grafton,	Guardianship,	33088
1835	Harriet	Southborough,	Guardianship,	33089
1838	Harriet W.	Worcester,	Guardianship,	33090
1769	Hopestill	Rutland,	Guardianship,	33091
1782	Israel	Worcester,	Administration,	33092
1872	James	Southbridge,	Administration,	33093
1753	John	Lunenburg,	Administration,	33094
1753	John	Lunenburg,	Guardianship,	33095
1828	John	Southborough,	Administration,	33096
1835	John	Phillipston,	Will,	33097
1753	Jonathan	Lunenburg,	Guardianship,	33098
1835	Joseph	Southborough,	Guardianship,	33099
1835	Joseph	Phillipston,	Guardianship,	33100
1864	Joseph	Southborough,	Will,	33101
1867	Joseph	Auburn,	Will,	33102
1849	Joshua	Templeton,	Administration,	33103
1841	Laura E.	Grafton,	Guardianship,	33104
1841	Levi	Grafton,	Administration,	33105
1863	Lucia N.	Templeton,	Guardianship,	33106
1873	Maria W.	Southbridge,	Administration,	33107
1842	Martha S.	Worcester,	Guardianship,	33108
1753	Mary	Lunenburg,	Guardianship,	33109
1761	Mary	Sutton,	Guardianship,	33110
1854	Mary	Auburn,	Will,	33111
1841	Mary A.	Oxford,	Guardianship,	33112
1876	Mary C.	Worcester,	Administration,	33113
1835	Mary E.	Southborough,	Guardianship,	33114
1867	Mary G.	Worcester,	Will,	33115
1842	Mary J.	Worcester,	Guardianship,	33116
1872	Maverick	Worcester,	Administration,	33117
1841	Miranda C.	Grafton,	Administration,	33118
1841	Miranda C.	Grafton,	Guardianship,	33119
1769	Nathaniel	Rutland,	Will,	33120

Year.	Name.	Residence.	Nature.	Case.
	JENNISON and JENISON,			
1803	Nathaniel	Barre,	Administration,	33121
1761	Olive	Sutton,	Guardianship,	33122
1878	Persis Ç.	Windham, Vt.,	Administration,	33123
1753	Rebecca	Lunenburg,	Guardianship,	33124
1761	Robert	Sutton,	Guardianship,	33125
1849	Sally	Sutton,	Will,	33126
1864	Sally, etc.	Worcester,	Administration,	33127
1874	Sally	Southborough,	Will,	33128
1790	Samuel	Oxford,	Administration,	33129
1815	Samuel	Worcester,	Will,	33130
1834	Samuel	Southborough,	Administration,	33131
1860	Samuel	Worcester,	Will,	33132
1830	Samuel, Jr.	Southborough,	Administration,	33133
1863	Samuel S.	Templeton,	Guardianship,	33134
1863	Samuel W.	Templeton,	Administration,	33135
1864	Sarah F.	Worcester,	Administration,	33136
1835	Silas	Southborough,	Guardianship,	33137
1841	Susan R.	Grafton,	Guardianship,	33138
1830	Sylvester	Southborough,	Will,	33139
1741	William	Worcester,	Administration,	33140
1761	William	Sutton,	Guardianship,	33141
1798	William	Brookfield,	Will,	33142
1835	William	Southborough,	Guardianship,	33143
1866	William	Worcester,	Will,	33144
1838	William C.	Worcester,	Guardianship,	33145
1758	JENO, Phillip	Lancaster,	Will,	33146
	JERAULD, JERAULT see GERALD.			
1864	JEROME, Elizabeth	Barre,	Administration,	33147
1871	JETTIM, Eliza, etc.	Worcester,	Guardianship,	33148
1873	Eliza, etc.	Worcester,	Will,	33148
	JEWELL and JEWIL,			
1778	Archibald	Dudley,	Administration,	33149
1856	Charles H.	Oakham,	Guardianship,	33150
1826	Esther	Dudley,	Will,	33151
1868	Frank D.	Worcester,	Guardianship,	33152
1868	Harvey H.	Worcester,	Guardianship,	33153
1832	Moses	Dudley,	Will,	33154
1781	Nathaniel	Dudley,	Will,	33155
1866	Sarah R.	Lancaster,	Administration,	33156
1854	Walter	Dudley,	Administration,	33157
1856	William C.	Oakham,	Guardianship,	33158
1854	William H.	Oakham,	Administration,	33159
1861	Zilpha	Dudley,	Administration,	33160

YEAR.	NAME.	RESIDENCE.	NATURE.	CASE.
	JEWELL AND JEWIL,			
1873	Zoradia W.	Worcester,	Administration,	33161
1872	JEWETT, Adaline M.	Leominster,	Will,	33162
1792	Amos	Sterling,	Will,	33163
1800	Amos	Sterling,	Will,	33164
1819	Anna	Sterling,	Administration,	33165
1874	Anna R.	Sterling,	Will,	33166
1802	Benjamin	Bolton,	Guardianship,	33167
1873	Benjamin	Sterling,	Guardianship,	33168
1873	Benjamin	Sterling,	Administration,	33168
1825	Caroline	Sterling,	Guardianship,	33169
1761	Daniel	Lunenburg,	Guardianship,	33170
1762	David	Lancaster,	Will,	33171
1767	David	Unknown,	Sale Real Estate,	33172
1825	David	Sterling,	Administration,	33173
1825	David, Jr.	Sterling,	Administration,	33174
1870	Ebenezer	Worcester,	Administration,	33175
1778	Elizabeth	Lancaster,	Guardianship,	33176
1858	Ella G.	Boxborough,	Adoption, etc.,	33177
1767	Enoch	Unknown,	Sale Real Estate,	33178
1784	Esther	Sterling,	Will,	33179
1825	Esther	Sterling,	Guardianship,	33180
1866	Esther	Worcester,	Administration,	33181
1868	Esther C.	Dudley,	Administration,	33182
1870	Forson Z.	Leominster,	Administration,	33183
1849	Hannah	Berlin,	Will,	33184
1851	Henry M.	Berlin,	Guardianship,	33185
1869	Henry M.	Newbury, Vt.	Guardianship,	33186
1869	Henry P.	Sterling,	Guardianship,	33187
1872	Henry P.	Bolton,	Administration,	33188
1829	Jesse	Berlin,	Will,	33189
1850	Jesse	Berlin,	Administration,	33190
1802	John	Bolton,	Administration,	33191
1868	John	Dudley,	Will,	33192
1855	Jonathan	Bolton,	Administration,	33193
1846	Joseph	Ashburnham,	Will,	33194
1846	Joseph	Ashburnham,	Pension,	33195
1875	Joshua A.	Sterling,	Administration,	33196
1834	Joshua C.	Berlin,	Guardianship,	33197
1851	Joshua C.	Clinton,	Administration,	33198
1872	Martha G.	Bolton,	Guardianship,	33199
1868	Mary A. B.	Grafton,	Will,	33200
1855	Mary H.	Sterling,	Will,	33201
1855	Merrick	Sterling,	Administration,	33202
1869	Milo A.	Newbury, Vt.,	Guardianship,	33203
1863	Mira	Berlin,	Will,	33204

YEAR.	NAME.	RESIDENCE.	NATURE.	CASE.
1767	JEWETT, Moses	Unknown,	Sale Real Estate,	33205
1878	Nathan B.	Hubbardston,	Administration,	33206
1860	Olive	Sterling,	Administration,	33207
1829	Oliver	Bolton,	Administration,	33208
1876	Pamelia	San Francisco, Cal.,	Partition,	33209
1868	Phebe	Bolton,	Administration,	33210
1838	Ruth	Sterling,	Administration,	33211
1825	Ruth S.	Sterling,	Guardianship,	33212
1776	Samuel	Princeton,	Administration,	33213
1778	Samuel	Lancaster,	Guardianship,	33214
1855	Samuel	Sterling,	Will,	33215
1767	Sarah	Winchendon,	Guardianship,	33216
1830	Sarah	Bolton,	Administration,	33217
1852	Sarah	Ashburnham,	Will,	33218
1856	Sarah W.	Sterling,	Administration,	33219
1806	Solomon	Sterling,	Will,	33220
1851	Sophia	Oxford,	Guardianship,	33221
1862	Stephen	Fitchburg,	Administration,	33222
1825	Susan	Sterling,	Guardianship,	33223
1758	Thomas	Lunenburg,	Will,	33224
1872	Walter S.	Bolton,	Guardianship,	33225
1872	Zenas	Princeton,	Administration,	33226
1844	JILLSON, George W.	Westminster,	Administration,	33227
1876	Gracie M.	Worcester,	Guardianship,	33228
1881	Harvey D.	Fitchburg,	Administration,	33229
1868	Uriah	Douglas,	Will,	33230
	JINKS see JENKS.			
1842	JITTIM, Charles	Worcester,	Administration,	33231
1871	Eliza, etc.	Worcester,	Guardianship,	33232
1873	Eliza, etc.	Worcester,	Will,	33232
1819	JOHNS, Samuel	Uxbridge,	Guardianship,	33233
1813	JOHNSON, Aaron	Hardwick,	Administration,	33234
1841	Aaron	Dana,	Administration,	33235
1852	Aaron	Dana,	Administration,	33236
1859	Abby B.	Millbury,	Guardianship,	33237
1863	Abiathar	Oakham,	Administration,	33238
1777	Abigail	Hardwick,	Guardianship,	33239
1784	Abigail	Leominster,	Administration,	33240
1792	Abigail	Southborough,	Administration,	33241
1815	Abijah	Western,	Guardianship,	33242
1841	Abner P.	Barre,	Administration,	33243
1868	Ada	Barre,	Guardianship,	33244
1825	Adaline	Worcester,	Guardianship,	33245
1837	Adaline B.	Oakham,	Guardianship,	33246
1845	Adelbert W.	Leominster,	Guardianship,	33247
1878	Albert A.	Milford,	Guardianship,	33248

YEAR.	NAME.	RESIDENCE.	NATURE.	CASE.
1849	JOHNSON, Albert P.	Westminster,	Guardianship,	33249
1853	Aleander S.	Worcester,	Administration,	33250
1858	Alfred	Athol,	Guardianship,	33251
1847	Alfred E.	Worcester,	Administration,	33252
1873	Alfred F.	Worcester,	Administration,	33253
1818	Alice	Hardwick,	Guardianship,	33254
1875	Alice M.	Hardwick,	Guardianship,	33255
1842	Alonzo W.	Charlton,	Guardianship,	33256
1809	Alvin	Milford,	Guardianship,	33257
1863	Alvin	Milford,	Will,	33258
1867	Amelia	Berlin,	Will,	33259
1825	Amos	Berlin,	Will,	33260
1825	Amos	Worcester,	Administration,	33261
1840	Amos	Petersham,	Administration,	33262
1827	Amos D.	Petersham,	Guardianship,	33263
1871	Amos D.	Petersham,	Administration,	33264
1872	Amy C. B.	Fitchburg,	Guardianship,	33265
1848	Anna	Southborough,	Will,	33266
1874	Anna	Worcester,	Will,	33267
1834	Anna H.	Grafton,	Will,	33268
1779	Anne	Sturbridge,	Guardianship,	33269
1880	Annie L.	Clinton,	Guardianship,	33270
1851	Apollos	Dana,	Will,	33271
1874	Arthur M.	Webster,	Guardianship,	33272
1821	Asa	Leominster,	Administration,	33273
1879	Asa	Petersham,	Administration,	33274
1831	Asa T.	Worcester,	Guardianship,	33275
1847	Asa T.	Worcester,	Guardianship,	33276
1847	Asa T.	Worcester,	Administration,	33276
1860	Asahel	Lawrence,	Will,	33277
1797	Asenath	Gerry,	Guardianship,	33278
1879	Bathsheba	Worcester,	Will,	33279
1805	Baxter	Mendon,	Administration,	33280
1874	Belinda H.	Leominster,	Administration,	33281
1771	Benjamin	Spencer,	Will,	33282
1788	Benjamin	Westborough,	Guardianship,	33283
1823	Benjamin	Lunenburg,	Will,	33284
1841	Benjamin	Lunenburg,	Administration,	33285
1856	Benjamin S.	Leominster,	Will,	33286
1778	Betsey	Harvard,	Guardianship,	33287
1790	Betsey	Grafton,	Guardianship,	33288
1831	Beulah	Leominster,	Administration,	33289
1766	Caleb	Shrewsbury,	Will,	33290
1845	Calista M.	Worcester,	Guardianship,	33291
1853	Carew	Sutton,	Guardianship,	33292

Year.	Name.	Residence.	Nature.	Case.
1870	JOHNSON, Caroline A.	Sturbridge,	Will,	33293
1808	Catharine	Shrewsbury,	Guardianship,	33294
1838	Catharine	Shrewsbury,	Will,	33295
1850	Catharine	Sturbridge,	Guardianship,	33296
1860	Catharine	Southborough,	Will,	33297
1877	Catherine	Milford,	Administration,	33298
1829	Charles	Leominster,	Guardianship,	33299
1845	Charles	Worcester,	Guardianship,	33300
1852	Charles	Auburn,	Guardianship,	33301
1864	Charles	Northborough,	Will,	33302
1872	Charles	Fitchburg,	Administration,	33303
1875	Charles A.	Worcester,	Guardianship,	33304
1878	Charles E.	Milford,	Guardianship,	33305
1872	Charles F. O.	Fitchburg,	Guardianship,	33306
1866	Charles H.	Barre,	Guardianship,	33307
1797	Charlotte	Gerry,	Guardianship,	33308
1828	Charlotte A.	Berlin,	Guardianship,	33309
1848	Chester	Dana,	Administration,	33310
1878	Clara A.	Milford,	Guardianship,	33311
1864	Clarissa	Warren,	Will,	33312
1824	Clark	Worcester,	Administration,	33313
1854	Cornelius	Grafton,	Guardianship,	33314
1870	Cornelius W.	Southborough,	Administration,	33315
1862	Cynthia	Worcester,	Will,	33316
1872	C. Hamilton	Fitchburg,	Guardianship,	33317
1853	Danforth	Sutton,	Guardianship,	33318
1763	Daniel	Shrewsbury,	Will,	33319
1777	Daniel	Harvard,	Administration,	33320
1802	Daniel	Worcester,	Administration,	33321
1806	Daniel	Southborough,	Will,	33322
1812	Daniel	Shrewsbury,	Will,	33323
1815	Daniel	Petersham,	Administration,	33324
1823	Daniel	Shrewsbury,	Administration,	33325
1825	Daniel	Worcester,	Guardianship,	33326
1847	Daniel	Athol,	Guardianship,	33327
1734	David	Lancaster,	Guardianship,	33328
1756	David	Southborough,	Administration,	33329
1797	David	Gerry,	Guardianship,	33330
1799	David	Leominster,	Will,	33331
1820	David	Shrewsbury,	Will,	33332
1866	David H.	Barre,	Guardianship,	33333
1854	David W.	Worcester,	Guardianship,	33334
1871	David W.	Elmira, N. Y.,	Guardianship,	33335
1869	Debby	Ashburnham,	Will,	33336
1861	Dexter D.	Southbridge,	Guardianship,	33337

Year.	Name.	Residence.	Nature.	Case.
1878	JOHNSON, Dexter W.	Leominster,	Administration,	33338
1858	Dianna M. L.	Upton,	Adoption, etc.,	33339
1752	Dillington	Southborough,	Guardianship,	33340
1745	Dole	Harvard,	Administration,	33341
1748	Dole	Harvard,	Guardianship,	33342
1865	Dolly	Leominster,	Will,	33343
1751	Dorothy	Shrewsbury,	Administration,	33344
1732	Eastor	Woodstock,	Guardianship,	33345
1767	Ebenezer	Southborough,	Administration,	33346
1784	Ebenezer	Charlton,	Guardianship,	33347
1836	Ebenezer	Barre,	Will,	33348
1788	Ebenezer B.	Westborough,	Guardianship,	33349
1784	Edward	Berlin,	Will,	33350
1827	Edward	Berlin,	Administration,	33351
1828	Edward	Sterling,	Administration,	33352
1869	Edward G.	Warren,	Guardianship,	33353
1865	Edward J. K.	Berlin,	Guardianship,	33354
1865	Edward L.	Worcester,	Guardianship,	33355
1854	Edward S.	Southborough,	Guardianship,	33356
1791	Eleazer	Berlin,	Will,	33357
1810	Eleazer	Milford,	Guardianship,	33358
1817	Eleazer	West Boylston,	Administration,	33359
1825	Eli	Worcester,	Guardianship,	33360
1860	Eli	Warren,	Administration,	33361
1767	Elijah	Southborough,	Guardianship,	33362
1832	Elisha	Southborough,	Will,	33363
1854	Elisha	Southborough,	Administration,	33364
1853	Elisha S.	Sutton,	Guardianship,	33365
1862	Eliza A.	Dana,	Administration,	33366
1793	Elizabeth	Shrewsbury,	Administration,	33367
1808	Elizabeth	Berlin,	Guardianship,	33368
1812	Elizabeth	Leominster,	Guardianship,	33369
1827	Elizabeth	Phillipston,	Guardianship,	33370
1831	Elizabeth	Phillipston,	Administration,	33371
1854	Elizabeth L.	Worcester,	Guardianship,	33372
1871	Ella	Worcester,	Guardianship,	33373
1854	Ellen A.	Southborough,	Guardianship,	33374
1859	Ellen E.	Millbury,	Guardianship,	33375
1845	Elvena E.	Leominster,	Guardianship,	33376
1875	Elvina M.	Worcester,	Guardianship,	33377
1838	Emily L.	Shrewsbury,	Guardianship,	33378
1862	Emma J.	Woodstock, Conn.,	Administration,	33379
1778	Ephraim	Leominster,	Guardianship,	33380
1864	Ephraim	Leominster,	Will,	33381
1876	Ephraim	Leominster,	Administration,	33382

YEAR.	NAME.	RESIDENCE.	NATURE.	CASE.
1869	JOHNSON, Ernest F.	Brookfield,	Guardianship,	33383
1875	Erving B.	Worcester,	Guardianship,	33384
1778	Esther	Leominster,	Guardianship,	33385
1779	Esther	Sturbridge,	Guardianship,	33386
1790	Esther	Grafton,	Guardianship,	33387
1809	Esther	Shrewsbury,	Administration,	33388
1876	Esther M.	Worcester,	Administration,	33389
1779	Eunice	Sturbridge,	Guardianship,	33390
1808	Eunice	Worcester,	Administration,	33391
1845	Evelina C.	Leominster,	Guardianship,	33392
1818	Fanny	Leominster,	Guardianship,	33393
1848	Fanny C.	Hardwick,	Guardianship,	33394
1862	Fanny E.	Dana,	Guardianship,	33395
1877	Flora A.	Worcester,	Change of Name,	33396
1845	Frederic	Leominster,	Administration,	33397
1859	Frederic A.	Millbury,	Guardianship,	33398
1858	Frederick	Worcester,	Administration,	33399
1868	Frederick	Barre,	Guardianship,	33400
1868	Frederick N.	Athol,	Guardianship,	33401
1874	Frederick W.	Webster,	Guardianship,	33402
1863	George A.	Upton,	Guardianship,	33403
1870	George A.	Fitchburg,	Administration,	33404
1841	George E.	Leominster,	Guardianship,	33405
1851	George E.	Berlin,	Guardianship,	33406
1865	George R.	Brookfield,	Administration,	33407
1859	George W.	Bolton,	Adoption, etc.,	33408
1871	George W.	Elmira, N. Y.,	Guardianship,	33409
1839	Gilman	Templeton,	Administration,	33410
1869	Grace V.	Brookfield,	Guardianship,	33411
1732	Hannah	Woodstock,	Guardianship,	33412
1748	Hannah	Harvard,	Guardianship,	33413
1850	Hannah	Sturbridge,	Guardianship,	33414
1831	Hannah B.	Worcester,	Guardianship,	33415
1845	Harriet	Rockford, Ill.,	Foreign Sale,	33416
1866	Harriet F.	Milford,	Adoption, etc.,	33417
1862	Harriet J.	Worcester,	Administration,	33418
1865	Harriet L.	Berlin,	Guardianship,	33419
1859	Harriet W.	Millbury,	Guardianship,	33420
1874	Helen M.	Ashburnham,	Administration,	33421
1852	Henrietta H.	Douglas,	Will,	33422
1811	Henry	Brookfield,	Guardianship,	33423
1818	Henry	Leominster,	Guardianship,	33424
1847	Henry	Athol,	Administration,	33425
1859	Henry	Millbury,	Administration,	33426
1869	Henry	Leominster,	Administration,	33427

YEAR.	NAME.	RESIDENCE.	NATURE.	CASE.
1880	JOHNSON, Henry	New Braintree,	Administration,	33428
1864	Henry A.	Lancaster,	Will,	33429
1844	Henry B.	Worcester,	Guardianship,	33430
1872	Henry J.	Woodstock, Conn.,	Administration,	33431
1852	Hervey B.	Auburn,	Guardianship,	33432
1742	Hezekiah	Woodstock,	Guardianship,	33433
1852	Hiram	Auburn,	Guardianship,	33434
1851	Huldah	Leominster,	Administration,	33435
1854	Ida L.	Dana,	Guardianship,	33436
1779	Isaac	Sturbridge,	Administration,	33437
1779	Isaac	Sturbridge,	Guardianship,	33438
1801	Isaac	Southborough,	Will,	33439
1769	Isaac, Jr.	Southborough,	Will,	33440
1837	Isaac T.	Upton,	Guardianship,	33441
1783	Israel	Southborough,	Guardianship,	33442
1827	Jaazaniah M. K.	Petersham,	Guardianship,	33443
1739	Jacob	Westborough,	Administration,	33444
1817	Jacob	Winchendon,	Administration,	33445
1869	Jacob N.	Brookfield,	Administration,	33446
1816	James	Sturbridge,	Will,	33447
1834	James	Templeton,	Will,	33448
1853	James	Dana,	Administration,	33449
1854	James	Templeton,	Guardianship,	33450
1860	James	Templeton,	Will,	33451
1862	James	Sturbridge,	Will,	33452
1871	James	Worcester,	Guardianship,	33453
1877	James	Webster,	Will,	33454
1850	James A.	Sturbridge,	Guardianship,	83455
1814	James D.	Sturbridge,	Guardianship,	33456
1880	James W.	Leominster,	Administration,	33457
1779	Jemima	Sturbridge,	Guardianship,	33458
1852	Jerome	Auburn,	Guardianship,	33459
1869	Jessie A.	Warren,	Guardianship,	33460
1778	Joanna	Harvard,	Guardianship,	33461
1813	Joel	Hardwick,	Will,	33462
1819	Joel	Dana,	Pension,	33463
1757	John	Worcester,	Administration,	33464
1762	John	Rutland,	Guardianship,	33465
1805	John	Western,	Administration,	33466
1807	John	Worcester,	Administration,	33467
1808	John	Shrewsbury,	Guardianship,	33468
1831	John	Shrewsbury,	Administration,	33469
1833	John	Southborough,	Will,	33470
1737	John, Jr.	Lancaster,	Administration,	33471
1866	John E.	Barre,	Guardianship,	33472

YEAR.	NAME.	RESIDENCE.	NATURE.	CASE.
1828	JOHNSON, John N. P.	Berlin,	Guardianship,	33473
1865	John N. P.	Berlin,	Administration,	33474
1838	John W.	Shrewsbury,	Guardianship,	33475
1756	Jonas	Leominster,	Administration,	33476
1769	Jonas	Southborough,	Guardianship,	33477
1809	Jonas	Sterling,	Will,	33478
1823	Jonas	Leominster,	Administration,	33479
1831	Jonas	Worcester,	Will,	33480
1812	Jonas, Jr.	Leominster,	Guardianship,	33481
1831	Jonas D.	Worcester,	Guardianship,	33482
1848	Jonas D.	Worcester,	Will,	33483
1740	Jonathan	Southborough,	Administration,	33484
1764	Jonathan	Worcester,	Guardianship,	33485
1776	Jonathan	Sturbridge,	Administration,	33486
1815	Jonathan	Petersham,	Administration,	33487
1779	Joseph	Southborough,	Guardianship,	33488
1815	Joseph	Leominster,	Administration,	33489
1817	Joseph	Milford,	Guardianship,	33490
1826	Joseph	Milford,	Administration,	33490
1830	Joseph	Southborough,	Administration,	33491
1848	Joseph	Leominster,	Administration,	33492
1859	Josephine	Worcester,	Guardianship,	33493
1784	Joshua	Berlin,	Administration,	33494
1827	Joshua	Dana,	Administration,	33495
1832	Joshua	Berlin,	Will,	33496
1827	Joshua, Jr.	Petersham,	Administration,	33497
1825	Joshua J.	Berlin,	Guardianship,	33498
1836	Josiah	Leominster,	Will,	33499
1840	Josiah	Fitchburg,	Guardianship,	33500
1864	Josiah	Southborough,	Will,	33501
1815	Jotham	Leominster,	Administration,	33502
1854	Julia A.	Worcester,	Guardianship,	33503
1869	J. Arthur	Sturbridge,	Administration,	33504
1768	Katharine	Southborough,	Guardianship,	33505
1810	Keziah	Medfield,	Guardianship,	33506
1825	Laban	Oakham,	Administration,	33507
1818	Laura	Leominster,	Guardianship,	33508
1847	Lawton A.	Douglas,	Will,	33509
1808	Levi	Mendon,	Guardianship,	33510
1815	Levi, 2d	Petersham,	Administration,	33511
1849	Levi	Milford,	Administration,	33512
1827	Levi J.	Petersham,	Guardianship,	33513
1842	Lewis	Charlton,	Administration,	33514
1849	Lewis	Milford,	Administration,	33515
1829	Livy J.	Dana,	Guardianship,	33516

YEAR.	NAME.	RESIDENCE.	NATURE.	CASE.
1830	JOHNSON, Lucius	Dana,	Administration,	33517
1774	Lucretia	Shrewsbury,	Guardianship,	33518
1821	Lucretia	Royalston,	Guardianship,	33519
1808	Lucy	Shrewsbury,	Guardianship,	33520
1811	Lucy	Brookfield,	Guardianship,	33521
1849	Lucy	Worcester,	Administration,	33522
1853	Lucy	Sturbridge,	Will,	33523
1838	Lucy A.	Shrewsbury,	Guardianship,	33524
1848	Lucy E.	Hardwick,	Guardianship,	33525
1828	Luke	Leominster,	Administration,	33526
1826	Luther	Lancaster,	Administration,	33527
1849	Luther, Jr.	Millbury,	Administration,	33528
1872	Luther S.	Lancaster,	Administration,	33529
1770	Lydia	Southborough,	Guardianship,	33530
1827	Lydia	Petersham,	Guardianship,	33531
1843	Lydia	Southborough,	Will,	33532
1837	Lydia H.	Upton,	Guardianship,	33533
1840	Lyman	Dana,	Will,	33534
1864	Lyman	Sturbridge,	Will,	33535
1865	Lyman	Webster,	Administration,	33536
1848	Lyman S.	Hardwick,	Guardianship,	33537
1790	Marcus J.	Grafton,	Guardianship,	33538
1871	Margaret	Worcester,	Guardianship,	33539
1880	Maria	Clinton,	Guardianship,	33540
1857	Marshall	Hardwick,	Will,	33541
1778	Martha	Holden,	Guardianship,	33542
1829	Martha	Shrewsbury,	Administration,	33543
1853	Martha	Worcester,	Will,	33544
1877	Martha	Milford,	Administration,	33545
1848	Martha M.	Hardwick,	Guardianship,	33546
1743	Mary	Southborough,	Administration,	33547
1785	Mary	Lunenburg,	Will,	33548
1815	Mary	Sturbridge,	Administration,	33549
1881	Mary	Lunenburg,	Administration,	33550
1828	Mary A.	North Brookfield,	Guardianship,	33551
1865	Mary A.	Mason, N. H.,	Guardianship,	33552
1872	Mary A.	Fitchburg,	Guardianship,	33553
1881	Mary C.	Northbridge,	Will,	33554
1859	Mary E.	Worcester,	Guardianship,	33555
1862	Mary E.	Dana,	Guardianship,	33556
1871	Mary E.	New Haven, Conn.,	Foreign Will,	33557
1879	Mary E.	Douglas,	Will,	33558
1869	Mary F.	Brookfield,	Guardianship,	33559
1879	Mary J.	Milford,	Adoption, etc.,	33560
1812	Mary P.	Westborough,	Guardianship,	33561

YEAR.	NAME.	RESIDENCE.	NATURE.	CASE.
1878	JOHNSON, Mary S.	Southborough,	Will,	33562
1842	Mary T.	Worcester,	Administration,	33563
1829	Mary W.	Dana,	Guardianship,	33564
1841	Mary W.	Leominster,	Guardianship,	33565
1873	Mary W.	Thompson, Conn.,	Administration,	33566
1746	Mathew	Westborough,	Administration,	33567
1868	Maude L.	Milford,	Adoption,	33568
1852	Meverick	Berlin,	Will,	33569
1802	Micah	Worcester,	Will,	33570
1869·	Micah	Worcester,	Will,	33571
1842	Mira A.	Templeton,	Guardianship,	33572
1865	Morga A.	Berlin,	Guardianship,	33573
1778	Nabby	Harvard,	Guardianship,	33574
1830	Nahum	Fitchburg,	Administration,	33575
1851	Nancy K.	Worcester,	Will,	33576
1848	Napoleon B.	Milford,	Guardianship,	33577
1768	Nathan	Southborough,	Guardianship,	33578
1771	Nathan	Leominster,	Administration,	33579
1778	Nathan	Leominster,	Administration,	33580
1790	Nathan	Grafton,	Guardianship,	33581
1822	Nathan	Grafton,	Administration,	33582
1825	Nathan	Worcester,	Guardianship,	33583
1831	Nathan	Berlin,	Guardianship,	33584
1833	Nathan	Berlin,	Administration,	33584
1833	Nathan	Berlin,	Pension,	33585
1851	Nathan H.	Milford,	Administration,	33586
1780	Nathaniel	Southborough,	Guardianship,	33587
1818	Nathaniel	Leominster,	Guardianship,	33588
1867	Nathaniel	Dana,	Will,	33589
1875	Nathaniel K.	Worcester,	Administration,	33590
1870	Nellie	Fitchburg,	Guardianship,	33591
1867	Nellie M.	Templeton,	Adoption, etc.,	33592
1812	Newell	Shrewsbury,	Guardianship,	33593
1870	Olive	Woodstock, Vt.,	Guardianship,	33594
1857	Oliver	Sterling,	Administration,	33595
1823	Orin	Sutton,	Guardianship,	33596
1854	Orrin T.	Worcester,	Guardianship,	33597
1847	Orville L.	Douglas,	Guardianship,	33598
1866	Orville L.	Douglas,	Administration,	33599
1814	Otis	Charlton,	Guardianship,	33600
1810	Parker	Brookfield,	Guardianship,	33601
1880	Parker	North Brookfield,	Will,	33602
1778	Patience	Leominster,	Guardianship,	33603
1778	Patty	Harvard,	Guardianship,	33604
1752	Paul	Southborough,	Guardianship,	33605

YEAR.	NAME.	RESIDENCE.	NATURE.	CASE.
1810	JOHNSON, Perley	Brookfield,	Guardianship,	33606
1827	Perley	North Brookfield,	Administration,	33607
1869	Permelia	Leominster,	Administration,	33608
1863	Perry	Barre,	Guardianship,	33609
1865	Perry	Barre,	Administration,	33609
1732	Peter	Woodstock,	Guardianship,	33610
1798	Peter	Worcester,	Administration,	33611
1799	Peter	Worcester,	Guardianship,	33612
1871	Peter	Worcester,	Administration,	33613
1836	Phebe	Shrewsbury,	Will,	33614
1847	Phebe H.	Douglas,	Guardianship,	33615
1811	Phebe W.	Brookfield,	Guardianship,	33616
1823	Philip	Shrewsbury,	Will,	33617
1875	Philip	Hardwick,	Administration,	33618
1815	Pliney	Western,	Guardianship,	33619
1853	Pliny	Sutton,	Will,	33620
1811	Polly	Brookfield,	Guardianship,	33621
1871	Polly	Webster,	Will,	33622
1732	Prudence	Woodstock,	Guardianship,	33623
1817	Prudence	Leominster,	Administration,	33624
1871	Rachel	Worcester,	Guardianship,	33625
1827	Rachel F.	Petersham,	Guardianship,	33626
1778	Rebecca	Leominster,	Guardianship,	33627
1814	Rebecca	Leominster,	Administration,	33628
1780	Rebekah	Spencer,	Will,	33629
1853	Relief	Barre,	Will,	33630
1859	Relief	Webster,	Administration,	33631
1878	Relief	Sterling,	Administration,	33632
1829	Relief A.	Dana,	Guardianship,	33633
1879	Reubin S.	Leominster,	Will,	33634
1756	Robert	Rutland,	Will,	33635
1869	Robert E.	Warren,	Guardianship,	33636
1845	Rodney A.	Worcester,	Guardianship,	33637
1880	Rodney A. M.	Worcester,	Administration,	33638
1864	Roxanna	Woodstock, Conm,	Administration,	33639
1836	Rufus	Upton,	Administration,	33640
1868	Rufus	Athol,	Administration,	33641
1868	Rufus H.	Athol,	Guardianship,	33642
1865	Rufus W.	Petersham,	Administration,	33643
1878	Ruhama	Milford,	Will,	33644
1790	Sally	Grafton,	Guardianship,	33645
1812	Sally	Westborough,	Guardianship,	33646
1833	Sally	Upton,	Will,	33647
1842	Sally	Northbridge,	Administration,	33648
1844	Sally	Worcester,	Administration,	33649

YEAR.	NAME.	RESIDENCE.	NATURE.	CASE.
1732	JOHNSON, Samuel	Shrewsbury,	Administration,	33650
1739	Samuel	Lancaster,	Administration,	33651
1765	Samuel	Lunenburg,	Will,	33652
1788	Samuel	Westborough,	Guardianship,	33653
1789	Samuel	Worcester,	Administration,	33654
1794	Samuel	Lunenburg,	Will,	33655
1807	Samuel	Worcester,	Administration,	33656
1811	Samuel	Westborough,	Administration,	33657
1812	Samuel	Westborough,	Guardianship,	33658
1814	Samuel	Worcester,	Administration,	33659
1815	Samuel	Winchendon,	Will,	33660
1847	Samuel	Hardwick,	Administration,	33661
1848	Samuel	Hardwick,	Guardianship,	33662
1872	Samuel	Hardwick,	Administration,	33663
1877	Samuel	Lunenburg,	Will,	33664
1878	Samuel	Milford,	Will,	33665
1838	Samuel H.	Shrewsbury,	Guardianship,	33666
1758	Samuel J.	Worcester,	Guardianship,	33667
1844	Samuel N.	Worcester,	Guardianship,	33668
1788	Sarah	Westborough,	Guardianship,	33669
1813	Sarah	Grafton,	Administration,	33670
1840	Sarah	Fitchburg,	Guardianship,	33671
1879	Sarah	Lunenburg,	Will,	33672
1841	Sarah A.	Leominster,	Guardianship,	33673
1838	Sarah E.	Shrewsbury,	Guardianship,	33674
1879	Sarah E.	Boston,	Adoption, etc.,	33675
1844	Sarah I.	Worcester,	Guardianship,	33676
1856	Sarah P.	Southborough,	Guardianship,	33677
1842	Sarah R. C.	Northbridge,	Guardianship,	33678
1763	Seth	Southborough,	Guardianship,	33679
1807	Seth	Hardwick,	Will,	33680
1839	Seth	Dana,	Administration,	33681
1752	Sheiah	Southborough,	Guardianship,	33682
1840	Silas	Hardwick,	Will,	33683
1748	Simeon	Harvard,	Guardianship,	33684
1736	Smith	Woodstock,	Administration,	33685
1811	Smith	Dudley,	Will,	33686
1773	Solomon	Worcester,	Guardianship,	33687
1793	Solomon	Worcester,	Administration,	33687
1808	Sophia	Shrewsbury,	Guardianship,	33688
1828	Sophia	Templeton,	Sale Real Estate,	33689
1852	Sophia	Leominster,	Guardianship,	33690
1853	Sophia	Leominster,	Administration,	33690
1853	Sophia	Sutton,	Guardianship,	33691
1864	Sophia	Lancaster,	Administration,	33692

YEAR.	NAME.	RESIDENCE.	NATURE.	CASE.
1870	JOHNSON, Sophia	Dana,	Administration,	33693
1850	Sophia G.	Milford,	Guardianship,	33694
1848	Sophia P.	Milford,	Guardianship,	33695
1845	Sophronia	Rockford, Ill.,	Foreign Sale,	33696
1867	Stedman	Templeton,	Will,	33697
1807	Stephen	Shrewsbury,	Administration,	33698
1808	Stephen	Leominster,	Will,	33699
1828	Stephen	Leominster,	Administration,	33700
1849	Stephen	Dana,	Pension,	33701
1877	Stephen	Woodstock, Conn.,	Foreign Will,	33702
1869	Susan B. M.	Athol,	Guardianship,	33703
1845	Susan M.	Rockford, Ill.,	Foreign Sale,	33704
1831	Thankful L.	Worcester,	Guardianship,	33705
1840	Theodore W.	Hardwick,	Guardianship,	33706
1797	Thomas	Gerry,	Administration,	33707
1871	Thomas	Worcester,	Guardianship,	33708
1751	Thyas	Southborough,	Guardianship,	33709
1768	Timothy	Southborough,	Administration,	33710
1790	Timothy	Grafton,	Administration,	33711
1790	Timothy	Grafton,	Guardianship,	33712
1815	Timothy	Shrewsbury,	Administration,	33713
1819	Timothy	Sutton,	Administration,	33714
1837	Truelove	Worcester,	Will,	33715
1752	Unis	Southborough,	Guardianship,	33716
1810	Uriah W.	Brookfield,	Will,	33717
1842	Uriel	Worcester,	Guardianship,	33718
1845	Uriel	Worcester,	Administration,	33718
1849	Voluntine H.	Westminster,	Guardianship,	33719
1811	Waldo	Brookfield,	Guardianship,	33720
1880	Waldo P.	Clinton,	Guardianship,	33721
1841	Walter	Worcester,	Administration,	33722
1850	Walter A.	Southborough,	Guardianship,	33723
1877	Walter E.	Milford,	Administration,	33724
1847	Warner	Athol,	Guardianship,	33725
1880	Wilber R.	Leominster,	Administration,	33726
1858	Willard	Leominster,	Will,	33727
1746	William	Western,	Administration,	33728
1756	William	Southborough,	Will,	33729
1757	William	Worcester,	Administration,	33730
1758	William	Worcester,	Guardianship,	33731
1768	William	Oakham,	Guardianship,	33732
1778	William	Holden,	Guardianship,	33733
1788	William	Westborough,	Guardianship,	33734
1811	William	Brookfield,	Guardianship,	33735
1818	William	Hardwick,	Guardianship,	33736

YEAR.	NAME.	RESIDENCE.	NATURE.	CASE.
1823	JOHNSON, William	Lunenburg,	Guardianship,	33737
1830	William	Westborough,	Will,	33738
1842	William	Worcester,	Administration,	33739
1842	William	Worcester,	Pension,	33740
1850	William	Hardwick,	Guardianship,	33741
1868	William	Barre,	Guardianship,	33742
1871	William	Hardwick,	Will,	33743
1871	William	Worcester,	Guardianship,	33744
1879	William	Worcester,	Administration,	33745
1880	William	North Brookfield,	Will,	33746
1867	William A.	Barre,	Administration,	33747
1868	William A.	Athol,	Guardianship,	33748
1843	William C.	Princeton,	Administration,	33749
1845	William E.	Rockford, Ill.,	Foreign Sale,	33750
1848	William H.	Hardwick,	Guardianship,	33751
1862	William H.	Athol,	Administration,	33752
1862	William H.	Leominster,	Administration,	33753
1878	William H.	Milford,	Guardianship,	33754
1848	William H. H.	Milford,	Guardianship,	33755
1854	William H. H.	Worcester,	Guardianship,	33756
1866	William L.	Barre,	Guardianship,	33757
1795	Zebadiah	Shrewsbury,	Will,	33758
1819	Zedekiah	Barre,	Will,	33759
1850	Zenas	Berlin,	Administration,	33760
1788	Zeruiah	Westborough,	Guardianship,	33761
1812	Zeruiah	Westborough,	Guardianship,	33762
1765	Zoeth	Shrewsbury,	Administration,	33763
1854	JOHNSTON, Cornelius	Grafton,	Guardianship,	33764
1732	James	Shrewsbury,	Guardianship,	33765
1732	Margaret	Shrewsbury,	Guardianship,	33766
1732	Mathew	Shrewsbury,	Guardianship,	33767
1732	Sarah	Shrewsbury,	Guardianship,	33768
1846	Thomas	Westminster,	Will,	33769
1732	William	Shrewsbury,	Guardianship,	33770
1854	William	Shrewsbury,	Administration,	33771
1828	JONES, Aaron	Templeton,	Administration,	33772
1833	Aaron	Templeton,	Guardianship,	33773
1839	Aaron	Lancaster,	Administration,	33774
1836	Abel	Winchendon,	Will,	33775
1760	Abigail	Mendon,	Guardianship,	33776
1877	Abigail	West Brookfield,	Administration,	33777
1879	Abijah	Templeton,	Will,	33778
1791	Abraham	Barre,	Administration,	33779
1825	Adam	Templeton,	Will,	33780
1881	Addie L.	Bolton,	Guardianship,	33781

Year.	Name.	Residence.	Nature.	Case.
1834	JONES, Alden	Milford,	Administration,	33782
1871	Alice A.	West Brookfield,	Guardianship,	33783
1828	Amasa	Leominster,	Will,	33784
1868	Amasa	Leominster,	Administration,	33785
1826	Amos	Royalston,	Will,	33786
1842	Amos, Jr.	Fitchburg,	Will,	33787
1853	Ann E.	Worcester,	Guardianship,	33788
1858	Ann E.	Worcester,	Adoption, etc.,	33789
1777	Anna	Princeton,	Guardianship,	33790
1774	Asa	Worcester,	Guardianship,	33791
1831	Asa	Spencer,	Will,	33792
1865	Asa T.	Spencer,	Will,	33793
1865	Asa T.	Spencer,	Guardianship,	33794
1855	Athna	Unknown,	Adoption, etc.,	33795
1758	Benjamin	Upton,	Administration,	33796
1778	Benjamin	Shrewsbury,	Administration,	33797
1866	Bethiah	Woodstock, Conn.,	Foreign Will,	33798
1785	Betsey	Princeton,	Guardianship,	33799
1777	Betty	Princeton,	Guardianship,	33800
1847	Catherine T.	Ashburnham,	Guardianship,	33801
1821	Charles	Lancaster,	Pension,	33802
1880	Charles	Webster,	Adoption, etc.,	33803
1857	Charles E.	Ashburnham,	Adoption, etc.,	33804
1839	Charles M.	Lunenburg,	Guardianship,	33805
1835	Charles P.	Westborough,	Administration,	33806
1876	Charles P.	Milford,	Guardianship,	33807
1868	Charles W.	Leominster,	Guardianship,	33808
1881	Charlotte	Milford,	Will,	33809
1843	Christopher	Ashburnham,	Administration,	33810
1871	Clara	Boston,	Adoption, etc.,	33811
1869	Clara A.	Worcester,	Adoption, etc.,	33812
1837	Clarissa	Lancaster,	Guardianship,	33813
1879	Cora B.	Athol,	Guardianship,	33814
1827	Cynthia	Charlton,	Will,	33815
1849	Cynthia	Ashburnham,	Administration,	33816
1843	Daniel	Ashburnham,	Will,	33817
1843	Daniel W.	Ashburnham,	Guardianship,	33818
1839	David	Lunenburg,	Will,	33819
1841	David	Milford,	Administration,	33820
1873	David	Worcester,	Will,	33821
1860	David N.	Milford,	Administration,	33822
1745	Dearing	Mendon,	Administration,	33823
1818	Dorothy	Berlin,	Will,	33824
1779	Ebenezer	Princeton,	Will,	33825
1789	Ebenezer	Sutton,	Administration,	33826

YEAR.	NAME.	RESIDENCE.	NATURE.	CASE.
1812	JONES, Ebenezer	Charlton,	Guardianship,	33827
1825	Ebenezer	Ashburnham,	Administration,	33828
1874	Edgar W.	Lunenburg,	Guardianship,	33829
1853	Edmund	Ashburnham,	Administration,	33830
1812	Eli	Charlton,	Will,	33831
1855	Eli	Spencer,	Administration,	33832
1875	Elijah	Boylston,	Will,	33833
1843	Eliza R.	Ashburnham,	Guardianship,	33834
1786	Elizabeth	Western,	Administration,	33835
1871	Elizabeth	Worcester,	Will,	33836
1873	Elizabeth	Royalston,	Guardianship,	33837
1875	Ella F.	Leominster,	Adoption, etc.,	33838
1868	Elliot B.	Leominster,	Guardianship,	33839
1849	Elnathan	Lunenburg,	Will,	33840
1857	Elnathan	Oxford,	Will,	33841
1880	Emily J.	Worcester,	Will,	33842
1825	Enos	Ashburnham,	Will,	33843
1784	Ephraim	Princeton,	Will,	33844
1881	Ephraim	Lunenburg,	Will,	33845
1812	Erasmus	Worcester,	Administration,	33846
1812	Erastus	Charlton,	Guardianship,	33847
1844	Erastus	Spencer,	Guardianship,	33848
1842	Evelina E.	Winchendon,	Guardianship,	33849
1875	Everett S.	Spencer,	Guardianship,	33850
1845	Ezekiel	Milford,	Administration,	33851
1846	Ezekiel	Milford,	Pension,	33852
1808	Ezra	Barre,	Will,	33853
1868	Ezra	Douglas,	Administration,	33854
1878	Fanny K.	Northborough,	Administration,	33855
1785	Farwell	Princeton,	Guardianship,	33856
1863	Flora M.	Worcester,	Change of Name,	33857
1837	Frances A.	Lancaster,	Guardianship,	33858
1839	Frances A.	Lunenburg,	Guardianship,	33859
1874	Frances A.	Lunenburg,	Guardianship,	33860
1871	Frances T.	Lunenburg,	Administration,	33861
1881	Frank	Bolton,	Guardianship,	33862
1869	Freddie A.	Douglas,	Guardianship,	33863
1824	Frederick W.	Leominster,	Administration,	33864
1808	George	Gerry,	Guardianship,	33865
1832	George	Phillipston,	Will,	33866
1875	George	Milford,	Will,	33867
1832	George H. G.	Phillipston,	Guardianship,	33868
1871	George R.	Sutton,	Guardianship,	33869
1857	George W.	Sutton,	Administration,	33870
1868	George W.	Leominster,	Guardianship,	33871

YEAR.	NAME.	RESIDENCE.	NATURE.	CASE.
1777	JONES, Hannah	Princeton,	Guardianship,	33872
1812	Hannah	Charlton,	Guardianship,	33873
1812	Hannah	Berlin,	Guardianship,	33874
1836	Hannah	Ashburnham,	Administration,	33875
1857	Hannah	Lunenburg,	Will,	33876
1861	Harriet	Worcester,	Will,	33877
1861	Harriet A.	Sutton,	Adoption, etc.,	33878
1874	Harriet K.	Brookfield,	Administration,	33879
1879	Harry L.	Athol,	Guardianship,	33880
1847	Homer S.	Ashburnham,	Guardianship,	33881
1872	Ira W.	Worcester,	Administration,	33882
1771	Isaac	Weathersfield, Conn.,	Guardianship,	33883
1785	Isaac	Western,	Administration,	33884
1874	Isabel T.	Lunenburg,	Guardianship,	33885
1873	Isedore	North Brookfield,	Administration,	33886
1808	James	Gerry,	Guardianship,	33887
1829	Jane	Athol,	Guardianship,	33888
1808	Jeffrey A.	Gerry,	Guardianship,	33889
1871	Jennie W.	West Brookfield,	Guardianship,	33890
1778	Jesse	Worcester,	Guardianship,	33891
1835	Jesse	Sutton,	Administration,	33892
1753	John	Mendon,	Will,	33893
1777	John	Princeton,	Administration,	33894
1777	John	Princeton,	Guardianship,	33895
1785	John	Princeton,	Guardianship,	33896
1851	John	Lunenburg,	Will,	33897
1876	John	Milford,	Will,	33898
1834	John E.	Leominster,	Administration,	33899
1865	John F.	Milford,	Guardianship,	33900
1767	Jonathan	Mendon,	Administration,	33901
1803	Jonathan	Gerry,	Will,	33902
1813	Jonathan	Berlin,	Administration,	33903
1796	Joseph	Milford,	Will,	33904
1799	Joseph	Milford,	Administration,	33905
1801	Joseph	Oxford,	Guardianship,	33906
1810	Joseph	Lunenburg,	Will,	33907
1778	Joseph B.	Worcester,	Guardianship,	33908
1851	Jude	Paxton,	Administration,	33909
1871	Julia E.	Sutton,	Guardianship,	33910
1875	Julia F.	Spencer,	Guardianship,	33911
1856	Junius A.	Carroll, N. Y.,	Guardianship,	33912
1875	Laura A.	Worcester,	Will,	33913
1868	Lewis F.	Leominster,	Guardianship,	33914
1812	Lory	Spencer,	Guardianship,	33915
1868	Louisa	Westminster.	Guardianship,	33916

YEAR.	NAME.	RESIDENCE.	NATURE.	CASE.
1869	JONES, Louisa	Westminster,	Administration,	33916
1879	Lucinda K.	Oakham,	Administration,	33917
1832	Lucinda S.	Phillipston,	Guardianship,	33918
1835	Lucy	Sutton,	Administration,	33919
1844	Lucy	Spencer,	Administration,	33920
1844	Lucy D.	Spencer,	Guardianship,	33921
1849	Luke	Worcester,	Will,	33922
1858	Luke	Leominster,	Will,	33923
1859	Luther	Leominster,	Will,	33924
1849	Luther P.	Milford,	Guardianship,	33925
1812	Lydia	Charlton,	Guardianship,	33926
1873	Marcus V. B.	Appleton, Wis.,	Administration,	33927
1849	Maria (L.)	Milford,	Guardianship,	33928
1751	Martha	Leicester,	Guardianship,	33929
1831	Martha	Berlin,	Will,	33930
1835	Martha	Southborough,	Administration,	33931
1813	Martin C.	Berlin,	Guardianship,	33932
1819	Martin C.	Berlin,	Administration,	33932
1751	Mary	Leicester,	Guardianship,	33933
1785	Mary	Princeton,	Will,	33934
1798	Mary	Shrewsbury,	Will,	33935
1841	Mary	Northborough,	Will,	33936
1866	Mary	Milford,	Will,	33937
1870	Mary	Lunenburg,	Will,	33938
1876	Mary C.	Southborough,	Will,	33939
1839	Mary E.	Lunenburg,	Guardianship,	33940
1853	Mary E.	Worcester,	Guardianship,	33941
1847	Mary M.	Ashburnham,	Guardianship,	33942
1875	Mary P.	Spencer,	Guardianship,	33943
1842	Mary S.	Winchendon,	Guardianship,	33944
1825	Matilda	Wayne, Me.,	Administration,	33945
1835	Mercy	Milford,	Will,	33946
1879	Milly	Worcester,	Will,	33947
1812	Mindwell	Spencer,	Guardianship,	33948
1879	Minerva L.	Athol,	Guardianship,	33949
1871	Minnie L.	Worcester,	Adoption, etc.,	33950
1876	Minnie L.	Worcester,	Guardianship,	33951
1881	Minnie P.	Bolton,	Guardianship,	33952
1798	Miranda	Berlin,	Guardianship,	33953
1830	Moses	Lancaster,	Will,	33954
1808	Nahum	Gerry,	Administration,	33955
1816	Nahum	Phillipston,	Guardianship,	33956
1803	Nathan	Berlin,	Will,	33957
1758	Nathaniel	Brookfield,	Administration,	33958
1795	Nathaniel	Charlton,	Will,	33959

YEAR.	NAME.	RESIDENCE.	NATURE.	CASE.
1832	JONES, Nathaniel	Barre,	Will,	33960
1758	Nathaniel, Jr.	Mendon,	Will,	33961
1879	Nathila	Athol,	Guardianship,	33962
1774	Noah	Worcester,	Guardianship,	33963
1781	Noah	Worcester,	Will,	33964
1852	Olivia G.	Lunenburg,	Administration,	33965
1816	Pamela L.	Phillipston,	Guardianship,	33966
1876	Persis G.	Spencer,	Will,	33967
1774	Peter	Salem,	Guardianship,	33968
1766	Phebe	Brookfield,	Guardianship,	33969
1874	Philip H.	Lunenburg,	Guardianship,	33970
1814	Phineas	Worcester,	Administration,	33971
1801	Polly	Oxford,	Guardianship,	33972
1785	Prescott	Concord,	Guardianship,	33973
1828	Prescott	Athol,	Administration,	33974
1820	Rebecca	Barre,	Administration,	33975
1874	Roger P. S.	Lunenburg,	Guardianship,	33976
1878	Rose M.	Worcester,	Guardianship,	33977
1867	Russell W.	Charlton,	Administration,	33978
1783	Ruth	Weston,	Guardianship,	33979
1812	Sally	Berlin,	Guardianship,	33980
1859	Sally	Worcester,	Administration,	33981
1797	Samuel	Berlin,	Administration,	33982
1808	Samuel	Berlin,	Guardianship,	33983
1811	Samuel	Berlin,	Administration,	33983
1819	Samuel	Milford,	Will,	33984
1835	Samuel	Barre,	Administration,	33985
1848	Samuel	Leominster,	Administration,	33986
1848	Samuel	Leominster,	Pension,	33987
1751	Sarah	Leicester,	Guardianship,	33988
1756	Sarah	Leicester,	Distribution,	33988
1838	Sarah A.	Westborough,	Guardianship,	33989
1842	Sarah K.	Winchendon,	Guardianship,	33990
1877	Sarah K.	Fitchburg,	Will,	33991
1763	Seth	Mendon,	Guardianship,	33992
1873	Silas	Royalston,	Will,	33993
1880	Silas	Royalston,	Administration,	33994
1768	Solomon	Mendon,	Guardianship,	33995
1770	Solomon	Wethersfield, Conn.,	Guardianship,	33996
1864	Solomon	Berlin,	Will,	33997
1871	Sophia	Milford,	Will,	33998
1758	Stephen	Upton,	Guardianship,	33999
1814	Stephen	Templeton,	Guardianship,	34000
1832	Sullivan	Lancaster,	Administration,	34001
1795	Susanna	Berlin,	Will,	34002

YEAR.	NAME.	RESIDENCE.	NATURE.	CASE.
1853	JONES, Susanna	Spencer, .	Will,	34003
1863	Theodore	Athol,	Will,	34004
1748	Thomas	Leicester,	Administration,	34005
1751	Thomas	Leicester,	Guardianship,	34006
1766	Thomas	Brookfield,	Guardianship,	34007
1774	Timothy	Worcester,	Guardianship,	34008
1785	Timothy	Princeton,	Guardianship,	34009
1822	Timothy	Berlin,	Will,	34010
1869	Walter E.	Douglas,	Guardianship,	34011
1871	Warren K.	West Brookfield,	Guardianship,	34012
1874	Willard	Worcester,	Will,	34013
1751	William	Leicester,	Guardianship,	34014
1761	William	Westborough,	Administration,	34015
1761	William	Lunenburg,	Will,	34016
1774	William	Worcester,	Guardianship,	34017
1777	William	Worcester,	Administration,	34018
1849	William	Berlin,	Administration,	34019
1854	William	Lunenburg,	Will,	34020
1876	William	Warren,	Will,	34021
1875	William H.	Lunenburg,	Administration,	34022
1837	Zophar	Lancaster,	Guardianship,	34023
1824	JOP, Benjamin	Winchester, Conn.,	Sale Real Estate,	34024
	JORDAN AND JOURDAN,			
1875	Alonzo P.	Worcester,	Administration,	34025
1750	Dudley	Hardwick,	Administration,	34026
1750	Dudley	Hardwick,	Guardianship,	34027
1869	Eliza B.	Oxford,	Administration,	34028
1870	Franklin T.	Millbury,	Guardianship,	34029
1867	Henry F.	Worcester,	Guardianship,	34030
1870	Jennie B.	Millbury,	Guardianship,	34031
1750	Marcy	Hardwick,	Guardianship,	34032
1872	Philip	Worcester,	Administration,	34033
1750	Phillip	Hardwick,	Guardianship,	34034
1750	Sarah	Hardwick,	Guardianship,	34035
1866	Stillman S.	Templeton,	Adminstration,	34036
1750	Susanah	Hardwick,	Guardianship,	34037
1870	Willie	Millbury,	Guardianship,	34038
1863	JORGENSON, Hans P.	Leominster,	Administration,	34039
	JOSELYN see JOSLIN.			
1851	JOSEPH, Joseph	Fitchburg,	Will,	34040
	JOSLIN, JOSELYN, JOSLYN			
	AND JOSSELYN,			
1819	Abigail	Western,	Administration,	34041
1777	Abraham	New Braintree,	Will,	34042
1861	Adelia M.	Leominster,	Guardianship,	34043

(783—SERIES A.)

	JOSLIN, JOSELYN, JOSLYN, AND JOSSELYN,			
1877	Almira D.	Oxford,	Guardianship,	34044
1851	Amanda M.	Webster,	Guardianship,	34045
1880	Asher	Webster,	Will,	34046
1864	Benjamin H.	Oakham,	Administration,	34047
1823	Betsey	Douglas,	Guardianship,	34048
1844	Betsey	Leominster,	Administration,	34049
1848	Betsey	New Braintree,	Will,	34050
1852	Betsey	Lancaster,	Administration,	34051
1857	Betsey	Fitchburg,	Administration,	34052
1867	Charles L.	Brookfield,	Guardianship,	34053
1823	Diantha	Douglas,	Guardianship,	34054
1825	Dorinda	Leominster,	Guardianship,	34055
1824	Earle	Douglas,	Guardianship,	34056
1806	Ebenezer	Hubbardston,	Administration,	34057
1861	Eddie F.	Leominster,	Guardianship,	34058
1817	Elbridge	Western,	Guardianship,	34059
1830	Elbridge G.	Western,	Guardianship,	34060
1855	Eldora E.	Blackstone,	Guardianship,	34061
1824	Elias	Leominster,	Administration,	34062
1874	Elias	Leominster,	Will,	34063
1850	Elisha C.	Webster,	Will,	34064
1808	Eliza	Hubbardston,	Guardianship,	34065
1808	Eliza	Lancaster,	Guardianship,	34066
1814	Eliza	Western,	Guardianship,	34067
1820	Eliza	Hubbardston,	Guardianship,	34068
1861	Ella M.	Leominster,	Guardianship,	34069
1876	Elliott	Thompson, Conn.,	Administration,	34070
1877	Elliott P.	Oxford,	Guardianship,	34071
1823	Elmer M.	Douglas,	Guardianship,	34072
1871	Erastus	Thompson, Conn,	Administration,	34073
1824	Esek	Douglas,	Guardianship,	34074
1861	Francis L.	Leominster,	Administration,	34075
1880	Fred M.	Gardner,	Administration,	34076
1861	Frederic A.	Leominster,	Guardianship,	34077
1861	George E.	Leominster,	Guardianship,	34078
1868	George H.	Brookfield,	Administration,	34079
1761	Hannah	Westborough,	Guardianship,	34080
1837	Hannah	Leominster,	Guardianship,	34081
1877	Hannah C.	Northborough,	Will,	34082
1855	Herbert A.	Blackstone,	Guardianship,	34083
1740	Israel	Southborough,	Will,	34084
1826	James	Leominster,	Administration,	34085
1841	Joel	Leominster,	Administration,	34086

YEAR.	NAME.	RESIDENCE.	NATURE.	CASE.
	JOSLIN, JOSELYN, JOSLYN AND JOSSELYN,			
1810	John	Leominster,	Will,	34087
1816	John	Western,	Administration,	34088
1825	John	Leominster,	Guardianship,	34089
1845	John	Leominster,	Administration,	34090
1864	John A.	Brookfield,	Guardianship,	34091
1863	John L.	Fitchburg,	Administration,	34092
1808	John R.	Western,	Administration,	34093
1838	Jonas	Lancaster,	Administration,	34094
1761	Joseph	Westborough,	Administration,	34095
1762	Joseph	Westborough,	Guardianship,	34096
1829	Joseph	Leominster,	Will,	34097
1847	Julia A.	Hubbardston,	Guardianship,	34098
1778	Katey	New Braintree,	Guardianship,	34099
1762	Katharine	Westborough,	Guardianship,	34100
1851	Lewis F.	Webster,	Guardianship,	34101
1778	Lovice	New Braintree,	Guardianship,	34102
1848	Lucina	Blackstone,	Will,	34103
1862	Lucinda	Blackstone,	Administration,	34104
1806	Lucy	Hubbardston,	Administration,	34105
1808	Lucy	Hubbardston,	Guardianship,	34106
1820	Lucy	Hubbardston,	Guardianship,	34107
1824	Luke	Leominster,	Administration,	34108
1877	Luke	Leominster,	Administration,	34109
1830	Martha	Leominster,	Will,	34110
1808	Mary	Hubbardston,	Guardianship,	34111
1814	Mary	Western,	Guardianship,	34112
1837	Mary	Leominster,	Guardianship,	34113
1871	Mary	Leominster,	Administration,	34114
1861	Mary A.	Hubbardston,	Guardianship,	34115
1877	Mary E.	Spencer,	Administration,	34116
1840	Mathew	Hardwick,	Will,	34117
1778	Mathews	New Braintree,	Guardianship,	34118
1808	Moses	Hubbardston,	Guardianship,	34119
1848	Moses	Hubbardston,	Administration,	34120
1844	Nathan	Mendon,	Administration,	34121
1876	Nathan	Webster,	Administration,	34122
1855	Otis	Blackstone,	Administration,	34123
1824	Palina	Douglas,	Guardianship,	34124
1778	Patty	New Braintree,	Guardianship,	34125
1771	Peter	Lancaster,	Administration,	34126
1777	Peter	New Braintree,	Administration,	34127
1778	Peter	New Braintree,	Guardianship,	34128
1802	Peter	Lancaster,	Will,	34129

YEAR.	NAME.	RESIDENCE.	NATURE.	CASE.
	JOSLIN, JOSELYN, JOSLYN AND JOSSELYN,			
1808	Peter	Lancaster,	Guardianship,	34130
1847	Peter	Hubbardston,	Administration,	34131
1872	Peter	Leominster,	Will,	34132
1778	Phebe	New Braintree,	Guardianship,	34133
1792	Phebe	New Braintree,	Will,	34134
1823	Phila	Douglas,	Guardianship,	34135
1814	Reed	Western,	Guardianship,	34136
1819	Reed	Western,	Administration,	34137
1811	Sally	Hubbardston,	Will,	34138
1822	Samuel	New Braintree,	Will,	34139
1826	Samuel	Lancaster,	Administration,	34140
1840	Samuel	Hardwick,	Guardianship,	34141
1845	Samuel	Hardwick,	Administration,	34142
1823	Sarah	Douglas,	Guardianship,	34143
1830	Sarah	Pelham,	Guardianship,	34144
1827	Silas	Thompson, Conn.,	Administration,	34145
1828	Silas	Hubbardston,	Will,	34146
1822	Silvanus	Douglas,	Administration,	34147
1876	Sophia	Barre,	Will,	34148
1855	Susan A.	Blackstone,	Guardianship,	34149
1831	Thomas	Leominster,	Guardianship,	34150
1837	Thomas	Leominster,	Administration,	34150
1807	William	Hubbardston,	Will,	34151
1808	William	Hubbardston,	Guardianship,	34152
1820	William	Hubbardston,	Guardianship,	34153
1873	William	Hubbardston,	Will,	34154
	JOURDAN see JORDAN.			
1850	JOUVET, William	Worcester,	Adminstration,	34155
1875	JOY, David	Mendon,	Will,	34156
1848	Ellen L.	Dudley,	Guardianship,	34157
1848	Esther	Dudley,	Guardianship,	34158
1871	Frank A.	Leominster,	Guardianship,	34159
1848	Samuel E.	Dudley,	Administration,	34160
1870	Sarah E.	Leominster,	Administration,	34161
1848	Sarah L.	Dudley,	Guardianship,	34162
1863	JOYCE, Eliza A.	Petersham,	Guardianship,	34163
1783	George	Sutton,	Administration,	34164
1861	George	West Brookfield,	Guardianship,	34165
1861	Hannah	West Brookfield,	Will,	34166
1866	Hannah	North Brookfield,	Guardianship,	34167
1866	John	North Brookfield,	Guardianship,	34168
1863	John P.	Petersham,	Guardianship,	34169
1863	Margaret E.	Petersham,	Guardianship,	34170

| --- | --- | --- | --- | --- |
1864	JOYCE, Martin	Worcester,	Administration,	34171
1863	Mary	Petersham,	Guardianship,	34172
1870	Mary	Worcester,	Guardianship,	34173
1870	Rose A.	Worcester,	Guardianship,	34174
1861	Thomas	West Brookfield,	Guardianship,	34175
1863	Thomas	Petersham,	Administration,	34176
1870	William J.	Worcester,	Guardianship,	34177
1862	JUDD, David S.	Sturbridge,	Administration,	34178
1866	JUDGE, Ellen	Athol,	Guardianship,	34179
1858	James	Worcester,	Administration,	34180
1866	James	Athol,	Guardianship,	34181
1866	Mary A.	Athol,	Guardianship,	34182
1864	Michael	Athol,	Administration,	34183
1832	JUDSON, Samuel	Uxbridge,	Will,	34184
1834	Sarah	Uxbridge,	Will,	34185
1833	Sarah E.	Southbridge,	Guardianship,	34186
1872	JULIAN, Catherine F.	Worcester,	Administration,	34187
	KAIN see KANE.			
	KALAHER see KELLIHER.			
1877	KALER, Harriet	Southborough,	Administration,	34188
1879	Jennie E.	Southborough,	Guardianship,	34189
	KANE AND KAIN,			
1869	Ellen M.	Worcester,	Guardianship,	34190
1869	George B.	Worcester,	Guardianship,	34191
1869	Henry V.	Worcester,	Guardianship,	34192
1866	Jeremiah	Worcester,	Administration,	34193
1877	John	Boylston,	Will,	34194
1859	John, Jr.	Worcester,	Guardianship,	34195
1877	Martin	Worcester,	Administration,	34196
1869	Mary E.	Worcester,	Guardianship,	34197
1863	Patrick	Milford,	Administration,	34198
1874	Patrick	Milford,	Partition,	34199
1878	Patrick	Gardner,	Will,	34200
1880	Terrence	Milford,	Will,	34201
1881	KARLE, Conrad	Paxton,	Guardianship,	34202
1859	KATING, Theresa	Berlin,	Guardianship,	34203
1872	KAY, Charles	Uxbridge,	Administration,	34204
1867	Josephine A.	Upton,	Guardianship,	34205
1867	Walter H.	Upton,	Guardianship,	34206
	KEACH AND KEECH,			
1859	Emeline	Blackstone,	Guardianship,	34207
1868	Emeline	Blackstone,	Administration,	34207
1853	George W., Jr.	Worcester,	Administration,	34208
1845	Lydia	Blackstone,	Administration,	34209
1866	Thomas J.	Smithfield, R. I.,	Administration,	34210

	KEALY see KEELY.			
	KEANE see KEENE.			
1880	KEARNAN, Catharine	Worcester,	Guardianship,	34211
1880	Sarah	Worcester,	Guardianship,	34212
1880	Thomas	Worcester,	Guardianship,	34213
1875	KEAVENY, Michael	Petersham,	Administration,	34214
	KEBBY see KIBBY.			
1863	KEBLER, George P.	Leicester,	Guardianship,	34215
	KEECH see KEACH.			
1871	KEEFE, Julia	Fitchburg,	Administration,	34216
1878	Richard	Leicester,	Will,	34217
1861	Timothy	Milford,	Administration,	34218
1874	KEEGAN, Margaret	Worcester,	Partition,	34219
	KEELEY and KEALY,			
1873	Bridget	Spencer,	Guardianship,	34220
1873	Daniel	Spencer,	Guardianship,	34221
1869	Dennis	Spencer,	Administration,	34222
1873	Ellen	Spencer,	Guardianship,	34223
1860	James	Blackstone,	Guardianship,	34224
1857	James, 2d	Blackstone,	Will,	34225
1873	Joanna	Spencer,	Guardianship,	34226
1875	John	Blackstone,	Will,	34227
1869	John A.	Spencer,	Guardianship,	34228
1873	Kate	Spencer,	Guardianship,	34229
1869	Margaret	Spencer,	Guardianship,	34230
1873	Mary	Spencer,	Guardianship,	34231
1860	Michael	Blackstone,	Guardianship,	34232
1869	Michael	Spencer,	Guardianship,	34233
1873	Michael	Spencer,	Guardianship,	34234
1869	William	Spencer,	Guardianship,	34235
1877	KEELTY, Peter	Williamstown, Vt.,	Administration,	34236
1866	KEENAN, Ellen M.	Milford,	Guardianship,	34237
1863	Hugh	Milford,	Administration,	34238
	KEENE and KEANE,			
1880	Belle H.	Milford,	Guardianship,	34239
1880	Belle Hallett	Milford,	Adoption, etc.,	34240
1872	John	Milford,	Will,	34241
1874	Margaret	Charlton,	Adoption, etc.,	34242
1869	Michael	Worcester,	Administration,	34243
1877	Rachel	New York, N. Y.,	Guardianship,	34244
1859	KEEP, Austin	Dana,	Administration,	34245
1872	Avery	West Brookfield,	Will,	34246
1838	Chelles	North Brookfield,	Administration,	34247
1859	Ellen M.	Dana,	Guardianship,	34248
1774	Jabez	Harvard,	Will,	34249

Year.	Name.	Residence.	Nature.	Case.
1859	KEEP, Maria M.	Dana,	Guardianship,	34250
1859	Mary E.	Dana,	Guardianship,	34251
1874	William S.	North Brookfield,	Administration,	34252
1873	KEHLER, Gustavus	Worcester,	Will,	34253
1876	KEHOE, Celia	Clinton,	Will,	34254
1872	KEIRNAN, Patrick	Blackstone,	Administration,	34255
1877	KEITH, Ada E.	Webster,	Guardianship,	34256
1839	Albert	Uxbridge,	Guardianship,	34257
1839	Andrew J.	Uxbridge,	Guardianship,	34258
1879	Anna H.	Oakham,	Will,	34259
1847	Apollos	Winchendon,	Administration,	34260
1842	Asa	Dudley,	Pension,	34261
1857	Charles	Oakham,	Will,	34262
1779	Chloe	Dudley,	Guardianship,	34263
1780	Chloe	Dudley,	Administration,	34263
1839	Chloe A.	Uxbridge,	Guardianship,	34264
1839	Daniel T.	Uxbridge,	Guardianship,	34265
1779	David	Dudley,	Will,	34266
1791	Deborah	Sutton,	Guardianship,	34267
1876	Edward H.	Worcester,	Guardianship,	34268
1842	Edwin O.	Winchendon,	Guardianship,	34269
1791	Eleazer	Sutton,	Guardianship,	34270
1775	Eunice	Uxbridge,	Guardianship,	34271
1791	Eunice	Sutton,	Guardianship,	34272
1876	Florence E.	Worcester,	Guardianship,	34273
1876	Frank M.	Worcester,	Guardianship,	34274
1774	George	Mendon,	Will,	34275
1770	Gershom	Uxbridge,	Will,	34276
1813	Gershom	Uxbridge,	Administration,	34277
1815	Hannah	Sutton,	Will,	34278
1866	Henry R.	Worcester,	Administration,	34279
1770	James	Uxbridge,	Will,	34280
1790	James	Uxbridge,	Guardianship,	34281
1877	Jason	Winchendon,	Will,	34282
1872	Jeremiah	Spencer,	Administration,	34283
1862	Joanna	Uxbridge,	Will,	34284
1815	Joseph	Dudley,	Will,	34285
1842	Joshua, 2d	Winchendon,	Administration,	34286
1833	Josiah	Douglas,	Administration,	34287
1853	Lucy	Dudley,	Will,	34288
1791	Luther	Sutton,	Guardianship,	34289
1775	Lydia	Uxbridge,	Guardianship,	34290
1839	Lyman	Uxbridge,	Administration,	34291
1777	Mary	Uxbridge,	Will,	34292
1872	Mary	Milford,	Will,	34293

Year.	Name.	Residence.	Nature.	Case.
1878	KEITH, Mary A.	Grafton,	Guardianship,	34294
1878	Mary A.	Grafton,	Administration,	34295
1854	Mary E.	Douglas,	Guardianship,	34296
1745	Micah	Mendon,	Administration,	34297
1775	Moses	Uxbridge,	Administration,	34298
1775	Moses	Uxbridge,	Guardianship,	34299
1806	Nathan	Mendon,	Will,	34300
1856	Nathan	Milford,	Will,	34301
1782	Noah	Sutton,	Administration,	34302
1800	Noah	Uxbridge,	Will,	34303
1864	Reuben	Webster,	Administration,	34304
1775	Reuel	Uxbridge,	Guardianship,	34305
1858	Royal	Grafton,	Will,	34306
1780	Ruth	Dudley,	Will,	34307
1874	Sabrina	Winchendon,	Administration,	34308
1867	Sarah	Burrillville, R. I.,	Administration,	34309
1741	Simeon	Mendon,	Administration,	34310
1744	Simeon	Mendon,	Guardianship,	34311
1776	Simeon	Northbridge,	Administration,	34312
1822	Stephen	Ward,	Administration,	34313
1835	Susanna	Warren,	Will,	34314
1836	Thomas	Webster,	Administration,	34315
1848	Timothy	Worcester,	Guardianship,	34316
1840	Wellington	Uxbridge,	Guardianship,	34317
1842	Willard B.	Winchendon,	Guardianship,	34318
1839	William E.	Uxbridge,	Guardianship,	34319
	KELLEHER, KELLIHER and KALAHER,			
1871	Francis	Worcester,	Guardianship,	34320
1861	Hannah, etc.	Worcester,	Administration,	34321
1880	Margaret J.	West Brookfield,	Adoption,	34322
1871	Mary E.	Worcester,	Guardianship,	34323
1871	Maurice	Worcester,	Guardianship,	34324
1874	Michael	Worcester,	Administration,	34325
1873	Thomas	Worcester,	Administration,	34326
1857	KELLER, Oliver R.	Bolton,	Administration,	34327
	KELLEY and KELLY,			
1783	Abigail	Charlton,	Guardianship,	34328
1783	Abner	Charlton,	Guardianship,	34329
1849	Alexander	Upton,	Pension,	34330
1849	Alexander	Upton,	Administration,	34331
1877	Ann	Worcester,	Administration,	34332
1858	Anna	Upton,	Will,	34333
1835	Aratus M.	Douglas,	Guardianship,	34334
1814	Aritus	Oakham,	Guardianship,	34335

KELLEY AND KELLY,

YEAR.	NAME.	RESIDENCE	NATURE.	CASE.
1852	Asa	Blackstone,	Will,	34336
1879	Aurelius M.	Charlton,	Administration,	34337
1856	Bartholomew	Westborough,	Administration,	34338
1867	Cassandra	Northborough,	Guardianship,	34339
1783	Chapin	Charlton,	Guardianship,	34340
1845	Charles E.	Barre,	Guardianship,	34341
1825	Daniel	Mendon,	Administration,	34342
1814	Daniel E.	Oakham,	Guardianship,	34343
1864	Daniel S.	Princeton,	Administration,	34344
1799	David	Mendon,	Guardianship,	34345
1860	David	Blackstone,	Will,	34346
1867	David	Blackstone,	Guardianship,	34347
1833	Dorcas	Mendon,	Will,	34348
1869	Edward	Sutton,	Administration,	34349
1788	Eleazer	Douglas,	Administration,	34350
1790	Eleazer	Douglas,	Guardianship,	34351
1854	Eli	Blackstone,	Administration,	34352
1865	Elizabeth	Spencer,	Guardianship,	34353
1866	Elizabeth	Southbridge,	Guardianship,	34354
1867	Elizabeth	Barre,	Guardianship,	34355
1869	Elizabeth	Spencer,	Adoption, etc.,	34356
1864	Ella H.	Princeton,	Guardianship,	34357
1845	Ellen M.	Barre,	Guardianship,	34358
1873	Emma J.	Thompson, Conn.,	Guardianship,	34359
1881	Esther T.	Gardner,	Administration,	34360
1857	Eunice	Blackstone,	Administration,	34361
1867	Evangeline	Blackstone,	Guardianship,	34362
1879	Fanny	Spencer,	Guardianship,	34363
1845	George	Barre,	Guardianship,	34364
1879	George	Spencer,	Guardianship,	34365
1819	Hannah	Oakham,	Administration,	34366
1835	Hannah	Milford,	Administration,	34367
1860	Harriet A.	Oxford,	Administration,	34368
1814	Harriot	Oakham,	Guardianship,	34369
1814	Hastings S.	Oakham,	Guardianship,	34370
1783	Henry	Charlton,	Guardianship,	34371
1825	Henry	Oakham,	Will,	34372
1826	James	Mendon,	Guardianship,	34373
1855	James	Blackstone,	Will,	34374
1879	James	Spencer,	Administration,	34375
1845	Jason B.	Barre,	Guardianship,	34376
1857	Jeremiah	Mendon,	Will,	34377
1783	Joel	Charlton,	Guardianship,	34378
1851	Joel	Barre,	Will,	34379

Year.	Name.	Residence.	Nature.	Case.
	KELLEY AND KELLY,			
1865	Joel	Northborough,	Administration,	34380
1845	Joel B.	Barre,	Administration,	34381
1863	John	Oxford,	Administration,	34382
1865	John	Southbridge,	Administration,	34383
1866	John	Blackstone,	Will,	34384
1874	John	Worcester,	Administration,	34385
1880	John	Blackstone,	Will,	34386
1814	Julia	Oakham,	Guardianship,	34387
1876	Julia	Worcester,	Administration,	34388
1777	Julia M.	Barre,	Guardianship,	34389
1864	Lavina A.	Princeton,	Guardianship,	34390
1867	Lizzie	Spencer,	Guardianship,	34391
1867	Lucina S.	Blackstone,	Guardianship,	34392
1859	Lucretia	Sutton,	Will,	34393
1835	Lucretia A.	Douglas,	Guardianship,	34394
1783	Lydia	Charlton,	Guardianship,	34395
1864	Lydia C.	Blackstone,	Will,	34396
1866	Margaret	Southbridge,	Administration,	34397
1873	Margaret	North Brookfield,	Administration,	34398
1879	Margaret	Spencer,	Guardianship,	34399
1838	Margaretta L.	Millbury,	Guardianship,	34400
1855	Maria	Blackstone,	Administration,	34401
1814	Mariot	Oakham,	Guardianship,	34402
1825	Mariot	Douglas,	Administration,	34403
1799	Mark	Mendon,	Guardianship,	34404
1783	Mary	Charlton,	Guardianship,	34405
1880	Mary	Worcester,	Will,	34406
1866	Mary A.	Southbridge,	Guardianship,	34407
1867	Mary J.	Spencer,	Guardianship,	34408
1870	Mary J.	Millbury,	Guardianship,	34409
1876	Mary J.	Spencer,	Administration,	34410
1855	Mary R.	Blackstone,	Guardianship,	34411
1878	Maud A.	Uxbridge,	Adoption, etc.,	34412
1844	Mercy	Charlton,	Pension,	34413
1858	Merrick T.	Oxford,	Administration,	34414
1875	Michael	Clinton,	Guardianship,	34415
1857	Nathan	Webster,	Administration,	34416
1874	Owen	Gardner,	Administration,	34417
1867	Patrick	Spencer,	Administration,	34418
1879	Peter	Sturbridge,	Will,	34419
1858	Rebecca	Lancaster,	Administration,	34420
1853	Rebeccah	Upton,	Will,	34421
1813	Richard	Oakham,	Will,	34422
1876	Richard	Worcester,	Administration,	34423

YEAR.	NAME.	RESIDENCE.	NATURE.	CASE.
	KELLEY AND KELLY,			
1783	Robert	Charlton,	Guardianship,	34424
1783	Robert	Charlton,	Will,	34425
1855	Rowland R.	Blackstone,	Guardianship,	34426
1783	Ruth	Charlton,	Guardianship,	34427
1863	Sally	Worcester,	Will,	34428
1790	Sarah	Douglas,	Guardianship,	34429
1870	Sarah J. C.	Gardner,	Adoption, etc.,	34430
1855	Sarah W.	Blackstone,	Guardianship,	34431
1790	Seth	Douglas,	Guardianship,	34432
1799	Seth	Mendon,	Will,	34433
1851	Seth-	Blackstone,	Will,	34434
1854	Seth	Blackstone,	Administration,	34435
1879	Seth	Auburn,	Administration,	34436
1870	Strickland	Douglas,	Will,	34437
1862	Thomas	Worcester,	Will,	34438
1869	Thomas	Millbury,	Administration,	34439
1854	Timothy	Clare Co., Ireland,	Guardianship,	34440
1783	William	Charlton,	Guardianship,	34441
1879	William	Spencer,	Guardianship,	34442
1866	William A.	Blackstone,	Administration,	34443
1873	William H.	Thompson, Conn.,	Guardianship,	34444
1867	William J.	Spencer,	Guardianship,	34445
1855	William R.	Blackstone,	Guardianship,	34446
1824	Wing	Milford,	Administration,	34447
1837	Wing	Millbury,	Administration,	34448
	KELLIHER see KELLEHER.			
1854	**KELLOGG,** Catherine G.	Sturbridge,	Administration,	34449
1808	Chester	Suffield, Conn.,	Guardianship,	34450
1855	Henry E.	Worcester,	Administration,	34451
1823	**KELSEY,** Aaron A.	Shirley,	Guardianship,	34452
1823	Albert	Shirley,	Guardianship,	34453
1868	Alvah	Webster,	Will,	34454
1823	Artemas	Shirley,	Guardianship,	34455
1850	Charles H.	Webster,	Administration,	34456
1868	Emma A.	Webster,	Guardianship,	34457
1737	**KELSO,** Hugh	Worcester,	Will,	34458
	KELTON AND KILTON,			
1879	Ann	Hubbardston,	Administration,	34459
1842	Calvin	Athol,	Will,	34460
1868	Calvin	Athol,	Will,	34461
1868	Charles H.	Fitchburg,	Will,	34462
1878	Elihu	Hubbardston,	Will,	34463
1858	George O.	Athol,	Administration,	34464
1859	Geraldine A.	Athol,	Guardianship,	34465

	KELTON AND KILTON,			
1837	Ira	Worcester,	Administration,	34466
1829	James	Athol,	Will,	34467
1828	John W.	Athol,	Administration,	34468
1869	Katie J.	Providence, R. I.,	Guardianship,	34469
1863	Lemuel	Gardner,	Administration,	34470
1818	Margáret	Athol,	Will,	34471
1841	Nabby	Gardner,	Will,	34472
1821	Samuel	Athol,	Administration,	34473
1879	Sophia	Gardner,	Administration,	34474
1844	Thomas	Athol,	Administration,	34475
1869	**KELTY,** Barney	Princeton,	Administration,	34476
1869	Jennie B.	Princeton,	Guardianship,	34477
1869	Martin J.	Princeton,	Guardianship,	34478
1814	**KEMP,** Aaron	Fitchburg,	Guardianship,	34479
1814	Abel W.	Fitchburg,	Guardianship,	34480
1871	Adelbert S.	Thompson, Conn.,	Administration,	34481
1814	Benjamin	Fitchburg,	Guardianship,	34482
1817	Benjamin	Fitchburg,	Will,	34483
1814	Daniel	Fitchburg,	Guardianship,	34484
1814	John R.	Fitchburg,	Administration,	34485
1814	Joseph	Fitchburg,	Administration,	34486
1873	Joseph A.	Clinton,	Adoption,	34487
1814	Joseph R.	Fitchburg,	Guardianship,	34488
1814	Polley	Fitchburg,	Guardianship,	34489
1839	Thomas, Jr.	Webster,	Administration,	34490
	KEMPTON AND KIMPTON,			
1870	Daniel	Blackstone,	Administration,	34491
1874	Eliza A.	Blackstone,	Guardianship,	34492
1749	Ephraim	Uxbridge,	Guardianship,	34493
1749	Ephraim	Uxbridge,	Administration,	34494
1853	Ezra	Uxbridge,	Will,	34495
1841	George	Uxbridge,	Administration,	34496
1787	John	Mendon,	Guardianship,	34497
1787	John	Uxbridge,	Will,	34498
1804	John	Mendon,	Guardianship,	34499
1749	Joseph	Uxbridge,	Guardianship,	34500
1871	Lucinda S.	Winchendon,	Administration,	34501
1863	Martin V.	Blackstone,	Will,	34502
1749	Mary	Uxbridge,	Guardianship,	34503
1874	Mary	Blackstone,	Administration,	34504
1749	Stephen	Uxbridge,	Guardianship,	34505
1863	**KENCHER,** Paulina	Clinton,	Adoption, etc.,	34506
	KENDAL, KENDALL AND KIN-DELL,			
1780	Aaron	Templeton,	Guardianship,	34507

(794)

YEAR.	NAME.	RESIDENCE.	NATURE.	CASE.
	KENDAL, KENDALL AND KINDELL,			
1780	Aaron	Templeton,	Will,	34508
1805	Aaron	Templeton,	Guardianship,	34509
1807	Aaron	Sterling,	Guardianship,	34510
1823	Abigail	Sterling,	Guardianship,	34511
1870	Addie E.	Worcester,	Guardianship,	34512
1789	Admonition	Lancaster,	Will,	34513
1854	Albert L.	Fitchburg,	Guardianship,	34514
1849	Alvan	Ashburnham,	Administration,	34515
1821	Amos E.	Sterling,	Guardianship,	34516
1829	Andrew	Royalston,	Will,	34517
1850	Andrew D.	Leominster,	Guardianship,	34518
1847	Ann A.	Worcester,	Guardianship,	34519
1850	Ann M.	Leominster,	Guardianship,	34520
1860	Anna E.	Sterling,	Guardianship,	34521
1821	Asa	Westminster,	Administration,	34522
1855	Asa G.	Westminster,	Guardianship,	34523
1860	Augustus W.	Sterling,	Guardianship,	34524
1800	Azubah	Sterling,	Guardianship,	34525
1800	Betty	Sterling,	Guardianship,	34526
1810	Betty	Sterling,	Guardianship,	34527
1806	Caleb	Boylston,	Administration,	34528
1857	Caleb	Holden,	Administration,	34529
1857	Caroline D.	Lancaster,	Administration,	34530
1780	Catharine	Lancaster,	Guardianship,	34531
1877	Charles B.	Brooklyn, N. Y.,	Administration,	34532
1866	Charles E.	Northbridge,	Guardianship,	34533
1867	Charles L.	Athol,	Administration,	34534
1816	Charles S.	Boylston,	Guardianship,	34535
1850	Charles W.	Leominster,	Guardianship,	34536
1843	Chester B.	Hubbardston,	Guardianship,	34537
1856	Clara	Gardner,	Guardianship,	34538
1875	Clara M.	Worcester,	Guardianship,	34539
1843	Crusoe	Hubbardston,	Administration,	34540
1807	David	Boylston,	Guardianship,	34541
1819	David	Phillipston,	Guardianship,	34542
1825	David	Leominster,	Administration,	34543
1826	David	Hillsborough, Ga.,	Administration,	34544
1863	David	Barre,	Administration,	34545
1749	Ebenezer	Lancaster,	Administration,	34546
1848	Edmund	Gardner,	Will,	34547
1776	Edward	Leominster,	Administration,	34548
1777	Edward	Leominster,	Guardianship,	34549
1846	Edward	Westminster,	Will,	34550

| --- | --- | --- | --- | --- |
	KENDAL, KENDALL and KINDELL,			
1847	Edward P.	Worcester,	Guardianship,	34551
1857	Edward W.	Westminster,	Administration,	34552
1860	Edwin	Sterling,	Administration,	34553
1860	Edwin M.	Sterling,	Guardianship,	34554
1876	Eliza L.	Worcester,	Administration,	34555
1825	Elizabeth	Leominster,	Administration,	34556
1850	Ellen	Leominster,	Guardianship,	34557
1807	Emily	Boylston,	Guardianship,	34558
1832	Enoch	Harvard,	Will,	34559
1868	Esther	Sterling,	Administration,	34560
1835	Ethan	Sterling,	Guardianship,	34561
1835	Ethan	Sterling,	Administration,	34561
1780	Eunice	Templeton,	Guardianship,	34562
1864	Eva	Cambridge,	Adoption, etc.,	34563
1740	Experience	Lancaster,	Guardianship,	34564
1828	Ezra	Sterling,	Administration,	34565
1868	Frances	Sterling,	Administration,	34566
1865	Francis	Phillipston,	Administration,	34567
1871	Frank	Holden,	Guardianship,	34568
1864	Frank M.	Leominster,	Change of Name,	34569
1866	Frederic A.	New Braintree,	Guardianship,	34570
1870	Frederick J.	Phillipston,	Change of Name,	34571
1830	George	Sterling,	Guardianship,	34572
1855	George	Westminster,	Administration,	34573
1875	George	Sterling,	Administration,	34574
1850	George F.	Leominster,	Guardianship,	34575
1880	George F.	Fitchburg,	Administration,	34576
1855	George M.	Westminster,	Guardianship,	34577
1815	George U.	Barre,	Guardianship,	34578
1807	Hannah	Boylston,	Guardianship,	34579
1851	Hannah	Templeton,	Administration,	34580
1880	Harriet H.	Worcester,	Administration,	34581
1800	Heman	Sterling,	Guardianship,	34582
1800	Heman	Sterling,	Administration,	34583
1857	Heman	Sterling,	Will,	34584
1826	Henry	Templeton,	Administration,	34585
1864	Henry	Northbridge,	Administration,	34586
1864	Henry H.	Northbridge,	Guardianship,	34587
1866	Henry H.	New Braintree,	Guardianship,	34588
1871	Horace	Phillipston,	Will,	34589
1855	Hubbard	Gardner,	Administration,	34590
1870	Huldah E.	Holden,	Administration,	34591
1755	Isaac	Lancaster,	Administration,	34592

YEAR.	NAME.	RESIDENCE.	NATURE.	CASE.
	KENDAL, KENDALL and KINDELL,			
1796	James	Sterling,	Will,	34593
1859	James B.	Worces'er,	Administration,	34594
1842	James W.	Leominster,	Guardianship,	34595
1847	James W.	Leominster,	Administration,	34596
1860	James W.	Sterling,	Guardianship,	34597
1864	Jane	Northbridge,	Guardianship,	34598
1797	Jesse	Petersham,	Administration,	34599
1817	Jesse	Phillipston,	Will,	34600
1834	Joel	Athol,	Administration,	34601
1850	Joel	Athol,	Will,	34602
1740	John	Lancaster,	Distribution,	34603
1776	John	Royalston,	Administration,	34604
1822	John	Leominster,	Will,	34605
1838	John	Athol,	Guardianship,	34606
1840	John	Athol,	Will,	34607
1851	John	Fitchburg,	Will,	34608
1826	John C.	Leominster,	Administration,	34609
1875	John G.	Worcester,	Administration,	34610
1854	John H.	Fitchburg,	Guardianship,	34611
1819	John L.	Phillipston,	Guardianship,	34612
1843	John N.	Hubbardston,	Guardianship,	34613
1863	John N.	Hubbardston,	Administration,	34614
1871	John O.	Phillipston,	Guardianship,	34615
1799	Jonas	Leominster,	Will,	34616
1845	Jonas	Leominster,	Administration,	34617
1862	Jonas H.	Leominster,	Will,	34618
1817	Jonathan	Athol,	Will,	34619
1777	Jonathan, Jr.	Lancaster,	Will,	34620
1834	Joseph	Sterling,	Will,	34621
1847	Joseph G.	Worcester,	Will,	34622
1845	Joseph S.	Fitchburg,	Guardianship,	34623
1768	Joshua	Westborough,	Will,	34624
1813	Joshua	Boylston,	Administration,	34625
1785	Josiah	Sterling,	Administration,	34626
1816	Josiah	Sterling,	Will,	34627
1826	Josiah	Sterling,	Will,	34628
1829	Josiah	Sterling,	Guardianship,	34629
1860	Josiah	Sterling,	Will,	34630
1826	Levi	Morgan Co., Ga.,	Administration,	34631
1878	Levi	Fitchburg,	Will,	34632
1854	Loring A.	Fitchburg,	Guardianship,	34633
1807	Lucy	Boylston,	Guardianship,	34634
1846	Lucy	Boylston,	Administration,	34635

KENDAL, KENDALL AND KINDELL,

1830	Lucy M.	Milford,	Guardianship,	34636
1843	Lucy M.	Hubbardston,	Guardianship,	34637
1859	Luther	Sterling,	Administration,	34638
1859	Luther, 2d	Sterling,	Administration,	34639
1856	Lydia	Templeton,	Will,	34640
1871	Lydia C.	Fitchburg,	Administration,	34641
1819	Lyman	Spencer,	Guardianship,	34642
1863	Lyman	Athol,	Administration,	34643
1875	Lyman	Milford,	Will,	34644
1871	Margaret	Worcester,	Administration,	34645
1866	Maro	Worcester,	Administration,	34646
1824	Martha	Mendon,	Guardianship,	34647
1740	Mary	Lancaster,	Guardianship,	34648
1816	Mary	Sterling,	Guardianship,	34649
1830	Mary	Sterling,	Guardianship,	34650
1864	Mary	Northbridge,	Guardianship,	34651
1871	Mary	Holden,	Guardianship,	34652
1855	Mary A.	Westminster,	Guardianship,	34653
1842	Mary E.	Leominster,	Guardianship,	34654
1850	Mary E.	Athol,	Guardianship,	34655
1850	Mary E.	Leominster,	Administration,	34656
1854	Mary J.	Fitchburg,	Guardianship,	34657
1850	Metaphor	Leominster,	Administration,	34658
1816	Miles	Templeton,	Will,	34659
1878	Minday B.	Boylston,	Administration,	34660
1845	Moses	Barre,	Administration,	34661
1867	Moses	Hubbardston,	Administration,	34662
1807	Myra	Boylston,	Guardianship,	34663
1846	Nancy	Leominster,	Administration,	34664
1850	Nancy J.	Leominster,	Guardianship,	34665
1780	Nathaniel	Templeton,	Guardianship,	34666
1845	Noah	Templeton,	Will,	34667
1846	Noah	Templeton,	Pension,	34668
1846	Noah, 2d	Templeton,	Administration,	34669
1816	Oliver S.	Boylston,	Guardianship,	34670
1880	Orrison	Gardner,	Administration,	34671
1859	Patty	Boylston,	Administration,	34672
1832	Paul	Templeton,	Will,	34673
1857	Paul	Templeton,	Administration,	34674
1800	Peter	Sterling,	Guardianship,	34675
1817	Peter, 2d	Sterling,	Administration,	34676
1847	Peter	Worcester,	Administration,	34677
1872	Pierson	Lunenburg,	Administration,	34678

YEAR.	NAME.	RESIDENCE.	NATURE.	CASE.
	KENDAL, KENDALL AND KINDELL,			
1865	Pierson T.	Clinton,	Administration,	34679
1860	Rebecca	Phillipston,	Administration,	34680
1842	Rufus	Leominster,	Administration,	34681
1823	Rufus W.	Sterling,	Guardianship,	34682
1845	Rufus W.	Fitchburg,	Guardianship,	34683
1863	Sally W.	Sterling,	Administration,	34684
1749	Samuel	Lancaster,	Will,	34685
1807	Samuel	Boylston,	Guardianship,	34686
1810	Samuel	Barre,	Administration,	34687
1854	Samuel L.	Fitchburg,	Administration,	34688
1855	Sarah L.	Westminster,	Guardianship,	34689
1850	Sarah R.	Athol,	Guardianship,	34690
1790	Seth	Athol,	Administration,	34691
1806	Seth	Athol,	Administration,	34692
1877	Smith	Worcester,	Administration,	34693
1777	Tabitha	Leominster,	Guardianship,	34694
1800	Tabitha	Sterling,	Administration,	34695
1844	Thirza	Leominster,	Administration,	34696
1825	Thomas	Athol,	Administration,	34697
1850	Thomas E.	Leominster,	Guardianship,	34698
1879	Thomas H.	Barre,	Will,	34699
1777	Timothy	Lancaster,	Guardianship,	34700
1780	Timothy	Leominster,	Will,	34701
1854	Vashti A.	Fitchburg,	Guardianship,	34702
1807	William	Boylston,	Guardianship,	34703
1835	William	Fitchburg,	Administration,	34704
1835	William	Fitchburg,	Pension,	34705
1866	William	Northbridge,	Administration,	34706
1870	William F.	Worcester,	Will,	34707
1866	William H.	Northbridge,	Guardianship,	34708
1842	William R.	Leominster,	Guardianship,	34709
1843	William R.	Leominster,	Administration,	34710
1835	Wyman	Sterling,	Guardianship,	34711
1807	Zipporah	Boylston,	Guardianship,	34712
	KENDRICK AND KINDRICK.			
1866	Abigail	Lancaster,	Will,	34713
1878	Almira W.	Sutton,	Will,	34714
1879	Bessie A.	Lancaster,	Guardianship,	34715
1849	Caroline W.	North Brookfield,	Guardianship,	34716
1872	Emma A.	North Brookfield,	Guardianship,	34717
1841	George	North Brookfield,	Guardianship,	34718
1879	Henry R.	Lancaster,	Guardianship,	34719
1872	James E.	North Brookfield,	Guardianship,	34720
1872	Joseph	North Brookfield,	Administration,	34721

KENDRICK AND KINDRICK.

YEAR.	NAME.	RESIDENCE.	NATURE.	CASE.
1849	Joseph E.	North Brookfield,	Guardianship,	34722
1841	Lucy A.	North Brookfield,	Guardianship,	34723
1841	Luke	North Brookfield,	Guardianship,	34724
1849	Mary L.	North Brookfield,	Guardianship,	34725
1849	Oliver P.	North Brookfield,	Guardianship,	34726
1841	Perley	North Brookfield,	Administration,	34727
1841	Sarah J.	North Brookfield,	Guardianship,	34728
1878	Susan A.	Lancaster,	Administration,	34729
1841	Susan B.	North Brookfield,	Guardianship,	34730
1832	Thomas	North Brookfield,	Administration,	34731
1852	Thomas	North Brookfield,	Administration,	34732
1867	KENDY, John	Worcester,	Administration,	34733
1875	KENESTON, Ida	Worcester,	Guardianship,	34734

KENIN see KENNAN.

1860	KENNA, James E.	Holden,	Guardianship,	34735
1860	Sarah C.	Holden,	Administration,	34736
1860	Sarah E.	Holden,	Guardianship,	34737

KENNADY see KENNEDY.

KENNAN AND KENIN.

| 1827 | Elijah | West Boylston, | Administration, | 34738 |
| 1857 | James | Winchendon, | Administration, | 34739 |

KENNEDY, KENNADY, KAN-ADY AND CANADA.

1757	Alexander	Lunenburg,	Guardianship,	34740
1869	Annie W.	Worcester,	Adoption, etc.,	34741
1865	Bridget	North Brookfield,	Administration,	34742
1870	Bridget T.	Worcester,	Guardianship,	34743
1871	Cornelius	Worcester,	Guardianship,	34744
1866	David	Hardwick,	Guardianship,	34745
1866	David	Hardwick,	Administration,	34746
1876	David	Northbridge,	Guardianship,	34747
1876	David	Northbridge,	Administration,	34748
1866	Ellen	Hardwick,	Guardianship,	34749
1824	James	Lansingburg, N. Y.,	Guardianship,	34750
1756	John	Lunenburg,	Guardianship,	34751
1866	John	Hardwick,	Guardianship,	34752
1871	John	Worcester,	Guardianship,	34753
1881	John	Fitchburg,	Will,	34754
1824	John Jr.	Lansingburg, N. Y.,	Guardianship,	34755
1875	Julia	Worcester,	Will,	34756
1824	Margarett	Lansingburg, N. Y.,	Guardianship,	34757
1875	Mary E.	Blackstone,	Guardianship,	34758
1877	Michael	Worcester,	Administration,	34759
1871	Michael P.	Worcester,	Guardianship,	34760
1871	Patrick	Worcester,	Guardianship,	34761

	KENNEDY, KENNADY, KAN-ADY AND CANADA.			
1880	Patrick	Uxbridge,	Administration,	34762
1881	Patrick	Worcester,	Administration,	34763
1757	Samuel	Lunenburg,	Administration,	34764
1876	Sarah J.	Northbridge,	Guardianship,	34765
1770	Thomas	Blanford,	Guardianship,	34766
1777	Thomas	Blanford,	Administration,	34766
1866	Thomas	Hardwick,	Guardianship,	34767
1765	William	Lunenburg,	Guardianship,	34768
1866	William	Hardwick,	Guardianship,	34769
	KENNY, KENNEY AND KINNEY.			
1789	Abigail	Sutton,	Will,	34770
1877	Albion P.	Milford,	Administration,	34771
1855	Alice	Sterling,	Guardianship,	34772
1848	Ann E.	Royalston,	Guardianship,	34773
1793	Artemas	Brookfield,	Administration,	34774
1760	Asa	Sutton,	Guardianship,	34775
1806	Asa	Sutton,	Administration,	34776
1801	Betty	Royalston,	Guardianship,	34777
1802	Beulah	Royalston,	Guardianship,	34778
1877	Bryen	Worcester,	Administration,	34779
1861	Catharine	Spencer,	Administration,	34780
1876	Catherine	Lowell,	Adoption, etc.,	34781
1753	Daniel	Sutton,	Administration,	34782
1758	Daniel	Sutton,	Administration,	34783
1878	Dennis	Sutton,	Administration,	34784
1874	Dorcas	Leicester,	Administration,	34785
1866	Edward	Clinton,	Will,	34786
1878	Elizabeth M.	Sutton,	Guardianship,	34787
1801	Enoch	Royalston,	Guardianship,	34788
1732	Henry	Sutton,	Will,	34789
1744	Henry	Sutton,	Guardianship,	34790
1802	Hosea	Royalston,	Guardianship,	34791
1801	Isaac	Royalston,	Administration,	34792
1755	Israel	Sutton,	Guardianship,	34793
1802	James	Royalston,	Guardianship,	34794
1801	Jenny	Royalston,	Guardianship,	34795
1819	John	Oxford,	Administration,	34796
1865	John	Milford,	Administration,	34797
1870	John	Milford,	Administration,	'34798
1870	John	Milford,	Guardianship,	34799
1764	Jonas	Sutton,	Guardianship,	34800
1731	Jonathan	Sutton,	Will,	34801
1757	Jonathan	Sutton,	Administration,	34802

KENNY, KENNEY AND KINNEY.

YEAR.	NAME.	RESIDENCE.	NATURE.	CASE.
1768	Jonathan	Sutton,	Administration,	34803
1870	Luke	Worcester,	Will,	34804
1767	Lydia	Sutton,	Guardianship,	34805
1855	Mary	Millbury,	Guardianship,	34806
1864	Mary F.	Leominster,	Will,	34807
1848	Mary J.	Royalston,	Guardianship,	34808
1801	Molly	Royalston,	Guardianship,	34809
1800	Moses	Royalston,	Administration,	34810
1802	Moses	Royalston,	Guardianship,	34811
1734	Nathan	Oxford,	Guardianship,	34812
1746	Nathan	Woodstock,	Administration,	34813
1757	Nathan	Sutton,	Administration,	34814
1767	Nathan	Sutton,	Guardianship,	34815
1865	Patrick	Milford,	Administration,	34816
1802	Rhoda	Royalston,	Guardianship,	34817
1765	Reuhiu	Sutton,	Guardianship,	34818
1802	Ruth	Royalston,	Guardianship,	34819
1803	Stephen	Sutton,	Guardianship,	34820
1770	William	Sutton,	Guardianship,	34821
1873	KENNINGTON, Alice	Worcester,	Will,	34822
1864	Henry	Worcester,	Administration,	34823
1868	KENSINGTON, John J.	Worcester,	Change of Name,	34824
1868	Milo L.	Worcester,	Change of Name,	34825
1849	KENT, Charlotte E.	Leicester,	Guardianship,	34826
1849	Daniel	Leicester,	Will,	34827
1871	Dolly	West Brookfield,	Will,	34828
1786	Ebenezer	Leicester,	Will,	34829
1806	Ebenezer	Leicester,	Administration,	34830
1849	Edward E.	Leicester,	Guardianship,	34831
1848	Emerson	Leicester,	Administration,	34832
1849	George E.	Leicester,	Guardianship,	34833
1825	Jacob	Brookfield,	Will,	34834
1847	Jacob	West Brookfield,	Will,	34835
1834	John	Spencer,	Administration,	34836
1767	Josiah	Harvard,	Administration,	34837
1861	Miranda	Leicester,	Guardianship,	34838
1807	Polly	Leicester,	Guardianship,	34839
1797	Sarah	Brookfield,	Will,	34840
1875	KEOUGH, Barnaby	Southbridge,	Administration,	34841
1871	James	Fitchburg,	Will,	34842
1872	James	Fitchburg,	Guardianship,	34843
1872	John	Southbridge,	Guardianship,	34844
1872	John Jr.	Fitchburg,	Guardianship,	34845
1873	KERBER, Amelia	Worcester,	Guardianship,	34846

Year.	Name.	Residence.	Nature.	Case.
1873	KERBER, Frank	Worcester,	Administration,	34847
1873	John	Worcester,	Guardianship,	34848
1873	Rosie E.	Worcester,	Guardianship,	34849
	KERLEY, see also CURLEY.			
1872	Johnson	Southbridge,	Administration,	34850
1872	Ralph	Southbridge,	Guardianship,	34851
1856	KERR, Harriet E.	Shrewsbury,	Administration,	34852
1865	KERSHAW, Elizabeth	Worcester,	Administration,	34853
1877	Emma	Worcester,	Administration,	34854
1863	KERVICK, Patrick	Worcester,	Administration,	34855
1873	KERWIN, Pierce	Worcester,	Administration,	34856
1876	KETT, Michael	Webster,	Administration,	34857
1859	KETTELL, Ann F.	Worcester,	Guardianship,	34858
1879	Elizabeth F.	Worcester,	Administration,	34859
1859	Ellen L.	Worcester,	Guardianship,	34860
1874	John P.	Worcester,	Will,	34861
	KEYES and KIES.			
1869	Abigail	Ashburnham,	Administration,	34862
1844	Adaline	Princeton,	Guardianship,	34863
1843	Adaliza M.	Northborough,	Guardianship,	34864
1827	Amasa	Lancaster,	Administration,	34865
1880	Amos	Princeton,	Administration,	34866
1855	Andrew S.	Dudley,	Guardianship,	34867
1843	Angelina A.	Northborough,	Guardianship,	34868
1848	Anna	Northborough,	Will,	34869
1857	Annah	Berlin,	Will,	34870
1851	Asa	Sterling,	Will,	34871
1808	Asenath	Princeton,	Guardianship,	34872
1844	Augusta	Princeton,	Guardianship,	34873
1801	Benjanin	Boylston,	Guardianship,	34874
1821	Benjanin	West Boylston,	Administration,	34875
1871	Benjanin F.	West Boylston,	Will,	34876
1875	Betsey	Woodstock, Conn.,	Administration,	34877
1782	Betty	Shrewsbury,	Guardianship,	34878
1767	Charles	Bolton,	Guardianship,	34879
1863	Charles B.	Sterling,	Administration,	34880
1877	Chester D.	Princeton,	Guardianship,	34881
1767	Christopher	Bolton,	Guardianship,	34882
1868	Cynthia	Warren,	Will,	34883
1802	Cyprian	Boylston,	Will,	34884
1757	Danforth	Western,	Guardianship,	34885
1826	Danforth	Western,	Will,	34886
1761	David	Western,	Administration,	34887
1879	David	Berlin,	Administration,	34888
1850	Dolly	Princeton,	Will,	34889

YEAR.	NAME.	RESIDENCE.	NATURE.	CASE.
	KEYES AND KIES.			
1767	Dolothea	Bolton,	Guardianship,	34890
1800	Eber	Mendon,	Administration,	34891
1854	Edward S.	Dudley,	Administration,	34892
1811	Elisha	Shrewsbury,	Will,	34893
1748	Elizabeth	Bolton,	Administration,	34894
1783	Elizabeth	Boylston,	Will,	34895
1809	Elizabeth	Princeton,	Administration,	34896
1810	Elizabeth	Princeton,	Guardianship,	34897
1853	Ellen L.	Berlin,	Guardianship,	34898
1799	Emerson	Shrewsbury,	Guardianship,	34899
1844	Emily S.	Princeton,	Guardianship,	34900
1756	Eunice	Shrewsbury,	Guardianship,	34901
1845	Everett	Worcester,	Guardianship,	34902
1876	Ezra S.	Princeton,	Administration,	34903
1877	Fannie A.	Princeton,	Guardianship,	34904
1848	Harriet M.	Northborough,	Guardianship,	34905
1756	Henry	Shrewsbury,	Will,	34906
1782	Henry	Shrewsbury,	Guardianship,	34907
1853	Henry F.	Berlin,	Guardianship,	34908
1848	Henry P.	Northborough,	Guardianship,	34909
1860	Henry P.	Northborough,	Administration,	34910
1764	Hepzibah	Western,	Guardianship,	34911
1782	Isaac	Shrewsbury,	Guardianship,	34912
1841	Israel	Princeton,	Will,	34913
1842	Israel	Princeton,	Pension,	34914
1746	James	Bolton,	Will,	34915
1763	James	Shrewsbury,	Will,	34916
1825	James	Northborough,	Administration,	34917
1844	James B.	Northborough,	Administration,	34918
1825	Joel	Boylston,	Administration,	34919
1753	John	Shrewsbury,	Will,	34920
1768	John	Shrewsbury,	Will,	34921
1853	John F.	Berlin,	Guardianship,	34922
1855	John M.	Dudley,	Guardianship,	34923
1736	Jonas	Shrewsbury,	Administration,	34924
1778	Jonathan	Shrewsbury,	Will,	34925
1767	Joseph	Bolton,	Guardianship,	34926
1872	Joseph H.	Fitchburg,	Administration,	34927
1866	Jotham	Fitchburg,	Administration,	34928
1871	Jotham	Princeton,	Will,	34929
1844	Julia B.	Princeton,	Guardianship,	34930
1798	Lewis	Shrewsbury,	Administration,	34931
1799	Lewis	Shrewsbury,	Guardianship,	34932
1878	Lois	West Boylston,	Will,	34933

YEAR.	NAME.	RESIDENCE.	NATURE.	CASE.
	KEYES AND KIES.			
1810	Lucinda	Princeton,	Guardianship,	34934
1837	Lucinda	Princeton,	Guardianship,	34935
1810	Lucretia	Princeton,	Guardianship,	34936
1870	Lucy A.	Rutland, Vt.,	Administration,	34937
1877	Luna F.	Princeton,	Guardianship,	34938
1845	Lyman	Worcester,	Guardianship,	34939
1845	Lyman	Worcester,	Administration,	34940
1757	Martha	Western,	Guardianship,	34941
1837	Mary	West Boylston,	Administration,	34942
1843	Mary E.	Ashburnham,	Guardianship,	34943
1801	Nahum	Mendon,	Guardianship,	34944
1875	Nancy H.	Dudley,	Administration,	34945
1880	Nellia S.	Princeton,	Guardianship,	34946
1827	Oren	Northbridge,	Administration,	34947
1861	Pardon	Warren,	Will,	34948
1810	Phebe	Princeton,	Guardianship,	34949
1794	Polly	Northborough,	Guardianship,	34950
1808	Polly	Princeton,	Guardianship,	34951
1842	Prentiss	Northborough,	Administration,	34952
1749	Rachel	Shrewsbury,	Guardianship,	34953
1782	Reuben	Shrewsbury,	Guardianship,	34954
1795	Robert	Princeton,	Will,	34955
1782	Ruth	Shrewsbury,	Guardianship,	34956
1824	Samuel	Brooklyn, Conn.,	Foreign Will,	34957
1856	Samuel	Ashburnham,	Guardianship,	34958
1868	Samuel	Ashburnham,	Administration,	34958
1843	Samuel H.	Ashburnham,	Administration,	34959
1764	Sarah	Western,	Guardianship,	34960
1831	Sarah	Western,	Will,	34961
1861	Sherburn	Worcester,	Administration,	34962
1756	Simeon	Shrewsbury,	Guardianship,	34963
1782	Simeon	Shrewsbury,	Guardianship,	34964
1782	Simeon	Shrewsbury,	Will,	34965
1755	Solomon	Western,	Administration,	34966
1808	Solomon	Princeton,	Will,	34967
1810	Stephen	Princeton,	Guardianship,	34968
1881	Susan J.	Warren,	Will,	34969
1782	Tabatha	Shrewsbury,	Guardianship,	34970
1794	Thomas	Northborough,	Guardianship,	34971
1813	Thomas	Boylston,	Will,	34972
1856	Thomas	West Boylston,	Administration,	34973
1831	Thomas Jr.	West Boylston,	Administration,	34974
1774	Titus	Northbridge,	Administration,	34975
1867	Warren S.	Louisa Co., Iowa,	Foreign Guard.,	34976

Year.	Name.	Residence.	Nature.	Case.
	KEYES and KIES.			
1852	Ziba	Berlin,	Administration,	34977
1869	KEYZER, Stillman	Lunenburg,	Administration,	34978
	KIBBY and KEBBY.			
1732	James	Reading,	Administration,	34979
1747	Seth	Hadley,	Administration,	34980
1878	KIBLING, Frank A.	Ashburnham,	Guardianship,	34981
1864	Franklin G.	Ashburnham,	Administration,	34982
1843	Henry 3rd.	Ashburnham,	Guardianship,	34983
1854	Susan	Ashburnham,	Administration,	34984
1878	Walter B.	Ashburnham,	Guardianship,	34985
1777	KIBLINGER, Elizabeth	Ashburnham,	Guardianship,	34986
1777	John	Ashburnham,	Will,	34987
1864	KIDDER, Abner C.	Westborough,	Administration,	34988
1862	Abram F.	Southborough,	Administration,	34989
1862	Albert A.	Oxford,	Adoption, etc.,	34990
1809	Almira	Winchendon,	Guardianship,	34991
1804	Benjamin	Dudley,	Will,	34992
1863	Charles A.	Sterling,	Will,	34993
1862	Charles H.	Southborough,	Guardianship,	34994
1865	Charles T.	Sterling,	Guardianship,	34995
1773	David	Dudley,	Administration,	34996
1774	David	Dudley,	Guardianship,	34997
1809	Elizabeth	Winchendon,	Guardianship,	34998
1836	Emeline	Oxford,	Guardianship,	34999
1852	Enoch	Winchendon,	Administration,	35000
1778	Ezhai	Dudley,	Guardianship,	35001
1763	Francis	Sutton,	Administration,	35002
1863	Helen M.	Sterling,	Guardianship,	35003
1807	Heywood	Winchendon	Administration,	35004
1869	Ida M.	Athol,	Guardianship,	35005
1836	Irena	Oxford,	Guardianship,	35006
1778	Jedidiah	Dudley,	Guardianship,	35007
1774	Jesse	Dudley,	Guardianship,	35008
1767	John	Sutton,	Guardianship,	35009
1853	John	Grafton, Vt.,	Foreign Will,	35010
1774	Jonathan	Dudley,	Guardianship,	35011
1809	Levi	Winchendon,	Guardianship,	35012
1862	Lizzie	Southborough,	Guardianship,	35013
1862	Marcia L. A.	Southborough,	Guardianship,	35014
1817	Mary	Oxford,	Will,	35015
1872	Mary A.	Westborough,	Administration,	35016
1809	Mary N.	Winchendon,	Guardianship,	35017
1778	Nathaniel	Dudley,	Guardianship,	35018
1836	Peter	Oxford,	Guardianship,	35019

|---|---|---|---|---|
1836	KIDDER, Peter	Oxford,	Administration,	35020
1836	Plina	Oxford,	Guardianship,	35021
1860	Pliny	Oxford,	Will,	35022
1778	Rebecca	Dudley,	Guardianship,	35023
1773	Richard	Dudley,	Will,	35024
1778	Richard	Dudley,	Guardianship,	35025
1862	Ruth	Sutton,	Will,	35026
1777	Samuel	Dudley,	Administration,	35027
1778	Samuel	Dudley,	Guardianship,	35028
1836	Sophia	Oxford,	Guardianship,	35029
1836	Susan	Oxford,	Guardianship,	35030
1861	KIERLIHY, Hannah, etc.	Worcester,	Administration,	35031
	KIES see KEYES.			
	KILBURN AND KILBOURNE.			
1878	Abby B.	Boston,	Partition,	35032
1876	Annie R.	Lunenburg,	Guardianship,	35033
1876	Asa	Lunenburg,	Administration,	35034
1852	Calvin	Princeton,	Will,	35035
1852	Calvin	Unknown,	Pension,	35036
1776	David	Lunenburg,	Will,	35037
1856	David	Lunenburg,	Administration,	35038
1754	Hannah	Mendon,	Guardianship,	35039
1803	Henry	Milford,	Administration,	35040
1778	Isaac	Lancaster,	Administration,	35041
1827	James	Sterling,	Administration,	35042
1828	James	Sterling,	Guardianship,	35043
1753	John	Mendon,	Administration,	35044
1840	John	Winchendon,	Pension,	35045
1880	John	Winchendon,	Administration,	35046
1806	Jonathan	Lunenburg,	Will,	35047
1789	Joseph	Sterling,	Will,	35048
1879	Katherine	Sterling,	Administration,	35049
1847	Levi	West Boylston,	Administration,	35050
1816	Lucinda	Wendell,	Sale Real Estate,	35051
1854	Lucy	Blackstone,	Administration,	35052
1759	Mary	Mendon,	Administration,	35053
1817	Mary	Sterling,	Administration,	35054
1857	Milton	Lunenburg,	Will,	35055
1754	Rachell	Mendon,	Guardianship,	35056
1781	Rebecca	Milford,	Guardianship,	35057
1828	Rebecca B.	Sterling,	Guardianship,	35058
1746	Robert	Woodstock,	Administration,	35059
1816	Sally W.	Wendell,	Sale Real Estate,	35060
1785	Samuel	Sterling,	Administration,	35061
1828	Samuel	Sterling,	Guardianship,	35062

YEAR.	NAME.	RESIDENCE.	NATURE.	CASE.
	KILBURN and KILBOURNE.			
1754	Sarah	Mendon,	Guardianship,	35063
1791	Sarah	Sterling,	Guardianship,	35064
1828	Sarah A.	Sterling,	Guardianship,	35065
1875	Sarah D.	Lunenburg,	Will,	35066
1842	Sumner R.	Lunenburg,	Administration,	35067
1843	Sumner R.	Lunenburg,	Guardianship,	35068
1861	Susan	Princeton,	Pension,	35069
1861	Susan	Princeton,	Will,	35070
1839	Timothy	Sterling,	Will,	35071
1869	Vanda L. W.	Charlton,	Will,	35072
1863	William	Holden,	Administration,	35073
1881	KILEY, Bridget A.	Worcester,	Guardianship,	35074
1881	Elizabeth A.	Worcester,	Guardianship,	35075
1881	Ellen M.	Worcester,	Guardianship,	35076
1881	Frances A.	Worcester,	Guardianship,	35077
1881	John W.	Worcester,	Guardianship,	35078
1875	Margaret	Worcester,	Guardianship,	35079
1875	Margaret L.	Worcester,	Will,	35080
1881	Margaret P.	Worcester,	Guardianship,	35081
1875	Mary	Worcester,	Guardianship,	35082
1881	Mary G.	Worcester.	Guardianship,	35083
1881	Michael E.	Worcester,	Guardianship,	35084
1881	Michael P.	Worcester,	Will,	35085
1868	Patrick	Worcester,	Will,	35086
1881	Patrick H.	Worcester,	Guardianship,	35087
1873	Patrick W.	Worcester,	Will,	35088
1875	William	Worcester,	Will,	35089
1872	KILLELEA, John	Leominster,	Administration,	35090
1877	KILLOM, Frederick D.	Berlin,	Administration,	35091
1864	KILMER, Carrie R.	Templeton,	Guardianship,	35092
1864	Harriet G. E.	Templeton,	Guardianship,	35093
1864	Jenny B. H.	Templeton,	Guardianship,	35094
1864	William G.	Templeton,	Will,	35095
1864	William H.	Templeton,	Guardianship,	35096
	KILTON see KELTON.			
	KIMBALL and KIMBLE.			
1777	Aaron	Brookfield,	Guardianship,	35097
1807	Aaron	Grafton,	Will,	35098
1833	Aaron	North Brookfield,	Will,	35099
1843	Aaron	Grafton,	Will,	35100
1866	Aaron	Brookfield,	Administration,	35101
1873	Aaron	Westborough,	Will,	35102
1811	Aaron B.	Lunenburg,	Guardianship,	35103
1788	Abigail	Brookfield,	Will,	35104

KIMBALL AND KIMBLE.

YEAR.	NAME.	RESIDENCE.	NATURE.	CASE.
1811	Abigail	Lunenburg,	Guardianship,	35105
1811	Abigail B.	Shrewsbury,	Guardianship,	35106
1821	Abigail B.	Shrewsbury,	Administration,	35107
1849	Abigail F.	North Boookfield,	Guardianship,	35108
1875	Alice E.	Peterboro, N. II.,	Adoption, etc.,	35109
1830	Almira M.	Millbury,	Guardianship,	35110
1859	Alpheus	Fitchburg,	Administration,	35111
1862	Amasa	Woodstock, Conn.,	Foreign Will,	35112
1774	Amos	Fitchburg,	Will,	35113
1806	Anna	Grafton,	Guardianship,	35114
1864	Anna F.	Blackstone,	Guardianship,	35115
1878	Archus S.	Winchendon,	Will,	35116
1873	Augusta	Oakham,	Will,	35117
1777	Benjamin	Brookfield,	Guardianship,	35118
1777	Benjamin	Brookfield,	Administration,	35119
1830	Benjamin	Harvard,	Administration,	35120
1849	Benjamin	North Brookfield,	Administration,	35121
1849	Benjamin G.	North Brookfield,	Guardianship,	35122
1806	Betsey	Grafton,	Guardianship,	35123
1873	Betsey A.	Fitchburg,	Will,	35124
1844	Betsy	Fitchburg,	Will,	35125
1816	Charles	Holden,	Guardianship,	35126
1819	Charles	Grafton,	Guardianship,	35127
1881	Charles E.	Southbridge,	Will,	35128
1830	Charlotte	Millbury,	Guardianship,	35129
1857	Charlotte E.	West Brookfield,	Guardianship,	35130
1881	Charlotte M.	Warren,	Will,	35131
1849	Charlotte S.	North Brookfield,	Guardianship,	35132
1815	David	Holden,	Administration,	35133
1816	David	Holden,	Guardianship,	35134
1857	David M.	West Brookfield,	Guardianship,	35135
1857	David M.	West Brookfield,	Administration,	35136
1778	Ebenezer	Fitchburg,	Guardianship,	35137
1868	Elijah	Grafton,	Will,	35138
1869	Elijah	Athol,	Administration,	35139
1816	Eliza	Holden,	Guardianship,	35140
1825	Ephraim	Fitchburg,	Will,	35141
1853	Ephraim	Fitchburg,	Administration,	35142
1857	Frederick W.	West Brookfield,	Guardianship,	35143
1790	George	Lunenburg,	Will,	35144
1800	George	Lunenburg,	Guardianship,	35145
1836	George	Holden,	Guardianship,	35146
1846	George	Holden,	Administration,	35147
1816	Hannah	Holden,	Guardianship,	35148

YEAR.	NAME.	RESIDENCE.	NATURE.	CASE.
	KIMBALL AND KIMBLE.			
1819	Hannah	Grafton,	Guardianship,	35149
1835	Hannah	Holden,	Administration,	35150
1860	Harriet	Millbury,	Guardianship,	35151
1874	Harriet L.	Fitchburg,	Will,	35152
1857	Harriot C.	West Brookfield,	Guardianship,	35153
1814	Henry	Princeton,	Guardianship,	35154
1854	Hiram	Worcester,	Will,	35155
1861	James	Oakham,	Will,	35156
1867	Jane E.	Milford,	Will,	35157
1879	Jefferson	Fitchburg,	Will,	35158
1777	John	Brookfield,	Guardianship,	35159
1800	John	Lunenburg,	Guardianship,	35160
1852	John	North Brookfield,	Will,	35161
1866	John C.	Brookfield,	Guardianship,	35162
1850	John S.	Worcester,	Administration,	35163
1823	Jonathan	Milford,	Administration,	35164
1777	Joseph	Brookfield,	Guardianship,	35165
1878	Joseph	Grafton,	Will,	35166
1849	Joseph E.	North Brookfield,	Guardianship,	35167
1777	Jude	Brookfield,	Guardianship,	35168
1879	Julia N.	Boston,	Adoption, etc.,	35169
1819	Katharine	Grafton,	Guardianship,	35170
1820	Lemuel	Sterling,	Guardianship,	35171
1816	Leonard	Holden,	Guardianship,	35172
1818	Leonard	Greenwich,	Guardianship,	35173
1872	Lloyd B.	Worcester,	Administration,	35174
1876	Lucy E.	Winchendon,	Partition,	35175
1777	Lydia	Brookfield,	Guardianship,	35176
1875	Lydia	Brookfield,	Administration,	35177
1830	Martha A.	Millbury,	Guardianship,	35178
1863	Martha A. B.	Leominster,	Administration,	35179
1877	Martha W.	Westborough,	Will,	35180
1819	Mary	Grafton,	Guardianship,	35181
1841	Mary	Lunenburg,	Guardianship,	35182
1864	Mary A.	Blackstone,	Will,	35183
1849	Mary A. II.	North Brookfield,	Guardianship,	35184
1844	Mary F.	Fitchburg,	Guardianship,	35185
1830	Mary J.	Millbury,	Guardianship,	35186
1819	Noah	Grafton,	Guardianship,	35187
1876	Noah	Westborough,	Will,	35188
1806	Noah B.	Grafton,	Administration,	35189
1819	Oliver	Grafton,	Guardianship,	35190
1819	Oliver	Grafton,	Administration,	35191
1788	Parnell	Boylston,	Administration,	35192

Year.	Name.	Residence.	Nature.	Case.
	KIMBALL and KIMBLE.			
1875	Phineas S.	Lunenburg,	Will,	35193
1816	Polly	Holden,	Guardianship,	35194
1851	Polly	Lunenburg,	Pension,	35195
1844	Porter M.	Fitchburg,	Guardianship,	35196
1866	Porter M.	Leominster,	Administration,	35197
1819	Richard	Sterling,	Administration,	35198
1857	Ruel R.	West Brookfield,	Guardianship,	35199
1860	Samuel G.	Millbury,	Will,	35200
1816	Sarah	Holden,	Guardianship,	35201
1851	Sarah	Winchendon,	Administration,	35202
1816	Sophia	Holden,	Guardianship,	35203
1840	Sophia	Holden,	Administration,	35204
1748	Thomas	Lunenburg,	Will,	35205
1789	Thomas	Holden,	Will,	35206
1816	Thomas	Holden,	Guardianship,	35207
1869	Thomas	Winchendon,	Administration,	35208
1857	Warren L.	West Brookfield,	Guardianship,	35209
1876	William	Oxford,	Will,	35210
1848	KIMBERLY, Albert T.	Grafton,	Guardianship,	35211
1848	Elizabeth G.	Grafton,	Guardianship,	35212
1848	Thompson, Jr.	Grafton,	Will,	35213
	KIMBLE see KIMBALL.			
	KIMMENS, KIMMEN and KIMMINS.			
1852	Abigail F.	Bolton,	Guardianship,	35214
1822	Amos	Bolton,	Guardianship,	35215
1822	Daniel	Bolton,	Guardianship,	35216
1871	Dinah	Berlin,	Will,	35217
1821	John	Bolton,	Administration,	35218
1852	John	Bolton,	Will,	35219
1850	Judith	Bolton,	Administration,	35220
1822	Kesiah	Bolton,	Guardianship,	35221
1822	Lydia	Bolton,	Guardianship,	35222
1822	Mary	Bolton,	Guardianship,	35223
1822	Phebe	Bolton,	Guardianship,	35224
1822	Sarah	Bolton,	Guardianship,	35225
	KINDELL see KENDALL.			
	KINDRICK see KENDRICK.			
1861	KINERY, Catherine	Spencer,	Administration,	35226
1828	KING, Adaline A.	Rutland,	Guardianship,	35227
1748	Adonijah	Brimfield,	Guardianship,	35228
1757	Adonijah	Brimfield,	Distribution,	35229
1827	Amasa W.	Leicester,	Guardianship,	35230
1875	Andrew	Charlton,	Administration,	35231

(811)

YEAR.	NAME.	RESIDENCE.	NATURE.	CASE.
1854	KING, Andrew P.	Oxford,	Guardianship,	35232
1880	Anna	Dudley,	Guardianship,	35233
1873	Annie L.	Worcester,	Guardianship,	35234
1879	Arthur N.	Fitchburg,	Guardianship,	35235
1831	Aurilla	Tyrone, N. Y.,	Sale Real Estate,	35236
1864	Baxter H.	Barre,	Administration,	35237
1739	Benjamin	Sudbury,	Guardianship,	35238
1880	Bertha	Dudley,	Guardianship,	35239
1860	Brigham T.	Leicester,	Guardianship,	35240
1812	Calvin	Rutland,	Administration,	35241
1881	Carl	Gardner,	Adoption, etc.,	35242
1828	Catharine A.	Rutland,	Guardianship,	35243
1807	Charles	Rutland,	Guardianship,	35244
1821	Charles	Rutland,	Administration,	35245
1831	Charles	Tyrone, N. Y.,	Sale Real Estate,	35246
1839	Charles	Leicester,	Administration,	35247
1877	Charles	Worcester,	Administration,	35248
1880	Charles A.	Dana,	Guardianship,	35249
1839	Charles B.	Leicester,	Guardianship,	35250
1849	Charles O.	Worcester,	Guardianship,	35251
1828	Charles W.	Rutland,	Guardianship,	35252
1856	Charles W.	Hardwick,	Guardianship,	35253
1836	Charlotte	Barre,	Guardianship,	35254
1877	Cyrus	Barre,	Administration,	35255
1774	Daniel	Rutland,	Administration,	35256
1833	Daniel	Charlton,	Administration,	35257
1834	Daniel	Rutland,	Will,	35258
1837	Daniel	Rutland,	Guardianship,	35259
1849	Daniel I.	Worcester,	Guardianship,	35260
1786	Ebenezer	Rutland,	Administration,	35261
1880	Eda	Dudley,	Guardianship,	35262
1792	Edmond	Sutton,	Administration,	35263
1875	Edward P.	Worcester,	Guardianship,	35264
1864	Edwin	Webster,	Adoption, etc.,	35265
1869	Eliza	Uxbridge,	Guardianship,	35266
1748	Elizabeth	Brimfield,	Guardianship,	35267
1857	Elizabeth	Sutton,	Will,	35268
1880	Elizabeth F.	Hardwick,	Administration,	35269
1831	Elmira	Tyrone, N. Y.,	Sale Real Estate,	35270
1880	Emma	Dudley,	Guardianship,	35271
1866	Etta E.	Phillipston,	Adoption, etc.,	35272
1863	Eveline E.	Sutton,	Administration,	35273
1859	Florence E.	Ashburnham,	Guardianship,	35274
1857	Frederick	Leominster,	Administration,	35275
1875	Frederick G.	Dudley,	Administration,	35276

YEAR.	NAME.	RESIDENCE.	NATURE.	CASE.
1861	KING, Frederick N.	Lancaster,	Guardianship,	35277
1877	George T.	Worcester,	Will,	35278
1880	Gustav	Dudley,	Guardianship,	35279
1834	Hannah	Hubbardston,	Administration,	35280
1863	Hannah	Barre,	Guardianship,	35281
1877	Hannah	Barre,	Administration,	35281
1807	Harriet	Rutland,	Guardianship,	35282
1828	Harriet E.	Rutland,	Guardianship,	35283
1837	Harriet N.	Rutland,	Guardianship,	35284
1879	Harvey A.	Fitchburg,	Guardianship,	35285
1854	Helen M.	Oxford,	Guardianship,	35286
1827	Henry	Leicester,	Administration,	35287
1831	Henry	Tyrone, N. Y.,	Sale Real Estate,	35288
1880	Henry	Dudley,	Guardianship,	35289
1852	Henry O.	Grafton,	Guardianship,	35290
1879	Herbert A.	Upton,	Administration,	35291
1840	Hiram N.	Ashburnham,	Administration,	35292
1859	Isaac	Sutton,	Will,	35293
1836	Jane	Barre,	Guardianship,	35294
1880	Jennie R.	Dana,	Guardianship,	35295
1855	Jesse W.	Hardwick,	Administration,	35296
1795	John	Sutton,	Administration,	35297
1807	John	Rutland,	Guardianship,	35298
1814	John	Barre,	Guardianship,	35299
1827	John	Sandersville, Ga.,	Administration,	35300
1858	John	Leicester,	Will,	35301
1863	John	Barre,	Will,	35302
1878	John	Sturbridge,	Administration,	35303
1859	John E.	Ashburnham,	Administration,	35304
1760	Jonathan	Sutton,	Administration,	35305
1827	Jonathan	Sutton,	Administration,	35306
1807	Joseph	Rutland,	Will,	35307
1836	Joseph	Barre,	Guardianship,	35308
1880	Joseph	Dana,	Administration,	35309
1841	Julia F.	Ashburnham,	Guardianship,	35310
1880	Lewis D.	Worcester,	Will,	35311
1857	Louisa	Leominster,	Guardianship,	35312
1837	Lovisa M.	Rutland,	Guardianship,	35313
1857	Lucy M.	Sutton,	Guardianship,	35314
1837	Lucy W.	Rutland,	Guardianship,	35315
1875	Martha E.	Athol,	Will,	35316
1836	Mary	Barre,	Guardianship,	35317
1862	Mary	Leominster,	Will,	35318
1880	Mary	Sutton,	Administration,	35319
1841	Mary A.	Ashburnham,	Guardianship,	35320

YEAR.	NAME.	RESIDENCE.	NATURE.	CASE.
1869	KING, Mary A.	Uxbridge,	Guardianship,	35321
1837	Mary J.	Rutland,	Guardianship,	35322
1858	Mary J.	Leominster,	Will,	35323
1871	Mary W.	Sutton,	Will,	35324
1879	Mercy	Southbridge,	Administration,	35325
1860	Michael	Worcester,	Will,	35326
1880	Minerva	Southborough,	Administration,	35327
1877	M. Jennie	Royalston,	Administration,	35328
1831	Nancy S.	Tyrone, N. Y.,	Sale Real Estate,	35329
1875	Nathaniel H.	Berlin,	Administration,	35330
1869	Nicholas	Uxbridge,	Guardianship,	35331
1866	N. Lizzie	Worcester,	Guardianship,	35332
1827	Pamela D.	Leicester,	Guardianship,	35333
1869	Paul	Uxbridge,	Guardianship,	35334
1818	Peter	Sutton,	Guardianship,	35335
1865	Rebecca P.	Rutland,	Administration,	35336
1879	Robert	Fitchburg,	Administration,	35337
1843	Roxanna L.	Leicester,	Administration,	35338
1856	Sally A.	Rutland,	Administration,	35339
1836	Samuel	Barre,	Guardianship,	35340
1836	Samuel	Barre,	Administration,	35341
1879	Samuel	Upton,	Administration,	35342
1879	Samuel	Oakham,	Administration,	35343
1846	Sarah	Barre,	Administration,	35344
1835	Sarah P.	Sutton,	Guardianship,	35345
1857	Sarah P.	Sutton,	Administration,	35346
1797	Simeon	Sutton,	Administration,	35347
1835	Solomon	Sutton,	Administration,	35348
1827	Stephen	Dana,	Administration,	35349
1837	Susanna H.	Rutland,	Guardianship,	35350
1825	Tarrant	Sutton,	Administration,	35351
1839	Thomas H.	Leicester,	Guardianship,	35352
1860	Walter C.	Leicester,	Guardianship,	35353
1743	William	Sutton,	Will,	35354
1813	William	Barre,	Administration,	35355
1826	William	Sutton,	Will,	35356
1874	William	Sutton,	Will,	35357
1827	William H.	Leicester,	Guardianship,	35358
1810	William P.	Rutland,	Will,	35359
1872	KINGMAN, Amos W.	Milford,	Administration,	35360
1867	Davis	Worcester,	Will,	35361
1788	Ebenezer	Harvard,	Will,	35362
	KINGSBURY AND KINGSBERY.			
1807	Adaline	Oxford,	Guardianship,	35363
1872	Alfred	Oxford,	Administration,	35364